Practical Guide to Estate Planning

Ray D. Madoff
Cornelia R. Tenney
Martin A. Hall
Lisa N. Mingolla

. Wolters Kluwer

Editorial Staff

Editor . . . . Barbara L. Post, J.D.

Production . . . . Jennifer Schencker, Manjula Mahalingam, Anbarasu Anbumani

This publication is designed to provide accurate and authoritative information in regard to the subject matter covered. It is sold with the understanding that the publisher is not engaged in rendering legal, accounting, or other professional services. If legal advice or other expert assistance is required, the services of a competent professional person should be sought. All views expressed in this publication are those of the author and not necessarily those of the publisher or any other person.

From the Authors: To ensure compliance with the requirements imposed by Internal Revenue Service Circular 230, the authors note that any tax advice contained in this book (or the accompanying URL) was not intended to be written to be used, and cannot be used, by any taxpayer for the purpose of avoiding tax-related penalties under the U.S. Internal Revenue Code of 1986, as amended.

ISBN: 978-0-8080-5737-6

No claim is made to original government works; however, within this publication, the following are subject to CCH Incorporated's copyright: (1) the gathering, compilation, and arrangement of such government materials; (2) the magnetic translation and digital conversion of data, if applicable; (3) the historical, statutory and other notes and references; and (4) the commentary and other materials.

Printed in Canada

Highlights of the 2023 Edition

Practical Guide to Estate Planning provides plain-English explanations of the law, together with practice-tested techniques for determining the approach best-suited to each client's specific circumstances. *Practical Guide to Estate Planning* is the only single-volume publication that includes fully annotated estate planning forms applicable to the needs of your clients.

The 2023 Edition of *Practical Guide to Estate Planning* covers the legislative, regulatory and judicial developments that are of most importance to estate planners, bringing you up to date in this constantly changing area. Highlights include:

- A discussion of a Supreme Court ruling, where a corporation redeemed a deceased shareholder's interest and the Internal Revenue Service (IRS) challenged the valuation on the basis that the Shareholder Agreement failed to satisfy the requirements of IRC Section 2703 and Section 2031 in order to fix the value of the decedent's interest;

- An analysis of CCA 202152018, where the IRS considered a transaction where a donor funded a two-year grantor retained annuity trust that appeared to satisfy the qualified interest requirements under IRC Section 2702;

- An overview of the proposed regulations for the Setting Every Community Up for Retirement Enhancement Act (SECURE Act) issued by the IRS in February 2022, which, if enacted, would clarify a number of outstanding questions and also would change the manner of distribution from inherited retirement accounts under the so-called "ten-year rule;"

- Updated discussion on the medical underwriting process, with special reference to those who tested positive for COVID-19 or a COVID-19 variant;

- An examination of the task of an estate planner who must educate the client about some of the components of a comprehensive estate plan;

- Updated discussion on the durable power of attorney, noting that provisions in some of the state statutes specifically provide that third parties cannot refuse to honor a document simply because of its age;

- Revised long-term care insurance deductibility limits for various age groups;

- Inflation adjustments resulting in revised rates of various federal estate and gift tax and exemption amounts;

- Updated unified credit exemption table;

- Updated forms; and

- Updated examples throughout.

About the Authors

Ray D. Madoff is a professor at Boston College Law School specializing in the areas of trusts and estates and estate planning. Prior to entering teaching, Professor Madoff practiced law in New York and Boston. She received her B.A. with honors from Brown University and her J.D. and LL.M. in Taxation from New York University School of Law. Professor Madoff has been a frequent lecturer on issues of tax and estate planning and is the author of numerous publications, including *Immortality and the Law: The Rising Power of the American Dead* (Yale 2010). Professor Madoff is an Academic Fellow of the American College of Trust and Estate Counsel, a member of the American Law Institute and past Chair of the Trusts and Estates Section of the American Association of Law Schools.

Cornelia R. Tenney is an attorney in the estate planning and nonprofit groups at Hemenway and Barnes in Boston, Massachusetts. She received a B.A. with honors and an M.L.S. from the University of Wisconsin-Madison, an M.A. from the University of Pennsylvania, a J.D. *magna cum laude* from Harvard Law School, and an LL.M. in taxation from Boston University. She served as a clerk to Justice Ruth Abrams at the Massachusetts Supreme Judicial Court. Her practice is focused on sophisticated estate tax planning, planning for business interests, and charitable organizations, and she has written and lectured frequently on these topics.

Martin A. Hall has been with the law firm of Ropes & Gray LLP, in Boston, Massachusetts, since 1986 and has been a partner since 1994. He is the current chair of the firm's Private Client Group. Martin graduated with an M.A. in law, first class honors (1981) from Cambridge University, England and earned a J.D., *summa cum laude* (1986) from Boston University School of Law. Martin is the co-author with Carolyn M. Osteen, also of Ropes & Gray, of the *Harvard Manual on Tax Aspects of Charitable Giving* (8th ed. 1999). Martin is a Fellow of the American College of Trust and Estate Counsel, and the current Chair of the Estate and Gift Tax Committee of the Tax Section of the American Bar Association.

Lisa Nalchajian Mingolla is a partner in the Trusts & Estates and Tax Departments at Sullivan & Worcester LLP in Boston, Massachusetts. Ms. Mingolla received her B.S.E., *magna cum laude*, from Princeton University, her J.D. from Boston College Law School, and her LL.M. in Taxation from Boston University School of Law. She is a member of the Estate Planning Committee of the Boston Bar Association and the Boston Probate and Estate Planning Forum.

Contributing Authors

Sarah M. Waelchli, Chapter 3: Basic Estate Planning Documents, Chapter 7: Issues in Planning for Children, and Chapter 8: Using Gifts in Estate Planning. Sarah Waelchli is a partner at the Boston firm of Hemenway & Barnes LLP, where she focuses on estate planning, probate, and trust administration. She works with families and individuals to develop and implement sophisticated plans tailored to the clients' personal and financial goals. She is a member of the American Bar Association, Massachusetts Bar Association, and Boston Bar Association (where she is a past Co-Chair of the Trusts & Estates Tax Law Updates Committee and CLE Committee). Ms. Waelchli graduated *cum laude* from Boston University School of Law and *summa cum laude* from Winona State University.

Georgiana J. Slade, Chapter 9: Generation-Skipping Transfer Tax Planning. Georgiana Slade is a partner in the Trusts & Estates Department of Milbank, LLP. Ms. Slade is the author or co-author of numerous publications on estate planning and estate administration, including the BNA Tax Management portfolios on *Personal Life Insurance Trusts* and *Partial Interests-GRATs, GRUTs QPRTs (Section 2702)*. Ms. Slade received her B.A. *summa cum laude* from Duke University, from which she graduated Phi Beta Kappa, and her J.D. from Harvard Law School. She is a member of the New York State Bar Association where she serves as Co-Chair of the Trusts and Estates Section's Tax Committee, a Fellow of the American College of Trust and Estate Counsel, and a member of the American Bar Association. She is also a member of the Duke University Estate Planning Council.

Nancy E. Dempze, Chapter 10: Charitable Giving. Nancy Dempze is a partner in the trusts and estates group of Hemenway & Barnes, LLC in Boston, Massachusetts. Her practice focuses on wealth transfer planning, charitable giving and trust and estate administration. Ms. Dempze is the author of Chapter 9, Powers and Duties of the Personal Representative, in the MCLE publication Massachusetts Probate Manual and the author of Chapter 10, Taxation Law and Conservation Gifts, in the MCLE publication *Massachusetts Environmental Law*. Ms. Dempze is a Fellow of the American College of Trust and Estate Counsel, and serves on its Massachusetts Committee, and is a past Co-Chair of the Boston Bar Association Trusts and Estates Section. Ms. Dempze is a Trustee of the Museum of Science, Boston where she serves on the Finance and Advancement Committees and Chairs the Washburn Society. She has served as President and Vice President of the Westwood Land Trust for many years, is an Honorary Trustee of Old Sturbridge Village, and Chairs the Board of Manomet, Inc.. Ms. Dempze graduated from the University of Wisconsin, *magna cum laude*, and from Boston University School of Law, *cum laude*, where she was an editor of the Boston University Law Review.

Robert P. Goldman, Chapter 10: Charitable Giving. Robert Goldman is an attorney in the trusts and estates group and a director of the law firm of Goulston & Storrs, P.C. in Boston, Massachusetts. Mr. Goldman is also general counsel of Philanthropic

Advisors, an affiliate of Goulston & Storrs that serves clients as their family foundation office, and he regularly advises family members on their fiduciary duties as foundation trustees and on best practices of grant making. His background in nonprofit organizations includes founding several successful public charities and serving as counsel to planned giving departments of national and international organizations. Mr. Goldman is a Fellow of the American College of Trust and Estate Counsel and a past chairperson of the Trusts and Estates Section of the Boston Bar Association, and a frequent lecturer on estate planning and charitable planning topics. He received his undergraduate degree from Dartmouth College and his law degree from New York University School of Law.

David Scott Sloan, Chapter 11: Planning for a Closely Held Business Interest. David Scott Sloan is a partner at Holland & Knight, where he is the Co-Chair of the firm's Global Private Wealth Services Practice Group. Mr. Sloan serves as general counsel to wealthy individuals and families as well as their businesses. High-net-worth individuals, particularly owners of substantial closely-held businesses, principals of private equity, venture capital and hedge fund firms, executives of public companies, and entrepreneurs, regularly turn to Mr. Sloan for advice in all aspects of succession planning, tax-efficient business structuring and wealth transfer.

Mr. Sloan would also like to acknowledge Brent Berselli who worked with him on this project:

> **R. Brent Berselli,** is a partner in Holland & Knight's Portland office and is a member of the firm's Private Wealth Services Practice Group. He often serves as outside general counsel for private companies and their owners, representing clients in an array of business, tax, business succession and estate planning matters, including business reorganizations, acquisitions and divestitures.

Tobe Gerard, Chapter 12: Insurance, Section 12.08: Long-Term Care Insurance. Tobe Lynn Gerard is the President of Tobe Gerard Insurance, LLC, an independent insurance agency specializing exclusively in long term care insurance (LTCi). Ms. Gerard has been in the insurance industry for more than 40 years and has specialized in LTCi for the last 20 years. She holds the CLTC (Certified in Long Term Care) designation. Ms. Gerard has been a national educator on the topic of LTCi, and an active champion of smart insurance reform on both the state and national levels. She has served as a Board member of the Massachusetts Association of Health Underwriters (MassAHU). As the chairperson of their LTCi Committee, Ms. Gerard lobbied energetically for LTCi rate stabilization in Massachusetts. Ms. Gerard also served on the LTC Advisory Committee for the National Association of Health Underwriters (NAHU). Ms. Gerard holds MLS and MBA degrees.

Stuart J. Hamilton, Chapter 13: Estate Planning with Retirement Benefits. Stuart J. Hamilton is the founder of Hamilton Law Office, P.C. in Sudbury, Massachusetts. Mr. Hamilton is a Phi Beta Kappa graduate of Hamilton College and a *magna cum laude* graduate of Boston College Law School, where he was an articles editor for the Boston College Law Review. Mr. Hamilton also holds an MBA from The Amos Tuck School of Business Administration at Dartmouth College. After clerking for the Hon. Justice Roderick Ireland of the Massachusetts Supreme Judicial Court, Mr. Hamilton joined the firm of Hill & Barlow, P.C. in Boston and also practiced at Ropes & Gray LLP in Boston. Mr. Hamilton is an adjunct faculty member of Boston College Law School. Mr. Hamilton gratefully acknowledges the contributions of Barbara Freedman Wand of Day Pitney LLP in Boston to prior versions of Chapter 13.

Acknowledgments

This project would not have been possible without the support of Boston College Law School, including intellectual and moral support from outstanding colleagues and students as well as generous contributions from alumni and alumnae to the Law School Fund. Finally, and most importantly, I have received endless support from my family: my husband, David Nicholas; my children, Gabriel, Jesse, and Amelia Nicholas. It is to them, and in memory of my parents, Janice Madoff and Dr. Irving Madoff, that I dedicate this book.

—Ray D. Madoff

The love and encouragement of Paul, Marion, and Reba have been invaluable to me.

—Cornelia R. Tenney

The documents incorporate the work product of many generations of Ropes & Gray lawyers to whom I am greatly indebted.

—Martin Hall

Thank you to John Emery (in memoriam), Tim Murray, Sue Betro and Steve Cunningham at Sullivan & Worcester, LLP, and to Willard and Lynne Nalchajian, Joe, Alex and Lindsay.

—Lisa Nalchajian Mingolla

Preface

This book is designed for the everyday use of individuals whose work requires an understanding of any aspect of estate planning. In writing the book, we made the text easily accessible to those with little background in estate planning who want to gain a more complete understanding of the tools of the estate planner while still addressing issues of concern to the more experienced estate planner. It was our feeling that although there are a number of excellent reference materials that provide detailed technical information, many of these assume a level of expertise that not all individuals involved in the estate planning process possess. We also felt that a clear, concise explanation of terms, concepts, and techniques would be a valuable resource to the sophisticated estate planner who often needs to provide explanations to clients in terms that a lay person can understand. Finally, a unique feature of this book that will be particularly valuable to estate planners at all levels of experience is the set of comprehensive annotations accompanying the form documents.

We had three goals in writing this book:

1. To de-mystify estate planning by providing an overview of estate planning principles with clear explanations of terms and concepts to serve as a guide to the forest as well as the trees;

2. To provide a clear sense of the range of available planning tools, from the simple to the sophisticated, together with guidance as to the specific circumstances in which they may be appropriate; and

3. To provide high-quality well-annotated forms that link the explanatory text to estate planning practice by illustrating exactly why specific provisions are used, which provisions are necessary, and what alternatives may exist.

The first section of the book (Chapters 1-4) provides an overview of estate planning: the estate planning process, how property passes upon death (including the different rules applicable to probate and nonprobate property), a description of the basic estate planning documents, and the role of trust in estate planning. These chapters apply to all estate plans regardless of whether tax planning is involved.

The second section in the book (Chapters 5-8) focuses on the tax principles involved in estate planning, as well as a description of how basic estate plans are structured to take advantage of tax saving opportunities. Chapter 5 outlines basic tax principles (including the changes brought about by the American Taxpayer Relief Act of 2012) and Chapters 6 and 7 provide more detailed explanation of the application of these rules in providing for the most common beneficiaries: spouses and nonmarital partners and children. Chapter 8 explains the advantages and varieties of techniques for making gifts.

The third section of the book (Chapters 9-14) addresses some of the more specialized topics in estate planning. Chapter 9 provides an overview of the complex principles of the generation-skipping transfer tax, an explanation of the specifics of its application, and a description of the various tax planning techniques available for minimizing this tax. Charitable planning, including the use of private foundations and split interest trusts, is covered in Chapter 10. Chapter 11 addresses issues of particular concern to the business owner and Chapter 12 provides a description of the various types of life insurance and its uses in estate planning. The increasingly important topic of retirement benefits is the subject of Chapter 13 which describes the various types of retirement benefits, explains the special rules for withdrawals, and discusses the problems and opportunities involved in passing on retirement benefits at death. Finally, Chapter 14 provides an explanation of the estate planning opportunities that are available after a person has died, which will be of special interest to individuals serving as executors and trustees.

The final section of this book is a set of estate planning forms with comprehensive annotations. The forms include a simple will and a codicil for changing a provision of the will that might be suitable for a client with a small estate or a client who did not need estate tax planning. The book also includes forms for a pour-over will and a living trust that can be used to reduce estate taxes, to provide for lifetime management of assets, and to hold assets in trust for a surviving spouse and children. The book also includes two forms of trusts that are particularly suitable for holding assets given to children or grandchildren (a minor's trust and a Crummey trust), a trust designed to hold life insurance, a charitable remainder trust, a qualified personal residence trust (QPRT) and a grantor retained annuity trust (GRAT). Finally, the book includes various forms that are useful for almost every client, including a durable power of attorney, a health care proxy, and a living will.

Whenever possible, we have included alternative drafting options in the forms in order to make them as flexible as possible. We hope that the extensive annotations accompanying each form will prove valuable in two respects. First, the annotations can be used as a tool in making choices as to how documents for a specific client should be drafted. Second, the annotations can serve as a quick reference to explain why particular provisions (including many often viewed as "boilerplate") are included in wills and trusts, and how those provisions work.

These forms do not take into account local law or the specific needs of any individual client. They should, therefore, not be used without the assistance of competent counsel. Neither the authors nor the publisher make any representation regarding the legal sufficiency or suitability of these forms for any particular person.

Ray D. Madoff
Cornelia R. Tenney
Martin A. Hall
Lisa N. Mingolla

July 2022

Contents

SUPPLEMENTAL MATERIAL

The supplemental material for Wolters Kluwer's 2023 *Practical Guide to Estate Planning* is provided at ***download.cchcpelink.com/PGEP2023.zip***

Chapter 14   POST-MORTEM ESTATE PLANNING

FORMS

1

The Estate Planning Process

---

§1.01 EDUCATING THE CLIENT REGARDING THE IMPORTANCE OF AN ESTATE PLAN

The majority of Americans die without any estate planning. The reasons for this are as varied as the individuals. For some, it is a result of a natural reluctance to contemplate and plan for their own deaths. For others, it is a belief that they do not have sufficient assets to warrant the time and expense of planning. Nonetheless, underlying most individuals' failure to plan their estates is the frequently misguided belief that the law will take care of things in a satisfactory manner. For example, most people assume that the law will provide a satisfactory plan of distribution for their property—even if they do not know precisely what that plan is. In relying on the law to take care of their estate planning needs, people usually underestimate the range of issues addressed by estate planning. Therefore, the first task of an estate planner is to educate the client about some of the components of a comprehensive estate plan. These include:

- A plan for the disposition of assets in a tax advantaged manner;
- A durable power of attorney to manage a client's finances without the expense and publicity of a guardianship hearing;
- A revocable trust to avoid probate, provide a unified plan of disposition for probate and nonprobate property and/or provide for management of a client's finances in the event of incapacity;
- Naming guardians to raise minor children;
- Naming fiduciaries to handle minors' assets;
- Directions regarding health care or the naming of an agent to make health care decisions in the event that the client cannot make those decisions herself and completing HIPAA release documents to enable the health care proxy and/or other individuals to receive health information;
- A plan for the succession or sale of a family business;
- A plan for charitable giving; and
- Planning for life insurance to support a family or provide liquidity for the estate.

§1.02 OBTAINING INFORMATION FOR AN ESTATE PLAN

[A] In General

The single most important factor in determining the likelihood of a successful estate plan is the level of information that the estate planner has regarding the client's property and dispositive plan. Many seemingly excellent estate plans have in reality been completely ineffectual due to the fact that the estate planner was missing some important piece of information. An estate planner can set an effective plan in place only if she has adequate information about the client's family, assets, and goals.

The amount of information that an estate planner needs to create a comprehensive estate plan covers a wide range of topics. An estate planner needs to obtain personal information about the client, including identifying members of his family and any other individuals who he may want to benefit, the client's relationships with these individuals, and any special needs that they may have. The estate planner should also get a complete picture of the client's financial situation: what property he currently owns and how title to that property is held, what property he expects to acquire in the future (by inheritance or otherwise), what liabilities the client currently has, and what financial needs the client anticipates in the future. Finally, the estate planner needs to understand how the client wants his property to be distributed upon his death, his choice of guardian for any minor children, and his choice of an individual to handle his property and make health care decisions for him in the event of disability. Most estate planners establish a system for collecting this information that includes both a written questionnaire for the client to fill out and a personal interview.

[B] Information That Needs to Be Collected: The "Who," "What," and "Where" of Estate Planning

All of the information that an estate planner needs to collect from a client can be summarized by three questions: "who?", "what?", and "where?"[1] "Who" refers to the personal information about the client and the other important people in the client's life, "what" refers to the property owned by the client, and "where" refers to the client's wishes about the disposition of his property in the future.

[1] Information About the Client

In gathering information about a person, the first thing the estate planner needs to learn is who this person is. Some of the facts that need to be collected are very mundane, but should nonetheless be collected at the beginning of the enterprise so that the estate planner has all of the information in one place. Other information that should be gathered is very sensitive and the estate planner needs to be tactful in making inquiries. Although the client may sometimes be reluctant to disclose his most personal information to the estate planner, such information may be useful in crafting a plan that accomplishes the client's goals. For example, if the estate planner knows that the client's children from his first marriage do not get along well with the client's second spouse, the planner will be better equipped to structure a plan that is less likely to produce disputes after the client's death.

The initial information that needs to be obtained is basic facts about the client. The following information should be obtained:

- The client's name (including any other names that he has gone by, either currently or in the past);
- Date of birth;

---

[1] **§1.02** Another way of thinking of this is in terms of the standards of mental competency for writing a will. The specific requirements are that the testator knows: (1) the persons who are the natural objects of the testator's bounty; (2) the nature and extent of his property; (3) the disposition that the testator is making; and (4) how these elements relate so as to form an orderly plan for the disposition of the testator's property. The requirements for writing a will are discussed in Chapter 3.

- Address and phone number;
- Social Security number;
- Occupation and, if the client works outside of the home, the client's business address and phone number;
- The citizenship of the client (and of the client's spouse, if the clients married); and
- The state of primary residence (if the client maintains more than one home, it is important for the estate planner to determine the state of domicile as that can determine where probate will occur as well as to which state taxing authorities the client is subject).

While gathering information about the client's home, it should also be determined whether the client has ever lived or owned real estate as a married person in any of the following community property states: Arizona, California, Idaho, Louisiana, Nevada, New Mexico, Texas, Washington, or Wisconsin (Wisconsin, while not technically a community property state, is functionally equivalent through its adoption of the Uniform Marital Property Act). Married individuals have special rights to community property, even if the individuals no longer live in a community property state, and as such it is important for the estate planner to be aware of such property in order to adequately plan the client's estate. There are also income tax advantages of community property, and these advantages can be lost if an estate planner fails to identify and preserve the identity of community property.[2]

The estate planner should also gather information about the general state of the client's health as this can have a significant impact on the planning of an estate.

[2] Information About Other People

There are two categories of people that the estate planner must learn about: those people whom the law presumes that the client wants to benefit (called the *heirs at law*) and those people whom the client actually wants to benefit. For many clients these two groups will be coextensive, but this is not always the case.

[a] Heirs at Law

Heirs at law are the people who would inherit the client's property in the event that he were to die without a will (called *intestate*).[3] It is important to determine who the heirs at law are, even for people who are not subject to the laws of intestacy, because the heirs at law (1) must be notified of the probate process and (2) will have standing to challenge the client's will.

The extent of the information that an estate planner must collect in this area depends upon the nature of the relatives. For example, if the client has children and/or grandchildren, then only the spouse and children (or grandchildren) will be heirs

---

[2] Community property is discussed in greater detail in Chapter 5.
[3] The law of intestacy is discussed in greater detail in Chapter 2.

at law. In this situation, absent special circumstances, the estate planner will generally not need to collect too much information about other collateral relatives. It is important to note, however, that a child need not be the product of a marriage in order to be considered an heir at law (and therefore have standing to challenge a will).[4] Since many states permit paternity to be established after death,[5] it is important that the estate planner know about *all* of the client's children, even those with whom he may not have an established relationship, so that he can plan accordingly.

In other situations, the client may not have any close blood relatives. If this is the case, the estate planner will need to pay close attention to identifying who the closest blood relatives are in order to be able to notify these future heirs at law and ward off fraudulent claims.

In gathering information about the client's relatives, it is helpful to prepare a family tree. It will often be sufficient to start with the client's parents and then establish all descendants of these parents (both living and dead), noting for each the person's name, age, address, and marital status. In the rare situation where the client has no living relative identified through this exercise, it will be necessary to go up to the client's grandparents and then establish all of the descendants of these ancestors.

The preparation of the family tree can be done either by the client alone or with the help of the estate planner. Although it may initially appear more efficient to have the client prepare the family tree on his own, there is a distinct advantage to the estate planner getting involved with this process. While collecting these family facts, the estate planner will have the opportunity to gather important information of a more personal nature. In particular, for each child the estate planner should note whether there are any disabilities or other special needs, problem marriages, creditor issues, or a problematic relationship with parents. It is also helpful to determine whose judgment the client feels most comfortable with for purposes of determining future fiduciaries for the client's estate plan. Knowledge of these matters will increase the likelihood of creating a plan that will not cause problems in the future that could have been avoided.

If the client is married, then in most cases it will be necessary for the estate planner to obtain extensive information about the client's spouse. Thus, all of the information that is obtained about the client (family members and property interests) should also be obtained about the client's spouse.

If the client was previously married and the marriage ended in divorce, then the estate planner should obtain copies of any divorce decrees or settlement agreements since they may impose other obligations regarding the disposition of the client's property upon death.

---

[4] Although children who have been put up for adoption will generally have all legal ties severed with the biological parent.

[5] *See* Alexander v. Alexander, 42 Ohio Misc. 2d 30, 537 N.E.2d 1310 (1988), in which the court allowed the exhumation of a body in order to establish paternity for purposes of determining who was entitled to take under intestacy.

[b] Other Beneficiaries

For many clients, it will be sufficient for the estate planner to gather information about the client's spouse and blood relatives. However, in a significant number of cases other people will be desired beneficiaries for the client's estate plan. These people may include:

- *Nonmarital Partners.* A client may be unmarried but nonetheless be in a committed relationship. If this is the case, it is important for the estate planner to gather additional information about this person and the client's intentions. If the client has plans to marry in the future, then that needs to be factored into the estate plan since a marriage can result in the complete or partial revocation of a premarital will by operation of law. If the client is unmarried, but in a committed relationship, then the estate planner may need to take this into account in order to prepare a plan that meets the client's needs. Although many of the traditional estate planning techniques for spouses are not available to unmarried couples, there are other available planning techniques and special issues to consider in planning for the nonmarital partner.[6]
- *Stepchildren.* Stepchildren are not provided for under most intestacy statutes. This makes sense in light of the fact that the relationship between a stepparent and a stepchild can vary dramatically from family to family. In some situations, typically when a parent with custody of the children remarries while the children are young, the relationship between stepparent and child is closely akin to any other parent-child relationship. In other situations, typically when a parent remarries after the children are grown up, the relationship between stepparent and stepchild can be very distant. If the client has stepchildren, it is important for the estate planner to determine the nature of the relationship, and the extent to which the client wants to benefit the stepchild.
- *Charitable Organizations.* Some clients have very close ties to particular charitable organizations. It may be a school that they or a member of their family attended, a religious organization, or an organization directed toward a particular cause or the curing of a disease. Whatever the organization, it is important for the estate planner to learn of any possible charitable intentions on the part of her client in order to provide information to the client about the tax advantages associated with charitable giving.[7]

[3] Information About the Client's Property

After learning who the client is, the next most important information to determine is what property the client owns. For each property interest that the client owns, the estate planner should establish what the property interest is, its value, and how

---

[6] *See* Chapter 6 for a detailed discussion of issues to consider in planning for a nonmarital partner.

[7] *See* Chapter 10 for issues to consider in charitable planning.

title to the interest is held. In collecting this information, it is important to realize that the client's understanding of his property interest may not always be accurate. Sometimes the inaccuracy may be related to the property's value, other times it may be related to the form of ownership (e.g., whether the property is owned outright, in trust, or in joint tenancy). Because of this possibility of error, whenever feasible, the estate planner should obtain copies of deeds and other records of ownership as well as any appraisals that have been done to confirm the client's understanding. Some of the documents that the estate planner should see in collecting information about the client's assets include real estate deeds, stock certificates, life insurance policies, mortgages, partnership agreements, buy-sell agreements, premarital agreements, retirement plans (including beneficiary designations), and property settlement agreements.

Property interests come in many forms and it is important to go over each category with the client to ensure that the client has accounted for all interests that he owns. Some of the most commonly held property interests include: real estate; investment interests, such as stocks, bonds, mutual funds, partnership interests, bank accounts, certificates of deposit; retirement benefits, including IRAs; insurance policies; automobiles and miscellaneous household property. In addition, some people will have significant tangible personal property, such as art work, valuable rugs, stamp or coin collections, or any myriad tangible property that people collect. Intangible interests must also be accounted for. Included in this category are powers of appointment, beneficial interests in trusts, accounts receivable, and other creditor claims.

For any real estate the client owns the estate planner should review the deed and determine in what state the property is located (since real estate is subject to probate in the state in which it is located), the amount of any mortgages to which the property is subject, the property's value, and the basis upon which the valuation has been made.

Life insurance policies should be reviewed to determine the owner of the policy, the named beneficiary, the face amount and the cash value (if any), as well as the name of the company issuing the policy. This is an area where the estate planner should be particularly wary of relying on a client's memory as many people confuse the beneficiary of the policy with the owner of the policy.[8]

If the client owns a business interest, then the estate planner must obtain a clear picture of the nature of the business, the client's interest therein and, if appropriate, plans for succession of the business. The specific information that needs to be collected will depend upon the nature of the business. If the business is a closely held corporation, then it may be appropriate to review the articles of incorporation, by laws, and shareholder agreements. If the business is a partnership, then a copy of the partnership agreement may be useful. In any event, the estate planner should get a copy of any applicable buy-sell agreement or other agreements entered into by the owners of the business.[9]

---

[8] *See* Chapter 12 for issues involving life insurance.

[9] *See* Chapter 11 for issues to consider in planning for a closely held business interest.

Finally, the estate planner should look to other property interests that, although not directly owned by the client, could nonetheless ultimately affect his estate plan. In particular, the estate planner should determine the value of any custodial interests or beneficial interests in trust for the client's children as well as the likelihood of future inheritances.

In reviewing the client's assets, the estate planner should always keep in mind the following questions for planning purposes:

- Is the property likely to become of sufficient value to warrant tax planning for either state or federal estate taxes?
- Is the property difficult to value?
- Is the value appreciating or depreciating?
- Does the property have sentimental value?
- Is the property relatively liquid or illiquid?

Finally, in order to complete the financial picture, the estate planner should get a sense of any liabilities that the client may have. Most typically these will be in the form of mortgages on real estate, automobile loans, and education loans. However, some clients may have personal loans or guarantees associated with their businesses.

[4] How the Client Wants His Property Distributed

The final step in gathering information from the client is in determining how the client wants his property distributed. In considering this question, it is important for the estate planner to understand both the amount that should be given to the beneficiary and the way it should be held (i.e., whether it should be distributed outright or in trust).

If the client is married or in a committed relationship, the first question to consider is the amount that the client wants to provide for his spouse or partner. A typical plan of disposition for smaller estates is for everything to go to the surviving spouse or partner. This is particularly the case when there are children of the union and neither spouse has children from outside the union. If the client is married, but has children from outside of the marriage, then special care may need to be taken to equitably provide for the spouse and children from outside the marriage.[10]

It should be noted that state law generally prohibits the complete disinheritance of a spouse. In community property states, the surviving spouse is entitled to her share of community property and in separate property states the surviving spouse is entitled to a minimum statutory share, called the elective share.[11] An estate planner should be mindful about how these rules apply to his or her client before preparing an estate plan.

---

[10] *See* Chapter 6 for a detailed discussion of issues to consider in planning for a spouse.

[11] *See* Chapter 6 for a discussion of community property and elective share laws.

[C] Collecting the Information

There are a variety of methods through which an estate planner can gather the information necessary to begin the estate planning process. The method chosen will depend in part upon the style of the planner as well as the personality of the particular client.

Since a wide variety of information must be collected from each client, many estate planners use a checklist to ensure that all relevant information has been obtained.

Some estate planners send clients a questionnaire to fill out prior to their first meeting. The advantage of this is that the client is informed as to what information he will need to provide and can have the time to gather and check bank statements, life insurance policies, deeds, and other relevant documents. This approach will work well with the client who is an organized do-it-yourselfer, since that person is likely to be able to gather the information without too much difficulty and will be more comfortable being actively engaged in the process. For this type of person, filling out a questionnaire in advance can provide the added advantage of keeping costs down by promoting an efficient exchange of information at the meeting.

Not all clients, however, react positively to a written request for information. If the client is approaching the estate planning process with reluctance (as many people do), the need to fill out complex questionnaires prior to meeting with an estate planner can provide just enough disincentive for him to abandon the project altogether. Also, the questionnaire will necessarily cover some questions that are not applicable to a particular client. The effect of this can be confusing and off-putting to the client. For this reason, most estate planners use some combination of written request and personal interview. Sending out a questionnaire merely gives the client the opportunity (but not the obligation) to collect material prior to the meeting.

2

Basic Rules of Property Transfers upon Death

---

§2.01 INTRODUCTION

There is a common misconception that a will provides for the disposition of all of a person's property upon death. In fact, for many people only a very small percentage of their property will pass by the terms of their will; instead, most of their property will pass outside of a will through nonprobate transfers, such as joint tenancies, retirement accounts with payable-on-death designations, and life insurance contracts. This chapter outlines the basic rules governing the way property is transferred upon death, and the implications for each method of transfer.

The way property is transferred upon death is dependent on whether the property is characterized as nonprobate property or probate property. Nonprobate property passes directly to the designated beneficiary. Probate property passes by will or, if there is no will, by the laws of intestacy.

Nonprobate property (also called "will substitutes") is a catchall category used to denote the variety of interests for which the law recognizes death beneficiary designations. There are many different kinds of nonprobate property, including life insurance, joint tenancies, beneficial interests in trusts, and retirement accounts. All other property is probate property. In general, probate property is all property directly owned by the person for which there is no legally recognized death beneficiary designation.

§2.02 IMPORTANCE OF UNDERSTANDING THE DISTINCTION BETWEEN PROBATE AND NONPROBATE PROPERTY

It is essential for an estate planner to understand the distinction between probate and nonprobate property in order to plan for the disposition of a person's property. Since nonprobate property provides for its own beneficiary designation, it does not pass under the terms of the will. Any attempt to transfer nonprobate property by will is void. An estate planner must be cognizant of this distinction, as failure to do so can result in unexpected disposition of a client's property as well as the failure of any tax planning that may have occurred.

[A] Unexpected Distribution of Assets

The most likely problem to be caused by failing to recognize the distinction between probate and nonprobate property is that a person will think that she is providing for the disposition of all of her property when she prepares a will, when in fact much of her property is going to be transferred at death without regard to the terms of her will.

EXAMPLE 2-1

Mother would like for her property to be distributed half to her husband and half to her son from a prior marriage. A will is prepared that provides that after payment of expenses, half of the property is to be paid to Husband and half is to be paid to Son.

Mother owns a house in joint tenancy with Husband, a joint bank account with Husband, and has a retirement account that names Husband as beneficiary, and personal property worth a nominal amount. Upon Mother's death, Son will only get half of Mother's personal property. Everything else—the house, bank account, and retirement account—will pass to Husband outside of the probate process.

[B] Failure of Tax Plan

The other significant risk that can arise from failing to recognize the distinction between probate and nonprobate property is that a person can have a perfectly constructed plan to minimize the estate tax that fails to take effect because there are insufficient assets passing through the probate estate.

EXAMPLE 2-2

Husband and Wife have an estate plan that provides for maximum federal and state estate tax savings by providing that, upon death, each spouse will transfer property having a value equal to the amount of the unified credit exemption equivalent to a credit shelter trust, and the remainder passes to the surviving spouse.[1]

Husband and Wife own real estate held in joint tenancy, joint bank accounts, retirement accounts, and life insurance policies that name each other as beneficiaries. When the first spouse dies all of the property will pass to the surviving spouse outside of the probate process. Since no property was available to fund the decedent's credit shelter trust, none of his or her unified credit exclusion amount will be used by the decedent spouse's estate.[2]

[C] Distinction Does Not Usually Affect Taxability of Transfer

Although the distinction between probate and nonprobate assets is of critical importance in determining how property is distributed upon death, the distinction does not usually affect the federal estate and gift tax liability associated with the transfer.

Federal taxes use the concept of gross estate to determine what interests are subject to tax. The concept of gross estate is a broad one that encompasses all interests

---

[1] § 2.02 This planning is discussed generally in Chapter 5 (Tax Tools of the Estate Planner) and in greater detail in Chapter 6 (Planning for a Spouse or Nonmarital Partner).

[2] While portability may ameliorate the situation for federal estate tax purposes, it is generally not available for state estate tax purposes.

for which the decedent controlled the disposition. Thus, most nonprobate property will be included within the concept of gross estate for purposes of calculating the decedent's tax liability.

EXAMPLE 2-3

Decedent's property consists of a house owned jointly with her son for which she provided the down payment and all mortgage payments, a joint bank account with her daughter for which she provided the money, a retirement account that names her son and daughter as beneficiaries, a life insurance policy that names her daughter as beneficiary, and a revocable trust for the benefit of her son and daughter. Upon decedent's death, the house, bank account, retirement account, life insurance policy, and revocable trust will all be included in the decedent's gross estate for purposes of calculating her federal estate tax liability, even though none of the property will be subject to the probate process.

[D] Distinction May Affect Creditors' Access to Assets

Although the distinction between probate and nonprobate assets usually has little effect on whether the property interest is subject to estate taxes, it may have a greater effect on whether the decedent's creditors can reach the assets to pay claims of the decedent. Thus, in advising a client regarding shifting assets between probate and nonprobate property, the estate planner should keep in mind the greater creditor protection often afforded to nonprobate assets.

The probate process provides a procedure for the payment of claims of a decedent and all probate assets are subject to claims of the decedent's creditors. The law regarding creditors' rights to nonprobate property is considerably more fragmented and complex.

The general rule is that nonprobate property is not subject to the claims of creditors. For example, assets held in joint tenancy are normally not subject to the creditors of the first joint tenant to die unless the surviving joint tenant had also assumed liability on the debt or unless the transfer into joint tenancy was done in fraud of creditors. In addition, if life insurance is payable to a named beneficiary other than the decedent's estate or executor, then state law frequently limits creditors' rights to those proceeds. However, each jurisdiction has its own panoply of statutory exceptions to this rule and courts have taken divergent approaches to interpreting these exceptions. Thus, in the absence of an applicable statute directly on point, it is often unclear to what extent a decedent's creditors may reach particular nonprobate assets. In any event, nonprobate assets are almost always more protected than probate assets since most states provide that nonprobate assets are only subject to creditor claims to the extent that the probate estate has insufficient assets to pay creditor claims.

§2.03 PROBATE PROPERTY

[A] What Is Probate Property?

Probate property is all property directly owned for which there is no legally recognized death beneficiary designation. Some examples of probate property typically owned include: real estate (owned outright or by tenancy in common); bank accounts (other than those that are held in joint tenancy or with a payable-on-death designation); interests in partnerships, corporations, or limited liability companies; and tangible personal property, such as automobiles.

[B] How Probate Property Passes upon Death

There are two ways in which probate property can pass upon death: by the laws of intestacy or by the terms of a validly executed will.

[1] Intestacy

[a] Defined

If a person dies without a will, then all of his probate property (i.e., all property for which there is no legally recognized death beneficiary designation) passes by the laws of *intestacy*. Intestacy is the statutorily created system for disposing of probate property at death that is not disposed of by will. In addition, intestacy provisions can sometimes apply even when the decedent had a will. If the will did not provide for the disposition of all of the decedent's property, then the property not so disposed is governed by the intestacy provisions. (A person who has died without a will is referred to as having died *intestate*.)

Each state has its own intestacy statutes (sometimes referred to as *statutes of descent and distribution*.) The decedent's domicile at the time of death determines which state intestacy statute is applicable, even if the person lived most of her life in a different state. Intestacy statutes vary in their particulars from state to state, but in general provide for property to pass to members of the decedent's family. If there are no family members, then the property passes to the state.

[b] Surviving Spouse and Issue

A typical intestacy statute provides that if the decedent is survived by a spouse and children, then a portion of his estate will go to his spouse and a portion will go to each of his children.[1] Adopted children are treated the same as biological children for

---

[1] §2.03 In some states, notably those that have adopted the Uniform Probate Code, if all of the children are products of the marriage to the spouse and if neither parent has children from outside

purposes of intestacy. However, stepchildren have no rights to inherit under most state intestacy statutes.

If any of the decedent's children have predeceased the decedent and are themselves survived by children, then all states provide that the share that the predeceased child would otherwise have taken be distributed to the children (or grandchildren) of the predeceased child. The decedent's children, grandchildren, great-grandchildren, etc., are referred to as the decedent's *issue* or *lineal descendants.*

EXAMPLE 2-4

Decedent's son, Sam, predeceased the decedent. Sam had two children, Alba and Bert, who survived the decedent. Alba and Bert will take Sam's share by representation.

All states provide that if the decedent is survived by a spouse and issue, then they will together inherit all of the decedent's property. This will cut off all other members of the decedent's family from inheriting the decedent's property. States vary in the relative portions allocated to the spouse and issue under their intestacy statutes. Under traditional intestacy statutes (still in place in many states), a spouse receives only between one-third and one-half of the decedent's probate estate, and the decedent's issue receive the rest. However, a large number of states now follow the Uniform Probate Code and provide that so long as all of the children are children of both spouses, the surviving spouse receives the decedent spouse's entire probate estate.

If the decedent is not survived by issue, then any share that does not go to a surviving spouse will be distributed to the decedent's parents and siblings. Some states prefer parents over siblings, while other states allow siblings to share the decedent's estate with the decedent's parents.

A person may be treated as a spouse for state law even if the couple is not married. This is because a number of states have adopted statutory provisions that allow two people to register their relationship with the state, creating a marriage-like relationship. Whether they are called "reciprocal beneficiaries," "civil unions" or "registered domestic partners," each of these statutory systems provides that the designated person will be treated as a spouse for purposes of the state intestacy statutes. These provisions were originally adopted as a way to allow same-sex couples, who had not been allowed to marry, to achieve some of the benefits of marriage. Now, due to the 2015 Supreme Court decision, the federal government and all state governments are required to recognize and grant all of the legal benefits of heterosexual marriages to same-sex marriages.[2] The effect of this change on these state provisions varies from state to state.

(Footnote Continued)

the marriage, then all property will pass to the surviving spouse. Unif. Probate Code § 2-102, 8 U.L.A. 274 (1998).

[2] Obergefell v. Hodges, 576 U.S. 644, 135 S. Ct. 2584 (2015).

[c] Collateral Relatives

If the decedent is not survived by any spouse, issue, parent, or siblings, then the decedent's property will be distributed to the decedent's more distant blood relatives, called *collateral relatives*. Collateral relatives are relatives who share a common ancestor with the decedent. For example, a first cousin is a collateral relative because she shares a grandparent with the decedent, whereas a brother-in-law is not a collateral relative because he does not share a common ancestor with the decedent (at least not in his role as brother-in-law).

States employ different methods to determine which collateral relatives are entitled to inherit the decedent's property. For purposes of understanding collateral relationships, it is valuable to have a consanguinity chart that depicts a family tree and the applicable designations for different blood relationships. Although most people know what a first cousin is, few people know the difference between a second cousin three times removed and a third cousin twice removed. A consanguinity chart is essential for applying the different intestacy provisions regarding collateral relatives.

There are basically two different methods for determining the hierarchy of collateral relatives for purposes of the intestacy statute: the *degree-of-relationship test* and the *parentelic test*. Under the degree-of-relationship test, the closest collateral relative is determined by counting the number of steps from the decedent up to the common ancestor and down to the collateral relative. The collateral relative connected by the fewest steps inherits the decedent's property. Under the parentelic test, the collateral relative who shares the closest common ancestor to the decedent inherits the decedent's property. Most states use the degree-of-relationship test, but many states (including those that have adopted the Uniform Probate Code) use the parentelic test and other states use a combination of these methods.

EXAMPLE 2-5

Decedent is survived by his first cousin once removed (i.e., the child of his first cousin) and his grand-aunt (i.e., the sister of his grandparent).

Under the degree-of-relationship test, decedent's property will pass to his grand-aunt since she is four degrees away from the decedent (three degrees up to their common ancestor, decedent's great-grandparent, and one degree down to decedent's grand-aunt). Decedent's first cousin once removed is five degrees away from the decedent (two degrees up to their common ancestor, decedent's grandparent, and three degrees down to decedent's first cousin once removed).

Under the parentelic test, decedent's property will pass to his first cousin once removed since their common ancestor (decedent's grandparent) is a closer relative to the decedent then the common ancestor shared by the decedent and his grand-aunt (decedent's great-grandparent).

State intestacy statutes differ as to how close a relative must be in order to be eligible to inherit. Some intestacy statutes, including those that have adopted the Uniform Probate Code, provide limitations on inheritance by remote collateral relatives by limiting inheritance to collateral relatives who are issue of the decedent's grandparents. Other states allow any blood relative, no matter how remote, to inherit the decedent's property. These relatives are often called *laughing heirs,* because it is assumed that their distant relationship makes it unlikely that they were saddened by the decedent's death.

If the decedent is not survived by a spouse or any blood relative who is eligible to inherit, then the decedent's property goes to the state.

Consanguinity Chart

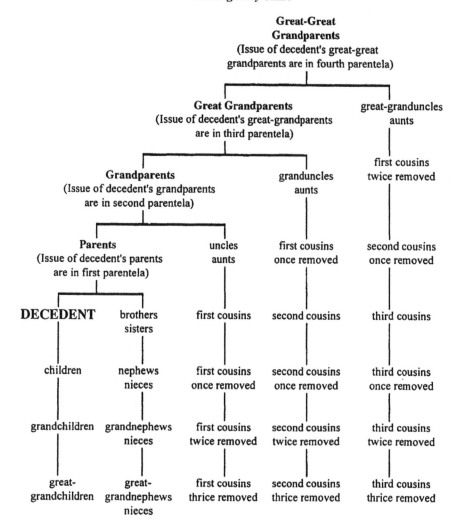

[2] **Wills**

Rather than relying on the intestacy provisions, a person may instead write a will directing the disposition of her property. In order for the will to be given effect, certain requirements must be met. The person writing the will (called a *testator*) must be at least 18 years old and have the mental capacity to write a will, and the will must be executed with the required formalities.[3]

A will may be changed or supplemented by the testator at any time prior to death, provided the testator has the prerequisite mental capacity to write in will. A document that adds or deletes a provision or otherwise changes a will is called a *codicil*.

[C] The Probate Process

Regardless of whether the decedent's property passes by the laws of intestacy or by the terms of a valid will, all probate property must go through the probate process. The probate process is a court supervised process through which a decedent's assets are collected, debts of the decedent (including estate tax liabilities) are paid, and the remaining property is distributed according to the terms of the will or the provisions of the intestacy statute. The probate process is necessary in order to legally transfer title to the appropriate beneficiaries, although some states have simplified affidavit procedures for small estates in which there is no real estate.[4]

The probate process occurs in the jurisdiction where the decedent was domiciled at the time of death, even if the decedent lived most of her life in another state. Real estate, however, must always be probated in the state in which it is located. Therefore, if the decedent owned real estate in another jurisdiction, then that property must go through a separate probate procedure called *ancillary probate*.

[1] Appointment of Personal Representative

The probate process begins with the appointment by the court of an estate representative, sometimes called the *personal representative*. The personal representative is the fiduciary responsible for overseeing the probate process. The personal representative is referred to as the *executor* if the decedent died with a will, or the *administrator* if the decedent died intestate.[5] An executor is named in the will and an administrator is appointed by the court as part of the appointment process. The personal representative must notify all interested parties of his petition for appointment. Interested parties typically include the beneficiaries of the will (if any) and the decedent's heirs at law (those who would inherit the decedent's property in the event of intestacy). Any interested party may challenge the appointment of the personal representative.

---

[3] The requirements for a valid will are discussed in Chapter 3. *See* Forms 7 and 8 for sample wills.

[4] Local rules of the applicable jurisdiction will outline any such procedure if it is available, as well as the jurisdiction's definition of small estate.

[5] Traditionally, the terms executor and administrator refer to a man, and a woman in this position is referred to as an executrix or administratrix. However, this distinction is out of favor in modern drafting, and the terms executor and administrator (or personal representative) are now used for both men and women.

[2] Marshalling Assets

Within a relatively short period of time after appointment, the personal representative must file an inventory of all of the decedent's assets with the court. This process is called *marshalling the assets.* The inventory will include all of the decedent's probate property, as well as all nonprobate property that names the decedent's estate or executor as the designated beneficiary.

The inventory should include a complete description of all assets, including, when relevant, account numbers, names and addresses of financial institutions, and legal and common descriptions of real property. In addition, the inventory should include the date-of-death value of all listed interests. Local law outlines the appropriate method for determining date-of-death values and many states require professional appraisers for particular assets.

[3] Payment of Liabilities

The personal representative is responsible for handling the estate's liabilities as well as its assets. The personal representative is also responsible for paying all valid creditor claims made against the estate. These can include routine claims, such as telephone and utility bills, as well as less usual claims, such as the settlement of lawsuits. The time period after the decedent's death in which a creditor may present claims for payment is relatively short and claims made after this time will be disallowed.

As part of the settlement of the estate's liabilities, the personal representative must also arrange for the preparation of the federal and state estate tax returns and the payment of those taxes within nine months of the decedent's death.[6]

[4] Distribution of the Estate

After all valid creditor claims have been paid, the personal representative can request permission from the court to distribute the estate. Once permission is granted, the personal representative distributes the estate according to the terms of the decedent's will or the applicable intestacy statutes. This may require the partial liquidation of estate assets in order to divide the estate or make cash disbursements.

In making the distributions, the personal representative must prepare receipts to be signed by the beneficiaries and filed with the court in order to provide documentation that the beneficiaries have in fact received the property. Until receipts for all property disposed of by the will have been filed with the court, the personal representative cannot be discharged.

---

[6] The Internal Revenue Code imposes personal liability on the personal representative for the estate taxes of the decedent. *See* IRC § 2002.

[5] Closing the Estate

Before the estate can be closed, the personal representative must prepare an accounting for presentation to the beneficiaries that details all receipts, disbursements, sales, and other changes that occurred during the period of estate administration. The accounting must be presented to the court. If the estate administration process lasts for more than one year, an accounting must be filed annually. Judicial approval of the personal representative's actions is required in order to relieve the representative from personal liability. Once the court approves all actions of the personal representative, she can be discharged from her fiduciary obligations and the estate can be closed.

[6] Disadvantages and Advantages

The probate process can be complicated and time consuming—sometimes lasting several years. During that time, much of the decedent's assets are frozen and the decedent's affairs are taken care of by a court appointed administrator. All of this oversight can make the probate process quite costly. Although the specifics of probate costs depend upon the size of the estate and vary from state to state, such costs usually include court fees, fees for a court appointed administrator, attorneys' fees, and sometimes the costs of appraisers and court appointed *guardian ad litem*. A *guardian ad litem* is a person appointed by the court to represent the interests of a minor during the course of a legal proceeding. Finally, since probate is a public process, it may expose the decedent or members of his family to unwanted publicity. The nature and amount of the decedent's probate assets, the terms of a will, as well as any will disputes are all a matter of public record. For all of these reasons, the probate process is very unpopular.

Despite the widespread unpopularity of the probate process, probate does provide some advantages that should not be overlooked. The probate process can afford greater protections to the beneficiaries by establishing a statutory period during which all creditor claims must be filed. Creditors that fail to file within that statutory period are generally barred from later bringing their claims. The probate process can also assure that the fiduciaries responsible for distributing the decedent's estate will do their job properly. People naturally like the idea of avoiding the expense of court oversight, however they sometimes forget the value that such oversight can provide in that trustees, left to their own, sometimes fail to understand the full extent of their obligations. Court oversight provided by the probate process can be helpful in facilitating the proper distribution of the decedent's estate.

§2.04 NONPROBATE PROPERTY

[A] In General

Nonprobate property is a single term used to describe the variety of property interests in which the law recognizes and gives effect to death beneficiary designations. This property bypasses the probate process and is distributed directly to the named beneficiary.

People commonly hold many different types of nonprobate property, including real estate held in joint tenancy, life insurance, retirement accounts, contracts with payable-on-death provisions, and interests in trusts.

In addition, due to the expense, delay, and publicity of probate, people frequently seek to convert their property to nonprobate assets in order to avoid the probate process. This can be accomplished by transferring property to a trust during the person's life.

Nonetheless, there is one instance in which nonprobate property passes through the probate process—when the designated beneficiary is the decedent's estate or executor of the decedent's will.[1] Sometimes this occurs by design in order to ensure that these assets pass under the terms of the decedent's estate plan as established in his will.[2] Other times, however, this is a result of the fact that the other named beneficiaries predeceased the decedent. Many nonprobate property interests, such as life insurance policies, provide that, in the event that the named beneficiaries predecease the decedent, the property passes to the decedent's estate. In this way, the probate process is used as a backstop to provide for the disposition of nonprobate assets.

[B] Types of Nonprobate Property

[1] Joint Tenancies and Tenancies by the Entirety

[a] Defined

A *joint tenancy* is a form of property ownership in which two or more people share undivided ownership of property during their lives, and, upon the death of one of the joint tenants, the ownership interest of the one who dies is extinguished, leaving outright ownership in the survivor. Because of this survivorship feature, neither joint tenant can dispose of his joint tenant interest by will. A tenancy by the entirety is a special type of joint tenancy available only to married couples.

[b] Creation of Joint Tenancy

A joint tenancy is created by two or more people taking title to property as joint tenants. In many jurisdictions, a joint tenancy must be created by a written instrument and not an oral agreement. Although many types of property can be held as joint tenants, the joint tenancy form of ownership is most commonly associated with real estate, bank accounts, investment accounts, and corporate stock.

---

[1] **§2.04** Assuming of course, that the executor is named in her capacity as executor and not in her individual capacity.

[2] In order to avoid probate for these assets, it is often preferable to establish a pour-over trust and name the trustee of the trust as the designated beneficiary in a will with a pour-over provision. Pour-over trusts are discussed in greater detail in Chapter 4. *See* Form 1 for a living trust and Form 7 for a simple will with pour-over provision.

[c] Dissolution of Joint Tenancy

A joint tenancy may always be dissolved by all of the joint tenants agreeing to dissolve the joint tenancy and replace it with a different form of ownership (e.g., as tenants in common). If one party is not willing to dissolve the joint tenancy, the other joint tenant may be able to sever the joint tenancy by unilateral action. In the case of a bank account, one joint tenant can easily destroy the joint tenancy (and gain entire ownership of the property) by withdrawing all of the money in the account. In the case of real estate, the process is a little more difficult. A joint tenant can sever the joint tenancy by conveying her joint interest to a third party, which effectively creates a tenancy in common, even if that person reconveys the interest back to the former joint tenant. A joint tenant may also bring an action for judicial partition. In a partition action, a court will either physically divide the land into separately owned parts or order the land sold and divide the proceeds among the tenants.

[d] Tenancy by the Entirety

Tenancy by the entirety is a form of joint tenancy only available to married couples. Tenancy by the entirety is similar to the usual form of joint tenancy in that both spouses have the right to undivided use of the property during life, and at death the property is owned outright by the surviving spouse. The main distinction between joint tenancy and tenancy by the entirety is that in a tenancy by the entirety neither husband nor wife has the ability to unilaterally sever joint title by transferring to a third party or by requesting a partition. In this way, tenancy by the entirety may provide greater creditor protections than joint tenancy. Another distinction is that divorce terminates the tenancy by the entirety since marriage is a requirement of this tenancy. Absent some special agreement, divorce usually results in the conversion of the tenancy by the entirety to a tenancy in common.

[e] Tenancy in Common Distinguished

A joint tenancy should not be confused with another form of property co-ownership—the *tenancy in common*. Tenancy in common is a form of co-ownership in which each co-owner has separate but undivided interest in property. There is no right of survivorship in a tenancy in common and a co-owner's ownership interest passes to her estate upon her death, not to the surviving co-owner. As such, it does not avoid probate. An interest as a tenant-in-common can be transferred by deed during life, and will pass by the terms of a will or intestacy at death.

[2] Insurance

Life insurance is another commonly held nonprobate property interest. Life insurance is a contract whereby the insurer agrees to pay a third party (called a *beneficiary*) a certain amount (called the *face amount* of the policy) in the event of the insured person's death.

Life insurance proceeds are paid directly to the beneficiary, and therefore do not pass through the probate process. An exception occurs when the decedent's estate or executor[3] is named as the beneficiary of the policy, in which case the proceeds go through the probate process and are distributed in accordance with the terms of the will or the relevant intestacy statute.[4]

[3] Qualified Retirement Accounts

Retirement accounts frequently constitute a significant portion of a decedent's estate. Retirement benefits can come in a number of forms—Individual Retirement Accounts (IRAs), pension plans, profit sharing plans, stock bonus plans, Keogh plans, simplified employment plans (SEPs), tax sheltered annuity and mutual fund arrangements under Sections 403(b), and 401(k) plans are all forms of qualified retirement benefits. Common to these forms is the fact that qualified retirement benefits provide for death beneficiary designations. Thus, unless the participant fails to designate a beneficiary, or unless the participant's estate or executor is designated as the death beneficiary, the plan will pass outside of the probate process.[5]

[4] Totten Trusts

A *Totten trust,* also known as a *savings account trust* or a *poor man's will,* is not a trust at all. Rather, a Totten trust is the name given to a special type of savings account in which the depositor opens an account with his name designated "as trustee for" someone else. In a Totten trust, the depositor can withdraw the funds for his own use at any time during his life, and upon his death any funds remaining are distributed to the "beneficiary." Despite the terminology, there is no trust relationship here because the so-called trustee is not obligated to hold the property for the benefit of the so-called beneficiary. Rather, this account functions the same as a payable-on-death account.[6]

Totten trusts, originally recognized in New York as a result of a case, *In re Totten,*[7] have been specifically recognized by statute in a number of jurisdictions. Where recognized, the proceeds of the account pass to the named beneficiary outside of the probate process.

[5] Deferred Compensation Contracts

A *deferred compensation contract* is a contractual agreement between an employer and an employee to pay a portion of the employee's compensation after the period in which it has been earned. One of the main reasons for doing this is to defer the employee's income tax liability, which may have the effect of shifting income to a

---

[3] In his role as executor, as distinguished from his individual capacity.

[4] Life insurance is discussed in greater detail in Chapter 12.

[5] Qualified retirement plans are discussed in greater detail in Chapter 13.

[6] *See* § 2.04[B][6] *infra.*

[7] 179 N.Y. 112, 71 N.E. 748 (1904).

year in which the employee will be in a lower income tax bracket (perhaps due to retirement or a reduction in income tax rates). Deferred compensation contracts typically provide for a designated beneficiary in the event that the employee dies prior to the time that the compensation is paid. If the designated beneficiary is other than the employee's estate or executor, then the proceeds will pass outside the probate process to the designated beneficiary.

[6] Payable-on-Death Accounts

Almost all jurisdictions now recognize payable-on-death (POD) designations for brokerage accounts, mutual funds, and securities. A POD account is an account that designates a beneficiary in the event of death. A POD account differs from a joint account because the designated recipient has no rights to the property while the person establishing the account is living. A POD account differs from a trust because no fiduciary relationship is created. The owner of a POD account is free to change the designated beneficiary at any time prior to death.

[7] Beneficial Interests in Trusts

Beneficial interests in trusts frequently pass outside of probate. Once property has been placed in trust, the terms of the trust dictate its distribution. Commonly, the effect of this is to take the interest out of probate. This is particularly likely to be the case when the individual has an interest that terminates upon death.

EXAMPLE 2-6

Sarah established a revocable *inter vivos* trust. The terms of the trust provide that during life Sarah is entitled to all income from the trust and has the power to invade the principle. The trust also provides that upon Sarah's death the trust principal will be distributed to Ben. Upon Sarah's death the interest in the trust will pass to Ben outside of the probate process.

If the decedent's interest in the trust is not terminated upon death (e.g., because it is a term of years lasting beyond the time of the decedent's death, or because it is a remainder interest), then the beneficial interest in the trust will pass through probate.

EXAMPLE 2-7

Sarah established a trust for the benefit of Alan and Ben. The terms of the trust provide that Alan is entitled to the income from the trust for ten years and that after ten years the remainder of the trust will pass to Ben. The trust names no other beneficiaries. Five years after the establishment of the trust, Alan and Ben die. Alan's remaining five-year income interest will pass through Alan's probate estate and Ben's remainder interest will pass through Ben's probate estate.

People wanting to avoid probate frequently accomplish this result by transferring their assets to a revocable *inter vivos* trust in which their interests terminate at death. In this way, they can retain unlimited access and control over the trust property during life, and can designate to whom the trust property will pass upon death.[8]

How Property Passes Upon Death

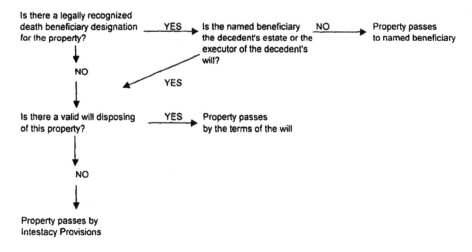

---

[8] Trusts, including revocable *inter vivos* trusts, are discussed in greater detail in Chapter 4. *See* Form 1 for a revocable *inter vivos* trust.

3

Basic Estate Planning Documents

§3.01 INTRODUCTION

Many people equate an estate plan with a will. While a will is an essential part of every estate plan, a complete estate plan usually also includes one or more trusts, a durable power of attorney, and a health care proxy or living will in addition to a will. Some of these instruments are effective during life; others are effective only at death. Together, these documents permit an individual to dispose of her property during life or at death, provide for the care of her minor children after death, minimize transfer taxes, and facilitate the continuing management of her affairs and care of her person during periods of incapacity.

Most of the instruments discussed in this chapter are governed by state law, and the law varies from state to state. Consequently, an estate planner always should bear in mind the state law requirements and default rules of the relevant jurisdiction and should draft the documents accordingly. Failure to conform to the specific requirements of state law can result in a document that is not effective to accomplish its purpose. For example, if state law requires three witnesses for a will, and a testator executes his will with only two witnesses, the will is invalid.

§3.02 WILLS

[A] Purpose of a Will

Every estate plan should include a will.[1] The most basic function of a will is to dispose of an individual's probate property at death. In addition, a will may appoint a guardian for the decedent's minor children, appoint an executor (also called a personal representative), and determine which beneficiaries will bear the burden of transfer taxes. Consequently, even estate plans for individuals with few assets or little probate property should include a will.

[1] Provide for the Distribution of Probate Assets

A will disposes of a decedent's probate property. Nonprobate property, such as life insurance proceeds and jointly held property, passes by its own terms and is not affected by the terms of a will.[2]

The law classifies bequests[3] under a will into several categories. A bequest of a particular item of property ("I give my gold engagement ring to my daughter") is

---

[1] §3.02 *See* Forms 7 and 8 for sample wills.

[2] The distinction between probate and nonprobate property is discussed in greater detail in Chapter 2.

[3] The term "bequest" is used to denote all dispositions under a will. Traditionally, the term "legacy" referred to a gift of cash, a "bequest" referred to a gift of other personal property, and the term "devise" referred to a gift of real property. These distinctions are no longer commonly observed, and these terms or the term "gift" are often used interchangeably. The Uniform Probate Code uses

known as a *specific bequest*.[4] A bequest of a certain amount of property that is not payable from identified property in the estate ("I give $10,000 to my son") is known as a *general* or *pecuniary bequest*.[5] The property that remains in the estate after the payment of specific and general bequests is known as the *residue* or *residuary*. The distinction among specific bequests, general bequests, and the residue of an estate can be important in determining which bequests will bear the burden of the estate tax and which bequests will be reduced (or possibly be eliminated) if the estate does not include enough assets to pay all of the estate's creditors and all of the bequests contained in the will. Issues relating to the payment of taxes (apportionment), the order in which bequests are paid (abatement), and the effect of a bequest of an item no longer in the decedent's estate (ademption) are discussed below.

The will may direct the executor to distribute a gift to an identified individual ("I give any real estate I may own at the time of my death to my spouse") or to a class of beneficiaries ("I give my tangible personal property to my children in equal shares"). A bequest to a class of beneficiaries should state clearly how the bequest is to be shared among the members of the class, and should provide for a mechanism to resolve any disputes among the beneficiaries. Leaving the final decision to the executor is one simple mechanism, but if the executor is a member of the class of beneficiaries, it may be preferable to take a more formal approach.

Often a testator wishes to leave specific tangible personal property, such as jewelry, books, furniture, or other household items, to family members or friends. The significance of these items may be primarily in their sentimental value, and the testator may find that he wishes to make frequent changes to the list of which beneficiary is to receive which item. Listing all such bequests in the will can become cumbersome, and will necessitate the execution of a new will or a codicil to the will each time the testator thinks of another small remembrance he would like to leave to a family member or friend. One alternative to listing small bequests in a will is for the testator to prepare a memorandum containing a detailed list of such gifts and then to refer to the memorandum in the will. In some states, the memorandum will be incorporated into the will (and so become a binding direction to the executor) only if the memorandum was in existence at the time the will was executed and is clearly identified in the will. This is referred to as *incorporation by reference*. The requirement that the list be in existence at the time of the execution of the will means that changes made after the execution of the will are not effective unless a codicil is subsequently executed.[6] This has the effect of limiting a testator's flexibility.

If the testator has not prepared the memorandum at the time the will is executed, or if he prefers to retain the flexibility of altering it after the execution of the will without observing additional formalities, then he can refer in the will to the possibility that he may leave a memorandum and express his desire that the executor act in

---

(Footnote Continued)

"devise" to denote gifts of real or personal property (Unif. Probate Code § 1-201(10) (last amended 2010)).

    [4] *See* Form 8 for examples of specific bequests.

    [5] *See* Forms 7 and 8 for examples of general bequests.

    [6] A codicil republishes the will as of the date of the codicil. *See* Form 9 for a sample codicil.

accordance with such memorandum. The executor will not be legally required to act in accordance with the memorandum, but generally an executor will do so absent a good reason to the contrary.

The Uniform Probate Code goes further in allowing a testator flexibility in disposing of items of tangible personal property (other than money) by allowing such a memorandum to be incorporated into a will even if it is not yet in existence at the time the will is executed.[7] In those states that have adopted this provision of the Uniform Probate Code, the dispositive provisions contained in the memorandum are binding on the executor and the testator can alter the memorandum at any time before death. Since the memorandum functions as part of the will in such case, the estate planner should instruct a testator to clearly identify any such memorandum, to date it, and to keep it in a safe place with other estate planning documents.

If the testator believes that certain items of tangible personal property will be sold in all events, thought should be given to including a provision directing the personal representative to sell those items. This has the advantage of making the selling expenses deductible for federal estate tax purposes as expenses of administration. If there is no such direction in the will, the Internal Revenue Service may determine that the assets were sold for the beneficiaries' convenience, in which case the associated expenses will not be deductible. A direction to sell is particularly valuable for those assets that may have substantial commissions associated with sale, including artwork, airplanes, and boats.

[2] Plan for Changes in Circumstances

A will may clearly provide for the disposition of the testator's assets at the time the will is executed, but changes in circumstances between the time of execution and the time of the decedent's death may make it impossible for the executor to follow the dispositive provisions of the will exactly. Changed circumstances could involve the death of a beneficiary or a change in the nature or amount of the assets in the estate. If the language of the will does not indicate the testator's intent in the event of such changed circumstances, then state law will provide a default rule. It is preferable, however, for the estate planner to raise the possibility of changed circumstances with the testator during the drafting process and to address them accordingly in the will.

[a] Changes Involving the Beneficiary: Lapse and Simultaneous Death

If a testator provides in his will, "I give John $10,000," and at the time of the testator's death John is no longer living, then the executor cannot transfer the $10,000 exactly as directed by the will. To avoid this situation, the estate planner should inquire as to what the testator wants to happen if a beneficiary under the will predeceases the testator. If the testator in the above example wants the bequest to

---

[7] Unif. Probate Code § 2-513 (last amended 2010).

pass to John's estate or children if John predeceases him, then he should so specify in the will. If the testator wants the bequest to go to other beneficiaries under the will if John predeceases him, then, again, the will should so specify.

If the will does not specify what should happen if a beneficiary predeceases the testator, then state law will determine who will receive the bequest. The common law provided that a gift would fail, or *lapse,* if the beneficiary died before the testator. A failed bequest passes to the residuary. This common law rule has been altered by state statutes. Almost all states have enacted statutes that prevent the lapse of a bequest if the predeceased beneficiary is a close relative of the testator. Generally, these *antilapse statutes* provide that the descendants of the predeceased beneficiary will receive the bequest. (The Uniform Probate Code protects gifts to the descendants of the donor's grandparents and stepchildren.)[8] The bequest passes directly to those descendants; it does not pass through the estate of the predeceased beneficiary. If the predeceased beneficiary does not fall within the group provided for under the state antilapse statute, the gift may fail.

A related issue arises if the beneficiary under a will dies simultaneously with, or within a short period of time of, the testator. The order of deaths can have great significance for the disposition of the testator's property. If the testator is deemed to have died first (i.e., if the beneficiary survives the testator), a bequest in the testator's will passes to the estate of the beneficiary, and ultimately will be distributed according to the estate plan of the (now) deceased beneficiary. It is likely that a testator, if faced with the question, would have preferred to have had a bequest intended for a predeceased beneficiary to pass under an alternate provision of her own will, rather than under the provisions of the predeceased beneficiary's will. Furthermore, if the testator is deemed to have died first, the property will be subject to the probate process in both the testator's estate and the predeceased beneficiary's estate.

A will can avoid these undesirable consequences of two deaths within a short period of time by including a provision that requires a beneficiary to survive the testator by some set period of time (generally at least 30 days) in order to be entitled to receive a bequest.[9] If the will does not contain such a provision, then state law may again fill the gap. Nearly every state has adopted a simultaneous death statute that addresses this issue. Under these statutes, if there is no evidence that two individuals died other than simultaneously, then the statute deems each individual to have survived for the purposes of determining the disposition of that person's estate. Many states have adopted a more recent version of a simultaneous death statute that requires a beneficiary to survive the testator by 120 hours (five days) in order to be treated as having survived the testator.[10]

In drafting will provisions intended to override or alter the effect of state antilapse or simultaneous death statutes, it is important for the estate planner to be familiar with the provisions of the statutes in the relevant jurisdiction, and to draft the language of the will with those statutes in mind.

---

[8] Unif. Probate Code § 2-603 (last amended 2010).

[9] *See* Form 8 for examples of bequests with survivorship provisions.

[10] *See also* Unif. Probate Code § 2-702 (last amended 2010).

[b] Changes in the Nature of Estate Assets: Ademption

If a testator's will provides, "I give my grand piano to John," and the testator then sells the piano to the local conservatory of music a few months before her death, the executor of her estate again will be unable to carry out the directions in the will. To avoid the uncertainty inherent in this situation, the estate planner should discuss with the testator what result she would want if the property described in a specific bequest is no longer in her possession at her death. In some circumstances, the testator may wish the beneficiary to receive a substitute for the property described in the bequest, such as the proceeds of the sale of such property. In other cases, the testator may not want the beneficiary to receive anything if the property described in the specific bequest is no longer in his possession at death. The will should specify which of these results is the one intended by the testator.

If the will does not specify the intended result if the property described in a specific bequest is not in the possession of the testator at his death, then state law will determine the result. The common law doctrine of *ademption* generally provides that if the property subject to a specific bequest was not in the possession of the testator at his death, then the bequest would fail, or *adeem,* and the beneficiary would receive nothing with respect to that bequest. Many states still follow this common law rule. However, some states have enacted statutes that prevent ademption in certain circumstances, and the Uniform Probate Code prevents ademption unless the facts and circumstances indicate that the decedent's intent was to the contrary.[11] In states that have adopted this rule, a beneficiary will receive the value of the specific property bequeathed to him unless the will indicates otherwise.

[c] Changes in the Amount of Estate Assets: Abatement

A third situation in which the executor will be unable to follow the dispositive provisions of a will as written arises when the will contains bequests that exceed the value of the estate assets available to satisfy those bequests.

EXAMPLE 3-1

The will contains bequests of $200,000 to one child, a commercial apartment building valued at $200,000 to a second child, and $10,000 to each of four nephews. The residue of the estate passes to the spouse. Shortly before the testator's death, one of his business ventures failed, and he incurred substantial debt. At the time of his death, the decedent owned the apartment building and $300,000 in liquid assets, and owed debts of $150,000. After payment of the debts, the executor will be left with $150,000 in liquid assets and instructions to pay bequests totaling $240,000.

---

[11] Unif. Probate Code § 2-606 (last amended 2010).

Since the estate in the above example does not contain sufficient assets to fund all of the bequests, some or all of the bequests will be reduced, or *abated*. The states have developed different rules governing the order in which bequests are abated if the will does not indicate the testator's intent. The most common pattern is that the residuary abates first, then general bequests, and, finally, specific bequests. Under this rule, the child receiving the apartment building would get his full bequest, whereas the other child and the nephews would have their bequests reduced proportionally and the spouse would receive nothing. The results of this rule are often problematic because people often provide for their primary beneficiaries under the residuary clause. Because of this, some states have altered this result by providing that bequests to the spouse, or spouse and descendants, abate after bequests to more distant relatives or unrelated persons.

A testator can avoid the application of state rules on abatement by specifying in the will the order of abatement. As a general rule, it is better to avoid large specific bequests if the residuary legacy is an important part of the testator's dispositive plan. When specific bequests are included in a will, the testator and planner should take the basic precaution of reviewing the estate plan at regular intervals, especially if the plan contains multiple specific legacies or the size of a testator's estate changes significantly.

[d] *Summary of Rules Applicable in Changed Circumstances*

The following chart summarizes the traditional rules governing changes in circumstance, as well as common statutory responses that alter the traditional rules in many states. It should be noted that there is tremendous variety among state statutes. Some states still follow the traditional rules, and other states have adopted different statutory responses. In all cases, however, the state rules only apply if the issue has not been directly addressed in the testator's will.

Doctrine	Traditional Rule	Statutory Response
Lapse	If the named beneficiary has predeceased the testator, the gift will lapse.	If the predeceased beneficiary is a close relative of the testator, the gift will pass to the beneficiary's descendants.
Ademption	If the property that is the subject of a specific bequest is not in the decedent's estate, the named beneficiary will receive nothing.	Ademption will not apply when circumstances show that the testator probably would not have wanted the gift to adeem.
Abatement	Gifts of residue abate first, general bequests next, and specific bequests are last to abate.	Bequests to a spouse, or spouse and descendants, abate after bequests to more distant relatives.

[3] Provide for Distribution of Property in Trust

It has become increasingly common for wills to provide for the bulk of the decedent's probate property to be distributed to one or more trusts created by the decedent during her life. The terms of the trust then dictate the ultimate distribution of the assets. One advantage of this type of will, commonly known as a *pour-over will,* is that it preserves the decedent's privacy. Only the will is submitted to the probate court; the trust (called a *pour-over trust*), which contains the dispositive provisions, need not become part of the public record.[12] Alternatively, a will can create a trust by establishing the terms of the trust in the will itself (a testamentary trust). In such a case, the terms of the trust become part of the public record.[13]

[4] Appoint Guardians

For a parent of a minor child, especially an unmarried parent, the most important function of a will may be to appoint a guardian for the child.[14] The appointment of a guardian of the person of a minor child in a will is not binding on a court, but a court will ordinarily respect the choice expressed in a will absent special circumstances. If the will does not appoint a guardian, the choice of a guardian will be left to the court.

[5] Appoint Executors/Personal Representatives

The function of an executor, referred to in many states and under the Uniform Probate Code as a personal representative,[15] is to carry out the terms of the will. In doing so, an executor is charged with multiple tasks: she must gather and inventory the decedent's assets, manage the assets during the course of estate administration, determine and pay the estate's creditors, including the state and federal income and estate taxes, and distribute the remaining assets in accordance with the will. The executor may be faced with difficult decisions involving the investment and management of the estate assets, especially if the decedent owned a family business. If the decedent owned assets that are difficult to value, the process of filing and paying income and estate taxes may be complex and time consuming. In addition, if the decedent owned property located in several states, then the executor may need to institute probate proceedings in different jurisdictions. Finally, the executor determines the timing of distributions of estate property, and frequently is called upon to divide the assets among beneficiaries. If the will is contested, it is the responsibility of the executor to be a proponent for the will. Serving as the executor of even a small estate can be a demanding job, especially if the assets of the estate are insufficient to pay the estate's creditors. Consequently, the choice of an executor deserves careful consideration.

---

[12] Form 7 is a sample pour-over will and Form 1 is a sample pour-over trust.

[13] Testamentary and *inter vivos* trusts are discussed in detail in Chapter 4.

[14] *See* Form 7 for an example of a guardian appointment. Guardianships for children are discussed in more detail in Chapter 7.

[15] Although the term "personal representative" is increasingly common, this chapter will continue to use the term "executor," mainly in the interest of conserving words.

An executor can be a family member or friend, an individual professional fiduciary (such as a lawyer or accountant), or an institution (such as a bank). Each has its advantages and drawbacks. For an individual with substantial assets, a professional fiduciary with extensive experience and expertise may be appropriate. In many cases a testator may choose to appoint the same professional fiduciary to act both as executor for the estate and as trustee of trusts established under the will or during life (indeed, some institutional fiduciaries will agree to act as executors only if the institution is also appointed as trustee). In some cases, the continuity provided by this arrangement may be helpful in maximizing the estate assets for the beneficiaries over the long term. In choosing between a professional fiduciary and a family member, a testator should consider the cost to the family. Professional fiduciaries typically charge a fee that consists of a fixed minimum amount plus a percentage of the estate assets.[16] Some states limit executors' fees by statute; in others states, the court determines the level of compensation that is reasonable according to local standards.

Professional fiduciaries may be either individuals or institutions. An institutional executor may be particularly appropriate when the testator has had a long-term business relationship with the institution, the estate includes substantial investment assets, or the plan includes *dynasty trusts* that will continue for many years of which the institution is the trustee. However, the testator will not know which employee of the institution will be handling her estate. A testator may be more comfortable appointing a lawyer or accountant with whom she has a personal relationship.

A family member, most often a surviving spouse, is the first choice for many testators. A family member has certain advantages as executor in that he is likely to be familiar with the decedent's affairs and to understand the decedent's wishes. The family member can engage an attorney, accountant, or investment advisor to provide professional services as needed. This alternative often offers the best of both worlds for the family since the family retains control of the process and can choose to purchase as much or as little professional advice as is necessary. This alternative is effective, however, only if the family members seek professional advice when necessary, as the cost of hiring a professional to clean up a mismanaged estate could equal or exceed the cost of having named the professional as executor in the first place.

A testator should be aware that special problems may arise with a family executor. The duties of an executor begin immediately after the decedent's death, a time at which family members may find it difficult to deal with the final disposition of the decedent's affairs. The choice of one child among several may create hurt feelings and suspicion on the part of the children not selected to act as executor. Furthermore, an executor frequently is called upon to make decisions that can create or aggravate existing family conflicts. An executor's decisions as to the timing of distributions or the division of tangible personal property could cause simmering family resentments to boil over, a result that might be avoided if those decisions were made by an independent executor. A testator may attempt to ward off family conflict by appointing multiple family members as coexecutors, such as all of her children.

---

[16] Nonprofessional fiduciaries may also be compensated. Compensation paid to a family member serving as executor will stay in the family, but will be taxable income to the executor.

Disagreements among coexecutors, however, may be more difficult to resolve than disagreements between an executor and a beneficiary, and may result in frequent, costly, and time-consuming requests to the probate court for instructions. Consequently, a testator should think carefully about appointing coexecutors, especially if the potential for conflict is inherent in the family structure. For example, it would rarely be advisable to appoint a second spouse and the children of a first spouse as coexecutors. In those circumstances, a professional may be the better choice.

[6] Apportion Taxes

A decedent may direct in her will how the executor is to fund the payment of death taxes. In the absence of a specific direction as to which beneficiaries are to bear the burden of death taxes, common law provides that death taxes are paid from the residue of the estate. Under the common law rule, specific legacies, jointly held property, and the proceeds of life insurance held in the decedent's estate would not be reduced by any portion of the estate tax attributable to their inclusion in the estate. If the testator did not take into account the effect of the estate tax on the residue of the estate, the result could be an unintended reduction of the amounts passing to the residuary legatees. Since the residuary legatees are often the prime objects of the testator's bounty, this rule could produce an unfortunate outcome. Most states have enacted tax apportionment statutes that change the common law rule to some extent if the will makes no provision for the payment of taxes. In some states, the general rule is that estate taxes are apportioned among all probate and nonprobate assets of the decedent. This general rule may contain exceptions providing that specific bequests of tangible personal property and bequests that do not generate estate tax (because the marital or charitable deduction protects them) do not share in the burden of the decedent's estate tax.

State apportionment statutes apply only if the decedent does not specifically direct the executor how to fund the tax liability. Generally, it is advisable to include an apportionment clause in a will rather than relying on the application of the state statute, especially since the testator may move to another state. In light of the substantial effect that estate tax liability can have on the net amount actually received by the various beneficiaries, the tax apportionment clause in the will should be carefully considered, especially if the estate contains substantial nonprobate property or if different beneficiaries will receive different types of assets. The estate planner should consider the tax apportionment provisions as akin to the dispositive provisions in importance due to their ability to significantly affect the amount received by the different beneficiaries. In addition, to avoid confusion, the tax apportionment clause in the will should be coordinated with the tax apportionment clause in any trust that forms part of the estate plan.[17]

---

[17] Sample tax apportionment clauses are in Form 1, Form 7, and Form 8.

[B] Requirements for a Valid Will

A court will recognize a will as valid if two requirements are met: (1) the decedent had the capacity to make a will at the time the will was executed, and (2) the actual execution of the will was conducted with the required formalities.

[1] Testamentary Capacity

An individual can make a valid will only if she has reached at least 18 years of age. In addition, she must have the requisite mental capacity to make a will, and the process must be free of fraud, undue influence, or the insane delusion of the testator. The standard for adequate mental capacity to make a will is different from, and generally less demanding than, the standard for mental capacity in other areas of the law. For example, an individual who is under a guardianship because she does not have the capacity to handle her day-to-day financial affairs may still meet the mental capacity standard for making a will. In order to have the mental capacity to make a will, an individual must meet the following criteria:

1. She must know the nature and extent of her property;
2. She must know who her family members are (traditionally denoted as the natural objects of her bounty); and
3. She must understand the basic plan for disposing of the assets that is contained in the will.

If there is doubt as to the testator's mental capacity, or if the planner has reason to believe that the will may be contested, it may be advisable to ask the testator questions that elicit answers sufficient to establish mental capacity in the presence of the witnesses to the execution of the will.

A will may be challenged even if the testator meets the above criteria for mental capacity on the grounds that the will was tainted by fraud, undue influence, or insane delusion. A will may be invalidated on the basis of fraud if the testator relied on false statements made by a third party who knew such statements were false and who made the statements with the intent to deceive the testator and for the purpose of persuading him to alter the provisions of the will. If, for example, a son intentionally induced his parent to disinherit his sister by convincing the parent, contrary to fact, that his sister had been convicted of a serious crime, the sister could contest the will on the grounds of fraud.

A court may invalidate a will on the grounds of undue influence if the testator was subject to someone's mental, moral, or physical influence to the extent that the will reflected the intent of the person exercising the influence rather than the intent of the testator. A classic situation in which a claim of undue influence may be made is when an elderly testator makes a new will shortly before his death that leaves his entire estate to his housekeeper upon whom he has depended for daily care during the past few months, while excluding his family.

Insane delusion can also form the basis for a challenge to a will. Courts have defined insane delusion as a persistent belief in purported facts contrary to all evidence and probability. Insane delusion is a basis for invalidating a will only if the delusion relates to the dispositive provisions of the will. A testator who believes that Abraham Lincoln is still the president might be capable of executing a valid will because this delusion might not affect his decisions as to how to dispose of his property at death. However, if the delusion involves a mistaken belief about a family member, it could render the will invalid. Claims to invalidate a will because the testator suffered from an insane delusion have been based on the testator's belief that he is not the biological father of his children, or that his wife has been unfaithful. Insane delusion is similar to fraud in that the will may be invalidated because the testator was acting on supposed facts that were false. In the case of insane delusion, however, there is no requirement that a third party be the source of the testator's mistaken beliefs.

Not all wills executed on the basis of a mistake of fact are susceptible to challenge on the basis of fraud or insane delusion. Consider the case of a testator who wrote a will giving everything to one child on the mistaken assumption that his other child was a drug addict. The disinherited child could challenge the will only if he could prove the specific elements of fraud, undue influence or insane delusion. A mistake of fact, without more, is insufficient to justify invalidating a will.

[2] Executed with Required Formalities

In order to be valid a will must meet certain formal requirements. Generally, the will must be in writing.[18] It must be signed by the testator, and the signature must be witnessed by at least two competent witnesses.[19]

The purpose of the signature requirement is to demonstrate that the testator intended to make the provisions of the will effective; consequently, a testator who is not capable of signing his full name may sign an initial or make another mark. The testator may be assisted if necessary, and if the testator is incapable of signing, another person may sign in his place if doing so at his request and in his presence.

At least two, and in some states three, competent witnesses must observe the testator signing the will. In general, a witness is competent to witness a will if she has the capacity to give testimony in court (i.e., she must understand the significance of the oath to tell the truth and must be able to distinguish between fact and fiction). In some states, the witnesses need to be at least 18 years of age as well. Many states provide that a bequest under a will to a witness (or her spouse) is invalid (or *purged*). Therefore, neither beneficiaries nor their spouses should be witnesses to the will. As part of the will execution ceremony, the witnesses must then sign the *attestation clause* on the will, which recites that the testator requested that they act as witnesses to his will and that he signed the will in their presence and that they are signing the will in his presence.[20]

---

[18] Those states that recognize oral wills (noncupative wills) do so only in certain very limited circumstances. Noncupative wills are not suitable for planning purposes.

[19] Some states and the Uniform Probate Code (§ 2-502) also recognize holographic wills. A holographic will is not witnessed, but, in order to be valid, the will must be entirely in the handwriting of the testator. Holographic wills, like noncupative wills, are not suitable for planning purposes.

[20] *See* Form 7 and Form 8 for a sample attestation clause.

Although not formally part of a validly executed will, a *self-proving affidavit* can make probating the will faster and easier. A self-proving affidavit is a notarized statement signed immediately after the will execution ceremony by the testator and the witnesses, affirming under oath that all of the requirements of a valid will have been complied with. Almost all states allow a self-proving affidavit to be substituted for in-court testimony of the witnesses to the will. This is a significant advantage in practical terms, since it eliminates the necessity of locating witnesses years after the execution of the will. In addition, a self-proving affidavit raises the presumption that the will was executed properly.[21]

The requirement that a will be executed with proper formalities applies with equal force to any additions or changes to a will. If a testator writes in additions to a will that has already been executed, those additions are not valid and do not affect the provisions of the will as executed. A testator can only add or alter specific provisions of a will by executing a valid *codicil*, which is an amendment to a will executed with the same formalities as a will.

[C] Revocations of Wills

A will is *ambulatory*, which means that the testator can revoke or alter it at any time before death. A will may be revoked by any of the following:

- A subsequent writing executed with the same formal requirements as, a valid will;
- A physical act with respect to the will; or
- By operation of law.

A validly executed will which has not been revoked in one of the above legally recognized ways remains effective regardless of testator intent.

[1] Revocation by Subsequent Writing

A testator can revoke a will by executing a new will that expressly revokes the prior will. Most wills begin with a clause that accomplishes this. In addition, a subsequent will revokes an earlier will, even if it does not do so expressly, if it provides for a plan of disposition that is inconsistent with the provisions of the earlier will. A will can be partially revoked by a *codicil*. A codicil is a subsequent writing executed with the necessary formalities that is intended to supplement rather than supplant an existing will. A codicil only affects those provisions of the prior will that are expressly addressed in the codicil or inconsistent with the terms of the codicil.[22]

---

[21] *See* Form 7 and Form 8 for sample self-proving affidavits.
[22] *See* Form 9 for a sample codicil.

[2] Revocation by Physical Act

All states provide that a will can be revoked by certain physical acts by the testator that are done with the intent of revoking the will. Most statutes provide that a testator can revoke a will by burning, tearing, canceling (i.e., making marks through the words of the will), or otherwise destroying the document with the intent to revoke the will. These actions must be done by the testator herself, or else in her presence and at her direction. Some states recognize partial revocation by physical act. In those states, a testator may partially revoke a will by canceling only certain provisions. However, it should be remembered that even if there is a valid partial revocation, provisions added to a will are not recognized unless executed with the required formalities. In order to avoid ambiguity, it is always preferable for the testator to revoke the entire will and replace it or to alter specific provisions by codicil.

[3] Revocation by Operation of Law

State law may revoke a will automatically in whole or part if the testator's family circumstances change in certain ways after the execution of the will.

Most states have enacted statutes that automatically revoke bequests to a former spouse after a divorce. Under these statutes, it is only the bequest to the spouse that is revoked; the rest of the will remains valid. Similarly, in some states a marriage revokes a premarital will unless the testator clearly made the will in anticipation of the marriage. In many states, a subsequent marriage does not revoke a will, but, rather, under *pretermitted spouse statutes,* the surviving spouse is given her intestate share from the decedent's estate. The Uniform Probate Code basically provides that if a will is signed before marriage and not clearly done in contemplation of the marriage, then the surviving spouse is entitled to receive an intestate share of the property that is not given to a child of the testator.[23] The birth of a child does not automatically revoke any portion of a will, but an after-born child generally would be considered a *pretermitted heir* (a child who has been unintentionally disinherited). Most states have enacted a pretermitted heir statute that gives an after-born child some portion of the parent's estate, which effectively reduces the shares of the other beneficiaries.

§3.03 TRUSTS

A trust is another basic estate planning tool. Trusts are extremely flexible and can be used to accomplish a wide variety of estate planning objectives. A trust can be created during the life of the creator (an *inter vivos trust*) or at death in the will itself (a *testamentary trust*). An *inter vivos* trust can be irrevocable or revocable, and can be funded either during the grantor's life or at the grantor's death. The types of trusts

---

[23] Unif. Probate Code § 2-301 (last amended 2010).

most commonly used in the estate planning context are described in detail in Chapter 4. Therefore, this section will address only the general purposes that a trust can serve in the estate planning context.

A trust is an arrangement in which the ownership of title to property is separated from the right to the economic benefit of the property. The trustee holds the legal title to the property and has both the right and the duty to manage the property. The beneficiary has no right to manage the property, but has the right to the economic benefit of the property. Most of the value of using trusts in estate planning springs from this severance of the economic benefit and the management and control of the property held in trust. A trust may serve one or more of the following purposes.

[A] Provide for Management of Assets

There are many circumstances in which a donor wishes to make a gift, but does not want the donee to manage the assets transferred. For example, parents and grandparents often make gifts to minor children or grandchildren who are not capable of managing investment assets. Placing the gift in trust is one method of transferring the benefit of the property to the minor children (and removing the property from the taxable estate of the donor) and providing for the management of the assets until the children are old enough to take on full ownership of the property. Similarly, if the first spouse to die has handled all of the family's financial affairs during life, she may wish to leave her bequest to the surviving spouse in trust so that the survivor will enjoy the economic benefit of the property without being burdened with the management of those assets. An elderly individual may choose to place her assets in a revocable trust, naming herself as beneficiary and someone else as trustee, for the same reason: The trustee will take on responsibility for managing the assets, and the donor/beneficiary can continue to enjoy the economic benefit of the assets.

[B] Provide for Split Interests

A trust can be used to create a number of different interests in a single piece of property.

EXAMPLE 3-2

Bob transfers property to a trust and directs the trustee to pay the income from the trust property to his sister during her lifetime. At her death, the trustee is directed to pay the trust income to Bob's children in equal shares for their lifetimes, the share of any deceased child to be paid to the surviving children. At the death of the last of the children, the trustee is to distribute the trust property in equal shares to Bob's grandchildren.

The use of a trust permits the donor to give partial interests (lifetime interests in income) to several beneficiaries, and then give the whole property to other beneficiaries at a later time. While it is possible to create split interests in property without the use of a trust, doing so is cumbersome and can create unnecessary complications.

[C] Postpone Dividing Up a Gift to a Class of Beneficiaries

Often a donor wishes to make a gift to a class of beneficiaries, such as her children or grandchildren, but would prefer to postpone the decision as to the portion of the gift that each individual will receive. For example, a grandparent may wish to make gifts to her grandchildren, to fund her grandchildren's education. The grandchildren are very young, however, and it is too soon to determine the financial resources that will be required by each individual child. One means of making a current gift, ensuring that the gift ultimately will be used for the intended purpose, but retaining the flexibility to determine at a later date how much each child will receive, is for the grandparent to establish a trust, naming another person as trustee.[1] The trust would direct the trustee to distribute income or principal to the grandchildren for their education according to the needs of each child as determined by the trustee. The trust would function as a "pot" to fund educational expenses for all of the beneficiaries in the class as needed in the future. Provided the grandmother is not the trustee, the gift would be complete when the trust was funded, but decisions as to how the gift will be divided among the children can be postponed until such time as the trustee can determine the differing needs of the individuals.

[D] Shelter Assets

A trust can also be used to limit access to the trust assets, and can protect those assets both from unwise use by the beneficiary and from the creditors of the beneficiary (which may include a former spouse in a divorce). A donor who is concerned that a beneficiary might rush to spend assets that were freely available to her can establish a trust and vest the authority to determine the amount and timing of distributions in the trustee. The terms of the trust could grant a trustee complete discretion to make distributions to the beneficiaries, or could limit distributions to the amount necessary for enumerated purposes, such as health, education, and support. The trustee can then prevent the beneficiary from squandering the trust assets on expenditures of which the donor would not approve.

Alternatively, a donor may have full confidence that a trust beneficiary would not use a power to withdraw assets from a trust unwisely. However, a creditor of a beneficiary generally can reach the assets in a trust to the same extent that the beneficiary can reach those assets. If the trust provides that the trustee has complete discretion to distribute income and principal to the beneficiary, and furthermore directs that no distribution can be made to creditors of the beneficiary and the beneficiary cannot assign her interest in the trust, then the assets held in the trust generally will be protected from the beneficiary's creditors as long as they remain in trust. This type of trust, known as a *spendthrift trust*, is discussed in more detail in

---

[1] **§ 3.03** If the grandparent established this type of trust during her lifetime and named herself as trustee, all of the trust assets would be included in her estate for estate tax purposes, and the gift might not be a completed gift under state property law.

Chapter 4. As discussed in Chapter 4, a spendthrift trust generally is effective to protect trust assets from the creditors of the beneficiary only if the trust was funded by someone other than the beneficiary.

[E] Avoid Probate

The probate process is public, and can be lengthy and cumbersome. All probate assets owned directly by a decedent must pass through the probate process, whereas assets held in trust generally pass by the terms of the trust and do not become part of the probate process. Therefore, one popular way for an individual to avoid the probate process is to transfer her assets to a revocable trust during life. The creator of the trust can be the trustee during her lifetime, and, in doing so, can retain complete control over the assets. At death, the trust will become irrevocable, and the assets will be distributed according to the terms of the trust, which are not public. This type of trust, often known as a *revocable living trust*, is discussed in more detail in Chapter 4.[2]

§3.04 DURABLE POWERS OF ATTORNEY

A durable power of attorney is an essential part of a complete estate plan because it permits someone to handle an individual's financial affairs even after the individual becomes incapacitated.[1] A *durable power of attorney* appoints a person as an agent for the person signing the power (the *principal*) and authorizes the agent (often called an *attorney-in-fact*) to step into the shoes of the principal in handling financial affairs. Unlike the trustee of a trust, an attorney-in-fact does not take title to the principal's property. The power of attorney simply authorizes the agent to act in place of the principal. A durable power of attorney can be used to handle the affairs of an incompetent person without the necessity of a court appointed guardian of the person's property.

[A] Effectiveness During Incapacity

A power of attorney is "durable" if it remains effective after the principal becomes incapacitated. In the past, a power of attorney could authorize the agent to do only what the principal could do, and therefore ceased to be effective as soon as the principal became incompetent. Since a power of attorney is often most needed at such a time, this rule severely limited the usefulness of this instrument in the estate planning context. Recognizing this problem, all states have now enacted statutes authorizing the creation of durable powers of attorney and setting limits on the powers and requirements for effectiveness. Under these statutes, a principal can create a durable power of attorney by expressly stating in the document that he

---

[2] *See* Form 1 for a sample revocable living trust.
[1] §3.04 *See* Form 10 for a sample durable power of attorney.

intends the power to continue to be effective notwithstanding his incapacity. In drafting a durable power of attorney, it is essential to conform to the requirements of the relevant state statute; if it fails to do so, the power may no longer be effective if the principal becomes incompetent.

[B] Actions Authorized

A durable power of attorney can be broad or narrow. The power could authorize the agent to act in the place of the principal with respect to only one type of transaction, such as banking transactions. Alternatively, a power may authorize the agent to act for the principal in all financial transactions, including buying and selling real property, tangible personal property, stocks, bonds and other investments; operating a business; handling digital assets; handling insurance claims, litigation claims, retirement benefits and governmental claims, such as Medicare and Social Security; and filing tax returns. While in theory a power of attorney could be drafted simply as a general statement that the agent is authorized to take any action that the principal could take, in practice, such documents generally enumerate the types of transactions included in the authorization in order to make the scope of the power clear to third parties.

A broad statement authorizing an agent to act for a principal generally does not include the power to make gifts. An agent can make gifts under a durable power of attorney only if the document expressly authorizes gifts, and can make gifts to himself only if the document contains a further specific authorization to do so. Since gifts are a basic estate planning tool, it is useful for a durable power of attorney to authorize an agent to make gifts for estate planning purposes. Powers of attorney that do authorize the agent to make gifts typically limit the power to some extent. For example, an agent might be authorized to continue the principal's previously established pattern of gifts made for estate planning purposes, or to make annual gifts to family members (possibly including the agent) that do not exceed the annual exclusion amount (the amount that a donor can give to a single donee without gift tax consequences). Including such limitations can reduce the agent's opportunity to make inappropriate gifts, and can also reduce the risk that the power to make gifts will create estate tax problems for the agent.[2]

The statutes governing durable powers of attorney in some states may allow the agent to undertake various estate planning tasks on behalf of the principal. The attorney-in-fact generally cannot change the principal's will, but may be allowed to establish new trusts, amend existing trusts, or fund previously existing trusts. Often, such powers to amend trusts must be conferred under both the durable power of attorney and any existing trust, but state laws vary.

In some states, the statute governing durable powers of attorney permits the principal to nominate a conservator or guardian for his property or person if a court finds it necessary to appoint one in the future. The court is not bound by the choice of the principal, but will respect it, unless there is good cause to do otherwise. Using a

---

[2] Some practitioners have concerns that an unlimited power to make gifts might be treated for estate tax purposes as a general power of appointment. Property subject to a general power of appointment is included in the taxable estate of the powerholder. IRC § 2041.

power of attorney to nominate a guardian permits an individual to exercise maximum control over both his person and his financial affairs in the event of future incapacity. In order to prevent a possible conflict between the attorney-in-fact and a guardian appointed later, the state statute may grant the guardian (who operates under court supervision) the authority to revoke the power of attorney.

[C] Choosing an Attorney-in-Fact

An attorney-in-fact need not be an attorney or other professional, although individuals may choose to appoint a family lawyer or accountant. Frequently the choice falls on a family member or friend. The most important factors to consider in choosing an attorney-in-fact are honesty and competence. An attorney-in-fact, unlike a guardian or conservator, is not supervised by a court. The potential for abuse, especially in the case of an attorney-in-fact who has been delegated full power to manage all of the principal's financial affairs, is evident. Competence is equally critical. Delegating the responsibility for managing the principal's financial affairs to a trusted family member or friend is an effective means of dealing with incapacity only if the agent selected can make competent financial decisions.

One means of dealing with concerns as to the honesty and competence of the agent is to require the signatures of two individuals on the power of attorney. The requirement of a second agent's concurrence can reduce the risk of mismanagement or misappropriation of the principal's assets. However, obtaining two signatures on every document can be cumbersome. Since one of the purposes of a power of attorney is to permit the handling of an incompetent's affairs as simply as possible, this alternative is often not appropriate. Moreover, as a practical matter, many financial institutions have expressed a hesitation or unwillingness to accept joint powers of attorney.

A final factor to be considered is whether other family members have confidence in the agent. For example, if the children in a family are hostile to one another, then appointing one child as an agent may aggravate existing tensions. An agent who is not a family member would be a better choice in such a case.

[D] Date of Effectiveness

A power of attorney may authorize the agent to begin acting for the principal immediately, or it may become effective only upon the occurrence of some future event (a *springing power*). The most common trigger for a springing power is the incapacity of the principal. Such powers generally require some evidence of incapacity, such as documentation by one or more physicians of the principal's incapacity. This type of trigger sounds appealing since many people are reluctant to give an agent the power to handle finances unless it is absolutely necessary. A springing power does have some drawbacks, however. Obtaining certification of incapacity can be cumbersome and may cause delays. Furthermore, the fact that a springing power becomes effective only on the incapacity of the principal may cause third parties, fearing that incapacity was not properly determined or documented, to hesitate to accept the power. For these reasons, many planners recommend the use of a power that is effective immediately rather than a springing power. The principal would execute the power and simply ask the agent to use it only in the case of incapacity. Some clients are concerned about giving these immediate powers when they do not want them immediately exercised. One way of addressing this concern is by using an escrow agreement. Under this arrangement, the drafting lawyer (or another party) retains the original power of attorney and enters into an agreement with the principal that the document will not be given to the attorney-in-fact until conditions set forth in the escrow agreement have been satisfied. For example, the document might be released when the lawyer is presented with a letter from a physician certifying that the principal is incompetent.

The issuance of regulations under the Health Insurance Portability and Accountability Act of 1996 (HIPAA) that took effect in 2003 makes the use of a springing power of attorney significantly less attractive. These regulations were promulgated to protect the privacy of a patient's health care records. The regulations impose sanctions on a health care provider who releases medical information without the proper authorization from the patient. As a result, health care providers are exceedingly cautious about releasing any medical information. This can make it difficult for an agent to obtain the necessary certification of incapacity in order to make a springing power of attorney effective. To address this issue, some practitioners now include a specific authorization to receive health care information, referencing HIPAA and tracking the language of the regulations, when drafting a springing power of attorney.

[E] Revocation and Reliance

The principal may revoke a power of attorney at any time, either by physically destroying or canceling the document or by a later writing. The death of the principal revokes a durable power of attorney automatically. In this respect, the ability of an agent to handle the principal's financial affairs is more limited than the power of a trustee, whose powers may not be affected by the death of the principal.

The concern that a durable power of attorney might have been revoked often led third parties, especially banks and mutual fund companies, to refuse to accept documents that were not executed recently. State statutes have reduced the risk for third parties relying on a durable power of attorney by providing that the death of the principal does not revoke a power of attorney with respect to persons who rely on the power in good faith and without actual knowledge of the principal's death. Many powers of attorney are drafted to offer to third parties further protection against the possibility that the principal may have revoked the power by some action by including a clause stating that a third party may rely on the power unless the third party has actual knowledge of revocation. Some state statutes even specifically provide that third parties cannot refuse to honor the document simply because of its age. Despite all such provisions, third parties may still hesitate to accept a power of attorney that has been signed several years previously, which can limit the efficiency of these instruments. The possibility that this problem will arise can be minimized by executing a new durable power of attorney every few years.

Often, powers of attorney provide that a third party may rely on a copy of the original document. Such a provision can be useful to an agent handling numerous financial transactions. However, the possibility that the original may have been revoked may cause a third party to refuse to accept a copy despite the terms of the instrument.

§3.05 HEALTH CARE PROXIES AND LIVING WILLS

Health care proxies and living wills are two different types of instruments designed to deal with a single issue: ensuring that the medical care provided at a time when the patient is no longer capable of expressing her wishes is consistent with those wishes. Some state statutes recognize health care proxies, some recognize living wills, and some recognize both. The use of these instruments can facilitate the medical care of an incompetent person and avoid the necessity of court intervention.[1]

The drafting of documents relating to medical care for an incapacitated person has been complicated by the issuance of regulations under HIPAA.[2] These regulations were issued in order to protect the privacy of medical records, and apply to virtually any health care provider who might be in the position of releasing health care information. One result of these regulations is that most health care providers are extremely cautious about releasing any health care information to anyone other than the patient. As a consequence, health care providers may be reluctant to accept a health care proxy that does not specifically reference HIPAA and then track the provisions in the regulations.

Some practitioners recommend a separate "HIPAA Release" document that authorizes named individuals ("representatives") to receive the principal's health information from doctors, pharmacies, insurance providers, and the like. Such documents do not authorize the representatives to make medical decisions, but can be quite useful if the principal needs help with bills or mental health issues that do not rise to the level of incapacity. Such a document, however, grants wide access, so the principal must trust the named representatives.

[A] Living Wills

The term *living will* has been used to refer to various types of instruments that memorialize an individual's wishes with respect to certain health care procedures and are intended to become effective if the individual is unable to communicate and is terminally ill or in an irreversible coma.[3] Only some states recognize living wills. Even in states that do not recognize living wills, however, individuals may execute a document explaining the circumstances in which they would choose to refuse certain health care procedures in the hope that their wishes will be respected. In the states that do recognize living wills, it is preferable to conform to the state statute; these vary widely.

---

[1] **§3.05** *See* Form 11 for a sample health care proxy and Form 12 for a sample living will.

[2] 42 U.S.C. §1320d.

[3] *See* Form 12 for a sample living will.

State statutes authorizing living wills, also called *advance medical directives*, generally permit an individual to direct that, in the event of terminal illness or irreversible coma, care providers should withhold certain life-sustaining procedures. A living will provides direct advance instructions to the medical care providers from the principal; no third party is involved. If the conditions specified in the instrument occur (terminal illness or irreversible coma), the instructions become effective. In this respect, a living will is inflexible because the principal can revoke a living will at any time, but, once he is no longer capable of communicating his wishes, no further modification is possible. Living wills and advance medical directives are different from a Do Not Resuscitate Order ("DNR"), Medical Order for Life-Sustaining Treatment ("MOLST"), or Physician's Orders on Scope of Treatment ("POST"). DNRs, MOLSTs, POSTs, and the like are documents completed with a medical doctor, not an estate planning attorney.

The inflexibility of a living will is in some respects an advantage and in some respects a disadvantage. Since a living will contains instructions directly from the principal to the health care providers, in theory family members will not be burdened with the decision to withhold treatment, and the instructions could be effective even if the family members disagree. (In practice, however, it is unlikely that health care providers would carry out the instructions contained in a living will over the objections of family members.)

The inflexibility of a living will also has drawbacks. It is impossible to draft an instrument that takes into account all possible circumstances, and even a detailed directive may not cover the circumstances actually encountered. A living will can be drafted in very general terms, directing simply that, in the event the principal is unable to communicate and is terminally ill or in an irreversible coma, all treatment except that necessary to alleviate pain should be withheld. However, a health care provider faced with such instructions may request more specific instructions from the family, which diminishes the usefulness of the document. The alternative method of drafting a living will is to provide a detailed list of procedures that the principal does or does not want provided. This approach has the advantage of reducing the discretion of the health care provider. However, questions may arise when the health care provider is faced with an issue not contemplated by the principal at the time the living will was executed.

In states recognizing living wills, a living will is valid only if the execution is witnessed. The state statutes authorizing living wills contain various different requirements as to the number and qualifications of the witnesses. Generally, two witnesses are required, and the witnesses must be disinterested (i.e., they cannot benefit from the estate of the principal). Some state statutes contain further requirements for execution if the principal is in a nursing home. Due to the wide variety in state statutes, it is important to check the relevant statute carefully before drafting or executing these instruments.

A living will is most likely to be effective if the principal has provided copies of the document to both her health care provider and to close family members, and has discussed her wishes in detail with these parties. Advance discussion can reassure both the health care providers and the family that the individual fully understands the importance of the document and is committed to her choice.

[B] Health Care Proxies

Some state statutes recognize a health care proxy in addition to, or instead of, a living will. A health care proxy appoints another individual as an agent to make decisions regarding health care if the principal is unable to make such decisions or unable to communicate decisions to health care providers. In this respect, a health care proxy is similar to a durable power of attorney. The theory underlying the health care proxy is that of substituted judgment; the agent is to make the decision that the principal would have made if able to do so. A health care proxy generally contains no specific instructions as to which health care measures should be provided or withheld. The document simply authorizes the agent to make all necessary decisions in accordance with the wishes that the principal has communicated to the agent.[4]

In states recognizing the validity of both, the health care proxy and living will can be incorporated into one document. In those states authorizing health care proxies but not living wills, it is possible to achieve a comparable result by incorporating specific directions in the health care proxy describing those actions the principal wants taken in the event of terminal illness or permanent unconsciousness. The advantage of combining a health care proxy with a living will is that it enables an individual to state her wishes regarding particular situations or procedures, while designating a person to make decisions other than those specifically contemplated.

In light of the general authorization granted to the agent in a health care proxy, it is essential that the principal engage in full and frank discussions with the agent so that the agent understands the wishes of the principal. Advance discussions with family members or friends and the health care professionals who will be providing services are also helpful in ensuring that the decisions of the agent are respected. In addition, it is essential to conform to the applicable state statute in drafting and executing a health care proxy.

§3.06 ORGAN DONATION

All states have enacted statutes that permit an individual to make anatomical gifts effective on death, and set out procedures for doing so. An individual desiring to make such a gift should comply with the state law procedures; a will is not an appropriate document to address anatomical gifts because the will may not be available in time to carry out the decedent's wishes. While following the procedures set out in the state law should be sufficient to accomplish such a gift, in practice hospitals generally ask for the permission of the family before proceeding. For this reason, an individual who wishes to make an anatomical gift should also clearly communicate her wishes to the family, even if she has followed the procedures mandated by state law for making the gift.

---

[4] *See* Form 11 for a sample health care proxy.

4

Trust Basics

§4.01 INTRODUCTION

The trust is an extremely flexible instrument that can be used for a wide variety of purposes. It has been said that "the purposes for which trusts can be created are as unlimited as the imagination of lawyers."[1] Although there is endless variety in the possible types of trusts, the types commonly used in estate planning are more limited. This chapter outlines the general requirements of a trust and describes the most common types of trusts used in estate planning. Finally, the chapter provides an overview of the income taxation of trusts and discusses issues to consider in choosing a trustee.

The trust is perhaps one of the most commonly misunderstood entities in estate planning. There is widespread misperception that if an individual wants to avoid taxes—be it income taxes, gift taxes, or estate taxes—he need only transfer his property to a trust. Although trusts can be very useful in structuring transactions to take advantage of tax saving provisions, it is not the trust per se that gives these advantages. Rather, it is the flexibility of the trust that makes it possible to impose some degree of control over the transferred property, while still conforming to the statutory requirements necessary to take advantage of tax saving provisions. For example, an irrevocable life insurance trust is typically used to avoid estate taxes on the proceeds of life insurance, yet it is not the trust that creates this result—the same result could be achieved by transferring the life insurance policy to an individual other than the insured. The advantage of the trust is that it enables the donor to impose restrictions on the use of the property while still meeting the requirements for keeping the property out of the donor's estate for estate tax purposes.

§4.02 WHAT IS A TRUST?

A trust is a device for holding property in which ownership is divided between a trustee and a beneficiary. The trustee holds legal title to the property and has both the right and the duty to manage the property for the benefit of the beneficiary. The beneficiary has an equitable interest in the property, which means that, although the beneficiary has no right to manage the property, he has the right to the economic benefit of the property.[1]

The trust instrument provides directions to the trustee regarding how she should manage and disburse the trust property. To ensure that these instructions are carried out, the law imposes obligations on the trustee to act fairly toward the beneficiary, and provides remedies for the beneficiary against the trustee for failing to carry out her responsibilities, as well as rights against the trust property itself.

---

[1] **§4.01** Frachter, 1 Scott on Trusts § 1, at 2 (4th ed. Little, Brown 1987).

[1] **§4.02** The beneficiary's interest is also a property interest, and is therefore capable of being transferred by the beneficiary or attached by the beneficiary's creditors unless there is a spendthrift provision that prevents the transfer of a beneficiary's interest. Spendthrift trusts are discussed in greater detail in § 4.05[C] *infra*.

§4.03 CREATING A TRUST

A trust is created when a property owner transfers property to a person with the intent that the recipient holds the property for the benefit of someone else. Thus, there are generally three parties to a trust: (1) the owner who transfers property (called the *settlor, donor,* or *grantor*), (2) the person receiving the property (called the *trustee*), and (3) the person for whose benefit the property is being held (called the *beneficiary*). Although a trust involves three parties, it does not require three people, as one person can wear more than one hat. For example, in a typical revocable *inter vivos* trust established to avoid probate, it is common for the person establishing the trust to be the initial trustee and the principal beneficiary of the trust—in that situation one person is the settlor, the trustee, and the beneficiary.

The one limitation to this rule of allowing one person to wear multiple hats is that the same person cannot be both the sole trustee and the sole beneficiary of the trust. In that event *merger* occurs and the trust is terminated.[1] The reason for this is that the essence of a trust is that it divides legal title from beneficial ownership, and merger ends this division. In practical terms, merger is rarely an issue because there is usually more than one beneficiary of a trust. Thus, although it might appear that a typical revocable *inter vivos* trust is subject to the doctrine of merger (due to the fact that the settlor is both the trustee and the principal beneficiary), this is not the case since revocable *inter vivos* trusts designate other beneficiaries who will benefit from the trust property after the settlor's death.

§4.04 ELEMENTS OF A TRUST

[A] Settlor

The person who creates a trust is the *settlor* (or *donor* or *grantor*). It is the intent of the settlor that determines whether a trust has been created. If a settlor transfers money to a recipient with the intent that the recipient hold the property for the benefit of someone else, then a trust has been created. If the settlor transfers property with the intent that the recipient use the property for the recipient's own benefit, then no trust has been created. On occasion a settlor may transfer property and convey the wish, though not impose the obligation, that the recipient use the property for the benefit of someone else. This is called a *precatory trust*, and it is not truly a trust (and therefore is not governed by the law of trusts), because the settlor is not imposing legal obligations on the recipient.[1]

---

[1] **§4.03** Merger does not apply when a person is trustee for herself and others or when the person is a trustee with others for herself alone. In addition, merger does not apply when an individual is a trustee for herself for life with a remainder interest for others. In none of these situations does the trustee-beneficiary have the entire legal and beneficial interest in the property.

[1] **§4.04** Precatory trusts are discussed in greater detail in §4.05[O][3] *infra.*

[B] Trustee

The trustee is the person who receives the property and accepts the obligation to hold the property for the benefit of the beneficiary. There can be one or several trustees.

A person or entity who has accepted the role of trustee has numerous duties. In particular, the trust arrangement imposes on the trustee the following duties:

1. The duty to be generally prudent (especially with respect to the investment of trust assets);
2. The duty to carry out the terms of the trust;
3. The duty to be loyal to the trust and administer the trust solely for the benefit of the beneficiaries;
4. The duty to give personal attention to the affairs of the trust; and
5. The duty to provide regular accounting to the beneficiaries.

Because of the onerous duties and liabilities imposed on a trustee, a person does not become a trustee unless she accepts the position. If the trustee chosen by the settlor is unable or unwilling to act, and if the settlor has not chosen a successor trustee, a court will appoint a trustee to carry out the terms of the trust—a trust will not fail for want of trustee.

A trustee can be an individual or a corporation. Most banks and financial institutions and many law firms have trust departments to manage trusts and carry out the duties of the trustee. These are professional trustees who charge fees for their service. On the other hand, there are no formal requirements for being a trustee, and individuals frequently serve as trustees for family members and friends.[2]

[C] Beneficiary

Every trust must have at least one beneficiary—a person[3] for whose benefit the trust property is being held and who therefore has a right to enforce the trust. The beneficiaries must be described with sufficient detail such that their identities can be ascertained. Thus, a trust can be held for the benefit of named beneficiaries or for the benefit of a class that is definite enough so that its membership can be determined (such as a trust for the settlor's then-living children). If the description of the beneficiaries is too vague or indefinite (such as a trust for the benefit of the settlor's friends), then the trust will fail and generally the property will be returned to the settlor or the settlor's estate. In some circumstances, the court may interpret this provision as granting a power of appointment.[4]

---

[2] Choice of trustee is discussed in § 4.07 *infra*.

[3] The term "person" does not include animals. Many times, people have attempted to establish trusts for the benefit of their dogs and other pets, and these attempted trusts have failed due to lack of a human beneficiary. Some states allow the creation of honorary trusts for the care of animals. These are not true trusts. Honorary trusts are discussed at § 4.05[O][2].

[4] *See* Leach v. Hyatt, 244 Va. 566, 423 S.E.2d 165 (1992).

There is one exception to the rule that the beneficiaries of a trust must be definitely ascertainable. Charitable trusts, i.e., those established for the purpose of fulfilling a recognized charitable purpose, can be for the benefit of an indefinite group. A charitable trust does not need ascertainable beneficiaries to enforce the trust because charitable trusts are enforced by the state attorney general.

Trusts commonly have more than one beneficiary. Sometimes, multiple beneficiaries will hold concurrent interests, and other times their interests will be successive. A common example of beneficiaries with successive interests is a trust in which one beneficiary has an interest for life or for a term of years, and the other beneficiary holds a future interest that becomes possessory after the present interest terminates (commonly called a remainder interest).

Beneficiaries have special remedies available to them under state law to protect their interest in a trust. First and foremost, if the trustee has committed a breach of trust, beneficiaries may be able to collect damages from the trustee's personal assets. In addition, if the trustee wrongfully disposes of the trust property the beneficiaries can, in certain situations, reclaim the property from a third party. If the trustee disposes of the trust property and acquires other property with the proceeds of the sale, the beneficiaries can enforce the trust against the acquired property.

[D] Property

Property is an essential element of the trust, as the trustee must be holding something for the benefit of the beneficiary. Trust property is sometimes referred to as the *res* or *corpus* or *assets* of the trust. Any transferable property interest may be the subject of a trust.

Previously, there had been some question as to whether an unfunded trust established to receive assets in the future (called a *pour-over trust*) was valid if it had no property in it at the time of creation. This issue was resolved by the Uniform Testamentary Additions to Trusts Act,[5] adopted in substance in all 50 states, which provides that a will may validly devise property to a trust established during the testator's lifetime regardless of the existence, size, or character of the corpus of the trust.[6]

[E] Trust Instrument

The trust instrument is the document that sets forth the terms of the trust.[7] Theoretically there is no requirement that a trust be in writing unless the law otherwise requires a writing. A writing is required in two situations: (1) if the trust holds an interest in real estate, the Statute of Frauds requires it to be in writing, and (2) if the trust involves the transfer of property upon death, the Wills Act requires it to

---

[5] 8 B.U.L.A. 451 (1991).

[6] Pour-over trusts are discussed in greater detail in § 4.05[B][3] *infra*.

[7] Sample trust instruments are provided in Forms 1–6.

be in writing. Thus, in many situations a legal trust can be created by simply transferring property and giving oral instructions to the trustee. Nonetheless, oral trusts should never be used in the estate planning context; it is always good form to memorialize the terms of the trust in writing rather than relying on good will and memories.

[F] Types of Beneficial Interests

Some trusts create two different types of beneficial interests: an income interest and a remainder interest. Income beneficiaries are entitled to all income (such as interest, rent, and dividends) produced by the trust for a set period of time (usually measured either by a term of years or by an individual's life), and remainder beneficiaries are entitled to the remaining principal at the end of the income beneficiaries' interest.

EXAMPLE 4-1

A trust provides that all income is to be paid to the settlor's second wife Wendy for life, with the remainder to Alice and Bob, the settlor's children from a prior marriage. Wendy is entitled to all of the income generated by the trust assets each year for so long as she lives, and Alice and Bob are entitled to receive the corpus, along with any appreciation, after Wendy's death.

Trustees are obligated to act for the benefit of all of the beneficiaries. However, traditional income and remainder trusts can create dilemmas for trustees because income beneficiaries will want the trustee to invest for maximum income (often produced by high-risk investments or those with little growth potential) while the remainderman will prefer the trustee to invest in low-risk, low-income producing assets yielding long-term appreciation. The law has traditionally addressed these conflicts by imposing tight controls on the types of investments in which trustees could invest. However, modern portfolio theory suggests that in order to provide maximum return for the beneficiaries as a whole, a trustee should not focus on individual investments or asset classes as they relate to each type of beneficiary, but rather on total return investing. Total return investing looks to the entire portfolio and encourages diversification to protect against market volatility.

In response to the recent emphasis on total return investing, there has been a trend toward drafting trusts with unitrust interests. The annual payment made to a beneficiary holding a unitrust interest is measured by a set percentage of the trust principal (often in the range of 3 to 5 percent) rather than the actual income of the trust. Under this type of provision, the interests of both the income beneficiary and the remainderman are tied to the overall performance of the trust.

Many states have also enacted statutes that encourage total return investing. The Uniform Prudent Investor Act encourages trustees to evaluate a portfolio as a whole, rather than as a series of individual investments.[8] Although the trustee still must consider the risk/return tradeoff of each class of beneficiaries, the Uniform Prudent Investor Act rejects absolute restrictions on certain types of investments and allows the trustee to delegate investment and management duties to financial professionals where their expertise will benefit the trust performance. The Uniform Prudent Investor Act applies only as a default rule and can be altered or eliminated by the terms of the trust.[9]

The Uniform Principal and Income Act helps avoid inequities that could potentially arise from the total return investing strategy proposed by the Uniform Prudent Investor Act by allowing the trustee to make adjustments to the allocation of returns between the income and principal beneficiaries or to employ a unitrust for the income beneficiary.[10] The Uniform Principal and Income Act, like the Uniform Prudent Investor Act, is a rule of construction and its terms do not apply to the extent that the trust provides otherwise.[11] The Uniform Principal and Income Act also provides the trustee with a power to allocate certain expenditures, such as agency fees and court costs, among the beneficiaries. Thus, if the income beneficiaries' interest accrues at a high rate while the remainder interest depreciates, the Uniform Principal and Income Act grants the trustee discretion to reallocate investment expenditures to the income interest and receipts to the corpus. Similarly, the trustee could allocate part of the appreciation of assets to income to ensure impartial treatment of the beneficiaries.

The Uniform Principal and Income Act raised significant fiduciary income tax concerns because, under the income tax statutes, it was unclear whether the income beneficiary would need to pay income tax on the income earned by the trust or the adjusted income actually received by the beneficiary. The Internal Revenue Service responded to these concerns by issuing regulations under IRC Section 643(b) which provide that state statutes permitting adjustments between income and principal or the use of unitrusts will be respected for federal tax purposes.[12] These regulations allow the trustee to use the alternative methods to allocate between income and principal approved by state statutes to treat the beneficiaries impartially.[13] Beneficiaries will not be taxed on the income earned prior to an adjustment. Instead, they will pay income taxes based upon the income received after adjustment or a switch to a unitrust. Furthermore, although capital gains have traditionally been categorized as principal, an allocation of capital gains to income will be respected if made pursuant to both the trust instrument and a state statute, or if the trust authorizes the trustee to do so.[14]

---

[8] Unif. Prudent Investor Act § 2 7B U.L.A. 289–90 (2004).

[9] Unif. Prudent Investor Act § 1 7B U.L.A. 286 (2004).

[10] Unif. Principal & Income Act § 104 (amended 1997), 7B U.L.A. 141 (2004).

[11] Unif. Principal & Income Act § 103 (amended 1997), 7B U.L.A. 141 (2004).

[12] Reg. § 1.643(b)-1.

[13] *Id.*

[14] T.D. 9102, 2004-5 I.R.B. 369.

§4.05 TYPES OF TRUSTS USED IN ESTATE PLANNING

Estate planning commonly involves the use of a variety of trusts. This section provides a general explanation of these different types of trusts and explains their role in estate planning. These trusts are described in greater detail in later chapters.

Before discussing the types of trusts used in estate planning, it is important to understand the nature of the terminology. The names for trusts refer to specific characteristics of a trust and one trust can have many characteristics. Thus, for example, a Crummey trust is also an *inter vivos* trust and an irrevocable trust, and could also be a spendthrift trust, depending on the trust's terms. The categories are not mutually exclusive.

All trusts used in estate planning can be categorized as either *inter vivos* or testamentary trusts and as either revocable or irrevocable trusts. Other categories are more specifically applicable to particular trusts.

[A] *Inter Vivos* and Testamentary Trusts

All trusts used in estate planning are either *inter vivos* or testamentary trusts. A trust established during the settlor's life is an *inter vivos* trust (sometimes referred to as a *living* trust). A trust that is established at death through a person's will is called a *testamentary* trust.

Any property held in an *inter vivos* trust is not part of the settlor's probate estate and is not subject to probate when the settlor dies. Instead, the property passes directly to the beneficiary designated in the trust. A settlor wishing to take advantage of gift tax exclusions (such as the $15,000 annual exclusion or the exclusion for medical and educational expenses) by making gifts in trust must make the transfer during life and, therefore, the trust must be an *inter vivos* trust.

A testamentary trust is created in a will and thus comes into existence only after the estate owner's death. Since it is a part of the will, the terms of a testamentary trust as well as the identity of the beneficiaries are a matter of public record. Also, since the trustee is required to file an inventory with the court listing the property used to fund the trust, the identity and value of the property initially transferred to the trustee are also matters of public record.

In many jurisdictions, a testamentary trust is subject to the continuing jurisdiction of the probate court. Although this can provide some additional safeguards for the beneficiaries, it will also frequently result in higher costs of administration.

[B] Revocable and Irrevocable Trusts

[1] Defined

A *revocable* trust is one in which the settlor retains the right to terminate the trust and reclaim the assets. An *irrevocable* trust is one in which the settlor has not retained the right to revoke the trust. Most states provide that a trust will be presumed to be irrevocable unless the settlor explicitly reserves the right to revoke.

An *inter vivos* trust can be either revocable or irrevocable, although all revocable *inter vivos* trusts become irrevocable upon the settlor's death. Since testamentary trusts only come into being upon the death of the settlor, they are, by necessity, irrevocable trusts.

As a general rule, in order to accomplish the tax planning goal of removing property from the settlor's estate, the trust must be an irrevocable trust. Thus, many of the common types of trusts used to save or reduce gift taxes—Crummey trusts, life insurance trusts, and qualified personal residence trusts—are irrevocable trusts. A transfer to a revocable trust, on the other hand, cannot be used to remove property from the settlor's taxable estate.[1] Nonetheless, a settlor may transfer property to a revocable trust during life in order to avoid probate and provide lifetime management of assets for the settlor, while maintaining maximum control over the assets in the trust.

[2] Revocable Living Trust

The revocable living trust (also called the *revocable inter vivos trust*) is one of the most widely used estate planning devices. A revocable trust funded during life avoids probate and a revocable trust funded at the settlor's death can provide a unified plan of disposition for the settlor's probate and nonprobate assets.[2]

As its name implies, a revocable living trust is a trust established during the settlor's life that may be revoked by the settlor. A revocable living trust typically provides that the trust property is to be used for the settlor's benefit during the settlor's life, and, upon the settlor's death, the trust assets are to be distributed to the settlor's chosen beneficiaries. To the extent that property is transferred to the trust during the settlor's life, it will not be subject to probate upon the settlor's death. For many years there was uncertainty regarding whether a revocable living trust could be used to transfer property at death. The issue has now been resolved in favor of revocable living trusts in all jurisdictions, although a small number of jurisdictions require that a revocable living trust be executed with the same formalities as a will in order to pass property at death.[3]

There is a common misperception that transferring assets to a revocable living trust can save taxes. This is not the case. The transfer of assets to a revocable trust does not provide any income or estate tax advantages to the settlor of the trust. Income earned by assets in a revocable living trust continues to be taxed to the settlor[4] and, upon the settlor's death, all assets in the trust will be subject to tax in the settlor's estate.[5] Similarly, a revocable living trust does not generally provide the settlor with any protections against creditors. The trend in the law is for creditors to be able to reach assets in the trust both during the settlor's life and after the settlor's death. Finally, a revocable living trust will generally not prevent a spouse from claiming her elective share against assets in the trust. Most states provide that when

---

[1] §4.05 IRC §2038.
[2] A sample revocable trust is provided in Form 1.
[3] *See, e.g.*, Fla. Stat. Ch. 737.111.
[4] IRC §676.
[5] IRC §2038.

claiming an elective share, a surviving spouse can reach assets in a revocable living trust established by the decedent spouse during marriage.

[3] Pour-Over Trust

A pour-over trust is a revocable living trust that is structured to receive and dispose of assets upon the settlor's death.[6] Assets may be directed to the trust by the settlor's will (called a *pour-over will*),[7] or by beneficiary designation for nonprobate assets (such as life insurance and retirement benefits).

A pour-over trust is similar to a testamentary trust in that both are designed to dispose of assets after the settlor's death. A testamentary trust, however, is contained in the settlor's will, whereas a pour-over trust is a separate document. This simple difference in form has several practical ramifications that provide numerous advantages for pour-over trusts over testamentary trusts.

The following are some of the most important advantages of pourover trusts over testamentary trusts:

- A pour-over trust is administered by a trustee without court supervision. This is different from a testamentary trust that in some states is subject to the continuing jurisdiction of the probate court. Since the trustee of a testamentary trust is likely to be required to file regular accountings with the probate court, this makes it more expensive to administer than a pour-over trust.

- A pour-over trust is a private instrument. This is in contrast to a testamentary trust, which, as part of the will, is a public record.

- A pour-over trust can provide a single consolidated plan of disposition for all of a person's assets—regardless of whether they are probate or nonprobate property—if the settlor names the trust as beneficiary of her nonprobate property. Although a testamentary trust can accomplish this same goal if the settlor names her estate or executor as the beneficiary of the nonprobate assets, this can only be done at the cost of subjecting the nonprobate assets to the expense, delay, and publicity of the probate process.

- A pour-over trust can be merged with another trust in certain circumstances to provide a unified plan of disposition for both spouses' assets after the death of the surviving spouse. In most states, this is not available for testamentary trusts.

---

[6] A sample pour-over trust is provided in Form 1.

[7] A sample pour-over will is provided in Form 7.

[C] Spendthrift Trust

[1] Defined

A *spendthrift trust* is a trust that has a provision limiting the beneficiary's ability to assign his interest in the trust and preventing the beneficiary's creditors from attaching the trust interest.[8]

A beneficiary's interest in a trust is a property interest that, absent other limitations, is capable of being assigned by the beneficiary or attached by the beneficiary's creditors. If the settlor has put the money in trust because she is concerned about the beneficiary's capacity to manage finances, then this ability of a beneficiary to transfer his interest can effectively eliminate the advantages sought in using a trust. In this situation, a spendthrift trust can be used to solve this problem.

A spendthrift trust specifically disallows the voluntary or involuntary transfer of a beneficiary's interest by including a *disabling restraint* on the beneficiaries and creditors. An example of a disabling restraint is as follows:

> The interest of each beneficiary, and all payments of income or principal to be made to or for any beneficiary, shall be free from interference or control by any creditor, spouse, or divorced former spouse of the beneficiary and shall not be capable of anticipation or assignment by the beneficiary.

Spendthrift trusts are very popular since they enable a donor to provide for a beneficiary while protecting that beneficiary against his own imprudence. However, spendthrift trusts are also very controversial because the fact that the equitable property interest is immune from the beneficiary's creditors enables the beneficiary to enjoy the advantages of wealth without bearing its responsibilities.

The validity of spendthrift trusts varies depending on the jurisdiction. Spendthrift trusts are not enforceable in some states as void against public policy. Nonetheless, spendthrift trusts are protected under federal bankruptcy law from creditor's claims[9] and are permitted in most states. While some states recognize these trusts absolutely, others only recognize spendthrift trusts to a limited extent (e.g., only up to a certain dollar amount).

Jurisdictions that allow spendthrift trusts often (but not always) provide that in order for a spendthrift trust to be valid it must restrict voluntary as well as involuntary transfers of the beneficiary's interest. Moreover, spendthrift provisions only protect the trust property until it is paid to the beneficiary. Once property has been distributed from the trust, the beneficiary holds full legal title and the property is no longer protected by the spendthrift provision.

---

[8] Form 4 includes a sample spendthrift trust provision.
[9] 11 U.S.C. § 541(c)(2).

Although spendthrift trusts are widely recognized, an increasing number of exceptions to the spendthrift trust doctrine have been carved out by case law and statute.

[2] Exception for Self-Settled Trusts

A longstanding principal of trust law is that a settlor may not create a spendthrift trust for his own benefit. The reason for this is that even if a settlor does not intend to defraud his creditors by creating a spendthrift trust, public policy will not allow a person to tie up his own property so as to ensure that he may enjoy it while preventing his creditors from reaching it. If a spendthrift trust is created for the benefit of the settlor, only the spendthrift provisions will be rendered invalid—the remainder of the trust will be upheld.

In recent years, offshore jurisdictions have begun offering self-settled spendthrift trusts. A number of states have followed suit, enacting statutes that permit settlors to establish spendthrift trusts for their own benefit in certain circumstances.[10] The effectiveness of these statutes has not been established.

[3] Exception for Alimony and Child Support

Spouses and children who have claims against a beneficiary for alimony, separate maintenance, and/or child support have generally been able to obtain the beneficiary's interest in a spendthrift trust. However, some jurisdictions have been more willing to allow trust assets to be reached for the payment of child support than alimony. The rationale for this distinction is that alimony merely represents a court-imposed adjustment of economic interests, while child support is a common-law duty and thus more readily recognized.

[4] Tort Creditor Exception

Based on the arguments applicable to alimony and child support creditors, some suggestion has been made that there should be a tort creditor exception to the

---

[10] The Alaska Trust Act allows an individual to create a trust in Alaska from which the grantor is eligible to receive distributions in the discretion of another person who is trustee without exposing the trust to claims of the grantor's creditors. Alaska Stat. § 34.40.110(a)-(b). Delaware has enacted a statute similar to Alaska, although the Delaware statute provides protections for certain creditors (such as those seeking alimony, child support, and claims for personal injury) seeking to enforce their claims from trust assets. Del. Code Ann. tit. 12 § 3570(8). Colorado, Nevada, and Rhode Island also have statutory provisions that are favorable to self-settled trusts. *See* Colo. Rev. Stat. § 38-10-111 (1999); Nev. Rev. Stat. Ann. § 166.010 (1999); R.I. Gen. Laws § § 18-9.2-2, 18-9.2-4, 18-9.2-5, 18-4-27 (1999) (amended 2000).

spendthrift trust doctrine.[11] Courts have generally rejected the claim that tort creditors should be able to reach a beneficial interest in a spendthrift trust.[12]

[D] A-B Trusts

The *A-B trust* is a common name for the two trusts (or one trust with two parts) used to provide for a spouse in a tax advantaged manner. The *"A" trust* (also called the *marital trust*) holds the portion of the estate designed to qualify for the marital deduction and the *"B" trust* (also called the *bypass* or the *credit shelter trust*) holds the portion of the estate designed to use the unified credit of the first spouse to die and to bypass the estate of the surviving spouse. By dividing the estate of the first spouse to die into these two shares, the married couple can (1) assure full use of both spouses' unified credits and (2) defer the payment of all estate taxes until the death of the surviving spouse.[13]

Bypass trusts are typically structured either as (1) discretionary trusts with an independent trustee or (2) trusts that give the trustee the right to distribute trust assets as limited by an ascertainable standard (typically for the beneficiary's health, education, support, and maintenance), in which case the beneficiary can be the sole trustee of the trust.[14]

The A-B Trust plan had been the most common form used in estate planning for spouses. However, with the increased unified credit exclusion amount and with the addition of portability, the A-B Trust plan is no longer so ubiquitous. That being said, the A-B trust plan is still advantageous in many situations and is an important part of the estate planner's arsenal.[15]

[E] Marital Trust

[1] In General

A marital trust is a trust that is designed to qualify for the marital deduction for estate and gift tax purposes.[16] A trust is not necessary for obtaining the marital

---

[11] Scott, 2A The Law of Trusts § 157.5 (4th ed. Little, Brown 1987).

[12] *See, e.g.,* Gibson v. Speegle, C.A. No. 134, 1984 Del. Ch. LEXIS 475 (Del. Ch. May 30, 1984). Although one court recognized a tort creditor exception, Sligh v. First Nat'l Bank, 704 So. 2d 1020 (Miss. 1997), the Mississippi legislature negated this result in cases through the Family Trust Preservation Act of 1998. Miss. Code Ann. §§ 91-9-501 *et seq.*

[13] The A-B trust structure and other issues involved in planning for a spouse are discussed in greater detail in Chapter 6. *See* Form 1 for a sample A-B trust.

[14] Bypass and credit shelter trusts are discussed in greater detail in Chapter 6.

[15] The A-B trust plan is discussed in greater detail in Chapter 6.

[16] The requirements of the marital deduction, and more information on marital trusts are discussed in Chapter 6. *See* Form 1 for a sample marital trust.

deduction as the marital deduction is available for outright transfers to a surviving spouse. However, trusts are commonly used in this context.[17]

There are a variety of types of marital trusts that qualify for the marital deduction.[18] The main difference between these different types of trusts is the degree of access and control over the trust assets given to the beneficiary spouse. The two most common types of marital trusts are the *power of appointment trust* and the *qualified terminable interest property trust* (QTIP). The *qualified domestic trust* (QDOT or QDT) is a special type of marital trust that is used in order to obtain the marital deduction for property transferred to a spouse who is not a citizen of the United States.

[2] Types of Marital Trusts

[a] *Power of Appointment Trust*

A power of appointment trust is a trust in which the beneficiary spouse is given an income interest for life and a power of appointment over the assets in the trust (a power of appointment is an ability to determine who will receive trust principal). The power of appointment can be exercisable either during life or at death or both, but it must otherwise be exercisable alone and in all events by the beneficiary spouse.[19]

The power of appointment trust can be drafted either narrowly or broadly. At one extreme, the power of appointment trust can be structured in such a way as to give the surviving spouse the substantial equivalent of outright ownership. For example, the beneficiary spouse could be given unlimited access to the trust assets through a general power of appointment exercisable at any time and control over the investment of the assets by naming her trustee. In addition, the property can pass at death the same way as if the surviving spouse had owned it outright by naming the surviving spouse's estate as the alternate taker in the event that the surviving spouse fails to exercise her power of appointment.

Alternatively, a power of appointment trust can be drafted in such a way as to give the surviving spouse only very limited rights to the trust assets. By giving the surviving spouse a power of appointment that is only exercisable upon death and by naming someone else as trustee, the surviving spouse will have no control over the management of the trust and no ability to access the trust assets during her life.

[b] *Qualified Terminable Interest Property (QTIP) Trust*

A *qualified terminable interest property* (QTIP) trust is a marital trust in which the beneficiary spouse is given an income interest for life payable at least annually.[20] The trust qualifies for the marital deduction if the executor of the decedent spouse's estate

---

[17] For a comparison of the relative advantages and disadvantages of transferring the marital share in trust, *see* Chapter 6.

[18] The requirements for qualifying for the marital deduction are discussed in Chapter 6.

[19] IRC § 2056(b)(5). Power of appointment trusts are discussed in greater detail in Chapter 6.

[20] IRC § 2056(b)(7). Form 1 has a sample QTIP trust.

files an election on the decedent's estate tax return for the trust to qualify for the marital deduction.[21] If no election is made, the trust does not qualify for the marital deduction.[22]

Although a QTIP trust is often thought of as limiting a surviving spouse's right to an income interest, this is not necessarily the case. If the donor spouse wants to provide additional benefits to the surviving spouse while still retaining the flexibility of tax planning available to the QTIP, the surviving spouse can be given any or all of the following in addition to the income interest: (1) the right to invade principal of the QTIP trust for her health, education, maintenance, and support; (2) the right to invade the greater of 5 percent of the trust principal or $5,000 from the QTIP trust each year; and/or (3) the right to receive discretionary payments from the QTIP trust (assuming there is an independent trustee).

The QTIP trust provides an estate owner the maximum control over a bequest while still qualifying for the marital deduction because it does not require that the surviving spouse be given the power of disposition over the trust assets. In addition, the QTIP trust provides a great deal of flexibility in tax planning because it allows the decision as to how much marital deduction to claim to be deferred until the time that the estate tax return is due (usually nine months after the decedent spouse's death). The QTIP trust will sometimes allow for more flexibly for state estate tax planning as many states allow special QTIP elections to be made for state estate tax purposes.[23]

[c] Reverse QTIP Trust

A *reverse QTIP trust* is a QTIP trust that is designed to use some or all of the transferring spouse's generation-skipping transfer tax (GSTT) exemption.

In 2022, each transferor is entitled to pass $12,060,000 free of generation-skipping transfer taxes (increased from $11,700,000 in 2021).[24] The transferor is generally that person who is subject to estate or gift taxes on the transfer. When a QTIP election is made with respect to property transferred to a QTIP trust, it is subject to estate taxes in the surviving spouse's estate and the surviving spouse is therefore treated as the transferor for GSTT purposes. This can result in underutilization of the exemption by the first spouse to die. However, there is a provision of the GSTT called a *reverse QTIP election*, that allows the estate of the first spouse to die to treat the property in a QTIP trust as if no QTIP election had been made (and therefore as if the property had been subject to tax in the decedent spouse's estate)—thereby allowing that spouse's GSTT exemption to be allocated to the assets in the QTIP trust.[25] A reverse QTIP election

---

[21] IRC § 2056(b)(7)(B)(1)(iii).

[22] QTIP trusts are discussed in greater detail in Chapter 6. The QTIP election is discussed in greater detail in Chapter 14.

[23] Planning with QTIP trusts is discussed in greater detail in Chapters 5 and 6.

[24] IRC §§ 2631 and 2010, *as amended by* the Tax Cuts and Jobs Act of 2017, Pub. L. No. 115-97, 131 Stat. 2060, 2091 (2017), title I, §§ 11002(d)(1)(CC), 11061(a). GSTTs are discussed in greater detail in Chapter 9.

[25] IRC § 2652(a)(3).

must be made with respect to *all* of the property in the trust.[26] However, the IRS will recognize the division of a single QTIP trust into two QTIP trusts in order to use the reverse QTIP election.[27] The trust that is intended to take advantage of the GSTT exemption of the first spouse to die is called a reverse QTIP trust.[28]

[d] Qualifying Domestic Trust

A *qualifying domestic trust* (QDOT or QDT) is a trust established for the benefit of a spouse who is not a citizen of the United States that qualifies for the estate tax marital deduction.[29]

The estate tax marital deduction is generally not available for transfers to a surviving spouse who is not a United States citizen. The one exception to this rule is for transfers to a qualifying domestic trust. A qualifying domestic trust is a trust (1) in which at least one trustee is a U.S. citizen or domestic corporation and (2) that provides that no distributions (other than income) can be made to the surviving spouse unless the trustee has the right to withhold special estate taxes imposed under Section 2056A.[30] The reason for these rules is to ensure that property passing tax free to a surviving spouse under the marital deduction does not evade taxation in the United States if the surviving spouse returns to her country of citizenship.[31]

[F] Family Pot Trust

A *family pot trust*, also called a *family trust*, is a trust designed to hold assets for minor children in the event of their parents' deaths. A pot trust typically gives a trustee discretion to distribute income and principal for the benefit of the children in accordance with their needs (as opposed to *pro rata*). A pot trust usually provides for the property to stay in a common fund until the youngest reaches a particular age (typically 22 or 25), at which point the property is divided into separate shares for each child.[32]

[G] Crummey Trust

A *Crummey trust* is a trust in which the beneficiary is given the right to withdraw property transferred to a discretionary trust for a limited period of time. The existence of this withdrawal right enables the donor to claim the annual gift tax exclusion with respect to property transferred to a discretionary trust. The withdrawal right is

---

[26] Reg. § 26.2652-2(a).

[27] Reg. § 26.2654-1(b)(1).

[28] Reverse QTIP trusts are discussed in greater detail in Chapter 9 and Chapter 14.

[29] IRC § 2056A(a).

[30] IRC § 2056A(a)(1)(B).

[31] Planning for a noncitizen spouse is discussed in greater detail in Chapter 6.

[32] *See* Form 1 for a sample family pot trust.

sometimes referred to as a *Crummey power*, named after the case, *Crummey v. Commissioner*,[33] which allowed the annual exclusion for assets transferred to a discretionary trust in which the beneficiaries had a right of withdrawal.[34]

[H] Minor's Trust

A *minor's trust* (also called a *Section 2503(c) trust*) is a trust established for the benefit of a minor that qualifies for the annual gift tax exclusion and the exclusion for generation-skipping transfer tax purposes.[35]

In order to qualify as a Section 2503(c) trust, the trust must provide (1) that the trustee has the unrestricted power to distribute income and principal to the beneficiary until the beneficiary reaches age 21; (2) if the beneficiary survives to age 21, then all accumulated income and all principal must be paid to the beneficiary; and (3) that the beneficiary must have a general power of appointment by will, or the remainder of the trust must pass to the beneficiary's estate if he dies before age 21.[36]

[I] Life Insurance Trust

A *life insurance trust* (also called an *irrevocable life insurance trust* or an *ILIT*) is a trust that is designed to hold a life insurance policy. The trust is structured in such a way that the insured has no incidents of ownership of the policy and the proceeds of the policy are therefore not subject to estate tax in the insured's estate.[37]

Life insurance trusts are commonly drafted as Crummey trusts so that premiums on the policy can be covered by contributions by the insured that qualify for the annual gift tax exclusion.

[J] Dynasty Trust

A *dynasty trust*, also called a *generation-skipping trust*, is a trust that is designed to hold assets that are not subject to the generation-skipping transfer tax. The principal beneficiaries of a dynasty trust are individuals who are more than one generation removed from the transferor, although these trusts often include the transferor's children as beneficiaries as well. Most dynasty trusts are exempt from the generation-skipping transfer tax because they fall within the exemption amount or because they were funded before the effective date of the generation-skipping transfer tax. Dynasty trusts are typically drafted to exist for a long period of time (often in perpetuity) in

---

[33] 397 F.2d 82 (9th Cir. 1968).

[34] Crummey trusts are discussed in greater detail in Chapter 7. *See* Form 4 for a sample Crummey trust.

[35] *See* Form 5 for a sample minor's trust.

[36] Section 2503(c) trusts are discussed in greater detail in Chapter 7.

[37] IRC § 2042. Life insurance trusts are discussed in greater detail in Chapter 12. *See* Form 4 for a sample insurance trust.

order to take maximum advantage of the opportunity to defer taxes.[38] In order to maximize the duration of dynasty trusts, they are frequently established in states that have repealed the Rule Against Perpetuities.

[K] Grantor Retained Interest Trusts

[1] Defined

A *grantor retained interest trust* (*GRIT*) is a trust in which the transferor retains an income interest in the property transferred. Grantor retained trusts are used for the purpose of transferring property at a reduced value for gift tax purposes since the value of the gift for gift tax purposes is the value of the property transferred minus the value of the interest retained by the grantor.[39] By having the grantor retain an interest, this reduces the value of the gift to the beneficiaries.

The Internal Revenue Code limits the availability of this technique for transfers to family members by providing that when property is transferred to a family member, the value of the retained interest will be treated as being zero, unless the retained interest meets one of the statutory exceptions.[40] The two most commonly used exceptions are for: (1) qualified personal residence trusts (known as QPRTs) and (2) grantor retained-annuity trusts (known as GRATs).

[2] Types of Grantor Retained Interest Trusts

[a] Qualified Personal Residence Trust

A *qualified personal residence trust* (*QPRT*) is a trust into which the donor has transferred a personal residence and retained the right to use the property for a set period of time. The transfer is subject to gift tax at the value of the property transferred into the trust, minus the value of the interest retained by the donor.[41] If the donor survives the time period of the retained interest (and the property is then held for the benefit of someone other than the donor), then the value of the property will not be included in the donor's gross estate at the time of death.[42]

[b] Grantor Retained Annuity Trust

A *grantor retained annuity trust* (*GRAT*) is a trust in which the donor has transferred property and retained the right to receive a fixed dollar amount from the

---

[38] Generation-skipping transfer trusts are discussed in greater detail in Chapter 9.

[39] Reg. § 25.2512-5T(d)(2).

[40] IRC § 2702.

[41] IRC § 2702(a)(3)(A)(ii); Reg. § 25.2512-5T(d)(2).

[42] QPRTs are discussed in greater detail in Chapter 8. *See* Form 15 for a sample QPRT.

trust each year.[43] The gift is valued for gift tax purposes at the value of the property transferred minus the value of the retained income interest.[44] If the donor survives the time period of the retained interest (and the property is then held for the benefit of someone other than the donor), then the value of the property will not be included in the donor's gross estate at the time of death.

[c] Grantor Retained Unitrust

A *grantor retained unitrust* (*GRUT*) is a trust in which the donor has transferred property and retained the right to receive a fixed percentage amount of the trust each year.[45] The gift is valued for gift tax purposes at the value of the property transferred minus the value of the retained income interest.[46] If the donor survives the time period of the retained interest (and the property is then held for the benefit of someone other than the donor), then the value of the property will not be included in the donor's gross estate at the time of death.[47]

[d] Common Law Grantor Retained Income Trust

A common law *grantor retained income trust* (*GRIT*) is a trust in which the grantor has retained an income interest that does not qualify for one of the statutory exceptions for QPRTs, GRATs, or GRUTs. Common law GRITs are only available for transfers to nonrelatives.[48]

[L] Charitable Trusts

[1] In General

A *charitable trust* is a trust that is established for a recognized charitable purpose, including, relief of poverty, advancement of education, advancement of religion, promotion of health, advancement of a governmental purpose, or the promotion of some other purpose beneficial to the community.[49]

Charitable trusts receive favored status in the law in a number of ways. Most importantly, charitable trusts that have been recognized as such by the IRS are tax exempt and (subject to limitations) are eligible to receive tax deductible contributions.

---

[43] IRC § 2702(b)(1). GRATs are discussed in greater detail in Chapter 8.

[44] Reg. § 25.2512-5T(d)(2).

[45] IRC § 2702(b)(2).

[46] Reg. § 25.2512-5T(d)(2).

[47] Id.

[48] Since the limitations imposed by IRC § 2702 only apply to transfers to family members (as defined in § 2702(e)), transfers to nonrelatives are subject to the regular valuation for partial interests, Reg. § 25.2512-5T(d)(2). GRITs are discussed in greater detail in Chapter 8.

[49] IRC § 501(c)(3).

In addition, charitable trusts can be of unlimited duration. This is unlike private trusts, which can only last as long as the applicable rule against perpetuities.

[2] Charitable Remainder Trusts

A *charitable remainder trust* is a trust in which a noncharitable beneficiary is given an income interest in the trust and a charity is given a remainder interest in the trust property. A donor to a charitable remainder trust can claim a charitable deduction for income, gift, or estate tax purposes only if the charitable remainder trust is structured as a charitable remainder unitrust (CRUT), or as a charitable remainder annuity trust (CRAT).[50]

[a] Charitable Remainder Unitrust

A *charitable remainder unitrust* (*CRUT*) is a trust in which a noncharitable benefici-ary is given an annual distribution of a fixed percentage (at least 5 percent) of the fair market value of the trust property for a term of years (not to exceed 20), or for the life of one or more individuals.[51] At the end of the period, the remainder interest passes to a charity.

The donor is treated as having made a charitable contribution for income, gift, and/or estate tax purposes generally equal to the value of the trust property minus the value of the interest passing to the noncharitable beneficiary.[52] If the transfer is made during life, the donor is treated as having made a gift of the income interest to the noncharitable beneficiary.

[b] Charitable Remainder Annuity Trust

A *charitable remainder annuity trust* (*CRAT*) is a trust in which a noncharitable beneficiary is given an annual distribution of a fixed dollar amount from the trust (equal to at least 5 percent of the initial value of the trust property) for a term of years (not to exceed 20), or for the life of one or more individuals. At the end of the period, the remainder interest in the trust property passes to a charity.[53]

The donor is treated as having made a charitable contribution for income, gift, and/or estate tax purposes equal to the value of the trust property minus the value of the interest passing to the noncharitable beneficiary. If the transfer is made during life, the donor is treated as having made a gift of the income interest to the noncharitable beneficiary.

---

[50] As defined under IRC § 664. Charitable remainder trusts are discussed in greater detail in Chapter 10.

[51] IRC § 664(d)(2). CRUTs are discussed in greater detail in Chapter 10.

[52] The value of the deduction is calculated under rules set forth in Reg. § 1.664-4.

[53] IRC § 664(d)(1). CRATs are discussed in greater detail in Chapter 10.

[3] Charitable Lead Trust

A *charitable lead trust* (*CLT*) is a trust in which a charity is given the right to receive current distributions of a fixed dollar amount or a fixed percentage of the value of the trust for a set period of time, and the remainder interest passes to a noncharitable beneficiary.[54]

The donor is treated as having made a charitable contribution for income, gift, and/or estate tax purposes equal to the value of the trust property minus the value of the remainder interest passing to the noncharitable beneficiary.[55] Alternatively, a charitable lead trust can be designed so that the donor receives no immediate deduction, and instead the trust receives an annual deduction as the income is actually paid to the charity.[56] If the transfer is made during life, the donor is treated as having made a gift of the remainder interest to the noncharitable beneficiary.

[M] Grantor Trusts and Intentionally Defective Grantor Trusts

A *grantor trust* is a trust over which the grantor has retained so much control, or in which the grantor has retained so great an interest, that the trust is disregarded for income tax purposes and all income and deductions associated with the trust are taxed directly to the grantor.[57] *Intentionally defective grantor trusts* are trusts that are intentionally drafted to be subject to the grantor trust rules in order to provide gift tax savings to the donor.

The grantor trust rules were originally enacted to prevent people from shifting the tax burden from income producing property to trusts that were taxed in a lower income tax bracket. However, since the rules were originally enacted, the relative tax rates have changed and now tax rates for trusts are more compressed than those that apply to other taxpayers. For example, in 2022, the maximum income tax rate applies to taxable income of trusts in excess of $13,450, whereas a married individual is only subject to the maximum rate for taxable income in excess of $647,850.[58] The effect of these changes in relative tax rates is that it is no longer advantageous for income to be taxed to the trust rather than the grantor.

While the grantor trust rules were originally enacted to prevent a perceived abuse, estate planners now often use these rules as a tax savings device. Estate planners intentionally draft trusts that will be classified as grantor trusts (sometimes called *intentional grantor trusts, defective grantor trusts,* or *intentionally defective grantor trusts*). The income of these grantor trusts is taxed to the grantor, while the benefit of the trust income passes to the beneficiaries unreduced by income taxes. The result is that the beneficiaries of a grantor trust can enjoy greater economic benefit from trust

---

[54] IRC §§ 170(f)(2)(B), 2055(c)(2)(B), and 2522(c)(2)(B). CLTs are discussed in greater detail in Chapter 10.

[55] IRC § 170(f)(2)(B).

[56] IRC § 642(c).

[57] The grantor trust rules are found in IRC §§ 671–679.

[58] IRC § 1(a) and (e); Rev. Proc. 2020-45, 2020-46 I.R.B. 1016.

assets than would be available to them if they owned the trust property directly. The Internal Revenue Service has expressed reservations about this use of the grantor trust rules,[59] but most commentators believe that a statutory change would be necessary to change this result.[60]

Many of the powers that trigger grantor trust status (such as the right to revoke or the retention of a reversionary interest that exceeds 5 percent of the value of the trust[61]) will also prevent a transfer from constituting a completed gift for gift tax purposes and/or cause the property to be included in the decedent's estate for estate tax purposes.[62] This could make the grantor trust unsuitable for some estate and gift tax planning purposes. However, because the income tax rules and the estate and gift tax rules are not identical, it is possible for a trust (1) to be a grantor trust for income tax purposes, (2) to be a completed gift for gift tax purposes, and (3) not to be included in the decedent's estate for estate tax purposes. For example, if a grantor establishes a trust with certain provisions for the benefit of his children, and names his spouse as trustee, then the gift may be completed for gift tax purposes and may take the property out of the decedent's estate for estate tax purposes, while still being treated as a grantor trust for income tax purposes. The effect of this is that any income earned by the trust will be a tax liability of the grantor, enabling the grantor to transfer additional value to the beneficiaries (in the form of paying the income taxes associated with the property), free of transfer taxes.

[N] Mallinckrodt Trusts

A *Mallinckrodt trust* (also called a *Section 678 trust* or a *beneficiary-owned trust*) is a trust over which someone other than the grantor (usually a beneficiary) has so much control or has been given so great an interest that the trust is disregarded for income tax purposes and the income and deductions associated with the trust are taxed directly to that person.[63] Although Mallinckrodt trusts derive their name from the case in which the rule was first elicited, *Mallinckrodt v. Nunan,*[64] the governing rules are now solely statutory in nature.[65]

In general, a person other than the grantor of a trust will be taxed on the income of the trust if that person has a power, exercisable alone, to vest the principal or

---

[59] The IRS ruled in Ltr. Rul. 9444033 that the grantor's payment of income taxes on the trust of a grantor trust effects an additional gift to the trust's remainder beneficiaries. The IRS amended that ruling in Ltr. Rul. 9543049, in which the IRS stated that it had reconsidered the language addressing the gift tax consequences from its earlier ruling and had decided to delete it.

[60] Intentionally defective grantor trusts are discussed in greater detail in Chapter 8.

[61] IRC §§ 676 and 673.

[62] IRC §§ 2038 and 2037.

[63] IRC § 678.

[64] 146 F.2d 1 (8th Cir. 1945), *cert. denied*, 324 U.S. 871 (1945). In that case, the beneficiary held broad management powers, the power to terminate the trust and receive the corpus, and the power to receive trust income upon request.

[65] IRC § 678.

income of the trust in himself.[66] A common example of this is a *Crummey* power, in which the beneficiary is given the right to withdraw principal for a short period of time in order for the transfer to qualify for the annual exclusion.[67] The Internal Revenue Service has ruled that in that situation the beneficiary is treated as the owner of the portion of the trust over which the beneficiary had the withdrawal right.[68] A person will also be treated as the owner of a trust if she has the power to cause trust assets to be used to discharge her legal obligation, other than the obligation to support a dependent.[69]

A person can avoid these rules by disclaiming a Mallinckrodt power within a reasonable period of time after she first becomes aware of its existence.[70]

[O] Nontrusts

The term *trust* is sometimes used for arrangements that are other than true trust arrangements. Totten trusts, honorary trusts, precatory trusts, and nominee trusts are all examples of the application of the term "trust" to an arrangement that is not truly a trust.

[1] Totten Trusts

A *Totten trust* (also called a *savings account trust*) is a form of ownership available for some savings bank accounts in which the depositor designates a person who will receive the property upon the depositor's death.[71] In form, the depositor opens the account in her own name "as trustee" for someone else. However, there is no trust relationship established; the account functions instead as a payable-on-death account in which the depositor can withdraw funds at any time for her own use. Upon the depositor's death the property passes to the person designated as beneficiary.[72]

[2] Honorary Trusts

An *honorary trust* is a purported trust that is established for a particular noncharitable purpose, rather than for the benefit of ascertainable beneficiaries.

---

[66] *Id.*

[67] Crummey powers are discussed in general in § 4.05[G] *supra,* and in Chapter 7 and in greater detail in Chapter 8.

[68] Rev. Rul. 81-6, 1981-1 C.B. 385.

[69] Special rules apply to determine when the ability to use trust assets to support a dependent will result in the holder of that power being treated as the owner of the trust assets. Reg. § 1.678(c)-1.

[70] IRC § 678(d); Reg. § 1.678(d)-1.

[71] The Totten trust is named for the case, *In re* Totten, 179 N.Y. 112, 71 N.E. 748 (1904).

[72] Totten trusts are described in greater detail in Chapter 2.

EXAMPLE 4-2

William transfers his cat and $1,000 to be used for the cat's care to his friend Ella. No trust has been created because a cat is not an ascertainable beneficiary.

Although no trust is created when there are no ascertainable beneficiaries and no charitable purpose, the law will sometimes allow the recipient to use the property for its designated purpose if the purpose is sufficiently definite. Honorary trusts have typically been respected when established for the care of pets, the building of monuments, and the maintenance of graves. If the recipient fails to use the property for the designated purpose, it is returned to the transferor or the transferor's estate. Some states have enacted statutory pet trusts to allow donors to provide funds and name a caretaker for their pets. These statutory provisions vary from state to state.

[3] Precatory Trusts

A *precatory trust* is a purported trust in which the transferor requests, rather than directs, that the transferee hold the property for the benefit of a designated beneficiary. Examples of language that is typically found to be precatory are statements such as, the transferor "hopes," "wishes," "would like," or "desires" that the recipient hold the property for the benefit of a third person.

No trust is created with precatory language and the recipient is legally free (and subject only to his conscience) to follow or ignore the transferor's request.

[4] Nominee Trust

In some states, there are arrangements for holding real property that go by the term "trust," although they are not truly trusts. The details vary from state to state, but typically the trustee in a nominee trust may only act as agent for the beneficiaries of the trust rather than having full legal authority to deal with the property. A nominee trust is commonly used to provide anonymity for the true owners of the property and to provide an easy mechanism for transferring ownership without the need to change title in the property.

§4.06 OVERVIEW OF INCOME TAXATION OF TRUSTS

[A] General Rules

The rules regarding the income taxation of trusts are exceedingly complex. Depending on the terms of the trust and applicable state law, the income tax liability associated with trust assets may be imposed on (1) the trust itself, (2) the beneficiaries, (3) the grantor, (4) a third person, or (5) any combination of the above. This section provides a broad overview of the rules regarding the income taxation of trusts.

The income taxation of trusts is best approached as a series of hurdles. The first hurdle is the grantor trust rules—has the grantor retained so much control such that the trust will be considered a grantor trust? If so, then the income and deductions associated with the trust (or with that portion of the trust that is treated as a grantor trust) is taxed directly to the grantor. The next hurdle involves the Mallinckrodt trust rules—has so much power been given to a beneficiary or third party such that the trust will be considered a Mallinckrodt trust?[1] If so, then the income and deductions associated with the trust (or with the portion of the trust that is treated as a Mallinckrodt trust) are taxed directly to that person. Finally, the third hurdle involves the rules for taxable trusts. If a trust is not treated as being owned directly by a grantor or third person (or where only a portion of the trust is deemed owned by its grantor or another person), a trust or any remaining portion of the trust is taxed under the rules applicable to taxable trusts. Taxable trusts are taxed under a complex set of rules in which trust income is reportable on the trust's own income tax return, the beneficiary's income tax return, or a combination of the two.

[B] Taxation of Grantor Trusts

A grantor trust is essentially disregarded as an entity for income tax purposes. Instead, the grantor must include those items of income, deductions, and credits attributable to that portion of the trust that she is treated as owning on her own income tax return.[2] Where only a portion of the trust is deemed owned by a grantor, any remaining portion of the trust is taxed under the rules applicable to taxable trusts.[3]

A trust will be treated as a grantor trust if any of the following powers or interests have been retained:

1. *Reversionary Interest in Trust Income or Corpus.* The grantor trust rules will apply if the grantor has retained a reversionary interest in the trust that, on the date of its creation, is worth more than 5 percent of the value of the trust property.[4]
2. *Power to Control Beneficial Enjoyment.* The grantor trust rules will apply if the grantor or a nonadverse party or both has the power, beyond specified limits, to dispose of a beneficial interest in trust income or corpus, regardless of whether the power is a fiduciary power, a power of appointment, or any other power.[5] A nonadverse party is generally anyone other than someone who has a substantial beneficial interest in a trust and whose interest would be adversely affected by the exercise or nonexercise of the power held by the grantor or nonadverse party.
3. *Certain Administrative Powers.* The grantor trust rules will apply if the grantor has administrative control of the trust property in such a way that the trust

---

[1] **§4.06** If the trust meets the definition of both a grantor trust and a Mallinckrodt trust, then the grantor trust rules will take precedence. IRC § 678(b); Reg. § 1.678(b)-1.

[2] IRC § 671.

[3] *Id.*

[4] IRC § 673.

[5] IRC § 674.

can be used for the grantor's, rather than the beneficiaries', interest.[6] These rules can apply, not only when the terms of the trust specifically allow the prohibited powers, but also when the terms of the trust are silent, but permissive of these powers. The trust will also be treated as a grantor trust if a nonadverse party holds these prohibited powers. Examples of the prohibited powers include the power to purchase the trust property for less than full and adequate consideration; the power to borrow the trust property without providing adequate security or paying adequate interest; the power to control voting power (in a nonfiduciary capacity) of stock in a corporation in which the grantor and trust have significant voting control, or to control the investment of the trust in a corporation in which the grantor holds a significant voting interest; or the power to reacquire the trust corpus by substituting other property of an equivalent value.

4. *Power to Revoke.* The grantor trust rules will apply if the grantor has the power to revoke the trust or the grantor or a nonadverse party has the power to return the trust corpus to the grantor.[7] Other powers, including a power of appointment or a power to amend the trust or the power to reacquire trust assets at less than fair market value, will also effectively be treated as a prohibited power.

5. *Power to Distribute Income to the Grantor.* The grantor trust rules will apply to any trust if the trust income is (or, at the discretion of the grantor or a nonadverse party, may be) (1) distributed to the grantor, (2) held or accumulated for future distribution to the grantor, or (3) applied to the payment of premiums on insurance on the life of the grantor, except policies irrevocably payable to charities.[8]

Under the spousal attribution rules, any powers or interests held by the grantor's spouse will be treated as being held by the grantor for purposes of determining whether the trust is a grantor trust.[9] Thus, for example, if the grantor's spouse is given a remainder interest in the trust that is worth more than 5 percent of the value of the trust on the date of its creation, then the grantor will be treated as the owner of the trust property. Similarly, if trust income is applied to payment of insurance on the life of the grantor's spouse, then the grantor will be treated as the owner of the trust property.

[C] Taxation of Mallinckrodt Trusts

A Mallinckrodt trust (also known as a Section 678 trust), like a grantor trust, is essentially disregarded as an entity for income tax purposes. Instead, the third person who is treated as the owner of the trust must include those items of income,

---

[6] IRC § 675.
[7] IRC § 676.
[8] IRC § 677.
[9] IRC § 672(e).

deductions, and credits attributable to that portion of the trust that she is treated as owning on her own income tax return.[10]

A third person will be treated as the owner of any portion of a trust as to which she has any of the following rights or powers:

1. A power exercisable alone to vest the corpus or income in herself;

2. A power exercisable alone to vest the corpus or income in herself, which has been partially released or modified and now constitutes a power that, had it been retained by the grantor, would have caused her to be taxed as the trust's owner under the grantor trust rules; or

3. A power exercisable solely by herself to apply income or principal for the satisfaction of legal obligations (other than certain legal obligations toward the support or maintenance of a person the third person is obligated to support).[11]

One of the most common examples of a power that will trigger Section 678 is when a person is given a power of appointment over assets in a trust. Thus, a Crummey trust, in which the beneficiary is given a right of withdrawal over trust principal, is also a Mallinckrodt trust, and the beneficiary who had the right of withdrawal will be taxed on the income attributable to that portion of the trust.

A person can avoid these rules by disclaiming a Mallinckrodt power within a reasonable period of time after she first becomes aware of its existence.[12]

[D] Taxation of Taxable Trusts

Trusts (other than grantor trusts or Mallinckrodt trusts) are taxed, along with estates, under a separate set of rules that treat them partially as separate entities and partially as conduits through which income tax liability is passed through to the trust beneficiaries.[13]

All income from a trust is reportable on the trust's income tax return, the beneficiary's income tax return, or a combination of the two. If a trustee makes no distributions from a trust to the beneficiaries during a tax year, then the trust will report all of the trust's income for that year. In contrast, if the trustee distributes income or property to beneficiaries, the trust is entitled to a deduction for that distribution, and the beneficiaries are required to include the value of the distributions in their gross income, to the extent of the trust's "distributable net income" (DNI).[14] DNI is a modified measure of the trust's net income that sets a cap on the amount of income that will be taxed to each beneficiary. DNI also preserves the

---

[10] IRC § 678.

[11] The rules regarding the application of Section 678 to support trusts are found in Reg. § 1.678(c)-1.

[12] IRC § 678(d); Reg. § 1.678(d)-1.

[13] The rules governing the income taxation of trusts and estates are found in IRC subsection J, §§ 641–682.

[14] IRC §§ 661, 662.

character of income so that the beneficiaries report the same character income that the trust would have reported if income had been accumulated rather than distributed.[15]

Each beneficiary receives a Schedule K-1 from the trustee, which tells the beneficiary how much and what type of income to report on her tax return. If the qualifying distributions are less than the trust's DNI, then the trust is taxed on the remaining income on its own return. If the qualifying trust distributions equal or exceed DNI, the trust, as an entity, will have no remaining taxable income.

Most trusts are required to use a calendar year for their tax year. Because most beneficiaries also use a calendar year, it is unlikely that any deferral of taxes will be obtained by using a trust.

[E] Net Investment Income Tax

In 2010, Congress enacted a new tax that went into effect on January 1, 2013.[16] This tax imposes, for the first time, a tax of 3.8 percent on net investment income.[17] Net investment income includes, among other things, interest, dividends, non-qualified annuities, royalties, rents, passive activity, income from businesses that trade in financial instruments or commodities, and capital gains.[18] The tax is imposed on individuals, trusts and estates.

For trusts, the 3.8 percent tax is imposed on the lower amount of either (1) the net investment income for the taxable year that has not been distributed and (2) the amount that adjusted gross income exceeds the threshold amount for the highest tax bracket for trusts in the taxable year. The threshold amount for the 2022 taxable year is $13,450.

EXAMPLE 4-3

In 2022, a trust earns $20,000 of investment income and incurs $4,500 of trustee fees. The trust's taxable income is $15,500. The 3.8 percent tax is imposed on the lower amount of either (1) the $15,500 undistributed investment income or (2) the amount that the trust's adjusted gross income, $15,500, exceeds the threshold amount of $13,450, which is an excess of $2,050. The tax would be 3.8 percent of $2,050, which is a little under $78.

The threshold amount for individuals is higher than the one for trusts. The threshold amount for individuals is $250,000 for married taxpayers filing jointly, $125,000 for married taxpayers filing separately, $250,000 for qualifying widowers

---

[15] *See* IRC § 643(a).

[16] Health Care and Education Reconciliation Act of 2010, 124 Stat. 1029.

[17] IRC § 1411.

[18] IRC § 1411(c).

with dependent child, and \$200,000 for other taxpayers.[19] Because the threshold amount is higher for individuals, they will owe less net investment income tax than trusts will owe on the same amount of net investment income. This encourages distributions to beneficiaries, whose individual threshold amounts will factor into how much tax is owed.

§4.07 CHOICE OF TRUSTEE

[A] Trustee's Duties

The choice of trustee can be a critical feature in the ultimate success or failure of an estate plan. Yet, the decision is one to which clients have frequently given little thought until faced with the issue in the estate planner's office.

The first step in advising a client as to choice of trustee is to explain clearly to the client what the position entails. A trustee takes legal title to the trust property and has numerous duties and responsibilities with respect to the property. First and foremost, the trustee is responsible for managing the property for the benefit of the beneficiaries. This means that the trustee will be responsible for making decisions regarding the investment of the trust assets and decisions as to whether and when to dispose of trust assets. In making these decisions, the trustee has a duty of fairness toward all beneficiaries—but this is more easily stated than accomplished since decisions that a trustee needs to make will frequently benefit one class of beneficiaries over another. For example, in making investment decisions, the income beneficiaries will want the trustee to invest in high-yield income-producing assets, whereas the remainder beneficiaries will want the trustee to be focused on preservation and growth of principal. Similarly, a trustee holding assets in a family business for the benefit of the settlor's family, facing the difficult issue as to whether to sell or keep the business, may have a difficult time acting for the mutual benefit of the child working in the business and the out-of-state child working as a dentist.

A trustee is also responsible for the distribution of trust assets to the beneficiaries in accordance with the trust instrument. Sometimes, a trust has mandatory provisions (e.g., requiring the distribution of all income from the trust), in which case, the trustee's job is relatively straightforward, once the investment decision has been made. Commonly, however, the trustee is given discretion to make distributions to some or all of the beneficiaries. This requires that the trustee take the time to learn about the situations of the beneficiaries, and have the ability to listen to their needs and respond in an empathetic manner.

A trustee also has numerous administrative duties with respect to trust property. A trustee is required to keep the trust property separate from the trustee's own property and prepare regular accountings for the beneficiaries. The trustee is also required to file all necessary tax returns for the trust.

---

[19] IRC § 1411(b).

Although a trustee is not required to personally perform all aspects of the trust office, and may hire professionals to give investment, legal, or accounting advice, the trustee must not abdicate the responsibilities of the office and remains ultimately responsible.

A trustee's job is difficult and requires the ability to do a wide range of tasks. A poor choice of trustee can have serious consequences for the preservation of trust assets and the well-being of the beneficiaries. Therefore, the choice of trustee should be made with great care. In addition, in choosing a trustee, the client must also be mindful of the tax implications of different choices.

[B] Choosing Between a Professional and a Nonprofessional Trustee

The first decision that must be made regarding the choice of trustee is whether to have a professional or nonprofessional trustee. Each has its advantages and disadvantages and the choice should be made with the settlor's particular goals for the trust in mind.

Any individual can serve as a nonprofessional trustee, provided she has the legal capacity to own and handle property. Thus, settlors often choose a family member, close friend, or business associate to act as a trustee of a trust. The advantages of a nonprofessional trustee are (1) the trustee is more likely to have personal knowledge of the beneficiaries and their needs, and (2) a nonprofessional trustee is likely to be significantly less expensive (even to the point of waiving her fees) than a professional trustee.

That being said, many of the same things that make a nonprofessional trustee desirable sometimes raise problems. The fact that the nonprofessional trustee is personally involved with the beneficiaries may make it difficult for the trustee to bring the appropriate level of impartiality to the job. In addition, even if the trustee truly acts impartially, the perception of favoritism may cause the destruction of the trustee's personal relationship in or with the family. Second, the cost savings achieved by naming a nonprofessional trustee may also be illusory. If the individual lacks the expertise to handle the many responsibilities of a trustee, it may end up being much more expensive to have a "free" trustee than to hire a professional. Finally, nonprofessional trustees are human and, therefore, are subject to illness and death. The longer the trust is intended to be in existence, the greater the need to take this into consideration. In any event, when naming an individual, it is always prudent to name a successor trustee in the event that the initial trustee becomes unwilling or unable to act.

A professional trustee could be either an individual (such as a lawyer, accountant, financial planner, or investment advisor) or a corporate trustee (such as a bank, law firm, or financial services company). An individual professional trustee may provide many of the advantages of a nonprofessional trustee in terms of enabling the settlor to choose an individual's judgment and having someone with personal knowledge of the beneficiaries and/or trust assets, while bringing a level of expertise that the nonprofessional rarely has. Of course, an individual professional trustee is subject to the same possibilities of illness and mortality as all individuals; therefore, a successor trustee should always be named.

A corporate trustee has many of the advantages that an individual lacks. If the individual trust officer of a corporate trustee dies, takes ill, or goes on vacation, another employee of the corporate trustee can be assigned to the case. In addition, the employee of a corporate trustee will generally have no other relationship to the beneficiaries and can therefore provide a degree of impartiality that is seldom available from a family friend or relative. Finally, the corporate trustee generally has greater resources at its disposal and typically employs a large number of trained individuals to make investment decisions, provide accounting services, and in-house counsel services to advise beneficiaries. That being said, a corporate trustee does have its own limitations. Corporate trustees are, by their nature, impersonal. By naming a corporation, the settlor is unable to choose the judgment of a particular individual. The settlor may be initially drawn to a corporate trustee due to the strengths of one of its officers, but there is no guarantee that that person will not leave the company or get promoted out of the job. Corporate trustees tend to be conservative in their investments, sometimes to the point of not even keeping pace with inflation. They also tend to be very conservative in making discretionary distributions and often move very slowly. In addition, corporate trustees frequently do not have the expertise to handle assets like a closely held business. Finally, corporate trustees charge significant fees for their services—usually a minimum amount plus a percentage of a trust's assets. This may make the choice of a corporate trustee prohibitively expensive for smaller trusts.

[C] Cotrusteeships

The relative advantages and disadvantages of professional and nonprofessional trustees (both corporate and individual) can sometimes be set off against each other by providing for cotrustees—a professional trustee to provide the services of a professional with a nonprofessional cotrustee to provide the human touch. However, these arrangements have their own problems, and should be adopted only after careful consideration.

Cotrusteeships can be very expensive since both trustees must act together in administering the trust. Both trustees must agree in order to take any action and this can result in costly delays. Moreover, if the cotrustees do not agree, then more problems can occur and any fees incurred in resolving the dispute will most likely come from the trust assets and therefore ultimately harm the beneficiaries.

One way of getting around some of these problems is by designating a professional trustee, but appointing an advisory committee (made up of family members, business associates, and/or close friends) to come in from time to time on a consulting basis. The corporate fiduciary could then be given the power to act with respect to the day-to-day affairs of handling the trust, while the advisory committee could be consulted as to general investment policies. In addition, to assure that the advisory committee is consulted or that their views are taken into consideration, the advisory committee could be given the power to remove the corporate trustee and replace it with a different corporate trustee.

[D] Tax Considerations in Choosing a Trustee

If a nonprofessional is named as either sole or cotrustee, then it is necessary to review the income, gift, and estate tax consequences of that designation. It is unlikely that there will be tax issues when a professional trustee is named.

[1] Settlor

If the purpose of a trust is to remove assets from the settlor's estate for estate tax purposes, or to assign income for income tax purposes, then the settlor should generally not be named as trustee of the trust. If a settlor transfers property to a trust, and retains controls over the disposition of the trust assets, then the trust property will generally be included in the settlor's estate for estate tax purposes.[1] This is so even if the settlor has given up all rights to reclaim the trust property himself. Similarly, if a settlor transfers property to a trust and retains control over the trust assets, then the income from the trust will be taxed to the settlor under the grantor trust rules.[2]

In order to give the settlor maximum control, the settlor of a revocable living trust is commonly named as sole trustee. This does not raise any tax issues, because the transfer of assets to a revocable living trust does not provide any income or estate tax advantages to the settlor of the trust. Income earned by assets in a revocable living trust continues to be taxed to the settlor,[3] and, upon the settlor's death, all assets in the trust will be subject to tax in the settlor's estate.[4]

[2] Settlor's Spouse

If the settlor's spouse is not a beneficiary of a trust, then she can be named as trustee of a trust without causing the trust assets to be included in the settlor's or the settlor's spouse's estate for estate tax purposes. However, under the grantor trust rules, any rights or powers held by a settlor's spouse are treated as being held by the settlor.[5] Therefore, if the spouse is named as trustee, the income from the trust will likely be taxable to the settlor.[6] This may, in fact, be desirable as it will enable the grantor to pass additional benefits to the beneficiaries free of gift tax.[7] However, it should nonetheless be taken into consideration in choosing a trustee.

---

[1] § 4.07 IRC § § 2036 and 2038.

[2] The grantor trust rules are discussed in § § 4.05[M] and 4.06[B] *supra*.

[3] IRC § 676.

[4] IRC § 2038.

[5] IRC § 672(e).

[6] *Id.*

[7] *See* the discussion of intentionally defective grantor trusts in § 4.05[M] *supra*.

[3] Beneficiary

If one of the goals of the trust is to keep the trust assets from being subject to tax in the beneficiary's estate, then particular care should be taken before naming a beneficiary as trustee of a trust. If the beneficiary-trustee has an unlimited power to distribute trust property to herself, her creditors, her estate, or creditors of her estate (called a *general power of appointment*), then the trust assets will be subject to tax in the beneficiary's estate.[8] However, a beneficiary can be named as the sole trustee of a trust, provided that her rights to the trust are limited. For example, a beneficiary can be given any or all of the following rights without the trust property being subject to tax in her estate:

1. All of the income from the trust;

2. The power to invade trust principal for her support, education, health, or maintenance; and

3. The power to appoint the trust principal either during life or at death to anyone other than herself, her estate, her creditors, or creditors of her estate.[9]

If a beneficiary is trustee of a trust, then, depending on the terms of the trust, the beneficiary may be subject to income tax on the trust assets. Under the Mallinckrodt trust rules, a person other than the grantor of a trust will be taxed on the income of the trust if that person has a power, exercisable alone, to vest the principal or income of the trust in himself.[10]

[4] Third Party

If a third party (someone other than the settlor, the settlor's spouse, or a permissible beneficiary of the trust) is named trustee, generally the assets in the trust will not be subject to estate tax in that person's estate. Nonetheless, depending upon how the trust is drafted, an issue could be raised as to whether the income from the trust is taxable to that person. That is because, under the Mallinckrodt trust rules, a third party nonbeneficiary could be subject to tax on the income from a trust if the trust assets could be used to pay that person's legal obligation.[11] For example, if a trustee is given the power to use trust principal to discharge the trustee's own legal obligation, the trust could be taxable to the trustee. This will not be an issue under the usual powers granted to a trustee.

---

[8] IRC § 2041.

[9] IRC § 2041(b). Bypass trusts are discussed in greater detail in § 4.05[D] *supra*.

[10] IRC § 678.

[11] *Id.*

5

Tax Tools of the Estate Planner

§5.01 INTRODUCTION

Understanding the basic tax rules applicable to transfers by gift and at death is an essential part of being an estate planner. This chapter provides an overview of the income tax rules and the estate and gift tax rules applicable to estate planning.

The chapter begins with an overview of the income tax aspects of gifts and inheritances—a topic of increased importance in recent years given the large exemption amount available for the federal estate and gift tax. The chapter then provides an overview of the rules of the estate and gift tax system, including a discussion of the exemptions, deductions and credits that comprise the tools of the estate planner. The chapter concludes with a general discussion of how these tax tools are used in structuring common estate plans. Later chapters illustrate the application of these rules to specific situations.

§5.02 INCOME TAX ASPECTS OF GIFTS AND INHERITANCES

Generally speaking, the income tax system is very favorable in terms of its treatment of transfers of property during life and at death. Property received by gift, inheritance or on payment of life insurance is not subject to income tax (although it may be subject to other tax, such as gift or estate tax). Thus, the recipient of the property can generally enjoy the full value of the property received, undiminished by income tax liability.

EXAMPLE 5-1

D gives his house, with a fair market value of $1,000,000, to his son S. S does not have any income tax liability as a result of the gift.

EXAMPLE 5-2

H inherits $50,000 from her grandmother. H does not have any income tax liability as a result of the inheritance.

EXAMPLE 5-3

I is named as a beneficiary on her father's $1,000,000 life insurance policy. I does not have any income tax liability as a result of the insurance payment upon her father's death.

Because of these rules, estate planners need not be concerned about income taxes in connection with transfers of cash. However, income taxes are relevant in the case where the recipient receives property other than cash and subsequently sells or exchanges the property. This disposition can result in income tax liability. The disposition of property will result in taxable gain or loss depending on the difference between the sale price and the property's basis. Basis is a technical tax term that generally refers to the cost of the property when acquired. However, there are special rules for determining basis for property acquired by gift or inheritance and these rules should be taken into account when planning for transfers of property during life or at death.

When property is acquired by gift the recipient takes the property with a carryover basis.[1] Carryover basis is the same basis that the donor had in the property.

EXAMPLE 5-4

D transferred a building to her daughter by gift. At the time of the transfer, the building had a fair market value of $800,000 and a basis in D's hands of $100,000. D's daughter takes the building with a basis of $100,000.

An important exception to this rule applies when the donor's basis is more than the property's fair market value at the time of transfer. If the recipient subsequently sells the property at a loss, then for purposes of calculating the loss, the property's basis is the fair market value at the time of transfer, not the donor's basis.[2]

EXAMPLE 5-5

D transferred a building to her daughter. At the time of the transfer, the building had a fair market value of $800,000 and a basis in D's hands of $900,000. D's daughter later sold the building for $750,000. D's daughter's loss on the sale is calculated using a basis of $800,000. Neither D nor D's daughter get to take advantage of the $100,000 loss in the property that took place while D owned the property.

The reason for this rule is to prevent taxpayers from transferring tax losses. However, this can also be a trap for the unwary as the effect of this rule is that use of the tax loss is lost forever. Thus, to ensure use of the loss, property with a built-in loss should not be transferred by gift or held until death (when the basis will be stepped down to the property's fair market value). In order to preserve the loss, the donor should consider selling the property (thereby allowing the donor to claim the loss) and then transferring the proceeds.

In contrast to gifts, when property is received by inheritance, the recipient takes the property with a basis equal to the fair market value of the property at the time of

---

[1] § 5.02 IRC § 1015.
[2] IRC § 1015(a).

the decedent's death.[3] If the fair market value of the property at the time of death is greater than the property's basis in the hands of the decedent, then the property's basis will be increased or stepped up. (If the fair market value of the property at the time of death is less than the property's basis in the hands of the decedent, then the property's basis will be decreased or stepped down.) Since property typically appreciates over time, it is usually advantageous from an income tax perspective to have property pass from the decedent at death rather than to pass by gift during life because the step-up in basis provided avoids capital gains taxes.

EXAMPLE 5-6

D transferred a building to her daughter through her will at death. At the time of transfer, the building had a fair market value of $800,000 and a basis in D's hands of $100,000. D's daughter takes the building with a basis of $800,000. If she sells the building for $800,000, she will have no tax liability. The $700,000 gain is never subject to capital gains taxes.

In order to ensure consistency in how property is reported for estate tax purposes and income tax purposes, the IRS now requires executors to file a Form 8971 basis statement.[4] These basis statements must be filed with the IRS and sent to estate beneficiaries within 30 days of the filing of an estate tax return (or the date the estate tax return is due).

§5.03 ESTATE AND GIFT TAXES

[A] Introduction

The modern estate and gift tax has gone through significant changes since it was first enacted in 1976. In its early years, the estate tax was applied fairly broadly. The exemption amount was only $120,667 and, as a result, about 10 percent of the individuals who died in 1977 were subject to estate taxes. In 2022, the picture is very different. The exemption amount is $12,060,000 (indexed for inflation, up from $11,700,000 in 2021) due to the Tax Cuts and Jobs Act ("TCJA"), passed at the end of 2017. The exemption is eligible for portability (the unused exemption amount can be transferred to the surviving spouse) and, as a result, it is expected that less than 0.1 percent of the individuals who die in 2022 will be subject to the estate tax. Due to the large exemption amount, the federal estate and gift tax has become a tax that is only applicable to the very wealthiest Americans.

---

[3] The valuation is the same as the value used for estate tax purposes. Thus, if the alternate valuation date is elected, then the recipient's basis will be determined with reference to those values. IRC § 1014(a).

[4] IRC § 6035.

Nonetheless, it is still important for the estate planner to understand the federal estate and gift tax system. The reason for this is that while wealthy Americans are a small percentage of the population at large, they are a sizeable percentage of individuals seeking estate planning advice. Moreover, once a taxpayer becomes subject to this tax, she does so at the rate of 40 percent for estate and gift tax purposes. If the transfer is also subject to generation-skipping transfer taxes, then an additional 40 percent tax may be imposed.[1] The interplay of these two taxes can result in a tax liability of 96 percent.

EXAMPLE 5-7

Donor D has used up all available credits (including the unified credit and the generation skipping transfer tax exemption). D makes a $100,000 taxable gift to his granddaughter in 2022.

As a result of this transfer, D has a gift tax liability of $40,000 (40 percent of $100,000), a generation-skipping tax liability of $40,000 (40 percent of $100,000), and an additional gift tax liability on the generation-skipping transfer tax paid of $16,000 (40 percent of $40,000), resulting in a combined gift tax and generation-skipping transfer tax liability of $96,000.

Finally, while federal estate taxes have become relevant for fewer Americans, state estate taxes have become increasingly relevant and many state estate tax systems simply track the federal legislation, with the exception of providing smaller exemption amounts.

[B] Recent History—And Possible Future—Of the Estate and Gift Tax

The unified estate and gift tax was enacted in its current form in 1976 in the Tax Reform Act of 1976. The 1976 Act provided the basic structure that we have today: the aggregation of transfers during life and at death subject to a single exemption amount and rate structure. The estate and gift tax system was thrown into a state of flux in 2001 when Congress passed the Economic Growth and Tax Relief Reconciliation Act of 2001 (the "2001 Act"). The purpose of the 2001 Act was to provide for the gradual repeal of the estate tax and the generation skipping transfer tax by providing for a ten-year phase-in of ever-larger exemption amounts (ranging from $1,000,000 to $3,500,000), and culminating in one year—the year 2010—with repeal of the estate tax. In order to meet budget constraints, the 2001 Act had a built-in sunset provision which provided that after 2010, the 2001 Act would no longer be effective, thereby repealing the repeal. Under this provision, the tax system was set to return to its pre-2001 Act state with a $1,000,000 exemption amount as of January 1, 2011. However, just two weeks before this was due to occur, Congress passed the Tax Relief, Unemployment Insurance Reauthorization and Job Creation Act of 2010 (the

---

[1] § 5.03 Generation-skipping transfer taxes are discussed in greater detail in Chapter 9.

"2010 Act") which deferred the sunset provision for another two years and which increased the amount of property that could pass free of estate taxes and generation-skipping transfer tax purposes to $5,000,000 (subject to an inflation adjustment for 2012, which raised the exemption amount to $5,120,000 for that year). Since the 2010 Act itself only applied for two years, the law was set to return to its pre-2001 Act state with a $1,000,000 exemption amount as of January 1, 2013.

Congress avoided the return to the pre-2001 Act by passing the American Taxpayer Relief Act of 2012 on January 2, 2013.[2] This law was thought to set the lifetime estate and gift tax exclusions, as well as the GST exemption amount, at $5,000,000, adjusted for inflation ($5,490,000 in 2017), with the maximum tax rate set at 40 percent.

The estate tax changed yet again in 2017. The TCJA effectively doubled the exemption amount to $10,000,000 ($12,060,000 for 2022 as adjusted for inflation). However, the TCJA carries a sunset provision that reverts the exemption amount to $5,000,000 (adjusted for inflation) for estates of decedents dying after December 31, 2025.[3]

As demonstrated by the sunset provision, it seems that nothing is truly permanent in the world of estate and gift taxes. An estate planner should exercise caution in advising clients and keep up-to-date on any future changes in the law.

§5.04 UNIFIED SYSTEM AND RATE STRUCTURE

[A] In General

Since 1976, transfers by gift and at death have been subject to a unified system of taxation.[1] A single unified rate schedule applies for both gift and estate tax purposes and the tax is imposed on the basis of cumulative lifetime and death transfers. The prescribed tax rate is nominally progressive in that it ranges from 18 percent (for transfers under $10,000) to 40 percent (for transfers over $1,000,000).[2] However, due to changes in the maximum tax rate and unified credit amount in recent years, the

---

[2] Pub. L. No. 112-240, H.R. 8, 126 Stat. 2313, enacted January 2, 2013.

[3] Tax Cuts and Jobs Act of 2017, Pub. L. No. 115-97, 131 Stat. 2060, 2091 (2017), applies to estates of decedents dying after December 31, 2017 and before January 1, 2026, and for qualified gifts made after December 31, 2017 and before January 1, 2026.

[1] **§5.04** The unified system was enacted as part of the Tax Reform Act of 1976, Pub. L. No. 94-455, 90 Stat. 1520 (1976), and applies to estates of decedents dying after December 31, 1976, and for gifts made after that date.

Prior to 1977 there were two separate systems of taxation for taxing gifts and transfers at death. Each system had its own exemptions and separate progressive rate schedule. The effect of these two systems was that people could achieve significant tax advantages by dividing the transfer of their property between lifetime transfers and transfers at death.

[2] Immediately prior to the 2001 Act, the maximum tax rate was 55 percent. Under the 2001 Act, the maximum rate was gradually reduced each year until it reached 45 percent for tax years 2007-2009. Under the 2010 Act, the maximum estate tax rate for the years 2010-2012 was set at 35 percent. In 2013, Congress signed the American Taxpayer Relief Act of 2012 into law, which set the maximum estate tax rate at 40 percent.

lowest marginal rate at which taxes are actually paid is 40 percent. Thus, although it appears from the rate table that the tax is progressive, the estate and gift tax has been imposed at a flat marginal rate of 40 percent since 2007. The rate table is reproduced in Appendix A.

The broad goal of the unified estate and gift tax system is generally to treat all gratuitous transfers in a similar manner, whether they occur during life or at death. Although as we will see later on, despite the unified system, there remain numerous differences between the tax consequences of transfers during life and those at death that must be taken into account.[3]

EXAMPLE 5-8

D makes a taxable gift of $1,000,000 in 2009, and dies in 2022 with a taxable estate of $12,000,000. D's tentative tax liability (i.e., his tax liability before applying any available credits, including the unified credit) is $5,145,800. This is the same tentative tax liability that would apply if D had died without making the gift and with a taxable estate of $13,000,000.

Not all gratuitous transfers result in a tax liability. There are a number of deductions, exclusions, and credits exempting certain transfers from tax, including unlimited deductions for transfers to a spouse or a charity.

EXAMPLE 5-9

D dies in 2022 with a taxable estate of $20,000,000. D transfers her entire estate to her husband. D's estate will not be subject to any estate or gift tax liability.

EXAMPLE 5-10

D dies in 2022 with a taxable estate of $10,000,000. D transfers her entire estate to charity. D's estate will not be subject to any estate or gift tax liability.

Most significantly, the estate and gift tax system provides a large unified credit of $10,000,000, indexed for inflation, through 2025, and with a reversion to $5,000,000, indexed for inflation, thereafter. This exempts most taxpayers from the federal estate and gift tax system. For the year 2022, the unified credit exemption amount for estate and gift tax purposes is $12,060,000.

---

[3] These differences are discussed in Chapter 8.

The unified credit exemption amount has been a political football which has changed significantly over the years. When the unified estate and gift tax system was first adopted in 1977, the unified credit only exempted the first $120,667 from tax. Over the next decade, this exemption amount gradually increased to $600,000, which applied for the years 1987-1997. In 1997, Congress increased the exemption amount to $1,000,000, providing for a ten-year phase in; however, before the phase-in was complete, Congress enacted the 2001 Act which provided for a more drastic increase to the unified credit exemption amount for estate (though not gift) tax purposes: $1,000,000 for years 2002-2003, $1,500,000 for years 2004-2005, $2,000,000 for years 2006-2008, and $3,500,000 for 2009. The estate tax was repealed for 2010. However, in 2010, Congress enacted the 2010 Tax Act which again increased the unified credit exemption amount, this time to $5,000,000, for estate tax purposes for years 2010-2012 and for gift tax purposes for years 2011-2012 (subject to inflation adjustment in 2012). If no new legislation had passed prior to January 1, 2013, the unified credit exemption amount would have returned to its pre-2001 Act levels with a $1,000,000 unified credit for gift and estate tax purposes. However, the American Taxpayer Relief Act of 2012 avoided this result, and set the unified credit exemption amount at $5,000,000, indexed for inflation. But then in 2017, Congress passed the TCJA, increasing that amount to $10,000,000 (indexed for inflation) through 2025, returning that amount to its pre-TCJA level thereafter. The applicable unified credit exemption amount for 2022 is $12,060,000. Table 5-1 shows the unified credit as well as the exemption equivalent amount (the amount of transfer exempted by the credit) for each year from 1977-2022.

TABLE 5-1
UNIFIED CREDIT

Year:	Amount of Credit:	Amount of Exemption Equivalent:
1977	$ 30,000	$120,667
1978	34,000	134,000
1979	38,000	147,333
1980	42,500	161,563
1981	47,000	175,625
1982	62,800	225,000
1983	79,300	275,000
1984	96,300	325,000
1985	121,800	400,000
1986	155,800	500,000
1987–1997	192,800	600,000
1998	202,050	625,000
1999	211,300	650,000
2000–2001	220,550	675,000
2002–2003	345,800	1,000,000
2004–2005	555,800*	1,500,000*
2006–2008	780,800*	2,000,000*

Year:	Amount of Credit:	Amount of Exemption Equivalent:
2009	1,455,800*	3,500,000*
2010	1,730,800**	5,000,000**
2011	1,730,800	5,000,000
2012	1,772,800	5,120,000
2013	2,045,800	5,250,000
2014	2,081,800	5,340,000
2015	2,117,800	5,430,000
2016	2,125,800	5,450,000
2017	2,141,800	5,490,000
2018	4,417,800	11,180,000
2019	4,505,800	11,400,000
2020	4,577,800	11,580,000
2021	4,625,800	11,700,000
2022	4,769,800	12,060,000

* For tax years 2004-2010, the unified credit remained at $345,800 (exempting $1,000,000) for gift tax purposes and the higher amounts are effective for estate tax purposes only. After 2010, the unified credit is re-unified with the same exemption amount for both gift and estate tax purposes ($5,000,000 for 2011, $5,120,000 for 2012, $5,250,000 for 2013, $5,340,000 for 2014, $5,430,000 for 2015, $5,450,000 for 2016, and $5,490,00 for 2017).

** Decedents who died in the year 2010 had the option of either being subject to the $5,000,000 exemption amount provided for in the 2010 Act or their executors could elect to have no estate tax, but be subject to modified carryover basis rules.

[B] Portability of the Unified Credit

Prior to the enactment of the 2010 Tax Act, the unified credit was personal to each taxpayer and was only available to the extent that it offset his or her tax liability. If a taxpayer failed to use all of his or her unified credit (either because the estate was smaller than the exemption amount or because the property passed to the surviving spouse or in some other way such that it was not subject to estate taxes), then the tax benefit of the unified credit for that taxpayer was lost. Married couples could easily lose some of the advantages of the unified credit by transferring all of their property to the surviving spouse.

EXAMPLE 5-11

H and W had simple wills that provided that upon death all property would go to the surviving spouse, if living, and, if not, the property would go to H and W's children. H and W each owned $3,500,000 in assets. H died in 2009, and W died later in the same year.

In 2009, the unified credit amount sheltered $3,500,000 in assets. Upon H's death all of the property went to W under H's will. Due to the marital deduction, there was no tax liability for H's estate and therefore none of H's unified credit was used. Upon W's death, she had $7,000,000 in her estate (her original $3,500,000 plus the $3,500,000 from H). The unified credit only sheltered the first $3,500,000 from tax, resulting in a tax liability in W's estate of $1,575,000.

The 2010 Act included a provision that, for the first time, allowed a surviving spouse to use the unused portion of a decedent spouse's unified credit. This is referred to as "portability."[4] Portability was made permanent in the American Taxpayer Relief Act of 2012. The portability provision significantly simplifies estate planning for many married couples by eliminating the need to plan to use each spouse's unified credit.

EXAMPLE 5-12

H and W had simple wills that provided that upon death all property would go to the surviving spouse, if living, and, if not, the property would go to H and W's children. H and W each owned $10,000,000 in assets. H died in 2022, and W died later in the same year.

In 2022, the unified credit sheltered $12,060,000 in assets. Upon H's death, all of the property went to W and, due to the marital deduction, none of H's unified credit was used. However, H's executor filed an estate tax return in which she made an election for H's unused unified credit amount to be available to W. Upon W's death, she had $20,000,000 in her estate (her original $10,000,000 plus the $10,000,000 from her husband). W's unified credit consisted of her unified credit amount of $12,060,000 plus H's unused unified credit exclusion amount of $12,060,000. As a result, this combined unified credit could shelter all $20,000,000 from tax and W's estate had zero tax liability.

Although portability has the potential to simplify estate planning, it is not without its limitations. Portability is only available if an election is made on a completed estate tax return filed at the time of the first spouse's death. Also, portability can be lost in the event that the surviving spouse remarries without first using the decedent spouse's unused unified credit. Portability does not apply to all situations as it is not available for the generation-skipping transfer tax and generally cannot be relied on for state estate tax purposes in those jurisdictions that have a state estate tax.[5]

---

[4] IRC § 2010(c), as amended by Pub. L. No. 111-312, 124 Stat. 3296, § § 301(a)(1) and 303(a).

[5] Portability is discussed in greater detail in Chapter 6.

§5.05 ASSETS SUBJECT TO TAX

The estate and gift tax casts a wide net. The estate tax is imposed on all property owned or controlled by the decedent at death, whether or not the property passes through the probate process. In addition, the estate tax is also imposed on some property that the decedent did not own at the time of death but, because of strings attached to lifetime transfers, is nonetheless treated as being owned at death for estate tax purposes. The gift tax serves as a backstop to the estate tax and is imposed on all transfers of property by gift, unless exempted.

§5.06 OVERVIEW OF THE GIFT TAX SYSTEM

This section provides an overview of the gift tax system. The gift tax system provides a backstop to the estate tax system by taxing transfers by gift prior to death. Although an individual's final transfer tax liability is determined in the estate tax return, gift taxes can be understood as down payments (analogous to quarterly estimated tax payments in the income tax context) on the taxpayer's ultimate unified estate and gift tax liability.

[A] Calculating Gift Taxes

Gift taxes are calculated on an annual basis. The starting point for determining gift liability is determining the taxable gifts for the current year. *Taxable gifts* are all property transferred by gift, excluding the portion of the gift that qualifies for the annual exclusion or the exclusion for educational and medical expenses, and subtracting the transfers that qualify for the marital and charitable deduction.

To calculate the gift taxes due, the taxable gifts for the current year are added to the taxable gifts for all prior years. The unified rate schedule is then applied to the total taxable gifts for all calendar years, including the year of current transfer (this amount is referred to as the *tentative tax on all transfers by gift*). The reason for adding all prior years' taxable gifts is to ensure that the current year's gift is taxed at the appropriate marginal tax rate. However, to avoid double taxation, this amount is next reduced by the tentative tax on the aggregate total adjusted gifts for all prior years excluding the current year (calculated using the current year rate tables). This gives the *tentative tax on the gifts made during the current year*. Finally, this amount is reduced by the unused portion of the unified credit to determine the transferor's current gift tax liability. Note that the unified credit is the amount that would offset the unified credit exemption amounts. For example, a credit of $4,769,800 would entirely offset the tax liability of a $12,060,000 estate.

EXAMPLE 5-13

D made his first taxable gift in 2009 of $1,000,000. In 2022, D made an additional taxable gift of $12,000,000.

The starting point for determining D's tax liability in 2009 is calculating the tentative tax on $1,000,000 (D's total lifetime taxable gifts through

2009). Applying the rate table, the tentative tax on $1,000,000 is $345,800. The next step is to reduce this amount by the tentative tax on all transfers prior to the current year. Since this was D's first taxable gift, that amount is zero. Finally, the $345,800 tentative tax liability is reduced by the unused portion of the unified credit. In 2009, the unified credit for gifts was $345,800. Since no prior taxable gifts had been made, the unified credit was fully available to offset the 2009 tax liability. Thus, the $345,800 tentative tax liability was totally offset by the unified credit, resulting in a zero-tax liability for that year.

As stated above, in 2022, D made a taxable gift of $12,000,000. The starting point to calculate D's tax liability for that year is to accumulate all of D's lifetime gifts (in this case, it is the $12,000,000 current gift and the $1,000,000 previous gift resulting in total lifetime taxable gifts of $13,000,000). The tentative tax liability on $13,000,000 (as determined by the 2022 rate table) is $5,145,800. The next step is to subtract the tentative tax liability on all prior year gifts (in this case, all prior year gifts are $1,000,000). The tentative tax liability on $1,000,000 (as determined by the 2022 rate table) is $345,800; thus, the tentative tax on all lifetime gifts ($5,145,800) minus the tentative tax on all prior year gifts ($345,800) results in a current tentative tax liability of $4,800,000. Finally, this amount is reduced by the unused portion of the unified credit. The unified credit amount in 2022 is $4,769,800; however, since $345,800 of this credit was already used in 2009 (to offset the gift tax liability on the transfer of $1,000,000), the remaining available credit is only $4,424,000. After applying this credit to the $4,800,000 tentative tax liability, D has a gift tax liability in 2022 of $376,000. (Note that this is the same tax liability that D would have had if she had transferred all $13,000,000 in 2022.)

[B] Transfers Subject to Gift Tax

The gift tax imposes a tax on transfers of property by gift. A *gift* is defined as a transfer of property for less than full and adequate consideration in money or money's worth.[1] Thus, even sales of property can constitute a gift if the property is sold for less than fair market value.

EXAMPLE 5-14

D sells her house to her son for $100,000. The fair market value of the house at the time of transfer is $800,000. D has made a gift to her son of $700,000 (the excess of the fair market value of the property over the consideration received by D).

---

[1] **§ 5.06** Reg. § 25.2512-8. What constitutes a gift is discussed in greater detail in Chapter 8.

If the sale occurs in the ordinary course of business and is free of donative intent, then it will not be treated as a gift for tax purposes.[2]

EXAMPLE 5-15

D sells her car to her neighbor for $10,000, a price she believes represents the car's fair market value. The fair market value of the car at the time of transfer is really $15,000. D has not made a gift to her neighbor if D was free of donative intent in making the sale.

[C] Valuation for Gift Tax Purposes

Property that is transferred by gift is subject to tax based on its fair market value measured at the time of transfer. The definition of fair market value for gift tax purposes is the same standard that applies for estate tax purposes. Fair market value is "the price at which such property would change hands between a willing buyer and a willing seller, neither being under any compulsion to buy or to sell, and both having reasonable knowledge of relevant facts."[3] Similar to the estate tax, this is an objective standard that looks to market values for purposes of establishing valuation. Inherent in this definition is the requirement that the property's "highest and best use" be considered. That is, property is valued at the use that would generate the largest market return, even if this use is different from the way the property is actually being used. However, unlike the estate tax system, there are no special-use valuation rules available for the gift tax.[4]

EXAMPLE 5-16

D has a family farm located in a wealthy residential suburb. As a farm, the property is worth $200,000. However, as a housing development the land would be worth $1,000,000.

D makes a gift of the farm to his son. The gift is valued at its $1,000,000 value based on its highest and best use (as a housing development), rather than its value as a farm, regardless of how D's son plans to use the property.

---

[2] *Id.*

[3] Reg. § 25.2512-1.

[4] The special-use valuation rules for estate tax purposes are found in IRC § 2032A and are discussed in greater detail in Chapter 11.

All transfers by gift are valued as of the date of transfer, regardless of any subsequent changes in the value of the property.[5] Thus, even if the value of the gifted property were to plunge shortly after transfer, the value of the property for gift tax purposes would still be the higher date of transfer value. This rule can also work to the taxpayer's advantage if the property appreciates in value after the date of gift. Because of the tendency of property to appreciate over time, it is often advantageous to transfer property by gift as early as possible in order to take advantage of the lower valuation.

[D] Exclusions and Deductions

The gift tax provides for a number of exclusions and deductions. The effect of these is to remove a number of transfers from the estate and gift tax system. In particular, the gift tax system provides for an annual exclusion of $16,000 per donee (for gifts made after December 31, 2021), an unlimited exclusion for transfers for certain educational and medical expenses, and unlimited deductions for marital and charitable transfers.

[1] Annual Gift Tax Exclusion

As of 2022, a taxpayer may make annual gifts of up to $16,000 to an unlimited number of donees.[6] This amount is scheduled to increase for inflation in $1,000 increments. A married taxpayer can transfer up to $32,000 per donee if his/her spouse consents to join in the gift.[7]

The purpose of the annual exclusion is to permit taxpayers to make small gifts without the necessity of filing gift tax returns. However, the size of the exclusion, combined with the fact that it is available annually for an unlimited number of donees, makes it a very valuable estate planning tool. Frequent use of the $16,000 annual exclusion enables a taxpayer to remove significant assets from his or her gross estate.

In order to be eligible for the annual exclusion, the interest must not be a future interest (this is sometimes referred to as the *present interest requirement*). A future interest is an interest that is "limited to commence in use, possession or enjoyment at some future date or time."[8] Under this rule, outright transfers of property will generally qualify for the annual exclusion, but interests in trusts will qualify for the annual exclusion only if specific requirements are met. All gifts of remainder interests, regardless of whether they are vested or contingent remainders, are future interests and therefore not eligible for the annual exclusion.[9] However, trusts are

---

[5] IRC § 2512(a).

[6] IRC § 2503(b).

[7] IRC § 2513.

[8] Reg. § 25.2503-3.

[9] The annual exclusion is discussed in greater detail in Chapter 8.

often drafted to give beneficiaries a right to withdraw principal for a limited period of time (called Crummey powers) and these withdrawal rights allow gifts in trust to qualify for the annual exclusion.

[2] Exclusion for Transfers for Educational and Medical Expenses

There is an unlimited gift tax exclusion for amounts paid on behalf of any individual for certain medical or educational expenses.[10] The exclusion is in addition to the annual exclusion and is unlimited as to amount. Moreover, the exclusion is available regardless of the relationship be the donor and the donee. However, in order to be eligible for the exclusion, the payment must be made directly to the provider of the educational or medical services.[11]

[3] Unlimited Gift Tax Deduction for Marital Transfers

An individual may make unlimited transfers of property to a spouse free of gift tax under the marital deduction provision.[12] However, in order to qualify for this deduction, the transfer must be in the form of a qualifying interest. These rules are the same as the estate tax rules applicable to transfers of property at death. In general, any outright transfer of property will constitute a qualifying interest, although transfers of less than the donor's entire interest in property must meet the requirements of the terminable interest rule in order to be eligible for the marital deduction.[13]

The *terminable interest rule* denies the marital deduction for transfers of interests that terminate or fail upon the lapse of time or the occurrence or nonoccurrence of an event if a person other than the spouse will receive the property from the donor after the termination of the spouse's interest.[14]

EXAMPLE 5-17

H transfers $1,000,000 to a trust for the benefit of W. The trust provides that, in the event of divorce, W's interest in the trust will instead be held for the benefit of H and W's children.

The $1,000,000 transfer by H to this trust will not qualify for the marital deduction. It violates the terminable interest rule because W's interest will terminate upon the occurrence of an event (divorce) and, after her interest terminates, someone else (H and W's children) will receive the property from the donor.

---

[10] IRC § 2503(e).

[11] The exclusion for educational and medical expenses is discussed in greater detail in Chapter 8.

[12] IRC § 2523.

[13] IRC § 2523(b).

[14] *Id.*

There are a number of exceptions to the terminable interest rule.[15] The two exceptions most commonly used in estate planning are the power of appointment trust and the QTIP trust. Under the power of appointment trust exception, a transfer will qualify for the marital deduction if the spouse receives all of the income from the property for life payable at least annually, and a power of appointment over the property exercisable either during life or at death.[16] Under the QTIP trust exception, a transfer will qualify for the marital deduction if the spouse receives all of the income from the property for life payable at least annually, and if the donor spouse makes the election to have the property treated as QTIP property.[17] The effect of the election is that all property remaining in the QTIP trust at the time of the donee spouse's death is taxed in the donee spouse's estate, even though the donee spouse's interest in the property was limited to an income interest for life.[18]

The marital deduction is not available in the case of transfers to spouses who are not U.S. citizens at the time of the gift. However, in that situation, the $16,000 annual exclusion is increased to $164,000 per year for transfers to spouses who are not U.S. citizens.[19] In order for the increased annual exclusion amount to apply, the gift in excess of $16,000 (the otherwise applicable annual exclusion amount) must be in a form that qualifies for the marital deduction.[20]

[4] Unlimited Gift Tax Deduction for Charitable Transfers

The gift tax provides for an unlimited charitable deduction for property transferred to qualifying charitable, religious, or governmental organizations.[21] If the donor transfers less than her entire interest in the property, then the transfer must be in a specifically permitted form in order to qualify for the charitable deduction. The charitable deduction is discussed in Chapter 10.

§5.07 OVERVIEW OF THE ESTATE TAX SYSTEM

This section provides an overview of the estate tax system. The estate tax is due nine months after the date of death and represents the final calculation of an individual's total lifetime transfer tax liability.

---

[15] These exceptions are discussed in greater detail in Chapter 6.

[16] IRC § 2523(e).

[17] IRC § 2523(f). Form 1 contains a sample QTIP trust.

[18] The taxes associated with this inclusion may be paid from the trust assets. IRC § 2207A.

[19] IRC § 2523(i); Rev. Proc. 2020-45, 2020-46 I.R.B. 1016.

[20] Reg. § 25.2523(i)-1(c). Planning for noncitizen spouses is discussed in greater detail in Chapter 6.

[21] IRC § 2522.

[A] Calculating Estate Taxes

The starting point for calculating the estate tax liability is determining what property is subject to the estate tax. This collection of property is referred to as the *gross estate*. The gross estate is reduced by the allowable deductions to arrive at the *taxable estate*. Because the estate tax system is unified with the gift tax system, all prior taxable gifts (except for those that are included in the gross estate under the *string provisions*) are added to the taxable estate. The sum of the taxable estate and the prior taxable gifts is called the *tax base*.[1] The *tentative tax is* computed by applying the unified tax rate table to the tax base. In order to avoid double taxation, the tentative tax is reduced by gift taxes paid on prior transfers. Finally, the tentative tax is further reduced by the unified credit amount for the year of death (and, if applicable, the unused unified credit amount of a deceased spouse) as well as the credits for state[2] and foreign death taxes, certain previously paid federal estate taxes, and credit for gift taxes paid on pre-1977 gifts.

The following examples illustrate estate tax calculations for different situations. The first example illustrates the calculation for the most simple situation in which the decedent died without having made any prior taxable gifts.

EXAMPLE 5-18

D died in 2022, with a gross estate of $15,000,000 and $1,000,000 of allowable deductions. D made no taxable gifts during her life.

D's estate tax liability is calculated by taking her gross estate of $15,000,000 and subtracting her allowable deductions of $1,000,000 to arrive at her taxable estate of $14,000,000. There are no prior taxable gifts, so there is nothing to add to the taxable estate to arrive at the tax base of $14,000,000. Applying the rate table to this amount, there is a tentative tax of $5,545,800. The tentative tax of $5,545,800 is reduced by the unified credit amount for the year of death (in 2022, the unified credit amount is $4,769,800). Assuming there are no other credits available to D's estate, D's final estate tax liability would be $776,000.

---

[1] **§ 5.07** Although it initially may appear that adding the taxable gifts will result in double taxation (once at the time of gift and later at the time of death), this is not the case since the estate tax will be offset by the full unified credit as well as any gift taxes paid. IRC § § 2010 and 2012.

[2] Many states had imposed *a sponge tax* (i.e., a state death tax equal to the amount of the federal estate tax credit allowable under IRC § 2011) that, prior to the 2001 Act, had the effect of allowing states to raise revenues without increasing a taxpayer's overall tax burden. The 2001 Act phased out the credit for state death taxes beginning in 2002 and replaced the credit with a deduction. IRC § 2011(b) as added by 2001 Act § 531. The effect of this federal change has been to erode state tax revenues. Some states have already responded by changing their estate tax provisions. In any event, state taxes are likely to become more relevant with the passage of time and the large scheduled increases in the federal exemption amount.

The next example illustrates the calculation for the situation where there have been prior taxable gifts, although no gift tax has been paid due to the fact that the total taxable gifts did not exceed the applicable unified credit.

EXAMPLE 5-19

D made a taxable gift in 2013 of $1,000,000. Since the gift tax liability was covered by the unified credit exemption equivalent amount, no gift tax was paid at that time. In 2022, D died with a gross estate of $14,000,000 and $1,000,000 of allowable deductions.

D's estate tax liability is calculated by taking her gross estate of $14,000,000 and subtracting her allowable deductions of $1,000,000 to arrive at her taxable estate of $13,000,000. The prior taxable gift of $1,000,000 is added to the taxable estate to produce a tax base of $14,000,000. Applying the rate table to this amount, there is a tentative tax of $5,545,800. The tentative tax of $5,545,800 is reduced by the unified credit amount for the year of death (in 2022, the unified credit is $4,769,800) as well as by any gift taxes actually paid on the prior gift (in this case, there were no gift taxes actually paid due to the fact that the transfers by gift were less than the unified credit amount applicable in the year of transfer). Assuming there are no other credits available to D's estate, D's final estate tax liability would be $776,000.

The final example illustrates how estate taxes are calculated when prior taxable gifts have been made and gift taxes have been paid.

EXAMPLE 5-20

D made a taxable gift in 2013 of $6,000,000. After taking into account her unified credit (which, in 2013, was $2,045,800), D paid a gift tax on the transfer of $300,000. In 2022, D died with a gross estate of $9,000,000 and $1,000,000 of allowable deductions.

D's estate tax liability is calculated by taking her gross estate of $9,000,000 and subtracting her allowable deductions of $1,000,000 to arrive at her taxable estate of $8,000,000. The prior taxable gift of $6,000,000 is added to the taxable estate to produce a tax base of $14,000,000. Applying the rate table to this amount, there is a tentative tax of $5,545,800. The tentative tax of $5,545,800 is reduced by the unified credit for the year of death (in 2022, the unified credit is $4,769,800), as well as by the $300,000 of gift taxes actually paid on the prior gift. Assuming there are no other credits available to D's estate, D's final estate tax liability would be $476,000.

Note that in all of the above examples, D transferred a total of $14,000,000 during life and at death (taking into account deductions), and had a combined gift and estate tax liability of $776,000.

The interplay between gift taxes and estate taxes in the unified system can be initially confusing since gifts are both subject to tax in the year of transfer and also added to the gross estate in determining the decedent's estate tax liability. The role of gift taxes becomes much clearer if you think of them as down payments (analogous to quarterly estimated tax payments in the income tax context) on the taxpayer's ultimate unified estate and gift tax liability. Although it appears that transfers by gift are being subject to tax twice (both in the year of transfer and at death), this is not really the case because, although the gifts are added back to the tax base in calculating the estate tax, the estate tax liability is offset by the full unified credit as well as any gift taxes actually paid.[3]

[B] Property Subject to the Estate Tax

The gift tax serves as a backstop to the estate tax. Therefore, the starting point for understanding the unified estate and gift tax system is the property subject to the estate tax. This is generally referred to as property in the *gross estate*. Many people confuse the gross estate with the probate estate.[4] However, the gross estate is a much broader concept. There are three general categories of property included in the gross estate: (1) property that was directly owned by the decedent (including property interests that pass outside of the probate process); (2) property whose disposition was subject to the decedent's control (through a general power of appointment); and (3) property that the decedent transferred by gift, but that is nonetheless subject to the estate tax, because the decedent did not give up complete control or ownership of the property at the time of transfer.[5]

[1] Property Directly Owned by the Decedent

[a] *In General*

The estate tax is imposed on all property interests owned by the decedent at the time of death.[6] Property is subject to the estate tax under this general provision if (1)

---

[3] After the 2001 Act, payment of gift taxes may result in the unnecessary payment of tax if the donor has made a taxable gift and subsequently dies with a taxable estate which, when combined with the taxable gifts, is equal to or less than the applicable exclusion amount for estate tax purposes. See § 5.02[B] *supra* for example.

[4] The probate estate is that property of the decedent that is subject to the probate process. It is generally property owned by the decedent at the time of death that does not have a legally recognized, designated death beneficiary. The probate estate is discussed in greater detail in Chapter 2.

[5] Property subject to the estate tax is described in IRC §§ 2031–2044 and 2046.

[6] IRC § 2033 provides that the gross estate includes "the value of all property to the extent of the decedent's interest therein at the time of his death."

the decedent owned the property interest immediately before death,[7] and (2) the decedent's property interest was transmittable at death.[8] This provision covers all probate property and many nonprobate property interests, such as accounts with payable-on-death provisions and Totten trusts. Some examples of property interests subject to tax under this general provision include: tangible property, such as real estate, automobiles, jewelry, and works of art; intangible interests, such as bank accounts, securities, patents, copyrights, stock, and other business interests; and future interests, including reversions and remainders. In addition, it also includes interests that one might not initially think of as property interests, including causes of action and rights of publicity.

Property interests that are not transmittable by the decedent at death are generally not subject to estate tax.[9] Thus, if the only interest the decedent ever owned in property was a life estate (the right to use of the property, or income from the property, for the life of the decedent), then nothing will be included in his gross estate because he owns no interest that can be transmitted at death.[10] Similarly, Social Security benefits are not subject to estate tax since the payment of death benefits is controlled by statute and not directed by the decedent.[11]

[b] Community Property

Community property is property acquired by either spouse, other than by gift or inheritance, during the course of a marriage while living in a community property jurisdiction.[12] Under the rules of community property, each spouse has the right to transmit only half of his or her community property at death. Because of this rule, when a spouse with community property dies, only half of the community property is subject to estate tax.

---

[7] The issue of whether the decedent had a property interest is determined by state law. State law is conclusively determined, if at all, only by the highest court of the state; decisions of the lower courts will only be given "due regard." Comm'r v. Estate of Bosch, 387 U.S. 456 (1967).

[8] IRC § 2033.

[9] There is an exception to this rule, however, for the situation in which the decedent had originally owned the entire interest in the property and then transferred by gift everything but the life estate. In that situation, the full value of the property will nonetheless be brought in to the decedent's gross estate under IRC § 2036. This is one of the "string" provisions discussed in greater detail in § 5.07[B][3] *infra*.

[10] *See, e.g.*, Rev. Rul. 66–86, 1966-1 C.B. 219.

[11] *See* Rev. Rul. 67-277, 1967-2 C.B. 322. Other interests that are similarly treated are Railroad Retirement Act benefits, Rev. Rul. 67-277, 1967-2 C.B. 322; veterans' benefits, Rev. Rul. 76-501, 1976-2 C.B. 267; U.S. Public Safety Officers' Benefits Act benefits, Rev. Rul. 79-397, 1979-2 C.B. 322; and state workers' compensation benefits, Rev. Rul. 56-637, 1956-2 C.B. 600.

[12] The community property system exists in Arizona, California, Idaho, Louisiana, Nevada, New Mexico, Texas, and Washington. In addition, Wisconsin, through its adoption of the Uniform Marital Property Act, has adopted a system that is very similar to the community property system. Community property is discussed in greater detail in Chapter 6.

EXAMPLE 5-21

H and W, a married couple, live in a community property state. H has $150,000 of separate property, and H and W have $800,000 of community property. At the time of H's death, his gross estate for tax purposes is $550,000, consisting of $150,000 separate property plus half of the $800,000 community property.

[c] Joint Tenancies

Property held in joint tenancy that was acquired by purchase is generally included in the decedent's gross estate, except to the extent that the executor can show that the surviving joint tenant contributed to the cost of the property.[13] Thus, absent proof of contribution, the entire value of joint tenancy property is subject to estate tax when the first joint tenant dies.

EXAMPLE 5-22

A and B own real estate as joint tenants. A paid the purchase price of $1,000,000. At the time of A's death, the property was worth $3,000,000. The full value of the property ($3,000,000) will be subject to estate tax in A's estate.

If B had predeceased A, then the full value of the property would be included in B's estate for estate tax purposes, unless the executor of B's estate submits facts sufficient to show that the property was not acquired with consideration furnished by B.

If it can be shown that the surviving joint tenant contributed to the cost of the property, then only a proportional share of the property will be subject to estate tax when the first joint tenant dies.

EXAMPLE 5-23

A and B own real estate as joint tenants. A paid $800,000 and B paid $200,000 toward the $1,000,000 purchase price. At the time of A's death, the property was worth $3,000,000. Of this amount, $2,400,000 (four-fifths of the date-of-death value of the property) will be included in A's estate for tax purposes.

---

[13] The estate tax treatment of joint tenancy property is governed by IRC § 2040. An exception to this rule is provided for joint tenancy property owned by married couples. IRC § 2040(b).

If B had predeceased A, then $600,000 (one-fifth of the date-of-death value of the property) would have been included in B's estate for tax purposes.

If the joint tenants are married at the time of the first joint tenant's death, then special rules apply. In that situation, only half of the value of the joint property is subject to estate tax upon the first joint tenant's death, regardless of contribution. This same rule applies if the property is held as tenants by the entirety.

EXAMPLE 5-24

H and W, a married couple, own real estate as joint tenants. H paid the entire purchase price of $1,000,000. At the time of H's death, the property was worth $3,000,000. Half of the date-of-death value of the property, or $1,500,000, will be subject to estate tax in H's estate.

If W had predeceased H, then half of the date-of-death value of the property, or $1,500,000, would be subject to estate tax in W's estate.

Although this rule superficially appears to benefit taxpayers (by limiting the amount included in the gross estate), the overall effect is detrimental because transfers to spouses are not subject to tax under the marital deduction, and this provision limits the income tax benefit to the surviving spouse of the full step-up in basis that could otherwise be available.[14]

If the joint tenants acquired the property by gift or inheritance, then a *pro-rata* share of the property is includable in each tenant's gross estate for tax purposes.

EXAMPLE 5-25

Father transfers real estate in joint tenancy to his daughters A, B, and C.

Upon A's death, one-third of the value of the property (her *pro-rata* share) is included in her gross estate, even though the property will pass by operation of law to B and C as joint tenants.

Upon B's death, half of the value of the property will be included in her gross estate, even though the property will pass by operation of law to C.

Upon C's death, the entire value of the property will be included in her gross estate. Since she was the last surviving joint tenant, she owned the property outright.

---

[14] This special basis rule is discussed in § 6.02[B][5] *infra*.

[d] Life Insurance

Proceeds of life insurance owned by the insured are generally subject to estate tax in the insured's estate.[15] Specifically, proceeds of life insurance are includable in the insured's estate for tax purposes if (1) the policy is payable to or for the benefit of the insured's estate, or (2) the policy proceeds are payable to someone else, but the insured possessed any of the incidents of ownership of the life insurance policy at the time of death.[16] Generally speaking, an *incident of ownership* is the ability to control any of the economic benefits of the property.[17]

A policy will be included in the insured's estate whenever the proceeds are payable to the estate or the executor of the estate.[18]

EXAMPLE 5-26

D was insured under a life insurance policy with a face value of $1,000,000. The policy named D's estate as beneficiary of the policy. At D's death, $1,000,000, the face value of the policy, will be subject to estate tax in D's estate.

The policy need not explicitly designate the estate or executor as the beneficiary in order for the policy to be treated as being payable to or for the benefit of the insured's estate. Rather, if the decedent's estate has the legal right to the proceeds of the life insurance policy, it will be treated as payable to the decedent's estate. Thus, if the policy names someone else as a beneficiary, but the beneficiary is legally obligated to pay taxes, debts, or other enforceable charges against the estate, then the amount of proceeds required for the payment of the obligation is subject to tax in the decedent insured's estate.[19]

Even if the decedent's estate has no legal right to the proceeds of the policy, a life insurance policy payable to someone else will nonetheless be included in the insured's estate if, at the time of death, the insured held any incidents of ownership of the policy.[20] An incident of ownership includes, among other things, the power to change the beneficiary, to surrender or cancel the policy, to assign the policy, to revoke an assignment, to pledge the policy for a loan, or to obtain from the insurer a loan against the surrender value of the policy.[21]

---

[15] IRC § 2042.
[16] *Id.*
[17] Reg. § 20.2042-1(c)(2).
[18] IRC § 2042(1).
[19] Reg. § 20.2042-1(b)(1).
[20] IRC § 2042(2).
[21] Reg. § 20.2042-1(c).

EXAMPLE 5-27

D was insured under a life insurance policy with a face value of $1,000,000. The policy named D's child, C, as beneficiary of the policy. D continued to own the policy and had the ability to change the beneficiary of the policy up until the time of D's death. At D's death $1,000,000 will be subject to estate tax in D's estate.

If the insured does not have any incident of ownership of the policy, and if the policy is not payable to or for the benefit of the insured's estate, then it will not be subject to tax in the insured's estate.

EXAMPLE 5-28

D was insured under a life insurance policy with a face value of $1,000,000. The policy named D's child, C, as beneficiary of the policy and the policy was owned by D's child, C. D has no incidents of ownership in the policy. At D's death none of the proceeds of the life insurance policy will be subject to estate tax in D's estate.

Finally, even if the insured did not have any incident of ownership of the life insurance policy at the time of death, proceeds from the policy will nonetheless be subject to tax in the insured's estate if the insured transferred ownership in the policy by gift within three years of death.[22]

EXAMPLE 5-29

D was insured under a life insurance policy with a face value of $1,000,000. The policy named D's child, C, as beneficiary of the policy. In 2020, D transferred ownership of the policy to C. In 2022, D died. Because D died within three years of making a gift of the life insurance policy, $1,000,000 will be subject to estate tax in D's estate.

[e] Retirement Benefits

Retirement benefits are generally subject to estate tax in the employee's estate, regardless of whether the benefits are from a nonqualified plan, qualified plan, or Individual Retirement Account (IRA).[23]

---

[22] IRC § 2035(a). The estate planning aspects of insurance are discussed in greater detail in Chapter 12.

[23] IRC § 2033. There is a limited exception to this rule for certain pre-1985 qualified retirement benefits. This exception is discussed in greater detail in Chapter 13. Retirement benefits in excess of a

EXAMPLE 5-30

At the time of D's death, D had an IRA that was worth $500,000. D's IRA is part of her gross estate for purposes of calculating her estate tax liability.

[2] Property Controlled by the Decedent—Powers of Appointment

The estate tax is also imposed on property that is controlled by the decedent, even if not owned directly by the decedent. In particular, the estate tax is imposed on property that was subject to a general power of appointment.[24]

A *power of appointment* is the right to select who will receive an interest in property. Since only certain powers of appointment are subject to estate tax, powers of appointment are extensively employed in trusts in order to give the holder considerable control over the trust property, while at the same time gaining some tax advantage. In addition, special powers of appointment are widely used to control a donee's disposition of property.

Powers of appointment have their own terminology. The person who creates the power of appointment is called the *donor* of the power. The person who holds the power is the *holder* or *donee* of the power. The persons in whose favor the power can be exercised are the *objects* of the power. When a power is exercised in favor of such person, that person is called the *appointee.* Finally, the instrument may provide for *takers in default of appointment,* people who will take the property if the holder fails to exercise the power.

A power of appointment can be exercisable during the holder's life (called an *inter vivos* power of appointment) or exercisable only upon death (called a *testamentary* power of appointment). If the power of appointment is testamentary, then it is exercisable through the holder's will.

A power of appointment is subject to estate tax in the holder's estate only if it is exercisable in favor of the holder, the holder's estate, the holder's creditors, or creditors of the holder's estate.[25] A power of appointment that is exercisable for the benefit of any of the above is a *general power of appointment.* If an individual holds a general power of appointment, then the property subject to the power is subject to estate tax in the individual's estate (regardless of whether the power is exercised).

(Footnote Continued)

certain amount were previously subject to an additional 15 percent excise tax, although this tax was repealed for distributions after December 31, 1996. IRC § 4980A, repealed by Taxpayer Relief Act of 1997, Pub. L. No. 105-34, 111 Stat. 788 (1997). The estate planning aspects of retirement benefits are discussed in detail in Chapter 13.

[24] IRC § 2041.

[25] IRC § 2041(b).

EXAMPLE 5-31

A trust is funded with $2,000,000. Under the terms of the trust, beneficiary B has the power to invade the principal for his own benefit. At the time of B's death, the full date-of-death value of the trust property will be included in B's gross estate for estate tax purposes because he could have withdrawn all of the trust property during his lifetime.

An important exception to this rule regarding general powers of appointment is the *ascertainable standard* exception. If the individual's power to appoint the property to himself is limited by an ascertainable standard relating to health, education, support, or maintenance (or any combination thereof), then it will not be treated as a general power of appointment.[26]

EXAMPLE 5-32

A trust is funded with $2,000,000. Under the terms of the trust, beneficiary B has the power to invade the principal only to the extent that it is required for his health, education, and support in his accustomed manner of living. None of the trust property will be included in B's gross estate for estate tax purposes because, although he could have withdrawn the property for himself, his right to do so was limited by an ascertainable standard.

When using the ascertainable standard exception, it is important for the estate planner to carefully draft the standard using only the language explicitly sanctioned in the regulations.[27] Use of additional language can cause the provision to no longer qualify for the ascertainable standard exception.

EXAMPLE 5-33

A trust is funded with $2,000,000. Under the terms of the trust, beneficiary B has the power to invade the principal as may be required for his health, education, support in his accustomed manner of living, and happiness. The entire value of the trust property will likely be included in B's gross estate for estate tax purposes, because "happiness" is not generally considered to be an ascertainable standard.

A power of appointment that is not exercisable in favor of the holder, the holder's estate, the holder's creditors, or creditors of the holder's estate is not subject to estate tax in the holder of the power's estate. A power of appointment that is not

---

[26] IRC § 2041(b)(1)(A).
[27] Reg. § 20.2041-1(c)(2).

exercisable in favor of any of those individuals is called a *special, limited,* or *nongeneral* power of appointment.[28]

EXAMPLE 5-34

A transfers $2,000,000 to a trust for the benefit of B. Under the terms of the trust, B has the power to distribute trust principal to anyone other than himself, his estate, his creditors, or creditors of his estate. B has a special power of appointment and, upon B's death, none of the trust property will be included in B's gross estate for estate tax purposes.

Special powers of appointment are commonly used in credit shelter trusts when the donor spouse wants to give the surviving spouse the ability to allocate trust property among their children, thereby retaining some degree of control, but not the ability to dispose of the property to someone else (e.g., to a new spouse).[29]

EXAMPLE 5-35

W funds a trust with $2,000,000. Under the terms of the trust, H has the power to distribute trust principal to H and W's children, A, B, and C, either during life or at death. In the event that H fails to appoint the trust property, it will be distributed equally to A, B, and C upon H's death. H can appoint any, none, or all of the property to any, none, or all of the children A, B, or C, either during his life or at death. None of the trust property will be included in H's gross estate for estate tax purposes.

[3] Certain Property Transferred by the Decedent by Gift During Life

The estate tax is also imposed on property that was transferred by the decedent during life by gift, if the decedent did not give up complete control or ownership of the property at the time of transfer.[30] The provisions of the Internal Revenue Code, which subject these property interests to estate tax, are commonly called *string provisions* because they have the effect of pulling the property back into the estate for estate tax purposes.

The string provisions apply generally to the transfer of property by gift when the donor has retained one of the following types of interests in the property:

---

[28] Reg. § 20.2041-1(c).

[29] Form 1 provides an example of a special power of appointment.

[30] These provisions apply to all transfers "except in the case of a bona fide sale for full and adequate consideration in money or money's worth." *See* IRC § § 2035-2039.

- A life estate or right to income (or the ability to determine who will enjoy the life estate or right to income);[31]
- Certain reversionary interests;[32] or
- The power to revoke, alter, amend, or terminate the gift.[33]

In addition, the estate tax will also apply if any of these retained interests are transferred by gift by the decedent within three years of the decedent's death.[34]

[a] Transfer with Retained Life Estate

The entire value of property transferred by gift is included in the decedent's gross estate if the decedent transferred the property by gift and retained the right to income from the property or the right to use the property for life or for a period that does not in fact end before the decedent's death.[35]

EXAMPLE 5-36

D transferred his house to his child, C, and retained the right to live in the house for life. At the time of D's death, the full value of the house will be subject to estate tax in D's estate because the right to use the property was retained for life.

EXAMPLE 5-37

D transferred $2,000,000 to a trust and retained the right to income from the trust for ten years. D died seven years later. At the time of D's death, the full value of the trust will be subject to estate tax in D's estate because the right to income from the property was retained for a period that did not in fact end before the date of D's death.

Even if the decedent did not retain the right to possession or income for his own purposes, the full value of the property will nonetheless be subject to estate tax in the decedent's estate if he retained the right (either alone or in conjunction with someone else) to determine who would possess or enjoy the property or its income.

---

[31] IRC § 2036.
[32] IRC § 2037.
[33] IRC § 2038.
[34] IRC § 2035.
[35] IRC § 2036.

EXAMPLE 5-38

D transferred $2,000,000 to a trust that provided that income was to be paid to A for ten years, and the remainder was to be paid to B. D retained the right to change the income beneficiary from A to C. D died seven years later. At the time of D's death, the full value of the trust will be subject to estate tax in D's estate because, even though D could not get the property himself, he could control whether A or C would get the income interest.[36]

The ability to control an income interest can appear in many forms. For example, if the decedent has the ability to accumulate income (either as a trustee or in his individual capacity), then he has the ability to determine who will possess or enjoy the income from the property.

This rule is subject to an important exception: If the decedent's control of the income interest is limited by an ascertainable standard, then the property is not subject to tax in the decedent's estate.[37]

EXAMPLE 5-39

D transferred $2,000,000 to a trust that provided that income was to be paid to A for ten years and the remainder was to be paid to B. D retained the right to accumulate income and pay the income to B for B's health and support in B's accustomed manner of living. D died seven years later. At the time of D's death none of the trust will be subject to estate tax in D's estate.

In order for this exception to apply, the standard must provide sufficient guidance for a state court to enforce the rights of the trust beneficiary. The standards provided in the regulations under Section 2041 will generally meet this requirement.[38]

[b] Transfer with Retained Reversionary Interest

The entire value of property previously transferred by gift may be included in the decedent's gross estate if the decedent retained certain reversionary interests.[39] In particular, property will be included in the decedent's gross estate under this rule if all of the following conditions are met:

---

[36] This should not be confused with a special power of appointment (discussed in § 5.07[B][2]) which is not subject to tax in the holder's estate. The difference in this example is that the decedent was the original transferor of the property and *retained* this interest.

[37] Jennings v. Smith, 161 F.2d 74 (2d Cir. 1947).

[38] Reg. § 20.2041-1(c)(2).

[39] IRC § 2037.

1. Possession or enjoyment of the property by another can only be obtained by surviving the decedent;

2. The decedent retained a possibility that the property would revert to the decedent or be subject to disposition by him; and

3. The value of the reversionary interest immediately before the decedent's death exceeded 5 percent of the value of the entire property.[40]

EXAMPLE *5-40*

D transferred $2,000,000 to a trust that provided that income was to be paid to A for ten years and the remainder was to be paid to B unless D was living at that time, in which case the remainder would revert to D.

D dies during the term of the trust. Assuming D's reversion valued immediately before D's death exceeded 5 percent of the value of the trust, the entire value of the trust property will be subject to estate tax in D's estate, since B can only possess the property by surviving D and there was the possibility that the property would revert to D (even if D's death negated that possibility).

If possession or enjoyment of the property can be obtained by means other than surviving the decedent, then the property will not be included in the decedent's gross estate under this provision, even if the decedent retained the possibility of a reversion.[41]

EXAMPLE *5-41*

D transferred $2,000,000 to a trust that provided that income was to be paid to A for ten years and the remainder was to be paid to B if B was married at that time. If B was not married at that time, then the remainder would revert to D or D's estate.

Since B could possess the property without surviving D, none of the trust property will be subject to estate tax in D's estate, even if D dies within the ten-year term of the trust.

---

[40] Reg. § 20.2037-1.
[41] Reg. § 20.2037-1(b).

[c] Transfer with Retained Right to Revoke

Property is included in the decedent's gross estate if the decedent transferred the property by gift and the property was subject to the right to alter, amend, revoke, or terminate the transfer.[42]

EXAMPLE 5-42

D transferred $2,000,000 to a trust for the benefit of A and retained the right to revoke the trust. At the time of D's death, the full value of the trust will be subject to estate tax in D's estate.

Property is included in the decedent's estate regardless of whether the decedent could have gotten the property back himself and regardless of whether the decedent held this power in his individual or fiduciary capacity.

EXAMPLE 5-43

D transferred $100,000 to a discretionary trust for the benefit of A and B. D was the trustee of the trust and had the power to make distributions to either A or B. Since D had the power to alter the interests of the beneficiaries, the full value of the trust will be subject to estate tax in D's estate, even though D could not get the property back for himself.

However, if the exercise of the power is governed by an ascertainable standard, then the property will not be included in the decedent's gross estate.[43]

EXAMPLE 5-44

D transferred $2,000,000 to a discretionary trust for the benefit of A and B. D was the trustee of the trust and had the power to make distributions to either A or B for their health, education, support, or maintenance. Since D's power is limited by an ascertainable standard, none of the trust will be subject to estate tax in D's estate.

[d] Certain Transfers Within Three Years of Death

Prior to 1982, all property that had been transferred by gift (except for those qualifying for the annual exclusion) within three years of death was brought back

---

[42] IRC § 2038.
[43] Jennings v. Smith, 161 F.2d 74 (2d Cir. 1947).

§ 5.07[B][3][c]

into the estate for tax purposes. This rule has been significantly modified over the years and now the three-year rule only applies to a very small category of property interests, namely, life insurance and those interests that would have invoked the string provisions (retained income interests, reversionary interests, and retained powers to alter, amend, revoke, or terminate) had they been retained by the decedent.[44]

EXAMPLE 5-45

D transferred $2,000,000 to a trust for the benefit of A and retained the right to revoke the trust. Subsequently, D released her right to revoke the trust. If D dies within three years of this release, the entire value of the trust will be subject to estate tax in D's estate.

EXAMPLE 5-46

D transferred ownership of a life insurance policy to a trust for the benefit of his son. At the time of transfer, the life insurance policy had a cash value of $50,000 and a face value of $1,000,000. If D dies within three years of the transfer of the policy, then the entire proceeds of the life insurance policy will be subject to estate tax in D's estate.

[e] Gift Taxes Paid Within Three Years of Death

Gift taxes paid by the donor for gifts made within three years of death are also brought back into the estate for estate tax purposes.[45]

EXAMPLE 5-47

In 2020, D made a gift of $13,000,000, generating a tentative tax of $5,145,800. After applying his unified credit of $4,577,800, D paid a gift tax of $568,000. D died in 2022. Included in his gross estate will be $568,000, the amount of the gift taxes paid by the decedent for transfers by gift within three years of death.

---

[44] IRC § 2035.
[45] IRC § 2035(b).

[C] Valuation for Estate Tax Purposes

[1] General Rule

Property included in the gross estate is subject to tax based on its *fair market value*.[46] The fair market value is defined as "the price at which the property would change hands between a willing buyer and a willing seller, neither being under any compulsion to buy or to sell and both having reasonable knowledge of relevant facts."[47] This is an objective standard that looks to market values for purposes of establishing valuation.

Inherent in this definition of fair market value is the requirement that the property be valued at its "highest and best use." That is, property is valued at the use that would generate the largest market return; this use may be different from the way the property is actually being used.

EXAMPLE 5-48

D's house is located on property that is zoned for residential or commercial use. Used for residential purposes, the land is worth $300,000. However, a developer would pay $700,000 for the land if he could tear down the house and build an office building. When D dies, the property will be valued at $700,000, the market value of the property as based on its highest and best use, rather than its value as based on its current use.

[2] Exception for Real Estate in a Business or Farm

The one exception to the rule that all property must be valued at its highest and best use instead of its actual use is that real property used in a family farm or closely held business may be valued at its actual current use instead of its highest and best use if certain requirements are met.[48] This exception is only available for transfers occurring at death and not for transfers by gift.

EXAMPLE 5-49

D owns farmland located in a wealthy residential area. Used as a farm, the land is worth $400,000. However, as a potential development for residential housing, the land is worth $1,000,000. If D dies owning this

---

[46] Reg. § 20.2031-1(b).
[47] *Id.*
[48] IRC § 2032A.

property, the land can be valued at its $400,000 farmland value, provided certain requirements are met.

If D gave the property by gift during his life, it would be valued at its highest and best use value (as a housing development) rather than at its farmland value.

There are very strict rules for the application of this provision. In general, in order to be eligible for the relief this section offers, a number of requirements must be met. In particular, the decedent (or a member of the decedent's family) must have been actively involved in the operation of the business for a significant period of time prior to the decedent's death, the property must constitute a significant portion of the decedent's estate, and the property must pass to family members of the decedent who continue to operate the business for a significant period of time following the decedent's death. Finally, even if all of the requirements are met, this provision allows for a maximum reduction of $1,230,000 in the value of the property in 2022 (the amount is indexed for inflation).[49]

[3] Valuation Date

Property that is included in the gross estate is generally valued as of the date of death (unless the executor elects to use the alternate valuation date, discussed below).[50] In determining this valuation, the fact of the owner's death is taken into account. This can have significant effect (both positive and negative) on the value of the decedent's property.

EXAMPLE 5-50

D was a painter with an established reputation. At the time of D's death, D owned a number of his own paintings. Due to the fact that D can no longer create new paintings, D's paintings have greater value after his death than they did before he died. D's estate tax liability will be based on the higher value of D's paintings, taking into account the fact of D's death.

EXAMPLE 5-51

D owned a business. Due to D's extensive knowledge of the business and goodwill with her customers, D's business was very valuable while she was living; however, D's business has a significantly lower value after her

---

[49] The special-use valuation rule for real estate used in a family farm or business is discussed in greater detail in Chapter 11.

[50] IRC §§ 2031(a), 2032.

death than it did while she was living. For estate tax purposes, D's business will be valued at the lower value, taking into account the fact of D's death.

EXAMPLE 5-52

D owned a business. One of the assets of the business was a $1,000,000 life insurance policy on D's life. At the time of D's death, D's business will be valued for estate tax purposes including the $1,000,000 proceeds of the life insurance policy on D's life.

[4] Alternate Valuation Date

Property is generally valued as of the date of death for estate tax purposes. However, in order to avoid hardships caused by reductions in market values during administration of the estate, the decedent's representative may elect to value the property as of the date that is six months after the date of the decedent's death.[51]

EXAMPLE 5-53

D died on January 30, 2022. At the time of D's death his property consisted of a substantial stock portfolio that was worth $1,000,000. On July 30, 2022, due to a fall in prices in his stock portfolio, D's property was worth $700,000. D's executor may elect to value D's property as of July 30 instead of January 30.

If the election is made, all property still in the estate six months after the date of the decedent's death must be valued as of the alternate valuation date and any property sold or disposed of during that period is valued as of its date of disposition.

The alternate valuation date may only be used if the election will reduce the value of the gross estate and reduce the total estate tax due.[52] The reason for this limitation is to prevent taxpayers from claiming a higher estate tax value for property, thereby increasing the property's basis in the hands of the recipients and decreasing the taxable gain for income tax purposes when the property is later sold.[53]

---

[51] IRC § 2032.
[52] IRC § 2032(c).
[53] *See* § 5.06 *supra* for a discussion of the basis rules and their effect.

[D] Estate Tax Deductions

The estate tax system provides for a number of deductions. The effect of these deductions is to remove certain transfers from the estate tax system. The two most significant deductions from a planning perspective are the unlimited marital deduction and the unlimited charitable deduction.

[1] Unlimited Marital Deduction

The estate tax allows for an unlimited marital deduction.[54] This is similar to the gift tax marital deduction applicable during life.[55] In order to qualify for the marital deduction, the transfer must be to a surviving spouse who is a U.S. citizen and must be in the form of a qualifying interest.[56] Any outright transfer of property constitutes a qualifying interest. But transfers of less than the decedent's entire interest in property must meet the terminable interest rule requirements in order to be eligible for the marital deduction.

The *terminable interest rule* provides that the marital deduction is not available for interests that terminate or fail upon the lapse of time or the occurrence or nonoccurrence of an event if a person other than the surviving spouse receives the property from the decedent after the termination of the surviving spouse's interest.[57]

EXAMPLE 5-54

W's will provides that upon her death $1,000,000 will pass to a trust for the benefit of H. However, in the event of H's remarriage, his interest in the trust will terminate and the trust will instead be held for the benefit of H and W's children.

The $1,000,000 transfer by W to this trust will not qualify for the marital deduction. It violates the terminable interest rule because H's interest will terminate upon the occurrence of an event (his remarriage) and after his interest terminates, someone else (H and W's children) will receive the property from the decedent.

There are a number of exceptions to the terminable interest rule.[58] The two exceptions most commonly used in estate planning are the power of appointment trust and the qualified terminable interest property (most commonly known by its

---

[54] IRC § 2056. The marital deduction became unlimited in 1982 with the enactment of the Economic Recovery Tax Act of 1981. Pub. L. No. 97-34, 95 Stat. 170 (1981). Prior to that, the marital deduction was limited to the greater of $250,000 or half of the value of the decedent's adjusted gross estate. Many old estate plans still refer to that formula in establishing the marital share.

[55] IRC § 2523.

[56] IRC § 2056(a). The marital deduction is discussed in greater detail in Chapter 6.

[57] IRC § 2056(b)(1).

[58] IRC § 2056(b). These exceptions are discussed in greater detail in Chapter 6.

acronym QTIP) trust. Under the power of appointment trust exception, a transfer will qualify for the marital deduction if the surviving spouse receives all of the income from the property for life payable at least annually and is given a general power of appointment over the property exercisable either during life or at death.[59] Due to the general power of appointment, the value of the assets in the trust will be included in the surviving spouse's estate at the time of her death. Under the QTIP trust exception,[60] a transfer will qualify for the marital deduction if the surviving spouse receives all of the income from the property for life payable at least annually and if the decedent spouse's executor makes the election to have the property treated as QTIP property on the decedent spouse's federal estate tax return. The effect of the election is that all property remaining in the QTIP trust at the time of the surviving spouse's death is taxed in the surviving spouse's estate, even though the surviving spouse's interest in the property was limited to an income interest for life.

If the surviving spouse is not a U.S. citizen, then the unlimited marital deduction is not available. However, an exception is provided if the property passes to the spouse in the form of a qualified domestic trust (commonly known by its acronym QDOT).[61]

[2] Unlimited Charitable Deduction

The estate tax provides for an unlimited charitable deduction for property transferred to qualifying charitable, religious, or governmental organizations.[62] This is similar to the gift tax unlimited charitable deduction for transfers during life.[63] If the decedent transfers less than her entire interest in the property, then the transfer must be in a specifically permitted form in order to qualify for the charitable deduction.[64]

§ 5.08 COMMON ESTATE PLANNING TECHNIQUES

To the uninitiated, and even to many more experienced estate planners, the variety and complexity of tax minimization techniques used in estate planning can seem overwhelming. Adding to the complexity is the large federal estate tax exemption, making some wonder whether tax planning is even necessary. This section provides an overview of the basic tax planning techniques of estate planners and how they apply to individuals with differing levels of net worth.

---

[59] IRC § 2056(b)(5).

[60] IRC § 2056(b)(7). Form 1 contains a sample QTIP trust.

[61] IRC §§ 2056(d) and 2056A. The rules regarding transfers to noncitizen spouses are discussed in greater detail in Chapter 6.

[62] IRC § 2055.

[63] IRC § 2522.

[64] Charitable deductions are discussed in greater detail in Chapter 12.

[A] Estate Planning for Those Not Subject to Federal or State Estate Taxes

The federal estate and gift tax exemption amount is $10,000,000, indexed for inflation, through 2025, and then reverts to $5,000,000, indexed for inflation. In 2022, the exemption amount is $12,060,000. In addition, the majority of states do not have state estate taxes. Therefore, if an individual lives in a state that does not have state estate taxes and has assets that are less than the federal exemption amount, estate and gift taxes may not be an issue.

Before an estate planner concludes that estate taxes are not an issue, it is important to consider all of the property that is subject to the estate tax. The estate tax casts a wide net. The tax is imposed on the "gross estate" which is much broader than the probate estate. It also includes non-probate transfers like jointly-held assets, retirement benefits, life insurance and, in some cases, property that was transferred by gift.

It is also important for the estate planner to be mindful of how an estate can change over time. It is seldom the case that a person's financial situation remains constant over the course of their lives. Individuals can change jobs, receive large inheritances or make profitable investments. All of this could make an otherwise exempt estate suddenly become subject to a large tax liability.

If estate taxes are not an issue, then it is particularly important for the estate planner to be mindful of the income tax rules. The reason for this is the differing basis rules applicable to transfers during life and transfers at death. If property is included in a decedent's estate, then the recipient of that property will receive the property with a tax basis equal to the property's fair market value at the time of death (called stepped-up basis). If property is instead passed by gift during life, then the recipient of that property will take the same basis that the donor had (called carryover basis). Assuming the property has gone up in value (as most, but not all, property does) stepped-up basis saves income taxes in the event that the recipient sells the property. If the decedent's estate is less than the unified credit, then making a lifetime gift of appreciated property will not save estate taxes but can result in an income tax liability that the donor could have avoided by instead transferring the property at death.

EXAMPLE 5-55

D's main asset is a house that he purchased in 1965 for $30,000. The house has a current fair market value of $1,000,000. D would like to eventually give his house to his child, C. If D makes a lifetime gift of the house, then C will take the house with a carryover basis of $30,000. If C sells the house for $1,000,000, he will have to pay taxes on the $970,000 of gain. If D passes the house at death, C will take the house with a stepped-up basis equal to the fair market value of the property at the time of death. If he sells the property shortly after receiving it, C will likely have no taxable gain on the sale.

[B] Estate Planning for Those Potentially Subject to Federal or State Estate Taxes

If an individual has substantial assets or lives in a jurisdiction with state estate taxes (which typically have lower exemption amounts), then the estate planner will need to be knowledgeable about the estate and gift tax system in order to be able to plan for tax minimization techniques.

While estate planning techniques may seem complex, the vast majority of these techniques flow from a small handful of basic principles.

The complex array of estate and gift tax rules can be distilled down to the following basic tax tools of the estate planner: (1) use tax-free gifts to reduce an individual's taxable estate, (2) secure the use of both spouses' unified credit and (3) provide financial security to an individual while keeping assets out of her estate for estate tax purposes. By mastering use of these tools, an estate planner will understand the bulk of common estate planning techniques.

[1] Reduce Transfer Tax Liability by Making Tax-Free Gifts

If an individual has substantial assets then one way of reducing estate and gift tax liability is by making tax-free gifts.[1] The annual exclusion[2] and the exclusion for payments of tuition and medical expenses[3] provide opportunities for the tax-free disposition of assets.

EXAMPLE 5-56

D has three children and five grandchildren, all of whom he wants to benefit. Using the annual exclusion, D can transfer $128,000 to his children and grandchildren ($16,000 to each), and, in addition, he can pay for all of their qualified educational and medical expenses, free of tax.

  If D is married and his spouse consents, D can transfer $32,000 tax free to each recipient, for a total of $256,000.[4]

Gifts are also valuable estate planning tools because, due to the valuation rules, transfers by gift may produce a significantly lower transfer tax than transfers at death for appreciating property.

---

[1] § 5.08 The value of gifts in estate planning is discussed in greater detail in Chapter 8.

[2] IRC § 2503(b). *See* § 5.04[D][1] *supra.*

[3] IRC § 2503. *See* § 5.04[D][2] *supra.*

[4] IRC § 2513. Gift splitting is discussed in greater detail in Chapter 8.

EXAMPLE 5-57

D owns stock that is rapidly appreciating in value. At the time of purchase the stock had a fair market value of $50,000. Due to appreciation, the stock was worth $200,000 at the time of D's death.

If D transferred the stock at the time of purchase, the tax liability would be calculated on the basis of its then-current market price of $50,000. Assuming D retained no control over the property, there would be no additional estate tax as a result of that stock.

If D retained the stock until D's death, the tax liability would be calculated on the basis of its date-of-death market price of $200,000. If D's estate was subject to tax at the highest marginal rate, this could result in an additional tax of $60,000.[5]

In calculating the tax benefits that may be associated with making gifts of appreciated property, it is important to take into account the offsetting disadvantage that occurs as a result of the carryover basis rules for gifts.

EXAMPLE 5-58

D owns stock that is rapidly appreciating in value. At the time of purchase the stock had a fair market value of $50,000. Due to appreciation, the stock was worth $500,000 at the time of D's death.

If D transferred the stock during life by gift, the recipient's basis in the stock would be $50,000 (the same basis that D had in the stock). If the recipient later sold the stock, she would pay income tax on the difference between the sale price and the $50,000 basis.

If D retained the stock until D's death, the recipient's basis in the stock would be $500,000 (the fair market value of the stock at the time of D's death). If the recipient later sold the stock, she would only pay income tax on the difference between the sale price and the $500,000 basis.

Given the large federal exemption amount, it is increasingly important for an estate planner to take into account this trade-off between state and federal estate taxes and income taxes. For many taxpayers, they will be better off passing the property at death with a stepped-up basis, rather than passing the property by gift with a carryover basis.

---

[5] Assuming D's estate was subject to tax at the highest marginal rate, 40 percent, D's additional estate tax liability would be calculated by multiplying 40 percent times $150,000 (the difference between the date-of-death value and the date-of-gift value).

[2] Ensure Use of Both Spouses' Unified Credit

The unified credit is the most important tax tool of the estate planner. The unified credit currently enables an individual to transfer $10,000,000, indexed for inflation, through 2025, then $5,000,000, indexed for inflation, tax-free either during life or at death.[6] In 2022, the unified credit exempts $12,060,000 of assets from tax for gift and estate tax purposes.

If a spouse fails to use his or her full unified credit, then his executor can elect to have that unified credit carried over for use by the surviving spouse.[7] This is referred to as portability. The American Taxpayer Relief Act of 2012 made the portability provision permanent and therefore available to all taxpayers dying after January 1, 2011.

Before the 2010 Tax Act, the unified credit was nontransferable and was only available to the extent that it offset a tax liability. If an individual failed to use the unified credit, the tax benefit was entirely lost. Married couples frequently lost some of the benefit of the unified credit because one spouse had either insufficient assets or an insufficient tax liability to cover full use of the credit. An important part of an estate planner's job in reducing taxes for a family unit was to ensure that each family member made maximum use of the unified credit.

In 2011, the Tax Relief, Unemployment Insurance and Job Creation Act of 2010 provided for portability for estates of decedents dying after December 31, 2010 and before January 1, 2013. Thus, for the first time, a surviving spouse was able to use the unused exemption amount of the deceased spouse, provided that certain requirements were met. Where portability works, it vastly simplifies estate planning for married couples by avoiding the need to plan in advance to use both spouse's unified credit.

However, portability is not a panacea. First, it requires that an election be made on a timely filed estate tax return of the first spouse to die. This requires a return to be filed even if no estate tax is due. If a return is not filed, the unused exemption amount can be lost. Second, the decedent spouse's unused exemption amount can also be lost if the surviving spouse remarries. Third, portability is not available for generation-skipping transfer tax purposes and is often not available for state estate tax purposes. Finally, since there is no inflation adjustment applied to the unused exemption amount, additional tax savings can be achieved by using traditional estate planning techniques designed to use the unified credit of the first spouse to die.[8]

[C] Bypass Trusts

Although much of an estate planner's work involves immediately reducing the gift and estate tax liability for the client at hand, longer-term tax savings can also be achieved by structuring transfers in such a way that the property transferred will not

---

[6] IRC § 2010.

[7] IRC § 2010(c).

[8] Planning to use both spouses' unified credit is discussed in greater detail in Chapter 6.

be included in the recipient's estate for tax purposes.[9] In particular, an individual can be given any or all of the following interests without having to worry about substantially increased estate tax liability: a right to income, a right to invade principal limited by an ascertainable standard, and a limited power of appointment. In addition, so long as the beneficiary is not the trustee of the trust, the individual can also be given payments out of a trust at the trustee's discretion. In all of these situations, the recipient beneficiary will only be subject to estate tax on any property actually distributed to the beneficiary to the extent it is held by the beneficiary at the time of death.

Bypass trusts are commonly formed for the benefit of the surviving spouse in order to give her access to trust assets without significantly increasing her subsequent estate tax liability. Bypass trusts can also be used for the benefit of other individuals. However, if the trust is for the benefit of the grantor's descendants or an individual more than 37^1/$_2$ years younger than the grantor, the planner must be mindful of the generation-skipping transfer tax that can significantly erode the benefits.[10] In that situation, the desired tax savings will only be achieved to the extent that the transfer fits within the exemption from generation-skipping transfer taxes.[11] The generation-skipping transfer exemption amount is $12,060,000 for transfers occurring in 2022.[12] Assuming that the trust is exempt from the generation-skipping transfer tax, a bypass trust can be used to benefit multiple individuals through several generations without subjecting the trust property to additional estate taxes.

EXAMPLE 5-59

D transfers $5,000,000 to a trust for the benefit of his lineal descendants. The trust is to continue in existence for the period allowed by the state's Rule Against Perpetuities. D allocates his generation-skipping transfer tax exemption to this trust.

The creation of this trust will be subject to gift tax, but no generation-skipping transfer tax. In addition, the trust assets will not be subject to estate tax in any of the beneficiaries' estates, except to the extent that the property is distributed to and held by the beneficiary at the time of the beneficiary's death.

---

[9] Due to the string provisions, these techniques cannot be employed for the transferor's own benefit.

[10] *See* Chapter 9 for a discussion of the generation-skipping tax.

[11] The generation-skipping transfer tax is discussed in Chapter 9.

[12] However, this is subject to the same sunset provision as the estate tax exemption amount and will revert to $5,000,000 adjusted for inflation after December 31, 2025. Pub. L. No. 115-97.

APPENDIX A ESTATE AND GIFT TAX RATE SCHEDULE

This chart reflects the gradual reduction in maximum rates for the years 2001–2009 enacted in the Economic Growth and Tax Relief Reconciliation Act of 2001 (the 2001 Act). The schedule does not apply in the year 2010 (the year for which the estate tax is repealed and gifts are taxed at a maximum marginal rate of 35 percent). Beginning in the year 2011, the 2001 rates are again effective for both estate and gift tax purposes.

If the Amount with Respect to Which the Tentative Tax to Be Computed Is:	The Tentative Tax Is:
Not over $10,000	18 percent of such amount
Over $10,000 but not over $20,000	$1,800, plus 20 percent of the excess of such amount over $10,000
Over $20,000 but not over $40,000	$3,800, plus 22 percent of the excess of such amount over $20,000
Over $40,000 but not over $60,000	$8,200, plus 24 percent of the excess of such amount over $40,000
Over $60,000 but not over $80,000	$13,000, plus 26 percent of the excess of such amount over $60,000
Over $80,000 but not over $100,000	$18,200, plus 28 percent of the excess of such amount over $80,000
Over $100,000 but not over $150,000	$23,800, plus 30 percent of the excess of such amount over $100,000
Over $150,000 but not over $250,000	$38,800, plus 32 percent of the excess of such amount over $150,000
Over $250,000 but not over $500,000	$70,800, plus 34 percent of the excess of such amount over $250,000
Over $500,000 but not over $750,000	$155,800, plus 37 percent of the excess of such amount over $500,000
Over $750,000 but not over $1,000,000	$248,300, plus 39 percent of the excess of such amount over $750,000
Over $1,000,000	$345,800, plus 41 percent of the excess of such amount over $1,000,000

For Tax Year 2001

Over $1,500,000 but not over $2,000,000	$555,800, plus 45 percent of the excess of such amount over $1,500,000
Over $2,000,000 but not over $2,500,000	$780,800, plus 49 percent of the excess of such amount over $2,000,000
Over $2,500,000 but not over $3,000,000	$1,025,800, plus 53 percent of the excess over $2,500,000
Over $3,000,000	$1,290,800, plus 55 percent of the excess over $3,000,000

| **If the Amount with Respect to Which the Tentative Tax to Be Computed Is:** | **The Tentative Tax Is:** |

For Tax Year 2002

Over $1,500,000 but not over $2,000,000	$555,800, plus 45 percent of the excess of such amount over $1,500,000
Over $2,000,000 but not over $2,500,000	$780,800, plus 49 percent of the excess of such amount over $2,000,000
Over $2,500,000	$1,025,800, plus 50 percent of the excess over $2,500,000

For Tax Year 2003

Over $1,500,000 but not over $2,000,000	$555,800, plus 45 percent of the excess of such amount over $1,500,000
Over $2,000,000	$780,800, plus 49 percent of the excess of such amount over $2,000,000

For Tax Year 2004

Over $1,500,000 but not over $2,000,000	$555,800 plus 45 percent of the excess of such amount over $1,500,000
Over $2,000,000	$780,800, plus 48 percent of the excess of such amount over $2,000,000

For Tax Year 2005

Over $1,500,000 but not over $2,000,000	$555,800, plus 45 percent of the excess of such amount over $1,500,000
Over $2,000,000	$780,800, plus 47 percent of the excess of such amount over $2,000,000

For Tax Year 2006

Over $1,500,000 but not over $2,000,000	$555,800, plus 45 percent of the excess of such amount over $1,500,000
Over $2,000,000	$780,800, plus 46 percent of the excess of such amount over $2,000,000

For Tax Years 2007–2009

Over $1,500,000	$555,800, plus 45 percent of the excess of such amount over $1,500,000

For Tax Years 2010–2012

Over $500,000	$155,800, plus 35 percent of the excess of such amount over $500,000

For Tax Year 2013 and Beyond

Over $1,000,000	$345,800, plus 40 percent of the excess of such amount over $1,000,000

6

Planning for a Spouse or Nonmarital Partner

§ 6.01 INTRODUCTION

Planning for a spouse or nonmarital partner is an important aspect of estate planning and, depending on the particular goals of the client, a variety of issues will need to be taken into account.

Both state property law and federal tax law favor transfers of property to a spouse. For the married individual, the estate planner needs to consider two areas in planning for a client's spouse: (1) state law provisions regarding the effect of marriage on the ownership of property, in particular, the role of community property law and the rights of a surviving spouse to claim a minimum share of the decedent spouse's estate under elective share statutes; and (2) federal tax law provisions enabling the surviving spouse to be provided for in a tax-advantaged manner, particularly in terms of qualifying for the marital deduction and bypassing the surviving spouse's estate.

Until recently estate planning for same-sex couples was complicated by the fact that many states refused to recognize same-sex marriages. However, on June 26, 2015, the Supreme Court issued a landmark decision recognizing marriage for same-sex couples as a fundamental right guaranteed by the Constitution.[1] As a result of this decision, all states are required to issue marriage licenses to same-sex couples and to recognize same-sex marriages validly performed in other jurisdictions.

Beginning in 1999, a number of states began adopting statutory provisions that allowed two people to register their relationship with the state. These provisions, like civil unions and registered domestic partnerships, were originally adopted as a way to allow same-sex couples, who had not been allowed to marry, to achieve some of the benefits of marriage. However, in many states these statutory provisions were also available to opposite sex couples. Each of these statutory systems differed in their details, but where these statutes existed, registered couples were generally treated like married couples for state, but not federal, law purposes.

Now that all states are required to allow and recognize same-sex marriages, the status of these types of non-marital partnerships are in flux. Some states have converted these statuses to marriage (by operation of law or by action of the couple), sometimes retroactively to the date of the civil union. Some states continue to make both statuses (civil marriage and spousal equivalent) available to couples, but the law is highly state-specific and subject to change. For federal law purpose, the law is also varied. The IRS and Department of Labor issued guidance after *Windsor* stating that for federal purposes, the various marriage equivalent statuses are not equivalent to marriage.[2] However, Social Security rules generally provide that legal relationships granting inheritance rights are treated as marriages. This will allow many couples in spousal equivalent relationships to be treated as married for purposes of Social Security.

---

[1] § 6.01 Obergefell v. Hodges, 576 U.S. 644, 135 S. Ct. 2584 (2015).

[2] Definition of Terms Relating to Marital Status, 81 Fed. Reg. 60,609 (Sept. 2, 2016) (codified at 26 C.F.R. § 301.7701-18). *See* United States v. Windsor, 570 U.S. 744, 133 S. Ct. 2675 (2013). *See also* DOL Tech. Release No. 2013-04; Rev. Rul. 2013-17, 2013-2 C.B. 201; Notice 2014-19, 2014-1 C.B. 979.

Different issues arise when planning for a nonmarital partner. Many couples (both same-sex and opposite sex) choose not to marry, making it more important for the couple to engage in estate planning in order to ensure that their wishes are effectuated. Traditionally, state property law treats a nonmarital partner no differently from any other person unrelated to the donor. For example, if an individual fails to write a will, the laws of intestacy will provide a portion of her estate to pass to her surviving spouse; nonmarital partners are generally not provided for under intestacy statutes. In addition, where state community property laws and elective share rights provide protections for the surviving spouse, there are no such protections for nonmarital partners. Indeed, when an individual transfers a significant portion of his estate to a person who is not legally a member of his family, the will is often more vulnerable to being successfully challenged by the family. Federal tax law lacks any special provisions favoring transfers to nonmarital partners, even where the couple has registered their relationship with the state. Where the federal tax law provides for a marital deduction for transfers to a spouse, there is no comparable deduction for transfers to a nonmarital partner. Therefore, if an unmarried individual wants to leave substantial assets to a nonmarital partner, the estate planner needs to consider a different array of issues, including (1) reducing the likelihood of a will dispute, and (2) working creatively with tax provisions in order to minimize tax costs.

§6.02 MARITAL PROPERTY RIGHTS

[A] Overview

There are two systems of marital property in the United States: the community property system, which exists in nine states primarily in southern and western parts of the country,[1] and the separate property system, which exists in the remaining 41 states and the District of Columbia. Each system provides its own mechanism for recognizing a spouse's contribution to assets acquired by the other spouse during marriage. An estate planner needs to understand the marital system(s) that applies to each client in order to (1) determine what property the client has a right to dispose of (and, conversely, what the surviving spouse can claim), and (2) accurately project the estate and income tax consequences of the estate plan. Community property law and elective share rights vary in their particulars from state to state. The following discussion provides a general overview and the estate planner should be certain to consider the laws of all relevant states when planning for a client.

---

[1] §6.02 Arizona, California, Idaho, Louisiana, Nevada, New Mexico, Texas, Washington, and Wisconsin.

[B] Community Property System

[1] In General

The community property system has long existed in Arizona, California, Idaho, Louisiana, Nevada, New Mexico, Texas, and Washington. More recently, Wisconsin adopted the Uniform Marital Property Act, which is substantially similar to the community property system.[2] Although community property only exists in a small number of states, due to the large populations in many of these states, over one-fourth of the population of the United States lives in community property jurisdictions.[3] In addition, since property acquired in a community property state retains its community property character even if the couple is no longer living in a community property state,[4] many married couples living in separate property states are at least partially subject to community property regimes. The following discussion provides a general overview of community property principles. However, community property laws vary considerably in their particulars from state to state, and the estate planner should be certain to consult the laws of a particular state when applicable.

Under the community property system, a husband and wife are deemed to be co-owners of all property earned by either spouse during the marriage. The community property system is based on the notion that a husband and wife are an economic partnership and they should jointly share the fruits of their joint labors. Each spouse is the owner of an undivided half interest in each item of community property. The death of a spouse dissolves the community, giving the surviving spouse outright ownership in his or her half.

EXAMPLE 6-1

H and W live in a community property state. H works outside the home earning $100,000/year. W is at home raising the children. Using his earnings, H has purchased, in his name, a house, a car, and investments worth $80,000. Assuming that all of their property was acquired with H's earnings since the time of the marriage, W will be considered the owner of half of the house, car, and investments.

This system stands in sharp contrast to the system in a separate property state in which ownership is determined solely by title.

---

[2] Wis. Stat. Ann. §§ 766.001-766.097 (1998). The Wisconsin Marital Property Act went into effect on January 1, 1986. The Wisconsin system is treated the same as community property for federal tax purposes. Rev. Rul. 87-13, 1987-1 C.B. 20.

[3] Texas and California alone contain almost 20 percent of the country's population.

[4] *See, e.g.,* Restatement (Second) of Conflict of Laws, § 259 (1971). The Uniform Disposition of Community Property Rights at Death Act, adopted in a significant number of separate property states, provides explicit statutory recognition of this result.

EXAMPLE 6-2

H and W live in a separate property state. H works outside the home earning $100,000/year. W is at home raising the children. Using his earnings, H has purchased in his name, a house, a car, and investments worth $80,000. H will be considered to be owner of all of the property titled in his name, regardless of his marital status at the time of the property's acquisition.

Community property rules only apply to married couples and therefore do not apply to couples who choose not to marry. However, some states give community property rights to putative spouses. A putative spouse is an individual who in good faith believes she has entered into a marriage, but the marriage is not valid due to some legal infirmity (e.g., the other party is legally married to someone else).

[2] What Constitutes Community Property?

Community property is generally defined as property earned by a husband or wife while the couple is domiciled in a community property state. A couple is considered domiciled in a particular state if they reside there and intend to remain there for the indefinite future. In addition, real estate located in a community property state may be considered community property regardless of the couple's domicile.

Community property includes all property acquired by either husband or wife during the marriage except that which is acquired by gift or inheritance. When it is difficult to determine the status of the property, there is a strong presumption that the property is community property. Thus, a married couple in a community property state is presumed to own all of their property as community property regardless of how the property is titled, unless there is affirmative proof that the property was

1. Brought into the marriage by either spouse;
2. Inherited by either spouse;
3. Given to either spouse; or
4. The separate property of one spouse before the couple became domiciled in a community property state.

In addition, a couple may contractually agree to treat community property as separate property.

Income from community property is treated as community property in all community property jurisdictions. However, states vary in their treatment of income from separate property earned during the course of a marriage in a community property state. Some states treat this income as separate property and other states treat it as community property. Moreover, states vary in their treatment of assets that are acquired over time, such as life insurance and employee benefits, which may have been purchased with a mixture of separate and community property or earned partially before and partially after marriage. Community property rights may be superseded by federal law. For example, the Supreme Court has held that the disposition of U.S. government bonds is controlled by federal law, which requires disposition to the named beneficiary, regardless of the community property character of the bonds.[5] In addition, although employee benefits acquired during marriage have generally been held to be community property, the Supreme Court has held that ERISA limits the rights of a nonemployee spouse to dispose of an interest in the employee spouse's qualified retirement benefits when the nonemployee spouse predeceases the employee spouse.[6]

Once property is classified as community property or separate property, it generally retains its status, regardless of subsequent changes in form.

EXAMPLE 6-3

> H and W live in a community property jurisdiction. W inherited stock worth $50,000 from her grandmother. Inherited property is classified as separate and not community property. W sold the stock and purchased a cabin with the proceeds. The cabin will be classified as separate property since the stock was classified as separate property.

However, there are two situations that can cause the classification of property to change: *commingling* and *transmutation*. The commingling doctrine provides that if community and separate property are mixed and the separate property contribution cannot be clearly proved, the whole mixture will be found to be community property. This doctrine is a function of the presumption in favor of community property. Commingling most commonly occurs when both separate property and community property are deposited in the same bank account. Commingling can also occur in the operation of a business when the business has some separate property, but growth of the business results from the work of one or both of the spouses during the course of the marriage.

The characterization of property can also be changed by transmutation. Transmutation refers to any agreement by contract or gift between a husband and wife that changes the characterization of property from separate to community or community to separate. Community property states generally provide that spouses can enter into an agreement to change the characterization of some or all of their property either prior to or during marriage. States vary in their requirements regarding the formality of these agreements. The character of property can also be changed by gift. Thus, a spouse can convert her separate property to community property or she can give her interest in community property to her spouse, essentially converting it to her spouse's separate property.

Community property generally retains its community property status regardless of how the property is titled. Therefore, community property can be titled in the name of either spouse individually or in the name of both spouses with the traditional community property designation: "as husband and wife." However, many (but

---

[5] Yiatchos v. Yiatchos, 376 U.S. 306 (1964); Free v. Bland, 369 U.S. 663 (1962). In these cases, the Court recognized an exception for the situation in which the designation on the bonds constituted a fraud on the spouse's interest.

[6] Boggs v. Boggs, 520 U.S. 833 (1997), *rev'g* 82 F.3d 90 (5th Cir. 1996).

not all) community property states provide that community property cannot be held in joint tenancy. The reason for this is that the survivorship provision of joint tenancy is inconsistent with the treatment of community property. Property held in joint tenancy automatically passes to the surviving spouse upon the decedent spouse's death, whereas in community property, each spouse has the ability to transfer half of the community property at death regardless of which spouse survives. If a couple uses community assets to purchase property in which title is taken as joint tenants (or tenants by the entirety) with the intention of creating a true joint tenancy, they may effect a transmutation of the property from community property to separate joint tenancy property. Since this can have negative repercussions, some community property states provide that the intention to create a joint tenancy must be expressly stated in the conveyance by which title is taken.

[3] Effects of Community Property Classification

Community property is subject to special rules regarding lifetime management and control, as well as the power to make testamentary dispositions. Traditionally husbands were granted the sole authority to manage and control community property. Now, all community property states provide that both husband and wife have management power. In the majority of states, each spouse may act alone to manage the community property. However, some actions, typically those involving real estate, require the consent of both spouses. Each spouse is free to dispose of his separate property by gift. Since both spouses have ownership interest in community property, a gift of community property by one spouse without the other spouse's consent can generally be set aside by the nonconsenting spouse. Some states provide an exception to this rule for small gifts or for gifts that do not injure or defraud the other spouse. To avoid potential conflict, both spouses should consent in writing to any significant gifts of community property.

Upon the death of a spouse, the surviving spouse gets outright ownership of her half interest in the community property. The decedent spouse is free to dispose of his half share of the community property at death, as well as his separate property.

EXAMPLE 6-4

H dies with a will that says: "I give all of my property to the Red Cross." All of H's separate property and half of H's community property will go to the Red Cross.

The first spouse to die has no right to dispose of the surviving spouse's share of the community property. However, he may effectively do so through the use of a *widow's election will*. Under a widow's election will, the decedent spouse's will provides a plan for the disposition of both halves of the community property. Upon the decedent spouse's death, the surviving spouse is given the choice of joining in the plan provided for under the will (usually by transferring her share of community property to a trust created under the will) or rejecting the will and taking her share of community property outright. The widow's election will typically provides for all of the community property to be transferred to a trust under which the surviving spouse is given an income interest for life and the remainder is given to the couple's children.

There is another device called a *voluntary widow's election will* where the first spouse to die attempts to dispose of both halves of community property, but his will permits the surviving spouse to receive benefits under his will even if she elects to take her half share of community property outright. This type of plan is designed to persuade, but not force, the surviving spouse to give up her rights of disposition over her half share of community property.

The advantage of the widow's election plan to the decedent spouse is that it enables the decedent spouse to direct the disposition of all the community property. If the surviving spouse agrees with the choice of beneficiaries, the widow's election can also be beneficial to that spouse by providing for management of the property during her life and avoiding probate upon her death (although these benefits could also be achieved by the surviving spouse creating her own revocable trust after the death of the decedent spouse).

[4] Estate Tax Consequences of Community Property

Community property can have a significant effect on estate taxes. Because each spouse has the ability to dispose of only half of the community property, a decedent spouse's gross estate for tax purposes will only include his half share of the community property as well as his separate property.

EXAMPLE 6-5

H and W, a married couple, live in a community property jurisdiction. H has $1,000,000 of separate property and H and W have $8,000,000 of community property. At the time of H's death, his gross estate for tax purposes will be $5,000,000: $1,000,000 of separate property plus half of the $8,000,000 of community property.

The marital deduction provides a way for couples in separate property states to achieve many of the estate tax advantages available to couples living in community property states, provided the decedent spouse is willing to transfer property to the surviving spouse.[7]

EXAMPLE 6-6

H and W, a married couple, live in a separate property jurisdiction. H has $9,000,000 of property in his name. H's will gives W $4,000,000 (the amount she would be entitled to in a community property state if

---

[7] IRC § 2056.

$1,000,000 of H's property was separate property). Although H's gross estate will be $9,000,000, after applying the marital deduction, H's taxable estate will only be $5,000,000 ($9,000,000 minus $4,000,000).

If one of the spouses is not a U.S. citizen, community property provides certain estate tax advantages over separate property. The marital deduction is only available on a limited basis if the surviving spouse is not a U.S. citizen.[8] However, in a community property state, the surviving spouse directly owns her half share of community property and thus there is no requirement to meet the special marital deduction rules that otherwise apply for transfers to non-citizen spouses with respect to her half share of community property.

[5] Special Basis Rules for Community Property

One of the most important tax advantages available only for community property is the special double step-up in basis rule. Under the general basis rules, property included in a decedent's gross estate receives a new basis at the time of the decedent's death equal to the property's fair market value (sometimes called a stepped-up basis).[9] This rule enables the recipient of the property to sell the property without income tax liability. However, owners of community property receive a double advantage because the stepped-up basis rule applies not only to the portion of the decedent's estate that was included in the decedent spouse's estate, but also applies to the surviving spouse's share of the community property.[10]

EXAMPLE 6-7

H and W, while living in a community property state, purchased stock for $100,000 with community property funds. At the time of H's death, the stock was worth $1,000,000. Under H's will, he transferred his half share in the stock to W.

Upon H's death, only $500,000 of the stock will be included in H's gross estate for tax purposes. However, both H's share and W's share of the stock will be given a new basis equal to the stock's fair market value at the time of H's death. If W were to sell the stock for $1,000,000, she would have no income tax liability from that sale of stock. This advantage is not available for quasi-community property[11] or for any other form of property ownership, including joint property.

---

[8] IRC § 2056(d). The marital deduction rules applicable to non-U.S. citizen spouses is discussed in § 6.03[G] *infra.*

[9] IRC § 1014. The basis rules for inherited property are discussed in § 5.06 *supra.*

[10] IRC § 1014(b)(6).

[11] Discussed in § 6.02[D][2] *infra.*

EXAMPLE 6-8

H and W, while living in a separate property state, purchased stock for $100,000. The property was held in joint tenancy. At the time of H's death, the stock was worth $1,000,000.

Upon H's death, only $500,000 of the stock will be included in H's gross estate for tax purposes under IRC Section 2040(b) (providing rules for the tax treatment of joint tenancies held by a husband and a wife). Since only $500,000 is included in H's gross estate, W's basis in the stock is only $550,000 ($500,000 from her husband's share and $50,000 from her half share). If she subsequently sells the stock for $1,000,000, she will be subject to income tax on $450,000 (the difference between the amount she received for the stock ($1,000,000) and her $550,000 basis in the stock).

[C] Separate Property System

[1] In General

The vast majority of states follow the separate property, also called the common law, system of marital property. Under the separate property system, marital status does not affect the ownership of property. Each spouse owns all he or she earns and has no ownership interest in the other spouse's earnings. If one spouse is the wage earner while the other spouse works at home, everything is owned by the wage earning spouse. Income from the separate property of each spouse is also separate property. The nonwage earning spouse has no ownership interest in any of the property held in the other spouse's name during life.[12] However, upon the death of a spouse, all separate property states, with the exception of Georgia, provide protections for the surviving spouse against disinheritance. The estate planner needs to be aware of these protections in order to avoid having the estate plan disrupted by a surviving spouse's election.

[2] Protections Against Disinheritance

[a] Common Law Protections

Common law protected surviving spouses in separate property states against disinheritance under the doctrines of *dower* (for wives) and *curtesy* (for husbands). The rights of dower and curtesy gave the surviving spouse a fractional interest in the decedent spouse's real property. Most separate property states have replaced or supplemented common law dower and curtesy with some form of an elective share

---

[12] Except in the event of divorce, in which case separate property states provide for "equitable distribution" of a couple's marital assets.

statute. Even states that have retained dower and curtesy seldom see these rights claimed due to the fact that elective share statutes almost always provide greater protection for the surviving spouse.

[b] Elective Share Statutes

Elective share (also called *forced share* or *widow's share*) statutes are designed to provide minimum protection against disinheritance for surviving spouses in separate property states. Elective share statutes apply to both husbands and wives. These statutes provide the surviving spouse with a choice: She can either (1) take under the will or (2) renounce whatever has been given to her under the will and take a fractional share of the decedent spouse's estate. Elective share statutes vary in their particulars from state to state, although an increasing number of states have adopted the elective share statute from the 1990 Uniform Probate Code.[13] The following discussion provides an overview of the law regarding elective shares. However, since the law is so state-specific and changes are occurring rapidly in this area, the estate planner should be certain to check the current laws of the relevant state when planning an estate.

[i] Traditional Elective Share Statutes. Under traditional elective share statutes, the surviving spouse is granted a right to claim between one-quarter and half of the decedent's estate (some states provide for an outright disposition; other states only provide for a life estate). Some states give a flat percentage share and others provide varying percentages, depending on the existence of other surviving relatives of the decedent. For those states providing varying percentages, the surviving spouse is typically given a smaller share if the decedent was also survived by issue. This provision gives the decedent spouse the option of providing generously for issue. It should be noted, however, that there is no obligation in any state (with the exception of Louisiana[14]) for a parent to provide anything to issue.

The percentage share allowed under traditional elective statutes does not take into account the length of marriage. Thus, the surviving spouse is entitled to the same portion of the decedent's estate, regardless of whether the marriage lasted for two weeks or 50 years. A surviving spouse is also entitled to claim her elective share even if the surviving spouse is wealthier than the decedent spouse. In addition, under many older elective share statutes a surviving spouse is entitled to claim her elective share even if the decedent provided generously for the spouse through nonprobate transfers.

Older elective share statutes calculate the surviving spouse's share based on the decedent spouse's probate estate. However, because these statutes are easily evaded

---

[13] Unif. Probate Code § 2-203 (amended 1993), 8 U.L.A. 103 (1998). Discussed in § 6.02[C][2][b] [ii] *infra*.

[14] Louisiana has a forced share for children, called a *legitime*, that protects children who are under the age of 23, mentally infirm, or disabled from disinheritance. La. Civ. Code Ann. art. 1493, 1494.

through nonprobate transfers, many states now include nonprobate property like revocable trusts, life insurance, and joint tenancy property in calculating the elective share.

[ii] 1990/2008 Uniform Probate Code Elective Share Statute. The Uniform Probate Code (UPC) amended its elective share statute in 1990, and again in 2008, and in doing so revolutionized the concept of the elective share.[15] The 1990/2008 elective share statute has been adopted with variations in a number of states. As many states are in the process of updating their elective share statutes, it is likely to be adopted in more states in the near future.

The elective share statute under the 1990/2008 UPC is designed more closely to approximate the results in a community property state, without requiring the difficult tracing of assets that is often necessary in community property states to distinguish community from separate property. Under the UPC, the surviving spouse's elective share percentage is based on the length of time that the decedent and the spouse were married to each other.[16] The percentage share ranges from 3 to 50 percent, depending on the length of the marriage. Thus, if the marriage lasted just one year, the surviving spouse is entitled to 3 percent of the augmented estate (defined below). If the marriage lasted 15 years or more, the surviving spouse is entitled to 50 percent of the augmented estate. In addition, the UPC provides for a minimum elective share of $50,000.

The UPC significantly broadened the basis of the calculation for the spousal share through its concept of the *augmented estate*. The augmented estate has four components:[17]

1. The decedent's probate estate;
2. The decedent's reclaimable estate consisting of other property that the decedent had control over during his or her life or gave away during the two-year period preceding his or her death (analogous to the string provisions applicable to calculating the gross estate for federal estate tax purposes);[18]
3. The value of property to which the surviving spouse succeeded by reason of the decedent's death; and
4. The value of property owned by the surviving spouse at the time of decedent's death (including assets that would have been includable in the surviving spouse's reclaimable estate had the spouse predeceased the decedent).

The effect of this is to combine the assets of both spouses (similar to the community property system, but including separate as well as community property)

---

[15] Unif. Probate Code, Part II, General Comment, 8 U.L.A. 93 (1998).

[16] Unif. Probate Code § 2-202, 8 U.L.A. 102 (1998).

[17] Unif. Probate Code § 2-203 (amended 1993), 8 U.L.A. 103 (1998).

[18] The string provisions are discussed in § 5.07[B] [3] *supra*.

so that if the surviving spouse had significant property in his or her name or was well provided for by transfers outside of the probate system, the elective share would not be available.

[iii] **Avoiding the Elective Share**. When a surviving spouse claims her elective share, there can be significant disruption to the plan of disposition for the decedent spouse's property. Therefore, the estate planner should take steps during the estate planning process to prevent this.

The simplest way to avoid application of an elective share statute is to provide the surviving spouse with a bequest equal to or greater than the elective share amount. Some states provide that this can be satisfied with a life estate, and many states (including those that have adopted the UPC) provide that the surviving spouse's share can also be satisfied by nonprobate assets (such as life insurance and joint tenancy property).

Elective share statutes can also be avoided by contractual agreement between the spouses. Some states require that the agreements be entered into prior to marriage (prenuptial agreements). However, an increasing number of states (including those that have adopted the UPC) allow agreements to be entered into after marriage, providing certain requirements are met.

Finally, in those states that calculate the surviving spouse's elective share based on the decedent spouse's probate estate, the elective share can sometimes be effectively evaded by acquiring assets that pass outside of the probate system. For example, under many traditional elective share statutes, the surviving spouse has no claim to life insurance or property that the decedent held in joint tenancy with someone other than the surviving spouse. Therefore, in those states a spouse may be able to evade elective share statutes by converting assets to these nonprobate assets. It should be noted, however, that courts have looked with disfavor on "fraud on the widow's share," and have included some of these nonprobate interests (particularly revocable *inter vivos* trusts) in calculating the surviving spouse's share even where not specifically provided by statute.[19]

[D] Issues Regarding Migrating Couples

We live in a highly mobile society. As such, it is very common for couples to move from separate property states to community property states and from community property states to separate property states. This section discusses issues that can arise as a result of these changes in domicile.

---

[19] *See, e.g.,* Sullivan v. Burkin, 460 N.E.2d 572 (Mass. 1984).

[1] Migration from Community Property to Separate Property State

When representing clients who have migrated from community property states to separate property states, the estate planner should work to ensure that community property status is preserved for the clients' community property. Property retains its classification as community property or separate property regardless of subsequent changes in a couple's domicile. Thus, if a couple moves from a community property state to a separate property state, the community property acquired in the community property jurisdiction will generally retain its community property character.[20] However, due to a lack of familiarity with community property in separate property states, the community property status may go unrecognized by personal administrators and courts. Moreover, estate planners in separate property states can cause the loss of community property classification by retitling the property as joint tenancy or by failing to maintain adequate records. Loss of community property status can pose hardships for a surviving spouse and can also cause loss of the double step-up in basis available for community property.[21] Therefore, it is important for estate planners in separate property states to help clients preserve community property character in such a way as will have the greatest chance of recognition. One of the best ways of accomplishing this is to have the husband and wife transfer their community property to a revocable living trust that explicitly states that the property will retain its community property character. To further the likelihood of recognition, the trust should provide that it is governed by the law of one of the community property states. Another possibility is to open a custody or agency account designated as community property. By doing so, the corporate fiduciary will provide the record keeping necessary for segregating the assets without the expense of setting up a trust. Some brokerage firms allow spouses to open accounts designated as community property, and if these are national firms the designation should be available for customers in separate property states as well (although convincing the account officer in the separate property state to open the account with the community property designation may involve a little work).

[2] Migration from Separate Property to Community Property State

If a couple moves from a separate property state to a community property state, the property acquired while the couple was domiciled in a separate property state will retain its separate property character. If the couple retires to a community property state (an increasingly common phenomenon given the temperate climate of many of the community property states), it is likely that they will have very little community property. This can leave a surviving spouse with no protection against disinheritance by a deceased spouse since the surviving spouse will no longer be protected by the elective share statute of their former domicile.

---

[20] Under the Uniform Disposition of Community Property Rights at Death Act, 8A U.L.A. 191 (1993), enacted in many separate property states, community property retains its character, despite changes in the couple's domicile, unless the spouses have agreed to convert it into separate property.

[21] The double step-up in basis is discussed at § 6.02[B][5] *supra*.

EXAMPLE 6-9

H and W lived in New York for most of their married lives. H worked outside the home and earned a large salary and W stayed home to raise the children. Upon H's retirement, H and W retired to Arizona. H died while the couple was living in Arizona. H's will disinherited W.

If H had died while a domiciliary of New York, W would have been entitled to claim a portion of H's estate through New York's elective share statute. However, since community property states, like Arizona, typically protect surviving spouses through community property (rather than elective share statutes), W may be left without any protection against disinheritance.

To address this problem, some community property states have adopted the concept of quasi-community property, which provides some, but not all, of the community property protections for the surviving spouse.[22] Quasi-community property refers to property acquired outside of a community property state that would have been community property if it had been acquired in a community property state. While both spouses are living, quasi-community property is treated as the separate property of the titled spouse. However, upon the death of the titled spouse, the surviving spouse is entitled to a portion of the quasi-community property. If the nonpropertied spouse dies first, she has no rights to dispose of the quasi-community property.

§6.03 TAX PLANNING FOR THE MARRIED COUPLE

[A] Overview

Prior to 2011, planning for the estate tax was of paramount importance in estate planning for many married couples. The reason for this is that (1) the amount of the unified credit exclusion was in a state of flux, making more taxpayers potentially subject to the tax, and (2) the unified credit exclusion amount operated on a use it or lose it basis. To the extent that a taxpayer failed to use his or her federal unified credit exclusion amount, it was lost. Because of these rules, much of estate planning involved securing use of both spouses' unified credits.

Beginning in 2011, the federal estate tax unified credit exclusion amount was increased to $5,000,000, indexed for inflation. In 2017, when the exclusion amount was $5,490,000, the Tax Cuts and Jobs Act ("TCJA") (Pub. L. No. 115-97), doubled that amount to $10,000,000, indexed for inflation, for estates of decedents dying after December 31, 2017 and before January 1, 2026. In 2022, the exclusion amount is $12,060,000. Under the TCJA, this amount is expected to rise annually with inflation adjustments until December 30, 2025, when it will revert to $5,000,000, indexed for

---

[22] *See* Cal. Prob. Code § § 66, 101 (West 1991); Wash. Rev. Code § § 26.16.220–250 (1997); Idaho Code § § 15-2-201, 202 (1979).

inflation. As a result of this increased exclusion, the vast majority of Americans no longer need to worry about federal estate taxes.

In addition to the increased unified credit exclusion amount, Congress abandoned the "use it or lose it" system that had been in place and replaced it with *portability*. Under portability, a surviving spouse is able to use his or her deceased spouse's unused unified credit exclusion amount, provided an election is made and certain technical requirements are met.

As a result of these changes, estate planning has become vastly simplified for the majority of Americans. Planning for the estate tax is now only necessary for: (1) couples whose combined assets are expected to be in excess of the unified credit exclusion amount at the time of death (in 2022, the exclusion amount is $12,060,000; but in 2026, the exclusion amount is scheduled to go down to $5,000,000, adjusted for inflation); and (2) people who live in jurisdictions with a state estate tax (since state estate taxes are often modeled on the federal system only with lower exclusion amounts).

[B] Non-Tax Planning for Small to Moderate Estates

If a couple is expected to have combined assets that are less than the unified credit exclusion amount indexed for inflation (the credit exempts $12,060,000 in 2022; in 2026, the exclusion amount is scheduled to go down to $5,000,000, adjusted for inflation) at the time of the couple's death, and if they live in a jurisdiction which does not have a state estate tax, then estate taxes need not be a factor in the couple's estate plan (although income taxes must always be considered).

Before an estate planner concludes that estate taxes are not an issue, it is important to consider all of the property that is potentially subject to the estate tax. The estate tax casts a wide net. The tax is imposed on the "gross estate" which is much broader than the probate estate. It includes non-probate transfers like jointly-held assets, retirement benefits, life insurance, as well as some property that was transferred during life.[1]

It is also important for an estate planner to be mindful of how an estate can change over time. It is seldom the case that a couple's financial situation remains constant over the course of their lives. Individuals can change jobs, make profitable investments or receive large inheritances. All of which could make an otherwise exempt estate, be suddenly subject to a large tax liability.

Because of these possibilities, the estate planner should remind the couple that an estate plan needs to be reviewed regularly in light of changes to an individual's situation and possible changes to the law.

The estate planner should not assume that tools that have been traditionally used for planning, such as a marital trust or a credit shelter trust, are inappropriate for an estate that will not be subject to estate taxes. Many individuals choose to create trusts for reasons that are unrelated to estate taxes. Some of the advantages of trusts include the following:

---

[1] § 6.03 *See* Chapter 5, *supra*, for a discussion of the estate tax and the gross estate.

- Property in trust can be protected from creditors of the surviving spouse;
- Property in trust will avoid probate in the surviving spouse's estate;
- Property in trust can be professionally managed either immediately or in the event of incapacity; and
- Property in trust can be subject to greater control as the decedent spouse will be able to impose conditions and/or name alternate or remainder beneficiaries. This is of particular value if the decedent spouse has children who are not children of the surviving spouse.

[C] Tax Planning Basics—The Marital Deduction

While the number of individuals subject to the estate tax has been drastically reduced, tax planning is still relevant for high net worth individuals and for people living in jurisdictions with a state estate tax. In these situations, an important aspect of estate planning for a married individual is providing for the spouse in a tax-advantaged manner. The most important aspect of this is in ensuring that transfers to the surviving spouse qualify for the marital deduction.

The estate and gift tax marital deductions allow for unlimited tax-free transfer of assets between spouses either during life or at death. These deductions are the most important estate planning tools available to married individuals as they allow for all federal wealth transfer taxes to be deferred until the death of the surviving spouse regardless of the size of the estate. This means that all of the couple's assets, undiminished by estate and gift taxes, can be made available for the support of the surviving spouse during her life. If a transfer between spouses does not meet the requirements for the marital deduction, then the property could be subject to estate taxes twice—first at the death of the first spouse, and then again at the death of the second spouse. For this reason, it is important that estate planners be mindful of the marital deduction rules.

[1] History of the Marital Deduction

The marital deduction has gone through a variety of permutations since it was first enacted in 1948. It is important for an estate planner to have a sense of this historical background as it can have an effect on interpreting the marital provisions in older wills.

The marital deduction was first enacted in the Revenue Act of 1948[2] as a means of enabling taxpayers in separate property states to take advantage of some of the estate tax benefits available to taxpayers in community property states. Without the marital deduction, a spouse who accumulated $1,000,000 of community property would only be subject to tax on $500,000 since under community property law he would only have a right to dispose of half of the community property and his spouse would control the disposition of the other half. This contrasts with a separate

---

[2] Pub. L. No. 80-471, 62 Stat. 110 (1948).

property state where a spouse who accumulated $1,000,000 of property would be subject to tax on the full $1,000,000. (Of course, he would also have the right to control the disposition of the full $1,000,000.) The marital deduction, as initially enacted, enabled the taxpayer in the separate property state to essentially opt into the community property system by allowing a deduction for transfers to a spouse of up to half of the individual's gross estate.

With the unification of the estate and gift tax in the Tax Reform Act of 1976,[3] the maximum marital deduction for both estate and gift taxes was increased to the greater of $250,000 or half of the decedent's adjusted gross estate. This gave decedents with estates smaller than $500,000 the ability to make larger tax-free transfers than were previously allowed.

The law regarding marital deductions was again made more generous in the Economic Recovery Tax Act of 1981,[4] which provided an unlimited marital deduction for individuals dying after 1981. The current unlimited marital deduction is substantially similar to the one enacted in 1981.

The 1981 Act provided a special transition rule that limited the marital deduction for certain wills and trusts executed prior to September 13, 1981. This limitation is applicable to pre-1982 wills and trusts containing formula clauses expressly providing that the spouse is to receive "the maximum amount of property qualifying for the marital deduction."[5] Congress was concerned that testators of these older wills may not have intended to give their spouses more than the amount that would have passed tax-free under the pre-1981 law (i.e., the greater of $250,000 or half of the adjusted gross estate) and therefore provided that the unlimited marital deduction would not apply to a such a will or trust unless (1) the formula clause was amended after September 12, 1981, to refer specifically to an unlimited marital deduction or (2) applicable state law was enacted that construed the formula clause as referring to the unlimited marital deduction. The issue of whether a pre-1982 will or trust is subject to this limitation is not always easy to determine as it may turn on subtle differences in how the formula clause was drafted.[6] Therefore, an estate planner involved in interpreting a pre-1982 will or trust should pay careful attention to the case law and rulings in this area.

[D] Qualifying for the Marital Deduction

A number of technical requirements must be met in order for a transfer to a spouse to qualify for the estate tax marital deduction:[7]

---

[3] Pub. L. No. 94-455, § 2002(a), 90 Stat. 1520 (1976).

[4] Pub. L. No. 97-34, § 403, 95 Stat. 170 (1981).

[5] Pub. L. No. 97-34, § 403(e)(3), 95 Stat. 170 (1981).

[6] For an example of a case that ruled that formula clause used in a pre-1982 will was not subject to the transitional rule, *see* Neisen Estate v. Comm'r, 89 T.C. 939 (1987), *aff'd*, 865 F.2d 162 (8th Cir. 1988).

[7] IRC § 2056.

1. The recipient of the property must be the decedent's surviving spouse;
2. The surviving spouse must be a U.S. citizen (or else additional requirements must be met);
3. The property must be included in the decedent spouse's gross estate;
4. The property must pass to the surviving spouse; and
5. The interest passing to the surviving spouse must not be a *non- deductible terminable interest.*

With the exception of the terminable interest rule, the requirements are relatively straightforward and will be discussed only briefly.

[1] Recipient of Property Is Decedent's Surviving Spouse

It should come as no surprise that in order for a transfer of property to qualify for the marital deduction, the transfer must be to the decedent's surviving spouse.[8] However, the issue of marital status and survivorship can, depending on the circumstances, sometimes be difficult to determine.

The determination of marital status is made under state law as of the date of death. Thus, a couple will still be considered married even if there has been a legal separation or an interlocutory decree of divorce that has not terminated the marriage at the time of the decedent's death. Moreover, if a couple was never legally married under state law (e.g., because one of the parties was already married), then the marital deduction is not available. The treatment of common-law marriages is similarly governed by state law.[9]

In order to be eligible for the marital deduction, the receiving spouse must survive the decedent spouse. Survivorship can sometimes be difficult to determine when the spouses die in a common disaster, such as a car accident or plane crash. This situation can be explicitly addressed by the terms of a will or trust. For example, a will could provide that if the testator and beneficiary under the will die in a common disaster, the testator will be presumed to survive the beneficiary.[10] In the absence of an express provision in the governing document, state law will determine the order of deaths. Most states have adopted some form of the Uniform Simultaneous Death Act, which generally provides that, when the deaths occur simultaneously,[11] each individual will be treated as having survived with respect to his or her own property.

---

[8] IRC § 2056(a).

[9] Rev. Rul. 76-155, 1976-1 C.B. 286.

[10] The advantage of this presumption is that it ensures that the property will go to the testator's second choice if the named beneficiary does not survive long enough to enjoy the property. It also keeps the property from being subject to probate twice within a short period of time.

[11] The Uniform Simultaneous Death Act has been adopted by states in two different forms that primarily differ in their determination of what constitutes "simultaneous death." The earlier version defines a simultaneous death as one where "there is no sufficient evidence that persons have died other than simultaneously" (U.S.D.A. 1990 Act) § 1, 8B U.L.A. 272 (1993). The later form defines simultaneous death as the situation in which the heirs or devisees fail to survive the decedent by more than 120 hours (U.S.D.A. 1991 Act) § 2, 8B U.L.A. 258 (1993). Both versions of the Uniform

EXAMPLE 6-10

H and W each had wills providing for all of their property to pass to the other. H and W died in a plane crash in which the order of their deaths could not be determined. In the absence of a contrary direction in their wills, H will be treated as having survived W with respect to his property and W will be treated as having survived H with respect to her property. Since no property will pass between the spouses, no marital deduction will be available.

Survivorship presumptions can be changed by the terms of a governing document. One common way this is done is to set the period of time required for survivorship (e.g., by requiring that a beneficiary survive the decedent by six months in order to inherit).[12] Another change that is sometimes made is to switch the survivorship presumption. Thus, if one spouse is wealthy and the other spouse is poor, then it may be advantageous to shift the presumption in the will of the wealthier spouse to provide that if it cannot be determined who survived it is presumed that the testator predeceased the named beneficiary.[13] The reason for doing this is to cause property to flow from the wealthier spouse to the poorer spouse's estate to increase the likelihood of the poorer spouse having sufficient assets to use her unified credit. (Note that this technique is not necessary to the extent that the couple is relying on portability.)

EXAMPLE 6-11

H and W each had wills providing for all of their property to pass to the other. H's will provided that if H and W died in circumstances in which it could cannot be determined who died first, W would be presumed to survive H. W's will also provided that if it cannot be determined who died first, W would be presumed to survive H.

H and W died in a plane crash in which it could not be determined who died first. Under the terms of their wills, W will be treated as having survived H with respect to H's property as well as her own property. The property passing from H to W's estate will be eligible for the marital deduction. W's estate can use these assets to take advantage of her unified credit.

(Footnote Continued)

Simultaneous Death Act provide that they will not apply if contrary directions were given by the decedent (U.S.D.A. 1990 Act) § 6, 8B U.L.A. 294 (1993); (U.S.D.A. 1991 Act) § 6, 8B U.L.A. 261 (1993).

[12] The length of time should not be longer than six months as that can affect eligibility for the minimal deduction. *See* § 6.03[D][1] *infra.*

[13] Form 1 contains an example of this type of switched survivorship presumption.

There are limitations, however, to what can be accomplished by the terms of a will. The Tax Court has ruled that a will or trust could not be used to modify the actual order of death of the couple for purposes of § 2056(b)(3). In this case, the decedent died 46 days after his wife. The decedent's will said that the husband would be deemed to predecease his wife if she died within six months of his death. The Tax Court held that the decedent was not eligible for the marital deduction.[14]

[2] The Surviving Spouse Is a U.S. Citizen

The marital deduction is not available for transfers to spouses who are not U.S. citizens, unless additional requirements are met.[15] The reason for this rule is to ensure that property passing tax free to a surviving spouse under the marital deduction does not evade taxation in the United States if the surviving spouse returns to her country of citizenship. The additional requirements are designed to ensure that the property passing to the non-citizen spouse is subject to gift or estate taxes in the United States.[16]

[3] The Property Is Included in the Decedent Spouse's Gross Estate

In order to be eligible for the marital deduction, the property passing to the surviving spouse must be included in the decedent spouse's gross estate. This ensures that the marital deduction is not used as a tax shelter.

EXAMPLE 6-12

H and W own their home in joint tenancy. The home has a fair market value of $3,000,000. Upon H's death, the home will pass to W as a result of the joint tenancy. H's estate is only eligible for a marital deduction with respect to $1,500,000 (50 percent of the value of the home) since that is the amount that will be included in H's gross estate under the rules regarding joint tenancy.[17]

[4] The Property Passes from the Decedent to the Surviving Spouse

A deduction is allowed only for interests that *pass* to the surviving spouse. There are numerous ways in which this passing requirement can be met, including the following methods:[18]

---

[14] Estate of Lee v. Comm'r, T.C. Memo 2007-371.

[15] IRC § 2056(d).

[16] Issues in planning for a non-U.S. citizen spouse are discussed in greater detail in § 6.03[E] *infra*.

[17] IRC § 2040(b).

[18] IRC § 2056(c); Reg. § 20.2056(c)-1. This list is not intended to be exhaustive.

- Bequest or devise
- Inheritance
- Dower, curtesy, or statutory elective share rights
- *Inter vivos* transfers
- Joint tenancy or other rights of survivorship
- The exercise or nonexercise of a power of appointment
- Proceeds of life insurance policies on which the surviving spouse is designated as beneficiary
- Survivorship interests in annuities
- Employee death benefits

An interest will also be treated as passing from the decedent spouse to the surviving spouse if it is assigned to the surviving spouse in settlement of a controversy involving the decedent's will.[19] However, in order to be deductible, the property must be transferred as a result of a bona fide recognition of the surviving spouse's enforceable rights in the decedent spouse's estate.[20] This requirement will be met if the transfer is pursuant to a decision of a local court upon the merits in an adversary proceeding following a genuine and active contest. However, if the transfer is made pursuant to an agreement of the parties, it will not necessarily be accepted as a bona fide evaluation of the spouse's rights.[21] In applying this rule, the Service is particularly suspicious of settlements of controversies in which the surviving spouse gives up interests that would not otherwise qualify for the marital deduction, in exchange for interests that are more likely to qualify.

EXAMPLE 6-13

H's will provides for W to receive $5,000/month for life or until she remarries. These payments would not be eligible for the marital deduction because they violate the terminable interest rule. W contests H's will and in settlement of the contest H's estate agrees to pay W $100,000 outright in exchange for W waiving her rights under the will. The Service is likely to challenge the deductibility of this payment on the theory that it is not in settlement of a bona fide recognition of the surviving spouse's enforceable rights in the decedent spouse's estate.[22]

The surviving spouse must actually receive the beneficial interest in the property in order for it to be eligible for the marital deduction. Thus, for example, if the surviving spouse waives her right to claim a spousal share, such amounts shall not be treated as having passed to the surviving spouse.

---

[19] Reg. § 20.2056(c)–2(d)(2).

[20] *Id.*

[21] *Id.*

[22] *See, e.g.,* Carpenter Est. v. Comm'r, 67 T.C.M. 2400 (1994), *aff'd,* 95-1 USTC ¶ 60,194 (4th Cir. 1995) and Ltr. Rul. 8236004 (May 23, 1982).

If the surviving spouse receives property encumbered by debt, only the net value of the property received will be eligible for the marital deduction.[23]

EXAMPLE 6-14

W's will provides for H to receive vacation property that is valued at $2,000,000, but is subject to a $500,000 mortgage. The full value of the property ($2,000,000) is included in W's estate. The marital deduction for this transfer is $1,500,000, the net value of the property passing to H. However, W's estate may also be able to deduct the $500,000 as a claim against the estate.

Similarly, if the surviving spouse is required to transfer property as a condition of receiving a bequest, the value of the property required to be transferred by the surviving spouse will reduce the marital deduction.[24] This most commonly occurs in community property jurisdictions when a spouse uses a *widow's election will*.[25] Under a widow's election will, the decedent spouse's will provides a plan for the disposition of both halves of the community property. Upon the decedent spouse's death, the surviving spouse is given the choice of joining in the plan provided for under the will (by consenting to the transfer of her share of the community property), or rejecting the will and taking her share of community property outright. If the surviving spouse elects to take under the will, the value of the marital deduction will be the value of the property transferred to the surviving spouse under the decedent spouse's will *minus* the value of the interest that the surviving spouse was required to surrender.

[5] Interest Passing to the Surviving Spouse Is Not a Nondeductible Terminable Interest

The marital deduction is not available for transfers of nondeductible terminable interests.[26] This requirement can be the most intimidating aspect of the marital deduction to both apply and understand. However, understanding the original reason for the terminable interest rule goes a long way toward making it more comprehensible.

The terminable interest rule has been part of the marital deduction since the deduction was first enacted in 1948.[27] At that time, the justification for the marital deduction was to enable taxpayers in separate property states to opt into the community property system by allowing the tax-free transfer of up to 50 percent of a decedent's property to a spouse. Under the community property system, a surviving

---

[23] IRC § 2056(b)(4)(B).

[24] United States v. Stapf, 375 U.S. 118 (1963).

[25] Widow's election wills are discussed in § 6.02[B][3] *supra*.

[26] IRC § 2056(b).

[27] The history of the marital deduction is discussed in § 6.03[C][1] *supra*.

spouse was given an outright interest in her share of community property. Therefore, with the goal of equalizing the treatment of separate property states with community property states, the terminable interest rule was enacted to ensure that the surviving spouse in the separate property state would receive, free of estate tax (with some notable exceptions), essentially what she would have received tax free in a community property state—an absolute and unqualified interest in up to 50 percent of the decedent spouse's property. The terminable interest rule was designed to limit the decedent spouse's ability to impose restrictions on the property interest given to the surviving spouse. Of course, this goal served another purpose as well—in assuring that the surviving spouse received an outright interest in property, this also assured that the property would be subject to tax in the surviving spouse's estate (to the extent the property was not consumed or disposed of by the surviving spouse during his or her lifetime). As time passed, the justification for the marital deduction changed and more exceptions to the terminable interest rule were added that allowed more limitations to be imposed on the surviving spouse's interest. However, all of these exceptions include mechanisms to insure that the property will be subject to tax in the surviving spouse's estate to the extent the property is not consumed or disposed of by the spouse during his lifetime.

The nondeductible terminable interest rule only disallows the marital deduction for transfers of certain terminable interests. Thus, to apply these rules, the estate planner must understand what a terminable interest is, and which terminable interests are nondeductible. In addition, because the Code provides for several exceptions to this rule (and because much estate planning involves use of these exceptions), the estate planner must have a good understanding of the statutory exceptions to the terminable interest rule.

An outright disposition of a decedent's property to his spouse will never violate the nondeductible terminable interest rule. Therefore, one easy way of qualifying for the marital deduction without worrying about the complexity of these rules is to provide for the decedent spouse's property to pass outright to the surviving spouse. However, if the decedent spouse wants to impose *any* conditions on the property passing to the surviving spouse, or wants the property to be held in trust, then the estate planner needs to have a firm understanding of the terminable interest rule and its exceptions.

[E] Terminable Interest Rule

[1] What Is a Terminable Interest?

A terminable interest is an interest that will fail or terminate due to the lapse of time or the occurrence or nonoccurrence of an event or contingency.[28] Classic examples of terminable interests include life estates, terms of years, interests subject to a condition (such as not remarrying), and interests in property having a limited life, such as an annuity, patent, or copyright.

---

[28] IRC § 2056(b).

The terminable interest rule is applied with reference to the interest provided for the surviving spouse by the decedent spouse. Thus, if the decedent provides for his wife to receive a life estate with remainder to his children, this will be a terminable interest even if the wife subsequently agrees with the children to take an outright distribution from the estate in lieu of her life estate.[29]

The determination of whether an interest is a terminable interest is made with reference to the date of the decedent's death. Thus, an interest is a terminable interest if there is the possibility (as determined at the time of death) that the surviving spouse's interest will terminate or fail.

EXAMPLE *6-15*

W's will named H as beneficiary, on the condition that he survive until her executor distributes her assets in the probate estate. H survives the period and all of W's assets are distributed to H. The interest passing to H is a nondeductible terminable interest (and therefore not eligible for the marital deduction) because at the time of W's death there was the possibility that H's interest would fail due to H not surviving the period of probate.

The terminable interest rule can cause problems for family allowance distributions qualifying for the marital deduction. Family allowance statutes enable probate courts to distribute assets of a decedent's estate to the decedent's spouse during the administration of the estate. Since many family allowance statutes provide limitations on these payments (e.g., that the payments cease upon the surviving spouse's death or remarriage), payments made to a spouse under a family allowance statute are often not eligible for the marital deduction due to the terminable interest rule.[30] This will not be a problem in those states where the family allowance statute creates an unconditional right upon the first spouse's death that is not defeated by the surviving spouse's death or remarriage, even if the amount of allowance is set by the court during the administration of the estate.

[2] Which Terminable Interests Are Nondeductible?

Not all terminable interests are nondeductible terminable interests. In general, a terminable interest will be nondeductible if it was either created by the decedent or acquired for the surviving spouse at the direction of the decedent.[31]

The first type of nondeductible terminable interest is a terminable interest that is created by the decedent. The Internal Revenue Code describes this type of nondeductible terminable interest as one in which (1) another interest in the same property

---

[29] Reg. § 20.2056(b)-1(e)(3).

[30] Jackson v. United States, 376 U.S. 503 (1964).

[31] IRC § 2056(b).

passes from the decedent to a person other than the surviving spouse for less than full and adequate consideration, and (2) that person will possess or enjoy the property after termination of the surviving spouse's interest.[32] An example of this type of nondeductible terminable interest is a life estate to a spouse with a remainder to the decedent's children. In that case, the decedent has transferred a remainder interest in the property to his children for less than full and adequate consideration (indeed for no consideration) and they will possess that interest after the termination of the surviving spouse's interest in the property.

The terminable interest rule only applies when the surviving spouse's interest is cut off by an interest going to someone other than a surviving spouse. Thus, for example, a surviving spouse can be given an interest in a trust over which there are no income distributions during life, but the property is paid to the surviving spouse's estate upon her death (an *estate trust*), and this will not violate the terminable interest rule since no one will receive the interest after the surviving spouse.[33]

Another example of a terminable interest that is not a nondeductible terminable interest is a 20-year annuity purchased by the decedent during his life. An annuity is a terminable interest because it will terminate upon the lapse of time (in this case, 20 years). However, it is not a nondeductible terminable interest under this rule because no one will possess or enjoy the annuity after the surviving spouse's interest expires. In other words, although the decedent spouse owned the terminable interest, he did not create the terminable interest and therefore it is not nondeductible.[34]

The second type of nondeductible terminable interest is a terminable interest that is acquired for the surviving spouse by the decedent's executor or trustee at the direction of the decedent.[35] Thus, for example, if the decedent directs his executor to purchase an annuity for his surviving spouse, this annuity will be a nondeductible terminable interest because it is a terminable interest acquired for the surviving spouse at the decedent spouse's direction.

The decedent need not provide explicit instructions in order for an interest to be nondeductible. Under the unidentified asset rule, the marital deduction will not be allowed to the extent that the surviving spouse's interest *may* be satisfied with interests that would violate the terminable interest rule if transferred by the decedent spouse.[36]

EXAMPLE 6-16

H's will provides for W to receive one-third of the residue of his estate. One of the assets in his estate is the right to receive rentals from an office building for a term of years, reserved by the decedent when he gave the building to his son. (The rentals would constitute a terminable interest if

---

[32] IRC § 2056(b)(1)(A) and (B); Reg. § 20.2056(b)-1(c)(1).

[33] Rev. Rul. 72-333, 1972-2 C.B. 530.

[34] Reg. § 20.2056(b)-1(g), Example (3).

[35] IRC § 2056(b)(1)(C); Reg. § 20.2056(b)-1(c)(2).

[36] IRC § 2056(b)(2); Reg. § 20.2056(b)-2.

they were transferred to the surviving spouse under the terms of the will, since the spouse's interest would terminate on the passage of time, and after the spouse's interest terminated the interest would be enjoyed by someone other than the surviving spouse—decedent's son—who received the interest from the decedent spouse without consideration.) The decedent did not make a specific bequest of the rentals. Therefore, it is possible for the surviving spouse's interest to be partially satisfied with the rentals from the office building.

The value of the marital deduction will be reduced by the value of the terminable interest that could be used to satisfy the spouse's interest (as determined under the decedent's will or local law), regardless of whether the interest is actually transferred to the surviving spouse.[37] Thus, for example, if one-third of the residue is valued at $80,000 and the rental income is valued at $60,000, and under the terms of the decedent's will the lease could be transferred to the surviving spouse in partial satisfaction of her interest, the marital deduction will be limited to $20,000.[38]

This rule ensures that the nondeductible terminable interest rule cannot be sidestepped by the decedent coming to an understanding with the executor to distribute terminable interest property to the surviving spouse. However, this rule poses a trap for the unwary as it applies regardless of testator intent. To avoid loss of the marital deduction due to inadvertent application of this rule, the will or other governing document should specifically provide that an executor may not satisfy a spousal bequest with assets that do not qualify for the marital deduction.[39]

[F] Exceptions to the Terminable Interest Rule

There are five statutory exceptions to the terminable interest rule. These exceptions specifically allow the marital deduction for certain interests passing to the surviving spouse, regardless of the fact that the interest would otherwise be a nondeductible terminable interest. Estate planning for married couples commonly involves use of one or more of these exceptions to the terminable interest rule. These exceptions are for:[40]

1. Interests conditioned on a spouse surviving for a particular period of time;
2. A right to income for life and a power of appointment over the principal;
3. Life insurance or annuity payments held by an insurer with the surviving spouse having a general power of appointment;

---

[37] Id.

[38] Reg. § 20.2056(b)-2(d).

[39] Form 1 includes this provision.

[40] IRC § 2056(b).

4. A right to income for life with an election by the executor to treat the interest as qualified terminable interest property; and
5. An interest in a charitable remainder trust in which the surviving spouse is the only noncharitable beneficiary.

[1] Survivorship Conditions

A transfer to a spouse conditioned on surviving the decedent by a specified period of time technically violates the terminable interest rule because the interest passing to the surviving spouse will terminate upon the occurrence of an event (the spouse's death), and upon termination of the spouse's interest the property will pass to the person named in the decedent's will as the alternative taker to the spouse. In recognition of the fact that survivorship conditions are a common element of estate plans, the Code provides an exception to the terminable interest rule for interests passing to a spouse conditioned on the spouse surviving the decedent spouse for a limited period of time.[41]

In order to be eligible for this exception, termination of the spouse's interest must be conditioned on one or both of the following: (1) the surviving spouse's failure to survive for a period of time not greater than six months after the decedent spouse's death; or (2) the surviving spouse and the decedent spouse dying as a result of a common disaster.[42] In addition, the marital deduction will only be allowed if the condition does not, in fact, occur.

EXAMPLE 6-17

W's will provides for everything to go to H, on the condition that he survive W by six months. H is still living six months after W's death. W's bequest to H will be eligible for the marital deduction provided the other requirements have been met.

This is not an area for creativity on the part of the estate planner as conditions that do not follow the terms of the exception will not be eligible for the marital deduction, even if the conditions are satisfied within the six-month period.

EXAMPLE 6-18

W's will provides for everything to go to H, on the condition that H survives the time during which W's estate is administered. H is still living at the time administration of W's estate is complete. The transfer to H will

---

[41] IRC § 2056(b)(3).
[42] IRC § 2056(b)(3); Reg. § 20.2056(b)-3.

not be eligible for the marital deduction even if administration of the estate occurs within six months of W's death because the condition is not specifically sanctioned under IRC Section 2056(b)(3).

[2] Life Estate with a Power of Appointment Trust

[a] General Rule

A transfer will qualify for the marital deduction if the surviving spouse is given a life estate and a general power of appointment over the property. From a tax perspective, a life estate with a general power of appointment is the equivalent of an outright transfer to the surviving spouse because all income earned by the trust will be taxed to the surviving spouse for income tax purposes,[43] and the trust principal will be taxed in the surviving spouse's estate for estate tax purposes.[44] Regardless of this tax parity, by placing property in a power of appointment trust, the decedent spouse can exert significantly more control over the property than would be the case if he had left the property outright to the surviving spouse. For example, by putting the property in trust and naming as trustee someone other than the surviving spouse, the decedent spouse can control the management of the funds. By limiting the power of appointment to exercise upon the surviving spouse's death, the decedent spouse can eliminate the surviving spouse's lifetime control over the property. Finally, the decedent spouse may even be able to provide for the ultimate disposition of the principal, because if the surviving spouse fails to exercise her power of appointment (which commonly occurs) the interest will pass to the alternate takers named by the decedent spouse.[45]

Alternatively, if the decedent spouse does not wish to maintain control of the trust property, the life estate with a power of appointment trust can be structured in such a way as to give the surviving spouse the substantial equivalent of outright ownership. For example, by naming the surviving spouse as the trustee, she can control the investment of the assets. By making the general power of appointment exercisable during life as well as at death, the surviving spouse can have unlimited access to the principal. Finally, by naming the surviving spouse's estate as the alternate taker in the event that the surviving spouse fails to exercise her power of appointment, the property will pass at death the same way as if she had owned it outright. Although there is very little difference between this and outright ownership of the trust assets from the spouse's perspective, use of the power of appointment trust can be advantageous over an outright bequest because the trust can provide management of the funds in the event of the surviving spouse's incapacity and can avoid probate in the surviving spouse's estate.

---

[43] IRC § 678.

[44] IRC § 2041. If the surviving spouse has a power to appoint the property during her life and exercises that power, the exercise of the power will be subject to gift tax under IRC § 2514.

[45] However, if this is the client's goal, then a QTIP trust would be a better option. QTIP trusts are discussed in greater detail in § 6.03[F][4] *infra*.

EXAMPLE *6-19*

H's will provides for property to be transferred to a trust. W is named trustee, and the trust provides that all income is to be paid to W annually or more frequently, and W has a general power of appointment exercisable at any time either during her life or at death. W exercises her power of appointment in favor of her child, C. The property will pass to C outside of the probate process.

Of course, the surviving spouse could accomplish the same goals by placing property that passed to her outright to a revocable trust during her lifetime. However, some couples enjoy the security of knowing that arrangements for management of their property are in place.

[b] Requirements for a Life Estate with a Power of Appointment Trust

In order to be eligible for the marital deduction under this exception, the trust must provide as follows:[46]

1. All trust income is payable to the surviving spouse at least annually for life;
2. The surviving spouse has a general power of appointment exercisable alone and in all events in favor of herself or her estate; and
3. No person other than the surviving spouse can be a beneficiary of the trust during the surviving spouse's life.

The following trust provision would qualify for the marital deduction as a life estate with a power of appointment trust:

The trustee shall pay all trust income to Spouse, at least annually, for Spouse's life. On the death of Spouse, the trustee shall distribute the trust principal (including any undistributed accrued income) to such persons, including Spouse's estate, as Spouse may appoint by will. In the event that Spouse fails to appoint the trust principal, on the death of Spouse the trustee shall distribute the trust assets to my then living descendants.

Nonetheless, careful attention should be paid to each of the requirements as it is easy to inadvertently run afoul of them (at a substantial cost in taxes) through other provisions in the trust:

[i] **Income.** In order to be eligible for the marital deduction, the surviving spouse must be entitled to all income from the trust, distributed at least annually.[47] The regulations explain that this requirement will be met if the surviving spouse is given (under either local law or the terms of the governing instrument) "substantially

---

[46] IRC § 2056(b)(5).

[47] IRC § 2056(b)(5); Reg. § 20.2056(b)-5(f). This is the same requirement for the QTIP trust discussed in greater detail in § 6.03[F][4] *infra.*

that degree of beneficial enjoyment of the trust property during her life which principles of the law of trusts accord to a person who is unqualifiedly designated as the life beneficiary of a trust."[48] In practical terms, this means that there can be no limitations on the surviving spouse's right to the regular payment of income. The requirements imposed by this rule can best be understood by examining possibilities of breach. Any of the following provisions will cause this "all income" requirement to *not* be met:[49]

- Income may be accumulated by the trustee;
- The income interest fails upon the spouse's incompetence, bankruptcy, or remarriage (or any other condition);
- The trustee can invade the principal or make income distributions to someone other than the surviving spouse; or
- The trustee is authorized to retain or acquire unproductive assets.

The restriction on retaining unproductive assets can be problematic when a large portion of the decedent spouse's estate consists of a closely held business interest with a poor history of paying dividends. The regulations provide that a power to retain unproductive property will not disqualify the interest if the applicable rules for the administration of the trust require, or permit the spouse to require, that the trustee either make the property productive or convert it within a reasonable time.[50] Often it may be undesirable to compel the trustee to sell unproductive assets as the spouse may be willing to have it retained in the trust, even if retention results in less income to her. In order to build in flexibility, it is often preferable to authorize the trustee to retain unproductive property, with the provision that it shall not be retained for more than a reasonable period of time without the consent of the surviving spouse.[51]

A power to retain a residence or other property for the personal use of the spouse will not disqualify the interest from the marital deduction.[52]

If qualified retirement benefits are being transferred to a trust, additional language may be required in order to ensure that the "all income" requirement is met.[53]

When drafting a trust that is intended to qualify for the marital deduction, the estate planner should be careful to avoid granting powers to the trustee that might be used in a manner that would deprive the surviving spouse the usual rights of an income beneficiary. For example, a power in the trustee's uncontrolled discretion to apportion receipts and expenses between principal and income may endanger the

---

[48] Reg. § 20.2056(b)-5(f).

[49] Reg. § 20.2056(b)-5(f)(7).

[50] Reg. § 20.2056(b)-5(f)(4).

[51] Form 1 includes language designed to address this issue in its QTIP trust. Another way of addressing this problem is through the use of an estate trust, discussed in § 6.03[E][2] *supra.*

[52] Reg. § 20.2056(b)-5(f)(4).

[53] Rev. Rul. 2000-02, 2000-1 C.B. 305. Form 1 includes an example of this language in its QTIP trust. Tax planning with retirement benefits is discussed in greater detail in Chapter 13.

deduction, at least where such provision is given a broad construction under local law.[54]

[ii] General Power of Appointment. The surviving spouse must be given a general power of appointment exercisable alone and in all events in favor of herself or her estate.[55] It is important to note that not all general powers of appointment will qualify for purposes of this rule. For example, a power of appointment exercisable in favor of the spouse's creditors or creditors of her estate meets the definition of a general power of appointment (and will thus be includable in the surviving spouse's gross estate),[56] but will not be eligible for the marital deduction in the decedent spouse's estate because it is not exercisable in favor of the surviving spouse or her estate. Similarly, if the surviving spouse can only exercise the power with the consent of another person, then that will not qualify for the marital deduction because it is not exercisable alone (although again it could still be subject to tax in the surviving spouse's estate).

The surviving spouse must not be obligated to appoint the property to anyone else. Thus, if the surviving spouse is legally obligated to appoint the property to the couple's children (or anyone else), the transfer would not qualify for the marital deduction under this provision.[57]

The general power of appointment must be exercisable by the surviving spouse in all events.[58] This requirement will not be met if there are conditions on the exercise of the power. For example, a power is not exercisable in all events if it can only be exercised for the surviving spouse's support or other limited purpose. However, the surviving spouse's rights to exercise the power of appointment can be limited to being exercisable only during her life or only by will.[59]

Originally there was some issue as to whether a power would be considered as "exercisable in all events" when the surviving spouse's interest was conditioned upon surviving for a period of time after the donor's death. The regulations now specifically provide that a survivorship clause will not affect qualification for the marital deduction if it is conditioned on (1) not dying in a common disaster or (2) surviving the decedent spouse by six months or less, and if the condition does not occur.[60]

[iii] No Person Other than the Surviving Spouse Can Be a Beneficiary of the Trust During the Surviving Spouse's Life. In order to ensure that property qualify-

---

[54] Reg. § 20.2056(b)-5(f). These rules are discussed in greater detail in Rev. Rul. 69-56, 1969-1 C.B. 224.

[55] IRC § 2056(b)(5); Reg. § 20.2056(b)-5(g).

[56] IRC § 2041.

[57] A better plan for that couple would have been to use a QTIP trust. These are discussed in greater detail in § 6.03[F][4] *infra*.

[58] IRC § 2056(b)(5); Reg. § 20.2056(b)-5(g).

[59] Reg. § 20.2056(b)-5(g).

[60] Reg. § 20.2056(b)-5(h). These rules provide for parity with the general survivorship exception found in IRC § 2056(b)(3) and the regulations in Reg. § 20.2056(b)-3.

ing for the marital deduction will be included in the surviving spouse's estate (except to the extent that it is either consumed or transferred by the surviving spouse), the statute requires that no person other than the surviving spouse can be a beneficiary of the trust during the surviving spouse's life. Thus, the marital deduction will not be available to the extent that a power is created in a trustee (or anyone other than the surviving spouse) to appoint an interest to any person other than the surviving spouse. This requirement does not preclude a provision that the property will pass to a designated beneficiary in the event that the surviving spouse fails to exercise the power of appointment, as that person does not have a beneficial interest during the surviving spouse's life.

[c] The Specific Portion Rule

A trust can qualify for the marital deduction in either whole or part. However, if only part of the trust is intended to qualify for the marital deduction, then under the *specific portion rule*, the part must be expressed as a fractional or percentile share of the entire interest (e.g., half, or 50 percent).[61] With respect to the income interest, the specific portion rule will be met if the surviving spouse is entitled to all of the income from a specific portion of the trust (e.g., all of the income from 20 percent of the trust) or a specific portion of the income from all of the trust (e.g., 20 percent of all of the income from the trust). With respect to the general power of appointment, the requirement will be met if the surviving spouse is given a qualifying general power of appointment over a specific portion of the trust assets. A partial interest will not qualify if it is stated in terms of a dollar amount (e.g., a provision that gives the surviving spouse income from and a general power of appointment over $500,000 of the trust). The reason for this restriction is to ensure that the appreciation in the property between the time of the decedent spouse's death and the surviving spouse's death will be subject to tax in the surviving spouse's estate.[62]

In cases of partial interests, the surviving spouse does not need to be given the same percentage share over the income interest and the power of appointment. However, the marital deduction will only be available to the extent of the smaller share.

EXAMPLE 6-20

W's will provides that H is to be given all of the income from the marital trust and a general power of appointment over 30 percent of the trust

---

[61] IRC § 2056(b)(10). This rule applies in general to decedents dying after October 24. 1992. However, the rule does not apply to a transfer under a will or trust executed before October 24, 1992, if either (1) the decedent died before October 24, 1995, or (2) on October 24, 1992, the decedent was under a mental disability to change the disposition of his or her property and did not regain competence to dispose of such property before death. Energy Policy Act of 1992, Pub. L. No. 102-486, § 1941(c)(1), 106 Stat. 2776 (1992).

[62] Reg. § 20.2056(b)-5(b)(2).

principal. W's estate will be eligible for a marital deduction with respect to 30 percent of the assets in the marital trust.

[3] Life Insurance, Annuity, and Endowment Proceeds with Power of Appointment

Life insurance proceeds or the proceeds of an annuity or endowment contract generally qualify for the marital deduction if the proceeds are payable to the surviving spouse in a lump sum, or other settlement option that provides that the unpaid balance, if any, is paid to the surviving spouse's estate upon her death. These dispositions do not violate the terminable interest rule since no one other than the surviving spouse has an interest in the property. However, if the policy provides for a secondary beneficiary who may be entitled to benefits after the surviving spouse's interest terminates (by death or otherwise), the deduction is not allowed unless the disposition fits into the insurance exception to the terminable interest rule.[63]

The insurance exception is closely analogous to the exception for the power of appointment trust. This exception permits the marital deduction for insurance proceeds held by an insurer if the following five conditions are met:[64]

1. The proceeds are held by the insurer on an installment or interest option with all amounts (or a specific portion thereof) payable only to the surviving spouse during her life;
2. Such installments are payable at least annually, beginning not later than 13 months after the decedent spouse's death;
3. The surviving spouse has the power to appoint all amounts (or a specific portion thereof) held by the insurer to herself or her estate;
4. The power of appointment is exercisable by the surviving spouse alone and in all events, although it may be exercisable only during her life or only by will; and
5. No other person has a power to appoint any part of the proceeds to any person other than the surviving spouse.

EXAMPLE 6-21

W has an insurance policy on her life that names H as the primary beneficiary. Under the settlement option chosen by W, upon W's death, the proceeds of the policy will be invested by the insurance company and interest will be paid monthly to H for H's life. H will also have the right, exercisable alone and in all events, to direct the insurance company to pay the entire proceeds at his death to his estate. The value of the life insurance policy will qualify for the marital deduction in W's estate.

---

[63] IRC § 2056(b)(6).
[64] IRC § 2056(b)(6); Reg. § 20.2056(b)-6.

These rules only apply to proceeds held by the insurer. If the proceeds are payable to a trustee, the terms of the trust instrument will determine whether the marital deduction will be allowed. Thus, the transfer of proceeds to a QTIP trust, a power of appointment trust, or an estate trust will all qualify for the marital deduction.

It is important to remember that the marital deduction will only be available to the extent that the life insurance or other policy was included in the decedent spouse's gross estate for tax purposes. Thus, if the policy on the decedent spouse's life was owned by an insurance trust and the decedent spouse had no incidents of ownership, no marital deduction would be available with respect to those proceeds since they would not have been included in the decedent spouse's gross estate.[65]

[4] QTIP Trust

[a] General Rule

A transfer will qualify for the marital deduction under the Qualified Terminable Interest Property (or QTIP) exception if the surviving spouse is given an income interest for life in the property, provided an election is made on the decedent spouse's estate tax return to treat the interest as a QTIP interest.[66] The effect of the QTIP election is to make the marital deduction available to the decedent spouse's estate and have the property in the QTIP trust subject to tax in the surviving spouse's estate. The marital deduction is available for (and the property is subject to tax in the surviving spouse's estate at) the full value of the property even though the surviving spouse is only given an income interest.

EXAMPLE 6-22

H's will provides for $3,000,000 to be transferred to a trust in which W is given an income interest for life and upon W's death, the remainder passes to H's children. Provided a QTIP election is made on H's estate tax return, H's estate will be entitled to a $3,000,000 marital deduction. Upon W's death, W's estate will be subject to tax on the full value of the property in the QTIP trust (although the tax liability will be paid from trust proceeds).

Because this type of bequest does not require that the surviving spouse be given the ultimate power of disposition over the trust assets, the QTIP trust provides an estate owner with an element of control not available for outright bequests, power of appointment trusts, or estate trusts. In addition, the QTIP trust provides a great deal of flexibility in tax planning because it allows the decision of how much marital

---

[65] *See* Chapter 12 for a discussion of life insurance trusts.
[66] IRC § 2056(b)(7).

deduction is going to be claimed to be deferred until the time that the estate tax return is due (usually nine months after the decedent spouse's death).

EXAMPLE 6-23

H's will provides for all of his property to be transferred to a trust in which W is given an income interest for life and upon W's death, the remainder passes to H's children. If H's executor makes the election to treat the property as QTIP property it will be eligible for the marital deduction in H's estate and subject to tax in W's estate. If H's executor does not make the QTIP election, the property will not be eligible for the marital deduction in H's estate (because it is a terminable interest) and it will not be subject to tax in W's estate (because the gross estate does not generally include interests in which the decedent only had a life estate). The decision of whether and how much marital deduction to claim can be deferred until nine months after H's death, when the estate tax return for H's estate is due.

It should be noted that, although the QTIP election is available for *some* terminable interests (namely those that terminate upon the surviving spouse's death), it is not available for interests granted for a term of years or ones that terminate upon the surviving spouse's remarriage or the occurrence of events other than the surviving spouse's death.[67]

[b] Requirements for a QTIP Trust

In order to be eligible for the marital deduction under the exception for the QTIP trust, the trust must provide as follows:[68]

1. All income is payable to the surviving spouse at least annually for life;
2. No one (including the surviving spouse) has the power to appoint any part of the property to any person other than the surviving spouse during the lifetime of the surviving spouse; and
3. The decedent spouse's executor makes the QTIP election on the federal estate tax return of the decedent spouse.

The following trust provision would qualify for the marital deduction, provided the appropriate election was made:

The trustee shall pay all trust income to Spouse, at least annually, for Spouse's life. Upon Spouse's death, the trustee shall distribute the trust assets to Children.

---

[67] Reg. § 20.2056(b)-7(b), Example 5.
[68] IRC § 2056(b)(7); Reg. § 20.2056. *See* Form 1 for a sample trust with QTIP provision.

As in the power of appointment trust, however, careful attention should be made to each of the requirements in order to ensure qualification for the marital deduction.

[i] Income. In order to be eligible for the marital deduction, the surviving spouse must be given all of the income payable at least annually for life. This is the same income requirement that is imposed for the power of appointment trust, and similar issues need to be addressed.[69]

The all income requirement is met if the effect of the trust is to give the surviving spouse "substantially that degree of beneficial enjoyment of the trust property during her life that the principles of the law of trusts accord to a person who is unqualifiedly designated as the life beneficiary of the trust."[70] In practical terms, this means that there can be no limitations on the surviving spouse's right to the regular payment of income. Thus, the payment of income must not be conditioned on the occurrence of any event (such as the need of the surviving spouse) or the non-occurrence of any event (such as the marriage, incompetence, or bankruptcy of the surviving spouse). In addition, the trustee must not have the right to accumulate income. Finally, the trustee must not be authorized to acquire or retain unproductive assets unless the surviving spouse has the ability to require that the trustee make the assets productive or convert them within a reasonable period of time.

For a time, it was thought necessary that in order to meet the "all income" requirement for the QTIP trust, the trust must provide that the surviving spouse be entitled to any accrued income that was undistributed at the time of the surviving spouse's death (called stub income). However, the regulations now provide that income earned between the last distribution date and the surviving spouse's death may be paid to other beneficiaries.[71]

[ii] No Person Can Have the Power to Appoint the Trust Property to Any Third Person During the Surviving Spouse's Life. The QTIP rules require that no person (including the surviving spouse) be given the power to appoint the trust property to any third person during the surviving spouse's life.[72] For example, the trustee cannot be given the power to make distributions from the trust property for the support of any children who the surviving spouse is not obligated to support. The reason for this rule is to ensure that the trust property will not escape taxation in the surviving spouse's estate.

The trustee can be authorized to make distributions for the benefit of the spouse. In addition, the surviving spouse may also be given the power to assign her income

---

[69] The regulations for the QTIP trust provision specifically refer to the principles found in the regulations regarding power-of-appointment trusts in Reg. § 20.2056(b)-5(f). Reg. § 20.2056(b)-7. This requirement is discussed in § 6.03[F][2][B][ii] *supra*.

[70] Reg. § 20.2056(b)-5(f)(1).

[71] Reg. § 20.2056(b)-7(d)(4). However, regardless of to whom it is paid, the stub income will be subject to tax in the surviving spouse's estate. Reg. § 20.2044-1(d)(2).

[72] IRC § 2056(b)(7)(8)(ii).

interest during her life, although such assignment will be treated for gift tax purposes as a gift of the entire interest, rather than just the income interest.

EXAMPLE 6-24

H was given a qualifying income interest from a trust valued at $3,000,000 for which the executor made the QTIP election. H transferred the income interest to his child, C. H will be treated as having made a gift of $3,000,000 even though C only received the income interest from $3,000,000.

For a time, there was an issue as to whether property would qualify as QTIP property when the surviving spouse's interest was dependent upon a QTIP election being made. The Internal Revenue Service took the position that when the surviving spouse's interest was contingent on a QTIP election being made, the effect of this was to give the executor (as the person responsible for making the election) the power to appoint the property to someone other than the surviving spouse.[73] However, after losing numerous cases on this issue, the Treasury conceded and issued regulations that provide that an otherwise qualifying income interest will not fail because it is contingent upon the executor's election to treat the property as QTIP property.[74]

EXAMPLE 6-25

H's will established a trust that provided that W was entitled to receive the income from that portion of the trust the executor elects to treat as qualified terminable interest property. W's interest in the trust otherwise meets the requirements for a qualifying interest for purposes of the QTIP rules. The executor may elect qualified terminable interest treatment for any portion of the trust.

[iii] **Election.** In order for a qualifying income interest to be eligible for the marital deduction, an election must be made on the decedent spouse's estate tax return.[75] This is in contrast to the power of appointment trust, which applies automatically if the statutory requirements are met. The QTIP election must be made by the court appointed executor. However, if no executor has been appointed, the election may be made by the person who is in possession of the property. For example, if an

---

[73] *See, e.g.,* Estate of Clayton v. Comm'r, 976 F.2d 1486 (5th Cir. 1992); Estate of Robertson v. Comm'r, 15 F.3d 779 (8th Cir. 1994); Estate of Clack v. Comm'r, 106 T.C. 131 (1996), *acq.* 1996-29 I.R.B. 4.

[74] Reg. § 20.2056(b)-7(d)(3).

[75] IRC § 2056(b)(7)(B)(v).

executor has not been appointed, the trustee of an *inter vivos* trust (that is included in the decedent spouse's gross estate) can make the election.[76]

The election must be made on the last estate tax return that is filed on or before the due date of the return (including extensions).[77] If a timely return is not filed, the election may be made on the first estate tax return filed by the executor after the due date.[78] Once an election is made, it is irrevocable (except to the extent that there is time for another return to be filed within the time a return can be filed).[79]

[c] Modifying the QTIP Trust

The QTIP requirements set the floor for the minimum provisions that must be made for the surviving spouse in order to enable the executor to claim the marital deduction. Under these minimum requirements, the surviving spouse need not be given any access or control over the principal either during her life or at death. However, because these rules establish a floor, a surviving spouse can be given additional rights over principal and income without risk of loss of the marital deduction.

In providing these additional rights, it is important for the estate planner to keep in mind that an important aspect of the QTIP trust is its flexibility since it allows the decision of how much of a marital deduction to claim to be deferred until nine months after the decedent spouse's death. Therefore, in order to maintain this flexibility, it is important that the surviving spouse not be given too much control over trust principal. If the donor wants to provide the surviving spouse with access to principal, the donor can give the surviving spouse any or all of the following while still maintaining the ability to choose whether or not to claim the marital deduction:

- Right to invade principal of the QTIP trust for her health, education, maintenance, and support;
- Right to invade the greater of 5 percent of the trust principal or $5,000 from the QTIP trust each year; and/or
- Right to receive discretionary payments from the QTIP trust (assuming there is an independent trustee).

[5] Charitable Remainder Trusts

The charitable remainder trust provides another alternative for structuring a bequest to a surviving spouse. Under the charitable remainder trust, the surviving spouse is given an income interest (for life or for a term of years) and a charitable organization is given the remainder. The decedent spouse's estate is entitled to a

---

[76] Reg. § 20.2056(b)(7)(b).
[77] Reg. § 20.2056(b)-7(b)(4)(i).
[78] *Id.*
[79] Reg. § 20.2056(b)-7(b)(4)(ii).

marital deduction for the income interest and a charitable deduction for the remainder interest.[80]

In order to qualify for this exception, the surviving spouse must be the only noncharitable beneficiary,[81] and the trust must otherwise qualify as a charitable remainder trust. In practical terms this means that the interest given to the surviving spouse must be either a fixed amount or a fixed percentage of the trust for life or for a term of years.[82]

[G] Marital Deduction for the Non-U.S. Citizen Surviving Spouse

The marital deduction is not available for transfers to spouses who are not U.S. citizens, unless additional requirements are met. In particular, in order to qualify for the estate tax marital deduction, either (1) the surviving spouse must become a U.S. citizen before the day on which the decedent's estate tax return is due and must have been a U.S. resident during the time from the date of the decedent's death to the date the surviving spouse became a U.S. citizen; or (2) the property must be transferred to a *qualifying domestic trust* (sometimes called a QDOT).[83] A QDOT is a trust in which at least one trustee is a U.S. citizen or domestic corporation and that provides that no distributions (other than income) can be made to the surviving spouse unless the trustee has the right to withhold special estate taxes imposed under IRC Section 2056A.[84]

The reason for these rules is to ensure that property passing tax free to a surviving spouse under the marital deduction does not evade taxation in the United States if the surviving spouse returns to her country of citizenship.

The marital deduction is also not available for lifetime gifts to a spouse who is not a U.S. citizen at the time of transfer.[85] Unlike transfers at death, there is no exception for transfers made to qualifying domestic trusts. However, the harshness of this rule is alleviated by another provision that increases the annual exclusion for gifts to non-U.S. citizen spouses to $164,000 (for 2022).[86] Thus, an individual may transfer up to $164,000 (indexed for inflation) each year tax free to her non-U.S. citizen spouse. In addition to the above provisions, it should be noted that the surviving spouse can also be provided for in a tax-advantaged manner through the use of a *credit shelter trust* (also called a *bypass trust*).[87] The estate planner should be

---

[80] IRC § 2056(b)(8).

[81] However, in the situation where there is another noncharitable beneficiary (e.g., where the trust gives a life estate to the surviving spouse and a secondary life estate to another noncharitable beneficiary), followed by a remainder interest to a charity, the bequest to the spouse may qualify under the QTIP trust provisions. Reg. § 20.2056(b)-8(b).

[82] *See* IRC § 664 for the rules regarding charitable remainder trusts. *See* Chapter 10 for a detailed discussion of charitable remainder trusts.

[83] IRC § 2056(d).

[84] IRC § 2056A(a).

[85] IRC § 2523(i).

[86] IRC § 2523(i); Rev. Proc. 2020-45, 2020-46 I.R.B. 1016.

[87] *See* § 6.05 *infra.*

certain to ask whether both spouses are U.S. citizens, as many clients don't realize that this is important and won't mention it unless asked.

[H] Qualifying for the Marital Deduction for Gift Tax Purposes

An individual can also make unlimited tax-free gifts to his spouse during life. The marital deduction for gift tax purposes tracks the requirements of the estate tax marital deduction.[88] Thus, the deduction is not available for transfers to non-U.S. citizen spouses (although the annual exclusion for those transfers is increased to $164,000 for 2022),[89] and the deduction is not available for most terminable interests.[90] As previously discussed, a terminable interest is generally an interest that will fail or terminate due to the lapse of time or the occurrence or nonoccurrence of an event or contingency. Classic examples of terminable interests are life estates, terms of years, and interests subject to a condition (such as not divorcing the transferring spouse).[91]

EXAMPLE 6-26

H transfers $2,000,000 to a trust for the benefit of W. The trust provides that W's interest terminates in the event that she divorces H. The transfer by H of the $2,000,000 is subject to gift tax and is not eligible for the marital deduction because it is a nondeductible terminable interest.

The gift tax marital deduction provides similar exceptions to the terminable interest rule as are provided in the estate tax. Thus, the gift tax marital deduction is available for the following types of transfers:

1. Outright transfers of property;
2. Creation of joint tenancies;
3. Transfers of interests in which the recipient spouse is given a qualifying income interest for life and a general power of appointment over the property exercisable either during life or at death;
4. Transfers of property in which the recipient is given a qualifying income interest for life and the donor spouse files an election to treat the property as Qualified Terminable Interest Property (*QTIP*);[92] and
5. Transfers of property in which the surviving spouse is the only noncharitable beneficiary of a charitable remainder trust.[93]

---

[88] IRC § 2523.

[89] IRC § 2523(i); Rev. Proc. 2020-45, 2020-46 I.R.B. 1016. The annual exclusion is discussed in greater detail in Chapter 8.

[90] IRC § 2523(b).

[91] IRC § 2056(b)(1). Terminable interests are discussed in greater detail in § 6.03[G] *supra.*

[92] IRC § 2523(f).

[93] IRC § 2523(g). Charitable remainder trusts are discussed in greater detail in Chapter 10.

[I] Comparison of Outright Marital Gift Versus Transfer to Marital Trust

When providing the marital share, many estate planners have the tendency to automatically transfer the funds into some form of a trust that qualifies for the marital deduction. Although trusts can be very useful in some circumstances, the estate planner should not automatically reach for a trust, when an outright distribution would be more satisfying for the parties involved.[94] There are many advantages to providing a spouse with an outright bequest of the decedent-spouse's property:

- An outright bequest is simple to draft and easy to understand;

- An outright bequest avoids the expense and hassle of administering the trust; and

- An outright bequest may most closely replicate the surviving spouse's access to the money prior to the decedent spouse's death.

The use of a trust to hold the marital share may pose its own advantages over an outright transfer. The advantages of a trust over an outright bequest are as follows:

- The money in the trust will avoid probate in the surviving spouse's estate;

- The money in the trust can be protected from creditors of the surviving spouse;

- The trust assets can be professionally managed;

- The decedent spouse will be able to impose greater control by either naming a remainder beneficiary (in the case of a QTIP trust) or naming a taker in the event that the surviving spouse fails to exercise her power of appointment (in a power of appointment trust);

- Transfer to a QTIP trust will enable the decision as to how much tax to pay in the estate of the first to die to be delayed until nine months after that spouse's death (a time when better information may be available for estimating the spouse's tax liabilities);

- Transfer to a trust will enable a reverse QTIP election for generation-skipping transfer tax planning purposes;

- Transfer to a trust may enable special QTIP elections to be made for state estate tax purposes; and

- A trust is necessary in order to qualify for a deduction for transfers to a non-U.S. citizen spouse.

---

[94] Form 1 provides for two alternative plans for disposition of the marital share—an outright bequest and a transfer to a QTIP trust.

§6.04 ENSURING USE OF BOTH SPOUSES' UNIFIED CREDITS

[A] Overview

While the marital deduction provides a *deferral* of taxes until the death of the surviving spouse, the unified credit provides an *exclusion* from taxes for up to $10,000,000, adjusted for inflation until 2026. After December 31, 2025, the amount is scheduled to revert to $5,000,000, adjusted for inflation. In 2022, the exclusion amount is $12,060,000. If a couple's combined assets fall within a single exclusion amount, the estate planner need not be concerned with federal estate taxes. However, if the couple is likely to have combined assets greater than a single exclusion amount, an important task for the estate planner is to secure the use of both spouses' unified credit exclusion amounts.

This section addresses the issue of how to ensure the use of both spouses' unified credit, either by relying on portability, or by using traditional credit shelter techniques: the optimal marital deduction bequest (also known as the A-B trust plan), the disclaimer plan or the all QTIP plan.

[B] Relying on Portability

[1] Portability in General

Prior to 2011, the unified credit was personal to each taxpayer and was only available to the extent that it offset his or her tax liability. If a taxpayer failed to use all of his or her unified credit (either because the estate was smaller than the exclusion amount or because the property passed to the surviving spouse in some other way such that it was not subject to estate taxes), then the tax benefit of the unified credit for that taxpayer was lost. Married couples could easily lose some of the advantages of the unified credit by transferring all of their property to the surviving spouse.

EXAMPLE 6-27

H and W had simple wills that provided that upon death all property would go to the surviving spouse, if living, and, if not, the property would go to H and W's children. H and W each owned $3,500,000 in assets. H died in 2009, and W died later in the same year.

In 2009, the unified credit amount sheltered $3,500,000 in assets. Upon H's death all of the property went to W. Because of the marital deduction, there was no tax liability for H's estate and therefore none of H's unified credit was used. Upon W's death, she had $7,000,000 in her estate (her original $3,500,000 plus the $3,500,000 from her husband). The unified credit only sheltered the first $3,500,000 from tax, resulting in a tax liability in W's estate of $1,575,000. This tax liability could have been avoided if H's estate plan had used a credit shelter trust.

Beginning in 2011, the law included a provision that, for the first time, allowed a surviving spouse to use the unused portion of a decedent spouse's unified credit. This is referred to as "portability."[1] The purpose of the portability provision was to simplify estate planning for married couples by eliminating the need to plan to use each spouse's unified credit.[2]

EXAMPLE 6-28

H and W had simple wills that provided that upon death all property would go to the surviving spouse, if living, and, if not, the property would go to H and W's children. H and W each owned $5,000,000 in assets. H died in 2011 and W died later in the same year.

In 2011, the unified credit sheltered $5,000,000 in assets. Upon H's death all of the property went to W and, due to the marital deduction, none of H's unified credit was used. However, H's executor filed an estate tax return in which she made an election for H's unused unified credit amount to be available to W. Upon W's death, she had $10,000,000 in her estate (her original $5,000,000 plus the $5,000,000 from her husband). W's unified credit consisted of her unified credit amount of $5,000,000 plus H's unused unified credit exclusion amount of $5,000,000. As a result, this combined unified credit could shelter all $10,000,000 from tax and W's estate had zero tax liability.

The advantages of portability can best be understood by contrasting it to the requirements of traditional credit shelter planning.

Traditional credit shelter planning (discussed in greater detail below) requires that (1) the first spouse to die owns sufficient assets to use the exclusion; (2) that these assets not be owned in such a way that they pass automatically to the surviving spouse, such as in joint tenancy, or in a retirement account or life insurance policy that names the spouse as a beneficiary; and (3) that those assets be transferred into an appropriately drafted trust, rather than outright to the surviving spouse.

Relying on portability can allow for the use of the unified credit of the first spouse to die where any of these three conditions are not met. This is particularly likely to be the case where the couple prefers for all property to pass outright to the surviving spouse rather than in trust.

In addition, using portability provides an important income tax advantage over traditional credit shelter planning. To the extent that property is included in the surviving spouse's estate, as it is when using portability, the property's basis is

---

[1] § 6.04 IRC § 2010(c), as amended by Pub. L. No. 111-312, § § 301(a)(1) and 303(a).

[2] Portability is now available to all taxpayers. However, when originally enacted, the portability provision was of limited application. When originally enacted in 2010, the portability provision was only available if both spouses died between January 1, 2011 and December 31, 2012. The American Taxpayer Relief Act of 2012 extended the portability provision to include taxpayers who died after December 31, 2012. Portability provides certain advantages over traditional credit shelter planning.

stepped up to its fair market value as of the time of the surviving spouse's death. This is in contrast to using the first spouse's unified credit in a credit shelter trust, in which case property is only stepped up to its fair market value as of the time of the first spouse's death. The later step-up in basis provided under portability will often save income taxes for the ultimate heirs of the estate.

That being said, there remain a number of drawbacks to relying on portability as opposed to using traditional credit shelter planning. The following are five reasons why a traditional credit shelter plan may be preferable to relying on portability.

(1) Portability only preserves the unified credit exclusion amount of the first spouse to die. There is no post-death inflation adjustment and, unlike the result with credit shelter trusts, a portability election will not shelter appreciation in value and/or accumulated income;

(2) The portability election does not apply to the decedent's GST exemption; thus, to the extent the decedent does not use his GST exemption, it will be lost;

(3) Under current law, only two states with state estate taxes currently recognize portability for state estate tax purposes (Delaware and Hawaii); therefore, a decedent who is domiciled in a state with an estate tax (other than Delaware or Hawaii) will need a bypass or credit shelter trust in order to take advantage of the state estate tax exclusion amount;

(4) In order to make the election, the personal representative must file an estate tax return for the decedent, even if the decedent would not otherwise be required to file a return. The deceased spouse's unused exclusion amount can be lost if no timely estate tax return is filed; and

(5) The deceased spouse's unused exclusion amount will not be available to the surviving spouse if the surviving spouse remarries and then survives his or her new spouse without first using the unused exclusion amount of the first spouse to die.

[2] Technical Requirements for Portability

Portability allows a surviving spouse to use her decedent spouse's unused exclusion ("DSUE") amount. However, in order to do so, the executor of the decedent's estate must elect portability of the DSUE amount on a timely filed estate tax return (Form 706, "United States Estate (and Generation Skipping Transfer Tax) Tax Return").

Estate tax returns are generally due nine months after the decedent's death, or the last day of the extension period provided an extension has been granted.

A surviving spouse is limited to using the DSUE amount of the last deceased spouse. This means that if a surviving spouse remarries, she runs the risk of losing use of the first decedent spouse's DSUE amount. In order to ensure use of the first decedent spouse's DSUE amount, the surviving spouse should make a taxable gift of the DSUE amount prior to remarrying.[3]

[C] Traditional Credit Shelter Techniques–In General

While portability allows a surviving spouse to use her deceased spouse's unused exclusion amount, traditional credit shelter techniques are instead based on the idea of each spouse using his or her own exclusion amount.

In general, a person uses his or her own exclusion amount by (1) owning property equal to the unified credit exclusion amount in his own name; and (2) transferring the property in such a way that it is not subject to tax in the surviving spouse's estate. As discussed above, this type of planning has several advantages over relying on portability.[4]

[1] Owning Sufficient Property to Use the Unified Credit Exclusion Amount

A married couple may have combined estates in excess of two unified credits, but their property may be held disproportionately such that one spouse will not have sufficient assets to fully use his unified credit.[5] This is not a problem if the wealthier spouse predeceases the less wealthy spouse, since both spouses will, at the time of death, have sufficient assets to use his unified credit. However, if the less wealthy spouse dies first, the couple will not be able to take full advantage of the credit shelter trust (although portability will still be available). Since it is impossible to guarantee the order of deaths, the estate planner should consider recommending a reordering of the couple's assets so that (1) each spouse owns assets at least equal to the unified credit amount and (2) the property is titled in such a way that it does not automatically pass to the surviving spouse at death. Sometimes, this can be accomplished by severing joint tenancies and creating tenancies in common, or by changing designations on retirement benefits or life insurance policies from the spouse to a trust for the benefit of the spouse. This reallocation of assets can also be accomplished by the wealthier spouse making a gift to the less wealthy spouse. Gifts between spouses are tax free, provided the requirements of the marital deduction are met.[6] If the wealthy spouse is concerned about giving up control of the property given to the less wealthy spouse, the gift can be in the form of a QTIP trust. Under a QTIP trust, the recipient is only given an income interest in the property for life, after which the property passes as designated by the spouse making the gift.[7]

---

[3] The technical requirements for electing portability are discussed in greater detail in Chapter 14, *infra*.

[4] *See* § 6.04[B][1] *supra*.

[5] This is less likely to be the case in community property states where community property laws typically result in a more even distribution of ownership of a couple's assets.

[6] IRC § 2523.

[7] IRC § 2523(f). *See* § 6.03[D][4] *supra* for a discussion of QTIP trusts.

If the couple does not have combined assets in excess of two unified credit exclusion amounts (and is not expected to have it at the time of the first spouse's death), then this reordering of assets only need occur with respect to the amount of property that exceeds one unified credit exclusion amount. For example, if a couple is expected to have $15,000,000 at the death of the surviving spouse, then an estate planner may want to plan for each spouse to own at least $3,000,000 in his or her own name (assuming a unified credit amount of $12,060,000). If state taxes are an issue, then the amount to look for in each spouse's name is the amount of the state estate tax exclusion or exemption.

[2] Avoiding Taxation in the Surviving Spouse's Estate

The key to using the unified credit exclusion amount of the first spouse to die is to provide in the estate plan for the unified credit exclusion amount to pass in such a way that it is not subject to tax in the surviving spouse's estate.

One way to accomplish this is to provide in the estate plan that assets equal to the amount of the unused unified credit exclusion amount (for federal or state estate tax purposes) passes to someone other than the surviving spouse (e.g., the decedent spouse's children). However, unless the couple has substantial assets, it is unlikely that the surviving spouse would be comfortable giving up access to these funds. Therefore, a better way of addressing this problem is by providing that the amount equal to the unified credit exclusion amount (or the state exclusion amount) passes to a credit shelter trust (also called a bypass trust, a "B" trust or a family trust).[8] A credit shelter trust is a trust that is structured to use the unified credit of the decedent spouse's estate and avoid taxation in the surviving spouse's estate.

Credit shelter trusts can be structured in a variety of ways. However, since the primary goal of the credit shelter trust is that it not be subject to tax in the surviving spouse's estate, it is necessary that the surviving spouse's degree of control and/or withdrawal powers be somewhat limited. In general, the rules provide a trade-off between control and access to principal. That is, if the surviving spouse is the sole trustee of the trust, the trust property will be included in her estate unless her access to principal is somewhat limited. If, on the other hand, there is an independent trustee exercising discretion over distributions of principal, the surviving spouse can be given unlimited benefits from the trust property. Many trusts mix and match these provisions to include some provisions which grant the spouse control and other provisions which give the spouse access to principal through an independent trustee.

The two most common forms for the credit shelter trust are the maximum spousal control trust and the discretionary trust. The maximum spousal control trust provides maximum benefits to a spouse while allowing the spouse to serve as the sole trustee. The discretionary trust requires an independent trustee with respect to the discretionary payments, but allows the entire amount to be available for distribu-

---

[8] These are described in greater detail throughout this section.

tion to the beneficiary spouse. A single credit shelter trust can include both the maximum spousal control provisions and the discretionary provisions.[9]

In addition, due to its shape-shifting nature, a QTIP trust can also be structured to function as a credit shelter trust.[10]

[a] Maximum Spousal Control Trusts

Under a maximum spousal control trust, a surviving spouse can be given maximum control by being the sole trustee and can be given any or all of the following interests in the trust while still keeping the trust assets from being subject to tax in her estate.

[i] All Income from the Trust Property for Life. A surviving spouse can be given the right to all of the income from the property in the credit shelter trust for life and it will not be included in her estate at the time of her death. In addition, if the property is real property or tangible personal property, she can be given use of the property for her life.

[ii] Power to Invade Subject to an Ascertainable Standard. Perhaps the most valuable right that can be given to the surviving spouse is the right to invade principal subject to an ascertainable standard relating to her support, maintenance, health, or education (sometimes referred to as a HEMS power).[11] If the spouse is trustee, she can have power to distribute trust property to herself subject to this standard. In order to avoid taxation in the surviving spouse's estate, the estate planner should consider drafting the standard using language explicitly sanctioned in the statute and regulations.[12] Any of the following provisions would be satisfactory: for her "health, maintenance, education and support," "support in reasonable comfort," "maintenance in health and reasonable comfort," "support in his accustomed manner of living," "medical, dental, hospital, and nursing expenses and expenses of invalidism." Use of additional language can cause the provision to no longer qualify for the ascertainable standard exception. For example, if the trust enables the spouse to appoint property for her "health, education, support, and happiness," the entire value of the trust property will likely be included in the spouse's gross estate for estate tax purposes because "happiness" is not generally considered to be an ascertainable standard.

[iii] Limited Power of Appointment. A surviving spouse can also be given a power to appoint property to anyone other than herself, her estate, her creditors, or creditors of her estate, without having the property become subject to tax in her

---

[9] Form 1 contains examples of both of these types of credit shelter trusts.

[10] This is discussed in greater detail below in the discussion of the all QTIP trust.

[11] IRC § 2041(b)(1)(A).

[12] Reg. § 20.2041-1(c)(2).

estate.[13] This power can be exercisable either during life or at death or both. The power can be very broad (e.g., it could state that it is exercisable in favor of anyone other than the spouse, her estate, her creditors, or creditors of her estate). Or, if the decedent spouse wants to maintain some control over the property, he can limit the power of appointment to being exercisable over a specific group of people (e.g., their children). In drafting the credit shelter trust, it is important that the surviving spouse is not given any power of appointment over property that has been disclaimed by the surviving spouse. This limitation is necessary in order for the disclaimer to not be treated as a taxable gift by the surviving spouse.

[iv] Five and Five Powers. A surviving spouse can also be given the ability to invade up to the greater of $5,000 or 5 percent of the trust property each year for any purpose (without being limited to an ascertainable standard).[14] This power is sometimes referred to as a five and five power. A five and five power can build flexibility into a plan by providing the option for the surviving spouse to obtain additional assets from the credit shelter trust without being limited by the ascertainable standard. If the surviving spouse holds a five and five power, the trust property will not be subject to tax in her estate except to the extent of any unexercised power held at the time of her death. The estate tax exposure in this situation can be reduced by providing that the power can only be exercised during a limited period of time (e.g., the last week in the calendar year). In that way, none of the trust property will be included in the surviving spouse's estate for estate tax purposes unless she dies during the exercise period.

[b] Discretionary Trusts

The most flexible credit shelter trust is a discretionary trust giving the trustee complete discretion in making distributions. In order to prevent the trust from being included in her estate, the surviving spouse cannot be the sole trustee of this trust. However, one of her relatives or close friends can be the trustee and the surviving spouse can be the co-trustee for purposes of making investment decisions for the trust property. Under a discretionary trust, the independent trustee makes the decision as to how much, if any, should be distributed to the surviving spouse. Since the surviving spouse is not the trustee of the trust, none of the trust principal is taxed in the surviving spouse's estate except to the extent that it has been distributed to the surviving spouse. A discretionary trust can be established with a number of beneficiaries (discretionary trusts are commonly established for the benefit of the decedent's spouse and children) and can provide greater flexibility than the maximum benefit trust. For example, under a discretionary trust, the surviving spouse can be given distributions of principal that are not limited to the ascertainable standard or the five and five power. The trust can instruct the trustee to give preference to the

---

[13] IRC § 2041(b)(1).
[14] IRC § 2041(b)(2).

surviving spouse if that is the donor's wish. Alternatively, if the surviving spouse is financially secure, greater tax savings can be achieved by distributing trust assets to individuals other than the surviving spouse (thereby avoiding increasing the surviving spouse's taxable estate at the time of her death).

[D] Three Ways to Structure an Estate Plan to Use the Credit Shelter Trust

Once property has been allocated between the spouses in such a way as to allow maximum use of the unified credit of the first spouse to die, and once the estate planner has chosen the form of credit shelter trust, the estate plan must be structured in such a way that assets get transferred from the decedent's estate to the credit shelter trust. The three most common plans for accomplishing this are: (1) the optimal marital deduction bequest (also called the A-B trust plan); (2) the disclaimer plan; and (3) the all QTIP trust.

[1] The Optimal Marital Deduction Bequest (Also Known as the A-B Trust Plan)

[a] *In General*

An optimal marital deduction bequest plan involves dividing the estate of the first spouse to die into two shares. The first share (sometimes called the "A" portion or the "marital share") gives the surviving spouse only that portion of the decedent spouse's estate that exceeds the unified credit exclusion amount available to the decedent spouse.[15] The second share (sometimes called the "B" portion, the "credit shelter trust," the "by-pass trust" or the "family trust") distributes the decedent spouse's unified credit exclusion amount to a credit shelter trust. Assuming the couple's property is appropriately allocated, this plan ensures that without further actions by the surviving spouse or the executor of the decedent-spouse, both spouses' unified credits are used and that no taxes are paid until the death of the surviving spouse. The optimal marital deduction bequest can also be used by couples who are not subject to federal estate taxes in order to preserve any available exemptions or exclusions for state estate tax purposes.

EXAMPLE 6-29

H and W have combined assets of $20,000,000—$17,000,000 owned by H and $3,000,000 owned by W. H dies in 2022. Under the optimal marital deduction bequest, $12,060,000 (the amount of H's unused exclusion

---

[15] *See* Chapter 5 for a discussion of the unified credit.

amount in 2022) passes to a credit shelter trust, and the remaining $7,040,000 passes to W either outright or in a marital trust.

No estate tax will be due upon H's death because the transfer to the credit shelter trust will be covered by H's unified credit, and the transfer to W will be excluded under the marital deduction.

W dies later that same year. Her estate will be subject to tax on the $3,000,000 of assets titled in her own name and the $7,040,000 of assets which passed to her in the marital transfer. Assuming the combined assets are not valued at the time of W's death at more than $12,060,000, there will be no taxes due in W's estate.

[b] Drafting an Optimal Marital Deduction Bequest

The optimal marital deduction bequest must be drafted carefully in order to achieve the goals of (1) obtaining full use of the unified credit and (2) avoiding paying taxes upon the death of the first spouse. It is extremely unlikely that these goals can be achieved absent use of a formula.[16] The two most common formulas used for splitting property between the marital share and the credit are (1) a formula pecuniary bequest (for either the marital or nonmarital portion), and (2) a formula fractional share of the residue bequest. Each formula will avoid federal estate taxes at the first death and will use the first-to-die's federal unified credit to full effect, thereby minimizing estate taxes at the second death.

A formula pecuniary bequest can be drafted for either (1) the marital portion, or (2) the nonmarital (or credit shelter) portion of the bequest. If the formula pecuniary bequest is drafted for the marital portion, then it provides that the surviving spouse is given "the smallest amount required to avoid estate taxes in the decedent spouse's estate" and the remainder of the estate passes to the credit shelter trust (or in some other manner that does not qualify for the marital deduction and will not be subject to tax in the surviving spouse's estate). If the formula pecuniary bequest is drafted for the credit shelter (or nonmarital) portion, then it provides that the credit shelter trust is given "the largest amount that will not result in any federal estate tax being payable by the estate" and the remainder of the estate passes to the surviving spouse in a transfer that would qualify for the marital deduction.

Regardless of whether the formula pecuniary bequest is drafted for the marital or nonmarital share, it will result in full use of the unified credit and avoiding payment of taxes upon the death of the first spouse. However, the choice of formula can have a significant impact on the distribution of estate assets. The reason for this is that a pecuniary bequest does not reflect any changes in value after the valuation date (the valuation date is usually the date of the decedent's death, unless the executor elects to use the alternate valuation date of six months after the decedent's death). Thus, if a formula pecuniary bequest is drafted for the marital portion, then the marital bequest will be established as of the valuation date and the nonmarital

---

[16] *See* Form 1 for a sample pour-over trust with a marital and credit share split set by formula.

portion will enjoy any increase in value (or suffer any decrease in value) of estate assets between the valuation date and the distribution date. If a formula pecuniary bequest is drafted for the nonmarital portion, then the nonmarital portion will be set as of the valuation date and the marital portion will enjoy any increase in value (or suffer any decrease in value) of estate assets between the valuation date and the distribution date.

Many practitioners prefer to use the pecuniary marital formula because it freezes the value of the marital share as of the date of death or the alternate valuation date. If assets appreciate in value between the date of death and the date of funding, all appreciation is shifted to the credit share. By shifting appreciation to the credit share, the appreciation is not subject to estate tax at the surviving spouse's death, thereby minimizing the overall estate tax burden as property passes ultimately to the children. If property depreciates in value after death, the depreciation is allocated similarly to the credit share, thereby protecting the surviving spouse against a market downturn. Of course, in the latter situation the credit share may be substantially underfunded as a result.

A formula fractional share of the residue bequest is a formula bequest under which both the marital and nonmarital share participate in any increase in value or suffer any decrease in value between the valuation date and the distribution date.[17] Neither share is fixed until actual funding. A fractional share of the residue bequest provides that the spouse is given "a fraction of the residuary estate that has a numerator equal to the smallest amount that, if allowed as a deduction, would result in the least possible federal estate tax, and that has a denominator equal to the value of the residuary estate."

EXAMPLE 6-30

H's estate is valued at $20,000,000 on the date of H's death and $24,000,000 at the time that the estate is distributed. At the time of H's death, the unified credit exclusion amount is $12,000,000.

If the will provides for a formula pecuniary bequest for the marital portion, then $8,000,000 will be distributed to H's spouse and $16,000,000 will be distributed to the nonmarital portion (all $4,000,000 appreciation will go to the nonmarital portion because that is the residuary taker under the will). If the will provides for a formula pecuniary bequest for the nonmarital portion, then $12,000,000 will be distributed to the nonmarital portion and $12,000,000 will be distributed to H's spouse (all $4,000,000 appreciation will go to the marital portion because that is the residuary taker under the will).

If the will provides for a fractional share of the residue bequest then H's spouse will be entitled to $8,000,000/$20,000,000 (or 40 percent) of

---

[17] Form 1 contains a formula fractional share of the residue bequest.

whatever is eventually distributed and the nonmarital portion will be entitled to \$12,000,000/\$20,000,000 (or 60 percent) of whatever is distributed.

In addition to selecting a formula for division of the trust property into a marital share and a credit share, the estate planner must also choose a method for funding those shares. This method must address the timing of valuation of the trust property (i.e., either valuing as of the date of distribution or using the federal estate tax value) and the manner in which assets are chosen to be allocated to the respective shares. If a pecuniary formula is used, the funding method merits careful consideration since some funding methods may result in the realization of capital gain.

[2] Planning for Disclaimer

[a] In General

As an alternative to providing a strict funding formula, disclaimer planning instead relies on a surviving spouse to determine the amount of property that will pass to the credit shelter trust.

A disclaimer is a refusal to accept property. If a named beneficiary disclaims an interest within nine months after the decedent's death, the disclaimed property passes as if the beneficiary had predeceased the decedent.[18] In the marital context, a disclaimer can be used to shift property that would otherwise go to the spouse (either outright or in trust) to a credit shelter trust. Under this plan, the surviving spouse would be advised to disclaim up to the amount of the federal or state exclusion amount.

EXAMPLE 6-31

H and W have wills that provide that, upon death, everything is to pass to the surviving spouse, unless the surviving spouse is not living or disclaims her interest, in which event the property is to be distributed to a credit shelter trust (specifically drafted to receive disclaimed property). The terms of the credit shelter trust are such that they allow the surviving spouse to benefit from the property in the trust, but the trust assets are not included in the surviving spouse's estate for estate tax purposes.

H dies in 2022 with a gross estate of \$20,000,000 and under H's will, all \$20,000,000 is to pass to W. If W disclaims \$12,060,000 (the amount covered by the unified credit in 2022), then she will ensure the use of H's unified credit. When W dies, her estate will not be taxed on the disclaimed property, regardless of its value at the date of W's death.

---

[18] IRC § 2518. Disclaimers are discussed in greater detail in Chapter 14.

A disclaimer trust can be used to preserve exclusion amounts for federal and/or state estate tax purposes. To achieve maximum benefit for federal tax purposes, the surviving spouse can disclaim an amount equal to the unused federal estate tax exclusion amount of the decedent spouse. If the couple is unlikely to be subject to federal estate taxes, then the disclaimer trust can be used to shelter property from state estate taxes. In that case, the surviving spouse would disclaim the amount allowed as an exclusion for state estate tax purposes.

EXAMPLE 6-32

H and W have wills that provide that, upon death, everything is to pass to the surviving spouse, unless the surviving spouse is not living or disclaims her interest, in which event the property is to be distributed to a credit shelter trust (specifically drafted to receive disclaimed property). The terms of the credit shelter trust are such that they allow the surviving spouse to benefit from the property in the trust, but the trust assets are not included in the surviving spouse's estate for estate tax purposes.

H dies in 2022 with a gross estate of $8,000,000 and under H's will, all $8,000,000 is to pass to W. H and W's combined estates are not likely to exceed $12,060,000. However, H and W reside in a state with a state estate tax that is imposed on estates that exceed $1,000,000. If W disclaims $1,000,000, then she will ensure the use of H's state estate tax exemption. When W dies, her estate will not be taxed on the disclaimed property, regardless of its value at the date of W's death.

Use of the disclaimer trust—like relying on portability—is likely to be particularly attractive for couples who ideally want to provide outright transfers of their property to the surviving spouse. The basic plan of disposition can be "all to spouse outright" and the spouse can then disclaim to the trust only to the extent necessary to preserve use of the state or federal exclusion amount. However, despite this apparent simplicity, the disclaimer plan will only work to save taxes if the surviving spouse actually files a qualifying disclaimer within nine months of the decedent spouse's death. This will likely require careful counseling by the advisors settling the first spouse's estate.

[b] *Drafting the Credit Shelter Trust for Disclaimer Purposes*

Generally speaking, any credit shelter trust that ensures that property is not subject to tax in the surviving spouse's estate will work for disclaimer purposes.[19] This is subject to one important limitation–in drafting a credit shelter trust for purposes of disclaimer the estate planner must be mindful of not giving the surviving

---

[19] Credit shelter trusts are discussed in § 6.04[C] and [D].

spouse a power of appointment over the disclaimed property as that could result in the disclaimer being treated as a taxable gift.[20]

[3] The All QTIP Trust

[a] *In General*

Another way of providing for the use of both spouses' unified credit is by using an all QTIP trust. The QTIP trust provides a great deal of flexibility in tax planning because it allows the decision of how much marital deduction is going to be claimed to be deferred until the time that the estate tax return is due (usually nine months after the decedent spouse's death).

EXAMPLE 6-33

H's will provides for all of his property to be transferred to a trust in which W is given an income interest for life and, upon W's death, the remainder passes to H's children. If H's executor makes the election to treat the property as QTIP property it will be eligible for the marital deduction in H's estate and subject to tax in W's estate. If H's executor does not make the QTIP election, the property will not be eligible for the marital deduction in H's estate (because it is a terminable interest) and it will not be subject to tax in W's estate (because the gross estate does not generally include interests in which the decedent only had a life estate). The QTIP election can be made with respect to part or all of the trust. The decision of whether and how much marital deduction to claim can be deferred until nine months after H's death, when the estate tax return for H's estate is due.

The all QTIP Trust has the advantage of providing flexibility with respect to the timing and use of the estate tax exemption of the first to die. This can allow for additional estate planning after the death of the first spouse to die, when presumably the estate planner will be able to make a better assessment of the likely size of the couple's estate at the death of the surviving spouse. This can result in greater overall tax savings. In particular, the QTIP election can be used to reduce estate taxes of the couple or to reduce income taxes of the heirs.

To reduce the estate tax liability of the couple, the election would be made in such a way as to make full use of the unified credit exclusion amount at the first death. A QTIP election would then only be made for federal estate tax purposes with respect to the QTIP trust to the extent that the first to die's assets exceeded the estate tax exemption ($12,060,000 in 2022). This would essentially have the effect of dividing

---

[20] Article THIRD (a) of Form 1 has an example of how to properly draft a trust to receive disclaimed property.

the estate into two trusts: one elected for the marital deduction and includable in the estate of the surviving spouse and the other not elected for marital deduction purposes and therefore not includable in the estate of the surviving spouse.

This approach also has the advantage in some states of allowing effective state death tax planning. Many states that still have their own estate tax systems permit a state-only QTIP election—that is, a QTIP election that is not identical to the election made for federal purposes and allow the decedent's estate to claim the benefit of the state estate tax marital deduction only. Such a provision may allow a personal representative to take advantage of the state estate tax exemption and then elect to qualify the balance of the trust property for the applicable state estate tax marital deduction.

To reduce the income tax liability of the heirs upon disposition of the property in the QTIP trust, the QTIP election could be made with respect to all of the property in the QTIP trust. Under this plan, none of the unified credit exclusion amount of the first spouse to die would be used at the first spouse's death. Instead, the estate tax exemption could then be ported to the surviving spouse. Making such a QTIP election to permit portability appears to be permitted under the marital deduction regulations and supported by Revenue Procedure 2001-38.[21] This alternative has the advantage of maintaining a trust structure (with creditor protection for the trust principal and control over the eventual disposition of the trust assets) while allowing for the property in the trust to receive a new stepped-up basis in the trust assets measured as of the property's fair market value at the death of the surviving spouse. This can save income taxes for the ultimate heirs of the trust. The potential downside is that all post-first-death appreciation in the trust assets will be includable in the estate of the surviving spouse for federal estate tax purposes.

[b] Drafting the QTIP Trust

In drafting a QTIP trust, a surviving spouse must be given all income from the trust payable at least annually and no one (including the surviving spouse) can have a power to appoint the property to anyone other than the surviving spouse. However, while these provisions set a minimum standard, the surviving spouse can be given other rights over the trust property as well while still preserving the flexibility of the QTIP structure.

In particular, the surviving spouse can also be given the:

- Right to invade principal of the QTIP trust for her health, education, maintenance, and support;

- Right to invade the greater of 5 percent of the trust principal or $5,000 from the QTIP trust each year (*Crummey* power); and/or

- Right to receive discretionary payments from the QTIP trust (assuming there is an independent trustee).

---

[21] Rev. Proc. 2001-38, 2001-1 C.B. 1335.

Sometimes, it is desirable to be able to give the surviving spouse a power of appointment over the trust assets so that she can control the ultimate disposition of the estate. This is generally not allowed under a QTIP trust since one of the requirements of the QTIP is that no one (including the surviving spouse) can have a power to appoint the QTIP property to anyone other than the surviving spouse. Moreover, it is also not allowed under the disclaimer plan since in order to have a qualified disclaimer the disclaimant must not have continued control over the property. The all QTIP trust can provide an answer to this problem as well. To address this problem, an alternative way of structuring the trust is to provide that a QTIP trust will be funded only to the extent that a QTIP election is actually made for estate tax purposes. Assets that are not covered by the QTIP trust would instead pass to the credit shelter trust. This is called a "Clayton" QTIP provision.

§6.05 PROVIDING FOR NONMARRIED PARTNERS

[A] Overview

A significant portion of our society consists of nonmarital partners—both same-sex and opposite sex—living together in committed relationships. However, the American probate and tax systems generally treat unmarried couples as unrelated individuals, which can create pitfalls if one partner wishes to leave substantial assets to the other. Without the legal association of marriage, many unmarried partners are left unprotected under intestacy systems and disadvantaged in terms of tax planning devices. In addition, end-of-life issues are also more complicated for unmarried couples since nonmarital partners are generally not afforded the same recognition as family members in health care decision making. Careful estate planning, however, can avoid some of these problems.

Beginning in 1999, a number of states began adopting statutory provisions that allowed two people to register their relationship with the state. These provisions were adopted as a way to allow same sex couples, who had not been allowed to marry, to achieve some of the benefits of marriage. However, in many states these statutory provisions were also available to opposite sex couples. Each of these statutory systems differ in their details, but where these statutes exist, registered couples are generally treated like married couples for state (but not federal) law purposes. Now that all states are required to allow and recognize same-sex marriages, the status of these types of non-marital partnerships are in flux. Some states have converted these statuses to marriage (by operation of law or by action of the couple), sometimes retroactively to the date of the civil union. Some states continue to make both statuses (civil marriage and spousal equivalent) available to couples, but the law is highly state-specific and subject to change. For federal law purpose, the law is also varied. The IRS and Department of Labor issued guidance after *Windsor* stating that for federal purposes, the various marriage equivalent statuses are not equivalent to marriage.[1] However, Social Security rules generally provide that legal relationships granting inheritance rights are treated as marriages. This will allow many couples in spousal equivalent relationships to be treated as married for purposes of Social Security.

Federal tax law lacks any special provisions favoring transfers to nonmarital partners, even where the couple has registered their relationship with the state. Where the federal tax law provides for a marital deduction for transfers to a spouse, there is no comparable deduction for transfers to a nonmarital partner. Therefore, if an unmarried individual wants to leave substantial assets to a nonmarital partner, the estate planner needs to consider a different array of issues, including (1) reducing the likelihood of a will dispute, and (2) working creatively with tax provisions in order to minimize tax costs.

[B] Planning for the Disposition of Property

In planning for a person in any committed relationship, regardless of whether it is marital or nonmarital, the estate planner must take into account the amount of financial sharing or separateness that exists in the relationship. For example, a couple could treat all of their assets as joint assets, all of their assets as separate assets, or some assets as joint and some as separate. However, whereas the law imposes certain minimum expectations of sharing for married couples (as evidenced by intestacy statutes, community property rules, and elective share rules), there are no such presumptions for nonmarried couples. Indeed, under the law, non-married couples are generally treated as strangers, regardless of their level of commitment to each other. This means that if the couple has a sharing relationship in which they treat some, most, or all of their assets as joint assets, and they wish the surviving partner to have access to all of those assets, then affirmative steps must be taken to assure that these wishes continue to be effected after one of the partners dies.

[1] Avoiding Will Disputes

A will is the essential document in any estate plan, regardless of the marital status of the client. However, when preparing a will that substantially benefits a person who is not legally recognized as a family member, such as a nonmarital partner, additional steps should be taken to avoid a will dispute. The reason for this is that when a will is probated, anyone who would be entitled to take under intestacy (the decedent's blood relatives) is notified of the probate proceeding and given an opportunity to object to the will. Since the people who are given an opportunity to object would also benefit financially in the event that the will were not given effect, the risk of a will dispute can be significant.

---

[1] §6.05 Definition of Terms Relating to Marital Status, 81 Fed. Reg. 60,609 (Sept. 2, 2016) (*codified at* 26 C.F.R. §301.7701-18). *See also* United States v. Windsor, 570 U.S. 744, 133 S. Ct. 2675 (2013); Obergefell v. Hodges, 576 U.S. 644, 135 S. Ct. 2584 (2015); DOL Tech. Release No. 2013-04; Rev. Rul. 2013-17, 2013-2 C.B. 201; Notice 2014-19, 2014-1 C.B. 979.

When gathering information from a client, the estate planner should ascertain the likelihood of a will dispute. One fact that will be central to this determination is the client's relationship with his biological family. If the family is close and knows of the client's nonmarital partner, then the risks of a will dispute are significantly less than in the situation where the client is estranged from his family. Indeed, the best prophylactic for a will challenge may be honest discussion between the client and his family regarding his estate plan.

The first step in avoiding a will challenge is in assuring that all of the requirements for a valid will have been met. In order to have a valid will, the testator must be of sound mind and free of fraud, duress, and undue influence, and the will must be executed with the requisite formalities. In most states, the formal requirements for a will are that the will be in writing and signed by the testator in the presence of two disinterested witnesses who also sign the will.[2] Although witnesses are commonly strangers to the decedent, if a will challenge is expected it may be advisable to use witnesses who could provide strong personal testimony that the decedent had testamentary capacity at the time the will was executed. However, in choosing witnesses, it is important to remember that the witnesses should not be beneficiaries under the will.

Finally, the estate planner may want to consider use of a *no-contest clause* in the will. A no-contest clause (also called an *in terrorem clause*) is a provision in a will that provides, in the event that a beneficiary in the will contests the validity of the will, that person will receive nothing. The goal of the no-contest clause is to serve as a deterrent to a will contest. However, in order for it to be effective, the beneficiary must be provided with a sufficiently large bequest such that risk of its loss will discourage a will challenge. This may make the no-contest clause unappealing to someone who wants to completely disinherit his family.

In a limited number of jurisdictions, a testator can assure the validity of a will through *ante mortem probate*. *Ante mortem* probate is a court proceeding available in Arkansas, North Dakota, and Ohio that effectively determines the validity of the testator's will while the testator is still living.[3] In order to be effective, the testator's family, as well as those who would take under the will, must be notified of the proceeding. Therefore, this proceeding may be of limited utility if the testator does not want to tell his family of his proposed will. On the other hand, if the testator goes forward with the proceeding, the testator's family may be less likely to object to a will in the presence of the testator than they would have after his death.

Adult adoption, in limited situations, may be an effective means of avoiding a will challenge. Most jurisdictions do not draw a distinction between adoption of a minor and adoption of an adult. If the testator is not otherwise survived by a spouse or issue, a will challenge can be avoided by adopting the primary beneficiary under the will. The reason for this is that the only people who can challenge a will are those

---

[2] The requirements for a valid will are discussed in greater detail in Chapter 3. In some states an interested (i.e., one who is named in the will) witness is purged of his bequest.

[3] Ark. Code Ann. § 28-40-202 (1997); N.D. Cent. Code § 30.1-08.1-01 (1997); Ohio Rev. Code Ann. § 2107.081 (1998).

who would take in the event of intestacy. By adopting the primary beneficiary, that person also becomes the only person who would take in the event of intestacy (since collateral relatives generally do not take if there are issue), and thus the only person who could challenge the will. Adult adoptions are extremely risky and should only be undertaken in rare circumstances. Once a person has been adopted, she may be much more difficult to extricate from in the event that the relationship turns sour. In addition, some states have disallowed these adoptions as against public policy.

[2] Use of Nonprobate Property

Sometimes, the best way of avoiding will disputes is by avoiding having property pass by will. This can be done by shifting assets into nonprobate property.

Nonprobate property is a single term used to describe the variety of property interests in which the law recognizes and gives effect to death beneficiary designations. This property bypasses the probate process and is distributed directly to the named beneficiary.[4] Nonprobate transfers are common devices for passing property at death. Indeed, although clients may not be aware of it, for most Americans, the majority of their property will pass outside the terms of their will and instead will pass to the designated beneficiary under a nonprobate transfer. Common examples of nonprobate transfers are:

- Joint tenancies;

- Life insurance;

- Accounts with payable-on-death designations (including retirement accounts); and

- Revocable *inter vivos* trusts.

Nonprobate transfers are very useful when transferring assets to a nonmarital partner. Since nonprobate transfers pass outside of the probate process, they are less susceptible to challenge. Moreover, many nonprobate transfers are revocable until death, making them functionally equivalent to passing property by will. However, an estate planner must pay careful attention when recommending nonprobate transfers since some confer a lifetime benefit on the designated beneficiary. Joint tenancies, life insurance, and revocable *inter vivos* trusts are the most common nonprobate methods for providing for a nonmarital partner.

The discussion in this section focuses on the use of nonprobate transfers in transferring assets to nonmarital partners. Nonprobate transfers are discussed generally in Chapter 2.

---

[4] The one instance in which nonprobate property passes through the probate process is when the designated beneficiary is the decedent's estate or executor of the decedent's will. Nonprobate property is discussed in greater detail in Chapter 2.

[a] Joint Tenancies

A *joint tenancy* is a form of property ownership in which two or more people share undivided ownership of property during their lives, and, upon death, the ownership interest of the one who dies is extinguished, leaving outright ownership in the survivor. A variety of interests can be held in joint tenancy, but the two most common types of interests held in joint tenancy are real estate and bank accounts.

Joint tenancies are a popular way for nonmarital partners to provide for the transfer of property. If the nonmarital couple owns a home, then it may be held in joint tenancy. If the couple shares finances, they may have joint checking, savings, or investment accounts. The advantage of joint tenancies are that they are relatively easy to create since they are created by merely taking title as joint tenants instead of individually, and they effectively transfer the property to the surviving partner upon death. However, there are certain disadvantages of joint tenancies that should not be underestimated. Joint tenancies create lifetime interests in property for both joint tenants. Thus, if one person transfers his real property from individual ownership to joint tenancy, then he is making a lifetime gift that may be difficult to revoke. If a bank account is held in joint tenancy, then either joint tenant has full access to all of the money in the account. This means that, regardless of the relative contributions, either joint tenant can withdraw all of the funds.

The creation of a joint tenancy in interests other than bank accounts may result in a taxable gift if the parties do not contribute equally to the purchase of the interest.[5]

EXAMPLE 6-34

A and B purchase a home. A contributes $200,000 to the purchase price and B contributes $100,000 to the purchase price. A and B take title to the property as joint tenants. A has made a taxable gift to B of $50,000.

This rule does not apply to joint tenancy bank accounts or other financial instruments unless and until one of the joint tenants withdraws more than her share of the contribution.[6]

EXAMPLE 6-35

A and B open a joint bank account. A deposits $200,000 and B deposits $100,000. B withdraws $200,000 from the account. At the time of withdrawal, A has made a taxable gift to B of $100,000 (the excess of the withdrawal over B's contribution).

---

[5] Reg. § 25.2511-1(h)(5).
[6] Reg. § 25.2511-1(h)(4).

[b] *Life Insurance*

Life insurance is an important component of many people's estate plans.[7] Life insurance is a contract whereby the insurer agrees to pay a third party (called a *beneficiary*) a certain amount (called the *face amount* of the policy) in the event of the insured person's death. Life insurance is very valuable when one partner is financially dependent on another, as it provides an additional source of funds for the support of the beneficiary partner. For nonmarital partners, like their married counterparts, life insurance is most critical when (1) the couple has minor children that will need money for their support, or (2) the nonmarital partners are financially dependent on each other for such things as making mortgage payments.

There are a variety of ways in which life insurance can be used to provide for a nonmarital partner. Most simply, an individual can purchase a policy on her life and name her nonmarital partner as a beneficiary under the policy. The insured retains control over the policy since she can always change the beneficiary designation. Since the insured retains control over the beneficiary designation, there are no gift tax consequences of naming a beneficiary.[8] Instead, the value of the policy will be included in the insured's estate at the time of her death.[9]

The proceeds of insurance policies originally acquired by a person other than the insured or transferred by the insured more than three years before the insured's death are generally not subject to tax in the insured's estate. Therefore, if the insured is prepared to relinquish control over the policy, additional tax savings can be achieved by having the policy owned by the nonmarital partner directly or by a life insurance trust held for the benefit of the nonmarital partner. If the insured has no incidents of ownership in the policy at the time of her death, none of the policy proceeds will be subject to estate tax in her estate.[10]

[c] *Revocable* Inter Vivos *Trusts*

A *revocable inter vivos trust* (also called a *living trust*) is the most flexible method for providing for a nonmarital partner through nonprobate transfers.

A revocable *inter vivos* trust is a trust created by transferring property to a trust during a person's life. The settlor retains access and control during her life and, upon the settlor's death, the property passes to the named beneficiary.

A revocable *inter vivos* trust provides all of the benefits of a will since

1. The settlor retains full lifetime use of the property;
2. The beneficiary designation is entirely revocable until the settlor's death;
3. The revocable *inter vivos* trust can be used for almost any type of property interest—ranging from real estate to securities to tangible personal property; and
4. There are no gift or estate tax liabilities until the time of the settlor's death.

---

[7] Life insurance is discussed in greater detail in Chapter 12.

[8] Reg. § 25.2511-2(c).

[9] IRC § 2042.

[10] Life insurance trusts are discussed in greater detail in Chapter 12.

In addition, a revocable *inter vivos* trust provides infinite flexibility for the disposition of the property. For example, the trust could be established for more than one beneficiary. This is particularly important if the settlor has children in addition to a nonmarital partner. Finally, revocable *inter vivos* trusts can be more advantageous than wills since (1) they can provide for lifetime management of the trust property in the event of the settlor's incapacity, and (2) they are less susceptible to challenge than wills since they are not subject to probate.[11]

[C] Providing for a Nonmarried Partner in a Tax Advantaged Manner

Transfers between spouses either during life or at death are free of tax under the unlimited marital deduction. This means that the surviving spouse can succeed to all of the couple's combined assets and those assets can be preserved until the death of the surviving spouse. The marital deduction does not apply to transfers to a nonmarital partner. There are, however, a variety of tax planning opportunities that should be considered when providing for a nonmarital partner.

[1] No Taxes Imposed on Many Estates

Due to the unified credit, each person can transfer a significant amount of money free of tax either during life or at death. In 2022, the unified credit enables an individual to transfer $12,060,000 free of tax either during life or at death.[12] Thus, if the nonmarital couple has combined assets of less than the unified credit amount and lives in a jurisdiction that does not have a state estate tax, then they may not need to worry about tax planning. In making this determination, keep in mind that fortunes change and that a couple with a smaller estate in one year could develop a significantly larger estate at a later time.

[2] Bypassing the Estate of the Surviving Partner

If a nonmarried couple has combined assets in excess of the unified credit amount, a *bypass* or *credit shelter trust* can be useful in minimizing the tax cost of passing on the combined assets at the death of the second to die. As previously discussed, a bypass trust is a trust that is structured in such a way that it is not subject to tax in the recipient's estate. These are the same types of trusts that are used in the marital context (although in that context they are more commonly referred to as *credit shelter trusts* because they must be structured in such a way that they do not qualify for the marital deduction).[13] The purpose of the bypass trust is to provide for the

---

[11] Revocable *inter vivos* trusts are discussed in greater detail in Chapter 4.

[12] *See* Table 5-1 for the scheduled increases for the unified credit.

[13] *See* § 6.05 *supra.*

nonmarital partner in such a way that the partner can benefit from the trust but the undistributed trust assets will not be included in the surviving partner's estate.

A nonmarital partner can be provided a range of access in a trust without subjecting the trust assets to taxes in the surviving partner's estate. In particular, a surviving partner can be given any or all of the following interests without having to worry about substantially increased estate tax liability: a right to income, a right to invade principal limited by an ascertainable standard, and a limited power of appointment. If the surviving partner's interest is limited to those listed above, then the surviving partner can be made the sole trustee of the trust. In addition, so long as the surviving partner is not the trustee of the trust, she can also be given payments out of a trust at the trustee's discretion. In all of these situations, the surviving partner will only be subject to estate tax on any interest actually distributed to her, and only to the extent that she holds it at the time of death.

If the surviving partner is more than $37^1/2$ years younger than the decedent partner, the planner must be mindful of the generation-skipping transfer tax, which can significantly erode the benefits of bypassing the partner's estate.[14]

[3] Annual Exclusion Gifts

The annual exclusion enables each taxpayer to make tax-free gifts of up to $16,000 (in 2022) to an unlimited number of donees. This amount is scheduled to increase for inflation in $1,000 increments.[15] The purpose of the annual exclusion is to permit taxpayers to make small gifts without the necessity of filing gift tax returns. However, the size of the exclusion, combined with the fact that it is available annually for an unlimited number of donees, makes it a very valuable estate planning tool. A significant amount of assets can be transferred to a nonmarried partner through yearly use of the annual exclusion.

[D] Planning for Incapacity and End-of-Life Issues

Planning for incapacity and end-of-life issues is an increasingly important aspect of estate planning, regardless of the marital status of the client. However, when the client has a nonmarital partner, particular care must be taken to address the problem of handling the financial and medical needs of an individual who no longer has the capacity to handle them herself if she wishes her partner to take care of her. The reason it is particularly important for nonmarital partners is that the apparent authority granted spouses is often not available to nonmarital partners. For example, the spouse of an incapacitated person is almost always consulted when medical decisions are being made. However, absent advanced planning, nonmarital partners are generally not afforded the same recognition as family members in health care decision making.

---

[14] The generation-skipping transfer tax is discussed in greater detail in Chapter 9.
[15] IRC § 2503(b). The annual exclusion is discussed in greater detail in Chapter 8.

The two most important documents for conferring authority over personal and financial decisions on a nonmarital partner in the event of incapacity are (1) the durable power of attorney and (2) the health care proxy.[16]

[1] Durable Power of Attorney

A durable power of attorney permits someone to handle an individual's financial affairs when the individual becomes incapacitated. A durable power of attorney is an essential part of a complete estate plan because it permits someone to handle an individual's financial affairs when the individual becomes incapacitated. A durable power of attorney appoints a person as an agent for the person signing the power (the *principal*) and authorizes the agent (often called an *attorney-in-fact*) to step into the shoes of the principal in handling financial affairs. Unlike the trustee of a trust, an attorney-in-fact does not take title to the principal's property. The power of attorney simply authorizes the agent to act in place of the principal. A durable power of attorney can be used to handle the affairs of an incompetent person without the necessity of a court appointed guardian of the person's property.

In some states, the statute governing durable powers of attorney permits the principal to nominate a conservator or guardian for his property or person if a court finds it necessary to appoint one in the future. The court is not bound by the choice of the principal, but will respect it unless there is good cause to do otherwise. Using a durable power of attorney to nominate a guardian permits an individual to exercise maximum control over both his person and his financial affairs in the event of future incapacity.[17]

[2] Health Care Proxy

The best way of providing a nonmarital partner with a voice in the medical decision-making process is to create a health care proxy. A health care proxy appoints another individual as an agent to make decisions regarding health care if the principal is unable to make such decisions or unable to communicate decisions to health care providers. Not all states recognize health care proxies and, where they do, states have different requirements. Therefore, it is important to check applicable state law.[18]

---

[16] The durable power of attorney and health care proxy are discussed in greater detail in Chapter 3. Form 10 is a sample durable power of attorney and Form 11 is a sample health care proxy.

[17] Durable powers of attorney are discussed in greater detail in Chapter 3. Form 10 is a sample durable power of attorney.

[18] Health care proxies are discussed in greater detail in Chapter 3. Form 11 is a sample health care proxy.

7

Issues in Planning for Children

§7.01 INTRODUCTION

The desire to provide for the care of minor children is often the primary factor motivating parents to seek out an estate planner. For most parents, planning for minor children is the most important aspect of estate planning because the plan will affect not only the disposition of property, but also the personal care of their children until they reach the age of majority. All parents, regardless of the size of their estates, need to set in place a plan that provides for the best possible home for their minor children in the event of the parents' premature death. In addition, parents need to take their children's minority into account in planning for the disposition of their property both during life and at death.

Three separate, though interrelated, issues arise in planning for minor children. First and foremost is the issue of providing for the personal care of the child in the event of the death of the parent. A parent wants to ensure that her child will have a safe, loving, and appropriate home if the parent should die during the child's minority. A parent can provide for the personal care of her child by appointing a guardian in her will. The second issue is the custody and management of the child's assets in the event of the parent's death. While planning for the child's property should be integrated with choosing a personal guardian for the person of the child, the two issues raise different concerns and it is useful to consider them separately. This section discusses problems raised by a minor's direct ownership of property and the preferred method of using trusts to hold property for the benefit of minor children.

In addition, parents and grandparents often wish to make *inter vivos* gifts to minor children for estate planning purposes and seek advice as to the best vehicle to hold such gifts. This chapter also discusses four of the vehicles most commonly used for estate planning gifts to minors: (1) custodianships; (2) Section 2503(c) minor's trusts; (3) Crummey trusts; and (4) Section 529 tuition plans.

§7.02 PLANNING FOR THE PERSON

[A] Duties of a Guardian

All minor children must have a *guardian* as the person responsible for their personal care. This is either a natural guardian (i.e., a custodial parent) or a court-appointed guardian. If a minor child is left without a custodial parent, a court will appoint a guardian to be responsible for the personal care and custody of the child. The guardian will have the responsibility for the daily care of the child, and will have the duty to make all decisions involving the child's residence, education, religious affiliation, and medical care, acting in this respect as a substitute parent. The guardian is not obligated to provide the financial support for the child, and is entitled to be reimbursed for the costs of support from any assets held for the benefit of the child.

[B] Appointment of a Guardian

Guardians derive their authority from the court. They must be court appointed, and remain under the supervision of the court until the child reaches the age of majority. If a deceased parent's will does not nominate an individual to be a guardian for his minor child, the judge will use her discretion in selecting a guardian. Some state statutes provide an order of preference, generally favoring close relatives.

A parent can nominate a guardian in his will, and should always take the opportunity to do so.[1] It is not advisable to leave the choice of a guardian to a judge who does not know the children or the families involved, and will have little basis for her decision. Furthermore, failure to name a guardian can provoke major family disruption, especially if relatives of both parents compete for custody of the child. A family dispute over custody could create a permanent rift in the extended family as well as delay the settlement of the child in a new home. The nomination of a guardian by will is the best way to minimize the risk of such disruptions. Although in most states the nomination is treated as an expression of the parent's wishes and is not binding on the judge who will make a final determination and appoint the guardian, a judge will generally appoint the guardian nominated by the deceased parent unless there is good reason to do otherwise. If the minor has reached age 14, the judge generally will consult the minor and will give the minor's preference significant weight.

[C] Choosing a Guardian

Choosing a guardian for minor children is a difficult process and parents should consider a variety of factors before reaching a final decision. Of primary concern, especially for very young children, is that the guardian and the children have a close and loving relationship. This factor often leads parents to think first of grandparents as guardians for their children. Grandparents, however, are rarely the best choice as guardians. Raising young children is a long and arduous job, and even grandparents who relish the opportunity to care for grandchildren on weekends or vacations may not be up to the physical and emotional challenges of serving as substitute parents. Some of the challenges of raising children increase as the children grow older, and it may be too much to ask grandparents in their seventies or eighties to take on the difficult issues of adolescence. Furthermore, naming a guardian of a generation older than the parents increases the chance that the guardian will die before the child reaches majority, thus leaving the child without a caretaker for the second time.

Siblings or close friends of the parents who share similar values are more likely to be suitable candidates for guardians. In choosing among such candidates, parents should consider how the other members of the potential guardian's family might react to the guardianship. If the potential guardian's spouse or partner is unwilling to take on the guardianship, another individual may be a better choice as guardian. If the potential guardians have children of their own, parents should consider how those children might react to having additional children in the family. The natural

---

[1] **§ 7.02** Some states allow for other documents by which a parent can appoint a guardian for minor children in the event of the parent's death or incapacity, but such documents typically require similar formalities as followed for wills.

tendency for children to resent additions to the family may be minimized if the children of the two families already share a close relationship.

As children approach the teenage years, friends and community connections take on increasing significance in their lives. Consequently, geography may be another factor to consider in choosing a guardian for older children. When the children reach age 14, parents may wish to consult the children as to their preferences, since a judge appointing a guardian would do so.

Before executing a will naming a guardian, a parent may want to ask the potential guardian if he or she is willing to take on the guardianship. This discussion also provides an opportunity for parents to communicate any special wishes they might have concerning the rearing of the children, and any special needs the children may have. It is also an opportunity to inform the potential guardians about the financial resources that would be left to the child, which might affect their willingness to take on the guardianship.

Choosing a guardian is usually the most difficult estate planning decision facing a parent, since most parents believe that they are the best caretakers for their children, and that no guardian could provide the same level of love and care. Because it is so difficult, many parents cannot force themselves to reach a decision, and simply postpone finalizing their wills. An important part of the estate planner's role is to emphasize to parents that any decision on this issue is probably better than no decision. It may be helpful to remind parents that the decision is not irrevocable because they can change their will at any time if they change their minds or if circumstances should change.

[D] Integrating the Care of the Minor's Person and Property

The job of caring for a minor's person is a legally separate function from the job of managing a minor's property and the person chosen for managing the minor's property need not be the same person who the parents choose to act as guardian of the minor's person.[2]

The qualities necessary to raise a child and those necessary to manage financial assets are quite different, and a parent should consider each role separately in planning for the child. If a single friend or family member qualified for both roles, then naming that individual as both trustee and guardian of the child will reduce the administrative burden associated with each role. Separating the functions of a trustee and a guardian of the child, however, also has advantages. If two individuals are responsible for different aspects of the child's care, each can serve as a check on the other's performance and as a source of support and consultation for the other. If a parent decides that the two functions should be separated, then the parent should consider and communicate to the fiduciary who will manage the child's assets how those assets are to be used to support the child in the care of the guardian.

A personal guardian is entitled to reimbursement for the expenses of a child's support from the child's assets. However, the economic impact of one or more

---

[2] Planning for a minor's property is discussed in § 7.03 *infra*.

additional children on the guardian's household often far exceeds the direct costs, such as food, clothing, and personal expenses. For example, a guardian taking on three young children as wards may need a larger home and additional household help in order to maintain the same level of comfort for the expanded family. Since it is in the best interests of all the parties involved to minimize the financial burden of a guardianship on the guardian's family, it may be appropriate to authorize the trustee holding the children's assets to apply some of those assets to expenses that will benefit the guardian's family as well as the children, where the assets left to the children are sufficient to do so. For example, depending on the level of assets available, the trust could permit the trust assets to be used for limited expenses of the family, such as vacations, or for major expenses, such as purchasing a larger home or providing the same educational opportunities to all of the children in the family. Using a portion of the child's assets for expenses that benefit the guardian's family as a whole can help to integrate the ward into the family by equalizing opportunities.

§7.03 PLANNING FOR A CHILD'S PROPERTY

In addition to providing for the personal care of a child, an estate plan should also address management of a child's property. While the necessity of appointing a guardian for a child's person generally arises only at the death of the child's parents, management of a child's property needs to be addressed whenever a child receives a gift of significant property. This is most likely to occur in two situations: (1) when parents die while the child is still a minor; or (2) when significant gifts are given to the child.

[A] Issues Raised by a Minor's Direct Ownership of Property

It is rarely desirable for a minor to own property directly. Two important reasons exist for avoiding direct ownership of property by a minor child. First, under state law a minor child is not competent to administer or manage her own property. While a child can hold title to property in her own name, state laws provide that a minor does not have the capacity to enter into a binding contract. As a result, a minor cannot sell, rent, or otherwise administer property she owns. In most instances, this inability to manage property will represent a serious handicap. The second issue related to direct ownership of property by minor children arises when the child reaches the age of majority, which is age 18 in many states. As soon as a minor child reaches the age of majority, she has full control over her property. While reaching the age of majority resolves the problem of the legal capacity to manage property, it can create other issues, given that many children only develop the wisdom and maturity to handle property at some age after the legal age of majority. For that reason, it is often desirable to have a third party manage and control distributions of the property until the child reaches at least 25 years of age.

[B] Legal Guardians of a Minor's Property

Since minors do not have the legal capacity to handle property, whenever a significant amount of property is transferred directly to a minor (as can happen in the event of the parents' deaths or upon receipt of a large gift), the court will appoint a legal guardian to handle property owned directly by the minor (sometimes referred to as a conservator). Generally, a legal guardian has the authority to enter into contracts with respect to the minor's property, and can sell, reinvest, rent, or develop the property. A parent may be appointed as the legal guardian of his child's property, but he will be obligated to follow the same procedures and his powers are subject to the same court oversight as would be the case if the guardian were unrelated.

The most significant drawback to the use of a legal guardian to manage a minor's property is that the guardian can act only under the supervision of the court that appointed him. The guardian must file annual accounts with the court to inform the court of his activities. In addition, the guardian must petition the court for permission before entering into certain types of transactions, such as a sale of the minor's real estate. In addition, a guardian often must post bond, and a surety on the bond is often required. The involvement of the court in a legal guardianship makes this arrangement cumbersome and expensive. Furthermore, the authority of a legal guardian ends when the minor reaches the age of majority. At that time, the guardian must turn over the minor's property directly to him, regardless of the child's emotional maturity. As a consequence of these drawbacks, legal guardianships rarely are used in a planning context. Trusts for minors and custodianships, described below, permit property to be held and managed for a minor without the expense and difficulties inherent in a legal guardianship.

[C] Planning for a Minor's Property in the Event of the Parents' Death: Using a Trust to Hold Minors' Property

If children inherit property upon their parents' death, and if the parents have made no provision for how that property is to be handled, then a court will appoint a guardian to manage the property while the children are minors. As discussed above, there are numerous disadvantages to having a minor's property handled through a legal guardianship. The best way to address the problems raised by guardianships is for parents to arrange instead for any substantial property transferred to their children to be placed in trust. The trustee of the trust will have full authority to manage the trust property, and the trust can be drafted to place appropriate restrictions on the child's access to the trust property.[1]

Trusts are the most flexible means of holding property for a minor. Trusts can hold property beyond the age of majority, can hold property for more than one beneficiary, and can distribute property to the beneficiaries for specifically designated purposes. As a consequence, trusts are an extremely valuable planning tool for minors, especially when a substantial amount of property or multiple children are involved. When preparing trusts to hold property for minor children after the death of the children's parents, the estate planner should pay careful attention to the issues of (1) if the trust is for the benefit of more than one child, whether each child should have a separate trust or whether the property should be kept together in a single trust (sometimes called a *pot trust* or a *family trust*); and (2) at what age the property should be distributed from the trust to the children.

---

[1] §7.03 A sample minority trust for children is provided in Form 5.

[1] Trusts for Multiple Children: Dividing the "Pot"

Trusts established on the death of a parent often begin as a single fund for multiple beneficiaries and then later divide into separate shares for each beneficiary. For example, a typical credit shelter trust funded at the death of one parent provides that the surviving spouse and the children are beneficiaries of the trust, and, at some point after the death of the surviving spouse, the trust will divide into separate shares for each of the children.[2] Parents establishing this type of trust need to consider two issues regarding the division of the trust assets among the beneficiaries: whether the trust will permit unequal distributions from the common fund, and at what point in time the trust will divide into separate shares. Parents may be drawn to a plan that favors equal distributions and divides trust assets into separate shares very early because they want to treat all the children fairly, and therefore want to ensure that ultimately each of the children will receive equal benefits from the trust. If the children's shares are separated early, then the trustee's decisions as to distributions affect only the timing of each child's receipt of his or her share. If the parents' estate is substantial and each child's share is fully adequate to support him or her, then an early separation into separate shares may be an appropriate way to divide the assets among the children.

While the concept of giving each child exactly the same amount from a trust has some appeal as a way to ensure that the family assets are divided fairly, this approach ultimately can have unintended results if the trust fund is of modest size and is the primary source of support for the children. Children are unlikely to have exactly the same needs, and a trust that provides for equal distributions to each child may not provide the children with equal opportunities in life. Parents planning for a trust that will supply the funds necessary to raise and educate minor children if the parents should die prematurely should recall that if no untimely death occurs, the family assets will be retained in one "pot" in the hands of the parents until long after the children reach majority. The amount that the parents expend on each child for health, education, and welfare will be determined by the particular needs of each individual child, not by the dollar amount expended on the previous child. If one child encounters medical or educational difficulties that require special treatment, the parents will devote a greater proportion of the family's resources to that child. It may be desirable for a trustee charged with determining how the family's assets are to be divided among the children to have the same flexibility to allocate resources according to need, at least until all of the children reach majority. A trust that permits the trustee to make unequal distributions from the "pot" and postpones separating the "pot" into separate shares until the youngest child has reached age 22 or 25 can help equalize the opportunities made available to each child. While this approach may result in some children receiving more assets from the trust than others, it is important to remember that treating children fairly does not necessarily mean treating them the same.

---

[2] Form 1 contains an example of this type of trust.

[2] Terminations and Withdrawals

Another decision that needs to be made when establishing a trust for minor children is when the beneficiaries should be given direct access to the trust assets. Relatively few trusts provide for outright distribution of the trust assets when a beneficiary reaches the age of 18 or 21, unless the trust is a "minor's trust," discussed below.[3] Grantors often prefer to postpone large distributions directly to a beneficiary based on four concerns. First, most grantors believe that age brings wisdom, and that a beneficiary is more likely to dissipate the trust assets on inappropriate expenditures if given access to them at too young an age. A second, related issue is competence to handle the continuing investment and management of the trust assets. The skills necessary to manage financial assets effectively take time to acquire. The third concern is that if the beneficiary knows that he will have access to all the trust assets at an early age, he will become dependent on support from the trust and will not have the incentive to establish himself as economically independent. Finally, grantors often wish to place a gift beyond the reach of any future creditors of the beneficiary, including claims pursuant to a divorce.

No plan for terminating a trust can ensure that the beneficiary will spend trust assets wisely, or invest them wisely, or avoid the temptation to rely on the trust for support. A few commonly used techniques, however, can increase the chances of a smooth transition. Often a trust provides that the beneficiary will receive the trust assets in installments, for example one-third at age 25, one-third at age 30, and one-third at age 35. In addition, a trust may provide that the beneficiary becomes a cotrustee (possibly with limited powers) upon reaching the age of majority. Participating in the management of the trust assets for several years before receiving them outright provides an opportunity to develop investment skills. Another technique is for the trust to substitute a withdrawal power for required distributions, so that the trust assets will be transferred to the beneficiary only if the beneficiary takes the initiative to request them.

EXAMPLE 7-1

A trust provides that when the beneficiary reaches age 30, he may withdraw some or all of the trust property. If the beneficiary makes no withdrawals, the property remains in trust. As a result, the trust assets are available to the beneficiary whenever he is prepared to undertake their management. If the beneficiary fails to request distribution of the assets, they will remain in the care of the trustee.

---

[3] A "minor's trust," or Section 2503(c) trust, discussed more fully in § 7.04[C], must either distribute all the trust assets or permit the beneficiary to withdraw the assets when the beneficiary reaches age 21. IRC § 2503(c). Form 5 includes a sample minor's trust.

[3] Planning for Children with Special Needs

Planning for a child with special needs puts many of the issues raised in planning for minors into high relief. A special needs child may need more of the family's financial resources than other children, even after reaching the age of majority; therefore, it may not be advisable to separate a family trust into separate shares for each of the children. In addition, any family trust that includes a child with special needs as a beneficiary should expressly permit unequal distributions.

In selecting a trustee for a trust for a special needs child, it is important to take into consideration that the trust may be in existence for many years. The trust should provide for successor trustees, preferably of a generation younger than the parents, and an institutional trustee should be considered in the interest of providing continuity. Similarly, in naming a guardian, special consideration should be given to the length of time that the guardian is likely to be required to serve.

Planning for a special needs child may also involve consideration of Supplemental Security Income (SSI), Medicaid, and other governmental aid programs. Integrating the planning for these programs into an estate plan requires specialized planning. This often involves the use of a *supplemental needs trust* (also called a *special needs trust*). The goal of a supplemental needs trust is to provide benefits to a disabled child without disrupting that child's eligibility to receive assistance under government needs-based programs. The assets of a supplemental needs trust are typically used to pay for education, counseling, recreation, and comforts beyond the basic necessities covered by public assistance.[4]

If parents are using their own assets to establish the supplemental needs trust (as opposed to the child's assets), then the trust will not affect eligibility provided that the trustee has discretion as to whether to distribute or accumulate income and principal. Each public benefit program has its own rules, but, in general, distributions from this type of trust will only affect eligibility if the beneficiary is entitled to receive income or if distributions are made directly to the beneficiary. In the case of SSI, payments made by the trust for food, clothing, or shelter are treated as "in kind" income and can cause a reduction in benefits. To make the trust purpose clear, the trust should state that it is the settlor's intention that the trust be used for supplemental benefits, and not for necessities. Unlike self-settled supplemental needs trusts (discussed below), a third-party supplemental needs trust can be revocable without affecting eligibility, provided the power of revocation is not held by the beneficiary.

There are some situations in which the disabled child's own assets must be used to fund a supplemental needs trust. These "self-settled trusts" are often set up on behalf of individuals who have become disabled through injury or medical malprac-

---

[4] Special accounts, called "ABLE accounts" (Achieving a Better Life Experience), are another method of allowing savings for and by disabled minors and young adults. ABLE accounts are similar in nature to 529 Plans (discussed in Section 7.04[E]), and allow tax-free earnings and payment of certain expenses More recent changes to the rules on ABLE accounts allow transfers from 529 Accounts to an ABLE account if the beneficiary is the same or in the same family.

tice and received settlement payments. Assets of a self-settled trust will not be counted in determining eligibility for SSI or Medicaid if the trust meets the requirements of one of two statutory safe harbors as either a *payback trust* or a *pooled trust.*

A *payback trust* (also called a "(d)(4)(A) trust") is an irrevocable trust established with the assets of a disabled individual under age 65 by a court or by the individual's parent, grandparent, or legal guardian.[5] In order to qualify for the safe harbor the trust must provide that upon the beneficiary's death, any remaining trust assets must first be used to reimburse the state for money spent on behalf of the beneficiary.[6]

A *pooled trust* (also called a "(d)(4)(C) trust") is a trust managed by a nonprofit association in which the assets of disabled individuals are pooled together for investment and management purposes but kept separate for accounting purposes.[7] Under federal law, pooled trusts need not provide that the trust assets be used to reimburse the state at the beneficiary's death, provided the funds are retained in trust to be used on behalf of other disabled beneficiaries.[8] However, contrary to federal law, some states do require reimbursement. A pooled supplemental needs trust is particularly useful when planning for a disabled person who has no family members who are willing or able to undertake the role of trustee.

§7.04 PLANNING FOR *INTER VIVOS* GIFTS TO MINORS

[A] Overview

Parents and grandparents (as well as other relatives and friends) often wish to make *inter vivos* gifts to minor children for estate planning purposes and seek advice as to the best vehicle to hold such gifts. The two vehicles most commonly used for having a third party hold and manage property for a minor without court supervision are custodianships and trusts.

A *custodianship* is the least complex and least expensive vehicle for holding property for a minor. Custodianships, however, are not suitable for all situations because they cannot be used for all types of property and must terminate when the minor reaches the age of majority. The most flexible vehicle for holding property transferred to minors is a trust. As discussed in Chapter 4, the variety of possible trusts is almost endless, and a trust can be designed to carry out almost any dispositive scheme. The two types of trust most commonly used to make *inter vivos* gifts to minors are Section 2503(c) trusts (also called minor's trusts) and *Crummey* trusts. In addition, Section 529 plans have become an increasingly popular device for funding education expenses for children and grandchildren.

---

[5] 42 U.S.C. § 1396p(d)(4)(A).

[6] *Id.*

[7] 42 U.S.C. § 1396p(d)(4)(C).

[8] *Id.*

[B] Custodianships

A *custodianship* offers a simple way of making an irrevocable gift to a minor and providing that someone else will manage the property until the minor reaches the age of majority. The simplicity of establishing and maintaining a custodianship has made this one of the most popular means of making a gift to a minor. All states have enacted a version of either the Uniform Gifts to Minors Act (UGMA)[1] or the Uniform Transfers to Minors Act (UTMA),[2] each of which provides a simple procedure by which a donor can transfer property to a custodian to be held for the benefit of a minor. The UGMA, which was enacted first by all 50 states, only permitted a donor to transfer money, securities, insurance policies, and annuity contracts to a custodian. The UTMA, enacted later by many states, broadened the categories of property that may be held in a custodianship. Under the UTMA, both tangible and intangible property, including real property located within or without the state, may be transferred to a custodianship. Due to the differences between the UGMA and the UTMA, and the variations of these statutes as enacted in the different states, it always is important to check the applicable state statute to determine exactly what type of property may be held, what powers a custodian holds, and when the custodianship terminates.

[1] Terms of Custodianships

A donor creates a custodianship by designating a custodian in the transfer documents. The exact form of designation is determined by state statute. Generally, a donor could establish a custodianship by transferring a security "to X as custodian for Y under the State Uniform Transfers to Minors Act." No additional documentation is required, and the duties and powers of the custodianship are determined by the state statute.

A custodian under the UTMA has broad powers to manage, sell, and reinvest the custodial property. Under the UGMA the powers of the custodian are generally more limited, although still include the power to buy, sell, and reinvest custodial property. A custodian must always exercise his powers for the exclusive benefit of the minor, but a custodian does not operate under the supervision of a court. A custodian must keep records, but the statutes do not require the custodian to submit regular accountings to the court or to post a bond.

A custodian has broad discretion to distribute or retain income and principal for the benefit of the minor, without regard to the minor's other income or sources of support.

When the minor reaches the age of majority, which is age 21 under the UTMA and varies between ages 18 and 21 under the UGMA, the custodian must distribute all of the custodial property to the beneficiary. This requirement that the custodianship terminate at the age of majority is the primary drawback of custodianships.

---

[1] § 7.04 U.G.M.A., 8A U.L.A. 375 (1993).
[2] U.T.M.A., 8B U.L.A. 497 (1993).

Distribution by age 21 may be appropriate if the custodial account is relatively small, or if the account was intended primarily as a vehicle to fund the minor's college education. Many parents, grandparents, and other donors feel, however, that it is too early to distribute substantial assets transferred as part of a family wealth transfer plan, especially if the assets include interests in a family business. For this reason, senior family members often prefer to transfer gifts to minors into a trust, which can be designed to maintain control of the transferred property as long as desired.

For income tax purposes, a transfer to a custodianship is treated as a transfer directly to the minor, and the minor is treated as an owner of the property for income tax purposes.[3] The minor's Social Security number is used to identify custodial accounts. The custodian is not required to file a fiduciary income tax return. The income of the custodial account is taxed directly to the minor, although the "kiddie tax" generally requires that a child under age 18 pay tax at his or her parents' rates.[4] A gift to a custodial account can qualify for the gift tax and generation-skipping tax present interest exclusion.[5] Thus, annual transfers of up to $15,000 can be made tax free to a minor by transferring it to a custodial account.

[2] Choosing a Custodian

In choosing a custodian it is always necessary to consider both honesty and competence. A custodian is not under court supervision, so that there will only be minimal oversight of the custodian's actions. Competence may not be a major issue if the custodian is holding only a bank account, but will be a greater concern if the custodian holds a portfolio of securities or other business interests requiring investment decisions.

Neither the UGMA nor the UTMA prohibits a parent from acting as custodian for her minor child. In order to avoid estate tax consequences to the transferor, however, a person who has transferred property to the custodial account should not act as custodian. A custodian has the power to determine when and how much property should be distributed from the account. If the donor is also the custodian, then he will control when the minor receives the transferred property. This control will cause the transferred property to be included in donor/custodian's estate for estate tax purposes under the "string provision" of IRC Section 2038 if he dies during the custodianship.[6] Since often one of the primary purposes of making gifts to a

---

[3] Rev. Rul. 59-357, 1959-2 C.B. 212; Rev. Rul. 56-484, 1956-2 C.B. 23.

[4] *Id.*; IRC §1(g). Under the Tax Cuts and Jobs Act of 2017 ("TCJA"), the kiddie tax was briefly changed to be imposed at the more compressed rates for estates and trusts. However, the Setting Every Community Up for Retirement Enhancement Act (the "SECURE Act") of 2019, basically removed those provisions and returned to taxation at the parents' rates. Pub. L. No. 116-94, 133 Stat. 2534 (Dec. 20, 2019).

[5] The gift tax annual exclusion is discussed in Chapter 8 and the generation-skipping transfer tax is discussed in Chapter 9.

[6] Rev. Rul. 70-348, 1970-2 C.B. 193. The "string" provisions of the estate tax are discussed in Chapter 5.

custodial account is to remove the property from the donor's estate, this result can defeat the purpose of the transfer.

[C] Section 2503(c) Trusts

A Section 2503(c) trust, or minor's trust, is named for the section of the Internal Revenue Code that describes a special type of trust for minors.[7] The Code section was enacted because many donors want to make gifts to minors by transferring property to a trust to be held until the minor reaches the age of majority, and further want such gifts to qualify for the present interest exclusion under the gift tax and generation-skipping tax rules. Under the general rules governing the annual exclusion, a gift to a trust to which the donee has no access until the age of majority would not qualify for the present interest exclusion.[8] Section 2503(c) permits gifts to minors in trust to qualify for the gift tax and generation-skipping tax present interest exclusion if the trust meets certain requirements.

In order to qualify as a Section 2503(c) trust, four requirements must be met. First, the trust must provide that the trustee has the unrestricted power to distribute income and principal to the beneficiary until the beneficiary reaches age 21. The second requirement is that if the beneficiary survives to age 21, then all accumulated income and all principal must be paid to the beneficiary. This requirement that the trust assets must be paid to the beneficiary at age 21 is the primary disadvantage of a Section 2503(c) trust. Often one of the donor's primary objectives in making a gift in trust is to keep control of the assets in the hands of a trustee until the beneficiary reaches an age past 21. Fortunately, the Internal Revenue Service takes the view that the trustee is not actually required to distribute the assets and terminate when the beneficiary reaches 21, as long as the beneficiary has the opportunity to withdraw all of the assets at that time.[9] The trust may provide that the trustee will notify the beneficiary when the beneficiary reaches age 21 that he has the right to withdraw all of the trust assets during a reasonable period of time, and if the beneficiary does not exercise this right, then the trust will continue. Thus, the trust may qualify as a Section 2503(c) trust even if the beneficiary has unfettered access to the trust assets for only a short period of time at his twenty-first birthday.

The third requirement of a Section 2503(c) trust is that the beneficiary must have a general power of appointment by will, or the remainder of the trust must pass to the beneficiary's estate if he dies before age 21. In most states a person cannot make a will or exercise a power of appointment before reaching age 18, but the beneficiary's inability to exercise the power of appointment will not affect the trust's qualification as a Section 2503(c) trust. The trust may provide for trust assets to pass to others if the beneficiary fails to exercise his power of appointment.

---

[7] *See* Form 5 for a sample annual exclusion trust with a Section 2503(c) provision.

[8] IRC § 2503(b) provides that the annual exclusion is not available for future interests.

[9] Rev. Rul. 74-43, 1974-1 C.B. 285.

Finally, a Section 2503(c) trust cannot have more than one minor beneficiary. Consequently, this type of trust cannot be used to establish a discretionary spray trust for a group of children.

A Section 2503(c) trust is a separate taxpayer for income tax purposes, and must obtain a separate federal tax identification number. The trustee must file fiduciary income tax returns, and the trust income will be taxed to the trust if the trustee retains the income in the trust or to the beneficiary, if the trustee distributes the income. If the trust continues after the beneficiary has reached age 21 because the beneficiary has failed to exercise a power to withdraw the assets, then the Internal Revenue Service takes the position that the trust will become a grantor trust for income tax purposes, and all of the trust income will be taxed to the beneficiary from that time forward.[10]

[D] Crummey Trusts

A Crummey trust is another trust structured to permit gifts to the trust to qualify for the present interest gift tax exclusion. Crummey trusts are not designed or used exclusively for gifts to minors, but they are commonly used for that purpose since it allows for an annual exclusion even when the beneficiaries' rights to the trust are limited. The term "Crummey trust" derives from the name of the case in which a court permitted a donee to claim a present interest exclusion for a gift to a trust of this type.[11]

A gift to a Crummey trust qualifies for the present interest gift tax exclusion because the beneficiary of the trust has the right to withdraw the gift from the trust. This right may be exercisable only for a limited period of time after the trust receives the gift. The trust may provide that if the beneficiary fails to exercise this withdrawal right, then the right will lapse and the trust will continue. The trust is not required to terminate when the beneficiary reaches age 21.

The IRS takes the position that in order for a gift to a Crummey trust to qualify for the present interest exclusion, the beneficiary must have reasonable notice of a gift to the trust and of his right to withdraw, and must be given a reasonable period of time to exercise the right.[12] The trustee should provide such notice in the form of a letter to the beneficiary (or to his or her guardian or parent, provided the latter is not the donor of the contribution) and should retain copies of the letters with the trust records in case the trust is audited. Most planners consider 30 days to be a reasonable period for the beneficiary's withdrawal right. It is not necessary, however, that a minor beneficiary have the capacity to exercise the withdrawal right, or that the guardian have been appointed for a minor beneficiary. In the case for which Crummey trusts are named, the beneficiary was a minor who was incapable of exercising the withdrawal right without appointment of a guardian, and no guardian had been

---

[10] Rev. Rul. 74-43, 1974-1 C.B. 285. The income taxation of trusts is discussed in Chapter 4.

[11] Crummey v. Comm'r, 397 F.2d 82 (9th Cir. 1954). *See* Form 5 for a sample annual exclusion trust with a Crummey provision.

[12] Rev. Rul. 81-7, 1981-1 C.B. 474.

appointed. It is advisable, however, to provide in the trust that the withdrawal power may be exercised by a legal or natural guardian of the minor, and to provide notice to any such guardians. A gift to a Crummey trust is eligible for the annual exclusion based on the beneficiary's legal right to withdraw the gift, even if the actual relationship among the parties makes it highly unlikely that the power will be exercised.

EXAMPLE 7-2

In the year of Allan's birth, each of his grandparents transfers a gift of $16,000 to a Crummey trust for his benefit. The trustee notifies Allan and Allan's mother that the gifts have been made and that Allan, or his mother, on Allan's behalf, can withdraw the gifts during the 30-day period following the receipt of the notice. None of the gifts are withdrawn. The trust continues until Allan reaches age 35. The gifts qualify for the present interest exclusion.

The primary advantage of a Crummey trust over a Section 2503(c) trust or a gift to a UGMA or UTMA account is that a Crummey trust is not required to terminate or to provide the beneficiary with another opportunity to withdraw the trust assets when the beneficiary reaches age 21. Consequently, the property can remain in the trust for as long as the donor wishes. Clients often prefer this form of trust because the beneficiary need not be given a right to withdraw the trust assets upon reaching age 21.

EXAMPLE 7-3

Eleanor creates a trust for each of her eight grandchildren. Each trust provides for discretionary distributions of income and principal to the beneficiary. When a gift is made to the trust, the trustee is required to notify the beneficiary (or the beneficiary's guardian, if any), and the beneficiary (or guardian) has the right to withdraw the property transferred to the trust for the following 30 days. If a beneficiary fails to withdraw the gift within 30 days of receiving notice of the gift, then the withdrawal power lapses. Any property that is not withdrawn remains in the trust. One-third of the trust property remaining in trust will be distributed when each beneficiary reaches age 35, one-third at age 40, and the remaining property at age 45. Each year Eleanor transfers $16,000 to each trust. At the end of 13 years, Eleanor will have transferred $1,664,000 to her grandchildren, free of gift and generation-skipping tax (without having used any of her unified credit or her GST exemption).

Not all gifts to a Crummey trust that qualify for the present interest exclusion to the gift tax will automatically qualify for the present interest exclusion to the generation-skipping tax. Under the generation-skipping rules, gifts to a Crummey trust will qualify for the present interest exclusion only if the trust has only one beneficiary during the life of the beneficiary or the term of the trust and the trust property will be included in the estate of the beneficiary at his death.[13] Consequently, a Crummey trust established for a class of beneficiaries (such as all of the donor's grandchildren) can qualify for multiple present interest exclusions for gift tax purposes, but will not be eligible for the present interest exclusion to the generation-skipping tax.[14]

[E] Section 529 Tuition Plans

Funding children's college education is a central part of the financial planning for many families. In some families, parents or grandparents can pay college expenses out of their current assets. Because payment of tuition (if the payment is made directly to the institution) is not subject to gift tax or to generation-skipping tax, having grandparents pay tuition can be a very simple way to fund college and save estate taxes at the same time. It is worth noting that the Tax Cuts and Jobs Act of 2017 (the "TCJA") expanded the use of 529 plans to allow for these plans to be used to pay a total of $10,000 of tuition per beneficiary for K-12 public, private, or religious schools. The SECURE Act of 2019 further expanded the use of 529 plans to include withdrawals of up to $10,000 to repay student loans, with an additional $10,000 to pay off student loans for each of the beneficiary's siblings.[15] It also expanded the use to include payments for certain apprenticeship programs.

For families that want to transfer assets to a separate "pot" earmarked for college education, there are a number of alternatives. Any of the vehicles described in this section (gifts to a custodian, to a minor's trust, or to a Crummey trust) can be used to create a college fund. In addition, a family can transfer assets to a "qualified tuition plan," which is a vehicle specifically designed to encourage families to save for college by offering federal income tax benefits. If the assets in the qualified tuition plan are used for educational expenses of the named beneficiary of the plan, no federal income tax will ever be paid on the earnings that accumulated while the assets were in the plan. These earnings may or may not be subject to state income tax, depending on the state sponsoring the plan and the state of residence of the beneficiary. The federal income tax benefits provided by qualified tuition plans are contained in Section 529 of the Internal Revenue Code; therefore, these plans are also called "Section 529 plans."

Section 529 plans are available for all taxpayers, regardless of their income levels. They have been widely publicized, and some employers now offer a program of automatic payroll deductions for funding a plan. However, although Section 529 plans can be useful to many families, it is important to understand exactly what such

---

[13] IRC § 2642(c)(2). *See* Chapter 9 for a discussion of the generation-skipping tax.

[14] Crummey trusts are discussed in greater detail in general in Chapter 8, and with respect to generation-skipping transfer taxes in Chapter 9.

[15] The Setting Every Community Up for Retirement Enhancement Act (the "SECURE Act") of 2019, Pub. L. No. 116-94, 133 Stat. 2534 (Dec. 20, 2019).

plans consists of and what advantages and disadvantages are involved before contributing funds.

Section 529 of the Internal Revenue Code sets forth certain basic requirements that a plan must meet in order to be treated as a qualified tuition plan. The plans themselves are created and administered either by colleges and universities or by states. The plans created by different institutions or states vary in important respects. In considering whether to use a qualified tuition plan, it is important to examine the details of the specific plan and to compare it to other alternative plans.

There are two basic types of qualified tuition plans:

- *Pre-Paid Tuition Plans,* which are organized by states or by colleges or universities, and
- *College Savings Plans,* which are organized by a state and administered through an investment house.

Pre-Paid Tuition Plans were the first type of qualified tuition plans authorized by Section 529, but they have declined in popularity since the advent of the more flexible *College Savings Plans*. In essence, a pre-paid tuition plan permits a family to pay tuition currently, at current rates, for a child who will attend college later. The effect is to protect the family against increases in tuition, at the cost of giving up the investment income on the cash transferred to the plan. Pre-paid tuition plans have an important limitation: the family must choose a specific institution when the plan is created. If the child ultimately decides not to attend that institution, the cash contributed to the plan will be returned to the family, but the family will not have derived any benefit from the plan.

College Savings Plans are more popular because they are far more flexible. Educational institutions do not have to agree to participate in the program—assets in a college savings plan can be used to fund expenses at virtually any postsecondary school.

A college savings plan consists of an account with a named beneficiary. The account owner contributes cash to the account. The contribution is a taxable gift and qualifies for the $16,000 annual exclusion from gift tax. Furthermore, a contributor may make a contribution of up to $80,000 in one year, and it will be treated as qualifying for the annual exclusion over five years.[16] The account owner cannot deduct the contribution for federal income tax purposes. When the account owner dies, the assets of the account are included in his or her taxable estate only to the extent that there has been a contribution that exceeded the annual exclusion amount and has not yet been prorated over the following four years. Each account can only be funded up to certain limits, which are intended to approximate the cost of a college education. The specific limitations vary from plan to plan.

The account owner chooses an investment program from among a limited number of programs. Under Section 529, the account owner cannot actively manage

---

[16] Contributing five years' worth of annual exclusions in Year 1 allows a "jump start" on the investment returns.

the account assets. The investment house administering the plan controls the management of the investments within the program. The plan, however, may permit account owners to change the investment program if the named beneficiary is changed, and otherwise no more than once a year.

The account owner controls the amount, timing, and recipients of distributions from the account. The account owner is not required by the terms of the plan to direct that distributions be paid only to the named beneficiary; he or she can withdraw cash and use it for his or her benefit if desired. However, if distributions are used for any purpose other than educational expenses of the named beneficiary, (1) the investment income on the account assets will be subject to federal income tax as ordinary income, and (2) an additional 10 percent income tax will apply to the investment income.

The account owner can change the beneficiary of the account without adverse consequences if the new beneficiary is a "family member" of the previous beneficiary. The definition of *family member* is fairly broad and includes a first cousin of the previous beneficiary. This permits a grandparent to name one grandchild as a beneficiary and then change the beneficiary to a grandchild who has different parents. If the new beneficiary is a generation or more lower than the previous beneficiary, however, a strange tax result follows. The change of beneficiary, which is controlled by the account owner, is treated for tax purposes as a taxable gift by the original beneficiary.

Some of the tax consequences of a college savings plan are uncertain. Among the open questions:[17]

- Are the plan assets includable in the taxable estate of the beneficiary at the beneficiary's death?
- Who pays the income tax if distributions are made to a beneficiary for a noneducational purpose, or if distributions are made to someone other than the account owner or the beneficiary?
- What are the tax consequences if the account owner is changed other than at the death of the original account owner?

The college savings plans established by the different states are not identical, and they vary in some important respects. There is no requirement for either the account owner or the beneficiary to be a resident of the sponsoring state, which means that families have a large number of plans from which to choose. In considering whether to create an account, and in choosing among plans, family members should investigate the following plan features:

- What fees does the plan charge? Fees may include a one-time startup fee or a flat annual fee, an annual percentage-based fee, a fee for changing beneficiaries, and extra fees for out-of-state account holders or beneficiaries.

---

[17] Although the Internal Revenue Service announced in February 2008 that it would issue proposed regulations that address some of the transfer tax issues and contain anti-abuse rules (Announcement 2008-17), no such regulations have yet been issued.

- What are the investment options? How often can an account owner change investment options? Do any options provide guaranteed returns?
- What is the limit on the account?
- Are there any state tax advantages or disadvantages?
- Are there any extra penalties for early withdrawals or other events?
- Are withdrawals required when a beneficiary reaches a certain age?

8

Using Gifts in Estate Planning

§8.01 INTRODUCTION

Individuals make lifetime gifts for many reasons. Some of these reasons are purely personal. For example, a donor may wish to provide financial assistance to the recipient or to be relieved of the responsibility of managing the transferred property. Another reason may be to protect the property against claims by the donor's future creditors. From an estate planner's perspective, however, one of the primary uses of gifts is to reduce the total estate and gift tax burden on the transfer of wealth from one generation to the next. For an individual whose taxable estate exceeds the amount that can be transferred free of federal estate tax (for 2022, $12,060,000),[1] or that will be subject to state estate tax, lifetime gifts may offer significant transfer tax advantages over transfers at death, and consequently are an important estate planning tool. If estate tax will be triggered at the death of members of an older generation, a planned giving program that begins early transferring wealth from the older generation to the younger generations can preserve the family wealth to an impressive extent. The transfer tax advantages of lifetime gifts result primarily from the following rules:

- An individual can give $16,000 each year to an unlimited number of people,[2] and may pay an unlimited amount of medical or tuition expenses for another completely free of both gift tax and generation-skipping tax.[3] All of the property that has been given away will be removed from the taxable estate of the donor.
- The effective rate of the gift tax is lower than the effective rate of the estate tax. The donor will pay gift tax only on the amount that the donee actually receives, and not on the amount of the gift tax paid. In contrast, the portion of the decedent's estate that is used to pay estate tax is itself subject to estate tax. The gift tax is "tax exclusive" and the estate tax is "tax inclusive."
- Property is valued for gift tax purposes at the time of the gift.[4] If the property appreciates in value after the gift has been made, that appreciation will benefit the recipient of the gift. The transfer of the appreciation will not be subject to either gift or estate tax.
- The income produced by property will generally be taxed to the recipient of the gift. If the recipient is in a lower income tax bracket, the family as a whole will pay less in income tax.[5]

---

[1] **§8.01** Under the Tax Cuts and Jobs Act, in 2018, the gift and estate exemption was increased to $11,180,000. This amount is indexed for inflation until 2026, at which time it is set to revert to the 2017 rate, adjusted for inflation (approximately $5,500,000). TCJA, Pub. L. No. 115-97 (December 22, 2017).

[2] IRC §2503(b).

[3] IRC §2503(e).

[4] IRC §2512(a).

[5] *See* IRC §1(g). Under the Tax Cuts and Jobs Act of 2017 ("TCJA"), the kiddie tax was briefly changed to be imposed at the more compressed rates for estates and trusts. The Setting Every Community Up for Retirement Enhancement Act (the "SECURE Act") of 2019, however, basically removed those provisions and returned to taxation at the highest marginal rate of their parent. Pub. L. No. 116-94, 133 Stat. 2534 (Dec. 20, 2019). Also, some gifts are structured in such a way that the

- In calculating the value of gifts for gift tax purposes, each gift is valued separately. If a donor gives 20 percent of a parcel of real estate to each of his children during life, the gift tax value of each gift will include a discount that reflects the fact that each gift was a fractional interest in property. If the donor retained the same property until death and then left it equally to his five children, the full value of the property would be subject to estate tax, unreduced by a discount.

As a result of the transfer tax advantages of lifetime gifts, estate planners often assume that gifts should be a part of every estate plan. In the current climate of gift, estate and income tax laws, however, it is crucial that an estate planner assess a client's total financial and tax situation before recommending a gift program. Beginning with the enactment of the American Tax Relief Act of 2012, which set the unified credit amount at $5,000,000 (indexed for inflation) for each individual and made the unified credit "portable" to the death of the second spouse, the number of families that could be subject to federal estate tax dropped dramatically. With the enactment of the Tax Cuts and Jobs Act of 2017 ("TCJA"), which raised the unified credit to $11,180,000 in 2018 (also indexed for inflation and currently at $12,060,000 for 2022), some estimate that less than 2,000 estates will be subject to federal estate tax.[6] While some states retain a separate state estate tax, the state estate tax rate is typically significantly lower than the federal estate tax rate. The result is that for many clients, the estate tax consequences of a gift program may be less important than the income tax consequences. If a couple living in a state with no state estate tax has combined assets of less than $24,120,000, making lifetime gifts may increase the total tax burden on the family due to adverse income tax effects. The income tax basis of property transferred by gift is the same in the hands of the recipient as it was in the hands of the donor. The income tax basis of property included in a decedent's estate will be adjusted to the fair market value of the property at the decedent's death. If the decedent's estate is less than the unified credit, then making a lifetime gift of appreciated property can result in an income tax liability that the donor could have avoided by transferring the property at death.

EXAMPLE *8-1*

Anna, who lives in a state with no state estate tax and whose husband died in 2009, gave her daughter, Jane, a gift of publicly-traded stock with a fair market value of $1,000,000 and an income tax basis of $200,000. Anna died in 2014, with a taxable estate of $3,000,000, at a time when the unified credit was $5,340,000. Jane sold the stock for $1,000,000. Jane has a gain of $800,000, subject to capital gains tax. If Anna had retained the

---

(Footnote Continued)

income continues to be taxed to the grantor after the gift under the grantor trust rules. The grantor trust rules are discussed in § 8.05[D][2] *infra*.

[6] Joint Committee on Taxation (www.jct.gov). The TCJA is set to sunset in 2026.

stock until her death, her estate would not have paid any estate tax, so the gift did not save estate tax. Jane's income tax basis in the stock would have been increased to $1,000,000, and Jane would not have recognized any taxable capital gains on the sale of the stock. The tax effect of the gift was to create $800,000 in taxable capital gain that could have been avoided if Anna had retained the stock until her death.

Finally, it is always important to remember not to let the tax tail wag the dog. Once a donor has given property away, that property is no longer available to him. It may be good tax planning for parents to reduce their taxable estates by giving income-producing assets to their children, but if the parents unexpectedly become disabled, or undergo some financial reverse, they may be left dependent on their children for support and may regret their earlier gift. The loss of control that results from a gift may similarly cause parents to regret making a gift. The distress caused by observing a child mismanage the business that parents spent their lifetimes building, or selling a family heirloom that has been given to her, can outweigh the transfer tax advantages of a lifetime gift. In addition, some parents feel strongly that giving a child too much too early will reduce his initiative and lessen the chances that the child will develop his personal resources. The story of King Lear is not the only description of the family disasters that can flow from parents passing control or cash to children too soon. To some extent, careful planning can address these issues, but the discussion that precedes the gifts should cover them in some detail to ensure that the client fully understands all the ramifications of making the gifts.

§8.02 WHAT CONSTITUTES A GIFT FOR FEDERAL TAX PURPOSES?

[A] Overview

As is the case with many other tax rules, the answer to this seemingly simple question is more complicated than one might expect. The nuances of the tax definition of a gift make it possible for an individual to make a taxable gift without intending to do so. Conversely, some transfers that appear to be gifts do not qualify as completed gifts for transfer tax purposes. An estate planner needs to have a firm grasp of the scope of the tax definition of a gift in order to avoid unintended tax consequences.

Many gifts are motivated by gift and estate tax objectives, such as removing the future appreciation of transferred property from the estate of the donor. However, if the transfer fails to qualify as a completed gift under the tax definition, the property will remain in the donor's estate and he will not realize the expected tax benefits. Furthermore, if an individual transfers property in a transaction that qualifies as a completed gift, but retains certain powers, the property may nonetheless be included in the estate of the donor at its date-of-death value. Again, the donor would not realize the expected tax benefits of the gift.

An unintended gift may generate equally unwelcome tax consequences. If an individual undertakes a transaction without realizing that it constitutes a gift, he will not file a gift tax return. A gift tax liability may arise and begin accruing interest.

When no gift tax return is filed, the limitations period for assessing gift tax will not expire, and the IRS could assess a gift tax, with interest and penalties, many years later.

To avoid the possibility of unexpected adverse tax consequences, an estate planner should analyze intrafamily transactions carefully to determine whether a gift has been made.

[B] Basic Definition

The definition of a gift for federal gift tax purposes is extremely broad:

> Any transaction in which an interest in property is gratuitously passed or conferred upon another, regardless of the means or device employed, constitutes a gift subject to tax.[1]

The Supreme Court has emphasized the breadth of the meaning of the term "gifts" for tax purposes:

> The term "gifts" was meant to be used in its broadest and most comprehensive sense . . . to reinforce the evident desire of Congress to hit all the protean arrangements which the wit of man can devise that are not business transactions within the meaning of ordinary speech, the Treasury Regulations make clear that no genuine business transaction comes within the purport of the gift tax. . . . Thus, on finding that a transfer in the circumstances of a particular case is not made in the ordinary course of business, the transfer becomes subject to the gift tax to the extent it is not made for "adequate and full consideration in money or money's worth."[2]

The regulations specifically identify some types of transfers as being outside the scope of the definition of a gift. A transfer of property in exchange for full and adequate consideration is not a gift.[3] If a parent sells property to a child, the transaction is not a gift if the purchase price is equal to the full fair market value of the property. However, if a parent sells property to a child for less than its fair market value, the difference between the purchase price and the value of the property is a taxable gift to the child. The regulations also specify that a transaction that is in the normal course of a business transaction is not a gift, even if it is not for full consideration.[4] Thus, selling property to an unrelated third party for less than its value is not a gift if it is in the ordinary course of business; it is simply a bad bargain.[5]

---

[1] **§ 8.02** Reg. § 25.2511-1(c)(1).

[2] Comm'r v. Wemyss, 324 U.S. 303, 306 (1945) (citations omitted).

[3] Reg. § 25.2511-1(g)(1).

[4] Reg. § 25.2512-8.

[5] Reg. § § 25.2511-1(g), 25.2512-8.

[C] Gift Must Be Complete and Irrevocable

A transfer will be recognized as a gift for federal gift and estate tax purposes only if the transfer is complete and irrevocable. The gift tax regulations provide that a gift is complete when "the donor has so parted with dominion and control as to leave in him no power to change its disposition, whether for his own benefit or for the benefit of another."[6] If a transfer is ineffective to transfer an interest in the property for state property law purposes, then the donor could go to court and recover the property. Consequently, the donor would not have so parted with dominion and control so as to leave him without the power to change the disposition of the gift, and the transfer would not be a completed gift for federal gift and estate tax purposes. Thus, there is a level of state property law that underlies the federal tax law regarding gifts.

Generally, state property law provides that a completed gift has been made when the following things have occurred:[7]

- The donor intended to make a gift;
- The gift was delivered to the donee; and
- The gift was accepted in some manner by the donee.

In addition, the donor must be competent at the time the gift was made, and the gift must not be the result of fraud, duress, or undue influence. If one of these elements is missing and the transfer is not a valid gift for state property law purposes, then the gift is not complete and irrevocable for federal gift and estate tax purposes.

EXAMPLE 8-2

Marion decided to give her son Paul an undeveloped parcel of land. She had her attorney prepare a new deed to the land, and put the deed in her safe deposit box without recording it. She never told Paul of her intent to make the gift. Under state law, if Marion had later sold the property to a third party and the third party had recorded the deed, Paul's claim to the property would have failed. The preparation of the deed to Paul is not a completed gift for gift and estate tax purposes because there was no delivery or acceptance, and under state law Marion could have revoked the gift by selling the property to someone else.

The question of when a gift is complete has been litigated frequently when the gift is in the form of a check delivered to the donee. Generally, under property law an individual can stop payment on a check until the bank on which the check was drawn has paid it. Thus, a donor could write a check to a donee, deliver the check,

---

[6] Reg. § 25.2511-2(b).

[7] *See, e.g.,* Murphy v. Kilimurray, 324 Mass. 707 (1949); In re Szabo's Estate, 176 N.E.2d 395 (N.Y. 1961).

and then revoke the gift by stopping payment on the check. For this reason, the IRS formerly took the position that a gift by check is not completed until the bank on which it is drawn has paid the check.[8] Following a loss in court, however, the IRS softened its position.[9] The IRS now takes the position that a gift of a check will be deemed to be complete at the earlier of (1) the date on which the donor no longer has any control over the check, or (2) the date on which the donee cashes or deposits the check, but only if all of the following conditions are satisfied:

1. The check was paid by the donor's bank when first presented;
2. The donor was alive when his bank paid the check;
3. The donor intended to make a gift;
4. The delivery of the check by the donor was unconditional; and
5. The check was cashed or deposited in the calendar year for which completed gift treatment is sought and within a reasonable time of issuance.

EXAMPLE 8-3

Sam gave each of his daughters a $10,000 check as a Christmas gift. Lucia deposited her check on Dec. 27, 2000, and Caroline deposited her check on Jan. 2, 2001. Assuming the other conditions were met, Sam's gift to Lucia was completed when she deposited the check. His gift to Caroline was not complete until the following calendar year.

It is important to note that a lack of donative intent is sufficient to make a gift incomplete for tax purposes only if the gift is incomplete for state property law purposes.[10] There is no separate federal tax law requirement that a donor have the intent to make a gift. In fact, the gift tax regulations specifically provide that:

donative intent on the part of the transferor is not an essential element in the application of the gift tax to the transfer. The application of the tax is based on the objective facts of the transfer and the circumstances under which it is made, rather than on the subjective motives of the donor.[11]

Thus, a donor may make a transfer that constitutes an indirect gift that is subject to gift tax without having considered the possibility that the transfer might be a gift. If the transfer is valid under state law, the gift is complete and subject to tax.

---

[8] See, e.g., Rev. Rul. 67-396, 1967-2 C.B. 351.

[9] See Metzger v. Comm'r, 38 F.3d 118 (4th Cir. 1994); Rev. Rul. 96-56, 1996-2 C.B. 161.

[10] See, e.g., Comm'r v. Berger, 201 F.2d 171 (2d Cir. 1953).

[11] Reg. § 25.2511-1(g).

EXAMPLE 8-4

Sue owns 50 percent of the stock of a family corporation and her children own the remaining 50 percent. The corporation could expand its business by expanding into a new line of business, but the corporation does not have sufficient cash flow to service a bank loan. Sue contributes $300,000 to the corporation and does not receive additional stock or a note from the corporation. Sue did not intend to make a gift to her children; she wanted to expand the corporation's business opportunities. However, her contribution to the corporation's capital increased the value of her children's stock as well as her own stock. Sue has made a taxable gift of $150,000 to her children.

The situation in the example above should be distinguished from the situation in which a parent signs a document transferring property by mistake, and the transfer is invalid under state law due to a lack of donative intent. In the latter case, the gift would be incomplete for federal tax purposes. This type of situation does not arise very often; consequently, in most situations the intent of the donor is not relevant for federal tax purposes.

[D] Gifts on the Creation of Joint Interests

In some circumstances, the creation of a joint interest is a completed gift, but in other circumstances, it is not. The result depends on two factors: the consideration furnished by each joint tenant and the rights of each of the joint tenants under state law. State laws are not uniform in defining the rights of joint owners; consequently, it is always necessary to check the relevant law to determine the gift tax results of the creation of a joint ownership.

Most states permit two individuals to own property as tenants-in-common, joint tenants, or tenants by the entirety.[12] Generally, the difference between a tenancy-in-common and a joint tenancy is that when one joint tenant dies, the property passes to the surviving joint tenant by operation of law, whereas when one tenant-in-common dies, the deceased tenant's interest in the property may be disposed of by will. A tenancy by the entirety is a special type of joint tenancy for married couples. State law permits a tenant-in-common to transfer his interest unilaterally, and some states permit either of the joint owners of property to sever the joint ownership. If one person provides all of the consideration for a purchase of property and takes title with another person as joint tenants or tenants-in-common, and either owner can unilaterally sever the joint ownership and receive a half interest in the property, then the individual providing the consideration has made a completed gift.

---

[12] The distinctions between tenants-in-common, joint tenants, and tenants by entirety are discussed in Chapter 2.

EXAMPLE 8-5

Mark purchases a vacation home for $200,000 and takes title with his son Nolan as joint tenants. Nolan does not provide any consideration for the purchase. Under state law, either joint tenant can unilaterally sever the joint tenancy. Mark has made a completed gift of a 50 percent interest in the property to Nolan.

A portion of the gift from Mark to Nolan will qualify for the gift tax annual exclusion as a present interest in property. If Mark had purchased the home with his wife, the gift on creation of the joint tenancy would have qualified for the marital gift tax deduction.

Another common situation in which the issue of whether the creation of a joint ownership results in a completed gift arises when one person deposits assets in a bank account held in joint names. If both persons listed on a joint account can withdraw any or all of the funds without participation of the other joint owner, then the opening of the account does not constitute a completed gift to the person who did not provide the deposited funds.[13] This result follows from the basic principle that a gift is complete for gift tax purposes only when it is irrevocable. Since the individual who deposited the assets in the account can recover them by withdrawing them from the account, there has not been an irrevocable transfer of an interest in those assets. If the person who did not deposit the funds makes a withdrawal that he is not obligated to return, then he has received a completed gift at that point.[14]

EXAMPLE 8-6

Mark deposits $200,000 in a joint bank account with Nolan. Under state law, both Mark and Nolan can withdraw funds from the account without being obligated to replace them. Mark has not made a completed gift by opening the account. The following year, Nolan withdraws $50,000 from the account. Mark has made a completed gift of $50,000 to Nolan at the time of the withdrawal.

[E] Indirect Gifts

Some gifts are indirect, in that they transfer an economic benefit to another, without actually transferring title to property. For example, if a parent loans cash to a child and then later forgives the loan, the loan forgiveness constitutes an indirect gift to the child. Similarly, if a parent pays a debt that her child owes to a third party, the payment is a gift to the child. If a parent contributes cash to a family corporation and

---

[13] Reg. § 25.2511(c).
[14] Reg. § 25.2511-1(h)(4).

fails to receive stock or a note in exchange, then the contribution will be treated as a gift to the other shareholders. In each of these situations the action of the parent provides some economic benefit to a family member, and therefore results in a taxable gift to that family member.

The Internal Revenue Code includes provisions that specifically identify certain transactions as gifts that do not fall within the usual understanding of the term. IRC Section 2514 provides that the exercise, release, or lapse of a general power of appointment is a gift for tax purposes. A general power of appointment is a power to dispose of property that may be exercised in favor of the holder, the holder's estate, the holder's creditors, or creditors of the holder's estate. The power to withdraw principal from a trust is a general power of appointment. The rule that a lapse of a general power of appointment constitutes a gift frequently comes into play when an individual creates a "Crummey" trust for multiple beneficiaries. A Crummey trust often gives each of the beneficiaries the right to withdraw a *pro rata* portion of any gift made to the trust during a limited period of time.[15] If the beneficiary fails to exercise the right to withdraw within the given time period, the right lapses. Under IRC Section 2514, the lapse of the power constitutes a gift to the other trust beneficiaries to the extent that the lapse exceeds $5,000 or 5 percent of the trust property.[16]

A second Code section that specifically identifies as a gift a transaction that does not fall within the usual understanding of the term gift is IRC Section 7872, which applies to below-market-rate loans between related parties. With certain exceptions, if one family member makes a loan to another family member and fails to charge interest at the applicable federal rate, the parties will be treated as if the borrower had paid interest to the lender at the applicable federal rate, and the lender had made a taxable gift of the interest amount to the borrower.[17]

[F] Gifts under a Power of Attorney

Individuals often execute a power of attorney as part of the estate planning process. The power of attorney authorizes the attorney-in-fact to act in financial matters on behalf of the person granting the power when he or she is incapacitated. If the principal has been making regular gifts to family members as part of an estate plan, the attorney-in-fact may determine that if the principal were not incapacitated, she would wish to continue her gift-giving program. A gift made by an attorney-in-fact may be a completed gift for gift tax purposes, but only if it is not revocable under state law. If state law permits a power of attorney to authorize gifts, and if the power of attorney specifically authorizes the attorney-in-fact to make gifts, then the gift will not be revocable under state law, and will be complete. If the power of attorney does

---

[15] *See* Crummey v. Comm'r, 397 F.2d 82 (9th Cir. 1968).

[16] Crummey trusts and the consequences of a lapse of a withdrawal right are discussed in more detail at § 8.06[D][3] *infra.*

[17] Intrafamily loans are discussed in more detail at § 8.09[F] *infra.*

not specifically authorize gifts, however, the IRS is likely to take the position that the gift is not complete because it is revocable under state law.[18]

§8.03 GIFT TAX CONSIDERATIONS

[A] Overview

Gifts are subject to the unified transfer tax system that applies to both lifetime transfers and transfers at death, discussed in detail in Chapter 5. In 2001, an individual could transfer the first $675,000 of property, either during life or at death, without gift or estate tax. In 2002, the amount that could be passed by lifetime gift free of gift tax increased to $1,000,000 and remained at that level until the end of 2010. In 2011, the gift tax exemption rose to $5,000,000, indexed for inflation, and that increase was made "permanent" in 2013. In 2018, the amount was increased to $11,180,000 (indexed for inflation), until 2026, at which time it is set to revert to $5,000,000 (adjusted for inflation). As of 2022, the amount is $12,060,000.

The marital deduction is available to shelter an unlimited amount of property transferred to a spouse during life or at death, as long as the interest transferred satisfies the requirements of the marital deduction rules contained in IRC Section 2523. The requirements for the marital deduction are discussed in more detail in Chapter 6.

At first glance, the unified nature of the gift and estate tax makes it appear that there would be little tax advantage to making lifetime gifts rather than retaining property until death and then making testamentary gifts. However, the gift tax rules offer a number of planning opportunities that can make a lifetime gift more tax efficient than a testamentary gift if the donor is likely to have a taxable estate. The most important of these planning opportunities are the following:

- An individual can make a tax-free gift of $16,000 to an unlimited number of people each year as long as the gifts are of a present interest;[1]
- An individual can pay an unlimited amount of tuition or medical expenses on behalf of others each year without gift tax consequences;[2]
- The cash used to pay gift tax is not itself subject to gift tax, while the cash used to pay estate tax is itself subject to estate tax; and
- All of the appreciation in property that occurs after the gift is complete benefits the recipient and is not subject to gift tax or to estate tax in the estate of the donor.

While these planning opportunities can make a gift program very attractive for individuals who will have estates large enough to be subject to estate tax, the estate planner should also be sensitive to the income tax consequences of gifts. In some

---

[18] *See* Casey v. Comm'r, 58 T.C.M. 176 (1989), *rev'd*, 948 F.2d 895 (4th Cir. 1991). Form 10, Durable Power of Attorney, includes a provision authorizing gifts.

[1] **§8.03** IRC § 2503(b).

[2] IRC § 2503(e).

circumstances, there are income tax disadvantages to passing property by gift rather than at death because the income tax basis of property transferred by gift generally remains the same as the property's basis in the hands of the donor, and is not adjusted to fair market value at the death of the donor. Before recommending any gift program, the estate planner should consider the income tax consequences to ensure that the gift does not result in avoidable income tax increases for the family.

[B] Gift Tax Annual Exclusion

The annual exclusion is an essential component of the use of gifts in an estate plan. This exclusion permits an individual to give $16,000 each year to an unlimited number of donees, free of both gift tax and generation-skipping tax, provided that the gift is of a present interest.[3] A married donor can give up to $32,000 each year to an unlimited number of donees if her spouse agrees to apply his annual exclusion amount to the gift by gift-splitting.[4] Annual exclusion gifts do not use up the donor's unified credit, and thus completely escape transfer tax. In most circumstances, for a donor who wishes to reduce her taxable estate by making lifetime gifts, the first step will be maximum use of the annual exclusion.

In order to qualify for the annual exclusion, the gift must be of a present interest in property. The regulations specify that a present interest in property is "[a]n unrestricted right to the immediate use, possession, or enjoyment of property or the income from property (such as a life estate or term certain)."[5] Most outright transfers of property qualify as present interests in property for purposes of the annual exclusion. When a gift is made in trust, however, the issue of whether a gift qualifies for the present interest exclusion is likely to arise. If the beneficiary of a trust does not have the right to possess the trust property immediately, a gift to the trust will not qualify for the present interest exclusion.[6]

EXAMPLE 8-7

John transfers $16,000 to a trust for the benefit of his son David, who is 18 years old. The trust permits the trustee to make discretionary distributions to David until David reaches age 30, at which point the property remaining in the trust will be distributed to David outright. The gift to the trust does not qualify for the present interest exclusion because David does not have the right to possess the trust property until he reaches age 30.

---

[3] IRC §§ 2503(b), 2642(c). If the gift is in trust and would otherwise be subject to generation-skipping tax, the trust must provide that, during the life of the beneficiary, distributions of principal or income can be made only to the beneficiary, and if the trust does not terminate before the beneficiary's death, the trust assets will be included in the beneficiary's estate.

[4] IRC § 2513.

[5] Reg. § 25.2503-3(b).

[6] Reg. § 25.2503-3.

Not all gifts to trusts fail to qualify for the present interest exclusion. Congress recognized that family members often wish to make gifts to children, but are reluctant to make outright gifts to a minor. A special section in the Internal Revenue Code permits a donor to claim a present interest exclusion for a gift in trust to a minor if the trust satisfies specific statutory requirements.[7] This type of trust, called a *Section 2503(c) trust*, or *minor's trust*, is described below.[8] Another type of trust that permits a donor to make a present interest gift in trust is a *Crummey trust*, named after the case in which the availability of the exclusion was first established.[9] Crummey trusts are also described below.[10]

While a gift of a future interest in property will not qualify for the annual exclusion, a gift of a fractional interest in property can qualify if the recipient receives a current right to possess the property. For example, a gift of a 50 percent interest in real property as a tenant-in-common could qualify for the annual exclusion if each of the cotenants has an unrestricted right to the use, enjoyment, and possession of the property.

The limit of $16,000 per donee applies year by year, and if an individual does not make any gifts in one year, that year's exclusion does not carry over to the following year. On occasion, a taxpayer has attempted to avoid this limitation by agreeing with another taxpayer to make reciprocal gifts. Such attempts are unlikely to be successful as the tax law generally looks to the substance rather than the form of a transaction.[11]

EXAMPLE 8-8

Sasha gives $16,000 to each of her two children and each of the two children of her sister Rosa. In the same year, Rosa gives $16,000 to each of her children and each of Sasha's children. Sasha and Rosa will be treated for tax purposes as if each had given $32,000 to her own children.

Another technique that taxpayers have used on occasion in the attempt to expand the limitations of the annual exclusion is to make a loan to a family member, then to forgive the loan in $16,000 annual increments. If the lender intends from the beginning to forgive the loan, then the IRS may recharacterize the loan as a gift of the entire loan principal in the first year, thus permitting the donor to shelter only $16,000 of the principal from gift tax.[12]

---

[7] IRC § 2503(c).

[8] *See* § 8.06[D][2] *infra.*

[9] Crummey v. Comm'r, 397 F.2d 82 (9th Cir. 1968).

[10] *See* § 8.06[D][3] *infra.*

[11] *See* Sather v. Comm'r, 251 F.3d 1168 (8th Cir. 2001); and Furst v. Comm'r, 21 T.C.M. 1169 (1962).

[12] Rev. Rul. 77-299, 1977-2 C.B. 343.

[C] Exclusion for Payment of Tuition or Medical Expenses

In addition to the annual exclusion for $16,000 in gifts per donee, a donor can pay an unlimited amount of medical or tuition expenses for the benefit of another, free of both gift tax and generation-skipping tax.[13] This special exclusion can serve as a particularly attractive estate planning tool for grandparents because:

- The amount of expenses is not limited: They could pay full primary, secondary, college, and graduate or professional school tuition, plus any medical expenses, for each of their grandchildren.

- Payments of tuition and medical expenses are free of generation-skipping tax as well as gift tax, so that there is no need to use generation-skipping tax exemption in order to benefit grandchildren.

- The donor controls the use of the gift by making the payment directly to the educational institution or medical provider.

- Payment of tuition provides an immediate benefit to the beneficiary, which is likely to be appreciated and acknowledged.

In order to qualify for this exception, the payments must be made directly to the educational institution or health care provider.[14] The exception will not apply if a donor transfers cash to a beneficiary, even if the beneficiary promptly uses the funds to pay qualifying expenses. Furthermore, only tuition expenses at an organization that maintains a regular faculty and student body qualify for the exception; expenses for room and board do not qualify.[15] With respect to medical expenses, health insurance premiums qualify for the exception, in addition to other payments made directly to a provider that are not reimbursed by insurance.[16]

[D] Future Appreciation of Property Removed from the Estate

Property that has been transferred by gift during the lifetime of the donor is not included in the taxable estate of the donor. The transfer will be a taxable gift, and the gift may result in a gift tax liability, but the amount of the tax will be calculated based on the value of the property at the time of the gift.[17] Thus, making lifetime gifts of property that is likely to appreciate significantly can reduce the amount of transfer tax that would otherwise be due if held until death.

---

[13] IRC § 2503.
[14] IRC § 2503(e)(2).
[15] Reg. § 25.2503-6(a)(2).
[16] Reg. § 25.2503-6(b)(3).
[17] IRC § 2512.

EXAMPLE 8-9

Deborah owned a parcel of undeveloped land. At a time when the land was valued at $1,000,000, she gave the property to a trust for her daughter Laura. Shortly after Deborah's death, the trust sold the land to a developer for $8,000,000, for development as a convention center and hotel. The trust assets were not included in Deborah's estate, and thus were not subject to estate tax. Deborah's taxable estate exceeded $12,060,000, and was subject to federal estate tax. If Deborah had retained the property until her death, the property would have been included in her estate at a value of $8,000,000. Assuming a 40 percent estate tax rate, the estate would have paid approximately $3,200,000 in estate tax, leaving $4,800,000 for Laura.

In assessing the tax consequences of a gift, it is important to take into account the income tax rules as well as the gift and estate tax rules. In the above example, Deborah's gift permitted all of the appreciation of the property that occurred after the gift to escape transfer tax. However, the appreciation will not escape income tax. The income tax basis of property transferred by gift generally is the same in the hands of the recipient as it was in the hands of the donor.[18] If Deborah's basis in the property had been $1,000,000 at the time of the gift, then the trust's basis in the property would also have been $1,000,000. When the trust sold the property, the gain of $7,000,000 would be subject to a capital gains tax of $1,400,000.[19] The amount remaining in the trust for Laura would be $6,600,000. The lifetime gift of the property in this case still saves a substantial amount of tax, but the benefit is less than it might appear if the income tax consequences of a sale were not taken into account.

[E] Gift Tax Is Tax Exclusive

One of the most significant differences between the estate tax and the gift tax is that the cash used to pay the estate tax is itself subject to estate tax, whereas the cash used to pay gift tax is not subject to gift tax. In other words, the estate tax is tax inclusive and the gift tax is tax exclusive. As a result, the gift tax rate is effectively lower than the estate tax rate, despite the fact that a single rate schedule applies for both taxes.

EXAMPLE 8-10

Ron makes a gift of $1,000,000 to his son Harry after he has used all of his lifetime gift tax exemption. Assuming a 40 percent tax rate, he would owe a gift tax of $400,000 and the cost of giving Harry $1,000,000 would be

---

[18] IRC § 1015.

[19] This figure assumes a 20 percent capital gains tax rate.

$1,400,000. If Ron had instead retained the cash used to make the gift and the cash used to pay the tax until his death and bequeathed all of the cash to Harry by will, his estate would have increased by $1,400,000. Assuming a 40 percent tax rate the estate tax would be approximately $560,000, and Harry would have received $840,000. By making a lifetime gift rather than a testamentary gift, Ron passed an additional $160,000 to Harry instead of to the government.

It should be noted that this tax advantage does not apply to gifts made within three years of the donor's death.[20] If the donor does not survive for three years after the gift, the gift tax paid will be included in his estate, and the tax exclusive feature of the gift tax will be lost.

[F] Tax Disadvantages of Making Gifts

When calculating the economic benefits of making a gift, it is important to take into account two additional factors:

1. If the gift is in excess of the donor's unified credit exemption amount, then the donor will be obligated to pay gift tax, and will lose the use of that cash; and

2. The income tax basis of the transferred property in the hands of the recipient generally will be the same as the donor's basis.

In some circumstances, one of these factors can have a significant impact on the economic benefits that a family may realize from a lifetime gift. For example, when analyzing the effects of making a gift in excess of the unified credit exemption amount, it is important to take into account that if the donor had not made the gift, he could have invested the cash used to pay the gift tax until his death. The comparative tax advantage of the lifetime gift and the testamentary gift will depend in part on the rate of return available to the donor on the cash that would otherwise be used to pay gift tax and on the rate of return available to the donee on the amount transferred as a gift. In preparing projections comparing the result of a lifetime gift to a testamentary gift, it is important to take this factor into account.

The rules governing the income tax basis of property transferred by gift should also be taken into account in preparing projections comparing a lifetime gift to a testamentary gift. Property that is given away during life retains the donor's tax basis, while property given at death has a tax basis equal to the property's fair market value at death. As a result, when property is given during life, all of the appreciation in excess of the donor's basis will be subject to income tax when the donee sells the property. When property is given at death, only the appreciation that occurred after the death of the donor will be subject to income tax when the donee sells the property. If the family's intention is to retain the transferred property for the indefinite future, as might be the case for a family farm, then the potential income tax

---

[20] IRC § 2035(b).

on the sale of the property may not be an important consideration. If, however, it is likely that the family will sell the property, then the potential income tax on the sale should be considered.

§8.04 VALUATION OF GIFTS

[A] General Rule

A gift is valued for gift tax purposes at the time that the gift becomes complete.[1] The value of the gift is its *fair market value,* which is the price at which the property would change hands between a willing buyer and a willing seller, neither being under any compulsion to buy or sell, and both having reasonable knowledge of the relevant facts.[2] The regulations specify that the deemed sale is in the market in which the property is most commonly sold to the public; thus, a used car would be valued at the price that a used car dealer would sell to the public, not at the price that a used car dealer would buy from an individual.[3]

The deemed sale is between a hypothetical buyer and a hypothetical seller, so that family relationships between the actual donor and the actual recipient are not taken into account.[4] This aspect of the rule becomes especially important when the gift in question is a minority interest in a family controlled entity or a partial interest in property owned by family members, because it permits the application of a *minority discount* in this situation.[5]

Special statutory valuation rules apply to some gifts, such as gifts of partial interests in property to family members, gifts of certain types of interests in family businesses, and gifts of property subject to restrictions on the use of the property. These rules, known as Chapter 14, are contained in Sections 2701 to 2704 of the Code. The effect of these rules is generally to establish a higher valuation for certain gifts to family members than would otherwise be applicable under the willing buyer-willing seller standard. An estate planner advising a client who intends to make gifts of this type should review both the statutory and regulatory provisions of Chapter 14 before the gifts are made.[6]

[B] Securities

The gift tax regulations provide detailed guidance with respect to the valuation of securities. The general rule is that if there is a ready market for the securities, the mean between the high and low selling prices on the date of the gift is the value of

---

[1] §8.04 IRC § 2512(a).

[2] Reg. § 25.2512-1.

[3] *Id.*

[4] *See* Rev. Rul. 93-12, 1993 C.B. 202.

[5] Minority discounts are discussed in Chapter 11.

[6] The rules of Chapter 14 are discussed in § § 8.07[C], 11.03[D][8], 11.06[C][2], 11.05[H] *infra.*

the security.[7] Securities of privately held companies for which there is no market are more difficult to value, and often an appraisal is necessary. In addition, special valuation rules for gifts of family business interests may apply.[8]

[C] Real Estate

The gift tax regulations do not contain special rules for valuing real estate, except to specify that the local property tax assessment is not the gift tax value unless the assessed value is the fair market value.[9] The fair market value of real property generally is its highest and best use, not its actual use. In most circumstances an individual making a gift of real estate should obtain an appraisal for gift tax reporting purposes.

[D] Valuation Discounts

The process of valuing many types of property will include the application of some kind of discount to reflect the special characteristics of the property. Among the discounts that are most commonly applied are:

1. A minority or fractional interest discount;
2. A lack of marketability discount; and
3. A blockage discount.

The applicability of any of these discounts, and the amount of the discount when applicable, depends on the unique features of the property being valued.

The *minority discount* and the *fractional interest discount* are similar in that both are applied when the donor does not own 100 percent of the property being valued. When the property involved is real estate, the term fractional interest discount is more commonly used; when the property involved is a business interest, the term minority discount is generally applied. A minority or fractional interest discount reflects the fact that the owner of a minority interest in a business or of a partial interest in real estate does not have full control over the property and cannot deal with it by herself. The owner of a partial interest in real estate generally cannot unilaterally choose tenants and set rents. The owner of a minority interest in a corporation cannot unilaterally elect directors or determine the company's dividend policy. As a consequence, courts generally permit a discount to account for such lack of control, and the IRS has recognized that such discounts may be appropriate.[10] For example, if two individuals own a piece of real estate as tenants-in-common and one of them makes a gift of her 50 percent interest in the property, the value of the gift probably would be reduced by a fractional interest discount such that it would be less than 50 percent of the value of undivided property. Similarly, a gift of 30 percent of

---

[7] Reg. § 25.2512(b).

[8] The valuation of closely held business interests is discussed in more detail in Chapter 11.

[9] Reg. § 25.2512-1.

[10] Minority interest discounts for closely held business interests are discussed in Chapter 11.

the stock in a closely held business would probably be reduced by a minority interest discount such that the value of the gift would be less than 30 percent of the value of the whole company.

The lack of marketability discount reflects the fact that property that does not have a readily available public market is more difficult to sell than publicly traded property. This discount is used in valuing closely held business interests, and is discussed in Chapter 11.

A *blockage discount* may be appropriate when the property being valued has a thin market, and the offer of all of the property at one time would depress the price. A blockage discount may be applied to publicly traded stock, or to other property, such as works of art.[11]

EXAMPLE *8-11*

A famous artist gave her niece a gift of 100 of her paintings. If all 100 paintings were to be put on the market at once, the prices for her art would fall. In valuing the gift, it would be appropriate to factor in a discount for blockage.

[E] Partial Interests

A partial interest in property, such as an annuity, a term of years, or a remainder interest, is valued by taking into account the following factors:[12]

- The value of the underlying property;
- An assumed interest rate that reflects the time value of money; and
- A time factor, which can be either a term of years or a mortality factor (when the extent of the gift is measured by an individual's life).

For example, the value of an annuity that provides annual payments for the lifetime of an individual will depend on the amount of the annual payment, the interest rate at the time the value is calculated, and the expected lifetime of the individual.

Section 7520 of the Code requires that in valuing partial interests, taxpayers use interest rates set monthly by the IRS and standard actuarial tables. The IRS has developed the factors necessary to value an annuity, a remainder interest, and a term interest based on these actuarial tables for a wide range of interest rates and has published them in two volumes, *Book Aleph* and *Book Bet* of *Pub. 1457, Actuarial Values*.[13] To use these tables, the first step for valuing any type of partial interest is to determine the relevant interest rate. The IRS publishes a revenue ruling each month,

---

[11] Reg. § 25.2512-2(e); Estate of O'Keefe v. Comm'r, T.C.M. 1992-210.

[12] IRC § 7520.

[13] These tables can also be found in the regulations under IRC § 2031.

which includes the applicable federal rate for valuing partial interests, known as the Section 7520 rate. The next step is to determine which of the tables in *Pub. 1457* is relevant.

EXAMPLE 8-12

A transfers property worth $100,000 to a trust that provides that the property is to be held for A's benefit for life, after which it is to pass to A's friend (and unrelated person) B. A is age 65 and the Section 7520 rate is 3.4 percent. The value of the remainder interest given to B can be determined by consulting Table S, contained in *Pub. 1457, Book Aleph*. Table S contains the remainder factors for a remainder interest after a single life for different interest rates. The page of Table S for an interest rate of 3.4 percent is headed Table S(3.4). The first column on this page lists ages, and the last column lists remainder factors. The remainder factor opposite age 65 is .57637. The value of the remainder interest is determined by multiplying the value of the property ($100,000) by the appropriate remainder factor. In this case, the value of the remainder is $57,637.

There are a number of commercial software products now available that will calculate values for partial interests. Most estate planners now use these products rather than IRS *Publication 1457*.

Certain partial interests in property, such as gifts in trust to a family member, are subject to special valuation rules under IRC Section 2702. One of the effects of Section 2702 is to prohibit the use of the actuarial tables to value certain partial interests unless specific requirements are met.

Taxpayers are not allowed to use the Section 7520 valuation tables in certain circumstances. If the partial interest to be valued is restricted in some manner such that using the tables would not be economically appropriate, then the tables cannot be used.[14] In addition, if the value of an interest depends on the life expectancy of an individual, then the tables cannot be used if the individual is terminally ill. For this purpose, an individual is considered to be terminally ill if there is at least a 50 percent probability that the individual will die within a year.[15]

§8.05 INCOME TAX CONSIDERATIONS

[A] No Income Tax Deduction for Donor

It is a common misperception that gifts to family members are deductible for income tax purposes. Making a gift reduces the assets of the donor, but the donor is not entitled to claim the gift as an income tax deduction unless the gift qualifies for the charitable deduction.

---

[14] Reg. § 25.7520-3(b)(2).
[15] Reg. § 25.7520-3(b)(3).

[B] No Income Tax to Recipient

The receipt of a lifetime gift is not treated as income to the recipient for income tax purposes.[1] This rule also applies to the receipt of a testamentary gift. Thus, property transferred by either gift or inheritance is received free of tax.

[C] Carryover Basis for Recipient

Generally, the tax basis of property received by gift is the same in the hands of the recipient as it was in the hands of the donor.[2] If the property had appreciated before the gift was made, and the recipient sells the property, the gain will be taxed to the recipient. This rule is different from the rule that determines the basis of property transferred at death. In the case of a testamentary transfer, the basis of the property transferred in the hands of the recipient is equal to the property's fair market value on the date of death (i.e., with a "stepped-up basis").[3]

EXAMPLE *8-13*

David gives his daughter Aliza stock with a fair market value of $10,000. David's tax basis in the stock was $1,000. Aliza's basis in the stock is also $1,000, and if she sells the stock immediately for $10,000, she will recognize a taxable gain of $9,000. If David had passed the stock to Aliza by will, on the same date, then Aliza's basis in the stock would have been $10,000. If she sold the stock immediately, she would not report any taxable gain.

In the case of a gift of property that has a basis higher than its fair market value on the date of the gift, a different rule applies. In such case, the basis of the property in the hands of the recipient can be finally determined only when the recipient disposes of the property. For purposes of determining gain, the recipient's basis will be equal to the donor's basis.[4] For purposes of determining loss, the recipient's basis will be equal to the fair market value as of the date of the gift.[5] For the situation in which the sale price is lower than the donor's basis, but higher than the property's fair market value at the time of the gift, neither gain nor loss is recognized on the sale by the donee.[6]

---

[1] **§8.05** IRC § 102.

[2] IRC § 1015.

[3] IRC § 1014. For decedents dying in 2010, there was a choice to be subject to the estate tax with a basis step-up or to have a limited basis step-up but not be subject to the estate tax. These provisions are set out in the 2001 Act and the 2010 Act and are discussed in more detail in Chapter 5.

[4] IRC § 1015(a); Reg. § 1.1015-1(a).

[5] *Id.*

[6] Reg. § 1.1015-1(a)(2).

EXAMPLE *8-14*

David gives his daughter Aliza stock with a fair market value of $10,000. David's basis in the stock is $15,000. If Aliza sells the stock for $20,000, her basis will be $15,000, and she will recognize a gain of $5,000. If Aliza subsequently sells the stock for $8,000, her basis will be $10,000, and she will recognize a loss of $2,000. If Aliza subsequently sells the stock for $13,000, no gain or loss will be recognized.

As a result of this rule, it is generally unwise to make a gift of property with a built-in loss. Instead, the donor should consider selling the property, recognizing the loss, and giving the proceeds to the donee.

If a donor pays a gift tax on a gift of appreciated property, the donee's basis in the property is increased by the portion of the gift tax paid that is attributable to the appreciation in the property.[7] To calculate the amount of the increase, the gift tax paid is multiplied by a fraction, the numerator of which is the appreciation in the property, and the denominator of which is the fair market value of the gift.

EXAMPLE *8-15*

David gives his daughter Aliza property with a fair market value of $100 and a basis of $50. He pays a gift tax of $40. Aliza's basis in the property is equal to David's basis ($50), increased by the gift tax he paid ($40) multiplied by a fraction the numerator of which is the appreciation in the property ($50) and the denominator of which is the fair market value of the property ($100). Aliza's basis is $50 plus $20, or $70.

In calculating a donee's holding period of property that he has received by gift for purposes of determining whether the property is short-term or long-term capital gain or loss property, the donor's holding period is added to the donee's holding period.[8]

[D] Special Rules

[1] Gifts of Encumbered Property

A gift of property that is subject to debt has different consequences than a gift of unencumbered property for both gift and income tax purposes. Generally, for gift tax purposes, the amount of the debt to which the property is subject is subtracted from the value of the property in determining the amount of the gift because the person

---

[7] IRC § 1015(d).
[8] IRC § 1223(2).

receiving the gift will be obligated to repay the debt.[9] For example, a gift of a building worth $100,000 subject to a mortgage of $80,000 will not confer an economic benefit of $100,000 on the donee, because the donee must use $80,000 of her own money to pay off the debt. For gift tax purposes the gift is of only $20,000.

For income tax purposes, a transfer of encumbered property is generally treated as if the donor had sold the property for the amount of the debt.[10] The reason for this rule is that the donor initially received the cash from the loan, and has now been relieved of the obligation to repay the loan. If the donor's basis in the property is lower than the amount of the debt, the donor will recognize taxable gain in the amount of the difference. Since most gifts do not have any income tax consequences, it is easy to overlook this rule, which may produce unintended results.

EXAMPLE *8-16*

David gives his son Mark a commercial building with a fair market value of $100,000. David's basis in the property is $50,000, and the building is subject to debt of $80,000. For gift tax purposes, the value of the gift is the fair market value of $100,000 less the debt of $80,000, or $20,000. For income tax purposes, David will be treated as if he had sold the building for $80,000, the amount of the debt that he will not be obligated to repay. David will recognize taxable gain on the transaction in the amount of $30,000, which is equal to the excess of the debt of $80,000 over his basis in the property of $50,000.

[2] Income Tax Consequences of the Grantor Trust Rules

A donor who has made a transfer in trust that qualifies as a completed gift for both gift and estate tax purposes may still be subject to income tax on the income of the property if she has retained certain powers. The income tax rules that have this effect are known as the grantor trust rules.[11] The grantor trust rules can be a window of opportunity for an estate planner. A trust that has been structured deliberately as a grantor trust used to be referred to often as an *intentionally defective grantor trust,* but such trusts are now so commonly utilized they may also simply be called *grantor trusts.* The primary opportunity that is presented by the grantor trust rules is the opportunity for a donor to transfer additional value to the donee, free of transfer tax, by paying the income tax on income that would otherwise be a liability of the donee of the property.

---

[9] *See, e.g.,* Laughinghouse v. Comm'r, 80 T.C. 425 (1983).

[10] *See* Levine v. Comm'r, 634 F.2d 12 (2d Cir. 1980).

[11] IRC §§ 671-679. The income taxation of trusts, including grantor trusts, is discussed in Chapter 4.

EXAMPLE *8-17*

Leon contributed $100,000 to a grantor trust of which his daughter Kate is the beneficiary. The contribution to the trust is a completed gift for gift and estate tax purposes, and the property will not be included in Leon's estate when he dies. In 2010, the trust earned $10,000, and distributed the income to Kate. Because the trust is a grantor trust, Leon is liable for the tax on the income, and pays $3,000 in income tax. Kate receives $10,000 in cash and is not subject to income tax on the receipt. If the trust had not been a grantor trust, Kate would have received $10,000 and paid $3,000 in tax, leaving her with $7,000 in after-tax proceeds. The effect of the grantor trust provisions is to permit Leon to make a $3,000 gift to Kate without transfer tax.

The opportunity to make an additional tax-free gift to the beneficiary of a trust is not the only opportunity offered by a grantor trust. Estate planners also deliberately create grantor trusts because a grantor trust is permitted to hold S corporation stock,[12] and because a sale or exchange between a grantor trust and the grantor is not treated as a taxable exchange.[13]

The grantor trust rules are detailed and complex. The following is a general summary of the circumstances that cause the income of a trust to be taxed to the grantor:[14]

- The grantor has retained a reversionary interest in the trust that exceeds 5 percent of the trust property;
- The grantor or a nonadverse party has the power to control the beneficial enjoyment of principal or income (subject to several important exceptions);
- The grantor or a nonadverse party has the power to deal with the trust for less than adequate and full consideration or to borrow from the trust without adequate interest or security;
- The grantor has borrowed corpus or income from the trust and has not repaid it before the end of the tax year;
- Any person has the power in a nonfiduciary capacity to vote the stock of a corporation in which the grantor and the trust hold a significant voting interest, or to control the investment of the trust in a corporation in which the grantor holds a significant voting interest, or to reacquire the trust corpus by substituting other property of an equivalent value;
- The grantor or a nonadverse party has the power to revest title to the property in the grantor;
- The income of the trust may be distributed, without the consent of an adverse party, to the grantor or the grantor's spouse, or held or accumulated for later

---

[12] Interests in closely held businesses are discussed in more detail in Chapter 11.

[13] Rev. Rul. 85-13, 1985-1 C.B. 184.

[14] Grantor trusts are discussed in greater detail in Chapter 4.

distribution to the grantor or the grantor's spouse, or used to pay premiums on policies of insurance on the life of the grantor or the grantor's spouse.

In structuring an intentionally defective grantor trust it is critical to analyze all of the tax consequences of the structure. Some of the powers that make a trust a grantor trust also would cause the trust property to be included in the estate of the grantor under the string provisions discussed below.[15] Since it is unlikely that it would be desirable to have property included in the grantor's estate under the string provisions, caution is necessary.

§8.06 GIFTS IN TRUST

[A] Overview

There are many situations in which a donor wishes to make a gift, but is reluctant to transfer the property outright to the donee. An outright gift may be undesirable because the recipient is a minor and so cannot manage or transfer the property, or because the donor fears that the recipient may spend the gift inappropriately, or because the donor wishes to protect the gift from the recipient's potential creditors, including a divorcing spouse, or because the donor feels that the recipient will not invest the property wisely. In some situations, a donor may wish to reduce her taxable estate by making gifts to children or grandchildren without deciding exactly how the gift will be divided among the members of the younger generations. In these situations, a gift in trust may be appropriate.

Trusts are extremely flexible vehicles, and may be drafted to include many different types of interests and limitations, as discussed more fully in Chapter 4. The type of trust that is appropriate will depend on the characteristics of the beneficiaries and the purposes of the donor. In drafting a trust, the estate planner should keep two separate considerations in mind:

1. The dispositive provisions of the trust should be designed to achieve the donor's personal goals, which may include:

   - Giving the trustee sufficient flexibility to make distributions to the beneficiaries most in need;
   - Giving the beneficiaries a limited withdrawal power; or
   - Ensuring that the trust assets are not subject to claims by creditors of the beneficiaries.

2. The trust should be structured to accomplish the donor's tax goals, which may include:

   - Ensuring that a transfer to the trust is a completed gift, such that the trust property will not be included in the donor's estate;

---

[15] The string provisions are discussed in §8.06[C].

- Ensuring that the donor does not retain any powers that would cause the trust property to be included in her estate under the "string provisions" of the Code;
- Qualifying a gift to the trust for the $16,000 present interest annual exclusion for gift tax, and possibly generation-skipping transfer tax purposes;
- Ensuring the income from the property is taxed to the desired party for income tax purposes (i.e., either to the beneficiary or to the grantor by establishing a grantor trust); and
- Avoiding the application of the generation-skipping tax.

The tax effects of a trust require close analysis because there are four separate taxes to consider: (1) gift tax, (2) estate tax, (3) income tax, and (4) generation-skipping tax. A provision that produces no adverse effects under three of the taxes may have significant negative effects under the fourth tax. For example, a transfer to a trust of which the donor is not a trustee may be a completed gift that removes the property from the estate of the donor, but may not qualify for the present interest exclusion for gift tax purposes, or may be subject to generation-skipping tax. In some instances, the apparent inconsistencies between the income tax and the gift and estate tax can be used to achieve beneficial results. For example, a planner can draft a trust such that a gift to the trust is removed from the donor's estate, but the donor will pay the income tax on the trust income (a grantor trust). The effect of using this type of trust is to permit the donor to transfer additional value to the trust beneficiary that is not subject to transfer tax.

[B] Completed Gifts to Trust

A gift in trust is a completed gift if the donor has parted with dominion and control of the transferred property.[1] In practical terms, this means that the trust should be drafted such that:

- The donor cannot revoke the trust or reacquire the beneficial interest in the trust property;
- The donor cannot amend the trust to change the beneficial interests of the beneficiaries;
- The donor cannot add beneficiaries;
- The donor cannot decide how discretionary distributions among beneficiaries are to be made, unless the power to distribute is limited by an ascertainable standard.[2]

Even if a transfer is a completed gift subject to gift tax when made, some or all of the property may be included in the donor's taxable estate at death under the "string provisions" of the Code if the donor retained certain powers.[3]

---

[1] § 8.06 Reg. § 25.2511-2(b).

[2] *See* Reg. § 25.2511-2.

[3] IRC § § 2035–2038.

[C] Powers That Have Estate Tax Consequences: The String Provisions

All of the gift tax advantages of making a gift can be lost if the donor retains certain powers over the transferred property or an interest in the property as a result of the *string provisions* contained in IRC Sections 2035 to 2038. Generally, the string provisions will have the effect of including transferred property in the taxable estate of a donor if the donor retains any of the following powers or rights:[4]

- The right to possess or enjoy the property;
- The right to the income from the property;
- The right to designate who will possess or enjoy the property or the income from the property;
- The right to vote shares of stock in a controlled corporation;
- The right to a reversion that exceeds 5 percent of the value of the property; or
- The right to alter, amend, revoke, or terminate the interest of the donee in the property.

Furthermore, even if a donor who retained one of these powers relinquishes the power, the property that was subject to the power will still be included in the donor's taxable estate if he dies within three years of the relinquishment.[5]

It is rare that it would be to the advantage of a donor to deliberately make a gift that would be included in his estate under the string provisions. As a consequence, these provisions often function as a trap for the unwary, and should be kept in mind in planning any family transfers. Special caution is required if a donor makes a gift to a trust and serves as trustee of the trust, because many trustee powers will cause trust property to be included in an estate of a trustee who is a donor of the trust.

EXAMPLE *8-18*

Ann transfers $100,000 to a trust for her son Ravi. Ann and her attorney are cotrustees of the trust. The trustees have discretion to distribute income and principal to Ravi during his lifetime, and at death any remaining trust property will be paid to his estate. The trustees do not distribute trust income, and at Ann's death the trust holds $800,000. The trust property will be included in Ann's taxable estate under Section 2038 because she had the power, with the other trustee, to affect the time and manner of Ravi's enjoyment of the trust property.[6]

---

[4] *Id.* The string provisions are discussed in Chapter 5.
[5] IRC § 2035.
[6] Reg. § 20.2038-1(a)(3).

[D] Gifts in Trust That Qualify for the Present Interest Exclusion

[1] Present Interest Exclusion

The present interest exclusion, which permits an individual to make annual $16,000 gifts to an unlimited number of donees, offers one of the most valuable estate planning opportunities. Outright gifts generally qualify for the present interest exclusion. Often, however, an individual would prefer to make gifts in trust rather than outright. Gifts to most types of trusts do not qualify for the present interest exclusion because generally the beneficiary of a trust does not have the right to possess or dispose of trust assets. (In fact, the purpose of making gifts in trust is often to ensure that the beneficiary does not have the right to possess or dispose of the gift.) A *Crummey trust* and a *Section 2503(c) trust* are two types of trust that permit a donor to claim a present interest exclusion for gifts to trust.[7]

[2] Section 2503(c) Trusts for Minors

A Section 2503(c) trust for minors is a special type of trust authorized by the Internal Revenue Code for the purpose of making annual exclusion gifts to a minor. The basic requirements that a trust must meet to qualify for the present interest exclusion under IRC Section 2503(c) are as follows:[8]

- The trustee must be free to distribute all of the principal and the income of the trust to or for the benefit of the beneficiary;
- The principal and any accumulated income must pass to the beneficiary at age 21; and
- If the beneficiary dies before reaching age 21, then the trust property must pass either as appointed by the beneficiary pursuant to a general power of appointment or to the beneficiary's estate.

[3] Crummey Trusts

[a] Requirements

The term *"Crummey trust"* derives from the name of the case in which a court permitted a donor to claim a present interest exclusion for a gift to a trust of this type.[9] Crummey trusts are frequently used as vehicles for making gifts to minors, and are discussed in that context in Chapter 3.

A gift to a Crummey trust qualifies for the present interest gift tax exclusion because the beneficiary of the trust has the right, which may be exercisable only for a

---

[7] Form 5 contains a sample Crummey trust and a sample 2503(c) trust.

[8] *See* § 7.04[C]for further details.

[9] Crummey v. Comm'r, 397 F.2d 82 (9th Cir. 1968).

limited period of time after the trust receives the gift, to withdraw the gift from the trust. The beneficiary's right to take possession of the gift is sufficient to qualify the gift for the present interest exclusion, even if the trust provides that if the beneficiary fails to exercise this withdrawal right, then the right will lapse and the trust will continue.

The IRS takes the position that in order to qualify a gift to a Crummey trust for the present interest exclusion, the beneficiary must be notified of a gift to the trust and of his right to withdraw, and must be given a reasonable period of time to exercise the right.[10] There is no bright line rule as to what constitutes a reasonable period of time to withdraw. The IRS has ruled on occasion that 30 days is enough, and that three days is not enough.[11] Most planners allow at least 30 days as a withdrawal period. There is no requirement that notification be in writing, but evidence of written notice will be extremely useful if the IRS challenges the applicability of the present interest exclusion. The beneficiary should not waive the right to withdraw or the right to receive notice in advance, or the IRS may assert that the present interest exclusion is not applicable.[12]

As long as a Crummey trust contains an appropriate withdrawal power for the beneficiary, a gift to the trust can qualify for the present interest exclusion, and the remaining trust terms may be as the donor desires. There is no requirement that a Crummey trust distribute to beneficiaries at any particular age.

[b] Income Tax Consequences of Withdrawal Rights from Crummey Trusts

If a Crummey trust permits a beneficiary to withdraw all gifts to the trust and the withdrawal right does not lapse, then the beneficiary will be treated as the owner of the trust assets for income tax purposes, and the beneficiary will report the income of the trust on her own tax return.[13] The result is less clear if the withdrawal right has lapsed. The Internal Revenue Service has taken the position in private letter rulings that a beneficiary who permits a withdrawal right to lapse is treated as if she had transferred the property to the trust as a grantor.[14] The grantor trust rules then apply to determine whether any powers held by the beneficiary over the property in the trust require that the trust income be taxed to the beneficiary as grantor. Under this theory, when a Crummey trust has only one beneficiary and the beneficiary has the right to withdraw all property transferred to the trust, then the beneficiary is taxable on all of the trust income after the withdrawal rights have lapsed.[15] In many instances this approach is ultimately favorable to the trust beneficiary because the alternative would be to tax undistributed income to the trust, and the income tax rates for trusts are far more compressed than the income tax rates for individuals. Some commenta-

---

[10] Rev. Rul. 81-7, 1981-1 C.B. 474.

[11] See Ltr. Rul. 9030005; Rev. Rul. 81-7, 1981-1 C.B. 474.

[12] Ltr. Rul. 9532001.

[13] IRC § 678(a)(1); Rev. Rul. 81-6, 1981-1 C.B. 385.

[14] See, e.g., Ltr. Ruls. 9504024, 9450014.

[15] Id.

tors disagree with the approach of the Internal Revenue Service on this issue, however, and take the position that a beneficiary should not be treated as the grantor of property that was subject to a withdrawal right that lapsed.[16] The question becomes more complex if the Crummey trust has multiple beneficiaries, and careful analysis of the income tax results of lapsed withdrawal rights is necessary in such trusts.

[c] Crummey Trusts for Multiple Beneficiaries

A Crummey trust need not be a trust for a single beneficiary; it can be a trust for multiple beneficiaries. Each of the beneficiaries can be given the right to withdraw a portion of any transfer of property into the trust, thereby permitting the donor to claim multiple present interest exclusions from the gift tax.

EXAMPLE 8-19

Parents create a trust of which all four of their children and the children's spouses are discretionary income and principal beneficiaries. Each of the beneficiaries has the right to withdraw his or her proportionate share of any property transferred to the trust. Parents transfer $240,000 to the trust. Each parent can claim eight present interest exclusions from the gift tax, and none of the gift will be subject to gift tax.

In the effort to benefit from the largest possible number of annual exclusions, some taxpayers have designed trusts that grant withdrawal powers not only to the primary beneficiaries of a trust, but also to contingent beneficiaries (e.g., beneficiaries who will receive trust assets only if their parents predecease them). The Internal Revenue Service took the litigating position that a withdrawal right held by a contingent beneficiary of a trust does not qualify for a present interest exclusion.[17] In the leading case in this area, *Cristofani v. Commissioner*,[18] a donor transferred assets to a trust of which his children were the income beneficiaries and his grandchildren were contingent beneficiaries. The trust provided that on the death of the donor the trust property would be distributed to the children. The donor's grandchildren would receive trust property only if the children did not survive the donor. Under the trust each child and each grandchild had a withdrawal right. The donor claimed a present interest exclusion for each child and each grandchild. The Internal Revenue Service argued that the donor could not claim a present interest exclusion for the withdrawal rights held by the grandchildren because they were only contingent beneficiaries of the trust. The court decided in favor of the donor, and permitted him

---

[16] For a discussion of this issue, *see* Lischer, Gifts for Minors, Tax Management, BNA Portfolio 846 at 58-60.

[17] 97 T.C. 74 (1991).

[18] *Id.*

to claim the present interest exclusions for the withdrawal rights held by the grandchildren.[19] The IRS did not appeal the *Cristofani* case. The IRS has announced, however, that it believes that the court's decision in the *Cristofani* case was too broad, and that it may challenge taxpayers who claim present interest exclusions for withdrawal rights held by contingent beneficiaries of a trust on the basis that such powers are illusory.[20]

[d] Additional Tax Issues with Crummey Trusts for Multiple Beneficiaries

While a Crummey trust for multiple beneficiaries can be extremely useful, it is important to address two additional tax issues that may be raised by such a trust: (1) the gift tax effects of the trust on the beneficiaries of the trust and (2) the application of the generation-skipping tax to such trusts.

The first issue relates to potential gift tax consequences for the beneficiaries (as opposed to the donor) of a Crummey trust for multiple beneficiaries. This issue arises when a beneficiary's withdrawal power lapses. A power to withdraw property from a trust is a general power of appointment under IRC Section 2041. The general rule is that the lapse of a general power of appointment constitutes a gift from the former holder of the lapsed power to the other beneficiaries of the trust that is potentially subject to gift tax.[21] This gift does not qualify for the gift tax present interest exclusion because the other beneficiaries cannot take immediate possession of the trust property. Fortunately, there is an exception to the general rule that the lapse of a general power of appointment constitutes a gift. This exception provides that a taxable gift results from the lapse of a general power of appointment only to the extent that the property subject to the power exceeds the greater of $5,000 or 5 percent of the property held in the trust (this is often referred to as the *five or five exception*).[22]

The simplest way to use the five or five exception to avoid a taxable gift when a Crummey power lapses is to limit each beneficiary's share of all gifts to the trust subject to the withdrawal power to the lesser of $5,000 or 5 percent of the trust corpus. If gifts to the trust are so limited, the beneficiary will never have the power to withdraw more than "five or five," and the lapse of the power will not result in a taxable gift by the beneficiary.[23] This approach, however, limits the donor's ability to fully use the annual gift tax exclusion for gifts to the trust, which, in 2022, is $16,000 per donee, or $32,000 if the donor's spouse elects to gift-split on the gift tax return.

---

[19] *Id.*

[20] AOD 1996-010.

[21] IRC § 2514.

[22] IRC § 2514(e).

[23] Form 4 provides an example of this type of limited withdrawal power.

EXAMPLE *8-20*

Emily creates a Crummey trust for her three children. The trust provides that when a gift is made to the trust, each beneficiary has the right to withdraw his or her proportional share of the gift. If the withdrawal right is not exercised, it will lapse 30 days after the beneficiary receives notice of the gift. Each year, Emily makes a gift of $16,000 to the trust, and the children allow their rights to withdraw to lapse. Each child had a right to withdraw $5,000. The lapse of that power is not a taxable gift to the other beneficiaries.

A second way to avoid making a taxable gift when a Crummey power lapses is to provide in the trust that the beneficiary may withdraw all of his or her share of any gift made to the trust, and that the withdrawal power lapses only to the extent of the greater of $5,000 or 5 percent of the corpus each year. A withdrawal power that lapses only to this extent is known as a *hanging Crummey power*.[24]

EXAMPLE *8-21*

Parents transfer $80,000 to a trust of which their four children are the beneficiaries. Each beneficiary has the power to withdraw all of his or her proportionate share of the gift. Each year the beneficiary's power to withdraw lapses to the extent of the greater of $5,000 or 5 percent of the trust corpus. When the gift is made, each beneficiary has the power to withdraw $20,000. During the first year, each beneficiary's power to withdraw lapses to the extent of the greater of $5,000 or 5 percent of the trust assets, in this case $5,000. At the beginning of the second year, each beneficiary has the power to withdraw $15,000. During the second year, each beneficiary's withdrawal power lapses to the extent of an additional $5,000, and at the beginning of the third year, each beneficiary has the power to withdraw $10,000. The withdrawal power will lapse to the extent of an additional $5,000 during the third year and the fourth year. At the end of the fourth year, the beneficiaries' power to withdraw will have lapsed completely, and no gifts will have resulted from the lapse.

A third way to prevent the lapse of a withdrawal power in excess of $5,000 or 5 percent of the trust is to provide that each of the beneficiaries retains either a general or limited testamentary power of appointment over the trust corpus subject to the lapsed withdrawal right to the extent that the withdrawal right exceeded $5,000 or 5 percent of the trust corpus. If the beneficiary retains such a testamentary power of appointment the lapse of the power will not be a completed gift, and therefore will not be subject to gift tax at the time of the lapse. The property over which the

---

[24] Form 4 provides an example of a hanging Crummey power.

beneficiary holds the power of appointment will, however, be included in the taxable estate of the beneficiary.[25]

The second set of issues raised by a Crummey trust that has multiple beneficiaries rather than a single beneficiary relates to the generation-skipping tax treatment of these trusts. First, a gift to a Crummey trust for multiple beneficiaries may qualify for present interest exclusions from the gift tax, but the gift will not qualify for the present interest exclusion from the generation-skipping tax.[26] Thus, a donor cannot claim present interest exclusions from the generation-skipping tax for a Crummey trust of which all his grandchildren are beneficiaries. If the donor does not assign enough of his generation-skipping exemption to the trust, it will be subject to generation-skipping tax.

The second generation-skipping tax complication raised by a Crummey trust for multiple beneficiaries is that after the withdrawal power has lapsed, it is the beneficiary and not the donor that is treated as the transferor of the property subject to the lapsed power to the extent that the lapse exceeded $5,000 or 5 percent of the trust property.[27] This rule makes a Crummey trust for multiple beneficiaries sometimes unsuitable for generation-skipping tax planning purposes if gifts to the trust are expected to exceed $5,000 or 5 percent of the trust corpus in a single year. However, this can also be used to the taxpayer's advantage by creating a cascading Crummey power.[28]

§8.07 SPECIAL GIFT-GIVING TECHNIQUES

[A] Valuation Discounts

Valuation discounts, such as the discount for a fractional or minority interest in property, can provide one of the simplest and most effective gift planning techniques.[1] A gift of property is valued according to the following basic principles:

- Each gift made by a donor is valued separately;
- The value of property is the value that a hypothetical buyer would pay to a hypothetical seller and does not depend on the actual identity of the donor and recipient; and
- A gift of a minority interest in property is generally worth less than the corresponding percentage of the whole property.

---

[25] Form 5 provides an example of a Crummey trust in which the beneficiary is given a general power of appointment.

[26] *See* IRC §2642(c). *See* Chapter 9 for a discussion of the generation-skipping tax and the annual exclusion as it applies to gifts in trust.

[27] *See* Reg. §26.2652-1(a)(5), Example 5.

[28] Cascading Crummey powers are discussed in Chapter 9.

[1] **§8.07** Valuation discounts are discussed at §8.04[D] *supra*, and in Chapter 11.

A donor can take advantage of these principles by dividing up property, such as the family business, and making gifts of minority interests at a discounted gift tax value.

EXAMPLE 8-22

Barbara owns 100 percent of the stock in the family business, which an appraiser has valued at $5,000,000. On January 1, she gives each of her five children 20 percent of the stock in the corporation. For gift tax purposes, each of the gifts is valued as a separate gift of a minority interest in the company. The appraiser determines that in valuing a 20 percent interest in the company, a hypothetical buyer would require a 25 percent discount to reflect the fact that the owner of 20 percent of the stock cannot control company management, payment of dividends, or sale or liquidation of the company. As a result, each of the gifts is valued for gift tax purposes at $800,000 ($4,000,000 for all of the gifts). If Barbara had died owning 100 percent of the stock and had left 20 percent of the stock to each child, the stock would have been valued for estate tax purposes at $5,000,000.[2]

The principles that (a) each gift is valued separately, and (b) the value reflects the price that a hypothetical buyer would pay apply even if an individual makes sequential gifts to the same family member. In the above example, Barbara might have been able to transfer 100 percent of the company at the same discounted gift tax value by making a series of five gifts of 20 percent of the stock to the same child.

Estate planning that incorporates the transfer of a minority interest is not limited to transfers of stock. Limited partnerships, discussed below, can be extremely useful in planning because limited partnership interests generally are treated as minority interests. Minority interest planning can also be used to dispose of real property. If a parent gives a 50 percent interest in real property to a child as a tenant-in-common, the valuation of the gift will take into account the fact that an unrelated buyer would hesitate to purchase that cotenancy for 50 percent of the value of the whole property. As a result, it is likely that the gift tax value of the gift would reflect a fractional interest discount.

While minority interest transfers can be highly effective as a means of reducing the gift tax value of property transferred to children, the IRS may challenge the taxpayer's valuation of the property if the transfer takes place solely for tax purposes and lacks economic substance. For example, in one well known case, a mother owned 51.41 percent of the stock in a family corporation.[3] After repeated urging by her tax advisor, she gave each of her two children a gift of 0.88 percent of the stock 18 days before her death. She remained as chairman of the board of directors until her death,

---

[2] *See* Rev. Rul. 93-12, 1993 C.B. 202.

[3] Estate of Murphy v. Comm'r, 60 T.C.M. 645 (1990).

at which point the remaining stock (49.65 percent) passed to two trusts for the children. The estate valued the lifetime gifts and the stock remaining in the estate as minority interests subject to a minority interest discount, and the IRS challenged the valuation. The court stated that a minority discount should not be applied when the explicit purposes and effect of fragmenting the control block of stock was solely to reduce federal tax, and rejected the use of any discount.[4]

[B] Family Limited Partnerships and Limited Liability Companies

[1] Use in Estate Planning

During the 1990s, the family limited partnership gained wide public attention as an estate planning tool. As more and more states enacted statutes authorizing the creation of limited liability companies, these entities became an alternative to the family limited partnership, and currently, estate planners prefer to use a limited liability company. Some of the differences between the two types of entity are outlined below, but generally the term limited partnership will be used here, since a limited liability company could be structured to resemble a limited partnership in most respects.

The appeal of family limited partnerships rests in part on the potential for reducing the transfer tax burden of passing property to children by placing it in a partnership and then claiming a minority discount for gifts of limited partnership interests.

EXAMPLE 8-23

Leon transfers several pieces of commercial real estate, interests in venture capital limited partnerships, and a portfolio of marketable securities with a total value of $990,000 to a Delaware limited partnership in exchange for a 1 percent general partnership interest and a 98 percent limited partnership interest. His daughter Kate transfers $10,000 in cash in exchange for a 1 percent limited partnership interest. Each year Leon gives Kate 5 percent of his limited partnership interest. In valuing the gifts of the limited partnership interest, the appraiser takes into account the provisions of the limited partnership agreement that prohibit a limited partner from withdrawing from the partnership before the end of the partnership term and vest control of the partnership in the general partner. The appraiser concludes that a minority discount of 25 percent should be applied to each gift of a limited partnership interest.[5]

---

[4] It may be useful to compare Estate of Frank v. Comm'r, 69 T.C.M. 2255 (1995), in which a minority discount was allowed for gifts of stock shortly before the decedent's death.

[5] If gifts of a limited partnership interest are intended to qualify for the $16,000 annual present interest exclusion, careful drafting is required. The Tax Court has held that restrictions on a partner's

Over the years, the IRS has challenged many estate and gift tax returns claiming valuation discounts for family limited partnership interests. The results vary, but a significant number of these challenges have been upheld in court. One factor the courts have continuously focused on is whether there was a genuine business purpose for the partnership. An estate planner should not assume that a valuation discount will be available for estate or gift tax purposes in the family context unless there is a demonstrable business purpose.

The usefulness of family limited partnerships in the estate planning context, however, extends beyond valuation planning. Family limited partnerships can serve numerous other wealth management functions, including protecting the partnership assets from the partners' creditors and centralizing the management of the family's investment assets. Creating a family limited partnership can simplify a gift program because a gift of a partnership interest transfers a "slice" of all of the partnership assets, and the donor is not required to choose specific assets to give to different donees. Many families find that a family limited partnership provides a useful structure for holding and managing an asset that many family members will share, such as a vacation home. In addition, a family limited partnership can serve a function similar to that of a trust in that a limited partner generally cannot control the partnership and cannot force distributions of the partnership income or assets. If family assets are held in a family limited partnership that includes a requirement that disputes be arbitrated, there is a chance that those assets may one day be reduced by litigation costs. As a consequence, the nontax advantages of a family limited partnership may be equally important, or more important, than the potential tax advantages.

[2] Requirements for Limited Liability Companies and Limited Partnerships

Both limited partnerships and limited liability companies are entities that are formed under state law, which sets out the rights, duties, and liabilities of the owners. These statutes vary from state to state. Some of the rights, duties, and liabilities are default rules, and can be changed by agreement of the parties (usually a limited partnership agreement in the case of a limited partnership and an operating agreement in the case of a limited liability company). For federal income tax purposes there is no difference between a limited partnership and a limited liability company: both are flow-through entities (i.e., the income and loss of the entity flows through to the owners and is reported on the owners' income tax returns[6]). In choosing between a limited partnership and a limited liability company, and in choosing the jurisdiction in which to form one of these entities, the estate planner should determine the

---

(Footnote Continued)

ability to withdraw from the partnership or to sell his partnership interest without consent of other partners may prevent a gift of a partnership interest from qualifying for the present interest exclusion. Hackl v. Comm'r, 118 T.C. 14 (2002), aff'd, 335 F.3d 664 (7th Cir. 2003). The court stated that a limited partner received only a future interest because he could not presently reach the economic value of the partnership interest. *See also* Fisher v. United States, 105 A.F.T.R.2d 2010-1347 (S.D. Ind. 2010).

[6] Under the "check the box" regulations, a limited partnership or limited liability company could elect to be treated as a corporation for federal income tax purposes. Reg. § 301.7701-3.

§ 8.07[B][2]

client's tax and nontax goals, and then choose the type of entity and jurisdiction that best suits those goals.

The formation of a limited partnership requires at least two partners, one of which is the general partner.[7] The partnership is formed by filing a certificate of limited partnership with the secretary of state. In addition, the partners may enter into a partnership agreement that defines their respective rights and duties in detail.

A limited partnership may have more than one general partner, and the same individual or entity may own both a general partnership interest and a limited partnership interest. The limited partners are not liable for the partnership's debts by reason of being limited partners.[8] The general partner, however, is personally liable for all of the partnership debts.[9] For this reason, an individual forming a limited partnership may choose to form a wholly owned corporation to act as the general partner rather than owning the general partnership interest directly. The corporation insulates the individual from the liabilities of the partnership.

The general partner controls the partnership business, although limited partners may have the right to participate in certain major partnership decisions, such as the decision to liquidate the partnership. The general partner is bound by a fiduciary duty to manage the partnership for the benefit of all the partners.

The owners of a limited liability company generally are referred to as members. A limited liability company may have one or more members. The members form the company by filing a certificate with the secretary of state, and in addition generally enter into an operating agreement that further defines their respective rights and duties.

One of the important differences between a limited partnership and a limited liability company is that a limited partnership is always managed by the general partner, whereas limited liability company statutes permit several different management structures. Under the limited liability company statutes, a limited liability company may be managed either by one or more managers or by the members. If it is managed by a manager, the manager may be a member, but need not be a member. The manager may be designated in the operating agreement or may be elected by the members. If the company is managed by the members, then the agreement may provide for different voting rights for different members or classes of members. As a result of the flexibility of limited liability company statutes, the owners of a company can structure the company to resemble a limited partnership by providing for a named manager who must be a member, or to resemble a corporation, by providing for members to elect a manager who need not be a member.

A second important difference between a limited liability company and a limited partnership is that no member of a limited liability company is liable for the debts of the company by reason of being a member, whereas the general partner of a limited

---

[7] The formation of a limited partnership is governed by state law. *See, e.g.,* Mass. Gen. Laws. ch. 109, § 1(7).

[8] *See, e.g.,* Mass. Gen. Laws. ch. 109, § 19.

[9] *See, e.g.,* Mass. Gen. Laws. ch. 109, § 24.

partnership is liable for the debts of the partnership.[10] This limitation on the liability of all members of a limited liability company may permit a simpler structure than would be the case in a limited partnership because it is possible to limit the liability of all of the owners without forming a separate corporation to act as general partner.

Since limited liability company statutes are relatively recent, the law governing them is less developed than the law governing limited partnerships. For this reason, some estate planners were initially cautious about using limited liability companies. Over the years, however, limited liability companies have gained wide acceptance, and are now the entity of choice for most planners.

[3] Valuing an Interest in a Family Limited Partnership or Limited Liability Company

The valuation of interests in a family limited partnership is important because one of the motivations in forming a family limited partnership may be to permit a senior family member to make gifts of limited partnership interests at a discounted gift tax value. The gift tax value of an interest in a family limited partnership may be subject to two sets of rules. As an initial matter, the basic principles of valuation apply, under which the gift tax value of a limited partnership interest is the price on which a hypothetical seller and hypothetical buyer would agree, both knowing the relevant facts and neither being under a compulsion to buy or sell. Under these principles, a minority discount will ordinarily be applicable because a limited partner does not control the partnership and cannot unilaterally liquidate it or withdraw from it. In the case of a partnership controlled by family members, however, an additional set of valuation rules may apply for gift tax purposes. These rules are in Sections 2704 and 2701 of Chapter 14 of the Code.

IRC Section 2704(b) and the accompanying regulations provide that for purposes of valuing an interest in a family partnership, if the partnership agreement contains restrictions on liquidation that are more restrictive than those under applicable state law, then the restrictions in the partnership agreement will be ignored for gift tax purposes. This rule could apply in the following situation:

EXAMPLE 8-24

A family limited partnership agreement provides that a limited partner may not withdraw from the partnership before the end of the partnership term without the consent of the general partner. The partnership term is 40 years. The relevant state law, however, permits a limited partner to withdraw from a limited partnership at any time upon six months' notice and requires the partnership to pay the withdrawing partner the fair market value of his interest (unless the partnership agreement provides

---

[10] State law governs the liabilities of limited partners and members of limited liability companies. *See, e.g.,* Mass. Gen. Laws. ch. 109, § 19; Mass. Gen. Laws. ch. 156C, § 22.

otherwise). The provision in the partnership agreement is more restrictive than the default state law rule, and therefore is disregarded for gift tax purposes under IRC Section 2704(b). The gift tax value of a limited partnership interest that can be liquidated on six months' notice is greater than the value of an equivalent interest that cannot be liquidated before the end of the partnership term without the consent of the general partner, and it is the greater value that will be used for gift tax purposes.

The effect of IRC Section 2704(b), when it applies, will be to increase the gift tax value of a limited partnership interest. Since IRC Section 2704(b) does not apply to restrictions on liquidation that are no more restrictive than applicable state law, a family limited partnership organized under one state statute may offer more gift tax benefits than a similar family limited partnership organized under a different state statute.[11]

IRC Section 2704(a) contains another rule intended to prevent the application of a minority discount in certain situations. Section 2704(a) provides that if there is a lapse of a voting or liquidation right in a family controlled partnership, then the lapse will be treated as a gift. This rule could apply in the following situation:

EXAMPLE 8-25

Lily owns a 40 percent general partnership interest in a family limited partnership. Her son Steve owns a 5 percent general partnership interest and a 25 percent limited partnership interest, and her daughter Melissa owns a 30 percent limited partnership interest. A general partner has both a voting right and a liquidation right, and a limited partner has neither a voting right nor a liquidation right. The partnership agreement provides that upon transfer of a general partnership interest, the interest automatically becomes a limited partnership interest. Lily gives her general partnership interest to Melissa, and the interest automatically becomes a limited partnership interest in Melissa's hands. Under IRC Section 2704(a), the lapse of Lily's voting right and liquidation right will be treated as a gift to Melissa, and no minority discount will be applied in valuing the gift received by Melissa.

Section 2701 contains another set of rules that affect the gift tax valuation of family limited partnership interests in certain circumstances. The rules of Section 2701 are extensive and complex, and a full analysis is beyond the scope of this discussion. The purpose of Section 2701 is to prevent families from artificially depressing the gift tax value of interests in family companies by creating two different classes of interests: a preferred interest and a nonpreferred or common interest. When Section 2701 applies, its effect is to increase the gift tax value of a gift

---

[11] *See* Kerr v. Comm'r, 113 T.C. 449 (1999); Estate of W.W. Jones III v. Comm'r, 116 T.C. 121 (2001).

of a nonpreferred or common interest. Section 2701 does not apply to a gift of a family limited partnership interest if the only difference between the general and the limited partnership interests is the general partner's management rights.[12] It is important to note that Section 2701 does not prevent the use of preferred distribution rights in the family limited partnership context; its effect is limited to special valuation rules for gifts of certain types of interests. In creating a family limited partnership that includes preferred interests, however, the estate planner should analyze carefully the effect of Section 2701 on the creation or transfer of partnership interests in order to avoid an unexpected taxable gift.

The case law on the valuation of interests in family limited partnerships or limited liability companies for gift and estate tax purposes continues to evolve. In a number of cases, the Internal Revenue Service has been successful in denying the discounts claimed by taxpayers for family limited partnership interests transferred by gift or at death.[13] In some of these cases the family members had commingled the partnership assets with assets owned by partners individually, made distributions from the partnership that were not pro-rata, or had otherwise failed to respect the terms of the partnership agreement. Few practitioners were surprised by the conclusion that a partnership should be disregarded for valuation purposes when the partners' actions suggested that they viewed the partnership property as their own personal property and did not view the partnership as a separate legal entity. These cases illustrate one reason why it is important to observe all of the formalities in administering a family limited partnership. Moreover, adverse estate and gift tax consequences are not the only potential negative repercussions of the partners' failure to respect the partnership as a separate legal entity. Casual administration of a family limited partnership could also encourage family disputes as well as jeopardize creditor protection.

Over the years, one of the most litigated aspects related to family limited partnerships is whether assets contributed to the limited partnership should be included in the donor's estate under IRC Section 2036. *Estate of Strangi v. Commissioner*, decided in 2003, attracted considerable attention in the estate planning community because the Internal Revenue Service prevailed using this legal theory.[14] In this case (often referred to as *"Strangi II"* to distinguish it from the first Tax Court decision in the case), the IRS was successful in arguing that the assets of a limited partnership were includable in a decedent's estate at their full undiscounted value because IRC Section 2036, one of the "string provisions," discussed in § 5.05[B][3],

---

[12] IRC § 2701(a)(2)(C).

[13] *See, e.g.,* Estate of Thompson, T.C.M. 2002-246; Estate of Harper, T.C.M. 2002-121.

[14] There are four decisions in this case. The first decision was in the Tax Court, Estate of Strangi v. Comm'r, 115 T.C. 478 (2000). The estate prevailed, and the IRS appealed to the Fifth Circuit. The Fifth Circuit upheld the Tax Court, but remanded the case to the Tax Court for consideration of an additional argument that the IRS had raised but the Tax Court had not considered. Estate of Strangi v. Comm'r, 293 F.2d 279 (5th Cir. 2002). On remand, the Tax Court held for the IRS. Estate of Strangi v. Comm'r, T.C.M. 2003-145 (2003), the case commonly referred to as "Strangi II." The estate appealed, and the Fifth Circuit again affirmed the Tax Court decision. Strangi v. Comm'r, 417 F.3d 468 (5th Cir. 2005).

applied. The court explained that when the decedent transferred assets to the partnership, he retained the following two "strings" to the transferred assets:

- The right to the income of the property; and
- The right, through the general partner, to determine who would enjoy the income of the property.

Either of these rights would be sufficient to cause the partnership property to be included in the decedent's estate at its full date-of-death value.

The aspect of the *Strangi II* decision that generated the most controversy was its holding that IRC Section 2036 applied because the decedent, through the general partner, controlled the enjoyment of the income of the partnership property. Given the fiduciary duty under state law that constrains the actions of a general partner, most practitioners had previously proceeded on the understanding that the powers of a general partner are not rights to which IRC Section 2036 apply.[15] In *Strangi II,* the decedent was not the general partner; the general partner of the partnership was a corporation of which the decedent owned 47 percent, and the decedent was not an officer of the corporation (although his son-in-law, who was also his attorney-in-fact, was an officer). These facts made the Tax Court's decision even more notable. In the subsequent appeal of the Tax Court decision, the Fifth Circuit affirmed the Tax Court's holding that Section 2036 applied because the decedent has retained the right to income from the property. The Fifth Circuit did not reach the question of whether the decedent also retained a second "string," the right to determine who would enjoy the income of the property, by virtue of his ownership interest in the general partner.

Another step in the evolution occurred in May 2004, when the Fifth Circuit Court of Appeals issued an important decision on the valuation of interests in family limited partnerships in *Kimbell v. United States.*[16] The Fifth Circuit's decision reversed a district court decision that had been highly unfavorable to the taxpayer. The taxpayer in the case had formed a family limited partnership shortly before her death. At her death, she retained a 99 percent limited partnership interest and 50 percent of the limited liability company that was the general partner. The trial court held that all of the assets the taxpayer had transferred to the partnership were includible in her estate at their full fair market value, without discount, because she retained IRC Section 2036 rights over the transferred assets.

In *Kimbell,* the Fifth Circuit rejected the application of Section 2036 in this context. The court explained that when a transfer of assets is made to a partnership and the transferor takes back a proportionate percentage interest in the partnership, the transaction is for "full and adequate consideration," and therefore is not subject to Section 2036. The court further held that the decedent's 50 percent interest in the

---

[15] Practitioners have relied on a Supreme Court case holding that the powers of a majority stockholder over corporate distributions do not cause IRC Section 2036 to apply because a majority shareholder is bound by fiduciary duty to respect the interests of the corporation and the other shareholders. Byrum v. U.S., 408 U.S. 125 (1972). The general partner of a limited partnership is similarly bound by fiduciary duty to respect the interests of the partnership and the other partners.

[16] Kimbell v. U.S., 244 F. Supp. 2d 700 (N.D. Tax 2003), *rev'd*, 371 F.3d 257 (5th Cir. 2004).

general partner was not sufficient control over the assets transferred to the partnership to cause Section 2036 to apply.

While the decision in *Kimbell* was a significant victory for the taxpayer, it did not eliminate the ability of the IRS to attack valuation discounts in family limited partnerships. The opinion in *Kimbell* indicated that the results would not have been the same if the transaction had been motivated solely for tax purposes without any business or corporate purpose, and after the *Kimbell* decision, the Tax Court has held that Section 2036 did apply in other cases to eliminate the valuation discounts in a family limited partnership.[17] There has been a steady flow of subsequent cases in which the IRS challenged discounts on family limited partnership valuations based on Section 2036, with varying results.

Estate of Powell v. Commissioner[18] is another important case regarding inclusion of family limited partnership interests under IRC Section 2036. This case involved facts that make it unsurprising that the taxpayer lost the case. What is notable, however, is that the Tax Court used Section 2036(a)(2) to find that the decedent's *limited* partnership interests nonetheless caused inclusion of her estate because she, in conjunction with all other partners, could dissolve the partnership, and she effectively controlled the other partners. While the decedent in this case owned a 99 percent limited partnership interest, the court's analysis did not focus on the amount. The result of *Powell* makes the bona fide sale exception important even for limited partnership interests.

Another decision affecting gifts of interests in family limited partnerships, *Hackl v. Commissioner*, was decided by the Tax Court in 2002 and affirmed by the Court of Appeals in 2003.[19] The court held that a gift of a limited partnership interest did not qualify for the $10,000 annual gift tax exclusion because the gift was of a future interest. The Tax Court noted that the general partner had complete discretion to make or withhold distributions of cash, and that the recipient could not sell his interest without the permission of the general partner. The IRS successfully challenged another taxpayer's claim of annual exclusions for gifts of limited partnership interests in *Price v. Commissioner*.[20] The court noted that the donees could not withdraw their capital accounts, they could not sell their interests without the consent of all other partners, and there was no steady flow of income.

The case law on the tax consequences of family limited partnerships has not always been consistent. Planning with limited partnerships and limited liability companies is complex, and a full analysis is beyond the scope of this discussion. One key aspect, however, is a focus on the business purpose of the partnership and the way that the partnership has been administered.[21] If the partnership structure and

---

[17] *See, e.g.*, Bongard Estate v. Comm'r, 124 T.C. 95 (2005).

[18] 148 T.C. 392 (2017).

[19] Hackl v. Comm'r, 118 T.C. 279 (2002), *aff'd*, 335 F.3d 664 (7th Cir. 2003).

[20] T.C.Memo 2010-2. *See also* Fisher v. United States, 105 A.F.T.R.2d 2010-1347 (S.D. Ind. 2010).

[21] Additional cases in this context to review with their non-tax purposes are: Estate of Mirowski v. Comm'r, T.C. Memo 2008-74 (joint management of pooled assets); Estate of Miller v. Comm'r, T.C. Memo 2009-119 (group investment philosophy and special investment methodology); Estate of Joanne Stone v. Comm'r, T.C. Memo 2012-48 (hold and manage family woodland parcels); Estate of

administration resembles a business deal between unrelated parties, it is likely to be respected for tax purposes. This makes it more important than ever to counsel clients to enter into a family limited partnership only if the partnership structure serves non-tax purposes and to respect the formalities of administration.

[C] Gifts of Partial Interests

[1] GRITS and Valuation of Partial Interest Gifts

In some circumstances an individual may wish to make a gift of property, but may not wish to give up all interest in the property immediately. In such a case, the individual may wish to make a gift of a partial interest in the property. It is possible to create a partial interest in property by separating the ownership of the property into two separate bundles of rights, each of which is a partial interest. The individual could then make a gift of one of the partial interests and retain the other partial interest for herself. One type of partial interest in property is the right to occupy real property for a term of years. Before 1990, gifts of partial interests in property were a standard estate planning technique used to minimize transfer taxes.

EXAMPLE 8-26

Katherine, age 50, owns an apartment building. She wishes to continue receiving rents, but realizes that at some point she will no longer want to manage the property. She eventually wants the building to pass to her daughter Rebecca. Katherine creates two partial interests in the building by retaining the right to receive rents for 20 years and giving Rebecca the right to take possession of the building at the end of that time. Katherine has given a *remainder interest* in the building to Rebecca. Under pre-1990 law, the gift tax value of the remainder interest was less than the current fair market value of the building. In addition, if Katherine survived the 20 years, the building would not be subject to tax in her estate and all appreciation that occurred over the 20 years would pass free of tax.

Another common type of partial interest is the right to receive the income from income producing property. Before 1990, some parents made gifts of an income interest in property by means of a trust, commonly known as a *grantor retained income trust (GRIT)*. A parent would transfer property to the GRIT, and would retain the right to receive the income from the trust property for a fixed term of years. At the end of the term of years, the assets remaining in the trust (the remainder interest) would be paid to the child (the remainder beneficiary). The creation of the trust

---

(Footnote Continued)

Kelly v. Comm'r, T.C. Memo 2012-73 (equal estate distribution and avoiding potential litigation); Estate of Purdue v. Comm'r, T.C. Memo 2015-249 (centralized management).

would be a taxable gift to the remainder beneficiary, but the gift would be valued by taking into account the fact that the child would not receive the property until the end of the term of years, and so would not receive the income from the property during those years. The gift tax value of the remainder interest given to the child would be calculated by subtracting from the value of the property the value of the income that would be paid to the parent during the term of years.[22] The value of the income stream would be determined by using an assumed interest rate. If the parent reserved the right to have the property pass to his estate if he died during the term of years (a *reversion*), the value of the reversion would also be subtracted from the initial value of the property in determining the gift tax value.[23] The assumed interest rate used to value the income stream is determined under IRC Section 7520, which mandates the use of the applicable federal rate, which is an interest rate determined monthly by the IRS. IRC Section 7520 also mandates the use of IRS tables to determine the value of a reversion.[24] Assuming the parent survived the term of the GRIT, none of the property would be subject to tax in the parent's estate.

Before the enactment of Section 7520 in 1988 and Section 2702 in 1990, parents were able to use a GRIT to minimize transfer taxes on gifts to their children by careful investment of the property held by the GRIT. The gift tax value of the remainder interest given to the child was determined by subtracting out the value of the retained income interest; consequently, by funding the GRIT with property that appreciated substantially but produced little income, the value received by the child would exceed the gift tax value of the remainder interest. The donor of the GRIT would have minimized transfer tax on the gift to the remainder beneficiary.

EXAMPLE 8-27

Mark created a GRIT for his son Alan in 1988. The trust provided that the trustee would pay all net income to Mark for a term of 15 years, and then distribute the remaining trust property to Alan. Mark's gift to Alan was valued for gift tax purposes by assuming that the trust property would generate 8 percent income annually. The property transferred to the trust was stock of a company that paid no dividends but increased in value by 15 percent per year. The actual value of the interest received by Alan was significantly greater than the gift tax value of that interest.

Congress perceived a potential for abuse in GRITs, and consequently moved to limit their use. Congress's first attempt to limit the use of GRITs was IRC Section 2036(c), which was soon judged to be overbroad and revoked retroactively to its enactment. In 1990, Congress enacted Chapter 14 of the Internal Revenue Code, which included IRC Section 2702, a provision that was specifically designed to prevent the abuse of GRITs and other partial interests in making gifts within the family.

---

[22] IRC § 7520.
[23] *Id.*
[24] IRC § 7520 was enacted in 1988.

§ 8.07[C][1]

The enactment of Section 2702 marked a sea of change in the use of partial interest gifts for estate planning purposes. Section 2702 did not, however, eliminate the use of partial interest gifts. Section 2702 contains special rules for valuing a gift of a partial interest. It does not *prevent* donors from making a gift of a partial interest in property at a reduced gift tax value; it simply requires that a gift of a partial interest to a close family member be structured so that the gift tax value of the gift more closely matches the economic value of the gift than was the case under former law. In some respects, it can be viewed as an aid to the use of partial interest gifts because it provides a road map for the design of a partial interest gift and a safe harbor for valuation of the gift.

Furthermore, the Section 2702 valuation rules for gifts of partial interests apply only to gifts to certain family members. The limitations in Section 2702 apply only to gifts to:

1. A spouse;

2. An ancestor or lineal descendant of the donor or the donor's spouse;

3. A sibling of the donor; or

4. A spouse of an ancestor, lineal descendant, or sibling of the donor.

Section 2702 does not apply to a gift to a niece or nephew, or to a friend or nonmarital partner. Consequently, it is still possible to create a GRIT for such gifts. The gift tax value of the gift of the remainder interest in the GRIT is determined under the rules of IRC Section 7520.

[2] Effect of the Special Valuation Rules of Section 2702 on Partial Gifts

[a] *In General*

When Section 2702 does apply to a gift of a partial interest, it is vital to structure the gift as one of the specific types of partial interest that fall within the exceptions provided by the statute. If the gift fits within one of the exceptions, then the gift is valued for gift tax purposes using the same general principles that apply to the valuation of any partial interest. The gift of a remainder interest is valued by subtracting the value of the retained interest from the current value of the property.[25] The value of the retained interest is determined under Section 7520, which mandates the use of the applicable federal rate as published monthly. If, however, the gift of a partial interest to which Section 2702 applies does not fit within the exceptions of the statute, then the gift is valued using a different rule. In such case, the donor is not permitted to subtract the value of the retained interest from the current value of the gift property.[26] The result is that the donor is subject to gift tax on the full value of the property, despite the fact that he has transferred only the remainder interest in the property.

---

[25] IRC § 2702(a)(1).
[26] IRC § 2702(a)(2).

EXAMPLE 8-28

In March 2001, Emma, age 50, creates a trust and funds it with investment assets with a current fair market value of $100,000. Emma retains the right to receive $10,000 from the trust each year for ten years. At the end of the ten years, the trustee will distribute the property remaining in the trust to Emma's son Aaron. The Section 7520 rate for March 2001 is 6.2 percent. If the trust is drafted to comply with one of the Section 2702 exceptions, then Emma's gift will have a gift tax value of $29,157. If the trust does not comply with the Section 2702 exceptions, then Emma's gift will have a gift tax value of $100,000, despite the fact that Aaron will not receive that amount.

The overall effect of Section 2702 is to put a premium on strict compliance with its terms in situations when it does apply. It is critical, therefore, for an estate planner advising families on gift programs (1) to determine whether the gift is the type of gift that falls under Section 2702, and (2) if Section 2702 does apply, to ensure that the gift is structured to qualify for one of the Section 2702 exceptions.

[b] Transfers to Which Section 2702 Applies

Section 2702 states that its special valuation rules apply to a "transfer in trust" to a family member if the transferor retains an interest in the trust. The term "a transfer in trust," however, has a very broad meaning in this context. Any transfer of property is treated as a transfer in trust if there is a term interest in the property.[27] A *term interest* is an interest for a term of years or a life interest.[28] Thus, if a parent gives a remainder interest in a house to a child and retains the right to live in the house for a term of years, the gift is subject to the rules of Section 2702. Neither a lease for full fair market rent, however, nor an interest in property as a cotenant, is treated as a term interest.

The scope of Section 2702 is not limited to transactions that obviously constitute gifts. A joint purchase of property by family members, which in economic terms does not involve any gift, also falls within the ambit of Section 2702.[29] If a parent purchases a life interest in real property, and simultaneously a child purchases the remainder interest, then the transaction is treated for gift tax purposes as if the parent had purchased the entire property and then transferred the remainder interest to the child in exchange for the portion of the purchase price paid by the child. In determining the gift tax consequences of the deemed transfer of the remainder interest, the principles of Section 2702 apply. The parent's retained life interest is valued at zero,

---

[27] IRC § 2702(c)(1).

[28] IRC § 2702(c)(3).

[29] IRC § 2702(c)(2).

and the parent will be treated as having made a gift of the difference between the value of the whole property and the price paid by the child.

Section 2702 applies only to transfers among certain family members. The rules apply only to a transfer for the benefit of: (1) the transferor's spouse; (2) an ancestor or lineal descendant of the transferor or the transferor's spouse; (3) a sibling of the transferor; or (4) a spouse of an ancestor, lineal descendant, or sibling of the transferor.[30] It does not apply to transfers to nieces and nephews.

The following chart summarizes the application and nonapplication of Section 2702 to some common transactions:

Section 2702 applies:	*Section 2702 does not apply:*
Parent transfers real property to a child and retains the right to occupy the property for a term of years.	Parent gives real property to a child and leases the property back for full fair market value rent.
Parent purchases a life interest in real property and child simultaneously purchases a remainder interest; both purchases are from an unrelated third party for full fair market value.	Parent and child purchase property as tenants-in-common, each pays full fair market value for his interest.
Parent transfers investment assets to a trust of which his child is the remainder beneficiary. Parent retains the right to the income from the trust for 20 years.	Parent transfers investment assets to a trust of which his nephew is the remainder beneficiary. Parent retains the right to the income from the trust for 20 years.

[c] Section 2702 Exceptions

The general rule of Section 2702 that treats a parent's retained interest in transferred property as having zero value does not apply to all transactions to which Section 2702 applies. If the retained interest is a "qualified interest" as defined in the regulations, then the retained interest is not valued at zero.[31] The regulations set out detailed requirements for a "qualified interest." Two popular planning vehicles have resulted from these regulations: a qualified personal residence trust, or QPRT, and a grantor retained annuity trust, or GRAT. These vehicles, both of which offer significant estate planning opportunities in the right circumstances are described below.

In analyzing Section 2702, it is important to review the regulations as well as the statute; many of the detailed requirements for compliance with the safe harbors are found in the regulations only.

---

[30] IRC §§ 2702(a)(1), 2702(e), 2704(c)(2).

[31] Reg. § 25.2702-1(b).

[3] Qualified Personal Residence

[a] *Overview*

Qualified personal residence trusts (QPRTs) had been very popular estate planning vehicles because they permit senior family members to accomplish two goals: They can retain the use of a family home for a term of years and then pass the home on to the younger generation at a reduced transfer tax cost. This arrangement comes close to letting a parent have his cake and eat it, too, from a gift tax perspective, because he can retain possession and control of the house for the term of years, but at the same time decrease the transfer tax that would be payable if he retained full ownership of the house and then made a gift of it in the future (or died owning the house). In many families of otherwise moderate means, the family home or vacation property is a major asset, and may cause such families to be subject to estate tax. A QPRT can be especially valuable for such families particularly if they wish to retain the property in the family.

A QPRT can be described in general terms as a gift of a personal residence that does not take effect until the end of a term of years. To create a QPRT, a parent typically would transfer a personal residence to a trust of which her children are the remainder beneficiaries. The parent would continue to use the property as a personal residence for a term of years. At the end of the term of years, the parent's right to use the property would terminate. At that point, the trust could terminate and distribute the residence to the child outright, or the trust could continue to hold the residence for the benefit of the child.

The effectiveness of a QPRT as an estate planning vehicle lies in the way that the parent's gift to the child of the remainder interest in the QPRT is valued. The gift tax value of the remainder interest is determined by subtracting the value of the parent's retained interest in the home from the value of the home at the time the trust is created.[32] Generally the parent will retain both the right to possess the house for the term of years and the right to have the house return to his estate if he should die during the term. The value of the parent's retained right to possess the house is determined by using the interest rate set monthly by the IRS under IRC Section 7520. The value of the parent's right to have the house revert to his estate if he dies during the term is determined using actuarial tables published by the IRS. The applicable interest rate plays an important part in the effectiveness of a QPRT as a gift tax planning vehicle. The higher the applicable federal interest rate, the greater the gift tax savings. When the applicable federal interest rate is low, as it has been in recent years, a QPRT is much less useful as an estate planning technique.

---

[32] IRC § 2036.

EXAMPLE 8-29

James, age 55, transfers the family vacation home to a QPRT for the benefit of his daughter Joanna. He retains the right to occupy the home for a term of 15 years. If James dies during the term, the house will be returned to his estate. The home is worth $400,000 at the time it is transferred to the QPRT. If the Section 7520 interest rate is 7.4 percent, the creation of the trust is a taxable gift to Joanna with a value of $112,412 (this discount is due to the fact that Joanna will not possess the property for 15 years). At the end of 15 years, when the house is worth $1,000,000, the QPRT terminates and the house passes to Joanna. No further gift tax is due, and when James dies the house will not be included in his taxable estate. If, however, the Section 7520 interest rate is 1.2 percent, then the creation of the trust is a taxable gift of $274,264 to Joanna, and the reduced discount may not justify the cost of establishing the QPRT and the burden of administering it.

The principal tax risk in creating a QPRT is that the donor may not survive the term of the trust. If the donor dies during the term, then the trust property will be included in his taxable estate,[33] and the QPRT will not have succeeded as a tax-saving vehicle. Most QPRTs provide that if the donor dies during the term, then the home reverts to the donor's estate. In such case, the donor's estate will be approximately in the same situation as it would have been if the QPRT had not been created: The taxable estate includes the home, and the executor could sell the home, if necessary, to pay the estate tax.

[b] Structuring a QPRT

The regulations under IRC Section 2702 contain lengthy and detailed requirements that a trust must fulfill in order to qualify as a QPRT.[34] In drafting a QPRT an estate planner must review these regulations carefully to ensure that the trust document complies with all requirements. The following discussion is a general outline of the basic terms of a QPRT, but does not include all of the requirements contained in the regulations. For example, the trust instrument must require that all trust income be distributed to the term holder at least annually, prohibit prepayment of the term holder's interest, and prohibit distributions of principal to anyone other than the donor prior to the expiration of the term.[35]

One of the most important decisions in structuring a QPRT is choosing the length of the trust term. If the donor dies during the trust term, then the property will be included in his taxable estate and the purpose of the trust will have failed. In choosing a term, therefore, a donor should take into account his general health and

---

[33] *Id.*

[34] Reg. § 25.2702-5.

[35] Reg. § 25.2702-5(b)(3), (4), (6).

life expectancy, and choose a term that he can reasonably expect to survive. This consideration militates toward a shorter term. As the term gets shorter, however, the value of the donor's retained interest decreases, and the value of the taxable gift of the remainder interest increases. This factor must be balanced with the donor's life expectancy to determine what term length is most appropriate for any individual donor.

The home transferred to the QPRT must be a personal residence, which means that the primary purpose of the home must be as a residence during the time that the donor occupies the home.[36] It is not necessary that the home be the primary residence of the donor; a vacation home that the donor uses only during a portion of the year can qualify as a personal residence.[37] A personal residence may include other structures on the property and adjacent land if it is not in excess of what is reasonably appropriate for a residence taking into account the neighborhood and the size of the house.[38] Furthermore, the IRS has issued some private letter rulings approving a QPRT holding a home that included a rental unit that was incidental to the taxpayer's use of the property as a residence.[39] Each individual may create a QPRT for her primary residence and an additional QPRT for one other residence.[40]

At the end of the QPRT term, the donor's interest in the home must terminate if the QPRT is to be effective in removing the home from the donor's taxable estate. This aspect of a QPRT may be troublesome for parents who are hesitant to give over control of the home to their children and fearful of being left homeless. A partial solution to this problem can be incorporated into a QPRT by providing that after the end of the QPRT term the home will remain in trust for the benefit of the children, and that the parents will have the right to rent the property from the trust for fair market value. This type of provision will offer the parents some assurance that they will be able to remain in the home (as long as they have sufficient assets to pay the market rent). This arrangement provides additional transfer tax savings also, because the rent paid by the parents to the trust for the children will benefit the children, but will not be subject to transfer tax. If the trust is structured as a grantor trust (i.e., the income of the trust is taxed to the donor under the rules of IRC Sections 671 to 677),[41] then the rental payment will not be subject to income tax when received by the trust.

While a parent may rent the residence after the end of the QPRT term, the trust must provide that the trustees are prohibited from selling the residence to the donor, the donor's spouse, or any entity controlled by the donor or the donor's spouse during the QPRT term or at any time that the residence is held by a trust that is a grantor trust with respect to the donor.[42] This requirement prevents a parent from

---

[36] Reg. § 25.2702-5.

[37] Reg. § 25.2702-5(c)(2).

[38] *See, e.g.*, Ltr. Rul. 9503025.

[39] Ltr. Ruls. 9609015, 199906014.

[40] Reg. § 25.2702-5(c)(2).

[41] *See* Chapter 4 for discussion of grantor trust rules.

[42] Reg. § 25.2702-5(c)(9).

contributing a residence to a QPRT, then repurchasing the residence from the QPRT just before the QPRT term expires.

The donor of a QPRT may serve as a trustee during the term of the QPRT. After the QPRT term has expired, however, the donor should not retain any powers that could cause the home to be included in his taxable estate under the string provisions of IRC Sections 2035 to 2038. If the home remains in trust for the benefit of the children after the initial QPRT term, then the donor should no longer serve as trustee (or his powers as trustee should be severely limited).

During the term of the QPRT, the donor generally pays the expenses that a life tenant would pay (i.e., property taxes, maintenance, and insurance). If the donor makes a capital improvement to the residence, however, the improvement would be an additional gift to the remainder beneficiaries.

If the personal residence held in a QPRT ceases to be the donor's personal residence (because it has been sold, destroyed, or the donor no longer uses the home), then one of three possible consequences must follow:

1. The original residence may be replaced by another personal residence within two years;

2. The house or the proceeds from the sale or insurance proceeds may be distributed back to the donor; or

3. The trust may convert to a grantor retained annuity trust, or GRAT, described below.[43]

The IRS has issued a sample QPRT Trust document, which provides for a term interest for a single individual. The sample trust agreement contains all of the required provisions for a QPRT, some optional provisions, and some annotations. The IRS will recognize a trust as a qualifying QPRT if it is substantially similar to the sample document, it is a valid trust under applicable local law, and it is operated in a manner consistent with the terms of the trust instrument. Adding additional substantive terms will not necessarily disqualify a trust as a QPRT, but qualification will not be assured. The sample trust is found in Revenue Procedure 2003-42.[44]

[4] Grantor Retained Annuity Trust

[a] In General

A *grantor retained annuity trust (GRAT)* is a special type of trust used to make gifts at a reduced gift tax cost. The donor, or grantor, creates an irrevocable trust and transfers property to the trust. The grantor retains the right to receive an annual annuity of a fixed amount for a term of years. At the end of the term of years, the property remaining in the trust passes to the remainder beneficiaries of the trust,

---

[43] Reg. § 25.2702-5(c).
[44] 2003-1 C.B. 993.

often the grantor's children or trusts for them. The creation of the GRAT is a taxable gift of the remainder interest to the remainder beneficiaries.[45]

EXAMPLE *8-30*

Lily creates a GRAT in June 2014, and funds it with $1,000,000 in closely-held stock. She retains the right to receive an annuity payment of $213,392 each year for five years. At the end of the five-year term, the remaining trust property will pass to the remainder beneficiaries, Lily's children. The creation of the GRAT is a taxable gift from Lily to her children. However, assuming the trust meets all of the requirements for a GRAT, the value of the gift (if calculated according to the regulations) will be $0.07 because it is calculated based on the value of the property transferred ($1,000,000) minus Lily's retained interest (the right to receive $213,392/year for five years). In December 2015, the company goes public and the stock in the trust appreciates in value to $5,000,000. The trustees pay Lily $213,392 each year for five years, then pay the remaining trust property to her children free of any additional transfer tax.

The special estate planning opportunity offered by a GRAT is a direct consequence of the method by which the gift of the remainder interest in the trust is valued for gift tax purposes. In valuing the remainder interest, the property in the trust is assumed to appreciate at a federally established rate, which is set monthly (known as the *7520 rate*). If the property in the trust actually appreciates at that rate, then the property remaining in the trust at the end of the trust term (and passing to the beneficiaries) will have the same value as the gift tax value, and the donor will not have achieved any gift tax savings. If, however, the property in the trust appreciates at a rate higher than the Section 7520 interest rate, then value of the property received by the remainder beneficiary will exceed the value on which the donor paid gift tax. The lower the 7520 rate, the greater the chance for gift tax savings. The historically low interest rates in recent years have made GRATs a very effective estate planning tool for families who will be subject to estate tax.

It is easiest to appreciate the power of a GRAT by examining a projection of economic results. The following table shows the economic results of a GRAT created by an individual funded with $1,000,000. This example assumes that the Section 7520 rate at the time the GRAT was created is 2.2 percent. The term of the GRAT is two years, and the donor retains the right to receive an annual annuity payment of $516,555. The property in the trust appreciates in value at an annual rate of 15 percent, well above the 7520 rate of 2.2 percent. At the end of the two-year term, the property remaining in the trust will be distributed to the remainder beneficiary of the trust. The activity in the trust will be as follows:

---

[45] IRC § § 2503, 2702.

Year:	Property in trust at beginning of year:	Actual appreciation (15 percent):	Annual annuity payment to donor:	Property remaining in trust at end of year:
One	$1,000,000	$150,000	$516,555	$633,444
Two	$633,444	$95,016	$516,555	$211,905

The creation of the GRAT will be a taxable gift by the donor to the remainder beneficiaries of the trust. For gift tax purposes, the value of the remainder interest will be calculated by assuming that the property in the trust appreciates at the 7520 rate of 2.2 percent, and the donor will be treated as having made a taxable gift of $0.1 (after taking into account the large retained annuity). In reality, however, the property in the trust appreciated at 15 percent, and the amount left in the trust at the end of the trust term for distribution to the trust beneficiaries is $211,905. By using a GRAT to make this gift, the donor was able to make a tax-free gift of $211,905 to the remainder beneficiaries. If the property in the trust had appreciated at a rate greater than 15 percent, the tax-free gift would be correspondingly larger. If the property in the trust had appreciated at a rate lower than 15 percent, the tax-free gift would have been correspondingly smaller.

Since a GRAT is a means to make a tax-free gift of the difference between the Section 7520 interest rate and the actual appreciation in the trust property, the Section 7520 rate is important to the success of a GRAT. As the 7520 rate rises, the required payments back to the donor rise, and the amount left in the remainder at the termination of the GRAT will be lower. If, in the above example, the 7520 rate were 7 percent instead of 2.2 percent, the activity in the trust would be as follows:

Year:	Property in trust at beginning of year:	Actual appreciation (15 percent):	Annual annuity payment to donor:	Property remaining in trust at end of year:
One	$1,000,000	$150,000	$553,097	$596,902
Two	$506,902	$89,535	$553,097	$133,340

The tax-free gift of the remainder interest is $133,340 when the Section 7520 rate is 7 percent, which is substantially less than the tax-free gift of $211,905 when the 7520 rate is 2.2 percent.

A GRAT will not produce transfer tax benefits if the grantor dies during the GRAT term. In such case, the property remaining in the trust will be included in the taxable estate of the grantor because the grantor has retained an income interest in the property that has not, in fact, ended before his death.[46] In such case, the GRAT will not have achieved the desired gift tax result. Consequently, it is important that the GRAT term be substantially shorter than the grantor's life expectancy. While the death of the grantor during the term of a GRAT will prevent him from realizing a gift tax benefit, it is possible to structure a GRAT such that the adverse gift tax results are minimal. This is accomplished by designing the GRAT such that the gift tax value of the remainder interest is either zero or very low. As long as the GRAT term is fixed (so that annuity payments will continue to be paid to the grantor's estate if he dies during the GRAT term) it is possible to reduce the gift tax value of the remainder almost to zero. If the property is included in the grantor's estate, then any gift tax paid prematurely or unified credit used to transfer the remainder interest will be minimal.

In short, in the right circumstances a GRAT is a high-reward, low-risk estate planning vehicle because:

- If the property transferred to the trust increases in value at a rate that is higher than the relevant federal rate, and the grantor outlives the term, then the grantor will get a transfer tax bargain; and

- If the property transferred to the trust fails to appreciate at a rate that is higher than the relevant federal rate, or the grantor dies during the term, then the adverse tax results are minimal.

[b] Structuring a GRAT: Term and Annuity Amount

A GRAT is a creature of statute; IRC Section 2702 and the accompanying regulations contain numerous detailed requirements for a GRAT. It is essential for an estate planner drafting a GRAT to follow those regulations closely. The following discussion covers only some of the major design features of a GRAT.

Since a GRAT may not accomplish the desired gift tax results if the trust property fails to appreciate faster than the Section 7520 rate or if the grantor dies during the term, most estate planners design a GRAT so that the gift tax value of the remainder interest is as close to zero as possible. Minimizing the tax value of the remainder interest minimizes the risk that the grantor will pay extra gift tax or waste unified credit.

Estate planners designing a GRAT minimize the gift tax value of the remainder interest by adjusting two variables: the length of the GRAT term and the amount of the annual annuity. In practical terms, most planners use commercial software to calculate the value of a GRAT remainder. The planner chooses a desired GRAT term, and the program will calculate the annuity payment that gives the lowest gift tax

---

[46] *See* IRC §§ 2036, 2039. The IRS regulations finalized in 2008 provide that the donor's estate will include only the amount necessary to generate the annuity retained by the donor under IRC § 2036. For a short-term GRAT, the amount required to generate the annuity, and thus includable in the donor's estate, is likely to be all property remaining in the GRAT. Even if the includable amount is less than all property remaining in the GRAT, the result will not be optimal.

value given that term and the Section 7520 rate. Thus, the choice of the GRAT term is one of the most important design features.

The most essential factor to consider in choosing a GRAT term is the life expectancy of the grantor since a GRAT will fail to accomplish its tax objective if the grantor dies during the term of the GRAT. It is generally advisable to structure a GRAT for a relatively short period of time. In fact, many planners recommend the use of a GRAT term that is as short as two or three years if the property transferred to the trust is expected to appreciate rapidly at some point in the future. The rationale for choosing a very short term has less to do with ensuring the survival of the grantor than with the expected performance of the trust investments. As illustrated above, a GRAT works best when the property in the trust appreciates rapidly, and the appreciation is captured for the remainder beneficiaries by the termination of the trust. If a rapid upswing in value is followed by low growth years during the trust term, then the extra growth in the early years will be used to pay out the annuity in the slow years, thereby diluting the desired effect of the GRAT. A short-term GRAT may offer the best opportunity for capturing a rapid upturn in value. If the GRAT terminates before the property has undergone a rapid increase in value, then the grantor can recontribute it to another GRAT and will have another opportunity to capture the upswing when it occurs. There is no certain way to determine the optimal term for a GRAT, however, since the results of the GRAT will depend on the performance of the trust assets and the survival of the grantor, both of which are always uncertain.

Planners who use commercial software as an aid in designing the GRAT generally choose a GRAT term and then use the software to obtain the annuity amount that will minimize the gift tax value of the remainder interest. If the GRAT provides that the full annuity will be paid to the estate of the grantor if the grantor dies during the GRAT term, then the gift tax value of the remainder can be reduced to zero.

One design feature that can make a GRAT even more tax efficient is to provide for annuity payments that increase over the term of the GRAT, thereby backloading the annuity payments. The rules permit the annuity to increase by no more than 20 percent each year.[47] If the trust property appreciates steadily during the trust term, it will generally be advantageous to keep the property in the trust as long as possible before making the annuity payments (since most annuity payments are paid in kind), and an annuity that increases at 20 percent per year may produce better tax results. There is no single best design, however, since the performance of any individual GRAT depends for the most part on the economic performance of the particular trust assets.

[c] Operational Issues

One issue that frequently arises is how the trustees will pay the annuity if the assets in the GRAT do not produce cash. The trustee cannot use a note to pay the

---

[47] Reg. § 25.2702-3(c)(1).

annuity.[48] Stock in a closely held company, which is often used to fund a GRAT because of its potential for rapid appreciation, may not pay dividends. In these circumstances the trustees would pay the annuity amount in stock, valued as of the time of the annuity payment. The use of trust assets to pay the annuity will not trigger taxable gain if the GRAT is structured as a grantor trust (i.e., all the income and losses of the trust are reported directly on the grantor's tax return).[49] If, however, the GRAT were not structured as a grantor trust, then the use of appreciated trust assets to pay the annuity would trigger taxable gain to the trust. For this reason, it is important that the estate planner draft the GRAT as a grantor trust.

The consequence of being a grantor trust is that the grantor will be taxed on all of the income of the GRAT, whether or not the annuity payment is large enough to include all of the trust income. From an estate planning perspective, this is a desirable feature, since it permits the grantor to pass additional economic benefit to the remainder beneficiaries without transfer tax. The grantor of a GRAT can serve as the trustee during the GRAT term. If the property continues in trust after the end of the GRAT term, however, the grantor should not continue as trustee, in order to avoid the possibility that trustee powers would cause the trust property to be included in the grantor's estate.

Since a donor will realize tax benefits from a GRAT only if the trust property outperforms the Section 7520 rate, it is clear that the potential for investment return is the most important factor to consider in selecting property to fund a GRAT. Assets such as stock of a closely held company that the donor expects to go public in the near future is one type of asset that can produce dramatic results in a GRAT. Other business interests can produce good results also, especially if the interest contributed to the GRAT is valued at a discount.

EXAMPLE 8-31

Lucia owns a well-established business that has been paying a steady return of 10 percent (calculated using a nondiscounted value for the company). She contributes 30 percent of the company to a GRAT at a time that the Section 7520 rate is 3 percent. For purposes of calculating the value of the remainder interest, combined discounts for lack of marketability and minority interest of 35 percent are applied. The GRAT will pay the annuity in cash received from the company. The return on the business interest held in the GRAT, when calculated as a percentage of the discounted value, is 15 percent. The difference between the 7520 rate and this rate of return based on the discounted value of the trust assets will cause the GRAT to produce a tax benefit.

---

[48] Reg. § 25.2702-3(d)(5). In the case of a GRAT created after September 20, 1999, the trust document must specifically prohibit the use of notes to make the annuity payments.

[49] Grantor trusts are discussed in Chapter 4.

Generally, it is preferable to fund a GRAT with a single asset rather than a mix of investments. A GRAT works best when the trust term captures an upturn in value, and the tax results are more or less neutral if the trust assets perform at or below the 7520 rate. If the trust is funded with a mix of assets, there is a significant chance that one of the assets will outperform the others. If the assets are in one GRAT, the superior performance of that asset will be diluted by lesser performance of the other assets. Consequently, most planners recommend using multiple GRATs, each funded with a different asset, rather than a single GRAT funded with a mix of assets.

In choosing the beneficiaries of a GRAT, it is important to note that generally it is not possible to allocate generation-skipping tax exemption to a GRAT at the time that the GRAT is created; therefore, the donor may wish to choose children rather than grandchildren as beneficiaries. Generation-skipping tax exemption cannot be allocated to property during any period in which the property would be included in the estate of the donor if the donor died.[50] During the term of the GRAT, the donor is an income beneficiary, and the GRAT property would be included in the donor's estate if the donor died. The donor could allocate generation-skipping tax exemption at the end of the GRAT term, but if the GRAT has been successful, the property will have appreciated substantially in value, and this may not be the most efficient use of the exemption.

§8.08 MISCELLANEOUS CONSIDERATIONS

[A] Gifts to Grandchildren

A gift to a grandchild or to a trust of which grandchildren are the only beneficiaries will be subject to generation-skipping tax unless the gift qualifies for one of the exceptions to the generation-skipping tax or is covered by an allocation of the donor's generation-skipping tax exemption.[1] The generation-skipping tax is a separate tax (in addition to the gift and the estate taxes) that applies to transfers to individuals (or trusts for individuals) who are more than one generation younger than the donor. The generation-skipping tax exemption permits a donor to make some gifts free of generation-skipping tax, but when this exemption has been used up, the tax kicks in at a flat rate. The exemption amount began at $1,000,000. In 2006, the exemption rose to $2,000,000; in 2009, it rose to $3,500,000; in 2011, it rose to $5,000,000, indexed for inflation; and in 2018, the exemption amount rose to $11,180,000 (subject to inflation). The GST exemption amount for 2022 is $12,060,000. The exemption, however, is set to revert to $5,000,000 (with an inflation adjustment) in 2026.[2] The tax rate in 2013 and beyond is 40 percent. The effect of the generation-

---

[50] IRC §§ 6501(a), 6601(g), 6665(a). *See* Chapter 9 for a discussion of the generation-skipping tax.

[1] §8.08 IRC §§ 2601 *et seq.*

[2] It is worth noting that the generation-skipping tax exemption, unlike the gift/estate tax exemption is <u>not</u> portable between spouses.

skipping tax should not be overlooked in planning for lifetime gifts. Planning for generation-skipping tax is discussed in detail in Chapter 9.

[B] The Gift Tax Statute of Limitations

The gift tax statute of limitations is helpful to taxpayers because it limits the length of time that the IRS can wait before assessing gift tax. After the limitations period has expired, the IRS can no longer assess gift tax, interest, or penalties with respect to past gifts. The statute of limitations will be determined under one of two sets of rules, depending upon the date of the gift. The gift tax statute of limitations was amended in 1997 and final regulations under the amended statute were promulgated at the end of 1999.[3] These rules apply to gifts made in 1997 and after, and the old rules continue to apply to gifts made before the effective date of these more recent rules.[4] Most estate planners will be dealing primarily with the more recent rules. The old rules, however, continue to be relevant in some circumstances because prior gifts must be listed on later gift tax returns and estate tax returns.

[1] Limitations Period for Gifts Made in 1997 and Thereafter

The limitations period begins to run when a gift tax return is filed.[5] Generally the limitations period expires three years after the return was filed.[6] There are three circumstances in which the limitations period does not start to run with respect to a particular gift (and consequently the IRS can assess gift tax at any time):

1. If the taxpayer does not file a gift tax return;[7]
2. If the return filed is fraudulent;[8] or
3. If the gift is not adequately disclosed on a gift tax return.[9]

The rule that the limitations period does not begin to run with respect to a gift unless it is adequately disclosed on a gift tax return makes the IRS interpretation of what constitutes adequate disclosure very important. Under the new regulations, a gift is adequately disclosed if the return includes all of the following information:[10]

- A description of the property transferred and any consideration received by the donor;
- The identity of the donor and the recipient and the relationship between them;

---

[3] Reg. § 301.6501(c)-1(f).

[4] Because they vary for different transactions, the regulations should be consulted for the exact effective dates.

[5] See IRC § 6501(a).

[6] *Id.*

[7] IRC § 6501(c)(3).

[8] IRC § 6501(c)(1).

[9] IRC § 6501(c)(2).

[10] Reg. § 301.6501(c)-1(f)(2).

- If the gift is made in trust, the trust's tax identification number and either a brief description of the terms of the trust or a copy of the trust instrument;
- One of the following: either (a) a qualified appraisal, or (b) a detailed description of the method used to value the gift, including any relevant financial data, any restrictions on the transferred property that were considered in determining the value, and any discounts that were applied; and
- A statement describing any position taken on the return that is contrary to any regulations or revenue rulings published at the time of the transfer.

If the gift is adequately disclosed on the gift tax return, then the limitations period will begin to run when the return is filed, and after the limitations period has expired the IRS will not be able to assess gift tax with respect to that gift. In addition, the expiration of the limitations period has the following other important effects:

- The IRS cannot revalue the gift when the gift is included as a prior taxable gift on a subsequent gift tax return or on an estate tax return (the revaluation would have the effect of increasing the gift or estate tax bracket applicable to the later transfer);[11]
- The IRS cannot assert that a gift failed to qualify for the present interest exclusion;[12] and
- If the transfer was reported as a completed gift, the IRS cannot assert that the transfer was an incomplete gift (thereby including the transferred property in the taxable estate of the donor).[13]

Given that the advantages resulting from the expiration of the limitations period are significant, and that the limitations period will not begin to run unless the gift is adequately disclosed, it is important for an estate planner filing a gift tax return to understand what constitutes adequate disclosure of a gift on a return. Of the five elements laid out in the regulations that are included as part of adequate disclosure, four are quite straightforward. One element, however, presents more difficulties, and that is the requirement of a detailed description of the method used to value the property. When the gift consists of property that requires a complex valuation process, such as an interest in a closely held company, it may not be clear how much information must be included on the return in order to adequately disclose the gift. As a result, many estate planners may choose to rely on an appraisal, which can be substituted for the detailed description of the method used to value the gift. Planners should note, however, that the appraisal must be a qualified appraisal. The regulations specify that an appraisal is a qualified appraisal only if it is done by an individual who is a professional appraiser, qualified by experience or education and who is not related to or employed by the donor or the recipient, and that the appraisal report must include a number of specific items of information.[14] As a consequence, it is important for an estate planner filing a gift tax return to review the regulations with care.

---

[11] IRC §§ 2001(f), 2504(c).

[12] Reg. § 20.2001-1(b).

[13] Reg. § 301.6501(c)-1(f)(5).

[14] Reg. § 301.6501(c)-1(f)(2).

[2] Limitations Period for Gifts Made Before 1997

The rules governing the limitations period for gifts made before 1997 may still be relevant for estate planners reporting gifts made before that date on current gift tax or estate tax returns, or on audit of a return. Some aspects of the prior rule are the same as the current rule: In both cases the basic limitations period is three years after the return was filed, and in both cases the limitation period does not begin if no return is filed or if the return is fraudulent. However, under the prior rule the effect of failing to adequately disclose a gift was to extend the limitations period to six years, if the value of the undisclosed gift was 25 percent or more of the total amount of the gifts reported on the return.[15] (Under the new rule the limitations period does not begin at all with respect to any gift not adequately disclosed on a return.)

The effect of the expiration of the limitations period is also different under the prior rules. Although the expiration of the limitations period does prevent the IRS from assessing gift tax for that particular gift, the expiration of the limitations period did not prevent the IRS from revaluing a gift for purposes of determining the gift or estate tax bracket applicable to a later gift.[16] Furthermore, the expiration of the limitations period did not prevent the IRS from raising other legal issues, such as the applicability of the present interest exclusion.

§8.09 ALTERNATIVES TO GIFTS

[A] Overview

While gifts are a very useful estate planning technique, there are many circumstances in which a gift is not appropriate. For example, a father who owns a family business and wishes to pass it to one of his children may be reluctant to make gifts of the business for any of the following reasons:

- He depends on the business for current income;
- He does not want to create family discord by making a major gift to only one child and does not have sufficient resources to make equalizing gifts to the other children;
- He believes that making major gifts to a child tends to diminish the child's ambition and focus; or
- He does not have sufficient liquid assets to pay the gift tax that would be due.

In any of these circumstances it may be preferable for the father to arrange a sale of the business to the child. He could take in exchange for the business either a simple installment note or a note that is canceled automatically on his death, or a

---

[15] IRC § 6501(e)(2).
[16] IRC § 2001 (before amendment).

private annuity. Any of these would provide the father with income for his retirement, defer the need to pay current tax, and avoid the need to equalize for a disproportionate gift and the possible negative effects of a gift. In addition, the sale would freeze the value of the business, because only the note (or the proceeds of the note, if it has been paid off) would be included in the seller's estate. Any appreciation in the business that occurred after the sale would benefit the child who purchased it.

There is a trade-off for the advantages of an intrafamily sale: The selling parent will be subject to income tax on any gain on the sale. If the seller's basis in the property is less than the sale price, then the gain will be taxable. In addition, if the seller receives payment over a term of years, the buyer will pay (or be deemed to pay) interest to the seller that is treated as ordinary income for income tax purposes.

There may also be an estate tax risk in an intrafamily sale. If the payments to the seller are recharacterized as a retained interest in the sold property, then the property would be included in the estate of the seller under IRC Section 2036 (one of the *string provisions*) if she dies before the payments are completed.[1] A 2013 Tax Court case, *Estate of Trombetta*,[2] illustrates this risk. An estate planner should check recent developments in this area before structuring an intrafamily sale.

An intrafamily sale is useful as a means of keeping a specific asset in the family and freezing the value of that asset for estate tax purposes. In other situations, a low interest loan or a joint purchase can be an effective way to pass value to another individual without triggering transfer tax. Some of the most useful alternatives to gifts are discussed below.

[B] Installment Sales and Bargain Sales

Most intrafamily sales are arranged as an installment sale of some type. The seller transfers title to the property in exchange for a note that provides for payments over a period of years. If the purchase price exceeds the seller's basis in the property, the seller will realize taxable gain. In most circumstances, however, the seller will be able to use the installment method of reporting the gain, and so will pay the tax on the gain in increments, as she receives the payments.[3]

EXAMPLE 8-32

Deborah sells all of the stock of her business to her daughter Laura in exchange for a note with a face amount of $100,000, payable in ten equal installments over ten years. The note provides for interest to be paid annually at 2.4 percent, which is the applicable federal rate in the month of the sale, and is secured by the stock. Deborah's basis in the stock is $10,000, and her gain on the sale is $90,000 (the purchase price of $100,000

---

[1] §8.09 The string provisions, including Section 2036, are discussed in Chapter 5.
[2] TCM 2013-234.
[3] IRC §453.

less her basis of $10,000). The portion of each principal payment that is taxable gain is $90,000/$100,000, or 90 percent. Each year, Deborah receives a principal payment of $10,000, of which $9,000 is taxable gain. The interest she receives is taxable as ordinary income. Laura's basis in the stock is $100,000.

Not all sales are eligible for installment sale treatment. A sale of marketable securities or inventory cannot be reported on the installment basis; consequently, all of the gain would be taxable to the seller in the year of the sale, even if the if the seller did not receive any payment in that year.[4] Similarly, a sale of depreciable property between related parties is not eligible for installment treatment.[5]

If the purchaser of the property is related to the seller and the purchaser resells the property within two years of the original purchase, then the seller will recognize the remaining taxable gain immediately.[6] This rule may apply even if the purchaser makes a gift of the purchased property.[7] Since the seller may not have received the balance of the payments on the note early, this rule can create difficulty for the seller. When there has been an installment sale between family members, or between a family member and a family business, these rules should be analyzed carefully before a second sale is made to avoid unintended acceleration of tax. For example, if in the example above Laura sold all of the stock one year later to a third party, Deborah's gain on the sale ($90,000) would be accelerated for tax purposes, even if Laura paid the note over ten years according to its terms.

If the seller disposes of the installment note or forgives payment of the note, the taxation of the gain to the seller will be triggered.[8] For example, if in the example above Deborah forgave each annual principal payment as it came due, she would report $9,000 in taxable gain each year. In addition, the forgiveness would be treated as a gift of $10,000 from Deborah to Laura. However, if Deborah died during the term of the note, the gain would not be accelerated unless the note passed to Laura. After Deborah's death, the person who received the note would report the gain as payments were received.

If an installment note does not carry interest at least equal to the applicable federal rate, then interest generally will be imputed to the seller, who will be obligated to report the imputed interest as if she had actually received it.[9] The rules that provide for imputed interest, known as the *original issue discount rules,* are complex and should be analyzed carefully before entering into an installment sale that provides for interest at a rate lower than the applicable federal rate. One exception to the general rule that may be useful in the estate planning context is the special rule that sets the maximum amount of interest that will be imputed at 6

---

[4] IRC § 453(k)(2).
[5] IRC § 453(g).
[6] IRC § 453(e).
[7] IRC § 453(e)(4).
[8] IRC § 453B(a).
[9] *See* IRC §§ 483, 1274.

percent for sales of land between family members that do not exceed $500,000.[10] The buyer may be entitled to deduct interest paid if the rules disallowing deductions for personal interest do not apply.[11]

If the seller dies before the note is paid, the note will be included in the seller's taxable estate at its fair market value.[12] As a consequence, while the sale has removed the sale property from the seller's estate, it has not necessarily reduced the seller's taxable estate. The sale, however, may result in a reduction in transfer tax because all of the postsale appreciation in the property will escape estate tax. In addition, the amount of the payments consumed by the seller to pay living expenses will not be subject to transfer tax.

If the price paid in an intrafamily sale is equal to the full fair market value of the property, then the transaction will not constitute a taxable gift. In the family context, however, individuals may wish to sell property for less than fair market value. When a bargain sale occurs between family members, the transaction is treated as two separate transactions: a sale of the property for the amount of the note, and a gift that is equal to the difference between the fair market value of the property and the sale price.

EXAMPLE 8-33

David sells the stock of his business to his daughter Margot for an installment note in the amount of $1,000,000. The fair market value of the business is $2,000,000, and David's basis in the stock is $500,000. David's taxable gain is equal to the purchase price less his basis in the stock, or $500,000. David will report the gain as he receives payments on the note. In addition, David is treated as having made a gift of $1,000,000, the amount equal to the excess of the fair market value of the stock ($2,000,000) over the purchase price ($1,000,000).

In arranging an installment sale in the estate planning context it is important that the transaction be structured so as to avoid unintended gift tax consequences. If the property is difficult to value, such as a closely held business, it may be necessary to get an appraisal in order to determine the fair market value of the property. In addition, the installment note should contain reasonable business terms, such that the seller could reasonably expect to be paid. If, for example, a parent sells property to a child for an installment note, and plans to forgive each installment as it comes due because the child has no means of meeting the payment, then the IRS may recharacterize the transaction as a gift rather than a sale of the property.[13]

---

[10] IRC § 483(e).

[11] *See* IRC § 163.

[12] IRC § 2031.

[13] *See* Rev. Rul. 77-299, 1977-2 C.B. 343.

[C] Sales to Intentionally Defective Grantor Trusts

One variation on the intrafamily installment sale is a sale to a special type of trust called a grantor trust. Such a trust is also referred to as an *intentionally defective grantor trust*, but is not defective in any real sense; it is simply a trust that has been designed to be treated for income tax purposes as a grantor trust. Under the grantor trust rules, all of the income and losses of the trust are reported on the income tax return of the grantor, whether or not the grantor is a beneficiary or otherwise receives any benefits from the trust.[14]

The advantage of selling property to an intentionally defective grantor trust is that a transaction between a grantor trust and the grantor is ignored for income tax purposes. As a consequence, the sale by the grantor to the grantor trust does not trigger gain on the sale, and the grantor will not pay income tax on the sale even if he receives cash.

EXAMPLE 8-34

Jim established a grantor trust with $5,000,000 in cash and income pro-ducing assets. He sells all of the stock in his company to the trust for a $2,000,000 installment note. Jim's basis in the stock is $1,000,000. The trust makes cash payments on the note. Jim will not report any gain on the sale, and will not report the interest paid on the note as income. The trust's basis in the stock is the same as Jim's basis in the stock.

In the above example, Jim has exchanged his stock for cash without paying income tax. In addition, he has frozen the value of the stock for estate tax purposes, so that all future appreciation in the stock will escape transfer tax. Only the note (or the proceeds of the note) will be included in his taxable estate at his death.[15]

A sale to an intentionally defective grantor trust will have the desired tax effects only if the installment note is recognized as genuine debt.[16] If the installment note does not have the indicia of real debt, the IRS may seek to recharacterize the transaction. If, for example, the trust has no assets other than the purchased property, the note might be recharacterized as a retained income interest. In such case, the trust property would be included in the grantor's estate under IRC Section 2036 if he died during the term of the note. Alternatively, the IRS might assert that the rules of IRC Section 2702 apply, and that the transfer should be treated as a gift of the entire property to the trust (i.e., without subtracting the value of the note from the gift). There are no bright line tax rules that distinguish "real debt" from other types of interests in this context. As a result, a sale to a defective trust should be undertaken

---

[14] IRC § 671.

[15] The income tax consequences that occur if the seller dies during the term of the note are very uncertain. *See, e.g.,* Nicholson, Frederic, Sale to a Grantor Controlled Trust: Better Than a GRAT?, Tax Management Memorandum, Feb. 22, 1996.

[16] IRC § 453.

with care. In particular, the trust should hold some assets other than the purchased property, so that there is a source for the note payments other than the income from the purchased property. Many practitioners counsel clients to fund the trust with "seed money" of at least ten percent of the value of the purchased property.

[D] Self-Canceling Installment Notes

A *self-canceling installment note*, or *SCIN*, is another variation on an installment sale. A SCIN is an installment note with one special feature: If the seller dies during the term of the note, the buyer's obligation to make future payments ceases automatically by the terms of the note. Since the buyer's obligation to pay ceases on the death of the seller, nothing will pass to the seller's estate. As a consequence, the note will not be included in the estate of the seller.

EXAMPLE 8-35

Bob sells property valued at $5,000,000 to his daughter Cassandra in exchange for a SCIN. Bob's life expectancy is 20 years. The SCIN provides for equal annual principal payments over a term of 15 years. In year two of the note term, Bob dies in an automobile accident and, under the terms of the note, no further payments are due. Neither the note nor the property sold to Cassandra is included in Bob's taxable estate.

The effect of Bob's premature death is to remove the value of all future payments on the note from his estate. A SCIN does not, however, eliminate all tax on the transfer of the property. Payments received by the seller are subject to income tax under the rules applicable to all installment notes.[17] In addition, any gain that remains at the death of the seller is triggered at that point, and is taxed to the estate of the seller as income in respect of a decedent.[18]

The self-canceling feature of the note clearly affects the value of the note; a note that is canceled on the death of the seller is worth less than a note with the same terms that does not include that feature. In order to avoid a taxable gift by the seller, the note must include a risk premium that reflects the risk that the seller may die prematurely. The risk premium generally is reflected in the interest rate, which will result in an interest rate that exceeds the market rate. One of the difficulties in drafting a SCIN is that the IRS has not issued any guidance as to how a risk premium should be calculated. The note is valued according to all the relevant facts and circumstances, which generally would include the actuarial life expectancy and the health of the seller. The lack of guidance with respect to valuation of the note makes a SCIN less certain in its gift tax effect than a private annuity, a similar vehicle that is described below.

---

[17] *See* Estate of Frane v. Comm'r, 998 F.2d 567 (8th Cir. 1993).

[18] *See* IRC § 453B(f); Estate of Frane v. Comm'r, 998 F.2d 567 (8th Cir. 1993).

It is uncertain how the buyer's basis in a SCIN will be determined if the seller dies during the term of the note. The IRS may take the position that only the amount actually paid can be included in the buyer's basis.

Since a SCIN must include a risk premium in order to avoid an immediate gift from seller to buyer, if the seller survives the term of the note, the buyer will have paid more than the fair market value of the property. In the family context, it may be acceptable if the seller needs the income for living expenses. However, if the goal of the transaction is primarily to minimize taxes, this feature may be a disincentive.

The use of a SCIN as a valid estate planning tool was upheld by the Sixth Circuit in *Costanza v. Commissioner*.[19] The Sixth Circuit, however, remanded the case to the Tax Court for further consideration of the IRS argument that the seller made a gift to the buyer because the purchase price was a bargain price.

In situations in which a SCIN appears appropriate, the estate planner should also consider the use of a private annuity, which is a similar vehicle in that it provides for payments that cease on the death of the seller. Each has slightly different advantages and disadvantages, compared below.

[E] Private Annuities

A private annuity is another variation on an installment sale that may be useful in the family context. In a sale for a private annuity, the seller transfers property to the buyer in exchange for the buyer's contractual promise to make a stream of payments to the seller that will continue until the seller's death, and then cease. As in the case of a SCIN, the seller's estate will not receive anything at the seller's death, and therefore the private annuity is not included in the seller's taxable estate (except to the extent of annuity payments that were made by the buyer and not consumed before the seller's death). A private annuity is well suited to a situation in which a senior family member wishes to pass a specific asset to a junior family member, but needs an income stream for living expenses during his lifetime. If the seller is in relatively poor health (but not so poor as to be terminally ill under the regulations), a private annuity can provide substantial transfer tax benefits.

EXAMPLE *8-36*

Roger, age 65, sells property worth $2,000,000 to his son Tim in exchange for Tim's promise to pay Roger $145,688 annually until Roger's death. The annuity has a fair market value equal to the value of the property. Roger uses the annuity payments to fund his living expenses. Roger dies two years later. Roger's estate does not include the transferred property or the private annuity (except to the extent that payments were previously made to Roger).

---

[19] 320 F.3d 595 (6th Cir. 2003), *rev'g* T.C.M. 2001-128.

It is important to note that while a private annuity provides tax benefits if the seller dies before reaching his life expectancy, the arrangement could have detrimental tax effects if the seller lives well beyond his life expectancy. In the above example, Tim will be obligated to continue making annuity payments until Roger's death. If Roger lives 20 years beyond his life expectancy, Tim will pay far more than the fair market value of the property to Roger. If Roger does not consume those payments during his lifetime, they will become part of his estate and will be subject to estate tax.

The income tax consequences of a sale of appreciated property in exchange for a private annuity remain somewhat uncertain. In October 2006, proposed regulations were issued that would significantly alter the income tax treatment of such a sale.[20] These proposed regulations state that, in general, they apply to sales that take place after October 18, 2006. Accordingly, while it is possible that these proposed regulations will never be adopted as final regulations, estate planners should take them into account in entering into any transaction involving a sale of appreciated property in exchange for a private annuity.

Under the rules in effect before the 2006 proposed regulations were issued, private annuity payments received by an individual in exchange for property were subject to income tax under the provisions of IRC Section 72.[21] Section 72 contains a formula that divides each payment into three parts: a nontaxable return of the seller's basis in the property; taxable gain on the sale of the property; and interest taxable as ordinary income. The effect of the formula was to spread the gain on the sale and the seller's recovery of her basis in the property over the life expectancy of the seller. If the seller outlived her life expectancy, all remaining payments would be ordinary income to her. The buyer was not permitted to deduct any portion of the annuity payment made as interest, even if the rules prohibiting deductions for personal interest would not apply.

Under the 2006 proposed regulations, an individual who sells appreciated property in exchange for an annuity would no longer be permitted to spread the gain on the sale over her life expectancy. The proposed rules provide that the seller is treated as if she had received cash equal to the value of the annuity (as determined under IRC Section 7520) at the time of the sale and had subsequently used the cash to purchase the annuity. The result is that any gain on the sale is subject to income tax in the year of the sale, despite the fact that the seller's actual receipt of cash payments will be spread out over her lifetime. If the property that was sold was highly appreciated, and the taxable gain is substantial, this would be an important disincentive to a private annuity sale.

The preamble to the 2006 proposed regulations indicates that the IRS is aware that some taxpayers use private annuity sales for valid non-tax reasons related to estate planning and family business succession planning and that the proposed regulations are not intended to frustrate these transactions. The preamble points out that it is possible to defer paying the income tax on the gain on such a sale under IRC

---

[20] Prop. Reg. §§ 1.1001-1(j), 1.72-6(e).
[21] *See* Rev. Rul. 69-74, 1969-1 C.B. 43; IRC § 72.

Section 453, which governs installment sales generally. The preamble invites comments from the public as to when a sale for a private annuity should be treated as an installment sale and subjected to income tax under Section 453. If the proposed regulations are finalized, there may be an exception that would allow family members to avoid triggering gain in the year of sale for some sales motivated by estate planning goals.

Generally, the buyer's initial basis in property purchased in exchange for a private annuity is equal to the fair market value of the annuity, and is adjusted up or down when the annuitant dies to reflect the amount actually paid.[22] The 2006 proposed regulations would not change this rule.

The 2006 proposed regulations would eliminate one important difference that currently exists between a private annuity and a SCIN. Under the existing rules, the gain on a sale for a private annuity is taxable in the year of the sale only if the annuity is secured by the property transferred.[23] To get the advantage of deferring income tax on the gain, the seller is required to rely on the promise of the buyer to make the annuity payments. If the seller receives a SCIN, however, the SCIN may be secured by the transferred property without changing the income tax consequences of the transaction. The 2006 proposed regulations would eliminate this difference between a private annuity and a SCIN in that the gain in a private annuity sale would be taxable in the year of the sale whether or not the annuity was secured.

Since one of the goals of a private annuity transaction is likely to be to remove the transferred property from the taxable estate of the seller, it is important that the buyer be in a financial position such that it is reasonable to expect that she will be able to meet the annuity payments. If the buyer's only source of income is the transferred property, the IRS may assert that the annuity payments constitute a retained right to the income of the transferred property, and the property will be includable in the seller's estate under IRC Section 2036.

While the 2006 proposed regulations may never be finalized, at this point practitioners assume that the gain on a private annuity sale will be subject to income tax in the year of the sale, and such sales are unattractive for sales of highly appreciated property. If the property to be transferred is not highly appreciated, however, a private annuity sale can be a useful estate planning tool.

EXAMPLE 8-37

Harold, the founder and sole owner of the Acme Company, died at age 65, leaving all of the company stock to his wife Maude. At the time of his death the company was worth $10,000,000. The following year, Maude, age 66, who was in frail health, although not terminally ill, sold the stock to her daughter Lily for a private annuity valued at $10,000,000 under IRC Section 7872. Maude's actuarial life expectancy was 18.7 years and the annual annuity payments were $753,210. The income tax basis of the stock

---

[22] Rev. Rul. 55-119, 1955-1 C.B. 352.
[23] *See* Estate of Bell v. CIR, 60 T.C. 469 (1973); 212 Corp. v. CIR, 70 T.C. 788 (1978).

was equal to the estate tax value of the stock, and so Maude will not recognize any taxable gain on the sale even if the 2006 proposed regulations are finalized. Two years later, Maude died, after receiving two payments totaling $1,506,420. The sale reduced Maude's taxable estate by approximately $8,500,000.

Some of the major features of a SCIN and a private annuity are contrasted and summarized below:

Private Annuity	*SCIN*
Method of valuing annuity provided by statute	Method of valuing note uncertain
No interest deduction for buyer	Interest may be deductible by buyer
Payments continue until the death of the seller	Payments cease at end of note term or death of seller, whichever comes first
Under existing rules, buyer's resale of property within two years will not trigger gain to seller; under 2006 proposed regulations, all gain is taxable in the year of sale	Buyer's resale of property within two years triggers seller's gain, if buyer does not resell, the income tax on the seller's gain may be stretched out
Under existing rules, seller's death does not trigger any remaining gain; under 2006 proposed regulations, seller's gain is triggered in year of sale	Seller's death during the term of the note triggers any remaining gain

[F] Loans

An intrafamily loan can be a useful way for senior members of a family to provide capital to younger family members without making a gift. It is no longer possible, however, to make an interest-free loan to a family member without tax consequences, except in limited circumstances. IRC Section 7872 now requires that for most loans in the family context, the lender will be treated as having received interest, and then transferred the interest amount to the borrower as a gift (or, depending on the circumstances, as a dividend or compensation).

Section 7872 contains a few important exceptions. It does not apply to a loan directly between individuals on any day on which the aggregate outstanding indebtedness between the individuals is $10,000 or less, except to the extent that the loan is attributable to the purchase or carrying of income producing assets. It does not apply to a compensation related or corporate-shareholder loan under $10,000 if it is not for tax avoidance purposes. (The OID rules also contain an exception to the rule that interest is imputed currently, and do not require interest to be imputed for loans of

$10,000 or less between individuals.)[24] In addition, there is a limitation on interest that will be imputed for income tax purposes on loans if the aggregate amount of the loans between the individual lender and the individual borrower is $100,000 or less. In such case, the amount of interest that will be imputed is limited to the borrower's net investment income for the year, and if the borrower's net investment income is $1,000 or less, it will be treated as zero.[25] Finally, certain term loans extended by an employer to an employee and used by the employee to purchase a principal residence in connection with the employee's employment are excepted from the operation of Section 7872, as are certain loans to a nursing home.[26]

While Section 7872 has limited the opportunities to use intrafamily loans as a means of transferring economic benefits to family members without transfer tax, Section 7872 requires only that interest be paid or accrued at the applicable federal rate, and the applicable federal rate may be substantially lower than alternative sources of capital. If the borrower can invest the borrowed funds in an investment that provides a return that exceeds the applicable federal rate, the loan can still be an effective estate planning tool.

EXAMPLE *8-38*

Rashmi lends $500,000 to her son Sahil and takes back a five-year note that provides for current payment of 2.2 percent interest, the applicable federal midterm rate. Sahil invests the cash in a venture capital company that produces an average annual yield of 20 percent. The loan from Rashmi has permitted Sahil to realize a substantial economic benefit from his investment and Rashmi has not incurred any gift tax.

If an intrafamily loan does not fall within one of the exceptions to Section 7872, then the interest rate on the loan becomes important. Section 7872 applies to loans that carry an interest rate that is less than the *applicable federal rate*. The IRS determines and publishes the applicable federal rate monthly. There are actually three applicable federal rates: (1) a short-term rate, for obligations of three years or less; (2) a midterm rate, for obligations of more than three years but less than nine years; and (3) a long-term rate, for obligations of nine years or more. For a demand loan (a loan that has no term) the short-term applicable rate, as compounded annually, applies.

The effect of Section 7872, when it applies to a loan between family members, is to treat the parties for tax purposes as if the borrower had paid the applicable rate of interest to the lender each year, and the lender had made a gift of that amount back to the borrower. These deemed payments have both income and gift tax consequences. The interest imputed to the lender will be taxable income to her, and may be deductible by the borrower if interest actually paid would have been deductible. In addition, the deemed retransfer of the interest amount to the borrower will be a

---

[24] IRC § 1272(a)(2)(e).

[25] IRC § 7872(d).

[26] IRC § 7872(g); Reg. § 1.7872-5T(c)(1).

taxable gift. If the loan is a term loan (as opposed to a demand loan), the entire amount of the foregone interest will be treated as a gift in the year that the loan is made.[27]

Section 7872 applies to any loan that provides for below-market interest if the inadequate interest is in the nature of a gift.[28] The scope of the rule, therefore, is broader than that of many other gift tax provisions that apply only to individuals having specific family relationships to each other. Section 7872 would apply, for example, to an interest-free loan from one member of unmarried couple to another. Section 7872 also applies to below-market loans between a corporation and a shareholder, and between an employer and an employee or independent contractor. The foregone interest in these situations would be treated as a dividend or as compensation, depending on the circumstances.

Section 7872 will not apply to an intrafamily loan if the note provides for interest at least at the applicable federal rate, even if the interest is not payable currently. Section 7872, however, is not the only tax provision that may apply to such loans. The *original issue discount* rules, or OID rules, are a complex set of rules intended to ensure that the tax consequences of loans or installment sales reflect the economic consequences or these transactions.[29] If a loan provides for adequate interest, but the interest is payable only at the end of the loan term, then the OID rules will require that the lender report the interest as received currently.

[G] Joint Purchases

Before 1990, families could employ a joint purchase of property as a means of transferring property to younger generations at a lessened transfer tax cost. In a typical joint purchase, a parent would purchase a life interest in property, and a child would simultaneously purchase a remainder interest in the property. The value of the life interest and the remainder interest would be calculated using the life expectancy of the parent. If each party paid the actuarial value of the respective interests, there would be no gift at the time of the purchase. The parent would have the right to occupy the property or receive all the income from the property during her lifetime. At her death, her life interest would expire, and the child would be entitled to the property as the remainderman. Since the parent's life estate terminated at her death, nothing would be included in her taxable estate.

In 1990, Congress enacted IRC Section 2702, which severely limited the opportunities to use joint purchases by family members for estate planning purposes. Under Section 2702, if a parent purchases a life estate and a child purchases the remainder interest, the transaction is recharacterized for gift tax purposes and is treated as if the parent had purchased the entire property and then had transferred the remainder interest to the child.

---

[27] IRC § 7872(d)(2).

[28] IRC § 7872(c)(1)(A).

[29] *See* IRC § § 1272–1275.

EXAMPLE *8-39*

Sharon purchases a life estate in property for $70 (the actuarial value of the life estate) and her daughter Peg purchases the remainder interest in the same property for $30. Under Section 2702, the transaction is treated for gift tax purposes as if Sharon had purchased the entire property for $100 and had transferred the remainder interest to Peg for $30. In determining the amount of any gift, Sharon's life estate is treated as having no value, and the remainder interest is treated as having a value of $100. As a consequence, Sharon will be treated under Section 2702 as having made a taxable gift of $70 to Peg.

Section 2702 contains certain limited exceptions, most notably the exceptions for a qualified personal residence trust and a grantor retained annuity trust, discussed above. Outside of these exceptions the rules of Section 2702 have effectively eliminated the usefulness of joint purchases as an estate planning advice in those situations in which they apply. Section 2702, however, applies only to transactions that involve certain family members. It would not apply to a joint purchase between an aunt and a nephew or niece. It would not apply to individuals who are not related by marriage or blood, and so could be used in planning for unmarried couples. In these situations, a joint purchase may remain a helpful estate planning tool.

§8.10 GIFT-GIVING STRATEGIES

[A] Factors Favoring a Gift-Giving Program

There are a number of different factors, both personal and financial, that favor a program of lifetime gifts:

- The donor will have the pleasure of receiving the beneficiary's gratitude during life;
- Beneficiaries may have the greatest need for additional assets in early years;
- The donor may wish to be free of the responsibility of managing the assets in her later years;
- The donor may wish to allow the beneficiary to take over the management of an asset such as family business while the donor is still alive to offer help and advice when needed;
- If the income from the property transferred is taxed to a beneficiary in a lower income tax bracket than the donor, the total income tax burden on the family may be reduced;
- Property given away is not subject to the donor's creditors (assuming that the gift was not a fraudulent transfer);
- Gifts can preserve the family's wealth by reducing the amount of transfer tax payable to pass assets to younger generations:
  - The donor can give $16,000 annually to any number of beneficiaries free of all estate and gift tax consequences;
  - All the appreciation in the transferred property that occurs after the date of the gift will be free of gift and estate tax;

— Any gift tax paid will be removed from the donor's estate if the donor survives for three years after the gift, and the tax amount will not be subject to estate tax; and

— The donor can reduce the transfer tax value of property given away by making gifts of minority interests or using special techniques such as a QPRT or GRAT.

While many factors favor an aggressive program of lifetime gifts for estate planning purposes, the estate planner should also remember that negative consequences can result from gifts:

- The donor's health or financial circumstances may deteriorate, and she may have a greater need for assets than she expected;
- Children may lose the incentive to care for elderly parents if they have already received a substantial part of the family's wealth as lifetime gifts;
- The beneficiaries may mismanage or sell transferred property;
- Children who receive gifts of significant assets early may lose the motivation to make their own way in the world;
- A disproportionate gift to one child can cause long-term resentment among other children, and the donor may not have sufficient asset to make equalizing gifts;
- Transferred assets may be subject to the creditors of the beneficiaries if the gift is not in trust;
- Property that is included in a decedent's estate receives a stepped-up basis for income tax purposes,[1] but gifts retain the donor's basis, so the beneficiary may have to pay income tax if she sells the gift.

[B] Gift-Giving for Maximum Tax Advantage

[1] Make Tax-Free Gifts First

Annual gifts that qualify for the $16,000 present interest exclusion should be one of the first steps in any gift program. A donor can make an unlimited number of annual exclusion gifts that are completely free of gift tax and generation-skipping tax. While $16,000 per year may seem relatively small to a very wealthy individual, using the annual exclusion to the fullest extent possible can provide a very significant tax benefit.

Paying tuition and medical expenses for family members can be another very powerful estate planning technique. A donor can pay any amount of such expenses without transfer tax consequences, and such payments do not affect the donor's ability to make $16,000 annual exclusion gifts.

---

[1] §8.10 In 2010, the year in which the estate tax was "repealed," there was a limitation on the basis step-up for assets included in a decedent's estate. These rules are discussed in Chapter 5. The basis step-up rule was reinstated in 2011.

EXAMPLE *8-40*

Jaden and Maria have seven grandchildren, all of college age. For each grandchild they make four $25,000 tuition payments, and in addition during each of the four years they add $32,000 to a Crummey trust for each grandchild. When all of the grandchildren finish college, Jaden and Maria will have passed $1,596,000 to their grandchildren, free of all transfer tax. Assuming that Jaden and Maria are in a 40 percent estate tax bracket, they have saved approximately $638,000 in estate tax by making these lifetime gifts rather than holding the assets until death.

[2] Choose Appreciating Property

Gifts are valued for gift tax purposes at the time the gift is made. If the gift increases in value after the gift is made the recipient benefits from the increase, without any further transfer tax. The higher the postgift appreciation, the greater the transfer tax advantage. Making gifts early, so that the appreciation or the income from the property has a long time to accrue to the benefit of the recipient of the gift, will also increase the advantage of a gift over testamentary bequest.

[3] Use Special Techniques

Gifts of partial interests (such as GRATs and QPRTs), fractional interests, and intrafamily loans and sales are not appropriate for every client. These techniques, however, can be remarkably powerful estate planning tools in the right circumstances, and an estate planner should be alert to the opportunity to use them.

[4] Consider Income Tax Basis

The income tax basis of property transferred by gift is generally the same as its basis in the hands of the donor. In some circumstances, it may be most tax efficient for a parent to make gifts of high-basis assets and to retain appreciated assets until death, when the income tax basis of the assets will be stepped up.

9

Generation-Skipping Transfer Tax Planning

§9.01 INTRODUCTION

The generation-skipping transfer (GST) tax provides an additional layer of complexity that an estate planner must take into consideration when planning for clients with significant wealth. Prior to the enactment of the GST tax, wealthy individuals could establish trusts to provide benefits for multiple generations while only paying one transfer tax. The potential for benefiting successive generations free of estate and gift taxes existed because the estate tax does not apply to life estates and other beneficial interests created by someone else and the gift tax does not generally apply to distributions from a trust. This allowed for significantly greater wealth to be passed through the generations than would have been the case if the property had been passed outright to each generation.

EXAMPLE 9-1

A mother had $10,000,000 that she wanted to pass down to her daughter, then to her granddaughter, and finally to her great-granddaughter. If the mother left the property outright to her daughter, and her daughter left the property outright to the granddaughter, and the granddaughter left the property outright to the great-granddaughter, and if a 40 percent estate tax applied at each death, then the property would be subject to estate tax three times before the great-granddaughter received it, reducing the size of the estate to $2,160,000.

	Tax Paid:	*Property After Tax:*
Mother's death	$4,000,000	$6,000,000
Daughter's death	$2,400,000	$3,600,000
Granddaughter's death	$1,440,000	$2,160,000

If, instead, the mother were to have established a trust from which money could be spent for her daughter and her granddaughter during their lives and then have the property pass outright to her great-granddaughter, only one transfer tax would have been due (at the time of the establishment of the trust), and at the termination of her daughter and her granddaughter's interests, her great-granddaughter would have been given the full $6,000,000 estate (plus any undistributed earnings) free of additional transfer taxes.

	Tax Paid:	*Property After Tax:*
Mother's death	$4,000,000	$6,000,000
Daughter's death	0	$6,000,000
Granddaughter's death	0	$6,000,000

The GST tax was designed to close this loophole by imposing a tax that approximates the estate and gift taxes that would have been imposed if the property had been transferred outright at each generation.

The GST tax is an expensive tax since it is applied at a flat (rather than progressive) tax rate (and is the maximum federal estate and gift tax rate, which is 40 percent).[1] The GST tax is imposed in addition to estate and gift taxes and the combined effect of these taxes is startling as they can result in tax rates of 100 percent of the value of the property transferred.

EXAMPLE 9-2

A grandfather has used up all available credits and exemptions and is in the 40 percent bracket for gift and estate tax purposes. The grandfather makes a $100,000 taxable gift to his granddaughter. As a result of this transfer, the grandfather has a gift tax liability of $40,000 (40 percent of $100,000), a GST tax liability of $40,000 (40 percent of $100,000), and an additional GST tax liability on the gift taxes paid of $16,000 (40 percent of $40,000),[2] resulting in a combined gift tax and GST tax liability of $96,000.

The GST tax system is extremely technical and complex. However, by understanding the tax and taking full advantage of the available exemptions and exclusions, the estate planner can reduce or eliminate a client's GST tax liability. In particular, the estate planner can advise a client how to take advantage of the following provisions:

- The education exclusion, by making tuition payments for skip persons for private day schools, college, and graduate school;
- The medical exclusion, by paying for the medical care of skip persons;
- The annual gift tax exclusion, by making annual exclusion gifts to skip persons either outright or through a trust that satisfies the requirements of IRC Section 2642(c)(2);
- The generation-skipping transfer tax exemption (GST exemption), by creating a dynasty trust or charitable lead trust that is funded with leveraged assets or structuring the testamentary plan to take advantage of any remaining exemption from the GST tax; and
- The predeceased ancestor exception, by making gifts to the children of a predeceased child, niece, or nephew.

In making use of these estate planning techniques, it is also important to select carefully the assets that will be given away. In order to achieve the greatest leveraging of the available exclusions and exemption, the donor should give away those assets that have the greatest potential for appreciation or assets that may be discounted. This chapter explains the rules of the GST tax and outlines planning techniques for minimizing GST tax liabilities.

---

[1] **§ 9.01** IRC § 2641.
[2] IRC § 2515.

§9.02 GST TAX BASICS

[A] Overview

One of the greatest obstacles to feeling comfortable with the GST tax is the fact that it involves a plethora of technical terms (often defined by other technical terms), and it is all too easy to get lost in the terminology. This section provides a general explanation of the tax as well as a roadmap through the terminology.

In general terms, the GST tax is imposed when there is a transfer to a person more than one generation below that of the transferor.[1] Each person is entitled to an exemption from the GST tax. In 2022, the exemption is $12,060,000.[2] In addition, some (but not all) transfers that are excluded from gift taxes are also excluded from the GST tax. To the extent that the transferor's exemption has not been allocated to a transfer, the GST tax is imposed at the highest federal estate and gift tax rate.

The GST tax is imposed on generation-skipping transfers. There are three types of generation-skipping transfers:

1. Direct skips;
2. Taxable distributions; and
3. Taxable terminations.

Each of these transfers involves a transfer of property to, or for the benefit of, an individual who is more than one generation below the transferor.

[B] Determining the Generations

[1] Skip Persons

The GST tax is generally imposed on transfers to individuals who are more than one generation removed from the transferor. The terms used to define generations are *skip persons*,[3] to denote persons who are considered to be more than one generation removed from the transferor and *non-skip persons*,[4] to denote persons who are not more than one generation removed from the transferor. It is only transfers to, or for the benefit of, skip persons that raise GST tax issues.

---

[1] **§ 9.02** The transferor is the person who was most recently subject to estate or gift tax on the transfer of the property. Thus, in the case of a gift subject to gift tax, the donor is the transferor. In the case of a transfer subject to estate tax, the decedent is the transferor. A person with a general power of appointment is treated as the transferor after the exercise or lapse of the power. IRC § 2652(a); Reg. § 26.2652-1(a)(1).

[2] IRC § 2631. The GST exemption equals the estate tax applicable exclusion amount which is $10,000,000 adjusted by a cost-of-living adjustment from 2010 forward ($12,060,000 in 2022). As of January 1, 2026, the estate tax applicable exclusion amount is scheduled to revert to $5,000,000 adjusted by a cost-of-living adjustment.

[3] IRC § 2613.

[4] *Id.*

There are two sets of rules for establishing generation assignments. The determination of which set of rules applies depends upon whether the recipient is related to the transferor.

[2] Generation Assignment for Relatives

For transfers to relatives, generations are determined along family lines. Thus, a transferor is considered to be in the same generation as her siblings, to be one generation removed from her children, nieces, and nephews, and to be more than one generation removed from grandchildren, grandnieces, and grandnephews.[5] It is transfers for the benefit of people in this last category that raise GST tax issues.

The rule for relatives also applies to transfers to relatives of the transferor's spouse.[6] Thus, a transferor is considered to be in the same generation as her spouse, to be one generation removed from her spouse's children (i.e., the transferor's stepchildren) and her spouse's nieces and nephews. A transferor is treated as more than one generation removed from her spouse's grandchildren, grandnieces, and grandnephews. It is transfers for the benefit of people in this last category that raise GST tax issues.

If an individual can be assigned to more than one generation under these rules, such individual is generally treated as being in the youngest of such generations.[7] Thus, adoption of an individual that already has a generation assignment based on a blood relationship will not move that individual to a higher generation.

EXAMPLE 9-3

Grandfather adopts a grandchild (such that now the grandchild is also grandfather's child). For generation-skipping transfer tax purposes, the grandchild will still be assigned to two generations below the grandfather.

When the transferee's parent is not living at the time of transfer, the transferee's generation assignment may be moved up under the *predeceased ancestor rule.*[8] This rule only applies if the transferee is a descendant of a parent of the transferor (or the transferor's spouse) and if the transferee's parent is dead at the time the transfer is subject to estate or gift tax.[9] If both of these requirements are met, then the transferee is treated as a member of the generation that is one generation below the lower of the transferor's generation or the generation assignment of the youngest living ancestor of such transferee who is also a descendant of the parent of the transferor.

---

[5] IRC § 2651.
[6] IRC § 2651(b)(2).
[7] IRC § 2651(f)(1).
[8] IRC § 2651(e).
[9] *Id.*

EXAMPLE 9-4

Grandfather makes a $3,500,000 gift to grandson. At the time of the gift, grandfather's daughter (who was grandson's mother) is dead. Grandson will be treated as being only one generation below grandfather, and therefore the gift to grandson will not be subject to generation-skipping transfer taxes.

This exception, however, does not apply to any individual who is not a lineal descendant of the transferor (or the transferor's spouse) unless, at the time of the transfer, the transferor has no living lineal descendants.[10]

EXAMPLE 9-5

Great-aunt makes a $3,500,000 gift to her great-nephew (the child of her deceased niece). If great-aunt has no lineal descendants at the time of transfer, then her great-nephew will be treated as being only one generation below great-aunt and the gift will not be subject to GST taxes. If great-aunt has lineal descendants of her own at the time of transfer, then her great-nephew will be treated as being two generations below great-aunt (and therefore a skip person) and the transfer to her great-nephew will potentially be subject to GST taxes.

The predeceased ancestor exception applies to taxable terminations and taxable distributions as well as direct skip transfers. However, in order to be applicable, the parent must have predeceased the beneficiary at the time of transfer (as opposed to at the time of termination or distribution).[11]

EXAMPLE 9-6

An individual (who has no descendants) creates an irrevocable trust for her sister, funding it with a $1,000,000 cash gift. The trust is to be held for the lifetime benefit of the sister, and thereafter to pass to the sister's descendants. All of the sister's children are living at the time the trust is created. However, before the sister dies, one of her sons (i.e., the transferor's nephew) dies leaving children of his own. His children do not assume the nephew's generation for GST tax purposes because the nephew was alive at the time the transfer to the trust was a completed gift. On the other hand, had the nephew died before the trust was created,

---

[10] IRC § 2651(e)(2).
[11] IRC § 2651(e)(1)(B).

his children would move up to his generation so that the transfer from the trust to them upon their grandmother's death would not be subject to GST tax.

The rules regarding relatives apply to people who:[12]

1. Are married to the transferor;
2. Are lineal descendants of the transferor's grandparents; or
3. Are lineal descendants of the transferor's spouse's grandparents.

Thus, people as remotely connected as the issue of the transferor's first cousins or the issue of the transferor's spouse's first cousins have their generation determined along family lines, as opposed to by reference to the transferor's age.

An individual who has been legally adopted is treated as if related by blood to the transferor.[13] In addition, individuals who are related by half blood (such as siblings who share one parent, but not both parents) are treated as if they are related by whole blood.[14]

[3] Generation Assignment for Nonrelatives

When transfers are made to people outside of the family (or to people more remotely connected to the transferor than first cousins and their issue), generations are determined by the age difference from the transferor. A generation is treated as occurring every 25 years.[15] Thus, individuals not more than $12^1/_2$ years younger than the transferor are treated as being in the same generation as the transferor, individuals more than $12^1/_2$ years younger and less than $37^1/_2$ years younger than the transferor are treated as being one generation below the transferor, and individuals more than $37^1/_2$ years younger than the transferor are treated as being more than one generation removed from the transferor. Again, it is only transfers for the benefit of people in this last category (i.e., nonrelatives more than $37^1/_2$ years younger than the transferor) that raise GST tax issues.

EXAMPLE 9-7

A decedent leaves her estate to a friend who is 40 years younger than the decedent. The friend is a skip person and therefore the transfer will potentially be subject to GST taxes.

---

[12] IRC § 2651(b).

[13] IRC § 2651(b)(3)(A). Although, as discussed above, a person cannot move up a generation by being adopted.

[14] IRC § 2651(b)(3)(B).

[15] IRC § 2651(d).

[4] Generation Assignment for Trusts

The generation assignment for a trust is dependent upon the generation assignment of the beneficiaries having a current interest in the trust. A trust will be treated as a skip person if (1) all interests in the trust are held by skip persons, or (2) no person holds an interest in the trust and at no time may a distribution be made to a non-skip person.[16]

Not all beneficial interests are treated as interests for purposes of the GST tax rules. In particular, an individual is treated as having an interest in the trust only if the individual (1) has a present right to receive principal or income, or (2) is a permissible current recipient of trust principal or income.[17]

EXAMPLE 9-8

A mother creates a trust with the income payable to her daughter and the remainder to her daughter's children. The daughter has an interest in the trust (because she has a right to current income), but the daughter's children are not treated as having an interest in the trust for GST tax purposes.

If the mother had created a trust that provided for income and principal to be distributed to both her daughter and her daughter's children with the remainder payable to her daughter's grandchildren, both her daughter and her daughter's children would have an interest in the trust. In both of these examples since an interest in the trust is held by a non-skip person (e.g., the daughter), the trust is a non-skip person.

EXAMPLE 9-9

Mother created a trust that provided that her daughter's children were eligible recipients of income and principal, with the remainder payable to her daughter's grandchildren. Only the daughter's children would have an interest in the trust for GST tax purposes. Since all interests in the trust are held by skip persons, the trust would be a skip person with respect to the transferor (the mother).

In order to avoid manipulation of these rules, an individual will not be treated as having an interest in a trust if (1) the probability that a distribution will be made to

---

[16] IRC § 2613; Reg. § 26.2612-1(d)(2).
[17] Reg. § 26.2612-1(e).

that person is so remote as to be negligible,[18] or (2) if the interest is granted to the individual for the principal purpose of postponing or avoiding the GST tax.[19]

An individual will also be treated as having an interest in the trust if trust income or principal must be used to satisfy the individual's support obligation.[20]

EXAMPLE 9-10

Grandfather established a trust for the benefit of his grandchild who is a minor. Under the terms of the trust, the trustee is obligated to use trust income and principal in satisfaction of father's support obligations to grandchild. Father will be treated as having an interest in the trust. Since father is a non-skip person, the trust will not be treated as a skip person.

An individual does not have an interest solely because trust property may be used within the discretion of a fiduciary, or pursuant to state law substantially similar to the Uniform Gifts to Minors Act (or Uniform Transfers to Minors Act) to satisfy a support obligation of the individual.[21]

EXAMPLE 9-11

Grandfather established a trust for the benefit of his grandchild who is a minor. Under the terms of the trust, the trustee has discretion to distribute property for the grandchild's support. The fact that the trust assets may be used to satisfy a support obligation of the beneficiary's parent does not mean that the beneficiary's parent (a non-skip person) has an interest in the trust.

PRACTICE NOTE

It is uncertain whether this "support obligation" exception will apply, as a practical matter, where the fiduciary is the person who has the obligation to support the beneficiary. Thus, when creating a trust for the benefit of skip persons, the beneficiary's parent should either not be designated as fiduciary or, if designated as fiduciary, should be precluded from exercising a discretionary power to discharge a support obligation.

---

[18] Reg. § 26.2612-1(d)(2)(ii).

[19] Reg. § 26.2612-1(e)(2)(ii).

[20] Reg. § 26.2612-1(f), Example 13.

[21] Reg. § 26.2612-1(f). The Uniform Gift to Minors Act and the Uniform Transfers to Minors Act are discussed in Chapter 7.

Once the individuals who have an interest in a trust are identified, it can be determined whether the trust is a skip person or a non-skip person. If all interests in the trust are held by skip persons, the trust is treated as a skip person. Also, if no person holds an interest in the trust for GST purposes (i.e., if the trust does not permit current distributions of income or principal), the trust will be treated as a skip person if no distributions, other than a distribution the probability of which occurring is so remote as to be negligible, may be made after the transfer to a person other than a skip person.[22] If any non-skip person holds an interest in the trust, then the trust is a non-skip person.

---

[22] IRC § 2613(a)(2)(B).

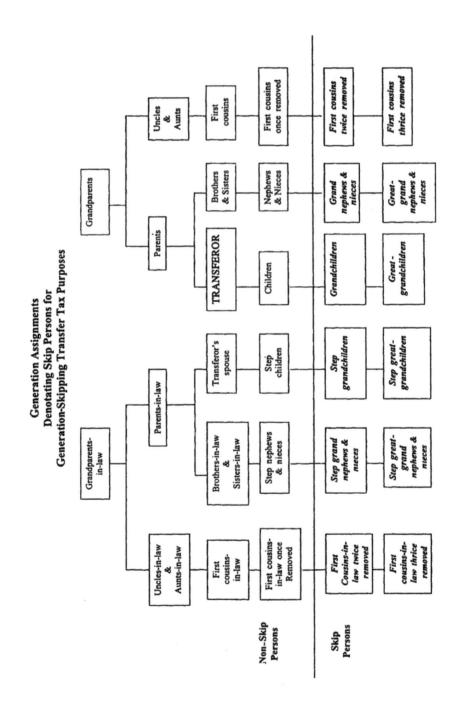

Generation Assignments Denotating Skip Persons for Generation-Skipping Transfer Tax Purposes

[C] Types of Generation-Skipping Transfers

There are three types of generation-skipping transfers:

1. Direct skips;
2. Taxable terminations; and
3. Taxable distributions.

All of these involve transfers for the benefit of a person who is more than one generation removed from the transferor. However, it is important to be able to categorize the different types of generation-skipping transfers since the type of transfer will determine who is liable for payment of the tax, the timing of the tax liability, as well as the amount on which the tax is imposed. In addition, the allocation of the exemption, as well as the availability of certain exclusions, depends upon the classification of the generation-skipping transfer.

[1] Direct Skips

A *direct skip* occurs when there is a transfer, subject to estate or gift taxes to a skip person.[23]

EXAMPLE 9-12

Grandfather makes a gift of $100,000 to his grandchild. The transfer is a direct skip since it is a transfer subject to gift taxes for the benefit of a skip person. Similarly, a direct skip would occur if the grandfather made a transfer to a trust, all the income of which was payable to his grandchild and the remainder passed to his great-grandchildren.

The taxable amount in a direct skip (i.e., the amount on which the GST tax liability is based) is the amount received by the transferee[24] and the tax is paid by the transferor.[25] Because of this, the GST tax on a direct skip is *tax exclusive,* which means that the GST tax is paid only on the amount of the gift and not on the dollars used to pay the GST tax.[26] For example, if the grandfather's gift of $100,000 to his grandchild was entirely subject to the GST, the tax would be calculated only on the basis of the $100,000 transferred to the grandchild. This is unlike the treatment of taxable terminations and taxable distributions—both of which are taxed on a tax inclusive basis (i.e., the tax is paid on both the amount of the transfer and the amount used to pay

---

[23] IRC § 2612(c)(1).
[24] IRC § 2623.
[25] IRC § 2603(a)(3).
[26] *Id.*

the GST tax).[27] In order to offset this advantage of direct skips, there is an additional gift tax imposed on the transferor on the amount of any GST tax imposed on the transferor of a direct skip.[28] As a result, the combined gift and GST tax on a direct skip is equivalent to the GST tax on taxable distributions and taxable terminations.

EXAMPLE 9-13

Grandfather made a $100,000 gift to his grandson in 2022. The gift was treated as a direct skip for GST tax purposes. None of grandfather's GST exemption was allocated to the transfer. As a result of this transfer, grandfather owes $40,000 of GST taxes, and grandfather's gift tax liability will be calculated on the sum of the amount transferred ($100,000) and the GST taxes paid ($40,000). If grandfather is subject to tax at the highest marginal rate, then the addition of this $40,000 to the tax base will result in an additional gift tax liability of $16,000 (40 percent of $40,000).

The transferor is liable for the payment of the GST tax on a direct skip.[29]

[2] Taxable Terminations

A taxable termination is any termination of an interest in a trust unless, (1) immediately after the termination, a non-skip person has an interest in the trust, or (2) no future distributions from the trust may be made to a skip person.[30]

EXAMPLE 9-14

Aunt creates a trust for her niece with income payable to the niece for her life and, upon the niece's death, the trust is to be distributed to the niece's children (who, under the generation assignment rules, are skip persons with respect to the aunt). The niece's death will be a taxable termination.

Only one taxable termination occurs upon the happening of a single event, even though the interests of more than one person may terminate as a result of that event resulting in the skipping of more than one generation.

---

[27] For taxable distributions this is accomplished by imposing the tax liability on the transferee (IRC § 2603(a)(1)), and imposing an additional tax if the GST tax is paid out of trust assets (IRC § 2621(b)). For taxable terminations this is accomplished by imposing the GST on the entire value of the trust, even though a portion of the trust must be used to pay the GST tax. IRC § 2622. The distinction between tax inclusive and tax exclusive transfers is discussed in the context of estate and gift taxes in Chapter 8.

[28] IRC § 2515.

[29] IRC § 2603(a)(3).

[30] IRC § 2612(a).

EXAMPLE 9-15

A trust is established for the benefit of the transferor's child, grandchild, and great-grandchild, and terminates on the death of the transferor's child in favor of the transferor's great-grandchild. Only one taxable termination occurs notwithstanding that the interests of both the transferor's child and grandchild terminated on the death of the child.[31]

This treatment as a single taxable termination where there are terminations of multiple interests may provide planning opportunities where a transferor wishes to benefit succeeding generations through a trust.

In order to avoid having remote interests added in order to keep a trust from having a taxable termination, the Code provides that in determining whether there is a taxable termination, any distribution the probability of which occurring is so remote as to be negligible is not considered.[32]

When a taxable termination occurs, the taxable amount for GST tax purposes is the value of the entire trust property.[33] A deduction is allowed for certain expenses, indebtedness, and taxes.[34] Since the tax is imposed on the entire value of the trust and the trust property is used to pay the GST tax,[35] the tax is imposed on a tax inclusive basis (i.e., the tax is imposed on the dollars used to pay the tax, as well as on that which eventually passes to the beneficiaries).

EXAMPLE 9-16

Grandmother established a trust for the benefit of her son for life and upon the son's death the property was to be held for her granddaughter until she reached age 35. Son dies. At the time of son's death, granddaughter was 28 years old and the trust was worth $1,000,000. Son's death is a taxable termination (since after the son's death no one has an interest in the trust for GST purposes and at no time will property be distributed to a non-skip person). The taxable amount is $1,000,000 and the tax will be paid from the trust assets. Granddaughter will receive $1,000,000 minus the GST taxes associated with the taxable termination.

In a taxable termination, the trustee is liable for the payment of the tax.[36]

---

[31] Reg. § 26.2612-1(f), Example 9.

[32] Reg. § 26.2612-1(b)(1)(iii).

[33] IRC § 2622(a).

[34] These are similar to the estate tax deductions allowed under IRC § 2053. IRC § 2622(b).

[35] IRC § 2603(a)(2).

[36] IRC § 2603(a)(2).

[3] Taxable Distributions

A taxable distribution is any distribution of income or principal from a trust to a skip person in a transaction that is not a direct skip or a taxable termination.[37]

EXAMPLE 9-17

Grandmother makes a transfer of $100,000 to an irrevocable trust that provides that income and principal may be distributed to her children and grandchildren. The trust will be a non-skip person (since her children are non-skip persons and have an interest in the trust) and, therefore, the transfer to the trust is not a direct skip and is not immediately subject to the GST tax. However, when distributions are made from the trust to a grandchild, such distributions will be taxable distributions.

The amount subject to the GST tax when a taxable distribution occurs is the value of the property distributed to the skip person.[38] This amount is reduced by any expenses incurred in connection with the determination, collection, or refund of the tax.[39]

The beneficiary receiving the distribution is personally responsible for paying the tax.[40] Because the beneficiary is liable for the tax (and therefore the tax is essentially paid out of the distributed property), the GST tax on taxable distributions is imposed on a tax inclusive basis. If the trustee pays any of the tax out of other trust assets, that tax payment is treated as being an additional taxable distribution subject to the GST tax.[41]

EXAMPLE 9-18

Grandfather established a trust for the benefit of his children and grandchildren. The trustee distributes $100,000 of the trust to one of the grandchildren for the purchase of a home. The transfer of property to the trust was not subject to the GST tax since a non-skip person (namely, grandfather's children) had an interest in the trust. However, the $100,000 distribution to grandchild was a taxable distribution. Grandchild is responsible for paying any GST taxes associated with this transfer. If instead the trustee pays the GST tax out of other trust assets, then that amount will be treated as an additional taxable distribution to grandchild.

---

[37] IRC § 2612(b).
[38] IRC § 2621(a).
[39] IRC § 2621(a)(2).
[40] IRC § 2603(a)(1).
[41] IRC § 2621(b).

[D] Determining the Tax Rate

The rules used to determine the tax rate imposed on a GST appear intimidating due to the seemingly complex mathematical computations that are required. However, the computations are quite easy to apply once the overriding framework is understood.

The GST tax rate applicable to any given transfer depends upon the extent to which the transferor has allocated some or all of her exemption (in 2022, $12,060,000) to the transfer.[42] If none of the exemption has been allocated, then the GST tax rate is the highest federal estate tax rate in effect (40 percent). If the amount transferred is completely covered by the allocated exemption, then the GST tax rate is zero. And if the amount transferred is partially covered by the allocated exemption, then the tax rate is between zero and the highest federal estate tax rate in effect. This result is accomplished through the concept of the inclusion ratio.

In specific terms, the GST tax is computed by multiplying the *taxable amount by the applicable rate*. The *applicable rate* is the highest federal estate and gift tax rate in effect at the time of the transfer,[43] multiplied by the *inclusion ratio* of the property transferred that is subject to tax.[44]

Applicable Rate = Highest Federal Estate Tax Rate in Effect × the Inclusion Ratio

The transferred property's inclusion ratio is equal to the excess of one over the transferred property's *applicable fraction*.[45] The *applicable fraction* has a numerator equal to the amount of GST tax exemption allocated and a denominator equal to the value of the property transferred (minus any federal and state estate taxes paid from the trust property plus and any charitable deduction allowed).[46] This can be expressed in the following mathematical formula:

$$\text{Inclusion Ratio} = 1 - \frac{\text{allocated GST tax exemption}}{\begin{array}{c}\text{value of property transferred} - \text{any federal and state} \\ \text{estate taxes paid from the trust property and any} \\ \text{charitable deductions allowed}\end{array}}$$

For direct skips the calculation is relatively straightforward since the charitable deduction and the deduction for federal estate taxes and state death taxes will usually not apply.

---

[42] The GST tax exemption is $10,000,000 adjusted by a cost-of-living adjustment beginning in 2010. In 2022, the adjusted GST exemption is $12,060,000.

[43] In 2022, the maximum federal estate and gift tax rate is 40 percent.

[44] IRC § 2641.

[45] IRC § 2642(a)(1).

[46] IRC § 2631. The GST exemption equals the estate tax applicable exclusion amount which is $10,000,000 adjusted by a cost-of-living adjustment from 2010 forward ($12,060,000 in 2022).

If a transferor makes a gift to a grandchild of $1,000,000 and allocates $1,000,000 of exemption to the transfer, then the inclusion ratio equals one minus $1,000,000 (the amount of exclusion allocated)/$1,000,000 (the amount transferred) or (1 – 1/1), which equals zero. The applicable rate is determined by multiplying this inclusion ratio (zero) by the highest federal estate and gift tax rate, which results in an applicable tax rate of zero. In this way, the transferor's GST exemption completely protects the transfer from the GST tax.

If the transferor does not allocate any GST exemption to the transfer, then the inclusion ratio equals one minus zero (the amount of exclusion allocated)/$1,000,000 (the amount transferred) or 1 – 0/1,000,000, which equals one. The applicable rate is determined by multiplying this inclusion ratio (one) times the highest federal estate and gift tax rate, which results in an applicable tax rate of the highest federal estate and gift tax rate (40 percent). In this way, by not allocating any of the transferor's exemption, the transfer is subject to the highest federal estate and gift tax rate currently in effect.

If the transferor allocates $500,000 of his exemption to the transfer, then the inclusion ratio equals one minus $500,000 (the amount of exclusion allocated)/ $1,000,000 (the amount transferred) or 1 – 1/2 which equals 1/2. Since the applicable rate is determined by multiplying this inclusion ratio (1/2) times the highest federal estate and gift tax rate (40 percent), this results, for example, in an applicable tax rate of 20 percent.

The calculation is done the same way for purposes of determining the GST tax rate applicable to taxable terminations and taxable distributions from trusts.[47] When a trust is established, the inclusion ratio is determined when property is first transferred to the trust. This inclusion ratio applies for the duration of the trust (unless there are future additions to the trust).[48] Subsequent taxable terminations and taxable distributions arising from that trust are subject to tax only to the extent required by the inclusion ratio. Thus, if the total funding of a trust is $1,000,000, a transferor can completely protect the trust from GST taxes for the life of the trust by allocating $1,000,000 of GST exemption to the trust. If the total funding of a trust is instead $2,000,000 and a transferor allocates $1,000,000 of GST exemption to the trust, the trust will have an applicable fraction of one-half and an inclusion ratio of one-half. Thus, any GST from the trust will be taxable at an applicable rate of one-half of the highest federal estate and gift tax rate. It should be noted that since the applicable fraction is determined at the time of the funding of the trust and continues throughout the life of the trust, a transferor can shelter much more through allocating GST exemption to a trust that will have future taxable distributions and taxable terminations, rather than to a transfer constituting a direct skip.

---

[47] Id.

[48] Transfers made to existing trusts may require a recomputation of the inclusion ratio. IRC § 2642(d).

EXAMPLE *9-19*

Grandmother transfers $1,000,000 to a trust for the benefit of her children, grandchildren, and great-grandchildren. Grandmother allocates $1,000,000 of her exemption to this trust.

Twenty-five years later (when the last non-skip person's interest in the trust terminates), the trust is worth $10,000,000 and numerous distributions have been made from the trust to skip persons. Neither the taxable termination, nor any of the distributions from the trust will be subject to GST taxes since the applicable tax rate for the trust will be zero times the highest federal estate and gift tax rate—which will always result in a tax rate of zero.

§9.03 EXEMPTIONS AND EXCLUSIONS

There are a number of exemptions and exclusions that limit the application of the GST tax. A direct skip, taxable distribution, or taxable termination may be avoided if the transfer to the skip person is eligible for one of the exclusions from the GST tax or if the transferor's GST exemption is allocated to the original transfer.

[A] Certain Lifetime Gifts

The GST tax provides exclusions for lifetime transfers that (subject to certain modifications) track the gift tax exclusions for:[1]

1. Educational expenses;
2. Medical expenses; and
3. Annual gifts of present interests.

In general, transfers that qualify for the exclusion for gift tax purposes will also qualify for the exclusion from the GST tax. The GST tax rules accomplish this by providing that these transfers will have an inclusion ratio of zero.[2] However, the GST nontaxable gift exclusion will not be available for annual exclusion transfers in trust unless two additional elements are provided for in the trust:

1. Trust principal or income can only be used for the benefit of a single individual during his or her life; and
2. The assets of the trust will be includable in the gross estate of the individual if the individual dies before the trust terminates.[3]

---

[1] **§9.03** IRC § 2503.

[2] IRC § 2642(c)(1).

[3] IRC § 2642(c)(2). The requirements for transfer in trust are discussed in greater detail in §9.03[B][3] *infra.*

[1] Exclusion for Educational Expenses

Tuition payments paid directly to an educational organization for the education or training of an individual are also not subject to the GST tax.[4] There is no dollar limit on the amount of the annual tuition payment. The payment, however, must be made directly to the educational organization and is limited to tuition. Tuition can cover private day school education, college education, and postgraduate education. However, tuition does not include room and board. Some educational organizations offer students the opportunity to prepay their tuition. These prepayments may qualify for the exclusion provided certain requirements are met.[5]

[2] Exclusion for Medical Expenses

Payments to any person for the medical care of an individual that are eligible for the exclusion from gift tax are also excluded for GST tax purposes.[6] Again, these payments must be made directly to the provider of the medical care. Medical care includes not only services rendered by a physician or hospital but also encompasses medical insurance.

[3] The Educational-Medical Exclusion Discretionary Trust

The educational and medical exclusions from the GST tax are applicable whether the source of the payment is the transferor or a trust created by the transferor, so long as the payment is made on behalf of a skip person directly to the educational organization or to the medical care provider. Thus, effective GST tax planning can be achieved by adding skip persons as discretionary beneficiaries of trusts that are otherwise not exempt from GST taxes and authorizing the trustee to make distributions to or for the benefit of such skip persons by making tuition payments directly to an educational organization or making medical payments directly to the medical care provider.

[B] GST Nontaxable Gift Exclusion

[1] General Rule

As a general rule, a gift that is eligible for the gift tax annual exclusion ($16,000 for the year 2022) is also exempt from the GST tax.[7] This is accomplished by a section that provides that, where there is a direct skip that is a nontaxable gift, the inclusion

---

[4] IRC § 2642(c)(1) and (3)(B). In order to qualify, the educational organization must be described in IRC § 170(b)(1)(A)(ii).

[5] Ltr. Rul. 200602002.

[6] IRC § § 2503(e) and 2642(c)(3)(B). Eligible medical care is described in IRC § 213(d).

[7] IRC § 2642(c)(1). The annual exclusion for gift tax purposes is in IRC § 2503(b)(1). Although the annual exclusion amount was $10,000 in 2001, the amount has increased since it is subject to

ratio is zero.[8] This exclusion is extremely valuable and can result in the transmission of substantial wealth if consistently used over a long period of time.

The annual exclusion allows a donor to make annual tax-free gifts of *present interests* of up to $16,000 (for the year 2022) to an unlimited number of donees. A present interest in property is "[a]n unrestricted right to the immediate use, possession, or enjoyment of property or the income from property (such as a life estate or term certain)."[9] In order to be eligible for the nontaxable gift exclusion for GST purposes, the transfer must (1) be a direct skip (i.e., a transfer subject to gift or estate tax to a skip person) and (2) qualify for the gift tax annual exclusion.[10] In addition, if the transfer is to a trust, additional requirements must be met.[11]

[2] Outright Transfers of Property

The simplest manner in which to take advantage of the non-taxable gift exclusion is to make an outright gift of $16,000 (for the year 2022) to a grandchild or other skip person. An outright transfer of property will qualify for the annual exclusion for both gift and GST tax purposes since the gift will be a direct skip (i.e., a transfer to a skip person that is subject to gift tax) and an outright transfer is a present interest and therefore qualifies under Section 2503(b).

If the grandchild is a minor, the transfer will also qualify for the exclusion (for both gift tax purposes and GST tax purposes) if the transfer is under a state Uniform Gifts to Minors Act or Uniform Transfers to Minors Act.[12]

[3] Gifts in Trust

If the transferor wants to make a gift in trust, several hurdles will need to be jumped in order for the gifts to qualify for the nontaxable gift exclusion. In particular, the transfer must meet the following three requirements:[13]

1. The trust must meet the special requirements imposed by Section 2642(c) on transfers in trust;
2. The transfer to the trust must qualify as a direct skip; and
3. The trust must meet the requirements for the annual exclusion under Section 2503(b).

(Footnote Continued)

adjustment for inflation (in $1,000 increments) for gifts made after 1998. IRC § 2503(b)(2). The annual exclusion amount is $16,000 in 2022.

[8] IRC § 2642(c)(1).

[9] Reg. § 25.2503-3(b). The annual exclusion is discussed in Chapter 8.

[10] IRC § 2642(c).

[11] *See* § 9.03[B][3] *infra.*

[12] Transfers under the Uniform Gifts to Minors Act and Uniform Transfers to Minors Act are discussed in Chapter 7.

[13] IRC § 2642(c).

First, the Code imposes special requirements for qualifying for the GST nontaxable gift exclusion when there is a transfer in trust. In order for such a transfer to qualify for the exclusion the trust must provide that, during the life of the individual, no portion of the corpus or the income of the trust may be distributed to or for the benefit of any person other than the skip person and, if the skip person dies before the trust is terminated, the assets of the trust will be includable in the skip person's gross estate (e.g., the skip person has a general power of appointment).[14] This means that the trust must be established for the benefit of a single skip person (e.g., one grandchild), or, if the trust is set up for multiple beneficiaries, that separate subtrusts be established for each skip person.

The other requirements are the same requirements for outright transfers of property to qualify for the nontaxable gift exclusion (i.e., the transfer must be a direct skip and must qualify for the annual exclusion for gift tax purposes). However, although these requirements are relatively easy to meet in the context of an outright distribution of property, they take on added complexity when the gift is in trust.

The second requirement is that the transfer must be a direct skip.[15] A direct skip is a transfer subject to estate or gift taxes to a skip person.[16] A trust is treated as a skip person if (1) all interests in the trust are held by skip persons or (2) if no person holds an interest in the trust and no distributions, other than a distribution the probability of which occurring is so remote as to be negligible, may be made to a person other than a skip person.[17] As noted above, an individual has an interest in the trust if the individual (1) has a present right to receive principal or income or (2) is a permissible current recipient of trust principal or income.[18] Therefore, to meet this direct skip requirement, the trust should be structured so that it is solely for the benefit of a skip person.

Is the "direct skip" requirement met by granting Crummey powers of withdrawal to skip persons? A common technique to make a transfer to a trust eligible for the gift tax annual exclusion is to grant a beneficiary of the trust a Crummey power of withdrawal. A Crummey power of withdrawal allows the beneficiary of the trust to withdraw property contributed to the trust in an amount typically that does not exceed the annual exclusion ($16,000 in 2022) for a limited period of time (e.g., 60 days).[19] Although it might appear that this withdrawal right is essentially the same as a direct skip to the holder of that right, this is not the position taken by the regulations. The regulations provide that a transfer to a trust subject to a beneficiary's right of withdrawal is treated as a transfer to the trust rather than a transfer to the beneficiary.[20] Thus, the granting of Crummey powers of withdrawal to a skip person

---

[14] IRC § 2642(c)(2).

[15] *Id.*

[16] IRC § 2612(c).

[17] IRC § 2613(a)(2).

[18] Reg. § 26.2612-1(e).

[19] Crummey powers are discussed in Chapter 8.

[20] Reg. § 26.2652-1(a)(5), Example 5, provides that a transfer to a trust subject to a beneficiary's right of withdrawal is treated as a transfer to the trust rather than a transfer to the beneficiary. Although the regulations, therefore, limit the ability to use the nontaxable gift exclusion to protect transfers to a

will not, on its own, secure the nontaxable gift exclusion. A transfer to a Crummey trust that has a skip person as the sole beneficiary may qualify, however, because then the trust would be a skip person.

Finally, in order for the nontaxable gift exclusion to apply, the transfer must meet the present interest requirement for the gift tax annual exclusion.[21] A present interest in property is "[a]n unrestricted right to the immediate use, possession, or enjoyment of property or the income from property (such as a life estate or term certain)."[22] Most outright transfers of property qualify as a present interest in property for purposes of the annual exclusion. However, a transfer in trust generally does not qualify as a present interest unless steps are taken to assure that the requirement is met. The two most common methods for qualifying a transfer in trust for the present interest requirement is either (1) structuring the trust as a Section 2503(c) minor's trust (a statutorily authorized exception to the present interest requirement),[23] or (2) granting the donee the immediate right to withdraw the annual exclusion amount ($16,000 for the year 2022) from the trust for a limited period of time (called Crummey withdrawal rights).

Transfers to an irrevocable trust (such as a traditional life insurance trust), where discretionary beneficiaries include not just one of the transferor's grandchildren but also the transferor's spouse, children, and other grandchildren, are not protected from GST taxation by reason of the non-taxable gift exclusion. The reason for this is that transfers to such trusts do not constitute "direct skips" because the spouse and children are not skip persons. Thus, taxable terminations and taxable distributions from these discretionary trusts will be subject to the GST tax unless (1) the transferor's GST exemption has been allocated to the trust, or (2) the transfer qualifies for the educational or medical exclusion.

EXAMPLE 9-20

G transfers a policy of insurance on G's life to an irrevocable sprinkle trust for the benefit of G's spouse and children. Transfers to the trust are not subject to gift tax due to the fact that G's spouse and children are granted

---

(Footnote Continued)

trust from the GST tax (i.e., by treating a transfer over which a skip person holds a Crummey power of withdrawal as a transfer to the trust), that treatment of Crummey powers allows practitioners to include skip persons (e.g., grandchildren or more remote descendants) as Crummey power holders without having to be concerned with immediate adverse GST tax consequences. Moreover, if all the property is used for the benefit of non-skip persons (e.g., the grantor's spouse and/or children), or for "exempt" purposes (e.g., tuition and health care for grandchildren), there might never be any GST tax imposed on the property in trust because there is no eventual taxable distribution or taxable termination in favor of skip persons who are the contingent remaindermen notwithstanding that such persons hold Crummey powers of withdrawal. Thus, where a skip person holds a power of withdrawal, the transfer under the regulations will not be treated as a direct skip, which would result in the imposition of an immediate GST tax or use of the transferor's GST tax exemption.

[21] IRC § 2503(b). The present interest requirement is discussed in greater detail in Chapter 8.

[22] Reg. § 25.2503-3(b).

[23] IRC § 2503(c).

Crummey withdrawal powers. Nonetheless, transfers to the trust will not qualify as "direct skips" because the spouse and children are not skip persons. Therefore, the transfer will not qualify as a nontaxable gift for GST tax purposes. If property is distributed from the trust to skip persons (e.g., the grandchildren), a taxable distribution or taxable termination will occur and a GST tax will be imposed (unless protected from the GST tax by reason of another exclusion or exemption).

If the primary reason for creating the trust is to benefit the transferor's grandchildren (and, perhaps, more remote descendants), a transferor may be able to take advantage of the nontaxable gift exclusion. However, in order to do so, it is critical that (1) the trust be drafted as a skip person (and, thus, that there must be no interests, including contingent interests, in non-skip persons) and (2) each trust must have only one skip person as a beneficiary. The latter requirement can be accomplished by drafting a trust agreement that provides for the creation of a subtrust for each skip person the grantor wishes to benefit, with each subtrust satisfying the requirements of IRC Section 2642(c)(2).

If a transferor makes a contribution to a trust that is in excess of the amount that is eligible for the annual exclusion, then the transfer is treated as consisting of two parts, one that qualifies totally for the GST tax nontaxable gift exclusion and one that does not qualify for the exclusion.

EXAMPLE 9-21

T transferred in 2022 $17,000 to an irrevocable trust for the benefit of T's grandchild, GC. Under the terms of the trust, the income is to be paid to GC for ten years or until GC's prior death. Upon the expiration of GC's income interest, the trust principal is payable to GC or GC's estate. $16,000 of the transfer qualifies for the annual exclusion for both gift tax and GST tax purposes. Solely for purposes of computing the tax on the direct skip, T's transfer is divided into two portions. One portion is equal to the amount of the nontaxable transfer ($16,000) and has a zero inclusion ratio; the other portion is $1,000 ($17,000 – $16,000). With respect to the $1,000 portion, the denominator of the applicable fraction is $1,000. Assuming that T allocates $1,000 of GST exemption, the numerator of the applicable fraction is $1,000 and the applicable fraction is one ($1,000/$1,000 = one) and the inclusion ratio is zero (1 – 1 = 0).[24]

---

[24] This example is taken from Reg. § 26.2642-1(d), Example 3.

[C] GST Tax Exemption

Under the Tax Cuts and Jobs Act of 2017 ("TCJA"), the GST exemption equals the estate tax applicable exclusion amount of $10,000,000 (adjusted for cost-of living from 2010). In 2022, the GST exemption is $12,060,000.[25]

[1] Allocating the GST Tax Exemption

Each individual may allocate his or her GST exemption to any transfer.[26] In the absence of an affirmation election, the Code provides *deemed* (or *automatic*) *allocation rules.* How the GST exemption is allocated depends on the form of the transfer.

Under the deemed allocation rules, any direct skip transfer (e.g., such as an outright transfer or a transfer to a trust of which all the current beneficiaries are skip persons) during the transferor's life automatically has GST exemption allocated to it unless the transferor affirmatively elects out of this automatic allocation.[27] As a general rule, if an election out is not made, the automatic allocation of GST exemption becomes irrevocable after the due date for reporting the transfer (including any extensions actually granted).[28]

The election out of the automatic allocation must be made on a timely filed gift tax return. A gift tax return is timely filed if it is filed on or before the date that would be the date for reporting the transfer if it were a taxable gift, including any extensions actually granted.[29] Once an election out has been made, the regulations indicate that the election is irrevocable.[30]

EXAMPLE 9-22

T transfers $10,000 to an irrevocable trust for the benefit of multiple skip persons on July 15, 2022. Because the transfer constitutes a direct skip, the GST tax exemption will automatically be allocated as of April 15, 2023 (assuming no extensions are granted), unless the transferor elects out by such date. This will be the case whether or not the transfer qualifies for the gift tax annual exclusion. Only if the transfer to the trust fell under the GST tax exception of IRC Section 2642(c)(2) (to a trust with only one skip person/beneficiary) would there be no automatic allocation of GST exemption.

---

[25] Tax Cuts and Jobs Act of 2017, Pub. L. No. 115-97.

[26] IRC § 2632(a).

[27] IRC § 2632(b)(1) and (3); Reg. § 26.2632-1(b)(1).

[28] Reg. § 26.2632-1(b)(1)(ii).

[29] Reg. § 26.2632-1(b)(1)(i).

[30] Reg. § 26.2632-1(b)(1)(ii).

In addition, a transferor's GST exemption is automatically allocated to an indirect skip. IRC Section 2632(c)(1) provides that if a transferor makes an indirect skip during the transferor's lifetime, the transferor's unused GST exemption will be allocated to the property to the extent necessary to make the inclusion ratio of such property zero (or, if the amount of the indirect skip exceeds the transferor's unused GST exemption, the entire unused GST exemption will be allocated to the property transferred).

An indirect skip is defined in IRC Section 2632(c)(3)(A) to include a transfer of property subject to gift or estate tax to a GST trust. The term GST trust is defined to include any trust that could have a generation-skipping transfer unless:

1. 25 percent of the trust corpus must be distributed to or may be withdrawn by non-skip person(s) (a) before the non-skip person attains age 46, (b) on or before one or more dates that will occur before the non-skip person attains age 46, or (c) upon the occurrence of an event that may reasonably be expected to occur before the non-skip person attains age 46;

2. 25 percent of the trust corpus must be distributed to or may be withdrawn by one or more individuals who are non-skip persons *and* who are living on the death of an identified person who is more than ten years older than such non-skip persons;

3. If non-skip person(s) die on or before a date or event set forth in paragraphs 1 or 2 above, more than 25 percent of the trust corpus must be distributed to the estate(s) of such non-skip person(s) or is subject to a general power of appointment held by such non-skip person(s);

4. The trust is includable in the gross estate of a non-skip person (other than the transferor) if such person died immediately after the transfer;

5. The trust is a charitable lead annuity trust, charitable remainder annuity trust, or a charitable remainder unitrust; or

6. The trust is a charitable lead unitrust that is required to pay principal to a non-skip person if such person is alive at the end of the unitrust term.

For purposes of applying the above exceptions, IRC Section 2632(c)(3)(B) provides that the value of the transferred property is not deemed to be considered includable in the gross estate of a non-skip person or subject to a right of withdrawal if such person is holding a right to withdraw the annual exclusion under IRC Section 2503(b) and it is assumed that powers of appointment held by non-skip persons will not be exercised.

As will be discussed in further detail below, if the transferor's GST exemption has not been effectively allocated because an estate tax inclusion period exists under IRC Section 2642(f) and an indirect skip has occurred, the indirect skip shall be deemed to have been made only at the close of the estate tax inclusion period and the fair market value of the transfer for the purposes of the allocation of the GST exemption is the fair market value of the trust property at the close of such estate tax inclusion period.

IRC Section 2632(c)(5) allows a transferor to elect out of these automatic allocation rules for indirect skips. An individual may elect to have the automatic allocation rules not apply to (1) an indirect skip, or (2) any and all transfers made by such transferor to a particular trust. In addition, an individual may elect to treat any trust as a GST trust for purposes of IRC Section 2632(c) with respect to any and all transfers made by such transferor to such trust, and therefore, have GST exemption automatically allocated to any such trust. These elections are deemed to be timely if made on a timely filed gift tax return for the calendar year in which a transfer was made or deemed to have been made.

These automatic allocation rules for indirect skips apply to any transfer subject to gift or estate tax made after December 31, 2000 and to an estate tax inclusion period ending after December 31, 2000.

When the transfer is not a direct skip or an indirect skip, an individual's GST exemption is not automatically allocated, but may be allocated any time on or before the date for the filing of the transferor's estate tax return either on the transferor's gift tax or estate tax return.[31] If the allocation is made on a timely filed return, including extensions, the allocation is effective as of the date of the transfer and, therefore, the amount of GST exemption to be allocated is based on the value of property transferred as of the date of the transfer; if the allocation is made on a late filed gift tax return, it is effective as of the date of its postmark.[32] Once made, an allocation of GST exemption on a timely return may be modified or revoked up to the due date of the return.[33] An allocation made on a late filed return is irrevocable.[34]

The regulations provide a special valuation rule for late allocations during life. If a transferor makes a late allocation of GST exemption to a trust, the transferor may, solely for purposes of determining the fair market value of the trust assets, elect to treat the allocation as having been made on the first day of the month during which the late allocation is made—such first day of the month to be known as the "valuation date."[35] Such an allocation becomes effective when filed with the IRS and is made by stating on the gift tax return on which the allocation is made that the election is being made, the applicable valuation date, and the fair market value of the trust assets on the valuation date.[36] This rule was enacted to recognize the practical difficulties of filing an allocation on the same day the property is valued.

EXAMPLE 9-23

A transferor transferred $500,000 of cash to a trust for his children and grandchildren in 2022. No other gifts were made to the trust. Although the transferor filed a timely gift tax return, none of the transferor's GST exemption was allocated to the transfer. In July 2023, the transferor decided to allocate GST exemption to the trust. The trust assets were invested in equities that vary in value substantially from day to day. Although on July 1, 2023, the transferor was able to ascertain that the

---

[31] Reg. § 26.2632-1(b)(2)(i).
[32] Reg. § 26.2632-1(b)(2)(ii)(A)(1).
[33] Reg. § 26.2632-1(b)(2)(i).
[34] IRC § 2631(b); Reg. § 26.2632-1(b)(2)(ii)(A)(2).
[35] Reg. § 26.2642-2(a)(2).
[36] *Id.*

value of the trust assets was $745,000, it was unclear on July 22, 2023, the date by which the return had been prepared and was going to be filed, what the value of the trust assets was since that value is ascertained by determining the mean between the highest and lowest selling prices on that date. To avoid this problem under the late allocation election, the transferor may elect to use the July 1, 2023 value of the trust assets for purposes of the allocation of GST exemption.

This special valuation rule for late allocation is not available with respect to life insurance or a trust holding a life insurance policy if the insured individual has died.[37] Presumably, this is to prevent a late allocation in the month that the transferor dies thereby requiring any such late allocation to cover the entire proceeds of the policy.

In order for an allocation to be effective, the allocation must clearly identify the trust to which the allocation is being made, the amount of GST exemption allocated to it, and the value of the trust principal at the time of the allocation.[38] The allocation must also state the inclusion ratio of the trust after the allocation.[39] The inclusion ratio, as discussed above, determines the effective rate of GST tax (called the "applicable rate"). Any such allocation of GST tax exemption is void to the extent the amount allocated exceeds the amount necessary to obtain an inclusion ratio of zero with respect to the trust.

An allocation of GST tax exemption is void if the allocation is made to a trust that has no GST tax potential with respect to the transfer for whom the allocation is being made, as of the date of the transferor's death.[40] This would occur, for example, where the remainder of a trust for a child will pass to charity upon the child's death. For purposes of determining whether such an allocation is void, the regulations provide that a trust has GST tax potential even if the possibility of a GST tax is so remote as to be negligible. This rule is beneficial to taxpayers as it will prevent the use of the GST tax exemption where no GST tax otherwise would be imposed.

[2] Deemed Allocation Rules

If the individual has not allocated his entire GST tax exemption by the date for filing his estate tax return, the individual's unused GST exemption will be deemed to be allocated first to property that is the subject of a direct skip at the individual's death, and then to trusts with respect to which such individual is the transferor and from which a taxable distribution or taxable termination might occur at or after the individual's death.[41]

---

[37] Reg. § 26.2642-2(a)(2).
[38] Reg. § 26.2632-1(b)(2).
[39] *Id.*
[40] Reg. § 26.2632-1(b)(2)(i).
[41] IRC § 2632(c); Reg. § 26.2632-1(d)(2).

EXAMPLE 9-24

The decedent created a testamentary sprinkle trust for his children and grandchildren that receives $500,000 proceeds of insurance policies on his life that are includable in his estate. The executor must allocate $500,000 of the decedent's GST tax exemption on the estate tax return to protect the proceeds from GST tax on later taxable distributions or taxable terminations.

[3] Effective Allocation and ETIP Rules

For property to be exempt from the GST tax by virtue of the GST tax exemption, an individual or the individual's executors must effectively allocate his or her GST tax exemption to the property. The GST tax exemption may not be allocated to property transferred *inter vivos* during the period that such property would be includable in the gross estate of the transferor or the transferor's spouse (other than by reason of IRC Section 2035).[42] This could occur if the transferor or the transferor's spouse retained an interest in the transferred property.[43] This period is known as the estate tax inclusion period, or *ETIP.*

Transferred property is not considered as being subject to inclusion in the gross estate of the transferor or the transferor's spouse for purposes of the ETIP rules if the possibility that the property will be included is so remote as to be negligible.[44] For purposes of this exception, the possibility of property being included in the transferor's or the transferor's spouse's gross estate is so remote as to be negligible if it can be ascertained by actuarial standards that there is less than a 5 percent probability that the property will be included in the gross estate.

Transferred property is not considered as being subject to inclusion in the transferor's spouse's gross estate if the spouse possesses with respect to any transfer to a trust the right to withdraw no more than the greater of $5,000 or 5 percent of the trust corpus and such withdrawal right terminates no later than 60 days after the transfer to the trust.[45]

An ETIP terminates on the first to occur of: (1) the death of the transferor; (2) the time at which no portion of property would be includable in the transferor's gross estate (other than by reason of IRC Section 2035) or, in the case of an individual who is a transferor solely by reason of an election under IRC Section 2513 (gift splitting with a spouse), the time at which no portion would be includable in the gross estate of the individual's spouse (other than by reason of IRC Section 2035); (3) the time of a GST; or (4) where the ETIP arises by reason of an interest held by the transferor's spouse, at the first to occur of (a) the death of the spouse or (b) the time at which no

---

[42] Section 2035 is applicable to certain transfers occurring within three years of death. IRC § 2642(f).

[43] IRC § § 2036–2042.

[44] Reg. § 26.2632-1(c)(2)(ii)(A).

[45] Reg. § 26.2632-1(c)(2)(ii)(B).

portion of the property would be includable in the spouse's gross estate (other than by reason of IRC Section 2035).[46]

An allocation of GST exemption on a gift tax return filed by the date the return would have been due, if the termination of the ETIP had been a taxable gift, is effective as of the date of the termination. An allocation of GST exemption made after that date is effective as of the earlier of the date the gift tax return on which the allocation is made is filed or the date of death of the transferor (or the transferor's spouse, if applicable).[47] In addition, an allocation of GST exemption to property subject to an ETIP that is made prior to the termination of the ETIP cannot be revoked.

If the ETIP property is includable in the transferor's estate, the value to be used for purposes of allocating GST exemption is the value for federal estate tax purposes. However, if the ETIP property is not includable in the transferor's gross estate, its value for purposes of determining the amount of GST exemption that must be allocated is the value of the property at the close of the ETIP if the allocation is made on a timely filed return or, if any allocation of exemption to such property is not made on a timely filed gift tax return for the calendar year in which the ETIP ends, its value is its fair market value at the time such allocation is filed with the secretary.[48]

An automatic allocation of GST exemption, or an allocation on a timely gift tax return, is not effective until the termination of the ETIP. The transferor can wait until the termination of the ETIP to make the allocation, when the exact amount of the property to which the GST exemption will be allocated is known. If the ETIP terminates during the transferor's life, an allocation of GST exemption may be made on a timely gift tax return for the taxable year in which the ETIP terminates, and the allocation will be effective as of the ETIP termination date.[49] If the ETIP terminates at the transferor's death, the allocation of GST exemption is made on a timely filed estate tax return and is effective as of the date of death.

Thus, for example, when there is a transfer of assets to an *inter vivos* revocable trust, GST exemption may not be effectively allocated at the time of the transfer to the trust since the trust would be includable in the transferor's gross estate due to the retained power to revoke.[50] However, if the transferor amends the trust to remove the transferor's power to revoke the trust (and any other power that would cause the trust to be includable in the transferor's gross estate other than by reason of IRC Section 2035), the GST exemption may be effectively allocated on: (1) a timely filed gift tax return for the calendar year in which the transferor releases the power to revoke, based on the value of the trust at that time; or (2) a late gift tax return, based on the value of the trust at the time such return is filed and the allocation made.[51]

---

[46] Reg. § 26.2632-1(c)(3).
[47] Reg. § 26.2632-1(c)(1).
[48] IRC § 2642(f)(2).
[49] Reg. § 26.2632-1(c)(1).
[50] IRC § 2038.
[51] Reg. § 26.2632-1(c)(1).

If, however, the transferor dies before releasing the power to revoke the trust, the transferor's GST exemption must be allocated on his or her estate tax return and the value of the trust for estate tax purposes will govern for purposes of determining how much of GST exemption must be allocated to protect it for GST tax purposes.

PRACTICE NOTE

Practitioners need to be particularly wary of the existence of an ETIP with Crummey trusts because the transferor's spouse could have an "interest" in the trust that will cause a portion of the trust to be includable in the spouse's estate. For example, the granting of a hanging Crummey power[52] to the transferor's spouse creates an ETIP because the power would be includable in the spouse's estate if the spouse were to die possessing the power because the power is a general power of appointment under IRC Section 2041 and because the power is not limited to the greater of $5,000 or 5 percent of the trust corpus as required by the exception contained in Regulation Section 26.2632-1(c)(2)(ii)(B). As a practical matter, this means that, if a transferor intends to allocate GST exemption to an irrevocable trust and wishes transfers to it to qualify for the gift tax annual exclusion by granting the spouse a Crummey power of withdrawal, the spouse should be granted a power of withdrawal that is limited to the greater of $5,000 or 5 percent of the trust corpus, which power should lapse in full in 60 days. Other beneficiaries may receive the "standard" $16,000/$32,000 Crummey powers, lapsing at a rate of the greater of $5,000 or 5 percent of the amount subject to withdrawal, with the balance of the withdrawal rights "hanging."

[4] Retroactive Allocation of GST Exemption to Certain Transfers

For transfers made after December 31, 2000, IRC Section 2632(d) permits a transferor to retroactively allocate the transferor's GST exemption to a trust in the case where a beneficiary of the trust who is related to the transferor predeceases the transferor. IRC Section 2632(d)(1) provides that a transferor may make an allocation of the transferor's unused GST exemption to any previous transfers (or transfers to a trust) if:

1. A non-skip person has an interest or a future interest[53] in the trust to which the transfer has been made;
2. Such non-skip person (i) is a lineal descendant of a grandparent of the transferor or of a grandparent of the transferor's spouse (or former spouse),

---

[52] Hanging Crummey powers are discussed in greater detail in Chapter 8.

[53] A person is considered to have a "future interest" in a trust if the trust may permit income or corpus to be paid to such person on a date or dates in the future.

and (ii) is assigned to a generation below the generation assignment of the transferor; and

3. Such non-skip person predeceased the transferor.

To the extent that the transferor makes a retroactive allocation to any previous transfer or transfer to the trust, such a retroactive allocation is to be made on a chronological basis.

If the retroactive allocation is made on a gift tax return filed on or before the date for timely filing a gift tax return within a calendar year within which the non-skip person dies, the value of such transfer or transfers for purposes of determining the amount of GST exemption to be allowed is determined as if the allocation had been made on a timely filed gift return for the calendar year in which each transfer was made, such allocation is effective immediately before such death, and the amount of the transferor's unused GST exemption available to be allocated is determined immediately before such non-skip person's death.

This retroactive allocation provision applies to any death of a non-skip person which occurs after December 31, 2000.

[5] Relief Provisions

Because of the complexity of the rules for the allocation of a transferor's GST exemption, Congress enacted IRC Section 2642(g) to provide relief for late elections in certain circumstances. This relief for late elections is applicable to requests pending on, or filed after, December 31, 2000. IRC Section 2642(g) authorizes the Secretary to issue regulations to prescribe certain circumstances and procedures under which extensions of time will be granted to make an allocation of GST exemption described in IRC Section 2642(b)(1) or (2), and to elect out of the automatic allocation rules for direct skips under IRC Section 2632(b)(3) or for indirect skips under IRC Section 2632(c)(5). In determining whether to grant relief, the Secretary is directed to take into account all relevant circumstances, including evidence of intent contained in the trust instrument or instrument of transfer, and such other factors as the Secretary deems relevant. For purposes of granting this relief, the time for making the allocation or election is directed to be treated as if not expressly prescribed by statute. This relief from late elections is applicable to requests pending on, or filed after, December 31, 2000.

IRC Section 2642(g)(2) also provides relief where there is substantial compliance with the GST provisions. This section provides that an allocation of GST exemption under IRC Section 2632 that demonstrates an intent to take advantage of the lowest possible inclusion ratio with respect to a transfer or a trust will be deemed to be an allocation of so much of the transferor's unused GST exemption as to produce the lowest possible inclusion ratio. For purposes of determining substantial compliance, the Secretary is directed to take into account all relevant circumstances, including evidence of intent contained in the trust instrument or an instrument of transfer and such other factors as the Secretary deems relevant. The relief for substantial compliance applies to transfers subject to gift or estate tax made after December 31, 2000.

§9.04 SPECIAL ISSUES IN PLANNING WITH THE GST TAX

[A] Cascading Crummey Power[SM]

In order to take advantage of the gift tax annual exclusion in a circumstance where the nontaxable gift exclusion requirements cannot be satisfied because, for example, both children and grandchildren are potential beneficiaries of a trust, an alternative is to consider using a specific form of double Crummey power that provides that, to the extent the Crummey power lapses in excess of the $5,000 or 5 percent threshold of IRC Section 2514(e), younger generation beneficiaries (such as grandchildren) in the trust are given a power of withdrawal over such excess.

For example, a married grantor gives $20,000 to the trust and grants her child the right to withdraw $20,000 for 30 days after the property is contributed. If there is at least one grandchild who is also a trust beneficiary, rather than having the power then lapse to the extent of $5,000, it would lapse to the extent of the full $20,000. Such grandchild would then become entitled upon the lapse to withdraw from the trust the amount that the child has allowed to lapse in excess of $5,000.[1]

As to the gift tax considerations when using Cascading Crummey Powers[SM], the grantor's initial transfer, with the use of gift splitting, qualified for the gift tax annual exclusion because the grantor's child had the power to withdraw $20,000. When the child's right to withdraw the $20,000 from the trust lapses, the child will be deemed to have made a gift of $15,000 (i.e., $20,000 minus the $5,000 threshold of IRC Section 2514(e)). However, because the grandchild will then be entitled to withdraw the amount of the child's $15,000 gift to the trust, the gift will qualify for the gift tax annual inclusion from the child to the grandchild, in the same way the original transfer to the trust qualified as annual exclusion transfers from the grantor and her spouse to the child.

Furthermore, for GST tax purposes, to the extent of the $15,000 gift deemed made (by reason of the lapse of the Crummey power that is a general power of appointment) from the child to the grandchild, the child becomes the transferor. That is, three-quarters (i.e., $15,000 of the $20,000 transferred) of what is in the trust is attributable to the child as the transferor for GST tax purposes. Thus, to that extent, transfers out of the trust to a grandchild are not subject to GST tax. (The grandchild is not a skip person with respect to transfers made by the child but only as to transfers made by the grantor or her spouse.) In fact, as explained in Regulation Section 26.2654-1(a)(2), the trustee may treat separate contributions from different transferors as separate trusts. Hence, the trustee can treat $5,000 of the $20,000 added to the trust as being attributable to a contribution by the grantor (and, perhaps, her spouse)[2] and $15,000 as being attributable to a contribution by the child. Presumably, the trustee,

---

[1] **§9.04** Even if there is more than one child, each may allow the power to lapse in excess of $5,000 (although such excess should not exceed the amount of exclusion available to each such child) without causing adverse gift tax consequences to the child and yet effecting a change of transferor for GST tax purposes so as to reduce or eliminate GST tax with respect to distributions to grandchildren.

[2] *See, e.g.,* Ltr. Rul. 9541029.

to the extent practicable, would make distributions to the child out of the trust of which the grantor is the transferor for GST tax purposes and would make distributions to the grandchild out of the trust of which the child is the transferor for GST tax purposes, thereby reducing or eliminating the tax.

Although by reason of the lapse in excess of $5,000, the child is deemed to have made a transfer to the trust for estate, gift, and GST tax purposes, the property deemed so contributed by the child should not be includable in the child's estate if the child holds no interest described in IRC Sections 2036(a), 2037, 2038, or 2041. Hence, if the child is only eligible (and not entitled) to receive income and principal from the trust in the discretion of a trustee other than the child, the child's creditors under applicable state law cannot reach the child's interest in the trust, and the child holds no power of appointment over (or another control over the beneficial enjoyment of) the part of the trust the child is deemed to have transferred to, and no part of the trust should be includable in the child's estate.

[B] Planning with the GST Tax Exemption

[1] Benefits of Lifetime Use

The GST exemption allows for the transfer of significant wealth free of GST taxes. By using the GST exemption for lifetime transfers, the donor can shift post-transfer appreciation, thereby leveraging the value of the exemption.[3] For example, assume an individual in 2022 transferred $12,060,000 to a grandchild. Even if the grandchild places the $12,060,000 into a fixed income account earning 1 percent annual interest, more will be transferred to the grandchild than if the transferor waits until death to give the $12,060,000 to the grandchild. Historically, though, assets invested in the stock market have grown an average of 10 percent a year. Accordingly, if a transferor made a gift of $12,060,000 to a grandchild in 2022 and the gift was invested in the stock market and grew 10 percent a year, in seven years the assets would be worth over $23,500,000, in 14 years worth over $45,790,000, and in 21 years worth over $89,240,000.

PRACTICE NOTE

In order to make the best use of an individual's GST exemption, not only should the assets be given away during life, but the assets given should be those that are expected to experience the most significant appreciation. Those assets could be interests in a newly formed company where there is a great potential for future growth or assets that can be discounted for lack of marketability or minority interest that results in the transfer of additional value as a result of such discount. Such leveraging of the GST exemption maximizes the potential benefit to skip persons.

---

[3] IRC § 2631. *See* § 9.03[C] *supra.*

[2] Creating a Dynasty Trust

An effective use of the GST exemption is to allocate exemption to a long-term trust for children, grandchildren, and more remote descendants of a transferor—sometimes called a *dynasty* or *descendants trust*. The transferor could fund a trust for descendants, in 2022, with up to approximately $12,060,000 ($24,120,000 if the transferor's spouse splits the gift) without incurring GST tax. The funding would be subject to gift tax to the extent it causes the transferor and the transferor's spouse each to exceed their respective estate and gift tax lifetime exemptions (in 2022, $12,060,000). The trust could be funded with cash, securities, or interests in closely-held businesses.

Typically, a dynasty trust would be structured to last for the maximum period of time permitted by law—or states with the common law rule against perpetuities, a period measured by lives in being at the creation of the trust plus 21 years, or, in Alaska, Delaware, New Jersey, South Dakota and many other states, perpetually. During this time, the trust corpus would not be subject to any further estate, gift, or GST tax.

The trustees of a dynasty trust are typically given broad authority to use the income and principal of the trust for the benefit of the transferor's descendants. The corpus of the trust is usually invested, especially in early years, for maximum appreciation, and income and gain are normally not paid out to beneficiaries but are retained in the trust and reinvested for many years.

It is not expected that the trustees would make distributions to the beneficiaries. To preserve corpus, rather than making distributions outright, the trustees would be authorized to acquire assets for the use of the beneficiaries. For example, if one of the transferor's children or grandchildren wished to acquire a vacation home, the trustees of the trust would purchase the home and allow the child or grandchild to use the home. The home, however, would always remain an asset of the trust and, therefore, any appreciation in the value of the home would inure to the benefit of the future beneficiaries of the trust. Moreover, because funds were not distributed to the child or grandchild to purchase the home, the home would not be includable in the child's or grandchild's estate on his or her death.

[3] Drafting Trusts to Maximize Use of GST Tax Exemption

[a] Only Skip Persons Have Interests

The best use of the GST exemption is a transfer directly to a skip person with non-skip persons having no interest whatsoever in the property transferred. In some estate plans this is not possible because there are insufficient assets to provide for non-skip persons. In such plans, a GST tax exempt trust may be established to take advantage of the GST exemption that allows for access to the property, if necessary, by non-skip persons. The GST tax exempt trust, however, should not require that all of the income be paid to the non-skip person for life with the balance on the child's death to the grandchildren. This would force the income to be distributed to the non-skip person regardless of whether the non-skip person needed the income, thereby reducing the effective use of the GST exemption. A trust that permits the trustee to make discretionary distributions of income and principal is preferable.

[b] Assets Available for Use of Beneficiary

Instead of making distributions to a non-skip person from a GST tax exempt trust, as noted above, it is preferable to make assets available for the non-skip person's use, thereby preserving the ability of the assets to pass without the imposition of any transfer tax to the skip persons. For example, suppose the non-skip person beneficiary wishes to receive a distribution from the GST tax exempt trust to purchase a business. The trustee, if authorized under the terms of the GST tax exempt trust to do so, may purchase the business and then operate the business with the non-skip person. The business, however, remains an asset of the GST tax exempt trust and, upon the non-skip person's death, may be held for the benefit of the skip person without the imposition of any GST tax. If, instead, the trustee had distributed the funds to the non-skip person to purchase the business, the business, at the non-skip person's death, would be includable in the non-skip person's estate requiring the payment of estate tax.

[c] Long-Term or Perpetual Trust

The GST tax exempt trust should also be drafted to last the maximum period of time permitted under applicable local law (e.g., the rule against perpetuities period or, if the rule against perpetuities has been repealed, perpetually). The GST tax exempt trust should not be drafted to pay outright to a skip person on the non-skip person's death. Such an outright distribution will force the assets in the GST tax exempt trust into the skip person's estate for estate tax purposes prematurely, potentially subjecting those assets to estate tax. If the, assets remain in the trust, the assets might be able to pass to the skip person's children without the imposition of any GST tax (assuming the trust has not terminated earlier as a result of the rule against perpetuities limitation on the trust).

[d] Broad Investment Authority

The trust should be drafted to grant the trustee broad and flexible investment authority to allow the trustee: (1) to invest for long-term growth; and (2) to enter into transactions that will leverage the GST tax exempt nature of the trust such as investments in newly formed businesses with great potential for future appreciation or purchases from senior generation family members of unmarketable minority interests in family companies. In addition, the trustee should be given broad enough authority to invest in assets for the use of the beneficiaries (such as vacation homes).

[e] Grantor Trust

During the life of the transferor, the trust should be structured as a grantor trust for income tax purposes. A *grantor trust* is a trust where all income, deductions, and credits are taxed to the grantor for income tax purposes under IRC Sections 671 through 677.[4] A trust will be treated as a grantor trust, for example, if the grantor's spouse is entitled or eligible to receive income from the trust,[5] a person (other than the grantor) in a nonfiduciary capacity has the power to add to the beneficiaries designated to receive income or corpus,[6] or the grantor has the power to reacquire the trust corpus by substituting other property of equivalent value.[7] From a gift and GST tax perspective, this payment by the grantor of the income taxes on a grantor trust should not be treated as a gift or addition to the trust provided that under applicable state law the grantor does not have a right to be reimbursed (which right should be able to be expressly negated in the trust agreement).[8]

The benefits of lifetime use of the GST exemption are enhanced if the trust is a grantor trust. Because the grantor will continue to be taxed on all of the trust income, the trust will, in effect, grow on a pretax basis as long as the grantor trust status continues (which can be until the death of the grantor). The leverage of this tax-free growth within a GST tax exempt trust is tremendous.

[4] Selecting Assets and Transactions to Maximize Leverage

[a] Initial Funding

Using cash for the initial funding of a GST tax exempt trust will provide the highest initial basis for income tax purposes. This should also minimize any risk that the initial transaction will be audited by the IRS.

[b] Subsequent Purchase of Assets

If senior generation family members own assets that are unmarketable, or represent minority interests, it may be appropriate for the trust to purchase those assets. For example, senior generation family members may own interests in a closely held business or a family holding company where interests may be valued at a significant discount because they are not marketable or represent a minority interest. A purchase of such interests may maximize the leverage of the GST exemption. To avoid an unintentional gift to the trust that would taint the GST tax exempt nature of

---

[4] Grantor trusts are discussed in greater detail in Chapter 4.

[5] IRC § 677(a)(1).

[6] IRC § 674(b)(5).

[7] IRC § 675(4)(C). *See* Rev. Rul. 2008-22, 2008-16 I.R.B. 796 (providing that, for estate tax purposes, the grantor's power of substitution will not, by itself, cause the value of the trust corpus to be includible in the grantor's gross estate, provided the trustee has a fiduciary obligation (under local law or the trust agreement) to ensure the grantor's compliance with the terms of this power by satisfying itself that the properties acquired and substituted by the grantor are in fact of equivalent value, and further provided that the substitution power cannot be exercised in a manner that can shift benefits among the trust beneficiaries).

[8] *But see* Ltr. Rul. 9444033 (suggestion that the payment of income tax by the grantor on income of a grantor trust may result in a gift to the trust), subsequently reissued as Ltr. Rul. 9543049 deleting discussion of this issue.

the trust, it is advisable for the trust to direct that any additional gifts in excess of the GST exemption amount will be held in a separate trust.

It should be noted that if interests in certain entities are sold by a decedent to a trust created by the decedent, such sale needs to be reported on the decedent's United States Estate (and Generation-Skipping Transfer) Tax Return (Form 706). Question 13(e) of Part 4 of Form 706 contains the following question: "Did the decedent at any time during his or her lifetime transfer or sell an interest in a partnership, limited liability company or closely-held corporation to a trust described in line 13a or 13b?" Question 13a appears to refer to trusts in existence at the decedent's death created by the decedent—"Were there in existence at the time of the decedent's death any trusts created by the decedent during his or her lifetime?"

[c] "Estate Freeze" Transactions with Trusts

The GST tax exempt nature of the trust may be leveraged by having the trust enter into, in effect, modified "estate freeze" transactions with senior generation family matters. An *estate freeze* is a transaction in which assets that might otherwise appreciate in value are converted to assets with a fixed value. For example, if a senior generation family member is considering making a new passive investment that is expected to appreciate greatly, the senior generation family member should loan the funds to the GST tax exempt trust, which would directly make the investment. In order to avoid the loan of the funds to the trust from being treated as a transfer subject to the gift and GST taxes, it is important to formalize the loan relationship. Where a loan relationship is not formalized and the facts and circumstances do not show that the transfer was made with a real expectation of repayment, the loan may be recharacterized as a gift. In addition, the loan must bear adequate interest.

[5] Allocating GST Tax Exemption to Life Insurance Trusts

For many individuals, a significant part of their assets consists of life insurance. Often, the issue will arise as to whether the life insurance should be given to a trust and the transferor's GST exemption allocated to the trust. The allocation of GST exemption to transfers to a trust that owns life insurance may be appropriate when the life insurance proceeds will be large compared to the amounts transferred to the trust by the grantor to pay the policy premiums. In such a case, a relatively large amount of property (the proceeds) is protected from tax through the allocation of a relatively small amount of GST exemption to the premiums. Whether a transferor will wish to allocate his or her GST exemption to a trust that holds life insurance will depend upon, in part, whether his or her GST exemption should be preserved to protect other assets and the aggregate tax savings by preserving the GST exemption.

There are a number of risks associated with having GST exemption allocated to a life insurance trust. For example, life insurance—particularly term insurance—often expires before the insured dies. The transferor should not waste his or her GST exemption on an insurance policy that will expire. Thus, if an insurance trust holds a term life insurance policy, it may be advisable to take a "wait and see" position on the allocation of GST tax exemption to the trust. Since the decision of whether to have GST tax exemption allocated to a trust does not have to be made until April 15 (or a later extended date) of the year following the year in which the transfer was made to the trust, there will be no need to have GST exemption allocated to the trust if the insured survived through the policy term. If, however, the insured dies during the term, it will still be possible to make a timely allocation of GST exemption in the following year, with the allocation being made in the amount of the transfer to the trust, rather than in the amount of the insurance proceeds. Although it may be possible to make a late allocation of GST exemption to an insurance trust after the due date of the gift tax return (assuming that GST tax exemption is not automatically allocated and an election out of such automatic allocation has not been made), any leveraging of the GST exemption will be lost if the late allocation is made after the insured's death. If a late allocation is made after the insured's death, the GST exemption must be allocated to the amount of the policy proceeds, rather than the amounts transferred to the trust to pay the policy premiums.[9]

[6] Allocating GST Tax Exemption to Charitable Lead Trusts

If a client is charitably inclined, a charitable lead trust may be an appropriate way to leverage the GST exemption. In a charitable lead trust, the interest paid to the charity precedes the interest of family members and must be in the form of either an annuity payment (i.e., a fixed sum of money) or a unitrust payment (i.e., a sum equal to a fixed percentage of the value of the assets determined annually).[10] The charitable interest in a charitable lead trust may last for a fixed term of years (such as 30 years), or until the death of a designated person or persons, or may terminate on the earlier of a fixed term or designated person's death.[11] When the charitable interest ends, the property may pass either outright or in further trust for the grantor's (or decedent's) descendants or others.

An essential difference between a charitable lead annuity trust (CLAT) and a charitable lead unitrust (CLUT) is that the unitrust payment in a CLUT participates in the increases and decreases in the value of the trust whereas the annuity payment in a CLAT is a fixed amount. The rules for allocating GST exemption to charitable lead trusts distinguish between CLATs and CLUTs. A CLUT usually offers a more tax efficient way to use the grantor's GST exemption to protect assets remaining in the trust (after the initial term for the benefit of charity) that will pass to skip persons. With a CLUT (unlike a CLAT), the grantor (or the decedent's executor) at the time of creation of the trust may allocate his or her unused GST exemption to the present value of the trust remainder, which is eventually payable to descendants. With a CLAT, the GST exemption is not in effect allocated until the end of the charitable term and hence cannot be leveraged.[12] With a CLAT, the GST exemption allocated to the trust at the time of its creation grows annually by the IRC Section 7520 rate until

---

[9] Reg. § 26.2642-2(a)(2).

[10] IRC §§ 170(f)(2)(B), 2055(e)(2)(B), 2522(c)(2)(B), and the regulations accompanying each of their Code sections. Charitable lead trusts are discussed in Chapter 10.

[11] *Id.*

[12] IRC § 2642(e).

the charitable interest ends.[13] This enhanced GST exemption is then compared to the then value of the trust to determine what part of the trust is exempt from the GST tax.

The reason for the difference in how a CLAT or a CLUT is treated for GST purposes stems from the way the inclusion ratios for a CLAT and a CLUT are determined. As discussed above, for purposes of determining the GST tax rate applicable to generation-skipping transfers from a trust, the trust's inclusion ratio must be calculated. A trust's inclusion ratio is equal to the excess of one over the trust's applicable fraction. A trust's applicable fraction has a numerator equal to the amount of GST exemption allocated to the trust and a denominator equal to the value of the property transferred to the trust reduced by (1) any federal or state estate taxes actually recovered from the trust attributable to such property and (2) any estate or gift tax charitable deduction allowed with respect to such property.[14]

However, where property is transferred to a CLUT, as noted above, the amount of any estate or gift tax charitable deduction allowable upon the transfer of the property to the trust reduces the value of the transfer.

EXAMPLE 9-25

Grantor created a CLUT with $1,000,000, which provided for an annual payment to charity for the lives of the grantor (age 60) and the grantor's spouse (age 55) of 8 percent of the annual value of the fund. At the time of creation, the applicable federal rate was 5 percent. Based on these figures 87.3 percent of the trust would be treated by the IRS as devoted to charity and 12.7 percent as devoted to the noncharitable remainder beneficiaries and, thus, subject to gift tax. Therefore, the gift tax charitable deduction would be approximately $873,000, and the denominator for purposes of determining the applicable fraction would be $127,000 ($1,000,000 (the value of the property transferred to the trust) less $873,000 (estate or gift tax charitable deduction allowed with respect to such property)). Although the grantor would have to pay a gift tax on (or use unified credit with respect to) this taxable gift portion of the gift, the grantor could allocate $127,000 of the unused portion of his or her GST tax exemption to the trust and protect the trust from ever being subject to further GST tax even if the trust lasts for several generations (or perpetually).

If the grantor wishes to structure a CLUT so that the noncharitable remainder exactly equals the individual's remaining GST tax exemption, a formula provision should be used to accomplish this.

The rule for determining the inclusion ratio of a CLAT differs from the rule described above for determining the inclusion ratio of a CLUT. For purposes of determining the inclusion ratio of a CLAT, the applicable fraction is a fraction the

---

[13] IRC § 2642(e).
[14] IRC § 2642(a)(2).

numerator of which is the "adjusted GST exemption" and the denominator of which is the value of all of the property in such trust immediately after the termination of the charitable lead annuity.[15] *Adjusted GST exemption* is the amount of GST tax exemption allocated to the trust increased annually for the charitable lead term by the interest rate under IRC Section 7520 used initially to value the annuity for gift or estate tax purposes.

EXAMPLE 9-26

> Using Example 9-25, if the grantor had, instead, created a CLAT of $1,000,000 that provided for an annual payment to charity for the lives of the grantor (age 60) and the grantor's spouse (age 55) of $80,000, and if the grantor allocated $27,100 (the value of the remainder interest) of his or her GST tax exemption, this allocation is increased at a rate equal to the assumed annuity rate of 5 percent for the full period of the trust and then is applied at the end of the lead period to determine the inclusion ratio.

Thus, with a CLAT, it is not certain until the end of the lead period whether the trust will be fully exempt from the GST tax. If the assets in the trust grow in excess of the assumed interest rate, the trust will not have an inclusion ratio of zero and generation-skipping transfers from the trust will be subject to GST tax. Consequently, a CLUT is preferable to a CLAT, if the grantor wishes to allocate GST exemption to the transfer.

[C] Structuring Wills for Married Couples—Reverse QTIP Election

Without consideration of the GST tax, most estate planners would structure the disposition of a client's property at death in a manner to take advantage of the applicable exclusion amount from gift and estate taxes (in 2022, $12,060,000) and the unlimited marital deduction. The credit shelter amount, as a general matter, would either be bequeathed directly to the testator's descendants or to a trust for the benefit of the testator's spouse and descendants (that would be structured in such a way as to bypass taxation in the surviving spouse's estate). The balance of the testator's estate would pass to the testator's spouse in a manner to pass free of estate tax under the protection of the marital deduction available for transfers to spouses.

If GST taxes are an issue (e.g., because more than $12,060,000 in 2022 will be transferred to skip persons), estate planners need to restructure the disposition of property in a testator's will to take advantage of not only the applicable exclusion amount but also the GST exemption.

A common way to take advantage of both has been the tripartite division of a testator's estate. With the tripartite division, the testator's property is divided into three portions:

---

[15] IRC § 2642(e).

- Portion A is equal to the testator's remaining applicable exclusion amount (e.g., $12,060,000 in 2022, assuming the testator has made no lifetime gifts), has the testator's exemption from the GST tax allocated to it on the testator's federal estate tax return (Form 706), and is structured not to be included in the testator's spouse's estate or testator's children's estates so as to pass free of additional transfer taxes to the testator's grandchildren and more remote descendants.

- Portion B is equal to the balance of the testator's GST exemption (i.e., the testator's GST exemption, less any amount allocated during life and to Portion A), is structured to pass to a trust for the testator's spouse that qualifies for the estate tax marital deduction (as qualified terminable interest property (QTIP) trust),[16] and is structured, upon the spouse's death, to continue in a form to pass free of additional transfer taxes to the testator's children, grandchildren, and more remote descendants. With respect to the Portion B trust, the estate of the testator will make what is known as a "reverse QTIP election." This election allows the testator to continue to be treated as the transferor for GST purposes even though the testator's spouse will be treated in effect as the owner of the trust property for estate tax purposes.[17] So, when the testator's spouse dies and the property in the QTIP trust is includable in her estate under IRC Section 2044, she will not be treated as the transferor for GST purposes. This election allows for the effective use of the transferor's GST exemption. The election is made on the testator's federal estate tax return (Form 709).

- Portion C equals the balance of the testator's property and will pass to the testator's spouse in a form to qualify for the marital deduction. To maximize the benefits of the allocation of the testator's GST exemption to Portion A and Portion B, the trust for descendants (after the testator's spouse's death with respect to Portion B) should be structured as a dynasty trust described above.

EXAMPLE 9-27

A testator, who has made $500,000 of lifetime gifts but has not allocated any GST exemption to transfers, dies in 2022 with a $30,000,000 estate. His will provides for a tripartite division: (1) Portion A equals $11,560,000 ($12,060,000 [applicable exclusion amount] less $500,000 lifetime gifts), is directed to be held in a discretionary trust for the testator's spouse and children, and $11,560,000 of the testator's GST exemption is allocated to the Portion A trust to produce an inclusion ratio of zero; (2) Portion B equals $500,000 (i.e., $12,060,000 − $11,560,000), is directed to be held in a QTIP trust for the benefit of the testator's spouse, has a reverse QTIP election made with respect to the property, and $500,000 of the testator's

---

[16] QTIP trusts are discussed in detail in Chapter 6.

[17] IRC § 2652(a)(3); Reg. § 26.2652-2.

GST exemption is allocated to Portion B; and (3) Portion C equals $17,940,000 (i.e., $30,000,000 – $12,060,000) and is directed to be held in a QTIP trust for the benefit of the testator's spouse. When the testator's spouse dies, both the Portion A trust and the Portion B trust continue in long-term trusts for the testator's children and grandchildren with discretionary distributions for the beneficiaries.

If the testator is in a state which has a state estate tax and the state exemption from the estate tax is less than the federal applicable exclusion amount, the tripartite division would result in a state estate tax. The testator instead may wish to consider either of the following alternatives: (1) The testator may instead structure Portion A as an amount equal to the state estate tax exemption amount and, thereby, eliminate any state estate tax. (2) In the alternative, the testator may bequeath the testator's entire residuary estate to a QTIP trust for the surviving spouse with liberal principal invasion provisions and direct the making of the portability election so the surviving spouse inherits the testator's unused applicable estate exclusion amount. After the testator's death, the surviving spouse would use distributions from the QTIP trust to create a lifetime trust for descendants using the federal applicable exclusion amount inherited from the testator. Since almost all states do not have a gift tax, this structuring would avoid any state estate or gift tax on transferring the property to the trust for the testator's descendants. It should be noted, however, that the GST exemption is not portable. Under this alternative, to use the testator's GST exemption, the residuary estate should be divided into two QTIP trusts, one of which will be GST exempt because of the allocation of the testator's GST exemption to such trust. The other QTIP trust will not be GST exempt and can be the source of the funds to make distributions to the surviving spouse to allow for funding of the lifetime trust. Also, this structuring could have the additional advantage of having the lifetime trust created by the surviving spouse structured as a grantor trust, allowing the surviving spouse to pay all income tax on the trust. Grantor trusts are discussed in detail in Chapter 4.

[D] Creation of Lifetime GST QTIP Trust

For donors who wish to use their GST exemption, but do not want to pay any gift tax for the difference between their GST exemption (in 2022, $12,060,000 as cost-of-living adjusted) and their remaining applicable exclusion amount from gift taxes, an option to consider is the creation during lifetime by the donor of a QTIP trust to be funded with the difference between the donor's GST exemption and the remaining applicable exclusion amount from gift taxes. The donor would fund the QTIP trust with this differential, would allocate GST exemption to the trust and would make a reverse QTIP election, which allows the donor to continue to be treated as the transferor for GST purposes even though the donor's spouse will be treated in effect as the owner of the trust property, upon her death, for estate tax purposes. Moreover, the donor spouse's Will will provide that, upon her death, the estate taxes that are payable as a result of the property in the QTIP trust being includable in her estate under IRC Section 2044 will be payable from her estate rather than the QTIP trust. This election is made on the donor's federal estate tax return (Form 709).

[E] Planning for Unmarried Individuals

The application of the GST tax is not limited to gifts and bequests to grandchildren and other lineal descendants. A gift or bequest to a great-nephew or great-niece or to an unrelated friend significantly younger than the donor may be subject to GST tax. As a consequence, an estate planner should remember to consider GST taxes when planning for individuals who are unmarried or who do not have children.

The GST tax can impose significant challenges when the client has a nonmarital partner who is more than $37^1/2$ years younger. For married persons, a person can make unlimited transfers to her spouse without worrying about the GST tax since an individual is always treated as being in the same generation as her spouse.[18] Since this advantage is not available for nonmarital partners, the estate planner should consider taking advantage of the opportunity for tax-free gifts and effective allocation of the GST exemption.

[F] Choosing Between Estate Tax and GST Tax—Jumping Generations

The estate planner may in some circumstances have the choice between an estate tax and GST tax upon the termination of a non-skip person's interest in a trust. For example, a trust for the benefit of children for life and then to grandchildren will be subject to GST tax if the children have a limited power of appointment and an estate tax if the children have a general power of appointment. In some circumstances, it may be advantageous to trigger an estate tax rather than a GST tax. For example, the estate tax may be lower than the GST tax. That may be the case if the property to be subject to an estate tax would be exposed to tax at less than the maximum rate of taxation, which may occur because credits are available. (No credits are available against the GST tax.) In addition, it also may be beneficial to expose property to estate tax if the decedent can shield it from future GST tax by allocating GST tax exemption to the property.

In other cases, however, the GST tax may be lower than the estate tax would be and it will be preferable to expose the property to the GST tax. That may occur, for example, if state death taxes exceed the maximum amount allowable under IRC Section 2011 as a state death tax credit.

Moreover, there are other cases where it will be preferable not to expose property to estate tax and risk the imposition of a GST tax since the GST tax might not ultimately be applicable. One situation is where the property is not transferred "down" to a younger generation, but only "over" to someone within the same generation. For example, a mother creates a trust for her son providing for the

---

[18] IRC § 2651(c)(1).

property upon the son's death to pass outright to the son's then-living descendants or, if he has none, to his sister, if living. If the property was exposed to estate tax, the tax would be imposed if the son died whether the property passed to his descendants or his sister. If the property was exposed to a GST tax, there would be no tax due if the assets passed to his sister because no generation-skipping transfer would have occurred.

Another case where it may be appropriate to expose property to the GST tax rather than the estate tax is where generations may be jumped and, thereby, the aggregate transfer taxes that will be paid will be reduced. For example, when a transferor's daughter dies, property in trust for her benefit passing to her descendants will be subject to the GST tax (if it is not subjected to estate tax at her generation and if another exception, exemption, or special rule does not apply). One GST tax will be due whether the property is transferred to her children, grandchildren, or even more remote descendants. For example, if the property is subject to GST tax and is transferred to the daughter's grandchildren, only one GST tax will be due even though two generations have been skipped (her generation and her children's generation).[19] If the property were subject to estate tax in the daughter's hands and the property then passed to her grandchildren, both estate tax and GST tax would be due. Unfortunately, one consequence of skipping the intermediate generations is the denial of benefits to the intermediate generation(s).

[G] Gift or Sale of Remainder Interests

In order to pass property free of GST tax to grandchildren, a strategy that is being advanced is the gift or sale of a remainder interest in a trust. Under this strategy, a child who is the remainderman of a trust created by her parent assigns by gift or sells her vested remainder interest in the trust to her children or more remote descendants (who are skip persons with respect to the grantor of the original trust), either outright or in trust. If the remainder interest is sold, the grandchildren or more remote descendants (or the trust created for their benefit) pay for the interest its full actuarial value using the normal valuation principles under IRC Section 7520. If the remainder interest is gifted, the child reports the gift using such valuation principles. The child's remainder interest is structured to have little value so the gift value or sale value is minimal. It is argued that the transfer should not be subject to GST tax because the child should be treated as the transferor of the remainder interest.

If this strategy is employed, the transaction should first be structured to avoid the imposition of a gift tax as a result of the application of IRC Section 2702. IRC Section 2702 would apply, as a general rule, to the gift or sale of a vested remainder interest in a trust. IRC Section 2702(a) provides that, for the sole purpose of determining whether a transfer of an interest in trust to (or for the benefit of) a member of the transferor's family is a gift (and the value of such transfer), the value of any interest retained by the transferor or any applicable family member shall be zero. A "transfer in trust" includes the sale, assignment, or transfer by an individual of a remainder

---

[19] Reg. § 26.2612-1(f), Example 9.

interest in property to a member of the transferor's family where the transferor or an applicable family member retains an interest that is not a qualified interest.[20] However, there are specific exceptions to the application for a qualified interest (e.g., a qualified annuity interest, a qualified unitrust interest, and a qualified remainder interest),[21] for certain transfers of a personal residence,[22] and for charitable lead trusts.[23] Thus, if the gift or sale of the vested remainder by the child is a remainder interest in a grantor retained annuity trust, a qualified personal residence trust, or a charitable lead trust, IRC Section 2702 should not apply.

Moreover, IRC Section 2702 applies only for gift tax purposes. The preamble to the final regulations under IRC Section 2702 specifically notes that IRC Section 2702 does not apply for GST tax purposes.[24]

Whether the gift or sale of the remainder interest in a trust will trigger a GST tax will depend upon whether there is a taxable termination when the property is distributed to the donee or transferee. Under IRC Section 2612(a), a taxable termination is any termination of an interest in a trust unless, immediately after the termination, a person other than a skip person has an interest in the trust or no future distributions from the trust may be made to a skip person. Whether a person other than a skip person has an interest in the trust for purposes of IRC Section 2702 will depend on whether the "transferor" for GST tax purposes is the original grantor or is the child. Thus, the issue is: Does the gift or sale of the vested remainder interest change the transferor from the original grantor parent to the child such that the termination of the trust in favor of the donee/transferee grandchild or more remote descendant is not a taxable termination?

Neither Chapter 13 of the Code nor the regulations deal directly with the issue of the treatment of a gift or sale of a vested remainder interest. Arguably, if the transfer is by gift, there should be no taxable termination because the gift by the child of his or her vested remainder interest should make the child the transferor of the property for GST tax purposes. The term "transferor" is defined for GST tax purposes as the donor, in the case of property subject to gift tax.[25] If the transfer of the remainder is by gift, the transferor should change under IRC Section 2652(a). However, this result is not as clear where the transfer is by sale.[26]

The IRS may also argue that the transferor does not change with respect to the entire property in trust because the sale value was based on the actuarial value of the

---

[20] Reg. §§ 25.2702-2(a)(2), 25.2702-4(d), Example 2.

[21] IRC § 2702(a)(2)(B).

[22] IRC § 2702(a)(3)(A)(ii).

[23] Reg. § 25.2702-1(c)(5).

[24] T.D. 8395, 1992-1 C.B. 316.

[25] IRC § 2652(a).

[26] First, Example 4 of Regulations Section 26.2652-1(a)(6) provides:

Effect of Transfer of an Interest in Trust on Identity of the Transferor: T transfer $100,000 to a trust providing that all of the net income is to be paid to T's child, C, for C's lifetime. At C's death, the trust property is to be paid to T's grandchild. C transfers the income interest to X, an unrelated party in a transfer that is a completed transfer for federal gift tax purposes. Because C's transfer is a transfer of a term interest in the trust that does not affect the rights of other parties with respect to the trust property, T remains the transferor with respect to the trust.

remainder interest determined using the normal valuation principles under IRC Section 7520. This position would be consistent with the IRS's position in *Gradow v. United States*.[27] However, *Gradow* has not been followed in other Circuits. Three more recent Federal Courts of Appeals cases have rejected *Gradow*.[28]

(Footnote Continued)

This example could be read to imply that if the interest in the trust that is transferred is not a "term interest," or does not "affect the rights of other parties with respect to the trust property," T will not remain the transferor. However, this result is not certain.

In 2000, the IRS issued a ruling concerning the consequences of the transfer by gift of a vested remainder interest in a charitable lead annuity trust (CLAT). In Private Letter Ruling 200107015 (Nov. 14, 2000), the IRS was requested to rule on the gift and generation-skipping transfer tax consequences of a proposed transaction involving the gift to the child's descendants of a vested remainder interest held by a child in a testamentary CLAT created by the child's deceased parent. The decedent, by will, had created a CLAT that provided that an annuity was to be paid to a designated charity for a term of 25 years. At the expiration of the term, the remaining trust property was to be divided into separate per *stirpital* shares for each child (or any descendants of any predeceased child of the decedent), with each such share to be held in further trust for such child (or the descendant of a predeceased child), his or her descendants, and charity. Such further trust provided for the payment of a stated percentage of the net income to the charity each year and for the balance of the net income and principal to be distributable to any beneficiary. The trust was to terminate on the earlier of the death of the child (or the descendant of a predeceased child) or the expiration of the applicable perpetuities period and was then to be distributable to such of the beneficiaries as the trustees determined. Under the will, the trustees also had the authority to amend the dispositive or administrative provisions of the trust. The trustees proposed (1) to amend the trust to provide that, upon the expiration of the 25-year term of the trust, one-sixth of the remaining principal of the trust would be vested in one of the children of the decedent and (2) to release their right to change that disposition. The child then proposed to assign gratuitously his remainder interest to his children.

The IRS in this ruling concluded that, for GST purposes, there would be two transferors with respect to the trust assets as of the date of the assignment: The child would be treated as the transferor with respect to the portion of the trust assets equal to the present value of the one-sixth remainder interest on the date of the gift, and the decedent would remain the transferor with respect to the balance of the trust. The IRS found that the proposed transaction would have the effect of avoiding the special rules enacted for allocating GST exemption to a CLAT in IRC Section 2642(e) (discussed above) and achieving the same leverage that prompted Congress to enact IRC Section 2642(e). The IRS noted that the legislative history to IRC Section 2642(e) states that, with a CLAT, by allowing the present value of the charitable interest at the creation of the CLAT to reduce the denominator of the applicable fraction for purposes of determining the inclusion ratio, tremendous leveraging of the GST exemption would occur. That is, if the trust assets sufficiently outperformed the rate of return assumed in computing the present value of the charitable interest (that is, the IRC Section 7520 rate), the amount passing to the individual beneficiaries would exceed the amount that would have passed to them if there had been no charitable interest in the trust.

Furthermore, the IRS noted that the transaction might also be disregarded in its entirety and the series of transactions viewed as the designation by the trustee of the child's children as the remainder beneficiaries, and, therefore, the decedent would remain the transferor of the entire trust for GST purposes.

Although this ruling appears to have a narrow application because it is based on the violation of the spirit of IRC Section 2642(e), which only applies to CLATs, it does suggest that the IRS does not like these transactions and will attempt to find that the transferor has not changed where there is a gift of a vested remainder interest. As noted above, this conclusion in the case of a gift seems unsupported by the Internal Revenue Code, which provides that the "transferor" is the donor in the case of property subject to gift tax. IRC § 2652(a).

[27] 11 Cl. Ct. 808 (1987), *aff'd*, 897 F.2d 516 (Fed. Cir. 1990).

[28] Estate of Cyril I. Magnin v. Comm'r, 184 F.3d 1074 (9th Cir. 1999); Estate of Wheeler v. Comm'r, 116 F.3d 749 (5th Cir. 1997); Estate of D'Ambrosia v. Comm'r, 101 F.3d 309 (3d Cir. 1996).

If the transfer caused the child to be the transferor of only the actuarial remainder interest but not the whole trust property, the termination of the trust would be a taxable termination in part for GST tax purposes.

If the transfer of the vested remainder interest is by means of a sale, the income tax consequences of such sale also need to be considered. If the interest in the property being sold has a below market value basis for income tax purposes, the sale will cause gain recognition. If gain recognition is a concern, it could be avoided, for example, if the trust in which the child holds the remainder interest is a grantor trust with respect to the parent grantor and the sale is to a trust created for the benefit of the grandchildren or more remote descendants, which is treated as a grantor trust with respect to the grantor parent. (A grantor trust is a trust all the income, deductions, and credits of which are attributed to the grantor. The IRS takes the position that the grantor is treated for income tax purposes as owning all of the assets owned by a grantor trust.)[29] If the sale is to such a trust, to achieve the GST tax advantages, the trust would need to be exempt from the GST tax.

---

[29] Rev. Rul. 85-13, 1985-1 C.B. 184.

10

Charitable Giving

§10.01 INTRODUCTION

Many individuals choose to make charitable giving an integral part of their estate plans. A variety of factors motivate individuals to give to charitable organizations, including the desire to benefit a particular cause or organization. In addition, there are significant income, gift, and estate tax benefits associated with charitable giving.

EXAMPLE *10-1*

Harry gives $1,000 to the American Red Cross. Generally, Harry can deduct the gift from his gross income before applying the income tax rates and paying income tax. If he is in a marginal 37 percent income tax bracket, his deduction saves him $370 in income taxes. If his gift and estate tax marginal bracket is 40 percent, then this gift also saves him $400 of gift or estate tax that would otherwise be due by the time of his death. At his death, Harry leaves the charity another $100,000, which his estate can deduct against the federal estate tax, saving $40,000. So, Harry's total charitable gifts of $101,000 saved a total of $40,770 in taxes and cost him and his heirs only $60,230. The charitable gift would provide additional estate tax savings if Harry were domiciled in a state with a state estate tax. Despite the various tax benefits associated with charitable giving, donors should always have as a primary motive the desire to benefit the charity, because the charity receives the money rather than the donor or the donor's family.

A small cash gift to a charitable organization does not usually give rise to any legal issues. However, clients frequently need an estate planner's advice in order to navigate the complex tax rules associated with larger gifts or gifts of property other than cash. In order to maximize the benefits of a charitable gift to both the donor and the charity, an estate planner's advice is often sought regarding (1) how much to give in a particular year, (2) if assets other than cash are being given, which assets to give, (3) when to make the gift, (4) whether to make the gift outright or in trust, and (5) which organizations to benefit. Accordingly, an estate planner should have a good working knowledge of the specific rules governing the income, gift, and estate tax deductions for charitable gifts. This will require the estate planner to understand:

- What constitutes a charitable donation;
- The distinctions between various types of public charities, private foundations, and donor-advised funds;
- The different rules applicable to charitable deductions for income, gift, and estate tax purposes;
- How to structure split-interest gifts, such as charitable lead trusts, charitable remainder trusts, and charitable gift annuities; and
- Ways to ensure that the donor's wishes are carried out by the charity.

§ 10.02 CHARITABLE CONTRIBUTIONS AND CHARITABLE ORGANIZATIONS

[A] What Constitutes a Charitable Contribution?

In order to achieve the tax benefits associated with charitable giving, the donor must generally make a *charitable contribution* to a *charitable organization*. Generosity does not always qualify for tax benefits. For example, if a donor provides direct financial support to a needy family, that may be a generous act inspired by a charitable intent, but it will not qualify as a deductible charitable contribution unless the money is given to a qualifying charitable organization.

To be deductible for federal income tax purposes, a charitable contribution must be a donation of cash or property to a charitable organization that has been recognized as such by the Internal Revenue Service and that has been created and organized under the laws of the United States, a state, or any political subdivision.[1] The contribution of services for charitable purposes is not deductible.

[B] What Is a Charitable Organization?

Charitable organizations are described in Section 501(c)(3) of the Internal Revenue Code and must have the following characteristics:

- The primary purpose of the organization, expressed both in organizational documents and in practice, is religious, charitable (such as social service organizations), educational, scientific, health-related, literary, the promotion of amateur sports competition, or the prevention of cruelty to children or animals;

- Private individuals may not be shareholders and may not benefit from the profits of the organization, and regulations provide that the prohibition against private benefit can include either economic or non-economic benefits, even if ostensibly reasonable;[2]

- The organization may not (except for an insubstantial amount) conduct any lobbying activities aimed at influencing legislation at local, state, or national levels;[3] and

---

[1] § 10.02 IRC § 170(c).

[2] Reg. § 1.501(c)(3)-1(d).

[3] Lobbying limited to time and effort of less than 5 percent of an organization's activities has been found to be insubstantial. Seasongood v. Comm'r, 227 F.2d 907 (6th Cir. 1955). Public charities that prefer to be judged by an expenditure test may make an election to limit lobbying expenditures, with permissible limits set by statute via a sliding scale with an upper limit of 20 percent of the organization's total expenditures (not to exceed $1,000,000), and only a portion of such permitted amounts being spent on grassroots lobbying.

- The organization may not participate in or intervene in any political campaign on behalf of (or in opposition to) any candidate for public office.[4]

EXAMPLE 10-2

Rachel wanted to start an organization dedicated to protecting children from the dangers of smoking. She did not expect the organization to have much income and wasn't too concerned about the organization paying income taxes. She was concerned, however, that the organization would not attract sufficient contributions unless donors could claim income tax deductions for those contributions. As a consequence, she decided that the organization should apply for tax-exempt status as an educational organization described in Section 501(c)(3). Although she had initially considered having the organization actively lobby for anti-smoking legislation and support anti-smoking candidates, Rachel decided (out of an abundance of caution, even though a limited amount of lobbying activities could have been permissible if structured appropriately) that charitable status was more important, and so she prohibited those activities in the organization's governing documents and limited the written purpose and actual activities of the organization to developing an anti-smoking curriculum to be used by elementary school teachers.

In order for donations to an organization to be tax deductible, the organization generally must be specifically recognized by the Internal Revenue Service as a charitable organization.[5] With a few exceptions, primarily pertaining to certain religious organizations,[6] each charitable organization that meets the requirements described in Section 501(c)(3) must also apply to the Internal Revenue Service for approval as a charitable organization.[7] The application is made on Form 1023, which requires the organization to disclose all of its planned activities, its affiliations, and

---

[4] *See* Rev. Rul. 2007-41, 2007-25 I.R.B. 1421 (describing various situations in which activities and communications by a 501(c)(3) organization are, and which are not, impermissible political activities).

[5] This requirement, found in IRC §508, does not apply to organizations (that are not §501(c)(3) organizations) to which contributions are deductible under IRC §170(c) (defining "charitable contribution"). Such organizations include certain governmental and quasi-governmental organizations (IRC §170(c)(1) and §115), war veterans organizations (IRC §170(c)(3)), fraternal organizations (IRC §170(c)(4), deductible only for gifts for certain purposes), and non-profit cemetery companies (IRC §170(c)(5)). Although an organization in one of these categories may not (unless it has affirmatively requested confirmation of its tax status, as many do) have a determination letter or be listed in Tax Exempt Organization Search (discussed below), contributions to the organization may nevertheless be eligible for an income tax charitable deduction. *See* IRS Publication 526, Charitable Contributions.

[6] IRC §508(c)(1)(A). This exception applies to churches, synagogues, temples and mosques, and also to certain entities under their control (referred to as "integrated auxiliaries"). Organizations under a "group exemption" may also be excused from these application procedures. Reg. §1.508-1(a)(3)(c).

[7] IRC §508(d)(2)(B) bars a charitable deduction for contributions to organizations that have not applied for approval as a charitable organization pursuant to IRC §508(a).

§10.02[B]

commercial obligations with other organizations, and its current and projected financial statements.[8] Once approved, the organization will receive a *determination letter* from the Internal Revenue Service stating that the organization is eligible to receive tax deductible contributions. So long as the organization files its application within 27 months of its creation, approval of its status under Section 501(c)(3) will be retroactive to the date of its formation.[9] The determination letter is a charitable organization's best proof of its tax-exempt charitable status,[10] and many donors will ask for a copy before making a gift. Although many religious organizations are not required to apply for a determination letter in order to receive tax deductible donations, some do so in order to have a determination letter to show to donors.

An estate planner who is assisting a client with a charitable gift should always check an official source to confirm that the organization is eligible to receive tax deductible donations. This has the added advantage of enabling the estate planner to make sure that the gift uses the charity's official name. Donors and their advisors can find a list of all qualified charitable organizations by using Tax Exempt Organizations Search which is available online at the IRS website.[11] Donors and Advisors can also check one of several private websites that have teamed up with the Internal Revenue Service to make this and other information available;[12] however, donors should be aware that the only online source on which they are officially entitled to rely is Tax Exempt Organization Search.[13]

Finally, gifts to foreign charitable organizations, even to a publicly supported institution such as the British Museum, are not deductible for U.S. income tax purposes.[14] This limitation does not apply to the estate tax deduction, so gifts to foreign as well as U.S. charitable organizations may be deducted in computing the donor's federal estate tax liability.[15]

It should be noted that charitable organizations described in Section 501(c)(3) are just one of many types of tax-exempt organizations. Organizations such as civic leagues are tax-exempt under Section 501(c)(4); labor organizations under Section 501(c)(5); trade associations and chambers of commerce under Section 501(c)(6); and

---

[8] Certain small organizations may be eligible to file the streamlined Form 1023-EZ.

[9] Reg. § 1.508-1(a)(2) sets the original 15-month deadline; Reg. § 301.9100-2 provides for an automatic 12-month extension.

[10] Donors are generally permitted to rely on a copy of an organization's exemption letter. *See* Reg. § 1.509(a)-7. However, once the IRS has issued public notice of a change in an organization's tax-exempt status (which it does by way of Tax Exempt Organization Search, discussed below), a donor can no longer rely on a copy of the organization's exemption letter. Accordingly, donors should never rely on an exemption letter without checking Tax Exempt Organization Search as well.

[11] Known as "Exempt Organizations Select Check" prior to May 2018, and originally known as "Publication 78." Tax Exempt Organization Search also includes copies of determination letters for many organizations created after January 1, 2014.

[12] One example can be found at www.guidestar.org.

[13] *See* Rev. Proc. 2011-33, 2011-25 I.R.B. 887.

[14] IRC § 170(c)(2)(A). Under treaties with Canada, Mexico, and Israel, there are a few limited exceptions under which a gift to a foreign charitable organization might allow for a U.S. income tax deduction. *See* IRS Publication 526, Charitable Contributions.

[15] *See generally* IRC § 2055.

social clubs under Section 501(c)(7).[16] However, generally only gifts to charitable organizations that are exempt under Section 501(c)(3) qualify for the charitable deduction.[17]

§ 10.03 THE DISTINCTION BETWEEN PUBLIC CHARITIES AND PRIVATE FOUNDATIONS

[A] In General

Each tax-exempt charitable organization is further classified by the IRS as either a public charity or a private foundation, and donors making a charitable contribution must be educated on the distinction between the two, because the charitable deduction rules are different depending upon whether a gift is to a public charity or to a private foundation. As discussed below, donors to public charities can receive somewhat more generous deductions than can donors to private foundations. In addition, charities themselves are subject to different rules, restrictions and penalties depending on whether they are public charities or private foundations.

In general, public charities receive funds from a broad group of donors and have boards that are responsive to such donors, while private foundations are often funded and controlled by one person or family. For example, the United Way and the American Cancer Society are public charities because they receive substantial support from the general public. The Ford Foundation is a private foundation because it received its funding from a single family. Federal tax law draws a distinction between the two because Congress saw more opportunity for abuse and a greater need for regulatory oversight for private foundations. Congress also decided that the charitable deductions for donations to private foundations should be more limited than donations to public charities.

When a new charitable organization is created and files Form 1023 to apply for tax-exempt status, it must set forth its case for being classified as a public charity. If an organization fails to prove that it qualifies as a public charity, it will be classified as a private foundation.

---

[16] Tax-exempt organizations must still pay income tax on business activities that are unrelated to their exempt purposes. IRC § 512. For example, a school, or an association of electrical engineers, or the League of Women Voters can apply to the IRS for tax-exempt status and, if granted, can invest its funds to earn interest, dividends, and capital gains, all of which will be tax-free to the organization. If any of these organizations decides to open a dry-cleaning shop, however, the proceeds from the shop will be subject to income tax (even if the organization uses the proceeds to further its exempt purposes). Also, some non-charitable organizations, such as social clubs, are exempt from tax on exempt function income (such as membership dues) but must pay income tax on investment income.

[17] A charitable deduction may also be allowed for a gift to a charitable trust that is described in IRC § 4947(a)(1).

[B] Public Charities

Section 509(a) of the Code sets forth four alternative categories of public charities, and provides that if a charitable organization is not described in one of these categories, it is automatically considered a private foundation.

- *Category 1.* An organization must either (i) be a religious organization, school, hospital, or a government branch or agency,[1] or (ii) show that it is sufficiently supported (see the public support tests below) by contributions from government units and/or the general public.[2]
- *Category 2.* This category also requires proof of sufficient support from government units and/or the general public and includes not only contributions but also receipts for the provision of charitable services.[3]
- *Category 3.* The third category, known as supporting organizations,[4] includes organizations that are dedicated to the support of organizations described in the first two categories.
- *Category 4.* The fourth category is for organizations that test for public safety.[5]

[1] Publicly Supported Organizations

As described above, two categories of public charities require that an organization prove that it receives significant support from government units and/or the general public. The tests are quite technical and discerning the difference between the two is challenging. An organization can attempt to meet either test, but will generally find one or the other is the better fit, depending upon whether the organization's support consists primarily of contributions, or whether it also has significant receipts from the performance of charitable activities. The organization will also need to consider the investment income it receives, as that affects each of the two tests in different ways.

[a] Significant Support from Contributions

Under the first category of public charities, an organization must show that it receives contributions from government units and/or the general public that, on average over its most recent five years of operation, make up at least one-third of its annual support.[6] For purposes of this public support test, the term "general public" is defined to include any individual or corporate donor except to the extent that donations from the donor (when aggregated with donations from related parties)

---

[1] § 10.03 IRC §§ 509(a)(1) and 170(b)(1)(A)(i)–(v).
[2] IRC §§ 509(a)(1) and 170(b)(1)(A)(vi).
[3] IRC § 509(a)(2).
[4] IRC § 509(a)(3).
[5] IRC § 509(a)(4).
[6] IRC §§ 509(a)(1) and 170(b)(1)(A)(vi).

exceed 2 percent of the organization's total support.[7] For organizations that cannot meet the "one-third support" test, there is an alternative "ten percent of support" test whereby the organization need only show that, on average over its most recent five years of operation, at least 10 percent of its support comes from government units and/or the general public, but must also show that certain facts and circumstances exist that prove the organization is in the nature of a publicly supported organization.[8] Organizations receiving significant support from contributions are not subject to an express limitation on investment income (but, because such income counts as part of the total support in the denominator of the public support fraction but not in the numerator, it will have the effect of lowering the percentage of public support).

EXAMPLE 10-3

An organization created to promote the history of women's achievements in America has plans to raise $1,000,000 over the next five years. It has several key backers who intend to donate a large portion of the funds, and those backers want the organization to qualify as a public charity so that they can receive the most beneficial deductions (*see* § 10.04 *infra*). To achieve public charity status, the organization must raise $333,333 from unrelated donors where no one donation is counted beyond $20,000 (2 percent of the total donations) (the goal could be reached by as few as 17 donors giving $20,000 each, or thousands of donors giving smaller amounts). The organization will work hard to meet the one-third public support test, not wanting to rely on the alternative 10 percent public support test (the organization is not optimistic that it could meet the required facts and circumstances that would compel the IRS to conclude that it is "in the nature of a publicly supported organization").

[b] Significant Support from Receipts for Charitable Services

Under the second category of public charities, an organization must show that it receives a combination of contributions from government units and/or the general public and/or receipts (received from the general public or from government units) for the conduct of its exempt activity that, on average over its most recent five years of operation, make up at least one-third of its annual support. For purposes of this public support test, the term "general public" is defined differently: it includes any individual or corporate donor, except that if the combined donations and receipts from the donor (when aggregated with donations and receipts from related parties) exceed 2 percent of the organization's total support (making such donor a "substan-

---

[7] Reg. § 1.170A-9(e)(6).

[8] Reg. § 1.170A-9(e)(3) (large number of donors; governing body representing broad interests of the public; services provided directly to the public; appeal for members designed to attract broad cross section of public; etc.).

tial contributor") then the donations and receipts from such donor will be entirely excluded.[9] In addition, when counting receipts from the conduct of its exempt activity (such as a museum's admission receipts or a social service organization's government reimbursements) as part of its one-third support fraction, receipts for services from any one person or any one government agency cannot be counted in any one year to the extent they exceed the greater of $5,000 or 1 percent of the organization's total support for that year.[10] Finally, an organization qualifying for this second category of public charity must not have investment income that exceeds one-third of its total support.

EXAMPLE *10-4*

A mental health counseling center has $1,000,000 of support during its most recent five years of operation, including receipts from patients for its delivery of counseling services, and hopes to preserve public charity status. Using the two alternative public support tests:

1. At least $333,333 must have come from government grants and/or contributions of no larger than $20,000 per donor (2 percent of total support) (aggregating gifts from the donor and his or her family members), or
2. At least $333,333 must have come from a combination of government grants and/or contributions and/or receipts for services not counting any contributions or receipts from one person (and related family) at all if such support exceeds $20,000 (2 percent of total support), and not counting any receipts for services from any person or government agency in excess of $10,000 (the greater of $5,000 or 1 percent of total support), all while no more than $333,333 of support comes from investment income.

[2] Supporting Organizations

A supporting organization is a charitable organization dedicated to the support of one or more other public charities. A supporting organization enjoys public charity status without the need to satisfy a public support test, so some donors may prefer to establish and fund a supporting organization rather than a private foundation. The tax code and regulations governing supporting organizations are very complex and have been subject to several changes over the past several years, including changes enacted with the Pension Protection Act of 2006 and regulations issued on December 28, 2012 and December 21, 2015. The supporting organization's governing documents

---

[9] Reg. § 1.509(a)-3; IRC § 4958(c)(3)(C) (defining a "substantial contributor").
[10] IRC § 509(a)(2)(A)(ii); Reg. § 1.509(a)-3.

must either specify the name(s) of the supported organization(s) or describe a class of charitable organization(s) that will be supported.[11] The supporting organization must support the specified organization(s) by either providing it/them with substantial financial resources or by conducting charitable activities that it/they would otherwise undertake directly.[12] The supporting organization may not be controlled (directly or indirectly) by a substantial donor,[13] and in fact is often controlled by the supported public charity with the participation of the donor and his or her family.

EXAMPLE 10-5

A donor wants to endow a program run by a specific public charity, but would prefer to retain some control over when and how the income from the fund is used, and would like to control the investment of the fund. A private foundation is not an acceptable solution because the donor intends to fund the endowment with appreciated property other than publicly traded stock, and wants a deduction for the full value of the property (*see* § 10.04 *infra*). The donor forms a supporting organization, giving a majority of the seats on the board to nominees of the supported public charity and keeping a minority of the seats for his family. The supporting organization's governing documents limit the use of funds solely for the benefit of the supported public charity.

The Treasury Regulations[14] provide that a supporting organization must meet each of the following four requirements:

1. *The Control Test.* A combination of statutes and regulations describe three alternative requirements for the control of a supporting organization, one of which must be met:

   - the supporting organization must be operated, supervised or controlled by the supported organization (commonly known as a "Type I supporting organization") (the regulations provide that the requirement is satisfied if the supporting organization has a majority of its directors appointed by the supported organization); or

   - the supporting organization must be supervised or controlled in connection with the supported organization (commonly known as a "Type II supporting organization") (the regulations provide that the requirement is satisfied if the control or management of the supporting organization is

---

[11] The class must be drawn narrowly enough that the qualifying members of the class are "readily identifiable." *See* Reg. § 1.509(a)-4(d)(2)(iii); Rev. Rul. 81-43, 1981-1 C.B. 350; Polm Family Foundation, Inc. v. United States, 644 F.3d 406 (D.C. Cir. 2011) (class of organizations which support, promote and/or perform public health and/or Christian objectives not readily identifiable).

[12] IRC § 509(a)(3); Reg. § 1.509(a)-4.

[13] IRC § 509(a)(3)(C).

[14] Reg. § 1.509(a)-4.

vested in the same persons that control or manage the supported organization); or

- the supporting organization must be operated in connection with the supported organization (commonly known and now defined in the Code as a "Type III supporting organization"); the regulations provide that the requirement is satisfied by complying with a notification requirement[15] and meeting *each* of the following two further tests:

    a. *Type III Responsiveness Test.* One of the following three relationships must result in the supported organization having a *significant voice* in the supporting organization's investment policies and the use of the supporting organization's income and assets: (i) the supported organization has the right to appoint or elect at least one officer, director or trustee of the supporting organization; or (ii) at least one officer, director or trustee of the supporting organization is in fact a member of the governing body of the supported organization; or (iii) the directors, officers or trustees of the supporting organization maintain a close and continuous relationship with the directors, officers or trustees of the supported organization.

    b. *Type III Integral Part Test.* A supporting organization must show that it has significant involvement in the operations of the supported organization and that the supported organization is dependent upon the supporting organization for support. Regulations provide that this requirement can be met in one of two ways: either (i) the supporting organization must show that it provides a certain amount of support each year[16] to the supported organization and the amount of support is sufficient to ensure the attentiveness of the supported organization to the supporting organization's operations;[17] or (ii) the supporting organization shows that substantially all of its activities consist of performing one or more important functions of the supported organi-

---

[15] For each taxable year, a Type III supporting organization must provide certain information to its supported organization(s). Reg. § 1.509(a)-4(i)(2) (requiring submission of a written notice following certain formalities and outlining support provided for the past year, a copy of the supporting organization's latest Form 990, and updated copies of its governing instruments if not previously provided).

[16] The required distribution amount is the greater of (i) 85 percent of the supporting organization's adjusted net income for the preceding taxable year, and (ii) 3.5 percent of the fair market value of its non-exempt-use assets in the preceding taxable year. Reg. § 1.509(a)-4(i)(5)(ii); Reg. § 1.509(a)-4(i)(6) (providing guidance on what distributions and expenses count toward this distribution requirement).

[17] At least one-third of the distributable amount must be distributed to one or more supported organizations that are attentive to the supporting organization and to which the supporting organization is responsive. A supported organization is "attentive" to the supporting organization if (i) the support provided amounts to at least 10 percent of the supported organization's total support (or, for a university, hospital, or church, of the total support of the particular department or school of the organization to which the distributions are made), (ii) the support is necessary to avoid the interruption of a particular substantial function or activity for which the funds are earmarked, or (iii) based on all of the facts and circumstances, there is evidence of actual attentiveness to the supporting organization's activities by the supported organization. Reg. § 1.509(a)-4(i)(5)(iii).

zation and that, but for its activities, the supported organization would have to conduct those activities itself.[18] Supporting organizations that satisfy the Integral Part Test in the latter way (by directly performing such functions of supported organizations) are called "functionally integrated Type III supporting organizations."[19] Those that satisfy this test by providing financial support are called "non-functionally integrated Type III supporting organizations," and (unlike functionally integrated Type III supporting organizations) are subject to many of the rules and restrictions applicable to private foundations.[20]

2. *The Organizational Test.* The supporting organization's organizational documents (articles of organization and by-laws) cannot empower the supporting organization to conduct activities beyond the scope of its support for the supported organization, and cannot permit the supporting organization to support any other organization.

3. *The Operational Test.* All of the supporting organization's activities must be in support of, or for the benefit of, the supported organization (or, if the supported organization is not specified by name in the documents, the class of organizations that is so specified). In addition, the supporting organization may not financially benefit any organization other than the supported organization (or the class of organizations that is so specified).

4. *The "No Control by Disqualified Persons" Test.* The supporting organization cannot be controlled (directly or indirectly) by any substantial contributors or persons or organizations related to substantial contributors. In addition, Type I and Type III supporting organizations will lose their status as supporting organizations if they accept any gift or contribution from a person who controls (alone or in conjunction with related parties) the *supported* organization.[21]

---

[18] *See* Reg. § 1.509(a)-4(i)(4)(ii) (defining "substantially all" and "directly further"). The aspects of the Integral Part Test (the "attentiveness" subtest and the "but for" subtest) have been litigated at the Tax Court by an organization seeking and failing to be found to be a supporting organization. *See* Lapham Foundation v. Comm'r, T.C. Memo 2002-293, where the court found that the supported organization would have conducted its own exempt activities whether or not the supporting organization helped out, and where, in any event, the support was too insignificant to guarantee the attention of the supported organization.

[19] IRC § 4943(f).

[20] Distributions from private foundations to non-functionally integrated Type III supporting organizations are not qualifying distributions for purposes of satisfying a private foundation's required annual distributions under IRC § 4942 and may be treated as taxable expenditures under IRC § 4945. Such organizations are also subject to the excess business holdings rules for private foundations (IRC § 4943), and are not eligible to receive direct charitable rollovers from IRAs.

[21] IRC § 509(f).

[3] Donor-Advised Funds

A donor-advised fund (DAF) is a charitable giving program sponsored by a public charity that gives a donor an ongoing role over the DAF even after the charitable contribution is complete.[22] Charitable community foundations (such as the Boston Foundation, the New York Community Trust, and the Silicon Valley Foundation) typically sponsor donor-advised funds, where they agree with a donor to hold and invest donated funds in separate accounts (bearing the donor's name, if the donor so wishes), with each donor advising the charity on how and when the funds in his or her separate account should be distributed among other charities.[23] Many financial service institutions also sponsor charitable organizations that host donor-advised funds.

Advantages of using a donor advised fund include:

- The ability to claim the donor's income tax charitable deduction in the year that the DAF is funded, even though the distributions to charities will be made over several years; this outcome is particularly attractive in years when the donor is otherwise facing large income tax obligations;

- Compared to a private foundation, a DAF is less expensive to create and maintain (a private foundation requires an initial application for tax-exempt status and annual federal and state filings);

- DAFs allow donors to give anonymously, whereas private foundation tax returns are readily available through services such as GuideStar and disclose not only the charitable organizations supported by the foundation but also the identity of, and amounts contributed by, each donor to the foundation.

- As a public charity, a DAF offers more favorable income tax deductions to donors than does a private foundation: first, gifts to a DAF of appreciated property (long-term gain) are deductible at fair market value, while gifts of such property to a private foundation generally provide a fair market value deduction only if the gift is of publicly-traded stock—otherwise the deduction is limited to the donor's basis in the gifted property; second, the limits on the amount of taxable income that may be offset by the charitable deduction in any one tax year are more generous for gifts to a DAF than for gifts to a private foundation;

- Community foundations and other DAF sponsors offer donors access to resources that can lead to satisfying and strategic philanthropy, including methods to facilitate family philanthropy.

In recent years, the IRS has tightened its oversight of DAFs. The rules impose penalties on both a DAF and its managers if a DAF distribution is made for non-charitable purposes.[24] In addition, a penalty is imposed where a DAF provides more

---

[22] IRC § 4966(d)(2).
[23] Reg. § 1.170A-9(e)(10)-(14).
[24] IRC § 4966(a).

than an incidental benefit to a donor of the DAF or to the grant advisors of a DAF.[25] The intermediate sanction rules have been expanded to include DAFs, bringing more scrutiny to transactions between a DAF and its donors, its grant advisors, and even its investment advisors.[26] In addition, the ban against excess business holdings applies to DAFs as well as private foundations.[27]

[4] Intermediate Sanctions

Public charities and donors to public charities should be aware of the so-called "intermediate sanctions," so dubbed because they are intended to curb the abuses that are not considered egregious enough to warrant a revocation of the organization's tax-exempt status. These provisions impose substantial penalties against any person "in a position to exercise substantial influence over the affairs of the organization" if such person engages in an "excess benefit transaction" with the organization.[28] Regulations indicate that being a substantial contributor (one who donates more than 2 percent of the organization's support in any one year) is a factor that tends to show substantial influence; and that such influence is held by a director or officer (and anyone else having similar powers and responsibilities) but only if such person is aware of the rule against excess benefit transactions and negligently fails to ascertain whether an excess benefit transaction exists in the face of facts sufficient for a reasonable person to conclude that there is in fact an excess benefit.[29] Excess benefit transactions include any compensation arrangement where the person with such influence receives from the organization compensation and any other economic benefits that exceed the fair market value of services provided to the organization; the term also includes any financial transaction where the person with such influence receives from the organization an economic benefit in excess of the fair market value of money or goods provided to the organization.[30]

Regulations also provide "safe harbor" protection to organizations (other than supporting organizations and donor-advised funds), providing that compensation and transactions will have a rebuttable presumption of reasonableness if (1) they are approved in advance by the organization's governing body (or authorized committee) composed of members not conflicted in the matter, (2) there is available to such

---

[25] IRC § 4967(a); Notice 2017-73, 2017-51 I.R.B. 562.

[26] IRC § 4958(c)(2).

[27] IRC § 4943(e).

[28] IRC § 4958.

[29] Reg. § 53.4958-3(c), (e).

[30] IRC § 4958(c); Reg. § 53.4958-4. The term "excess benefit transaction" includes any grant, loan, compensation or similar payment from a supporting organization to a substantial contributor (or related person), or from a donor-advised fund to any donor or donor-designated advisor (or related person), regardless of whether the payment is reasonable and not in excess of the value of the services provided by such person; similarly, there is an automatic excess benefit transaction regarding any loan from a supporting organization to its other disqualified persons (anyone in a position to exercise substantial influence over the supporting organization). IRC § 4958(c)(2)-(3).

decision makers some data of comparable compensation or fees incurred by unrelated organizations, and (3) the basis for the decision made is documented.[31]

Even if compensation is reasonable and is sufficiently supported, under new rules the organization may be subject to tax on that compensation if it is in excess of $1,000,000, or is in the nature of a severance payment and is more than three times the employee's base salary over the previous five years (an "excess parachute payment").[32] This excise tax is independent of and in addition to the intermediate sanctions rules.

Regulations provide that the IRS has discretion to impose intermediate sanction penalties, revoke an organization's tax-exempt status, or both, and that facts relevant to such determination include whether there have been repeated excess benefit transactions, the size and scope of such transactions, whether safeguards against future violations have been put into place, and whether there has been compliance with other applicable laws.[33]

[5] Limitations on Global Funding

The U.S. Department of Treasury maintains a list of countries in which it is illegal to conduct business or even make charitable grants.[34] In addition, the Treasury Department has issued an advisory entitled "Anti-Terrorist Financing Guidelines: Voluntary Best Practices for U.S.-based Charities,"[35] which contains suggestions that are much-criticized for being overbearing and effectively discouraging global philanthropy by anyone but the largest of grant-making foundations. The Guidelines recommend that before funding a foreign organization, donors (including U.S.-based public charities) must collect basic information, conduct basic vetting of the grantee's personnel, and review the grantee organization's financial operations, all as summarized below:

(i) Collect basic information about the grantee:

- organization's name in English and in its language of origin, any acronyms used in jurisdictions in which it operates, with addresses and local phone numbers;
- copies of the grantee's governing documents and information about its founders;
- a detailed report of the organization's purposes, projects and goals;
- names and addresses of the organizations to which the grantee organization provides (or proposes to provide) funds, services, or material support, to the extent reasonably discoverable;

---

[31] Reg. § 53.4958-6.

[32] IRC § 4960, effective for taxable years beginning after December 31, 2017; Notice 2019-09, 2019-04 I.R.B. 403.

[33] Reg. § 1.501(c)(3)-(1)(g).

[34] *See* www.treas.gov/offices/enforcement/ofac/sdn.

[35] *See* www.treasury.gov/resource-center/terrorist-illicit-finance//Documents/guidelines_charities.pdf.

- names and addresses of any subcontracting organizations used by the grantee organization;
- copies of any of the grantee organization's public filings and annual reports;
- financial data of the grantee organization, including sources of income.

(ii) Conduct basic vetting of the grantee:

- research public information about the grantee to determine any connection to terrorism or terrorist financing;
- the grantee must not be on any OFAC prohibited parties' lists; consider similar lists of other nations created pursuant to United Nations Security Council Resolution 1373;
- obtain names, nationality, citizenship, and place and date of birth of grantee organization's board members and key staff in every field office; check to be sure these names are not on the above lists;
- get certification from the grantee organization that it is in compliance with United States laws regarding OFAC prohibited parties' lists; if the grantee is a foreign organization, the certification should state that the grantee does not deal with any individuals, entities or groups on OFAC prohibited parties lists or who support terrorism.

[6] Annual Reporting Requirements

Public charities (except for religious organizations) must annually file a federal tax return, which may be a Form 990, Form 990-N, or Form 990EZ, depending on the organization's gross receipts and, in most states, must file some form of report with the Charities Division of the office of the Attorney General of the state in which the organization is based, and possibly other states in which the organization is raising funds or performing activities. These returns contain information concerning the organization's activities and accomplishments, information on officers and directors and their compensation, and financial statements. These forms are open to public inspection, and donors considering a charitable contribution often review such reports as part of their investigation of an organization. In addition, if the charity has any "unrelated business taxable income" (e.g., income from regularly operating a commercial business, advertising revenue, income from certain debt-financed property and the cost of certain fringe benefits provided to employees which, under the Tax Cuts and Jobs Act of 2017 ("TCJA"),[36] are now treated as deemed unrelated business taxable income[37]), federal income tax must be paid with Form 990-T (and

---

[36] Pub. L. No. 115-97.

[37] *See* IRC § 512(a)(7), enacted as part of the TCJA, treating costs pertaining to certain transportation, parking and fitness benefits provided to employees as deemed unrelated business taxable income to the organization incurring those costs. This rule requires many organizations that did not previously file the Form 990-T to now file that form to report this deemed "income" and pay the resulting tax. *See also* Notice 2018-99, 2018-52 I.R.B. 1067, and Notice 2018-100, 2018-52 I.R.B. 1074.

most states collect such tax as well).[38] Further, if the charity is a corporation, an annual report listing the current directors and officers must be filed with the Secretary of State's office for the state in which the organization is incorporated (and possibly for other states in which the organization is active). In general, a charitable organization should keep its records on hand for several years in order to comply with any requests for information by state or federal regulatory authorities.

[C] Private Foundations

[1] Overview

If a charitable organization cannot meet one of the tests for public charity status, it is automatically considered a private foundation.[39] Most private foundations are created by design to receive contributions from only one donor or one family or one corporation, and so their founders simply acknowledge private foundation status on Form 1023 and accept the consequences of private foundation status:

- Donors to private foundations follow different income tax deduction rules for their contributions;[40]
- Private foundations pay an excise tax on net investment income;
- Several penalty taxes apply to private foundations that fail to meet certain requirements; and
- Public disclosure rules are slightly different for private foundations.

[2] Excise Tax on Net Investment Income

Although private foundations are exempt from federal income tax, they nevertheless pay tax under a special "excise tax"[41] intended to collect funds sufficient for the IRS to cover the costs of policing private foundations and enforcing the penalty tax system described below. Effective for tax years starting in 2020, including 2020 estimated tax payments, the tax is applied at a flat rate of 1.39 percent on the foundation's net investment income (including interest, dividends, rents, realized capital gains, less deductions for depreciation and expenses paid or incurred for the production of the income). The new flat excise tax rate simplifies tax reporting for private foundations. It eliminates the need to do a separate calculation that was

---

[38] Under IRC § 512(a)(6), enacted as part of the TCJA, an organization can no longer use losses in one unrelated trade or business to offset unrelated income from a separate trade or business. This rule has the effect of increasing the unrelated business income tax exposure of many organizations. *See* Notice 2018-67, 2018-36 I.R.B. 409.

[39] IRC §§ 508(b), 509(a).

[40] *See* § 10.04 *infra.*

[41] IRC § 4940. The flat 1.39 percent excise tax rate was enacted on December 20, 2019 as part of the Further Consolidated Appropriations Act, 2020.

required under the former law to determine the amount that the foundation needed to distribute in order to qualify for the 1 percent excise tax rate rather than the 2 percent excise tax rate.

[3] Minimum Distribution Requirement

Private foundations must annually distribute 5 percent of the net fair market value of the foundation's assets to accomplish one or more charitable purposes.[42] The computation of the 5 percent minimum distribution for a given fiscal year begins after the close of the fiscal year when it is possible to value the foundation's assets using the average monthly value of marketable securities and average monthly cash balance and an annually updated appraisal of other assets (real estate may be revalued every five years).[43] The value of the foundation's assets does not include cash on hand equal to 1.5 percent of the value of all foundation assets, in acknowledgement of the need to use cash for charitable distributions and miscellaneous operating expenses, nor the value of any assets used by the foundation in directly conducting its charitable purpose, such as kitchen equipment used by a foundation that operates a soup kitchen.[44] The 5 percent minimum distribution, once computed, is reduced by the amount of any excise tax on investment income. The resulting minimum distribution amount computed for a tax year must actually be distributed for charitable purposes by the end of the following tax year.[45] Distributions to public charities and private operating foundations will satisfy the distribution requirement, but distributions to other private foundations will not count toward satisfaction of the distribution requirement.[46] A private foundation's grant to a Type III supporting organization will count toward satisfaction of the distribution requirement only if the supporting organization is functionally integrated. Grants to Type I, Type II and Type III functionally integrated supporting organizations will not count toward satisfaction of the distribution requirement if a disqualified person with respect to the private foundation controls such supporting organization or if such a disqualified person controls any supported organization supported by such supporting organization.[47] A distribution to a foreign charity that is the equivalent of U.S.-based public charity or operating foundation will also satisfy the requirement if the equivalency is determined in good faith by the organization reasonably relying on a current opinion of a qualified tax practitioner (attorney, CPA or enrolled agent).[48] The distribution requirement can also be satisfied by certain foundation expenses incurred to support

---

[42] IRC § 4942.

[43] IRC § 4942(d), (e); Reg. § 53.4942(a)-2(c).

[44] Reg. § 53.4942(a)-2(c)(3).

[45] IRC § 4942(d)(2).

[46] IRC § 4942(g); Reg. § 53.4942(a)-3.

[47] IRC § 4942(g)(4).

[48] Reg. § 53.4942(a)-3(a)(6); Reg. § 53.4945-5(a)(5); Reg. § 53.4945-6(c)(2)(ii); Rev. Proc. 2017-53, 2017-40 I.R.B. 263. An organization is no longer permitted to rely on an affidavit of the foreign charity.

charitable activity (salary or fees paid for administration of the foundation's charitable programs, travel and conference fees regarding a charitable strategy of the foundation, or legal fees associated with the foundation's grant making).[49] Shortfalls in the 5 percent minimum distribution must still be paid and will be subject to a 15 percent tax.[50]

EXAMPLE *10-6*

The Green family funds a private foundation with $1,000,000 on October 15, 2021. They select the longest fiscal and tax year possible, ending on the following September 30, 2022. Before this first fiscal year is over, the foundation distributes $20,000 to charitable organizations. After the close of the fiscal year, the Greens value the foundation's assets for the fiscal year that has just ended, being sure to use the average monthly balances for cash (reduced as permitted) and marketable securities. The value is $1,060,000. The foundation also computes an excise tax of $1,000 on its net investment income for the year that has just ended. So, with respect to the fiscal year that has just ended on September 30, 2022, the Greens must distribute (or spend on certain charitable expenses) at least $53,000 (5 percent of $1,060,000), less $1,000 of taxes due, which is $52,000; they have already distributed $20,000 of that amount, and the balance of $32,000 must be distributed to public charities or paid for charitable expenses before September 30, 2023.

[4] Prohibitions on Self-Dealing

One of the most significant of the private foundation rules is the rule that prohibits self-dealing.[51] Self-dealing is described as virtually any transaction, direct or indirect, between a private foundation and a disqualified person. Disqualified persons generally include substantial contributors and the foundation's managers (directors, trustees, officers, key employees), and any person or entity related to such persons.[52] Prohibited transactions specifically listed include selling, leasing (except a rent-free lease to the foundation), lending (except an interest-free loan to the foundation), furnishing of goods or services (except the donation of goods or services to the foundation), and payment of compensation by the foundation (except reasonable, "not excessive," compensation).[53] The rule against self-dealing generally provides no exceptions for a prohibited transaction, even if the transaction was fair or even

---

[49] IRC § 4942(g)(4).
[50] IRC § 4942(a).
[51] IRC § 4941.
[52] IRC § 4946(a).
[53] IRC § 4941(d)(1), (2).

favorable to the foundation.[54] The penalty assessed to a disqualified person who engages in self-dealing with a foundation is 5 percent of the amount involved in the self-dealing.[55] A foundation manager who participates in an act of self-dealing is subject to an excise tax of 5 percent of the amount involved in the self-dealing if the manager's participation was wilful and without reasonable cause.[56] An additional tax of 200 percent of the amount involved in the self-dealing is imposed on the disqualified person, and 50 percent of such amount on the foundation manager, if the self-dealing is not corrected in a timely fashion.[57]

EXAMPLE *10-7*

Marge and Bob funded their foundation with cash and have invested in a diverse portfolio of securities. Their investment advisor suggests that the foundation's portfolio should have some real estate investments as a hedge against inflation. Their son Tim just bought a fully leased office building in a negotiated deal for $10,000,000 but would be willing to sell it to the foundation for only $5,000,000 and take a charitable contribution deduction for the difference. However, any sale between Tim and the foundation, regardless of price, is prohibited self-dealing.

[5] Prohibition on Excess Business Holdings

A private foundation is generally not permitted to control, together with disqualified persons, more than 20 percent of certain active businesses,[58] which becomes an issue when an individual wishes to contribute a substantial interest in a family business to a private foundation and have that interest retained by the foundation. However, the foundation is given five years within which to dispose of gifts and bequests of business interests that would otherwise cause an excess business holding problem.[59]

Under a special exception to these rules enacted on February 9, 2018, a private foundation can hold certain business interests that under prior law would have been treated as excess business holdings as long as the following conditions exist:

---

[54] *But see* Reg. § 53.4941(d)-1(b) for a rule permitting an estate in administration to deal with disqualified persons prior to distributing estate assets to a foundation. Interestingly, the IRS ruled that the pro rata partition of undivided interests in real estate among a private foundation and disqualified persons is not self-dealing, Ltr. Rul. 200350022, and that an early termination of a charitable remainder trust, with the disqualified person receiving payment for the sale of his income interest to the charitable remainderman, is not self-dealing, Ltr. Rul. 200552015.

[55] IRC § 4941(a)(1).

[56] IRC § 4941(a)(2).

[57] IRC § 4941(b).

[58] IRC § 4943.

[59] IRC § 4943(c)(6). In addition, the IRS may extend this period for an additional five years. IRC § 4943(c)(7).

- One hundred percent of the voting stock is held by the private foundation, all of which was acquired by gift or bequest, not purchase;
- All of the net profits of the business (other than a reasonable reserve) are distributed to the foundation no later than 120 days after the close of the taxable year; and
- The business is operated independently of the foundation.[60]

[6] Limitations on High-Risk Investment of Foundation Assets

A private foundation must not invest its assets in such a manner that jeopardizes the carrying out of its exempt purpose.[61] An investment is considered to jeopardize the carrying out of exempt purposes if the foundation manager, in making the investment, has failed to exercise ordinary business care and prudence in providing for the long-term and short-term financial needs of the foundation to carry out its exempt purposes, under the facts and circumstances then prevailing.[62] Without giving certain examples of imprudent investments, the regulations state that methods of investment which will be closely scrutinized include trading in securities on margin, trading in commodity futures, investments in working interests in oil and gas wells, the purchase of derivative securities such as puts, calls, and straddles, the purchase of warrants, and selling short.[63]

A program-related investment that furthers a private foundation's exempt purpose is not a jeopardizing investment.[64] An investment is program-related if: (i) its primary purpose is to accomplish one or more religious, educational, or other charitable purposes; (ii) no significant purpose of the investment is the production of income or the appreciation of property; and (iii) no purpose of the investment is attempting to influence legislation or intervening in any political campaign.[65] On May 9, 2016, the IRS issued final regulations providing guidance on program-related investments.[66] The regulations include several detailed examples and provide that an investment is made primarily to accomplish one or more exempt purposes if it significantly furthers the accomplishment of the foundation's exempt activities and would not have been made but for the relationship between the exempt activities and the investment. For example, a foundation committed to combat inner-city deteriora-

---

[60] IRC § 4943(g), enacted as part of the Bipartisan Budget Act of 2018 (Pub. L. No. 115-123 (2018)). A business is treated as operated independently of the foundation where (1) no substantial contributor to the foundation (or family member) is a director, officer, manager, employee or contractor of the business, (2) at least a majority of the foundation's directors are persons who are not directors or officers of the business (or family members of a substantial contributor to the foundation), and (3) there is no loan outstanding from the business to a substantial contributor to the foundation (or any family member).

[61] IRC § 4944.

[62] Reg. § 53.4944-1(a)(2).

[63] Reg. § 53.4944-1(a)(2).

[64] IRC § 4944(c).

[65] Reg. § 53.4944-3.

[66] Reg. § 53.4944-3.

tion could invest in a company located in a distressed area that provides jobs and training to economically disadvantaged people.

Many foundations participate in investments that may not meet the definition of a program-related investment, but that nevertheless have a purpose (in addition to generation of returns) that is consistent with the foundation's charitable mission. These sorts of investments are often referred to as "mission-related" investments. While there are no regulations or other forms of guidance on which an organization may rely regarding when a mission-related investment may run afoul of the jeopardizing investment rules, the IRS has acknowledged that a private foundation may consider the relationship of a particular investment to the foundation's exempt purposes in determining whether the investment is prudent.[67]

[7] Taxable Expenditures

A private foundation must avoid certain "taxable expenditures."[68] Taxable expenditures are amounts paid by a private foundation:

- For influencing legislation or public elections or for other noncharitable purposes;[69]
- As grants to individuals for travel or study unless they are awarded on an objective and non-discriminatory basis in accordance with procedures approved in advance by the IRS;[70] or
- As grants to other private foundations, foreign charities or noncharitable organizations without exercising *expenditure responsibility*.[71]

"Expenditure responsibility" requires the foundation to exert all reasonable efforts and establish adequate procedures: (1) to see that the grant is spent solely for the purpose for which it was made; (2) to obtain full and complete reports from the grantee on how the funds are spent; and (3) to make full and detailed reports on the expenditures to the IRS.[72] To avoid the extra complications of exercising expenditure responsibility, many private foundations make grants only to public charities.

Also excused from the definition of taxable expenditure is a distribution to a foreign charity that is the equivalent of a U.S.-based public charity or operating foundation where the equivalency is determined in good faith by the organization reasonably relying on a current opinion of a qualified tax practitioner (attorney, CPA or enrolled agent).[73]

---

[67] Notice 2015-62, 2015-39 I.R.B. 411.

[68] IRC § 4945.

[69] IRC § 4945(d).

[70] IRC § 4945(g).

[71] IRC § 4945(h).

[72] Reg. § 53.4945-5. The expenditure responsibility procedures can be set forth in a grant agreement between the private foundation and the non-public charity grantee. Ltr. Rul. 200603031.

[73] Reg. § 53.4945-5(a)(5); Reg. § 53.4945-6(c)(2)(ii); Rev. Proc. 2017-53, 2017-40 I.R.B. 263. An organization is no longer permitted to rely on an affidavit of the foreign charity. In addition, a distribution to a foreign organization treated as a partial or complete termination of a private foundation under

[8] Limitations on Global Funding

Private foundations are subject to the same scrutiny with respect to funding global organizations as are public charities.[74]

[9] Annual Reporting Requirements

Private foundations are subject to the same reporting requirements as are public charities, except that they file IRS Form 990-PF, rather than Forms 990, 990-EZ or 990-N.

[D] Private Operating Foundations

[1] In General

Some private foundations directly conduct the charitable activity that constitutes their exempt purpose, either in addition to or in lieu of making grants to public charities. If a substantial portion of a foundation's income or assets is devoted to such direct conduct of charitable activity, the foundation can qualify as an "operating foundation"[75] and it will not be subject to the five percent minimum distribution rule.[76] In addition, donations to operating foundations will qualify the donor for the more attractive income tax deduction rules that normally apply only for gifts to public charities.[77]

To qualify as an operating foundation, an organization must satisfy the "income test" and any one of three other tests, known as the "asset test," the "endowment test," and the "support test."

[2] Income Test

To satisfy the income test, a foundation must make *qualifying distributions* that are *directly for the active conduct* of its exempt purpose which are equal to *substantially all* of the lesser of (i) its *adjusted net income,* or (ii) its *minimum investment return.*[78]

(Footnote Continued)

the rules of IRC § 507 and Reg. § 1.507-3(c) (i.e., a distribution or series of related distributions amounting to 25 percent or more of the fair market value of the organization's assets) must be held in a separate fund by the grantee devoted exclusively to purposes described in IRC § 170(c)(2)(B), and must comply with the expenditure responsibility rules regardless of whether an equivalency determination is made. *See* Reg. § 53.4945(a)-6(c)(2)(ii) and Rev. Proc. 2017-53, 2017-40 I.R.B. 263.

[74] *See* § 10.03[B][4] *supra.*

[75] IRC § 4942(j)(3).

[76] IRC § 4942(a)(1).

[77] IRC § 170(b)(1)(F). *See* § 10.04 *infra.*

[78] Reg. § 53.4942(b)-1.

- *Qualifying Distributions* are distributions and expenditures made to accomplish a charitable purpose;
- *Directly for the active conduct* of the foundation's own exempt purposes and programs means, generally, that the foundation administers and provides the charitable activity itself instead of funding others to do it. Examples of qualifying distributions directly for the active conduct of exempt purposes include:
  — Wages paid to staff, including program specialists, researchers, teachers, administrators, or other personnel who supervise, direct, and carry out the foundation's programs on a continuing basis;
  — The cost of acquiring and maintaining assets used in the foundation's programs, such as buildings, collections of specimens and art objects, research laboratories, books and other publications, computer programs and hardware, and other project supplies, such as food to feed the poor;
  — The cost of administering the foundation's programs, such as telephone and utilities bills, insurance premiums, and professional advisors' fees attributable to active (non-grantmaking) programs;
- *Adjusted Net Income* is gross income for the year, including investment income and other revenues from charitable and non-charitable activities but excluding long-term capital gains, reduced by ordinary and necessary expenses paid or incurred for the production or collection of gross income;
- *Minimum Investment Return* is roughly equal to 5 percent of the value of the foundation's assets (but *not* counting assets that are used directly for the active conduct of the foundation's exempt purpose);
- *"Substantially all"* of adjusted net income or minimum investment return means at least 85 percent of such amounts.

[3] Asset, Endowment, and Support Tests

In addition to the income test, an operating foundation must meet one of three alternative tests: the asset test, the endowment test, or the support test.

- *Asset Test*: The asset test requires that substantially more than half of the foundation's assets be devoted directly to the active conduct of either (i) activities constituting the foundation's exempt purpose, or (ii) functionally related businesses.[79]
- *Endowment Test*: A foundation satisfies the endowment test when it makes qualifying distributions directly for the active conduct of its tax-exempt activities in an amount equal to at least two thirds of its minimum investment return. All definitions and requirements in the endowment test parallel those of the income test, so that an organization that satisfies the income test by

---

[79] Reg. § 53.4942(b)-2(a).

expending at least 85 percent of its minimum investment return on the direct conduct of charitable activity will always satisfy the endowment test.[80]

- *Support Test*: The support test requires that (i) at least 85 percent of the foundation's *support* (when such support is computed not counting gross investment income) be from the *general public* and/or exempt organizations, (ii) not more than 25 percent of the foundation's *support* (again when such support is computed not counting gross investment income) be from any one exempt organization, and (iii) not more than 50 percent of all *support* be from gross investment income. The support test would appear to be applicable to an organization that fails to qualify as a public charity only because a substantial part of its public support includes gross receipts from admission to an exempt activity while it receives more than one third of its support from gross investment income.[81]

[E] Pass-through Foundations

Donations to a private foundation that is a pass-through foundation can qualify for the more attractive income tax deduction normally applicable only to gifts to public charities.[82] Pass-through foundations, which are still generally subject to the excise tax and penalty taxes applicable to private foundations, must pay out to public charities, within two and a half months of the close of a tax year, 100 percent of the contributions received during the year.[83]

[F] Giving to Existing Charities or Creating Your Own Charity

An individual who intends to make a charitable gift has the opportunity to develop a philanthropic strategy. Sometimes, the strategy simply calls for outright gifts to charitable organizations that can (or at least are attempting to) accomplish the donor's philanthropic wishes. Other times, however, the donor must first create the charity to meet the strategic goals. Common reasons for creating a charity are: no other charity is addressing the selected issue in the donor's preferred manner; part of the donor's vision of philanthropy is to conduct it as a family with thoughtful meetings and decision making by consensus, so a private foundation or one of its alternatives may be appropriate; the donor wants to give away and deduct more cash or property today than he or she is prepared to actually hand over at one time to charities—parking such gifts in a private foundation or donor-advised fund may be the answer; or the donor would part with the funds (say, to a charity's endowment fund), but wants to retain control over investment decisions. In each case, the donor must determine the degree of control desired after the gift is made. If control is

---

[80] Reg. § 53.4942(b)-2(b).

[81] Reg. § 53.4942(b)-2(c).

[82] IRC § 170(b)(1)(E)(ii).

[83] IRC § 170(b)(1)(E)(ii).

important, the donor must then decide whether to abide by the rules governing private foundations, or whether an alternative public charity is warranted.

§10.04 INCOME TAX DEDUCTION

[A] Overview

Gifts of cash and other property to U.S.-based charitable organizations are generally deductible for income tax purposes, as itemized deductions.[1] However, as discussed below, the deduction is subject to numerous limitations depending on whether cash or appreciated property is donated, whether the charity receiving the gift is a public charity or private foundation, and the amount of the donor's adjusted gross income.

When speaking to a client regarding the planning of a charitable gift, an estate planner must gather the following information:

- What is the donor receiving in return for the gift?
- Is the donor giving cash, appreciated property, or depreciated property?
- Would a sale of any donated property be eligible for long-term capital gain treatment?
- What is the donor's adjusted gross income and marginal tax bracket?
- Is the donor taking the standard deduction or itemizing deductions?
- Is the charitable organization classified as a public charity or a private foundation, and if it is a new organization to be established, is it possible to design it to qualify as a public charity?

[B] Qualification for Deduction

[1] Receipt of Value in Return for Gift

It has long been the rule that a donor may not deduct a gift to charity to the extent that the donor receives value back from the charity.[2] Certainly (and this may come as news to many donors and even some charitable organizations) if a donor buys a painting at a charitable auction for half of the painting's fair market value, there is no charitable deduction to the donor because she received back more than she paid to the charity (and it is irrelevant that the charity may have received the painting

---

[1] **§10.04** IRC §63(d). In 2021, taxpayers who do not itemize deductions, but instead elect the standard deduction, can also deduct up to $300 for charitable contributions (single filers) or up to $600 for charitable contributions (joint filers). The standard deduction amounts for 2022 are as follows: $12,950 for single filers (or married filing separately), $19,400 for head of household, and $25,900 for married filing jointly (in each case, to be adjusted for inflation in future years). Consolidated Appropriations Act, 2021 (Pub. L. 116-260, 134 Stat. 1182); IRC §63(c)(2); Rev. Proc. 2019-44, 2019-47 I.R.B. 1093.

[2] Reg. §1.170A-1(h).

as a donation for the auction). Similarly, if an individual pays $100 to attend a benefit performance for a charity and tickets to such a performance would sell for $25, then her charitable contribution is limited to $75. A perception of rampant neglect of this rule led to stricter regulations. For gifts as small as $75, charitable organizations must now inform a donor of the estimated value of any goods or services received in return for the gift.[3] Under a special rule enacted as part of the TCJA, contributions to higher education institutions in exchange for the right to purchase tickets for seating at athletic events are no longer deductible.[4]

[2] Substantiation of Gift

In order to deduct any gift of $250 or more, taxpayers must have a receipt from the charitable organization acknowledging the donation (a cancelled check is not sufficient), and the acknowledgment must describe and state the value of any goods or services received by the donor in return for the contribution.[5] There is an exception for goods or services having a value of less than 2 percent of the amount of the gift (capped at an amount that is indexed for inflation each year—for 2022, the limit is $117); in addition, certain token "low-cost" ($11.70 or less in 2022) gifts to donors may also generally be disregarded.[6] The acknowledgment must be received on or before the earlier of the date the donor files his tax returns for the calendar year of the donation or the due date for filing such return.[7]

[3] Required Description and Appraisal of Gift

For contributions of property valued at more than $500, in order to substantiate the claim of an income tax deduction, the tax return must adequately describe the property.[8] For contributions of property valued at more than $5,000, the taxpayer must obtain a "qualified appraisal." A qualified appraisal is a formal written valuation by an appraiser who has earned an appraisal designation from a recognized professional organization or has otherwise met minimum education and experience requirements, who has qualifications to make an appraisal of the type of property

---

[3] IRC § 6115.

[4] IRC § 170(l). Previously, a donor could deduct up to 80 percent of such amounts (effectively valuing the ticket purchase rights received in exchange for the contribution as worth 20 percent of the total contribution).

[5] IRC § 170(f)(8). For all charitable donations, including gifts under $250, the taxpayer must have some form of substantiation—a cancelled check, a credit card statement, or a receipt from the charity. IRC § 170(f)(13).

[6] Reg. § 1.170A-13(f); Rev. Proc. 90-12, 1990-1 C.B. 471 (*as amplified by* Rev. Proc. 92-49, 1992-1 C.B. 987, and *modified by* Rev. Proc. 92-102, 1992-2 C.B. 579); Rev. Proc. 2019-44, 2019-47 I.R.B. 1093, § 3.34 (establishing *de minimis* low-cost articles, payment and benefit thresholds below which amounts need not reduce the charitable deduction).

[7] IRC § 170(f)(8)(c).

[8] IRC § 170(f)(11).

being valued, who holds herself out to the public as an appraiser and regularly performs appraisals for compensation, and who is not related to the donor or donee.[9]

[C] Limitations Affecting Gifts of Appreciated Property

Donors to charity often like to contribute appreciated property (long-term gain) rather than cash, because the charity can sell the appreciated property and, being tax-exempt, it will not pay any income tax on realized gain.[10] This can often produce significant tax benefits.

EXAMPLE 10-8

A donor has $1,000 of cash and $1,000 of stock for which she paid $400. If the donor needs some funds for her own use, she could either:

- Donate the cash and keep the stock, which she sells:

Amount realized on sale	$1,000
Donor's basis in stock	(400)
Donor's gain on sale	$600
Donor's tax on gain	$120
(20% federal and state combined rate)	
Net proceeds	$ 880

- Keep the cash and donate the stock, which the charity sells:

Amount realized on sale	$1,000
Donee's basis in stock	(400)
Donee's gain on sale	$600
Donee's tax on gain (donee is tax-exempt)	0
Net proceeds	$1,000

Note: There are limitations on a donor's ability to fully deduct the value of appreciated property that apply with respect to gifts of short-term capital gain property and some gifts of long-term capital gain property.

---

[9] IRC § 170(f)(11)(C)-(E).

[10] Donors of appreciated property that will be subject to a sale in the hands of a charity must part with control early enough to avoid the assignment of income doctrine that will apply if the realization occurs only after the donor already has a fixed right to the gain. In Ferguson v. Comm'r, 174 F.3d 997 (9th Cir. 1999), the donor contributed stock to charity too late, after a tender offer had been announced by an acquiring corporation and after the acquiring corporation had acquired a majority of the target corporation's stock, thus removing any meaningful contingency prior to the tender of the remaining stock.

[1] Gifts of Short-Term Capital Gain Property

With respect to gifts of appreciated property that, if sold, would result in short-term capital gain (the donor has held the property for one year or less), only the donor's basis (generally, the amount paid by the donor) is deductible, not the portion of the property's value representing the gain.[11] There are exceptions for gifts of inventory and computer equipment used for certain purposes.[12]

EXAMPLE *10-9*

Maura is a day-trader in stocks and has a talent for buying and selling quickly to make a profit. She would like to donate one of her short-term holdings that she bought for $1,000 and that has gone up to $10,000, to avoid the ordinary income tax on short-term capital gain of $9,000 that she would pay if she were to sell the stock. Her income tax charitable deduction, however, will be limited to her $1,000 basis in the stock.

[2] Gifts of Long-Term Capital Gain Property

With respect to gifts of appreciated property that, if sold, would result in long-term capital gain (the donor has held the property for more than one year), the full fair market value of the property may be deducted if the gift is to a public charity, donor-advised fund or private operating foundation.[13] However, if the gift is to a private non-operating foundation, the full fair market value of the property may be deducted only if the gift is of publicly traded stock.[14] The income tax deduction for gifts to a private non-operating foundation of long-term capital gain property consisting of closely held stock, or of bonds, real estate, or partnership interests, is limited to the donor's basis in the property.[15]

EXAMPLE *10-10*

Steve bought a commercial building ten years ago for $200,000 and he is thinking of selling it now for $500,000, and wonders whether he should first give it to a charity and have the charity sell it, so that the $300,000 gain will not be taxed to him or to the charity (the charity is tax-exempt). Steve would like to maintain some control over the charity's investments

---

[11] IRC § 170(e)(1)(A).
[12] IRC § 170(e)(3), (6).
[13] IRC § 170(e)(1) by inference.
[14] IRC § 170(e)(1)(B), (e)(5).
[15] IRC § 170(e)(1)(B)(ii).

and disbursements and is thinking of setting up a family foundation to receive the gift. While such a gift may avoid the capital gains tax on the sale, Steve's income tax deduction will likely be limited to his basis in the building of $200,000 because his new charity will be a private foundation. An alternative to a private foundation may permit Steve to deduct the building's full fair market value of $500,000, such as a gift to a supporting organization or a donor-advised fund.

[3] Limitations on Gifts of Tangible Personal Property

One exception to the above rule that long-term capital gain property is fully deductible if given to a public charity arises with a gift of tangible personal property. The deduction for a gift of tangible personal property is limited to the donor's basis in the property even if the organization is a public charity unless the organization's use of the property is related to its tax-exempt purpose.[16] For gifts of tangible personal property to a private foundation, the same rules applicable to any gift of appreciated property apply: the deduction is limited to the donor's basis (even if the foundation were to use the property in accomplishing its charitable purpose).[17]

EXAMPLE *10-11*

Julia bought a painting for $200,000 that has appreciated to $1,000,000. She is thinking of donating it either to the American Red Cross (which will sell it) or to the Museum of Fine Arts (which will keep it for its permanent collection). Her income tax charitable deduction will be limited to her basis in the painting ($200,000) if she gives it to the Red Cross. Julia may deduct the painting's full fair market value of $1,000,000 if she gives it to the Museum of Fine Arts.

---

[16] IRC § 170(e)(1)(B)(i). The rules take aim at abuse in this area: if the public charity disposes of the related-use tangible personal property within the same year as the contribution, the deduction is limited to the donor's basis (IRC § 170(e)(1)(B)(i)(II)); and if the disposition by the charity takes place within three years of the donation, the donor will have recapture of a portion of the deduction relating to gain in the property (IRC § 170(e)(7)(A)). In both cases the result can be avoided if the charity certifies that the property's use was in fact related to the charity's exempt purposes. IRC § 170(e)(7)(B).

[17] IRC § 170(e)(1)(A).

[D] Limitations on Deductions

[1] General Limitations

Once the amount of the charitable deduction is established, additional limitations may affect whether the whole deduction may be taken in one tax year, or whether only part of the deduction may be taken for the year of the gift with the balance being carried forward to future tax years. Congress did not intend for taxpayers to completely wipe out their adjusted gross income through the charitable deduction, so it limited the charitable deduction to certain percentages of the donor's contribution base each year.[18] The donor's *contribution base* is the donor's adjusted gross income without regard to any net operating loss carry-back.[19] The annual limitation is either 20 percent, 30 percent, 50 percent, or 60 percent of the donor's contribution base, with the percentage depending upon what kind of property is being given and what kind of charity is receiving it.[20] Excess contributions generally may be carried forward for up to five tax years.[21]

Special Note:

For 2020 and 2021, the Coronavirus Aid, Relief, and Economic Security Act (the "CARES Act") and the Consolidated Appropriations Act, 2021, allow donors to deduct up to 100 percent of their contribution base for cash gifts to public charities (other than donor-advised funds and supporting organizations). Unlike the subparagraph G gifts described below in which 100 percent of charitable gifts must be in cash in order to qualify for the 60 percent deduction limitation, in 2020, donors can take advantage of the 100 percent deduction limitation by deducting up to 30 percent of their contribution base for non-cash gifts to charity and then topping off those gifts with cash gifts to public charities totalling up to 70 percent of their contribution base. The CARES Act also allows taxpayers who do not itemize their deductions to take the standard deduction and also deduct "above the line" up to $300 of their 2020 contributions to public charities (other than donor-advised funds and supporting organizations). For 2021, the Consolidated Appropriations Act, 2021, extended the "above the line" charitable deduction for taxpayers who do not itemize, allowing single filers to claim up to $300 in charitable deductions and joint filers to claim up to $600 in charitable deductions.

---

[18] IRC § 170(b).
[19] IRC § 170(b)(1)(H).
[20] IRC § 170(b)(1).
[21] IRC §§ 170(d), 170(b), and Reg. § 1.170A-10.

[2] Subparagraph G Gifts—Gifts of Cash to a Public Charity

Under a new temporary rule enacted as part of the TCJA, for tax years after 2017 and prior to 2026, an individual donor may deduct up to 60 percent of her contribution base for gifts of cash to a public charity.[22] To qualify for the 60 percent threshold, such gifts must be "to" the public charity, not "for the use of" the public charity.[23] We will refer to cash gifts qualifying for the 60 percent limitation as "subparagraph G" gifts (with reference to IRC § 170(b)(1)(G)).

[3] Subparagraph A Gifts[24]—Gifts to a Public Charity (Other than Subparagraph G Gifts, and Subject to Subparagraph C)

Traditionally, all gifts to (not "for the use of") a public charity are subparagraph A gifts, provided that deductibility of gifts of short-term capital gain property is limited to the donor's cost basis, and deductibility of subparagraph C gifts (gifts of long-term capital gain property) is limited as described below. Under the new law, deductibility of cash gifts to public charities is now provided for primarily under subparagraph G. Other gifts to public charities fall under subparagraph A. An individual donor may deduct up to 50 percent of her contribution base, reduced by the amount of any subparagraph G deduction allowed, for subparagraph A gifts.[25]

[4] Subparagraph B Gifts[26]—Gifts of Cash and Short-Term Capital Gain Property to a Private Foundation, or Gifts "For the Use of" Public Charities

For gifts of cash or short-term capital gain property to a private foundation, and for gifts that are "for the use of" rather than "to" a public charity, an individual donor may deduct up to the lesser of (i) 30 percent of her contribution base or (ii) the excess of 50 percent (not 60 percent) of the donor's contribution base for the year over the combined amount of subparagraph G gifts and subparagraph A gifts (remember, the deduction for short-term capital gain property is limited to the donor's basis).

---

[22] IRC § 170(b)(1)(G) (increasing annual limitation to 60 percent for certain gifts, enacted as part of the TCJA but expiring on December 31, 2025). In addition, Congress occasionally passes disaster relief bills which suspend these annual limitations entirely for qualifying cash gifts to support affected disaster areas. *See, e.g.,* Section 20104 of the Bipartisan Budget Act of 2018 (suspending adjusted gross income limitations for cash gifts made during a certain time period for the purpose of relief efforts in the California wildfire disaster area).

[23] Reg. § 1.170A-8(a)(2). Many gifts in trust, including gifts to charitable lead trusts, are treated as contributions "for the use of" the recipient charity rather than "to" the charity, and therefore are subject to the lower 30 percent limitation for subparagraph B gifts. However, gifts to public charities of remainder interests in charitable remainder trusts are generally treated as gifts "to" the charity and therefore may take advantage of the higher 50 percent limitation for subparagraph A gifts (but not the 60 percent limitation under subparagraph G, which is available only for cash gifts).

[24] IRC § 170(b)(1)(A).

[25] IRC § 170(b)(1)(G)(iii)(II).

[26] IRC § 170(b)(1)(B).

[5] Subparagraph C Gifts[27]—Gifts of Long-Term Capital Gain Property to a Public Charity

Subparagraph C of IRC Section 170(b)(1) operates as a limitation on deductibility of subparagraph A gifts involving long-term capital gain property. Except for gifts of qualified conservation easements, an individual donor may deduct up to 30 percent of her contribution base for gifts of long-term capital gain property to a public charity.[28] Donors of qualified conservation easements may deduct up to 50 percent or, in certain circumstances, up to 100 percent of their contribution base.

[6] Subparagraph D Gifts[29]—Gifts of Long-Term Capital Gain Property to a Private Foundation

For gifts of long-term capital gain property to a private foundation, an individual donor may deduct up to the lesser of (i) 20 percent of her contribution base and (ii) the excess of 30 percent of the donor's contribution base for the year over the amount of subparagraph C gifts (remember, only basis in long-term capital gain property is deductible unless the gift is of publicly traded stock).

[7] Charitable Planning and Income Tax Planning

Individuals should plan charitable gifts in conjunction with other income tax planning in order to ensure that the full benefit of an income tax deduction for the gift can be enjoyed.

The following chart summarizes the percentage limitation rules described above:

PERCENTAGE OF CONTRIBUTION BASE AVAILABLE FOR CHARITABLE DEDUCTION

	Gifts to Public Charities	*Gifts to Private Foundations*
Cash and Short-term Capital Gain Property	60 percent[30]	30 percent
Long-term Capital Gain Property	30 percent	20 percent

---

[27] IRC § 170(b)(1)(C).

[28] In 2015, the limitation was permanently increased to 50 percent of the donor's contribution base for gifts of qualified conservation easements, and any such contribution in excess of this expanded limit can be carried forward for up to 15 years. IRC § 170(b)(1)(E); Protecting Americans from Tax Hikes Act of 2015 (Pub. L. No. 14-113).

[29] IRC § 170(b)(1)(D).

[30] Reverts to 50 percent as of January 1, 2026, when IRC § 170(b)(1)(G) expires. Note that because the statutes regarding limitations on deductions for gifts to private foundations were not updated, the effect of the higher 60 percent limitation is lost in many cases (see below). Unlike cash gifts, gifts of short-term capital gain property to public charities are subject to the 50 percent limitation. For 2020 and 2021, see discussion above regarding deduction limitation increases enacted as part of the CARES Act and the Consolidated Appropriations Act, 2021.

EXAMPLE *10-12*

Don has always given to charities, but never in such large amounts as compared to his income that he needed to worry about percentage limitations. This year he became a real estate investor and will have depreciation deductions that substantially reduce his adjusted gross income. He is thinking of donating to a hospital a building that he has held for more than one year. The full fair market value of the building will be deductible because the hospital is a public charity, but the deduction this year is limited to 30 percent of his contribution base since it is long-term capital gain property. Don's contribution base is $100,000 and the building is worth $200,000. Only $30,000 can be deducted this year. The remaining $170,000 can be carried forward and deducted over the next five years (again, subject to the donor's 30 percent limitations in those years).

[8] Multiple Gifts in One Year

If an individual makes multiple charitable gifts in one year it will be necessary to determine the order in which different limitations apply to the contributions. Deductions for gifts to both public charities and private foundations generally cannot in the aggregate exceed 60 percent of the donor's contribution base, and in many cases will be effectively limited to an aggregate of 50 percent of the donor's contribution.

Because this temporary increase in the threshold for gifts to public charities to 60 percent was accomplished by a statute (subparagraph G) that interacts with the pre-existing threshold rules of subparagraphs A through D in a variety of ways, the new law has introduced considerable confusion regarding how mixed gifts are treated. Here are two examples of how this would work under the new tax law:

Examples Involving Cash and Short-Term Capital Gain Property Gifts Only

EXAMPLE *10-13*

Mary has adjusted gross income of $100,000 and contributes $30,000 cash to a public charity (a subparagraph G gift), $10,000 of high-basis short-term capital gain property to a public charity (a subparagraph A gift, but with a deduction limited to cost basis), and $10,000 cash to a private foundation (a subparagraph B gift).

- The $30,000 cash contribution to the public charity is deductible in full during the year of the gift under subparagraph G, as it is less than 60 percent of Mary's contribution base.
- The $10,000 contribution of short-term capital gain property to the public charity is deductible in full under subparagraph A, as it is equal to the difference between $50,000 (50 percent of Mary's contribution base, the maximum under subparagraph A) and the subparagraph G contribution of $40,000 (which, under the rules of subparagraph G, reduces the subparagraph A deductible amount).

- The $10,000 contribution to the private foundation is also deductible in full under subparagraph B, as that amount is within the permitted limits (the lesser of $30,000, or 30 percent of Mary's contribution base, and $10,000, the difference between the 50 percent aggregate limit under subparagraph B ($50,000) and the combined subparagraph G and subparagraph A deductible amounts ($40,000)).
- In all, the entire $50,000 contributed is allowed as a deduction in the tax year of the contribution.

EXAMPLE *10-14*

Mary has adjusted gross income of $100,000 and contributes $35,000 cash to a public charity (a subparagraph G gift), $20,000 of short-term capital gain property to a public charity (a subparagraph A gift), and $10,000 cash to a private foundation (a subparagraph B gift).

- The $35,000 cash contribution to the public charity is deductible in full during the year of the gift under subparagraph G, as it is less than 60 percent of Mary's contribution base.
- The $20,000 contribution of short-term capital gain property to a public charity is only deductible in the year of the gift up to $15,000, as the subparagraph A maximum ($50,000, or 50 percent of Mary's contribution base) is reduced under the subparagraph G rules by the $35,000 subparagraph G deduction, leaving only $15,000 of subparagraph A deduction left to be used.
- The $10,000 contribution to the private foundation is not deductible *at all* in the year of the gift under subparagraph B, even though the public charity donation is $5,000 below the 60 percent threshold.
- This is because the rule for mixed gifts to public charities and private foundations in subparagraph B limits deductibility of the private foundation gift to the lesser of $30,000 (30 percent of Mary's contribution base) and $0 (the difference between (i) Mary's combined subparagraph G and subparagraph A gifts and (ii) 50 percent, not 60 percent, of Mary's contribution base).
- In all, only $50,000 of the $65,000 contributed is allowed as a deduction in the tax year of the contribution.
- The unused subparagraph A and subparagraph B contributions may be rolled over and used as subparagraph A and subparagraph B deductions, respectively, for up to five subsequent years.

After applying the limitations in the order described above, the gifts to public charities must be revisited to be sure that any gifts of long-term capital gain property (subparagraph C gifts) do not exceed 30 percent of the contribution base.[31] If such gifts of long-term capital gain property are less than the 30 percent limit, then gifts to private foundations must also be revisited to be sure that gifts of long-term capital gain property (up to the lesser of (i) 20 percent of the contribution base and (ii) the excess of 30 percent of the donor's contribution base for the year, over the allowed amount of subparagraph C gifts) do not push total gifts of long-term capital gain property beyond that 30 percent limit.[32]

Examples Involving Mixed Gifts of Cash and Capital Gain Property

EXAMPLE *10-15*

Mary has adjusted gross income of $100,000, and contributes $20,000 cash to a public charity (a subparagraph G gift), $20,000 of long-term capital gain property to a public charity (a subparagraph C gift), $5,000 cash to a private foundation (a subparagraph B gift), and $5,000 of long-term capital gain property in the form of publicly traded stock to a private foundation (a subparagraph D gift).

- The $20,000 in cash contributions to the public charity is deductible in full under subparagraph G, as it is well below $60,000 (60 percent of Mary's base contribution amount).
- The $20,000 of long-term capital gain property to the public charity is deductible in full under subparagraph A as modified by subparagraph C (providing limits on how much of the subparagraph A limitation may be used by long-term capital gain property), as the amount is less than both the 50 percent limitation of subparagraph A reduced by the subparagraph G gifts (or $30,000) and the 30 percent limitation on gifts of long-term capital gain assets to public charities under subparagraph C (also $30,000).
- The $10,000 in cash contributions to the private foundation is also deductible in full under subparagraph B, as that amount is within the permitted limits (the lesser of $30,000, or 30 percent of Mary's contribution base, and $10,000, the difference between the 50 percent aggregate limit in subparagraph B ($50,000) and the combined subparagraph A and subparagraph G gifts ($40,000)).
- The $5,000 capital gain contribution to the private foundation is deductible in full, as that amount is within the permitted limits (the lesser of $20,000, or 20 percent of Mary's contribution base, and $10,000, or the excess of 30 percent of the donor's contribution base ($30,000) over the amount of subparagraph C gifts ($20,000)).
- In all, the entire $50,000 contributed is allowed as a deduction in the tax year of the contribution.

---

[31] IRC § 170(b)(1)(C)(i).
[32] IRC § 170(b)(1)(D)(i).

EXAMPLE *10-16*

Mary has adjusted gross income of $100,000, and contributes $20,000 cash to a public charity (a subparagraph G gift), $35,000 of long-term capital gain property to a public charity (a subparagraph C gift), $5,000 cash to a private foundation (a subparagraph B gift), and $5,000 of long-term capital gain property in the form of publicly traded stock to a private foundation (a subparagraph D gift).

- The $20,000 in cash contributions to the public charity is deductible in full under subparagraph G, as it is well below $60,000 (60 percent of Mary's base contribution amount).
- The $35,000 of long-term capital gain property is deductible only up to $30,000 in the year of the gift. Subparagraph A only allows up to $30,000 of additional deductibility for gifts to a public charity, as the 50 percent limitation of subparagraph A ($50,000) must be reduced by the amount of any subparagraph G deduction ($20,000). Separately, the subparagraph C limitation (30 percent of Mary's contribution base) would also limit this deduction to $30,000.
- The $5,000 cash contribution to the private foundation is not deductible at all in the year of the gift, as subparagraph B limits that deduction to the lesser of $30,000 (30 percent of Mary's contribution base) and $0 (the excess of 50 percent of Mary's contribution base, or $50,000, over the combined subparagraph G and subparagraph A gifts, or $55,000).
- Similarly, the $5,000 contribution of long-term capital gain property to the private foundation is not deductible in the year of the gift, as subparagraph D limits that deduction to the lesser of $20,000 (20 percent of Mary's contribution base) and $0 (the excess of $30,000, or 30 percent of Mary's contribution base, over $30,000, the amount of allowed subparagraph C deductions).
- In all, only $50,000 of the $65,000 contributed is allowed as a deduction in the tax year of the contribution.
- The unused contribution amounts may be rolled over and used as deductions for up to five subsequent years, subject to the same contribution limits for such gifts in those future years.

For planning purposes, as long as a donor is willing to forego the higher 60 percent threshold established by the TCJA for subparagraph G gifts (cash gifts to public charities), a donor can maximize tax benefits and control over the charitable gifts by giving as much appreciated property as can be deducted to a private foundation, and then giving as much appreciated property as can be deducted to public charities, and then giving as much cash as can be deducted to the private foundation, and, finally, giving as much cash as can be deducted to public charities. However, donors seeking to take advantage of the higher 60 percent threshold should emphasize gifts of cash to public charities (which may include donor-advised funds).

[9] Gifts by Corporations

For gifts by corporations of cash and appreciated property to any type of tax-exempt charitable organization (i.e., both public charities and private foundations), the percentage limitation is 10 percent of taxable income (computed after several adjustments).[33] However, contributions to charities by corporate donors are often deductible as business expenses rather than as charitable contributions.

Note:

For 2020 and 2021, the CARES Act and the Consolidated Appropriations Act, 2021 increase the percentage limitation for corporate contributions to charities to 25 percent of taxable income.

[E] Overall Limitation on Itemized Deductions for Individuals ("Pease Limitation")

Prior to 2006, and again from 2013 through 2017, federal tax law set an additional limitation on the amount of charitable deduction that a donor could enjoy in one tax year. Individuals with adjusted gross income over a threshold amount were required to reduce their itemized deductions (including the charitable deduction) by the lesser of one-third of: (i) 3 percent of the amount by which their adjusted gross income exceeds the threshold amount; or (ii) 80 percent of the itemized deductions otherwise allowable.[34] The threshold amount is inflation-adjusted, and in 2017, it was $313,800 in the case of a joint return or surviving spouse's return ($261,500 if unmarried or married, filing separately). This limitation has been suspended until 2026.[35] Under the 2001 Tax Act, this limitation was phased out beginning in 2006, and completely repealed in 2010. The Tax Relief, Unemployment Insurance Reauthorization, and Job Creation Act of 2010 (Pub. L. No. 111-312) extended the phase-out of the limitation on itemized deductions through 2012. The limit on itemized deductions returned on January 1, 2013. However, under the TCJA, this limitation has been suspended until 2026.

---

[33] IRC § 170(b)(2).
[34] IRC § 68.
[35] Rev. Proc. 2015-35, 2015-26 I.R.B. 1142.

[F] Denial of Deduction for Gift of Partial Interests

Generally, a donor must give his or her entire interest in property (or a fraction of the entire interest) to a charity in order to qualify for a deduction.[36] For example, a donor owning a parcel of land may deduct a gift of the entire parcel to charity, and may also deduct a gift of a 20 percent undivided interest in the parcel.[37] But (subject to the exceptions described below), there is no deduction for a gift of a temporal interest in the property (charity gets the parcel only for the next five years, or only for the rest of the donor's lifetime) or for any other partial use of the property (charity can use the parcel for harvesting timber but otherwise the donor keeps the right to use or to sell the parcel).[38] Further, in an attempt to reduce abuse with gifts of fractional interests in tangible personal property (especially works of art that are likely to appreciate), rules provide that no deduction is available for a contribution of an undivided fractional interest in tangible personal property unless immediately before the contribution all interests in the property are held either by the donor or by the donor and the donee-charity.[39] Therefore, a taxpayer will be permitted to deduct an initial contribution of an undivided fractional interest in an item of tangible personal property ("initial contribution"), and to deduct gifts of further undivided fractional interests in the same item in future years ("additional contributions"), but only so long as the charity still retains the interests it has received. The rules also provide that if a deduction is claimed for an initial contribution of an undivided fractional interest in tangible personal property and later a deduction is claimed for an additional contribution of an undivided fractional interest in such property, the donor may not value the item of property at the time of an additional contribution any higher than its value at the time of the initial contribution.[40] Therefore, the donor's aggregate deductions for a series of gifts of interests in the same item can no longer be greater than the deduction would have been if a gift of the entire item had been made initially. Finally, the rule provides for recapture of a charitable deduction claimed by the donor for all contributions of such interests if the donor has not completely donated all of his interests in the property to the charitable donee (or if the initial charitable donee is no longer in existence, to any other charitable donee) by the earlier of ten years after the initial contribution or the donor's death, and there is also recapture if during such period the charitable donee has not had substantial

---

[36] IRC § 170(f); Reg. § § 1.170A-6 and 1.170A-7.

[37] IRC § 170(f)(3)(B). In a Field Service Advice, Ltr. Rul. 200149007, the IRS Chief Counsel set forth a detailed analysis of the criteria for establishing a fraction of an entire interest in property, including: (1) the donee must receive a portion of every substantial right owned by the donor, (2) the gifted interest must run for the same term as the donor's interest, and (3) the donor must give the donee the right, as a tenant in common, to possession, dominion and control over the property for the time period commensurate with the fractional interest.

[38] Reg. § 1.170A-7.

[39] IRC § 170(o)(1).

[40] IRC § 170(o)(2).

possession of the property and has not used such property in a manner related to its exempt purposes.[41]

EXAMPLE *10-17*

Rick donates the use of his ski condominium for one week to his daughter's school for its annual fundraising auction. The ski condominium is usually rented out at $500 for a week. Nonetheless, Rick receives no deduction for the gift because it is a gift of a partial interest.

There are several important exceptions to this prohibition of deductions for partial interests:

- *Charitable Remainder Trusts.* A donor may deduct the present value of the remainder interest in a charitable remainder trust, where the income is paid to noncharitable beneficiaries (such as the donor and her family members) for a term of years or for one or more lifetimes, at which time the remainder passes to charities. The income interest must be in the form of a fixed annuity or a unitrust interest (a fixed percentage of the value of the trust principal, revalued annually).[42]

- *Charitable Lead Trusts.* For a gift to a charitable lead trust where charities receive the income interest for some period of time, after which individuals receive the remainder interest, the donor could receive an income tax deduction for the present value of the income that is predicted to pass to charity. Alternatively, a charitable lead trust can be designed so that the donor receives no immediate deduction and instead the trust receives an annual deduction as the income is actually paid to charity.[43] The trust will qualify as a charitable lead trust only if the lead interest is in the form of a fixed annuity or a unitrust interest.[44]

- *Pooled Income Funds.* A donor may deduct the present value of the remainder interest in a gift to a pooled income fund sponsored by a charitable organization.[45]

- *Remainder in Personal Residence or Farm.* A donor may deduct the gift of a remainder interest in a personal residence or farm.[46]

- *Qualified Conservation Easement.* A donor may deduct the gift of a conservation easement limiting the use of property to certain qualified purposes.[47]

---

[41] IRC § 170(o)(3).

[42] IRC § 170(f)(2)(A).

[43] IRC § 642(c).

[44] IRC § 170(f)(2)(B).

[45] IRC § 170(f)(2)(A).

[46] IRC § 170(f)(3)(B).

[47] IRC § 170(f)(3)(B) and § 170(h).

§10.05 GIFT AND ESTATE TAX DEDUCTIONS

Gifts and bequests to charitable organizations are fully deductible for gift and estate tax purposes regardless of whether the organization is a public charity or private foundation.[1] In addition, the amount of the deduction is equal to the full fair market value of the bequest or gift, regardless of whether the property has appreciated in value.[2] Thus, the distinction under the federal income tax law between public charities and private foundations is not present with respect to estate and gift taxes. A donor may make unlimited lifetime or testamentary gifts to a private foundation free of estate and gift taxes. However, the rule against deductibility of a gift of a partial interest in property does apply in the gift and estate tax context, so that, generally, the gift or bequest of a remainder or term interest in trust will qualify for the gift or estate tax charitable deduction only if the trust is a charitable remainder annuity trust or unitrust, or a charitable lead annuity trust or unitrust, or a pooled income fund.[3]

Many donors are motivated to give to charity because each dollar will get to the charity free of estate tax, while the same dollar passing to family members will be greatly reduced by gift or estate tax. For a donor in the 46 percent estate tax bracket (state and federal combined), only 54 cents of every dollar gets to the children. All dollars left to charity at death will be available to accomplish the donor's charitable wishes.

Some donors gain further comfort with dollars passing to charity rather than to family by selecting as the charity a family foundation or one of its alternatives,[4] so that the family stays involved with the wealth and is empowered in that regard.

EXAMPLE *10-18*

Elena believes that she is leaving sufficient bequests to her children to help them be comfortable, even after considering the estate taxes that her estate must pay. She decides to leave the residue of her estate to a family foundation, which can be funded without any diminution for estate taxes. By naming her children as trustees of the foundation, Elena has provided them with the opportunity to make charitable grants to organizations that they support.

---

[1] §10.05 IRC §§2055(a) and 2522(a). However, similar to the income tax rules, no gift tax deduction is available for a contribution of an undivided fractional interest in tangible personal property unless immediately before the contribution all interests in the property are held either by the donor or by the donor and the donee charity. IRC §2522(e).

[2] IRC §§2055(a) and 2522(a). Unlike the income tax rules, if a donor makes a lifetime charitable gift of a fractional interest in an item of tangible personal property, and subsequently makes a gift or bequest of the balance of the interest in the item to the same charity, the value of the additional contribution for purposes of the gift or estate tax charitable deduction is not limited to the value of such item at the time of the initial contribution.

[3] IRC §§2055(e), 2522(c).

[4] See §10.03 supra.

§10.06 SPECIAL TYPES OF CHARITABLE GIFTS

Donors will often inquire of estate planners whether it is possible to donate property to charity but keep the income (rent, dividends, interest) generated by the property, and still qualify for tax deductions. Other donors want to restrict the use of real property for conservation or historic preservation purposes, but otherwise keep the ownership of the property, and again are interested in any available tax deductions. These special issues are discussed below.

[A] Gifts of Income or Remainder Interests

Donors may wish to retain for themselves or their family members partial interests in gifts otherwise intended for charity. Some donors want to keep the use of property or the income from property for a term of years or for one or more lifetimes, but also want to ensure that the remainder interest will pass to charity. Other donors are pleased to commit the use of property or the income from property to a charity for a specific period of time, after which the use or the income will revert to family members. These *split-interest* gifts also provide opportunities for reducing or deferring capital gains tax and for passing property to children at reduced gift and estate taxes. The common split-interest gift vehicles include:

- A gift of a remainder interest in a personal residence or farm;
- A gift to a pooled income fund;
- A gift to a charitable remainder trust;
- A bargain sale to a charity with payment in the form of a charitable gift annuity; and
- A gift to a charitable lead trust.

[1] Computation of Charitable Deduction for Split-Interest Gifts

In computing income, gift, and estate tax charitable deductions with respect to split-interest gifts, a deduction is allowed only for the present value of the amount that is expected to pass to charity.[1] In addition, the charitable deduction is only permitted if the income interest is for a fixed term of years or for the lifetime of one or more individuals.[2]

The present value computation is based on (1) the term of the interest (with IRS life expectancy tables used to determine the term of an interest for an individual's

---

[1] **§10.06** Reg. §§ 1.170A-6, 1.170A-7, 20.2055-2, 25.2522(a)-2.
[2] *Id.*

life[3]), and (2) discount rates established by the IRS.[4] The IRS publishes applicable rates each month (generally 120 percent of the average market yield on midterm U.S. Treasury obligations determined just prior to the applicable month), and the donor may use the rate that applies for the month in which the gift is made or for either of the preceding two months.[5] There is commercial software available that contains these factors and computes the present value of the charitable interest for various types of split-interest gifts.

[2] Remainder Interest in Personal Residence or Farm

Income tax rules specifically permit a charitable deduction for the present value of a gift to charity of a remainder interest in a personal residence or in a farm, allowing homeowners and farmers to keep the use of their property for their lifetimes and enjoy an income tax deduction during life for the irrevocable transfer of the remainder interest to charity.[6] A special rule for gifts of a remainder interest in real property requires that, when computing the present value of the remainder, the depreciable portion of the gift (the value of the house alone less its salvage value following its estimated useful life) must be subject to a special factor that will decrease the value of the gift, while the nondepreciable portion of the gift (the land and the salvage value of the residence following its estimated useful life) is not subject to such factor.[7]

EXAMPLE *10-19*

John lives in a large house that his grown children do not wish to inherit. He signs a deed in which he keeps a life interest in the house and conveys the remainder interest to his church. He receives an income tax deduction equal to the present value of the remainder interest, which takes into consideration John's actuarial life expectancy and an assumed interest rate that the IRS publishes on a monthly basis. Because the gift includes depreciable property, the value of the deduction also considers depreciation of the house (but not the land) prior to the time when the church will receive it. If John is 72 and the IRS published rate is 8 percent, the present value of the remainder of the nondepreciable portion (land plus salvage value of house) is 0.43666 times its current value. If the house has an

---

[3] On April 30, 2009, the IRS issued mortality Table 2000CM which affects charitable deduction computations for gift annuities, charitable remainder trusts, retained life estates and charitable lead trusts. Donors must use Table 2000CM to value any gift made on or after July 1, 2009. *See* IRS Publications 1457 (Remainder, Income and Annuity Examples) and 1458 (Unitrust Remainder and Life Estate Examples).

[4] IRC § 7520.

[5] IRC § 7520(a). There is an exception to this rule for pooled income funds.

[6] IRC § 170(f)(3)(B)(i).

[7] Reg. § 1.170A-12.

estimated useful life of 40 years, the present value of the remainder of the depreciable portion (house less its salvage value) is only 0.33851 times its current value. And if the depreciable portion is two-thirds of the total value of the house and land, then John's income tax deduction is 37 percent of the current value of the house and land.

[3] Pooled Income Funds

A charitable organization is authorized to sponsor its own pooled income fund to which many donors contribute, each donor retaining the income attributable to his or her contributed share of the fund principal.[8] A pooled income fund is in some respects similar to a mutual fund, except that capital gains are not distributed and the charity receives the principal after the deaths of the donor and/or any other named beneficiaries.

A pooled income fund is particularly valuable when a donor contributes appreciated capital gain assets because the fund can sell the assets tax free (although the fund is taxable, it receives a charitable deduction for long-term capital gains as they are permanently set aside for the use of the charity).[9] This enables the donor to enjoy income from the full value of the gift. The income can be paid to the donor or other individuals for one or more lifetimes, after which the charity can remove and keep the principal attributable to the contributed share. The donor's income, gift, and estate tax deduction is the present value of the remainder interest, computed using IRS actuarial tables and a discount rate equal to the fund's highest yearly rate of return during the three years preceding the gift.[10] Distributions from the fund are taxed as ordinary income to the recipient.[11]

[B] Charitable Remainder Trusts

[1] Requirements

A *charitable remainder trust* is defined by statute and regulations as a trust arrangement where a donor retains an interest for him or herself and/or other individuals that can be objectively valued, prior to a charitable organization receiving the remainder interest (which can also be objectively valued).[12] The rules governing charitable remainder trusts were enacted because Congress was concerned that some split-interest charitable arrangements could be manipulated through the choice of

---

[8] IRC § 642(c)(5).
[9] IRC § 642(c)(3).
[10] IRC § 642(c)(5) and Reg. § 1.642(c)-6.
[11] IRC § 652(a).
[12] IRC § 664.

investments to produce less for charity than was predicted using the published discount rates.

EXAMPLE *10-20*

A donor contributed $100,000 to a trust, retaining an income interest for life and giving the remainder interest to charity. The trust property was invested solely in high-yield junk bonds. Based on the presumed interest rate, the donor would get a large charitable deduction. However, the income paid to the donor would be more than presumed by the published discount rate, while the principal of the trust that passed to the charity at the donor's death would not have enjoyed the capital appreciation presumed by the published discount rate.

To avoid this outcome, Congress now generally requires that split-interest gifts (other than a gift of a remainder interest in a personal residence or farm) state the income interest in the form of either a fixed dollar amount (an "annuity interest") or a fixed percentage of the principal as that principal is redetermined annually (a "unitrust interest").[13] Requiring that fixed sums be paid during the term of a split-interest trust ensures that the trust earns income and capital appreciation initially predicted, the amount allowed as a deduction will match (on a present value basis) the amount actually received by the charity.

The value of the deduction to the donor will correlate inversely to the interest retained by the donor.

EXAMPLE *10-21*

Jack would like to contribute some of his savings to the hospital that cared for his wife during her illness but is not sure that he can afford to give up the income from the property. Jack is considering creating a charitable remainder trust, in which he will retain for his lifetime annual distributions equal to a percentage (Jack is considering distributions of 5 percent, 6 percent, and 7 percent) of the fair market value of the trust on the first day of each year. Upon Jack's death, any remaining trust property would be distributed to the hospital. If Jack is 70 and the published discount rate is 2.2 percent, and if he contributes $100,000 to the trust, then the present value of his retained income interest (paid to him in quarterly installments) and the present value of what is predicted to pass to the hospital (and therefore deductible) are as follows:

---

[13] IRC §§ 170(f), 2055(e), 2522(c). The rules governing charitable remainder trusts are found in IRC § 664 and the accompanying regulations.

Jack's retained interest in the trust as it is revalued annually	Present value of Jack's retained interest	Present value of remainder passing to charity (amount of deduction)
5 percent	$47,700	$52,300
6 percent	$53,400	$46,600
7 percent	$58,300	$41,700

Note that the greater the percentage retained by Jack, the less that is predicted to pass to charity. If Jack were 80 years old rather than 70, the value of his retained life income interest would decrease and the value of the charitable remainder interest would increase.

[2] Why Fund a Charitable Remainder Trust?

Charitable Remainder Trusts (CRTs) are funded by donors who wish to retain for themselves (or give to family members or other individuals) the income from property for some duration of time, but who are also willing to transfer the remainder interest to charity. Donors to CRTs can claim an income tax deduction for the present value of the remainder interest in the year that the CRT is funded, even though the donor retains the right to receive payments from the trust. In addition, estate planners often recommend the use of a CRT when a donor owns appreciated property that, if sold, would give rise to a capital gains tax. If, instead, the donor gives the appreciated property to a CRT and the CRT sells it, there is no immediate capital gains tax. The taxable gain is suspended inside the CRT (which is exempt from income tax) and is taxed to the beneficiary over time as distributions are made.[14]

EXAMPLE *10-22*

Donna is nearing retirement and will need more income than her investment portfolio now produces. She would like to sell some of the growth stocks that have done well and which now represent too much of the portfolio and diversify the investments to include more bonds and stocks that pay better dividends. If she sells the growth stocks, however, the capital gains tax will diminish the portfolio by 25.25 percent of the long-term gain in those stocks (assuming combined state and federal capital gains tax rate of 25.25 percent). Donna would receive the earnings on only the remaining 74.75 percent of the portfolio. Instead of selling the growth stock, Donna donates the growth stock to a CRT. The CRT sells the stock

---

[14] IRC § 664(c). Distributions from the CRT to the beneficiary will be taxable to the beneficiary (and will reflect this capital gain).

and, being tax-exempt, is able to keep 100 percent of the proceeds and diversify them into income-producing assets. The CRT pays Donna the enhanced income for her lifetime (in the form of a fixed annuity interest or a unitrust interest). On her death the remainder passes to Donna's favorite charities.

[3] CRATs and CRUTs

[a] *CRATs Versus CRUTs*

Donors to CRTs must decide if the income interest they retain or give to family members will be in the form of an annuity interest (a fixed amount) under a charitable remainder annuity trust (CRAT) or a unitrust interest (a fixed percentage of the trust assets as the assets are revalued annually) under a charitable remainder unitrust (CRUT). There are various factors to consider in choosing between a CRAT and a CRUT. The primary advantage of a CRUT (and indeed the reason that it is chosen more often by donors) is that the distribution is more likely to keep pace with inflation since the amount of the annual distributions from the CRUT will rise and fall with the value of the assets in the trust. However, a donor might nonetheless choose to fund a CRAT if he wants to be assured of a fixed annuity regardless of the performance of the trust, or if he wants to avoid the expense of revaluing the trust property every year.

[b] *Rules Applicable to CRATs and CRUTs*

In order for a trust to qualify as a CRAT or a CRUT, the noncharitable interest retained by the donor (or given by the donor to one or more individuals) must be paid annually for a term of years (not to exceed 20) or for one or more lifetimes (provided that the measuring lives are of beneficiaries receiving an income interest).[15] A CRAT must pay a minimum annuity of 5 percent (and may not exceed 50 percent) of the initial value of the trust property, and no further additions may be made after the initial funding of a CRAT.[16] A CRUT must pay a minimum distribution of 5 percent (and may not exceed 50 percent) of the value of the trust property determined each year, but there is no restriction on additional contributions.[17] With both a CRAT and a CRUT, the present value of the remainder interest passing to charity must be at least 10 percent of the value of the property contributed.[18] As a result of this rule, young donors wishing to retain a life interest in a CRAT or CRUT will have to keep

---

[15] IRC § 664(d); Reg. § § 1.664-2(a)(5) and 1.664-3(a)(5).

[16] IRC § 664(d); Reg. § 1.664-2.

[17] IRC § 664(d); Reg. § 1.664-3.

[18] IRC § § 664(d)(1)(D) and 664(d)(2)(D).

the payments at a low level. The IRS has released sample forms for CRATs[19] and CRUTs[20] which, in most circumstances, ought to be carefully followed in order to be sure a trust will qualify as a charitable remainder trust.

EXAMPLE *10-23*

A 30-year-old seeking to create a CRUT for her lifetime could keep a 5 percent unitrust interest; but increasing the retained interest to a 6 percent unitrust interest means that, on a present value basis, less than 10 percent of the gift is passing to charity, so the trust would not qualify as a CRUT. A couple who are both 30 could not create a CRUT for their joint lifetimes because a retention of the minimum 5 percent unitrust amount would leave less than 10 percent (on a present value basis) for charity.

[c] Income Taxation of CRTs and Beneficiaries

A CRT is exempt from income tax. However, the beneficiaries of a CRT do pay tax on the income of the CRT under rules quite different from the usual rules applicable to beneficiaries of trusts.[21] When the trust makes annual distributions to the individual beneficiaries, the distributions are taxed to the beneficiaries

1. First, as ordinary income to the extent the trust earned ordinary income that year (or in a prior year if not fully carried out to the beneficiaries in any prior year); within this category, for different classes of ordinary income that are subject to varying tax rates, a class taxed at a higher rate (such as taxable interest) is deemed to pass out before a class taxed at a lower rate (such as taxable dividends);

2. Second, as capital gain to the extent the trust realized capital gain in that year (or in a prior year if not fully carried out to the beneficiaries in any prior year); within this category, for different classes of capital gain that are subject to varying tax rates, a class taxed at a higher rate (such as short-term capital gain) is deemed to pass out before a class taxed at a lower rate (such as long-term capital gain);

3. Third, as tax-exempt income to the extent the trust earned tax-exempt income that year (or in a prior year if not fully carried out to the beneficiaries in any prior year); and

4. Fourth, as tax-free return of principal.[22]

---

[19] Rev. Procs. 2003-53 to 2003-60, 2003-31 I.R.B. 230–274.

[20] Rev. Procs. 2005-52 to 2005-59, 2005-34 I.R.B. 326–412.

[21] The income taxation of trusts is discussed in Chapter 4.

[22] IRC § 664(b); Reg. § 1.664-1(d)(1).

Notwithstanding the foregoing, if the CRT earns any unrelated business taxable income, the CRT must pay an excise tax equal to the amount of such unrelated business taxable income.[23]

EXAMPLE *10-24*

Sophia owns zero-basis stock held for more than one year, which she contributes at the beginning of 2018 to a CRUT that distributes a 5 percent unitrust payment to her for her lifetime. The CRUT trustee sells the stock for $1,000,000, and invests the proceeds in a diversified portfolio of bonds and stocks that, for year 2018, yield $15,000 in taxable interest and $8,000 in dividends. Of the total $50,000 distribution to Sophia in 2018, the first $15,000 is taxed to her as interest, the next $8,000 is taxed to her as dividends, and the remaining $27,000 is a portion of the suspended long-term capital gain and is taxed to her as such.

[d] NICRUTs, NIMCRUTs, and FLIPCRUTs

The requirement to make annual distributions under a traditional CRT may be problematic in the situation where the donor transfers assets that, at the time of transfer, do not produce sufficient income to meet the annual payments. This commonly occurs when the donor transfers an interest in a closely held business or non-income-producing land.

There are a variety of permissible variations on the traditional CRUT that are used to address this problem. One variation is to set the income distribution to the noncharitable beneficiaries at the *lesser of:* (1) a fixed percentage of the principal; and (2) the net income earned by the trust (NICRUT). The problem with the NICRUT is that the noncharitable beneficiary will lose some of the income (for the period where the percentage amount is less than the actual income earned by the trust) to which she would otherwise be entitled. To address this problem, there is another permissible variation on a NICRUT that enables the trustee to *make up* to the noncharitable beneficiary the underpayment attributable to years in which the net income of the trust is in fact less than the standard unitrust amount, by distributing to her such underpayment in subsequent years when the net income may exceed the standard unitrust amount (NIMCRUT).[24] NICRUTs and NIMCRUTs are popular vehicles when the unitrust is unlikely to have sufficient income and principal liquidity to be able to make the required distributions to noncharitable beneficiaries. In such situations, most donors would prefer a NIMCRUT, which gives the donor at least a possibility of making up for early low income years during later high income years; however, more charitably inclined donors (or donors who don't want to track the make-up amounts)

---

[23] IRC § 664(c)(2).
[24] IRC § 664(d)(3); Reg. § 1.664-3(a)(1)(i)(b).

might choose a NICRUT and forego the make-up amounts. NIMCRUTS are also used by some estate planners (albeit in the face of IRS criticism) to hold partnership interests that intentionally distribute little or no income in years when the beneficiary is in a high income tax bracket but that distribute lots of income in later years when the beneficiary is in a lower bracket.

There is a way to give relief to donors who use a NICRUT or NIMCRUT because the asset contributed to the CRT is illiquid and pays little or no income, but who desire to receive the standard unitrust amount at such time as the CRT has the liquidity to pay it. Regulations permit the governing instrument of a NICRUT or a NIMCRUT to authorize a flip (hence named a FLIPCRUT) into a standard CRUT upon certain events or dates (e.g., upon the beneficiary attaining a certain age, and even upon the sale of certain "unmarketable assets"[25]). A FLIPCRUT can be useful because an individual can contribute illiquid, non-income-producing property to the CRT, and then receive the higher standard unitrust amount once the trust has sufficient liquidity.

EXAMPLE *10-25*

Marie and Marvin contribute their respective interests in a parcel of undeveloped real estate to separate 5 percent CRUTs, with hopes that the trustees will eventually sell the property and invest the proceeds to create an income stream. Due to market conditions, they do not expect any sale to occur in the near future and they are concerned that until such sale occurs, the trustees will be unable to make the required distributions. Marie makes her trust a NICRUT with an automatic flip into a standard CRUT in five years, so the trustee need not make any distribution in the first five years if in fact there is no net income. Marvin makes his trust a NIMCRUT with the same flip provision, accomplishing the same thing, with the exception that he may get some extra distributions during the first five years if the property is sold and thereafter the net income actually exceeds the 5 percent unitrust amount. Their tax deductions are computed as if they retained straight 5 percent unitrusts, so there is no deduction for the extra funds that may go to charity on account of the lower distributions they may receive before the flip occurs. After the five years have passed, both trusts become standard CRTs paying out a 5 percent unitrust amount each year.

---

[25] Reg. § 1.664-3(a)(1)(i)(c).

[C] Bargain Sale to Charity with Payment in the Form of a Charitable Gift Annuity

Some donors want to receive (or want their beneficiaries to receive) a life annuity in return for a charitable gift, and do not care about establishing a charitable remainder trust to hold their gift and secure their income stream. Instead, they transfer cash or sell appreciated property directly to a charity, with the payment back in the form of a charitable gift annuity backed by the general credit of the charity. Charities benefit from these contracts with donors because the present value of the life annuity paid by the charity (computed using IRS actuarial and interest rate assumptions) is less than the fair market value of the cash or property received from the donor. In such a "bargain sale" of appreciated property, the donor's gain is computed by reducing the sales proceeds (the present value of the life annuity) by a *pro rata* portion of the donor's basis in the sold property. The donor's income tax deduction is the difference between the sold property's fair market value and the sales proceeds received in return (the present value of the annuity). The payments to the donor or other beneficiary are taxed a bit more favorably than payments from a CRT, because each payment is considered to carry out a proportionate amount of tax-free return of capital as well as taxable income.[26]

EXAMPLE *10-26*

Millie would like to increase her income and support a major university. She is familiar with the benefits of a charitable remainder trust and is thinking of creating one and funding it with $200,000 of appreciated stock that pays no current dividend. Her plan is for the trustee to sell the stock without paying capital gains tax, reinvest the proceeds, and annually distribute $12,000 to her for her lifetime. At her death any remaining balance would pass to the university. The university suggests she not bother with a CRT and instead just sell the stock to the university in return for a charitable gift annuity—the university's promise to pay her $12,000 a year for her lifetime. Millie likes the thought of not needing a lawyer to draft a CRT and not needing an accountant to file annual tax returns for a CRT. If she is willing to become a general creditor of the university (which she may well be since this is a large, creditworthy institution) and give up the ability to oversee the investment of an identifiable trust portfolio, then she should consider the charitable gift annuity.

From the donor's point of view, charitable gift annuities are simpler than CRTs because there is no need for a trust instrument or a trustee. The sponsoring charity gets immediate use of the funds (with a CRT, the charity has to wait until the

---

[26] IRC § 72.

payments to individual beneficiaries have terminated), but the charity must be aware of any state regulations that might require it to keep sufficient reserves to pay the annuity.

[D] Charitable Lead Trusts

A charitable lead trust (CLT) is the opposite of a CRT in that it makes annual income distributions to a charitable organization for a term of years or for one or more persons' lifetimes, after which the remainder of the trust passes to individuals (or trusts for individuals) such as the donor's children.[27] To achieve any income, gift, or estate tax deduction, the income interest must be in the form of either a fixed annuity (a charitable lead annuity trust or CLAT) or a fixed percentage of the trust assets as the assets are revalued annually (a charitable lead unitrust or CLUT).[28]

An important motivation for most donors to fund a CLT is that rapidly appreciating assets can be donated to a CLT and, after the termination of the charitable term, passed on to children or grandchildren at reduced gift or estate tax costs. In this respect, a CLAT is similar to a GRAT.[29] In both a CLAT and a GRAT, much of the value of the donated property generally is represented (on a present value basis) by the stream of annuity payments (retained by the donor in a GRAT, or given to charity in a CLAT, in either case at no gift tax cost). In both a CLAT and a GRAT, the value of the remainder interest passing to children or grandchildren (or to trusts for their benefit) represents none or only a small part of the value of the property transferred to the trust, and, as a consequence, funding a GRAT or a CLAT gives rise to little or no gift tax. If the property in the CLAT (or GRAT) appreciates at a rate greater than the prescribed discount rate, then the amount of assets passing to children at the end of the trust term will exceed the amount that was subject to gift tax.

A CLT can be structured in one of two ways for income tax purposes. If the donor is willing to design the CLT as a *grantor trust* (in which case all of the CLT's income would be taxed to the donor),[30] then the donor can receive an income tax deduction up front for the present value of the amount predicted to pass to charity.[31] Each year the donor will report the trust income on her return, and she will not be entitled to any further income tax deduction for the amount paid each year to the charity. If the donor to a grantor trust dies during the term of the CLT (or the trust otherwise ceases to be a grantor trust as to the donor) there is a recapture of all or a part of the charitable income tax deduction that was allowed to the donor on funding the CLT.[32] As an alternative, the donor may create a *nongrantor trust* and forego an

---

[27] *See* IRC §§ 170(f)(2)(B), 2055(e)(2)(B), 2522(c)(2)(B), and the regulations accompanying each of these Code sections.

[28] Reg. §§ 1.170A-6(c), 20.2055-2(e)(2), 25.2522(c)-3(c)(2).

[29] GRATs are discussed in greater detail in Chapter 8.

[30] Grantor trusts are discussed in greater detail in Chapter 4.

[31] To the extent that a lesser amount is distributed to charity than the donor deducted, there will be recapture of the excess charitable income tax deduction. *See* IRC § 170(f)(2)(B).

[32] IRC § 170(f)(2)(B).

upfront income tax deduction. In that case the CLT will be subject to income tax on its income but the income generally will be offset by a charitable income tax deduction each year for the amount that it distributes to charity.[33] It should be noted that a CLT is not tax exempt and, unlike a CRT, is not a technique for capital gain deferral. The IRS has released sample forms for CLTs which, in most circumstances, ought to be carefully followed in order to ensure that a trust will qualify as a CLT.[34] The sample forms confirm that CLUTs can provide for varying percentage payouts from year to year, for example, increasing the percentage that must be paid to charity in later years after the CLUT has had time to appreciate. Similarly, the sample forms confirm that CLATs can provide for varying annuity amount payments from year to year. Estate planners may want to use the software programs now available to compare potential remainder amounts passing to the CLT remaindermen using straight annuity or unitrust payments versus unitrust or annuity payments that increase over the lead term.

EXAMPLE *10-27*

Susan is charitably inclined, but is also interested in passing the future appreciation in her company stock (which may go public) to her children at reduced gift and estate tax costs. She establishes a CLAT with $1,000,000 of stock, which will make distributions to her donor-advised fund at the local community foundation, with the remainder passing to trusts for her children. Assuming that the applicable IRS interest rate is 2.2 percent, the annual annuity that would be required to go to charity in order for the value of the remainder to be zero (and hence the gift tax to be zero), assuming the lead term lasts five, ten, or fifteen years, is calculated as follows:

---

[33] IRC § 642(c). The IRS has issued regulations that disregard income ordering provisions in a CLT designed to treat the most highly-taxed income as being distributed to charity first, before other types of income or principal, unless the ordering provision has economic effect independent of income tax consequences. Reg. §§ 1.642(c)-3 and 1.643(a)-5. The regulations give an example of a CLAT which provides that the annual annuity will be deemed to be paid first from ordinary income, second from short-term capital gain, third from 50 percent of the UBTI, fourth from long-term capital gain, fifth from the balance of UBTI, sixth from tax-exempt income, and last from principal, and states that such provisions lack economic effect and would be disregarded.

[34] Testamentary CLTs: Rev. Proc. 2007-46, 2007-29 I.R.B. 102 (6/22/07); Rev. Proc. 2008-46, 2008-30 I.R.B. 238 (7/30/08). Intervivos CLTs: Rev. Proc. 2007-45, 2007-29 I.R.B. 89 (6/22/07); Rev. Proc. 2008-45, 2008-30 I.R.B. 224 (7/30/08).

Term of charity's interest in the CLAT	Required annual annuity to charity in order to create a remainder with a zero value
5	$213,400
10	$112,500
15	$79,000

Susan selects the five-year CLAT, and two years later she sells the company and the CLAT assets increase substantially. At the end of the five-year term, the donor-advised fund has received over $1,000,000 from the CLAT, and the trusts for her children receive substantial funds remaining in the CLAT. There are no further gift and estate tax consequences, since the taxable gift was completed at the time the CLAT was funded.

Note that a special rule under the generation-skipping transfer tax[35] makes it difficult for Susan to make the trusts for her children fully exempt from that tax, even though the gift tax value was successfully established at zero. Under this rule, the generation-skipping tax exemption is allocated at the time of the gift and such allocation is then deemed to grow at the rate determined under IRC Section 7520 during the lead term. The trust's inclusion ratio is not finally determined until the end of the lead term, and if, at that time, the trust property has grown at a rate better than the IRC Section 7520 rate, then the trust's inclusion ratio will be greater than zero. Donors would not usually fund a CLT if they felt that the assets could not appreciate at a rate in excess of the IRC Section 7520 rate.

[E] Conservation Easements

Another type of partial interest in property that qualifies for an income, gift, and estate tax charitable deduction is a *qualified conservation contribution*. A qualified conservation contribution must be in the form of an easement for real estate deeded to a qualified conservation organization (one whose purpose is land conservation or preservation) for one of the following purposes: (1) use of the land by the public for outdoor recreation or education; (2) to protect a natural ecosystem; (3) to preserve open space, farmland, or forest land for significant public benefit (including scenic enjoyment of the general public); or (4) to protect an historic landmark.[36] Generally, the amount of the deduction is equal to the difference between the fair market value of the property before the easement was placed on the property and its fair market value with the easement. As noted in § 10.04[D][4], qualified conservation easement donations of long-term capital gain property can be deducted up to 50 percent of the donor's contribution base, or up to 100 percent of the donor's contribution base if the donor is a qualifying farmer or rancher, and the unused deduction may be carried forward for to up to 15 years.

---

[35] IRC § 2642(e). The generation-skipping transfer tax and its application to charitable lead trusts is discussed in Chapter 9.

[36] IRC § 170(h).

§ 10.07 FUNDING CHARITABLE GIFTS

[A] Lifetime Gifts Versus Testamentary Gifts

One advantage of a lifetime gift to charity is that a lifetime gift provides the donor with a double tax benefit. The donor is entitled to claim an income tax deduction, and, in addition, the property is no longer in his estate and will not be subject to estate tax. Bequests to charity at the donor's death are not subject to estate tax, but neither the estate nor the beneficiaries are entitled to a deduction for income tax purposes. For this reason, some donors who have been planning to fund charities at death decide to accelerate their bequests through lifetime gifts, especially when they reach an age at which they are comfortable that their remaining wealth is sufficient for their support.

Alternatively, a client who does not want a charitable gift paid until his death can arrange for his surviving spouse to make such a gift after he dies and obtain an income tax deduction at that later date.

EXAMPLE *10-28*

A married couple is considering a charitable bequest to the husband's alma mater at the death of the husband. In order to build flexibility into the plan, the husband's will could provide for a bequest to the school in the event the husband is the second to die, but also provide that, if his wife survives him, the bequest goes instead to her (qualifying for the estate tax marital deduction) with the suggestion that she use the bequest to make a gift to the school, for which she will get an income tax deduction.

[B] Use of Retirement Benefits to Fund Charitable Bequests

Using qualified retirement benefits or IRAs to fund a charitable bequest can be a very tax-efficient way to make a charitable gift.[1]

Qualified retirement funds, such as Section 401(k) plans, and deductible IRAs[2] are subject to income tax at the time that funds are distributed because income tax has not yet been paid on the initial amounts funded or on the income earned since

---

[1] § 10.07 Retirement benefits generally, and the use of retirement funds for charitable giving, are discussed in greater detail in Chapter 13.

[2] The rules are different for Roth IRAs. Roth IRAs are discussed in greater detail in Chapter 13.

funding. In addition, such funds are included in their owners' estates, and thus are subject to estate taxes. The double taxation of retirement benefits is somewhat ameliorated because the estate tax attributable to the benefits is deductible against the income taxed to the beneficiary.[3] If such funds pass to a charity, the estate tax charitable deduction and the charity's income tax exempt status would eliminate the impact of both the federal estate tax and the federal income tax, but possibly not state income tax.

Owners of retirement benefits and IRAs may be interested in giving their beneficiaries the option of accepting a bequest of such assets (subject to taxes) or disclaiming such bequest, in which case such assets would pass free of such taxes to a charity such as a family-controlled private foundation. Care should be taken to ensure that the rules governing qualified disclaimers[4] are satisfied, including the rule that the person disclaiming cannot retain any right to control the disposition of the disclaimed assets.[5]

EXAMPLE *10-29*

Ian has an IRA worth $100,000. If he left it to his daughters in 2022, the total federal estate tax on the fund could be as high as $40,000. The beneficiaries may deduct the estate tax attributable to the IRA ($100,000 × 40% federal estate tax bracket = $40,000). Therefore, the $37,000 of income taxes on the IRA withdrawal (assuming the top federal rate of 37 percent) would be entirely offset by the deduction for federal estate taxes paid on the IRA. Note that IRA withdrawals are not subject to the 3.8 percent Medicare surtax. Ian decided that designating his daughters to inherit the IRA where they kept only $60,000 after federal taxes without factoring in any state income or estate taxes was not an efficient use of his money, so he designated a family foundation as the beneficiary of the IRA. If the IRA still has $100,000 in it at the time of his death, Ian will be leaving his daughters in charge of a $100,000 foundation.

Taxpayers age 70^1/$_2$ or older can do a "charitable rollover" and distribute up to $100,000 per year directly from a traditional IRA or Roth IRA to certain public charities.[6] The 70^1/$_2$ age requirement applies to "the individual for whose benefit the plan is maintained," and refers to both the original owner of an IRA and to a beneficiary of an inherited IRA (provided that the beneficiary was 70^1/$_2$ or older). The charitable distribu-

---

[3] IRC § 691(c).

[4] *See* § 14.06 *infra*.

[5] In Ltr. Rul. 200420007, the IRS ruled that a disclaimer is qualified where the disclaimed funds passed to a family foundation and the foundation undertook to reform its bylaws to provide that funds passing to it by disclaimer would be held in a segregated account over which only directors other than the disclaimant had control.

[6] IRC § 408(d). The IRA charitable rollover was made permanent by the Protecting Americans from Tax Hikes Act of 2015 (Pub. L. No. 114-113).

tion counts toward satisfaction of the owner/beneficiary's required minimum distribution under Section 401(a)(9). Specifically excluded from the class of permissible charities are supporting organizations and donor-advised funds. Charitable distributions excluded from the taxpayer's income are not deductible by the taxpayer and do not count when applying limitations on the taxpayer's charitable deduction. However, the *quid pro quo* receipt of value and substantiation rules of Section 170 do apply, reducing the exclusion to the extent that the IRA owner/beneficiary receives value in return for the contribution, and requiring that the owner/beneficiary obtain a tax receipt from the charity.

11

Planning for a Closely Held Business Interest

§11.01 BEGINNING THE PROCESS OF PLANNING FOR A CLOSELY HELD BUSINESS INTEREST

Estate planning for the owner of a family or closely held business presents many special challenges, including income and transfer tax considerations, business planning concerns, retirement planning, and personal and psychological issues. Often, the business represents a very large percentage of the owner's estate and is not readily marketable. A family business often presents valuation challenges, so estimating the potential estate tax liability may be difficult and time consuming. Special gift and estate tax provisions may be available to ease the tax burden of passing the business to heirs, but these provisions are detailed and complex, and careful planning is necessary to achieve proper compliance. When the business owner has one or more children that participate in the operation of the business and other children who do not, he or she will need to decide whether to pass a portion of the business to the nonparticipating children, and, if not, how to provide for the children who are not receiving the business. This may require consideration of equalizing distributions to nonparticipating children using non-business assets. In many instances, however, there are insufficient non-business assets to provide equal bequests to all children. The business owner must decide how to appropriately divide the estate, while achieving the objective of successfully transitioning the business to the next generation for continued operation. Additionally, many business owners have not put in place a plan for retirement income for themselves and their spouses, which may become an issue if the owner's estate plan involves transferring the business during his or her lifetime. Finally, many business owners, especially those who founded and built their businesses, find it extremely difficult to relinquish ownership or control of the business. This reluctance often presents a substantial obstacle when developing and implementing a tax efficient estate plan for the business owner.

When approaching a first meeting with a family business owner, it is helpful to consider three preliminary steps that are of particular importance. First, the estate planner should assist the business owner in developing realistic goals for the business while taking into account his or her personal and family circumstances. A threshold question is whether the business owner's primary goal is to pass the business itself to the next generation, or if passing maximum value is preferred, regardless of the future of the business. If the primary goal is passing on maximum value, then a lifetime sale of the business may be a better plan than leaving the business to beneficiaries upon the business owner's death. This may be particularly true if there is no heir apparent to the continued operation of the business. If the business owner wishes to preserve the business for future generations to operate, it will be necessary to develop a comprehensive business succession plan. This type of plan must address such issues as who should have control of the business, how to allocate ownership interest, and how to determine the best way to equalize the shares of the estate that the various beneficiaries will receive. A successful business succession plan will also envision the integration of the successor generation into a meaningful operational capacity while the current generation remains at the helm. The current generation rarely wishes to pass the business to the next generation without first affirming that the successors will have the adequate preparation and technical skills to maintain and grow the business.

Second, the estate planner should help the business owner understand that planning for a family business is a dynamic process that necessarily evolves over time. Starting as early as possible will often maximize the planning opportunities, but the plan should be continually revisited and re-evaluated. Over time the owner's goals will likely evolve, the preferences and skills of the owner's intended successors may be different, the value or nature of the business may be significantly different, and the applicable transfer tax rules and strategies may change.

Finally, the business owner (and his or her advisors) should understand that planning for a family business requires an iterative team effort. Corporate counsel and the accountant for the business should be part of the team, especially if the plan involves a restructuring of the business or a transfer of an interest in the business. These advisors may offer valuable insight as to the effect of state, corporate, or partnership laws, potential corporate or partnership income tax issues, the effect of a proposed plan on business contracts or financing arrangements (particularly if a lender has the ability to call a loan if the current business owner does not maintain a required percentage of ownership, or voting control, in the business), and any transfer restrictions on the business interest. Another aspect of the team approach to planning for a family business is to encourage the business owner to involve other members of the family in the process, particularly if the plan is to pass the business on to the next generation. Countless family businesses have been ruined as a result of heirs feuding over ownership and control of the business. A comprehensive plan that all of the beneficiaries understand and agree to in advance may prevent prolonged and expensive litigation.

As is the case in planning for other types of assets, the planning process begins with the collection of information from the client. When a business is the primary asset, specific questions that should be posed by the estate planner should include the following:

- What is the form of the business? Is the business organized as a general partnership, a limited partnership, a limited liability company, a C corporation, an S corporation, or a sole proprietorship?
- In what state is the business organized? In what other states is the business registered to do business? In what other states, if any, does the business operate without formal registration?
- How is voting control of the business held? It is critical to obtain and review the provisions of the by-laws governing shareholder voting, and possibly state law governing shareholder voting.
- Are there any restrictions on transfer of the business interest? Such restrictions might be in the form of shareholder agreements (a buy/sell agreement) or provisions in corporate by-laws, an LLC Operating Agreement, or a partnership agreement.
- Are there any options or warrants outstanding, and if so, what are the terms?
- Has the business ever been the subject of a formal valuation? If so, for what purpose and what valuation methodology was utilized?
- Have there been prior transfers of the business interests? If so, how, when, and at what price (and how was that price established)?
- Does the business have a retirement plan that will provide retirement income for the business owner and spouse?

- Does the business own insurance on the business owner's life, or provide life insurance benefits for him or her?
- Do any family members work in the business? If so, what are their positions and what training did they receive for such roles? Are any other family members expected to join the business in the near term?
- Are there key employees who are not family members? If so, do they have an ownership interest in the company? If not, are there any safeguards in place (i.e., attractive executive compensation benefits, etc.) to ensure that these key employees are likely to remain with the business after a transition of ownership to the next generation? How would they react to a transfer of ownership of the business to the next generation? Do they get along with family members who one day may be their boss?
- Has the owner had any offers to purchase the business? Does the owner anticipate any such offers? Advance knowledge of a potential liquidity event is crucial to appropriately planning for the potential income tax liability that may result from a sale. Planners must educate clients that their options may be severely limited if they are brought in only after the letter of intent is received.
- What are the owners' views of the future prospects for the business? Are there plans for expanding into new areas?
- What are the business-related challenges, independent of any transition of ownership, that the current owners expect the next generation to face?

The above list is not exhaustive, but should provide a starting point for the planning process.

§11.02 FORMS OF CLOSELY HELD BUSINESS INTERESTS

When planning with an interest in a closely held business, it is critical for the estate planner to ascertain how the business and any subsidiaries or other related entities are organized for state law purposes and how such entities are classified for federal income tax purposes. The form and tax attributes of the business will be a primary factor in determining which planning techniques are appropriate.

Closely held business are most often organized as sole proprietorships, corporations, partnerships, or limited liability companies. This section provides a brief overview of the particular characteristics of each form of entity that an estate planner should be aware of when working with a closely held business.

[A] Sole Proprietorship

In a sole proprietorship, the assets of the business are held directly by the owner, the employees of the business are employed by the owner, and the owner reports the profit and loss of the business directly on his or her personal income tax return. The owner has no protection from the liabilities of a sole proprietorship; consequently, most owners at some point choose to restructure their business as an entity that offers liability protection.

[B] Corporation

Historically, many closely held businesses have been organized as corporations under state law. The shareholders of a corporation are not liable for the liabilities of the corporation. For federal income tax law purposes, a corporation may be classified as either a "C corporation" (governed by subchapter C of the Internal Revenue Code)[1] or an "S corporation" (governed by subchapter S of the Internal Revenue Code).[2] Most states recognize a similar distinction for state tax purposes. The distinction between a C corporation and an S corporation is relevant only for tax law purposes; for state corporate law purposes there is no difference between the two types of corporations. In this chapter, the term "corporation" will be used to refer to all state law corporations or to C corporations and material that applies only to S corporations will be separately identified.

The primary difference between a C corporation and an S corporation is that the net profits of a C corporation are subject to two levels of income tax, and the net profits of an S corporation generally are subject to only one level of income tax.[3] A C corporation is treated for federal tax purposes as a separate taxpayer, and pays tax on its net income at corporate income tax rates, which have been reduced to 21 percent under the Tax Cuts and Jobs Act of 2017 ("2017 Tax Act").[4] When the C corporation distributes the after-tax net profits of the corporation to the shareholders as a dividend, the shareholders are subject to a second level of tax at individual income rates on the dividend they receive.[5] The shareholders of a C corporation are not permitted to deduct the net losses of the C corporation. An S corporation is not treated as a separate taxpayer, in that the income and loss of an S corporation flows through to the personal income tax returns of its shareholders, who pay income tax on their attributable share of the net income at individual tax rates, and can deduct any net loss.[6] Generally the shareholders of an S corporation are not subject to an additional level of tax when the S corporation distributes a cash dividend. In fact, as a pass-through entity, the shareholders are generally taxed on the net income of an S corporation, whether or not it is received as a dividend distribution. Consequently, the cash received by the shareholders of an S corporation as dividends is only taxed once for income tax purposes.

---

[1] **§ 11.02** Subchapter C is contained in IRC § § 301–385.

[2] Subchapter S is contained in IRC § § 1361–1379.

[3] *See* IRC § 1366. However, an S corporation may be subject to tax at the corporate level on certain passive investment income under IRC § 1375. In addition, a corporation that was a C corporation before electing S corporation status may be subject to corporate level tax during the first five years after the election on gains that were built-in at the time of the election. IRC § 1374.

[4] Pub. L. No. 115-97; originally titled the Tax Cuts and Jobs Act, but changed to comply with the Senate's reconciliation rules by dropping the short title, and is now known as the "2017 Tax Act."

[5] IRC § 301. Dividends are taxed as ordinary income (i.e., compensation) to the individual shareholders.

[6] IRC § 1366.

EXAMPLE 11-1

Acme Corporation is organized as a C corporation. Acme earns a profit of $100,000 in 2022, and pays a federal income tax of $21,000. It distributes the remaining cash ($79,000) to its sole shareholder as a dividend. The shareholder reports the dividend on his tax return as ordinary income, and pays a federal income tax on the dividend of $17,380 (at a 24 percent rate). After tax, the shareholder is left with $61,620 in cash. If Acme Corporation were an S corporation, it would file an information return but would not pay any federal income tax. The shareholder would report the corporation's income of $100,000 on his or her personal return and would pay federal income tax of $24,000. When the corporation distributes the $100,000 to the shareholder as a dividend, the shareholder will not pay any additional tax. After tax, the shareholder is left with $76,000.

Not all corporations are qualified to become S corporations for federal tax purposes. The Internal Revenue Code sets strict requirements that a corporation must meet in order to obtain and maintain S corporation status.[7] The most important qualifications relate to the number and type of shareholders of the corporation and the type of stock issued by the corporation.[8] An S corporation may not have more than 100 shareholders.[9] All of the shareholders must be U.S. citizens or resident individuals, with exceptions for estates, certain specific types of trusts, and certain charities.[10] Partnerships, for example, are not eligible S corporation shareholders; however, a limited liability company may own S corporation shares if such entity is disregarded for tax purposes (if it is a single member LLC).[11] An estate planner dealing with S corporation stock must be careful to prevent inadvertent termination of the corporation's S status due to a transfer of stock to an ineligible shareholder. In addition, an S corporation may not have more than one class of stock, although differences in voting rights are disregarded, meaning that an S corporation can offer both voting and non-voting stock, but all shareholders must share identical distribution and liquidation rights. Accordingly, S corporation stock may not be bifurcated, for example, into common and preferred interests.[12] While the economic interests of all shares of S corporation stock must be identical, creative tax planning can be done to create bifurcated interests using interim disregarded entities between the shareholder and the S corporation.

---

[7] IRC § 1361.

[8] *Id.*

[9] IRC § 1361(b)(1).

[10] *Id.*

[11] Ltr. Rul. 200513001. Practitioners should carefully coordinate the estate plan to address potential consequences arising on the death of the individual who is the single member of the LLC. For example, while a disregarded entity is a permissible shareholder of an S corporation, if the decedent's estate plan provides for the LLC membership interest to be distributed to multiple family members, the S corporation's election may be invalidated.

[12] IRC § 1361(c)(4).

[C] Partnership

Under state law, a partnership may be formed as either a general partnership (under a form of the Uniform Partnership Act or Revised Uniform Partnership Act, as appropriate) or a limited partnership (under a form of the Uniform Limited Partnership Act or the Revised Uniform Limited Partnership Act). Some states also allow for the formation of limited liability limited partnerships. State law (including both statutes and common law), and the terms of any partnership agreement entered into by the partners define the powers and duties of the partners. The rights and duties of the partners are governed by the state law of the state in which the entity was formed as well as by the terms of the limited partnership agreement. General partnerships typically differ from limited partnerships in the following ways:

- A limited partnership must be formed by filing a certificate of limited partnership with the secretary of state, but a general partnership can be formed by any agreement among the partners, whether written or oral, and it is not necessary to file any documentation with the state to create a general partnership;
- All general partners are personally liable (in the form of joint and several liability) for the liabilities of the partnership, but limited partners are not liable for partnership liabilities;[13] and
- All general partners in either a limited or general partnership have the right to manage the partnership, but limited partners do not have management rights.

Only the general partners are liable for the liabilities of a limited partnership. Consequently, it is common to form a corporation to act as the general partner of a limited partnership in order to provide maximum creditor protection for all parties. For federal income tax purposes, partnerships are not treated as separate taxpayers, and the net partnership income passes through to the partners who then report their share of net partnership gains and losses on their individual income tax returns.[14] The fact that an entity is formed as a general or limited partnership for state law purposes does not necessarily mean that the entity will be taxed as a partnership for federal income tax purposes. Under the "check the box" regulations, an entity formed under one of the uniform partnership acts may elect to be treated for federal income tax purposes as either a corporation or as a partnership.[15] In most instances, the partners

---

[13] Typically, a creditor must first exhaust the assets of the partnership before seeking recovery against the individual partners, unless it is clear that doing so would be inadequate to recover on the debt. Thereafter, partners are jointly and severally liable on all obligations of the partnership, and creditors may seek recovery from any partner. Each such partner who is required to pay a partnership debt would then have a claim for contribution against the other partners.

[14] IRC § 701.

[15] Reg. § 301.7701-3. Not all states have adopted the 1997 federal rules that permit an entity to elect whether to be treated as a corporation or as a partnership for income tax purposes. In those states an entity will be treated as a partnership for state income tax purposes only if it meets the historic test for partnership status in that it does not have more than two of the following corporate characteristics: unlimited life, free transferability of interests, centralized management, and limited liability for the owners.

want the entity to be treated as a partnership for tax purposes in order to avoid the two levels of tax (at both the entity and owner level) imposed on C corporations. Partnerships are more flexible than S corporations in that they do not have restrictions on the number and qualification of shareholders, and they may offer different classes of interest to their partners.

[D] Limited Liability Company

A limited liability company (LLC) is a popular type of state law entity that combines certain liability benefits of a corporation with the tax benefits of a partnership. The state laws governing LLCs provide that none of the owners of the company (generally referred to as members) is liable for the liabilities of the company. This provides the members with the liability protection that is one of the most important characteristics of a corporation. For federal tax law purposes, an LLC can choose to be taxed as a partnership,[16] thus providing the benefits of a single level of tax on company profits and the ability of members to deduct net losses on their individual tax returns. Generally, LLC statutes permit wide latitude with regard to management structure; thus, an LLC can be managed by one or more members, a third-party manager, officers and directors, and any combination thereof. An LLC may have multiple classes of membership interests, with each class having varied voting and/or economic rights, and there are no state law restrictions on the type or number of underlying members.

Note that a new type of state law entity has emerged in a handful of states, that of the Series LLC.[17] While the Series LLC has been in existence since Delaware enacted its legislation in 1996, it is still not definitive that Series LLCs will be treated as separate legal entities for purposes of creditor protection in all states. The purpose of the Series LLC is to allow for an LLC to be subdivided into separate Series with varying ownership and management with respect to each Series. The debts and liabilities of each Series are enforceable against only that Series and not other Series established by the same LLC. As was the case with the LLC in the 1990s, one disadvantage of Series LLCs is that the law governing them is still relatively underdeveloped. As a consequence, it will take time before many of the current uncertainties with regard to Series LLCs are resolved. Note that generally those states that allow for a Series LLC also allow for a Series LP or Series LLLP.

---

[16] Reg. § 301.7701-3.

[17] The Series LLC exists in Alabama, Delaware, District of Columbia, Illinois, Iowa, Kansas, Minnesota, Missouri, Montana, Nevada, North Dakota, Oklahoma, Tennessee, Texas, Utah, Wisconsin, and Puerto Rico. Some states, like California, do not allow for series LLCs to be formed under state law but series LLCs formed in other states can register with the state and do business in the state.

[E] Taxation of Pass-Through Entities and the IRC Section 199A Deduction

The 2017 Tax Act contained numerous income tax related provisions, including the addition of new Internal Revenue Code Section 199A ("Section 199A"). Section 199A is effective for tax years beginning January 1, 2018, through its sunset after December 31, 2025. Treasury issued the Final Regulations on January 18, 2019. A detailed discussion of Section 199A is beyond the scope of this chapter but following is a general overview of the application of this provision and various planning opportunities available to clients owning pass-through entities.

The 2017 Tax Act reduced the tax rate applicable to C corporations to 21 percent. Owners of flow-through entities remain subject to federal income tax at up to the highest marginal rate of 37 percent. The 2017 Tax Act enacted Section 199A to address this potential 16 percent rate discrepancy and reduce the tax burden on income earned from flow-through trades or businesses, including entities taxed as partnerships, S corporations and sole proprietorships. Section 199A allows a deduction for up to 20 percent of the qualified business income ("QBI") that passes through to the owner of the business.

Assuming no state income tax and no application of the net investment income tax to the owner of a flow-through entity (also assuming the QBI deduction is not limited to something less than 20 percent, as discussed below), a taxpayer in the top marginal federal tax bracket of 37 percent will be subject to an effective tax rate of 29.6 percent on flow-through income. $100 of QBI would result in net, after-tax funds of $70.40 to the taxpayer. In contrast, if a C corporation has $100 of taxable income, the corporation will pay $21 in tax (the C corporation 21 percent rate), then if the remaining $79 is distributed as a qualified dividend taxed at the highest dividend rate, the shareholder would pay 23.8 percent (20 percent capital gain plus the 3.8 percent net investment tax) on that amount, resulting in a net $60.20 remaining for the taxpayer. This illustrates the very real economic value of qualifying for the QBI deduction, if possible.

The QBI deduction is subject to certain income limitations, determined by the taxable income of the owner receiving the flow-through income. The QBI income limitation is determined at the taxpayer, rather than the entity, level. Taxable income is based on all income sources for the taxpayer, not only the amount derived from the qualifying pass-through business. The threshold on the low end is $170,050 for a single taxpayer ($340,100 for a married couple filing jointly or $170,050 for a married taxpayer filing a separate return) and is $220,050 for a single taxpayer ($440,100 for joint filers or $220,050 for married filing separately) on the high end.[18] Note that the threshold amounts will be increased for taxable years after 2022 by the cost-of-living adjustment under IRC Section 1(f)(3).

Taxpayers below the bottom threshold are permitted to claim the 20 percent QBI deduction, regardless of whether their trade or business is an SSTB. For taxpayers

---

[18] *See* Reg. § 1.199A-1(b)(12).

with income above the minimum threshold, the applicable limitations will depend on whether the trade or business is a Specified Service Trade or Business (an "SSTB").

[1] "W-2 Wages" and "Qualified Property"

For the purpose of determining the QBI deduction limitations imposed on taxpayers with taxable income in excess of the lower end of the threshold ($170,050/$340,100), it is important to define the terms "W-2 wages" and "qualified property." While the calculation of a taxpayer's taxable income is based on taxpayer's income from all sources, each flow-through business, and any corresponding limitation that may apply to the deduction available, is analyzed on an individual basis. Likewise, the W-2 wage calculation and amount of qualified property available for determining the QBI deduction limitations is determined based solely on the respective amounts for the specific business in question.

The Treasury Regulations do permit the aggregation of QBI across multiple trades or businesses. Where a taxpayer has multiple businesses, QBI must be determined separately for each business. If a taxpayer's QBI from at least one trade or business is negative, the taxpayer must offset the QBI attributable to each trade or business that produced net positive QBI with the QBI from each trade or business that produced net negative QBI in proportion to the relative amounts of net QBI in the trades or businesses with positive QBI. This "adjusted QBI" is then compared with the W-2 wages and UBIA of qualified property in calculating the QBI deduction. If the net QBI for all businesses in a year is a negative number, the negative amount is treated as QBI from a separate business, and is carried over to subsequent years to offset the positive QBI of businesses in subsequent years.[19]

IRC Section 199A(b)(4)(A) defines W-2 wages as wages paid by the pass-through entity with respect to the employment of employees during the calendar year ending during that taxable year. Wages include those amounts that are paid to all employees of the pass-through entity, including but not limited to the individual taxpayer/owner. W-2 wages include salary, bonuses and elective profit sharing plan deferrals paid by the qualifying business.[20] It does not include amounts paid to independent contractors, paid to the taxpayer by any source other than the specific pass-through business in question, or amounts subject to self-employment taxes. Guaranteed payments paid to a partner are subject to self-employment taxes, and, similar to payments to independent contractors, are not W-2 wages and are not counted for purposes of the W-2 limitation.

Qualified property is defined as tangible property subject to the allowance for depreciation under IRC Section 167 which is: (1) held by, and available for use in, the qualified trade or business at the close of the taxable year; (2) used at any point during the taxable year for the production of QBI; and (3) the depreciable period for the property has not ended before the close of the taxable year.[21] Interestingly, for the

---

[19] *See* Reg. § 1.199A-1(d)(2)(iii)(B).

[20] Reg. § 1.199A-2(b)(2).

[21] *See* IRC § 199A(b)(6)(A); Reg. § 1.199A-2(c)(1).

purposes of Section 199A, the end of the depreciable period for qualified property is defined as the later of its applicable recovery period under IRC Section 168 (without regard to subsection (g) thereof) or ten years from the date the property was placed into service by the taxpayer.[22]

[2] Non-SSTB versus SSTB

If the taxpayer's taxable income in a non-SSTB is lower than the bottom end of the threshold ($170,050/$340,100 adjusted annually after 2022), then there is no limitation on the deduction. If the taxpayer's taxable income exceeds the upper threshold ($220,050/$440,100), then the deduction available is limited to the lesser of (1) or (2):

(1) 20 percent of the taxpayer's QBI with respect to the qualified trade or business; or

(2) The greater of: (A) 50 percent of the W-2 wages with respect to the qualified trade or business; or (B) the sum of (i) 25 percent of the W-2 wages with respect to the qualified trade or business plus (ii) 2.5 percent of the UBIA of qualified property for that trade or business.[23]

If the taxpayer's taxable income falls between the lower and upper threshold, then his or her deduction is determined in the same fashion as for those who exceed the top end, but is phased out depending how far along the threshold spectrum the taxpayer's income falls.

If the pass-through business is an SSTB, then the threshold amounts are the same, but the limitation imposed on the QBI deduction for the taxpayer may differ. If the pass-through business is an SSTB, the entire Section 199A deduction is available for taxpayers with taxable income below the lower ($170,050/$340,100) threshold. For SSTB taxpayers with taxable income above the higher ($220,050/$440,100) threshold, the deduction is denied entirely, regardless of the W-2 wages paid or qualified property owned by the business. If the taxpayer's taxable income falls between the two benchmarks, the deduction is subject to the W-2/UBIA limitation, but also is phased out by the amount the taxable income exceeds the bottom threshold, divided by $50,000 for a single taxpayer and $100,000 for joint filers.[24]

The Treasury Regulations define the types of businesses that are considered an SSTB. In this regard, the Treasury Regulations addressed at least one prevalent concern among tax practitioners, in that they are narrowly tailored to specific business ventures as opposed to more broadly defined categories of businesses. Treasury Regulations Section 1.199A-5(b)(1) and (2) define the performance of services in the fields of: (1) health, (2) law, (3) accounting, (4) actuarial science, (5) performing arts, (6) consulting, (7) athletics, (8) financial services, (9) brokerage

---

[22] *See* Reg. § 1.199A-2(c)(2).

[23] Reg. § 1.199A-1(d)(iv)(A).

[24] Reg. § 1.199A-1(d)(iv)(B).

services, (10) investing and investment management, (11) trading, (12) dealing in securities, (13) dealing in commodities, and (14) any trade or business where the principal asset of such trade or business is the reputation or skill of one or more of its employees or owners.

Fortunately, the Treasury Regulations interpret the final, catch-all SSTB classification (i.e., any trade or business where the principal asset is the reputation or skill of one or more of its employees or owners) narrowly and provide that a business is an SSTB under this rule if it is a business in which a person receives fees, compensation or other income for: (a) endorsing products or services; (b) the use of a person's image, likeness, name, signature, voice, trademark or any other symbols associated with the individual's identity; or (c) appearing on radio, television or another media format.[25] This avoids the concern expressed by tax practitioners that nearly any business closely associated with a particular name (i.e., "Joe's Pizza") could be treated as an SSTB.

§11.03 VALUATION OF A CLOSELY HELD BUSINESS

[A] Overview

The estate planner may be faced with the issue of determining the value of the business on several occasions while developing an estate plan for the owner of a closely held business. If the owner retains ownership in the company until his or her death, then the company must be valued for estate tax purposes. If the owner makes gifts of interests in the company during life, the value of such interests must be determined for gift tax purposes. If the owner decides to sell interests in the company to descendants, trusts, or other estate planning vehicles, then it will be important to determine the value of the interest in order to ensure that the sale price is equal to the fair market value of the interest.

The valuation of a closely held business is a complex and technical task, which requires consideration of numerous factors including the structure of the business, the relevant industry, the geographic area, and the general economy. In almost all cases, it is advisable to engage a professional appraiser to prepare a formal valuation, as this will provide the best evidence if the IRS challenges the value reported on a gift or estate tax return.[26] The appraiser should be asked to prepare a written appraisal that sets out in detail each of the following:

- The appraiser's qualifications;
- The characteristics of the company that are relevant to value;
- Other external factors on which the appraisal is based, including facts relating to the industry, comparable sales, and any market studies; and
- A description of the methodology used by the appraiser
- The purpose of the appraisal, i.e., sale, gift transaction, estate tax return, etc.

---

[25] Reg. § 1.199A-5(b)(2)(xiv).

[26] With respect to contemplated lifetime transfers, a professional appraisal is likely required to satisfy the adequate disclosure requirements of Reg. § 301.6501(c)-1 and to commence the statute of limitations period.

While the estate planner will unlikely be preparing the appraisal itself, estate planners are often called upon to review professional appraisals or to defend an appraisal in a gift or estate tax audit. Consequently, an understanding of the general principles of valuing a closely held business is important.

[B] General Rules: Fair Market Value

The fair market value of an interest in a family or closely held business for both estate and gift tax purposes is the price at which the interest would change hands between a willing buyer and a willing seller, neither being under any compulsion to buy or sell and both having reasonable knowledge of the relevant facts.[1] The gift and estate tax regulations provide relatively little guidance as to how the fair market value of a family business interest is to be determined, but the IRS has issued a revenue ruling—Revenue Ruling 59-60—that lists the factors to be considered in valuing a closely held business.[2] This revenue ruling applies by its terms only to stock in a corporation, but a later revenue ruling confirmed that these principles are to be applied equally to any type of family business, including sole proprietorships and partnerships.[3] Consequently, Revenue Ruling 59-60 is the starting point for the valuation of any closely held business.

In Revenue Ruling 59-60, the Service acknowledged that valuation is not an exact science, and that no formula exists that is uniformly applicable to all closely held businesses. The revenue ruling states, however, that the following factors are fundamental and should be analyzed in each case:

- *Nature and History of the Business.* This factor includes an analysis of the products or services produced by the company, the assets of the company, the capital and management structure, the production records, gross income and net profits, and pattern of dividend payment. Generally, the appraiser should give more weight to events close in time to the appraisal, but the revenue ruling suggests that a long history of income, profits, and dividend payments is highly desirable.

- *Outlook of the General Economy and Specific Industry.* The value of a business depends in part on the state of the general economy in the sense that when the economy is booming it is more likely that a business owner could find a willing buyer. The position of the specific industry in comparison to other industries is also significant, as is the company's ability to compete with other companies in the same industry. The appraiser should consider both current conditions and reasonably foreseeable changes related to competition and

---

[1] § 11.03 Reg. § § 20.2031-3, 25.2512-3.

[2] Rev. Rul. 59-60, 1959-1 C.B. 237, *as modified by* Rev. Rul. 65-193, 1965-2 C.B. 370, Rev. Rul. 68-609, 1968-2 C.B. 327, Rev. Rul. 77-287, 1977-2 C.B. 319, Rev. Rul. 80-213, 1980-2 C.B. 101, Rev. Rul. 83-120, 1983-2 C.B. 170.

[3] Rev. Rul. 68-609, 1968-2 C.B. 327.

management stability. If, for example, the success of the business depends largely on the services of a single individual, then the value of the company may drop when that individual dies or retires.

- *Book Value.* The revenue ruling recommends that appraisers obtain balance sheets for at least two years preceding the appraisal. The appraiser should determine the type and condition of the company's assets, the amount of working capital and long-term indebtedness, and the capital structure. If the company has more than one class of interest, the voting rights and any preferences in allocations and distributions are relevant to the value of each class.

- *Earning Capacity.* The appraiser should examine detailed profit and loss statements for five or more years to determine gross income, expenses, capital expenditures, net income available for dividend payments, and amounts carried to surplus. The revenue ruling notes that potential future income is a major factor in the valuation of many companies, and that prior earnings are usually the most reliable guide to expected future earnings. The revenue ruling cautions against resorting to average earnings to determine the company's potential for future earnings when the company exhibits a pattern of increasing or decreasing earnings because in such case the most recent years will be more relevant than earlier years.

- *Capacity to Pay Dividends.* The revenue ruling distinguishes between a company's capacity to pay dividends and its actual record of past dividend payments. The amount of dividends paid may be influenced by the company's need to retain working capital, and, in a family-controlled business, by the owner's income needs and desire to avoid payment of income taxes on dividends. The ruling specifies that, when a controlling interest in a company is being valued, dividend payments are not a material factor because the owners have discretion to withhold dividends or to move cash out of the company in the form of salaries or bonuses.

- *Presence of Goodwill.* The revenue ruling recognizes that goodwill is essentially based on earning capacity. Other factors such as the reputation of the business, the ownership of a trade or brand name, and long-term operation in a particular locale may support the conclusion that the business has intangible value in excess of the value of its tangible assets.

- *History of Sales of Interests in the Company and the Size of the Interest Being Valued.* Actual sales of interests in the company are indicative of the value of the company, but the revenue ruling warns that the appraiser should investigate such sales to determine whether they represent arm's length transactions. The revenue ruling recognizes that a minority interest is more difficult to sell than a controlling interest, and a controlling interest may be valued at a premium.

- *Market Price of Traded Stocks in a Similar Line of Business.* If the stock of a comparable company is publicly traded, then the trading price of that company's stock may be taken into account. The appraiser should be cautious to ensure that the companies are truly comparable and should not rely on this factor alone.

Revenue Ruling 59-60 does not describe how an appraiser should weigh the factors listed above, and does not recommend any particular method of valuation. The ruling does note, however, that if the company sells products or services, then earnings generally are the most important factor. If the company holds primarily investment assets or real estate, then the value of the company is closely related to its assets, and earnings should be accorded a lesser weight. The revenue ruling also states that using an average of values derived from earnings and from assets does not serve a useful purpose.

While Revenue Ruling 59-60 provides the starting point for valuing a closely held business, it fails to describe how an appraiser should analyze the factors in order to reach a final conclusion as to value. Also note that the standard of valuation under U.S. generally accepted accounting principles, which is used for purposes of completing a Black Scholes analysis as well as certain other valuation strategies for options, is not fair market value, but rather "fair value." Fair value goes beyond the objective factors and takes into account "the respective advantages or disadvantages that each will gain from the transaction."[4] While fair market value is still the predominately accepted approach, fair value is becoming more commonly used, and some commentators hypothesize that the IRS will eventually transition this way.

Qualified business valuations are necessary to determine the fair market value for multiple testamentary and lifetime transfers. Recent IRS guidance considered the absolute necessity of a contemporaneous gift tax appraisal while taking advantage of one strategy that has long been favored as an "estate freeze" transaction, known as the "zeroed-out GRAT."[5] In CCA 202152018, the IRS considered a transaction where a donor funded a two-year grantor retained annuity trust (a "GRAT") that appeared to satisfy the qualified interest requirements under IRC Section 2702. However, the IRS noted that:

- The value of the transferred shares was based on a dated appraisal (dated approximately seven months prior to the date of transfer) that had originally been commissioned to report stock value under a nonqualified deferred compensation plan under IRC Section 409A.
- Prior to the donor's transfer to the GRAT, the donor had entered into substantial discussions regarding the sale and/or merger of his business interests. These offers were not contemplated in the Section 409A valuation.
- A few weeks prior to transferring shares to the GRAT, the donor gifted shares to a charitable remainder trust and valued the shares at a higher value based on offers received for a third-party purchase of the shares. This value was approximately three (3) times higher than the Section 409A valuation.

While the Treasury Regulations include various savings provisions related to valuations for GRATs, the IRS determined that the understated valuation in CCA 202152018 was so substantial that it "casts more than just doubt upon the bona fides of the transfer to the GRAT." Ultimately, the IRS determined that the GRAT was not a qualified interest and the donor was treated as making a gift equal to the fair market value of the shares to the GRAT, as finally determined for federal gift tax purposes, with no offset for the value of the donor's retained annuity payments. This is an

---

[4] International Valuation Standards 2007.
[5] *See* CCA 202152018.

abysmal result, and, while the CCA addresses valuation in the context of a GRAT structure, we note that the lessons of CCA 202152018 should extend to many other valuation engagements. Namely, it is vital for any qualified appraisal to be commissioned for the specific purpose for which it will be used, i.e., a "fair market value appraisal for federal gift tax purposes," and to be dated as of the date of the transaction. Further, the client and the advisors must provide all relevant information to the appraiser, such as ongoing sale negotiations/offers received, and the appraisal must take into account such information that would be relevant to a third party, arms-length purchaser in making an offer to buy the subject interest.

In practice, appraisers use a wide variety of methods, many of which involve complex economic and financial analysis. Generally, these methods fall into three broad categories: methods that focus on the value of the company's assets, methods that focus on the company's earnings, and methods that focus on comparison of the company to other, marketable companies. Each of these categories is described in general terms below.[6]

[C] Valuation Methods

[1] Valuation Based on Assets

The easiest way to value a business is to subtract the company's liabilities on its balance sheet from the assets on its balance sheet. Unfortunately, this method will rarely produce an accurate value for appraisal purposes, as the value of the assets appearing on the balance sheet frequently does not reflect the current fair market value of those assets. In addition, intangible assets such as goodwill, customer lists, and trademarks generally do not appear on the balance sheet. If the values appearing on the balance sheet are adjusted to reflect fair market value, then the net value of the assets may be a reasonable indication of the company's value in the absence of any intangible assets. Revenue Ruling 59-60 suggests the use of this valuation method for investment or real estate holding companies. However, if the business sells products or services, the net value of its balance sheet assets is likely to represent only the value that would be realized on liquidation, not the value of the company as a going concern. For this reason, appraisers generally rely primarily on methods based on earnings to value such companies, although an appraisal may use the net asset value as a "floor" value.

An alternative way to use a company's book value in an appraisal is to compare the ratio between the book value and the trading price of a publicly traded company to determine the price of a company that is not publicly traded. This method is described briefly as one of the methods based on comparable companies.

---

[6] For a further description of appraisal methodology, it is useful to consult John A. Bogdanski, Federal Tax Valuation (Warren, Gorham & Lamont 1996). A more detailed treatise that deals exclusively with the valuation of closely held businesses is Shannon P. Pratt, Robert F. Reilly, and Robert P. Schweihs, Valuing a Business, The Analysis and Appraisal of Closely Held Companies (McGraw-Hill, 3d Ed.). The training manual for Appeals Officers used by the IRS, IRS Valuation Guide (CCH 1994), also contains chapters on valuing a closely held business.

[2] Valuation Based on Income Stream

Another method of determining the value of a business is to view the business as the opportunity to receive a stream of income in the future, and to ask how much a hypothetical investor would pay to receive that income stream. This approach to valuing a business is referred to generally as the *capitalization of income* or *discounted future earnings method*. There are many variations of this method, but all variations are based on the principle that the value of a company is the present value of the future income that the company will produce. The appraiser assumes that each year the company will produce a certain amount of income, and calculates the value of the company by applying a capitalization rate, or a discount rate, to the future income. In essence, this method of valuation answers the question "What would an investor pay today for the right to receive the future income of this company?"

Put simply, there are two components to the calculation of the capitalized income of a company: the expected income of the company in future years and the discount rate to be applied to that income to determine the present value of the income. The discount rate is determined by considering the current interest rates and the relative risk of the investment in the business. The value of a perpetual income stream is determined by dividing the expected annual income by the discount rate.

EXAMPLE *11-2*

Acme Company can reasonably be expected to produce annual income of $100,000 per year in the future. The appropriate discount rate for Acme is determined to be 10 percent. Under the capitalization of earnings method of valuation, the value of the company is $100,000/10%, or $1,000,000.

The measure of income of the company that is used in this calculation may vary significantly. An appraiser may use the company's net profits, cash flow, or gross revenues, depending on the circumstances of the company. The capitalization rate will differ according to the measure of income that is used.

Since the capitalization of income method values the stream of future income, it is necessary to project the company's income into the future. Projected income is based on past performance as well as material indicators of change such as new products or industry trends.

The discount rate can be thought of as the rate of return that an investor would require in order to invest in the company. The appropriate discount rate to be used to value a particular company depends primarily on two basic factors:

- *The Time Value of Money.* The profits of the company will not be available to the owner until they are earned in the future. A dollar payable in the future is worth less than a dollar paid today. A dollar paid today can be immediately invested to earn a return; consequently, a delay in payment produces a lost opportunity to receive investment returns. Furthermore, inflation may reduce the value of a dollar payable in the future.

- *Risk.* The risk that the company will not succeed in producing the expected profits will always exist.

In determining the discount rate to be applied to the earnings of a particular company, an appraiser generally begins by determining the *risk-free rate of return*. The risk-free rate of return is the rate of return that an investor would require to invest in an investment that the investor feels is virtually certain to pay off as expected, and reflects prevailing interest rates. Investments in U.S. Treasury obligations are generally considered to be risk-free investments.

After determining the risk-free rate, the appraiser will increase that rate to reflect the risk inherent in investments that are less stable than U.S. Treasury obligations. The amount of the increase will depend on the risk inherent in any equity (as opposed to debt) investment, the volatility of the market, the economic prospects for the relevant industry, and the characteristics of the particular company being valued. As the risk increases, the discount rate increases, as an investor would require a higher rate of return in order to make the investment. The higher the discount rate, the lower the value of the company.

In determining the appropriate discount rate for a particular company, appraisers often rely on published studies that survey the market generally or particular industry segments for guidance. The ultimate determination of how a particular company compares to the market generally or to an industry segment, however, is largely a matter of judgment.

[3] Valuation Based on Comparables

A simple and direct way of determining the value of a business interest is to look to the actual sale price of a similar interest. An arm's length sale of an interest in the same company to an unrelated third party may provide the best evidence of the value of the company. In many instances, such sales will not have occurred, and it will be necessary to seek sales of comparable interests in other companies. The statutory provisions governing valuation of untraded securities and both the estate and gift tax regulations include comparable sales of publicly held companies in the same or similar business as a factor to be considered in valuing a closely held business.[7] The difficulty lies in locating a publicly traded company that is similar enough to the company being valued to be useful. Differences in size, geographic location, market share, financial security, and diversification are factors that can cause significant disparities in the values of companies in the same line of business.

Rather than make a direct comparison between the share price of a publicly traded company and the share price of a closely held company, appraisers may look to the relationship between the price of a publicly traded company's stock and its earnings and dividends. For example, an appraiser might use the price/earnings ratio of one or more publicly traded companies to determine the appropriate price for a closely held company, given that company's earnings.

---

[7] IRC § 2031(b); Reg. § § 20.2031-2(f), 25.2512-2(f).

[D] Discounts and Premiums

[1] In General

The valuation methods described above serve as the starting point for valuation but in most cases the initial results must be further adjusted in order to reach fair market value. For example, an investor who would pay $1,000,000 for all of the stock in a company would not pay $100,000 for 10 percent of the stock in the same company because the 10 percent minority interest would not permit the investor to control the management, dividend payments, and other business affairs of the company. In order to value a 10 percent interest in the company, it is usually necessary to apply a discount to reflect the fact that a 10 percent interest does not convey control of the company. Similarly, if an appraiser has determined the value of a company by comparing its price/earnings ratio to a publicly traded company, the result may overstate the fair market value of the company if there is no discount to reflect the fact that an investor in the public company could sell her stock at any time, whereas there is no ready market for an interest in a closely held company. These adjustments to value can have a very substantial effect on the fair market value of a closely held company, and often play an important role in the estate planning for a business owner.

The most common adjustments that an estate planner may encounter in the context of a closely held business are:

- Minority discount;
- Control premium;
- Lack of marketability discount;
- Key person discount; and
- Blockage discount.

In assessing whether it is appropriate to apply one or more of these discounts or premiums, it is first essential to understand exactly how the preliminary valuation has been done. If the preliminary valuation is based on the value of the company as a whole, then the value of 20 percent of the company may be eligible for a minority discount. On the other hand, if the preliminary valuation is based on a comparison with the price per share of a publicly traded company, then the result will be a value of the interest as a minority interest in a publicly traded company. In such case, a minority discount would not be appropriate, because the share price of a publicly traded company already encapsulates any minority discount. A discount for lack of marketability could nonetheless be appropriate, because the price of publicly traded stock reflects the fact that shareholders have a ready market for their stock, and the owner of a closely held company has no ready market.

[2] Minority Discount

The minority discount reflects the fact that a minority owner cannot control the management of the business. The majority owner will select the management of the company. The management of the company determines who will be hired as employees, what the salaries will be, how much of the business profits will be paid out as dividends or partnership distributions, how the business should be conducted, and when the company should be liquidated. Consequently, a share of stock that is part of a controlling block is more valuable than a share of stock that is part of a minority block. Similarly, a general partnership interest is generally more valuable than the same percentage of limited partnership interest, depending on the corresponding economic rights.

A minority discount is justified only when the interest being valued does not control the business entity.[8] The control of an entity depends in part on state law and in part on the governing documents of the company (generally articles of organization and by-laws of a corporation, partnership agreement of a partnership, and operating agreement of a limited liability company). State law sets out basic rules as to the percentage of owners who are entitled to vote on certain basic issues such as liquidation. In many instances, these statutory provisions may be altered or waived by including different provisions in the company's governing documents. In determining whether a minority discount is appropriate, it is necessary to check both the relevant state law and the governing documents of the company, as well as any side agreements affecting the rights of the owners, in order to assess fully who controls company decisions.

The amount of discount that is appropriate is a factual issue that depends on the circumstances of the company being valued. Minority discounts claimed by taxpayers are frequently challenged by the IRS, and the case law in which this issue has been litigated illustrates the wide range in the amount of minority discount applied to similar companies. It is not unusual for a court to permit a minority discount in the range of 20 to 30 percent, although aggregate minority and marketability discounts have been decided as high as 66 percent.[9]

The special importance of the minority discount in the estate planning context stems from the fact that the IRS has now taken the position that there is no attribution of ownership from one family member to another in determining control of the business. The IRS announced this position in Revenue Ruling 93-12,[10] as relied upon in TAM 9449001, in which the IRS determined the value of each gift of stock from a donor to his eleven children separately, despite the stock being for the same corporation and the gifts being made simultaneously.

EXAMPLE 11-3

Father owns 30 percent of the stock of Acme Corporation, mother owns 30 percent, and their child owns 40 percent. All three family members work together in the business. Father and Mother give their stock to child, who now owns 100 percent of the stock. In valuing the two gifts, each gift will be considered separately; the stock ownership of the other members of the

---

[8] *See, e.g.*, Rev. Rul. 59-60, 1959-1 C.B. 237; Rev. Rul. 78-367, 1978-2 C.B. 249.

[9] *See, e.g.*, Ward v. Comm'r, 87 T.C. 78 (1986); Carr v. Comm'r, 49 T.C.M. 507 (1985); Frank v. Comm'r, 69 T.C.M. 225 (1995). A summary of selected cases appears as Worksheet 1 in *Summary of Discounts and Premiums in Selected Cases* (Tax Management Portfolio 831).

[10] 1993-1 C.B. 202.

family will not be attributed to the donor. The value of each gift is the value of a minority (30 percent) interest in the company and may be eligible for a minority discount.

EXAMPLE *11-4*

Father owns 100 percent of the stock of Acme Corporation. If he gives 20 percent of the stock to each of his five children, each gift will be separately valued as a 20 percent interest in the company and may be eligible for a minority discount. If father had instead died owning 100 percent of the stock and had bequeathed 20 percent of the stock to each child, the value of the stock for estate tax purposes is the value of the whole company, and no minority discount could be applied.

EXAMPLE *11-5*

Mother owns 100 percent of stock of ACME Corporation that she would like to pass on to daughter. In year one, mother gives 30 percent of the stock to daughter, and in year two she makes another gift of 30 percent of the stock. When mother dies, she leaves 40 percent to daughter in her will. Each of the gifts, as well as the bequest of the remaining 40 percent, will be eligible for a minority discount.

As the examples above illustrate, under Revenue Ruling 93-12, there can be a substantial transfer tax advantage to transferring a family business by lifetime gift rather than waiting until the death of the owner. Planners should recall, however, that there is a basic principle applicable to all of tax law that provides that it is the substance of a transaction, and not the form, that governs for tax law purposes. For example, in *Estate of Murphy v. Commissioner*,[11] a woman owned 51.41 percent of the stock in a closely-held company, and was the chairman of the board of directors. She became terminally ill, and her accountant repeatedly advised her to transfer some of her stock to her children in order to reduce her ownership of the company to less than 50 percent. Eighteen days before she died, she gave 0.88 percent of the stock to her children, reducing her stock ownership to 49.65 percent. The court held that evidence showed that the sole purpose of the gifts was to avoid transfer taxes, and nothing of substance had changed after the gifts. Citing the doctrine of substance over form, the Tax Court held that no minority discount should be applied to the stock left in the decedent's estate.

---

[11] 60 T.C.M. 645 (1990).

Similarly, the Service has also attacked gifts of minority interests as sham transactions. In *Estate of Cidulka v. Commissioner*,[12] the Tax Court found indication of an implicit understanding of future transactions and found it appropriate to step certain actions of the transaction together as the evidence showed that such actions were clearly part of a plan to eliminate the controlling shareholder's estate and gift taxes and the consideration paid was less than fair market value.

While not addressing *Murphy* directly, in the subsequent case of *Estate of Frank v. Commissioner*,[13] two days before the decedent's death, the decedent's son, acting under a power of attorney, caused roughly 18.2 percent of the decedent's 50.3 percent in corporate stock to be transferred from the decedent to the decedent's wife. Following the transfer, each of the decedent and the decedent's wife owned roughly 32 percent of the corporation's stock. The decedent died two days after the transfer, and the decedent's wife died 15 days later. Both the decedent and his wife were allowed to take a minority discount on their respective ownership.

Another way in which the Service challenges the application of a minority discount is by asserting that a minority interest has additional value as a "swing vote." In the *Estate of Winkler*,[14] the decedent owned 10 percent of the stock of a company. One family group held 40 percent of the stock and another family group held 50 percent. The Tax Court held that the decedent's 10 percent interest should be valued at a premium because the 10 percent interest could be a swing vote. The swing vote theory has not been asserted frequently by the IRS in the past, and would seem to conflict in theory to the conceptual standards of "willing buyer" and "willing seller," but may become more significant as more taxpayers claim minority discounts for gift and estate tax purposes.

It is important for estate planners to remember that if a minority discount is appropriate, it will be applied whenever the business interest is being valued for tax purposes. Taxpayers generally think of the discount as working to their advantage, which is true if the interest is being valued as a gift or part of a gross estate. The same discount will be applied, however, if the taxpayer makes a gift of a business interest to a charity and claims a charitable deduction, or if the interest is used to fund a marital trust and the estate claims a marital deduction. In certain circumstances this can be a trap for the unwary.

EXAMPLE 11-6

Jessica owns 80 percent of a corporation at her death. She leaves 40 percent of the stock to her husband, Lewis, and 40 percent of the stock to a charity. The stock will be valued as a controlling interest in valuing her gross estate. For purposes of calculating the marital deduction and the charitable deduction, however, the two 40 percent blocks of stock will be treated as minority interests and may be subject to a minority discount. In

---

[12] T.C. Memo 1996-149.

[13] T.C. Memo 1995-132.

[14] 57 T.C.M. 373 (1989).

such case, the marital and charitable deductions would not fully offset the value of the stock included in Jessica's gross estate.

[3] Control Premium

A control premium is the inverse of the minority discount. They are both based on the concept that a share of stock that is part of a controlling block is worth more than a share of stock that is not part of a controlling block.[15] A minority discount would be used when the preliminary value reflects the value of the whole company, and the interest to be valued is a noncontrolling interest.[16] A control premium may be used when the preliminary value is based on a single share or a minority interest in the company, and the interest being valued is a controlling interest.[17] The Treasury Regulations indicate that a control premium should be applied in valuing a controlling interest in a business.[18] Revenue Rule 59-60 states that "control of a corporation, either actual or in effect, representing as it does an added element of value, may justify a higher value for a specific block of stock." A control premium is most likely to be appropriate when the preliminary value was based on comparison with shares of a publicly traded company. Publicly traded shares are minority interests; therefore, if the interest being valued is a controlling interest, a control premium may be applicable. It is critical to understand fully how the preliminary value was reached in order to determine whether a control premium is warranted.

Note that while a decedent's controlling interest in a corporation shall be valued as controlling regardless of the identity of the subsequent owner or owners following administration of the decedent's estate, the per share value for purposes of estate inclusion does not necessarily determine the value of the shares for purposes of determining deductions. In *Estate of Chenoweth v. Commissioner,*[19] the decedent owned 100 percent of the stock in a corporation and left 51 percent of such stock to his wife. The Service accepted the reporting of the 100 percent interest on the decedent's federal estate tax return, but concluded that a marital deduction under IRC Section 2056 could not exceed 51 percent of the total value included for estate tax purposes. The estate argued that the 51 percent interest passing to the spouse should have a greater value due to its controlling interest. The Tax Court held that nothing prevents a different value being applied for the marital deduction than was included for gross estate purposes.

In 2020, the Tax Court sided with the taxpayers in a contested valuation case in which the IRS expert, employing a "theoretical application" approach, assessed a

---

[15] For an interesting case discussing the magnitude of a control premium, *see* Estate of Simplot, 112 T.C. 130 (1999). The Tax Court decision was reversed by the Ninth Circuit, 249 F.3d 1191 (9th Cir. 2001).

[16] *See* Bogdanski, *Federal Tax Valuation,* ¶ 4.03[1][c] (Warren, Gorham & Lamont 1996).

[17] *Id.*

[18] Reg. §§ 20.2031-2(f), 25.2512-2(f).

[19] 88 T.C. 1577 (1987).

sizeable control premium with respect to a closely held business interest that was not part of the donor's gift transaction.[20] In *Grieve v. Commissioner*, the taxpayer created two LLCs. Each LLC was funded with cash, cash equivalents, and marketable securities. In each LLC, a 0.2 percent voting interest was held by a corporation owned by the taxpayer's daughter. This interest was acquired by the corporation upon the formation of each LLC; it was not transferred from taxpayer to daughter in the form of a gift or sale transaction. Thereafter, the taxpayer transferred his 99.8 percent membership interest in each LLC to a series of estate planning vehicles, including a zeroed-out GRAT and an irrevocable trust, in exchange for a lifetime annuity. The taxpayer reported the transactions on a timely filed gift tax return, and claimed a combined 35 percent lack-of-marketability and lack-of-control discount. The IRS denied the discounts and in the ensuing litigation, the IRS expert applied a theoretical analysis in which he stated that a hypothetical purchaser would also acquire the 0.2 percent voting interest to maximize the return on his investment at a substantial control premium.

The Tax Court rejected the IRS argument, stating that the court does not "engage in imaginary scenarios as to who a purchaser might be." *Grieve* represents a significant taxpayer victory against the IRS's use of hypotheticals that are not part of the actual transaction.

[4] Lack of Marketability Discount

The discount for lack of marketability is based on the principle that a business interest that can be readily traded on a public market is worth more than a business interest that has no ready market. For example, stock of a closely held family business that is not traded on an established exchange is less valuable than stock of a publicly traded corporation.[21] In valuations of minority interests in closely held businesses, the lack of marketability discount is often combined with the minority discount to arrive at one discount that reflects both lack of control and lack of marketability. The two discounts are theoretically distinct, however, and in many instances only one of the discounts is appropriate. Further, a control analysis is independent of a lack of marketability discount. As such, marketability discounts are appropriate even for a controlling interest in a closely held business.[22]

The amount of marketability discount that is appropriate is a factual issue, and must be determined by examining the circumstances of the business in question. Appraisers frequently refer to published studies that compare the prices of readily marketable interests to the prices of interests with restricted marketability for guidance, but it is the facts relevant to the particular company that ultimately determine the appropriate discount. As in the case of minority discounts, the opinions of appraisers may differ widely as to the amount of the discount. A useful discussion of

---

[20] *See* Grieve v. Comm'r, T.C. Memo 2020-28 (Mar. 2, 2020).

[21] *See, e.g.,* Estate of Desmond v. CIR, T.C. Memo 1999-76; Rev. Rul. 77-287, 1977-2 C.B. 319; Rev. Rul. 80-213, 1980-2 C.B. 101.

[22] Estate of Desmond v. CIR, T.C. Memo 1999-76; Estate of Andrews v. CIR, 79 T.C. 938 (1982).

the factors to be considered in determining the appropriate amount of a lack of marketability discount can be found in an often cited case *Mandelbaum v. Commissioner*.[23] In *Mandelbaum*, the taxpayer's appraiser opined that a 70 to 75 percent discount for lack of marketability was justified; the court allowed a 30 percent discount. The Tax Court accepted higher discounts, including a 50 percent discount in *Estate of Huber v. Commissioner*[24] when it is determined that the appraisal is at arms-length and is the "best reference" for determining the value of gifts in question.

In some instances, the lack of marketability of a business interest may result in part from restrictions on the interest, such as a buy-sell agreement among owners or with the company or provisions in the company's governing documents that restrict transferability of the interest. As a practical matter, such restrictions may have a significant impact on the value of the business interest. These restrictions, however, are not always taken into account in valuing the interest for tax purposes in a family-owned company. For buy-sell agreements entered into before October 8, 1990 (and not modified since), the agreement will be taken into account for tax purposes only if it meets all of the following criteria:[25]

- The estate must be obligated to sell;
- The agreement must have been binding during life as well as at death;
- The agreement must set a fixed or determinable price; and
- The agreement must be a bona fide business arrangement and cannot be a device to pass the interest to the natural objects of the decedent's bounty for less than adequate consideration.

In the case of any agreement entered into (or modified) after October 8, 1990, that obligates the holder of an interest to sell at less than fair market value or otherwise restricts the use or transferability of an interest, the restriction will not be taken into account for tax purposes unless the agreement also meets the additional requirements set out in IRC Section 2703:

- The agreement is a bona fide business arrangement;
- The agreement is not a device to transfer the interest to members of the decedent's family for less than full consideration; and
- The terms of the agreement are comparable to similar arrangements entered into by persons in an arm's length transaction.

These rules are discussed more fully below in the context of buy-sell agreements.

With respect to the IRC Section 2703 substantial modification rules, on April 2, 2020, the IRS released PLR 202014006 through PLR 202014010. These PLRs addressed whether certain previous modifications to grandfathered shareholder agreements were "substantial" for purposes of IRC Section 2703. Each prior modification involved adding certain family members to the shareholder agreement upon the death of a member of an older generation. Citing Treas. Reg. § 25.2703-1(c), the Service determined that such modifications to the shareholder agreement were not "substan-

---

[23] T.C. Memo 1995-255, *aff'd*, 91 F.3d 123 (3d Cir. 1996).

[24] T.C. Memo 2006-96.

[25] *See* Rev. Rul. 59-60, 1959-1 C.B. 237; Reg. § 20.2031-2(h); Bischoff v. Comm'r, 69 T.C. 32 (1977).

tial" since they met two criteria: (i) the modification was mandated under the terms of the original, grandfathered shareholder agreement, and (ii) the added family member(s) were assigned to a generation no lower than the lowest generation occupied by individuals already party to the right or restriction.

Additionally, PLRs 202014006 through 202014010 addressed a further proposed modification in which the shares of the impacted companies would be recapitalized such that each share of common stock would be exchanged for a share of voting common stock and a certain number of nonvoting shares. Once the recapitalization was complete, certain family members would next transfer nonvoting shares to GST trusts. The intent of this transaction was to centralize voting control in family members who were active in the business while allowing wealth transfers to be made with respect to the nonvoting shares. The Service found that the recapitalization would not be a substantial modification because: (i) the recapitalization was pro rata to the shareholders' existing shares of common stock; and (ii) none of the family members to be added to the revised shareholder agreement was assigned to a lower generation.

[5] Key Person/Key Employee Discount

In many family-owned businesses, the value of the business depends largely upon the knowledge, skills, and personal contacts of one key employee. When that person dies, the value of the business may decline substantially if there is no plan for a succession in management. In such case, it may be appropriate to reduce the value of the business interest in the estate of the deceased owner by a key person discount.[26] If the company has purchased key person insurance, the amount will be taken into account in valuing the company. The court does not grant this discount when the employee's loss can be otherwise mitigated by other factors, including use of competent employees or receipt of insurance proceeds.[27]

[6] Blockage Discount

In some instances, the stock of a company may have some market, but that market can absorb only a limited amount of the stock at one time. If a large block of stock were to come onto the market at one time, the price would be depressed. In such case, a blockage discount might be appropriate. If the executor can show that the block of stock to be valued is so large in relation to the actual sales in the marketplace that it could not be liquidated in a reasonable time without depressing the market, the price at which the block could be sold as such outside the usual market may be a more accurate indication of value than market prices.[28] Blockage discounts are more frequently applied to valuations of publicly traded stock or real estate than closely held companies. On occasion, however, courts have allowed a

---

[26] *See, e.g.,* Estate of Furman v. Comm'r, 75 T.C.M. 2206 (1998).

[27] *See, e.g.,* Estate of Huntsman v. Comm'r, 66 T.C. 861 (1976), *acq.,* 1977-2 C.B. 1.

[28] Reg. § 20.2031-2(e).

blockage discount in the context of a closely held company.[29] The case of *Estate of Sawade v. Commissioner*[30] offers an excellent example of the type of data considered persuasive by the courts in determining whether a blockage discount should apply, including showing actual market sales near the valuation date that are not representative of the value of the stock, that the large size of the block precludes its sale on the market at quoted prices, and the fact that brokers could not obtain quoted prices over a reasonable time period.

[7] Other Discounts

In determining the fair market value of corporate stock, an independent third-party purchaser may consider any built-in gain on the corporation's assets. If the corporation were to sell or distribute assets with built-in gain, a corporate -level income tax on that gain would be triggered. In a few cases, courts have permitted a discount in valuing corporate stock in this situation.[31] Another factor that may result in a discount is the effect of securities laws that restrict the owner's ability to sell stock.[32]

Historically, practitioners have been wary of "multi-tiered" discounts where there is a holding company/subsidiary structure and valuation discounts are determined at each level. The Tax Court addressed one such structure favorably in *Nelson v. Commissioner*, indicating that in appropriate circumstances, multi-tiered discounts may be warranted.[33] In *Nelson*, the family had created a holding company with multiple subsidiaries, each acting as a separate operating business. The taxpayer received a 27 percent interest in the holding company upon the death of taxpayer's father. Thereafter, the taxpayer contributed the 27 percent interest to a Family Limited Partnership ("FLP") and gifted and sold the FLP to an irrevocable trust. The IRS did not challenge the taxpayer's claimed discounts at both the holding company and FLP level. Commentators have noted that this structure had several good facts, including: (i) the holding company had been established well over a decade in advance of the taxpayer's gift of the FLP interest to the irrevocable trust; and (ii) the holding company and each of its subsidiaries clearly served a legitimate business purpose. Therefore, while the FLP and subsequent transfers of FLP interests to the irrevocable trust occurred within a relatively short three-month time frame, the fact that the holding company structure had long been in place provided some additional justification for the claimed multi-tiered discounts. *Nelson* should not be viewed as the IRS blessing multi-tiered discounts—particularly where the structure is clearly created for the purpose of generating additional discounts. However, *Nelson* is

---

[29] Estate of Frank v. Comm'r, 78 T.C.M. 78 (1999).

[30] T.C. Memo 1984-626.

[31] *See, e.g.*, Eisenberg v. Comm'r, 155 F.3d 50 (2d Cir. 1998); Estate of Dunn v. Comm'r, 301 F.3d 339 (5th Cir. 2002); and Jelke v. CIR, 507 F.3d 1317 (11th Cir. 2007).

[32] *See, e.g.*, McClatchy v. CIR, 147 F.3d 1089 (9th Cir. 1998).

[33] Nelson v. Comm'r, T.C. Memo 2020-81 (June 10, 2020).

encouraging for the proposition that multi-tiered discounts are not inherently suspect and susceptible to an IRS challenge.

[8] Judicial Acceptance of "Tax-Affecting"

Tax-affecting is a valuation concept that seeks to address the inherent disparate income tax treatment between pass-through entities and C corporations. In effect, tax-affecting involves reducing the earnings of pass-through entities to account for an assumed corporate tax rate. The IRS has historically taken the position that the earnings of pass-through entities should not be tax-affected because pass-throughs pay no entity-level tax. The IRS view was embraced by the Tax Court for decades.

Two 2019 decisions significantly weakened the position of the IRS.[34] *Estate of Jones v. Commissioner* is of particular importance as it has precedential authority as a U.S. Tax Court decision. *Estate of Jones* involved a gift tax deficiency with respect to the decedent's 2009 gift tax return. The decedent (who died before trial, thus being replaced by his estate) reported gifts of closely held business interests in an S corporation and limited liability company valued at $21,000,000. The estate's valuation expert tax-affected the earnings of the S corporation and the limited liability company by applying a combined state and federal income tax rate to the earnings as if the entities were taxed as C corporations. This tax-affecting adjustment properly allowed the two subject entities to be properly contrasted with the public companies used for comparison in the valuation. The IRS, using a net asset approach, valued the transferred interests at $120,000,000 and assessed a gift tax deficiency of approximately $45,000,000.

The IRS asserted that there was no showing that the two pass-through entities at issue would lose their pass-through status and maintained that there was no judicial authority supporting tax-affecting in such valuations. In rejecting the IRS position, the Tax Court's opinion, noting that the IRS valuation experts were silent with respect to the tax-affecting discussion, held that adjusting earnings of pass-through entities to account for a corporate-level tax can be appropriate and that each such determination will depend on the facts and circumstances of the case.

[9] Valuation Impacted by Subsequent Events

It is important to note that post-valuation events can, in certain circumstances, affect the valuation. For example, in *Estate of Dieringer v. Commissioner*,[35] the decedent devised a majority interest in a closely held family corporation to a Private Family Foundation, taking a charitable deduction on the estate tax return. The estate tax valuation considered the decedent's interest in the closely held corporation on a controlling basis.

---

[34] *See, e.g.,* Kress v. United States, 382 F. Supp. 3d 820 (E.D. Wis. 2019); Estate of Jones v. Comm'r, T.C. Memo 2019-101 (Aug. 19, 2019).

[35] 917 F.3d 1135 (9th Cir. 2019), *aff'g* 146 T.C. 117 (2016).

After filing the estate tax return, the company elected to redeem the Private Foundation's interest in exchange for a series of promissory notes. A separate valuation was completed as part of the redemption transaction, in which the valuation firm was directed to value the shares on a minority basis. The Tax Court, as affirmed by the Ninth Circuit, held that this direction to utilize a minority discount materially impacted the value of the asset that ultimately was distributed to charity. Based on this change in value, the IRS reduced the estate tax charitable deduction and assessed a deficiency and accuracy related penalty against the estate.

Estate of Dieringer presents a unique case, with notably bad facts. However, it should serve as caution that, in valuing closely held business interests, planners should be cognizant of certain post-valuation circumstances that could be viewed to impact the valuation.

[10] The Effect of Lapsing Voting Rights and Restrictions on Liquidation: IRC Section 2704

[a] Principles Underlying IRC Section 2704

IRC Section 2704 is a provision of the Internal Revenue Code that can affect the valuation of an interest in a family business for gift and/or estate tax purposes. IRC Section 2704 was added to the Code in 1990 as part of Chapter 14, and, like the rest of Chapter 14 and the accompanying regulations, is highly technical.[36] Note that the effect of IRC Section 2704(b) depends on applicable state law, and thus may have different consequences in different states. As a result, in any situation in which IRC Section 2704 might apply, the estate planner should analyze the particular facts of the transaction in light of IRC Section 2704 and applicable state law to determine what the result will be. This discussion is intended primarily to flag those circumstances in which IRC Section 2704 might apply.[37]

In addition, founders should be sure to monitor any Treasury regulations aimed at curtailing the valuation discounts related to family businesses, including family limited partnerships. With this issue on the IRS's radar, founders and their advisors should pay particular attention to ensuring that each entity has a legitimate business purpose, and that senior family members do not retain control over the management of an entity that has been transferred to the next generation.

Before addressing the technical provisions of IRC Section 2704, it is helpful to review the principle that underlies the perceived problem that Congress was trying to correct when it enacted this provision. The root of IRC Section 2704 is the valuation principle that a controlling interest in a business is worth proportionately more than a

---

[36] The other parts of Chapter 14 are IRC § 2701 (which may apply to a gift of a business interest when the business has both preferred and common interests), IRC § 2702 (which may apply to split-interest gifts in trust), and IRC § 2703 (which applies primarily to buy-sell agreements).

[37] On August 2, 2016, the U.S. Treasury Department unveiled its proposed regulations targeting common valuation discounts used in estate planning. The proposed regulations were formally withdrawn on October 20, 2017.

noncontrolling interest in the same business. The minority discount and control premium discussed above result from this basic principle.

EXAMPLE 11-7

The partnership agreement of the ACK Limited Partnership provides that a limited partner has no right to participate in the management of the partnership, and cannot transfer a limited partnership interest or withdraw from the partnership without the consent of the general partner, which can be withheld in the sole discretion of the general partner. The general partner manages the partnership and can withdraw from the partnership and liquidate the partnership at any time. Generally, a 1 percent general partnership interest in ACK Limited Partnership will be worth more than a 1 percent limited partnership interest because the general partner controls the partnership.

IRC Section 2704 was enacted because the IRS believed that applying this principle in certain family situations resulted in gift and estate tax loopholes. The statute was not meant, however, to eliminate all minority discounts in the family context; its effect is limited to those situations that fall within its technical requirements.[38]

IRC Section 2704 is divided into two parts, IRC Section 2704(a), which comes into play when a right to vote or to liquidate a business interest lapses, and 2704(b), which affects the value of a business interest that involves certain restrictions on liquidation that are more limiting than applicable state law. The two parts of IRC Section 2704 are discussed separately below. Both parts of the statute apply only to interests in entities "controlled" by a family. "Controlled" is defined to mean family ownership of at least 50 percent (by vote or value) of a corporation and ownership of at least 50 percent of the capital or profits interest in a partnership, or a general partnership interest in a limited partnership.[39] Attribution rules of IRC Section 2701 apply in determining family ownership.[40]

[b] IRC Section 2704(a): Deemed Gift on the Lapse of Certain Rights

IRC Section 2704(a) was enacted to ensure that the extra value inherent in the control of a family company does not escape gift or estate tax when voting rights or the right to liquidate the company lapses instead of passing by gift or through an estate. The loophole that Congress perceived is best understood by means of an example.

---

[38] Conf. Rep. H.R. Rep. 964, 101st Cong., 2d Sess. 1137.

[39] IRC §§ 2704(c), 2701(b)(2).

[40] IRC § 2704(c)(1).

EXAMPLE *11-8*

Sara owns a 1 percent general partnership interest and an 89 percent limited partnership interest in the Sara Family Partnership. The partnership agreement provides that a general partner can liquidate the partnership. The limited partnership interest is valued at $59,000,000 if it is held by an individual who also holds the general partnership interest, and so could liquidate the partnership and obtain the liquidation value. The limited partnership interest is valued at $33,000,000 if it is held by an individual who does not also hold a general partnership interest, and so could not liquidate the partnership. On Sara's death, her general partnership interest automatically converts to a limited partnership interest, and her estate receives a 90 percent limited partnership interest. Her executor reports the partnership interest included in his estate as having an estate tax value of approximately $33,000,000, and takes the position that the value attributable to her lifetime power to liquidate the partnership escapes estate taxation because it lapsed at death.

IRC Section 2704(a) was enacted to close this perceived loophole by taxing a lapse of a liquidation right. IRC Section 2704(a) applies when

- A voting right or a liquidation right in a corporation or partnership lapses; and
- The individual who held the right, together with members of her family, controlled the company both before and after the lapse.

When these conditions are met, the effect of IRC Section 2704(a) is to increase the gift or estate tax value of an interest in the business that has been transferred, or, in some circumstances, to deem a gift to have been made. The value of the gift is the excess of the value of the interests held by the individual before the lapse over the value of the interests after the gift. This is a rather abstract notion that is best understood by another example.

EXAMPLE *11-9*

Melissa and her two children are partners in Family Retreat Limited Partnership. Each holds a 3.33 percent general partnership interest, and a 30 percent limited partnership interest. Under the partnership agreement, a general partner can liquidate the partnership. If the general partner dies, the general partnership interest will be converted to a limited partnership interest. A limited partner cannot liquidate the partnership and will be paid for his partnership interest only when the partnership is liquidated. A limited partnership interest held together with a general partnership interest is more valuable than a limited partnership interest held alone because the general partnership interest carries the liquidation right. Melissa dies and leaves her limited partnership interest to her husband. There has been a lapse of a liquidation right since, prior to Melissa's death, she could liquidate the partnership, and her husband received a limited partnership interest that does not carry that right. Under IRC

Section 2704(a), Melissa's estate includes the excess of the value of all of her interests in the partnership before her death over the interests received by her estate. In essence, the limited partnership interest will be valued for estate tax purposes as if it carried a liquidation right.

It is important to note that IRC Section 2704(a) applies only when a voting right or liquidation right is restricted or eliminated. If an individual gives away interests in a company that carry with them control of the company, IRC Section 2704(a) will not apply.

EXAMPLE *11-10*

Rachel holds 75 percent of the voting common stock of Marathon Inc. Both the by-laws of the corporation and state law provide that a two-thirds vote of shareholders is required to liquidate the corporation. Rachel gives 25 percent of the stock to each of her two children. After the gift, Rachel no longer possesses the power to liquidate the corporation, but the voting rights inherent in the stock have not lapsed. The gifts are valued for gift tax purposes without regard to IRC Section 2704.

Note that the application of IRC Section 2704(a) can result in a mismatch when the value for estate tax purposes is different from the value desired by beneficiaries. For example, if IRC Section 2704(a) is applied to include the value of a lapsed voting right in the decedent's estate, there will be a mismatch in the value actually received by the estate and the value for estate tax purposes.

[c] IRC Section 2704(b): Disregarding Certain Restrictions on Liquidation

IRC Section 2704(b) was enacted to address a different perceived loophole in the gift and estate tax valuation of family business interests. The concern that underlies IRC Section 2704(b) is that taxpayers may claim a discounted value for business interests on the basis of restrictions on liquidation that have little real economic effect in the family context. Again, the purpose of this Code section is best understood through an example.

EXAMPLE *11-11*

Lily owns 75 percent of the voting stock of Cisco Corporation and her sons own the remaining 25 percent. State law requires a vote of two-thirds of the shareholders for liquidation of a corporation, but the by-laws of Cisco require a unanimous vote. Lily dies, and her executor claims a minority discount for the stock included in her estate, citing the restriction in the by-laws that would prevent her from unilaterally liquidating the corporation: Immediately after Lily's death, her sons, who inherited the stock, vote to amend the by-laws and conform them to state law.

IRC Section 2704(b) addresses this perceived problem by disregarding certain *applicable restrictions* on liquidation in valuing a family business. A restriction on liquidation is an applicable restriction that is disregarded for transfer tax purposes if:

- The restriction is a limitation on liquidation that is more limiting than the state law applicable to the entity; and
- Either the transferor or the transferor's family can remove the restriction after the transfer or the restriction lapses by its own terms.[41]

In the above example, IRC Section 2704(b) would disregard the provision in the by-laws of Salvia Corporation that requires a unanimous vote for liquidation in valuing Lily's interest. Lily's 75 percent of the stock would be valued as a controlling interest in the corporation, and no minority discount would apply.

Since IRC Section 2704(b) is relatively new, there is little case law interpreting it, and the full ramifications of the IRC Section are not yet clear. Proposed Treasury Regulations under IRC Section 2704 were issued in 2016 but were formally withdrawn on October 27, 2017. Treasury has taken no action with respect to any further Proposed Regulations and no additional guidance is presently anticipated.

One area that is currently at the center of some debate is the differing effects of IRC Section 2704(b) on the valuation of limited partnership interests in various states.[42] An estate planner forming a limited partnership for estate planning purposes, or planning for a transfer of an interest in a limited partnership, should analyze the applicable state law, current developments in the case law, and the current position of the IRS before finalizing plans for any transfer.

[E] Special Use Valuation for Real Estate Used in Farming or Business: IRC Section 2032A

[1] Requirements

[a] In General

Prompted by fears that the estate tax would force farming families to sell off farmland in order to pay taxes, in 1976 Congress enacted a special Code section providing estate tax relief for family farms and real estate used in other family businesses. This provision, IRC Section 2032A, was drafted narrowly to remedy a specific concern about the effect of the estate tax rules on family farms (and certain other real property used in a trade or business).[43] Under the usual estate tax rules,

---

[41] Reg. § 25.2704-2(b).

[42] *See* TAMs 9723009, 9725002, 9730004, 9735003, 9842003; Mulligan, Michael, *Dealing with the IRS's Arguments Against Family Limited Partnerships*, 26 Estate Planning 195 (June 1999); Kerr v. Comm'r, 113 T.C. 449 (December 23, 1999) (discussing Texas law); Harper v. Comm'r, T.C.M. 2000-202 (discussing California law).

[43] While IRC § 2032A can apply to real property used in a trade or business other than farming, its primary use is for farms. For convenience, this discussion refers only to farms.

real property is valued at its "highest and best use" (i.e., the use that produces the highest value). Often "highest and best use" of farmland is for development, and this valuation method may produce an estate tax value that far exceeds the value of the land for farming purposes. IRC Section 2032A is intended to reduce the estate tax for families in which the next generation wishes to continue farming the land, so that the heirs are not forced to sell off land to pay estate taxes. IRC Section 2032A provides this relief by permitting an executor to elect to value farmland for estate tax purposes using a formula based on the returns actually received from farmland in the geographic area rather than on the "highest and best use" of the land. This valuation method generally will result in a lower estate tax value, and thus a lower estate tax liability. The amount by which the estate tax value of land owned by a decedent can be reduced is limited to $750,000 (indexed for inflation), or $1,230,000 in 2022.[44] If the family disposes of the land after the election has been made, or fails to continue actively farming the land, a recapture tax may apply that eliminates the prior benefit of the election.

As IRC Section 2032A was enacted to address this one particular concern, it contains numerous technical requirements to ensure that it is applicable only in the situation it was intended to address. Furthermore, the IRS tends to take a strict approach to compliance with the various requirements. As a result, if it appears that a client's estate may be eligible to elect special valuation under IRC Section 2032A, an estate planner should review the client's position and the technical requirements of the statute with great care at all stages of the estate planning and estate administration process.[45] The following discussion of IRC Section 2032A is intended primarily to assist an estate planner in determining when the provision may be applicable to a particular client.

An executor may elect to use the special valuation rules of IRC Section 2032A to value land for estate tax purposes only if all of the following requirements are met:

- The decedent was a U.S. citizen or resident;
- The property is "qualified real property," i.e.:

  — the property is located in the United States,
  — the property was "acquired from or passed from" the decedent to a "qualified heir,"
  — the property was used for a "qualified use" at the time of the decedent's death by the decedent or a member of the decedent's family;
- Fifty percent or more of the "adjusted value" of the decedent's gross estate consists of the "adjusted value" of real property that was:

  — used by the decedent or a member of the decedent's family for a "qualified use" on the date of death, and
  — was "acquired from or passed from" the decedent to a "qualified heir";

---

[44] IRC § 2032A(a)(3); Rev. Proc. 2021-45, 2021-48 I.R.B. 764, § 3.42.

[45] A good description of the technical requirements of IRC Section 2032A and the special planning opportunities and pitfalls that it presents is found in Steven E. Zumbach, Wayne E. Reames, and Dean V. Krishna, *IRC Section 2032A—Special Use Valuation Tax Management* (BNA Portfolio 833).

- Twenty-five percent or more of the "adjusted value" of the gross estate consists of real property:
  - that was "acquired from or passed from" the decedent to a "qualified heir," and
  - with respect to which the decedent or a member of the decedent's family "materially participated" during at least five of the eight years prior to retirement, disability, or death, and
  - for at least five of the eight years prior to death there was ownership and "qualified use" by the decedent or a member of the decedent's family;
- The property was owned and used for a "qualified use" by the decedent or a member of the decedent's family for at least five of the eight years prior to death;
- There was "material participation" by the decedent or a member of the decedent's family with respect to the property for at least five of the eight years prior to death, retirement, or disability;
- The executor files an election; and
- Everyone who has an interest in the property signs an agreement in which they agree to be personally liable for any recapture tax that may become due if the recapture tax applies.

The above list is a simplified version of the requirements; the regulations under IRC Section 2032A elaborate on these requirements and the numerous defined terms add an additional layer of complexity.[46] In making an initial determination as to whether land might qualify for IRC Section 2032A, most planners begin by examining the so-called "fifty percent test" and "twenty-five percent test" as a threshold matter. These two tests are described in detail below.

[b] Fifty Percent Test

The fifty percent test looks to the proportion of the decedent's estate that consists of the type of property that IRC Section 2032A is designed to protect (i.e., land that is actively used as farmland by family members). To pass the fifty percent test, at least 50 percent of the "adjusted value of the gross estate" of the decedent must consist of the "adjusted value" of property that is used for a "qualified use" by the decedent or a member of the decedent's family and that was acquired from or passed from the decedent to a "qualified heir."[47]

The "adjusted value of the gross estate" of the decedent is the gross estate (valued using the usual rules) less unpaid mortgages and debts secured by the property.[48] For purposes of this test, gifts made within three years of death (other than annual exclusion gifts) are added back into the estate.[49]

---

[46] Reg. §§ 20.2032A-1 *et seq.*
[47] IRC § 2032A(b)(1)(A).
[48] IRC § 2032A(b)(3).
[49] IRC § 2032A(d)(3).

The "adjusted value" of property is the value of the property using the usual rules, reduced by mortgages and debts secured by the property.[50]

A "qualified use" of the property is use as a farm for farming purposes, including timber, as well as other agricultural activities.[51] In order to constitute a "qualified use," the decedent or a family member must have held "an equity interest in the farm operation."[52] An issue that has arisen frequently is whether there was a "qualified use" of property if the decedent rented the land to someone else for farming purposes. If the rental is a crop sharing arrangement where the owner shares in the risk of the farming activity, then the rental generally can be a "qualified use." However, if the rental is for cash, then the arrangement generally is a "qualified use" only if it is a rental to a member of the decedent's family before the decedent's death.[53]

To pass the fifty percent test, the "qualified use" must be by the decedent or a "member of the decedent's family." For these purposes, a member of the decedent's family includes only the decedent's spouse, ancestors, a lineal descendant of the decedent's parents or a spouse of such descendant, and a lineal descendant of the decedent's spouse or a spouse of such descendant.[54]

The property at issue must be "acquired from or pass from" the decedent to a "qualified heir."[55] Property is acquired from or passes from the decedent if its basis is determined under IRC Section 1014(b) (governing the basis of property acquired from a decedent's estate), or it was acquired from the decedent's estate (which includes property purchased by a qualified heir from the decedent's estate), or it was acquired from a trust, to the extent that the property was included in the decedent's gross estate.[56] Additional complications arise if the property is held in trust. In such case the qualified heir must have a present interest in the trust. If all the income beneficiaries of a discretionary trust are qualified heirs, they will be considered to have present interests in the trust.[57] If the trust provides for successive interests, then under the regulations the special use valuation may be elected only if all of the interests in the trust are held by qualified heirs (and they all join in the election).[58] A "qualified heir" is a member of the decedent's family.

---

[50] IRC § 2032A(b)(3).

[51] IRC § 2032A includes other business uses as "qualified uses." However, the primary importance of IRC § 2032A is in its application to farming, and this description will be limited to that context.

[52] Reg. § 20.2032A-3(b).

[53] The term "qualified use" is also used in determining when the recapture tax is triggered. In that context, a "qualified use" includes a cash rental by a surviving spouse or lineal descendant to a family member. IRC § 2032A(c)(7)(E).

[54] IRC § 2032A(e)(2).

[55] IRC § 2032A(b)(1)(A).

[56] IRC § 2032A(e)(9).

[57] IRC § 2032A(g).

[58] Reg. § 20.2032A-8(a).

[c] Twenty-Five Percent Test

Another requirement for eligibility for special use valuation is the twenty-five percent test. At least 25 percent of the decedent's adjusted estate must consist of the net value of real property that (1) was "acquired from the decedent" by a "qualified heir," and (2) meets the "qualified use" and "material participation" tests described below.[59] The definitions of "acquired from the decedent" and "qualified heir" are as described above.

[d] Qualified Use Test

Another requirement for special use valuation is that both on the date of death and during at least five of the eight years preceding the decedent's death, the real property involved was owned and used for a "qualified use" by the decedent or a member of the decedent's family.[60] For these purposes, a "qualified use" means farming or use in another trade or business.[61] A residence may be included if it is occupied on a regular basis by the owner, lessee, or an employee of the owner or lessee for the purpose of operating the farm or business.[62] There has been much litigation and discussion concerning when a lease arrangement is a "qualified use." In general, a lease in which the decedent or a family member shared in the economic risk of the farming operation through a crop sharing arrangement may be a qualified use, but a cash lease to an unrelated party will not be a qualified use.[63]

[e] Material Participation Test

During periods aggregating five of the eight years preceding the decedent's death, the decedent or a member of the decedent's family must have "materially participated" in the operation of the farm.[64] This requirement is intended to ensure that the benefits of IRC Section 2032A are limited to families who are actively engaged in farming on a full-time basis rather than families that hold land as a passive investment. If the decedent or a family member is directly involved in the farming activity, then the requirement is met if the individual is engaged in the business 35 or more hours per week, or such fewer number of hours as is sufficient to fully manage the operation.[65] If this standard for direct involvement is not met, then material participation can be established by an arrangement providing for actual participation in the production or management of production if the standards under

---

[59] IRC § 2032A(b)(1)(B).

[60] IRC §§ 2032A(b)(1)(A)(i) and (b)(1)(C)(i).

[61] IRC § 2032A(b)(2).

[62] IRC § 2032A(e)(3).

[63] Reg. § 20.2032A-3(b). *See* Zumbach, Reames, and Krishna, *IRC Section 2032A—Special Tax Valuation, Tax Management* (BNA Portfolio 833).

[64] IRC § 2032A(b)(1)(C).

[65] *See* Reg. § 20.2034A-3(e)(1).

the IRC Section 1402 regulations (governing the definition of self-employment) are met.[66] The principal factors to be considered in determining whether the material participation test has been met are physical work and participation in management decisions.

[f] Recapture Tax

In order to ensure that the benefits of IRC Section 2032A are available only to families who continue a family farming operation, the statute provides for a recapture of estate tax benefits if the family ceases to operate the farm within ten years after the decedent's death. The recapture tax may be triggered if:[67]

- The qualified heir disposes of the property to someone other than a member of the qualified heir's family;
- There is a cessation of the "qualified use" by a qualified heir holding an equity interest in the property; or
- For any eight-year period that ends after the decedent's death there are periods of time aggregating three years during which there was not material participation by the decedent or a member of the decedent's family (for periods before the death) or a qualified heir or a member of the qualified heir's family (for periods after the death).

The qualified heir is personally liable for the recapture tax.

§11.04 STATUTORY RELIEF TO AID IN PAYMENT OF ESTATE TAX

One concern that many business owners share is reconciling their desire to retain their businesses until death while also avoiding the need to sell the business to pay estate taxes. Such a forced sale is not aligned with their business succession goals. To address this paradox, there are several tools available to the estate planner.

[A] Installment Payments of Estate Tax

Often, the value of a closely held business is disproportionately large in relation to all other assets of the owner's estate. If the family does not wish to sell the business, payment of estate tax can create a difficult cash flow issue. The Code, however, provides a measure of statutory relief designed to assist those inheriting a family business. This provision, IRC Section 6166, permits the executor to defer the payment of estate taxes for up to five years after the due date of the estate tax. During this initial time period, the estate is required to pay only the interest on the deferred tax. Thereafter, the executor can then pay the tax in up to ten annual installments. The interest rate on the deferred tax attributable to the first $1,000,000, adjusted for

---

[66] Reg. § 20.2032-3(e).
[67] IRC § 2032A(c).

inflation, of the taxable value of the business interest is 2 percent. The interest rate on the remaining deferred tax is 45 percent of the rate applicable to underpayments of tax.[1]

The effect of an IRC Section 6166 election is to permit the estate to, in essence, borrow from the government on favorable terms so that the business does not need to be immediately sold to pay the estate taxes due. In such situations, the business ultimately will be the source of the cash necessary to pay the estate tax. Making an IRC Section 6166 election permits the business to use its capital for business purposes, rather than estate tax payment, during the deferral period.

The election to defer payment of estate taxes is only available if certain requirements are satisfied. In order to qualify for estate tax deferral under IRC Section 6166, (1) the decedent had to be a U.S. citizen or resident, and (2) more than 35 percent of the decedent's adjusted gross estate had to have consisted of an interest in a closely held business. The business interest may be in the form of a proprietorship, a partnership (if 20 percent of the partnership capital interest is included in the decedent's estate or the partnership has no more than 15 partners), or a corporation (if 20 percent of the value of the voting stock of the corporation is included in the decedent's estate or the corporation had no more than 15 shareholders). For decedents dying after December 31, 2001, the maximum number of partners or shareholders is 45.[2] It is important to note that the company must carry on an active trade or business; as a general rule, passive assets are excluded in determining whether the 35 percent test is satisfied.[3] For example, a family investment portfolio of marketable securities housed in an LLC is unlikely to qualify as an active trade or business and is ineligible for IRC Section 6166 deferral.

The amount of estate tax that can be deferred under IRC Section 6166 is limited to a proportionate share of the total tax due. Such amount which qualifies for deferral is equal to the value of the business interest included in the estate divided by the adjusted gross estate. Thus, if the business interest constitutes 40 percent of the adjusted gross estate, then the executor can elect to defer 40 percent of the total estate tax due.[4]

EXAMPLE *11-12*

Kevin died leaving an adjusted gross estate of $10,000,000. One of the assets included in his estate was his wholly owned business, which had a

---

[1] **§ 11.04** The interest is no longer deductible for either estate or income tax purposes. Amendments to IRC § 6166 enacted in the 1997 Taxpayer Relief Act lowered the interest rate on deferred payments and denied the deduction for interest paid.

[2] 2001 Act, § 571(a); IRC § 6166(b)(1).

[3] IRC §§ 6166(b)(8)(D), 6166(b)(9). For decedents dying after December 31, 2001, certain finance and lending businesses may be treated as active trades or businesses that qualify for installment payments under IRC § 6166. The initial five-year deferral of tax is not available to a finance or lending business, however, and installment payments must be made over five years rather than over ten years. 2001 Act § 572, IRC § 6166(b)(10).

[4] IRC § 6166(a)(2).

fair market value of $6,000,000. The estate tax due is $4,000,000. Since the business constitutes 60 percent of his adjusted gross estate, his executor can elect to defer payment of 60 percent of the tax, or $2,400,000.

Payment of estate taxes deferred under IRC Section 6166 will be accelerated if a portion of the business interest is sold or disposed. Additionally, the deferral terminates if cash or assets are withdrawn from the business and the aggregate of the sales, dispositions, and withdrawals is at least 50 percent of the business interest.[5] Payments may also be accelerated if the estate fails to make a scheduled payment of principal or interest. Finally, if the estate has undistributed net income in any year in which an installment payment is due, the estate must apply the undistributed net income to payment of the estate tax.

In addition to qualification under IRC Section 6166, another method of deferring payment of estate tax over an extended period of time is through a "Graegin note," so named based upon the case *Estate of Graegin v. Commissioner.*[6] In *Graegin*, the estate consisted primarily of stock in a family-owned company held in a revocable trust. In order to avoid selling the company stock, the executors borrowed funds from a wholly owned subsidiary. The court allowed deduction of loan interest by the estate as a reasonable and necessary expense of estate administration. The use of similar "Graegin notes" has survived multiple IRS challenges.[7] Among several requirements, the Graegin note must be in writing, provide for a market rate of interest, be payable over a specific term, and the estate must be able to show that it was necessary to borrow these funds to meet its obligations. Graegin loans can be preferable to an IRC Section 6166 deferral in some situations. For example, the estate may not meet the 35 percent test required by IRC Section 6166, and there is greater flexibility with regard to both the time period of payments and the payment terms. In today's high income tax rate environment, it is critical to "run the numbers" to analyze which strategy is most beneficial to an estate, taking into account income and estate taxes, when considering both a Graegin loan and an election under IRC Section 6166.

[B] Redemptions of Stock to Pay Estate Tax

[1] In General

One source of cash to pay the estate tax of a decedent whose estate consisted primarily of stock in a closely-held corporation may be cash held in the corporation. In some situations, an executor can raise the cash necessary to pay estate taxes by redeeming all or a portion of the stock held by the estate in a manner that does not generate income tax consequences. This is due to the fact that any stock included in the estate of the decedent will have an income tax basis equal to its fair market value

---

[5] IRC § 6166(g).

[6] T.C. Memo 1988-477.

[7] *See* Estate of Thompson v. Comm'r, T.C. Memo 1998-325; Estate of Sturgis v. Comm'r, T.C. Memo 1987-415; and Estate of Gilman v. Comm'r, T.C. Memo 2004-286.

on the date of death (or the alternate valuation date). This is commonly referred to a step-up in basis. Consequently, a sale of the stock at that price will not generate an income tax liability for the estate, provided that the transaction is treated for tax purposes as a sale or exchange. The problem that may occur in a family held corporation is that the cash distributed from the corporation may be treated as a dividend rather than as a sale for income tax purposes. If the corporation is organized as a C corporation, there could be significant income tax consequences. In such circumstance, instead of a tax-free sale of the stock, the entire cash distribution would be treated as a dividend under IRC Section 302, which is taxed as ordinary income to the estate. (The rules that govern the income tax treatment of redemptions of stock in a family corporation contained in IRC Section 302 are discussed below.)

To address this potential problem, a special Code section was enacted to permit an estate holding stock in a family corporation to raise cash for payment of federal or state estate taxes (as well as interest thereon, and funeral and administrative expenses allowable as deductions under IRC Section 2053) without adverse income tax consequences. IRC Section 303 provides that a distribution from a corporation in exchange for stock will be treated for income tax purposes as a sale (and not a dividend) if certain requirements are satisfied. IRC Section 303 will treat a redemption of stock as a sale and not a taxable dividend if the following criteria are met:

- More than 35 percent of the decedent's estate (after deductions) consists of stock in the redeeming corporation;

- The proceeds of the redemption do not exceed the decedent's estate and inheritance tax liability, plus funeral and administration expenses allowable as deductions; and

- The stock is redeemed within a requisite time period.

Life insurance can be an ideal funding mechanism to provide the redemption payment. That being said, practitioners need to document the transaction accordingly. Life insurance proceeds received by the entity on the death of the shareholder can cause an increase in the value of the entity (reportable on the decedent shareholder's estate tax return, potentially increasing the liability); therefore, it is imperative that any insurance owned by the entity must be committed in a valid buy-sell, redemption or similar agreement obligating the entity to use the insurance proceeds to purchase the interest in the entity held by the decedent's estate. This should avoid the life insurance proceeds being viewed as an asset of the entity (thus, increasing the value of the entity for estate tax reporting purposes) due to the offsetting liability owed to the decedent shareholder's estate.

Further, practitioners advising with respect to entity owned life insurance must also plan for any attendant income and gift consequences depending on the payment of the life insurance premiums (i.e., paid by the shareholder or the entity during the shareholder's lifetime). Depending on the nature and source of the premium payments, the decedent and the entity may be in a deemed "split-dollar" life insurance arrangement, which could cause the shareholder to make a gift to the entity and/or receive phantom compensation income on the payment of insurance premiums.

[2] More Than 35 Percent of Estate Must Consist of Stock

The benefits of IRC Section 303 are available to an estate only if more than 35 percent of the decedent's estate consisted of stock in the redeeming corporation. In determining the percentage test, the value of the stock is considered in relation to the value of the decedent's gross estate reduced by deductions allowable under IRC Sections 2053 (debts and expenses of the estate) and 2054 (losses of the estate).[8] If the decedent owned stock in two or more corporations, then the stock of the corporations may be consolidated and treated as stock of a single corporation for purposes of the 35 percent test if the decedent owned at least 20 percent of the value of the outstanding stock of each corporation.[9]

EXAMPLE *11-13*

Nancy's estate consists of 50 percent of the stock in Alpha Corporation, worth $2,000,000, and 50 percent of the stock of Beta Corporation, worth $5,000,000. The value of Nancy's estate, after deductions, is $17,000,000, and 35 percent of that amount is $5,950,000. Nancy's estate does not include enough of the stock of either Alpha or Beta to qualify for IRC Section 303 treatment under the general rule. However, since Nancy owns more than 20 percent of each of Alpha and Beta, the stock of the two corporations is aggregated in applying the 35 percent test. When the stock of the two companies is aggregated, the resulting value exceeds 35 percent of Nancy's estate. As a result, a redemption of stock by either Alpha or Beta is eligible for IRC Section 303 treatment. The amount of redemption proceeds that is eligible for IRC Section 303 treatment will be limited by the amount of estate tax and funeral and administration expenses.

[3] Limits on the Amount of Stock Redeemed

IRC Section 303 limits the amount of stock that is eligible for special treatment to the funds needed to pay the decedent's estate taxes as well as funeral and administration expenses allowable as estate tax deductions.[10]

EXAMPLE *11-14*

Laurence's gross estate is valued at $800,000 which consists of stock in a family corporation worth $450,000 and other assets worth $350,000. His taxable estate is $500,000, and estate taxes and funeral and administration

---

[8] IRC § 303(b)(2).
[9] *Id.*
[10] IRC § 303(a).

expenses total $225,000. If his estate sells all of his stock back to the corporation, $225,000 of the proceeds will be treated as proceeds of a sale under IRC Section 303. The remaining $225,000 will be taxed either as a dividend or as proceeds of a sale as determined under the traditional rules in IRC Sections 301 and 302.

IRC Section 303 does not require that the proceeds of a redemption actually be applied to payment of estate tax. However, the benefit of IRC Section 303 is limited to the amount actually paid within one year in the case of redemptions occurring more than four years after the date of death.[11]

[4] Seller of Stock Must Bear the Burden of Estate Tax

The estate is not the only shareholder who is eligible to apply the benefits of IRC Section 303. For example, if stock is received by a beneficiary as part of the residuary estate that bears the burden of taxes, then a redemption by a residuary legatee may qualify for IRC Section 303 treatment. A redeeming shareholder who does not bear the burden of any of the estate taxes or expenses, however, is not eligible for IRC Section 303 treatment.[12] Thus, if a beneficiary of an estate receives stock as a specific bequest that does not bear the burden of estate tax or expenses, then IRC Section 303 will not apply to a redemption from that beneficiary.

[5] Time Limitations on Redemptions

Generally, IRC Section 303 treatment is available only for redemptions made:[13]

- Within the three-year statute of limitations period applicable to the estate tax return as filed; or
- Within the period for payment of estate tax under IRC Section 6166, if an election has been timely made by the executor.

If estate tax is being paid under the special deferral provisions of IRC Section 6166, and redemptions occur more than four years after the decedent's death, the amount eligible for IRC Section 303 treatment is limited to the amount of tax and/or estate expenses actually paid within one year of distribution.[14] Note that, if the corporation issues an installment note as part of the redemption proceeds, the receipt of the note is treated as the date of redemption.[15]

---

[11] IRC § 303(b)(4).
[12] IRC § 303(b)(3).
[13] IRC § 303(b)(1).
[14] IRC § 303(b)(4).
[15] Rev. Rul. 65-289, 1965-2 C.B. 86.

§11.05 BUY-SELL AGREEMENTS

[A] In General

A buy-sell agreement is a contractual agreement among the owners of a business entity, or among the owners and the entity itself, that provides for the purchase of an owner's interest in the entity under specified circumstances. Buy-sell agreements take many different forms and serve many purposes. In the estate planning context, most business owners are motivated by two principal goals. First, owners often wish to control the future ownership of the business. For example, some owners believe that ownership of the business should remain with those individuals who are active in the business. A buy-sell agreement that obligates an owner (or the owner's estate) to sell upon death or retirement to the continuing owners/managers of the business can accomplish this goal. Moreover, if the founder of a business has made gifts of business interests to his or her children and their spouses in order to reduce his or her estate, he or she may wish to set in place a buy-sell agreement that obligates the spouses of his or her children to sell their interests to family members in the case of a divorce, thus avoiding the possibility of a hostile ex-spouse as a part owner of the family business.

The second principal reason to establish a buy-sell agreement is to provide a market for the sale of the owner's interest in the business upon death or retirement. It may be necessary for an owner's estate to sell a portion or all of the owner's business interest in order to raise cash for payment of estate taxes. An agreement that obligates the remaining owners or the entity itself to purchase the interest of a deceased owner can ensure liquidity for the estate. The need to provide for a market for an interest in a closely held business may arise aside from a need for estate taxes. For example, instead of paying dividends, many family businesses pay the owner/managers substantial salaries, and any extra cash is reinvested in the business. A retired owner, or an heir who does not work in the business, may wish to sell his or her interest in order to reinvest the proceeds in a vehicle that will produce current income. If the heir or retired owner is a minority owner, there may be little incentive for the other owners to pay a fair price to cash out the minority interest. A buy-sell agreement that permits the retired owner or heir to exercise the right to require the company to purchase the interest can avoid inequities in bargaining power in this situation.

In planning for a buy-sell agreement, the estate planner should explore with the client in some detail the operations and future prospects of the company, the roles played in the company by other owners and family members, the financial situation of potential purchasers of the client's interest, and the projected liquidity needs of the client's estate. The estate planner can use this information to design a buy-sell agreement that best suits the client's goals.

Once the buy-sell agreement has been negotiated, established, and funded, it is crucial that all parties monitor the terms on a regular basis because circumstances change. For example, the value of the company may change, the company may change its form, certain key employees may leave and others may join, partners may become incapacitated or die, and relevant state and federal laws may change. For these reasons, it is critical to include amendment provisions in the buy-sell agreement. It may also be beneficial to include provisions requiring the parties to reapprove the terms after specified periods of time and/or following certain key events such as those cited above.

[B] Form of Agreement

The basic choices that a client needs to make in designing a buy-sell agreement are:

- What event or events will trigger a sale;
- Whether the buyers or sellers have an obligation, or are given the option of buying or selling the interest;
- Whether the other owners or the company will be the purchaser;
- How the purchase will be funded; and
- What the purchase price will be.

[C] Triggering Events

The trigger for the obligation to buy or sell is dependent on the purpose of the agreement. If the parties wish to limit ownership of the business to those who are active in the business, then any separation from the company should trigger the sale. If the agreement is intended to provide liquidity at retirement for a founder of the company, then retirement would be an appropriate trigger. If the agreement is intended to provide liquidity for payment of estate taxes, then death might trigger the obligation. If the parties simply want to keep ownership of the company within the family, then triggers might include any attempted transfer to a third party, bankruptcy, foreclosure, and transfer by court order or by operation of law.

[D] Mandatory Versus Optional Sales

One of the important design features to consider is whether parties will have the right to act or rather whether they will be obligated to act. In structuring buy-sell agreements, buyers and sellers need not be subject to the same rules. Thus, the agreement could provide that a retiring owner or his or her estate has the option to require the company or other owners to buy the business interest, but that the owner (or the owner's estate) is not obligated to sell. Alternatively, an agreement could provide that the company or the other owners have the option to require a retired owner (or the owner's estate) to sell his or her interest, but that the company or other owners are not obligated to buy. A third alternative is an agreement that mandates all parties to complete the sale transaction when the relevant conditions are met. Finally, an agreement could simply provide that each owner of the business must offer to sell his or her interest in the business to the other owners or the company before selling it to a third party. The purposes of the agreement and the circumstances of the parties will determine which of these options is most suitable. An agreement may also provide that a sale is mandatory under certain conditions (such as an attempted transfer to a third party) but optional in other circumstances (such as retirement). In many instances the agreement may provide for differing options upon varying triggering events.

[E] Identifying the Purchaser

One of the central decisions in designing a buy-sell agreement is whether the company or the other owners of the business will be the purchasers. If the company will be the purchaser, the agreement is typically called a redemption agreement. If the other owners will be the purchasers, the agreement is termed a cross-purchase agreement. Redemption agreements and cross-purchase agreements have different tax and business implications. Depending on the circumstances, one may be more desirable than the other. Each of these is discussed separately below.

[1] Cross-Purchase Agreement

Under a cross-purchase agreement it is the remaining owners of the business who purchase the interest of the retiring or deceased owner. For income tax purposes the transaction is treated as a sale or exchange, and the purchasers take the acquired interest with a basis equal to the purchase price paid.[1] If the remaining owners plan to sell their interests at some point, the increase in basis in the acquired interest may be a significant advantage of a cross-purchase agreement over a redemption agreement. In a partnership or an S corporation, the increase in basis may be advantageous to the remaining owners even if they do not intend to sell the interest because an increase in basis increases the distributions they can receive without tax.[2]

The seller of the interest generally recognizes capital gain on the sale. If the sale takes place after the death of the owner, however, the basis of the interest will have been stepped-up to its fair market value as of the date of the decedent's death.[3] In these circumstances the estate will likely recognize little or no gain.

A cross-purchase agreement can be more flexible than a redemption agreement. The agreement may be limited to only specific business owners rather than providing for all of the owners to acquire the selling owner's interest proportionately. If the company redeems the selling owner's interest, there is no way to avoid a proportionate increase in the ownership of each of the remaining owners, which is not always the most desirable result.

EXAMPLE *11-15*

Scott and Lesli founded a corporation and each initially owned 50 shares of stock. Over the years, each sold ten shares of stock to key employees, and gave shares of stock to a family trust for which there is an independent trustee. Currently Scott and Lesli each hold 30 shares, the two employees each hold ten shares, and each of the trusts holds ten shares. If

---

[1] **§11.05** IRC §1012.

[2] A shareholder of one S corporation and a partner of a partnership generally are not subject to income tax on the receipt of cash distributions that do not exceed his or her basis in the stock or the partnership interest.

[3] IRC §1014.

on Scott's death, Lesli can purchase Scott's stock directly, then Lesli will own 60 of the 100 shares outstanding, and will therefore control the company. If the company purchases Scott's stock, Lesli will own only 30 of 70 shares outstanding, or 43 percent, and will not control the company.

In a cross-purchase agreement, the selling owner depends on the credit of the other owners rather than the company to pay the purchase price. This may be either an advantage or a disadvantage, depending on the financial condition of the other owners and of the company. If the purchase will be funded with life insurance, a cross-purchase arrangement can become very cumbersome if there are more than two owners, as further discussed below.

[2] Redemption Agreement

[a] Advantages and Disadvantages

Under a redemption agreement, the company is the purchaser of the ownership interest. Clients often find the concept of a redemption agreement attractive because it can be simpler than a cross-purchase agreement, especially if the purchase is to be funded by insurance. Redemptions, however, have clear drawbacks in certain circumstances and the situation should be carefully analyzed before the parties commit themselves to a redemption agreement.

One appealing feature of a redemption agreement is that it is the company's credit that will support the purchase. The co-owners of a business generally know more about the financial status of the company than they do about the other owners' personal financial status, and therefore are more comfortable with relying on the company's credit. If a loan will be used to finance the purchase it may be easier for the company than for individual owners to secure advantageous loan terms. State law, however, can affect the company's ability to repurchase an owner's interest; for example, some state statutes prohibit a corporation from redeeming stock if the corporation does not have adequate capital reserves or does not meet the statutory test for solvency.

A redemption agreement can be substantially simpler than a cross-purchase if the purchase will be funded by insurance. In order to fund a cross-purchase agreement, each of the owners must purchase insurance on the life of each of the other owners. If the company will purchase the interests, it is necessary to buy only one policy on the life of each shareholder (to be owned by the company). Furthermore, in a redemption agreement, the cost of the policies will be allocated among all the owners, which can be an advantage if insurance on one owner is significantly more expensive than the policies on the other owners.

If the company is a C corporation (or is an S corporation that formerly was a C corporation) then a redemption can have serious negative income tax consequences to the selling shareholder. A distribution from a corporation to a shareholder in exchange for stock can be classified for income tax purposes either as a shareholder sale of the stock or as a dividend paid by the corporation.[4] If the transaction is treated as a sale, the selling shareholder will recognize capital gain in an amount equal to the amount received for the stock less his basis in the stock. If the selling shareholder is the owner's estate, the basis of the stock will be equal to its value for estate tax purposes, and in most circumstances the estate will recognize little or no gain. If, however, the distribution is characterized as a dividend as opposed to a sale, then the entire distribution will be treated as dividend income to the selling shareholder. Even if the tax rates applicable to capital gains and dividend income are the same, the difference in the amount of taxable income can be significant because in a dividend transaction, the selling shareholder (or his or her estate) does not enjoy the benefit of any tax-free recovery of basis.

EXAMPLE *11-16*

> Amy's estate holds 50 percent of the stock in Concord Corporation (a C corporation), and A's children hold the remaining 50 percent. Amy's stock was valued at $1,000,000 for estate tax purposes. One year after Amy's death, in 2022, the corporation purchases Amy's stock from Amy's estate for $1,200,000, its fair market value at the time of the sale. If the transaction is treated as a sale, Amy's estate will recognize $200,000 in long-term capital gain. If the transaction is treated as a dividend, Amy's estate will recognize $1,200,000 in dividend income.

The magnitude of the differential in tax treatment makes it essential for an estate planner to determine the likely tax consequences of a redemption before recommending use of a redemption agreement.

[b] Rules for Classifying a Distribution from a Corporation

The rules for classifying a distribution from a corporation as a dividend or a sale or exchange of the shareholder's stock are contained in IRC Section 302. IRC Section 302 provides that a distribution will be treated as a dividend unless it meets one of three statutory tests. Two of these tests, known as the substantially disproportionate test and the complete termination test, are used commonly in the estate planning context because they are quantitative tests and the outcome is predictable. Estate planners rarely rely on the third test, known as the dividend equivalence test, because it sets out a vague standard and it is impossible to be certain of the outcome.

While an estate cannot avoid family attribution of stock ownership for purposes of the tests for classification as a dividend, Congress did enact IRC Section 303, a special relief provision that permits a redemption from an estate to qualify for sale treatment to the extent that the estate needed to cover estate taxes.[5]

---

[4] IRC § 302.
[5] IRC § 303 is discussed in § 11.04[B] *supra*.

[i] Substantially Disproportionate Test. Under the substantially disproportionate test, a distribution will not be treated as a dividend if after the transaction the shareholder holds less than 50 percent of the combined total voting power of the corporation and the shareholder's percentage interest in the corporation is 80 percent or less of the shareholder's interest in the corporation before the transaction.[6]

EXAMPLE *11-17*

Heidi owns 500 shares of the stock of a corporation and Bob owns the remaining 500 shares. Heidi agrees to sell half of her shares to the corporation at her retirement. Before the sale, Heidi owned 500/1,000 shares, or 50 percent of the stock. After the transaction, Heidi will own 250/750 shares, or 33.3 percent of the stock. Her stock ownership after the transaction is 66.6 percent of her stock ownership before the transaction, and therefore the transaction will be treated as a sale and not as a dividend.

It is easier to satisfy the substantially disproportionate test if all of the shareholders of a corporation are unrelated. It becomes much more difficult to qualify a distribution as a sale under this test if the shareholders are related because the Internal Revenue Code contains special provisions that attribute stock ownership from one family member to another for purposes of applying this test.[7] For example, all of the stock owned by a shareholder's spouse, parents, children, and grandchildren (but not siblings) is attributed to the shareholder. This rule cannot be circumvented by transferring stock to an entity, because stock held by a trust or estate, and, in certain circumstances, stock held by a corporation or partnership, is attributed to the beneficiaries of the trust or estate and the owners of the corporation or partnership.[8] In addition, stock held by a shareholder may be attributed to a trust, estate, corporation, or partnership of which the shareholder is a beneficiary or owner.[9] The attribution rules are detailed and complex, and can produce results that seem counterintuitive.

EXAMPLE *11-18*

Jon owns 500 shares of the stock of a corporation, his mother owns 100 shares, and each of his four children own 100 shares. At Jon's retirement, the corporation redeems 250 of his shares. Before the transaction, Jon owned 500/1000 shares, or 50 percent of the corporation. After the transaction Jon owns outright 250/750 shares, or 33.3 percent of the corpora-

---

[6] IRC § 302(b)(2).
[7] IRC §§ 302(c), 318(a).
[8] IRC § 318(a)(1).
[9] IRC § 318(a)(2).

tion. If the attribution rules did not apply, the transaction would satisfy the substantially disproportionate test because Jon has reduced his outright ownership to 66.6 percent of what he owned before the transaction. The attribution rules, however, will treat Jon as owning all of the stock held by his mother and children. Consequently, he is treated as holding 1,000/1,000 shares, or 100 percent of the corporation before the transaction, and 750/750 shares, or 100 percent of the corporation after the transaction. The transaction will be treated as a dividend.

[ii] Complete Termination Test. The second test for nondividend classification, the complete termination test, may be easier to meet in some family situations. The complete termination test classifies a transaction as a sale rather than as a dividend if after the transaction the selling shareholder no longer holds any interest in the corporation. Again, the attribution rules apply, which makes this test very difficult to satisfy if the shareholders of the corporation are related. Congress recognized, however, that if there were not exceptions to this rule, a shareholder could never qualify for sale treatment when a family corporation redeemed all of the shareholder's stock. Therefore, an exception to the general rule was enacted that permits a shareholder to avoid family attribution if the shareholder sells all of his or her stock to the corporation and terminates all connections to the corporation, including employment, and does not reacquire any interest in the corporation for the following ten years.[10]

EXAMPLE *11-19*

Steven owns 500 shares of the stock of a corporation, his mother owns 100 shares, and each of his four children own 100 shares. At Steven's retirement, the corporation redeems all of his shares and terminates all of his positions with the company. The transaction will be treated as a sale of his stock for tax purposes.

The exception that permits a redemption of all of the stock of a retiring shareholder to qualify for sale treatment if the shareholder terminates all other connections to the corporation does not apply when a family corporation redeems all the stock held by estate of which the remaining family shareholders are the beneficiaries.

EXAMPLE *11-20*

Jack's estate holds 500 shares of stock in a family corporation, and his five children own the remaining 500 shares. Jack's wife and children are the

---

[10] IRC § 302(b)(3), (c)(2).

beneficiaries of his estate. The corporation redeems all of the stock from Jack's estate. The stock held by Jack's children is attributed to the estate, and the estate is treated as if it still owned 50 percent of the stock. The special exception that prevents attribution in some instances does not apply to attribution to an estate. The transaction does not qualify as a sale, and money received by the estate will be taxed as a dividend.

[F] Setting the Price

There are many alternatives for setting the selling price in a buy-sell agreement. In choosing among them the estate planner should consider:

- The economic effect on the parties (i.e., will the seller receive fair market value for the interest);
- Whether the agreement will fix the estate tax value of the interest (IRC Section 2703, discussed below, may apply for this purpose); and
- The transaction costs of applying the pricing method.

Three of the most common methods for setting the purchase price in a buy-sell agreement are a fixed price, a formula price, and a requirement that an appraisal be obtained. Each has its own advantages and disadvantages.

Under a fixed price method, the parties set the sale price at the time of the agreement. The primary advantage of using a fixed price in a buy-sell agreement is that it is simple and certain. As a result, the transaction costs in setting the price and applying it are low. However, as most businesses fluctuate significantly in value over time, a fixed price is unlikely to reflect the fair market value of the business interest at the time it takes effect. As a further consequence, a fixed price may be disregarded for estate tax purposes under IRC Section 2703, particularly in the context of a buy-sell agreement between related parties under IRC Section 267, which could lead to the unfortunate situation of an estate that is obligated to sell at a low price but required to pay estate tax based on a higher value of the business interest.[11] One means of dealing with potential changes in value of the business is to require the parties to reset the purchase price periodically, though this may still not address the potential for the IRS revaluing the business interest in a transaction between related parties. This can provide a simple solution, but only if the parties remember to do so on a regular basis.

Some business owners tie the purchase price in a buy-sell agreement to the book value of the business at the time of the sale. A method of this type again has the advantage of relative simplicity. A valuation method based on book value, however, will not reflect the fair market value of many types of businesses because it does not take into account certain factors such as the earning potential of the business. This methodology is more likely to be appropriate if the value of the company is closely tied to the value of its assets (such as, e.g., a company whose primary assets consist of

---

[11] *See* § 11.05[H] *infra.*

real estate). Even in such a case, however, the value obtained may be distorted because book value generally is based on original cost of the assets less depreciation rather than the fair market value of the assets. As a result, there may be a mismatch between book value and estate tax value.

A formula price is one where the parties do not establish a dollar amount, but instead choose a formula by which the price can be determined. The formula method can be a good means of determining the value of the company at the time of sale if an appropriate formula can be established. A formula price that is based on the earnings of the company is more likely to reflect the fair market value of many companies than a fixed price on a book value. A capitalization of earnings approach provides some automatic adjustment for changes in the business. The formula will still require periodic re-examination and adjustment, however, because the capitalization rate that is appropriate for the company may change as the company's business and economic conditions change. An additional source of distortion in using a capitalization of earnings approach in a family business is the calculation of the company's earnings. In a family or closely held business the compensation and distribution policies of the company may be influenced by the personal needs of family members and key employees rather than purely by objective business factors.

The appraisal method sets the purchase price as an amount to be determined by an appraisal at the time of the sale. This type of provision is simple to draft, but clearly involves transaction costs at the time that it is applied. The primary advantage of a price set by appraisal is that it is likely to reflect fair market value. When drafting a buy-sell agreement that requires an appraisal, the method for choosing the appraiser should be specified in the agreement (including a method for choosing one if the parties cannot agree at the time).

Note that mismatch can arise when the purchase price established under the buy-sell agreement is disregarded for purposes of IRC Section 2703. This will result in the purchase of the deceased owner's interest for less than what the IRS determines to be fair market value. Consider, for example, the Court's ruling in *Connelly v. U.S.*,[12] in which two brothers entered into a Shareholders' Agreement containing buy-sell provisions with respect to their interests in their closely held business. The Shareholders' Agreement required the value of a deceased shareholder's interest to be determined based upon either: (i) an executed Certificate of Value, or (ii) two or more appraisals. The shareholders failed to execute any Certificates of Value while both were living, and upon the death of one of the shareholders, the remaining shareholder and the decedent's estate ignored the appraisal requirement under the buy-sell and valuation provisions of the Shareholders' Agreement.

In *Connelly*, the corporation ultimately redeemed the deceased shareholder's interest for $3,000,000, and the IRS challenged the valuation on the basis that the Shareholder Agreement failed to satisfy the requirements of IRC Section 2703 and Section 2031 in order to fix the value of the decedent's interest. Importantly, and as discussed in § 11.05[G][2], *infra*, the Court found that the Shareholders' Agreement failed to satisfy the IRC Section 2703(b) safe harbour for the reason that the agree-

---

[12] Connelly v. U.S., 128 AFTR 2d 2021-5955 (2021).

ment did not satisfy the device test, in part due to the fact that the purchase price did not include the life insurance proceeds in determining the value of the company.

[G] Funding the Purchase

[1] Installment Sale

If the selling owner does not need the proceeds of a sale of the business interest immediately (e.g., to pay the estate tax) then providing for an installment sale (for example, with an initial lump sum and the remainder to be paid over 36 or 60 months) may be an appropriate means of funding the purchase. An installment note that provides for payments over a period of years permits the company or the remaining owners to use the company profits to fund the purchase. The business interest can serve as security for the note. In some instances, a selling shareholder may be uncomfortable with an installment sale because the shareholder (or the shareholder's heirs) will be unable to terminate his or her investment in the company and diversify his or her holdings until the note is paid. When the business is established and stable, however, an installment sale is often appropriate. Generally, IRC Section 453 will require the seller of a family business interest to report any gain on the sale for income tax purposes as the payments are received, unless the seller affirmatively elects out of such installment sale reporting.

[2] Insurance

Life insurance is a common way to fund a buy-sell agreement when the purchase is triggered by the death of the owner. Life insurance used to fund a redemption agreement raises concerns that differ from those that arise when insurance is used to fund a cross-purchase; consequently, redemptions and cross-purchases are discussed separately.

If the company will be the purchaser, it can buy a single life insurance policy on each of the owners subject to the buy-sell agreement. If the proceeds of the policy are payable to the company (as opposed to a shareholder), the company cannot deduct the premiums. Generally, the death benefits paid on a life insurance policy are not subject to income tax.[13] When life insurance proceeds are received by a C corporation, the corporation may be subject to income tax on the life insurance proceeds under the alternative minimum tax.[14]

The shareholder of a corporation will not be treated as holding incidents of ownership in a policy owned by the corporation if the proceeds are payable to the corporation, even if the shareholder controls the corporation.[15] Consequently, the full

---

[13] IRC § 101.

[14] Reg. § 1.56(g)-1(c). In addition, the increase in cash surrender value on a corporate-owned life insurance policy may be subject to alternative minimum tax. IRC § 56(g)(4)(ii).

[15] IRC § 2042-1(c)(6); Rev. Rul. 82-85, 1982-1 C.B. 137.

dollar value of the policy will not be included in the estate of the controlling shareholder under IRC Section 2042. In *Blount v. CIR*, the 11th Circuit reversed the Tax Court's inclusion of life insurance proceeds in the fair market value of the corporation, reasoning that when there is an enforceable contractual obligation to offset a non-operating asset, such asset should not be included in the fair market valuation of a company.[16] Note, however, that the Eighth Circuit court in *Connelly* recently disagreed with the ruling in *Blount* and held that the life insurance proceeds were included in the valuation of the company. Planners should carefully consider each buy-sell agreement funded with life insurance. In crafting formula valuation clauses and appraisal clauses, it may be advisable to include the anticipated value of the life insurance proceeds in the purchase of the deceased shareholder's interest. Failure to do so appeared to have been a critical concern for the *Connelly* Court in finding that the arrangement did not satisfy the IRC Section 2703(b) safe harbour on the basis that it was merely a device to transfer value to members of the decedent's family as opposed to a bona fide business arrangement.

The use of insurance to fund a cross-purchase agreement raises more issues than does the use of insurance in conjunction with redemption agreements. Since it is impossible to know which owner will die first, each owner will need to purchase an insurance policy on each of the other owners. Prices for policies on the different owners may vary substantially. If the company owns the insurance, all of the owners will share in the total expense in proportion to their ownership. If each owner is paying premiums on each of the other owners, a differential in premiums may place a disproportionate burden on some of the owners. Owners should take particular care not to name themselves as the insured of the policy on their own lives, which would not only thwart the goals of the buy-sell agreement, but would also result in estate tax inclusion of the policy proceeds for that owner under IRC Section 2042.

The need for each owner to purchase a policy on each of the other owners raises an additional problem not present in a redemption arrangement. When an owner dies, the owner's estate will be left with insurance policies on the lives of the surviving owners. It is also critical to continue to coordinate the purchase price and related funding provisions with the fair market value of the company. Failure to coordinate these provisions will result in unintended and problematic results for all parties. For example, if the value of the company has increased, the deceased shareholder's estate may have an estate tax liquidity issue if the estate tax value of the company is greater than the value of the sale proceeds received pursuant to the buy-sell agreement. Conversely, if the company has decreased in value, the surviving partners and/or the business may be forced to liquidate company assets to fund the value stipulated in the buy-sell agreement.

---

[16] 428 F.3d 1338 (11th Cir. 2005).

EXAMPLE *11-21*

Tyler, Caroline and Meredith each own one-third of Family Business, Inc. and have entered into a cross-purchase agreement under which the surviving shareholders will purchase a proportionate share of a deceased shareholder's interest. Each shareholder purchases an insurance policy on the lives of the other two shareholders in an amount sufficient to cover one-sixth of the value of the company. When Tyler dies, each of Caroline and Meredith use the proceeds of their insurance policies on Tyler to purchase his stock. Caroline and Meredith now each hold a policy on the life of the other, but each policy will cover only one-sixth of the value of the company, and each of them now owns half of the company. Tyler's estate holds policies on the lives of Caroline and Meredith, which the estate may not want to keep, but if the estate sells the policy on Caroline's life to Meredith and the policy on Meredith's life to Caroline, the proceeds of the insurance will become subject to income tax under the transfer for value rule.

When cross-purchase agreements are funded with life insurance, the individuals may want the company to provide the cash for premium payments. When the owners are employees, the company may be able to make such payments as bonuses, which would be treated as additional compensation by both the company and the individuals. This would provide a deduction to the corporation and would be taxable as ordinary income to the employed shareholders. If payments by the company are not treated as bonuses, such payments will likely be treated as corporate distributions. If the company is a C corporation, such distributions will be taxed as dividends, which will not be favorable from an income tax perspective. Split dollar arrangements, in which the company effectively advances the cash for payment of premiums to employees as a no-interest loan, can be a useful means of using company funds to pay premiums on policies owned by the employees in some circumstances. Split dollar arrangements are discussed in more detail in Chapter 12.

The Pension Protection Act of 2006 included a trap for the unwary when the company owns insurance on the life of an officer, director, or highly compensated employee. This provision, codified at IRC Section 101(j), reverses the general rule that the death benefits paid on an insurance policy are excluded from taxable income. When the provision is applicable, the result is that the entire proceeds of a life insurance policy payable to the company are subject to income tax. This provision was aimed at curbing a practice that the IRS considered abusive, in which large corporations purchased life insurance on many employees. The statute, however, applies by its terms to any "employer-owned" life insurance policy, not just insurance policies purchased by large corporations for tax purposes. There are exceptions to the rule that are available for insurance policies purchased to fund buy-sell agreements, but these exceptions are available only if the parties meet certain requirements. Given the draconian effect of the rule when the company fails to qualify for an exception, it is crucial for any advisor working with clients on an insurance-funded buy-sell agreement to be fully aware of IRC Section 101(j) and to ensure that the requirements for the exception to the rule are met if the company owns the insurance policy.

To qualify for an exception to the rule, the company-owned insurance policy must be (1) paid to the estate of the deceased employee or the employee's family or a trust for family members, or (2) used to purchase an equity interest in the company from the employee's estate, family, or family trusts. However, this exception is available only if the employee receives written notice that the company intends to insure the employee and the maximum face amount for which the employee could be insured, and the employee consents in writing to the purchase. In the context of a closely-held company in which all parties are fully aware of the arrangements, it would be all too easy to overlook this requirement of a written notice and formal consent. Thus, it is often best practice to include this language in any buy-sell agreement that might involve company-owned life insurance.

It is important to be aware of applicable timing requirements of the required notices and the completion of the required equity acquisition to satisfy the exception. In Notice 2009-48,[17] the IRS provided guidance regarding the employer-owned life insurance rules of IRC Sections 101(j) and 6039I. This guidance was provided in the form of questions and answers, some of which directly address these timing considerations. For example, in response to the question of "how soon after the death of an employee must an amount be used to purchase an equity (or capital or profits) interest in the applicable policyholder, in order to qualify for the exception set forth in § 101(j)(2)(B)(ii)," the IRS concluded: " . . . an amount must be so paid or used by the due date, including extensions, of the tax return for the taxable year of the applicable policyholder in which the applicable policyholder is treated as receiving a death benefit under the contract."[18]

[3] Sinking Fund

One way for a company to fund an obligation to repurchase ownership interests is for the company to set aside a portion of its annual profits as a reserve earmarked for this specific purpose (commonly known as a "sinking fund"). In the case of a corporation, establishment of a sinking fund will decrease the chances that the corporation will be prevented by state law from redeeming stock due to inadequate surplus. As a practical matter, however, it is unlikely that the company will be able to set aside cash sufficient to fully fund a redemption agreement, and a sinking fund is more likely to serve only as a partial funding mechanism. If the company is a C corporation, accumulating funds in a sinking fund could subject the corporation to the accumulated earnings tax under IRC Sections 531 to 537.

[H] Effect on Estate Tax Value

In some circumstances, a buy-sell agreement will fix the estate tax value of the business interest subject to the agreement.[19] The estate planner needs to ascertain

---

[17] Notice 2009-48, 2009-24 I.R.B. 1085 (June 15, 2009).

[18] *Id.*, Q-6, A-6.

[19] Reg. § 20.2031-2(h); Rev. Rul. 59-60, 1959 C.B. 237, 244.

whether the agreement will fix the valuation because failure to do so can have disastrous results. An agreement may bind the estate of the business owner and require the estate to sell at one price, but may not prevent the Internal Revenue Service from asserting that the business interest has a higher value for estate tax purposes.

EXAMPLE *11-22*

Laura's estate holds 100 shares of stock subject to a binding agreement to sell the stock to the corporation at $100 per share. The estate receives $10,000 in cash from the corporation, and reports the stock on the estate tax return as having a value of $10,000. The Internal Revenue Service determines that the agreement is not binding for estate tax purposes and that the fair market value of the stock is $1,000 per share. The estate will have received only $10,000 in cash pursuant to the agreement, but will be liable for estate tax on a value of $100,000.

The rules for determining when the price set in a buy-sell agreement will determine the estate tax value come from two sources. There is a long series of case law interpreting a regulation that developed four basic criteria that an agreement must satisfy in order to fix estate tax value.[20] In addition, in 1990, Congress enacted IRC Section 2703 of the Internal Revenue Code, which provides that a buy-sell agreement among family members will be ignored in determining the estate tax value of property unless the agreement meets three specific criteria.[21] Two of the statutory requirements in IRC Section 2703 overlap the pre-existing common law requirements, but the third IRC Section 2703 requirement was not part of the common law requirement. An estate planner analyzing the potential estate tax effects of a buy-sell agreement will need to work through the four factors in the regulations and older case law and the three IRC Section 2703 factors.

The first three of the four traditional requirements that a buy-sell agreement must meet in order to have the effect of fixing the estate tax value are straightforward. First, the agreement must obligate the estate to sell. If the estate has the option but not the obligation to sell, the agreement will not fix estate tax value. The second requirement that the agreement must meet is that the agreement must have restricted the owner's ability to sell the interest during life.[22] If the owner could have sold the interest for any price during life, an agreement that obligates the owner's estate to sell at a fixed price at death functions to set the minimum but not the maximum the

---

[20] Reg. § 20.2031-2(h). *See, e.g.,* Bischoff v. Comm'r, 69 T.C. 32 (1977). For a detailed review of the factors that courts consider in determining whether a buy-sell agreement fixes estate tax value, *see* Estate of True v. Comm'r, T.C.M. 2001-167, 390 F.3d 1210 (2004).

[21] IRC § 2703 does not apply if more than 50 percent of the value of the company is owned by persons unrelated to the decedent and those interests are subject to the same agreement. Reg. § 25.2703-1(b)(3).

[22] Reg. § 20.2031-2(h).

owner could have gotten for his interest and consequently such an agreement will not fix estate tax value. Third, the agreement must set a price that is fixed or determinable by a formula. These requirements are objective, and it is not difficult to ensure that an agreement fulfills them.

The fourth traditional requirement that an agreement must meet in order to fix estate tax value is that the agreement must represent "a bona fide business arrangement and not a device to pass the decedent's shares to the natural objects of his bounty for less than adequate and full consideration in money or money's worth."[23] In most instances, a buy-sell agreement is drafted to fulfill bona fide business reasons, and the estate would not have difficulty in establishing this. The courts have found the following to be bona fide business arrangements: agreements whose purpose is to provide continuity of management and preservation of family control, agreements necessary to retain the services of a family employee, and agreements meeting the desire of the decedent's conservator to mitigate the risks of a minority discount and to plan for future liquidity needs of the decedent's estate.[24] Conversely, the courts have found that estate planning, tax reduction, wealth transference, protection against dissipation by children, and education for children are not bona fide business purposes.[25]

It is far more difficult to show that an agreement among the owners of a family business is not a device to transfer the interest to members of the transferor's family at less than fair market value. For purposes of IRC Section 2703(b)(2), "members of the transferor's family" include the transferor's spouse, ancestors of the transferor or the transferor's spouse, or the spouse of any such ancestor, lineal descendants of the parents of the transferor or the transferor's spouse, and natural objects of the transferor's bounty.[26] The regulations do not offer any guidance as to when an agreement will be treated as a "device." Recent case law suggests that where the agreement provides for a fixed price, the agreement may be considered a "device" if the family members subject to the agreement do not negotiate over the price and do not seek the advice of a professional appraiser in setting the price.[27]

When Congress enacted IRC Section 2703 it picked up the regulatory requirement that a buy-sell agreement must be a bona fide business arrangement and not a device to pass on the property for less than full consideration. The concepts contained in the regulation are repeated as two separate requirements in IRC Section 2703, and the regulations under IRC Section 2703 emphasize that each of the IRC Section 2703 factors is separate and must be separately satisfied.[28] Thus, at least for agreements executed or modified after October 8, 1990, the estate must be able to show both that: (1) the agreement had a bona fide business purpose, and (2) that it was not a device to

---

[23] *Id.*

[24] Slocum v. United States, 256 F. Supp. 753, 66-2 U.S.T.C. ¶12410, 18 A.F.T.R.2d 6213 (S.D. N.Y. 1966); Bensel v. C.I.R., 316 B.T.A. 246, 1937 WL 325 (B.T.A. 1937); Amlie v. C.I.R., T.C. Memo 2006-76, 91 T.C.M. 1017 (2006).

[25] Holman v. C.I.R., 130 T.C. 170, Tax Ct. Rep. (CCH) 57455 (2008).

[26] Reg. § 25.2703-1(b)(3).

[27] Estate of Lauder, 390 F. 3d 1210, 64 T.C.M. 1643 (1992); Estate of True, T.C.M. 2001-167(2004).

[28] Reg. § 25.2703-1(b)(2).

pass assets to the decedent's family for less than fair market value. In addition, Congress added another, completely new requirement that an agreement must meet in order to fix estate tax value: The agreement must be comparable to similar arrangements entered into by unrelated third parties.[29] This requirement caused consternation in the estate planning community because it is so difficult to satisfy. Family businesses tend to be idiosyncratic, and it is often difficult to locate a comparable company. Furthermore, if a truly comparable company could be located, it is highly unlikely that the owners would agree to reveal the terms of their buy-sell agreement. The regulations under IRC Section 2703 contain some discussion about the requirement that the terms of an agreement be comparable to third party agreements, but the discussion does not offer much practical advice.[30] The regulations provide that an agreement will meet the requirement if it conforms to the general practice of unrelated parties under negotiated agreements in the same business, but that isolated comparables are not sufficient to establish general business practice.[31] The most concrete advice in the regulations is that the factors to be considered generally will include the expected term of the agreement, the current fair market value of the property, anticipated changes in value during the term of the agreement, and the adequacy of any consideration given in exchange for the rights granted in the agreement.[32] An estate planner drafting or reviewing a buy-sell agreement should consider the role of these factors in the proposed agreement.

As a result of the IRC Section 2703 requirement, it is now very difficult to ensure that a buy-sell agreement will fix the estate tax value of a business interest if the agreement calls for a fixed price or a formula price that does not clearly reflect fair market value. Many estate planners now advise clients to draft buy-sell agreements in which the purchase price is fair market value as determined by appraisal.

§11.06 RECAPITALIZATIONS

[A] Defined

A recapitalization is a change in the capital structure of a company. The term is most often used to refer to the creation of a preferred or nonvoting interest. Preferred stock typically is entitled to a preferential share of the company's profits but does not share in the future appreciation of the company, which will benefit only the common stock, and nonvoting stock is entitled to a *pro rata* share of the economic benefits of other stock but does not participate in the control of the company. The decision to recapitalize may be based on particular family situations. For example, the senior members of the family may need a steady stream of retirement income but want to limit the future appreciation of the business interests in their estates that will be

---

[29] IRC § 2703(b)(3).

[30] Reg. § 25.2703-1(b).

[31] *Id.*

[32] Reg. § 25.2703-1(b)(4)(i).

subject to estate tax, while junior family members will have the strongest incentive to take over and maintain the business if they will benefit from all of the appreciation produced by their efforts. Until 1990, a recapitalization was a standard method of restructuring interests in a family corporation in order to permit the senior generation to retain some interest in the corporation while reducing the value of the stock in their estates. The planning possibilities of recapitalizations were drastically restricted by the enactment in October of 1990 of IRC Sections 2701 to 2704, often referred to as Chapter 14. Chapter 14 did not eliminate the usefulness of recapitalizations as an estate planning tool, but it did limit many of the advantages that could previously be obtained by a recapitalization. An estate planner should analyze the potential effect of Chapter 14 on the transaction before advising a client to undertake a recapitalization.

[B] Voting and Nonvoting Interests

Due to the numerous tax advantages of transferring property by gift, it is frequently advantageous for an owner of a family business to retain control of the business while transferring some economic benefits of the business to other family members. For example, the founder of the company may wish to make annual exclusion gifts of stock in the family corporation to trusts for the founder's children in order to reduce his or her taxable estate, but may want to retain voting control of the corporation until his or her retirement. If the founder recapitalizes the corporation to create voting and nonvoting common stock, the founder can make gifts of the nonvoting stock and retain the voting stock until he or she is ready to pass control of the company to the next generation. Similarly, at the time the founder is ready to begin passing control of the company to the next generation, he or she may wish to give each of his or her children an equal share of the economic benefit of the company, but pass the control of the corporation only to those children who work in the business. Creating a class of nonvoting stock can help to accomplish this goal. The founder can make gifts of voting common stock to the children who work in the business, thereby gradually transferring control of the company to them. The founder can make gifts of the same number of shares of nonvoting stock to the other children. All of the children will be entitled to equal dividends and liquidation proceeds of the company, although the nonvoting stock is worth less per share than the voting stock, and if the company is sold to a third party the children holding the nonvoting stock will receive less per share.

In a C corporation, nonvoting stock may be either common stock or preferred stock. Even S corporations, which are permitted to have only one class of stock, can issue nonvoting stock (provided the stock is all treated identically in all other respects) because a difference in voting power alone is not treated as a separate class of stock for purposes of the S corporation rules. If a business owner wants to give away economic ownership while retaining voting control, favorable transfer tax consequences can only be achieved by creating a separate class of nonvoting stock. Although it may seem that the same results could be achieved by giving common stock to a trust of which the donor is trustee (and thus votes the stock), this type of transfer to trust will not remove the stock from the decedent's estate for estate tax purposes. A special provision of the Internal Revenue Code includes in the estate of the donor all corporate stock that the donor gave away over which she retained the voting rights, as a trustee or otherwise.[1]

Interests in a partnership or a limited liability company can be created that are functionally equivalent to voting and nonvoting corporate stock. A common example is the creation of Class A (voting) membership units and Class B (non-voting) membership units. A common tactic in recapitalizing a limited liability company is to segregate the voting and non-voting interests as follows: (1) 10 percent of the total ownership will consist of Class A (voting) units; and (2) 90 percent will consist of Class B (non-voting) units. This structure provides an opportunity for the founder to gift, sell, or otherwise transfer non-voting Class B units to the successor generation (and, in the process, move substantial equity out of his or her estate) while retaining voting control of the entity.

An interest in a company that is not entitled to vote is often worth less than the same interest with a voting right, depending on the associated economic rights. In a corporation, this differential has been found to be in the range of 3 to 10 percent.[2] When the founder of a company creates a class of nonvoting stock to give to children in annual exclusion gifts, this differential will be an advantage, allowing the founder to pass more nonvoting shares while remaining under the annual exclusion limitation. However, in other circumstances this differential can create unintended tax consequences. For example, if the parents exchanged their voting common stock in a family corporation for the same number of shares of nonvoting common stock, so that control of the company passed to their children who owned the balance of the common stock, the parents would have made a gift to the children in an amount equal to the difference in value between the parent's voting stock and the nonvoting stock they received in exchange.

Practitioners must carefully consider the Tax Court's ruling in *Estate of Powell v. Commissioner*,[3] in analyzing any proposed gifting strategy of a corporate, limited liability company or partnership interest to subsequent generations of a family. In *Powell*, the decedent made gifts of significant interests to a family limited partnership ("FLP"), retaining some minority interests in the FLP. Based solely on the decedent's retention of an interest in the FLP, the Tax Court held that the full value of the FLP was includable in her taxable estate under IRC Section 2036. In this holding, the Tax Court reasoned that the decedent, with her retained minority interest, could join in with the holders of the majority interests to exercise sufficient control over the FLP to affect beneficial enjoyment of the property. For example, the Tax Court speculated that the decedent and her children could have agreed to terminate the FLP, thereby accelerating distributions of the FLP property to the partners.

Cases following from *Powell* have continued to indicate that the IRS will aggressively challenge estate inclusion under IRC Section 2036 where the decedent retained any interest, even if a minority interest, that may allow him or her to affect beneficial enjoyment of the gifted property. Consider, for example, *Estate of Moore v. Commis-*

---

[1] **§ 11.06** IRC § 2036(b).

[2] *See, e.g.*, Kosman v. Comm'r, T.C. Memo 1996-112.

[3] 148 T.C. 392 (May 18, 2017).

sioner,[4] in which the Tax Court—again, in the context of a deathbed transaction—disregarded lifetime transfers the decedent made to irrevocable trusts for the benefit of his children upon finding that the decedent was "effectively" in control over the entity. The *Powell* Section 2036 analysis has also been applied in the context of intergenerational split-dollar life insurance arrangements to disregard transfer restrictions where any modification to the arrangement required the mutual consent of all parties, including the donor. In *Estate of Cahill v. Commissioner,*[5] while the decedent did not possess unilateral ability to terminate the split-dollar agreement, the fact that his revocable trust, acting together with the donee, had the power to cancel the arrangement by agreement, was sufficient to disregard the restrictions inherent in the arrangement.

A complete discussion of *Powell* and subsequent cases is beyond the scope of this chapter, but practitioners are encouraged to exercise caution to work within the confines of the *Powell* analysis to eliminate, to the extent possible, a donor's retained interest in the entity.

[C] Common and Preferred Interests: The Estate Freeze

[1] How an Estate Freeze Works

Prior to the enactment of Chapter 14 of the Internal Revenue Code in 1990, one of the standard tools in planning for a family or closely held business was an estate freeze using a recapitalization into common and preferred stock. In a traditional estate freeze, the founders of the company would recapitalize their common stock in the family corporation into separate classes of common stock and preferred stock. The preferred stock would carry a high dividend rate, but the dividends would not be cumulative, so that if dividends were not actually paid in a given year the right to that year's dividend would lapse. In addition, the preferred stock might have other preferential rights such as a "put right," entitling the holder to require the company to redeem the stock for a high price at the option of the stockholder. The reason for providing preferential rights to the preferred shareholders was to shift the value away from the common stock and toward the preferred stock. The preferred stock would absorb most of the value of the company due to the preferential rights of the preferred stockholders, but would not share in the future appreciation of the company. The founders then would make gifts of the common stock, which would have little value (and thus generate little gift tax), to their children. The company often would retain excess cash flow rather than pay dividends on the preferred, and since the right to dividends is noncumulative, the right to receive each year's dividends would lapse at the end of that year. The founders generally would not exercise any of

---

[4] Estate of Moore v. Comm'r, T.C. Memo 2020-40 (Apr. 7, 2020). *Estate of Moore* contained many bad facts and the transaction was clearly implemented directly in anticipation of the donor's death. IRC Section 2036 was but one issue addressed by the Tax Court; there were many additional concerns and potential causes of inclusion in the donor's estate.

[5] Estate of Cahill v. Comm'r, T.C. Memo 2018-84 (June 18, 2018).

their optional rights, such as the right to put the stock to the company. As a result, the value of the common stock in real economic terms would not be depleted by the optional preferential rights held by the preferred stock.

The result of the traditional estate freeze was to permit the founders to freeze the value of the preferred stock remaining in their estates at a value approximately equal to the value of the company at the time of the recapitalization. The founders would have passed all of the future appreciation in the company (the common stock) to the next generation at minimal transfer tax cost.

The 2017 Tax Act increased the basic exclusion amount for estate, gift, and generation-skipping transfers from $5,000,000 to $10,000,000 per person, indexed for inflation. Revenue Procedure 2021-45 provides that the basic exclusion amount for 2022, calculated using the chained CPI inflation adjustment specified in the 2017 Tax Act, is $12,060,000. Taxpayers may wish to use their increased exemption to make additional lifetime transfers of common (and even preferred) stock through the use of gifting and/or sales of the shares to irrevocable dynastic grantor trusts for the benefit of their descendants. The increased basic exclusion amount is set to sunset as of December 31, 2025, so this is a "use-it-or-lose-it" proposition, and taxpayers—even those of more moderate wealth—should consider mechanisms to avail themselves of the increased exemptions while available.[6]

The enactment of IRC Section 2701 of the Internal Revenue Code in 1990 restricted, but did not eliminate, the ability of estate planners to use a recapitalization as an estate freezing device. The intent of IRC Section 2701 is to ensure that when any recapitalization into common and preferred interests is used in the family context, the preferential rights retained by the senior family members will have real economic significance. IRC Section 2701 works in two ways. First, it establishes a special way of determining the gift tax value of the common interests transferred to junior family members when senior family members retain preferred interests in the company, and may artificially increase the gift tax value of the common interests. Second, the statute requires a re-examination of the transfer at the time that the senior family members die or transfer their retained preferred interests, and may artificially increase the gift or estate tax value of the preferred interest at that time. IRC Section 2701 is an exceedingly complicated and technical provision, consisting in large part of interrelated definitions of specialized terms. In considering a recapitalization for a family company the estate planner should work through each of these definitions and the prescribed valuation process. A detailed description of the technical provisions of IRC Section 2701 is beyond the scope of this book.[7] The following discussion of IRC Section 2701 provides a general overview of the major elements and effect of the statute.

---

[6] On November 26, 2019, the Treasury Department and the IRS issued final regulations, 84 FR 64995, confirming that taxpayers use of the increased gift and estate tax exclusion amounts in effect from 2018 to 2025 will not be subject to clawback with respect to any portion of the gift when the exclusion amount reverts to pre-2018 levels after December 31, 2025.

[7] *See, e.g.,* Mezullo, Chapter 14, Tax Management (BNA Portfolio 835).

[2] Effect of IRC Section 2701

IRC Section 2701 may apply upon transfer of common interests by senior family members to junior family members. If applied, IRC Section 2701 sets out a specific method for determining the gift tax value of common interests transferred to junior family members when senior family members retain preferred interests.[8] This method requires that the taxpayer first value all family-held interests immediately before the transfer (in the case of a family-owned business, this will be the value of the company as a whole), and second, value the preferred interests retained by senior family members. In valuing the preferred interests, only those rights that must be exercised at a specified time in a specified amount are "qualified payments" that will be taken into account.[9] Any rights of the preferred interest are ignored to the extent that those rights are optional rather than mandatory because they are not "qualified payment" rights. The gift tax value of the common interests is determined by subtracting the value of the preferred interests (taking into account only the qualified payment rights) from the value of the whole company.[10] In effect, this provision assumes that in the family context senior family members will not exercise any discretionary right that would increase the value of the preferred and reduce the value of the common stock.

EXAMPLE *11-23*

Kathy and David own all 100 shares of the common stock of Searenity, Inc., a C corporation, which has been appraised at $5,000,000. Kathy and David recapitalize the corporation and exchange their common stock for 50 shares of common and 50 shares of preferred stock. The preferred stock is entitled to a 15 percent annual dividend that is noncumulative, and the preferred stockholders have the right to put their stock to the company at any time for $2,500,000. Kathy and David give all the common stock to their children and retain the preferred stock. Since the transfer is to a family member, IRC Section 2701 applies for purposes of establishing the gift tax value of the common stock. The gift tax value of the common will be determined by subtracting the value of the preferred from the value of the whole company. Since the dividend on the preferred stock is not cumulative, the right to the dividend is disregarded in valuing the pre-ferred. Similarly, the right of preferred shareholders to put the stock to the company is ignored because it is an option and is not mandatory. When the optional rights of the preferred are ignored, the value of the preferred will be drastically reduced. Under these circumstances, since the value of the preferred stock under these special valuation rules will be very low, the gift tax value of the common stock may be almost $5,000,000.

---

[8] IRC § 2701(a).

[9] IRC § 2701(c)(3).

[10] Reg. § 25.2701-3.

Nonqualified dividend rights may be taken into account in valuing a gift of common stock by making an election.[11] However, if this election is made, failure to pay the dividend may result in a deemed increase in the value of the preferred stock.[12] When the senior family members die or transfer their preferred stock, an additional gift or estate tax may be due, as discussed further below.

Section 2701 may also apply upon the transfer of preferred stock retained by the senior family members. If a right to dividends was taken into account as a qualified payment right in valuing the preferred stock (and the common stock) under IRC Section 2701, then the statute looks to the dividends that were actually paid. If the company failed to pay the dividends for more than four years, then IRC Section 2701 applies to artificially increase the gift or estate tax value of the preferred stock currently being transferred. The statute accomplishes this by adding to the value of the preferred stock the value of the dividends that should have been, but were not paid, increased by an interest factor to reflect the time value of money since the time the dividends were due.[13] As a result, the senior family members transferring the preferred stock may be faced with a gift or estate tax on phantom value, which could have a serious adverse effect in an illiquid estate. The amount of the increase in the value of the preferred under IRC Section 2701 is limited to the amount of the increase in the value of the common;[14] consequently if the common stock has not increased in value since it was transferred to junior family members, then no additional value will be added to the preferred retained by the parents, even if required dividends were not paid.

IRC Section 2701 has functioned as a significant disincentive to use recapitalizations in estate planning both because it can produce substantial and unexpected increases in gift or estate valuation and because the complexity of the provision makes it difficult to determine exactly what the tax consequences of a recapitalization will be. It is important to remember, however, that there are many circumstances in which IRC Section 2701 does not apply, and when it does not apply, significant tax savings can still be achieved through recapitalization.

IRC Section 2701 does not apply to recapitalizations if the only difference between the classes of interests created is a difference in voting power.

EXAMPLE 11-24

Charlie and Mary own all of the stock of a corporation, and exchange their voting common shares for voting and nonvoting shares. They give all of the nonvoting shares to their children and retain the voting shares. IRC Section 2701 will not apply to the valuation of the nonvoting shares.

---

[11] IRC § 2701(c)(3)(C)(iii).
[12] IRC § 2701(d).
[13] IRC § 2701(d)(2).
[14] IRC § 2701(d)(2)(B).

- To companies that are not controlled by one family (using attribution rules). A company is controlled by one family if one family owns at least 50 percent of the vote or value of the company.

EXAMPLE 11-25

Jim, Craig and Peter who are unrelated, each own 33.3 percent of the stock in a corporation. They recapitalize the corporation into common and preferred stock and give all of the common stock to their respective children, retaining the preferred stock. IRC Section 2701 does not apply to the valuation of the common stock for gift tax purposes.

- To some transfers to family members who are not direct descendants of the transferors.
- If the senior family member transfers a proportional amount of both common and preferred stock.

EXAMPLE 11-26

Greg owns 50 shares of common stock and 50 shares of preferred stock that is entitled to a noncumulative dividend of 15 percent. There are no other stockholders. A gives 25 shares of common and 25 shares of preferred stock to his daughter. IRC Section 2701 will not apply to the gift tax valuation of the stock.

- If the senior family members transfer preferred stock to the junior family members and retain the common stock.

EXAMPLE 11-27

Father and mother own all of the common stock and all of the preferred stock of a corporation. They give the preferred stock to their children. IRC Section 2701 does not affect the gift tax value of the preferred stock.

Note that there is some variance in the language of IRC Section 2701 and its corresponding Regulations with regard to those transactions which are exceptions. IRC Section 2701 provides for a broad exception for transfers "of the same class as or proportional to the transferred interest" while the Regulations provide an exception for transactions in which each family member holds "substantially the same interests" before and after the transaction. Both exceptions can apply concurrently.[15] For purposes of IRC Section 2701, the "substantially identical" exception is a complete exception from the definition of "transfer." The "substantially identical" test looks to the holdings of each individual party to the family transfer as opposed to the "same class as or proportional" exception in Section 2701 which looks exclusively to the holdings of the transferring party.

As a result, a reading of IRC Section 2701 should also include its Regulatory language to appropriately appreciate its scope. For example, a literal reading of IRC Section 2701 would apply if there has been a transfer "to or for the benefit of the transferor's family" and if after the transfer, "the transferor or an applicable family member still holds" an applicable retained interest that is neither of the same class as nor proportional to the transferred interest. Many transactions, reorganizations for example, do not include a transferor in the traditional sense, nor are many transactions "to or for the benefit" of the transferor's family. Thus, the inclusion of the Regulatory language regarding capital structure transactions serves to appropriately broaden the interpretation of IRC Section 2701.

§11.07 SPECIAL PLANNING FOR SUBCHAPTER S STOCK

Planning for an estate that includes stock in a corporation that has elected to be treated as an S corporation requires special attention. A corporation's election to be treated as an S corporation will terminate automatically if the stock is transferred to an ineligible shareholder or if the transfer results in the corporation having more than 100 shareholders.[1] Given the substantial income tax advantage of S corporation status over C corporation status (the net profits of an S corporation are subject to only one level of income tax when distributed to a shareholder, while the net profits of a C corporation are subject to two levels of tax when distributed to a shareholder), careful planning to avoid inadvertent termination of S corporation status is necessary.

Some of the changes made by the American Taxpayer Relief Act of 2012, including the increase of the top income tax rate for individuals and the increase of the top rate on most capital gains from 15 percent to 20 percent have been viewed as having a negative impact on the use of S corporations. However, one of the advantages of structuring operations as an S corporation is that, if certain tests are met, the income is not subject to the 3.8 percent surtax imposed under The Patient Protection and Affordable Care Act, which took effect on January 1, 2013.[2]

---

[15] Ltr. Rul. 9843010 (1998).

[1] **§ 11.07** IRC § 1361.

[2] Note that, at the time of this writing, President Trump has released his administration's proposal for the overhaul of the Internal Revenue Code. One of President Trump's proposals is the creation of a flat 15 percent tax on corporations. If this legislation were adopted as proposed, practitioners would once again need to consider the relative benefits and burdens of operating as a C corporation (with a flat 15 percent federal corporate tax rate) versus a pass-through entity (S corporation, partnership, limited liability company), which will cause the entity's net income to be taxed to the individual owners at their effective marginal rate.

A corporation can retain its status as an S corporation only if it meets all of the following criteria:[3]

- The corporation has no more than 100 shareholders;
- No shareholder is a nonresident alien individual;
- No shareholders are entities other than estates, certain charities, and certain specific types of trusts described below; and
- The corporation has only one class of stock.[4]

The estate planner needs to consider all of these requirements in planning for a client who owns S corporation stock, particularly if transfers of the stock are contemplated during the shareholder's lifetime or at death. To the extent S corporation stock will be owned by a trust, it is critical that the terms of the trust comply with the S corporation requirements, and the beneficiaries of the trust must be qualified shareholders.

[A] Number of Shareholders

The number of shareholders in an S corporation is limited because the S corporation rules were intended to benefit small businesses. In determining the number of shareholders of an S corporation, a husband and wife who are U.S. citizens or residents are treated as a single shareholder.[5] Further, all members of a family will be treated as a single shareholder if an election to that effect is made.[6] If unmarried individuals hold S corporation stock as joint owners, each of the joint owners is considered a shareholder.[7] An estate or a charitable organization holding S corporation stock counts as a single shareholder; however, certain "look through" rules apply to trusts and agency arrangements for purposes of determining the number of shareholders.[8] Various types of trusts may qualify as S corporation shareholders. How the beneficial interests in such trusts are structured have a direct impact on determining which beneficiaries are counted as shareholders.

[B] Qualified Shareholder

[1] Individuals as Shareholders

Only U.S. citizens and resident aliens qualify as individual S corporation shareholders.[9] This requirement can be a trap for the unwary in two respects. First, shareholders may change their residency without realizing that this affects the ability

---

[3] *Id.*

[4] IRC § 1361(b)(1).

[5] IRC § 1361(c)(1).

[6] IRC § 1361(c); Reg. § 1.1361-1(e)(3).

[7] Reg. § 1.1361-1(e)(1).

[8] Reg. § 1.1361-1(h).

[9] IRC § 1361(b)(1).

of the corporation to continue to qualify as an S corporation. Second, when S corporation stock is held by a trust, the beneficiaries of the trust may be treated as the shareholders. It is easy to overlook a beneficiary of a trust who is a nonresident alien, particularly where the terms of the trust provide discretionary benefits to a broad class of beneficiaries (such as the issue of the donor and the spouses of such issue).

[2] Estates as Shareholders

An estate is eligible to be an S corporation shareholder for a limited period of time after the decedent's death.[10] The estate, and not the beneficiaries, is treated as the shareholder; therefore, the presence of a nonresident alien beneficiary of the estate will not terminate the S corporation status. The estate remains an eligible shareholder for the length of time reasonably necessary to complete the administration of the estate.[11] When the executor distributes the stock to the beneficiaries of the estate, those beneficiaries then become the shareholders. For the S election to remain effective, each inheriting beneficiary must, in his or her own right, be an eligible S corporation shareholder.

[3] Voting Trusts and Agents as Shareholders

A voting trust may hold S corporation stock.[12] In such circumstances, each trust beneficiary is treated as a separate shareholder in determining the number and nationality of shareholders.[13] Similarly, when an agent or custodian holds S corporation stock, each of the principals is treated as a separate shareholder.[14]

[4] Grantor Trusts as Shareholders

A grantor trust is a trust that is treated for income tax purposes as if the trust assets were owned by the creator of the trust. As described in Chapter 4, a trust is treated as a grantor trust if the grantor retains certain powers over the trust property, such as the power to revoke the trust, the power to substitute assets, or the power to borrow from the trust without adequate interest or security.[15] An income beneficiary may also be treated as the grantor of the trust for income tax purposes if the beneficiary has certain powers. The IRS has ruled privately that a "Crummey" trust (discussed in Chapter 8) is a grantor trust, and is therefore eligible to be an S corporation shareholder.[16]

---

[10] *Id.*

[11] IRC § 1361(c)(3).

[12] IRC § 1361(c)(2).

[13] Reg. § 1.1361-1(h).

[14] Reg. § 1.1361-1(e).

[15] *See, e.g.,* IRC §§ 671–679.

[16] *See, e.g.,* Ltr. Rul. 199942037.

A grantor trust is an eligible S corporation shareholder as long as the deemed owner is alive, and the trust continues to be an eligible shareholder for two years after the death of the deemed owner.[17] The deemed owner is considered to be the S corporation shareholder during his life. During the two-year period following the death of the deemed owner, the deemed owner's estate is treated as the shareholder.[18]

EXAMPLE *11-28*

Brad owns 100 shares of stock in an S corporation that has a total of 70 shareholders. As part of his estate plan, Brad transfers his stock to his revocable trust. The trust provides that during Brad's lifetime the trustee can make discretionary distributions from the trust to Brad, his six children, and the spouses of those children. One of Brad's children is married to a nonresident alien. The trust is eligible to be an S corporation shareholder during Brad's lifetime and for two years following Brad's death because the trust is a grantor trust. Accordingly, for income tax purposes, during Brad's lifetime, he will be treated as the shareholder, and during the two years following Brad's death, his estate will be treated as the shareholder.

[5] Qualified Subchapter S Trusts as Shareholders

A *qualified Subchapter S trust*, or *QSST*, is a trust that meets specific requirements set out in IRC Section 1361. In order for the trust to qualify as an S corporation shareholder, the income beneficiary must file an election for the trust to be treated as a QSST.[19] The requirements that the trust must meet in order to qualify to make the QSST election are as follows:[20]

- The trust must have only one current income beneficiary;
- The current income beneficiary must be a U.S. citizen or resident;
- All of the trust income must be distributed currently to the income beneficiary (this requirement will be met if the trustee actually distributes all of the income currently, even if the trust instrument does not require the distributions);
- During the lifetime of the income beneficiary, the income beneficiary must be the only person who can receive distributions of principal;
- The beneficiary's income interest must terminate upon the earlier of the death of the income beneficiary or the termination of the trust; and
- If the trust terminates during the lifetime of the income beneficiary, all of the trust assets must be distributed to the income beneficiary.

---

[17] IRC § 1361(c)(2)(A).
[18] IRC § 1361(c)(2)(B)(ii).
[19] Reg. § 1.1361-1(j).
[20] *Id.*

If the QSST requirements are met and an election is timely made, the income beneficiary of the trust is treated as the shareholder of the corporation for income tax purposes.[21]

EXAMPLE *11-29*

Meredeth owned all of the stock of an S corporation, and at her death the stock was transferred to a marital trust for the benefit of her husband Frank. The trust provided that all of the trust income must be distributed to Frank at least annually, that during Frank's lifetime, principal distributions can be made only to Frank, and that if the trust terminates during Frank's lifetime, the trust assets will be distributed to Frank. Upon Frank's death, the trust provides that the stock will be distributed among Meredeth and Frank's children. If Frank files an election for the trust to be treated as a QSST, the trust will be eligible to be an S corporation shareholder.

[6] Electing Small Business Trusts as Shareholder

Until 1996, the strict limitations on the types of trusts that could qualify as S corporation shareholders created difficulties for estate planners attempting to integrate S corporation stock into a traditional estate plan. For example, a credit shelter trust providing for discretionary distributions of income and principal to the decedent's surviving spouse and children could not qualify as a QSST and therefore was not eligible to be an S corporation shareholder. In 1996, Congress significantly expanded the S corporation rules by enacting legislation authorizing a discretionary trust to elect to be treated as an *electing small business trust,* or *ESBT,* and thereby become eligible to be an S corporation shareholder. This change provided the estate planner with a broader range of planning opportunities when representing a client who owns S corporation stock.

Any trust may elect to be treated as an ESBT for income tax purposes if the following two requirements are met:[22]

- All of the beneficiaries are individuals who are U.S. citizens or resident aliens, estates, or certain types of charitable organizations; and

- None of the beneficiaries has acquired her interest in the trust by purchase or taxable exchange.

---

[21] *Id.*
[22] IRC § 1361(e).

While the statutory requirements to qualify as an ESBT appear very simple, specific rules apply regarding the nationality of the trust beneficiaries and determining whether each beneficiary of the trust is considered a shareholder. For purposes of determining whether all holders are U.S. individuals, all beneficiaries of a trust, including beneficiaries holding a remainder or reversionary interest, are taken into account. However, a person in whose favor a power of appointment could be exercised is not considered a beneficiary for purposes of determining nationality unless the power of appointment has been exercised. Further, a trust will still satisfy the requirement that all the beneficiaries of an ESBT be U.S. individuals if the trust contains provisions for certain future distributions to trusts.[23]

EXAMPLE *11-30*

A trust provides that during Liam's lifetime, the trustee must distribute all income to Liam, and has discretion to distribute principal to him. After Liam's death, the trust divides into separate shares for each of Liam's children. For purposes of determining whether all of the beneficiaries of the trust are U.S. individuals, Liam and his children (as opposed to the trusts for Liam's children) are considered to be the beneficiaries. Under these facts, the trust is eligible to elect to be an ESBT.

For purposes of counting the number of shareholders of the S corporation, all of the "potential current beneficiaries" of the ESBT are treated as shareholders.[24] A beneficiary is a "potential current beneficiary" if the trustee is required, or has the discretion, to make current distributions to the beneficiary of income or principal.[25] A beneficiary who is entitled to distributions only after the happening of some event is not a potential current beneficiary and is not counted as a shareholder. Additionally, if an ESBT "disposes of all of the stock which it holds in an S corporation, then, with respect to such corporation, the term 'potential current beneficiary' does not include any person" to whom the trustee had the authority to make distributions to "during the 1-year period ending on the date of such disposition."[26] Therefore, if an ESBT disposes of its S corporation stock, those individuals whose interest vested within the one-year period prior to the disposition are not considered potential current beneficiaries. For example, suppose a nonresident alien became a potential current beneficiary on February 1 of Year 1. If the ESBT disposes of its S corporation stock prior to February 1, Year 2, the nonresident alien should not be considered a potential current beneficiary, and the corporation's S election should continue to be valid.

---

[23] Reg. § 1.1361-1(m).
[24] IRC § 1361(c)(2)(B).
[25] IRC § 1361(e)(2).
[26] *Id.*

EXAMPLE *11-31*

An ESBT provides that during Shari's lifetime, the trustee must distribute all income to Shari, and has discretion to distribute principal to her. After Shari's death, the trustee has discretion to make distributions of income and principal to Shari's children and grandchildren. Until Shari's death, only Shari is a potential current beneficiary treated as a shareholder of the S corporation.

The election to be treated as an ESBT permits a trust to hold S corporation stock without disqualifying the corporation, but carries important income tax consequences for the trust. In an ESBT, all of the S corporation income is taxed to the ESBT (not to the beneficiaries), whether or not the trust makes distributions to the beneficiaries.[27] Additionally, the ESBT will pay income tax on the S corporation income at the highest rate applicable to individuals.[28] If all of the beneficiaries of the trust are not in the highest income tax bracket, this rule provides a potentially significant income tax disadvantage to the ESBT election.

EXAMPLE *11-32*

An ESBT receives a distribution of $20,000 in taxable income from S corporation stock in 2000. The ESBT pays income tax on the distribution at a current rate of 39.6 percent. Assume that the trustee distributes all cash remaining after payment of taxes to the two beneficiaries, Chuck and Barbara, who are in the 15 percent tax bracket. If Chuck and Barbara were direct shareholders of the S corporation, the distributions received by them would be subject to income tax at a 15 percent rate. However, since the shareholder is an ESBT, the distributions are taxed at the trust level and are subject to income taxes at a 39.6 percent rate.

[7] Trusts Receiving Stock under a Will as Shareholders

Any trust that receives S corporation stock as the result of the death of the shareholder qualifies as an S corporation shareholder for the two-year period following the transfer of the stock to the trust.[29] This grace period permits the trustee, the beneficiaries, and the corporation to properly plan for the S corporation stock.

---

[27] IRC § 641(c).
[28] *Id.*
[29] IRC § 1361(c)(2)(A)(ii).

[8] Limited Liability Company as Shareholder

Due to the limitation in Section 1361(b)(1)(B) that precludes entities other than an individual, an estate, certain trusts, and certain nonprofit organizations from being a shareholder of an S corporation, it has been commonly understood that a limited liability company cannot own stock in an S corporation. However, several private letter rulings have permitted the acquisition of S corporation stock by entities organized as limited partnerships and limited liability companies.[30]

While it is clear that a disregarded entity is an eligible shareholder of an S Corporation, planners must exercise caution in structuring S corporation ownership through an LLC, particularly where that LLC may only be qualified as a "disregarded entity" due to the fact that it is owned by multiple trusts, each treated as a grantor trust. A frequent estate freeze tactic is to structure sales and/or gifts of LLC membership interests to grantor trusts in order to avoid capital gain recognition on the sale as well as the taxation of interest payments received on any installment obligation. If, however, that LLC (now owned by more than one grantor trust) acquires an S Corporation membership interest, there is a risk that the LLC becomes an ineligible shareholder of the S corporation on the grantor's death, or at any such earlier time when the trusts owning LLC membership interest no longer qualify as grantor trusts.

In that event, the LLC would then have multiple members for federal tax purposes and would be taxed as a partnership. This may well immediately make the LLC an ineligible shareholder, terminating the corporation's S election with no two-year cure period that may have otherwise applied in the event a grantor trust owned the S Corporation shares directly.

§11.08 DISPOSING OF A CLOSELY HELD BUSINESS INTEREST DURING LIFE

[A] Overview

Often the founder of a business who has spent his or her lifetime building the company will not consider parting with ownership and control of the business during his or her lifetime. As a result, when an estate planner raises the possibility of transferring ownership, either to family members or to third parties, the planner may encounter significant resistance notwithstanding the many practical advantages of lifetime transfers of interests in the business. Additionally, in some instances retaining business interests until death can be an effective tax planning technique. For example, retaining all of the business interest may permit the founder to postpone the payment of estate tax under IRC Section 6166 and/or to step up the income tax basis of the stock. For many family businesses, however, the most effective estate plan (and business succession plan) will include some transfers of business interests during the founder's lifetime. This creates a natural tension between a founder wishing to

---

[30] *See, e.g.,* PLRs 200107025, 200816002, 200816003 and 200816004.

maintain control, as well as a steady source of cash flow, and implementing sophisticated wealth transfer strategies.

For business owners who are willing to transfer the business to their children, the estate planner should always consider some type of gift program. As discussed in Chapter 8, *inter vivos* gifts can reduce transfer taxes substantially in circumstances where estate taxes will otherwise be due upon the death of the business owner. Many of the techniques discussed in Chapter 8 for making gifts or as alternatives to gifts are suitable for transferring interests in a family business. To the extent a strategy can be structured which enables utilizing valuation discounts for business interests, the family can benefit from significant transfer tax savings. Discussed below are some of the special considerations that arise in the context of transfers of a family business.

[B] Division of the Business

A common dilemma estate planners encounter is related to the equitable division of the estate of a family business owner when the business represents the bulk of the potential estate and some, but not all, of the owner's children want to continue in the business. A plan that divides the business interests equally among all the children may provide each child the same economic interest in the estate, but may create resentments that threaten the continuing prosperity of the company or the relationships among the siblings. Family members who are employed in the business and depend upon it for their livelihood are rarely content to share control of the business with siblings who are employed elsewhere and view the business principally as an investment. The family members not involved in the business may be equally unhappy if the business uses its available cash to pay compensation to the children active in the business and then reinvests any remaining cash in the business. An entirely different set of issues may arise if all of the heirs are involved in the business. For example, children may be able to work together effectively while a parent is at the helm of the business, but upon death or retirement of the parent, there is potential for a power struggle among the remaining children seeking to fill the void left by the parent.

In some instances, the estate planner can work with the company's business advisors to develop a plan to divide the business as a partial solution to this challenge. There are several methods of dividing a business. If the business includes more than one product line or activity, it may be possible to divide the company into separate divisions or separate companies, each to be controlled by a different family member. For example, if the company manufactures both athletic shoes and athletic clothing, it may be possible to create two separate companies and pass them to different children. Similarly, if the business consists of a series of stores in different locations, the parent may be able to divide the company by geographic location. If the company's business does not lend itself to either of these types of division, it may be possible to pass the real estate on which the company is located to the child who is not active in the business, and to pass the operating company to the children who are employed by the business. The inactive child can then lease the real estate to the company. This arrangement permits the inactive child to receive some cash from the business without participating in the control of or the future appreciation in the value of the company. Another method of dividing a company is to recapitalize the stock into common and preferred interests. The preferred interest can be designed so that it does not participate in the management of the company or in the future appreciation of the business. This preferred interest could be passed to a child who is not active in the business, and would provide him or her with a current return on the assets. The common interest could be passed to the child who is active in the business, who could control the management of the company and receive current cash through payment of compensation. If his or her efforts in managing the business increase its value, his or her common stock ownership will reap the benefits.

In planning for any division of a business or for the distribution of assets from a business it is crucial to consider the income tax consequences of any proposed transaction. Depending upon the corporate structure, a division of the corporation could trigger both a corporate level tax and a shareholder level tax. Similarly, distributing an asset from a corporation could generate a corporate level tax, and receipt of the asset could be treated as a taxable dividend to the shareholder. Recapitalizing a corporation into common and preferred stock in some circumstances changes the character of the gain realized by the preferred shareholder on the sale of the preferred stock. Consequently, this type of estate/business planning should be a team effort that includes the company's business and tax advisors.

[C] Sale to a Family Trust

Many family business owners begin the process of planning to pass the business to the next generation without ever considering a sale of the company. To the extent that there are family members who are both capable and eager to continue the business, if the owner can plan for future transfer taxes appropriately, avoiding a sale is appropriate. However, estate planners can recount many stories of successful family businesses that did not survive when transferred to family members.

One option for the founder who wants to keep the business in the family is the sale of the business to an irrevocable trust for the benefit of the founder's children and/or further descendants. Such a trust could be structured to be multi-generational to which a generation-skipping transfer ("GST") exemption may be applied. Depending upon the state in which the trust is created, it could be a dynasty trust, which lasts forever. A transfer, in the form of a completed gift, to an irrevocable trust is designed to avoid the imposition of estate tax at the founder's death on the assets transferred to such trust, including any realized post-transfer date appreciation on such assets. By structuring such trust to be multi-generational, the trust assets can benefit future generations without any diminution of value by payment of estate tax or GST tax.

This strategy can provide even greater benefit to the family business owner as a result of passage of the 2017 Tax Act, which increased the basic exemption amount to $12,060,000 in 2022, subject to further inflation increases after 2022. Planners must, however, advise their clients that the basic exclusion amount is scheduled to sunset after 2025 (or earlier if President Biden's administration is successful in repealing the increased exemption; recall that Congress introduced the Build Back Better Act in September 2021, which, had it been enacted, would have caused the basic exclusion amount to sunset as of January 1, 2022). Clients who wish to avail themselves of the increase should consider taking advantage of the higher exemption amount as soon as possible. The IRS previously confirmed there will be no "clawback" of the exemption for gifts made prior to 2026 (while the exemption is increased to $10,000,000 per person, subject to inflation adjustments) and dies after the exemption increase sunsets after December 31, 2025.[1] Treasury issued Final Regulations in 2019, codified at Treas. Reg. § 20.2010-1(c)(2), to confirm the "use it or lose it" nature of the increased basic exclusion amount and confirmed that this anti-clawback rule applies for purposes of portability. Accordingly, if a surviving spouse elects portability on the death of the first spouse, the federal estate tax exemption available to the deceased spouse will be carried over to the surviving spouse, and will be available to offset the future estate and gift tax liability of the surviving spouse.[2] This alleviates practitioners' concerns upon a technical reading of IRC Section 2001(g)(2) which could have supported the potential clawback of lifetime gifts made at the higher exemption level.

A further complicating factor in considering substantial lifetime gifts in 2022 to utilize the balance of a client's remaining federal gift and GST exemption is the concern that Congress could introduce tax legislation that could seek to retroactively reduce a taxpayer's exemption. Consider, for example, the "For the 99.5 Percent Act" introduced by Senator Bernie Sanders, which would, among its many provisions:

- Reduce the estate tax exemption to $3,500,000 per person, indexed for inflation;
- Reduce the gift tax exemption to $1,000,000 per person;
- Change the estate and gift tax rate from a 40 percent flat rate to a progressive system, with a top rate of 65 percent for estates in excess of $1 billion;
- Eliminate valuation discounts for nonbusiness assets, including family LLCs funded with cash or marketable securities;
- Eliminate much of the effective grantor trust planning that practitioners have undertaken for clients to facilitate leveraged gift and sale transactions of assets to an estate planning vehicle outside of the donor's taxable estate.

Additional legislation introduced in 2021, such as the "Sensible Taxation and Equity Promotion Act of 2021," would further create a taxable recognition event where none exists under current law. For example, the Sensible Taxation and Equity Promotion Act would cause recognition of capital gains, in excess of certain threshold amounts, upon a donor's lifetime gift of appreciated assets or the death of the donor.

---

[1] **§ 11.08** 26 C.F.R. Part 20, "Estate and Gift Taxes: Difference in the Basic Exclusion Amount," Notice of Proposed Rulemaking and Notification of Public Hearing.

[2] With respect to the increased basic exclusion amount, the Final Regulations clarify that donors cannot use only the increased exemption prior to 2025 and then hope to still have the original $5,000,000 exemption available to them after the sunset of the increased exemption amount after 2025. For example, an individual who makes $5,000,000 of taxable gifts prior to 2025 will have no basic exclusion amount (ignoring inflation adjustments) once the exemption increase sunsets. For more modestly wealthy clients, planners should consider the possibility of avoiding gift splitting. In that scenario, a husband and wife could make lifetime gifts of $10,000,000 prior to 2025, fully using the basic exclusion amount of one spouse, and, upon sunset of the increased exemption after 2025, the other spouse would still have his or her original $5,000,000 exemption. In contrast, had these same spouses elected to gift split all pre-2025 gifts, each spouse would have been deemed to use his or her entire exemption once the increased amounts sunset after 2025.

This would have the result of imposing two layers of tax on the same asset class—both an income tax in the form of the capital gain tax as well as a separate estate tax.

A traditional GST exempt trust has the advantage of continuing for the benefit of the founder's descendants for the longest period permitted under state law (often 21 years after the death of the last surviving beneficiary of the trust living at the time it is established, or approximately 100 years) while avoiding the imposition of estate tax or GST tax during the trust's existence. The terms of a GST trust generally provide that the trust property will be held for the benefit of the founder's grandchildren and further descendants, although distributions to the founder's spouse and children could be permitted at the discretion of the trustees. For instance, the trust could provide that during the founder's lifetime, the trustees may, at their discretion, distribute income and principal from the GST trust to or for the benefit of any one or more of the founder's spouse and descendants for any purpose or could highlight certain specific purposes such as education, the purchase of a first home, or an entrepreneurial endeavor.

There are also many states that do not require trusts to have a finite end. Trusts in these jurisdictions are commonly referred to as "dynasty trusts." A dynasty trust is simply a version of a GST trust that is permitted under state law to remain in existence in perpetuity. Popular dynasty trust jurisdictions include New Hampshire, Delaware, Nevada, South Dakota, and Alaska.

In considering the option of making a sale to a trust, founders should be aware that there is no statutory guidance on this technique, and therefore, it is susceptible to IRS scrutiny. For example, the IRS could claim that the sale price of the company does not accurately reflect fair market value. If the sale is for less than fair market value, the difference between the sale price and fair market value would be treated as a gift from the founder to the trust, which may require the payment of gift taxes and unintended allocation of GST tax exemption. To avoid such a result, practitioners may wish to use a *Wandry*-type formula transfer clause in the relevant sale document.[3] In its simplest form, a formula transfer clause fixes the value of an interest transferred (whether by sale or gift) and, if the valuation of the entity is later challenged, there is an automatic adjustment of the amount of the business interest (i.e., shares of the company, units of the limited liability company, etc.) transferred to the recipient. Such clauses have been "analogized to asking for $10 worth of gasoline . . . rather than a certain number gallons of gas. . . ."[4] A *Wandry* clause is an effective mechanism to fix the sale price and provide for the automatic adjustment of the amount of the interest sold in the event of a subsequent challenge by the IRS. This can prevent the potential for an unintended gift by the seller to the trust, as the *Wandry* clause will reduce the business interest sold to match the sales price.

While transferring the business to a single heir or a trust for such heir may eliminate intrafamily disputes over management, other siblings who feel that they have not received a fair share of the estate have been known to challenge such a

---

[3] *See* Wandry v. Comm'r, T.C. Memo 2012-88.

[4] Steve R. Akers, *Wandry v. Commissioner,* T.C. Memo 2012-88 (March 26, 2012), BESSEMER TRUST, March 2012.

testamentary disposition, often asserting that the recipient child exercised undue influence over the business owner. In some of these situations, the family might have been better off both financially and emotionally if the founder of the business had sold it to a third party during his or her lifetime and simply divided the proceeds equally among children or further descendants.

[D] Sale to a Third Party

[1] Advantages and Disadvantages

If the founder desires to sell the company to a third party, he or she should consider making the sale before he reaches the age at which he wants to retire. Generally, the founder of a business is a "key person" who adds significant value to the company. A sale that includes an agreement providing for the founder to remain as an employee or consultant during a transition period often helps him or her maximize the price received for the company. One of the advantages of selling a business when the founder is near retirement age is that the sale will provide the founder with liquid assets for retirement. Often a founder builds a business by reinvesting profits and has taken only the compensation necessary to support current living expenses. In such circumstances, providing a mechanism for retirement income can be a significant consideration.

An important disadvantage to selling the family business during one's lifetime is that the sale will likely be subject to significant capital gains taxes. If, instead, the founder retains the business interests until death, the beneficiaries of the estate will receive the interests with a stepped-up basis.[5] As a result, the business could then be sold without generating any capital gains taxes. Another approach the business owner may want to consider, if the business is in a corporate form, is disposing of the business through a tax-free corporate merger. If the founder receives stock in an acquiring corporation instead of cash, he may not be subject to income tax on the appreciation in his stock until a subsequent sale of the stock received. If such stock is held until death, the basis of the acquired stock will be stepped up and a subsequent sale will not generate capital gains. This result can be achieved, however, only if the founder does not need to sell the stock to raise cash for retirement. If retirement income is needed, and the business is structured as a C corporation, the founder may wish to consider a sale of the business to an employee stock ownership plan ("ESOP").

[2] Exclusion for Small Business Capital Gains

The Protecting Americans from Tax Hikes (PATH) Act of 2015, established on December 18, 2015, included a valuable provision which made permanent IRC

---

[5] The basis step up is achieved because the business interest is included in the founder's estate and estate tax is paid on the asset.

Section 1202, which allows certain taxpayers to exclude from taxation 100 percent of capital gains associated with Qualified Small Business stock ("QSBS"). The capital gain exclusion is capped at the greater of: (i) $10,000,000, reduced by the aggregate amount of eligible gain taken into account by the taxpayer in prior years from the same issuing corporation; or (ii) ten times the aggregate adjusted bases of QSBS issued by the corporation and disposed of by the taxpayer during the taxable year.[6]

Small business owners who sell all or a portion of a company organized as a C corporation, as well as owners who are in the process of forming a business should be mindful of the requirements of Section 1202. The following criteria must be met by both the owner (Taxpayer) and his or her company:

Owner (Taxpayer) Criteria:

- Taxpayer must not be a corporation.[7]
- Taxpayer may hold the QSBS through an interest in a pass-through entity. For example, a partner in a venture capital fund can qualify if the fund holds the QSBS. However, the Taxpayer must have held the interest in the entity on the same date the entity acquired the QSBS and until the earlier of the sale or other disposition.
- To obtain an exclusion of 100 percent of the capital gains Taxpayer must have acquired the QSBS after September 27, 2010.[8]
- If the Taxpayer acquired the QSBS between August 10, 1993 and September 27, 2010, it is possible to qualify for a 50 percent or 75 percent exclusion, depending on the date of the QSBS acquisition.[9]
- Taxpayer must have held the QSBS for more than five years.[10]
- The QSBS must be "originally issued" to the taxpayer, either directly or through an underwriter, for money, property or services provided to the issuing corporation.[11] This means, for example, that the taxpayer cannot purchase his or her stock from an existing shareholder. However, IRC Section 1202(h) is clear that a gift of QSBS is permissible, as long as the donor received the shares through an original issuance. In such event, the donee is treated as acquiring the shares in the same manner as the original issuant and is permitted to tack the donor's holding period in the shares.[12]

---

[6] IRC § 1202(b)(1).

[7] IRC § 1202(a)(1).

[8] IRC § 1202(a)(4).

[9] IRC § 1202(a)(1) and (3).

[10] IRC § 1202(a)(1).

[11] IRC § 1202(c)(1).

[12] This raises the possibility of creating one or more non-grantor trusts to receive gifts of shares in the qualified small business, thereby permitting the use of multiple QSBS exclusions. Planners adopting this strategy should carefully consider the reciprocal trust doctrine and other potential sources of IRS scrutiny.

Company Criteria:

- The company must be a domestic C Corporation.
- Prior to and subsequent to the Taxpayer's investment, the company's gross assets must never have exceeded $50,000,000.[13]
- The company must use 80 percent of its assets in the active conduct of one or more active trades or businesses (as distinguished from several nonqualifying businesses, which include a financial institution, farm, professional service firm, hotel, or restaurant).[14]

Certain redemption transactions which occur shortly before or after the issuance of stock may deprive the newly issued shares of the qualified small business stock status. There are three types of redemption transactions that disqualify stock from QSBS status, as follows:

- Any redemptions from the holder or persons related to the holder of the stock within a window extending two years on either side of its issuance;
- Any significant redemptions from any persons within a window extending one year on either side of the issuance of the stock; and
- Certain redemptions of stock through parties related to the issuer of the stock that are subject to IRC Section 304. A complete discussion of the effect of corporate redemptions on eligibility for QSBS status is beyond the scope of this chapter.

Business owners who have not yet legally formed their companies should also be mindful of the IRC Section 1202 requirements. In addition, owners seeking to eventually reap the benefits of IRC Section 1202 should consider obtaining a third-party valuation, both to establish their personal basis in the company and to ensure the company's assets are under the $50,000,000 threshold.

The Build Back Better Act, passed by the U.S. House of Representatives on November 19, 2021, included provisions that limited the gain exclusion to 50% for: (i) those taxpayers with an adjusted gross income of $400,000 or more, or (ii) trusts or estates. While the Build Back Better Act failed to be adopted by the Senate, this provision is worth noting as it indicates the potential for future Congressional action. If the Build Back Better Act had been adopted, the QSBS-related limitation would have substantially impacted planning for owners of certain closely-held businesses that would otherwise qualify to exclude up to $10 million (or 10 times basis) of capital gain on the sale of shares in a qualified small business.

[3] Sale to an ESOP

A family business owner willing to sell all or part of a family business that is organized as a C corporation should consider selling to an ESOP. In the appropriate

---

[13] IRC § 1202(d)(1).

[14] IRC § 1202(e); *see also* PLR 201436001 (May 22, 2014) (IRS stated that "the thrust [of Section 1202] is that businesses are not qualified trades or businesses if they offer value to customers in the form of services, [such as] in the form of individual expertise (law firm partners)").

circumstances, a sale of stock to an ESOP can be an attractive exit strategy for the owner of a family business.[15]

An ESOP is a qualified retirement plan for employees, subject to federal regulation under ERISA[16] (as are other qualified retirement plans such as 401(k) plans and defined benefit pension plans), which is designed to invest in stock of the employer corporation. If a family business owner sells at least 30 percent of the stock in a C corporation to an ESOP and reinvests the proceeds in qualified "replacement securities" which consists of securities of U.S. operating corporations, the business owner can enjoy all of the following benefits:

- By forming an ESOP, the owner of a family corporation can create a market for an otherwise unmarketable minority interest in the company;
- The selling owner will not pay any capital gains tax on the gain on the sale as long as he or she continues to hold the replacement securities;[17]
- If the selling owner holds the replacement securities until death, the basis of the securities will be stepped up to fair market value as of the date of death, and the gain on the sale of the family corporation stock may then escape income tax altogether;[18]
- By choosing a diversified group of publicly traded securities (or high-grade long-term corporate bonds that can be pledged as security for a loan) as replacement securities, the seller can reduce the investment risk that otherwise results from owning a concentrated position in non-marketable private company stock;
- The selling owner can select replacement securities that provide investment income for retirement;
- The employees of the company who are beneficiaries of the ESOP will share in the ownership of the company;
- The selling owner or a company officer can act as the ESOP trustee, and can then vote the stock held in the ESOP with respect to most corporate issues;
- The company can make tax deductible contributions to the ESOP; and
- The employees will not be subject to income tax with respect to contributions to the ESOP for their benefit until they receive distributions from the ESOP (generally upon retirement, disability, or death).[19]

---

[15] This discussion considers the use of ESOPs in the estate planning context only. ESOPs can also be used to accomplish various corporate goals.

[16] 29 U.S.C. §§1101–1114. ERISA is the Employee Retirement Income Security Act of 1974, as amended, which governs qualified employee retirement plans. The rules governing qualified retirement plans provide a tax incentive to both employers and employees to participate in a retirement plan by permitting the employer to deduct a contribution to a qualified plan when paid, and deferring the corresponding income tax of the employee until the employee receives cash from the plan at retirement. A qualified plan is subject to numerous detailed rules regarding participation by employees, the amount of employer contributions, and timing of withdrawals by employees. Planning for qualified retirement benefits is discussed in more detail in Chapter 13.

[17] IRC §1042(a).

[18] IRC §1014.

[19] *See* IRC §402.

A sale of stock to an ESOP can be structured in many different ways. In a typical sales transaction, the company first adopts an ESOP plan. Thereafter, an ESOP trust that will hold the company securities for the participants (employees) will be established and the employer appoints the ESOP trustee. The ESOP then borrows funds from a bank necessary to purchase stock from the selling business owner. The loan from the bank to the ESOP is often guaranteed by the company and will be secured by the purchased stock. The bank may sometimes insist that the loan be secured by a pledge of the seller's proceeds. The ESOP uses the borrowed funds to purchase stock from the selling business owner. The company will then make annual contributions (limited in amount by the ERISA rules applicable to qualified retirement plans) to the ESOP. The contributions to the plan are deductible by the corporation. The ESOP can use such contributions for debt service on the bank loan. As each loan payment is made, a portion of the shares that were held as security for the loan are released and are allocated to individual accounts for the employees participating in the ESOP. When an employee becomes entitled to benefits under the ESOP, the ESOP may distribute either the stock held in his or her account or cash in an amount equal to the value of the stock. The following chart illustrates this type of ESOP purchase transaction.

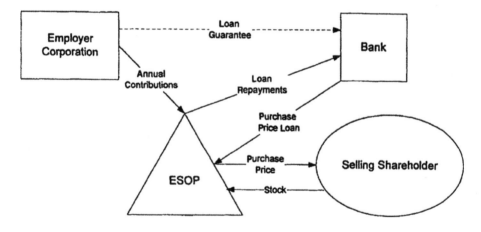

EXAMPLE 11-33

Briahnna owns 100 percent of a manufacturing company that she founded many years ago. Her other assets consist of a house, tangible personal property, and an investment account of $200,000. The company has a stable group of 50 employees and has enjoyed steady profits for the last ten years. At age 55, Briahnna is beginning to think about retirement. She would like to retain control of the company for at least ten years, but would also like to begin to diversify her assets. As president of the company, Briahnna forms an ESOP. She is the initial ESOP trustee. A bank loans enough cash to the ESOP to enable the ESOP to purchase 30 percent of Briahnna's stock. The company guarantees the bank loan. The ESOP uses the borrowed cash to purchase 30 percent of Briahnna's stock, and Briahnna uses the sale proceeds to purchase a diversified portfolio of stocks and bonds in U.S. operating companies. Briahnna will pay no income tax on the sale of her stock unless she sells the replacement securities. The company will make tax deductible contributions to the ESOP that the ESOP will use to repay the bank loan. When employees retire, become disabled, or die, they receive benefits from the ESOP.

One common variation on this ESOP structure is referred to as a leveraged ESOP, where the company, rather than the ESOP, borrows from the bank. The company would first create the ESOP and then borrow the required funds from the bank. Thereafter, the company would lend the funds to the ESOP. The company would then make deductible contributions to the ESOP, and the ESOP would use the cash to repay the loan to the company. The company, in turn, would use such funds for debt service on the loan. The following chart illustrates this variation on an ESOP transaction.

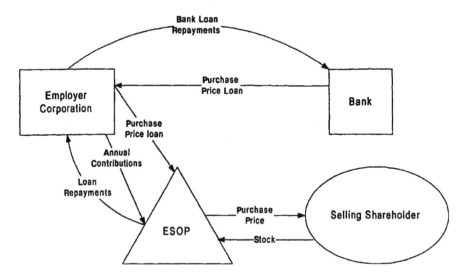

[4] ESOP Requirements

An ESOP is a qualified plan that is subject to extensive, complicated ERISA and Internal Revenue Code rules. A detailed discussion of these rules is beyond the scope of this chapter.[20] In practical terms, however, the overlay of federal tax and labor laws applicable to ESOPs requires consultation with an attorney specializing in qualified retirement benefit plans. The following description of these rules is intended to provide a general overview.

---

[20] 29 U.S.C. §§ 1101–1114; IRC §§ 401–420.

An ESOP requires adoption of an ESOP plan and a trust to hold the ESOP assets. The written ESOP plan describes which employees are entitled to be ESOP participants and their rights. Since an ESOP is a qualified plan, the employee's interest in the plan, vesting as well as the amount and timing of distributions will be dictated by law.

An ESOP trust holds the assets contributed under the plan. The trustee of the ESOP trust has the ultimate responsibility for protecting the interests of the participants in the ESOP, and is subject to strict fiduciary duties. An officer of the company can, and often does, serve as the ESOP trustee. In such circumstances, the employee/trustee should be mindful of the potential for a conflict of interest and should seek independent advice when participating in certain transactions. In any situation in which the trustee must determine the fair market value of the company stock (e.g., when the ESOP purchases stock from a selling shareholder or pays benefits to a participant based on the value of the stock held in the participant's account) the trustee is required to engage an independent appraiser to value the stock.

A recent decision from the Fifth Circuit Court of Appeals highlights the dangers of a trustee failing to adhere to his or her fiduciary duties and ignoring potential (or actual) conflicts of interest.[21] In *Perez v. Bruister*, an ESOP purchased 100 percent of the stock of a closely held corporation over a three-year period. The three ESOP trustees (one of whom was the seller) used a third-party valuation to establish the purchase price. In an apparent effort to avoid an impermissible conflict in his role as trustee, the seller did not vote on any matters related to the ESOP transaction. Despite his abstention, the Fifth Circuit found that the seller/trustee was still a functional fiduciary with respect to the transactions because he (1) fired the original ESOP appraiser, (2) hired a new ESOP appraiser, (3) influenced the outcome of the second appraiser's valuations, (4) made his personal preferences regarding the transaction known to other ESOP trustees, and (5) actively participated in trustee meetings considering the transaction.[22] Ultimately, the Fifth Circuit held that the trustees breached their fiduciary duties and imposed personal liability on the fiduciaries in the sum of nearly $6,500,000, including nearly $2,000,000 of post-judgment interest imposed against the seller/trustee, individually.

An ESOP is a defined contribution plan (as opposed to a defined benefit plan).[23] Accordingly, the benefit that each participant will receive is determined primarily by the amount contributed to the ESOP by the employer and the earnings generated within the plan. An ESOP differs from other types of defined contribution plans in that it is designed to invest primarily in stock of the employing company. As a consequence, the amount that an individual participant will receive from the ESOP on retirement depends on the success of the employer company.

---

[21] Perez v. Bruister, 823 F.3d 250 (5th Cir. 2016).

[22] *See* Christopher K. Buch and Louis L. Joseph, "Fifth Circuit Decision Includes Important Holdings for ESOP Fiduciaries," available at https://www.hklaw.com/Publications/Fifth-Circuit-Decision-Includes-Important-Holdings-for-ESOP-Fiduciaries-05-13-2016/.

[23] *See* IRC § 4975(e). The difference between defined contribution plans and defined benefit plans is discussed in Chapter 13.

When a participant is entitled to receive benefits from the ESOP, the trustee may distribute the amount held in the participant's account in cash or in stock. If a participant receives stock and the company is not publicly traded, the participant has the right to put the stock to the company (i.e., require the company to repurchase the stock.) The practical result of the distribution rules is that, if the company is not publicly traded, it will generally be required to supply cash in the amount of any distributions made to a participant. In effect, the company will supply the cash to purchase the stock held in the ESOP twice: first as contributions to the ESOP so that it may purchase the stock from the selling shareholder, and again when the ESOP makes distributions to participants.

[5] Qualifying for Deferral of Gain on Sale: IRC Section 1042

Family business owners who sell stock to an ESOP are often motivated in large part by the opportunity to defer or potentially avoid the income tax on the sale of the stock. The selling shareholder can qualify for this tax benefit if the requirements of IRC Section 1042 are met, which include the following:

- The company must be a U.S. corporation that is classified as a C corporation;[24]
- The company stock must not be publicly traded for at least one year before and one year after the sale;
- The seller may not have acquired the stock in a distribution from a qualified retirement plan or through the exercise of an option or other right to acquire stock granted by the company;
- The seller must have held the stock for at least three years;
- After the sale, the ESOP must, for at least three years, hold at least 30 percent of either each class of stock or the total value of all outstanding stock (with certain exceptions);
- The seller must purchase *qualified replacement securities* (stock, bonds, or long-term notes issued by a U.S. operating corporation) during the 15-month period that begins three months before the date of the sale; and
- The seller must make timely notarized designations of her qualified replacement securities and an election of deferral under IRC Section 1042 on his or her tax return for the year of the sale to the ESOP.

The deferral of the gain on a sale of stock to an ESOP is available only for as long as the selling shareholder retains the qualified replacement securities.[25] If the shareholder disposes of the replacement securities, the deferred gain is accelerated and will be reported as taxable income in the year of the disposition.[26] As a result, a business owner should exercise great care in selecting the qualified replacement securities. This is particularly important since some types of securities that are

---

[24] A C corporation is a corporation that has not elected to be subject to the special income tax provisions of subchapter S of the Code. Some of the differences between a C corporation and an S corporation are outlined in the beginning of this chapter.

[25] *See* IRC § 1042(a).

[26] IRC § 1042(e).

generally available to investors, such as U.S. government bonds, mutual funds, or holding company stock, are not qualified replacement securities. One strategy that a selling shareholder can employ if he or she wants to retain the ability to alter investments in the replacement securities is to choose high-grade, long-term corporate notes as replacement securities. The selling business owner can then pledge these notes as collateral and use the resulting cash to invest in government securities, short-term investments, or for current consumption, without triggering an income tax on the sale.

One important exception to the rule that disposing of qualified replacement securities generates a taxable gain involves gifts. A gift of qualified replacement securities is not treated as a disposition, and, therefore, does not trigger gain.[27] In a Technical Advice Memorandum, the Service has interpreted this exception as applying to a gift to a charitable organization, which could provide significant planning opportunities.[28]

[6] Sale of S Corporation Stock to an ESOP

As a result of the S corporation changes enacted in 1997, an ESOP is a qualified shareholder of S corporation stock.[29] A sale of S corporation stock to an ESOP carries an extra tax benefit not available if the company is a C corporation. The income of an S corporation is not taxed to the company, but rather passes through directly to the shareholders. The S corporation's income is therefore subject to only one level of income tax (as opposed to the income of a C corporation, which is subject to tax at the corporate level when earned, then subject to an additional level of tax when distributions are made to shareholders). An ESOP, however, is a tax exempt entity; thus, any taxable income flowing from an S corporation to the ESOP will not be subject to current income tax.[30] To the extent that an S corporation is owned by an ESOP, no one will pay current income tax on the company's taxable income.

There is a trade-off for lack of current income tax on S corporation income with respect to shares owned by an ESOP. A shareholder selling stock to an ESOP is not eligible to defer the gain on the sale under IRC Section 1042, discussed above.[31]

EXAMPLE *11-34*

Roseline owns all of the stock of Enterprise Corp., which is an S corporation. Her tax basis in the stock is $100,000. She sells 50 percent of the stock to an ESOP for $2,000,000. Roseline has a taxable gain on the sale equal to

---

[27] IRC § 1042(e)(3).

[28] TAM 9515002. A technical advice memorandum is issued to a particular taxpayer and is binding on the Service only with respect to that taxpayer.

[29] The distinction between an S corporation and a C corporation is discussed above.

[30] IRC § 501(a).

[31] IRC § 1042(c).

the amount received ($2,000,000), less her basis in the stock ($50,000). She will pay current income tax on the gain, even if she reinvests the proceeds in U.S. securities. After the sale, half of the company's profits and losses will flow through to her, and half will flow through the ESOP. Roseline will report her share of the net income on her tax return each year. The share of the company's income that flows through to the ESOP will not be subject to current income tax because the ESOP is tax exempt.

Congress recognized that there was a possibility that S corporation owners might take advantage of the rules permitting deferral of income tax through the use of an ESOP in ways that benefit a small group of family members rather than a substantial group of unrelated employees.[32] To ensure that the use of an ESOP is attractive only to S corporations that sponsor an ESOP covering a broad group of employees, the 2001 Act contains provisions that have the effect of prohibiting the allocation of ESOP benefits to individuals who are deemed to own substantial portions of the S corporation stock.[33] These rules generally are applicable when a family or a small group of individuals own, or historically owned, at least 50 percent of the S corporation stock. Family attribution is used to determine who is deemed to own stock. If the S corporation has a broad group of employees who participate in the ESOP, the tax deferral benefits of an ESOP may remain attractive, even if the S corporation was owned by a single individual or family. If, however, a family-owned S corporation has mostly family employees, then there will no longer be a tax advantage to a sale to an ESOP. If a sale of S corporation stock to an ESOP is being contemplated, a member of the advisory team should work through the new rules to see how they will affect the parties to the transaction.

[7] Other Considerations in Selling to an ESOP

A sale of stock to an ESOP can provide significant tax benefits for a family business owner, but before engaging in such a sale, the business owner should understand that ESOPs are not always an unqualified success in the long-term, especially from the perspective of the employees. While ESOPs have been promoted as a special opportunity for employees to participate in ownership of the employing company, in fact some employees do not want their retirement benefits to be tied up in employer stock. Instead, many employees may prefer to have their retirement benefits invested in a diversified portfolio. It is important to note that an ESOP participant who has been in the plan for at least ten years and is over age 55 has the right to direct that his ESOP account be diversified. Until that time, however, the participants' accounts are likely to be invested only in employer stock.

The choice to adopt an ESOP limits the employer's ability to provide other types of qualified retirement benefits. The contributions made by the company to the ESOP may reduce the amount that the company and the employees can contribute to a

---

[32] H.R. Rep. No. 107-51.

[33] 2001 Act § 656; IRC § § 409(q), (p), 4975(e)(7), 4975A.

401(k) plan or other qualified plan if those plans are designed to provide maximum benefits. Employees may not view the replacement of an existing qualified plan with an ESOP as an improvement in their benefits.

The adoption of an ESOP can also result in pressure on the company's cash flow in the long-term. If the ESOP has borrowed funds to purchase stock, then the company must continue to make contributions to the ESOP to permit the ESOP to repay the loan, even if the value of the purchased stock has declined. In addition, if the company is not publicly traded, the company will be obligated to make additional cash payments when employees become entitled to benefits, because the employee can require the company to repurchase any stock distributed to the employee (and in any case, the company would not want its stock to become widely dispersed). This obligation to repurchase the stock can put a strain on the company's cash flow.

If the company's stock value decreases after the ESOP purchases the stock, the employees will receive less in benefits than the amount that the company paid to the selling shareholder. While this result is not inconsistent with the goal of providing employees with an equity stake in the employer, it can become a source of resentment among employees.

Finally, a family business owner contemplating a sale of stock to an ESOP should realize that the company will no longer be entirely family owned. The ESOP participants will become indirect shareholders in the company, and the company must be operated for their benefit as well as the benefit of any remaining family shareholders. The selling shareholder or a family member may serve as the ESOP trustee, but an ESOP trustee is subject to a strict fiduciary duty to the ESOP participants and the trustee's actions are subject to regulation by the Department of Labor and the Internal Revenue Service. This is not often a practical concern when the trustee is voting the ESOP shares to elect directors on a routine basis, but may become an important issue if the question of selling the company arises.

§11.09 FAMILY OFFICE PLANNING

[A] Overview

Family offices have long been desired by ultra-high-net worth, multi-generational families. No one definition can encompass the various functions served by different family offices, but in the broadest sense, a family office is an organization that assumes the day-to-day administration and management of a family's affairs. In addition to the centralized governance structure afforded by a family office, clients often wish to structure such enterprises in an effort to seek deductibility of expenses related to the operation of the family office.

Two events in December 2017 presented new tax challenges and planning opportunities for family offices and provide a reason to evaluate the family office structure and classification of expenses.

- The 2017 Tax Cuts and Jobs Act suspended the rules that previously permitted individual income tax deductions for expenses incurred for the production of income under IRC Section 212 for 2018 through 2025. Accordingly, the distinction between business expenses and investment expenses has assumed a greater significance.

- The Tax Court released its decision in *Lender Management v. Commissioner*,[1] which provides guidance in structuring a family office enterprise to qualify for ordinary and necessary business expense deductions under IRC Section 162.

[B] *Lender* Analysis

The *Lender* Tax Court held that the family office, Lender Management, LLC ("Lender Management"), carried on a trade or business under IRC Section 162. During the tax years in issue, Lender Management provided direct management services to three Lender family limited liability companies (the "Investment LLCs"), each of which was taxed as a partnership for federal income tax purposes. Lender Management directed the investment and management of assets held by the Investment LLCs for the benefit of their owners—all of whom were members of the Lender family. It is important to review the facts in *Lender* when establishing family offices and preserving income tax benefits.

The Investment LLCs were created as part of a reorganization of Lender Management with a goal of accommodating greater diversification of the managed investments and more flexible asset allocation at the individual investor level. As part of the restructuring, Lender Management shifted from a cost-based office model to a profit-based model. Lender Management engaged a hedge fund specialist to help it restructure its affairs and its managed portfolio using a hedge fund, or "fund of funds," manager model. Pursuant to the restructuring strategy, Lender Management divided its managed portfolio into the three Investment LLCs, each formed for the purpose of holding investments in a different class of assets. Investment LLC # 1 invested in private equities, Investment LLC # 2 in hedge funds, and Investment LLC # 3 in public equities.

The terms of Lender Management's Operating Agreement permitted it, without limitation, to engage in the business of managing the "Lender Family Office" and to provide management services to Lender family members, related entities, and "other third-party nonfamily members." The Operating Agreements for the Investment LLCs designated Lender Management as the sole manager for each entity. Lender Management held the exclusive rights to direct the business and affairs of the Investment LLCs.

Members understood that they could withdraw their investments in the Investment LLCs at any time, subject to liquidity constraints, if they became dissatisfied with how the investments were being managed. The Operating Agreements for certain of the Investment LLCs provided that members could withdraw all or a portion of their capital accounts on specified dates of each year or on any other date approved by the Manager.

---

[1] § 11.09 T.C. Memo 2017-246 (2017).

[1] Compensation of Lender Management

Lender Management received a profits interest in each of the Investment LLCs in exchange for the services it provided to the Investment LLCs and their Members. These profits interests were designated "Class A" interests in the Operating Agreements for the Investment LLCs. The Class A interests were structured concurrent with Lender Management's reorganization and its shift to a profit-based model.

Under the terms of the initial Operating Agreement, effective August 1, 2005, Lender Management was entitled to receive for its Class A interests the following percentages: (1) from Investment LLC # 1, 1 percent of Net Asset Value annually, plus 5 percent of any increase in net asset value from the prior fiscal period; (2) from Investment LLC # 2, 5 percent of gross receipts annually, plus 2 percent of any increase in Net Asset Value from the prior fiscal period; and (3) from Investment LLC # 3, 2 percent of Net Asset Value annually, plus 5 percent of net trading profits. Lender Management received income from the Class A interests only to the extent that the Investment LLCs generated profits. Net Asset Value was defined as the amount by which the fair market value of the investment LLC's assets exceeded its liabilities.

As of December 31, 2010, the Operating Agreements for Investment LLC # 1 and Investment LLC # 2 were amended to provide Lender Management with increased profits interests. The Class A interests for Investment LLCs # 1 and # 2 were increased to equal the aggregate of 2.5 percent of Net Asset Value, plus 25 percent of the increase in Net Asset Value, annually. Similar to the initial terms of the Operating Agreements, Lender Management received payments for its Class A interests only to the extent that Investment LLCs # 1 and # 2 generated net profits. The increased profits interests were intended to more closely align Lender Management's goal of maximizing profits with that of its clients and to create greater incentive for Lender Management and its employees to perform successfully as managers of the invested portfolios. During the tax years in issue, any payments that Lender Management earned from its profits interests were to be paid separately from the payments that it would otherwise receive as a minority member of each of the Investment LLCs.

[2] Management Services

During the tax years in issue, Lender Management made investment decisions and executed transactions on behalf of the Investment LLCs. It operated for the purpose of earning a profit, and its main objective was to earn the highest possible return on assets under management. Lender Management provided individual investors in the Investment LLCs with one-on-one investment advisory and financial planning services.

Lender Management employed five employees during each of the tax years in issue. It had a total payroll for its employees of $333,200, $311,233, and $390,554 during the tax years in issue, respectively. For tax year 2011, the payroll included a $123,249 guaranteed payment to its Chief Investment Officer ("CIO"). For tax year 2012, the payroll included a $206,417 guaranteed payment to the CIO. Lender Management's CIO worked about 50 hours a week. The Tax Court favorably noted the extent of the CIO's activities, as follows:

- The CIO retained the ultimate authority to make all investment decisions on behalf of Lender Management and the Investment LLCs. Most of his time was dedicated to researching and pursuing new investment opportunities and monitoring and managing existing positions.
- The CIO personally reviewed approximately 150 private equity and hedge fund proposals per year on behalf of the Investment LLCs. He met with and attended presentations of hedge fund managers, private equity managers, and investment bankers. Lender Management was not an active trader, but in a typical year, the firm would enter into multiple new private equity deals and make one or two hedge fund investments.
- Lender Management arranged annual business meetings, which were for all clients in the Investment LLCs. These group meetings were held so that Lender Management could review face-to-face with all of its clients the performance of their investments at least once per year. Because of conflicts, the CIO had difficulty getting all of Lender Management's clients to attend these meetings. He would conduct additional face-to-face meetings with clients who were more interested in the status of their financial investments at times and locations that were convenient for them.
- The CIO interacted directly with Lender Management's clients. He collected information from and worked with these individuals to understand their cash flow needs and their risk tolerances for investment, and Lender Management engaged in asset allocation based on these and other factors. Lender Management devised and implemented special ventures known as eligible investment options (EIOs), which allowed clients to participate in investments more directly suited to their age and risk tolerance. The CIO developed and maintained a number of computer models, including a model that projected the cash needs of individual investors and a model that tracked and forecasted the cash flows associated with the Investment LLCs' private equity investments.

[3] Trade or Business Analysis

The *Lender* Tax Court distinguished several previous cases which addressed the act of managing a taxpayer's own funds versus operating a trade or business. The Court correctly noted that an investor is not, by virtue of his activities undertaken to manage and monitor his own investments, engaged in a trade or business.[2] While the taxpayer's activities as an investor may produce income or profit, profit from investment is not taken as evidence that the taxpayer is engaged in a trade or business.

A common factor distinguishing the conduct of a trade or business from mere investment has been the receipt by the taxpayer of compensation other than the normal investor's return.[3] Compensation other than the normal investor's return is income received by the taxpayer directly for his or her services rather than indirectly

---

[2] *See* Whipple v. Comm'r, 373 U.S. 193 (1963).

[3] *See, e.g., id.* at 202-203.

through the corporate enterprise.[4] If the taxpayer receives not just a return on his or her own investment but compensation attributable to his or her services provided to others, then that fact tends to show that he or she is in a trade or business.[5] The trade-or-business designation may apply even though the taxpayer invests his or her own funds alongside those that are managed for others, provided the facts otherwise support the conclusion that the taxpayer is actively engaged in providing services to others and is not just a passive investor.[6]

In discussing the scrutiny associated with family enterprises, the *Lender* Court found that Lender Management satisfied the heightened level of review. Notwithstanding the family ownership of Lender Management and the Investment LLCs, as well as the fact that the CIO of Lender Management was a family member, the Court was satisfied that there was no requirement or understanding among members of the Lender family that Lender Management would remain manager of the assets held by the Investment LLCs indefinitely. Lender Management's investment choices and related activities were driven by the needs of clients, and its clients were able to withdraw their investments if they became dissatisfied with its services.

Although each investor in the Investment LLCs was in some way a member of the Lender family, Lender Management's clients did not act collectively or with a single mindset. Lender Management's clients were geographically dispersed, many did not know each other, and some were in such conflict with others that they refused to attend the same business meetings. Their needs as investors did not necessarily coincide. Lender Management did not simply make investments on behalf of the Lender family group. It provided investment advisory services and managed investments for each of its clients individually, regardless of the clients' relationship to each other or to the managing member of Lender Management.

---

[4] *Id.* at 203.

[5] Dagres v. Comm'r, 136 T.C. 263, 281-282 (2011).

[6] *Id.* at 282, 285-286.

12

Insurance

§12.01 INTRODUCTION

Life insurance is a common component in many estate plans. This chapter provides a general discussion of estate planning with life insurance, including the various uses of life insurance in estate planning and the distinction between different types of life insurance policies as well as an analysis of the income, estate, and gift tax consequences of life insurance. The discussion includes a description of one of the most popular estate planning techniques—keeping life insurance out of the insured's estate.

The chapter concludes with a discussion of another type of insurance that has become increasingly popular in recent years: long-term care insurance.

§12.02 WHAT IS LIFE INSURANCE?

[A] In General

Life insurance is a contract in which an insurance company (the *insurer*) promises to pay a specified amount (the *face value*) to a designated person (the *beneficiary*) upon the death of the insured.

The purchaser of a life insurance policy need not be the insured, but she does need to have an insurable interest in the insured. An *insurable interest* is a relationship between the purchaser and the insured in which the purchaser stands to experience a loss upon the death of the insured. The reason for the insurable interest rule is to avoid having life insurance used for gambling purposes. Individuals have insurable interests in themselves. Family members typically have insurable interests in each other. Similarly, businesses are considered to have insurable interests in their employees.

The owner of a life insurance policy generally has the power to name or change the beneficiary and the right to assign the policy. In addition, if the policy is a cash value policy, the owner also has the right to cash the policy in for its cash surrender value or use the policy as collateral to obtain a loan.

The beneficiary of a life insurance policy is designated by the owner of the policy. This designation is not permanent, however, since the owner of the insurance policy generally has the right to change the beneficiary at any time before the death of the insured without the consent of any previously named beneficiary. Since the designated beneficiary has no ability to prevent the owner of the policy from changing the designation, the named beneficiary has no property interest in a life insurance policy before the death of the insured.

[B] Definition of Life Insurance for Tax Purposes

Prior to 1982, there had been no formal definition of life insurance for purposes of the Internal Revenue Code. However, as the focus for life insurance products began shifting away from protecting against the risk of mortality and toward providing tax advantaged investment vehicles, Congress began to question whether such policies should be accorded the tax advantages of life insurance. In response to this concern, Congress enacted a variety of provisions designed to limit the tax advantages of life insurance to those products that are truly insurance in nature.[1]

The rules are extremely complex and their application requires technical actuarial calculations that are beyond the scope of most estate planners' expertise. Therefore, it is generally recommended that if a policy has a strong investment element, is for a very large amount, or is issued by a less-well-known insurance company, then before purchasing a policy the policyholder should obtain written assurances from the insurance company that the policy will be treated as life insurance for tax purposes and will not be treated as a modified endowment contract.

§12.03 USES OF INSURANCE IN ESTATE PLANNING

[A] Income Replacement

The most common use of insurance is to provide a source of support for the insured's family (and other dependents of the insured) in the event of the insured's premature death.

For people with little savings, insurance proceeds are often the largest asset in the estate. If the insured is the primary provider, then the insurance proceeds may be necessary in order to support the family, educate the children, or satisfy the mortgage on the family home. If the insured did not work outside the home, insurance on that person's life may be necessary in order to provide the resources to hire people to do work previously done without compensation by the at-home spouse.

Even for families with sufficient assets, life insurance can be valuable insofar as it is payable to the beneficiaries without going through the probate process. This can provide an immediate source of support during a time that much of the decedent's estate may be tied up in the probate process.

[B] Providing Liquidity to Pay Estate Taxes

Life insurance is a valuable tool for providing liquidity to pay estate taxes and other expenses incurred by reason of the insured's death. An insured may have an estate large enough to generate an estate tax liability, but still have insufficient liquid assets to pay the liability or other expenses of administration. This is particularly likely to be the case if the insured owned a family business, vacation home, or other valuable asset that the family wants to retain. Life insurance can obviate the need to sell assets in order to pay this liability.

---

[1] §12.02 In 1984, Congress enacted IRC §7702, which establishes a definition of life insurance that is applicable to policies issued after 1984. Policies that fail to meet the definition of insurance set out in IRC §7702 lose much of the favorable tax treatment afforded insurance. In 1998, Congress enacted IRC §7702A, introducing the concept of the "modified endowment contract." This provision adds an additional hurdle for purported life insurance contracts to meet in order to be taxed under the rules applicable to life insurance.

[C] Providing Liquidity to Fund Buy-Sell Agreements

For clients who own a business, life insurance can play an important role by providing the cash necessary to fund buy-sell agreements. Buy-sell agreements are agreements in which co-owners of a business (or the business entity itself) agree to purchase the interest in the business held by the decedent upon her death. Buy-sell agreements provide a ready purchaser for a partial interest in a business that may otherwise be difficult to sell. This is important both in terms of providing liquidity to pay estate taxes as well as providing a source of revenue to the heirs. Many closely held businesses do not pay dividends and instead pay out revenues in the form of salaries. An heir who does not work in the business will likely want to sell the business interest in order to reinvest the proceeds in a vehicle that will produce current income.

In order for a buy-sell agreement to be effective, the people or entity obligated to purchase the decedent's interest must have the cash necessary to make the purchase. By purchasing life insurance on each other's lives, the co-owners of the business can be certain to have sufficient assets to carry out the promises made in the buy-sell agreement at the time that the agreement becomes operative.[1]

[D] Equalizing Distributions

Insurance can be useful in enabling a client to distribute her property equitably among her family members or other desired beneficiaries. If a client's estate consists largely of an asset that is not easily divisible and that the client does not want the heirs to have to sell (such as a business interest, vacation home, or other valuable tangible asset), life insurance can provide an additional asset to facilitate an equitable distribution of the client's property. In addition, sometimes the people who the client wants to benefit do not get along well and their differences can cause disruption in the administration of the estate. By providing one party with a life insurance policy and the other party with assets of the decedent's estate, potentially destructive conflicts after the client's death can be avoided.

[1] Business Interests

Life insurance can be a valuable tool for equalizing bequests for business owners. When a client's estate consists largely of a business interest, and some children participate in the business while others do not, the client will need to decide whether to pass the business on to all of the children, or only those that participate in the operation of the business.[2] If the client decides to give the business only to the participating children, insurance can be used to provide an equivalent bequest to the nonparticipating children.

---

[1] § 12.03 Buy-sell agreements are discussed in greater detail in Chapter 11.
[2] Planning for a client with a closely held business is discussed in Chapter 11.

[2] Second Marriage

One situation in which insurance can be very useful is when the client wants to benefit a new spouse as well as children from a prior marriage. A common estate planner's response to such a situation is the QTIP trust in which the surviving spouse is given a life estate in some or all of the decedent's estate and the remainder is given to the client's children from the prior marriage.[3] However, if the new spouse and children do not get along well, the QTIP trust can escalate tensions in the relationship since the spouse's interest (for the trust to produce the maximum annual income) is in direct conflict with the children's interest (for the trust to be invested for long-term growth, rather than for current income). In addition, if the second spouse is close in age to the children from the prior marriage, the children may not live long enough to enjoy the remainder interest under the QTIP. Taking these factors into account, a decision may be made that the parties' relationship will be more amicable in the long run by foregoing use of the QTIP and instead providing either the spouse or the children with the proceeds of a life insurance policy.[4]

[E] Investment Vehicle

Life insurance policies that generate a cash value, such that the owner has the ability to cash in or borrow against the policy, are sometimes used as a source of savings for the owner of the policy. Due to the tax advantages associated with life insurance (in particular tax-free build-up and the ability to avoid estate taxes by giving up all incidents of ownership), life insurance policies have increasingly been developed and marketed as investment vehicles.

[F] Employee Benefit

Life insurance is often provided as an employee benefit. As such, even a client who hasn't planned for the purchase of insurance may have group life insurance, a split dollar policy, or life insurance benefits under a pension or profit sharing plan.

§ 12.04 TYPES OF INSURANCE

There are numerous types of insurance policies. It is important that the insured purchase the right type of life insurance to accomplish the desired goals. All life insurance policies provide that the designated beneficiary will be paid a certain amount at the time of the insured's death in exchange for premium payments, but

---

[3] *See* Chapter 6 for a discussion of QTIP trusts.

[4] In advising a client in this situation, it is important to keep in mind that the spouse's right to an elective share may not be satisfied by designating the surviving spouse as beneficiary of a life insurance policy. The reason for this is that many states do not count nonprobate transfers in calculating the amount to which the surviving spouse is entitled. The elective share is discussed in Chapter 6.

policies vary regarding their period of coverage and the length and amount of premium payments and death benefits. The most significant difference between life insurance policies is that some policies, namely *term insurance,* provide pure insurance protection against the risk of premature death, whereas other policies (such as whole life, variable life, and universal life insurance) have an investment component that can provide lifetime benefits as well. These types of policies are known as *cash value policies.*

[A] Term

Term life insurance is pure insurance that protects against the risk of death for a specific period of time. If the insured dies during that period, the insurer will pay the face amount of the policy to the beneficiary. Term policies typically run for one year, but are often renewable at the insured's option, albeit at a higher cost reflecting the insured's increased age (with its attendant increased risk of mortality). Some policies provide for level premiums for an initial period of years, after which the premiums may increase annually. With term insurance, all of the premium goes toward the insurance coverage and administration expenses and no cash value builds up. Term insurance policies do not pay dividends.

Term life insurance is very popular because it has the lowest premium for a given age. Thus, it enables an individual with relatively few assets to have a sufficient estate for her family in the event of an untimely death. However, as the insured grows older, and the risk of mortality goes up, the premiums also go up, making it increasingly uneconomical for the individual to maintain term insurance.

[B] Whole Life

Whole life insurance, also known as *ordinary life insurance,* differs from term insurance in that it lasts for the entire life of the insured unless the policy is canceled by the insured or lapses due to failure to pay premiums. Whole life typically provides for level premium payments throughout the insured's life (although some policies, called *limited payment policies,* only require premium payment for a set number of years). Annual premiums on a whole life insurance policy are larger than for a term insurance with the same face amount. This excess premium allows for the creation of a reserve, which is accumulated and eventually supports lower premiums in later years. A portion of this cash reserve is accessible to the owner of the policy who is typically given the option to borrow against or cash out the policy.

[C] Variable Life

Variable life insurance is a form of whole life in that it is intended to last for the lifetime of the insured, provides for level payments of premiums, and also provides a cash value benefit to the owner of the policy. The difference between variable life insurance and whole life is that, in variable life insurance, the policy owner controls the investment portion of the insurance (and typically can choose to invest the cash reserve in stocks, bonds, or money market portfolios) and the death benefit is a combination of a minimum fixed benefit and the value of the investments at the time of the insured's death. The owner of the policy thus bears the risk (and enjoys the rewards) of the investment portion of the policy. A variable life insurance policy is sometimes described as term insurance combined with a mutual fund. The difference is that, unlike most mutual funds, this one is held by an insurance company and therefore grows tax free. Due to the perceived potential for abuse, these policies (along with universal life policies) have given rise to rules that restrict the favorable income tax treatment normally applicable to life insurance to policies that meet the statutory definition of insurance. Before purchasing a variable life insurance policy, the owner should make certain that the policy will receive the tax-favored treatment generally afforded life insurance.

[D] Universal Life

Universal life insurance, also called *flexible premium adjustable life insurance,* is a form of whole life in that it provides insurance over the life of the insured. However, unlike traditional whole life policies, in a universal life policy the premiums, cash value, and death benefits are all flexible. Each premium payment on a universal life policy is credited to the cash value account and deductions are made from the account to cover the death benefit. The owner may choose not to make premium payments so long as the cash value of the policy is sufficient to cover the risk of mortality and expenses each month. Alternatively, the owner can make large premium payments in order to build up the cash reserve.

The death benefit in a universal life insurance policy is either a fixed benefit or a fixed benefit that automatically adds to it the current cash value of the reserve. The universal life insurance policy thus most resembles a term policy combined with a savings account. The difference is that, unlike most savings accounts, this one is held by an insurance company and therefore grows tax free. Due to the perceived potential for abuse, these policies (along with variable life policies) have given rise to rules that restrict the favorable income tax treatment normally applicable to life insurance to policies that meet the statutory definition of insurance. Before purchasing a universal life insurance policy, the owner should make certain that the policy will receive the tax-favored treatment generally afforded life insurance.

[E] Second to Die

Second to die life insurance (also called survivorship life insurance) is a life insurance policy that pays a death benefit upon the death of the second of two insured lives. Second to die policies are typically less expensive than a comparable policy on one person's life due to the lower risk of mortality for two people rather than for one.

Second to die policies are often used when planning for a husband and wife since, due to the unlimited marital estate tax deduction, it is often the case that no taxes are due until the death of the second spouse. Thus, a second to die policy can provide liquidity when it is needed—at the death of the surviving spouse.

[F] Split Dollar

Split dollar life insurance is not a type of insurance, but rather an arrangement whereby the payment of premiums and the death benefit are allocated between two parties. Split dollar arrangements are commonly used in the employment context as an employee benefit. Under the most common type of split dollar arrangement (sometimes called an equity split dollar plan) the employer pays all of the premiums on the policy while the agreement is in effect. In exchange for its agreement to pay the premiums on the policy, the split dollar agreement gives the employer the right to recover the amount it paid toward premiums (without interest) from the death benefit of the policy.[1] Thus, the effect of the arrangement is an interest-free loan from the employer to the employee. The employee designates the beneficiary of the policy who receives the balance of the death benefits.

If the arrangement is terminated prior to the employee's death, the employee is entitled to keep the cash surrender value of the policy in excess of the employer's contribution.

EXAMPLE *12-1*

An employee participates in a split dollar plan with her employer in which the employer pays a $25,000 annual premium for a $1,000,000 whole life insurance policy on the employee's life. The employee designates the beneficiary of the policy. Upon the death of the employee, the employer will recover the amounts that it paid on the policy. Thus, if the employee dies during the first year of the arrangement, the designated beneficiary would receive $975,000 and the employer would receive $25,000. If the employee dies during the second year of the arrangement, the designated beneficiary would receive $950,000 and the employer would receive $50,000. If the arrangement is terminated prior to the employee's death, the employer will recover the amounts that it paid on the policy and the employee would recover the remaining cash value of the policy.

Split dollar arrangements are useful because they enable an employee to purchase a large amount of insurance at a time when the employee's income may not be high enough to pay the full premiums. Each year that the agreement is in effect, however, the employee is required to report as additional compensation income the value of one year of term insurance protection.[2] As the employee gets older, and the cost of obtaining insurance is greater, the amount of phantom compensation income

---

[1] **§ 12.04** This amount can be recovered from the cash value of the policy if the policy is surrendered prior to the employee's death.

[2] The amount to be included is the annual value of the benefit received by the employee. This is generally an amount equal to the one-year cost of life insurance protection. The method of valuing current life insurance protection under a split dollar arrangement has received much attention in

that must be reported on her income tax return will increase. At some point the employee may want to terminate the agreement in order to avoid paying income tax on the phantom income. She can do this by borrowing against the cash value of the policy and using that cash to annually repay the employer on the premiums paid.

In July 2002, the Internal Revenue Service issued proposed regulations that provided comprehensive rules for the income, gift, and employment taxation of split dollar life insurance arrangements. These rules were amended in May 2003 when the Internal Revenue Service issued supplemental proposed regulations and were finalized and became effective on September 17, 2003.

The regulations provide two mutually exclusive regimes for the taxation of split dollar arrangements depending generally upon who owns the policy. If the policy is owned by the employee (or a trust for the employee's family), known as a *collateral assignment split dollar arrangement,* then the premiums paid by the employer are treated as a series of loans by the employer to the employee. Under this regime, the loans are subject to the rules governing below market loans found in IRC Section 7872.[3]

EXAMPLE *12-2*

An employee participates in a split dollar plan with her employer in which the employer pays a $25,000 annual premium for a $1,000,000 whole life insurance policy on the employee's life. The policy is owned by the employee, although the employer is entitled to be reimbursed for the premiums paid by the employer. Each year the employer will be treated as having made a $25,000 interest free loan to the employee. Under Section 7872 the transaction will be treated as if the employee had paid the employer interest on the loan at the applicable federal rate, and as if the employer had transferred the amount of that deemed interest payment back to the employee as additional compensation income. Thus, if the applicable federal rate is 5 percent, it will be treated as if the employer had paid and the employee had received an additional $1,250 of compensation income.

If the employer is formally designated the owner of the policy, known as an *endorsement split dollar arrangement,* then the employer will be treated as providing a current economic benefit to the employee. The regulations provide guidance for the valuation of these economic benefits for purposes of federal income, employment, and gift taxes. These rules generally provide that the value of the economic benefits provided under the arrangement equals the cost of any current life insurance protec-

---

(Footnote Continued)

recent years. *See* Rev. Rul. 2001-10, 2001-1 C.B. 459; Notice 2002-8, 2002-4 I.R.B. 398; and Notice 2002-59, 2002-36 I.R.B. 481.

[3] Reg. § 1.7872-15.

tion, plus the amount of policy cash value to which the non-owner has current access and the value of any other economic benefits provided to the non-owner.[4]

These rules apply to arrangements entered into, or materially modified, after September 17, 2003 (the effective date of the final regulations). Arrangements entered into prior to this date are governed by the rules outlined in Notice 2002-8.[5] In many cases, these transition rules allow taxpayers to continue with their prior treatment of split dollar arrangements. In particular, the notice provides as follows:

1. For split dollar insurance arrangements entered into before January 28, 2002, the Service will not assert that there has been a taxable transfer of property upon termination of the arrangement if either (1) the arrangement is terminated prior to January 1, 2004, or (2) for all periods after January 1, 2004, all payments by the sponsor from the inception of the arrangement are treated as loans for federal tax purposes. As loans they would also be subject to IRC Sections 1271 through 1275 (original issue discount rules) and 7872 (rules governing below-market loans).

2. For split dollar arrangement entered into before September 17, 2003 where the value of current life insurance protection has been treated as an economic benefit provided by the employer to the employee, the parties may continue to treat and report the arrangement that way and it will be accepted. If the arrangement continues after January 1, 2004, the parties may be required to treat payments after that date as loans for federal tax purposes.

3. For split dollar arrangement entered into before September 17, 2003, the parties to the arrangement may treat the premium or other payments by the employer as loans, and the Service will not challenge such treatment provided that reasonable efforts are made to comply with the requirements of IRC Sections 1271 through 1275 (original issue discount rules) and 7872 (rules governing below-market loans).

§12.05 TAX CONSEQUENCES OF INSURANCE

One of the reasons that life insurance plays such a central role in estate planning is that there are numerous tax advantages associated with life insurance. In particular, the following tax attributes make life insurance a very attractive investment:

1. The build-up in cash value of life insurance generally occurs free of income tax;

2. Amounts received by a beneficiary of a policy paid by reason of the death of the insured are generally received free of income tax; and

3. Estate taxes on proceeds of life insurance can be avoided by having the insured give up all incidents of ownership on the policy during life. Since

---

[4] Reg. § 1.61-22.

[5] Notice 2002-8, 2002-4 I.R.B. 398.

the value of life insurance during the insured's life is usually relatively small in comparison with the death benefit, this can usually be done with little or no gift tax liability.

[A] Income Tax

[1] Income Tax Consequences to the Policy Owner

When the cash value of a life insurance policy increases in value, such increases generally occur free of income tax. This increase in value is only subject to tax if the owner of the policy surrenders the policy for its cash value.[1] If the owner merely borrows against the policy, there is no income tax liability associated with the increase in value, even if the loan is not paid back during the insured's life. This opportunity for tax-free build-up is one of the features that have made life insurance a valuable investment vehicle.

Due to concern about possible abuses by insurance companies selling what essentially constitutes investment vehicles under the name insurance, Congress enacted rules that subject the policyholder to current income tax on increases in a policy's cash surrender value if the policy does not meet the statutory definition of life insurance.[2]

[2] Income Tax Consequences to the Beneficiary

When the insured dies and life insurance proceeds are paid to the beneficiary, the beneficiary generally receives the proceeds free of income tax.[3] In this way, life insurance is treated the same as amounts received under a will or by intestacy.[4]

EXAMPLE 12-3

B is the named beneficiary in a $2,000,000 insurance policy on I's life. I dies. B receives the $2,000,000 free of income tax.

The one exception to this rule is the *transfer for value* rule. Under this rule, if the transferee of a life insurance policy received the policy for valuable consideration, the

---

[1] **§ 12.05** IRC § 1001.

[2] IRC § 7702.

[3] IRC § 101(a).

[4] IRC § 102. Again, this tax advantage is only available to the extent that the policy meets the statutory definition of life insurance in IRC § 7702. In addition, if a settlement option is chosen by the beneficiary in which the proceeds are kept with the insurance company under an agreement to pay interest on those amounts, the interest portion of any benefits paid to the beneficiary are subject to income tax. IRC § 101(d)(1).

proceeds of the policy are subject to income tax when received by the named beneficiary.[5]

When a beneficiary is paid under a policy that is subject to the transfer for value rule, the proceeds are subject to income tax to the extent that the amount received exceeds the sum of (1) the amount of valuable consideration paid by the transferee and (2) the premiums paid by the transferee.

EXAMPLE 12-4

I owns a $100,000 insurance policy on her life. A purchases the policy for $15,000. A then pays another $5,000 in premiums on the policy. When I dies, A will have taxable income in the amount of $80,000, the face amount of the policy minus A's $20,000 investment in the policy.

The transfer for value rule does not apply when:[6]

1. The policy was acquired directly from the insurance company;
2. The transferee obtains the policy by gift or in any situation in which the recipient takes the same income tax basis in the property as the transferor (such as a tax-free disposition from a partnership to a partner);[7] or
3. The policy is transferred to the insured, a partner of the insured, a partnership in which the insured is a partner, or a corporation in which the insured is a shareholder.

This exception is not available to transfers from one shareholder to another shareholder.[8] Thus, the transfer for value rule can apply when the owners of a corporation use life insurance as part of a buy-sell agreement, but subsequently attempt to restructure the ownership of the policies.[9]

[B] Estate Tax

Life insurance proceeds are subject to estate tax in the insured's estate if:

1. The policy is payable to or for the benefit of the insured's estate;[10]
2. The policy proceeds are payable to someone else, but the insured possessed any "incidents of ownership" of the life insurance policy at the time of death;[11] or

---

[5] IRC § 101(a)(2).

[6] IRC § 101(a)(2)(B).

[7] IRC § 101(a)(2)(A).

[8] *Id.*

[9] Buy-sell agreements are discussed in Chapter 11.

[10] IRC § 2042(1).

[11] IRC § 2042(2).

3. Ownership of the policy was transferred from the insured to someone else within three years of the insured's death.[12]

[1] Policy Payable to the Insured's Estate

A policy will be included in the insured's estate whenever the proceeds are payable to the estate of the insured or the executor of the estate of the insured.[13]

EXAMPLE *12-5*

D was insured under a life insurance policy with a face value of $2,000,000. The policy named D's estate as beneficiary of the policy. At D's death, $2,000,000, the face value of the policy, will be subject to estate tax in D's estate.

The policy need not explicitly designate the estate or executor as the beneficiary of the policy in order to be treated as being payable to or for the benefit of the insured's estate. Rather, if the decedent's estate has the legal right to the proceeds of the life insurance policy, it will be treated as payable to the decedent's estate. Thus, if the policy names someone else as a beneficiary, but the beneficiary is legally obligated to pay taxes, debts, or other enforceable charges against the estate, then the amount of proceeds required for the payment of the obligation is subject to tax in the decedent insured's estate.[14] Thus, insurance purchased as collateral security for a loan to the insured will be included in the decedent's estate, even if the lender is the owner and named beneficiary of the policy.[15]

EXAMPLE *12-6*

D purchased a car and obtained a car loan of $25,000. As a condition of the loan, D was required to purchase a $25,000 life insurance policy on his life that named the lender as the beneficiary. D died several years later, when the loan was still outstanding. The $25,000 life insurance policy is includable in D's estate (although D's estate may be able to deduct the outstanding amount due on the loan).

This issue can also arise in connection with life insurance trusts. If the trust instrument requires the trustee to pay debts, taxes, or expenses of the decedent's

---

[12] IRC § 2035(a).

[13] IRC § 2042(1).

[14] Reg. § 20.2042-1(b)(1).

[15] In that situation, the estate may also be entitled to a deduction for amounts of the policy used to pay off the loan. Reg. § 20.2053-4.

estate, the policy proceeds will be included in the decedent's estate to the extent of the obligation.[16] In order to avoid this, a life insurance trust should include a provision that the trustee is not obligated to pay debts, taxes, or expenses of the decedent's estate. In order to provide liquidity to the insured's estate without raising estate tax issues, the trustee could be authorized to (1) loan the insurance proceeds to the decedent's estate and (2) use the proceeds to purchase assets from the insured's estate.[17]

If the life insurance policy is community property, then only half of the proceeds will be includable in the decedent's estate even if the proceeds are payable to the decedent's estate. This reflects the fact that the insured's spouse has a half ownership interest in the property under community property laws.[18]

[2] Retention of Incidents of Ownership

[a] *In General*

Even if the decedent's estate has no legal right to the proceeds of the policy, a life insurance policy payable to someone else will nonetheless be included in the insured's estate if, at the time of death, the insured held any *incidents of ownership* of the policy.[19]

EXAMPLE 12-7

D was insured under a life insurance policy with a face value of $2,000,000. The policy named D's child C as beneficiary of the policy. D continued to own the policy and had the ability to change the beneficiary of the policy up until the time of the decedent's death. At D's death, $2,000,000 will be subject to estate tax in D's estate.

The term *incidents of ownership* is not limited to the concept of ownership in the legal sense; rather, it refers to the right of the insured to any of the economic benefits of the policy.[20] An incident of ownership includes, among other things:[21]

- The power to change the beneficiary;
- The power to surrender or cancel the policy;
- The power to assign the policy or to revoke an assignment;

---

[16] Reg. § 20.2042-1(b)(1). *See* § 12.07 *infra*, for a discussion of life insurance trusts.

[17] These provisions are included in the Form 4 life insurance trust.

[18] Reg. § 20.2042-1(b)(2). Community property is discussed in greater detail in Chapter 6.

[19] IRC § 2042(2).

[20] Reg. § 20.2042-1(c)(2).

[21] Reg. § 20.2042-1(c).

- The power to pledge the policy for a loan; or
- The power to obtain from the insurer a loan against the surrender value of the policy.

This list is not exhaustive and interests as minimal as the right to affect the timing of payments to the beneficiary (e.g., through choosing settlement options) have been found to be incidents of ownership for purposes of subjecting the insured's estate to tax on insurance proceeds.[22]

The fact that it may be impossible for the insured to actually exercise any of the incidents of ownership before death does not keep the proceeds from being taxable in the insured's estate. All that matters is that the insured had a general legal power to exercise ownership, regardless of the owners' ability to exercise it at a particular moment.[23] For example, even if the insured was declared incompetent and therefore unable to exercise any incident of ownership, she could still be treated as possessing an incident of ownership in the policy at the time of her death.

If the insured does not have any incident of ownership of the policy and if the policy is not payable to or for the benefit of the insured's estate, then it will not be subject to tax in the insured's estate.

EXAMPLE *12-8*

D was insured under a life insurance policy with a face value of $2,000,000. The policy named D's child, C, as beneficiary of the policy and was owned by a life insurance trust for the benefit of C. D is not a trustee of the trust and has no incidents of ownership in the policy. At D's death none of the proceeds of the life insurance policy will be subject to estate tax in D's estate.

[b] *Reversionary Interests*

A reversionary interest may also be treated as an incident of ownership.[24] A reversionary interest is the possibility that the policy or the proceeds of the policy may be returned to the decedent or his estate or may be subject to a power of disposition by him. The possibility that the insured might receive the policy or proceeds of the policy by inheritance through the estate of another, however, is not considered a reversionary interest.

A reversionary interest will only be treated as an incident of ownership if the value of the reversionary interest exceeds five percent of the value of the policy immediately before the death of the insured.[25] The value of a reversionary interest is

---

[22] Estate of Lumpkin, Jr. v. Comm'r, 474 F.2d 1092 (5th Cir. 1973). *But see* Estate of Connelly v. United States, 551 F.2d 545 (3d Cir. 1977).

[23] Comm'r v. Noel Estate, 380 U.S. 678 (1965).

[24] IRC § 2042(2); Reg. § 20.2042-1(c)(3).

[25] IRC § 2042(2); Reg. § 20.2042-1(c)(3).

determined by use of the actuarial tables issued by the IRS. These tables are based on life expectancy, without taking into account the fact of the insured's death.

EXAMPLE *12-9*

Under the terms of a divorce agreement, Husband was required to maintain a life insurance policy on his life for the benefit of Wife for so long as she lived and remained unmarried. The divorce agreement also provided that in the event that Wife predeceased Husband or married prior to his death, the policy would return to Husband or his estate.

Husband died and the insurance proceeds were payable to Wife. Although Husband did not own the policy at the time of his death, the proceeds would nonetheless be subject to tax in Husband's estate if the value of his reversionary interest (as based on the possibility that Wife would predecease him or remarry prior to his death) exceeded 5 percent of the value of the policy immediately prior to his death.[26]

PRACTICE NOTE

This rule is a trap for the unwary as it can cause inclusion in the insured's estate even when the insured did not explicitly retain any control over the policy. In order to avoid application of this rule, the trust or other instrument governing ownership of the policy should explicitly state that in no event will ownership of the policy revest in the insured.

[c] *Jointly Held Interests*

An insured will be treated as having an incident of ownership if the interest is held jointly with another individual. Even the right to veto the exercise of an incidence of ownership by another is sufficient to treat the insured as having an incident of ownership in the policy.

EXAMPLE *12-10*

Husband transferred ownership of a life insurance policy on his life to Wife. Under the terms of the policy, Husband had the right to prevent Wife from transferring the policy to anyone not having an insurable interest in Husband's life. This interest is sufficient to treat Husband as

---

[26] Rev. Rul. 76-113, 1976-1 C.B. 277.

having an incident of ownership in the policy such that the proceeds will be subject to tax in Husband's estate upon his death.[27]

[d] Indirect Interests

An indirect interest can also be treated as an incident of ownership. For example, a shareholder who is the sole or controlling shareholder of a corporation may be treated as having the interest held by the corporation.[28] This attribution rule will not apply to the extent that the proceeds of the policy are payable to the corporation or to a third party for a valid business purpose (e.g., in satisfaction of a business debt of the corporation).[29]

[e] Fiduciary Interests

What if the insured is the trustee of a trust holding life insurance on her life—will those fiduciary powers be treated as an incident of ownership? Powers held by an insured in her fiduciary capacity (i.e., as trustee of a trust) will not constitute incidents of ownership in the policy so long as the following conditions are met:[30]

1. The powers are not exercisable for the insured's own benefit;
2. The insured did not transfer the policy or any of the consideration for purchasing or maintaining the policy to the trust; and
3. The insured did not retain these powers as settlor of the trust.

EXAMPLE 12-11

Insured acquired a life insurance policy on his life in 2014. In 2016, Insured transferred ownership of the policy to his wife who named their child as beneficiary of the policy. In 2020, Wife died. Her will provided for her property (including the insurance policy) to be transferred to a trust for the benefit of her child. The insured was named trustee of the trust. Insured died in 2022. Under the terms of the trust, the insured could not benefit from any of the terms of the trust. The insured will not be treated as having any incident of ownership in the insurance policy and, therefore, the policy will not be included in the insured's estate at the time of his death.[31]

---

[27] Rev. Rul. 75-70, 1975-1 C.B. 301.

[28] Reg. § 20.2042-1(c)(6).

[29] Id.

[30] Rev. Rul. 84-179, 1984-2 C.B. 195. This ruling reflects a reversal from the service's previous position in Rev. Rul. 76-261, 1976-2 C.B. 276, that treated all powers held in a fiduciary capacity as incidents of ownership.

[31] Rev. Rul. 84-179, 1984-2 C.B. 195.

An insured will still be deemed to have incidents of ownership over an insurance policy held in trust where these requirements are not met. Thus, the insured-trustee will be treated as having an incident of ownership in a policy held by the trust if (1) the insured has transferred the policy or any of the consideration for purchasing and maintaining the policy to the trust or (2) the insured-trustee can exercise the trustee powers for her own benefit. In addition, the insured may be treated as having an incident of ownership in the policy if the insured-trustee has a support obligation toward the beneficiary and if the proceeds could be used to satisfy the trustee's support obligation. Thus, as a practical matter, the insured should generally not be named trustee of a trust holding a policy on the insured's life.

[f] Payment of Premiums

The payment of premiums is not, in and of itself, treated as an incident of ownership. Moreover, the insured's right to receive dividends on a life insurance policy owned by another has been found not to be an incident of ownership on the theory that the right to dividends is nothing more than a reduction of the amount of premiums paid.[32] However, as noted above, if the insured pays the premiums of a policy on her life and is the trustee of a trust that owns the policy on her life, she will be treated as having an incident of ownership in the policy.[33]

[3] Transfers of Policies within Three Years of Death

Even if the insured did not have any incident of ownership of the life insurance policy at the time of death, proceeds from the policy will nonetheless be subject to tax in the insured's estate if the insured transferred ownership in the policy by gift within three years of death.[34] This rule will apply even if the transfer of the life insurance policy was excluded from gift tax and the requirement for filing gift tax returns because the policy had a fair market value of less than $15,000.

EXAMPLE 12-12

D was insured under a life insurance policy with a face value of $2,000,000. The policy named D's child, C, as beneficiary of the policy. In 2020, D transferred ownership of the policy to C. D died in 2022. Because D died within three years of making a gift of the life insurance policy, $2,000,000 will be subject to estate tax in D's estate.

---

[32] Estate of Bowers v. Comm'r, 23 T.C. 911 (1955).

[33] *See* § 12.05[B][2][e] *supra.*

[34] IRC § 2035(a).

This rule applies to policies that were transferred by the insured within three years of the insured's death. However, the rule does not apply if the insured merely made premium payments on the policy within three years of death.[35]

EXAMPLE *12-13*

D was insured under a life insurance policy with a face value of $2,000,000. The policy named D's child, C, as beneficiary of the policy. In 2016, D transferred ownership of the policy to C. D continued to make premium payments on the policy until the time of his death in 2022. The proceeds of the policy are not subject to tax in D's estate because D did not have any incidents of ownership in the policy at the time of his death nor in the three years prior to his death. The payment of premiums by D does not change this result.

What if the policy was purchased by someone other than the insured within three years of the insured's death? The law in this area has undergone some changes in recent years, but it is now clear that the proceeds of the policy will not be subject to tax in the insured's estate, provided that the insured did not have any incidents of ownership in the policy within the three years prior to the insured's death.[36]

EXAMPLE *12-14*

In 2010, C purchased a life insurance policy on his father, D's, life. Although C owned the policy, D paid premiums on the policy until the time of his death in 2022. The proceeds of the policy are not subject to tax in D's estate because D did not have any incidents of ownership in the policy at the time of his death nor in the three years prior to his death. The payment of premiums by D does not change this result.

[C] Gift Tax

The designation of a beneficiary on a life insurance policy does not constitute a gift since the owner of the policy is free to change the beneficiary designation.

---

[35] Rev. Rul. 71-497, 1971-2 C.B. 29.

[36] Prior to the 1981 revisions to Section 2035, both the IRS and the courts took the position that if the insured paid the premiums and named someone else as owner of the policy, which was effectively the same as if the insured had purchased the policy herself and then transferred ownership of the policy to the new owner. *See, e.g.,* Bel v. United States, 452 F.2d 683 (5th Cir. 1971). After changes to Section 2035 in 1981, the IRS continued to litigate this position, albeit unsuccessfully. *See, e.g.,* Leder Est. v. Comm'r, 89 T.C. 235 (1987), *aff'd,* 893 F.2d 237 (10th Cir. 1989). In 1991, the IRS reluctantly acquiesced and stated that it would no longer litigate this issue. AOD 1991-012 (July 3, 1991).

However, there are generally three situations involving life insurance that can result in the imposition of a gift tax:

1. The transfer of ownership of a life insurance policy;[37]

2. The payment of premiums of a life insurance policy owned by someone else;[38] and

3. The death of the insured can be treated as a gift from the policy-holder to the beneficiary if the policy is owned by someone other than the insured (including under community property laws).[39]

[1] Transfer of Ownership of Policy

The complete transfer of ownership of a life insurance policy constitutes a gift for gift tax purposes. This assignment can be outright to an individual or, more commonly, to a trust (assuming that the transferor has not retained control of the trust).[40]

[a] Valuation

Like all gifts, a transfer of a life insurance policy is taxed at its fair market value as of the date of transfer.[41] The regulations provide specific valuation rules for life insurance.[42] In particular, the value of a life insurance policy for gift tax purposes depends upon whether the policy is a new policy or has been fully or partially paid up. If the policy is a newly issued policy (either issued directly to a third party or issued to the insured and immediately transferred to a third party), the value of the policy is the amount that was paid for the insurance contract.[43] If it is a fully paid up policy (either because it is a single pay policy or because all of the premium payments have been made with respect to the policy), then the value of the policy for gift tax purposes is the amount that the company would charge for a policy of the same specified amount on the life of a person who is the age of the insured. Finally, if the policy is not a new policy, and not yet fully paid up, then the value of the policy is the *interpolated terminal reserve*. The *interpolated terminal reserve* is the amount that the insurance company lists on its books of account and is roughly equivalent to the cash value.[44]

---

[37] IRC § 2511; Reg. § 25.2511-1(h)(B).

[38] *Id.*

[39] Reg. § 25.2511-2(f); Rev. Rul. 81-166, 1981-1 C.B. 477.

[40] The requirements of a completed gift for gift tax purposes are discussed in Chapter 8.

[41] IRC § 2512.

[42] Reg. § 25.2512-6(a).

[43] Reg. § 25.2512-6(a), Example 1.

[44] An example of the calculation is found in Reg. § 25.2512-6(a), Example 4.

[b] Availability of Annual Gift Tax Exclusion

The annual exclusion permits an individual to give $15,000 each year to an unlimited number of donees, free of both gift tax and generation-skipping tax, provided that the gift is of a present interest.[45] In order to qualify for the annual exclusion, the gift must be of a present interest in property. The regulations specify that a present interest in property is "[a]n unrestricted right to the immediate use, possession, or enjoyment of property or the income from property (such as a life estate or term certain)."[46] The fact that the purpose of life insurance is to provide a benefit in the future (i.e., upon the death of the insured) does not, in and of itself, prevent the policy from meeting the general present interest requirement.[47]

The outright transfer of a life insurance policy to a single donee meets the present interest requirement. However, a gift of a life insurance policy to more than one donee will generally not meet the present interest requirement since no single owner can exercise all of the rights of ownership without the consent of the other co-owners.[48] One way of addressing this problem would be to purchase smaller policies for each donee or request the insurance company to split a pre-existing policy into several policies for each donee.

If the gift of the policy is to a minor, it can qualify for the present interest exclusion by making a transfer to a custodian under the Uniform Gifts to Minors Act or Uniform Transfers to Minors Act.[49]

A transfer of a life insurance policy to a trust will generally not qualify for the annual exclusion unless additional steps are taken. The most common way of meeting the present interest in a trust holding insurance is to create a Crummey trust.[50] A Crummey trust gives the trust beneficiaries the right to withdraw a *pro rata* portion of any gift made to the trust during a limited period of time. This withdrawal right is a present interest and therefore enables transfers to the trust to qualify for the annual exclusion.

[2] Payment of Premiums

The payment of insurance premiums by an insured on a policy in which he has no interest is a gift.[51] However, if the transfer of the underlying life insurance policy qualifies or would qualify for the annual exclusion (because it is to a single donee or

---

[45] IRC §§ 2503(b) and 2642(c). The annual exclusion for gift tax purposes is discussed in Chapter 8. The annual exclusion for generation-skipping transfer tax purposes is discussed in Chapter 9. There are additional requirements for the annual exclusion for GST purposes when the transfer is in trust.

[46] Reg. § 25.2503-3(b).

[47] Reg. § 25.2503-3(a).

[48] *See* Skouros Est. v. Comm'r, 188 F.2d 831 (2d Cir. 1951).

[49] The Uniform Gifts to Minor Act, 8A U.L.A. 375 (1993), and Uniform Transfers to Minors Act, 8B U.L.A. 497 (1993), are discussed in Chapter 7.

[50] A Crummey trust is named after Crummey v. Comm'r, 397 F.2d 82 (9th Cir. 1954). Crummey trusts are discussed in Chapter 8.

[51] Reg. § 25.2511-1(h)(8).

because it is to a trust that otherwise qualifies for the annual exclusion), then the payment of premiums on the policy will qualify for the annual exclusion as well.[52]

EXAMPLE *12-15*

Mother transferred a life insurance policy on her life to her daughter. Thereafter, Mother continued to pay the annual premiums of $15,000 per year. The annual premium payments will qualify as a present interest since the daughter owns the policy outright.

[3] Death of the Insured

The death of the insured can sometimes result in a gift if the policy is owned by someone other than the insured and a third party is named as the beneficiary of the policy. In that case the death of the insured completes the gift from the owner of the policy to the named beneficiary for gift tax purposes.[53]

EXAMPLE *12-16*

Mother transferred a life insurance policy on her life to Daughter. The policy named Grandson (Daughter's child) as beneficiary of the policy. Upon Mother's death, there will be a completed gift from Daughter to Grandson.

§12.06 KEEPING LIFE INSURANCE OUT OF THE INSURED'S ESTATE

[A] In General

Life insurance provides a unique opportunity for wealthy individuals to provide substantial benefits to desired beneficiaries with very little tax cost. The reasons for this are (1) if the insured has no incidents of ownership in the policy, it will not be subject to estate tax in the insured's estate; (2) the value of a life insurance policy or the premiums necessary to support it during the life of the insured may be relatively small in comparison to the death benefit and gifts of premiums can be spread out over many years using the annual exclusion, making it possible to transfer a policy during life with little or no gift tax liability; (3) the nature of insurance is such that it is unlikely that the insured will feel that she is giving up use of an asset with

---

[52] Reg. § 25.2503-3(c), Example 6.
[53] Rev. Rul. 77-48, 1977-1 C.B. 292; Reg. § 25.2511-2(f).

substantial lifetime value; (4) the named beneficiary will receive the insurance proceeds free of income tax; and (5) unlike other assets that appreciate in value between the time of transfer by gift and the time of death, the beneficiary will not have a problem of built-in gain often caused by carryover basis.

In planning for the maximum tax advantages available for insurance, the estate planner must address a number of issues:

- Which life insurance policies should be transferred?
- Who should be the owner of the policy? If a trust is the owner of the policy, who should be the trustee?
- Who should be the named beneficiary of the policy?
- Who should pay the premiums on the policy?

[B] Which Life Insurance Policies Should Be Transferred?

The first decision that needs to be addressed in this area is whether the insured is going to transfer new or existing policies. If existing policies are transferred, there may be a question as to which of the insured's existing policies should be transferred. If new policies are going to be purchased on the insured's life, there may be a question as to whether the insured or someone else should be the initial purchaser of the policy.

[1] New or Existing Policies

The surest way of keeping an insurance policy out of the insured's estate is by purchasing a new policy on the insured's life. However, other factors may work against this. The insured may already own several policies on her life and it may not make financial sense to purchase new ones. In addition, if the insured is in ill health, he may no longer be insurable or it may be prohibitively expensive to purchase a new policy on the insured's life.

[a] Existing Policies

It is not unusual for an individual to have more than one life insurance policy on her life. In that case, the question may come up as to which, if any, of these policies should be transferred. In advising this decision, the estate planner should consider (1) the benefits, if any, to the insured of retaining ownership of the policy, and (2) the tax costs of assigning the policy.

Some policies, such as policies with a significant cash value, are able to provide significant lifetime benefits to the insured, whereas other policies are valuable solely or primarily for their death benefit. In deciding which policy to transfer, the insured should first consider transferring those policies that provide little lifetime benefit to the insured.

The tax cost of assigning the policy is another factor that should be taken into account in making the decision as to which policy to transfer. Life insurance policies carrying the same death benefit may have very different current fair market values depending upon the existence and extent of the policy's cash value. This can have a significant impact on the gift tax liability associated with the transfer of the policy. Thus, to limit gift tax liability, consideration should be given first to transferring term policies in favor of cash value policies, and, second, to transferring recently purchased cash value policies in preference to older cash value policies.

If the insured is transferring ownership of an existing policy, it is important that the insured transfer all incidents of ownership in the policy. Transfer of the policy is accomplished by (1) completing the insurance company forms regarding transfer of ownership; (2) delivering physical possession of the policy to the new owner; and (3) reviewing to make certain that all ownership rights have been transferred. If any incidents of ownership are retained, no matter how seemingly insignificant, the insured runs a substantial risk that the proceeds of the policy will be subject to tax in the insured's estate.

[b] New Policies

If a new policy is going to be purchased for the purpose of passing outside of the insured's estate, a question may arise as to whether the insured or someone else should purchase the policy. From a tax-planning standpoint, it is always preferable to have someone other than the insured purchase the policy. The reason for this is that if the donee purchases the policy directly from the insurer, then there has not been a transfer of the policy from the insured and the three-year rule doesn't apply.[1]

[C] Designating the Recipient

[1] In General

It is generally advisable to have the owner of the policy be the same person or entity as the desired beneficiary. The reason for this is twofold: (1) the new owner will have the power to change the beneficiary and could therefore change to benefit someone other than the person or entity the insured wants to benefit; and (2) if the owner of the policy is someone other than the insured and other than the beneficiary, then the death of the insured will result in a taxable gift from the owner of the policy to the named beneficiary.[2]

[2] Outright to Spouses

Prior to 1981 it was common for spouses to be made owners of each other's life insurance policies. However, after the adoption of the unlimited marital deduction, this device no longer provides any tax benefits since the same benefits can be achieved by having the insured spouse retain ownership of the policy and then

---

[1] **§ 12.06** *See, e.g.,* Leder Est. v. Comm'r, 893 F.2d 237 (10th Cir. 1987). The three-year rule is discussed in § 12.05[B][3] *supra.*

[2] Reg. § 25.2511-2(f); Rev. Rul. 81-166, 1981-1 C.B. 477.

transfer the proceeds of the policy to the spouse in a way that qualifies for the unlimited marital deduction.[3]

[3] Outright to Nonmarital Partners

If the insured has a nonmarital partner, then significant tax savings can be achieved by having that person own a life insurance policy on the insured's life. The transfer of the policy to a nonmarital partner should qualify as a present interest for purposes of the $15,000 annual exclusion. In addition, so long as the policy is owned by a single donee, any payment of premiums by the insured will also qualify as a present interest for purposes of the $15,000 annual exclusion. As long as the insured did not have any incidents of ownership in the policy within three years of death, the proceeds of the policy will be paid to the nonmarital partner free of estate tax liability.

[4] Outright to Children and Other Beneficiaries

Ownership of the policy could also be transferred outright to the children of the insured or to other beneficiaries that the insured wants to benefit. These transfers will qualify as a present interest for purposes of the $15,000 annual exclusion as long as the policy is transferred to a single beneficiary. If the transfer is to more than one person, the transfer will not be eligible for the annual exclusion because the fact that the owners must work together will cause the present interest requirement not to be met. If the insured wants to transfer the policy to more than one beneficiary, it is usually preferable to transfer the policy to a trust with Crummey powers so that it will qualify for the annual exclusion.[4]

The payment of premiums by the insured on a policy owned by another will also qualify as a present interest for purposes of the $15,000 annual exclusion as long as the transfer of the underlying policy qualifies as a present interest (e.g., because the policy was transferred to a single donee or to a trust with Crummey powers). If there is more than one owner of the policy, then the payment of premiums will generally not qualify as a present interest since the transfer of the policy itself did not qualify. In that case, the insured could still provide the funds for premium payments in a way that qualifies as a present interest by making cash gifts during the year to the beneficiaries that could then be used to pay the premiums on the policy. Another way to avoid any gift tax problems would be for the owners of the policy to pay the premiums themselves.

An outright transfer of a life insurance policy may be the simplest manner for getting the policy out of the insured's estate for tax purposes. However, before transferring a policy outright to children or other beneficiaries, there are several potential problems the insured should consider:

---

[3] The marital deduction is discussed in greater detail in Chapter 6.

[4] *See* Chapter 8 for a discussion of Crummey powers. Form 4 is a sample life insurance trust with Crummey powers.

1. The owners of the policy will have the ability to cash in the policy prior to the insured's death, thus foregoing the benefit intended by the insured;
2. After the death of the insured, the children or other designated beneficiary may choose not to use the proceeds for estate liquidity purposes;
3. If the insured's children own the policy outright, the proceeds cannot be used for the benefit of the insured's spouse without the children making a taxable gift to the spouse; and
4. The proceeds of the policy will be subject to tax in the estate of the beneficiary-owners.

Many of these problems can be addressed by transferring the policy to a trust for the benefit of the desired beneficiaries.

§12.07 LIFE INSURANCE TRUSTS

[A] Transfers in Trust

The *life insurance trust* (sometimes called the *personal life insurance trust* or an *irrevocable life insurance trust*, or *ILIT*) is the most common device for keeping an insurance policy from being subject to tax in the insured's estate.[1]

A life insurance trust is created either (1) for existing policies, by having the insured-owner transfer the policy to a trust, or (2) for new polices, by having the insured create a trust with cash and having the trustee purchase life insurance on the settlor's life. In either case, the trust is designated both the owner of the policy and the beneficiary of the policy. The trust instrument provides the plan of disposition for the proceeds of the policy.

In order to obtain the maximum advantage of a life insurance trust, the trust should be structured in such a way that (1) the proceeds are not subject to tax in the insured's estate for estate tax purposes and (2) the transfer of the policy and any premium payments qualify for the annual exclusion for both gift and generation-skipping transfer tax purposes. The estate planner should also be mindful of the income tax issues arising from a life insurance trust to both the grantor of the trust as well as to the beneficiaries.

[B] Estate Tax Issues with Life Insurance Trusts

The life insurance trust should be structured in such a way that the life insurance is not subject to estate tax in the insured's estate. In doing so, the estate planner should be mindful of the rules applicable to life insurance policies as well as the rules applicable to trusts. It should also be noted that the tax goals of keeping insurance out of the insured's estate are more easily achieved by purchasing a new policy, as opposed to transferring an existing policy, since in the latter case the insured must

---

[1] § 12.07 Form 4 is a sample life insurance trust.

also survive three years after the date of transfer in order to keep the policy from being subject to tax in the insured's estate.[2]

In order to avoid inclusion in the insured's estate, the insured must be careful not to retain any incidents of ownership in the policy or any beneficial interest in the trust itself. In transferring an existing policy the insured should be certain to (1) complete and file the applicable insurance company forms for the change of beneficiary and transfer of ownership of the policy, naming the trust as the owner of the policy; (2) physically transfer the life insurance policies to the trustee; and (3) prepare a schedule for the trust listing all assets transferred to the trust and state explicitly that the insured is transferring "all right title and interest, including any and all incidents of ownership of the [described] policy." It is also important that the assignment of the policy be effective for state law purposes as well as under the terms of the policy, as the ineffective assignment of a policy could result in the proceeds being subject to tax in the insured's estate.

The trust must also be drafted in such a way that it is not inadvertently subject to tax in the insured's estate. In particular, the following should be kept in mind:

- The trust must be an irrevocable trust;[3]

- The insured should not be the trustee of the trust.[4] Although there is some flexibility for the situation in which the insured did not transfer ownership of the policy or consideration for the purchase of the policy and the powers are not exercisable for the insured's benefit, the safer course is to provide that the insured is not the trustee and that in no event will the insured be named successor trustee; and

- The trust should not permit trust assets to be used in satisfaction of any legal obligation of the insured, although the trustee could be given authorization to loan the proceeds to the insured's executor or to use the trust assets to purchase assets from the insured's estate.

The life insurance policy may be purchased by the trust or an existing policy can be transferred into the trust. It is preferable to have the insurance policy acquired by the trustee rather than be transferred into the trust. If the existing policies are transferred into the trust by the insured, the insured must survive the transfer by three years or more or the insurance proceeds will be included in the insured's estate.[5]

---

[2] IRC § 2035.

[3] IRC § 2038 includes assets in a revocable trust in the settlor's gross estate. The insured should be reminded that the effect of this requirement is that the insured will not have the power to change beneficiaries should his relationships with them change. However, this can be ameliorated in part by having the trust purchase term insurance on the insured's life. In the event that the insured later regrets having established the trust, he can stop payment on the policies and thereby effectively terminate the trust.

[4] Reg. § 20.2042-1(c)(4).

[5] IRC § 2035(a)(2).

[C] Gift Tax Issues with Life Insurance Trusts

The life insurance trust may also be structured in such a way that transfers to the trust (of the insurance policy or of cash to purchase the policy or pay premiums) qualify for the annual exclusion for gift tax purposes.

A transfer to a trust will generally not qualify for the annual exclusion for gift tax purposes unless additional steps are taken. The most common method of making transfers to an insurance trust qualify for the annual exclusion is to create a Crummey trust in which the trust beneficiaries are given the right to withdraw a *pro rata* portion of any gift made to the trust during a limited period of time.[6] This withdrawal right is a present interest and therefore enables transfers to the trust to qualify for the annual exclusion.[7]

The Internal Revenue Service has questioned whether the Crummey withdrawal power will constitute a present interest when the only asset owned by the trust is the life insurance policy. The reasoning behind this is the assumption that should the power be exercised, the trustee could not pay it off.[8] This argument appears to have little merit so long as it is clear under the terms of the withdrawal right that the policy itself can be withdrawn and the policy's value is sufficient to support the withdrawal obligation.[9] Although the merit of this issue is questionable, to be on the safe side, it is advisable to provide the trust with other, more liquid, assets that can be used to fulfill the withdrawal right obligations.

The payment of premiums by someone other than the trustee of the trust will also constitute gifts to the beneficiaries.[10] However, if the trust is structured as a Crummey trust, the premium payments should also be eligible for the present interest exclusion.

There is an additional gift tax issue that must be taken into account when planning a Crummey trust. If everything goes as planned, the beneficiaries will not in fact exercise their withdrawal powers and, under the terms of the trust, the powers will then lapse. This lapse of Crummey powers can, in some situations, be treated as a taxable gift by one beneficiary to the other beneficiaries.[11] Since this gift will not meet the present interest requirement, the effect of this will be to eat away at the beneficiaries' unified credit exclusion amount. In order to avoid this result, the Crummey powers should be drafted to fit within the so-called five or five exception to this rule.[12] Under the *five or five* exception, a lapse of a general power of appointment will only be treated as a gift to the other beneficiaries to the extent that the property subject to the power exceeded the greater of $5,000 or 5 percent of the

---

[6] Rev. Rul. 81-7, 1981-1 C.B. 474.

[7] Crummey trusts are discussed in greater detail in Chapter 8.

[8] *See, e.g.,* Ltr. Ruls. 8103074 and 8118051.

[9] *See, e.g.,* Ltr. Ruls. 8006109, 8021058, and 8111123.

[10] Reg. § 25.2511-1(h)(8).

[11] IRC § 2514(b).

[12] IRC § 2514(e).

property held in the trust.[13] The simplest way to use the five or five exception to avoid a taxable gift when a Crummey power lapses is to limit each beneficiary's share of all gifts to the trust subject to the withdrawal power to the lesser of $5,000 or 5 percent of the trust corpus. If gifts to the trust are so limited, the beneficiary will never have the power to withdraw more than "five or five," and the lapse of the power will not result in a taxable gift by the beneficiary. This approach will often work well in the insurance trust context since the value of the policy transferred is often within this five or five limitation. In situations in which the value of the policy or annual premiums are in excess of these amounts, the trust should be drafted with a hanging power (in which the right of withdrawal only lapses to the extent protected under the five or five exception) or the beneficiaries should be given either a general or limited testamentary power of appointment over the trust corpus subject to the lapsed withdrawal right to the extent that the withdrawal right exceeded $5,000 or 5 percent of the trust corpus.[14]

[D] Income Tax Issues with Life Insurance Trusts

Many irrevocable life insurance trusts are treated as grantor trusts for income tax purposes.[15] Under the grantor trust rules, the trust is disregarded for income tax purposes and all income and deductions associated with the trust are taxed directly to the insured. Similarly, the Service has taken the position that the lapse of Crummey powers may result in the beneficiaries of the trust being treated as grantors for purposes of the grantor trust rules.[16]

In practical terms, the grantor trust status of an insurance trust for either the insured or the beneficiaries should not be problematic since the increase in value of a life insurance policy is not subject to income tax.

§12.08 LONG-TERM CARE INSURANCE[1]

[A] Introduction

In fundamental terms, insurance is the transfer of risk from the policyowner/insured to the insurance company in exchange for the payment of a premium. Long-term care insurance (LTCI) is the insurance coverage that specifically funds the risk of long-term care. LTCI covers a range of services designed to help clients when they are

---

[13] *Id.*

[14] Form 4 contains samples of both a five or five Crummey power and a hanging Crummey power. These issues are discussed in greater detail in Chapter 8.

[15] IRC §677(a)(3) provides that a trust will be a grantor trust if the trust income can be and is used to pay premiums on the life of the grantor and/or the grantor's spouse. Grantor trusts are discussed in Chapter 4.

[16] The Service takes the position that the lapse of a Crummey withdrawal power will cause the power holder to be subject to income tax on that lapsed amount under IRC §678(a)(2).

[1] **§12.08** Section 12.08 was written by Tobe Gerard, CLTC, MBA, MLS, LIA.

no longer able to complete everyday tasks, oftentimes referred to as the activities of daily living (ADLs). Long-term care can be received in any of the following settings: home care, assisted living, adult day, skilled nursing, and hospice.

Deciding to purchase an LTCI policy is a big decision; deciding not to purchase a policy also has its ramifications. Not every client will want to insure for this risk, but it can be an extremely useful financial and estate preservation tool for more affluent clients.

While this chapter will focus exclusively on LTCI as a planning strategy, there are different options to consider for clients who have limited assets and limited income and might be better served with Medicaid planning.

[B] Who Should Purchase LTCI?

When LTCI was first introduced, it was marketed predominantly to seniors who were 65 and older, with premiums that were within the reach of many middle-income Americans. We now hear the expression: "This is not your Grandma's LTCI!" Today's products are significantly more expensive. They cater to a younger, more affluent audience. We find that most buyers today are high wage earners who own their own homes and who have assets between $1,500,000 and $5,000,000. We are now seeing advisors recommend LTCI to some of their clients who have assets above $5,000,000 if there has been already been a long-term care event in these clients' families.

Many advisors start the LTCI conversation proactively with clients who are in their 50s, and some advisors engage their clients at even younger ages if there is a family history of some significant health issue or disease. In some cases, clients have competing priorities for their expense stream dollars and are not able to consider LTCI when they are in their 50s. These clients may have children who have not graduated from college yet, or they may be helping to support aging parents. These clients may need to wait to explore LTCI until they are in their 60s. It is important to know that LTCI is still affordable for people in their 60s as long as they are in good health.

Besides the asset protection side of mitigating long-term care risk, the other facet of LTCI is the emotional side that comes into play when a loved one needs care. It can create punishing emotional and physical stress for spouses, partners, children, and siblings. Clients who have had a personal experience with a loved one needing care are excellent candidates for LTCI.

[C] What Factors Go into LTCI Policy Design?

An overall comment regarding policy design is that the trend today is toward policies that are referred to as "short and fat" rather than "long and lean." This means that it is more advantageous to buy a policy with a monthly benefit of $6,000 per month for a three-year period of time than to buy a policy with a monthly benefit of $4,000 per month for a five-year period of time. The rationale for "short and fat" is that a policyholder does not lose the benefit if he or she does not use it in full; the benefit remains as part of the lifetime maximum and extends the benefit period beyond the number of years that had been anticipated. With "long and lean," the policyholder may have to substantially supplement the monthly benefit on the front end and may never get to use the full lifetime maximum on the back end.

There is no "one size fits all" when it comes to LTCI. All clients are encouraged to customize their LTCI policies. The premium can be dialed up or down depending upon whether the policy design will be more basic or more robust.

There are four main component parts of an LTCI policy. The remaining features fall into the category of optional benefits known as riders.

[1] Daily or Monthly Benefit

LTCI policies offer either a "daily" or a "monthly" benefit. Many LTCI policies today are designed using a monthly platform. The daily or monthly amount is the maximum that the policy will pay out based upon the actual charges that are incurred for care on a daily or a monthly basis.

Most LTCI policies today are "comprehensive" in nature, which means that they can be used to access care at home, at an adult day care center, in an assisted living facility, in a skilled nursing facility, as well as for hospice services.

One example of how the monthly benefit works is a scenario where an LTCI policy has a benefit of $6,000 per month. Care at an assisted living facility costs $7,000 per month. The policy would pay the full benefit of $6,000 per month, and the policyholder would need to self-fund the remaining monthly balance of $1,000.

Another example of how the monthly benefit works is a scenario where an LTCI policy has a benefit of $7,500 per month. Care at an assisted living facility costs $7,000 per month. The policy would pay the full benefit of $7,000 per month, and the remaining $500 per month that was not accessed would remain in the policy as part of the lifetime maximum, which is described below.

[2] Benefit Period/Lifetime Maximum

In the early days of LTCI, it was common to be able to purchase a "lifetime" (or "unlimited") benefit period. At the present time, there is only one traditional and one linked benefit LTCI company that offer a lifetime benefit.

Most LTCI policies sold today have a defined benefit duration that is expressed in a variety of ways, depending upon the LTCI company. Some companies use a number of days (i.e., 730, 1095, 1460, or 1825); some use a number of months (i.e., 24, 36, 48, or 60); and some use a number of years (i.e., 2, 3, 4 or 5). All of these also use a lifetime maximum. The lifetime maximum is a pool of money that is calculated using the daily or monthly benefit multiplied by the number of days, months, or years.

For example, an LTCI policy that has a monthly benefit of $6,000 per month and a three-year benefit period will have a pool of money with a $216,000 lifetime maximum.

[3] Elimination Period

All LTCI policies have an elimination period. The elimination period is the waiting period that has to be satisfied before benefits can begin to be paid. An elimination period is similar to a deductible. The difference is that with auto, home, personal umbrella, and other property and casualty coverages, clients select a flat dollar amount as a deductible (i.e., $250, $500, $1,000, etc.); with LTCI, clients select a number of days as the elimination period (i.e., 0, 30, 60, 90, 180, or 365).

The most common elimination period is 90 days. While a 180-or 365-day elimination period may sound attractive to more affluent clients, sometimes there is not much of a savings to consider beyond a 90-day elimination period.

It is important to note that not all elimination periods are created equal. The client needs to understand the nuances of coverage based upon the various ways that elimination periods are satisfied. Most of the earlier LTCI policies had a "Service Day" elimination period. Most of the LTCI policies today have a "Calendar Day" elimination period. A calendar day elimination period is far more flexible than a service day elimination period and may require less of a cash outlay to satisfy it.

a. Service Day Elimination Period

A service day elimination period is based upon the number of days that the insured/policyholder receives qualified long-term care services. Only those days when qualified long-term care services are received count toward satisfaction of the elimination period. Days when services are received do not need to be consecutive. If you have a 90-service-day elimination period and you don't receive qualified long-term care services every day of the month, it can often take much longer than 90 days to satisfy a 90-service-day elimination period.

b. Calendar Day Elimination Period

A calendar day elimination period is only concerned with the days on the calendar. While some companies may require that you start a calendar day elimination period by receiving one day of qualified long-term care services, the remaining days are counted and satisfied simply by going through the days on the calendar; there is no requirement that qualified long-term care services be received. With a calendar day elimination period, it will never take longer than 90 days to satisfy a 90-calendar-day elimination period.

EXAMPLE *12-17*

I receive qualified long-term care services in any given week on Monday, Wednesday, and Friday. With a service day elimination period, I would have satisfied three days. With a calendar day elimination period, I would have satisfied seven days.

[4] Inflation

Inflation is technically a rider, but we always consider it as one of the four component parts of an LTCI policy because it is the leverage that allows a client's policy to keep up with the rising cost of long-term care services over time.

The average age of claim with most LTCI policies is around 85 or 86. With that in mind, it becomes critical for clients who are in their 40s, 50s, and early to mid-60s to consider some amount of inflation protection. A five percent compound inflation used to be the gold standard, but because of the dramatic increase in its cost, many clients now purchase 3 percent compound instead. Compound inflation is the best inflation that can be purchased. It is similar to interest. Where simple inflation is interest that is calculated based upon going back to the original daily or monthly benefit, compound inflation is interest that is calculated based upon going back to the previous year. The saying is that "3 percent is the new 5 percent," as 3 percent compound inflation has become the most common inflation purchased today. Other inflation options are available that range from 1 percent to 5 percent.

EXAMPLE *12-18*

Assume that a 50-year-old client purchases an LTCI policy with a monthly benefit of $6,000, a lifetime maximum of $216,000, and with 3 percent compound inflation. The value of that policy in 24 years when the client is 74 will have doubled, making the monthly benefit approximately $12,000 and the lifetime maximum approximately $432,000. The leverage that compounding provides is essential.

[5] Riders

Riders are optional benefits. Riders are ways to personalize an LTCI policy, but they also increase the premium. If budget is the main concern for the client, you may decide not to recommend any riders. If having robust and more customized coverage is the client's goal, then there are three riders that we see purchased on a regular basis that may be worthy of consideration:

[a] Shared Care

Sharing is available to couples only. This option assumes that both members of the couple have purchased identical individual policies. Sharing allows the policies to be linked in some fashion. Depending upon the LTCI company, Sharing will be structured in one of two ways. Both options are well designed with neither being better than the other:

1. If one spouse/partner exhausts the benefits in his or her policy, he or she is able to access most, or with some companies all, of the benefits in the other spouse/partner's policy; or
2. If one spouse/partner exhausts the benefits in his or her policy, he or she is able to access the benefits in an extended joint third pool, but he or she is not able to access the benefits in the other spouse/partner's policy.

[b] "0" Day Elimination Period for Home Care

This rider, also known as the "waiver of elimination period for home care," allows the policyholder to receive home care benefits from day one without having to satisfy any elimination period. Many advisors look at this rider as a gift to the family knowing that care will be available from the first day while the family is grappling with all of the other issues surrounding the impairment of a loved one.

[c] Joint Waiver of Premium

The industry standard is that when a policyholder is on claim and receiving benefits under the policy, then the premium is waived. This rider waives the premium for both spouses/partners if one spouse/partner is on claim and receiving benefits under the policy.

[D] What Factors Go into the Pricing of LTCI?

When LTCI was first introduced, the pricing platform was unrealistic. With no actuarial data available at that time, there was no information available on lapse rates, claims frequency and severity, the impact of a low interest rate environment, the significance of increasing mortality, and other key pieces of information. LTCI companies now have that data available. The products that are being sold today are sounder actuarially than they have been at any other time in the history of the LTCI industry. We are hopeful that pricing has finally stabilized and that it will be sustainable going forward with only minor rate increases.

[1] Age

The younger your client is, the lower the premium will be.

[2] Marital/Partner Status

There are discounts available when your clients are a "couple." The definition of a "couple" is slightly different from one LTCI company to another, but in most cases, it will be one of the following: (1) two people who have been living together and are either married to each other, have a civil union in place with each other, or have a domestic partnership in place with each other, or (2) two people who are either of the opposite sex or of the same sex and are in a committed relationship with each other and have been living together and sharing expenses with each other for at least three years. Neither of these people may be married to someone else. Couple's discounts have historically been in the 30 percent range, but more recently, a number of companies have been lowering the percentage of that discount. Discounts may also be available if only one member of a couple applies, or if only one member of a couple is approved. These discounts used to be in the 15 percent range, but more recently have been lowered as well.

[3] Gender

LTCI was initially introduced as a unisex product. At the present time, all LTCI companies charge higher premiums for women than for men. Actuarial data shows that two-thirds of all LTCI claims are attributable to women, so LTCI companies decided that the pricing structure should represent that fact. Single women who live alone now pay higher rates than anyone else.

[4] Health

When it comes to LTCI, health trumps everything else. Clients can be young or old, male or female, part of a couple or single, but if the client is not in good health, nothing else matters. As part of the initial sales process, insurance agents should take the time to prequalify a prospective client's health history to potentially ward off a declination.

There are various health rate classes that are available depending upon the LTCI company. While most applicants are approved with the equivalent of the "standard" health rate class, there is usually a category for the optimal LTCI applicant, and there is usually a category for the LTCI applicant who has been prequalified as being in substandard health, but who is still insurable. With traditional LTCI, the optimal LTCI applicant may take advantage of a discount of 10 to 15 percent less than the standard rate class, the applicant with the substandard health rate will receive a surcharge of 25 to 50 percent.

[E] What Is the Medical Underwriting Process?

How we each define being in "good health" is not the same as how an insurance company underwriter would. Underwriters are concerned with how the applicant's health at the time of application could potentially develop into the insurance company having to pay a claim in the future. With that in mind, medical underwriting today is less casual than it was in the early years of LTCI.

  (1) The list of conditions noted below is not a complete list of conditions that would make someone uninsurable, but it contains many of the more common conditions that LTCI underwriters categorize as "knock outs." A "knock out" makes someone unable to be considered for LTCI:

  - AIDS
  - ALS (Lou Gehrig's Disease)
  - Alzheimer's
  - Cerebral Palsy
  - Chronic Hepatitis
  - Cirrhosis
  - Crest Syndrome
  - Cystic Fibrosis
  - Dementia
  - Down's Syndrome
  - Hydrocephalus
  - Kidney Failure
  - Memory Loss
  - Multiple Myeloma
  - MS (Multiple Sclerosis)
  - Muscular Dystrophy
  - Organ Transplant

- Oxygen use
- Paralysis
- Psychosis
- Schizophrenia
- Systemic Lupus
- Von Willebrand's Disease
- Walker use
- Wheelchair use

While having any of the specific conditions noted above makes someone uninsurable, having more mainstream health issues is acceptable and does not stand in the way of a policy being issued. The docket below is by no means exhaustive. The particular conditions listed are generally medically underwritten with favourable results:

- Angioplasty
- Anxiety (mild)
- Arthritis (mild)
- Atrial Fibrillation (asymptomatic)
- Cancer (except Stage IV)
- Cholesterol
- Crohn's (in remission)
- Depression (mild)
- Diabetes (Type II)
- Gastric Bypass/Banding/Sleeve
- Gout
- Heart Valve
- High Blood Pressure
- Joint Replacement
- Osteopenia
- Pacemaker
- Psychotherapy
- TIA

Any discussion of medical underwriting merits a comment on how underwriters view physical therapy, occupational therapy, and cortisone injections as forms of treatment. If someone is presently having either physical therapy, occupational therapy, or cortisone injections as a form of treatment, he/she would not be eligible to apply for LTCI. Once someone has completed physical therapy or occupational therapy and an "adjustment period" of time has passed, he/she would be eligible to apply for LTCI. Cortisone injections are looked at a bit differently. Generally speaking, if someone has had one cortisone injection, the problem has been resolved, and no further injections are anticipated, he/she would go through an "adjustment period" of time and would then be eligible to apply for LTCI. The underwriting guidelines are different if someone has had multiple cortisone injections, or additional cortisone injections are anticipated in the future. In cases such as these, there could be some challenges.

An additional conversation is now taking place regarding how those who have tested positive for COVID-19 or a COVID-19 variant will be medically underwritten. While the guidelines are still evolving, the sense is that the insurance companies will treat a positive test for COVID-19 in the same manner that they would treat other health conditions where there has been a recent diagnosis in someone's medical records. In the submitted application, the insurance company underwriter would want to see that the person not only tested negative for COVID-19, but also that a specific period of time had passed before they could be considered. For someone who has experienced more minor symptoms and has not been hospitalized, there could be a one to three month wait depending upon the LTCI company. If someone has been hospitalized for COVID-19 or a COVID-19 variant, the guidelines could extend to six months. For someone who has been diagnosed with "Long COVID," he/she may be uninsurable. To put this in context, if someone is diagnosed with Shingles, they cannot apply for traditional LTCI without being fully recovered from Shingles with no residuals and also having completed a required wait time which could be three to six months. If someone is diagnosed with Lyme's Disease, they too cannot apply for traditional LTCI without first having no residuals and then having passed through a required wait time that could be anywhere from three months to twelve months depending upon the insurance company. Things should loosen up over time, but right now the underwriting guidelines for COVID-19 are quite strict.

(1) Once a person has been prequalified for LTCI and the results appear to be positive, the application process comes next. Applications can be done in person, by mail, or as an e-application by phone. Most companies do not require that a deposit be made with the application. With traditional LTCI, a request will usually be made for a copy of the applicant's medical records. This request is made through a vendor that is contracted with the LTCI company. The request for medical records starts with the applicant's Primary Care Physician, but records may also be requested from Specialists that the applicant may have seen if the records from the Primary Care Physician are not complete or do not provide sufficient information. Depending upon the age of the applicant, traditional LTCI companies also do either a prescheduled phone interview with the applicant, or a face-to-face assessment with a nurse at the applicant's home. The face-to-face assessment is generally a requirement for applicants who are age 65 and older, though some companies start this evaluation at age 70. A cognitive acuity screen will be requested based upon the applicant's age. With hybrid LTCI, the underwriting process is generally less invasive. An application can be done in person, by mail, or as an e-application. There is usually no request for the applicant's medical records unless there is "cause." Most hybrid companies try to gather the applicant's full health profile during a prescheduled phone interview.

(2) The final part of the medical underwriting process takes place when everything that has been requested above is handed off to an underwriter who makes a business decision. With traditional LTCI, there are a number of different health rate classes that an applicant can be approved for. This information was mentioned previously in Section D. While there is one hybrid LTCI company that approves applicants with various health rate classes, most hybrid LTCI companies either approve or decline an application with no modifications.

(3) Once the application has been approved, the LTCI company will notify its agent. The agent will then reach out to the applicant with the good news.

Policies can be delivered in person or by mail. The balance of the premium is due upon acceptance of the policy.

(4) If the applicant initially completed a form giving the agent the authority to be notified of an adverse underwriting decision, the agent will then be notified prior to the applicant receiving a letter. If an application has been declined, the applicant will be notified of this decision in writing and he/she will generally have the right to appeal.

There are some cases where an appeal will not be allowed based upon the particular reason for the declination. An appeal usually takes the form of a letter written by the applicant's Physician responding specifically to the reasons for declination by stating why the underwriting decision to decline was not correct and why it should be overturned. The applicant's file will then be reviewed again and a decision will be made whether or not to accept the appeal. If the appeal is accepted, a policy will be issued. If the appeal is not accepted, the process ends.

[F] How Much LTCI Is Enough?

When LTCI was inexpensive, many clients purchased policies that allowed them to insure the full cost of care. As mentioned earlier in this chapter, those policies included a "lifetime" (or "unlimited") benefit period and 5 percent compound inflation. With the price of LTCI today being significantly higher than it was in the past, advisors have found themselves embracing a new perspective and approaching LTCI from a co-insurance model. Many advisors are recommending that their clients consider purchasing policies that will cover 50 percent of the risk and that they be prepared to self-fund the other 50 percent should it be necessary. Using that protocol, agents are fundamentally selling policies that are a "coupon" toward the cost of care.

Knowing where clients are planning to live if and when they may need care is just as important as knowing where they reside now. Care in Alabama, Florida, Louisiana and New Mexico will cost substantially less than care in California, Connecticut, Massachusetts and New Jersey. We are fortunate that a few LTCI companies publish cost-of-care surveys. This allows advisors and clients to obtain current countrywide information on the cost of home care, assisted living, adult day care, and skilled nursing. Two of these are:

1. https://www.genworth.com/aging-and-you/finances/cost-of-care.html

2. http://www.mutualofomaha.com/long-term-care-insurance/calculator

Clients vary widely. They are different ages and different genders. They have different financial profiles, estate profiles, health profiles, and family profiles. While some clients may be comfortable with more basic coverage that pays out $3,000 per month for two years with 3 percent compound inflation and a 365-day elimination period, other clients will want their policies to pay out $7,500 per month for four years with 4 percent compound inflation and a 90-day elimination period. It is always best for clients to customize their policies to suit their own individual needs rather than to mirror what friends, colleagues, or family members have purchased.

[G] Growth of Linked Benefit Products

Linked benefit products, otherwise known as "hybrid" products, "combo" products, or "asset-based" products, were originally introduced more than 25 years ago, but have only gained traction within the last few years. While sales of traditional LTCI have waned, sales of linked benefit products have experienced double-digit growth.

There is no right or wrong; there is no better or worse. Once clients have been presented with the various products that can fund the risk of long-term care, they will self-select which product is the better fit for them.

Linked benefit products are products that link one kind of insurance with another kind of insurance. In most cases, LTCI is linked with life insurance, but there are also products that link LTCI with annuities, as well as a number of other options. Some advisors refer to these products as "hybrid" products, "combo" products, or "asset-based" products, but for the purposes of this chapter, we will refer to them as "linked benefit" products.

The linked benefit product that has captured the lion's share of the market links LTCI with life insurance. Some of these products are built on a universal life chassis and some are built on a whole life chassis. These products allow your client to leverage three things:

1. An LTCI policy;
2. A life insurance death benefit; and
3. A predetermined amount of surrender value or cash value.

While many sales are funded with a single premium (i.e., $100,000), some clients select the limited payment options that range from two to fifteen years, and some clients select the option for a recurring payment where available.

The structure of these products is fairly straightforward. If a 60-year-old married male contributes $100,000 to fund a policy that links LTCI with life insurance, this premium might leverage the following policy design:

- $5,400 per month benefit for long-term care;
- Six-year benefit period;
- 3 percent compound inflation; and
- 90-day elimination period.

There are some common traits among those clients who have chosen to purchase traditional LTCI in comparison to those clients who have chosen to purchase the linked benefit product of LTCI with life insurance.

In general, clients who purchase traditional LTCI:

- Are comfortable having a recurring premium similar to what they have with the other insurance coverages that they pay premiums for;
- View insurance as nothing more than paying a premium to have "peace of mind";
- Are not looking to get anything back if they never use their policies; and
- Are willing to accept a potential future rate increase should one be approved.

In general, clients who purchase the linked benefit product of LTCI with life insurance:

- Are usually affluent and can reposition some of their assets to create an LTCI bucket without difficulty;
- Are looking for their beneficiaries to get something back if they don't use their policies;
- Are seeking protection from any potential future rate increases; and
- Want to be guaranteed that they can get some or all of their money back if they change their mind.

Two important features of traditional LTCI that may not available with the linked benefit products:

- If your client is looking for deductibility, traditional LTCI offers that without question. On the other hand, only some of the linked benefit products are designed where a portion of the premium may be deductible. If deductibility is a priority, it is recommended that clients speak with their tax advisor before purchasing a linked benefit product. We will discuss deductibility later in this section.
- If your client is looking for a "Partnership" policy, only traditional LTCI qualifies. We will discuss "Partnership" later in this section.

[H] Eligibility for Benefits

Both traditional LTCI and the linked benefit products described above use the same criteria for determining "eligibility for benefits." This eligibility was standardized as part of the Health Insurance Portability and Accountability Act of 1996 (HIPAA). Prior to HIPAA, it was not uncommon to see LTCI policies that could be triggered based upon "medical necessity" as determined by the policyholder's physician. With the advent of HIPAA, policyholders now need to meet the definition of being "chronically ill." The words used to describe being chronically ill can vary slightly from one LTCI company to another, but regardless of the subtle differences in policy language, one of the following must exist:

1. The policyholder is unable to perform at least two out of six activities of daily living (ADLs) without substantial assistance from another person for a period that is expected to last at least 90 consecutive days. The six ADLs are: bathing, continence, dressing, eating, toileting, and transferring; or
2. The policyholder requires substantial supervision due to severe cognitive impairment.

[I] Deductibility

HIPAA was implemented on January 1, 1997. Among other things, this legislation allowed for the favorable tax treatment of "qualified" LTCI. Qualified policies must meet the guidelines in the regulations that were implemented by the National Association of Insurance Commissioners (NAIC). When talking about deductibility, qualified LTCI means that the benefits received from an LTCI policy are not considered taxable as income. In addition, qualified LTCI means that LTCI premiums may be deductible for those individuals who itemize their medical expenses, as well as for those who are self-employed, partnerships, LLCs, S corporations, and C corporations. The chart below displays the deductibility limits for 2022 based upon the taxpayer's age at the end of the year. This is the first time that the IRS has not raised these limits, and the first time that for one age group (ages 61 to 70), the limit was actually lowered by $10:

Long-Term Care Insurance Deductibility Limits for 2022

Age 40 or less	$450
Ages 41 to 50	$850
Ages 51 to 60	$1,690
Ages 61 to 70	$4,510
Over age 70	$5,640

In addition to the federal deductibility of LTCI, many states offer tax incentives in the form of either credits or deductions to encourage the purchase of LTCI. As it is with all matters regarding taxability of expense, it is best to consult with a tax advisor.

[J] Rate Increases

While today's LTCI products are believed to be "right" priced, the products of yesteryear were not. An LTCI company that makes the decision to file for a rate increase is not a "bad" company, and the policy that the client purchased was not a "bad" policy. A number of LTCI companies have never filed for a rate increase. This has lulled their policyholders into believing that they are the lucky ones who will not be affected, though actuarial data presents a different story. There have already been some aggressive rate increases on older blocks of business, and that trend is likely to continue, especially from those companies that have either not sought a rate increase to date or that have not had approval of a rate increase to date.

If a client is notified of an impending rate increase, he or she will usually be offered some "landing spots." Landing spots are options that will generally keep the premium at or near the level that the policyholder has been paying. The most common landing spots are a reduction in benefit (i.e., from $200 per day to $150 per day, or from $6,000 per month to $4,500 per month), a reduction in benefit period (i.e., from six years to five years, or from five years to four years), or a decrease in the percentage of compound inflation (i.e., from 5 percent to 3.5 percent, or from 5 percent to 2.8 percent). Some LTCI companies may make other options available, which could include removing inflation, increasing the elimination period, removing riders, etc. It is always best for a client to consult with his or her agent before making any changes. If the client is not able to locate the agent of record, then calling the insurance company to discuss all available options would be the next best course of action.

For clients who are still working, we recommend that they pay the rate increase if they are able. Recommending that clients pay the rate increase is a bit of protection against a potential future rate increase when they may not be able to pay it.

[K] Partnership

One of the main reasons that clients purchase LTCI is for protection of assets. The term "Partnership" evolved in the late 1980's when a public policy initiative was launched that was supported by the federal government and operated by state governments. This initiative allowed insurance companies to market LTCI policies which contained specific criteria so that policyholders would not need to deplete all of their assets before relying upon Medicaid to pay for their long-term care needs. Policies which met these standards would be qualified for Partnership status. Policies which did not meet these standards would hold the status of non-Partnership.

For many years, there were four states which had Partnership programs in place: California, Connecticut, Indiana, and New York. As part of the Omnibus Budget Reconciliation Act of 1993 (OBRA), any new Partnership programs were halted. With the signing of the Deficit Reduction Act (DRA) in February 2006, states were once again allowed to establish Partnership programs.

At the present time, there are approximately 40 states that have Partnership programs. The DRA Partnership states use the "dollar for dollar" approach, whereas the original four Partnership states have different requirements. The "dollar for dollar" platform enables a Partnership policyholder to protect one dollar of assets for every dollar that his/her policy pays out in LTCI benefits. The total assets that your client is able to retain as a result of owning a Partnership-qualified LTCI policy is in addition to the regular allowances that are available under Medicaid. Purchasing a Partnership-qualified LTCI policy allows your client to identify and protect a portion of his/her assets from what would normally have to be used for a "spend down" to become eligible for Medicaid benefits.

For a LTCI policy to have DRA Partnership status, the following must be in place:

- The policy must be qualified under federal tax law;
- The policy must be issued with an effective date that is after the date that the Partnership program in the respective state was implemented;
- The policy must have certain consumer protections in place; and
- The policy must meet the requirements of age-based inflation.[2] The original DRA requirements are that:

  — Ages 61 and younger are required to have compound inflation protection;
  — Ages 61 to 75 are required to have some amount of inflation protection;
  — Ages 76 and older are not required to have inflation protection.

In addition, your client must be a resident of the state where he/she is applying for a Partnership policy. Residency is determined based upon where your client has his/her primary residence. As an example, if your client's primary residence is in Massachusetts, which is not a Partnership state, but he/she has a second home in

---

[2] Some states are allowing CPI or another form of indexed inflation for policyholders who are age 61 and younger. This was not allowed as part of the original DRA Partnership requirements.

Florida, which is a Partnership state, your client cannot purchase a Partnership policy in Florida.

Because DRA Partnership programs are still relatively new, we can expect that they will evolve over time with some states integrating their own unique requirements. Many states include updated information about their Partnership program on their state insurance department's website.

[L] Ten Common Questions in and around LTCI

Discussed below are the common questions that prospective clients ask on an ongoing basis.

(1) What is the "right" age to purchase LTCI?

While there is no "right" age, we do find that most of our clients are between the ages of 50 and 66. There are occasions where someone younger than 50 may consider LTCI if they have a family history of a dread disease—i.e., ALS, MS, Parkinson's, Alzheimer's, etc. There are also occasions where someone older than 66 may consider LTCI if they have only recently become aware of this important insurance protection.

(2) What happens if I move to another state? Does my LTCI policy go with me or do I need to purchase another policy?

You do not need to purchase another policy. Your policy is fully portable and goes with you from state to state. Most LTCI policies also include a specified amount of international coverage which can be extremely important for those clients who are citizens of the world.

(3) What if I'm approved for an LTCI policy but my partner/spouse is declined?

The partner/spouse who is approved for coverage should definitely accept his/her policy. When one spouse/partner is uninsurable, it becomes even more important for the insurable spouse/partner to own a LTCI policy.

(4) I've heard that there is a product out there that pays out the full monthly benefit in "cash." Is that true?

At the present time, there are at least three linked benefit products that pay out 100 percent of their monthly benefit in "cash." With traditional LTCI, there are no longer any companies that offer a 100 percent "cash" benefit, but at least two companies offer a "cash" benefit that is limited to a percentage of the daily or monthly benefit, with that percentage being no more than 30 to 40 percent of the benefit. Most LTCI companies use the traditional "reimbursement" method. This method requires that bills and/or receipts be forwarded to the insurance company for the actual charges that were incurred and reimbursement will be based upon those actual charges. A "cash" benefit means that the policyholder will receive the full monthly benefit with no bills and/or receipts required to be submitted as long as the policyholder remains benefit eligible.

(5) Our best friends just purchased LTCI. My husband and I are the same age as them. Should we consider purchasing LTCI as well?

We refer to this as "keeping up with the Joneses!" The fact that your best friends purchased LTCI doesn't mean that LTCI is right for you. Every couple is unique. Every couple has a different financial profile; some couples are high wage earners and others aren't. Every couple has a different estate profile; some couples have inherited money and others haven't. Every couple has a different health profile: some couples are in excellent health and others have challenges. Every couple has a different family profile: some couples have children and others don't. Our recommendation is to have the LTCI conversation with your own trusted advisors and then to go with their recommendations.

(6) I hear that LTCI companies give you a hard time when it comes to paying claims?

We always say that legitimate insurance companies pay legitimate claims. There will always be a few companies that have poor financial ratings and that will do their very best to try to get out of paying a legitimate LTCI claim, but these companies are rare. The majority of the LTCI companies intend to pay any legitimate claim. For a claim to be legitimate, the policyholder must meet the definition of being "chronically ill" according to the contract language in the policy. It is not the policyholder or the policyholder's family who decides if benefits should be paid; rather, the claims department of the LTCI company makes that determination. Some LTCI companies will have a nurse perform a face-to-face assessment to determine eligibility for benefits, while other LTCI companies will rely heavily upon the policyholder's medical records.

(7) If I buy LTCI and pay my premium for 25 or 30 years and never use my policy, will I get anything back?

The answer is no. Traditional LTCI has no cash value. It is what we refer to as "pure" insurance. By paying the premium on an ongoing basis, you gain the peace of mind of knowing that if you have a long-term care event your policy will respond and pay out benefits. If you are looking to get something back, you may want to consider a linked benefit policy rather than a traditional LTCI policy.

(8) Do I continue to pay my LTCI premium while I am receiving benefits?

With most of the LTCI companies who are selling policies today, once you are "eligible for benefits" and have satisfied your elimination period, you will no longer pay your premium whether you are receiving care at home, at an adult day care, at an assisted living, or at a skilled nursing facility. Back in the early days of LTCI, there were companies which didn't automatically waive the premium specifically for home care claims. Some companies offered a rider that you could purchase to waive the home care premium and other companies didn't. For those companies that didn't waive the home care premium, you would find that the policyholder would be receiving reimbursement under his/her policy, but he/she would still be paying his/her premium. Today, there is only one company that doesn't automatically waive the home care premium, but they offer a rider for a minimal cost.

(9) Is there any way that I can purchase a LTCI policy that I can "pay up" so that I don't have a premium that continues into retirement?

Yes, while most of the traditional LTCI insurance companies no longer offer the option of a "paid up" policy, there is one company that still offers both a single pay and a 10 pay option. With the linked benefit policies, there are a number of "paid up" options available ranging from making a single payment, often referred to as "one and done," to making payments for up to 25 years. There are also a variety of options in between. Based upon the person's age and income level, an accelerated payment option may make good financial sense.

(10) We are both 57. We're still working and we're in really good health so we are leaning toward waiting another ten years until we are retired. What are your thoughts?

This is never a wise decision: (1) In ten years, from age 57 to age 67, your health could change dramatically and one or both of you could become uninsurable. (2) The product that you are considering now will not be the same product that will be on the market in ten years. Any time a LTCI company introduces a new product, it is always more expensive than their previous product. (3) The difference in premium today between a 65-year-old and a 55-year-old is approximately 45 percent.

[M] Conclusion

Clients who purchase LTCI do so because they are looking for the peace of mind that only this specialized insurance can provide. Clients do not have a crystal ball, so they do not know if they will need extended care, but they will not want to deal with the grave consequences to their loved ones if they do. The costs associated with extended care can be significant. Though LTCI is not the panacea, it is the best funding source that we have available today. With that in mind, clients should explore LTCI with an agent who specializes in LTCI and is aware of the distinctions from one company to another, and from one product to another.

13

Estate Planning with Retirement Benefits

§13.01 INTRODUCTION

Retirement benefits often represent a significant proportion of a client's wealth. Indeed, it is not uncommon for retirement benefits to represent the single largest asset in a client's estate. Yet, the rules regarding retirement benefits are both unique and exceedingly complex. Therefore, even someone with a good understanding of estate planning strategies may need to take some time to understand the rules applicable to retirement benefits. This chapter will explore the major issues faced by the estate planner in advising clients with respect to retirement plan assets.

There are a number of situations in which the estate planner may be called upon to advise a client with respect to retirement benefits. The client may seek assistance in completing a beneficiary designation during a client's employment, in directing the disposition of plan benefits upon changing jobs, in selecting a payment option for the benefits at retirement, or in determining how retirement benefits should be disposed of at death. In addition, a beneficiary may need advice regarding the payment or rollover options upon the death of the retirement plan owner.

In dispensing advice to clients regarding retirement benefits, the estate planner must become familiar with the myriad special rules that apply to such assets. The federal government protects the interest of spouses of participants in certain retirement plan assets, and decisions regarding beneficiary designations must be made taking such rules into account. Retirement plan assets often involve income tax deferral, and therefore basic strategies regarding the costs and benefits of income tax deferral are relevant to decision making. In addition, excise taxes may be imposed on retirement plan distributions actually taken (or which should have been taken) if the timing or amount of such distributions is outside of limits prescribed by law. The estate planner therefore needs to know how to help a client avoid these taxes.

A variety of issues also must be addressed when directing the disposition of retirement plan assets upon death. Retirement plan assets are nonprobate property, and their disposition upon death accordingly is governed by the beneficiary designation, rather than under the terms of the will. The estate planner therefore will need to coordinate the disposition of the retirement benefits with the client's other assets in order to achieve the client's overall dispositive goals. Moreover, choices that a client makes during lifetime, such as the choice of the designated beneficiary and the choice of the form of the benefit, can have continuing impact upon the disposition of those assets following the death of the owner. An integrated approach to advising the client that considers both lifetime and testamentary objectives is necessary to insure that all the client's objectives are accomplished. Commonly encountered estate planning dilemmas such as how to fund the credit shelter trust fully or how to qualify a disposition for the marital deduction take on added complexity when the major asset available is a retirement plan.

The fact that many retirement plan assets are *income in respect of a decedent* (IRD) also will have to be taken into account when advising a client. Income in respect of a decedent, unlike many other categories of property passing at death, is subject to income tax when received by a beneficiary.[1] The income tax is in addition to the estate tax that is payable with respect to the transfer of that property at the owner's death. This double layer of taxation will have an impact upon appropriate advice regarding the disposition of retirement benefits.

A number of the rules governing retirement plans were changed by the Setting Every Community Up for Retirement Enhancement Act (hereinafter the "SECURE Act"), which was enacted on December 20, 2019, and went into effect on January 1, 2020.[2] In particular, new rules began in 2020 with respect to the minimum age at which withdrawals from retirement plans must begin[3] and the time period over which the beneficiary of an inherited retirement account must make withdrawals.[4]

On February 24, 2022, the Internal Revenue Service issued proposed regulations for the SECURE Act (hereinafter the "2022 Proposed Regulations").[5] If enacted, the 2022 Proposed Regulations would clarify a number of outstanding questions, as discussed in the following sections of the chapter. The 2022 Proposed Regulations, however, also would change the manner of distribution from inherited retirement accounts under the so-called "ten-year rule."[6]

§ 13.02 GENERAL ESTATE PLANNING OBJECTIVES WITH RESPECT TO RETIREMENT PLANS

[A] Income Tax

[1] Special Income Tax Rules

The special income tax rules that apply to most retirement plan assets set the backdrop that propels much of the estate and retirement planning with respect to retirement plan assets. Most contributions to retirement plans are deductible for income tax purposes at the time the contribution is made.[1] During the time the contributions remain in the plan, the earnings on those contributions are not subject to income tax.[2] Thus, retirement plan assets can earn interest or dividends or generate capital gains without being subject to income tax. However, when distributions from the retirement plan are eventually taken, both the deductible contributions themselves and the earnings thereon are taxed as ordinary income.[3] Moreover, when

---

[1] **§ 13.01** IRC § 691. Income in respect of a decedent is discussed in Chapter 14.

[2] IRC § 401(a)(9)(H).

[3] *See* § 13.05[B][3] *infra*.

[4] *See* § 13.05[D] *infra*.

[5] *See generally* Prop. Reg. § 1.401(a)(9).

[6] *See* § 13.05[D][2] *infra*.

[1] **§ 13.02** IRC § 404. These rules do not apply to contributions to Roth Individual Retirement Accounts, which are discussed in § 13.04[B][2] *infra* or to contributions to Qualified Roth Contribution Programs, which are discussed in § 13.04[C] *infra*.

[2] IRC §§ 501(a), 511.

[3] IRC § 402(a).

retirement plan assets are transferred at death, they are taxed as income in respect of a decedent, and the recipient is responsible for income taxes on the plan assets when distributed.[4] These basic income tax aspects of retirement plans underlie many of the strategic decisions that estate planners must make in connection with retirement plans.

[2] Extending Income Tax Deferral Opportunities

For many clients, providing the maximal continued income tax deferral opportunities for those receiving the benefits at the client's death is an important planning objective. However, in some situations maximum tax deferral may conflict with the client's dispositive goals. In that situation, the goal of tax deferral must be analyzed in light of other objectives of the client to determine the best course of action. For example, in a blended family situation, the objective of providing maximal income tax deferral opportunities, which might be best preserved by naming the spouse as beneficiary of the retirement benefit (thereby allowing for a spousal rollover) may conflict with the client's wish that the remaining benefits at the spouse's death cannot be diverted from the client's own children or more remote issue if the spouse remarries. Similarly, naming children or grandchildren as the beneficiaries of a portion of retirement benefits to possibly extend income tax deferral may conflict with the client's wish to have all the benefits available to the spouse for the spouse's use. Only by fully exploring these competing considerations can a recommended course of action be plotted.

[B] Estate Tax

[1] In General

The full value of all retirement plans owned by an individual as of the date of his or her death is included in the individual's gross estate for federal estate tax purposes.[5] No discount is available for the amount of income taxes that would be owed if the assets in the retirement plans were distributed.[6]

There is a potentially valuable estate tax exclusion for individuals who separated from service with respect to an employer before 1983, and who subsequently die without having changed the form of the retirement benefit. For such individuals, 100 percent of the retirement benefit will be excluded from the decedent's estate for federal estate tax purposes.[7] A lesser (but nevertheless still valuable) federal estate tax exclusion is available with respect to individuals who separated from service after

---

[4] IRC §§ 501(a), 511.

[5] IRC § 2039.

[6] *See, e.g.,* Estate of Smith v. Comm'r, 267 F.3d 366 (5th Cir. 2001). *But see* the discussion in § 13.12[B], *infra,* about the possible availability of an income tax deduction attributable to any federal estate tax paid as the result of the inclusion of an IRA in the taxable estate under IRC § 691(c).

[7] Deficit Reduction Act of 1984, Pub. L. No. 98-369, § 525(b), 98 Stat. 494 (1984) (DEFRA).

1982 but before 1985. For such individuals, if they have not changed the form of benefit between the time they separated from service and the date of death, a federal estate tax exclusion limited to $100,000 is available.[8] These exclusions are available regardless of whether the form of benefit of the decedent was irrevocable or in pay status. What is determinative is whether or not any change was made to the *form* of benefit between the time of separation from service and date of death. In order to take full advantage of these exclusions, the estate planner should obtain information regarding a client's employment history. An estate planner should also be careful to advise a client not to change a form of benefit in a situation where the exclusion for federal estate tax purposes might otherwise be available without careful consideration of the costs of doing so.

[2] Qualifying Retirement Benefits for the Marital Deduction

Qualifying retirement benefits for the marital deduction presents special challenges. Where the spouse is named as the outright beneficiary of the retirement plan or IRA and has the ability to select the form of benefit, the marital deduction generally will be available. However, when a plan owner wishes instead to make those benefits payable to a Qualified Terminable Interest Property (QTIP) trust for the benefit of the spouse, great care must be taken in order to qualify the retirement plan benefits for the marital deduction.[9]

[3] Funding the Credit Shelter Trust

In many cases, a client's retirement plan assets constitute the bulk of the client's estate, and the other assets may not be sufficient to fund the credit shelter trust. In such a case, the benefits and disadvantages of using retirement benefits to fund the credit shelter trust must be explored. However, there are significant disadvantages to using retirement benefits to fund the credit shelter trust. Therefore, special care must be taken when planning for an individual with large retirement benefits and with few other assets available to fund the credit shelter trust.[10]

[4] Disclaimers and Retirement Benefits

As in other aspects of estate planning, qualified disclaimers can be a valuable tool for accomplishing the client's estate planning objectives. Disclaimers with respect to retirement benefits have been allowed by the IRS and can be used in appropriate cases to direct retirement benefits to a spouse for purposes of a spousal rollover, to direct sufficient assets to the credit shelter trust, or to accomplish other estate

---

[8] *Id.*

[9] *See* § 13.08 *infra*, for a discussion of retirement benefits and QTIP trusts. QTIP trusts are discussed in Chapter 6.

[10] *See* § 13.07 *infra*, for a discussion of retirement benefits and credit shelter trusts. Credit shelter trusts are discussed in Chapters 5 and 6.

planning objectives.[11] Under the regulations issued in 2002, disclaimers have taken on added significance because they can be used to eliminate named beneficiaries in order to secure the existence of a designated beneficiary after the participant's death. Nonetheless, disclaimers must be used with great care to achieve the intended result.[12]

§ 13.03 GATHERING INFORMATION FROM CLIENTS ABOUT RETIREMENT PLAN ASSETS

The first step in planning for a client's retirement benefits is to obtain accurate information regarding the nature, extent, and status of a client's retirement plan assets. Clients often have limited understanding of these assets. For that reason, it is important not to rely on the client's memory or sketchy understanding, but instead to insist that the client provide documentation regarding these assets. The following information should be obtained with respect to *each* of the client's retirement plan assets:

- *Type of Retirement Plan.* There are a number of types of retirement plans, and different rules may apply with respect to these different types of plans. For example, a traditional IRA is taxed very differently from a Roth IRA. Therefore, it is important to know the type or types of retirement plans in which the client has an interest.[1]

---

[11] The proposed regulations issued in January 2001 made it clear for the first time that disclaimers can be used to change the designated beneficiary after the death of the participant. The final regulations issued in April 2002 clarify this concept by making specific reference to the use of disclaimers that satisfy Section 2518 of the Internal Revenue Code. Reg. § 1.401(a)(9)-4, Q&A 4(a). In Rev. Rul. 2005-36, 2005-26 I.R.B. 1368, the IRS further clarified the use of disclaimers by concluding that an IRA beneficiary who accepted the participant's required minimum distribution (*see* discussion in § 13.05[C] *infra*) in the year of the participant's death did not violate Section 2518(b)(3) (requiring that the disclaimant not accept the interest or any of the benefits of the disclaimed property) and thus was not precluded from disclaiming the balance of the IRA. Qualified disclaimers are discussed in more detail in Chapter 14.

[12] For example, in Ltr. Rul. 200327059, a surviving wife disclaimed a portion of her deceased husband's IRA, so that the disclaimed portion passed under the residuary clause of the husband's will to his trust, with the intention of stretching out the IRA distributions over the life expectancy of the oldest trust beneficiary (*see* discussion in § 13.06 *infra*). The IRS ruled, however, that as a result of the disclaimer, the husband's *estate* was the beneficiary of the disclaimed portion of the IRA, not the trust, because the trust was not named as the beneficiary of the IRA, but only became the recipient of the disclaimed portion of the IRA benefits by operation of the will's residuary clause. Accordingly, the distributions from the disclaimed portion of the IRA were subject to a shorter time period than if the trust itself had been named as the beneficiary, or even if the disclaimer had not been made at all (*see* discussion in § 13.05[C] *infra*). In Ltr. Rul. 201202042, however, a careful use of a disclaimer resulted in a much more favorable outcome. A husband designated a trust as the beneficiary of his IRA. Upon his death, his wife became the sole beneficiary of the trust for her lifetime. The trust met all of the "look through" requirements (*see* discussion in § 13.06 *infra*), so that the distributions from the IRA could be made over the wife's life expectancy. The wife died 11 days after the husband, leaving their daughter and a grandchild as the beneficiaries of the trust. The executor of the wife's estate disclaimed her interest in the trust, so that the IRA distributions then could be made over the much longer life expectancy of the daughter under the distribution rules that were then in effect.

[1] § 13.03 The major categories of retirement plans are discussed in § 13.04 *infra*.

- *Current Balance in and History of Contributions to Retirement Plan.* As with any asset, an estimate of current value is an important piece of information for the estate planner to have. With retirement plan assets, it is also important to know the breakdown of employee and employer contributions to the plan, whether a portion of the employee contributions were post-income tax (as opposed to pre-income tax), whether any portion of the plan balance represents a rollover from another plan, and whether there have been any withdrawals from the plan. All of these facts can have an effect on planning opportunities available with respect to the plan assets.

- *Beneficiary Designation.* The client should provide the estate planner with a copy of the beneficiary designation currently in force with respect to the plan. The memory of the client should *not* be relied upon, because it is often the case that the actual beneficiary designation differs from the client's memory of it.[2] If the client is married and the primary beneficiary is not the client's spouse, a copy of the spousal waiver under the Retirement Equity Act also should be obtained.[3]

- *Copy of the Plan or Summary Plan Description.* The most complete information regarding retirement plans, including benefit and payment options, can be obtained by reviewing an actual copy of the plan, which the employee can obtain from the employer. Another document that the employer must make available to the employee is the Summary Plan Description, a shorter document that summarizes the terms of the plan. The Summary Plan Description is only updated periodically. Therefore, before relying on the summary document, the estate planner should ascertain that it reflects all changes that have been made to the plan.

- *Qualified Domestic Relations Orders.* A Qualified Domestic Relations Order (QDRO) is a court order issued pursuant to a divorce or separation under

---

[2] Mays-Williams v. Williams, 777 F.3d 1035 (9th Cir. 2015), demonstrates the need for the estate planner's diligence in dealing with client beneficiary designations. In this case, a husband designated his wife as the beneficiary of various retirement plans administered by his employer. The husband and wife subsequently divorced. On several occasions, the husband called the administrative office for the retirement plans, each time saying that he wanted to change the beneficiary designation for each plan to his son. The administrative office each time sent the husband new beneficiary designation forms, which the husband never filled out, signed or returned. After the husband died, the ex-wife and the son both filed claims as the beneficiary of the retirement plans. The United States District Court granted the ex-wife's motion for summary judgment. On appeal from the son, a panel of the Ninth Circuit reversed, concluding that, because of particular language in the retirement plan documents, the determination of whether the husband had strictly or substantially complied with terms of those documents was a matter of factual determination and thus was not appropriate for summary judgment. The panel remanded the case back to the District Court for further proceedings. Upon remand, the District Court determined that the son had not presented sufficient factual evidence that the father had strictly or substantially complied with the plan's requirements for changing a beneficiary designation and awarded the full amount of the plan's benefits to the ex-wife (168 F. Supp. 3d 1325 (W.D. Wash. 2016)). On the subsequent appeal, the Ninth Circuit affirmed the District Court (712 Fed. Appx. 682 (9th Cir. 2018)). The general holding of the Ninth Circuit remains intact, namely that under certain circumstances, a telephone call alone may be sufficient to change the beneficiary designation of a retirement plan.

[3] Pub. L. No. 98-397, Retirement Equity Act of 1984 (August 23, 1984).

which a former spouse or dependent of a plan participant can become entitled to a portion of the participant's benefit.[4] It is important to know whether any QDRO has been entered with respect to any of a client's plan benefits.

§13.04 TYPES OF RETIREMENT PLANS

The estate planner must become familiar with the various types of retirement plan assets in which their clients may have an interest. It is not uncommon for an individual to have interests in a number of retirement plans, and each of these plans may be subject to its own rules.[1]

[A] Qualified Retirement Plans

[1] In General

Qualified retirement plans are employer-sponsored retirement plans that meet the strict requirements established by the Internal Revenue Code and by the Employee Retirement Income Security Act of 1974 (ERISA).[2]

These plans provide tax benefits to both the employer and to the employee. The employer may deduct its contributions to the plan, while the employee can defer income taxation on contributions made on the employee's behalf and on the earnings on those contributions until they are distributed from the plan. In addition, qualified retirement plans provide extensive creditor protections. Plan assets are not subject to the claims of the employer's creditors and generally are protected from the employee's creditors as well. Numerous regulations apply to the maintenance of qualified plans, establishing the amount of contributions that can be made to the plan, the extent of employee participation that must occur, minimum vesting schedules, and record-keeping requirements.

Qualified plans can appear under a variety of names. Regardless of the name of the plan, qualified retirement plans generally take the form of either a defined benefit plan or a defined contribution plan.

---

[4] *See generally* IRC § 414(p).

[1] **§ 13.04** So-called education individual retirement accounts were created in 1997 with the addition of Section 530 of the Internal Revenue Code. These accounts, which were renamed Coverdell education savings accounts in 2001, share some common features with Roth IRAs (which are discussed in § 13.04[B][2] *infra*), in that contributions to the accounts are not tax deductible, but all earnings accumulate tax free. In addition, distributions can escape income taxation altogether if used to pay for qualified education expenses of the account beneficiary. However, the account must be distributed in full to the beneficiary within 30 days of the beneficiary's 30th birthday (or the beneficiary's estate within 30 days of the beneficiary's death, if earlier). Accordingly, such accounts—despite formerly being called "retirement" accounts—are not properly considered as retirement benefits and will not be discussed further in this chapter.

[2] Pub. L. No. 93-406, Employee Retirement Income Security Act of 1974 (September 12, 1974).

[2] Defined Benefit Plans

A defined benefit plan is a plan under which an employee is paid a set benefit as determined by a formula in the plan. The formula usually is based upon the employee's salary level and the number of years of the employee's service. The employer is required to make sufficient contributions to the plan to yield the defined benefit, but the amount of the employer's contributions will vary from year to year. The benefit usually is payable in the form of an annuity for the employee's lifetime, with survivor benefits to the employee's spouse. Defined benefit plans—such as traditional pension plans—have largely fallen out of favor at private sector employers in recent years.

[3] Defined Contribution Plans

The other basic form of qualified retirement plan is the defined contribution plan. Under a defined contribution plan the employee makes contributions to a separate account maintained by the employer for each employee. The benefit received by the employee is the balance in the employee's account, which will vary depending upon the amount of the contributions and the market performance of the particular investments held in the plan. Examples of defined contribution plans include profit-sharing plans (including 401(k) plans, which are a type of profit-sharing plan under which the employee can choose the level of contribution to be made to the plan within certain IRS limits), money purchase plans, and Employee Stock Ownership Plans (ESOPs). For example, an individual may make annual contributions of up to $20,500 to a 401(k) plan in 2022. An individual who has reached age 50 also may make an additional annual "catch-up" contribution of $6,500.

As defined benefit plans have waned in popularity, defined contribution plans have become increasingly commonplace.

[4] Keogh Plans

A Keogh plan (also known as an H.R. 10 plan) is a qualified retirement plan that is maintained by self-employed persons, such as sole proprietors and partners. It may be any type of qualified plan.

[5] 403(b) Plans

Retirement plans sponsored by tax-exempt employers are known as 403(b) plans. These plans offer the same tax advantages for participants as qualified retirement plans, with some minor exceptions. For example, 403(b) plan participants cannot qualify for the favorable tax treatment afforded some lump sum distributions under qualified retirement plans.[3] Furthermore, money in the 403(b) plan can only be invested in mutual funds or annuity contracts issued by an insurance company.[4]

[B] Individual Retirement Accounts (IRAs)

[1] Traditional Individual Retirement Accounts

Traditional individual retirement accounts maintained by individuals are similar to qualified plans in the respect that contributions to these accounts are tax deductible and earnings on the accounts are not taxed until distributions are made from the account.[5] Virtually any person who receives income for personal services may establish an individual retirement account. Contributions to an IRA must be made in cash.[6] The contribution limit is $6,000 for 2022 and will be adjusted for inflation in subsequent years (in $500 increments).[7] An individual who has reached age 50 also may make an additional annual "catch-up" contribution of $1,000. However, the *deductibility* of IRA contributions is phased out for a single (or head of household) taxpayer whose adjusted gross income exceeds $68,000 in 2022 and is eliminated altogether if adjusted gross income exceeds $78,000. For a married taxpayer filing jointly, the deductibility of IRA contributions is phased out if adjusted gross income exceeds $109,000 in 2022 and is eliminated if adjusted gross income exceeds $129,000.[8] A married taxpayer filing separately is not eligible to make deductible contributions to a traditional IRA if his or her adjusted gross income exceeds $10,000.[9]

Historically, IRA contributions could only be made by individuals who had not yet attained age 70 1/2. Starting in 2020, the age limitation has been eliminated.[10]

Although traditional IRAs are subject to similar tax treatment as qualified retirement plans, there are a number of differences. For example, the mechanism of a Qualified Domestic Relations Order is not necessary for the transfer of an IRA upon a divorce. If a divorce or separation instrument so provides, an IRA may be transferred upon a divorce. In addition, there are no federally mandated spousal benefits for IRAs. Therefore, an owner of an IRA can freely designate the beneficiary, even where the IRA contains amounts rolled over from a qualified plan (which do have mandated spousal benefits).

In addition, IRAs are not governed by ERISA (with the exception of IRAs that are sponsored by an employer under a Simplified Employer Pension, called a SEP IRA).

---

[3] IRC § 402(e)(4)(D)(i).

[4] IRC § 403(b).

[5] Traditional IRAs are to be contrasted with Roth IRAs, to which clients may make post-tax contributions. Roth IRAs are discussed in § 13.04[B][2] *infra*.

[6] IRC § 408(a)(1). This rule does not apply to certain rollover contributions. *Id.*

[7] *Id.*; IRC § 219(b)(1), (5)(A). In addition, the annual contribution limit is increased by $1,000 to allow so-called catch-up contributions for any individual who has attained age 50 before the end of the particular tax year. IRC § 219(b)(5)(B).

[8] *Id.*

[9] *Id.*

[10] IRC § 401(a)(9)(H).

Historically, this meant that the creditor protections of qualified plans provided under ERISA did not apply to IRAs.[11]

[2] Roth Individual Retirement Accounts

As of 1998, another form of IRA became available to individuals—the Roth IRA.[12] Unlike traditional IRAs, contributions to Roth IRAs are not tax deductible. However, as is the case with contributions to a traditional IRA, earnings on the contributions are not taxed, and qualified distributions from a Roth IRA have the additional advantage of not being subject to income tax.[13] *Qualified distributions* are those distributions made after the end of a five year "nonexclusion" period after the participant first made a contribution to a Roth IRA *and* are one of the following: (1) made after the date upon which the participant attained age 59^1/$_2$, (2) made to a beneficiary after the participant's death, (3) attributable to the participant's being totally disabled, or (4) a qualified special purpose distribution, such as the purchase of a first home.[14] Because Roth IRAs are funded with after-tax dollars, they are not subject to many of the limitations imposed on qualified plans or traditional IRAs. Thus, there are no minimum distribution requirements during the participant's lifetime and no early withdrawal penalties to the extent that the withdrawals do not exceed the aggregate amount of the contributions.[15]

The maximum amount that can be contributed to a Roth IRA for any tax year is equal to the maximum contribution allowable for a traditional IRA less any amounts actually contributed to such traditional IRAs for that tax year.[16] However, to be eligible to make the maximum contribution, a single individual's adjusted gross income cannot exceed $129,000 in 2022 and the income of married taxpayers filing jointly cannot exceed $204,000.[17] The amount that can be contributed to a Roth IRA phases out for individuals with incomes higher than these amounts, with no contribution available to a single taxpayer with an adjusted gross income that exceeds $144,000 in 2022 or to married taxpayers filing jointly with an adjusted gross income

---

[11] Creditor protection issues for IRAs are discussed in more detail in § 13.11, *infra*.

[12] *See generally* IRC § 408A.

[13] IRC § 408A(d)(1); Reg. § 1.408A-1.

[14] IRC § 408A(d)(2), (5). The five-year nonexclusion period begins on the first day of the tax year to which the participant's first Roth IRA contribution applies and ends on the last day of the fifth tax year thereafter. IRC § 408A(D)(2)(B); Reg. § 1.408A-6. For example, if a participant first made a Roth IRA contribution on April 15, 2005, pertaining to the 2004 tax year, the nonexclusion period would begin on January 1, 2004 and end on December 31, 2008, such that the qualified distributions could not be made until 2009 at the earliest.

[15] IRC § 408A(c), (d)(4). Minimum distribution requirements for traditional IRAs are discussed in § 13.05[B] *infra*. Deductible contributions cannot be made to traditional IRAs after the IRA holder has reached age 70^1/$_2$. IRC § 219(d)(1). Early withdrawal penalties for traditional IRAs are discussed in § 13.05[A] *infra*.

[16] IRC § 408A(c)(2). Contribution limits for traditional IRAs are discussed in § 13.04[B][1] *supra*.

[17] IRC § 408A(c)(3)(A). The income limits are indexed each year for inflation. Pub. L. No. 109-280. The Pension Protection Act of 2006 (August 17, 2006).

that exceeds $214,000.[18] A married taxpayer filing separately is not eligible to make contributions to a Roth IRA if his or her adjusted gross income exceeds $10,000.[19]

In addition to advising clients on establishing a Roth IRA, the estate planner may be called upon to advise clients on converting a traditional IRA to a Roth IRA. Historically, this conversion option had only been available for individuals whose adjusted gross income did not exceed $100,000.[20] As a practical matter, this limit had been a substantial barrier to such conversions.[21] However, under rules enacted in 2006, the $100,000 limit was eliminated altogether beginning in 2010, thus making the conversion option available to everyone with a traditional IRA.[22]

Upon conversion, the taxpayer must pay income tax on the amount converted.[23] Thereafter, earnings on the converted Roth IRA will not be taxed, and qualified distributions will not be subject to income tax. For example, assuming all of the requirements discussed above for conversion and for qualified distributions are met, if a 55-year-old client rolls over $400,000 from a traditional IRA to a Roth IRA, the client will have to pay income tax on the $400,000 in the year of the rollover. When the client later retires, any distributions will be tax free and no income tax will ever be paid on any increase in the value of the rollover amount, regardless of whether the money is paid to the client or the client's beneficiaries after the client's death.

In making the determination as to whether it is advisable to convert a traditional IRA to a Roth IRA, the accelerated payment of the income tax must be balanced against the elimination of future income taxes on qualified distributions. Generally speaking, the conversion is most valuable for those individuals who do not foresee the need to access the benefits in an IRA for retirement, whose life expectancy is such that a substantial period of continued tax deferral is expected, and who have sufficient assets outside of the IRA to pay the income tax liability that arises from the conversion. The conversion, which will generate an income tax liability, also permits the removal of the income tax amount from the participant's taxable estate for estate tax purposes.

Beginning in 2008, it became possible for the first time to make a direct rollover from a qualified retirement plan to a Roth IRA.[24] Prior to this date, such a rollover could be accomplished only by first rolling over all or part of the qualified retirement plan to a traditional IRA and then converting the traditional IRA to a Roth IRA.

---

[18] *Id.*

[19] *Id.*

[20] IRC § 408A(c)(3)(B).

[21] Beginning in 2005, the amount of any required minimum distribution from a traditional IRA did not count against the $100,000 limit for purposes of determining an individual's eligibility for conversion. IRC § 408A(c)(3)(C)(i)(II). Accordingly, the conversion option became available to more individuals, for example, those individuals whose adjusted gross income consisted primarily of such required minimum distributions. Required minimum distributions are discussed in § 13.05[B], *infra.*

[22] Pub. L. No. 109-222, Tax Increase Prevention and Reconciliation Act of 2005 (May 17, 2006). For conversions that occur in 2010 only, the taxpayer may elect to defer one-half of the income resulting from the conversion until 2011 and one-half until 2012. *Id.*

[23] IRC § 408A(d)(3); Reg. § 1.408A-4.

[24] IRC § 408A(e), which was added to the Internal Revenue Code by Pub. L. No. 109-280, The Pension Protection Act of 2006 (August 17, 2006).

Eliminating the need for the interim step is expected to reduce the possibility for errors and expedite the timeliness of a conversion to a Roth IRA. Note that the rules discussed above for conversions from a traditional IRA to a Roth IRA also apply to conversions from a qualified retirement plan.[25]

[C] Qualified Roth Contribution Programs

The Economic Growth and Tax Revenue Reconciliation Act of 2001 (EGTRRA) added a new Section 402A to the Internal Revenue Code, which, beginning in 2006, allows employers to designated some or all contributions under a 401(k) or 403(b) defined contribution plan to a designated Roth account.[26] As discussed above for Roth IRAs, the employee will not be able to deduct any such "designated Roth contributions" for income tax purposes, but any earnings on the contributions will not be taxed and qualified distributions from the designated Roth account also will not be subject to income tax.[27]

Under regulations that were finalized in 2007, the treatment of distributions from designated Roth accounts generally will be the same as for Roth IRAs, but with one major exception. Because designated Roth accounts are part of a 401(k) or 403(b) plan, the accounts will be subject to the same lifetime and post-death required minimum distribution rules that apply to those plans.[28]

[D] Nonqualified Plans and Arrangements

There are a variety of fringe benefits that may be provided to employees outside of the qualified plan context. Often these arrangements are provided to high-level executives and are negotiated individually by the employee with the employer. These arrangements may include deferred compensation plans of various types or supplementary pension plans above the limits permitted by qualified plans. These plans are often less secure for the employee than qualified plans, because they may be subject to the claims of the employer's creditors. The rules relating to the distribution of the plan benefits both during the lifetime of the employee and at the employee's death are generally set forth in the individual contracts between the employee and the employer, rather than regulated by statute.

---

[25] *Id.*

[26] Pub. L. No. 107-16, Economic Growth and Tax Revenue Reconciliation Act of 2001 (June 7, 2001).

[27] IRC § 402A(b)–(d). The definition of qualified distributions is essentially identical to the definition of qualified distributions for Roth IRAs as discussed in § 13.04[B][2] *supra.* IRC § 402A(d)(2).

[28] *See generally* Reg. § 1.402A-1.

§ 13.05 RULES RELATING TO DISTRIBUTIONS FROM QUALIFIED RETIREMENT PLANS AND TRADITIONAL IRAs

Clients may seek assistance in understanding their obligations with respect to withdrawals from their retirement plans during their lifetimes. A client may have a need for funds, with the only source of funds being the retirement plans. Alternatively, a client may have received a notice from a plan administrator or IRA custodian or trustee notifying the client of the obligation to begin receiving benefits and requiring the client to make choices regarding how those benefits are to be taken. Clients may look to estate planners for assistance with these decisions, which will have an impact not only on the client's current income tax situation, but also on the size and nature of the estate to be disposed of at death. While it is advisable to work with the client's accountant in charting the appropriate course with respect to lifetime distributions, an estate planner nonetheless should have a basic knowledge of the rules relating to lifetime distributions from retirement plans, as well as distributions at death.

[A] Penalty for Early Withdrawals from Retirement Plans

[1] General Rule

Generally speaking, a participant in a qualified plan or IRA may not take a distribution from the plan before attaining age 59½ without incurring an early withdrawal penalty equal to 10 percent of the amount of the withdrawal.[1] This penalty is in addition to the ordinary income tax that will be due with respect to the withdrawal.

EXAMPLE 13-1

Amy, who is 30 years old and in the 24 percent marginal federal income tax bracket, needs $26,400 to buy a new car. If she is considering accessing the funds through a withdrawal from her IRA, she will need to withdraw $40,000 altogether. Unless the withdrawal qualifies for one of the exceptions to the early withdrawal penalty (as discussed below), it will be subject to an early withdrawal penalty of $4,000 ($40,000 × 10 percent) and to federal income tax of $9,600 ($40,000 × 24 percent), thus reducing the net amount of the withdrawal to the $26,400 needed for the purchase.[2]

---

[1] § 13.05 IRC § 72(t)(1).

[2] This example assumes that there are no state income tax consequences to the IRA withdrawal. However, many states will subject such withdrawal to state income tax.

[2] Exceptions to the Early Withdrawal Penalty

In the following circumstances, withdrawals from qualified plans or from IRAs (or, in some cases, from both) are not subject to the early withdrawal penalty, *but are still subject to ordinary income tax*:[3]

1. Withdrawals from qualified plans and from IRAs up to the amount of the participant's deductible medical expenses paid during that tax year.[4]
2. Withdrawals from qualified plans for participants who have attained age 55 and who have separated from service (i.e., left their employment with respect to the employer who sponsored the plan).[5]
3. Withdrawals from qualified plans (if the participant has separated from service) and from IRAs that are substantially equal periodic payments calculated with reference to the participant's life expectancy and that are taken annually or more frequently for a period of at least five years or until the participant attains age 59½, whichever occurs later.[6]
4. Withdrawals from IRAs up to $10,000 (over the lifetime of the IRA owner) if the withdrawal is used within 120 days for the costs of acquiring, constructing, or reconstructing a principal residence for first-time home buyers.[7]
5. Withdrawals from IRAs for certain "qualified higher education expenses" with respect to the taxpayer, spouse of the taxpayer, or any child or grandchild of the taxpayer or the taxpayer's spouse.[8] Qualified expenses

---

[3] *See generally* IRC § 72(t). Except as noted in note 6 *infra*, the IRS and the courts have tended to construe the exceptions enumerated in IRC § 72(t) strictly and have shown little or no flexibility in cases where the taxpayer did not follow the rules precisely. *See, e.g.,* Barbee v. Comm'r, T.C. Summary Op. 2006-71 (2006); Reese v. Comm'r, T.C. Summary Op. 2006-23 (2006); Ahmud v. Comm'r, T.C. Summary Op. 2005-103 (2005).

[4] IRC § 72(t)(2)(B). As with all of these exceptions, great care must be taken to follow rules precisely. In Evers v. Comm'r, T.C. Summary Op. 2008-140 (2008), the taxpayer borrowed money in 2003 to pay for medical expenses incurred during that year. In 2004, the taxpayer took an early withdrawal from a qualified retirement plan and used most of the withdrawal amount to repay the loan. The Tax Court upheld the imposition of the early withdrawal penalty for multiple reasons, not the least of which was that the medical expenses were not paid in the same year in which the early withdrawal occurred.

[5] IRC § 72(t)(2)(A)(v).

[6] IRC § 72(t)(4). Recent IRS rulings have provided some additional flexibility with respect to this exception. In Revenue Ruling 2002-62, the IRS laid out procedures for reducing the ongoing amount of the periodic payments under certain circumstances. These procedures can be particularly helpful in situations where the value of the retirement plan has decreased substantially (for example, because of a prolonged decline in the stock market), such that continuing to receive the original payment amounts would exhaust the plan's assets prematurely. In addition, the IRS has, in past rulings, allowed taxpayers to reduce periodic payments proportionately to reflect the reduction in the value of a retirement account following a property settlement incident to the taxpayer's divorce. In Ltr. Rul. 200225040, the IRS also allowed a taxpayer to recalculate the ongoing post-divorce periodic payments based not only on the reduced balance of the retirement accounts of the date of the property division, but also the interest rates then in effect and the taxpayer's then current single life expectancy. *See also* Ltr. Rul. 201030038 for a similar result.

[7] IRC § 72(t)(2)(F).

[8] IRC § 72(t)(2)(E).

generally include tuition, room and board if the student is enrolled at least half time, fees, books, supplies and equipment required for enrollment at an accredited public, nonprofit, or proprietary postsecondary institutions.

6. Stock distributions paid on stock held by an ESOP (Employee Stock Ownership Plan).[9]

7. Distributions from qualified plans made to alternate payees under Qualified Domestic Relations Orders.[10]

8. Distributions from IRAs to unemployed persons to pay health insurance premiums.[11]

9. Distributions from qualified plans and from IRAs to individuals who are totally disabled.[12]

The early withdrawal penalty also does not apply to distributions paid to a participant's beneficiaries (or the participant's estate) in the event of the participant's death or to distributions attributable to the participant's total disability.[13] Here again, though, the distributions are subject to income tax.[14]

In addition to the above exceptions, a withdrawal from an IRA will not be subject to the early withdrawal penalty, *nor will it be subject to income taxes*, to the extent that the withdrawal is rolled over to another IRA or retirement plan within 60 days from the date of the withdrawal.[15] The IRS also may allow a tax- and penalty-free rollover after the expiration of the 60-day period if the failure to do so would be "against equity or good conscience."[16]

---

[9] IRC § 72(t)(2)(A)(vi).

[10] IRC § 72(t)(2)(C).

[11] IRC § 72(t)(2)(D).

[12] IRC § 72(t)(2)(A)(iii). The individual's disability must satisfy the provisions of IRC § 72(m)(7), which defines disability as being "unable to engage in any substantial gainful activity by reason of any medically determinable physical or mental impairment which can be expected to result in death or to be of long-continued and indefinite duration." Thus, in Dollander v. Comm'r, T.C. Memo 2009-187 (August 19, 2009), a taxpayer who was unable to continue with his previous job responsibilities after developing certain mental health issues was nonetheless subject to the early withdrawal penalty because he was able to carry on other gainful activity and could not demonstrate that his impairment was irremediable. By contrast, an individual who was unable to work at all because of multiple sclerosis was not subject to the early withdrawal penalty. Ltr. Rul. 201011036.

[13] IRC § § 72(t)(2)(A)(ii), (iii), 72(m)(7).

[14] In El v. Comm'r, 144 T.C. 140 (March 12, 2015), the Tax Court concluded that the 10 percent amount is actually an additional tax, rather than a penalty. At issue is who has the initial burden of proof concerning whether the 10 percent amount should be assessed or not. If the 10 percent amount is a penalty, the initial burden is on the Internal Revenue Service. IRC § 7491(c). If the 10 percent amount is an additional tax (as the Tax Court concluded), the initial burden is on the taxpayer. IRC § 7491(a)(1).

[15] *See generally* IRC § 408(d)(3).

[16] IRC § 408(d)(3)(I). In Revenue Procedure 2003-16, 2003-4 I.R.B. 359, the IRS enumerated conditions under which the 60-day deadline would be waived automatically. The IRS also has issued a series of letter rulings (both before and after issuing Revenue Procedure 2003-16) in which it has shown considerable leniency in waiving the 60-day requirement. *See, e.g.*, Ltr. Ruls. 200521036, 200407023, 200406050, 200403098, 200402028, and 200327064. However, in more recent rulings, such as Ltr. Rul. 200809043, the IRS appeared to have tightened the circumstances under which it would waive the 60-day rollover requirement, limiting it to cases in which a financial institution involved in

[B] Minimum Distribution Rules

Most participants in qualified retirement plans and traditional IRAs must begin withdrawals from their plans by their "required beginning date" and must take "required minimum distributions" each year thereafter. Under previous rules, the existence of a "designated beneficiary" was an important factor in determining required minimum distributions. Under the 2002 regulations, the identity (or even the existence) of a "designated beneficiary" generally will not be a factor in determining required minimum distributions *during the participant's lifetime*, but remains an important factor in determining such distributions after the participant's death.[17]

The Worker, Retiree, and Employer Recovery Act of 2008 added new subparagraph 401(a)(9)(H) to the Internal Revenue Code, the general effect of which was to eliminate required minimum distributions from retirement plans and traditional IRAs for 2009.[18] This provision has not been extended to any subsequent years.

[1] The Designated Beneficiary

[a] *Choosing the Designated Beneficiary*

The term "designated beneficiary" is a defined term that refers to an individual who under the provisions of the plan is entitled to a benefit contingent on the participant's death. A designated beneficiary can be entitled to benefits either by being affirmatively designated by the participant as required by the plan, or by the default beneficiary provision established in the plan.[19] A "designated beneficiary" must be an individual, which means that an estate, corporation, partnership, or charity cannot be a designated beneficiary. Although a trust generally will not qualify as a designated beneficiary (because it is not an individual), if certain requirements are met, one can "look through" a trust and consider one of the beneficiaries of the trust as the designated beneficiary for purposes of the minimum distribution calculations.[20]

(Footnote Continued)

the rollover made an error or to cases in which the rollover was not completed due to death, disability or illness of the owner. The IRS was seemingly ignoring any other circumstances that might be considered "equity or good conscience." *See, e.g.*, Ltr. Ruls. 201311037, 201025084, and 201022025 for more recent cases in which the IRS waived the 60-day rollover requirement because of medical reasons. The IRS clarified its position considerably in Revenue Procedure 2016-47, 2016-37 I.R.B. 346, under which the IRS will now allow a taxpayer to "self-certify" that the 60-day requirement will be waived if the taxpayer meets any one of 11 enumerated conditions and completes the rollover as soon as practicable after the condition that prevented the taxpayer from completing the rollover within the 60-day period is no longer present.

[17] IRC §§ 72(t)(2)(A)(ii), (iii), 72(m)(7).

[18] Pub. L. No. 110-458, Worker, Retiree, and Employer Recovery Act of 2008 (December 23, 2008).

[19] Reg. § 1.401(a)(9)-4.

[20] A detailed discussion of the requirements for "looking through" a trust to use one of its beneficiaries as the designated beneficiary can be found in § 13.06[C] *infra*. *See generally* Reg. § 1.401(a)(9)-4, Q&A 5, 6.

If a client's objectives include keeping his or her retirement plan assets tax deferred as long as possible, it is extremely important to ensure that the client has a designated beneficiary. While the 2002 regulations made several significant changes in the rules governing designated beneficiaries, it is still important for the client to have a designated beneficiary, because without a designated beneficiary, the assets remaining in the plan or IRA must be withdrawn within five years of death (if the client died before his or her required beginning date) or over the client's remaining life expectancy (if the client died after his or her required beginning date).[21] In some circumstances, having a designated beneficiary at death will permit the beneficiary to stretch out withdrawals from the plan or IRA, thus deferring the income tax on the withdrawals.

The date on which the client names the designated beneficiary is not significant. The client can name the designated beneficiary at any time before the client's death, and can change the designation at any time without affecting lifetime distributions.

The estate planner should examine the client's existing beneficiary designations to determine whether they will allow for tax deferral opportunities with respect to the plan benefits. A common estate planning technique is to name the estate as a beneficiary of nonprobate property in order to achieve a unified estate plan. However, while naming the client's estate as the beneficiary of a retirement plan may be viewed as a shortcut mechanism for ensuring that the plan benefits are directed to the individuals named in the client's will, this "shortcut" can preclude maximum income tax deferral after the client's death.

[b] Protection of Spousal Rights: Spousal Consent

When advising a client regarding appropriate beneficiary designations for qualified plans, it should be kept in mind that the Retirement Equity Act of 1984 (REA)[22] may require spousal consent for beneficiary designations other than the spouse.[23] For plans covered by the REA, the form of benefit must be a "qualified joint and survivor annuity" for distributions beginning during the lifetime of the participant and a "qualified pre-retirement survivor annuity" for a spouse of a participant who dies before retirement.[24] These required forms of benefits can only be deviated from where the spouse has consented to a waiver of the form of benefit in a writing meeting the requirements of the REA.[25] The REA requirement does not apply to IRAs or to certain profit-sharing plans.[26]

---

[21] Reg. §§ 1.401(a)(9)-3, Q&A 4(a)(2), 1.401(a)(9)-5, Q&A 5(a)(2).

[22] Pub. L. No. 98-387, 98 Stat. 1426.

[23] IRC §§ 401(a)(11), 417.

[24] *Id.*

[25] *Id.*

[26] In Charles Schwab and Company v. Chandler, 593 F.3d 916 (9th Cir. 2010), the Ninth Circuit Court of Appeals rejected the argument that a surviving spouse had a statutory claim under the REA to an IRA that had been funded by a rollover from a qualified plan.

[2] Penalty for Failure to Take Required Minimum Distributions

Failure to take required minimum distributions subjects a participant to a *50 percent* tax on the minimum distributions that should have been taken, but were not.[27] The effect of the 50 percent tax on top of the ordinary income tax payable with respect to plan distributions can be disastrous.

EXAMPLE *13-2*

Robert, who has attained age 80, fails to take his required minimum distribution of $4,950 in 2022 from his $100,000 IRA. When Robert discovers in a subsequent year that this minimum distribution should have been taken, he then must take the distribution, pay ordinary income tax on the distribution, and pay a penalty tax of 50 percent of the distribution, or $2,475, *in addition to* the income tax.

The IRS may waive the additional tax if the taxpayer can demonstrate that the failure to take the required minimum distribution was due to reasonable error and that reasonable steps have been taken to remedy any shortfall.[28]

[3] Required Beginning Date for Required Minimum Distributions

An employee's "required beginning date" is the date upon which the employee must take the first minimum distribution from the qualified plan or IRA.[29] That date differs depending upon (1) whether the plan in question is a qualified plan or an IRA; and (2) if the plan in question is a qualified plan, whether the employee is a 5 percent owner of the employer sponsoring the plan, determined according to IRS criteria.[30]

[a] *Required Beginning Date from Qualified Plans for Non-5 Percent Owners*

For those qualified plans as to which the employee is not a 5 percent owner, the employee's required beginning date is April 1 of the calendar year following the later of:[31]

---

[27] IRC § 4974(a).

[28] IRC § 4974(d). Until recently, the IRS required any taxpayer seeking a waiver of the 50 percent tax to pay the tax first and then seek a refund. Though the IRS stated this requirement in its Publication 590 and in the instructions to the relevant tax form (Form 5329), the Internal Revenue Code and the Regulations do not expressly address this subject. Following numerous complaints as to the potentially onerous nature of this requirement, the IRS apparently has changed its position, as there is no mention of having to pay the tax first in the most recent Publication 590 or the instructions to Form 5329.

[29] IRC § 401(a)(9)(C).

[30] IRC §§ 401(a)(9)(C)(ii)(I), 416(i)(1)(B)(i), 318.

[31] IRC § 401(a)(9)(A), (C).

1. The calendar year in which the employee attains age 72; or

2. The calendar year in which the employee retires.

[b] *Required Beginning Date from Traditional IRAs and from Qualified Plans for 5 Percent Owners*

Individuals born after June 30, 1949, must begin distributions from IRAs and from qualified plans as to which the employee is a 5 percent owner must begin distributions by April 1 of the year following the calendar year in which the employee attained age 72, even if the employee remains employed.[32] The employee cannot delay distributions until retirement if the employee continues to work beyond age 72.

[4] Calculating Required Minimum Distributions

Required minimum distributions are calculated in a manner that is intended to distribute the entire retirement plan benefits over the lifetime of the plan participant or over the lifetimes of the participant and the participant's designated beneficiary or beneficiaries.[33] It is neither required nor anticipated that the actual amounts of the distributions will be equal (or substantially equal) from year to year.

The amount of a client's required minimum distribution will be based on the size of the client's plan balance at the end of the year prior to the year for which the required minimum distribution must be taken.[34] For example, if a client is retired and reaches the required beginning date in 2022, the client may wait until April 1, 2023, to take the first required minimum distribution, but that payment will be for the year 2022, and the balance of the plan at the end of 2021 will be used in determining that distribution. The required minimum distribution for the year 2023 will be based upon the plan balance at the end of 2022 and must be made on or before December 31, 2023, and so on in each subsequent year.

The required minimum distribution then is calculated by dividing the plan's balance by an applicable distribution period, which is an actuarially determined life expectancy.[35] Depending on the exact circumstances, the life expectancy to be used may be the single life expectancy of the participant, the single life expectancy of the beneficiary, or the joint life expectancies of both. The life expectancies to be used are contained in various IRS tables, which are updated periodically to reflect changing mortality rates.

In calculating required minimum distributions for all years after the first year for which such distributions are required, a new applicable distribution period must be determined by one of two methods. Under the *fixed term method*, the new applicable

---

[32] IRC §§ 401(a)(9)(A), (C), 408(a)(6).

[33] IRC § 401(a)(9)(A)(ii).

[34] Reg. § 1.401(a)(9)-5, Q&A 1(a), 3.

[35] Reg. § 1.401(a)(9)-5, Q&A 1(a), 4.

distribution period is arrived at each year by subtracting one from the applicable distribution period used in the preceding year. Under the *recalculation method* the new applicable distribution period is redetermined each year using the IRS tables based on the ages reached by the participant and/or the beneficiary, as applicable, in that year.

The exact calculations will depend primarily on whether the distributions are being made during the client's lifetime and, if not, (1) whether the client died before or after reaching the required beginning date, and (2) the exact identity of the designated beneficiary or beneficiaries.[36]

PRACTICE NOTE

Qualified retirement plans are *not* required to offer payouts based on life expectancy distributions.[37] In practice, many qualified plans in particular will offer only a lump sum distribution upon the employee's retirement or death. It thus is imperative to obtain information from the client concerning the distribution options that are available from each of the client's retirement plans.

[5] Strategy Regarding the Timing of the First Required Distribution

The estate planner should not be misled by the fact that the required beginning date for distributions is defined in terms of April 1 following the calendar year in which the client attains age 72 or retires, because a client must take a minimum distribution *for* the calendar year in which the applicable event occurs, even though the timing of that distribution can be delayed until April 1 of the following calendar year. If the client waits until April 1 of the calendar year following the applicable event, the client will be required to take two minimum distributions in that year, because the client also will have to take a distribution for the calendar year subsequent to the applicable event. Whether it is advisable to delay the first required minimum distribution until the year following the applicable event depends upon the client's income needs and the comparative income tax brackets the client expects to be in during each of the years in which the first required minimum distribution could be taken. Delaying the first required minimum distribution causes two such distributions to be received in one calendar year and could cause the client to be subject to a higher income tax bracket. On the other hand, if the client expects income to be significantly reduced in the second year for which a required minimum distribution must be taken, the delay in taking the first required minimum distribution could result in the tax rate applied to that distribution being lower than if the distribution had been taken earlier. Taking the first required minimum distribution as

---

[36] The exact calculations are discussed in § 13.05[C], [D] *infra.*

[37] Reg. § 1.401(a)(9)-3, Q&A 4(b).

late as possible also will maximize the period during which the required minimum distribution remains tax deferred. Distributions for each calendar year after the first required minimum distribution *must* be taken by December 31 of that year.[38]

[C] Required Minimum Distributions During Participant's Lifetime

The 2002 regulations contained several important new rules with respect to distributions from IRAs and defined contribution plans such as 401(k) plans and 403(b) plans.[39] These regulations are effective for years beginning on or after January 1, 2003.[40] Under the 2002 regulations, almost everyone will use the same life expectancy table, known as the Uniform Lifetime Table, to determine the amount of required minimum distributions during the participant's lifetime.[41] This table is based on the joint life expectancy of the participant and a designated beneficiary who is presumed to be ten years younger than the participant.[42] A participant will use this table to calculate required minimum distributions based on the age attained by the participant in the year for which the distribution is required to be made, regardless of whether the participant has a designated beneficiary who is less than ten years younger or has a designated beneficiary who is older. A participant also will use this table even if he or she has no designated beneficiaries at all.

The life expectancies for the Uniform Lifetime Table had not been updated since the 2002 regulations went into effect. The 2002 life expectancies were updated effective January 1, 2022.[43] The new Uniform Lifetime Table, effective January 1, 2022, is shown in Appendix A at the end of the chapter.

The only participant who will use a different table to determine lifetime required minimum distributions is a participant whose sole designated beneficiary is a spouse who is more than ten years younger than the participant.[44] Those participants will use the Joint and Last Survivor Table, which is an IRS table based on the actual joint life expectancies of the two spouses, and will use the recalculation method for redetermining life expectancy each year.[45] The life expectancies for these tables also were updated effective January 1, 2022.[46]

Accordingly, to determine required minimum distribution during the lifetime of a client (other than a client with a spouse more than ten years younger) only two pieces of information are needed: the account balance at the end of the prior year, and the client's age (or, more specifically, the age that the client will reach in the calendar year for which the required minimum distribution is being determined).

---

[38] Reg. § 1.401(a)(9)-5, Q&A 1(c).

[39] Reg. §§ 1.401(a)(9)-0 to -9, 1.403(b)-3, 1.408-8.

[40] *Id.*

[41] *Id.*

[42] Reg. § 1.401(a)(9)-9, Q&A 2.

[43] Reg. § 1.401(a)(9)-5, Q&A 4(a).

[44] Reg. § 1.401(a)(9)-5, Q&A 4(b).

[45] Reg. § 1.401(a)(9)-9, Q&A 3.

[46] Reg. § 1.401(a)(9)-5, Q&A 4(a).

EXAMPLE *13-3*

Deborah, who has long since retired, will reach age 74 on her birthday in 2024. On December 31, 2023, the value of her IRA account is $1,000,000. Deborah's designated beneficiary is her husband, David, who also will reach age 74 in 2024. To determine her required minimum distribution for the year 2024, Deborah will refer to the Uniform Lifetime Table. Based on the joint life expectancy of 25.5 years determined from this table, Deborah will divide the account balance by the joint life expectancy, and the result will be the required minimum distribution that she must take before December 31, 2024:

$1,000,000/25.5 = $39,216

This figure would be the same regardless of David's age (unless he was more than ten years younger than Deborah), or if Deborah had no designated beneficiary at all.

To determine Deborah's required minimum distribution for 2025, divide the balance in the IRA as of December 31, 2024 by 24.6, which is the joint life expectancy determined from the Uniform Lifetime Table based on Deborah reaching age 75 in 2024.

In the updated Uniform Life Table, the life expectancies at the younger ages (such as the early 70s), are almost two years greater than the 2002 life expectancies. The differences in the life expectancies diminish over time. But even at age 87, the difference is still an entire year.

The effect of the longer life expectancies can be seen by revisiting Example 13-3. If this example had occurred in 2021, Deborah would have used a life expectancy of 23.8. Correspondingly, the required minimum distribution would have been $42,017, or almost $3,000 more than the distribution using the longer life expectancies.

The longer qualified plan benefits can remain in the plan, the longer the income taxes on those assets can be deferred. This income tax deferral has a significant impact on the growth of the plan assets.[47]

---

[47] Under the rules in effect prior to 2001, if a participant did not have a "designated beneficiary" as of the required beginning date, the plan benefits had to be withdrawn over a period determined by the participant's life expectancy. If, on the other hand, the participant had a designated beneficiary, the participant could withdraw his plan assets over the *joint* life expectancy of himself and that designated beneficiary, provided, however, that if the designated beneficiary was someone other than the participant's spouse, that designated beneficiary would be deemed to be no more than ten years younger than the participant for purposes of calculating the joint life expectancy. This limitation on the deemed age of a nonspouse designated beneficiary was called the "minimum distribution incidental benefit" rule (MDIB). Because the joint life expectancy of a participant and another person always will be at least as long as the participant's life expectancy alone, having a designated beneficiary under the old rules resulted in the required minimum distribution being lower than if there were no designated beneficiary and the distribution were calculated solely by reference to the participant's life expectancy.

In addition, the required minimum distribution could be determined using a variety of calculation methods and using unisex life expectancy tables published by the Internal Revenue Service in

[D] Required Minimum Distributions Following Death of Participant

Under the Internal Revenue Code, required minimum distributions also must be taken from retirement plans following the death of the participant. The rate at which distributions must be taken from the plan after the participant's death depends upon whether the participant had a designated beneficiary, the identity of the beneficiary, and, to a lesser extent, whether the participant died before or after reaching his or her Required Beginning Date.

One of the important changes in the 2002 regulations is that the identity of the designated beneficiary is not fixed until the "designation date" which is September 30 of the calendar year following the year of employee's death.[48] Although new beneficiaries cannot be added after the participant's death, the participant's executor

---

(Footnote Continued)

Section 1.72-9 of the Regulations (designated as Table V for single life expectancy and as Table VI for joint life expectancy). Although the use of these tables was mandated, participants had a choice as to how their life expectancy and that of their spouse (if the spouse was the designated beneficiary) was to be determined in years following the initial required minimum distribution. Plans were permitted, but not required, to give participants a choice whether or not to "recalculate" their life expectancies (and that of their spouse if the spouse was the designated beneficiary) each year. A careful examination of a client's retirement and estate planning goals was required to assist a client in making the appropriate choices regarding the calculation method for life expectancy because, once made at the required beginning date, this decision was irrevocable.

If participants did not choose to recalculate life expectancy, then after the tables were consulted to determine the initial life expectancy used to calculate the first required minimum distribution, those tables were not consulted again. Rather, each subsequent year, one year was subtracted from the previous year's life expectancy to determine the remaining life expectancy and hence the size of the required minimum distribution. Under this approach, if the initial life expectancy had been 15.3 years, 1/15.3 of the plan balance would have to be distributed in the first year. The next year, the life expectancy would be 14.3 years (15.3 minus 1.0), and 1/14.3 of the plan balance would have to be distributed for that year. Upon the expiration of the initial life expectancy, the entire remaining balance would have to be distributed. If participants died before the expiration of their life expectancy, the retirement benefits would continue to be distributed over that life expectancy, as initially determined by the tables.

The alternative method of calculating annual distributions under the old rules was to recalculate the participant's life expectancy each year under the IRS tables. As the tables make clear, an individual's life expectancy is not reduced by a whole year for each year of life, because each year that a person survives increases the individual's total life expectancy. For example, the life expectancy of a 71-year-old under Table V is 15.3 years, thus predicting that the individual will reach age 86.3 years. Recalculating that person's life expectancy at age 72, the life expectancy has decreased by less than one year to 14.6 years, thus predicting that the person will live to age 86.6 years.

The effect of recalculating life expectancy was to slow down the rate at which the required minimum distribution had to be made. Continuing with the example from above, under the recalculation method, if in the first year 1/15.3 of the plan had to be distributed, in the next year only 1/14.6 of the plan would have to be distributed, as opposed to the larger 1/14.3 fraction of the plan, if the life expectancy had not been recalculated. The "catch" was that under the recalculation method, a participant's life expectancy was reduced to zero in the year the individual died, thus potentially accelerating the required minimum distributions.

If a participant's designated beneficiary was the participant's spouse, then the participant could choose whether to recalculate both the participant's and the spouse's life expectancies, neither of their life expectancies, or one or the other of their life expectancies. If the designated beneficiary was not the spouse, recalculation of the designated beneficiary's life expectancy was not permitted.

[48] Reg. § 1.401(a)(9)-4, Q&A 4(a).

or heirs can, in effect, change the designated beneficiaries by using disclaimers or by cashing out a beneficiary prior to the designation date. In turn, this may allow the remaining beneficiaries to stretch out the retirement plan distributions over a longer time period.

If a participant dies before reaching the required beginning date, there is no required minimum distribution for the year of the participant's death.[49]

[1] Death of Participant: No Designated Beneficiary

If the participant dies *before* reaching the required beginning date and does not have a designated beneficiary on September 30 of the year following the participant's death (for example, the participant's estate is designated as the beneficiary), the so-called "five-year rule" will apply and all assets in the retirement plan must be distributed by December 31 of the calendar year that contains the fifth anniversary of the participant's death.[50] The withdrawals do not have to be made ratably during the five-year period, so long as the distribution is complete by the end of the prescribed period.

If the participant dies *after* reaching the required beginning date and does not have a designated beneficiary on September 30 of the year following the participant's death, required minimum distributions must be made over the remaining single life expectancy of the *participant* (determined as if the participant had not died) using the fixed term method.[51]

The SECURE Act did *not* change the rules concerning the death of a participant who does not have a designated beneficiary.

[2] Death of Participant: Designated Beneficiary

Under the SECURE Act, if a participant dies and has a designated beneficiary, the designated beneficiary must withdraw the entire amount of the plan by December 31 of the year in which the *tenth* anniversary of the participant's death occurs, unless the designated beneficiary is an Eligible Designated Beneficiary (the "ten-year rule").[52] Prior to the issuance of the 2022 Proposed Regulations, many practitioners had anticipated that the withdrawals would not have to be made ratably over the ten-year period, so long as the distribution was completed by the end of the prescribed period. Under the 2022 Proposed Regulations, however, minimum distri-

---

[49] Reg. § 1.401(a)(9)-3, Q&A 2, 3.

[50] IRC § 401(a)(9)(B)(ii); Reg. § 1.401(a)(9)-3, Q&A 2. Under Pub. L. No. 110-435, Workers, Retirees and Employer Recovery Act of 2008 (December 23, 2008), the "five-year rule" effectively becomes a "six-year rule" as the year 2009 is disregarded in terms of determining the end of the prescribed period for which withdrawals must be made.

[51] Reg. § 1.401(a)(9)-5, Q&A 5(a)(2).

[52] IRC § 401(a)(9)(H).

butions will be required annually for some beneficiaries, with a final distribution of the entire remaining balance at the end of the prescribed period.[53]

Distributions can be extended beyond the ten-year period if the designated beneficiary is an Eligible Designated Beneficiary. There are five categories of Eligible Designated Beneficiaries.

[a] Surviving Spouse

The SECURE Act did not change the rules concerning the treatment of a surviving spouse as a designated beneficiary.

If a surviving spouse is named as the outright beneficiary of a retirement plan, the spouse has the option of rolling over the plan balance into an IRA in his or her own name.[54] The spouse then can defer distributions until reaching his or her required beginning date, which may permit a longer deferral opportunity than if the plan remained in the name of the participant. Further, having rolled over the participant's plan into his or her own IRA, the surviving spouse then can name a new designated beneficiary and use the Uniform Lifetime Table (which is based on joint life expectancies of the surviving spouse and a presumed beneficiary who is ten years younger) in calculating required minimum distributions. Also, if the surviving spouse remarries someone who is more than ten years younger and names the new spouse as the designated beneficiary, required minimum distributions can be stretched out even further, using the actual joint life expectancies of the surviving spouse and the new spouse. The ability of the spouse to roll over the deceased spouse's retirement benefits is one of the most important tax planning options available upon the death of a plan participant.

EXAMPLE 13-4

Andrew, who has reached age 75, has started to receive minimum distributions from his IRA at his required beginning date. Andrew has named his 50-year-old wife, Erin, as his beneficiary. Andrew dies four years later. During the four years prior to his death, Andrew received distributions based on the joint life expectancy of himself and Erin. Following Andrew's death, instead of continuing to receive distributions based on the couple's joint life expectancy, Erin elects to roll over the benefits to her own IRA. As a result, Erin (who then has reached age 54) is able to defer taxation for another 18 years, until she reaches her own required beginning date. Once Erin reaches her required beginning date, her minimum distribution will be based on the joint life expectancy of herself and an individual ten years younger. Finally, following the death of Erin, the distribution can be spread out over another ten years, unless her benefici-

---

[53] Prop. Reg. § 1.401(a)(9)-5(e).
[54] IRC § 402(c)(9); Reg. § 1.408-8, Q&A-5(b).

ary is an Eligible Designated Beneficiary, in which case, it may be possible to stretch out the distribution further still.

There is one circumstance in which a surviving spouse may not wish to roll over a deceased spouse's retirement benefits. If the surviving spouse is *under* age 59$1/2$, any distributions taken by the surviving spouse from the deceased spouse's plan would not be subject to the early distribution penalty if the plan is not rolled over into the surviving spouse's own IRA. By contrast, once a plan is rolled over into the surviving spouse's own IRA, any distribution taken from the IRA before the surviving spouse reached age 59$1/2$ would be subject to the early distribution penalty. Therefore, if a surviving spouse will need to access some of the deceased spouse's retirement benefits, the portion of the benefits reasonably anticipated to be withdrawn prior to the surviving spouse's reaching age 59$1/2$ should be retained in the deceased spouse's IRA and not rolled over. Because there is no requirement that all of a plan or IRA be rolled over, the estate planner can be creative in recommending which portion of a deceased spouse's retirement benefits should be rolled over by the surviving spouse. There is no time limit on the rollover decision.

If the designated beneficiary is the spouse of the participant, an additional tax deferral opportunity is available. The spouse is permitted to defer any distributions from the plan until December 31 of the year in which the participant would have reached age 72 and then to make annual distributions on the basis of recalculating the spouse's life expectancy each year.[55]

[b] Minor Child of the Participant

If a minor child of the participant is named as the designated beneficiary, the child is an Eligible Designated Beneficiary and distributions can be made to the child using the child's life expectancy during the term of the child's minority.[56] When the child reaches the age of majority, distributions then become subject to the ten-year rule.[57] The SECURE Act does not define "minor"—it apparently leaves the exact definition up to the law of the minor's domicile. Under the 2022 Proposed Regulations, however, "majority" is defined as age 21.[58]

Note that the minor child must be a child of the *participant*. The treatment of a minor child as an Eligible Designated Beneficiary does *not* apply to a grandchild (or more remote descendant) of the participant or to a minor child that is unrelated to the participant.

---

[55] IRC § 401(a)(9)(B)(iv).

[56] IRC § 401(a)(9)(e)(ii)(II).

[57] *Id.*

[58] Prop. Reg. § 1.401(a)(9)-5(e).

[c] Disabled Beneficiary

If an individual who is disabled within the meaning of IRC Section 72(m)(7) is named as the designated beneficiary, the disabled individual is an Eligible Designated Beneficiary and distributions can be made using the disabled individual's life expectancy.[59]

[d] Chronically Ill Beneficiary

If an individual who is chronically ill within the meaning of IRC Section 7702B(c)(2) is named as the designated beneficiary, the chronically ill individual is an Eligible Designated Beneficiary and distributions can be made using the chronically ill individual's life expectancy.[60]

[e] Beneficiary Less than Ten Years Younger

If an individual who is not in any of the other classification for being an Eligible Designated Beneficiary is named as the designated beneficiary and is not more than ten years younger than the participant, the individual is an Eligible Designated Beneficiary and distributions can be made using such individual's life expectancy.[61]

[3] Death of Eligible Designated Beneficiary

Upon the death of an Eligible Designated Beneficiary, distributions from any remaining portion of the plan are subject to the ten-year rule.[62]

[4] Special Issues for IRAs

Although the required minimum distributions must be calculated separately for each IRA, the total of the required minimum distributions generally can be distributed from a single IRA or disproportionately among different IRAs.[63] This gives added flexibility to the estate planner in accomplishing the client's dispositive goals.

The 2002 regulations added certain reporting requirements. For each year beginning in 2003, the trustee, custodian, or issuer of an IRA must either (i) report the

---

[59] IRC § 401(a)(9)(e)(ii)(III). IRC § 72(m)(7) provides that "an individual shall be considered to be disabled if he is unable to engage in any substantial gainful activity by reason of any medically determinable physical or mental impairment which can be expected to result in death or to be of long-continued and indefinite duration."

[60] IRC § 401(a)(9)(e)(ii)(IV). IRC § 7702B(c)(2) provides that an individual shall be considered to be chronically ill if *inter alia* the individual cannot perform "at least 2 activities of daily living for a period of at least 90 days due to a loss of functional capacity" or requires "substantial supervision to protect such individual from threats to health and safety due to severe cognitive impairment."

[61] IRC § 401(a)(9)(e)(ii)(V).

[62] IRC § 401(a)(9)(H)(iii).

[63] Reg. § 1.408-8, Q&A 9.

amount of the required minimum distribution to any IRA owner who is required to take such a distribution for that year; or (ii) report to any IRA holder who is required to take a required minimum distribution for that year that such a distribution is required and offer to calculate the amount of the distribution at the request of the IRA owner.[64] Beginning in 2004, the trustee, custodian, or issuer of an IRA also must report to the IRS that a minimum distribution is required to be made to the IRA owner, but is not required to report the amount of any such distribution.[65]

[5] Non-Spousal Rollovers from Qualified Retirement Plans

Historically, if a qualified plan participant designated his or her spouse as the beneficiary, the spouse would be allowed to roll over the plan benefits to his or her own IRA upon the participant's death.[66] However, for a non-spouse beneficiary, the rollover option was not available. Instead, the plan generally would require that the full amount of the plan benefits be distributed to the non-spouse beneficiary shortly after the participant's death, thus triggering an income tax liability on the full amount of the distribution.[67] In fact, from the perspective of the plan participant, one of the advantages of rolling over a qualified plan into an IRA upon retiring or (otherwise separating from the employer's service during the participant's lifetime) was to preserve the ability of any non-spouse beneficiaries to stretch out distributions over their own life expectancies.[68]

The Pension Protection Act of 2006[69] added Section 402(c)(11) to the Internal Revenue Code, which permits a direct rollover of plan benefits from a qualified retirement plan to an inherited IRA in the name of the deceased plan participant. The inherited IRA then is subject to required minimum distributions each year.[70] Section 402(c)(11) is effective for plan distributions made after December 31, 2006, regardless of the date of the plan participant's death.

In Notice 2007-7,[71] the Internal Revenue Service issued guidance concerning the application of Section 402(c)(11). For example, Notice 2007-7 confirms that a trust may be treated as a designated beneficiary for purposes of a plan rollover, so long as the trust meets the "look through" requirements.[72] Notice 2007-7, however, left many

---

[64] Reg. § 1.408-8, Q&A 10.

[65] *Id.*

[66] IRC § 402(c)(9).

[67] Under Reg. § 1.401(a)(9)-3, Q&A 4, qualified retirement plans were permitted to adopt provisions under which all of the plan benefits had to be distributed either under the so-called "five-year rule" (as discussed in § 13.05[D][1] *infra*) or over the life expectancy of the beneficiary designated by the plan participant. As a practical matter, most plans chose the former.

[68] *See generally* the discussion on determining required minimum distributions following the death of a plan participant in § 13.05[D] *infra*.

[69] Pub. L. No. 109-280, The Pension Protection Act of 2006 (August 17, 2006).

[70] IRC § 402(c)(11). A rollover is not permitted if there is no "designated beneficiary" as that term is defined in Reg. § 1.401(a)-4. *Id.*

[71] 2007-1 C.B. 395 (January 10, 2007).

[72] The "look through" requirements are discussed in § 13.06[C] *infra*.

questions unanswered, including what procedures need to be followed for a qualified retirement plan to adopt the provisions of Section 402(c)(11). Also left unanswered was when—or if—employers would be required to incorporate provisions allowing non-spousal rollovers from their qualified plans. Section 402(c)(11) provides only that such provisions are permissible. The Workers, Retirees and Employer Recovery Act of 2008 amended Section 402(c)(11) to make non-spousal rollover provisions mandatory.[73]

§ 13.06 NAMING A TRUST AS THE BENEFICIARY OF A QUALIFIED RETIREMENT PLAN OR IRA

There are a number of circumstances in which it may be appropriate to name a trust as the beneficiary of a qualified retirement plan or IRA. Doing so, however, may jeopardize the opportunity to achieve maximum income tax deferral following the death of the plan owner, because a trust generally does not qualify as a designated beneficiary.[1] Nonetheless, if certain requirements are met, it is possible to "look through" the trust so as to use a trust beneficiary for purposes of calculating required minimum distributions.[2]

[A] Reasons for Naming a Trust as the Beneficiary of a Retirement Plan

The reasons for naming a trust as the beneficiary of a retirement plan asset are generally the same reasons why a client would choose to leave any assets in trust rather than outright to a beneficiary. A trust severs legal title and control of property from the property's economic benefit; this makes trusts a useful device for providing management of property or for controlling the disposition of property.

[1] Investment Management

A trust is commonly used to provide management of assets for the benefit of the named beneficiaries. When a client has a self-directed retirement plan of significant value and a spouse or other beneficiaries with no interest or expertise in financial matters, the client may decide that a trust vehicle should be used to remove the burden of investment decisions from the ultimate beneficiary. When the beneficiaries are young children, similar considerations may lead to naming a trust as the beneficiary.

---

[73] Pub. L. No. 110-458, Workers, Retirees and Employer Recovery Act of 2008 (December 23, 2008).

[1] **§ 13.06** Reg. § 1.401(a)(9)-4, Q&A 5, 6.

[2] *See* § 13.06[C] *infra.*

[2] Protecting Assets from a Spendthrift

In situations where a client has concerns about a beneficiary's good judgment in making spending decisions, naming a trust with a spendthrift provision as the beneficiary of retirement plan assets creates a buffer between the ultimate beneficiary and the retirement account. A spendthrift provision generally provides that the beneficiary cannot sell, pledge, or otherwise alienate his or her interest in the trust. The trust interest held for that beneficiary is also not subject to the claims of the beneficiary's creditors.[3]

[3] Second Marriage Situations

While naming a spouse as the outright beneficiary of a retirement plan has several significant advantages, including the spouse's ability to roll over the retirement plan benefits into an IRA of his or her own (thus providing potential for additional tax deferral), naming a spouse as the outright beneficiary also gives the spouse the ability to dispose of the plan assets to whomever he or she chooses, both as to distributions taken during the lifetime of the spouse and by beneficiary designation with respect to the remaining plan benefits at the spouse's death. This result may be acceptable in the case of a first marriage where the husband and wife both are likely to want to ultimately benefit their children. However, in a situation where a participant has a second spouse and children from a first marriage, the participant may want the surviving spouse to benefit from the plan assets during his or her lifetime, but also may want to assure that the children from the first marriage will receive the remaining plan assets following the death of the surviving spouse. Directing plan benefits to a marital trust for the benefit of the spouse with the remainder passing to the children of the first marriage at the death of the surviving spouse can accomplish the goals of a client in such a situation. In situations where qualifying benefits for the marital deduction is necessary for estate tax deferral, special care must be taken when naming a trust as beneficiary, because obtaining the estate tax marital deduction for the full value of the retirement plan asset requires compliance with a number of requirements.[4]

[4] Making Full Use of the Unified Credit

A primary goal of estate planning for many clients is to make full use of the unified credit that permits assets to pass free of estate taxes upon the death of an individual.[5]

A frequently used vehicle to allow full use of the applicable exclusion amount upon the death of the first spouse to die is the credit shelter trust, also often known as

---

[3] *See* Chapter 4 for a discussion of spendthrift trusts.

[4] *See* § 13.08 *infra.*

[5] *See* Chapter 5 for a discussion of the unified credit.

the bypass trust.[6] The beneficiaries of this type of trust can be the spouse and issue of the decedent and any other individuals (such as parents of the decedent) or institutions whom the decedent wishes to benefit. The use of a trust for the applicable exclusion amount allows a surviving spouse to benefit from the assets in the trust, without giving the surviving spouse so much control over the trust as to subject the trust property to estate taxation at the death of the surviving spouse.

As will be discussed below, retirement assets are not the optimal assets for the use of the applicable exclusion amount. There may be situations, however, in which a client does not have sufficient nonretirement assets with which to use the applicable exclusion amount fully. In such a situation, the client may need to consider naming the credit shelter trust as the beneficiary of some of the retirement benefits.

[B] Disadvantages to Naming a Trust as the Beneficiary of Retirement Plan Assets

There are a number of potential disadvantages to naming a trust as the beneficiary of a retirement plan.

[1] Potential Loss of Maximal Income Tax Deferral

One of the important advantages of qualified retirement plan assets derives from the fact that the growth on plan assets is not taxed until distributions are taken from the plan or account. Having a "designated beneficiary" is one mechanism for maximizing the income tax deferral opportunities of retirement plan assets. However, unless the requirements for looking through a trust are met, a trust will not qualify as a designated beneficiary, thereby foreclosing some of these deferral opportunities.

[2] Loss of Maximum Benefit of Unified Credit by Allocating Plan Benefits to Credit Shelter Trust

Because qualified plan benefits are *income in respect of a decedent*, they will be subject to income tax when distributed from the plan.[7] Therefore, if a retirement plan is directed to a credit shelter trust as a means of utilizing the applicable exclusion amount, the amount of property that will pass to the ultimate beneficiaries will be substantially less than the pre-tax value of the plan's assets after the income taxes on distributions have been paid. If, instead, the identical amount of cash or marketable securities were shielded from estate taxation through the applicable exclusion amount, the full amount could pass to the beneficiaries. For that reason, if there are other assets to direct to the credit shelter trust, it is usually preferable to use those benefits rather than retirement benefits.

---

[6] The credit shelter trust is discussed in greater detail in Chapters 5 and 6.
[7] IRC § 691.

[3] Loss of Maximum Tax Deferral Opportunities from Naming a Marital Trust as the Beneficiary of Retirement Plan Benefits

Naming a marital trust as the beneficiary of retirement plan benefits may result in a loss of maximum income tax deferral opportunities after the death of the plan participant. This can occur even when the "look through" requirements are met so that the spouse who is the beneficiary of a marital trust is deemed the designated beneficiary for purposes of the minimum distribution rules.

As discussed above, the spouse's ability to roll over a decedent's retirement plan benefits where the spouse has been named as the outright beneficiary is a valuable tax planning option. However, when a QTIP trust is named as a beneficiary, the advantages of rolling over to the spouse's IRA will likely not be available. The 2002 regulations specifically state that rollover is not available when a trust is named as beneficiary of an IRA, even if the spouse is the sole beneficiary of the trust.[8]

The general rule for qualifying retirement benefits for the estate tax marital deduction when the beneficiary of the plan is a marital trust has been that all the income on the undistributed portion of the plan (i.e., the portion of the plan that is not distributed to the marital trust through required minimum distributions or otherwise) be distributed from time to time to the marital trust and from there to the surviving spouse each year.[9] The consequence of this rule was that if the income on the undistributed portion of the plan exceeded the required minimum distribution, this additional income also had to be distributed to the marital trust and then to the surviving spouse. Accordingly, the income would become subject to income tax at a faster rate than if only the required minimum distribution needed to be distributed from the plan. Revenue Ruling 2000-2, which is discussed in more detail below, provides an alternative method for qualifying an IRA for the marital deduction that does not require all income from the plan to be distributed to the trust if the income exceeds the required minimum distribution.[10] This alternative method, however, may raise additional income tax and gift tax problems and thus has not gained widespread acceptance as a viable alternative to the annual distribution of all income from the IRA to the marital trust.

[4] Spousal Consent May Be Required

As previously discussed, the Retirement Equity Act of 1984 (REA)[11] requires spousal consent for beneficiary designations for qualified plans other than to a surviving spouse. This requirement does not apply to IRAs or to certain profit-sharing plans. The spousal consent requirement adds another layer of administrative

---

[8] Reg. § 1.408-8, Q&A 5(a).

[9] *See* Rev. Rul. 89-89, 1989-2 C.B. 231. Qualifying retirement benefits for the estate tax marital deduction is discussed in § 13.08 *infra*.

[10] Rev. Rul. 2000-2, 2000-1 C.B. 305.

[11] Pub. L. No. 98-397, 98 Stat. 1426. *See also* IRC §§ 401(a)(11), 417.

complexity to obtaining a valid beneficiary designation to a trust, as there are numerous requirements governing how and when the spousal waiver is to be obtained.[12]

[5] Effect of SECURE Act

The SECURE Act does not change the requirements for naming a trust as the beneficiary of a retirement plan. However, the plan owner needs to be mindful of the new limitations on the time period over which distributions from such plans must be made after the owner's death. A typical use of a trust is to protect assets from a spendthrift beneficiary or to otherwise limit the beneficiary's direct access to the plan assets, perhaps until the beneficiary reaches a certain age. Under the SECURE Act, the plan will have to be fully distributed over ten years for many beneficiaries.[13] That may be a shorter period than the duration of the trust.

[C] Requirements for Naming Trust as Designated Beneficiary

Provided certain requirements are met, the beneficiary of a trust may be considered the designated beneficiary for purposes of computing required minimum distributions. The requirements for "looking through" a trust for purposes of using the trust beneficiary as the designated beneficiary for computing required minimum distributions are:

1. The trust must be valid under state law,

2. All beneficiaries of the trust must be individuals,

3. All beneficiaries must be identifiable as of the date of the participant's death, and

4. The trust must be irrevocable by its terms upon the participant's death.

In addition, there is a requirement that certain documentation be provided to the administrator of the retirement plan. These requirements are discussed in greater detail below.

[1] The Trust Must Be Valid Under State Law

The trust must be valid under state law.[14] This will be the simplest of the requirements to satisfy for the experienced estate planner.

---

[12] *See* § 13.05[B][1] [b] *supra,* for a discussion of the spousal consent requirement.

[13] *See* § 13.05[D] *supra.*

[14] Reg. § 1.401(a)(9)-4, Q&A 5(b)(1).

[2] All Beneficiaries of the Trust Must Be Individuals

No corporations, estates, trusts, or charities can be beneficiaries of the trust.[15] This presents a trap for the unwary because small provisions for non-individuals can have significant negative ramifications. For example, if a trust includes a $10,000 legacy to a charity, with the remainder of the estate left to the spouse and children of the plan participant, all the beneficiaries of that trust are not individuals for purposes of the rule, and the "look-through" requirements will not be met. Similarly, trusts that leave remainder interests to charity have been held to preclude the application of the "look through" rules on the ground that remainder beneficiaries must be considered in determining whether all beneficiaries are individuals. Under the 2002 regulations, charitable legatees may be cashed out by September 30 of the year following the participant's death, thus curing this impediment to the use of the "look through" rules.[16]

The 2002 regulations, most especially Section 1.409(a)(9)-5, Q&A 7(c), left unanswered questions about which potential beneficiaries of a trust must be considered for purposes of determining if all such beneficiaries are individuals. Prior to these regulations, estate planners generally assumed—though without any express provision in the Code or regulations—that beneficiaries who could take only after a series of individuals lived to their normal life expectancies could be disregarded. For example, a trust for the benefit of the participant's issue, but with a back-up beneficiary designation that included one or more charitable organizations in default of all such issue, generally was thought to meet the requirement of all beneficiaries being individuals. Under the 2002 regulations, it was no longer clear that such charitable beneficiaries could be ignored, regardless of how remote the possibility of the charities actually receiving any benefit from the trust.[17] The 2022 Proposed Regulations, however, may finally provide some long-needed clarification. The 2022 Proposed Regulations classify beneficiaries into three different categories and provide rules for which category of beneficiaries must be included in determining whether the trust meets the "look through" requirements or not, and which category of beneficiaries can be ignored.[18]

The regulations clearly provide, however, that any such successor beneficiaries can be ignored if the trust requires that all distributions received from the retirement plan be distributed immediately to the individual beneficiaries, rather than giving the

---

[15] IRC § 401(a)(9)(E); Reg. § 1.401(a)(9)-4, Q&A 3.

[16] Reg. § 1.401(a)(9)-4, Q&A 4(a).

[17] Letter Ruling 200708084 has added clarity for situations in which a trust is designated as the beneficiary of a retirement plan, but the trust must be distributed immediately to identifiable individuals. The decedent had designated a trust as the beneficiary of her IRA. Upon the decedent's death, the trust split into two sub-trusts, one for each of the decedent's children. Each child's sub-trust was to be distributed to that child upon reaching age 45. At the time of the decedent's death, both children had already reached age 45. The IRS concluded that, so long as the trust satisfied the remaining "look though" requirements, the only beneficiaries that needed to be considered were the two children, and that minimum required distributions could be made from their respective shares of the IRA based on the life expectancy of the older child.

[18] Prop. Reg. § 1.401(a)(9)-4(f)(3)(i).

trustee any power to retain the distributions in the trust.[19] Such trusts are commonly referred to as "conduit" trusts, though this term does not appear in the Code. The 2022 proposed regulations add a definition of "conduit" trusts that conforms to the common usage of the term.[20]

[3] All Beneficiaries Must Be Identifiable from the Trust Instrument as of the Date of Participant's Death

To comply with this requirement, it is not necessary that all beneficiaries be identified by name, so long as at the applicable time (usually September 30 of the year following the participant's death) it is possible to ascertain which of the beneficiaries is the oldest, and thus has the shortest life expectancy.[21] Therefore, a description of beneficiaries by class (e.g., the "Donor's children") may be acceptable. Where there are several beneficiaries of a trust, the life expectancy of the oldest of the beneficiaries will be used in determining the required minimum distribution, and the regulations require that there be an identifiable oldest beneficiary for this requirement to be satisfied.[22]

It is not clear, however, how strictly the IRS might interpret the possibility of adding new (and older) members to a class. For example, a trust for the benefit of the participant's "issue and their spouses" clearly fails the test of all individuals being identifiable because of the possibility that, after the designation date, one of the participant's issue could marry an individual who is older than all of the participant's issue.[23] But if the trust is for the benefit of the participant's "issue living from time to time" could the IRS argue that the beneficiaries of the trust are not identifiable because of the possibility (however remote) of one issue of the participant adopting an individual who was older than the oldest issue of the participant who was living

---

[19] Reg. § 1.401(a)(9)-5, Q&A 7(c)(3), Example 2.

[20] Prop. Reg. § 1-401(a)(9)-4(f)(1)(ii)(A).

[21] Reg. § 1.401(a)(9)-4, Q&A 5(b)(3).

[22] Reg. § § 1.401(a)(9)-4, Q&A 5(c), 1.401(a)(9)-5, Q&A 7(a)(1). The changes under the 2002 regulations concerning which beneficiaries can be disregarded (as discussed in the previous section) have led to some unusual results in identifying the oldest possible beneficiary. In Letter Ruling 200228025, the decedent designated a trust as the beneficiary of her IRA. The trust beneficiaries were two children, then ages 5 and 6. The trust provided that if either child died before reaching age 30, that child's share would pass to the child's issue, or, if there were none, to the other child. If both children died without issue prior to reaching age 30, the trust beneficiary would be a named individual, who then was age 67. The IRS ruled that the required minimum distributions from the IRA must be made based on the life expectancy of the 67-year-old, notwithstanding the extremely remote statistical likelihood that the individual ever would receive any benefit under the trust.

[23] The problem of having beneficiaries who are not identifiable can sometimes be cured with the use of a disclaimer. In Ltr. Rul. 200438044, the decedent designated a trust as the recipient of his retirement benefits. The decedent's spouse was the beneficiary of the trust for her lifetime. Upon her death, the trust became payable to the decedent's issue, subject, however, to the spouse's power to appoint the trust principal to the decedent's issue and their spouses. As the trust was written, it failed the "look through" requirements because of the inclusion of the spouses of the decedent's issue as possible beneficiaries. The spouse, however, disclaimed the power of appointment, so that the only possible beneficiaries of the trust were the decedent's spouse and his issue. Accordingly, all of the possible beneficiaries then were identifiable

on the designation date? One possibility for eliminating this potential problem is to limit any class of beneficiaries to individuals who are younger than the oldest possible beneficiary as of the designation date. Another possibility is to expressly state in the trust that an adoptee can only be a beneficiary of a retirement plan if his or her adoption had been completed prior to reaching a certain age (for example, age eighteen).

In situations where there are multiple individual beneficiaries of a trust, it also may be possible to split the retirement benefits into separate shares during the participant's lifetime and designating a separate trust for each share, with each trust then benefiting a separate individual.[24] This could be beneficial in situations in which one or more beneficiaries might fall under one of the exceptions to the ten-year rule and be able to stretch out distributions over a longer period of time.

Where a trust is named as a beneficiary of a retirement plan and the trustee has discretion to allocate trust property among subtrusts within that trust (such as a pour-over trust in which a formula will divide trust property between a marital trust and a credit shelter trust, with the allocation of particular assets between subtrusts to be made by the trustee), the IRS may conclude that the beneficiaries of the plan are not identifiable.[25] For that reason, a direction within the trust as to which subtrust retirement assets should be allocated may be advisable. Alternatively, a formula for dividing retirement plan assets between a marital trust and a credit shelter trust may be included directly in the beneficiary designation to satisfy the "identifiability" requirement.

[4] The Trust Must Be Irrevocable by Its Terms upon the Participant's Death

At one time, the trust had to be irrevocable as of the required beginning date in order for the "look through" treatment to apply. The current requirement is that the trust be irrevocable by its terms upon the participant's death.[26] This change has simplified estate planning for plan owners, because previously, when the owner approached the required beginning date, a revocable trust that had been named as the beneficiary of the plan had to be made irrevocable, or, alternatively, a separate irrevocable trust established and designated as the beneficiary in order to permit the plan owner to use the life expectancy of a beneficiary of the trust in determining the required minimum distribution. Because the current requirement appears to require that the terms of the trust specify the trust's irrevocability after the death of the participant, it may be advisable to include a statement to that effect in the trust. Trustee amendment powers in trusts that give the trustees the ability to amend the trust after the death of the donor should be scrutinized to determine whether the

---

[24] Reg. §§ 1.401(a)(9)-4, Q&A 5(c), 1.401(a)(9)-5, Q&A 7. It does not appear possible to use the separate life expectancy of each beneficiary if the designated beneficiary of the retirement plan is a single trust for the benefit of the multiple beneficiaries, even if the trust splits into separate shares, one share for each beneficiary, upon the death of the participant. Ltr. Ruls. 200317041, 200317043, 200317044.

[25] *See, e.g.,* Ltr. Rul. 9501044.

[26] Reg. § 1.401(a)(9)-4, Q&A 5(b)(2).

retention of that power casts any doubt upon the irrevocability of the trust following the death of the participant. In cases in which testamentary trusts are created in wills, there has been a question whether it is the terms of the will or the applicability of state law that renders the trust irrevocable. The 2002 regulations confirm that testamentary trusts can qualify for the look through rules.[27]

[5] Delivery of Documentation Regarding the Trust to the Plan Administrator Is Required

In order to treat the beneficiaries of a trust as designated beneficiaries for purposes of calculating required minimum distributions, the trust must provide the plan administrator with the documentation required by the regulations. In the case of postdeath distributions, the trustee must furnish the plan administrator with either:

1. A final list of all beneficiaries of the trust (including contingent and remainder beneficiaries with a description of their entitlement) as of September 30 of the year following the year of the employee's death; and a certification that the list is complete with an agreement to furnish a copy of the trust instrument if requested; or,
2. A copy of the actual trust document.[28]

For predeath transfers, the documentation rules are the same as above except that there is an additional requirement that if the trust instrument is amended at any time in the future, that the participant will, within a reasonable time, provide to the plan administrator a copy of such amendment.[29] The regulations do not give a specific time for complying with this documentation requirement, though as a practical matter, it appears likely that the requirement should be met no later than the participant's required beginning date. There is only one circumstance in which it would be desirable to treat the beneficiaries of a trust as designated beneficiaries for purposes of calculating required minimum distributions during a participant's life (thereby requiring compliance with these documentation rules), and that is when the beneficiary is a spouse who is more than ten years younger than the participant. In all other cases, lifetime required minimum distributions do not depend on the existence or identity of designated beneficiaries.

While providing the list of beneficiaries and certifications to the plan administrator preserves some degree of privacy for the participant (in that other provisions of the trust not relevant to the required information need not be disclosed), the burden on the person making the certification to reflect accurately the interests of all beneficiaries and to update certifications when necessary may make the provision of the trust document itself a more attractive option. It is possible that a plan administrator may require one or the other of the methods to be complied with, and it is therefore important to check with the administrator before complying with the disclosure requirements.

---

[27] Such confirmation is not expressly stated in the regulations, but appears in examples in the regulations. *See* Reg. § 1.401(a)(9)-5, Q&A 7(c), Example 2.

[28] Reg. § 1.401(a)(9)-4, Q&A 6(b).

[29] Reg. § 1.401(a)(9)-4, Q&A 6(a).

§ 13.07 FUNDING THE CREDIT SHELTER TRUST WITH RETIREMENT BENEFITS

Estate plans for married couples typically involve the use of a credit shelter trust.[1] A credit shelter trust is a trust that is funded with a portion of the decedent's estate equal to the amount of property that can be sheltered by the unified credit.[2] A credit shelter trust is drafted in such a way that it is not subject to tax in the estate of the decedent's spouse, while still giving the surviving spouse an interest in trust assets. There may be situations in which a client has insufficient nonretirement plan assets with which to fund a credit shelter trust. In such situations, a portion of the retirement benefits may need to be directed to such a trust. Because lifetime gifts and other dispositions at death may have used a part of the unified credit, and further because the level of the unified credit has often changed from year to year, it is likely that a formula may need to be used to direct the appropriate amount of the retirement plan assets to the credit shelter trust.[3] One approach to directing plan assets to the credit shelter trust is to include that formula in the retirement benefit beneficiary designation, rather than in the client's trust document itself. This approach may be used when the client wishes the plan assets in excess of what is needed to fund the credit shelter trust to pass outright to the surviving spouse or children, rather than to be held in trust for them. If the formula is to be included in the beneficiary designation itself, the plan administrator, custodian, or trustee should be consulted about the acceptability of a formula in the beneficiary designation. The inclusion of language in the beneficiary designation that puts the burden of calculating the formula amount on the trustees of the recipient trust or upon the decedent's executor will render the formula designation much more likely to be acceptable to the administrator of the plan.

Another method for directing retirement plan assets to a credit shelter trust is through the use of a qualified disclaimer. In order to use this option, the beneficiary designation for the plan assets should name the spouse as primary beneficiary, with the credit shelter trust as secondary beneficiary. Following the death of the plan owner, the spouse could disclaim so much of the retirement benefits as were necessary to fully fund the credit shelter trust. Alternatively, the credit shelter trust could be named as the primary beneficiary, with the spouse as secondary beneficiary. In that case, the trustees would disclaim the excess of the plan benefits not sheltered from estate taxation by the unified credit to the spouse outright.

If the client is willing to give the spouse the freedom to choose whether and how much of the benefits to disclaim, the disclaimer method has several advantages over including the formula in the beneficiary designation or directing the entire plan to the

---

[1] § 13.07 Credit shelter trusts are discussed in Chapters 5 and 6.

[2] The amount used to fund a credit shelter trust may have to be reduced to take state estate taxes into consideration. A discussion of state estate taxes is beyond the scope of this chapter.

[3] Formula bequests are discussed in Chapter 6.

trust and including a formula in the trust. Where the spouse is the primary benefici-ary, no consultation with the plan administrator is necessary to obtain approval for including a formula in the beneficiary designation. In addition, where the spouse is the primary beneficiary, there is no question that the spouse's life expectancy may be used together with the participant's in calculating required minimum distributions (if the spouse is more than ten years younger than the participant). When a trust is named as the beneficiary, there are a number of requirements that must be complied with in order that the life expectancy of the trust's beneficiaries may be used in calculating the required minimum distribution.[4] Where the disclaimer route is to be used, however, the estate planner, should make sure that there is in place a power of attorney for the surviving spouse that specifically gives the attorney-in-fact the ability to disclaim retirement benefits. This precaution will permit disclaimer in the situation where the surviving spouse is not competent to effect the disclaimer on his or her own.

§13.08 RETIREMENT BENEFITS AND THE QTIP TRUST

One of the most common vehicles for providing for the spouse is through the use of a Qualified Terminable Interest Property Trust, or QTIP trust.[1] Under a QTIP trust, the surviving spouse is given an income interest for life and, upon the surviving spouse's death, the property passes to the one or more beneficiaries chosen by the donor spouse. However, when a QTIP trust is funded with retirement benefits, a number of factors needs to be taken into consideration.

[A] Spousal Consent to Trust as Beneficiary

One threshold matter to discuss with any client considering naming a trust as the beneficiary of retirement benefits is the necessity for obtaining the consent of the spouse to such a beneficiary designation. Under the Retirement Equity Act of 1984,[2] except in the case of individual retirement accounts and certain (but not all) profit sharing and stock bonus plans,[3] spousal consent is necessary where someone other than the spouse is to be named as the beneficiary of the plan or account. For some married couples, obtaining this consent will not be a problem, but in other family situations, broaching this subject may be more problematic. The required consent must be in writing, either notarized or witnessed by a plan representative, and limited to the particular alternative beneficiary designation being consented to unless by its specific terms the consent applies to future changes as well.

---

[4] *See* discussion in § 13.06 *supra.*

[1] **§ 13.08** QTIP trusts are discussed in Chapter 6. Form 1 contains a sample QTIP trust.

[2] Pub. L. No. 98-397, 98 Stat. 1426.

[3] *See generally* IRC § § 401(a)(11) and 417.

[B] Qualifying for the Marital Deduction

[1] General Requirements

Assuming that spousal consent can be obtained or is unnecessary, the estate planner's task is to insure that the designation of the marital trust as the beneficiary of the retirement plan will qualify for the marital deduction, to the extent that the marital deduction is necessary for the proper operation of the estate plan in question. Before turning to the special issues that must be addressed in qualifying a retirement benefit made payable to a marital trust for the estate tax marital deduction, it is important to understand the basic rules for obtaining the marital deduction for a QTIP trust generally, because these requirements are the backdrop against which the special issues for retirement benefits must be examined.[4]

The requirements for obtaining the estate tax marital deduction for property in a QTIP trust are as follows:[5]

1. The property in the trust must pass from the decedent;
2. The spouse beneficiary must have a qualifying income interest for life;
3. A QTIP election must be made on the decedent's federal estate tax return electing to treat the trust property as QTIP property, the effect of which is the inclusion of the QTIP property in the estate of the surviving spouse upon his or her death.

Where a client owns an interest in a retirement plan and names a marital trust as the beneficiary, the requirement of the property passing from the decedent generally will be satisfied. The latter two requirements, namely that the spouse receive a qualifying income interest for life and that the QTIP election be made on the decedent's federal estate tax return electing to treat the trust property as QTIP property, demand special consideration when a trust is named a beneficiary.

[2] Qualifying Income Interest for Life

The surviving spouse will have a qualifying income interest in property for purposes of the marital deduction if the spouse is entitled to all the income from the property, payable annually or more frequently for life, and no person has a power to appoint any part of the property to any person other than the spouse during the spouse's lifetime.[6]

Satisfying the requirement that the surviving spouse receives all the income from the trust at least annually is a relatively simple when the QTIP property is held entirely within the QTIP trust. Special challenges arise when the QTIP property consists of retirement benefits for which the trust is named as the beneficiary. The benefits will grow without being subject to income tax so long as they are not

---

[4] The marital deduction and the requirements for a QTIP trust are discussed in Chapter 6.

[5] IRC § 2056(b)(7). *See generally* IRC § 2056; Reg. § § 20.2056(a)(1)–(d)(3).

[6] IRC § 2056(b)(7)(B)(ii).

distributed from the plan. Depending upon the income needs of the surviving spouse, the optimal strategy from an investment perspective may be to allow the benefits to remain in the plan for as long as possible. Minimum distribution rules may not require that any distributions be made from the plan for many years (e.g., until the deceased plan owner would have attained age 72). In such a case, any income earned on the retirement plan benefits would remain in the plan, and would not pass to the QTIP trust and, in turn, to the spouse. Even if minimum distribution rules required that some distribution be made from the plan, depending upon the applicable life expectancies upon which the distribution was calculated and the actual income earned within the plan, it is possible that the required minimum distribution could be less than the plan's annual income.

At one time, the retention in the plan of some or all of the plan's annual income was problematic where a QTIP trust had been named as the designated beneficiary of the plan and where the marital deduction was sought, because the IRS had held that under such circumstances, the requirement that the spouse be entitled to all the income from the property had not been satisfied.[7] The IRS position had been that in order for plan benefits to qualify for QTIP treatment, the spouse must actually receive all the income earned by the plan annually. Achieving this goal required that the client's beneficiary designation and the terms of the QTIP trust be coordinated to insure that the spouse would actually receive all the annual income earned in the plan.

In Revenue Ruling 2000–02, the IRS relaxed the requirements for qualifying an IRA made payable to a QTIP trust for the marital deduction.[8] The following requirements must be met for the IRA to qualify for the marital deduction:

1. The terms of the QTIP trust must provide that:

   a. All income from the trust is payable at least annually to the spouse;
   b. No one has the power to appoint trust principal to any person other than the spouse; and
   c. The spouse has the power exercisable annually to compel the trustee to withdraw from the retirement plan an amount equal to the income earned on the assets held by the plan during the year and to distribute that amount through the trust to the spouse.

2. The retirement plan document must not contain any prohibition on the withdrawals that the spouse is given the right to compel under the terms of the QTIP trust.

Revenue Ruling 2006-26 offered additional guidance concerning the definition of the "income" of the retirement plan as to which the spouse must have the right to compel withdrawal.[9] However, the existence of the right to compel withdrawal may raise unanswered issues of constructive receipt for income tax purposes. In addition, the failure of the spouse to exercise the right to compel withdrawal may be deemed a

---

[7] Rev. Rul. 89-89, 1989-2 C.B. 231.
[8] Rev. Rul. 2000-2, 2000-1 C.B. 305.
[9] Rev. Rul. 2006-26, 2006-1 C.B. 939.

gift to the remainder beneficiaries to the trust, and thus have gift tax consequences for the spouse. Therefore, the estate planner should proceed with caution in attempting to qualify retirement plan benefits payable to a QTIP trust for the marital deduction.

[C] Electing QTIP Treatment for Qualified Retirement Plan Benefits

There are special requirements for electing QTIP treatment for qualified retirement benefits.[10] While an executor ordinarily would elect QTIP treatment with respect to all or a portion of a trust, rather than for specific assets held within the trust, in the case where QTIP treatment is sought for a retirement plan of which the QTIP trust is designated as beneficiary, the QTIP election must be made for both the QTIP trust and for the retirement plan asset itself.[11]

§ 13.09 NON–U.S. CITIZEN SPOUSES AND THE MARITAL DEDUCTION FOR RETIREMENT PLAN BENEFITS

Where the surviving spouse is a non–U.S. citizen, marital deduction rules differ substantially from those applicable to citizen spouses.[1] Outright transfers to a noncitizen spouse at death are not entitled to the estate tax marital deduction.[2] In order to obtain the marital deduction for a non–U.S. citizen spouse, the property must be transferred to a Qualified Domestic Trust (QDOT) either by terms of the decedent's estate plan or by the surviving spouse after the decedent's death.[3] Where a participant has not named a QDOT as the beneficiary of a retirement plan for a non–U.S. citizen spouse, the process of obtaining the marital deduction is somewhat more complicated than with respect to other assets due to the anti-alienation provisions applicable to qualified plan assets, which may prohibit a surviving spouse from transferring a qualified plan benefit to a QDOT. In this situation, alternative avenues have been established to permit the plan benefits to qualify for the marital deduction.[4] The marital deduction is available if the surviving spouse either agrees to roll over the corpus portion of distributions from the plan to a QDOT as they are received or agrees to pay the estate tax on the corpus portion of distributions as they are received.[5]

---

[10] These requirements are spelled out in Rev. Rul. 89-89, 1989-2 C.B. 231.

[11] *Id.*

[1] **§ 13.09** *See generally* IRC § § 2056(d) and 2056A. Estate tax planning for non-citizen spouses is discussed in Chapter 6.

[2] IRC § 2056(d)(1).

[3] IRC § 2056(d)(2). Alternatively, the marital deduction will be available if the surviving spouse becomes a U.S. citizen before the date on which the deceased spouse's estate tax return is due and the surviving spouse has been a U.S. resident from the date of the deceased spouse's death until the date the estate tax return is due.

[4] The marital deduction available in the case of a non-U.S. citizen spouse differs markedly from the ordinary marital deduction, with any principal distributions to the surviving spouse during the spouse's lifetime generally being subject to estate taxes, paid at the marginal estate tax rate of the deceased spouse. *See* IRC § 2056A.

[5] Reg. § 20.2056A-4(b)(7).

§13.10 CHARITABLE GIVING AND RETIREMENT BENEFITS

For clients who have charitable inclinations, the use of retirement benefits for charitable giving can be advantageous, but great care must be taken to prevent unintended consequences.[1]

The 2002 regulations permit a client to name a charity as the beneficiary of retirement benefits without adversely affecting the client's lifetime tax deferral opportunities with respect to the benefits.[2] In addition, the provision in the regulations that delays the time for fixing the identity of designated beneficiaries until September 30 of the year following the year of death is useful when a participant wishes to leave retirement benefits to a charity.[3] If a charity is one of multiple designated beneficiaries at the death of the participant, the participant will be deemed to have no designated beneficiary, and individual beneficiaries will not be permitted to use their own life expectancies in determining required minimum distributions. This result can be altered by cashing out the charity before the designated beneficiaries are finally determined on September 30 of the year following the year of death. Once the charity has been cashed out, it is no longer a beneficiary, and the remaining beneficiaries will be permitted to use the life expectancy of the oldest individual in withdrawing their shares of the retirement benefits (or if the beneficiaries are able to satisfy the "separate share" rule, each individual will be able to use his or her own life expectancy in withdrawing the benefits).

---

[1] **§13.10** Perhaps being mindful of the potential difficulties, the IRS has demonstrated considerable flexibility with respect to using retirement benefits to satisfy charitable bequests, both under a trust and under a will.

Ltr. Rul. 200218039 allowed the judicial reform of a trust that was the beneficiary of an IRA of a decedent who died before the 2002 regulations were issued. As originally written, the trust was for the benefit of the surviving spouse for the spouse's lifetime. Upon the spouse's death, 10 percent of the trust property passed to charity and the remaining 90 percent passed to the decedent's children and grandchildren. Absent reformation, the entire trust would not have had a designated beneficiary because of the charitable beneficiary. As reformed, the trust was separated into two trusts, each of which benefited the spouse for life. Upon the spouse's death, the one trust (representing the 10 percent share) passed to charity, while the other trust (representing the 90 percent share) passed to the children and grandchildren. As a result, only the trust with the 10 percent share did not have a designated beneficiary.

In Ltr. Rul. 200234019, the IRS allowed an executor to assign the estate's interest in several retirement plans to various charities to satisfy bequests in the decedent's will to those charities. The will left a certain percentage of the estate (after debts and expenses) to named charities and the remaining percentage to named individuals. Because the decedent's estate was the beneficiary of all the retirement plans, allowing the assignment of those plans directly to the charities—rather than distributing the retirement plans to the estate and then making the distributions from the estate to the charities—resulted in a significant income tax savings to the estate. Among the factors the IRS took into consideration was the fact that the decedent's will gave the executor power to make distributions in kind and to make income tax elections with respect to such distributions.

These rulings underscore the particular need for careful drafting of estate planning documents where charities are intended to be the beneficiaries of retirement benefits.

[2] Reg. §§ 1.401(a)(9)-5 (for defined contribution plans), 1.408-8 (for IRAs).

[3] Reg. § 1.401(a)(9)-4, Q&A 4(a).

As previously mentioned, naming a charity as a beneficiary of a plan could adversely affect income tax deferral after the participant's death because a charity is not a "designated beneficiary" for minimum distribution purposes. Therefore, if a client wishes to name a charity as a beneficiary of a portion of an IRA, an alternative may be to divide the IRA into two separate IRAs, with the charity named as the beneficiary of only one of them. Under this alternative, the client's total required minimum distributions from the IRAs will be the same as if the separate IRAs had not been created. Also, although the required minimum distributions with respect to each IRA must be calculated separately, the actual distributions can be taken disproportionately from the separate IRAs, or even entirely from one IRA.[4] Thus, the client could keep the level of the assets passing to the charity in line with his or her intentions, by taking disproportionately large or small distributions from the IRA intended for the charity.

Putting aside the complications related to required minimum distributions, if a client wishes to leave money to charity, using retirement benefits for that purpose is advantageous because if noncharitable beneficiaries receive the retirement benefits, withdrawals will be subject to income tax, thus decreasing the after-tax funds they will have at their disposal. If non-IRA assets are directed to individuals, with the retirement benefits directed to fulfill charitable intentions, then the individuals will be left with greater after-tax funds, while the charity will not be subject to income taxes on withdrawals.

Under the Pension Protection Act of 2006,[5] it became possible to make direct contributions—known as Qualified Charitable Distributions—from an IRA to one or more charitable organizations. This provision applied only to individuals who had reached age 70½ at the time of making any such contributions, and the total amount of the contributions was limited to $100,000 per year. The contributions were not included in the individual's gross income, but the individual also was not allowed to take an income tax deduction for the contributions. The contributions counted toward the individual's required minimum distribution for the year, and could be made to almost all types of charitable organizations except donor advised funds, supporting organizations and some private foundations. Contributions also could not be in the form of split-interest gifts, such as a charitable remainder trust. In addition, contributions could only be made from IRAs (including inherited IRAs); contributions could not be made from qualified plans.[6] Despite these limits, there were some significant advantages to making Qualified Charitable Distributions from an IRA, especially for individuals who did not need the income from any required minimum distributions.

---

[4] Reg. § 1.401(a)(9)-1, Q&A D-2A(a).

[5] Pub. L. No. 109-280. The Pension Protection Act of 2006 (August 17, 2006).

[6] *Id.*

The Pension Protection Act of 2006 allowed Qualified Charitable Distributions only for 2006 and 2007.[7] Subsequent legislation extended this provision on a piecemeal basis. Under the Emergency Economic Stabilization Act of 2008, Qualified Charitable Distributions were allowed for 2008.[8] After lapsing for a year, Qualified Charitable Distributions were reinstated for 2010 and 2011 under the Tax Relief, Unemployment Insurance Reauthorization, and Job Creation Act of 2010.[9] The American Taxpayer Recovery Act of 2012 created retroactive rules for making Qualified Charitable Distributions effective for the 2012 tax year and extended the provisions for 2013, but not beyond.[10] A further extension for 2014 was enacted in December 2014.[11]

The Protecting Americans from Tax Hikes Act of 2015[12] finally made the provisions for making Qualified Charitable Distributions permanent.[13]

The SECURE Act did not change the minimum age for making Qualified Charitable Distributions, but eliminated the age restriction for making contributions to an Individual Retirement Account—which formerly had been age $70^1/_2$.[14] Beginning in 2020, the maximum amount of an individual's Qualified Charitable Distributions for any year is reduced by the amount of *deductible* contributions made to an Individual Retirement Account in that year.[15]

§13.11 CREDITOR PROTECTION ISSUES FOR IRAs

Because IRAs generally are not governed under ERISA, creditor protection under federal law that is available for qualified plans was not historically available to IRA owners. Instead, IRA owners had to look to state law to determine whether and to what extent an IRA was protected from creditors. The Bankruptcy Abuse Prevention and Consumer Protection Act of 2005, enacted on April 20, 2005, eliminated much of the difference in creditor protections between qualified plans and traditional or Roth IRAs that were funded *with the creditor's own funds*.[1]

---

[7] *Id.*

[8] Pub. L. No. 110-343, Emergency Economic Stabilization Act of 2008 (October 3, 2008).

[9] Pub. L. No. 111-312, Tax Relief, Unemployment Insurance Reauthorization, and Job Creation Act of 2010 (December 17, 2010).

[10] Pub. L. No. 112-240, American Taxpayer Recovery Act of 2012 (January 2, 2013).

[11] Pub. L. No. 113-295, Tax Increase Prevention Act of 2014 (December 19, 2014).

[12] Pub. L. No. 114-113.

[13] IRC § 408(d)(8).

[14] *See* § 13.04[B] *supra*.

[15] IRC § 408(d)(8)(A).

[1] §13.11 In Rousey v. Jacoway, 544 U.S. 320 (2005), released just 16 days before the Bankruptcy Abuse Prevention and Consumer Protection Act of 2005 was enacted, the United States Supreme Court also eroded much of the distinction between creditor protections for qualified plans and for IRAs, though only to the extent that the IRA holder could demonstrate that the IRA was necessary for the support of the holder and the holder's dependents. Although *Rousey* remains good law, its applicability is likely to be limited given the broader scope of the Bankruptcy Abuse Prevention and Consumer Protection Act of 2005.

It has long been less certain, whether an IRA that an individual *inherited* from a deceased IRA owner was subject to the same protection in bankruptcy cases. In recent years, bankruptcy courts, in a number of jurisdictions, have held that inherited IRAs are exempt from the claims of bankruptcy creditors,[2] and this result has been codified in at least one state.[3]

However, in *In re Clark*,[4] the United States Bankruptcy Court for the Eastern District of Wisconsin came to the opposite conclusion, holding that an inherited IRA was not exempt from claims of bankruptcy creditors because the funds in the IRA "were no longer segregated to meet the needs of, nor distributed on the occasion of, any person's retirement" and thus no longer could be considered "retirement funds" within the meaning of Section 522(b)(3) of the Bankruptcy Code.[5] After reversal at the federal district court,[6] the United States Court of Appeals for the Seventh Circuit reversed again and the case came before the United States Supreme Court. Writing for a unanimous court, Justice Sotomayor affirmed the underlying rationale of the bankruptcy court that inherited IRAs are not "retirement funds" within the definition of Section 522(b)(3) of the Bankruptcy Code because the holder of the inherited IRA is not permitted to invest additional funds in the inherited IRA, the holder is required to withdraw funds from the account each year no matter how many years away from retirement the holder may be and the holder may withdraw the entire balance of the inherited IRA without any penalty, again regardless of whether the holder of the inherited IRA had reached retirement age or not.[7]

The *Clark* ruling leaves unanswered questions. It seems clear that if a surviving spouse treats an IRA from the deceased spouse as an inherited IRA (for example, if the spouse had not yet reached age 59$\frac{1}{2}$ and expected to need access to the deceased spouse's retirement benefits on an ongoing basis), the assets in the inherited IRA would not be protected from the surviving spouse's creditors. By contrast, if a surviving spouse chooses instead to roll over the IRA into his or her own IRA, it

---

[2] A leading case in this regard appeared to be *In re* Nessa, 105 A.F.T.R.2d 2010-609 (January 11, 2010), in which the United States Bankruptcy Court for the District of Minnesota held that assets in an inherited IRA were exempt from the claims of bankruptcy creditors under the plain meaning of the Bankruptcy Code. The United States Bankruptcy Appellate Panel for the Eighth Circuit affirmed the lower court ruling in *In re* Nessa, 426 B.R. 312 (BAP 8th Cir. 2010). Bankruptcy courts in Florida and Arizona have reached the same result after citing *Nessa*. *See In re* Mathusa, No. 6:10-bk-13336-KSJ (March 28, 2011); *In re* Thiem, 107 A.F.T.R.2d 529 (Bankr. Ct. AZ 2011). In *In re* Chilton, 105 A.F.T.R.2d 2010-1271 (Bankr. Ct. E.D. Tex. March 5, 2010), the United States Bankruptcy Court for the Eastern District of Texas came to the opposite conclusion. The Appeals Court in *Nessa* cited *Chilton*, saying (albeit in a footnote) that the Chilton court's conclusion was erroneous, and the United States District Court for the Eastern District of Texas agreed, reversing *Chilton* on appeal, largely following the reasoning of *Nessa*. Chilton v. Moser, 107 A.F.T.R.2d 1391 (E.D. Tex. March 16, 2011).

[3] On May 31, 2011, the governor of Florida signed House Bill 469 into law, amending Section 222.21(2) of the Florida Statutes so as to exempt inherited IRAs from creditor's claims. The statute applies retroactively and thus overturns an earlier contrary ruling from the state's Second District Court of Appeals in Robertson v. Deeb, 16 So. 3d 936 (Fla. 2009).

[4] *In re* Clark, 2011 WL 1814209 (Bankr. E.D. Wis. May 10, 2011).

[5] *Id.*

[6] *In re* Clark, Case No. 11-CV-482 (USDC W.D. Wis. March 14, 2012).

[7] Clark v. Rameker, 573 U.S. 122, 134 S. Ct. 2242, 189 L. Ed. 2d 157 (2014).

seems that the funds from the rollover are protected from the surviving spouse's creditors. But what if the surviving spouse had been insolvent or subject to actions from his or her own creditors at the time of the rollover? Could the rollover be construed as a fraudulent transfer because the surviving spouse had the option to treat the IRA as an inherited IRA? Will the Supreme Court's logic for determining that an inherited IRA can no longer be considered to be retirement funds be applied elsewhere? For example, could the rules for stretching out distributions over the lifetime of the beneficiary of an inherited IRA be eliminated? Further guidance will be required.

The *Clark* ruling, however, has not been the final word on this subject. In *In re Pacheco*,[8] the United States Bankruptcy Court for the District of Arizona concluded that (1) Arizona has permissibly opted out of the exemption provisions of the Federal Bankruptcy Code on which the *Clark* case was decided; (2) *Clark* does not require debtors in opt-out states to use the federal exemption provisions, nor does it preempt state law in such states; and (3) under the broader Arizona statute, inherited IRAs are exempt from the claims of bankruptcy creditors. The United States Bankruptcy Court for the District of New Jersey reached the same conclusion in *In re Andolino*[9] and *In re Norris*.[10] Because a substantial number of states have opted out of the federal exemption provisions (or allow debtors to choose between the federal or the state provisions), *Pacheco* and the New Jersey cases raise the prospect that the uncertainty surrounding creditor protection issues has returned.[11]

By contrast, in *Lerbakken v. Sieloff & Associates, P.A.*,[12] the debtor had permissibly relied upon *federal* law to support his claim that retirement funds that he had received from his wife as part of a divorce settlement were exempt from the claims of his creditors. The United States Bankruptcy Appellate Panel for the Eighth Circuit disagreed, concluding that under federal law, the accounts were not retirement funds as defined in *Clark*, but were "nothing more than a property settlement" and thus were not exempt from creditors' claims.[13]

---

[8] 537 B.R. 935 (Bankr. D. Ariz. 2015).

[9] 525 B.R. 588 (Bankr. D.N.J. 2015).

[10] 550 B.R. 271(Bankr. D.N.J. 2016). The court in *Norris*, though finding that the Supreme Court ruling in *Clark* did not apply because of New Jersey statutes, reached its conclusion with some reluctance, stating that "it is difficult to envision a reasonable policy explanation for such a result." *Id.* at 278.

[11] For another example, in *In re Kara*, the United States Bankruptcy Court for the Western District of Texas followed the reasoning in *Pacheco* to conclude that *Clark* was not applicable under Texas law and that an inherited IRA was exempt from creditors under the broader Texas exemption statute. *In re Kara*, 573 B.R. 696 (Bankr. W.D. Tex. 2017). *See also In re* Arehart (Case No. 17-01678-TLM, Bankr. D. Idaho Jan. 10, 2019) for a similar result. For another approach, Florida (which has opted out of the exemption provisions of the Federal Bankruptcy Code) amended the statute governing the state exemptions to expressly include inherited IRAs. Fla. Stat. § 222.21(2)(a).

[12] 590 B.R. 895 (B.A.P. 8th Cir. 2018), *aff'd*, 949 F.3d 432 (8th Cir. 2020).

[13] *Id.*

§13.12 SPECIAL INCOME TAX ISSUES RELATING TO RETIREMENT PLAN ASSETS

While a comprehensive treatment of income tax issues relating to retirement plan assets is beyond the scope of this chapter, the estate planner should be aware that in certain situations, special income tax benefits may be available with respect to distributions from retirement plans.

[A] Lump Sum Distributions

For clients taking lump sum distributions[1] from retirement plans, income averaging, capital gains treatment of a portion of the distribution, or special income tax treatment for net unrealized appreciation on distribution of employer stock may be available.[2] By gathering full information on the history and holdings in a client's retirement plan benefits, the estate planner can alert the client to the possible applicability of favorable income tax treatment and work with the client's accountant or other advisors on these issues.

[B] Income Tax Deduction for Estate Taxes Paid

The draconian effect of the payment of both estate taxes and income taxes with respect to a decedent's retirement plan benefits is somewhat alleviated by the availability of an income tax deduction available to those receiving retirement plan assets for the federal estate taxes paid with respect to those assets.[3] If more than one person receives retirement plan assets as a result of the decedent's death, the beneficiaries share the benefit of the deduction, and the deduction is amortized over the course of receipt of distributions where they are not received in a lump sum.

EXAMPLE 13-5

Charles died in 2016 with a taxable estate of $6,450,000, which required the estate to pay federal estate taxes of $400,000.[4] The estate included an IRA worth $1,000,000. Charles's daughter, Gail, is the designated beneficiary of the IRA. When Gail takes distributions from Charles's IRA, she will be entitled to an income tax deduction in the amount of the estate taxes in Charles's estate attributable to the inclusion of the IRA in the estate. For these purposes, the amount of the estate tax that is attributed to the IRA is

---

[1] **§13.12** *See* IRC § 402(d)(4) for the definition of a lump sum distribution.

[2] *See* IRC § 402(e)(4).

[3] IRC § 691(c).

[4] State estate taxes are ignored for purpose of this example. The federal estate tax exemption amount in 2016 was $5,450,000.

taken in the manner most favorable to the beneficiary, which means that the entire $400,000 of estate taxes paid is attributed to the IRA and can be used by Gail as an income tax deduction against her distributions from the IRA.

[C] Avoidance of Acceleration of IRD

The satisfaction of a pecuniary marital bequest with retirement plan benefits will accelerate the income tax due with respect to the plan benefits. This result can be avoided by choosing a fractional formula, rather than a pecuniary formula, for the funding of marital and credit shelter trusts, or, alternatively, specifically by directing the disposition of the retirement plan benefits within the trust so they will not be available to satisfy a pecuniary bequest.

[D] Disqualification of Subchapter S Election

It has long been settled that traditional IRAs are not eligible shareholders of an S corporation.[5] In 2009, the Tax Court held that a Roth IRA is also not an eligible shareholder of an S corporation.[6] It is important to keep these rules in mind because a corporation's election to be treated as an S corporation will be terminated automatically if the stock is held by an ineligible shareholder.[7]

---

[5] Rev. Rul. 92-73, 1992-2 C.B. 224.

[6] Taproot Administrative Services, Inc. v. Comm'r, 133 T.C. 9 (2009).

[7] Subchapter S corporations are discussed in Chapters 11 and 14.

APPENDIX A UNIFORM LIFE TABLE

Uniform Life Table (Effective January 1, 2022)

Age	Divisor	Age	Divisor	Age	Divisor
70	29.1	87	14.4	104	4.9
71	28.2	88	13.7	105	4.6
72	27.4	89	12.9	106	4.3
73	26.5	90	12.2	107	4.1
74	25.5	91	11.5	108	3.9
75	24.6	92	10.8	109	3.7
76	23.7	93	10.1	110	3.5
77	22.9	94	9.5	111	3.4
78	22.0	95	8.9	112	3.3
79	21.1	96	8.4	113	3.1
80	20.2	97	7.8	114	3.0
81	19.4	98	7.3	115	2.9
82	18.5	99	6.8	116	2.8
83	17.7	100	6.4	117	2.7
84	16.8	101	6.0	118	2.5
85	16.0	102	5.6	119	2.3
86	15.2	103	5.2	120	2.0
				Thereafter	2.0

14

Post-Mortem Estate Planning

§14.01 INTRODUCTION[1]

Although most estate planning occurs prior to a person's death, the personal representative and the beneficiaries of a decedent's estate often have certain opportunities to minimize estate and income taxes and to reform defects in the decedent's estate plan after the decedent has died.[2] These planning opportunities are commonly referred to as "post-mortem estate planning." Post-mortem estate planning occurs by (1) making elections on the tax returns filed for the decedent or the decedent's estate, (2) executing disclaimers, and (3) regulating the distribution of income and assets to the beneficiaries.

This chapter will discuss the tax returns that a personal representative must file after a person's death and the various elections available to a personal representative or beneficiary. Each election is discussed in the context of each required return. However, in certain instances the personal representative is given a choice of returns on which to claim a deduction. The following chart provides a summary of the various elections that may be reported on the different tax returns:

---

[1] §14.01 In United States v. Windsor, 570 U.S. 744, 133 S. Ct. 2675 (2013), the United States Supreme Court ruled that same-sex married couples would be recognized for federal purposes. In Rev. Rul. 2013-17, 2013-38 I.R.B. 1, the IRS ruled that, for federal tax purposes, the terms "husband and wife," "husband," and "wife" include an individual married to a person of the same sex if they were lawfully married in a state whose laws authorize the marriage of two individuals of the same sex, and the term "marriage" includes such marriages of individuals of the same sex. For purposes of this chapter, any direct or indirect references to the terms "husband," and "wife" shall be interpreted accordingly.

For ease of illustration, examples regarding income taxation ignore personal exemptions, deductions, and the alternative minimum tax. Examples regarding estate taxation ignore deductions other than the marital deduction.

[2] Unless otherwise noted, the use of the term "personal representative" shall include an executor, administrator, trustee, person in possession of the decedent's property, or any other person in charge of the administration of the decedent's estate under the relevant probate laws.

Post-mortem Elections on Tax Returns

	Decedent's Final Income Tax Return (Form 1040)	Estate Income Tax Return (Form 1041)	Estate Tax Return (Form 706)
Option to File Joint Return with Surviving Spouse	X		
Deduction for Decedent's Medical Expenses	X		X
Recognition of Savings Bond Interest	X	X	
Deduction of Income Tax Liability on Estate Tax Return			X
Calendar Year Versus Fiscal Year for Estate		X	
Option to Combine Revocable Trust and Estate		X	
Distributions from the Estate		X	
Deduction for Estate Administration Expenses		X	X
Alternate Valuation Date			X
Special Use Valuation			X
QTIP Election			X
GST Election			X
Reverse QTIP Election			X
Election to Defer Payment of Estate Tax			X
Redemption of Stock to Pay Estate Tax			X
Election to Transfer Deceased Spousal Unused Exclusion Amount to Surviving Spouse			X
Conservation Easements			X
Disclaimers			X
Income in Respect of a Decedent		X	X
Retirement Benefits			X
Partnership Interests	X	X	X
S Corporation Stock	X	X	X

§ 14.02 TAX RETURN REQUIREMENTS

The personal representative of a decedent's estate must file certain tax returns for a decedent if the value of a decedent's assets, the income generated by these assets, or the income earned by the decedent in the year of his death exceeds specified minimum levels.

[A] Final Individual Income Tax Return

The personal representative of a decedent's estate must file a final income tax return for the period from January 1 of the year of death through (and including) the date of the decedent's death.[1] In 2022, the personal representative of a decedent's estate does not need to file this return if the decedent's gross income for the period is less than $12,950 for an individual and $25,900 for a married couple filing jointly.[2] A tax return will need to be filed if the gross income exceeds this amount even if, due to deductions, no tax is actually due.

The appropriate federal tax form on which to file the final individual income tax return is generally either Internal Revenue Service Form 1040, Form 1040A, or Form 1040EZ, depending on the amount and types of income generated during the year.[3] The due date for the final individual tax return is April 15 of the year following the year of the decedent's death, which is the same day that the return would have been due if the decedent had not died.[4] If a spouse survives the decedent, the decedent's personal representative may elect to file a separate return for this period, or may file a joint return with the surviving spouse.[5]

[B] Estate Income Tax Return

Upon the death of the decedent, a new taxable entity comes into existence—the decedent's "estate." The decedent's estate for income tax purposes consists of all property owned by the decedent in the decedent's name alone at the time of his or her death that passes to beneficiaries under the decedent's will or under a state intestacy statute.[6] The personal representative of an estate must file a federal income

---

[1] **§ 14.02** *See* Reg. § 1.443-1(a)(2).

[2] IRC § § 6012(f), 6012(b)(1), 63(c), 151(d); Rev. Proc. 2021-45, 2021-48 I.R.B. 764, 769. The personal exemption was eliminated by the Tax Cuts and Jobs Act (An Act to Provide for Reconciliation Pursuant to Titles II and V of the Concurrent Resolution on the Budget for Fiscal Year 2018) ("TCJA"). Pub. L. No. 115-97, 131 Stat. 2504. Instead, for the years 2018 through 2025, the filing threshold is equal to the standard deduction.

[3] All references to a specific form are references to Internal Revenue Service forms.

[4] *See* Reg. § 1.6072-1(b). If the decedent had been filing his income tax returns on a fiscal-year rather than calendar-year basis, then the return is due on the 15th day of the fourth month following the 12-month fiscal year that would have been the decedent's tax year had he or she not died.

[5] *See* § 14.03[A], *infra*.

[6] Income from the decedent's assets that are in joint name with another person, such as a house owned as joint tenants with right of survivorship with a spouse, or assets that pass directly to a

tax return for the estate for each year that the estate has more than $600 of income.[7] The personal representative files a federal estate income tax return on Form 1041. The tax return is due on the 15th day of the fourth month after the close of the estate's tax year.[8] The personal representative may choose a calendar year or a fiscal year for the estate.[9] The personal representative may also have the option of filing a combined income tax return for the estate and a revocable trust established by the decedent.[10]

[C] Estate Tax Return

[1] Estate Tax Return

The personal representative of a decedent's estate must file a federal estate tax return listing all of the decedent's assets and liabilities as of the date of the decedent's death if the decedent's gross estate plus taxable gifts during life exceed the basic exclusion amount for the year of death.[11] In 2022, the basic exclusion amount is $12,060,000 ($10,000,000 indexed for inflation, for estates of decedents dying between 2018 and 2025).[12]

The personal representative must file an estate tax return on Form 706 within nine months of the decedent's death, or request an extension of time from the Internal Revenue Service to file this return using Form 4768.[13] An extension of time to file will not operate as an extension of time to pay, and vice versa.[14]

[2] Form 8971 and Schedule A

The personal representative of an estate that is required to file a federal estate tax return must also file Form 8971 and the associated Schedules A to report the estate

---

(Footnote Continued)

named beneficiary under a contract, such as life insurance, is taxed to the beneficiaries rather than the decedent's estate.

[7] IRC § 6012(a)(3); Reg. § 1.6012-3(a); IRC § 641(b).

[8] IRC § 6072.

[9] *See* § 14.04[A], *infra.*

[10] *See* § 14.04[B], *infra.*

[11] IRC § 6018(a).

[12] IRC § 2010(c)(3)(A); Rev. Proc. 2021-45, 2021-48 I.R.B. 764, 771. Additional options existed for decedents who died in 2010. The Tax Relief, Unemployment Insurance Reauthorization, and Job Creation Act of 2010, enacted on December 17, 2010 (the "2010 Act"), permitted the personal representative of the estate of a decedent who died in 2010 to elect to opt out of the estate tax and have the modified carryover basis rules under Section 1022 apply to the estate. The estates of 2010 decedents that opted out of the estate tax were not required to file an estate tax return; rather they were required to file a Form 8939 to report certain transfers at death and to allocate allowable increases to basis for assets passing to a surviving spouse and others. IRC § 6018, as in effect before the 2010 Act.

[13] IRC § § 6075(a), 6081; Reg. § 20.6081-1. An automatic six-month extension will be granted if the correct procedure is followed.

[14] *See* Reg. § § 20.6081-1(c) and 20.6161-1(c).

tax value of certain property to the Internal Revenue Service.[15] In addition, the personal representative must furnish each beneficiary who has acquired or will acquire property from the decedent's estate with the Schedule A from Form 8971 specific to such beneficiary to identify the property the beneficiary will receive and to report the value of that property.[16] The personal representative must file Form 8971 and the corresponding Schedules A with the Internal Revenue Service and the beneficiaries on or before the earlier of the date that is 30 days after the due date of the estate tax return (including extensions) or the date that is 30 days after the date on which that return is filed with the Internal Revenue Service.[17]

Proposed Treasury regulations provide an illustrative list that identifies who qualifies as a beneficiary.[18] Where a trust, another estate, or a business entity is a beneficiary, the personal representative must furnish Schedule A to the trustee of the trust, the personal representative of the estate, or the business entity itself, rather than to the beneficiaries of the trust or estate or the owners of the business entity.[19]

[D] Final Gift Tax Return

If the decedent made any taxable gifts in the calendar year of his or her death and died before filing a gift tax return, the personal representative must file a final gift tax return for the decedent on Form 709.[20] Form 709 for a decedent is due on April 15 of the year following the decedent's death (unless an extension is approved), provided, however, that such gift tax return may not be filed later than the due date, including extensions, for filing the decedent's estate tax return.[21]

[E] State Tax Returns

The states in which a decedent resided, earned income, or owned real estate may impose their own requirements for income and estate tax returns.

---

[15] Prop. Reg. § 1.6035-1(a)(1); Instructions for Form 8971 and Schedule A (September 2016), p. 1. The personal representative of an estate that is not required to file an estate tax return because the decedent's gross estate plus adjusted taxable gifts is below the filing threshold is not required to file a Form 8971, even if the personal representative files an estate tax return to make a portability election as discussed in § 14.05[E], *infra*, an election for GST purposes as discussed in § 14.05[C], *infra*, or an allocation of GST exemption as discussed in § 14.05[C], *infra*. Prop. Reg. § 1.6035-1(a)(2).

[16] Prop. Reg. § § 1.6035-1(a)(1), (c)(1); Instructions for Form 8971 and Schedule A (September 2016), p. 4.

[17] Prop. Reg. § 1.6035-1(d)(1). A personal representative must file a supplemental Form 8971 and Schedules A with the Internal Revenue Service and furnish supplemental Schedules A to the beneficiaries whenever there is any change to information required to be reported that causes the information as reported to be incorrect or incomplete. Prop. Reg. § § 1.6035-1(e)(1), (e)(2).

[18] Prop. Reg. § 1.6035-1(c)(1).

[19] Prop. Reg. § 1.6035-1(c)(2).

[20] IRC § 6019; Reg. § 25.6019-1.

[21] IRC § 6075(b)(3); Reg. § 25.6075-1(b)(2).

§ 14.03 DECEDENT'S FINAL INDIVIDUAL INCOME TAX RETURN ELECTIONS

The personal representative of a decedent's estate must file a final federal income tax return for the decedent unless the decedent's income for the period is less than the specified exemption amount.[1] The final return includes the decedent's gross income and deductions from the first day of the decedent's final tax year through the date of the decedent's death.[2] Issues to consider when completing the decedent's final income tax return include:

1. Whether to file a joint income tax return with the surviving spouse or a separate income tax return reporting only the decedent's income;
2. Whether to deduct medical expenses incurred by the decedent prior to death on the final individual income tax return or on the estate tax return; and
3. Whether to recognize or defer income from certain types of savings bond interest.

[A] Option to File Joint Income Tax Return with Surviving Spouse

If a decedent is survived by a spouse, the personal representative has the option of either (1) filing a separate return for the decedent's final income tax period, or (2) filing a joint return with the surviving spouse.[3] If the personal representative elects to file a separate return, the tax return will include only the decedent's income and deductions through the date of death.[4] If the personal representative elects to file a joint return with the surviving spouse, the tax return will include the decedent's income and deductions through the date of death and the surviving spouse's income and deductions for the entire tax year.[5]

EXAMPLE 14-1

Husband H died on May 8, 2022. H's wife W survives H. The personal representative may elect to file either separate or joint returns for H for 2022. A joint return in 2022 would include H's income and deductions from January 1, 2022, through (and including) May 8, 2022, as well as W's income and deductions from January 1, 2022 through December 31, 2022.

---

[1] **§ 14.03** IRC § 6075(b)(3); Reg. § 25.6075-1(b)(2).

[2] Reg. § 1.443-1(a)(2).

[3] Reg. § 1.6013-(1)(d)(2).

[4] Reg. § 1.443-1(a)(2).

[5] Reg. § 1.6013-1(d)(1). The personal representative and the surviving spouse may not file a joint return if the surviving spouse remarries during the tax year, or if the decedent and the surviving spouse do not have the same tax year, or if either the decedent or the surviving spouse were nonresident aliens at any time during the year. IRC § 6013(a).

The personal representative, along with the surviving spouse, must sign a joint tax return for the decedent and his or her spouse if the court has officially appointed a personal representative prior to the due date of the tax return.[6] If the court has not yet appointed a personal representative, the surviving spouse may file the joint return. However, the personal representative will have the option to disaffirm this joint return by filing a separate return within one year of the initial filing deadline for the joint return.[7]

The decision whether to file a separate tax return or a joint tax return will turn primarily on which alternative results in the least tax. A joint return will often produce a more favorable result because the joint return effectively allows income and deductions to be split equally between the spouses, and thus the tax due on a joint return is generally less than the combined tax imposed on married individuals filing separately.[8] In addition, some deductions (such as charitable deductions and capital losses) must be used on the decedent's final income tax return or else they are lost.[9] The filing of a joint return can increase the likelihood of having enough income to use those deductions.

There are situations, however, when it is more advantageous to file a separate tax return. First, filing a separate tax return may decrease the total amount of tax due. For example, certain expenses, such as medical expenses, must exceed a percentage of the taxpayer's adjusted gross income before qualifying as a deduction.[10] The decedent might reach this floor individually and thus have the opportunity to use the deductions on a separate return, but might not reach the required percentage on a joint return if the surviving spouse had significant income during the year. Second, if the personal representative has any concerns about the surviving spouse's finances, or if the surviving spouse is reluctant to cooperate in filing the return, the personal representative may elect to file a separate return because filing a joint return makes the personal representative jointly and severally liable for the tax due on the joint return.[11] Third, if a personal representative hopes to close an estate quickly, the personal representative may file a separate return for the decedent's final, partial tax year before the spouse's tax year has ended. Even if the personal representative files a separate return for the decedent, the surviving spouse may still have the option to use the more favorable joint rate tables under certain circumstances.[12]

---

[6] IRC § 6013(a)(3); Reg. § 1.6013-1(d)(4).

[7] IRC § 6013(a)(3).

[8] *See* IRC § 1. For example, when a couple files separately, they may not maximize the use of the lower tax brackets on both returns if one spouse has significantly more income than the other spouse.

[9] Rev. Rul. 74-175, 1974-1 C.B. 52.

[10] For example, deductions for medical expenses for a taxpayer under age 65 must exceed 10 percent of the taxpayer's adjusted gross income. IRC § 213.

[11] IRC § 6013(d)(3). A personal representative may qualify for the relief afforded to an "innocent spouse" under Section 6015 of the Internal Revenue Code, which limits exposure for liabilities unknown to one of the two spouses.

[12] IRC § 1(a)(2). A surviving spouse may use the joint tax return rate tables for two years following the decedent's death if the spouse (1) has not remarried before the close of the tax year; (2) heads a household that is the principal residence of a dependent child; (3) furnishes more than half the

[B] Deduction for Decedent's Medical Expenses

A personal representative often must pay the bills for medical and prescription drug expenses that a decedent incurred just prior to his or her death. The personal representative may elect to deduct such medical and drug expenses on either the decedent's final income tax return as a medical expense, or the decedent's federal estate tax return as a debt of the estate.[13] The marginal tax rates and the amounts deductible on the two tax returns often differ; thus, the best choice depends on the particular circumstances.

The first option is for a personal representative to deduct medical expenses paid from the decedent's estate during the one-year period following the date of death on the decedent's final income tax return.[14] The Internal Revenue Service treats these bills as paid by the decedent at the time the decedent incurred the charges. One drawback to deducting the expenses on the final income tax return is that the personal representative may only deduct medical expenses to the extent that they exceed 10 percent of the decedent's adjusted gross income for the tax period.[15]

The second option is for a personal representative to deduct medical and drug expenses that the decedent incurred before death but did not pay prior to death on the decedent's estate tax return as a debt of the decedent.[16] The full amount of each medical bill is deductible on the estate tax return.[17] If the decedent owes a federal estate tax, the estate often receives a greater benefit from the estate tax deduction than the income tax deduction because the medical and drug bills are fully deductible and the marginal estate tax rate generally exceeds the marginal income tax rate.

(Footnote Continued)

support for the child during the year; and (4) qualified to file a joint return with the deceased spouse in the year of the deceased spouse's death. IRC § 2(a).

[13] IRC § § 213(c), 2053(a)(3).

[14] IRC § 213(c). To qualify for this deduction, the personal representative must file in duplicate (1) a statement that the medical expenses have not been allowed as a deduction on the estate tax return of the decedent; and (2) a waiver of the right to have such amounts allowed at any time as a deduction on the estate tax return. Reg. § 1.213-1(d)(2). This procedure protects against a double deduction.

[15] IRC § 213(a). All medical expenses paid during the period covered by the income tax return count toward this 10 percent floor. If the decedent has already reached the 10 percent floor due to other medical expenses during the year, the full amount of the unpaid, pre-death medical expenses will be deductible. For tax years beginning after December 31, 2016 and ending before January 1, 2019, medical expenses are deductible to the extent that they exceed 7.5 percent of the decedent's adjusted gross income for the tax period. IRC § 213(f).

[16] IRC § 2053(a)(3).

[17] Where the personal representative claims medical expenses that exceed the threshold percentage of the adjusted gross income on the estate's income tax return, the personal representative cannot deduct the balance of such expenses (the amount below the threshold percentage of the adjusted gross income) on the decedent's estate tax return. *See* Rev. Rul. 77-357, 1977-2 C.B. 328.

EXAMPLE *14-2*

Decedent D died in 2022 and had adjusted gross income of $40,000 in the year of death. D was 72 years old at the time of his death. D had unpaid medical expenses of $5,000, which were D's only medical expenses during the year. D was not married, had made no taxable gifts during life, and had a gross estate of $13,000,000 (the basic exclusion amount in 2022 is $12,060,000). The personal representative could deduct $5,000 on D's estate tax return, which would save $2,000 of estate tax at the 40 percent marginal estate tax rate. Alternatively, the personal representative could deduct $1,000 (the amount that exceeds 10 percent of $40,000) on D's final income tax return, which, at a 22 percent marginal income tax rate, would save $220 of income tax.

If the decedent does not have a taxable estate, it is more advantageous to claim the income tax deduction.

EXAMPLE *14-3*

Decedent D died in 2022 and had an adjusted gross income of $40,000 in the year of death. Unpaid medical expenses of $4,000 were D's only medical expenses during the year. D was not married, had made no taxable gifts during life, and had a gross estate of $750,000. No estate tax will be due on D's estate, and thus the personal representative should claim any deduction available on the decedent's final income tax return.

If the decedent has a large estate but no tax due because of a full marital deduction, the personal representative should assess the potential for future estate tax savings for the surviving spouse if the medical and drug bills are taken as an estate tax deduction.[18] However, even if the estate tax deduction results in a potential significant tax savings at the time of the surviving spouse's death, the beneficiaries may prefer a smaller, immediate income tax deduction.

[C] Recognition of Savings Bond Interest

A taxpayer may defer reporting the interest income on Series E or Series EE bonds until the bonds mature or are redeemed.[19] Alternatively, a taxpayer may report all of the accrued interest to date in any year.[20] If a decedent did not exercise the

---

[18] A deduction on the estate tax return might reduce the amount of property included in the spouse's estate upon the spouse's death if the property were held in a QTIP trust (the funds of which will ultimately be taxed in the spouse's estate if not consumed). *See* § 14.05[B], *infra*.

[19] IRC § 454(c).

[20] IRC § 454(a). *See* Reg. § 1.454-1(a)(4), Example 1.

option to report the accrued interest annually before death, the personal representative of the decedent's estate has four choices:

1. To recognize the accrued interest on the decedent's final income tax return;
2. To recognize the accrued interest on the estate's income tax return;
3. To redeem specific bonds (thus triggering the recognition of income); or
4. To distribute the bonds to the beneficiaries of the estate without recognizing any accrued interest income.[21]

At least two reasons exist for electing to recognize all accrued interest on the decedent's final income tax return. First, if the decedent has little income for the final partial tax year, the accrued interest will be taxed at a comparatively low rate and, depending upon the available exemptions or deductions, may escape income tax altogether. Second, the election increases the decedent's final income tax liability, which the personal representative may deduct as a claim against the estate on the estate tax return.[22]

If the personal representative does not choose to make the election on the decedent's final income tax return, the personal representative may make the election on any income tax return filed for the estate, or may redeem specific bonds during years with low taxable income rather than making the election.[23] If the income levels for the final individual return and the estate income tax returns are high, the personal representative may elect to distribute the bonds without paying any income tax, thereby deferring the income tax liability until a future date. The different techniques and timing of taxation may alter slightly the interests of the beneficiaries of the estate, depending on the ultimate recipient of each bond and the other terms of the estate plan.

EXAMPLE *14-4*

Decedent D died on January 31, 2022, owning Series E bonds with accrued interest of $1,400. No spouse survived D, and D's sole source of income had been securities that generated approximately $10,000 per month. D had significant medical expenses in the month before his death. D's personal representative may choose to recognize the $1,400 of accrued E bond interest on the decedent's final income tax return, because that return will have either no tax due or a tax at the lowest marginal rate. Assuming that the estate remains open for several months, generates significant amounts of income, and the beneficiaries are in high income tax brackets, recognizing the income on the decedent's final individual income tax return will result in less tax than recognizing the income on the estate's income tax return.

---

[21] Rev. Rul. 68-145, 1968-1 C.B. 203; Rev. Rul. 64-104, 1964-1 C.B. 223.

[22] Reg. § 20.2053-6(f).

[23] The personal representative cannot make the election on a bond-by-bond basis. Once made, the election applies to all qualifying bonds. IRC § 454(a).

[D] Deduction of Income Tax Liability on Estate Tax Return

Regardless of whether the personal representative files a joint return or an individual return for the decedent's final individual income tax return, the personal representative may deduct a decedent's accrued state and federal income tax liability at his or her death on the decedent's federal estate tax return as a claim against the estate.[24] If the personal representative elects to file a joint final income tax return, the Treasury Regulations set forth a formula that allocates the tax liability between the surviving spouse and the estate for the purpose of this deduction.[25]

§14.04 ESTATE INCOME TAX RETURN ELECTIONS

A personal representative must file a federal income tax return for a decedent's estate if the estate has over $600 of income for the applicable period.[1] The estate's first income tax year begins on the day after the date of the decedent's death. The personal representative reports on the estate's income tax return only income generated by assets held in the probate estate (which were held in the decedent's name alone on the date of the decedent's death), and not income generated by assets that pass automatically to a beneficiary upon the decedent's death. Issues to consider when preparing the estate's income tax return include:

1. Whether to establish a fiscal tax year or a calendar tax year for the estate;
2. Whether to file a combined return for the estate and a qualified revocable trust;
3. How to time estate distributions to beneficiaries to minimize the tax; and
4. On which tax return to deduct certain administrative expenses.

[A] Calendar Year Versus Fiscal Year for Estate

The personal representative of an estate may adopt either a calendar or a fiscal taxable year for the purpose of the estate's income tax return.[2] This election is significant because the choice of tax year can affect the timing and amount of the estate's income tax.

If the personal representative selects a calendar year, the first tax year will run from the day after the date of the decedent's death until December 31 of that year. The following tax year will run from January 1 through December 31. Alternatively, the personal representative may elect a fiscal year that will run from the day after the

---

[24] IRC § 2053(a)(3).

[25] Reg. § 20.2053-6(f).

[1] **§ 14.04** IRC § 6012(a)(3). The Internal Revenue Service form for an estate income tax return is Form 1041. Reg. § 1.6012-3.

[2] IRC § 441; Reg. § 1.441-1.

decedent's death until the last day of any month other than December, as long as such ending date is not more than one year after the date of death.[3] The personal representative adopts a tax year by filing a tax return by the 15th day of the fourth month following the close of the selected tax year.[4] A personal representative who has not established a fiscal year must submit the estate income tax return on the basis of a calendar year.[5] After the personal representative fixes the tax year, the personal representative cannot change the tax year without prior approval from the Internal Revenue Service.[6]

EXAMPLE 14-5

Decedent D died on February 18, 2022. The personal representative of D's estate could elect a calendar tax year, in which case the first tax year would run from February 19, 2022 to December 31, 2022. The personal representative would select this calendar year by filing a tax return by April 15, 2023. Alternatively, the personal representative could choose a fiscal year ending on the last day of any other month that ends within one year of the date of D's death. The longest tax year would end on January 31, 2023. The personal representative would select this fiscal year by filing a tax return by May 15, 2023.

The personal representative's ability to elect a fiscal year presents a number of planning opportunities. The choice of the estate's taxable year may affect the following:

- The due date of the estate's income tax return and the related tax payment;
- When beneficiaries of the estate need to report the taxable income associated with distributions made to them; and
- The number of taxable years occurring during the administration of the estate.

A fiscal year that ends after the calendar year allows the estate to defer the payment of income tax. Unless a decedent dies in January, the longest possible fiscal year will end later than the end of a calendar tax year. Given that the income tax return is due on the 15th day of the fourth month following the close of the tax year, an extended year will defer the payment of any tax by the estate for up to 11 months.[7] As an alternative to a long fiscal year to defer the initial tax payment, a personal representative who anticipates the receipt of a substantial item of income may select a

---

[3] *Id.* The first tax year may not cover a period of more than 12 months, but it may cover a period of less than 12 months. After the first tax year, all subsequent tax years except the final year must be 12 months in length.

[4] Reg. § 1.441-1(c); Reg. § 1.6072-1.

[5] Reg. § 1.441-1(b)(4).

[6] Reg. § 1.441-1(e).

[7] The personal representative does not need to make estimated tax payments for an estate's federal income tax return if the tax year ends within two years of the decedent's death. IRC § 6654(1)(2). Individual states may require estimated tax payments during this period.

short first year and end the fiscal year prior to the receipt of that income, which would defer payment of the tax on that particular item of income until the following tax year.

EXAMPLE *14-6*

Decedent D died on June 22, 2022. The personal representative of D's estate could elect a fiscal tax year ending May 31, 2022, which would result in a year beginning June 23, 2022, and ending May 31, 2023. The tax payment for the estate's first year would not be due until September 15, 2023, rather than April 15, 2023, if a calendar year was selected. If, instead, the personal representative expected to generate significant income for the estate in October 2022 (for example, by the sale of a business), by choosing a fiscal tax year ending September 30, 2022, the personal representative could defer income taxes associated with the sale until January 15, 2024.

Second, the choice of the estate's taxable year can also affect the timing of income tax payments by a beneficiary. A beneficiary reports distributions from an estate in the calendar year in which the estate's tax year ends.[8] Therefore, the choice of the estate's tax year may allow a calendar year beneficiary to defer payment of tax on any receipts from the estate until the beneficiary's next tax year.

EXAMPLE *14-7*

Decedent D died on February 18, 2022, leaving Child C as the sole beneficiary. The estate adopts a fiscal year ending January 31, 2023. The personal representative makes several distributions of income to C during 2022. C will report all income from D's estate that C receives between February 18, 2022, and January 31, 2023, as received by C on January 31, 2023, which is the last day of the estate's tax year. Thus, C will report this income on C's tax return for 2023. C has effectively deferred the payment of tax on distributions received from the estate in 2022 until April 15, 2024.

Third, the choice of the tax year will dictate the number of tax years that occur during the administration of the estate. A personal representative may prefer to have more tax years to increase the total number of exemptions available and to tax more of the income at lower marginal rates.[9] Alternatively, the personal representative may

---

[8] IRC § 662(c).

[9] An estate is allowed a deduction of $600 per year. IRC § 642(b). Increasing the number of tax years subjects some of the income to tax at lower marginal rates. *See* IRC § 1(e).

choose to have fewer tax years to decrease the administrative costs associated with the preparation of tax returns.[10]

EXAMPLE *14-8*

Decedent D died on January 31, 2022. The personal representative anticipates that the estate will receive a substantial amount of income on July 15, 2022, and also anticipates that the entire estate will be closed by November 30, 2023. The personal representative elects to have the first fiscal year for the estate run from February 1, 2022, through June 30, 2022. The second fiscal year will run from July 1, 2022, through June 30, 2023. The final fiscal year will run from July 1, 2023, to November 30, 2023. By electing a fiscal year, the estate will defer taxation on the income received in July of 2022, until the second taxable year. The personal representative has also structured the tax year to allow the estate to have three taxable years within the two-year period, which permits use of the lowest tax brackets three times and may increase the number of deductions and exemptions available to the estate.

[B] Option to Combine Revocable Trust and Estate

If a decedent has a qualified revocable trust, the personal representative of the decedent's estate and the trustee of the decedent's revocable trust may elect to treat the revocable trust as part of the estate for income tax purposes.[11] The election allows taxpayers to use funded or unfunded revocable trusts in their estate plan without having to accept potentially less favorable tax rules if assets are held in a revocable trust rather than in the taxpayer's probate estate. A trust qualifies for this election if the decedent is deemed to own the trust for income tax purposes during the decedent's lifetime due to a retained power to revoke the trust.[12]

By making this election, the trust is eligible for certain benefits otherwise reserved for estates only. Differences between the tax rules for trusts and estates include:

- An estate can elect a fiscal tax year, but a trust must use a calendar tax year;
- An estate will receive a charitable deduction for amounts permanently set aside for charitable purposes, while a trust will only receive a charitable

---

[10] A calendar year may also reduce costs because custodians of certain assets send tax information on a calendar year basis. This may make it simpler, and thus less costly, to prepare a calendar year tax return. However, a personal representative can often calculate the fiscal year information with relative ease.

[11] IRC § 645; Reg. § 1.645-1. This election must be made jointly by the personal representative of the estate and the trustee of the revocable trust. Reg. § 1.645-1(c)(1).

[12] IRC § § 645(b)(1), 676.

deduction for amounts actually paid to charity in the current tax year (or the succeeding tax year if an election is made);

- An estate may recognize a loss if a pecuniary bequest is satisfied with assets that have a basis that exceeds the fair market value, while a trust cannot recognize this loss; and
- An estate can waive the active participation requirement under the passive loss rules for two years after the date of death, but a trust cannot.[13]

Both the personal representative and the trustee must elect to combine the estate and the trust for income tax purposes no later than the date for filing the estate's first income tax return, including extensions.[14] To make the Section 645 election, the personal representative and the trustee must complete Form 8855 and attach it to the first estate income tax return, or else make the election pursuant to any other published guidance from the Internal Revenue Service. The form requires the name, address, and taxpayer identification number of the decedent, the estate, and the revocable trust, the decedent's date of death, and a representation that the revocable trust qualifies for the election. The election is irrevocable once made.[15] The election begins at the time of the decedent's death. If no estate tax return is required, the election continues for those tax years ending after the date of the decedent's death and before the date that is two years from the date of the decedent's death. If the personal representative does file an estate tax return, the election continues until six months after the date of the final determination of estate tax liability.[16] The probate estate and each electing revocable trust are treated as separate shares for the purpose of computing distributions to beneficiaries.[17]

EXAMPLE *14-9*

A funded revocable trust will ultimately pay 50 percent of its net assets to charity, but the trust makes no distributions of income or principal in the year following the donor's death. By combining the donor's estate and revocable trust for income tax purposes, the combined entity will receive a deduction for the revocable trust income set aside for charity, even if it has not yet been paid to charity.

Factors that may dissuade the personal representative or a trustee from making the election to combine the estate with one or more revocable trusts include the possible complexity of combining the entities for tax purposes but following the

---

[13] IRC §§ 644(a), 642(c), 267(b)(13), 469(i)(4). A trust with rental real estate, qualified timber property, or subchapter S corporation stock may also benefit from more favorable rules for estates.

[14] IRC § 645(c). It is possible to make the election even if there is no personal representative. Reg. § 1.645-1(c)(2).

[15] IRC § 645(c); Reg. § 1.645-1(e)(1).

[16] IRC § 645(b)(2).

[17] Reg. § 1.663(c)-4(a). Separate shares allow the economic interests of the beneficiaries of the estate and the revocable trust to remain distinct.

separate share rules, a potential lack of state law conformity, and a possible loss of income tax deferral that could be achieved if a fiscal year estate distributes property to a calendar year trust.[18]

[C] Distributions from the Estate

Decisions made by a personal representative regarding the timing and amounts of distributions from the estate can affect who bears the tax burden associated with the estate's income. There are several planning opportunities involving distributions from the estate:

- Certain distributions from the estate to the beneficiaries will result in a distribution deduction for the estate and will require the beneficiaries to report some or all of the estate's income on the beneficiaries' income tax returns.[19]
- The personal representative may elect to treat a beneficiary distribution that the estate makes in the first 65 days of a tax year as having been made in the estate's prior tax year.[20]
- The personal representative may elect to recognize gain or loss when the estate distributes appreciated or depreciated property to a beneficiary.[21]
- Excess deductions flow through to the beneficiaries only in the estate's final year; thus, the personal representative's decisions about when to incur certain costs and when to make final distributions from the estate affect the beneficiaries' ability to use any excess deductions from the estate.[22]

Reviewing several basic concepts relating to the income taxation of estates will help put these planning opportunities in context. All income from an estate is reportable on the estate's income tax return, the beneficiary's income tax return or a combination of the two. In general, if a personal representative makes no distributions from an estate to the beneficiaries during a tax year, then the estate will report all of the estate's income for that year. In contrast, if the personal representative has distributed income or property to beneficiaries, the estate receives a deduction for the distributions, and the beneficiaries must include the value of these distributions in their gross income, to the extent of the estate's "distributable net income" (DNI).[23] DNI is a modified measure of the estate's net income.[24] Each beneficiary receives a Schedule K-1 from the personal representative, which tells the beneficiary how much and what type of income to report on her federal income tax return. If the qualifying distributions are less than the estate's DNI, then the estate is taxed on the remaining

---

[18] *See* § 14.04[A], *supra*, regarding the deferral of income tax when an estate on a fiscal tax year distributes income to a beneficiary (which would include a trust) with a calendar tax year.

[19] IRC §§ 661, 662.

[20] IRC § 663(b).

[21] IRC § 643(e)(3).

[22] IRC § 642(h).

[23] IRC §§ 661, 662.

[24] *See* IRC § 643(a).

income on its own return. If the qualifying estate distributions equal or exceed DNI, the estate, as an entity, will have no remaining taxable income. The same rules apply to trusts (other than grantor trusts).[25]

Based on these rules, the first planning opportunity available to a personal representative is that the timing of distributions from an estate to one or more beneficiaries may shift the tax burden from the estate to those beneficiaries who receive distributions. For a trust or estate, the top 37 percent bracket in 2022 begins when taxable income reaches $13,450, whereas the top 37 percent bracket for a single individual does not begin until taxable income reaches $539,000 ($647,850 for married individuals filing jointly).[26] Thus, distributions to beneficiaries can save a significant amount in income taxes if the beneficiaries are not in the top income tax bracket.[27] In addition, distributions can avoid the additional 3.8 percent surtax on undistributed net investment income (as described below) if the beneficiaries do not have adjusted gross income greater than the threshold amounts ($250,000 for married individuals filing jointly and $200,000 for single individuals).[28]

In the case of an estate, the 3.8 percent surtax is imposed on the lesser of (1) the undistributed net investment income for the taxable year, or (2) the excess, if any, of (a) the estate's adjusted gross income for the taxable year over (b) the dollar amount at which the highest trust and estate tax bracket begins for the taxable year ($13,450 for 2022).[29] Net investment income includes the following three categories of income, reduced by the deductions which are properly allocable to such income:[30]

1. Gross income from interest, dividends, annuities, royalties, and rents, but excluding all such income derived in the ordinary course of an active trade or business other than financial instruments or commodities businesses;

2. All other gross income derived from a trade or business that is either (a) a passive activity with respect to the estate, or (b) a financial instruments or commodities business; and

3. Net gain (to the extent taken into account in computing taxable income) attributable to the disposition of property, but excluding all net gain attributable to the disposition of property held in an active trade or business other than a financial instruments or commodities business.

---

[25] Income taxation of trusts and grantor trusts are discussed in Chapter 4.

[26] IRC §§1(a), (c), (e). Note that only certain types of income are taxed at the top 37 percent rate; income from sources such as qualified dividends and long-term capital gains are not taxed at this rate.

[27] In making distribution decisions, it is important to consider the state income tax consequences of distributions; if an estate in a state with no state income tax makes a distribution to a beneficiary who lives in a state with a state income tax, the state income tax incurred by the beneficiary may offset the federal income tax savings as a result of the distribution.

[28] IRC §1411(b).

[29] IRC §§1411(a)(2), 1(e). For individual taxpayers, the amount subject to the 3.8 percent surtax is the lesser of (1) the taxpayer's net investment income (generally determined in the same manner as for estates) or (2) the taxpayer's modified adjusted gross income over an applicable threshold amount. IRC §1411(a)(1).

[30] IRC §1411(c). Net investment income does not include any distribution from certain qualified retirement plans. IRC §1411(c)(5).

The undistributed net investment income of an estate is the estate's net investment income, reduced by (1) the amount of net investment income included in the estate's distribution deduction under Section 661, and (2) the charitable contribution deduction under Section 642(c).[31] Undistributed net investment income and the 3.8 percent surtax are calculated using Form 8960.

EXAMPLE *14-10*

An estate's sole item of income in 2022 is $50,000 of interest income. The estate has a sole beneficiary, B, who is an unmarried taxpayer with no income for 2022. If the estate retains the interest income, the estate will owe $16,763 of income tax. In addition, $36,550 of this income will be subject to the 3.8 percent surtax ($50,000 interest income – $13,450 threshold) and the surtax payable by the estate will be $1,389, resulting in a total tax of $18,152. If the estate distributes this $50,000 of interest income, the estate will not be subject to the $18,152 tax on this income. Instead, B will pay only $6,617 tax on the income and will not be subject to the 3.8 percent surtax on the income because his total income does not exceed the $200,000 threshold applicable to an unmarried individual.

One significant exception to the general rule regarding the distribution deduction is that the distribution deduction does not apply to bequests of a specific sum of money or specific property.[32] Thus, these distributions do not result in taxable income to the beneficiary and are not deductible by the estate when distributed.[33]

EXAMPLE *14-11*

An estate has $3,000 of dividend income in its first year. The decedent's will left $10,000 in cash to the decedent's nephew. The $10,000 distribution from the estate to the nephew is the only estate distribution during the year. The estate will report the $3,000 of dividend income. The nephew will not report any estate income.

The personal representative has a second, related tool at her disposal to shift the tax burden from the estate to the beneficiaries. If the personal representative finds that the estate income exceeds the distributions to beneficiaries during a tax year, the personal representative may elect to have distributions made in the first 65 days of the following tax year count as distributions made on the last day of the prior tax

---

[31] Reg. § 1.1411-3(e)(2), (3), (4).

[32] IRC § 663(a)(1). A specific bequest will not be eligible for this exception if, under the terms of the trust or the will, the property is required to be distributed or credited to the beneficiary in more than three installments. Reg. § 1.663(a)-1(c) explains how this installment rule is applied.

[33] IRC § 663(a)(1).

year.[34] The personal representative makes this election on Form 1041. The personal representative does not need to elect this treatment for all amounts distributed during the 65-day period; instead, the personal representative may select specific distributions or amounts for this election.[35] The amount to which this election applies cannot exceed the greater of the estate's accounting income, or the DNI in the prior year reduced by payments made, credited, or required to be made in the prior year.[36] This election is important if the beneficiaries are in a lower tax bracket than the estate. A post year-end distribution to a beneficiary after the estate's income for the tax year is calculated could result in the beneficiary paying the tax at a lower rate rather than the estate paying the tax at a higher rate due to the compressed income tax brackets that apply to estates.

EXAMPLE *14-12*

An estate has $60,000 of dividend and interest income in 2022. Some of this income will be taxed at the top income tax rate of 37 percent (an estate reaches this marginal rate in 2022 if it has $13,450 of taxable income). The estate makes no distributions to Beneficiary B, an unmarried taxpayer and the sole beneficiary of the estate, in 2022. B has $92,000 of salary income, subjecting B to a 24 percent marginal income tax bracket for 2022. If the estate is subject to income tax on the $60,000 of dividend and interest income, the estate will owe $20,463 of income tax on this income. In addition, $46,550 of the estate's income will be subject to the 3.8 percent surtax ($60,000 − $13,450) and the surtax payable by the estate will be $1,769 (3.8 percent × $46,550), resulting in a total tax of $22,232. If the personal representative distributes $60,000 from the estate to B on January 31, 2022, and elects to have the distribution treated as a 2022 distribution under the 65-day rule, the estate will not be subject to the $22,232 tax on this income. Instead, B will pay only a $14,400 tax on the income and will not be subject to the surtax on the income because his total income does not exceed the $200,000 threshold applicable to an unmarried individual.

Third, a personal representative can select whether the estate or the beneficiaries will recognize gain or loss when the estate distributes property to the beneficiaries that has appreciated or depreciated between the date of death and the date of distribution. The basis of property acquired from a decedent is equal to its fair market value as of the decedent's date of death (or as of the alternate valuation date).[37] However, property can appreciate or depreciate between the date of death and the

---

[34] IRC § 663(b).

[35] *See* Reg. § 1.663(b)-1(a)(1), (2)(ii).

[36] *See* Reg. § 1.663(b)-1(a)(2).

[37] IRC § 1014(a). The alternate valuation date is discussed in § 14.05[A], *infra.* Note that under the 2010 Act, the estates of decedents dying in 2010 that elected to have the estate not subject to estate tax will be subject to the modified carryover basis rules under IRC § 1022.

date of transfer. Unless an election is made, when a personal representative distributes appreciated or depreciated property other than in satisfaction of a specific pecuniary amount, the beneficiary takes the property with its date of death basis and will recognize gain or loss upon the ultimate disposition of the property.[38] However, if the property distributed from the estate qualifies for a distribution deduction for the estate and as income for a beneficiary, the personal representative may elect to recognize any built-in gain or loss prior to distributing the asset to the beneficiary.[39]

The election allows the beneficiary to take the property with a basis equal to the fair market value of the property as of the distribution date.[40]

If made, the election is irrevocable and it applies to all property distributions during the taxable year.

EXAMPLE 14-13

In 2022, the personal representative of Decedent D's estate distributes ten shares of Corporation C stock to Beneficiary B. The shares of stock were worth $5,000 on the date of D's death, and $7,500 on the date of distribution to B. If the personal representative elects to recognize the gain, the estate will have $2,500 of capital gain and B will take the asset with a basis of $7,500. If the personal representative does not elect to recognize the gain, B will take the asset with a basis of $5,000.

This election to recognize gain or loss may shift the tax burden between the property recipient and the estate, which indirectly affects the residuary beneficiaries of the estate.

EXAMPLE 14-14

In 2022, the personal representative of Decedent D's estate distributes stock that was worth $2,000 at the date of D's death and $5,000 at the time it was distributed to Beneficiary B. The personal representative does not elect to realize the $3,000 of built-in capital gain. The estate has $5,000 of interest income and makes no other distributions. The estate will receive a distribution deduction of $2,000 for the property distributed to B. If the estate has no other deductions, B will report $2,000 of interest income on B's income tax return, and the estate will be taxed on the remaining $3,000. The tax paid by the estate (which is greater than if the distribution deduction to B was a full $5,000 and the estate paid a capital gains tax on the $3,000 built-in capital gain) will ultimately reduce any amounts payable to other beneficiaries who receive a percentage of the remainder of the estate.

---

[38] *See* IRC §§ 643(e)(1), 1001.
[39] IRC § 643(e)(3), (4).
[40] IRC § 643(e)(3).

The election may also result in differences in the income allocated among multiple beneficiaries who receive distributions in a given year if certain beneficiaries receive cash while other beneficiaries receive appreciated or depreciated property.

Factors that a personal representative may consider when deciding whether to make the election include the tax brackets of the estate and the beneficiary, whether the estate has previously recognized losses that may offset the gain recognized if the election is made, and whether the beneficiary is in a lower tax bracket than the estate or has prior recognized losses.

Fourth, the beneficiaries of an estate will only receive the benefit of excess estate deductions in the estate's final tax year.[41] In all other years, excess deductions such as attorney's fees and investment fees will not pass to the beneficiaries for their use. A personal representative often has some discretion as to when to pay a deductible bill. When possible, the personal representative should try to avoid having tax years (other than the final year of the estate) with deductions in excess of income where the excess deductions could have passed to the beneficiaries if they had occurred in the estate's final tax year.

[D] Deduction for Estate Administration Expenses

The personal representative of an estate may deduct estate administration expenses on either the estate's income tax return (Form 1041) or on the estate tax return (Form 706).[42] Deductible estate administration expenses include those expenses that are actually and necessarily incurred in the administration of the decedent's estate, such as expenses incurred in the collection of assets, payment of debts, and distribution of property to the beneficiaries.[43] Examples of administration expenses include personal representative's commissions, attorney's fees, accountant's fees, and miscellaneous expenses, such as court costs and appraisal fees.[44] The personal representative may also deduct expenses incurred to preserve the estate, such as the cost of storing or maintaining estate property, if it is impossible to effect immediate distribution to the beneficiaries. However, the personal representative may not deduct expenditures for the individual benefit of the heirs, legatees, or devisees that are not essential to the proper settlement of the estate.[45]

---

[41] IRC § 642(h); Reg. § 1.642(h)-2.

[42] IRC § § 2053(a)(2), 67(e), 642(g). Note that the personal representative may only deduct many of the other items listed in Section 2053-funeral expenses, debts, and unpaid mortgages-on the estate tax return, and not on an income tax return. *See* § 14.03[B], *supra*, for options relating to medical expenses.

[43] Reg. § 20.2053-3(a).

[44] Reg. § 20.2053-3.

[45] Reg. § 20.2053-3(a). If the estate's selling expenses are not deductible because the decedent's will or trust did not require the sale of the item and the asset did not need to be sold to meet the estate's cash needs, the personal representative may be able to increase the basis of the asset on the income tax return that reports the sale. Examples of selling expenses that may be added to the basis of an asset include realtor's fees, broker's commissions, and auction commissions.

EXAMPLE *14-15*

The personal representative of Decedent D's estate incurred brokerage fees in an effort to alter the mix of securities to reflect the personal preferences of the beneficiaries who would ultimately receive the securities. The personal representative may not deduct the brokerage fees as administration expenses because the expenses were primarily for the benefit of the beneficiaries and not necessarily incurred for the administration of the decedent's estate.

In addition, no deduction in excess of any amount permitted by local law will be allowed.[46] Thus, if the probate court disallows all or part of an expense, the deduction will be disallowed for federal tax purposes as well.[47]

The personal representative may also deduct certain administrative expenses that relate to property included in a decedent's gross estate, but are not included in the decedent's probate estate (e.g., property held in a revocable trust, proceeds of life insurance that were subject to tax in the decedent's estate, or property held by joint tenancy).[48] To receive a deduction, the expenses must relate to the decedent's death and be incurred in settling the decedent's interest in property or vesting good title to the property in the beneficiaries.[49] In addition, the expenses must be paid within three years of the due date of the estate tax return.[50] Expenses of this type include trustees' fees or distribution charges incurred in connection with a trust established by a decedent during his or her lifetime, the collection of miscellaneous assets such as insurance policies payable to third parties, or the transfer or clearance of title to property included in the decedent's gross estate for estate tax purposes but not included in his or her probate estate, such as real estate held by joint tenancy.

The personal representative may deduct administration expenses on either the decedent's estate tax return or the estate's income tax return. On the decedent's estate tax return, a personal representative may deduct the actual amount paid for a given expense, or an estimate of the expected liability, provided that the expected liability is ascertainable with reasonable certainty and will be paid.[51] If the personal representative deducts an estimated expense and the Internal Revenue Service audits the estate tax return, the Service may disallow any part of the expense that the estate has not actually incurred by the conclusion of the audit.[52] If an expense subsequently becomes ascertainable with reasonable certainty and is certain to be paid (or is paid),

---

[46] IRC § 2053(a).

[47] Reg. § 20.2053-1(b)(3).

[48] IRC § 2053(b).

[49] Reg. § 20.2053-8(b).

[50] Reg. § 20.2053-8(a)(2); IRC § 6501.

[51] Reg. § 20.2053-1(d)(4)(i). To the extent that an expense is contested or contingent, the expense is deemed not to be ascertainable with reasonable certainty. *Id.* There is no affirmative duty to report amounts that were claimed as deductions on the estate tax return but were subsequently not paid or not paid in full. Preamble to T.D. 9468 (10/20/09).

[52] Reg. § 20.2053-1(d)(4)(ii).

the personal representative may file a claim for refund.[53] In order to preserve the estate's right to claim a refund for amounts that become deductible after the expiration of the period of limitations for filing a claim for refund, the personal representative may file a protective claim for refund.[54] The Internal Revenue Service has released detailed guidance on the procedures relating to protective claims for refund.[55]

In the alternative, most administration expenses will also qualify as itemized deductions on the estate's income tax return.[56] The personal representative may not deduct administration expenses on the estate's income tax return unless the personal representative files a statement that the amounts have not been allowed as an estate tax deduction.[57] In addition, the estate must have actually paid an administrative expense within the income tax year to receive an income tax deduction. The personal representative does not need to make a global decision; it is possible to deduct some expenses on the estate tax return and other expenses on an income tax return.[58]

The primary consideration in deciding whether to claim deductions for administrative expenses on an estate tax return or an income tax return is the amount of tax ultimately owed on each return.[59] The personal representative may choose to deduct certain expenses on the estate's income tax return and other expenses on the estate tax return.[60] The personal representative may also elect to deduct part of an expense on the estate's income tax return if the appropriate statement is filed and another part on the estate tax return.[61]

EXAMPLE *14-16*

The personal representative of Decedent D's estate incurred expenses in the administration of the estate, including attorney's fees and appraiser's fees. The personal representative may deduct the attorney's fees and

---

[53] *Id.*

[54] *Id.* A protective claim for refund may be filed at any time before the later of three years after the estate tax return was filed or two years after the payment of the estate tax. Reg. § 20.2053-1(d)(5)(i). The protective claim for refund must identify each claim or expense and describe the reasons and contingencies delaying actual payment of the claim or expense; it is not necessary to state a particular dollar amount or demand an immediate refund. *Id.* The Service will consider the protective claim after the personal representative has notified the Service within a reasonable period that the contingency has been resolved and that the amount deductible has been established. *Id.*

[55] Rev. Proc. 2011-48, 2011-42 I.R.B. 527; Instructions for Form 706 (Rev. September 2021), pp. 16, 49-51. A deduction will be allowed when the claim is resolved and paid. *Id.*

[56] IRC § 67(e).

[57] IRC § 642(g); Reg. § 1.642(g)-1. Once the statement is filed, it is irrevocable. *Id.*

[58] Reg. § 1.642(g)-2.

[59] In 2013 and thereafter, the maximum rate for the estate and gift tax is scheduled to exceed the maximum stated rate for the income tax; however, the 3.8 percent surtax on undistributed net investment income could cause the total tax rate for an estate to exceed the estate and gift tax rate.

[60] Reg. § 1.642(g)-2.

[61] *Id.*

appraiser's fees as expenses of administration. If D died in 2022, had a taxable estate that exceeded $12,060,000, was not subject to any state estate tax, and D's estate had no undistributed net investment income subject to the 3.8 percent surtax (as described in §14.04[C], *supra*), then the personal representative will likely elect to deduct the administration expenses on the estate tax return because of the 40 percent federal marginal estate tax rate. If D instead had a $400,000 estate and was therefore not subject to estate tax, then the personal representative should take the deduction on the income tax return.

A second consideration is the fact that the personal representative may only deduct expenses actually incurred on the income tax return, whereas the personal representative can deduct an estimate for future expenses on the estate tax return. This may allow a larger deduction at an earlier date if estimated future expenses are deducted on the estate tax return. Third, in all years other than the final year of the estate, the estate may not pass excess deductions on an income tax return through to the beneficiaries. Thus, if in the estate's first year the deductions exceed the income, the personal representative should deduct at least some administrative expenses on the estate tax return if this is at all useful, because the excess deductions will be neither used nor carried forward on the income tax return. Finally, depending on the state of residence, an estate tax or income tax deduction may or may not result in tax savings at the state level.[62]

§14.05 DECEDENT'S ESTATE TAX RETURN ELECTIONS

A personal representative of the estate of a decedent whose date of death occurs in 2018 must file a federal estate tax return if the decedent's gross estate plus adjusted taxable gifts during life has a value in excess of the basic exclusion amount for the year of death.[1] The gross estate generally consists of property owned and controlled by the decedent at the date of death.

The basic exclusion amount for 2022 is $12,060,000[2] ($10,000,000 indexed for inflation, for estates of decedents dying in 2018 through 2025).[3] The federal estate tax return is filed on Form 706 and is due nine months after the date of the decedent's death (unless the Internal Revenue Service grants an extension of time to file the return).[4]

---

[62] In some states, for example, in Massachusetts, the state income tax structure would not allow a deduction for most estate administration expenses, but the deduction would benefit the estate on the state estate tax return.

[1] **§14.05** IRC §6018(a).

[2] IRC §2010(c)(3)(C); Rev. Proc. 2021-45, 2021-48 I.R.B. 764, 771.

[3] IRC §2010(c)(3). *See* Chapter 5 for a table showing the exclusion amount for each year since 1977.

[4] IRC §§6075(a), 6081. An automatic six-month extension may be obtained by filing Form 4768 prior to the nine-month due date of the return).

Issues to consider when preparing the federal estate tax return include: (1) the method of valuation of property included in the gross estate, including special elections for farm and business property; (2) to what extent the marital deduction should be claimed for any property eligible for a QTIP election that is set apart for the surviving spouse; (3) the allocation of generation-skipping transfer tax exemption; (4) estate tax payment options for owners of closely held businesses; (5) the election to transfer the decedent's unused basic exclusion amount to the decedent's surviving spouse; and (6) other deductions and exclusions relating to family businesses and conservation easements.

[A] Valuation Elections

[1] Alternate Valuation Date

In general, a decedent's estate is valued as of the date of death for estate tax purposes.[5] However, under certain circumstances the personal representative may elect an alternate valuation method that values assets as of the date that is six months after the date of death (the "alternate valuation date").[6] The personal representative may select the alternate valuation date only if the alternate valuation decreases the value of the gross estate, and the alternate valuation decreases the sum of the estate tax and the generation-skipping transfer tax due (reduced by allowable credits).[7] If the aggregate value of a decedent's gross estate decreases in value in the six months following the date of the decedent's death, the use of the alternate valuation date will result in a reduction in the amount of estate tax due.[8] This reduces the potential for payment of estate tax on amounts greater than the amounts that the beneficiaries will ultimately receive.

EXAMPLE *14-17*

Decedent D died on July 2, 2022, with $12,500,000 of X Corporation stock as D's only asset. On January 2, 2023, the stock's value has decreased to $12,100,000. The stock is distributed to the estate's beneficiaries on January 3, 2023. The personal representative may elect to value the stock for

---

[5] IRC § 2031(a).

[6] IRC § 2032.

[7] IRC § 2032(c). If the alternate valuation is desirable but there is no requisite decrease in the tax due because the estate will receive a full marital deduction, the surviving spouse may want to consider executing a qualified disclaimer (*see* § 14.06[B], *infra*) to generate a small tax.

[8] Reg. § 20.2032-1(b)(1).

estate tax purposes at its $12,100,000 value, which will save approximately $160,000 of estate tax at a 40 percent marginal tax rate (if D's estate had no deductions), and will more accurately reflect the actual asset value transferred to the beneficiaries.

The alternate valuation date does not apply to all assets. Although the personal representative will value most assets in the estate on the date that is six months after the date of the decedent's death, three exceptions to the six-month alternate valuation date exist.[9] The three exceptions are:

1. Assets that the estate has distributed, sold, exchanged, or otherwise disposed of before the six-month alternate valuation date are valued as of the date of distribution, sale, exchange, or disposition;[10]
2. Assets that decrease in value based only on the passing of time, such as life estates, remainders, reversionary interests, and patents, are valued as of the date of death;[11] and
3. The alternate valuation rules disregard interest that accrues after the date of death and before the six-month alternate valuation date.[12]

EXAMPLE *14-18*

Decedent D died on March 18, 2022. At the time of D's death, D owned securities valued at $7,600,000, and a house valued at $4,650,000, which, absent alternate valuation, would result in a $12,250,000 gross estate. D's personal representative sold the house on August 20, 2022, for $4,000,000. On September 18, 2022, D's securities were worth $7,000,000. D's personal representative may elect to value D's estate at the alternate valuation date. The alternate valuation method would result in a gross estate of $11,000,000 ($7,000,000 of securities as of the date that is six months after the date of the decedent's death, and $4,000,000 for the house, which was sold after death but prior to the six-month valuation date).

Proposed Treasury regulations provide a non-exclusive list of transactions that would constitute a distribution, sale, exchange or other disposition for purposes of alternate valuation.[13] These proposed Treasury regulations also set forth an aggregation rule that eliminates the application of fractional interest discounts when, during

---

[9] IRC § 2032(a). The six-month period is counted by calendar months, not by days. Thus, if the decedent dies on February 25, 2022, the alternate valuation date is August 25, 2022. If there is not an equivalent day in the sixth month, the valuation date is the last day of the sixth month. For example, if the decedent dies on August 30, 2022, the alternate valuation date will be February 28, 2023. Rev. Rul. 74-260, 1974-1 C.B. 275.

[10] IRC § 2032(a)(1); Prop. Reg. § 20.2032-1(a)(1).

[11] IRC § 2032(a)(3); Reg. § 20.2032-1(f); Prop. Reg. § 20.2032-1(f)(2).

[12] Reg. § 20.2032-1(d)(1), (f); Prop. Reg. § 20.2032-1(c)(1)(iii)(A).

[13] Prop. Reg. § 20.2032-1(c)(1)(i) and (ii).

the alternate valuation period, part of an interest owned by a decedent is distributed, sold, exchanged, or otherwise disposed of.[14] Under this rule, the value of each part subject to such a transaction is determined on the respective transaction date and the value of the decedent's remaining interest is determined on the alternate valuation date, all without any fractional or minority interest discounts.[15]

EXAMPLE *14-19*

Decedent D died on March 1, 2022. At the time of D's death, D owned 100 percent of a parcel of undeveloped real estate referred to as Blackacre. D's will directs that an undivided 70 percent interest in Blackacre is to pass to Trust A for the benefit of D's surviving spouse, and an undivided 30 percent interest is to pass to Trust B for the benefit of D's surviving child. On June 1, 2022, the personal representative of D's estate distributed a 70 percent interest in Blackacre to Trust A. On July 1, 2022, the personal representative of D's estate distributed a 30 percent interest in Blackacre to Trust B. The fair market value of the 70 percent interest in Blackacre for alternate valuation purposes is determined by calculating 70 percent of the fair market value of all (100 percent) of Blackacre as of June 1, 2022. The fair market value of the 30 percent interest in Blackacre for alternate valuation purposes is determined by calculating 30 percent of the fair market value of all (100 percent) of Blackacre as of July 1, 2022.

A personal representative elects alternate valuation on an estate tax return (Form 706) filed no later than one year after the date the estate tax return is due, including extensions.[16] If the personal representative makes the election, it applies to all property included in the gross estate; the personal representative may not elect alternate valuation for selected assets only.[17] If the personal representative elects to value the estate using alternate valuation, references to "the value of property at a decedent's death" in contexts such as the marital and charitable deductions will mean the value as of the alternate valuation date.[18] In addition, a recipient of a decedent's property will have a basis equal to the alternate valuation of the property.[19]

---

[14] Prop. Reg. § 20.2032-1(c)(1)(iv).

[15] *Id.*

[16] IRC § 2032(d). Thus, the personal representative may make the election on a late estate tax return, but not on a return filed more than one year after the last valid extension date. If the personal representative files a return within such time, but fails to make the election on the return, the personal representative may request and receive a discretionary extension of time to make the election. Reg. § 20.2032-1(b)(3).

[17] Reg. § 20.2032-1(b)(1).

[18] IRC § 2032(b).

[19] IRC § 1014(a)(2). The alternate valuation election is optional, not mandatory. The personal representative may consider factors such as a lower basis for a beneficiary for a particular asset (which will produce more taxable income for the beneficiary upon the sale of the asset) when

[2] Special Use Valuation

There is a special valuation rule that is available for real estate used in a family farm or business.[20] Property included in a decedent's gross estate is usually valued at fair market value, which is the price at which a willing buyer would purchase the property from a willing seller.[21] Inherent in this definition of fair market value is the requirement that the property's "highest and best use" be considered.[22] That is, property is valued at the use that would generate the largest market return, even if this use is different from the property's actual use. One exception to this rule is that real property used in a family farm or closely held business may be valued at its actual use instead of its highest and best use if certain requirements are met.[23] The goal of this provision is to allow families to pass farms and businesses to the next generation rather than having to sell the farms and businesses to pay estate taxes. To be eligible for this special valuation rule, the farm or business must meet a detailed set of requirements relating to the size of the farm or business relative to the entire estate and the family's level of participation in the farm or business, and the property must pass to persons who constitute qualified heirs under the statute.[24] The eligibility requirements for special use valuation require the following:[25]

1. 50 percent or more of the adjusted value of the gross estate consists of real or personal property that the decedent or a member of the decedent's family used for farm or business purposes at the time of the decedent's death and that a qualified heir acquired from the decedent;

2. During the eight-year period ending on the date of the decedent's death, periods aggregating five years or more have existed during which the decedent or a member of the decedent's family owned such property and materially participated in the farm or business; and

3. 25 percent or more of the adjusted value of the gross estate consists of real property that a qualified heir acquired from the decedent and that meets the requirements set forth in (2). Qualified heirs include ancestors, spouses, lineal descendants of the decedent's parents, lineal descendants of the decedent's spouse, or the spouses of any such lineal descendants.

(Footnote Continued)

deciding whether or not to make the election, but in general such factors will not outweigh the estate tax savings realized from the alternate valuation election if it is available.

[20] IRC § 2032A.

[21] Reg. § 20.2031-1(b).

[22] *See* Reg. § 20.2032A-3(a).

[23] IRC § 2032A.

[24] IRC § 2032A(b). Section 2032A is also discussed in Chapter 11.

[25] IRC § 2032A(b).

If the requirements are met, the personal representative may value the qualifying property at its actual use value, but the decrease from fair market value as a result of this provision cannot exceed $1,230,000 in 2022.[26]

EXAMPLE *14-20*

Decedent D died in 2022. D's gross estate consisted of farm property valued at $3,800,000 as a farm but $4,500,000 if sold to a developer to build ten houses on the property. The associated farm buildings and equipment had a value of $250,000. D's only other asset was a securities account valued at $8,000,000. D has run the farm operations for the past ten years. D's son S plans to operate the farm for the next ten years. The personal representative of D's estate may elect special use valuation and value the farm at $3,800,000 on the estate tax return.

To elect special use valuation, the personal representative must file Schedule A-1 on the decedent's estate tax return, which includes a written agreement signed by each person who has an interest in the subject property consenting to the special-use valuation rules.[27] Once made, the election is irrevocable. If a qualified heir disposes of the property within ten years or fails to operate the property for its qualified use, certain recapture provisions apply that require the repayment of some or all of the estate tax saved.[28]

[B] QTIP Election

Most direct transfers to a spouse automatically qualify for the marital deduction on the decedent's estate tax return.[29] Such property will be subject to estate tax in the surviving spouse's estate unless it is consumed by the surviving spouse during her life. However, only certain transfers to a spouse in trust qualify for the marital deduction. If the surviving spouse has been given an interest in a Qualified Terminable Interest Property (QTIP) trust, then this interest will qualify for the marital deduction in the decedent spouse's estate (and be subject to estate tax in the surviving spouse's estate) only to the extent that an election is made on the decedent spouse's estate tax return to have the interest qualify for the marital deduction.[30] The use of a QTIP trust in an estate plan rather than a direct transfer to a spouse provides a unique post-mortem planning opportunity because the personal representative may

---

[26] IRC § 2032A(a)(2). An inflation amount will increase the $1,190,000 figure to take into account future cost of living increases. IRC § 2032A(a)(3).

[27] IRC § 2032A(d).

[28] IRC § 2032A(c).

[29] IRC § 2056(a). Special rules apply if the spouse is not a citizen of the United States. IRC § 2056(d). *See* Chapter 6 for a more detailed discussion regarding estate planning for a surviving spouse.

[30] IRC § 2056(b)(7); Reg. § 20.2056(b)-7. QTIP trusts are discussed in greater detail in Chapter 6.

affirmatively elect how much of the property in the QTIP trust receives a marital deduction, and how much property will not receive the marital deduction and will instead be subject to estate tax in the decedent's estate.

A QTIP trust is a trust in which a surviving spouse is given an interest for his or her lifetime. The interest terminates at the surviving spouse's death, at which time the property passes to a third party pursuant to the estate plan of the first spouse to die.[31] To obtain a marital deduction for part or all of the property in a QTIP trust, the trust must meet the following requirements:[32]

    1. The surviving spouse must receive the income from the trust property;

    2. No person may have the power to appoint the property to anyone other than the surviving spouse during the spouse's life; and

    3. The personal representative must make a QTIP election on the estate tax return of the first spouse to die.

The election must be made by the personal representative of the decedent's estate on the last estate tax return filed on or before the due date of the return (including extensions) or, if a timely return is not filed, the first estate tax return filed after the due date.[33] The election, once made, is irrevocable; however, an election may be revoked or modified on a subsequent estate tax return filed on or before the due date of the return (including extensions actually granted).[34] The regulations also provide detailed guidance for making a protective election which, once made, cannot be revoked.[35]

For the decedent's federal estate tax return, if less than the entire value of the QTIP property is entered on Schedule M, the personal representative is considered to have made an election only as to a fraction of the QTIP property; the numerator of the fraction is equal to the amount of the QTIP property deducted on Schedule M and the denominator is equal to the total value of the QTIP property.[36]

An interest that otherwise qualifies for a QTIP election will not fail to qualify for the election if the interest is contingent on the personal representative making the QTIP election, and the portion of the property which is not subject to the election passes to or for the benefit of persons other than the surviving spouse (a so-called "Clayton QTIP").[37] For example, if a decedent's revocable trust established a marital trust (with provisions qualifying the marital trust for QTIP treatment) and also a credit shelter or bypass trust, and then provided that the marital trust will receive all property for which the personal representative makes the QTIP election and the

---

[31] IRC § 2056(b)(1). Although the original decedent controls the disposition of the QTIP trust after the spouse's death, the decedent may give the spouse the right to control the ultimate distribution of the property by granting the spouse a testamentary power of appointment.

[32] IRC § 2056(b)(7); Reg. § 20.2056(b)-7. The requirements for a QTIP trust are discussed in Chapter 6. Form 1 contains a sample QTIP trust.

[33] Reg. § 20.2056-b(7)(4)(i).

[34] Reg. § 20.2056-b(7)(4)(ii).

[35] Reg. § 20.2056-(b)(7)(c).

[36] Instructions for Form 706 (Rev. September 2021), pp. 36-37.

[37] Reg. § 20.2056(b)-7(d)(3)(i).

balance of the trust property will pass to the credit shelter or bypass trust, the property passing to the marital trust would qualify for QTIP treatment.[38]

Property with a QTIP election will not be subject to estate tax in the decedent's estate because of the marital deduction, but any property not consumed by the surviving spouse will, by statute, be taxed in the spouse's estate, regardless of the ultimate disposition of the property.[39] Depending on the circumstances, the personal representative may choose to make a full QTIP election, a partial QTIP election, or no QTIP election for terminable interest property passing to the surviving spouse.

If the personal representative makes a QTIP election for all of the property in the QTIP trust (a full QTIP election), none of the property will be subject to estate tax in the estate of the first spouse to die due to the marital deduction, but all remaining property will be subject to estate tax in the surviving spouse's estate. Before making a full QTIP election, the personal representative should confirm that the decedent has a sufficient amount of taxable property to use at least his full applicable exclusion amount. Otherwise, to the extent that the decedent's applicable exclusion amount is not used in the decedent's estate, its benefit will be entirely lost unless the personal representative of the decedent's estate elects to transfer the decedent's unused applicable exclusion amount to the decedent's surviving spouse.[40]

In the absence of such an election, if the surviving spouse then dies with a taxable estate, the personal representative of the first decedent's estate could have reduced or eliminated the tax at the surviving spouse's death by having more property included in the taxable estate of the first spouse to die.

The personal representative also has the option to select only a specific amount for QTIP treatment, such as 50 percent of the property, which would result in a partial QTIP election.[41] Under this scenario, the assets for which a QTIP election has been made would be taxed at the death of the second spouse, and all other assets would be taxed in the estate of the first spouse to die. A third alternative is for a personal representative to choose not to elect QTIP treatment for any property that would otherwise qualify for such treatment. Not electing QTIP treatment will cause all assets in the QTIP trust to be subject to estate tax in the estate of the first spouse to die.

At least two reasons could exist for a personal representative to make either a partial QTIP election or no QTIP election. First, partial QTIP treatment or no QTIP treatment may make optimal use of the first decedent's applicable exclusion amount in that it can provide for full use of the applicable credit amount of the first spouse to die, while still deferring all estate tax until the death of the surviving spouse.

---

[38] Reg. § 20.2056(b)-7(h), Example (6). Form 2 contains a sample trust with a Clayton QTIP.

[39] IRC § § 2056(b)(7)(A), 2044.

[40] This election is discussed in § 14.05[E], *infra*.

[41] Reg. § 20.2056(b)-7(b)(2). Any partial election must be made with respect to a fractional or percentage share of the property. Reg. § 20.2056-7(b)(2)(i).

EXAMPLE *14-21*

Husband H who died in 2009 had a $500,000 house owned jointly with his wife W, $100,000 of tangible personal property that passes to W under the will, and $5,000,000 of other assets that pass to a QTIP marital trust for W's benefit. H's personal representative may choose to elect QTIP treatment for only the amount of trust property that exceeds the applicable exclusion amount for the year of the decedent's death ($3,500,000 in 2009). Thus, of the $5,000,000 trust, $1,500,000 would have a QTIP election and would ultimately be included in W's estate, and $3,500,000 would be included in H's estate but, due to H's applicable credit amount, it would not be subject to estate tax in either H's or W's estate. Upon W's death, $1,500,000 of the trust assets, the $500,000 house, and the $100,000 of tangible personal property will be taxed in W's estate. If W died later in 2009 with no other assets, having only $2,100,000 of assets taxed in W's estate rather than $5,600,000 if a full QTIP election had originally been made will save H and W, as a couple, $945,000 of federal estate tax. Note that the amount saved would differ in a year (such as 2022) where the personal representative had the opportunity to make a portability election with respect to any unused portion of the decedent's applicable exclusion amount, but this type of planning remains important because the GST exemption is not portable (*see* § 14.05[C][4], *infra*).

A second reason not to make a full QTIP election is to equalize the amount taxed in each of the two spouses' estates. If there is a graduated rate structure for the estate tax, a married couple will pay less estate tax if each spouse's estate bears the tax on approximately half of the couple's combined assets. Equalizing the estates will allow the use of all lower tax brackets when the first spouse dies, rather than having the same dollars taxed at a higher marginal rate when the second spouse dies.[42] One drawback is that the surviving spouse will lose the use during his or her life of any estate tax payments made earlier than necessary, and any appreciation on these amounts. The reduction in the top estate tax rate to a flat 40 percent for years after 2012 reduced the desirability of this technique.

[C] GST Election

[1] In General

A generation-skipping transfer (GST) is a transfer to a beneficiary at least two generations younger than the transferor.[43] GSTs may occur through an outright transfer or under a trust or similar arrangement. The tax on GSTs exists as a backstop

---

[42] Under current law, the maximum tax rate in 2013 and thereafter is a flat 40 percent, but in certain prior years a graduated rate structure has been in effect.

[43] IRC §§ 2611, 2612, 2613. GST tax planning is discussed in greater detail in Chapter 9.

to the gift and estate tax; it prevents taxpayers from avoiding the estate tax upon the death of their children by passing assets directly to their grandchildren. Each person is entitled to a GST exemption in an amount equal to the basic exclusion amount.[44] The GST exemption is $12,060,000 ($10,000,000 indexed for inflation, for estates of decedents dying in 2018 through 2025) in 2022.[45] If a decedent has not allocated his or her GST exemption during life, the personal representative may allocate the decedent's GST exemption on the decedent's estate tax return.

If the decedent's personal representative does not allocate the decedent's remaining GST exemption, the Internal Revenue Service provides rules for automatic allocation.[46] In most cases, it is preferable for the taxpayer or his or her personal representative to make the allocation to ensure that the final allocation produces the best possible tax and administrative result, rather than to rely on the default allocation rules. Allocating the exemption to certain transfers may save tax dollars, and dividing a trust into sub-trusts that are either wholly GST exempt or wholly GST nonexempt is often advantageous for administrative convenience and potential future tax savings.

[2] Default Allocation Rules

The default allocation rules allocate generation-skipping transfer exemption based on the type of GST transfer. As discussed in Chapter 9, three types of GSTs exist: taxable distributions, taxable terminations, and direct skips.[47] All three types of transfers require an understanding of the concept of a "skip person," which is defined as an individual assigned to a generation more than one generation below the transferor (e.g., a grandchild or great-grandchild), or a trust if all interests in the trust are held by skip persons (e.g., a trust for grandchildren).[48] A direct skip is an outright transfer to a skip-person (either an individual or a trust) that is subject to federal estate or gift tax.[49] A taxable termination occurs upon the termination of an interest in property held in a trust unless immediately after such termination a non-skip person has an interest in such property or at no time after such termination may a distribution be made from such a trust to a skip person.[50] For example, a trust for a child continuing after the child's death for grandchildren is a taxable termination at the child's death because there is then no non-skip person with an interest in the trust. Finally, a taxable distribution is a distribution of income or principal from a

---

[44] IRC § 2631(c).

[45] IRC § 2010(c)(3); Rev. Proc. 2021-45, 2021-48 I.R.B. 764; IRC § 2631(a), (c).

[46] IRC § 2632(b), (c), (e).

[47] During an individual's lifetime, an automatic allocation of GST exemption may also occur for an indirect skip, which is defined as a transfer of property subject to gift tax and made to certain types of trusts that could have a generation-skipping transfer with respect to the transferor. IRC § 2632(c). An individual may elect out of such an allocation on a timely filed gift tax return. IRC § 2632(c)(5).

[48] IRC § 2613.

[49] Reg. § 26.2612-1(a).

[50] Reg. § 26.2612-1(b).

trust to a skip person that does not qualify as a taxable termination or a direct skip.[51] At a transferor's death the rules automatically allocate any of the decedent's remaining GST exemption not otherwise allocated by the decedent's personal representative first to property subject to a direct skip, and second, *pro rata* to trusts with respect to which such individual was the transferor and from which a taxable distribution or a taxable termination might occur at or after such individual's death.[52]

EXAMPLE 14-22

Decedent D's revocable trust creates trusts for each of D's two children, C1 and C2. C1's trust is distributable outright to C1 once C1 reaches the age of 50, or it passes to C1's descendants if C1 dies before age 50. C2's trust terminates at C2's death and the principal is distributable to C2's children. D did not use any GST exemption during D's lifetime. At D's death in 2022, each trust is valued at $12,060,000. At the time of D's death, C1 is 49 years old and C2 is still living and has children.

Under the automatic allocation rules, D's GST exemption, $12,060,000 for decedents dying in 2022, will be applied *pro rata* between the two trusts (each $12,060,000 trust will have $6,030,000 of GST exemption). However, the personal representative may want to alter this allocation. It is unlikely that a GST tax will be imposed on C1's trust because the property will pass outright to a child within one year. Therefore, the $6,030,000 of GST exemption allocated to C1's trust will not provide any tax benefit. Under the automatic allocation rules, the distributions to C2's children (D's grandchildren) will be only partially protected from GST tax. The personal representative may instead want to allocate all $12,060,000 of exemption to C2's trust, fully protecting the distributions to C2's children, who are skip persons.

[3] Avoiding Fractional Inclusion Ratios

Situations often arise in which the amount of property potentially subject to a generation-skipping tax exceeds a decedent's remaining GST exemption. Under the automatic allocation rules, insufficient GST exemption for the property in question results in a fractional inclusion ratio; each distribution to a skip person from a trust with a fractional inclusion ratio will be subject to GST tax, but at a reduced rate.[53] When an insufficient amount of GST exemption exists, personal representatives and trustees often divide the trust into two sub-trusts (if authorized by the instrument), in

---

[51] Reg. § 26.2612-1(c)(1).

[52] IRC § 2632(e)(1).

[53] The applicable rate of tax for a GST is the maximum federal estate tax rate (40 percent in 2022) multiplied by the inclusion ratio relating to the transfer. IRC § 2641.

such proportions that one sub-trust is fully subject to GST tax and one sub-trust is not subject to GST tax.

EXAMPLE 14-23

A sub-trust for children and grandchildren within a revocable trust created by a decedent who died in 2022 will be funded with $900,000 after the decedent's estate is closed. The decedent has $600,000 of GST exemption remaining at her death. Assuming that authority for such a division exists, the sub-trust may be divided into two parts, one part with $600,000 that will be fully exempt from GST tax, and one part with $300,000 that will not be exempt from GST tax.

At least two benefits exist to having no fractional inclusion ratios. First, trusts often include both children and grandchildren as beneficiaries. If the trust remains as one trust with a fractional inclusion ratio, distributions to grandchildren will require the payment of some GST tax, and distributions to children will waste the benefit of any GST exemption applied. The tax efficiency improves if the trustees distribute property to children from a nonexempt portion, and make distributions to grandchildren from an exempt portion. Second, the trustees may have the opportunity to refine their investment strategies. Appreciating, long-term investments in the exempt sub-trust may pass the maximum amount of property to the grandchildren free of tax, while more conservative, income-producing assets with less growth potential can provide additional security for older children.

[4] Reverse QTIP Election

The reverse QTIP election is an important element of GST tax planning because it can avoid wasting a decedent's remaining GST exemption.[54] Under the common "optimum" or "reduce to zero" marital deduction clause, a portion of the decedent's estate equal to the decedent's applicable exclusion amount is allocated to the *credit shelter* or *bypass trust* and the balance of the decedent's estate is allocated to a QTIP trust, in order to take advantage of the decedent's applicable exclusion amount and reduce the federal estate tax to zero. The QTIP trust will be includable in the surviving spouse's gross estate for estate tax purposes and the surviving spouse will therefore be treated as the transferor for GST tax purposes.[55] If the decedent's available GST exemption exceeds the value of the decedent's bypass trust, a portion of the decedent's available GST exemption will not be used. If a personal representative makes a reverse QTIP election in this situation, the decedent will be treated as the transferor of the QTIP trust for GST tax purposes, and the decedent's GST

---

[54] IRC § 2652(a)(3).
[55] IRC § § 2044, 2056(b)(7)(A), 2652(a)(1).

exemption can be allocated to the property in the QTIP trust.[56] The election is made on the return on which the QTIP election is made.[57] A partial reverse QTIP election is not permitted; the election must be made with respect to all of the property in the QTIP trust.[58] Therefore, if the personal representative would like to make a reverse QTIP election, the property that will be subject to the reverse QTIP election must be held in a separate trust prior to the election. The IRS will recognize the severance of a QTIP trust into two QTIP trusts, one of which will be subject to the election and the other of which will not be subject to the election.[59] Thus, the decedent's revocable trust should expressly authorize the trustees to sever the QTIP trust into two separate trusts to allow the reverse QTIP election.

EXAMPLE 14-24

> Husband H died in 2022, having made a total of $2,000,000 in lifetime taxable gifts to which no GST exemption was allocated and having a taxable estate of $15,000,000. Under H's estate plan, (1) property equal in value to H's remaining $10,060,000 applicable exclusion amount ($12,060,000 basic exclusion amount less $2,000,000 lifetime taxable gifts) is allocated to a Family Trust for the benefit of H's issue and W, and $10,060,000 of H's $12,060,000 GST exemption is allocated to the Family Trust, and (2) the balance of the property is held in a QTIP Trust for wife W, with the ability to divide the QTIP Trust into sub-trusts for tax purposes. If no reverse QTIP election is made, the remaining $2,000,000 of H's GST exemption will never be used. Assuming that at least some of the property will continue in trust for family members after W's death, a more tax-efficient plan is to segregate $2,000,000 of the QTIP Trust assets into a separate sub-trust, and make a reverse QTIP election with respect to this sub-trust. H's remaining $2,000,000 GST exemption will be applied to the property, and the assets will be exempt from GST tax for future generations.

[D] Tax Payment Elections for Owners of Closely Held Businesses

[1] In General

As previously discussed, estate taxes are generally due nine months after the date of the decedent's death. If the estate consists largely of illiquid assets (such as real estate used in a business), it may be difficult for the personal representative to

---

[56] IRC § 2652(a)(3).

[57] Reg. § 26.2652-2(b).

[58] Reg. § 26.2652-2(a).

[59] Reg. §§ 26.2652-2(a), 26.2654-1(b)(1).

generate sufficient cash to pay the estate taxes. Two provisions provide some tax relief to an estate if a closely held business constitutes a significant part of the estate.[60] First, certain estates may defer the payment of estate tax on the closely held business for up to five years, and then pay the tax over the next nine years.[61] Second, redemptions of stock to pay death taxes may receive more favorable capital gain treatment rather than having the proceeds taxed as ordinary income.[62]

[2] Election to Defer Payment of Estate Tax

If over 35 percent of a decedent's adjusted gross estate consists of a closely held business interest, the personal representative may elect to defer the payment of any estate tax that is attributable to the business interest.[63] For the purpose of this election, "adjusted gross estate" means the gross estate reduced only by any estate expenses, debts, taxes, or losses.[64] A closely held business interest exists if the decedent held an interest in a proprietorship, a partnership where the decedent's estate includes 20 percent or more of the capital interest, a corporation where the decedent's estate includes 20 percent or more of the voting stock value, or a partnership or corporation that has 45 or fewer partners or shareholders.[65] Interests equal to or greater than 20 percent in two or more closely held entities can be added together to reach the 35 percent of the adjusted gross estate requirement for this provision.[66]

If the estate qualifies for a deferral of the payment of the estate tax, the personal representative may elect this deferral on the decedent's estate tax return (Form 706).[67] The maximum possible deferral is an initial payment five years after the due date for the tax return, and then nine additional annual installments over the next nine years.[68] The estate must pay interest during the deferral period.[69] The rate of interest on a calculated amount (depending on the year) is only 2 percent, and the rate of interest on the remaining amount is only 45 percent of the otherwise prescribed rate, but the estate will not receive a deduction for any interest paid.[70]

---

[60] Tax planning for closely held businesses is discussed in greater detail in Chapter 11.

[61] IRC § 6166.

[62] IRC § 303.

[63] IRC § 6166(a). Section 6166 is also discussed in Chapter 11.

[64] IRC § 6166(b)(6). Certain passive assets not used in the trade or business may not count toward the 35 percent threshold. IRC § 6166(b)(9).

[65] IRC § 6166(b)(1).

[66] IRC § 6166(c).

[67] IRC § 6166(d).

[68] IRC § 6166(a)(3). The balance will be due immediately if 50 percent or more of the business is sold, exchanged, or distributed. IRC § 6166(g).

[69] IRC § 6166(f).

[70] IRC § § 2053(c)(1)(D), 6601(j).

[3] Redemption of Stock to Pay Estate Tax

If stock of a closely held business exceeds 35 percent of a decedent's estate and the personal representative redeems some of the stock to pay death taxes, the redemption may be treated as a sale of the stock, rather than a dividend, for tax purposes.[71] A partial redemption of closely held stock is often taxed as a dividend that results in a tax to the recipient on the full amount received (without any offset for the stock's basis).[72] This special provision allows a redemption of stock to pay death taxes to be treated as a sale of the stock, allowing an offset of basis. This treatment will frequently produce little taxable gain for the estate (or the beneficiary) because in most instances the basis of the stock will have been increased to fair market value at death, which, absent unusual circumstances, will be close to the redemption value.[73] The redemption amount that receives this favorable treatment cannot exceed the sum of the estate tax due and the estate's allowable funeral and administration expenses.[74]

[E] Election to Transfer Deceased Spousal Unused Exclusion Amount to Surviving Spouse

The personal representative of the estate of a decedent whose date of death occurs in 2011 or thereafter can elect to allow the decedent's surviving spouse to take advantage of any unused portion of the decedent's applicable exclusion amount. This amount is in addition to the surviving spouse's basic exclusion amount (the "portability" election).[75] The portability election allows the surviving spouse to use the decedent's unused applicable exclusion amount against the gift tax as well as the estate tax.[76] However, the portability election does not allow the surviving spouse to use the decedent's unused GST exemption.[77] Furthermore, the portability election is not available to the estate of a nonresident decedent who was not a citizen of the United States at the time of his death, and the timely filing of such a decedent's estate tax return will not constitute the making of a portability election.[78]

---

[71] IRC § 303. As with Section 6166, the stock must exceed 35 percent of the decedent's gross estate reduced by expenses, debts, taxes, and losses. Two or more corporations in which the decedent held a 20 percent or greater interest may also qualify. A person other than a personal representative who acquires the decedent's stock and redeems stock to pay death taxes will similarly be eligible for this favorable tax status. Section 303 is also discussed in Chapter 11.

[72] IRC § § 301, 302.

[73] See IRC § 1014.

[74] IRC § 303(a).

[75] IRC § 2010(c)(2), (4), (5); Reg. § § 20.2010-1 through 20.2010-3 and 25.2505-1 through 25.2505-2.

[76] IRC § 2505(a)(1); Reg. § § 20.2010-3(a), 25.2505-2(a).

[77] The 2010 Act changed the definition of GST exemption under Section 2631(c) by substituting the words "the basic exclusion amount" for the "applicable exclusion amount." This indicates Congress's intention to exclude the portability election for GST purposes.

[78] Reg. § § 20.2010-2(a)(5) and 20.2010-3(e).

EXAMPLE 14-25

Husband H died in 2022, having made a total of $6,000,000 in taxable transfers and having no taxable estate. The personal representative of H's estate files an estate tax return for H's estate and makes the portability election. At the time of H's death, Wife W has made no taxable gifts. Following the portability election, W's applicable exclusion amount is $18,120,000 (her $12,060,000 basic exclusion amount plus the $6,060,000 applicable exclusion amount she received from H as a result of the portability election). W may use her $18,120,000 applicable exclusion amount for lifetime gifts or for transfers at death.

More specifically, under current law, a person's applicable exclusion amount is defined as the sum of (1) the basic exclusion amount, and (2) in the case of a surviving spouse, the deceased spousal unused exclusion amount (DSUE Amount).[79] If a surviving spouse is predeceased by more than one spouse, the DSUE Amount that is available for use by the surviving spouse is limited to the lesser of the basic exclusion amount in effect at the death of the last such deceased spouse or the unused applicable exclusion amount of the last such deceased spouse.[80] If the last such deceased spouse paid a gift tax on prior gifts, regulations provide that those gifts are excluded from the calculation of the DSUE Amount.[81]

EXAMPLE 14-26

In 2002, having made no prior taxable gifts, Husband, H1 makes a $2,000,000 taxable gift and reports the gift on a timely-filed gift tax return. Since the amount of H1's gift is greater than the applicable exclusion amount for 2002 ($1,000,000), H1 owes gift tax on $1,000,000 (the amount of H1's gift in excess of the applicable exclusion amount for 2002), and H1 pays the gift tax due on the gift. H1 dies in 2022, survived by Wife W, with a $1,000,000 taxable estate. H1 and W are U.S. citizens and neither was previously married. The personal representative of H1's estate timely files an estate tax return for H1's estate and makes the portability election, thereby allowing W to benefit from H1's DSUE Amount. The personal

---

[79] IRC § 2010(c)(2).

[80] IRC § 2010(c)(4); Staff of Joint Committee on Taxation, 111th Cong., 2d Sess., "Technical Explanation of the Revenue Provisions Contained in the 'Tax Relief, Unemployment Insurance Reauthorization, and Job Creation Act of 2010' Scheduled for Consideration by the United States Senate," p. 52 (Dec. 10, 2010) (Comm. Print 2010) (the "2010 Technical Explanation"). Reg. § 20.2010-2(c)(1)(i) confirms that the term "basic exclusion amount" referred to in Section 2010(c)(4)(A) means the basic exclusion amount in effect in the year of the death of the decedent whose DSUE Amount is being computed. Reg. § 20.2010-1(d)(5) explains that the term "last such deceased spouse" referred to in Section 2010(c)(4)(B)(i) means the most recently deceased individual who, at that individual's death after December 31, 2010, was married to the surviving spouse.

[81] Reg. § 20.2010-2(c)(2).

representative of H1's estate computes H1's DSUE Amount to be $10,060,000 (the lesser of the $12,060,000 basic exclusion amount in 2022, or the excess of H1's $12,060,000 basic exclusion amount over the sum of H1's $1,000,000 taxable estate and H1's $1,000,000 adjusted taxable gift). H1's adjusted taxable gift of $2,000,000 was reduced for purposes of this computation by $1,000,000, the amount of H1's taxable gift on which gift taxes were paid.

The last deceased spouse limitation applies whether or not the last deceased spouse has any unused applicable exclusion amount, and whether or not the last deceased spouse's estate makes a timely election.[82] Therefore, if the surviving spouse's last deceased spouse had no DSUE Amount, or if the personal representative of such last deceased spouse's estate did not make a portability election, the surviving spouse's estate has no DSUE Amount to be included in determining the surviving spouse's applicable exclusion amount, even if the surviving spouse previously had a DSUE Amount available from a prior marriage.[83] The regulations clarify that if the surviving spouse remarries, the DSUE Amount from the surviving spouse's deceased spouse will still be available to the surviving spouse as long as the surviving spouse's new spouse is still living.[84]

EXAMPLE *14-27*

Husband, H1 died in 2022, having made a total of $6,000,000 in taxable transfers and having no taxable estate. The personal representative of H1's estate files an estate tax return for H1's estate and makes the portability election. At the time of H1's death, Wife W has made no taxable gifts. W subsequently marries Husband, H2. H2 also predeceases W in 2022, having made a total of $8,000,000 in taxable transfers and having no taxable estate. The personal representative of H2's estate files an estate tax return for H2's estate and makes the portability election. Although the combined unused applicable exclusion amount of H1 and H2 is $10,120,000 ($6,060,000 for H1 and $4,060,000 for H2), only H2's $4,060,00 applicable exclusion amount is transferrable to W, because the DSUE Amount is limited to the lesser of the basic exclusion amount in effect in the year of the deceased spouse's death ($12,060,000) or the unused applicable exclusion amount of the last deceased spouse of W (H2's $4,060,000 unused applicable exclusion amount). Following the portability election on the estate tax return for H2's estate, W's applicable exclusion amount is $16,120,000 (her $12,060,000 basic exclusion amount plus the $4,060,000 DSUE Amount she received from H2 as a result of the

---

[82] IRC § 2010(c)(4)(B)(i); Reg. § § 20.2010-3(a)(2), 25.2505-2(a)(2).

[83] *Id.*

[84] Reg. § § 20.2010-3(a)(3), 25.2505-2(a)(3).

portability election). W may use her new applicable exclusion amount for lifetime gifts or for transfers at death.

The regulations contain an ordering rule, which provides that if a surviving spouse makes a taxable gift with a DSUE Amount from the surviving spouse's last deceased spouse at the time of the gift, the surviving spouse will be considered to apply such DSUE Amount to the taxable gift before the surviving spouse's own basic exclusion amount.[85]

The election must be made by the personal representative of the decedent's estate on a timely filed estate tax return (including extensions) that computes the decedent's unused applicable exclusion amount.[86] The due date of an estate tax return required to elect portability is nine months after the decedent's date of death or the last day of the period covered by an extension (if an extension of time for filing has been obtained).[87] The portability election is deemed to be made upon the timely filing of a complete and properly prepared estate tax return.[88] The election is effective as of the decedent's date of death, so a surviving spouse may apply the DSUE Amount received from the surviving spouse's last deceased spouse to any transfer occurring after the decedent's death.[89]

If a personal representative making the portability election is not required to file an estate tax return for the estate of a decedent (because the total value of the decedent's estate and the decedent's adjusted taxable gifts does not exceed the basic exclusion amount), the personal representative is not required to report the value of most assets that qualify for the marital or charitable deduction.[90] The personal representative needs only to exercise due diligence to estimate the value of the

---

[85] Reg. § 25.2505-2(b). If the surviving spouse had multiple spouses, the surviving spouse made taxable gifts using the DSUE Amount from one or more last deceased spouses, and if any of those last deceased spouses is different from the surviving spouse's last deceased spouse at the time of the surviving spouse's death, then the DSUE Amount which will be included in determining the applicable exclusion amount of the surviving spouse at the surviving spouse's death is equal to the sum of the DSUE Amount of the surviving spouse's last deceased spouse plus the DSUE Amount of each other deceased spouse of the surviving spouse, to the extent that such amount was applied to one or more taxable gifts of the surviving spouse. Reg. § 20.2010-3(b). The regulations provide a similar rule for purposes of calculating the surviving spouse's applicable exclusion amount for gift tax purposes. Reg. § 25.2505-2(c).

[86] IRC § 2010(c)(5)(A); Reg. § 20.2010-2(a)(1) and (b)(1). If there is no appointed personal representative, any person in actual or constructive possession of any property of the decedent (a "non-appointed personal representative") may file the estate tax return on behalf of the decedent and, in so doing, make the portability election. Reg. § 20.2010-2(a)(6)(ii).

[87] Reg. § 20.2010-2(a)(1), (7)(i). If a personal representative is not required to file an estate tax return for the estate of a decedent (because the total value of the decedent's estate and the decedent's adjusted taxable gifts does not exceed the basic exclusion amount) and fails to make the portability election within the requisite time period, the personal representative may apply for relief under Reg. § 301.9100-3 by filing a private letter ruling request. *See* Reg. § 20.2010-2(a)(1) (last sentence).

[88] Reg. § 20.2010-2(a)(2). The final regulations provide that a personal representative who is not required to file an estate tax return for the estate of a decedent may seek relief under Section 9100 for an extension of time to elect portability. Reg. § 20.2010-2(a)(1).

[89] Reg. §§ 20.2010-3(c)(1), 25.2505-2(d)(1).

[90] Reg. § 20.2010-2(a)(7)(ii)(A).

decedent's gross estate (including the value of property that qualifies for the marital or charitable deduction).[91] The instructions for the estate tax return provide ranges of dollar values, and the personal representative must identify on the estate tax return the range within which falls the personal representative's best estimate of the total gross estate.[92] The personal representative must include the personal representative's best estimate, rounded up to the next highest multiple of $250,000.[93] However, the personal representative must still provide detailed values for marital deduction property or charitable deduction property if:

1. The value of such property relates to, affects, or is needed to determine, the value passing from the decedent to another recipient;
2. The value of such property is needed to determine the estate's eligibility for the provisions relating to alternate valuation, special-use valuation for farm-land and certain other real property, or the election to defer payment of estate tax if the estate consists largely of a closely held business interest;
3. Less than the entire value of an interest in property includible in the decedent's gross estate is marital deduction property or charitable deduction property; or
4. A partial disclaimer or partial QTIP election is made with respect to a bequest, devise, or transfer of property includible in the gross estate, part of which is marital deduction property or charitable deduction property.[94]

While there is no procedure to make a protective election to allow the DSUE Amount to be recalculated based upon subsequent events affecting the decedent's estate tax return, the Internal Revenue Service has indicated that it is sufficient if the decedent's estate tax return is properly prepared in a manner that would advise the Service of the uncertainty.[95]

The election, once made, becomes irrevocable once the due date of the estate tax return (including extensions actually granted) has passed.[96] If a personal representative makes a portability election on the decedent's estate tax return, the statute of limitations on the decedent's estate tax return will remain open for the sole purpose of confirming the surviving spouse's DSUE Amount, even though the statute of limitations for assessing estate or gift tax with respect to the predeceased spouse may

---

[91] Reg. § 20.2010-2(a)(7)(ii)(B). This special rule does not apply to assets whose valuation is required for eligibility under Sections 2032 (alternate valuation date), 2032A (special use valuation), 2652(a)(3) (reverse QTIP election), 6166 (election to defer payment of estate tax), or other provision of the Code or Regulations. Instructions for Form 706 (Rev. September 2021), p. 17.

[92] *Id.*

[93] *Id.* Instructions for Form 706 (Rev. September 2021), pp. 17-18.

[94] Reg. § 20.2010-2(a)(7)(ii)(A).

[95] *See* Reg. §§ 20.2010-2(a)(7) and -2(b). Section 2 of the preamble to the regulations provides an example involving an estate tax return where the DSUE Amount was listed as zero, the box "Opting Out of Portability" was not checked, and a protective claim for refund was reported based upon a claim against the estate. Subsequent to the filing of the estate tax return, a payment was made in satisfaction of the claim against the estate, which reduced the estate tax and resulted in unused applicable exclusion amount. The Service stated that the regulations automatically recalculate the DSUE Amount so that no protective portability election is necessary in the example.

[96] Reg. § 20.2010-2(a)(4).

have expired.[97] The Internal Revenue Service may adjust or eliminate the DSUE Amount reported on an estate tax return after the statute of limitations for assessing estate or gift tax with respect to the predeceased spouse has expired, but it can assess additional tax with respect to the deceased spouse's return only if that tax is assessed within the statute of limitations on assessment applicable to the deceased spouse's estate tax return.[98]

If a personal representative does not want portability to apply, the personal representative must either check the box, "Opting Out of Portability," in Section A of Part 6 of the decedent's Form 706 or not file an estate tax return (if the estate is not otherwise required to file).[99]

A notable reason for a personal representative to make a portability election would be if the decedent's estate plan or the decedent's assets do not permit full use of the decedent's applicable exclusion amount. Under such circumstances, making the election would permit full use of the decedent's applicable exclusion amount with little downside.

If, based on the structure of the decedent's estate plan, the personal representative has discretion as to whether to make a portability election, factors that the personal representative should consider when deciding whether to make a portability election include federal and state estate taxes, income taxes and generation-skipping transfer taxes, preservation and management of assets, and protection against creditors.

Portability can provide at least three major advantages. As noted above, if the decedent's estate plan or the decedent's assets do not permit full use of the decedent's applicable exclusion amount, making the election would permit full use of the decedent's applicable exclusion amount with little downside. Second, for married couples with combined assets that are well under $24,120,000 in 2022, assets passing to or for the benefit of the surviving spouse (either outright or in a marital trust) will receive a second step-up in basis on the surviving spouse's death; this additional basis step-up is not available with a bypass or credit shelter trust. Third, if the decedent wants the surviving spouse to receive all of the decedent's assets outright rather than in a trust, the decedent's estate can accomplish this non-tax goal without foregoing the use of the decedent's applicable exclusion amount.

However, if the decedent has sufficient assets in his name to make use of his applicable exclusion amount, there are at least six reasons for a personal representative not to make a portability election. First, unlike using a bypass or credit shelter trust in an estate plan, a portability election will not shelter appreciation in value and accumulated income if the surviving spouse lives for several years after the decedent's death and the combined assets of the decedent and the surviving spouse appreciate to a value in excess of the applicable exclusion amount on the surviving

---

[97] IRC § 2010(c)(5)(B); Reg. §§ 20.2001-2(a), 20.2010-2(d), and 20.2010-3(d). Any revaluations of assets on the decedent's estate tax return can only result in a recalculation of the decedent's unused applicable exclusion amount; they cannot result in any additional assessment of estate taxes because the statute of limitations on assessment will have already closed.

[98] Reg. §§ 20.2001-2(a), 20.2010-2(d), 20.2010-3(d), and 25.2505-2(e).

[99] Reg. § 20.2010-2(a)(3).

spouse's death. Note that this appreciation in value will likely be subject to capital gains tax and the 3.8 percent surtax on net investment income. Second, the portability election does not apply to the decedent's GST exemption; thus, to the extent the decedent does not use his GST exemption, it will be lost. Third, unlike a bypass or credit shelter trust, a portability election will not protect the decedent's assets from creditors of the surviving spouse and the decedent's descendants, or from consumption or diversion by the surviving spouse in the case of a second marriage situation. Fourth, under current law, only three states with state estate taxes currently recognize portability for state estate tax purposes (Delaware, Hawaii, and Maryland); therefore, a decedent who is domiciled in a state with an estate tax (other than Delaware, Hawaii, and Maryland) will need a bypass or credit shelter trust in order to take advantage of the state estate tax exclusion amount (which may be significantly less than the federal applicable exclusion amount). Fifth, in order to make the election, the personal representative must file an estate tax return for the decedent, even if the decedent would not otherwise be required to file a return. If the combined estates of the decedent and the surviving spouse are well below $24,120,000 in 2022 and the decedent's estate contains several hard-to-value assets, filing an estate tax return for the decedent may bring the valuation of the assets to the attention of the IRS. Sixth, the DSUE Amount of a deceased spouse will be lost if the surviving spouse remarries and then survives his or her new spouse.

[F] Conservation Easements

A personal representative may exclude from a decedent's taxable estate a percentage of the value of any land subject to a qualified conservation easement.[100] Conservation easements present a post-mortem estate planning opportunity because the easement may be placed on the property by parties other than the decedent after the date of the decedent's death. A member of the decedent's family, the decedent's personal representative, or a trustee of a trust that holds the land may place the conservation easement on the land, and it will qualify for the deduction as long as the easement has been granted prior to the date that the estate tax return is filed (including extensions) and no income tax charitable deduction is allowed to any person with respect to the grant of the easement.[101] Easements for valid conservation purposes will generally satisfy the requirements under this provision if the decedent or a family member owned the property for at least three years prior to the decedent's death.[102]

The amount excluded from a decedent's gross estate is the lesser of (1) the value of the land subject to the qualified conservation easement multiplied by a calculated percentage; or (2) the maximum exclusion allowed in the year of the decedent's

---

[100] IRC § 2031(c). Conservation easements are also discussed in Chapter 10.
[101] IRC § 2031(c)(8)(C), (c)(9).
[102] IRC § 2031(c)(8)(A)(ii).

death.[103] The maximum possible percentage of the value excluded is 40 percent, but this percentage is reduced by 2 percent for each percentage point by which the value of the qualified conservation easement is less than 30 percent of the value of the subject land prior to the easement.[104] Thus, easements that more significantly reduce the value of the encumbered land receive a larger deduction. The exclusion limitation is $500,000 for decedents dying in 2002 or thereafter.[105] The personal representative must elect to have the exclusion apply on Schedule U of a timely filed estate tax return.[106] If the easement is granted by the personal representative after the date of the decedent's death and before the estate tax return is due, the personal representative may claim a charitable deduction on the estate tax return in addition to the property valuation exclusion associated with the easement.[107]

EXAMPLE 14-28

Decedent D died in 2022. D owned for 15 years prior to her death a parcel of vacant land with a value of $400,000. Within five months of D's death, D's personal representative placed a conservation restriction limiting development on the parcel of land, which reduced the value of the property by 25 percent to $300,000. The personal representative may claim a $100,000 charitable deduction for the easement on the estate tax return. In addition, the net value of the property on the estate tax return will be $310,000, calculated as follows (using Schedule U):

$300,000	Value of land reduced by the charitable deduction
× 30%	40 percent applicable percentage reduced by 10 percent because the easement is only 25 percent of the value of the subject land
$ 90,000	Exclusion
$310,000 =	400,000 (value listed) minus $90,000 (exclusion)

---

[103] IRC § 2031(c)(1). Prior to the application of the percentage limitation, the value of the land is reduced by the amount of any estate tax charitable deduction with respect to such land. *Id.*

[104] IRC § 2031(c)(2). For purposes of determining the applicable percentage, the values of the easement and the land (and the value of any retained development right) as of the date of the contribution of the qualified conservation easement are to be used. *Id.*

[105] IRC § 2031(c)(3).

[106] IRC § 2031(c)(6).

[107] IRC §§ 2031(c)(9), 2055(f). The personal representative may not claim a charitable estate tax deduction for an easement granted after death if a charitable income tax deduction is allowed with respect to the easement. IRC § 2031(c)(9).

§14.06 DISCLAIMERS BY BENEFICIARIES

[A] Reasons to Disclaim

A person entitled to some or all of a decedent's property may not want to accept the property for tax reasons or otherwise. A named beneficiary has the option to refuse (or "disclaim") such property. Unfortunately, if the beneficiary does not follow certain rules when disclaiming the property, the beneficiary may be treated for tax purposes as having accepted the property and then making a taxable gift of the property to the ultimate recipient. The Internal Revenue Code provides a procedure that permits a named beneficiary to disclaim an asset without making a taxable gift. A *qualified disclaimer* is a written refusal by a beneficiary to accept an interest in property that meets certain requirements set forth in the Code.[1] When an individual (the "disclaimant") executes a qualified disclaimer with respect to an interest in property that would otherwise pass to him or her, such interest is treated as never having been transferred to the disclaimant, and the disclaimant has not made a gift to the ultimate recipient for gift tax purposes.[2]

A named beneficiary may execute a disclaimer if he or she does not want to own the property, or to improve the tax result for a particular beneficiary or the family as a whole. One example of a situation in which a beneficiary may use a disclaimer to improve a tax result is when a spouse executes a disclaimer to increase the utilization of a decedent's applicable exclusion amount or GST exemption. With respect to the decedent's applicable exclusion amount, if all property included on a decedent's estate tax return is held in joint name with a spouse, the property will pass directly to the spouse and will receive a full marital deduction. Assuming that the decedent made no taxable lifetime gifts and the personal representative of the decedent's estate did not elect to transfer the decedent's applicable exclusion amount to the surviving spouse through a portability election, the decedent's applicable exclusion amount will never be used. A disclaimer that results in some property passing to persons or entities other than the surviving spouse allows for the use of some or all of the decedent's applicable exclusion amount.

As discussed in §14.07[A][1], *infra*, given the inflation-adjusted applicable exclusion amount and portability, many estates will not be subject to the federal estate tax but will be subject to federal and state income taxes on capital gains when assets are sold. As a result, many estate plans are being drafted to provide significant post-mortem flexibility through the potential use of qualified disclaimers by the surviving spouse. These plans generally leave the assets of the first spouse to die outright to the surviving spouse or in a QTIP trust for the benefit of the surviving spouse and include provisions which state that if the surviving spouse disclaims any portion or all of the assets passing outright to her or to the QTIP trust, the disclaimed assets will pass to a QTIP trust (in the case of a disclaimer of property passing outright to the surviving spouse) or to a bypass or credit shelter trust (in the case of a disclaimer of

---

[1] **§14.06** IRC §2518.
[2] IRC §2518(a); Reg. §25.2518-1(b).

property passing to the QTIP trust). If the surviving spouse disclaims an outright bequest under one of these plans, the personal representative of the decedent's estate would need to decide whether to make a QTIP election for the QTIP trust (as discussed in § 14.05[B], *supra*), a reverse QTIP election (as discussed in § 14.05[C][4], *supra*), and, depending upon the value of the disclaimed property, a portability election (as discussed in § 14.05[E], *supra*).

EXAMPLE *14-29*

Wife W died in 2022. Husband H is the named beneficiary of a $500,000 painting under W's will, and H is the joint owner with W of all other property on W's estate tax return (total value $2,000,000). W's only Child, C, is the contingent beneficiary of the painting. If H does not want to own the painting, H may choose to execute a qualified disclaimer. The painting will then pass directly to C from W's estate without any adverse tax consequences to H or to W's estate (due to W's applicable credit amount). This will decrease the size of H's future estate, and may save estate tax at H's death if H has a taxable estate.

[B] Qualified Disclaimer

[1] Definition of a Qualified Disclaimer

For a person to make a qualified disclaimer of an interest in property, the disclaimer must meet four criteria. It must be:[3]

1. An unqualified and irrevocable written refusal to accept the property;
2. Received by the personal representative within nine months of the later of either the date of the transfer creating the interest or the date on which the disclaimant reaches age 21;
3. The disclaimant must not have accepted the interest in or any benefits from the disclaimed property; and
4. The property disclaimed must pass without any direction from the disclaimant to someone other than the disclaimant (unless the disclaimant is the spouse of the decedent, in which case the disclaimed property can pass to the disclaimant).

[2] Written Refusal to Accept Property

A qualified disclaimer must be in writing. The writing must identify the interest in the property disclaimed. The Treasury Regulations require either the disclaimant

---

[3] IRC § 2518(b).

or the disclaimant's legal representative to sign the disclaimer.[4] Cases and rulings have also allowed a person holding a power of attorney to sign a disclaimer in certain circumstances.[5]

In order to have a qualified disclaimer, the disclaimant must irrevocably and without qualification refuse to accept the ownership of an interest in property. A named beneficiary may disclaim the entire interest in the subject property or only a partial interest in the property.[6] One option for disclaiming a partial interest in the property is to disclaim a specific portion of severable property, such as a disclaimer of 50 shares of stock where the decedent bequeathed 100 shares of stock to the beneficiary.[7] It is also possible to disclaim a specific pecuniary amount if the amount disclaimed and any income attributable to the amount disclaimed is segregated from the portion of the gift or bequest that was not disclaimed, or to disclaim a portion determined by means of a formula.[8]

A disclaimer will not constitute a qualified disclaimer if the disclaimant receives actual consideration for the disclaimer. The Internal Revenue Service may determine that consideration existed if the disclaimant receives property similar to the property disclaimed from a different source.[9] However, a disclaimer is not invalid if the disclaimant merely has an expectation that he or she might ultimately benefit indirectly from the disclaimer.[10]

EXAMPLE 14-30

Husband H died in 2022 leaving a $1,000,000 bequest to his nephew. Wife W is the personal representative of the estate. W promises nephew that if the nephew disclaims the $1,000,000 bequest, she will pay the nephew $1,000,000 from her own bank account. W believes that this will produce a better tax result for W by reducing the estate tax due at H's death. Nephew accepts the offer and disclaims the $1,000,000 bequest. The nephew's disclaimer is not qualified because he received $1,000,000 from W in exchange for his disclaimer.

---

[4] Reg. § 25.2518-2(b)(1).

[5] Estate of Allen v. Comm'r, T.C. Memo 1989-111; Ltr. Rul. 9015017 (Jan. 10, 1990).

[6] Reg. § 25.2518-3(a)(1)(i).

[7] Reg. § 25.2518-3(a)(1)(ii). The beneficiary may similarly disclaim severable interests in a trust. For example, a beneficiary could retain an income interest in a trust and disclaim a remainder interest in the same trust. Reg. § 25.2518-3(d), Example 8.

[8] Reg. § 25.2518-3(c); Reg. § 25.2518-3(d), Example 20. For example, a beneficiary can disclaim a fractional share of the residuary estate, with the numerator of the fraction equal to the smallest amount that will allow the beneficiary's estate to pass free of federal estate tax and the denominator of the fraction equal to the value of the residuary estate. *Id.*

[9] *See* Estate of Monroe v. Comm'r, 124 F.3d 699 (5th Cir. 1997), *rev'g* 104 T.C. 352 (1995). This issue becomes more significant when a named beneficiary who is not in the immediate family of the ultimate recipient executes a disclaimer, which calls into question the motivation for the disclaimer.

[10] *Id.*

[3] Disclaimer Must Be Made Within Nine Months

The disclaimant must deliver the disclaimer to the transferor of the interest or the transferor's legal representative by the date that is nine months after the later of (1) the date on which the transfer creating the interest in the disclaimant is made, or (2) the date on which the disclaimant reaches age 21.[11] Although in the estate context the transfer creating the interest is generally the decedent's death, other dates may apply for property held in trust or by a joint tenancy.

With respect to transfers made by a decedent at death or transfers that become irrevocable at death, the transfer creating the interest occurs on the date of the decedent's death.[12] The named beneficiary must therefore file the disclaimer within nine calendar months of the date of death. Neither the date the decedent's will is probated nor any extensions of time to file the decedent's estate tax return or any other probate or tax deadline associated with the decedent's estate extends the nine-month disclaimer deadline.

For property held by a joint tenancy with right of survivorship, the general rule is that a person must disclaim an interest received in a joint tenancy within nine months of the creation of the joint tenancy. However, a surviving joint tenant may disclaim a deceased joint tenant's share of a joint tenancy that the survivor receives by operation of law as a result of the decedent's death within nine months of the deceased joint tenant's date of death.[13]

EXAMPLE *14-31*

Decedent D died on January 1, 2022. D purchased his primary residence with his wife W as joint tenants with right of survivorship on January 1, 1980. W cannot disclaim her original interest in the residence after D's death, but W may disclaim D's half interest that passes to W by operation of law upon D's death so long as W executes a qualified disclaimer by October 1, 2022.

---

[4] No Acceptance of Benefits

A disclaimer will not be a qualified disclaimer if the disclaimant has expressly or impliedly accepted the property interest or any of its benefits.[14] A beneficiary has accepted the property if an affirmative act consistent with ownership of the interest in

---

[11] IRC § 2518(b)(2). A timely mailing of a disclaimer qualifies as a timely delivery. Reg. § 25.2518-2(c)(2).

[12] Reg. § 25.2518-2(c)(3).

[13] Reg. § 25.2518-2(c)(4). Special rules applicable to certain joint bank accounts, brokerage accounts, and investment accounts prohibit the surviving joint tenant from disclaiming any portion of the joint account originating from consideration furnished by the surviving joint tenant.

[14] IRC § 2518(b)(3).

property has occurred.[15] Acts indicating acceptance include using the property, accepting interest, dividends or rent from the property, or directing others to act with respect to the property.

EXAMPLE *14-32*

> Decedent D bequeaths his car to Child C. D's personal representative transfers the title to the car into C's name. C drives the car for one month, and then decides that she does not want the car. The transfer of the title alone will not prevent C from disclaiming the property. However, C cannot make a qualified disclaimer because C's use of the car for one month constituted an acceptance of the car.

However, the acceptance of one interest in property will not, by itself, constitute an acceptance of other separate interests created by the transferor and held by the disclaimant in the same property.[16]

EXAMPLE *14-33*

> Decedent D died on January 1, 2022. On this date, D's funded revocable trust became irrevocable. The trust provides for quarterly distributions of trust income to Child C, and the distribution of all of the trust principal to C when C attains the age of 40 years. C receives a quarterly income distribution on March 31, 2022. C decides on May 15, 2022, that he wants to disclaim his interest in the trust. C cannot make a qualified disclaimer of his income interest because he accepted an interest payment on March 31, 2022. However, C can still disclaim his interest in the trust principal (that C would otherwise receive at age 40) within nine months of the decedent's death. The trust principal is considered a separate property interest from the trust income.

[5] Property Passes with No Direction from Disclaimant

A disclaimer is not a qualified disclaimer unless the disclaimed interest passes (1) to a person other than the disclaimant, and (2) without any direction on the part of

---

[15] Reg. § 25.2518-2(d)(1). With respect to a disclaimant who received an interest prior to her twenty-first birthday, any actions taken with regard to the interest prior to the disclaimant's twenty-first birthday will not constitute an acceptance by the beneficiary. Reg. § 25.2518-2(d)(3).

[16] Reg. § 25.2518-2(d)(1).

the disclaimant.[17] Thus, the property must pass to the contingent beneficiary named on a beneficiary designation form, listed in the decedent's will or trust, or mandated under the applicable state statute that regulates the disposition of a decedent's property and the disclaimant must not have an interest in the property after the disclaimer.

EXAMPLE *14-34*

Under the will of Decedent D, Child C1 is named to receive a vacation residence. A trust for Child C1 receives the residue of D's estate. C1 disclaims the vacation residence. The will contains no direction regarding the disposition of disclaimed property, so the disclaimed property will pass with the residue of the estate to a trust in which C1 has an interest. The disclaimer is not qualified, unless Cl executes additional disclaimers with respect to C1's interest in the trust.

The only exception to this rule is that if the disclaimant is the surviving spouse, the spouse may not direct the disposition of the property, but he or she may be the ultimate recipient of the property.

EXAMPLE *14-35*

The primary beneficiary listed on Decedent D's IRA beneficiary designation form is D's wife W. The contingent beneficiary is D's revocable trust, of which W is a beneficiary. W may disclaim her interest as primary beneficiary of D's IRA. The IRA benefits will pass to the contingent beneficiary listed on the IRA beneficiary designation form, without any direction from W. The disclaimer will be a qualified disclaimer despite the fact that W as a beneficiary of D's revocable trust may indirectly receive some of the IRA proceeds.

---

[17] IRC § 2518(b)(4). Precatory language in the disclaimer stating who the disclaimant would like to have receive the property will not invalidate the disclaimer if the relevant state law gives the language no legal effect. Reg. § 25.2518-2(e)(4).

§ 14.07 OTHER POST-MORTEM ESTATE PLANNING ISSUES

[A] Basis Planning

[1] Property Acquired from an Estate Not Subject to Federal Estate Tax

The current tax environment with the $10,000,000 applicable exclusion amount for federal estate tax purposes (inflation-adjusted to $12,060,000 in 2022), a 20 percent federal capital gains tax rate for taxpayers in the 37 percent federal income tax bracket, and state capital gains taxes has changed the post-mortem planning land-scape for many decedents' estates, which will no longer be subject to the federal estate tax. While the parties should not lose sight of non-tax goals, an important tax issue for these estates and their beneficiaries will be the taxes on any capital gains when assets are sold. Therefore, post-mortem planning for the estates of these decedents will focus on planning to increase the basis of these assets, such as making a Section 754 election as discussed in § 14.07[C], *infra*.

For estates that are not subject to estate tax, personal representatives should still obtain appraisals for purposes of income tax basis. The basis of property acquired from a decedent is equal to its fair market value as of the decedent's date of death (or as of the alternate valuation date).[1] If a federal estate tax return is filed, the value listed on such return is deemed to be the fair market value.[2] If no estate tax return is required to be filed, the value of the property appraised as of the date of the decedent's death for purposes of state inheritance or transmission taxes will be deemed to be its fair market value and no alternate valuation date will be applicable.[3] However, in the past, the Internal Revenue Service has ruled that an asset's value as determined by the personal representative is only a presumptive value which an estate beneficiary may rebut with clear and convincing evidence to the contrary, unless the beneficiary is otherwise estopped by his previous actions or statements.[4] Therefore, beneficiaries of estates that are not subject to the federal estate tax should consider reviewing appraisals of hard-to-value assets (such as closely held securities), determine whether the appraised values are undervalued and, if so, obtain new appraisals for support in claiming a higher basis upon any subsequent sale of the assets.

In basis planning, beneficiaries of estates that are not subject to estate tax should keep in mind that they may nevertheless be subject to the judicial doctrine of consistency. Under this doctrine, the duty of consistency can bind a beneficiary of an

---

[1] **§ 14.07** IRC § 1014(a). The alternate valuation date is discussed in § 14.05[A], *supra*. Note that under the 2010 Act, the estates of decedents dying in 2010 that elected to have the estate not subject to estate tax will be subject to the modified carryover basis rules under Section 1022.

[2] Reg. § 1.1014-3(a).

[3] *Id.*

[4] Rev. Rul. 54-97, 1954-1 C.B. 113. In Tech. Adv. Mem. 199933001 (Jan. 7, 1999), the Internal Revenue Service ruled that a beneficiary of a decedent's estate who had inherited stock of a closely held corporation was not estopped from claiming a higher basis for income tax purposes than the value used on the decedent's federal estate tax return.

estate to a representation made on an estate tax return if the beneficiary was a fiduciary of the estate.[5]

[2] Property Acquired from an Estate Subject to Federal Estate Tax

For estate tax returns filed after July 31, 2015, the initial basis of property acquired from a decedent whose estate was subject to estate tax cannot exceed the value of the property as finally determined for estate tax purposes or, if the value of the property has not been finally determined, the value reported by the personal representative of the decedent's estate on Form 8971.[6]

This initial basis consistency rule applies to property that is includible in the decedent's gross estate for estate tax purposes and that increases the federal estate tax payable by the estate.[7] It also applies to property the basis of which is determined in whole or in part by reference to the basis of such includible property (for example, as the result of a like kind exchange or involuntary conversion).[8]

Property is not subject to the initial basis consistency rule if:

- It qualifies for an estate tax charitable or marital deduction;[9]
- It is reported on an estate tax return and no estate tax was payable due to allowable credits (such as the applicable exclusion amount) other than a credit for prepayment of the estate tax; or[10]
- It is tangible personal property for which an appraisal is not required.[11]

If, after the application of all allowable credits as discussed above, no estate tax is payable, the decedent's entire gross estate is excluded from the application of the initial basis consistency rule.[12]

---

[5] In Janis v. Comm'r, T.C. Memo 2004-117, *aff'd*, 461 F.3d 1080 (9th Cir. 2006), the court applied a duty of consistency where the sole beneficiaries were also co-personal representatives of an estate with a large art collection. The court held that the beneficiaries had a duty of consistency to use the discounted value that had been used on the estate tax return when calculating their cost of goods sold for income tax purposes.

[6] IRC § 1014(f)(1). Form 8971 is discussed in § 14.02[C][2], *supra*. Proposed Treasury regulations provide detailed rules regarding when the value of property subject to the initial basis consistency rule is finally determined for estate tax purposes. Prop. Reg. § 1.1014-10(c)(1). Such final determination generally occurs once the statute of limitations has expired, once a final agreement has been signed, or once a court's determination is final.

[7] IRC §§ 1014(f)(1), (2); Prop. Reg. § 1.1014-10(b)(1). Proposed Treasury regulations provide special rules for the basis of property that is discovered after the filing of the estate tax return or that is otherwise omitted from the estate tax return. These proposed regulations provide that after-discovered or omitted property has a final value (and therefore initial basis) of zero in two situations: (i) if an estate tax return is filed and no supplemental return reporting the property is filed before the expiration of the statute of limitations on assessment; and (ii) if no estate tax return is filed as required by the Internal Revenue Code. Prop. Reg. § 1.1014-10(c)(3).

[8] Prop. Reg. § 1.1014-10(b)(1).

[9] Prop. Reg. § 1.1014-10(b)(2).

[10] IRC § 1014(f)(2); Prop. Reg. §§ 1.1014-10(b)(1), (b)(3).

[11] Prop. Reg. § 1.1014-10(b)(2).

[12] Prop. Reg. § 1.1014-10(c)(3).

EXAMPLE *14-36*

Decedent D died on July 5, 2022 with a gross estate of $28,000,000 which included $30,000 of tangible personal property for which an appraisal was not required. The estate had an allowable $1,900,000 charitable deduction, an allowable $10,600,000 marital deduction for property passing to D's Wife W, and $500,000 allowable miscellaneous estate tax deductions. The only credit for which D's estate was eligible was the applicable credit amount. Because D's taxable estate is greater than the applicable exclusion amount of $12,060,000, all of the property in D's gross estate is subject to the initial basis consistency rule except for the $1,900,000 of property passing to charity, the $10,600,000 of property passing to W, and the $30,000 of tangible personal property for which an appraisal was not required.

The initial basis consistency rule applies whenever a beneficiary who receives property subject to the rule reports a taxable event with respect to the property (such as depreciation or amortization) and continues to apply until the property is sold, exchanged, or otherwise disposed of in one or more transactions that result in the recognition of gain or loss for federal income tax purposes, regardless of whether the owner on the date of the sale, exchange, or other disposition is the same taxpayer who acquired the property from the decedent or as a result of the decedent's death.[13] A beneficiary's initial basis in property received from a decedent's estate may be subsequently adjusted due to the operation of other provisions of the Internal Revenue Code without violating the initial basis consistency rule.[14] Such adjustments could include, for example, gain recognized by the decedent's estate upon distribution of the property as discussed in § 14.04[C], *supra*, post-death capital improvements and depreciation, and post-death adjustments to the basis of an interest in a partnership as discussed in § 14.07[D], *infra*.[15]

[B] Income and Deductions in Respect of a Decedent

[1] Income in Respect of a Decedent

In general, property received by a beneficiary from a decedent is exempt from income tax.[16] One exception to this rule is income owed to the decedent on the date of death, on which the decedent would have paid an income tax had the decedent received the income during his or her life. The Code refers to this category of property as "income in respect of a decedent" (IRD).[17] Examples of IRD include

---

[13] Prop. Reg. § 1.1014-10(a)(1).

[14] Prop. Reg. § 1.1014-10(a)(2).

[15] *Id.*

[16] IRC § 102(a).

[17] IRC § 691(a).

certain retirement plan benefits, accrued interest on Series E savings bonds, salary payments not received prior to death, and other accounts receivable. The recipient of an item of IRD must include any income attributable to the item of IRD on his or her income tax return in the year that the income is received.[18] The income from an item of IRD has the same character for income tax purposes that it would have had if it had been received by the decedent.[19] The recipient will receive a deduction for any federal estate tax paid that is attributable to the property so that the property is not subject to a full estate tax and a full income tax.[20] However, this deduction does not cover any estate or inheritance taxes paid to a state.

EXAMPLE 14-37

Decedent D died before receiving all of the benefits from his retirement plan. Some estate tax was due at D's death. D's child C is the named beneficiary of the retirement plan. Based on the method in which funds were contributed to the retirement plan, the distributions of income from the plan after D's death will constitute an item of IRD. C must pay income tax on any income that she receives from the retirement plan. However, she is entitled to a deduction for the amount of federal estate tax that is attributable to the distribution.

Depending on the estate plan, the personal representative may or may not have control over the disposition of an item of IRD or the timing of the distribution from the estate. If the personal representative has any discretion, the personal representative should consider that: (1) fully tax-exempt charitable organizations do not pay income tax upon the receipt of IRD; (2) the beneficiary who receives the IRD will receive the benefit of the IRD deduction for the estate tax paid, regardless of which beneficiaries bore the actual burden of the estate tax; and (3) the recipient of an item of IRD may have a preference regarding the tax year in which the recipient receives the item of IRD, with its additional taxable income.

[2] Deductions in Respect of a Decedent

Section 691 allows a decedent's estate and, in some circumstances, a decedent's successors in interest, to take certain deductions and credits that the decedent would have been entitled to take had the decedent survived.[21] These deductions are referred to as "deductions in respect of a decedent" (DRD). There are five classes of deduc-

---

[18] Reg. § 1.691(a)-2.

[19] Reg. § 1.691(a)-3(a).

[20] IRC § 691(c); Reg. § 1.691(c)-1. The deduction is available even if the estate tax has not yet been paid.

[21] IRC § 691(b).

tions and one class of credits that can be treated as DRD: (1) Section 162 deduction for trade or business expenses; (2) Section 163 deduction for interest; (3) Section 164 deduction for taxes; (4) Section 212 deduction for expenses for the production of income; (5) Section 611 deduction for depletion; and (6) Section 27 foreign tax credit.[22] A DRD is deductible only in the taxable year when paid.[23] A DRD with respect to expenses, interest, and taxes is limited to those items for which the decedent was liable.[24] A DRD is claimed by the decedent's estate, or if the decedent's estate is not liable to pay the obligation to which the DRD relates, the DRD may be claimed by the person who acquires, subject to that obligation, an interest in the decedent's property from the decedent by reason of the decedent's death or by bequest, devise, or inheritance.[25]

EXAMPLE *14-38*

Beneficiary B receives a right to IRD (by reason of the death of Decedent D), which is subject to an income tax imposed by a foreign country during D's life and which must be satisfied out of the item of IRD. B is entitled to claim the Section 27 foreign tax credit when B pays the tax.

The prohibition of double deductions under Section 642(g) (discussed in § 14.04[D], *supra*) does not apply to DRD.[26] Items of DRD, when paid, are properly deductible on both the estate's federal income tax return and the federal estate tax return.[27]

EXAMPLE *14-39*

During his life, Decedent D incurred a liability for $50,000 in business expenses. The personal representative of D's estate pays these business expenses after D's death. D's estate may claim a DRD for $50,000 on the estate's federal income tax return and also claim a $50,000 deduction on the federal estate tax return as a claim against the estate paid during the administration of the estate.

---

[22] *Id.*

[23] IRC § 691(b)(1).

[24] Reg. § 1.691(b)-1(a).

[25] IRC § 691(b)(1)(B).

[26] IRC § 642(g), last sentence.

[27] Reg. § 1.642(g)-2.

[C] Retirement Benefits

When a decedent dies with retirement plan assets, the personal representative should ascertain the types of retirement plans, the beneficiaries of the plans, and any required distribution amounts and payment dates.[28] The required distribution amounts and the applicable dates for qualified plans depend on: (1) the beneficiary named; (2) whether the decedent died before or after he or she began receiving benefits from the plans; and (3) what elections and distributions the decedent made during his or her lifetime with respect to the plan.[29] Penalties exist if the minimum required distributions from these accounts are not made. The personal representative should determine soon after the decedent's death whether a disclaimer of the retirement benefits would be beneficial, since this option may be foreclosed if the beneficiary accepts distributions from a given retirement plan.

When the beneficiary of a retirement plan is a spouse, the spouse often has a choice either to receive benefits from the existing account or to roll over the full amount into a new Individual Retirement Account (IRA) where the spouse is named as the owner.[30] In most cases the spouse will want to roll over the retirement plan into a new IRA, because the spouse will then have the opportunity to name new beneficiaries, which can extend the payout period. In addition, if the spouse has not yet attained the age of 72 ($70^1/_2$ if the spouse reached $70^1/_2$ before January 1, 2020), the spouse may defer all distributions until after he or she reaches such age.[31]

[D] Partnership Interests

At the time of a decedent's death, the decedent may own an interest in a partnership. Under rules enacted in 1997, the death of a partner terminates the tax year of the partnership with respect to the deceased partner.[32] Thus, the income and deductions attributable to the period running from the beginning of the partnership's tax year through and including the date of the decedent's death are included on the decedent's final individual income tax return. The income and deductions attributable to the period from the day after the decedent's death to the end of the partnership's tax year are reported on the tax return of the estate or the beneficiary succeeding to the partnership interest.

One significant partnership election that could benefit the estate of a deceased partner is an election that effectively adjusts the basis of a deceased partner's interest in the underlying partnership assets to match the valuation of the partnership interest

---

[28] Planning with retirement benefits is discussed in greater detail in Chapter 13.

[29] *See* IRC § 401(a)(9); Reg. § 1.401(a)(9)-1.

[30] IRC § 402(c)(9); Reg. § 1.402(c)-2, A-12.

[31] IRC § 401(a)(9). In certain instances, the required beginning date may be even later than age 72.

[32] IRC § 706(c)(2)(A). Issues involving partnership interests are discussed in greater detail in Chapter 11.

reported on the estate tax return.[33] If the basis in the underlying assets is increased, the estate's taxable gain on the sale of an appreciated partnership asset will decrease.

This is an election that the partnership (not the estate) must make, by attaching a statement to a timely-filed income tax return for the partnership for the taxable year during which the decedent's death occurs.[34] Once the election is in place for the partnership, it cannot be revoked without the consent of the Internal Revenue Service.[35] The election will affect the estate's basis in the underlying partnership assets upon all future partners' deaths, all sales of partnership interests, and all liquidations of partners' interests. It may also complicate the partnership's accounting, because the partnership must keep separate records for all transferees and new partners. Thus, although it is often beneficial for the decedent, the partnership may not be willing to make the election, or the partnership agreement may explicitly prohibit the election.[36]

[E] S Corporation Stock

The transfer of stock in an S corporation after the death of a shareholder may affect the corporation's status as an S corporation.[37] An S corporation is a small business corporation that meets certain statutory requirements and has an "S election" in effect for the given year.[38] When a person dies owning stock in an S corporation, the personal representative of the decedent's estate should confirm that the stock will continue to be held by a person or entity that is eligible to hold such stock. Several restrictions limit the types of entities that may hold S corporation stock after the death of an original shareholder. In general, after the death of a shareholder, two categories of acceptable dispositions to entities exist: (1) a transfer to the estate of the deceased shareholder; or (2) a transfer to certain qualifying trusts.

The estate of the deceased shareholder may continue to own the stock after the shareholder's death for the duration of the administration of the estate.[39] The estate

---

[33] IRC §§ 754, 743(b). The basis adjustment will not "step-up" the basis of partnership assets that would be considered income in respect of a decedent if held by the deceased partner individually and unrealized receivables of the partnership. IRC §§ 1014(c), 691(a)(1); Reg. § 1.691(a)-1(b); Rev. Rul. 66-325, 1966-2 C.B. 249.

[34] Reg. § 1.754-1(b).

[35] Reg. § 1.754-1(c).

[36] If the partnership does not make the election under Section 754 but does distribute the partnership assets in kind within two years after the decedent's death to the person entitled to the deceased partner's partnership interest, the recipient may make a similar basis adjustment under Section 732(d). Both true partnerships and limited liability companies (LLCs) that are taxed as partnerships qualify for these basis adjustments.

[37] Issues involving S corporation stock are discussed in greater detail in Chapter 11.

[38] IRC § 1361(a)(1), (b). A "small business corporation" is a domestic corporation that does not (1) have more than 100 shareholders; (2) have as a shareholder a person who is not an individual (other than an estate, certain trusts, and certain exempt organizations); (3) have a nonresident alien as a shareholder; or (4) have more than one class of stock. A common ancestor, lineal descendants of the common ancestor, and spouses and former spouses of the common ancestor or such lineal descendants will be treated as a single shareholder. IRC § 1361(c)(1)(A)(ii), (c)(1)(B)(i); Reg. § 1.1361-1(e)(3)(i).

[39] IRC § 1361(b)(1)(B).

may remain open for the period required to perform the typical duties of administration, including the collection of assets and the payment of debts, taxes, and bequests.[40] An estate that holds the S corporation stock is counted as one shareholder.[41]

Certain qualifying trusts are also permitted to be S corporation shareholders. Qualifying trusts include:[42]

1. A voting trust;
2. A trust all of which is treated as owned by one individual for income tax purposes (a grantor trust);
3. A trust holding stock transferred to it pursuant to the terms of a will;
4. A qualified subchapter S trust (QSST); and
5. An electing small business trust (ESBT).

The first type of trust that could qualify is a voting trust. The beneficiaries of the trust are counted in determining the number and nationality of shareholders.

The second type of trust that is a permitted S corporation shareholder is a grantor trust, which for income tax purposes is treated as owned by one individual. To qualify as a trust owned by one individual (whether or not the grantor), an individual must be treated as owning both the income and the principal of the trust.[43] The deemed owner is considered the shareholder and, as such, must be a U.S. citizen or resident.[44] In most cases, these trusts are only eligible shareholders for a two-year period from the date of the grantor's death.[45]

The third type of trust that may hold S corporation stock is a trust that obtains subchapter S stock pursuant to the terms of a will. This type of trust may only hold the S corporation stock for the two-year period beginning on the day that such stock is transferred to the trust.[46]

EXAMPLE *14-40*

Decedent D died on July 1, 2022, owning an interest in two S corporations, O Corp. and P Corp. D owned his stock in P Corp. directly, but his shares in O Corp. were held by a grantor trust, of which D was the deemed owner. Although the trust holding O Corp. stock continues after D's death, it is no longer a grantor trust. On August 1, 2023, D's shares in P

---

[40] Reg. § 1.641(b)-3(a). The IRS will consider the estate terminated after the personal representative has had a reasonable period of time to perform his, her, or its duties. However, if the estate has validly elected to defer the payment of estate taxes, the estate may remain open during the period of deferral, and continue to be an eligible shareholder during that time. Rev. Rul. 76-23, 1976-1 C.B. 264.

[41] Reg. § 1.1361-1(e)(1). The estate is the shareholder, not the beneficiaries.

[42] IRC § 1361(c), (d). These trusts are discussed in greater detail in Chapter 11.

[43] IRC § 1361(c)(2)(A)(i). This may be achieved through the use of either a grantor trust or a Section 678 trust (under which an individual other than the grantor is deemed to own the trust). IRC §§ 671-679.

[44] IRC § 1361(c)(2)(B)(i), (b)(1)(C).

[45] IRC § 1361(c)(2)(A)(ii).

[46] IRC § 1361(c)(2)(A)(iii).

Corp. are transferred to a trust under the terms of D's will. The last day the trust under D's will is an eligible shareholder of P Corp. stock is July 31, 2025 (two years after the date of the transfer to the trust). The last day on which the grantor trust is an eligible shareholder of O Corp. stock is June 30, 2024 (two years after the date of death).

A fourth type of trust that is permitted to be an S corporation shareholder is a qualified subchapter S trust (QSST).[47] To qualify as a QSST, the trust must have only one beneficiary to whom all of the current income, and any principal, is distributed during the beneficiary's lifetime.[48] The trust must not distribute income or principal to anyone other than the current income beneficiary, and upon the termination of the trust during the beneficiary's lifetime (i.e., other than by reason of his or her death), the income beneficiary must receive the trust corpus. Some trusts commonly used in estate planning, such as a QTIP trust or a Section 2503(c) trust for the benefit of a minor, may qualify as QSSTs.

EXAMPLE 14-41

A puts S corporation stock into a trust for the benefit of Beneficiary B, who is not related to A. The terms of the trust provide that the trust will terminate upon the earlier of B's death or B's twenty-first birthday. Upon the termination of the trust, the corpus will revert to A. This trust does not qualify as a QSST because the trust corpus will not be distributed to B upon the termination of the trust.

The beneficiary of a QSST must file an election for the trust to qualify as a QSST.[49] The election applies to successive income beneficiaries unless any of them affirmatively refuses to consent.[50] For purposes of determining the qualification and number of shareholders of the S corporation, the QSST beneficiary is treated as the shareholder.

An electing small business trust (ESBT) is a fifth type of trust that is a permissible S corporation shareholder.[51] Unlike a QSST, an ESBT may have multiple beneficiaries, may accumulate income, may distribute income and principal among all of the beneficiaries, and may serve as a generation-skipping trust. The requirements of an

---

[47] IRC § 1361(d).

[48] IRC § 1361(d)(3); Reg. § 1.1361-1(j). There are some exceptions to the sole beneficiary requirement. First, separate shares in a single trust that are "substantially separate and independent" (as though two separate trusts were created) are treated as separate trusts and may qualify. Reg. § 1.1361-1(j)(3). Second, successive beneficiaries are permitted, but there may be only one current beneficiary at a time. Reg. § 1.1361-1(j)(9).

[49] IRC § 1361(d)(2); Reg. § 1.1361-1(j)(6).

[50] IRC § 1361(d)(2)(B)(ii); Reg. § 1.1361-1(j)(9), (10). It is important to note that every time there is a new income beneficiary of a QSST, the new beneficiary may refuse to consent to the trust being treated as a QSST, which would disqualify the trust.

[51] IRC § 1361(c)(2)(A)(v).

ESBT are: (1) all of the beneficiaries must be individuals, estates, or charities; (2) no interest in the trust may be acquired by purchase; and (3) the trustee must make an election.[52] For a discussion of how the rules governing the number of shareholders and the qualification of shareholders apply to an ESBT, see Chapter 11.[53] Although the ESBT is a more flexible device than the QSST for holding subchapter S corporation stock, the trust's income is taxed to the trust, whether or not the trust distributes income to beneficiaries. The tax is at the highest income tax rate for individuals.[54]

---

[52] IRC § 1361(e)(1)(A).

[53] IRC § 1361(c)(2)(B)(v), (e)(2). When drafting an ESBT, the number of potential beneficiaries should be taken into account so that the 100-shareholder limit is not exceeded.

[54] IRC § 641(c). Only the portion of the trust consisting of S corporation stock is taxed at the highest rate. The remainder of the trust is taxed under normal rules.

Forms

Each form listed below is also available electronically in RTF (Rich Text Format), with and without Practice Notes (comments).

These electronic forms are available at the following URL:

*download.cchcpelink.com/**PGEP2023**.zip*

Form 1:   Living Trust with Traditional Marital Trust and Credit Shelter Trust
Form 2:   Living Trust with Multiple QTIP Marital Trust Options
Form 3:   Living Trust Amendment
Form 4:   Irrevocable Life Insurance Trust
Form 5:   Annual Exclusion Trusts
Form 6:   Additional Annual Exclusion Trust
Form 7:   Will with Pour-Over Provision
Form 8:   Will with Outright Dispositions
Form 9:   Codicil
Form 10:   Durable Power of Attorney
Form 11:   Health Care Proxy
Form 12:   Living Will
Form 13:   HIPAA Authorization Form
Form 14:   Charitable Remainder Unitrust
Form 15:   Qualified Personal Residence Trust (QPRT)
Form 16:   Grantor Retained Annuity Trust (GRAT)

FORM 1

Living Trust with Traditional Marital Trust and Credit Shelter Trust

Overview

This form establishes a revocable trust, which is sometimes referred to as a *living trust.* It contains provisions for the donor during lifetime and creates trusts for the donor's family after the donor's death.

While the donor is alive, the donor remains in complete control of the trust. The donor can amend any and all of its terms or can revoke the trust in its entirety. It is not necessary that the donor fund the trust during lifetime, but if assets are held in the name of the trust, the donor may withdraw them at any time. The donor can also serve as the sole trustee. A living trust can be a useful device during lifetime to plan for incapacity and the management of property. Lifetime funding of such a trust does not provide income tax savings or estate tax savings. Any assets that are transferred to the trust during the donor's lifetime will pass outside of the probate process, which varies from state to state.

At the donor's death, the living trust provides for the disposal of all assets held in the trust while the donor was alive and the disposal of all assets transferred to the trust as a result of the donor's death. Assets may be transferred to the living trust by a provision in the donor's will (a "pour-over" clause as in Form 7) or by a contractual beneficiary designation (for assets such as life insurance death benefits and retirement plan assets).

The model form assumes that the donor is married and has children. After the donor's death, the trust assets are disposed of in favor of the spouse and children. If the spouse survives, the trust property is split into two shares. One share is identified as the Credit Share and has a value equal to the donor's so-called "applicable exclusion amount." In more understandable terms, this is the amount of property that can pass free of federal estate tax at the donor's death regardless of who is the recipient. This share could be distributed immediately to the donor's children without federal estate tax liability. In the model form, however, it passes into a trust of which the donor's spouse is either the sole beneficiary or one of several discretionary beneficiaries. This trust is structured in such a way that the surviving spouse is not treated as the owner of the trust property, with the result that whatever remains in the trust at the spouse's later death passes tax-free to the children at that time. The other share is identified as the Marital Share. It consists of the balance of the trust property. It passes to the surviving spouse either outright or in trust; in all events, however, the disposition qualifies for the estate tax marital deduction. Whatever remains of the Marital Share at the surviving spouse's later death is part of the survivor's estate for tax purposes, whether it passed outright at the first death or is held in a marital trust during the survivor's lifetime.

This two share plan is generally referred to as an *optimal marital deduction plan.* It avoids all federal estate taxes at the first death and minimizes estate tax liability at the second death because both spouses' applicable exclusion amounts are used. As mentioned above, whatever remains in the Credit Share trust passes tax-free to the children at the second death and the survivor can apply her own applicable exclusion amount to the assets that are includable in her estate for tax purposes. The two share plan has been common since 1981 when the unlimited marital deduction was first introduced. It remains an appropriate technique in 2022 and thereafter, even with the new portability of a deceased spouse's unused exclusion amount (as discussed in Section 14.05[E]).

A practitioner suggesting this approach to clients should be mindful of several considerations. First, optimal tax planning may not be optimal estate planning from the clients' perspective; the tax tail should not wag the planning dog. Making use of both spouses' applicable exclusion amounts under this approach means that the surviving spouse cannot have outright ownership of all the decedent spouse's property. Even if the surviving spouse is the only beneficiary of the Credit Share trust, and even if the trust is structured so that the survivor can serve as sole trustee, the surviving spouse does not have legal or psychological ownership of the assets. This may be particularly important in the case of a younger couple.

Second, as the applicable exclusion amount has changed over the years, the amount allocated to the Credit Share and the Marital Share has also changed, which can produce unexpected results for clients who do not review their estate plans regularly. During the period 2001 through 2009, the Credit Share equivalent amount increased in uneven steps from $675,000 to $3,500,000. Following one year in 2010 with no federal estate tax, the amount continued to increase. The Credit Share equivalent amount is $12,060,000 ($10,000,000 indexed for inflation) in 2022. As a consequence, in many estate plans, the amount passing in 2022 to the Credit Share has grown larger and the Marital Share amount has decreased. If an estate plan provides for the Credit Share to be given to the children immediately, this could have the effect of disinheriting the spouse. If, as in option two in the model document, the Credit Share passes into a discretionary trust of which the spouse is one of several beneficiaries, the spouse will not be disinherited but will receive less property outright or less property in the trust of which she is the sole beneficiary. It might be appropriate, therefore, to reconsider the scheme provided for in the model and, for example, impose a dollar limit on the amount used to fund the Credit Share trust (even if this results in the applicable exclusion amount not being used in full at the first death) or to provide that part of the Credit Share passes into a discretionary trust and the balance passes into a trust of which the spouse is the sole beneficiary.

Third, it is difficult to plan now for all possible eventualities. A client may be best advised to plan for the next several years and understand that revisions will be necessary to his documents in the near future. Alternatively, a practitioner could suggest the option of a disclaimer plan. Under this plan, all assets will pass outright to the surviving spouse. However, the spouses will have a back-up trust drafted while they are both alive to which assets will pass under the will of the first spouse to die to the extent that the survivor disclaims those assets within nine months after the first spouse's death. This back-up trust could have provisions identical to either of the alternative Credit Share trusts in the model document with one important exception; the surviving spouse cannot have a power of appointment to vary the disposition of the remaining trust assets at her later death. Such a plan puts the burden on the survivor to effect an appropriate tax plan and requires careful counseling by the advisors settling the first spouse's estate. It has the advantages, however, of superficial simplicity and flexibility.

Finally, where a married couple has combined wealth of many millions of dollars, there was previously a concern that use of the optimal marital deduction plan could lead to a larger overall estate tax liability. This would have resulted from bunching more assets in the survivor's estate and subjecting a greater amount of the couple's combined wealth to higher marginal rates of federal estate tax at the second death. The overall tax liability in such a situation might be reduced by paying some tax at the first death. This is not a consideration (at least at the federal level) for 2022 and thereafter, given that all estates are now subject to a flat 40 percent federal estate tax rate.

The optimal marital deduction plan will only work to full advantage if the married couple's assets are held appropriately. Specifically, each spouse must have a taxable estate equal to the unused applicable exclusion amount or be able to reach this amount following the death of the first spouse to die using a qualified disclaimer. If the first spouse dies in 2022 with too few assets in his name, then, absent an election to transfer his unused basic exclusion amount to the surviving spouse, the decedent's basic exclusion amount cannot be used fully. This means that it is always necessary for the practitioner to review how assets are owned. In some instances, property held in a joint tenancy by the spouses will need to be divided into separate property or a cotenancy in order to ensure adequate funding of the Credit Share at the first death. Beneficiary designations for life insurance and possibly retirement plans may need to be amended, naming the living trust as the beneficiary as opposed to the surviving spouse.

After the death of the surviving spouse, the model form provides for remaining property to be distributed ultimately to the donor's then living children (with the children of any child who has predeceased the survivor of the donor and his spouse taking that child's share). If the donor has stepchildren (that is, children of the donor's spouse who are not children of the donor), the stepchildren would not be beneficiaries under the trust as drafted. The document defines child and issue to include adopted descendants (the default rule in most states) and descendants born out of wedlock, provided, in the case of inheritance through the father, that the father has acknowledged paternity voluntarily or paternity has been established by a court adjudication. The practitioner should always be certain that the donor's dispositive wishes are captured accurately when designating beneficiaries, particularly when by class or generic descriptions.

The model document assumes that both spouses are citizens of the United States. If they are not, the marital deduction provisions must be in special form in order to defer any federal estate tax until the second death. The model document also does not deal with (i) state estate or inheritance tax issues, which are quite varied and beyond the scope of this general analysis, or (ii) generation-skipping transfer tax issues, save to structure trusts for children and others in a way that a generation-skipping transfer tax would not be payable at the trust beneficiary's death prior to the termination of the trust.

THE SAM SAMPLE [*YEAR*] TRUST

Practice Note

The opening paragraph identifies the maker of the trust (the "donor"). All variations on the donor's name should be stated to ensure that all property owned by the donor can be transferred to the trust without complication. The statement of the donor's residence should correspond to the residency claimed for state income tax purposes.

The opening paragraph should identify the initial trustee or trustees by name and describe the funding assets. Such trusts are generally established to receive assets at death under the terms of a "pour-over" will. However, if the trust is to be funded with property other than a nominal cash amount, a separate schedule may be used to describe the assets.

SAM SAMPLE (also known as SAMUEL ARTHUR SAMPLE), of [*ADDRESS*] (the "Donor"), herewith transfers the sum of One Dollar ($1) to himself and his wife, SARAH SAMPLE, as trustees hereunder; and the trustees hereby acknowledge receipt of said sum and agree, for themselves, any additional trustees and all successors in office, to hold and manage it, together with any additions to it, IN TRUST, upon the following terms and provisions:

Practice Note

Article FIRST sets forth the name of the trust. This is the name that should be used when designating the trust as a beneficiary under a will or of nonprobate assets (such as a life insurance policy or retirement benefits).

This article provides expressly that the donor retains the right to revoke the trust. This is essential because in many jurisdictions a trust cannot be amended or revoked unless that power is reserved explicitly on the face of the trust document. Here, the power is reserved by the donor and is exercisable during lifetime; changes cannot be effected by will. The trust also provides that alterations or amendments will become effective upon the trustee's consent. Requiring the consent of the trustee to an amendment is appropriate, since a trustee cannot be forced to manage a trust on terms unacceptable to the trustee. Should a trustee refuse to consent to an amendment, the donor has the option of removing the trustee (*see* Article ELEVENTH) or revoking the trust in its entirety.

The language of this Article would permit the trust to be amended or revoked under a durable power of attorney or by a court appointed guardian or conservator. If the donor wants the right to be personal, the document should provide that the right is not exercisable by any person in a representative capacity.

In some circumstances, it might be appropriate to authorize the trustee or a third person to amend or revoke the trust, either during the donor's lifetime or after his death. Such a power may be limited to specific purposes or circumstances or to revisions that would not alter the beneficial interests created by the trust after the donor's death. An example of such a provision might state that, after the donor's

---

death, the disinterested trustee may alter or add to the administrative provisions of the trust, including the powers of the trustees, provided that any such amendment or addition does not alter or shift any beneficial interest or the time of enjoyment of any beneficial interest.

FIRST: Revocation or Amendment. This trust shall be known as "THE SAM SAMPLE [*YEAR*] TRUST." The Donor shall have the right at any time or times, by a writing or writings (other than a will or a codicil) signed by him and delivered to the trustees during the Donor's lifetime, to revoke the trust hereunder, or to alter or amend this trust instrument, in whole or in part. If this trust is revoked in its entirety, the revocation shall take effect upon the delivery of the required writing to the trustees, who shall thereupon pay or transfer to the Donor, or as he directs, all of the trust property. Any alteration or amendment of this trust instrument shall take effect when consented to in writing by the trustees.

Practice Note

If the trust is funded during the donor's lifetime other than with the nominal initial funding, most donors will want to be the primary or sole beneficiary of the trust so long as they are living. This trust accomplishes that objective by permitting the donor to withdraw trust property on demand and by directing the trustee to use the trust property for the donor's benefit.

Much is made of avoiding the probate process by funding a revocable trust of this type during lifetime. As probate laws are relaxed, however, and probate court fees reduced, this advantage becomes less pressing. Perhaps the most useful function of a funded revocable trust is as a planning tool in the event of the donor's incapacity. With this in mind, the model document grants broad authority to a trustee other than the donor to use the trust assets for the donor's benefit. To increase flexibility and prevent any disruption in accessibility to the donor's assets, the trust could also authorize the trustee to make distributions to support the donor's spouse, dependent children, or others dependent on the donor, and to continue or initiate gift-giving programs on behalf of the donor. If broader powers are granted, care must be taken to ensure that the trustee vested with the powers will not have a potential tax problem by virtue of these rights. For example, if the trustee can exercise discretion to distribute in favor of herself, the trustee may have a sufficient interest in the trust property to cause the property to be includable in her estate for estate tax purposes. To avoid this problem, wider ranging distribution powers should only be given to an independent or disinterested trustee and not, for example, to the donor's spouse or one of his children acting as trustee.

The standby provision in the second paragraph permits a donor-trustee to continue to administer the trust property almost as if the property were not in the trust, while providing the safeguard of having an appointed "back-up" trustee should the donor become incapacitated or not be available to act.

SECOND: Provisions Applicable During Donor's Lifetime. During the lifetime of the Donor, the trustees shall distribute to him, or as he directs, all or such part of the net income and principal as he from time to time requests; and without any request, at any time or times during the Donor's lifetime, the trustee other than the Donor may distribute to, or apply in such manner as such trustee thinks advisable for the benefit of, the Donor such amounts or all of the net income and principal as the trustee other than the Donor, in such trustee's discretion, thinks advisable for any purpose. Any net income not so distributed or applied may be added to principal at any time or times, and any net income remaining at the death of the Donor shall be added to principal at that time.

So long as the Donor is serving as trustee hereunder, any trustee in office other than the Donor (unless directed to the contrary in writing by the Donor) shall have no responsibility whatsoever to consider the advisability of retaining, disposing of or acquiring investments for the trust hereunder, or to make investment decisions, but shall act in these respects solely as directed from time to time by the Donor in his capacity as trustee. Any action by the Donor as trustee pursuant to this provision shall be binding on the trust. In addition, any person or entity shall be entitled to rely conclusively on the sole signature or execution by the Donor as trustee as the act and deed of the trust with respect to all matters relating to the administration of the trust property, and the signature or execution by any or all other trustees then in office shall under no circumstances be required. No co-trustee shall be liable in connection with any action taken by the Donor as trustee unless the particular co-trustee shall join affirmatively in that action.

Practice Note

Article THIRD disposes of all property held in the trust on the date of the donor's death, together with all property added to the trust as a result of the donor's death. Probate property may be added by a pour-over provision in the donor's will (as provided in the residuary clause of the will in Form 7); and life insurance proceeds or retirement plan benefits may be added by naming the trust as the beneficiary of the policy or retirement plan benefits.

If the donor's spouse survives the donor, the trust provides that the property will be divided into two shares. The first share qualifies for the federal estate tax marital deduction (known as the Marital Share) and is disposed of under Article FOURTH. The second share takes advantage of the donor's federal estate tax applicable exclusion amount (known as the Credit Share) and is disposed of under Article FIFTH. If the donor's spouse does not survive the donor, all trust property is disposed of under Article FIFTH.

There are several different formulae for splitting property between the Marital Share and the Credit Share. The formulae are either "pecuniary" or "fractional." Each formula will avoid federal estate taxes at the first death and will use the first-to-die's federal applicable exclusion amount to full effect, thereby minimizing estate taxes at the second death. The model determines the Credit Share by reference to the "federal estate tax." If the donor lives in a state that still has a state estate tax, the formula provision may need to be adjusted to avoid the imposition of a state estate tax at the first death.

A straight pecuniary formula sets aside a Marital Share as a specific dollar amount, with the residue passing as the Credit Share. An example of a straight pecuniary formula is

> The trustees shall set aside that amount equal to the maximum federal estate tax marital deduction allowable to the donor's estate less (a) the greatest amount that will not increase the donor's federal estate tax (after taking into account all available credits) and less (b) the value of any property passing to the donor's spouse other than under this trust instrument and that qualifies for the federal estate tax marital deduction. The amount so set aside (the "Marital Share") shall be held in trust under Article FOURTH below.

A reverse pecuniary formula sets aside the Credit Share first as a specific dollar amount, with the residue passing as the Marital Share. An example of a reverse pecuniary formula is

> The trustees shall set aside that amount equal to the maximum amount (if any) that, as a result of all credits and exemptions available to the donor's estate, could pass to beneficiaries other than the donor's spouse or charity without causing the donor's estate to be subject to any federal estate taxes. The Credit Share shall be held in trust under Article FIFTH below.

The difference between these formulae is that the share set aside is a fixed amount as of the date of death, and any appreciation or depreciation between the date of death and the date of distribution is allocated to the other share. Thus, in a straight pecuniary formula the Marital Share is fixed and the Credit Share is affected by fluctuations in value between the date of death and the date of distribution; in a reverse pecuniary formula, the Credit Share is fixed and the Marital Share is affected by fluctuations in value between the date of death and the date of distribution.

Many practitioners prefer to use the straight pecuniary marital formula because it freezes the value of the Marital Share as of the date of death or the alternate valuation date. If assets appreciate in value between the date of death and the date of funding, all appreciation is shifted to the Credit Share. By shifting appreciation to the Credit Share, the appreciation is not subject to estate tax at the surviving spouse's death, thereby minimizing the overall estate tax burden as property passes ultimately to the children. If property depreciates in value after death, the depreciation is allocated similarly to the Credit Share, thereby protecting the surviving spouse against a market downturn. Of course, in the latter situation, the Credit Share may be substantially underfunded as a result.

The model form does not use either of the pecuniary formulae described above, but instead uses a fractional share formula to determine the Marital Share. The numerator of the fraction is the amount of the deduction sought (the smallest amount that would result in the lowest possible net federal estate tax), and the denominator is the value of all assets available for funding. By using a fractional share formula, the Marital Share and the Credit Share both participate in any appreciation or depreciation in the value of trust assets between the date of death and the date of funding and neither share is fixed until actual funding.

In addition to selecting a formula for division of the trust property into a Marital Share and a Credit Share, the estate planner must also choose a method for funding those shares. This method must address the timing of valuation of the trust property (i.e., either valuing as of the date of distribution or using the federal estate tax value) and the manner in which assets are chosen to be allocated to the respective shares. If a pecuniary division formula is used, the funding method merits careful consideration since some funding methods may result in the realization of capital gain.

The model form uses a "pick and choose" funding method (see paragraph (k) of Article TENTH). This approach provides the utmost flexibility in selecting assets and avoids the realization of capital gain when funding the Marital Share. The disadvantage to using this type of funding method is that every asset held in the trust must be revalued each time a distribution is made in order to maintain the appropriate fraction. This can create an administrative burden if funding takes place in stages.

The model form also provides that the Credit Share will be increased, and the Marital Share decreased, by any amount of the Marital Share disclaimed by the surviving spouse. A disclaimer is a refusal to accept property and, if it meets the statutory requirements for a qualified disclaimer, its effect on the disclaimed property is as if the disclaimant predeceased the donor. A surviving spouse may choose to disclaim a portion of the Marital Share in order to cause some estate taxes to be payable in the estate of the donor spouse, rather than deferring all taxes to the survivor's estate. Under current law, while the federal estate tax has a flat estate tax rate structure in 2022 and beyond, state estate tax considerations continue to make a disclaimer a relevant tool to reduce the spouses' total estate tax liability in large estates. This technique does not provide a benefit if a consistent, flat estate tax rate structure is in effect for both federal and state estate taxes. In order for a disclaimer not to be treated as a gift by the disclaiming spouse, the disclaiming spouse must not be able to control the disposition of the disclaimed property. For this reason, the model form provides that, if the surviving spouse disclaims and if the first alternative Article FIFTH is used, the surviving spouse will not have the power to appoint the disclaimed property and thereby affect its disposition at her later death. This language should be deleted if the second alternative to Article FIFTH is used since the surviving spouse has no control over the disposition of the trust property under this option.

Paragraph (c) of Article THIRD sets out a number of issues to take into consideration when deciding which assets to use to fund the Credit Share and the Marital Share. For example, whatever type of formula is used—pecuniary or fractional—the trust should provide that assets that do not qualify for the marital deduction should not be allocated to the Marital Share. The so-called *unidentified asset rule* disallows the marital deduction to the extent that the spouse's interest *could have been* funded with property that does not qualify for the marital deduction. This provision avoids this trap for the unwary. Property that may be subject to foreign death taxes (such as real estate located in a foreign country) should not be allocated to the Marital Share. This will ensure full use of the credit available for the payment of foreign taxes. Such a direction should be inserted in the model form in cases where it might be applicable.

The model form also provides that assets constituting items of income in respect of a decedent for federal income tax purposes (such as retirement plan assets) should be allocated to the Marital Share. This is good practice since, if such items are allocated instead to the Credit Share, the value of the Credit Share will be reduced by the income tax liability built in to the value of the funding assets.

The model trust includes a presumption that all property that may be elected to qualify for the marital deduction is so elected. This provides added assurance that the formula will achieve its objective of producing a quantifiable Marital Share that qualifies for the federal estate tax marital deduction.

A second presumption included in the model document concerns the order of death of the donor and the donor's spouse when this cannot be determined by proof. Under the laws of most states, it is presumed that the decedent survives the beneficiaries of his estate, unless the governing documents provide otherwise. In the situation when one spouse is wealthier than the other, it may be desirable—as in the model form—to reverse the statutory presumption. As a result, the wealthier spouse's estate can be used to fund the less wealthy spouse's estate and make use of the less wealthy spouse's federal applicable exclusion amount. The statutory presumption for simultaneous death should not be changed in the case of beneficiaries other than the spouse. The donor will expect that property would pass to her own specified default beneficiary if the primary beneficiary died at the time of the donor's death. In drafting trust distributions for beneficiaries other than a surviving spouse, thought should be given to adding a requirement that the beneficiary survive the donor by a minimum number of days.

THIRD: Disposition Upon the Donor's Death. Upon the death of the Donor, the then trust principal (as augmented by all property transferred to the trustees from any source as a result of the Donor's death) shall be disposed of as follows:

(a) *If the Donor's Wife Shall Survive the Donor.* If the Donor's said wife survives him, the trustees shall first set aside, to be disposed of as provided in Article FOURTH below, the smallest fractional share, if any, of the trust principal that will result in there being payable by reason of the Donor's death the lowest possible net federal estate tax (the "Marital Share"). The balance of the trust principal shall be disposed of as provided in Article FIFTH below. Further, the Marital Share shall be reduced, and the property to be held in trust for the Donor's said wife under Article FIFTH below, shall be increased, to the extent of any disclaimer executed by or on behalf of the Donor's said wife of all her interest in all or any portion of that share. [*the following language should be added if Option 1 of Article FIFTH is used,* except that the Donor's said wife shall not have the power of appointment set forth in paragraph (c) of said Article FIFTH over such disclaimed property].

(b) *If the Donor's Wife Shall Not Survive the Donor.* If the Donor's said wife does not survive the Donor, the trust principal shall be disposed of as provided in Article FIFTH below.

(c) *Provisions Applicable to Marital Share.* Only assets that are includable in the Donor's gross estate for federal estate tax purposes and that qualify for the federal estate tax marital deduction shall be allotted by the trustees to the Marital Share. To the extent possible, assets that constitute items of income in respect of a decedent for federal income tax purposes shall be allotted to the Marital Share if such assets otherwise qualify for such share as provided in the preceding sentence. In determining the Marital Share, it shall be presumed that the Donor's personal representative elects to qualify for the federal estate tax marital deduction all property for which such an election is available, regardless of whether such an election is actually made. In addition, the determination of such share shall be made subject to any election to claim debts, losses, or expenses of administration as income tax deductions and to pay certain expenses from income or from principal as provided in Article EIGHTH below. If the order of death of the Donor and his said wife cannot be established by proof, it shall be presumed, for all purposes of this trust instrument, that the Donor's said wife survived him.

Practice Note

Article FOURTH provides two options for the disposition of the Marital Share. The first option is to transfer the Marital Share outright to the surviving spouse's own revocable trust. The second option is to transfer the Marital Share to a QTIP (qualified terminable interest property) trust in which the surviving spouse is given an income interest for life and the remainder passes to the one or more beneficiaries designated by the donor spouse. These are by no means the only options available, but are the most common ones used.

[OPTION ONE—OUTRIGHT MARITAL]

Practice Note

In the first alternative, the model document provides for the Marital Share to be distributed to the surviving spouse's own revocable trust unless requested otherwise by the surviving spouse or unless the distribution to the revocable trust would not qualify for the estate tax marital deduction (in which case the property is to be distributed outright to the surviving spouse). Assuming that the surviving spouse is the sole trustee of her revocable trust, this will give her the same degree of control as she would have had if the property were distributed to her directly. This formulation is preferable to a straightforward outright distribution since it may keep the Marital Share out of the surviving spouse's probate estate upon the surviving spouse's later death. In addition, if the surviving spouse is incapacitated at the time of the first death, the Marital Share will not have to be delivered to a guardian for her benefit. This first option is suitable if the spouses want to give the survivor maximum access to and control of the Marital Share. It is also the easiest type of provision for clients to understand. Potential drawbacks may, however, result for state estate tax planning, or if the married couple plan to have long-term trusts for their children's descendants and want to take full advantage of their exemptions from the federal generation-skipping transfer tax.

FOURTH: Disposition of Marital Share. Any Marital Share provided in Article THIRD above, to be disposed of as provided in this Article FOURTH shall be distributed to the trustees then in office of THE SARAH SAMPLE [*YEAR*] TRUST, established today by the Donor's said wife, with herself and the Donor as trustees ("SARAH'S [*YEAR*] TRUST"), to be added to the principal of SA-RAH'S [*YEAR*] TRUST and administered in accordance with its provisions, as from time to time amended. If SARAH'S [*YEAR*] TRUST is not then in existence, or if such distribution would not qualify for the federal estate tax marital deduction, or if requested by the Donor's said wife, the Marital Share shall instead be distributed outright to the Donor's said wife.

[OPTION TWO—QTIP TRUST MARITAL]

Practice Note

The second alternative form of marital disposition is to a qualified terminable interest property trust, or QTIP Trust. Under a QTIP trust, the surviving spouse is given an income interest for life and, upon the surviving spouse's death, the property passes to the beneficiaries chosen by the donor spouse (in the model form the property passes to the Credit Share portion of the trust in Article FIFTH). A QTIP trust provides flexibility for post-mortem estate planning because it only qualifies for the marital deduction to the extent that an election is made on the decedent's estate tax return. This allows the decision regarding whether to pay taxes upon the donor spouse's death to be deferred until the return is due (nine months after the death of the donor spouse). In addition, a QTIP trust also provides the donor spouse with maximum control over the disposition of the Marital Share.

A QTIP Trust is generally appropriate if the client wants to limit the surviving spouse's control of the Marital Share. This is often the situation where the surviving spouse is not a parent of the donor's children. The QTIP trust addresses concerns of subsequent remarriage and the redirection of trust assets to the new spouse or the new spouse's family. It may also be appropriate if the surviving spouse has a lack of financial expertise or is engaged in a high-risk business and it is desired to protect the trust principal from her creditors.

In order for this type of trust to qualify for the marital deduction, numerous technical requirements must be met. The surviving spouse must be the sole beneficiary during her surviving lifetime and she must receive a distribution of all income earned by the trust assets at least as often as annually. The Code does not require that the surviving spouse be given any access to trust principal during her surviving lifetime or that she have any control over the disposition of the principal at her later death. However, various discretionary rights or entitlements may be granted to the surviving spouse without losing the flexibility of QTIP treatment.[1] For example, during the surviving spouse's lifetime, the trust could provide for no distribution of principal, principal to be distributed as needed for health, maintenance, education, or support, or, as in the model document, principal to be distributed to the surviving spouse for any reason and in any amount in the discretion of a disinterested trustee. At death, the surviving spouse can be given a limited power of appointment exercisable, for example, in favor of the donor's issue (as provided in the model document if the first version of Article FIFTH is used) or the surviving spouse can have no control over the distribution of principal. In either situation, assuming an election has been made to treat the property as QTIP property, the property remaining in the QTIP trust at the survivor's death is includable in the survivor's estate for federal estate tax purposes. Taxes attributable to the QTIP trust property are payable from the property itself unless the surviving spouse provides otherwise by an explicit provision in her will or pour-over trust. If the QTIP election is not made in the estate of the donor spouse, the property will be taxable in the donor spouse's estate and will not be subject to tax in the estate of the surviving spouse.

Paragraph (c) sets forth various provisions designed to ensure that the regulatory requirements applicable to QTIP trusts are met (particularly with regard to the surviving spouse's entitlement to income from the trust assets).

Paragraph (d) addresses the possibility that a QTIP election will not be made for all the property of the Marital Share. A full election may not be made if it is decided after the first death that complete tax deferral is not advantageous. If an election is only made with respect to a portion of the assets in the Marital Share, this provision authorizes the trustee to split the Marital Share into two separate trusts for convenience of administration and estate and income tax planning. If a full election is not made, the separate nonelected Marital Share trust will not be includable in the surviving spouse's estate at the time of her later death.

---

[1] The QTIP requirements set the floor for the minimum provisions that must be made for the surviving spouse in order to be able to make the election to claim the marital deduction. A surviving spouse can be given an unlimited amount of additional rights without risk of loss of the marital deduction. However, if the surviving spouse is given too much control over the property, the trustee may lose the ability to elect *out of* marital deduction treatment.

FOURTH: Marital Trust. Any Marital Share provided in Article THIRD above to be disposed of as provided in this Article FOURTH shall be administered in a separate trust as follows:

   (a) *Distributions During Lifetime of Donor's Wife.* The net income shall be paid to the Donor's said wife at least as often as quarterly during her lifetime. In addition, all or any part of the principal may be paid to her in such amounts and at such time or times as the disinterested trustee, in the disinterested trustee's discretion, thinks advisable for any purpose. The Donor hopes, without limiting the discretion of the disinterested trustee, that, in the exercise of this authority to make payments of principal, the disinterested trustee will give primary consideration to the welfare of the Donor's said wife during her lifetime.

   (b) *Disposition on Death of Donor's Wife.* On the death of the Donor's said wife, the then remaining principal shall be administered and disposed of as provided in Article FIFTH below.

   (c) *Qualification for Marital Deduction.* The Donor intends that the value for federal estate tax purposes of the property of the trust under this Article shall be available for any marital deduction allowable by the federal estate tax laws applicable to his estate; and all questions applicable to the trust shall be resolved accordingly. To this end it is directed that in making elections for any periodic payments to the trust from the Donor's account or other interest in any pension plan, Keogh plan, individual retirement account, or other employee benefit plan, whether qualified or nonqualified (in each case, the "Donor's Plan"), the trustees shall select a method that ensures that the aggregate payments to the trust for any year are at least equal to the income earned by the Donor's Plan for the year and such payments shall, in turn, to the extent of the income earned by the Donor's Plan for the year, be treated as current income of the trust; any income earned during the period of administration of the Donor's estate that is transferred to the trustees (whether under the provisions of the Donor's will or otherwise) and allocable to the trust shall be treated as income of the trust; if directed by the Donor's said wife, the trustees shall convert any trust property that is not producing a periodically distributable income as is consistent with the value of the trust property and with its preservation into property that does produce such an income; and the powers and discretions of the trustees and of the disinterested trustee with respect to the property in the trust shall not be exercised or exercisable during the period that the Donor's said wife survives him except in a manner consistent with the Donor's intention as expressed in the preceding sentence.

(d) *Partial QTIP Election.* If an election is made to qualify a specific portion (but not all) of the trust hereunder for the federal estate tax marital deduction, the trustees shall divide the trust into two separate trusts, one of which shall consist of the portion so qualified and the other of which shall consist of the balance of the trust principal, and each such trust shall be administered as provided in this Article. Any such division shall be made in accordance with Reg. Section 20.2056(b)-7(b)(2)(ii), or any successor regulation.

Practice Note

Article FIFTH provides two options for the disposition of the Credit Share. There are no statutory requirements concerning the disposition of the Credit Share and the tax goals could be achieved by any plan that does not subject the trust property to tax in the surviving spouse's estate. Thus, the property could be distributed immediately to the donor's children or to other family members. In the model form, it is assumed that the married couple wants the survivor to retain a beneficial interest in the assets allocated to the Credit Share. As a consequence, the Credit Share is held in one of two forms of trust with the surviving spouse as a beneficiary. It is important that the surviving spouse not be given any powers or discretion over the administration or distribution of this trust that would cause the property to be included in the surviving spouse's estate at her later death. One significant difference in the two alternative trust structures offered in the model form is that, in the first, the surviving spouse could be the sole trustee without causing potential estate tax issues in her estate, and, in the second, there must be an independent trustee.

[OPTION ONE—MAXIMUM BENEFIT TRUST]

Practice Note

Under the first alternative, the surviving spouse is the sole beneficiary of the trust during her lifetime. All income is distributable quarterly to the surviving spouse and principal may be distributed to the surviving spouse for her health, education, maintenance, or support. Under such a structure, the surviving spouse can serve as the sole trustee because the power to distribute under an ascertainable standard is not considered a general power of appointment causing estate tax inclusion in the surviving spouse's estate. The trust is also structured so that if there is a disinterested trustee in office, that trustee may distribute principal to the surviving spouse for any reason.

Further control is given to the surviving spouse in the form of a withdrawal power. The spouse can withdraw $5,000 at any time during the calendar year and is then permitted to withdraw an extra amount at the end of the year equal to 5 percent of the value of the then trust assets less the amount of any prior withdrawals during the same calendar year. For example, if the trust has a value at year-end of $700,000 and the spouse has withdrawn no amounts for herself during the year, the spouse could withdraw $35,000 on December 31. The power is noncumulative. If not exercised in any year, it is not carried forward to the next.

This type of withdrawal power is a so-called five and five power. It is not treated as a general power of appointment under the Internal Revenue Code and, therefore, it does not cause the entire trust to be subject to estate tax in the surviving spouse's estate upon her death. If, however, the surviving spouse dies at the time the withdrawal power is exercisable, the amount of the property that could be withdrawn will be treated as includable for tax purposes in the surviving spouse's estate. This is the reason that the right to withdraw 5 percent of the trust is limited to a small window of time (the last day of the calendar year). So long as the surviving spouse does not die on that day, she will have at most $5,000 subject to tax in her estate by virtue of this right. Furthermore, because of the "five and five" limitation, the surviving spouse is not treated as making a gift for federal gift tax purposes in favor of the remainder beneficiaries of the trust if she fails to exercise the power. An unexercised five and five power may cause income tax complications, however, under the grantor trust rules.

The surviving spouse is also given control over the disposition of the trust property at her later death. This control is in the form of a limited power of appointment and, therefore, will not subject the trust property to estate tax in her estate. In the model form, the surviving spouse may dispose of the trust property in favor of any one or more of the issue of the donor of the trust. If desired, the power could be expanded to include collateral relatives, other individuals, or charitable organizations. In order to provide maximum flexibility, the power could be expanded to be exercisable in favor of "any person or entity other than the surviving spouse's estate, creditors, or the creditors of the surviving spouse's estate." Under the terms of Article THIRD (a), this limited power of appointment will not apply with respect to any property transferred to this trust by virtue of the surviving spouse's disclaimer. A surviving spouse may disclaim a portion of her Marital Share to cause some estate taxes to be payable at the death of the first spouse. This limitation is necessary in order for the disclaimer not to be treated as a taxable gift by the surviving spouse.

The final paragraph of the Article deals with the disposition of the trust property at the surviving spouse's later death if she does not exercise the power of appointment. It also disposes of the trust property in the event that the donor to the trust is the survivor of the married couple. In the model form, the trust assets are divided into equal shares among the donor's then living children. Should a child predecease the survivor of his or her parents, the deceased child's share is further divided among his or her own children. Any distributions to beneficiaries who are under the age of 25 are directed to be held in simple management trusts (set forth in Article SIXTH) for the benefit of the individual beneficiaries.

FIFTH: Credit Shelter Trust. All principal provided under any Article of this trust instrument to be disposed of as provided in this Article FIFTH shall be administered in a separate trust and disposed of as follows:

(a) *Distributions During Lifetime of Donor's Wife.* If the Donor's said wife survives him, the net income shall be paid to her at least as often as quarterly during her lifetime. In addition, the trustees shall distribute to her such amounts or all of the principal and at such time or times as the trustees, in their discretion, think advisable for her health, maintenance, education, and support, and any disinterested trustee may distribute to the Donor's said wife such amounts or all of the principal and at such time or times as the disinterested trustee, in the disinterested trustee's discretion, thinks advisable for any purpose.

(b) *Right of Withdrawal.* During the surviving lifetime of the Donor's said wife she shall have the right at any time or times by a writing or writings delivered to the trustees to withdraw from the trust principal any amount or amounts up to Five Thousand Dollars ($5,000) in the aggregate in each calendar year and, if the Donor's said wife is living on the last day of the calendar year, she shall have the additional right by a writing delivered to the trustees on or before such day to withdraw from the trust principal the excess, if any, of five percent (5%) of the value of the trust principal as of such day over the value of any prior withdrawals (as of the date of each such withdrawal) in the calendar year; *provided* that the aggregate of all withdrawals in any calendar year shall not exceed the greater of Five Thousand Dollars ($5,000) and said five percent (5%) of the trust principal valued on the last day of the calendar year. This right of withdrawal shall be noncumulative.

(c) *Power of Appointment.* Upon the death of the Donor's said wife if she survives the Donor, the then remaining principal (as augmented in any way) shall be disposed of as she shall appoint by a will, executed at any time after the Donor's death, and referring specifically to this power of appointment, to or for the benefit of any one or more of the Donor's issue, in such amounts or proportions, for such estates, on such trusts, and subject to such terms, conditions, general or special powers of appointment and restrictions as the Donor's said wife shall appoint. This power of appointment shall not be exercisable, directly or indirectly, in favor of the Donor's said wife, her estate, her creditors, or the creditors of her estate.

(d) *Disposition Upon Death of Survivor of Donor and Donor's Wife.* In default of or subject to appointment by the Donor's said wife as aforesaid, upon her death if she survives the Donor, or upon the Donor's death if she does not survive him, the then remaining principal shall be distributed in equal shares, one share to each child of the Donor who is then living and one share by right of representation to the then living issue of each child of the Donor who is then deceased with issue then living; *provided* that any principal thus distributable to a beneficiary who has not then reached the age of twenty-five (25) shall be held in trust for the particular beneficiary as provided below in Article SIXTH, instead of being distributed outright.

[OPTION TWO—DISCRETIONARY SPRINKLE TRUST]

Practice Note

The second alternative creates a sprinkling trust for the benefit of the surviving spouse and the donor's children and other issue (meaning grandchildren and more remote descendants). This structure provides maximum flexibility. Funds can be distributed based on relative needs or in a tax-advantaged way by directing income to beneficiaries in low-income tax brackets. A sprinkling trust, however, requires a disinterested trustee. If a family member beneficiary serves as trustee and holds the sprinkling discretion, that family member is likely to be taxable on all the income of the trust regardless of who receives it and is likely to be deemed to have a general power of appointment over the trust assets, causing estate tax inclusion or potential gift tax liability.

The first paragraph includes a precatory direction to the disinterested trustee that primary consideration be given to the welfare of the surviving spouse during her lifetime. Alternatively, the donor may wish to provide more detailed guidance to the disinterested trustee in exercising the discretion, although, to preserve flexibility, such guidance is usually better contained in a separate memorandum rather than being stated on the face of the trust instrument.

The sprinkling trust continues until the later of the death of the surviving spouse or when the youngest child reaches the age of 22. This enables the trust to continue as a single fund until the children have likely completed their undergraduate education. After both spouses have died and the youngest child reaches age 22, the property is divided into shares, with one share for each child of the donor who is then living or who has predeceased the termination date of the trust but is survived by issue of her or his own. Any distributions to beneficiaries who are under the age of 25 are directed to be held in simple management trusts (as provided in Article SIXTH) for the benefit of the individual beneficiaries.

The precise terms of the trust should be tailored to suit the circumstances of the donor and his family. The model form provides for equal division of the trust property on termination. No adjustments are made for prior distributions of trust income or principal to the donor's children or other issue. If the client is concerned that this may

---

produce unfair results—as where extraordinary distributions are made to one child but not the others—the trust could require that uneven distributions be treated as advancements of the share to which the child is entitled on termination. The terminating distribution would then be adjusted to take into account the earlier distribution activity.

The family pot approach is particularly appropriate when the overall level of family wealth is limited. If the combined assets of the married couple exceed several million dollars, it may be preferable to adopt a structure that establishes separate shares or trusts for each child immediately after both parents have died, particularly if there is a meaningful difference in age from the youngest to the oldest child.

FIFTH: Family Trust. After the death of the Donor, all principal provided under any Article of this trust instrument to be disposed of as provided in this Article FIFTH shall be administered in a separate trust and disposed of as follows:

(a) *Distributions During Lifetime of Donor's Wife.* All or any part of the net income and principal may be paid to any one or more of the Donor's said wife, the Donor's children, and the Donor's more remote issue, in such amounts and proportions and at such time or times as the disinterested trustee, in the disinterested trustee's discretion, thinks advisable for any purpose. Any net income not so paid may be added to principal at any time or times. The Donor hopes, without limiting the discretion of the disinterested trustee, that in the exercise of this authority to make payments of net income and principal, the disinterested trustee will give primary consideration to the welfare of the Donor's said wife during her lifetime.

(b) *Disposition Upon Death of Survivor of Donor and Donor's Wife.* When both the Donor and his said wife have died and no child of the Donor is living and under the age of twenty-two (22), any balance of net income shall be added to principal and the then remaining principal shall be distributed in equal shares, one share to each child of the Donor who is then living and one share by right of representation to the then living issue of each child of the Donor who is then deceased with issue then living; *provided* that any principal thus distributable to a beneficiary who has not then reached the age of twenty-five (25) shall be held in trust for the particular beneficiary as provided below in Article SIXTH, instead of being distributed outright.

Practice Note

Article SIXTH sets forth a simple discretionary trust to manage assets that would otherwise be distributed to a beneficiary under age 25 after the deaths of the donor and his spouse. It can be used with either variant of Article FIFTH. A disinterested trustee is given discretion to distribute income and/or principal to the beneficiary for any reason and at any time. In the alternative, specific limitations could be imposed on the disinterested trustee's discretion (such as distribution for health, maintenance, support, or education only). When the beneficiary reaches age 25, the trust terminates and the assets are distributed outright to the beneficiary. Should the beneficiary die before reaching that age, the beneficiary has a general power to dispose of the remaining trust assets exercisable by will. The existence of this power will cause the trust property to be includable in the beneficiary's estate for purposes of the federal estate tax. For this reason, and in appropriate circumstances, the practitioner may wish to omit the power, or cut it back to a limited power of appointment. Taking either such course may, however, cause a liability for generation-skipping transfer tax at the beneficiary's death. If the general power is not exercised, the remaining trust property is distributed in equal shares to the beneficiary's own children, or, if none, in equal shares to the beneficiary's siblings, with the issue of any deceased sibling taking the deceased sibling's share by right of representation.

The trust includes a provision in paragraph (c) designed to ensure that the trust does not violate the rule against perpetuities. The common law rule against perpetuities provides that, in order for a trust to be valid, all interests must vest or fail no later than 21 years after the death of some life in being at the creation of the interest. In some jurisdictions, the rule against perpetuities can also be satisfied by a fixed term of years (ranging generally from 80 to 110 years). In other jurisdictions, the rule has been eliminated entirely. The form conforms to the most onerous common law rule against perpetuities by providing that, in all events, the trust will terminate no later than 20 years after the date of death of the survivor of the donor, his spouse, and any of the donor's issue (including children and grandchildren) living at the time of the death of the first to die of the donor and his spouse. Lives in being are fixed as of the date of the first death in order to permit trusts created under each spouse's separate trust instrument for the same beneficiary to be combined into one trust.

SIXTH: Trusts for Persons Under Age Twenty-Five. All principal provided under any Article of this trust instrument to be held in trust under this Article SIXTH for a particular beneficiary who has not reached the age of twenty-five (25) shall be combined and administered, in each case, in a single, separate trust for the beneficiary as follows:

(a) *Discretionary Distributions.* All or any part of the net income and principal may be paid to the beneficiary from time to time as the disinterested trustee, in the disinterested trustee's discretion, thinks advisable for any purpose. Any net income not so paid may be added to principal at any time or times.

(b) *Mandatory Distribution of Principal at Age Twenty-Five; Power of Appointment.* When the beneficiary reaches the age of twenty-five (25), the then remaining principal and any balance of net income shall be distributed to the beneficiary. If the beneficiary dies before reaching the age of twenty-five (25), any balance of net income remaining at the beneficiary's death shall be added to principal and the then remaining principal shall be disposed of as the beneficiary appoints by will, executed at any time after the Donor's death and referring specifically to this power of appointment. This power is exercisable in favor of the beneficiary's estate or in favor of any one or more persons or objects; it is exercisable by appointment outright or in trust, and subject to such terms, conditions, general or special powers and restrictions as the beneficiary shall so appoint. In default of or subject to appointment as aforesaid, upon the beneficiary's death before reaching the age of twenty-five (25) the then remaining principal shall be distributed by right of representation to the beneficiary's then living issue, or if none, by right of representation to the then living issue of the beneficiary's ancestor of the nearest degree who has issue then living and who is the Donor or one of his issue; *provided* that any principal thus distributable to a beneficiary who has not then reached the age of twenty-five (25) shall be held in trust for the particular beneficiary as provided in this Article, instead of being distributed outright.

(c) *Rule Against Perpetuities.* If not sooner terminated as provided in paragraph (b), above, the trust shall terminate, and the trust property shall thereupon be distributed to the beneficiary, twenty (20) years after the death of the survivor of the Donor, his said wife, and the issue of the Donor living at the death of the first to die of the Donor and his said wife.

Practice Note

Article SEVENTH provides for the ultimate disposition of trust property upon the failure of all other named beneficiaries. Since there is always a possibility that all of the donor's children and other issue will die before all trusts created under the document terminate, it is prudent to cover this situation. If there is no contingent disposition, the undisposed property would likely be distributed in accordance with the intestacy laws of the donor's domicile.

Typically, a contingent disposition will provide for the disposition of trust property to siblings or nieces and nephews of the donor and the donor's spouse. Alternatively, it may provide for distributions to charities. In the latter event, care must be taken to identify the charity by its correct legal name and to specify the charitable purposes, if any, for the gift (e.g., a gift to a college to establish a scholarship fund).

Care should also be taken to coordinate the contingent dispositions in the pour-over trusts of a married couple if it is anticipated that trusts created after both deaths will be combined and administered together. If the pour-over trust of the husband has a different ultimate disposition from that of the wife, the option of merging the two trusts may not be available.

SEVENTH: <u>Contingent Disposition.</u> If at any time after the death of the survivor of the Donor and his said wife no issue of the Donor is living, any balance of net income and principal that is not otherwise disposed of in accordance with the provisions of this trust instrument shall be distributed as follows:

[ADD DESCRIPTION OF CONTINGENT DISPOSITION]

Practice Note

A pour-over trust should ordinarily provide for the payment of debts and ex-penses and for the method of paying estate taxes. Although not dealt with in the model form, the trust may also provide for the discretionary payment of any legacies contained in the will that the personal representative is not otherwise able to satisfy.

There are many options for dealing with the payment of taxes. The trust property could be used to pay all taxes occasioned by the donor's death. This might be appropriate if all property is passing to the same beneficiaries in accordance with the same general dispositive scheme. Alternatively, the tax clause could provide for the payment of taxes with respect to certain types of property only. For example, it might specifically exclude the payment of taxes on life insurance proceeds unless those proceeds are added to the pour-over trust. The clause in the model document directs that all of the donor's death taxes, whether federal or state, will be paid from the trust property, unless the taxes are attributable to property held in other trusts (with certain exceptions) or property held in trust-form retirement accounts, IRAs, or charitable split-interest trusts. For example, if the donor was a beneficiary of a QTIP trust at his death, the taxes on the QTIP trust property would not be payable from the donor's own trust under this formulation.[2]

Since state death taxes are now deductible for purposes of determining the federal taxable estate, the tax Article provides that they are paid "off the top" even if there is a surviving spouse. As a deductible item, their payment cannot affect the amount of the marital deduction and cause a possible federal estate tax liability. The tax Article also specifically overrides reimbursement rights that may be granted by federal or state law with respect to taxes paid on property held outside the pour-over trust.

The model document does not mandate that all debts and expenses be paid but rather only those requested by the personal representative. The disinterested trustee is given discretion to allocate the payment of debts and expenses to income or principal. The trust should provide that the trustee may rely on the personal repre-sentative's certification that the taxes, debts, and expenses are owing. This provides the trustee protection in the event of dispute. In the event that retirement accounts are made payable to the trust, this Article finally provides that these accounts can only be used to pay debts, expenses, and taxes through September 30 of the year following the year of the donor's death. This is the final date on which the designated beneficiary of a retirement account can be determined for purposes of calculating future minimum distributions. If a retirement account can be used for tax, debt, or expense payments after this date, current regulations appear to prevent there being a designated beneficiary, which as a consequence may accelerate distributions from the account and limit income tax deferral.

---

[2] IRC § 2207A and, in general, state apportionment statutes provide that the taxes attributable to QTIP trusts are to be paid from the QTIP trust property itself at the death of the beneficiary spouse, unless the beneficiary spouse provides other-wise in her will or pour over trust.

EIGHTH: Debts, Expenses and Taxes—in General. Notwithstanding the provisions of Article THIRD above, the trustees shall pay out of the trust principal disposed of thereunder as a whole all death taxes occasioned by the Donor's death, except any such death taxes with respect to property held in any trust other than (i) the trusts hereunder, (ii) any qualified trust described in Section 401(a) of the Internal Revenue Code of 1986, as amended (or any successor provisions thereto) (the "Code"), and any individual retirement account described in Sections 408(a) or 408A of the Code, and (iii) any trust to which the Donor has contributed and under which an annuity, unitrust or remainder interest is intended to qualify for the federal estate tax charitable deduction; all without requiring any reimbursement to the trust from the Donor's personal representative or other persons receiving property as a result of the Donor's death.

In addition, the trustees shall pay out of the trust property as a whole on the Donor's death such of the Donor's debts, funeral and burial expenses, and expenses of administering the Donor's estate as may be requested by the Donor's personal representative. All payments of debts and expenses shall be made from and charged against trust income or principal as the disinterested trustee considers appropriate, or if there is no disinterested trustee for the time being in office, in accordance with the laws of [*SPECIFY STATE GOVERNING LAW*]. Any payments of deductible death taxes shall be made from and charged against principal.

The trustees may rely upon a certificate from the Donor's personal representative to the effect that all such death taxes, debts, or expenses are payable; and the trustees need not inquire into the legality or amount of any death taxes, debts, or expenses so certified. Payments under this Article may be made to or upon the order of the Donor's personal representative or in such other manner as the trustees think advisable. All payments under this Article shall be made only out of property (or proceeds from property) otherwise includable in the Donor's gross estate for federal estate tax purposes, or from the income on such property (or the proceeds therefrom).

Any payments under this Article made by withdrawal from a qualified retirement plan, individual retirement account, or annuity contract or custodial account described in Section 403(b) of the Code of which any trust hereunder is the beneficiary shall be made on or before September 30 of the year following the year of the Donor's death.

References in this Article to "death taxes" mean all federal and state taxes in the nature of estate, inheritance, succession or like taxes, but do not include federal or state generation-skipping transfer taxes.

Practice Note

Article NINTH includes several general administrative provisions. The first is a so-called "facility of payment" provision. It authorizes a trustee to make distributions for a beneficiary's benefit, rather than to the beneficiary directly. This is of particular importance if the beneficiary is incompetent or if it is undesirable to distribute property directly to the beneficiary (e.g., if the beneficiary is a spendthrift). It also allows the trustee to obtain a valid discharge in making a distribution to a minor beneficiary without going through a legally appointed guardian. Instead, the distribution can be made to a parent of the beneficiary or to a custodian under the Uniform Transfers to Minors Act or Uniform Gifts to Minors Act.

The second provision is a "spendthrift clause." It provides that creditors cannot reach the interests of the beneficiaries in the various trusts. It also prohibits voluntary assignments of beneficial interests.

The third provision defines the terms "child" and "issue." Adopted descendants are included, as are all natural born descendants, including the children of unmarried mothers and the children of unmarried fathers where the father has acknowledged paternity. If the donor desires a different result, the clause should be modified.

The term "by right of representation" is defined to state how the shares are to be determined whenever that means of distribution is employed. The children of the person whose issue are to be benefited are considered the stocks for purposes of determining the number of distributive shares, whether or not any of those children are alive at the time of distribution. This overrides the laws of several states. For example, if the donor of the trust had three children (Alice, Betty, and Charles) who all predeceased the donor and four grandchildren (one from Alice, one from Betty, and two from Charles), all of whom survived the donor, a distribution by right of representation to the donor's issue would result under the model form in the donor's property being divided into three parts (one part for each child who had predeceased the donor, but was survived by issue), and Alice's and Betty's children would each get one-third, and Charles's two children would each get one-sixth. In some states, the default rule would provide that if all of the donor's children have predeceased the donor, each grandchild would receive one-quarter of the donor's property.

Finally, the fourth provision states that, although each of the trusts created under the instrument is a separate trust, the trustees are nonetheless authorized to commingle the investments of the separate trusts. Under most state laws, this is not permitted absent a specific provision authorizing it, even when the same instrument creates the trusts. Economic sense will often dictate that this is the most reasonable course. In some situations, commingling will not be possible because of the income, estate, or generation-skipping transfer tax consequences of such action.

NINTH: General Administrative Provisions. Each trust hereunder is subject to the following provisions:

(a) *Distributions to Minors; Impracticable Distributions.* Whenever a payment of income or principal is to be made to any beneficiary, and the beneficiary has not reached the age of twenty-one (21) or is ill or away, or because of other circumstances it is impracticable or undesirable, in the opinion of the disinterested trustee, to make such payment directly to the beneficiary, the disinterested trustee, in the disinterested trustee's discretion, may apply such payment for the beneficiary's benefit in such manner as the disinterested trustee thinks best for the beneficiary, regardless of the beneficiary's other resources. Such application for the beneficiary's benefit, and any payment to a beneficiary who has not reached the age of twenty-one (21), may be made in any amount, either directly or through a guardian, custodian, or member of the family of the beneficiary, or by payment to the beneficiary in person even though he or she has not reached the age of twenty-one (21) or is incapacitated; and the receipt of the payee shall, with respect to each such payment, be a sufficient discharge to the trustees so that they need not see to the further application thereof. No payment may be made that discharges a legal obligation of an individual serving as a disinterested trustee.

(b) *Spendthrift Clause.* The interest of each beneficiary, and all payments of income or principal to be made to or for any beneficiary, shall be free from interference or control by any creditor, spouse, or divorced former spouse of the beneficiary, and shall not be capable of anticipation or assignment by the beneficiary.

(c) *Definitions.* In this trust instrument, references to "child" or "children" mean descendants in the first degree only, and references to "issue" mean descendants in the first, second, or any other degree; in each case meaning lawful descendants of the ancestor designated, whether by blood or by adoption and whether living on the date of this trust instrument or born or adopted thereafter. For purposes of the preceding sentence, a person born out of wedlock and those claiming through that person shall be treated as lawful descendants (i) of the natural mother and her ancestors, and (ii) if the natural father acknowledges paternity, of the natural father and his ancestors, in each case unless a decree of adoption terminates such natural parent's parental rights. Whenever property is to be distributed by right of representation to the then living issue of a designated ancestor, the ancestor's children shall be considered the stocks for purposes of determining the respective shares of such issue.

(d) *Investment in Common Fund.* Each of the trusts hereunder shall constitute a separate and distinct trust, but for convenience of administration the trustees may, in their discretion, mingle or combine any of the investments or property of said trusts in a common fund in which the several contributing trusts shall have undivided proportionate interests.

Practice Note

State law grants many powers of administration to trustees. To eliminate the need to refer to statutes and case law and to explicitly set forth the donor's intent, it is good drafting practice to set forth the powers expressly. This will also serve to eliminate problems arising from ambiguities in local law, expand the scope of the trustees' authority, avoid the need for court approval of certain actions, and, in some circumstances, minimize estate taxes. The list of powers contained in the model article is general and should cover most situations. If, however, a client wishes to fund the trust and open a margin account with a broker, the brokerage house will typically require specific authority in the document for such action.

TENTH: Trustees' Powers. In extension and not in limitation of the powers given them by law or other provisions of this trust instrument, the trustees of each trust hereunder shall have the following powers with respect to the trust and its property, in each case to be exercised from time to time in the discretion of the trustees and without order or license of court:

(a) To retain indefinitely, and to invest and reinvest in, stocks, shares, obligations, partnership interests, and other securities or any other kind of personal or real property, even though any or all of the investments made or retained are of a character or size that, but for this express authority, would not be considered proper for trustees;

(b) To sell, to exchange, to lease, and to make contracts concerning real or personal property for such consideration and upon such terms as to credit or otherwise as the trustees consider advisable, which leases and contracts may extend beyond the term of the trust; to give options on real or personal property of the trust; to establish depreciation, depletion, tax, or any other reserves; to execute deeds, transfers, leases, and other instruments of any kind; and to deal with themselves or one of them as freely as with a stranger;

(c) To hold securities or other property in bearer or unregistered form or in the name of one or more of the trustees or of any other person, firm, or corporation, without indication of any fiduciary capacity;

(d) To give general or special proxies or powers of attorney (which may or may not be discretionary and with power of substitution) for voting or acting with respect to securities; to deposit securities with, or transfer them to, protective committees, voting trustees, or similar bodies; to join in any reorganization; and to pay assessments or subscriptions called for in connection with securities held by the trustees;

(e) To receive additions to the trust by gift or will or under any policy of insurance on the Donor's life or otherwise, and to hold and administer the same under the provisions hereof;

(f) To compromise or submit to arbitration and to pay before due any tax, claim, or matter in dispute;

(g) If in the opinion of the trustees it is necessary or advisable to do so, to borrow money for such time and at such rate of interest or discount as the trustees deem proper; to give notes or obligations therefor binding the trust property; and as security therefor to mortgage or to pledge real or personal property with or without power of sale; but the Donor recommends that such borrowing be limited to cases in which, in the judgment of the trustees, it is necessary or advisable to provide for the payment of taxes or indebtedness or to meet emergencies;

(h) To improve or develop real estate; to construct, alter, repair, or demolish buildings or structures; to settle boundary lines and easements and other rights; to partition; and to join with co-owners or others in dealing with real estate in any way;

(i) To employ investment counsel and consult with them concerning the investments of the trust and to delegate to such counsel such powers as the trustees deem appropriate; to employ agents and to delegate to such agents such powers as the trustees deem appropriate; to employ legal counsel, accountants, and any special services; to employ a custodian of any funds or securities and to delegate to the custodian such powers as the trustees deem appropriate; and, in addition to the compensation and expenses of the trustees, to pay the compensation and expenses of all such services even if rendered by a trustee;

(j) To credit particular receipts or gains, and to charge particular disbursements or losses or charges, to income or to principal of the trust or to apportion them between income and principal, whether such credits or charges relate to bonds acquired at a premium, to reserves or to any other matter, all as the disinterested trustee considers fair and reasonable in each case, or if there is no disinterested trustee for the time being in office, all in accordance with the laws of [*SPECIFY STATE GOVERNING LAW*]; and

(k) To make any division or distribution of, or payment from, the trust, in kind by the fair and reasonable allotment and transfer of specific securities or other personal or real property or undivided interests therein, at then current values, in lieu of cash, as a part or the whole of any one or more shares or payments.

Practice Note

Article ELEVENTH addresses issues regarding the identity of the trustees. It clarifies that any reference to the term "trustees" refers to whoever occupies the position at that time, regardless of whether he or she is an original, additional, or successor trustee. This provision also deals with the manner in which trustees may resign voluntarily, and the circumstances in which trustees are deemed to resign or retire. It also gives the donor and then his spouse the right to remove trustees. Until 1995, there was some concern that giving a surviving spouse the right to remove trustees of the Credit Share trust and appoint their successors would give the surviving spouse a sufficient degree of control of the trust assets to cause their inclusion in her estate for tax purposes at her later death. A published ruling from that year dispels this concern, provided that if in removing a disinterested trustee the spouse is prohibited from appointing someone who is related or subordinate to her, as those terms are defined under the grantor trust rules.

The model document includes a general mechanism for appointing successor and additional trustees. It is not necessary for successor trustees to be named specifically in the document but a donor will frequently want to identify who would act as trustee in the event that both he and his spouse die leaving minor children. This form makes a provision for such a designation. The trustee so appointed will be responsible for managing the children's assets through the termination date of the trust. In choosing a successor trustee, the donor should consider whether he would like her to be the same person or a different person from whoever is named in the will to be the personal guardian of the children. The advantage of having it be the same person is that it is less cumbersome. On the other hand, there is frequently some comfort in dividing these roles and setting up a system of checks and balances.

Where there are different classes of trustees, the distinctions should be carefully delineated in order to avoid unexpected tax problems. The model document uses the concept of a disinterested trustee and defines the disinterested trustee to exclude any individual who has a beneficial interest in the trust. The disinterested trustee is vested with those discretions—primarily over the distribution of trust assets—that, if held by a beneficiary trustee, would produce gift and estate tax problems. An alternative and perhaps simpler definition could require that the disinterested trustee be a professional fiduciary or a national bank or a trust company.

This article authorizes the trustees to delegate authority to each other and waives bond or surety. Other provisions that might be included would cover a limitation on trustee liability in the absence of gross negligence or willful default, and trustee compensation.

ELEVENTH: Trustees. With respect to each trust hereunder, references in this trust instrument to the "trustees" mean the one or more trustees, whether original, additional, or successor, for the time being in office; and references to the "disinterested trustee" mean the one or more trustees having no beneficial interest, whether vested or contingent, in the income or principal of any trust hereunder.

Any trustee may resign by giving written notice to the Donor, if he is then living, or if not, to his said wife, if she is then living, or if not, to the remaining trustee, if any, or if none, to the one or more persons to whom the trustees would then render accounts of the particular trust as provided below in Article TWELFTH. Any individual trustee shall be deemed to have resigned and any named individual successor trustee shall be deemed unable to serve upon the first to occur of the following: (i) the appointment of a legal guardian or similar legal representative for such individual; and (ii) the receipt by the one or more persons then entitled to appoint successor trustees of a writing signed by the individual's regularly attending physician certifying that, in the physician's opinion, such individual is mentally or physically incapable of discharging the responsibilities of a trustee.

During his lifetime, the Donor may remove any trustee by giving the trustee written notice. After the Donor's death, any trustee may be removed in a writing delivered to the trustee and signed by the Donor's said wife, if she is then living and of full legal capacity; *provided* that no such removal of a disinterested trustee shall take effect until a successor disinterested trustee who is not a "related or subordinate party" within the meaning of Section 672(c) of the Code with respect to the Donor's said wife has been appointed in a writing signed by the Donor's said wife and has accepted such appointment.

There need not be more than one trustee for the time being in office of each trust hereunder, but [after the death of the Donor] OR [after the death of the survivor of the Donor and his said wife] there shall regularly be at least one disinterested trustee for the time being in office of each trust hereunder. After the death of the survivor of the Donor and his said wife, [*NAME OF SUCCESSOR*

TRUSTEE], of [ADDRESS], shall become a trustee of each trust hereunder, upon written acceptance of the office. If for any reason the said [NAME OF SUCCESSOR TRUSTEE] fails to accept the appointment or, having accepted, later ceases to serve, and in case of any other vacancy in the office of trustee of any trust hereunder, a successor trustee may be appointed in a writing signed by the Donor, if he is then living and of full legal capacity, or if not, by his said wife, if she is then living and of full legal capacity, or if not, by the remaining trustee, if any, or if none, by the one or more persons to whom the trustees would then render accounts of the particular trust as provided below in Article TWELFTH.

Whenever there are fewer than three (3) trustees for the time being in office, one or more additional trustees may be appointed at any time or times, to take office presently or at any future time and upon such other terms and conditions, by a writing signed by the Donor, if he is then living and of full legal capacity, or, if not, by his said wife, if she is then living and of full legal capacity, or, if not, by the trustees for the time being in office. Any such appointment may be revoked in writing at any time before it becomes effective.

Unless otherwise provided in the instrument of appointment, each appointment of a successor or additional trustee shall take effect upon written acceptance of the office.

By a writing or writings, any trustee may delegate all or any of that trustee's powers and discretions to any other trustee for a period specified in such writing, and may revoke or successively renew such delegation; *provided* that the powers and discretions given to the disinterested trustee, as such, shall be exercised by the disinterested trustee alone, exclusive of any other of the trustees, and may be delegated only to another disinterested trustee.

No trustee named herein or appointed as above provided need furnish any bond or surety. No one dealing with the trustees need inquire concerning the validity of anything the trustees purport to do or need see to the application of any money paid or property transferred to or upon the order of the trustees.

Practice Note

The trust should deal with the manner in which trustees account to beneficiaries so that the trustees' obligations are clear. In the model form, accounts are rendered to all beneficiaries who are entitled either as of right or in the discretion of the disinterested trustee to income distributions. Accounts would not be rendered to contingent remainder beneficiaries. The provision also attempts to bring finality by providing protection to the trustees once accounts are assented to. However, it should be noted that, in some jurisdictions, such a provision might not be sufficient to insulate the trustees from complaints later raised by remainder beneficiaries.

TWELFTH: Accounts. During the Donor's lifetime, the trustees shall render an account of the trust hereunder to him or, if he is not then of full legal capacity, to his said wife, if she is then living and of full legal capacity, or, if not, to the Donor's legal guardian or similar legal representative, upon request. After the

Donor's death, the trustees of each trust hereunder shall render an account of the trust at least as often as annually to each beneficiary of the trust to whom in the period covered by such account current income from the trust was payable or could have been paid in the discretion of the disinterested trustee and who is living and of full legal capacity and, if any such beneficiary is not of full legal capacity, to his or her legal guardian or similar legal representative, if any, or, if none, to either of his or her parents if he or she is a minor. In the case of each trust hereunder, the written assent to any such account by the one or more persons of full legal capacity to whom it is rendered as provided above shall fully protect the trustees as to all matters or transactions stated in such account or shown thereby, even if such person is serving as a trustee hereunder. Any person who is not of full legal capacity shall be deemed to assent to such account if his or her legal guardian or similar legal representative assents in writing to the account or if (such beneficiary being a minor and having no such legal guardian or representative) the parent to whom the account was rendered assents in writing to the account. Nothing in this Article shall be deemed to give anyone the power to modify the terms of this trust instrument or to alter or shift any beneficial interest created hereunder.

Practice Note

An *inter vivos* pour-over trust is frequently named as the beneficiary of life insurance proceeds. This provision makes it clear that the trustees have no responsibility for the maintenance or selection of the policy merely by reason of the beneficiary designation. All ownership rights and responsibilities remain with the donor-insured. The trustees' responsibilities would increase, however, if the policy ownership were assigned to them. This would be unusual in the case of an *inter vivos* revocable trust, however, because the assignment would have no estate tax benefits. If an assignment is to be made, it should be made to an irrevocable trust designed specifically to own the policy and dispose of the death benefit. A model of such a trust is set forth in Form 4.

THIRTEENTH: Life Insurance. Unless any policy of life insurance made payable to the trustees is assigned to them, the owner of the policy shall retain, as against the trustees, all incidents of ownership thereof, and the trustees shall have no responsibility for the payment of premiums thereon. The trustees shall be entitled to indemnification from the trust principal for the expense of any legal proceedings taken to collect the proceeds of any such policy.

Practice Note

The trustees should make secure arrangements for the custody of all trust documentation. It is general practice today, in light of photocopying technology, to sign only one original counterpart of the trust instrument. This provision allows outside parties to rely on certified copies of original documentation rather than requiring access to the original document itself.

FOURTEENTH: Trust Documentation. The original of each alteration or amendment of this trust instrument, each resignation, removal, or appointment of a trustee, each acceptance of appointment and each instrument of delegation shall be kept attached to the original trust instrument, which shall be held by the trustees. Anyone may rely on a copy certified by a notary public of this trust instrument or of any writings attached thereto as fully as on the original document; and anyone may rely fully upon any statements of fact certified by anyone who appears from the original document or a certified copy thereof to be a trustee hereunder.

Practice Note

Spouses typically have mirror image estate plans. This provision authorizes the trustees after the death of the surviving spouse to merge substantially identical trusts under both instruments. This should permit costs savings.

FIFTEENTH: Combination and Termination of Trusts. If at any time after both the Donor and his said wife have died a trust is being administered hereunder for one or more beneficiaries on terms substantially identical to those on which a trust is then being administered for the same one or more beneficiaries under the provisions of [THE SARAH SAMPLE [*YEAR*] TRUST, established today by the Donor's said wife, with herself and the Donor as trustees ("SARAH'S [*YEAR*] TRUST")], the trustees in their discretion may terminate the trust under this instrument by distributing any balance of net income and the then remaining principal to the then trustees of SARAH'S [*YEAR*] TRUST to be added to the trust thereunder for the same beneficiaries.

Practice Note

Conflict of law problems can arise when the donor, the trust beneficiaries, and the trustees are not all resident in the same jurisdiction. Article SIXTEENTH states which jurisdiction will govern the operation of the trust. A governing law clause will generally be upheld as long as the state chosen has some logical connection to the trust. Consideration should be given to permitting the trustees to change the governing law with respect to the administration of the trusts created by the trust instrument. This might be appropriate if all connections with the original chosen jurisdiction cease.

SIXTEENTH: Governing Law. This trust instrument and the trusts hereunder shall be governed, construed, and administered in accordance with the laws of [*SPECIFY GOVERNING STATE LAW*] from time to time in force.

Practice Note

The document should be dated and signed by the donor and trustees at the end. It is good practice in most jurisdictions to have the donor's signature notarized. This may be particularly relevant if real estate will be held in the trust and the trust document recorded. Care should be taken that a trust is executed in accordance with all required local formalities. In some jurisdictions, the signatures of the donor and trustees should be witnessed. In other jurisdictions, all signatures must be notarized. In yet others, an *inter vivos* pour-over trust should be executed with the same formalities as a will. In general, the document should be executed in accordance with the requirements of the donor's state of domicile. Where, however, out-of-state real estate may be held in the trust, consideration should be given to the execution requirements of those other jurisdictions as well.

SIGNED and SEALED this ＿＿ day of ＿＿＿, 20＿.

———————————————————
SAM SAMPLE, Donor and Trustee

———————————————————
SARAH SAMPLE, Trustee

STATE/COMMONWEALTH OF [*NAME OF STATE*]

_____, ss.

On this ____ day of _____, 20__, before me, the undersigned notary public, personally appeared the above-named SAM SAMPLE, known to me personally or proved to me through _____ as satisfactory evidence of identification, to be the person whose name is signed on the preceding document, and acknowledged to me that he signed it voluntarily for its stated purpose.

_____
Notary Public
My Commission Expires:

FORM 2
Living Trust with Multiple QTIP Marital Trust Options

Overview

This form also establishes a revocable or living trust. In many respects, it incorporates and follows the provisions of Form 1. For that reason, it is strongly urged that you review that form first and its related overview and practice notes before looking at this form. In particular, the practice notes in Form 1 relating to the overview, Article FIRST, and Articles SIXTH through SIXTEENTH have not been repeated in Form 2. The critical difference between the two forms is in the provisions that apply if the donor spouse is the first of the married couple to die.

As outlined in detail in various sections of the text of this book, the American Taxpayer Relief Act of 2012 has prompted reconsideration of the traditional approaches to estate planning for a married couple. The Act itself contained no radical changes to the estate tax law. However, it made permanent two important provisions that had been included in legislation at the end of 2010: (1) a higher level of exemption from the federal estate tax, with each person having a $5,000,000 basic exclusion amount, indexed for inflation beginning in 2011; and (2) portability of the applicable exclusion amount between spouses. The basic exclusion amount was again raised in 2018 to $10,000,000, which indexed for inflation is $12,060,000 in 2022.

Under portability, if the first spouse to die does not use his or her applicable exclusion amount in full, the unused portion, referred to as the "Deceased Spousal Unused Exclusion Amount" or the "DSUE Amount," can be transferred or ported to the surviving spouse. The surviving spouse then has an exclusion, for both gift and estate tax purposes, equal to the sum of his or her own basic exclusion amount and the DSUE Amount of the first spouse to die.

There are numerous requirements for portability to be effective and restrictions on its applicability. *See* Section 14.05[E]. However, it has introduced a new set of considerations to the planning process, as well as provided a mechanism for the correction of mistakes that may have been made in the planning process (e.g., where assets are not held in a way that facilitates use of the applicable exclusion amount of the first spouse to die or where the estate plan itself does not contain optimal provisions to use both applicable exclusion amounts).

It may be tempting to conclude that planning of the type outlined in Form 1 has been rendered redundant by portability. In some cases, this may be true, particularly where simplicity – achieved either by owning all assets jointly or by having "I-love-you" wills (that is, wills that leave everything outright to the surviving spouse) – is the goal and meets the family's critical needs. However, there are both advantages and disadvantages to relying exclusively on portability and moving away from prior core planning concepts. The following is a list of the more significant considerations:

- *Asset appreciation between deaths.* If a trust is funded at the first death and shielded from estate taxes by use of the first to die's applicable exclusion amount, all subsequent appreciation in those assets is also shielded from estate taxes at the surviving spouse's death. In contrast, if all assets pass to the surviving spouse at the first death and the first to die's applicable exclusion amount is ported, those assets will be included in the survivor's estate at their value at the time of the survivor's death, thereby subjecting the appreciation to potential estate tax liability. In addition, the DSUE Amount is fixed at the time of the first death; it is not adjusted by an inflation factor for the period between the first death and the second death.

- *Generation-skipping transfer tax exemption.* Portability only applies to the estate tax exemption; there is no portability of the exemption from the federal generation-skipping transfer tax. Accordingly, a plan that leaves all assets outright to the surviving spouse would not be an optimal plan if, after both deaths, the desired distribution provisions involve the use of long-term trusts for the benefit of children, grandchildren and more remote issue.

- *State death taxes.* Although the number of states that continue to have a state estate tax is dwindling, certain key states have maintained their death taxes. For the most part, those taxes have not been amended to increase the state exemption in line with the federal exemption, or to permit portability of the state estate tax exemption between spouses. Accordingly, a simple plan that relies exclusively on portability may increase the overall level of state estate taxes due after both spouses' deaths by wasting the state estate tax exemption of the first to die.

- *Income tax considerations.* Under a traditional plan, assets held in the Credit Share trust established by the first to die do not get a new basis at the death of the surviving spouse because they are not includable in the estate of the surviving spouse. Any unrealized appreciation in those assets attributable to the period between the two deaths would then be subject to an income tax liability when the assets are sold by the children or others receiving them. In contrast, with a portability plan, all assets are includable in the estate of the survivor and receive a new basis, thereby side-stepping the built-in capital gains tax liability. This difference can be significant if the combined level of federal estate tax exemptions was adequate to cover the entire asset base of the couple, meaning that a full portability plan would result in no federal estate tax.

- *Asset protection.* Assets passing to a Credit Share trust that is funded at the first death can include the surviving spouse as a discretionary beneficiary and can be shielded from estate taxes at the survivor's later death and from the survivor's creditors during the survivor's lifetime and at his or her death. In contrast, a simple outright portability plan will place all assets in the ownership of the surviving spouse and subject all assets to the claims of his or her creditors.

- *Control.* A simple portability plan will leave the surviving spouse in control of all assets owned by the married couple. This means that the distribution of all property will be determined by the survivor's will. If the survivor remarries, assets may not pass at the survivor's death to the children of the first marriage or other individuals or organizations that the original couple had intended to benefit. In contrast, a traditional plan involving a Credit Share trust will ensure that the assets remaining in that trust at the survivor's death pass as the couple had agreed when both were alive.

- *Reduced expenses.* A simple portability plan will likely produce lower administrative expenses during the surviving spouse's lifetime. There will be no need for trust tax returns and trustee fees will be avoided.

As these points illustrate, while portability may superficially appear to have simplified the estate planning process, in reality it has created further complications in many situations. It has provided a new set of options, with uncertainty – at least at the initial planning stage – as to which of those options may prove the most advantageous. With this in mind, the task for the planner will frequently be to build in flexibility, so that decisions are not preordained by the documents themselves but can instead be determined at the time of the first death. This form incorporates two possible "flexible" approaches, as will be outlined in the practice note to Article THIRD.

THE SAM SAMPLE [*YEAR*] TRUST

SAM SAMPLE (also known as SAMUEL ARTHUR SAMPLE), of [*AD-DRESS*] (the "Donor"), herewith transfers the sum of One Dollar ($1) to himself and his wife, SARAH SAMPLE, as trustees hereunder; and the trustees hereby acknowledge receipt of said sum and agree, for themselves, any additional trustees and all successors in office, to hold and manage it, together with any additions to it, IN TRUST, upon the following terms and provisions:

FIRST: Revocation or Amendment. This trust shall be known as "THE SAM SAMPLE [*YEAR*] TRUST." The Donor shall have the right at any time or times, by a writing or writings (other than a will or a codicil) signed by him and delivered to the trustees during the Donor's lifetime, to revoke the trust hereunder, or to alter or amend this trust instrument, in whole or in part. If this trust is revoked in its entirety, the revocation shall take effect upon the delivery of the required writing to the trustees, who shall thereupon pay or transfer to the Donor, or as he directs, all of the trust property. Any alteration or amendment of this trust instrument shall take effect when consented to in writing by the trustees.

SECOND: Provisions Applicable During Donor's Lifetime. During the lifetime of the Donor, the trustees shall distribute to him, or as he directs, all or such part of the net income and principal as he from time to time requests; and without any request, at any time or times during the Donor's lifetime, the trustee other than the Donor may distribute to, or apply in such manner as such trustee thinks advisable for the benefit of, the Donor such amounts or all of the net income and principal as the trustee other than the Donor, in such trustee's discretion, thinks advisable for any purpose. Any net income not so distributed or applied may be added to principal at any time or times, and any net income remaining at the death of the Donor shall be added to principal at that time.

So long as the Donor is serving as trustee hereunder, any trustee in office other than the Donor (unless directed to the contrary in writing by the Donor) shall have no responsibility whatsoever to consider the advisability of retaining, disposing of or acquiring investments for the trust hereunder, or to make investment decisions, but shall act in these respects solely as directed from time to time by the Donor in his capacity as trustee. Any action by the Donor as trustee pursuant to this provision shall be binding on the trust. In addition, any person or entity shall be entitled to rely conclusively on the sole signature or execution by the Donor as trustee as the act and deed of the trust with respect to all matters relating to the administration of the trust property, and the signature or execution by any or all other trustees then in office shall under no circumstances be required. No co-trustee shall be liable in connection with any action taken by the Donor as trustee unless the particular co-trustee shall join affirmatively in that action.

Practice Note

Article THIRD disposes of all property held in the trust on the date of the donor's death, together with all property added to the trust as a result of the donor's death (through the donor's will or by beneficiary designation).

If the donor's spouse survives the donor, two approaches are offered. Under the first approach, all assets pass into a QTIP Marital Trust for the benefit of the surviving spouse. The QTIP Marital Trust is set forth in Article FOURTH and is for the sole benefit of the surviving spouse. The Family Trust under Article FIFTH, which can include others as beneficiaries during the surviving spouse's lifetime, would be funded only if the surviving spouse or her legal representative chooses to disclaim some part or all of the property passing to the QTIP Marital Trust through a qualified disclaimer. If the Family Trust were funded in this way, it should be noted that the surviving spouse cannot be given a power of appointment to dispose of the Family Trust assets at his or her later death. The existence of such a power would prevent the disclaimer from being treated as a qualified disclaimer and would result in a taxable gift by the surviving spouse.

Under the second approach, the assets of the first to die pass into the QTIP Marital Trust to the extent that a QTIP election is actually made for estate tax purposes by the first spouse to die's personal representative. Assets that are not covered by the QTIP election would pass instead into the Family Trust. This type of planning is often referred to as a "Clayton" QTIP provision. See Section 6.03[D][4][b][ii]. If the Family Trust is funded because a QTIP election is not made with respect to all the trust property, the surviving spouse can have a power of appointment at his or her later death to vary the disposition of the remaining assets then held in the Family Trust.

Both of these approaches have the advantage of providing flexibility with respect to the timing and use of the estate tax exemption of the first to die. Under the first approach, a decision can be made to use the first to die's exemption at the first death. A QTIP election would then only be made for federal estate tax purposes with respect to the Marital Trust to the extent that the first to die's assets exceeded the estate tax exemption. Two Marital Trusts would then exist: one elected for the marital deduction and includable in the estate of the surviving spouse; and the other not elected for marital deduction purposes and therefore not includable in the estate of the surviving spouse.

At the other end of the tax spectrum, the first approach would allow a QTIP election to be made with respect to all assets passing to the Marital Trust. The first to die's unused applicable exclusion amount could then be ported to the surviving spouse. Making such a QTIP election to permit portability appears to be permitted under the marital deduction regulations and is supported by Revenue Procedure 2016-49. It has the advantage of maintaining a trust structure (with creditor protection for the trust principal and control over the eventual disposition of the trust assets) while securing a new basis in the trust assets at the death of the surviving spouse. The potential downside is that all post-first-death appreciation in the trust assets will be includable in the estate of the surviving spouse for federal estate tax purposes.

The first approach also has the advantage in some states of allowing effective state estate tax planning. Many states that still have their own estate tax systems permit a state only QTIP election – that is, a QTIP election that is not identical to the election made for federal purposes and allows the decedent's estate to claim the benefit of the state estate tax marital deduction only. Such a provision may allow a personal representative to take advantage of the state estate tax exemption and then elect to qualify the balance of the trust property for the applicable state estate tax marital deduction.

The second approach – the "Clayton" QTIP – provides similar planning opportunities with respect to portability and potential state estate tax planning. Since the decision to elect marital deduction treatment may change the nature of the interest of the surviving spouse (a net income Marital Trust versus a discretionary interest under a spray Family Trust), the surviving spouse should not be the personal representative of the first-to-die's will (or the personal representative who is charged with making tax election decisions). If the spouse were a personal representative, it could be argued that he or she was making a gift (for example, foregoing an automatic income interest). As a consequence, Clayton planning may add to the cost of estate settlement by requiring a disinterested fiduciary.

THIRD: Disposition Upon the Donor's Death. Upon the death of the Donor, the then trust principal (as augmented by all property transferred to the trustees from any source as a result of the Donor's death, and as reduced by payment of the Donor's death taxes, debts and expenses as directed below in Article EIGHTH) shall be disposed of as follows:

[OPTION ONE — SINGLE QTIP MARITAL TRUST]

(a) *If the Donor's Wife Shall Survive the Donor.* If the Donor's said wife survives him, the then trust principal shall be set aside as the Marital Share and shall be held in the Marital Trust as provided below in Article FOURTH.

[OPTION TWO — MARITAL/FAMILY SPLIT TURNS ON QTIP ELECTION — MARITAL IN QTIP TRUST]

(a) *If the Donor's Wife Shall Survive the Donor.* If the Donor's said wife survives him, the then trust principal shall be set aside as the Marital Share and shall be held in the Marital Trust as provided below in Article FOURTH, except if any portion of the Marital Share is not elected to qualify for the federal estate tax marital deduction and is not treated as marital deduction property for purposes of calculating any state estate tax, then such portion instead shall be held in the Family Trust as provided below in Article FIFTH.

(b) *If the Donor's Wife Shall Not Survive the Donor.* If the Donor's said wife does not survive the Donor, the then trust principal, or any other property directed to be disposed of as provided in this paragraph, shall be distributed in equal shares, one share to each child of the Donor who is then living and one share by right of representation to the then living issue of each child of the Donor who is then deceased with issue then living; *provided* that any principal thus distributable to a beneficiary who has not reached the age of twenty-five (25) shall be held in trust for the particular beneficiary as provided below in Article SIXTH, instead of being distributed outright.

(c) *If the Donor's Wife Shall Survive the Donor but Shall Disclaim All or Any Portion of the Marital Share.* If the Donor's said wife survives the Donor but she or her legal representative disclaims all her interest in all or any portion of the Marital Share, the Marital Share (or the disclaimed portion thereof, as the case may be) shall instead be held in the Family Trust as provided below in Article FIFTH. If the Donor's said wife or her legal representative disclaims all her interest in all or any portion of the property to be held in the Family Trust, such disclaimed portion shall instead be disposed of as provided above in paragraph (b) of this Article THIRD as if the Donor's said wife had predeceased the Donor.

Practice Note

Article FOURTH sets forth the terms of the Marital Trust. The Marital Trust is set up as a QTIP Trust, the broad requirements of which are discussed above in Form 1. Note the following:

- The options for paragraph (a) concern the ability to distribute principal. The QTIP Trust must provide for the surviving spouse to receive all the trust net income at least annually. It is not necessary for the trust to permit principal distributions. Under the second option, the spouse can serve as the sole trustee and also distribute principal to himself or herself under an ascertainable standard. The first option requires a disinterested trustee, since the discretion to distribute principal is not limited to an ascertainable standard.

- Including a withdrawal right is entirely optional. The structure included is simple and permits up to 5 percent of the trust principal to be withdrawn on the last business day of the calendar year. Five percent is the maximum amount withdrawable in any year to avoid gift tax problems to the surviving spouse if the right is allowed to lapse.

- The form includes a limited power of appointment exercisable by the surviving spouse at his or her later death. The power of appointment is not mandatory and can be omitted. It is exercisable in favor of the donor's issue, their spouses and charities. This class of appointees could be expanded or contracted.

> The language in clause (ii) of the final paragraph is optional and could be omitted if the couple lives in a state without a state estate tax.

FOURTH: <u>Marital Trust</u>. Any Marital Share provided in Article THIRD above to be disposed of as provided in this Article FOURTH shall be administered in a separate trust as follows:

[OPTION ONE — DISCRETIONARY PRINCIPAL]

(a) *Distributions During Lifetime of Donor's Wife.* The net income shall be paid to the Donor's said wife at least as often as quarterly during her lifetime. In addition, all or any part of the principal may be paid to her in such amounts and at such time or times as the disinterested trustee, in the disinterested trustee's discretion, thinks advisable for any purpose. The Donor hopes, without limiting the discretion of the disinterested trustee, that, in the exercise of this authority to make payments of principal, the disinterested trustee will give primary consideration to the welfare of the Donor's said wife during her lifetime.

[OPTION TWO — ASCERTAINABLE STANDARD FOR PRINCIPAL DISTRIBUTIONS]

(a) *Distributions During Lifetime of Donor's Wife.* The net income shall be paid to the Donor's said wife at least as often as quarterly during her lifetime. In addition, all or any part of the principal may be paid to her in such amounts and at such time or times as the trustees, in their discretion, think advisable for her health, maintenance or support, and whenever there is a disinterested trustee for the time being in office, all or any part of the principal not so used may be paid to the Donor's said wife in such amounts and at such time or times as the disinterested trustee, in the disinterested trustee's discretion, thinks advisable for any purpose.

[OPTION — WITHDRAWAL RIGHT]

(b) *Withdrawal Right.* Notwithstanding the provisions of paragraph (a) above, in each calendar year after that of the Donor's death, if the Donor's said wife is living on the last day of the calendar year, she shall have the right by a writing delivered to the trustees on or before such day to withdraw from the trust principal any amount up to five percent (5%) of the value of the trust principal as of such day.

(b) /(c) *Power of Appointment.* Upon the death of the Donor's said wife, the then remaining principal shall be disposed of as the Donor's said wife shall appoint by a will, executed at any time after the Donor's death, and referring specifically to this power of appointment, to or for the benefit of any one or more of the Donor's issue, the spouses of such issue and charitable organizations or purposes, in such amounts or proportions, for such estates, on such trusts, and subject to such terms, conditions, general or special powers of appointment and restrictions as the Donor's said wife shall appoint. This power of appointment shall not be exercisable, directly or indirectly, to or in favor of the Donor's said wife, her estate, her creditors, or the creditors of her estate.

(c) /(d) *Disposition Upon Death of Survivor of Donor and Donor's Wife.* In default of or subject to appointment by the Donor's said wife as aforesaid, upon her death the then remaining principal shall be distributed in equal shares, one share to each child of the Donor who is then living and one share by right of representation to the then living issue of each child of the Donor who is then deceased with issue then living; *provided* that any principal thus distributable to a beneficiary who has not then reached the age of twenty-five (25) shall be held in trust for the particular beneficiary as provided below in Article SIXTH, instead of being distributed outright.

(d) /(e) *Division of Marital Trust.* The trustees, in their discretion, may divide the Marital Trust into two or more separate trusts of equal or unequal value, to be administered on the same terms as the original trust. Such a division may be made (i) to reflect an election to qualify a specific portion (but not all) of a trust for the federal estate tax marital deduction, in which case such division shall be made in accordance with Section 20.2056(b)-7(b)(2)(ii) of the Treasury Regulations; (ii) to reflect a marital deduction election made or deemed to be made for state estate tax purposes; or (iii) for any other reason the trustees, in their discretion, think advisable.

Practice Note

This Article sets forth the terms of the Family Trust. Four options have been provided for the administration of the trust during the survivor's lifetime. These options differ based on whether there will be a disinterested trustee in office and based on the scope of the interest in the trust to be provided to the surviving spouse.

The Article contains a withdrawal right in the surviving spouse and a power of appointment, both of which can be omitted if desired. The power of appointment should be omitted if the Family Trust will only be funded by a disclaimer. This would happen if the single marital trust option were selected. In this situation, the funding of the Family Trust can only arise if the spouse or his or her legal representative disclaims part of the Marital Share.

FIFTH: Family Trust. All principal provided under Article THIRD above to be disposed of as provided in this Article FIFTH shall be administered in a separate trust and disposed of as follows:

[OPTION ONE — SPRAY INCOME AND PRINCIPAL]

(a) *Distributions During Lifetime of Donor's Wife.* All or any part of the net income and principal may be paid to any one or more of the Donor's said wife, the Donor's children, and the Donor's more remote issue, in such amounts and proportions, and at such time or times, as the disinterested trustee, in the disinterested trustee's discretion, thinks advisable for any purpose. Any net income not so paid may be added to principal at any time or times, and any net income remaining upon the death of the Donor's said wife shall be added to principal at that time. The Donor hopes, without limiting the discretion of the disinterested trustee, that, in the exercise of this authority to make payments of net income and principal, the disinterested trustee will give primary consideration to the welfare of the Donor's said wife during her lifetime.

[OPTION TWO — NET INCOME TO SPOUSE AND SPRAY PRINCIPAL]

(a) *Distributions During Lifetime of Donor's Wife*. The net income shall be paid to the Donor's said wife at least as often as quarterly during her lifetime. In addition, all or any part of the principal may be paid to any one or more of the Donor's said wife, the Donor's children and the Donor's more remote issue, in such amounts or proportions and at such time or times as the disinterested trustee, in the disinterested trustee's discretion, thinks advisable for any purpose. The Donor hopes, without limiting the discretion of the disinterested trustee, that, in the exercise of this authority to make payments of principal, the disinterested trustee will give primary consideration to the welfare of the Donor's said wife during her lifetime.

[OPTION THREE — NET INCOME TO SPOUSE AND PRINCIPAL TO SPOUSE SUBJECT TO ASCERTAINABLE STANDARD]

(a) *Distributions During Lifetime of Donor's Wife*. The net income shall be paid to the Donor's said wife at least as often as quarterly during her lifetime. In addition, all or any part of the principal may be paid to her in such amounts and at such time or times as the trustees, in their discretion, think advisable for her health, maintenance or support, and whenever there is a disinterested trustee for the time being in office, all or any part of the principal not so used may be paid to the Donor's said wife in such amounts and at such time or times as the disinterested trustee, in the disinterested trustee's discretion, thinks advisable for any purpose.

[OPTION FOUR — NET INCOME TO SPOUSE AND PRINCIPAL TO SPOUSE AND ISSUE SUBJECT TO ASCERTAINABLE STANDARD]

(a) *Distributions During Lifetime of Donor's Wife*. The net income shall be paid to the Donor's said wife at least as often as quarterly during her lifetime. In addition, all or any part of the principal may be paid to any one or more of the Donor's said wife, the Donor's children and the Donor's more remote issue, in such amounts or proportions and at such time or times as the trustees, in their discretion, think advisable for the health, education, maintenance or support of the particular beneficiary, and whenever there is a disinterested trustee for the time being in office, all or any part of the principal not so used may be paid to any one or more of the Donor's said wife, the Donor's children and the Donor's more remote issue, in such amounts or proportions and at such time or times as the disinterested trustee, in the disinterested trustee's discretion, thinks advisable for any purpose.

[OPTION — WITHDRAWAL RIGHT]

(b) *Withdrawal Right.* Notwithstanding the provisions of paragraph (a) above, in each calendar year after that of the Donor's death, if the Donor's said wife is living on the last business day of the calendar year, she shall have the right by a writing delivered to the trustees on or before such day to withdraw from the trust principal any amount up to five percent (5%) of the value of the trust principal as of such day.

(b) /(c) *Power of Appointment.* Upon the death of the Donor's said wife, the then remaining principal shall be disposed of as the Donor's said wife shall appoint by a will, executed at any time after the Donor's death and referring specifically to this power of appointment, to or for the benefit of any one or more of the Donor's issue, the spouses of such issue and charitable organizations or purposes, in such amounts or proportions, for such estates, on such trusts, and subject to such terms, conditions, general or special powers of appointment or restrictions as the Donor's said wife shall appoint. This power of appointment shall not be exercisable, directly or indirectly, to or in favor of the Donor's said wife, her estate, her creditors, or the creditors of her estate.

CAUTION

If the plan includes only a single QTIP Trust and the Family Trust will only be funded as a result of disclaimer, do not the include Power of Appointment.

(c) /(d) *Disposition Upon Death of Survivor of Donor and Donor's Wife.* In default of or subject to appointment by the Donor's said wife as aforesaid, upon her death the then remaining principal shall be distributed in equal shares, one share to each child of the Donor who is then living and one share by right of representation to the then living issue of each child of the Donor who is then deceased with issue then living; *provided* that any principal thus distributable to a beneficiary who has not then reached the age of twenty-five (25) shall be held in trust for the particular beneficiary as provided below in Article SIXTH, instead of being distributed outright.

SIXTH: Trusts for Persons Under Age Twenty-Five. All principal provided under any Article of this trust instrument to be held in trust under this Article SIXTH for a particular beneficiary who has not reached the age of twenty-five (25) shall be combined and administered, in each case, in a single, separate trust for the beneficiary as follows:

(a) *Discretionary Distributions.* All or any part of the net income and principal may be paid to the beneficiary from time to time as the disinterested trustee, in the disinterested trustee's discretion, thinks advisable for any purpose. Any net income not so paid may be added to principal at any time or times.

(b) *Mandatory Distribution of Principal at Age Twenty-Five; Power of Appointment.* When the beneficiary reaches the age of twenty-five (25), the then remaining principal and any balance of net income shall be distributed to the beneficiary. If the beneficiary dies before reaching the age of twenty-five (25), any balance of net income remaining at the beneficiary's death shall be added to principal and the then remaining principal shall be disposed of as the beneficiary appoints by will, executed at any time after the Donor's death and referring specifically to this power of appointment. This power is exercisable in favor of the beneficiary's estate or in favor of any one or more persons or objects; it is exercisable by appointment outright or in trust, and subject to such terms, conditions, general or special powers and restrictions as the beneficiary shall so appoint. In default of or subject to appointment as aforesaid, upon the beneficiary's death before reaching the age of twenty-five (25) the then remaining principal shall be distributed by right of representation to the beneficiary's then living issue, or, if none, by right of representation to the then living issue of the beneficiary's ancestor of the nearest degree who has issue then living and who is the Donor or one of his issue; *provided* that any principal thus distributable to a beneficiary who has not then reached the age of twenty-five (25) shall be held in trust for the particular beneficiary as provided in this Article, instead of being distributed outright.

(c) *Rule Against Perpetuities.* If not sooner terminated as provided in paragraph (b), above, the trust shall terminate, and the trust property shall thereupon be distributed to the beneficiary, twenty (20) years after the death of the survivor of the Donor, his said wife, and the issue of the Donor living at the death of the first to die of the Donor and his said wife.

SEVENTH: Contingent Disposition. If at any time after the death of the survivor of the Donor and his said wife no issue of the Donor is living, any balance of net income and principal that is not otherwise disposed of in accordance with the provisions of this trust instrument shall be distributed as follows:

[ADD DESCRIPTION OF CONTINGENT DISPOSITION]

EIGHTH: Debts, Expenses and Taxes—in General. Notwithstanding the provisions of Article THIRD above, the trustees shall pay out of the trust principal disposed of thereunder as a whole all death taxes occasioned by the Donor's death, except any such death taxes with respect to property held in any trust other than (i) the trusts hereunder, (ii) any qualified trust described in Section 401(a) of the Internal Revenue Code of 1986, as amended (or any successor provisions thereto) (the "Code"), and any individual retirement account described in Sections 408(a) or 408A of the Code, and (iii) any trust to which the Donor has contributed and under which an annuity, unitrust or remainder interest is intended to qualify for the federal estate tax charitable deduction; all without requiring any reimbursement to the trust from the Donor's personal representative or other persons receiving property as a result of the Donor's death.

In addition, the trustees shall pay out of the trust property as a whole on the Donor's death such of the Donor's debts, funeral and burial expenses, and expenses of administering the Donor's estate as may be requested by the Donor's personal representative. All payments of debts and expenses shall be made from and charged against trust income or principal as the disinterested trustee considers appropriate, or if there is no disinterested trustee for the time being in office, in accordance with the laws of [*SPECIFY STATE GOVERNING LAW*]. Any payments of deductible death taxes shall be made from and charged against principal.

The trustees may rely upon a certificate from the Donor's personal representative to the effect that all such death taxes, debts, or expenses are payable and the trustees need not inquire into the legality or amount of any death taxes, debts, or expenses so certified. Payments under this Article may be made to or upon the order of the Donor's personal representative or in such other manner as the trustees think advisable. All payments under this Article shall be made only out of property (or proceeds from property) otherwise includable in the Donor's gross estate for federal estate tax purposes, or from the income on such property (or the proceeds therefrom).

Any payments under this Article made by withdrawal from a qualified retirement plan, individual retirement account, or annuity contract or custodial account described in Section 403(b) of the Code of which any trust hereunder is the beneficiary shall be made on or before September 30 of the year following the year of the Donor's death.

References in this Article to "death taxes" mean all federal and state taxes in the nature of estate, inheritance, succession or like taxes, but do not include federal or state generation-skipping transfer taxes.

NINTH: <u>General Administrative Provisions</u>. Each trust hereunder is subject to the following provisions:

(a) *Distributions to Minors; Impracticable Distributions.* Whenever a payment of income or principal is to be made to any beneficiary, and the beneficiary has not reached the age of twenty-one (21) or is ill or away, or because of other circumstances it is impracticable or undesirable, in the opinion of the disinterested trustee, to make such payment directly to the beneficiary, the disinterested trustee, in the disinterested trustee's discretion, may apply such payment for the beneficiary's benefit in such manner as the disinterested trustee thinks best for the beneficiary, regardless of the beneficiary's other resources. Such application for the beneficiary's benefit, and any payment to a beneficiary who has not reached the age of twenty-one (21), may be made in any amount, either directly or through a guardian, custodian, or member of the family of the beneficiary, or by payment to the beneficiary in person even though he or she has not reached the age of twenty-one (21) or is incapacitated; and the receipt of the payee shall, with respect to each such payment, be a sufficient discharge to the trustees so that they need not see to the further application thereof. No payment may be made that discharges a legal obligation of an individual serving as a disinterested trustee.

(b) *Spendthrift Clause.* The interest of each beneficiary, and all payments of income or principal to be made to or for any beneficiary, shall be free from interference or control by any creditor, spouse, or divorced former spouse of the beneficiary, and shall not be capable of anticipation or assignment by the beneficiary.

(c) *Definitions.* In this trust instrument, references to "child" or "children" mean descendants in the first degree only, and references to "issue" mean descendants in the first, second, or any other degree; in each case meaning lawful descendants of the ancestor designated, whether by blood or by adoption and whether living on the date of this trust instrument or born or adopted thereafter. For purposes of the preceding sentence, a person born out of wedlock and those claiming through that person shall be treated as lawful descendants (i) of the natural mother and her ancestors, and (ii) if the natural father acknowledges paternity, of the natural father and his ancestors, in each case unless a decree of adoption terminates such natural parent's parental rights. Whenever property is to be distributed by right of representation to the then living issue of a designated ancestor, the ancestor's children shall be considered the stocks for purposes of determining the respective shares of such issue.

(d) *Investment in Common Fund.* Each of the trusts hereunder shall constitute a separate and distinct trust, but for convenience of administration the trustees may, in their discretion, mingle or combine any of the investments or property of said trusts in a common fund in which the several contributing trusts shall have undivided proportionate interests.

TENTH: Trustees' Powers. In extension and not in limitation of the powers given them by law or other provisions of this trust instrument, the trustees of each trust hereunder shall have the following powers with respect to the trust and its property, in each case to be exercised from time to time in the discretion of the trustees and without order or license of court:

(a) To retain indefinitely, and to invest and reinvest in, stocks, shares, obligations, partnership interests, and other securities or any other kind of personal or real property, even though any or all of the investments made or retained are of a character or size that, but for this express authority, would not be considered proper for trustees;

(b) To sell, to exchange, to lease, and to make contracts concerning real or personal property for such consideration and upon such terms as to credit or otherwise as the trustees consider advisable, which leases and contracts may extend beyond the term of the trust; to give options on real or personal property of the trust; to establish depreciation, depletion, tax, or any other reserves; to execute deeds, transfers, leases, and other instruments of any kind; and to deal with themselves or one of them as freely as with a stranger;

(c) To hold securities or other property in bearer or unregistered form or in the name of one or more of the trustees or of any other person, firm, or corporation, without indication of any fiduciary capacity;

(d) To give general or special proxies or powers of attorney (which may or may not be discretionary and with power of substitution) for voting or acting with respect to securities; to deposit securities with, or transfer them to, protective committees, voting trustees, or similar bodies; to join in any reorganization; and to pay assessments or subscriptions called for in connection with securities held by the trustees;

(e) To receive additions to the trust by gift or will or under any policy of insurance on the Donor's life or otherwise, and to hold and administer the same under the provisions hereof;

(f) To compromise or submit to arbitration and to pay before due any tax, claim, or matter in dispute;

(g) If in the opinion of the trustees it is necessary or advisable to do so, to borrow money for such time and at such rate of interest or discount as the trustees deem proper; to give notes or obligations therefor binding the trust property; and as security therefor to mortgage or to pledge real or personal property with or without power of sale; but the Donor recommends that such borrowing be limited to cases in which, in the judgment of the trustees, it is necessary or advisable to provide for the payment of taxes or indebtedness or to meet emergencies;

(h) To improve or develop real estate; to construct, alter, repair, or demolish buildings or structures; to settle boundary lines and easements and other rights; to partition; and to join with co-owners or others in dealing with real estate in any way;

(i) To employ investment counsel and consult with them concerning the investments of the trust and to delegate to such counsel such powers as the trustees deem appropriate; to employ agents and to delegate to such agents such powers as the trustees deem appropriate; to employ legal counsel, accountants, and any special services; to employ a custodian of any funds or securities and to delegate to the custodian such powers as the trustees deem appropriate; and, in addition to the compensation and expenses of the trustees, to pay the compensation and expenses of all such services even if rendered by a trustee;

(j) To credit particular receipts or gains, and to charge particular disbursements or losses or charges, to income or to principal of the trust or to apportion them between income and principal, whether such credits or charges relate to bonds acquired at a premium, to reserves or to any other matter, all as the disinterested trustee considers fair and reasonable in each case, or if there is no disinterested trustee for the time being in office, all in accordance with the laws of [*SPECIFY STATE GOVERNING LAW*]; and

(k) To make any division or distribution of, or payment from, the trust, in kind by the fair and reasonable allotment and transfer of specific securities or other personal or real property or undivided interests therein, at then current values, in lieu of cash, as a part or the whole of any one or more shares or payments.

ELEVENTH: Trustees. With respect to each trust hereunder, references in this trust instrument to the "trustees" mean the one or more trustees, whether original, additional, or successor, for the time being in office; and references to the "disinterested trustee" mean the one or more trustees having no beneficial interest, whether vested or contingent, in the income or principal of any trust hereunder.

Any trustee may resign by giving written notice to the Donor, if he is then living, or if not, to his said wife, if she is then living, or if not, to the remaining trustee, if any, or if none, to the one or more persons to whom the trustees would then render accounts of the particular trust as provided below in Article TWELFTH. Any individual trustee shall be deemed to have resigned and any named individual successor trustee shall be deemed unable to serve upon the first to occur of the following: (i) the appointment of a legal guardian or similar legal representative for such individual; and (ii) the receipt by the one or more persons then entitled to appoint successor trustees of a writing signed by the individual's regularly attending physician certifying that, in the physician's opinion, such individual is mentally or physically incapable of discharging the responsibilities of a trustee.

During his lifetime, the Donor may remove any trustee by giving the trustee written notice. After the Donor's death, any trustee may be removed in a writing delivered to the trustee and signed by the Donor's said wife, if she is then living and of full legal capacity; *provided* that no such removal of a disinterested trustee shall take effect until a successor disinterested trustee who is not a "related or subordinate party" within the meaning of Section 672(c) of the Code with respect to the Donor's said wife has been appointed in a writing signed by the Donor's said wife and has accepted such appointment.

There need not be more than one trustee for the time being in office of each trust hereunder, but [after the death of the Donor] OR [after the death of the survivor of the Donor and his said wife] there shall regularly be at least one disinterested trustee for the time being in office of each trust hereunder. After the death of the survivor of the Donor and his said wife, [*NAME OF SUCCESSOR TRUSTEE*], of [*ADDRESS*], shall become a trustee of each trust hereunder, upon written acceptance of the office. If for any reason the said [*NAME OF SUCCESSOR TRUSTEE*] fails to accept the appointment or, having accepted, later ceases to serve, and in case of any other vacancy in the office of trustee of any trust hereunder, a successor trustee may be appointed in a writing signed by the Donor, if he is then living and of full legal capacity, or if not, by his said wife, if she is then living and of full legal capacity, or if not, by the remaining trustee, if any, or if none, by the one or more persons to whom the trustees would then render accounts of the particular trust as provided below in Article TWELFTH.

Whenever there are fewer than three (3) trustees for the time being in office, one or more additional trustees may be appointed at any time or times, to take office presently or at any future time and upon such other terms and conditions, by a writing signed by the Donor, if he is then living and of full legal capacity, or, if not, by his said wife, if she is then living and of full legal capacity, or, if not, by the trustees for the time being in office. Any such appointment may be revoked in writing at any time before it becomes effective.

Unless otherwise provided in the instrument of appointment, each appointment of a successor or additional trustee shall take effect upon written acceptance of the office.

By a writing or writings, any trustee may delegate all or any of that trustee's powers and discretions to any other trustee for a period specified in such writing, and may revoke or successively renew such delegation; *provided* that the powers and discretions given to the disinterested trustee, as such, shall be exercised by the disinterested trustee alone, exclusive of any other of the trustees, and may be delegated only to another disinterested trustee.

No trustee named herein or appointed as above provided need furnish any bond or surety. No one dealing with the trustees need inquire concerning the validity of anything the trustees purport to do or need see to the application of any money paid or property transferred to or upon the order of the trustees.

TWELFTH: <u>Accounts</u>. During the Donor's lifetime, the trustees shall render an account of the trust hereunder to him or, if he is not then of full legal capacity, to his said wife, if she is then living and of full legal capacity, or, if not, to the Donor's legal guardian or similar legal representative, upon request. After the Donor's death, the trustees of each trust hereunder shall render an account of the trust at least as often as annually to each beneficiary of the trust to whom in the period covered by such account current income from the trust was payable or could have been paid in the discretion of the disinterested trustee and who is living and of full legal capacity and, if any such beneficiary is not of full legal capacity, to his or her legal guardian or similar legal representative, if any, or, if none, to either of his or her parents if he or she is a minor. In the case of each trust hereunder, the written assent to any such account by the one or more persons of full legal capacity to whom it is rendered as provided above shall fully protect the trustees as to all matters or transactions stated in such account or shown thereby, even if such person is serving as a trustee hereunder. Any person who is not of full legal capacity shall be deemed to assent to such account if his or her legal guardian or similar legal representative assents in writing to the account or if (such beneficiary being a minor and having no such legal guardian or representative) the parent to whom the account was rendered assents in writing to the account. Nothing in this Article shall be deemed to give anyone the power to modify the terms of this trust instrument or to alter or shift any beneficial interest created hereunder.

THIRTEENTH: <u>Life Insurance</u>. Unless any policy of life insurance made payable to the trustees is assigned to them, the owner of the policy shall retain, as against the trustees, all incidents of ownership thereof, and the trustees shall have no responsibility for the payment of premiums thereon. The trustees shall be entitled to indemnification from the trust principal for the expense of any legal proceedings taken to collect the proceeds of any such policy.

FOURTEENTH: Trust Documentation. The original of each alteration or amendment of this trust instrument, each resignation, removal, or appointment of a trustee, each acceptance of appointment and each instrument of delegation shall be kept attached to the original trust instrument, which shall be held by the trustees. Anyone may rely on a copy certified by a notary public of this trust instrument or of any writings attached thereto as fully as on the original document; and anyone may rely fully upon any statements of fact certified by anyone who appears from the original document or a certified copy thereof to be a trustee hereunder.

FIFTEENTH: Combination and Termination of Trusts. If at any time after both the Donor and his said wife have died a trust is being administered hereunder for one or more beneficiaries on terms substantially identical to those on which a trust is then being administered for the same one or more beneficiaries under the provisions of [THE SARAH SAMPLE [*YEAR*] TRUST, established today by the Donor's said wife, with herself and the Donor as trustees ("SARAH'S [*YEAR*] TRUST")], the trustees in their discretion may terminate the trust under this instrument by distributing any balance of net income and the then remaining principal to the then trustees of SARAH'S [*YEAR*] TRUST] to be added to the trust thereunder for the same beneficiaries.

SIXTEENTH: Governing Law. This trust instrument and the trusts hereunder shall be governed, construed, and administered in accordance with the laws of [*SPECIFY GOVERNING STATE LAW*] from time to time in force.

SIGNED and SEALED this ___ day of _____, 20___.

_____
SAM SAMPLE, Donor and Trustee

_____
SARAH SAMPLE, Trustee

STATE/COMMONWEALTH OF [*NAME OF STATE*]

—————————, ss.

On this ___ day of _____, 20__, before me, the undersigned notary public, personally appeared the above-named SAM SAMPLE, known to me personally or proved to me through _____ as satisfactory evidence of identification, to be the person whose name is signed on the preceding document, and acknowledged to me that he signed it voluntarily for its stated purpose.

_____

Notary Public
My Commission Expires:

FORM 3
Living Trust Amendment

Overview

This form makes amendments to an existing revocable living trust. A trust may be amended as permitted by the terms of that trust.

If the desired amendments to an existing trust instrument are extensive, it may be preferable to restate the entire trust. In the alternative, the earlier trust may be revoked and an entirely new trust created. If the existing trust has been funded, an amendment and restatement in their entirety permit the current account arrangements to continue in place. If, instead, a new trust is created, the client will need to transfer all trust assets into the name of the new trust. In addition, if the trust has been named as a beneficiary of life insurance proceeds or retirement plan benefits, no change in the beneficiary designations will be required if the trust is amended and restated in its entirety. If the trust is revoked, however, and replaced with a new trust, the client must execute new beneficiary designation forms.

A client with a funded living trust or with a living trust designated as beneficiary of life insurance proceeds and retirement account benefits may, nevertheless, prefer to execute a new trust if she does not want the beneficiaries of her estate plan to see the provisions of the prior plan.

THE SAM SAMPLE [*YEAR*] TRUST

First Amendment

Practice Note

Any amendment to an existing revocable trust should specifically refer to the provision in the original trust document containing the power to amend. The amendment should also recite the full title of the original trust, the names of the donor and of the current trustees, and the date of the establishment of the trust. If the trust has been amended previously, the current amendment should make reference to all prior amendments.

Pursuant to the provisions of Article FIRST of THE SAM SAMPLE [*YEAR*] TRUST established [*INSERT DATE*] by SAM SAMPLE, of [*ADDRESS*], as Donor, with himself and his wife, SARAH SAMPLE, as trustees, the Trust is hereby amended in the following respects:

Practice Note

The amendment should clearly designate which sections are being revised. This form provides sample language for referring to different parts of the trust.

---

1. Articles THIRD through FIFTH are hereby deleted and the following new Articles THIRD through FIFTH are hereby inserted in their place:

   "[NEW LANGUAGE]."

2. The first unnumbered paragraph of Article SEVENTH (which begins with the words "[WORDS]" and ends with the words "[WORDS]") is hereby changed to read as follows:

   "[NEW LANGUAGE]."

3. Paragraph (a) of Article TENTH is hereby deleted and the following new paragraph (a) is inserted in its place:

   "[NEW LANGUAGE]."

SIGNED this _____ day of _____, 20 __.

_____
SAM SAMPLE, Donor

Practice Note

In the model trust document, the trustees are required to consent in writing to the amendment before it is effective. This consent should be set forth after the text of the amendment.

The undersigned trustees of THE SAM SAMPLE [*YEAR*] TRUST hereby acknowledge receipt of and consent to the foregoing First Amendment, as of the date last above written.

_____
SAM SAMPLE, Trustee

_____
SARAH SAMPLE, Trustee

STATE/COMMONWEALTH OF [*NAME OF STATE*]

————————, ss.

On this ——— day of ———, 20—, before me, the undersigned notary public, personally appeared the above-named SAM SAMPLE, known to me personally or proved to me through ——— as satisfactory evidence of identification, to be the person whose name is signed on the preceding document, and acknowledged to me that he signed it voluntarily for its stated purpose.

————————————————
Notary Public
My Commission Expires:

FORM 4
Irrevocable Life Insurance Trust

Overview

This form establishes an irrevocable trust designed to be funded with a life insurance policy. An existing policy could either be transferred to the trust, or the trustees of the trust could apply for a new policy on the life of the donor. If life insurance is purchased by a third party, such as an irrevocable trust, the policy proceeds are not subject to estate tax when the insured dies (assuming that the insured has no control or "incidents of ownership" over the policy through the trust). If an existing policy is transferred to an irrevocable trust, the donor must survive the transfer by three years in order to avoid estate tax on the policy proceeds.

The model form creates a discretionary spray trust to hold the life insurance policy during the lifetime of the donor. The donor's ongoing contributions to the trust—which enable the trustees to pay premiums or otherwise service the insurance policy—are qualified in whole or in part for annual exclusion treatment because the trust beneficiaries are given the power to withdraw part or all of the contributions. After the donor's death, the policy proceeds are divided among the donor's children and held in simple management trusts for each child until the child reaches age 35. An irrevocable trust of this type could include the donor's spouse as a beneficiary. It could also provide for generation-skipping or dynasty trusts, which will ultimately benefit grandchildren or more remote generations.

THE SARAH SAMPLE [*YEAR*] IRREVOCABLE TRUST

Practice Note

The opening paragraph identifies the settlor of the trust (the "donor"). The trust could also be used for two settlors (e.g., a husband and wife), in which case both settlors should be listed. This would be appropriate if the trust were to hold "second to die" insurance, paying a death benefit at the death of the survivor of the two insureds.

The opening paragraph should also identify the initial trustee or trustees by name. As outlined in more detail below, the insured should not be named as a trustee. The initial trust property should also be described. If the trust is to be funded with an existing policy, details of the policy should be listed. Otherwise, the funding assets need not be more than a nominal amount of cash.

The trust must be irrevocable if the insurance policy proceeds are to be excluded from the donor insured's estate. Under the law of most states, trusts are deemed to be irrevocable unless an express right of revocation or amendment is reserved. Nevertheless, it is good practice to state in the opening paragraph that the instrument cannot be revoked.

SARAH SAMPLE, of [*ADDRESS*] (the "Donor"), herewith transfers the sum of Ten Dollars ($10) [*or DESCRIPTION OF LIFE INSURANCE POLICY*] to [*NAME OF TRUSTEE #1*], of [*ADDRESS*], and [*NAME OF TRUSTEE #2*], of [*ADDRESS*], as trustees hereunder; and the trustees hereby acknowledge receipt thereof and agree, for themselves, any additional trustees and all successors in office, to hold said sum [*or* said policy], together with any other property transferred to them, IRREVOCABLY IN TRUST, upon the following terms and provisions:

Practice Note

Article FIRST identifies the trust instrument by name. Care should be taken to ensure that the life insurance company accurately names the trust in designating the owner of the policy. This article also sets forth the terms of the irrevocable trust during the donor's lifetime. Under the terms of the trust, the disinterested trustee is authorized to use net income and principal of the trust to purchase and pay premiums on policies of insurance on the donor's life. Any net income and principal not so used may then be distributed by the disinterested trustee for any purpose to any one or more of the donor's children or other issue. The trustee is also authorized to distribute all or any part of the net income and principal to trusts for the benefit of the donor's issue provided that those trusts do not violate the perpetuities rule. This document makes reference to a statutory perpetuities period of 90 years. In those states in which the perpetuities rule has been abolished, this reference may be deleted. In other states, which have different statutory perpetuity periods or still use the common law rule of lives-in-being plus 21 years, this reference should be revised.

Article FIRST then includes two optional forms of withdrawal powers (also known as Crummey powers). These withdrawal powers enable contributions to the trust to qualify for the federal gift tax annual exclusion under IRC Section 2503 since the beneficiary's power to make an immediate withdrawal qualifies as a present interest. The "Crummey" power is named for the case of Crummey v. Commissioner (397 F.2d 82 (9th Cir. 1968)), in which the Ninth Circuit Federal Court of Appeals held that gifts to a discretionary trust subject to a beneficiary's immediate right of withdrawal qualified for the gift tax annual exclusion. The Internal Revenue Service has accepted the holding of the case but has added several glosses. In particular, the Service has required that the trust beneficiaries receive actual notice of each contribution and their resulting withdrawal rights and be given a reasonable period of time to exercise those rights. The trustees should provide such notice in the form of a letter to each beneficiary (or to his or her guardian or parent, provided the latter is not the donor of the contribution) and should retain copies of the letters with the trust records. These issues are addressed in both optional provisions.

While Crummey powers have potentially beneficial transfer tax consequences for the donor to the trust, the lapse of Crummey powers can raise tax problems for the beneficiaries of multiple beneficiary trusts. The reason for this is that a power to withdraw property from a trust is treated as a general power of appointment under IRC Sections 2041 and 2514. The lapse of a general power of appointment ordinarily constitutes a gift from the holder of the lapsed power to the other beneficiaries of the trust. Such a gift is potentially subject to gift tax and does not qualify for the annual exclusion because the other beneficiaries cannot take immediate possession of the trust property (in other words, they do not have a present interest). Fortunately, there is an exception to the general rule that the lapse of a general power constitutes a gift. This exception, set forth in IRC Section 2514(e), provides that a taxable gift results from a lapse only to the extent that the property subject to the power exceeds the greater of $5,000 or 5 percent of the property held in the trust. The model form provides two alternatives for using the "five or five" exception. The first option limits the amount of the beneficiaries' withdrawal rights and the second option limits the annual lapse of those rights.

FIRST: During the Donor's Lifetime. This trust shall be known as "THE SARAH SAMPLE [*YEAR*] IRREVOCABLE TRUST." During the lifetime of the Donor, so much or all of the net income and principal as the disinterested trustee, in the disinterested trustee's discretion, thinks advisable may be used to purchase and pay premiums on policies of insurance on the life of the Donor. Any net income and principal not so used may be paid to any one or more of the Donor's children, [*NAMES OF CHILDREN*], and the Donor's other issue, in such amounts or proportions and at such time or times as the disinterested trustee, in the disinterested trustee's discretion, thinks advisable for any purpose. In addition, all or any part of the net income and principal may be paid by the disinterested trustee to any trust for the benefit of any one or more of the Donor's issue that terminates in all events no later than ninety (90) years from the date of execution of this trust instrument. Any net income not so used or paid may be added to principal at any time or times, and any net income remaining at the death of the Donor shall be added to principal at that time.

Practice Note

The simplest way to use the five or five exception is set forth in Option One. To avoid a taxable gift when a Crummey power lapses, each beneficiary's withdrawal rights are limited during each calendar year to the amounts referenced in IRC Section 2514(e) (i.e., the greater of $5,000 or 5 percent of the value of the trust property). By including this limitation, each beneficiary will never have the power to withdraw in any calendar year more than "five or five," and, therefore, the lapse of the power will not result in a taxable gift by the beneficiary. This approach, however, may limit the donor's ability to use the annual exclusion in full. For 2022, that exclusion is $16,000 per donee, or $32,000 per donee if the donor and the donor's spouse elect to split gifts on a gift tax return. If the only amount that can be withdrawn by a beneficiary of a multiple beneficiary Crummey trust is $5,000 or 5 percent of the value of the trust assets, then that will serve as a limit on the donor's annual exclusion amount. This limitation will not be a problem if the assets in the trust are of such value that 5 percent of that value covers the annual exclusion amount. For example, if the donor is a single individual (and therefore can only transfer $16,000 to each donee per year under the annual exclusion), then this limitation will not be a problem if the trust assets equal at least $320,000, because 5 percent of $320,000 is $16,000. If the donor is married and is planning on gift splitting in order to make annual tax-free gifts of $32,000, then the trust must have assets equal to at least $640,000 in order to take full advantage of the annual exclusion under this option. Of course, depending on the size of the life insurance policy and the age and health of the insured, the donor may not need the full annual exclusion amount in order to cover the annual premiums.

[OPTION ONE: Five or Five Crummey Power]

Notwithstanding the foregoing provisions, with respect to the initial and each subsequent contribution made to the trust hereunder by *inter vivos* gift during the lifetime of the Donor, each of the Donor's said children and her other issue who is living at the time of the particular contribution shall have the noncumulative right, exercisable by a writing or writings delivered to the trustees within thirty (30) days after the date of the contribution, to withdraw so much of the particular contribution as the donor thereof may designate with respect to the particular beneficiary in a written notice delivered to the trustees prior to the making of the contribution. In the absence of such written designation, each beneficiary shall have the right to withdraw an amount equal to a fraction of the contribution, the numerator of which is one and the denominator of which is the number of such beneficiaries who are then living; *provided* that no beneficiary shall have the right to withdraw in any calendar year an aggregate amount that exceeds the maximum amount over which a beneficiary may have rights of withdrawal the lapse of which in the same calendar year are not treated as a taxable release of a general power of appointment under Section 2514(e) of the Internal Revenue Code of 1986 (as amended, or any successor provisions thereto) (the "Code"). Any withdrawal right exercisable by a beneficiary who is not of full legal capacity may be exercised by his or her legal guardian or similar legal representative who is not the donor of the particular contribution, if any, or if none and the beneficiary is a minor, by either of his or her parents who is not such donor.

Any asset of the trust under this Article, including any policy of life insurance, may be used by the trustees to satisfy any such withdrawal. During the period that any such right of withdrawal is exercisable the trustees shall not make any distributions to a beneficiary under the first paragraph of this Article that would reduce the value of the trust property below that which would be necessary to satisfy such right, if exercised to the maximum extent. The trustees, in advance of or upon receipt of the initial and each subsequent contribution by *inter vivos* gift to this trust, shall notify each beneficiary, if any, who has the right to withdraw any portion of such contribution of its date and the amount that the beneficiary may withdraw; and if any such beneficiary is not of full legal capacity, such notice shall be given to his or her legal guardian or similar legal representative, if any, or, if none, and the beneficiary is a minor, to either parent of the beneficiary.

Premiums on any policy of life insurance held in the trust hereunder that are paid by the Donor or by any other person or entity other than this trust and that, for federal gift tax purposes, are deemed to be gifts to the trust hereunder shall, for purposes of this Article, be considered contributions to the trust at the time such premiums are paid.

Practice Note

An alternative way to use the five or five exception is set out in Option Two. This option gives the beneficiary full withdrawal powers equal to a fraction of the contribution. The fraction is determined by dividing the amount of the contribution by the number of beneficiaries who have current withdrawal rights. This enables the donor to take full advantage of the annual exclusion even if the trust assets are less than $320,000, or $640,000 in the case of a split gift. However, Option Two avoids the problem of a taxable gift by the beneficiary upon lapse by limiting the lapsing of the withdrawal right. Each withdrawal right that has been outstanding for 30 days and has not been exercised lapses only to the extent of the greater of $5,000 or 5 percent of the value of the trust property. To the extent that rights of withdrawal remain outstanding after the 30-day period, the rights are aggregated with any prior outstanding rights and are continuing or hanging. These rights then lapse (if not exercised) on the first day of the succeeding calendar year, again only to the extent of the five or five exception. This type of withdrawal power is commonly referred to as a "hanging Crummey power."

The advantage of using a hanging power is that it enables a donor to make full use of the annual exclusion, even when the trust has relatively few assets. However, hanging powers present more complicated issues in administering the trust. The trustee must keep careful records of (1) the contributions made, (2) the amount that may lapse within 30 days after the contribution, and (3) the amount that continues to hang until it can be treated as lapsing at the beginning of future calendar years.

[*OPTION TWO: Hanging Crummey Power*]

Notwithstanding the foregoing provisions, with respect to the initial and each subsequent contribution made to the trust hereunder by *inter vivos* gift during the lifetime of the Donor, each of the Donor's said children and her other issue who is living at the time of the particular contribution shall have the right, exercisable by a writing or writings delivered to the trustees, to withdraw so much of the particular contribution as the donor thereof may designate with respect to the particular beneficiary in a written notice delivered to the trustees prior to the making of the contribution. In the absence of such written designation, each beneficiary shall have the right to withdraw an amount equal to a fraction of the contribution, the numerator of which is one and the denominator of which is the number of such beneficiaries who are then living. Any withdrawal right exercisable by a beneficiary who is not of full legal capacity may be exercised by his or her legal guardian or similar legal representative who is not the donor of the particular contribution, if any, or, if none, and the beneficiary is a minor, by either of his or her parents who is not such donor.

Any asset of the trust under this Article, including any policy of life insurance, may be used by the trustees to satisfy any such withdrawal. During the period that any such right of withdrawal is exercisable the trustees shall not make any distributions to a beneficiary under the first paragraph of this Article that would reduce the value of the trust property below that which would be necessary to satisfy such right, if exercised to the maximum extent. The trustees, in advance of or upon receipt of the initial and each subsequent contribution by *inter vivos* gift to this trust, shall notify each beneficiary, if any, who has the right to withdraw any portion of such contribution of its date and the amount that the beneficiary may withdraw; and if any such beneficiary is not of full legal capacity, such notice shall be given to his or her legal guardian or similar legal representative, if any, or, if none, and the beneficiary is a minor, to either parent of the beneficiary.

Each right of withdrawal held by any beneficiary that has been outstanding for thirty (30) days and has not been exercised by the particular beneficiary shall terminate upon the expiration of such period to the extent that the value of such unexercised right of withdrawal, together with the aggregate value of all unexercised rights of withdrawal held by the beneficiary under this trust that have terminated earlier in the same calendar year, does not exceed the greater of (i) the amount then specified in Section 2514(e)(1) of the Internal Revenue Code of 1986 (as amended, or any successor provisions thereto) (the "Code") (currently Five Thousand Dollars ($5,000)) and (ii) the percentage then specified in Section 2514(e)(2) of the Code (currently five percent (5%)) of the fair market value of the assets of this trust upon such termination date. To the extent that any unexercised right of withdrawal held by a particular beneficiary remains outstanding beyond such thirty (30) day period, such right shall be aggregated with any other outstanding rights of withdrawal held by the same beneficiary that arose earlier under the terms of this trust instrument, and the aggregate of such rights of withdrawal held by a particular beneficiary that have not been exercised shall terminate on the first day of each succeeding calendar year to the extent of the greater of (i) the amount then specified in Section 2514(e)(1) of the Code and (ii) the percentage then specified in Section 2514(e)(2) of the Code of the fair market value of the assets of this trust on such date.

Premiums on any policy of life insurance held in the trust hereunder that are paid by the Donor or by any other person or entity other than this trust and that, for federal gift tax purposes, are deemed to be gifts to the trust hereunder shall, for purposes of this Article, be considered contributions to the trust at the time such premiums are paid.

Practice Note

At the death of the donor, the trust under Article FIRST terminates. The trust property (which will then consist of the death benefit under the insurance policy as well as any other assets transferred to the trustees as a result of the donor's death) is divided into equal shares for the donor's children. In the event that any child should predecease the donor, that child's share will be further divided among his or her own children. These shares are distributed outright to the beneficiary unless the beneficiary has not reached age 35 at the donor's death, in which case the property will be held in a simple management trust (as described in Article THIRD.)

Article SECOND includes a savings clause in the event that any part of the life insurance proceeds is includable in the donor's estate. As indicated at the outset, the planning objective is to avoid estate tax on the life insurance proceeds. This result may not be achieved, however, if an existing policy is transferred to the trust and the

---

donor dies within three years after the transfer or if the donor has retained any "incidents of ownership" in the policy. If the policy proceeds are includable in the donor's estate, for whatever reason, they are instead distributed to the donor's personal representatives to be disposed of as part of the donor's probate estate. Alternatively, the proceeds could be added to an existing living trust or, if appropriate, be distributed outright to a surviving spouse. In this way the insurance proceeds will be available to pay any applicable estate taxes imposed with respect to the policy death benefit.

SECOND: Upon the Death of the Donor. Upon the death of the Donor, the then trust principal (as augmented by all property transferred to the trustees from any source as a result of the Donor's death and subject to any outstanding rights of withdrawal granted under Article FIRST above) shall be distributed in equal shares, one share to each of the Donor's said children who is then living and one share by right of representation to the then living issue of each of the Donor's said children who is then deceased with issue then living; *provided* that any principal thus distributable to a beneficiary who has not then reached the age of thirty-five (35) shall be held in trust for the particular beneficiary as provided below in Article THIRD, instead of being distributed in its entirety outright.

Notwithstanding the foregoing provisions of this Article, in the unlikely event that any portion of the trust principal disposed of hereunder is includable in the Donor's gross estate for federal estate tax purposes, the portion so includable shall be distributed to the Donor's personal representatives to be disposed of as part of the Donor's estate. The balance of the trust principal, if any, shall be distributed as provided in the immediately preceding paragraph.

Practice Note

Article THIRD sets forth a simple discretionary trust to manage assets that would otherwise be distributed to beneficiaries under the age of 35 after the death of the donor. The disinterested trustee is given discretion to distribute income and/or principal to the beneficiary for any reason and at any time. In the alternative, specific limitations could be imposed on the disinterested trustee's discretion (such as distribution for health, maintenance, support, or education only). When the beneficiary reaches age 35, the trust terminates and the assets are distributed outright to the beneficiary. Should the beneficiary die before reaching that age, the trust property remaining at the beneficiary's death is distributed in equal shares to the beneficiary's own children, or, if none, in equal shares to the beneficiary's siblings, with the issue of any deceased sibling taking the deceased sibling's share by right of representation. If a federal generation-skipping transfer tax (GST tax) would be payable on the distribution of the trust property following the beneficiary's premature death, the beneficiary is also given a general power of appointment that would allow the beneficiary to dispose of the trust property to any person or entity, including the beneficiary's estate. The inclusion of this power will subject the trust property to estate taxes in the beneficiary's estate, but will avoid the GST tax. In most cases, this will lead to a lower tax liability. In general, the GST tax is assessed at a flat rate equal to the highest marginal rate of estate tax on all property that constitutes the generation-skipping transfer. If, instead, the trust property is includable in the beneficiary's estate, it will be aggregated with the beneficiary's other assets and be subject to estate taxes with the beneficiary's applicable exclusion amount available to offset the estate tax liability. However, given recent changes in estate tax laws and particularly the elimination of the credit for state death taxes, it is possible that combined federal and state estate tax liability will exceed GST tax liability. For this reason, the trust instrument might include authority in the disinterested trustee to eliminate or reduce the scope of the general power. Finally, if the intention is to allocate the donor's GST tax exemption to all contributions made by the donor to the trust, so that the trust property will be fully exempt from the GST tax, the latter provision should be omitted.

The trust includes a provision in paragraph (d) designed to ensure that it does not violate the rule against perpetuities. The perpetuities rule included here is a statutory one set at 90 years after the date of the execution of the trust instrument. In some jurisdictions, the rule against perpetuities has been eliminated entirely so that this provision may be deleted. In other jurisdictions, the rule against perpetuities has a different fixed term or is governed by the common law rule that requires trusts to terminate no later than 21 years after the date of death of the survivor of lives in being at the time the irrevocable trust instrument is created.

THIRD: Trusts for Persons Under Age Thirty-Five. All principal provided under any Article of this trust instrument to be held in trust under this Article THIRD for a particular beneficiary who has not reached the age of thirty-five (35) shall be combined and administered, in each case, in a single separate trust for the beneficiary as follows:

(a) *Discretionary Distributions.* All or any part of the net income and principal may be paid to the beneficiary from time to time as the disinterested trustee, in the disinterested trustee's discretion, thinks advisable for any purpose. Any net income not so paid may be added to principal at any time or times. Without limiting the discretion of the disinterested trustee, the Donor hopes that, in exercising this authority to make payments of net income and principal, the disinterested trustee will ensure that the basic needs of the beneficiary are provided for adequately.

(b) *Distribution of Principal at Age Thirty-Five.* When the beneficiary reaches the age of thirty-five (35), the then remaining principal and any balance of net income shall be distributed to the beneficiary. If the beneficiary dies before reaching the age of thirty-five (35), any balance of net income remaining at the beneficiary's death shall be added to principal and the then remaining principal shall be distributed by right of representation to the beneficiary's then living issue, or, if none, by right of representation to the then living issue of the beneficiary's ancestor of the nearest degree who has issue then living and who is the Donor or one of her issue; *provided* that any principal thus distributable to any beneficiary who has not then reached the age of thirty-five (35) shall be held in trust for the particular beneficiary as provided in this Article, instead of being distributed outright.

(c) *Power of Appointment.* Notwithstanding the provisions of paragraph (b) above, if the beneficiary dies before reaching the age of thirty-five (35), the beneficiary shall have a power of appointment, exercisable by will executed at any time and referring specifically to this paragraph, to or for the benefit of any one or more persons or objects (including the beneficiary's estate), with respect to any portion of the remaining principal that would pass under paragraph (b) above in such a way as to give rise to a federal generation-skipping transfer tax at the beneficiary's death. In default of or subject to appointment as aforesaid, upon the beneficiary's death the portion of the then remaining principal subject to this power shall be disposed of as provided in paragraph (b) above.

(d) *Rule Against Perpetuities.* If not sooner terminated as provided above, each trust for a beneficiary under this Article shall terminate, and the trust property shall thereupon be distributed to the beneficiary, ninety (90) years after the date of execution of this trust instrument.

Practice Note

Article FOURTH provides for the ultimate disposition of trust property upon the failure of all named beneficiaries. Since there is always a possibility (however remote) that all of the donor's children and other issue will die before the trust or trusts created under the document terminate, this situation should be addressed. This is because the undisposed of property would likely revert to the donor's estate if there is no contingent disposition. The possibility of reversion could be treated as an incident of ownership, causing the policy to be subject to tax in the donor's estate. The issue of reversion is also expressly addressed in Article TENTH.

Typically, a contingent disposition will provide for the disposition of trust property to siblings or nieces and nephews of the donor and the donor's spouse. Alternatively, it may provide for the distribution of property to charities. In the latter event, care must be taken to identify the charity by its correct legal name and to specify the charitable purposes, if any, for the gift (e.g., a gift to a college to establish a scholarship fund). In the case of an irrevocable trust, it is important that the donor not retain any control over the disposition of the assets. Sometimes such control can arise unexpectedly through a contingent disposition. For example, if a donor has established a private foundation and the donor is a trustee of that foundation, having the ability to determine foundation distributions, the donor may have unwittingly retained control of the assets of the irrevocable trust for purposes of IRC Section 2036 if the donor names the foundation as the contingent beneficiary. This will undo the transfer tax planning inherent in establishing the irrevocable trust and funding it with the life insurance policy.

FOURTH: Contingent Disposition. If at any time after the death of the Donor no issue of the Donor is living, any balance of net income and principal that is not otherwise disposed of in accordance with the provisions of this trust instrument shall be distributed [*DESCRIBE TERMS OF CONTINGENT DISPOSITION*].

Practice Note

Article FIFTH includes several general administrative provisions. The first is a so-called "facility of payment" provision. It authorizes a trustee to make distributions for a beneficiary's benefit, rather than to the beneficiary directly. This is of particular importance if the beneficiary is incompetent or if it is undesirable to distribute property to the beneficiary (e.g., if the beneficiary is a spendthrift). It also allows the trustee to obtain a valid discharge in making a distribution to a minor beneficiary without going through a legally appointed guardian. Instead, the distribution can be made to a parent of the beneficiary or to a custodian under the Uniform Transfers to Minors Act or the Uniform Gifts to Minors Act. It should be noted that this provision does not apply with respect to the beneficiaries' withdrawal rights. A trustee cannot apply for a beneficiary's benefit any amount that the beneficiary decides to withdraw under the Crummey powers. The withdrawal payment must be made directly to the beneficiary.

The second provision is a "spendthrift clause." It provides that creditors cannot reach the interests of the beneficiaries in the various trusts. It also prohibits voluntary assignments of beneficial interests. The Crummey powers may limit the extent of creditor protection provided by the spendthrift clause.

The third provision defines the terms "child," "children," and "issue." Adopted descendants are included as are all natural born descendants, including the children of unmarried mothers and the children of unmarried fathers where the father has acknowledged paternity. If the donor desires a different result, the clause should be modified. The term "by right of representation" is defined to state how the shares are to be determined whenever that means of distribution is employed. The children of the person whose issue are to be benefited are considered the stocks for purposes of determining the number of distributive shares, whether or not any of those children are alive at the time of distribution. This overrides the laws of several states. For example, if the donor of the trust had three children (Alice, Betty, and Charles) who all predeceased the donor and four grandchildren (one from Alice, one from Betty, and two from Charles) all of whom survived the donor, a distribution by right of representation to the donor's issue would result under the model form in the donor's property being divided into three parts (one part for each child who had predeceased the donor but were themselves survived by issue), and Alice's and Betty's children would each get one-third and Charles's two children would get one-sixth. In some states, the default rule would provide that, if all of the donor's children have predeceased the donor, each grandchild would receive one-quarter of the donor's property.

Finally, the fourth provision states that although each of the trusts created under the instrument is a separate trust, the trustees are nonetheless authorized to commingle the investments of the separate trusts. Under most state laws, this is not permitted absent a specific provision authorizing it, even when the same instrument creates the trusts. Economic sense will often dictate that this is the most desirable course. In some situations, commingling will not be possible because of the income, estate, or generation-skipping transfer tax consequences of such action.

FIFTH: General Administrative Provisions. Each trust hereunder is subject to the following provisions:

(a) *Distributions to Minors; Impracticable Distributions.* Except as provided in the second paragraph of Article FIRST above, whenever a payment of income or principal is to be made to any beneficiary, and the beneficiary has not reached the age of twenty-one (21) or is ill or away, or because of other circumstances it is impracticable or undesirable, in the opinion of the disinterested trustee, to make such payment directly to the beneficiary, the disinterested trustee, in the disinterested trustee's discretion, may apply such payment for the beneficiary's benefit in such manner as the disinterested trustee thinks best for the beneficiary, regardless of the beneficiary's other resources. Such application for the beneficiary's benefit, and any payment to a beneficiary who has not reached the age of twenty-one (21), may be made in any amount, either directly or through a guardian, custodian, or member of the family of the beneficiary or by payment to the beneficiary in person even though he or she has not reached the age of twenty-one (21) or is incapacitated; and the receipt of the payee shall, with respect to each such payment, be a sufficient discharge to the trustees so that they need not see to the further application thereof. No payment may be made that discharges a legal obligation of an individual serving as a disinterested trustee.

(b) *Spendthrift Clause.* The interest of each beneficiary, and all payments of income or principal to be made to or for any beneficiary, shall be free from interference or control by any creditor, spouse, or divorced former spouse of the beneficiary and shall not be capable of anticipation or assignment by the beneficiary.

(c) *Definitions.* In this trust instrument, references to "child" or "children" mean descendants in the first degree only, and references to "issue" mean descendants in the first, second or any other degree; in each case meaning lawful descendants of the ancestor designated, whether by blood or by adoption and whether living on the date of this trust instrument or born or adopted thereafter. For purposes of the preceding sentence, a person born out of wedlock and those claiming through that person shall be treated as lawful descendants (i) of the natural mother and her ancestors and (ii) if the natural father acknowledges paternity, of the natural father and his ancestors, in each case unless a decree of adoption terminates such natural parent's parental rights. Whenever distribution is to be made by right of representation to the then living issue of a designated ancestor, the ancestor's children shall be considered the stocks for purposes of determining the respective shares of such issue.

(d) *Investment in Common Fund.* Each of the trusts hereunder shall constitute a separate and distinct trust, but for convenience of administration the trustees may, in their discretion, mingle or combine any of the investments or property of said trusts in a common fund in which the several contributing trusts shall have undivided proportionate interests.

Practice Note

State laws grant many powers of administration to trustees. To eliminate the need to refer to statutes and case law and to explicitly set forth the donor's intent, it is good drafting practice, however, to set forth the powers expressly. This may also serve to eliminate ambiguities in local law, to expand the scope of the trustees' authority, and to avoid the need for court approval of certain actions.

The list of powers contained in the model Article is general and should cover most situations. Paragraph (h) includes the power to purchase assets out of the donor's estate and from other trusts established by the donor and to make loans to the donor's estate and other trusts. Paragraph (i) provides for express powers to deal with life insurance policies.

SIXTH: Trustees' Powers. In extension and not in limitation of the powers given them by law or other provisions of this trust instrument, the trustees of each trust hereunder shall have the following powers with respect to the trust and its property, in each case to be exercised from time to time in the discretion of the trustees and without order or license of court:

(a) To retain indefinitely, and to invest and reinvest in, stocks, shares, obligations, partnership interests, and other securities or any other kind of personal or real property, even though any or all of the investments made or retained are of a character or size that, but for this express authority, would not be considered proper for trustees;

(b) To sell, to exchange, to lease, and to make contracts concerning real or personal property for such consideration and upon such terms as to credit or otherwise as the trustees consider advisable, which leases and contracts may extend beyond the term of the trust; to give options on real or personal property of the trust; to establish depreciation, depletion, tax or any other reserves; to execute deeds, transfers, leases and other instruments of any kind; and to deal with themselves or one of them as freely as with a stranger;

(c) To hold securities or other property in bearer or unregistered form or in the name of one or more of the trustees or of any other person, firm, or corporation, without indication of any fiduciary capacity;

(d) To give general or special proxies or powers of attorney (which may or may not be discretionary and with power of substitution) for voting or acting with respect to securities to any person other than a donor; to deposit securities with, or transfer them to, protective committees, voting trustees, or similar bodies; to join in any reorganization; and to pay assessments or subscriptions called for in connection with securities held by the trustees;

(e) To receive additions to the trust by gift or will or under any policy of insurance on the Donor's life or otherwise, and to hold and administer the same under the provisions hereof;

(f) To compromise or submit to arbitration and to pay before due any tax, claim, or matter in dispute;

(g) If in the opinion of the trustees it is necessary or advisable to do so, to borrow money for such time and at such rate of interest or discount as the trustees deem proper; to give notes or obligations therefor binding the trust property; and as security therefor to mortgage or to pledge real or personal property with or without power of sale;

(h) To purchase assets from the estate of the Donor, or from any other trust established by the Donor, at the then fair market value of such assets, and to make loans to the estate of the Donor or any other trust established by the Donor upon such reasonable terms as to interest, security, term, and payment as the disinterested trustee, in the disinterested trustee's discretion, thinks advisable;

(i) To exercise all rights of ownership over any insurance policy held hereunder, including but not limited to rights to assign or surrender the policy, to change the beneficiary thereof, to borrow on the policy and to pledge it as security for a loan or loans, to convert it into paid-up insurance or whole life insurance and to exercise any options inuring to the trustees as owner or beneficiary or otherwise in connection with any policy;

(j) To improve or develop real estate; to construct, alter, repair, or demolish buildings or structures; to settle boundary lines and easements and other rights; to partition; and to join with co-owners or others in dealing with real estate in any way;

(k) To employ investment counsel and consult with them concerning the investments of the trust and to delegate to such counsel such powers as the trustees deem appropriate; to employ agents and to delegate to such agents such powers as the trustees deem appropriate; to employ legal counsel, accountants and any special services; to employ a custodian of any funds or securities and to delegate to the custodian such powers as the trustees deem appropriate; and, in addition to the compensation and expenses of the trustees, to pay the compensation and expenses of all such services even if rendered by a trustee;

(l) To participate as seller or purchaser in private placements, secondary offerings or other regulated or special transactions, and to execute and deliver such instruments and take such action as is customary or, in the opinion of the trustees, appropriate in connection therewith, including investment representations, indemnity agreements, pledges, and guarantees binding the trust property; and

(m) To make any division or distribution of, or payment from, the trust, in kind by the fair and reasonable allotment and transfer of specific securities or other personal or real property or undivided interests therein, at then current values, in lieu of cash, as a part or the whole of any one or more shares or payments.

In addition, the disinterested trustee of each trust hereunder shall have the power, exercisable from time to time in the disinterested trustee's discretion and without order or license of court, to credit particular receipts or gains, and to charge particular disbursements or losses or charges, to income or to principal of the trust or to apportion them between income and principal, whether such credits or charges relate to bonds acquired at a premium, to reserves or to any other matter, all as the disinterested trustee considers fair and reasonable in each case.

Practice Note

Article SEVENTH deals with trustee liability in connection with the life insurance policy held in the trust and the exercise of withdrawal rights by the beneficiary. In particular, it states that the trustees are under no personal obligation to satisfy the carrying costs of an insurance policy or to satisfy a withdrawal right. Instead, the trustees are authorized to borrow against policies, surrender paid-up additions, and exercise other rights of ownership in order to raise assets to meet carrying costs and withdrawals. Ordinarily, of course, it is anticipated that the donor will make cash contributions from time to time to the trust to enable the trustees to maintain the insurance coverage.

SEVENTH: Life Insurance. If at any time or times the assets of the trust under Article FIRST above are insufficient to pay premiums on all policies of insurance held thereunder and any interest, expense, or other cost of maintaining such policies and the trust and to satisfy any exercise of a right of withdrawal provided for in the second paragraph of Article FIRST above, the trustees shall be under no personal obligation to pay such premiums and costs or to satisfy such exercise nor shall the trustees be liable in case if any such premium, cost, or exercise is not paid in full. The trustees, however, may borrow against the cash value (if any) of any such policy in order to pay such premiums or costs and to satisfy such exercise, may apply such cash value to the purchase of paid-up insurance, may accept such cash value in the event of forfeiture of the policy, and may otherwise exercise any or all of the incidents of ownership of any such policy, whether to keep it in force or limit the coverage or cancel or otherwise deal with it. The trustees shall be entitled to indemnification from the principal of the trust for the expense of any legal proceedings taken to collect the proceeds of any such policy.

Practice Note

Article EIGHTH addresses issues regarding the identity of the trustees. It clarifies that any reference to the term "trustees" refers to the one or more trustees occupying the position at any time, regardless of whether those trustees are original, additional, or successor trustees. It also identifies the different classes of trustees and defines the concept of a "disinterested trustee." A disinterested trustee is defined as a trustee having no beneficial interest, whether vested or contingent, in any trust created or to be created under the trust instrument. This will exclude any of the donor's children or other issue from being considered a disinterested trustee, together with any individual—such as a niece or nephew—named or provided for in the contingent disposition provision. It should also be noted that the trust instrument prohibits any person who donates property to the trust or any person whose life is insured by a life insurance policy owned by the trust from being a trustee. The latter is an important prohibition to ensure that the policy proceeds are not included in the insured's estate at the time of her death.

This Article also deals with the manner in which trustees may resign voluntarily and the circumstances in which trustees are deemed to resign. It gives the donor and then the donor's spouse the right to remove trustees. A removal does not take effect unless a successor trustee (who is both a disinterested trustee—whether or not the removed trustee is disinterested—and a person or entity not related or subordinate to the person effecting the removal) is appointed and has accepted the office. The grant of such a removal power to the donor does not cause the donor to have incidents of ownership in the insurance policy on her life held in the trust.

Additional trustees may be appointed by the donor or by the donor's spouse, or, if not, by the trustees for the time being in office whenever there are fewer than three trustees. Terms and conditions can be attached to any such appointment. While it is not necessary to name successor trustees specifically, the model document provides a space for the naming of the first successor. Further successor trustees may be appointed first by the donor, then by the donor's spouse, then by the one or more remaining trustees, or, if none, by those of the donor's children who are living and of full legal capacity, or, if none, by the persons to whom the trustees would then render accounts.

The Article authorizes the trustees to delegate authority to each other, although powers and discretions vested in the disinterested trustee may only be delegated to another disinterested trustee. The Article waives the requirement of bond or surety, and provides that trustees are not liable for any act or omission with respect to insurance policies acquired by the trustees or transferred to the trust in the absence of gross negligence. Finally, trustees are not liable or responsible for the acts or omissions of any former trustees or of any co-trustees or of any agents selected with reasonable care. Local law should be checked for the effectiveness of all types of indemnification and liability restriction provisions.

EIGHTH: Trustees. References in this trust instrument to the "trustees" mean with respect to each trust hereunder the one or more trustees, whether original, additional, or successor, for the time being in office; and references to the "disinterested trustee" mean the one or more trustees having no beneficial interest, whether vested or contingent, in the income or principal of any trust hereunder.

Any trustee may resign by giving written notice to the Donor, if she is then living, or, if not, to her husband, [*HUSBAND'S NAME*], if he is then living, or, if not, to the remaining trustee, if any, or, if none, to the persons to whom the trustees would then render accounts of the particular trust as provided below in Article NINTH. Any individual trustee shall be deemed to have resigned and any named individual successor trustee shall be deemed unable to serve upon (i) the appointment of a legal guardian or similar legal representative for such individual or (ii) the receipt by the one or more persons (other than the particular trustee) who are then entitled to appoint successor trustees of a writing signed by the individual's regularly attending physician certifying that, in the physician's opinion, such individual is mentally or physically incapable of discharging the responsibilities of a trustee. In addition, any individual trustee who transfers property to any trust hereunder or upon whose life a policy of insurance is acquired to be held in trust hereunder shall be deemed to have resigned immediately before the transfer or the acquisition of the policy of life insurance, as the case may be.

Any trustee may be removed by a writing delivered to the trustee and signed by the Donor, if she is then living and of full legal capacity, or, if not, by her said husband, if he is then living and of full legal capacity; *provided* that no such removal of a trustee shall take effect until a successor disinterested trustee who is not a "related or subordinate" party (within the meaning of Section 672(c) of the Code) with respect to the person effecting the removal has been appointed as a successor trustee by the person effecting the removal and has accepted the office in writing.

Whenever there are fewer than three (3) trustees for the time being in office, an additional trustee may be appointed, to take office presently or at any future time and upon such other terms and conditions, all as specified in a writing signed by the Donor, if she is then living and of full legal capacity, or, if not, by her said husband, if he is then living and of full legal capacity, or, if not, by the trustees for the time being in office. Any such appointment of an additional trustee may be revoked at any time before it becomes effective.

There need not be more than one trustee for the time being in office of each trust hereunder, but there shall be at all times at least one disinterested trustee in office of each trust hereunder. In the case of the first vacancy in the office of trustee, [*TRUSTEE #3*], of [*ADDRESS*], shall become a successor trustee, upon written acceptance of the office. If for any reason [*TRUSTEE #3*] fails to accept the appointment or, having accepted, later ceases to serve, and in case of any other vacancy in the office of trustee of any trust hereunder, a successor trustee may be appointed in a writing signed by the Donor, if she is then living and of full legal capacity, or, if not, by her said husband, if he is then living and of full legal capacity, or, if not, by the one or more remaining trustees, if any, or, if none, by those of the Donor's children who are then living and of full legal capacity, or, if none, by one or more persons to whom the trustees would then render accounts of the particular trust as provided below in Article NINTH.

All appointments of additional and successor trustees shall, unless otherwise specified in the instrument of appointment, take effect upon written acceptance of the office; *provided* that no donor and no insured under a policy of insurance held in trust hereunder may be appointed a trustee.

Whenever there is more than one trustee in office, by a writing or writings, any trustee may delegate all or any of that trustee's powers and discretions to any other trustee for a period specified in such writing, and may revoke or successively renew such delegation; *provided* that the powers and discretions given to the disinterested trustee, as such, shall be exercised by the disinterested trustee alone, exclusive of any other of the trustees, and may be delegated only to another disinterested trustee.

No trustee named herein or appointed as above provided need furnish any bond or surety. No one dealing with the trustees need inquire concerning the validity of anything the trustees purport to do or need see to the application of any money paid or property transferred to or upon the order of the trustees. No trustee shall be liable for any act or omission with respect to any insurance policy acquired by the trustees or transferred to and retained by the trustees in the absence of a showing of gross negligence by the trustee. No trustee shall be liable or responsible for the acts or omissions of any former trustee or of any co-trustee or of any agent, custodian, or depositary selected with reasonable care.

Practice Note

A trust should deal with the manner in which the trustees account to the beneficiaries so that the trustees' obligations are clear. In the model form, accounts are to be rendered after the donor's death to the beneficiary of each age 35 trust. If the beneficiary is not of full legal capacity, the accounts will be rendered to his or her legal guardian or parents. This provision attempts to bring finality to the accounting procedure by providing protection to the trustees once assent has been given. However, it should be noted that in some jurisdictions such a provision might not be sufficient to insulate the trustees from complaints later raised by remainder beneficiaries.

NINTH: Accounts. After the Donor's death, the trustees of each trust hereunder shall render an account of the trust at least as often as annually to the beneficiary of the trust to whom in the period covered by such account current income from the trust could have been paid in the discretion of the disinterested trustee if he or she is living and of full legal capacity and, if the beneficiary is not of full legal capacity, to his or her legal guardian or similar legal representative, if any, or, if none, to either of his or her parents if he or she is a minor. In the case of each trust hereunder, the written assent to any such account by the person of full legal capacity to whom it is rendered as provided above shall fully protect the trustees as to all matters or transactions stated in such account or shown thereby, even if such person is serving as a trustee hereunder. Any person who is not of full legal capacity shall be deemed to assent to such account if his or her legal guardian or similar legal representative assents in writing to the account or if (such beneficiary being a minor and having no such legal guardian or representative) the parent to whom the account was rendered assents in writing to the account. Nothing in this Article shall be deemed to give anyone the power to modify the terms of this trust instrument or to alter or shift any beneficial interest created hereunder.

Practice Note

Article TENTH emphasizes that the trust instrument and the trusts created by the instrument are irrevocable and cannot be altered or amended. It also states that no donor shall have the power to control in any manner the administration of any trust created under the document, and that no part of the principal or income of the trust may be used to satisfy the legal obligations of the donor or her estate or shall revert to the donor or her estate. These provisions are designed again to avoid estate tax issues for the donor. It should be noted that the model form does not deal with grantor trust issues for federal income purposes. This is because, by most readings of the grantor trust provisions, the ability to use and the actual use of trust income and principal to pay life insurance premiums makes the trust a grantor trust for income tax purposes during the donor insured's lifetime. However, to ensure that the trust is treated in all respects as a grantor trust, additional provisions might be added (including, for example, authority in the disinterested trustee to add beneficiaries to the trust, such as spouses of the donor's children or charities).

TENTH: Irrevocable. This trust instrument and the trusts hereunder shall be irrevocable and shall not be subject to alteration or amendment. No donor shall have the power to control in any manner the administration of any trust hereunder. No part of the income or principal of any trust hereunder shall ever revert to the donor thereof or his or her estate (except as otherwise provided in Article SECOND above) or be used for the satisfaction of any legal obligation of the donor thereof or his or her estate. References in this trust instrument to a "donor" include the Donor.

Practice Note

The trustees should make secure arrangements for the custody of all trust documentation. It is general practice today, in light of photocopying technology, to sign only one original counterpart of the trust instrument. This provision allows outside parties to rely on certified copies of the original documentation rather than requiring access to the original document itself.

ELEVENTH: Trust Documentation. The original of each resignation, removal, or appointment of a trustee, each acceptance of appointment, and each instrument of delegation shall be kept attached to the original trust instrument, which shall be held by the trustees. Anyone may rely on a copy certified by a notary public of this trust instrument or of any writings attached thereto as fully as on the original document; and anyone may rely fully upon any statements of fact certified by anyone who appears from the original document or a certified copy thereof to be a trustee hereunder.

Practice Note

This provision authorizes the trustees after the donor's death to merge substantially identical trusts under this instrument with trusts established by the donor or by the donor's spouse under any other trust instrument or declaration. This should permit administrative cost savings.

TWELFTH: Combination and Termination of Trusts. If at any time after the death of the Donor a trust is being administered hereunder for one or more beneficiaries on terms substantially identical to those on which a trust is then being administered for the same beneficiaries under any other trust instrument or declaration established by or on behalf of the Donor or her said husband, the trustees, in their discretion, may terminate the trust for the one or more beneficiaries under this trust instrument by distributing any balance of net income and the then remaining principal to the then trustees of such other instrument or declaration to be added to the trust thereunder for the same beneficiaries.

Practice Note

Conflict of law problems can arise when the donor, the trust beneficiaries, and the trustees are not resident in the same jurisdiction. This provision states which jurisdiction will govern the operation of the trust. A governing law clause will generally be upheld as long as the state chosen has some logical connection to the trust. Consideration should be given to permitting the trustees to change the governing law in the future. This might be appropriate, for example, if all connections with the original chosen jurisdiction cease. This provision also sets forth a general savings clause, concerning the estate tax treatment of the trust. Such a clause is helpful if there is later found to be any other provision in the instrument that might be construed to cause estate tax inclusion of part or all of the trust property.

THIRTEENTH: Governing Law. This trust instrument and the trusts hereunder shall be governed, construed, and administered in accordance with the laws of [*SPECIFY GOVERNING STATE LAW*] from time to time in force, and shall also be construed and administered in all respects so as to further the Donor's intent that no property contributed to the trusts hereunder by *inter vivos* gift shall be includable in the estate of the particular donor for federal estate tax purposes.

Practice Note

The document should be dated and signed by the donor and by the trustees at the end. It is good practice in most jurisdictions to have the donor's signature notarized. Care should be taken that a trust is executed in accordance with the requirements of the donor's state of domicile. In some jurisdictions, the signatures of the donor and trustees should be witnessed. In other jurisdictions, all signatures must be notarized. In yet others, a trust that has testamentary consequences—i.e.,

---

one that provides for the management and distribution of trust property after the donor's death—should be executed with the same formalities as a will.

SIGNED and SEALED as of the ___ day of _____ 20___.

_____

SARAH SAMPLE, Donor

_____

[*TRUSTEE #1*], Trustee

_____

[*TRUSTEE #2*], Trustee

STATE/COMMONWEALTH OF [*NAME OF STATE*]

——————, ss.

On this —— day of ——, 20—, before me, the undersigned notary public, personally appeared the above-named SARAH SAMPLE, known to me personally or proved to me through ———— as satisfactory evidence of identification, to be the person whose name is signed on the preceding document, and acknowledged to me that she signed it voluntarily for its stated purpose.

_____

Notary Public
My Commission Expires:

Form 5
Annual Exclusion Trusts

Overview

Forms 5 and 6 contain two types of irrevocable trusts that can be used by a donor to make gifts in trust to a family member or third party. One form can be used only for the benefit of minors and must give withdrawal rights at the age of 21. The other form can be used for any beneficiaries. The trusts are structured so that gifts transferred to the trusts qualify for the annual exclusion from federal gift tax under Code Section 2503. Outright gifts and gifts to custodial accounts (under the Uniform Transfers to Minors Act or the Uniform Gifts to Minors Act) also qualify for the annual exclusion. However, outright gifts are rarely appropriate for younger donees since minors do not have the legal capacity to manage property, and custodial accounts may not be the best device to transfer significant amounts of property to minors because the accounts must generally terminate when the beneficiary reaches either age 18 or 21. A trust provides the most flexible alternative for managing and conserving property for the benefit of a minor. The model form contains two alternative trust structures that each give the trustee discretion to make distributions to or for the benefit of the named beneficiary. As a general rule, a gift made to a discretionary trust is treated as a gift of a "future interest" and does not qualify for the gift tax annual exclusion. These two trust forms represent exceptions to that rule. The first form meets the statutory requirements of Code Section 2503(c), and is commonly referred to as a *2503(c) trust*. The second form meets the annual exclusion requirements by creating an immediately exercisable withdrawal right over the property added to the trust. This second type of trust is commonly referred to as a *Crummey trust.*

THE SARAH SAMPLE CHILDREN'S TRUSTS

Practice Note

The opening paragraph identifies the settlor of the trust (the "donor"). The trust could have two settlors; for example, both parents or one set of grandparents of the trust beneficiaries could be listed. The opening paragraph should identify the initial trustee or trustees by name and describe the funding assets. The funding assets need not be more than a nominal amount.

In order to qualify for the annual exclusion, the trust must be irrevocable. Under the law of most states, trusts are deemed to be irrevocable unless the settlor expressly reserves a right of revocation or amendment. Nevertheless, it is good practice to state in the opening paragraph that the trusts created are irrevocable.

SARAH SAMPLE, of [*ADDRESS*] (the "Donor"), herewith transfers the sum of One Dollar ($1) to [*TRUSTEE #1*], of [*ADDRESS*], and [*TRUSTEE #2*], of [*ADDRESS*], as initial trustees hereunder; and the trustees hereby acknowledge receipt thereof and agree, for themselves, any additional trustees and all successors in office, to hold and manage said sum, together with any additions thereto, IRREVOCABLY IN TRUST, upon the following terms and provisions:

Practice Note

Article FIRST identifies the trust instrument by name and also titles each of the separate trusts created under the document. The model form assumes that only one trust will be created initially. If trusts for more than one child are to be established at the outset, the Article should be revised accordingly. This Article contemplates and authorizes the creation of additional trusts (e.g., for future born children) after the original document is signed. An additional trust is established formally by signing a simple, one-page document stating that a trust is created for the new child in accordance with the provisions of Article FIRST. A model document establishing an additional trust is provided in Form 6.

Any property transferred to "The Sarah Sample Children's Trusts" will be divided equally among each of the then existing trusts under the instrument. If this is not the donor's intention (e.g., the donor wants to make a gift to one child's trust but not to the others), the instrument of transfer should identify the separate trust as the donee.

FIRST: Creation of Separate Trusts. The trusts hereunder may be known collectively as "THE SARAH SAMPLE CHILDREN'S TRUSTS," and individually as "THE SARAH SAMPLE TRUST FOR [*NAME OF PARTICULAR BENEFICIARY*]." The trustees shall hold the initial trust property in a separate trust for the Donor's daughter, SAMANTHA SAMPLE (born [*DATE OF BIRTH*]), as provided below in Article SECOND.

Transfers to the trustees of cash, securities, or other property may be made by the Donor or by any other person or persons from time to time, by gift or will or otherwise, either to establish one or more separate trusts under Article SECOND below for one or more additional children of the Donor, or as additions to one or more of the separate trusts already existing thereunder. Any such additional property received by the trustees at any time shall (except as may be otherwise specified by the donor thereof at the time of transferring such additional property to the trustees) be added equally to and made a part of the principal of each of the then existing trusts under Article SECOND below or, if only one such trust is then in existence, shall be added to that one.

[OPTION ONE]

[Use the Following Article to Create Section 2503(c) Trusts]

Practice Note

Code Section 2503(c) provides that a transfer in trust for the benefit of a beneficiary who is under the age of 21 will not be considered a gift of a future interest (and thereby disqualified for the gift tax annual exclusion) provided that several conditions are met.

Under the first of these conditions, the trust must permit the trust principal and the income therefrom to be distributed to or used for the benefit of the beneficiary while under the age of 21 without substantial restrictions on the trustee's discretion. For example, a trust will not qualify for the annual exclusion if the trustee can only make distributions for the beneficiary's education. However, a precatory statement outlining the donor's wishes (which is not binding and which does not create a limit on the trustee's discretion) is permissible. If desired, the Internal Revenue Service has stated that the discretion can be limited to amounts necessary for the "support, care, education, comfort and welfare" of the beneficiary.

The second condition is that the principal of the trust and any accumulated income must pass to the beneficiary when the beneficiary reaches the age of 21. This does not mean, however, that the trust must terminate at the beneficiary's twenty-first birthday. A trust qualifies if, upon reaching age 21, the beneficiary has either a continuing right to compel distribution of all trust assets and accumulated income or a right for a limited period of time to terminate the trust and require distribution of all the trust assets. The model form satisfies the second condition by giving the beneficiary a 60-day right to withdraw the trust property upon reaching age 21. In its rulings, the Internal Revenue Service has accepted a 30-day period as sufficient. The beneficiary must be notified in writing of the existence of the with-drawal right. If the beneficiary fails to exercise the withdrawal right, the property will continue to be held under the terms of the trust until the beneficiary reaches age 35.

The third condition concerns the beneficiary's premature death. In order to qualify for the annual exclusion, the trust must provide that, if the beneficiary dies before the trust is distributed in full, all remaining principal and accumulated income must either be payable to the beneficiary's estate or be payable to those one or more persons as directed by the beneficiary in the exercise of a general power of appointment. The model document satisfies this condition by granting the beneficiary a general power of appointment. The document then sets forth default distribution provisions if the beneficiary dies and does not exercise the power (or cannot exercise the power because the beneficiary is not old enough to make a will).

Paragraph (d) limits the existence of any trust created under the document to a period of 90 years from the date of execution of the original instrument. This provision conforms to many statutory rules against perpetuity. In those states in which the perpetuities period has been abolished, this provision may be eliminated. In those states which have different statutory periods or still use the common law rule of lives-in-being plus 21 years, this provision should be revised. A provision that conforms to the common law rule against perpetuities can be found in Article SIXTH(c) of Form 1.

Gifts to the model form of trust also qualify for the annual exclusion from the federal generation-skipping transfer tax. This exclusion is available for transfers to trusts for the exclusive benefit of a grandchild or other skip person, where the assets of the trust will be subject to estate tax in the beneficiary's estate should the beneficiary die before the trust terminates. The existence of the general power of appointment (or, in the alternative, providing for the trust assets to be distributed directly to the beneficiary's estate) satisfies the latter requirement.

> In establishing a trust of this nature, it is important to consider not only the transfer tax but also the income tax consequences. Each Section 2503(c) trust is treated as a separate taxable entity, requiring its own tax identification number and separate annual returns. For federal purposes, income is taxable to the trust provided that the income is accumulated and not distributed. The tax rates applicable to trusts are highly condensed, with the highest income tax bracket applying at a very low threshold. In addition, there is a 3.8 percent surtax on undistributed net investment income. Thus, it is unlikely that significant income tax savings can be achieved by accumulating and reinvesting income in the trust. If income is distributed to the trust beneficiary, the income is not taxed to the trust but is instead reportable on the beneficiary's own income tax return. If the beneficiary is under a certain age, the "kiddie tax" rules will apply. The effect of these rules is that the child's income (in excess of a threshold amount) will be subject to tax at the parents' marginal tax rate. Note that the kiddie tax rules include dependents under age 19, and dependent full-time students under age 24.
>
> It is important to note that the income tax treatment of a Section 2503(c) trust changes once the beneficiary reaches age 21 (assuming the trust continues in existence because the child has not exercised the limited or continuing withdrawal right). Because of the withdrawal right, once the beneficiary has reached age 21, all income from the trust is taxable to the beneficiary and should be reported on the beneficiary's personal income tax return. This rule applies whether or not the income is distributed. It also applies with respect to capital gains earned in the trust. For this reason, although not provided in the model form, the trust might be drafted so that all income is required to be distributed to the beneficiary upon reaching the age of 21. Alternatively, the trust could provide that the trustee is required to distribute an amount sufficient to cover the beneficiary's income tax liability associated with the trust's income and capital gains.

SECOND: Child's Trust. All principal provided under any Article of this trust instrument to be held in trust under this Article SECOND for a child of the Donor shall be combined and administered, in each case, in a single, separate trust for the child as follows:

(a) *Discretionary Distributions.* So long as the child is living and has not reached the age of thirty-five (35), all or any part of the net income and principal may be paid to the child from time to time as the disinterested trustee, in the disinterested trustee's discretion, thinks advisable for any purpose. Any net income not so paid shall be added to principal at the end of each calendar year. [Without limiting the discretion of the disinterested trustee, the Donor hopes that in the exercise of this authority to make payments of income and principal the disinterested trustee will give primary consideration to the child's education.]

(b) *Right of Withdrawal.* Notwithstanding the foregoing, the child (or if the child is not then of full legal capacity, the child's legal guardian or similar legal representative other than the donor of any contribution to the trust) shall have the right, by a writing or writings delivered to the trustees during the sixty (60) day period beginning with the date on which the child reaches the age of twenty-one (21), to withdraw any amount or all of the then trust principal and any balance of net income.

Any amount not so withdrawn shall continue to be held in trust hereunder. The disinterested trustee shall, on or before such date, notify the child in writing of the child's right to withdraw the trust property under this paragraph (b); and if the child is not then of full legal capacity, such notice shall be given to the child's legal guardian or similar legal representative, if any.

(c) *Distribution of Principal at Age Thirty-Five; Power of Appointment.* When the child reaches the age of thirty-five (35), the then remaining principal and any balance of net income shall be distributed to the child. If the child dies before reaching the age of thirty-five (35), any balance of net income remaining at the child's death shall be added to principal and the then remaining principal shall be disposed of as the child shall appoint by will, referring specifically to this power of appointment, to or for the benefit of the child's estate or to or for the benefit of any one or more other persons or objects, all in such amounts or proportions, for such estates, on such trusts, and subject to such terms, conditions, general or special powers and restrictions as the child shall so appoint. In default of or subject to appointment as aforesaid, upon the child's death the then remaining principal shall be distributed in equal shares to the child's then living children, or, if none, by right of representation to the Donor's then living issue, or, if none, to the child's personal representative or administrator to be disposed of as part of the child's estate; *provided* that any principal thus distributable to a child of the Donor who has not then reached the age of thirty-five (35) shall be held in trust for the child as provided in this Article, instead of being distributed outright.

(d) *Rule Against Perpetuities.* If not sooner terminated as provided above, each trust under this Article shall terminate, and the trust property shall thereupon be distributed to the person then living in respect of whom such trust was set apart, ninety (90) years after the date of execution of this trust instrument.

[OPTION TWO]

[Use the Following Article to Create Crummey Trusts]

Practice Note

Gifts made to a Crummey trust satisfy the annual exclusion requirements of Code Section 2503 because the beneficiary has the power to demand from the trust the amount of the gifted assets. The demand right arises at the time of contribution and lapses after an adequate time period (the Service has approved withdrawal periods of 30 to 90 days) with no continuing rights. Clients often prefer this form of trust because, except for the initial withdrawal right, the beneficiary need not be given a right to withdraw the trust assets upon reaching age 21. This trust is also appropriate for gifts to beneficiaries who are no longer minors.

The Crummey trust is named for the case of *Crummey v. Commissioner,* decided in 1968 (397 F.2d 82), in which the Ninth Circuit Federal Court of Appeals held that gifts to a discretionary trust subject to a beneficiary's immediate right of withdrawal qualified for the gift tax annual exclusion. The Internal Revenue Service has accepted the holding of the case but has added several glosses. In particular, the Service has required that the trust beneficiary receive actual notice of each contribution and the beneficiary's resulting withdrawal rights. The trustee should provide such notice in the form of a letter to the beneficiary (or to his or her guardian or parent, provided the latter is not the donor of the contribution) and should retain copies of the letters with the trust records.

Once withdrawal rights have been granted, there are no additional requirements concerning the distribution of income or principal from a Crummey trust. A Crummey trust can be drafted giving the trustee broad discretion as in the model form. Alternatively, restrictions could be placed on the trustee's discretion (e.g., for the limited purpose of education prior to the beneficiary reaching a certain age). A Crummey trust can last as long as the donor desires. The model form terminates at age 35.

The model form of Crummey trust gives the beneficiary a general power of appointment to dispose of the trust property should the beneficiary die before the trust is distributed in full. The existence of this power means that the property will be includable in the beneficiary's estate for estate tax purposes (although even without the general power the property would likely be includable for estate tax purposes because of the lapsed annual withdrawal rights). The inclusion of the general power of appointment also prevents the beneficiary from having any gift tax problems as a result of allowing the withdrawal rights to lapse. Finally, the general power means that gifts to the trust will qualify for the generation-skipping transfer tax annual exclusion. This is particularly relevant if grandparents intend to fund the trust.

The Internal Revenue Service has routinely taken the position that, in the absence of language causing the donor to be treated as the grantor for federal income tax purposes, a Crummey trust should be treated as a grantor trust for federal income tax purposes, in which the beneficiary is the grantor (other names for this type of trust are Mallinckrodt trust and Section 678 trust). If correct, and if the beneficiary has had the right to withdraw the total amount of all contributions to the trust, this means that all income and capital gains earned and realized by the trust must be reported on the beneficiary's own income tax return. While the beneficiary is under age 19 (or under age 24 depending on the beneficiary's status as a full-time student), the taxation of the income would be subject to the "kiddie tax" rules.

SECOND: Child's Trust. All property provided under any Article of this trust instrument to be held in trust under this Article SECOND for a child of the Donor shall be combined and administered, in each case, in a single, separate trust for the child as follows:

    (a) *Discretionary Distributions.* So long as the child is living and has not reached the age of thirty-five (35), all or any part of the net income and principal may be paid to the child from time to time as the disinterested trustee, in the disinterested trustee's discretion, thinks advisable for any purpose. Any net income not so paid shall be added to principal at the end of each calendar year.

(b) *Right of Withdrawal.* Notwithstanding the foregoing, with respect to the initial and each subsequent contribution made to the trust by *inter vivos* gift by any donor, the child shall have the noncumulative right during his or her lifetime, exercisable by a writing or writings delivered to the trustees within sixty (60) days after the particular contribution is made, to withdraw such amount of the contribution as the donor thereof may designate in a written notice delivered to the trustees prior to making the particular contribution, or, in the absence of such a written designation, all of the particular contribution. If the child is not of full legal capacity when a contribution is made, this right of withdrawal shall be exercisable on his or her behalf by a legal guardian or similar legal representative, if any, who is not the donor of the contribution, or, if none and the child is then a minor, by either of the child's parents who is not the donor of the contribution. Any asset of the trust may be used by the trustees to satisfy any such withdrawal. The trustees, in advance of or upon receipt of each contribution to the trust that is subject to any extent to the aforesaid right of withdrawal, shall notify the child of its date and the amount, if any, the child may withdraw. If the child is not then of full legal capacity, such notice shall be given to his or her legal guardian or similar legal representative, if any, or, if none, to either of his or her parents if he or she is a minor, in each case provided that the representative or parent is not the donor of the contribution.

(c) *Distribution of Principal at Age Thirty-Five; Power of Appointment.* When the child reaches the age of thirty-five (35), the then remaining principal and any balance of net income shall be distributed to the child. If the child dies before reaching the age of thirty-five (35), any balance of net income remaining at the child's death shall be added to principal and the then remaining principal shall be disposed of as the child shall appoint by will, referring specifically to this power of appointment, to or for the benefit of the child's estate or to or for the benefit of any one or more other persons or objects, all in such amounts or proportions, for such estates, on such trusts, and subject to such terms, conditions, general or special powers and restrictions as the child shall so appoint. In default of or subject to appointment as aforesaid, upon the child's death the then remaining principal shall be distributed in equal shares to the child's then living children, or, if none, by right of representation to the Donor's then living issue, or, if none, to the child's personal representative or administrator to be disposed of as part of the child's estate; *provided* that any principal thus distributable to a child of the Donor who has not then reached the age of thirty-five (35) shall be held in trust for the child as provided in this Article, instead of being distributed outright.

(d) *Rule Against Perpetuities.* If not sooner terminated as provided above, each trust under this Article shall terminate, and the trust property shall thereupon be distributed to the person then living in respect of whom such trust was set apart, ninety (90) years after the date of execution of this trust instrument.

Practice Note

Article THIRD sets forth general administrative provisions. The first is a so-called "facility of payment" provision. It authorizes the trustees to make distributions for a beneficiary's benefit, rather than to the beneficiary directly. This is of particular importance while the beneficiary is under the age of 21. It is not, however, limited to that situation and could be exercised after the beneficiary's twenty-first birthday. The provision also allows the trustees to obtain a valid discharge in making a distribution to a beneficiary who is a minor without going through a legally appointed guardian. The distribution can be made to a parent of the beneficiary or to a custodian under the Uniform Transfers to Minors Act or the Uniform Gifts to Minors Act. This section includes a provision that no payment may be made that discharges a legal obligation of an individual serving as a disinterested trustee. The purpose of this provision is to avoid making trust income taxable to the trustee under the grantor trust rules. It should be noted that the facility of payment provision does not apply to any amounts that may be withdrawn by the trust beneficiary. Withdrawal payments, whether at age 21 under the Section 2503(c) option, or at the time of contribution under the Crummey option, must be made directly to the beneficiary.

The second provision is a "spendthrift clause." It provides that creditors cannot reach the beneficiary's interest in the trust. It also prohibits a voluntary assignment by the beneficiary of his or her beneficial interest. (In order to protect trust assets against involuntary attachment by creditors, most states require that voluntary assignment be prohibited as well.) The existence of the withdrawal right at age 21 in the Section 2503(c) trust and the annual withdrawal rights in the Crummey trust may limit the protection provided against third party creditors by the spendthrift provision.

The third provision defines the terms "child" and "issue." Adopted descendants are included, as are all natural born descendants, including the children of unmarried mothers and the children of unmarried fathers where the father has acknowledged paternity. If a different result is desired, the clause should be modified. The term "by right of representation" is defined to state how the shares are to be determined whenever that means of distribution is employed. The children of a person whose issue are to be benefited are considered the stocks for purposes of determining the number of distributive shares, whether or not any of those children are alive at the time of distribution. This overrides the law of several states.

Finally, the fourth provision states that, although each of the trusts created under the instrument is a separate trust, the trustees are authorized to commingle the investments of each of the trusts in one common fund. Under most state laws, this is not permitted absent a specific provision authorizing it even when the same instrument creates the trusts. Economic sense will often dictate that this is a most reasonable course.

THIRD: General Administrative Provisions. Each trust hereunder is subject to the following provisions:

    (a) *Distributions to Minors; Impracticable Distributions.* Except as provided in paragraph (b) of Article SECOND above, whenever a payment of income or principal is to be made to any beneficiary, and the beneficiary has not reached the age of twenty-one (21) or is ill or away, or because of other circumstances it is impracticable or undesirable, in the opinion of the disinterested trustee, to make such payment directly to the beneficiary, the disinterested trustee, in the disinterested trustee's discretion, may apply such payment for the beneficiary's benefit in such manner as the disinterested trustee thinks best for the beneficiary, regardless of the beneficiary's other resources. Such application for the beneficiary's benefit, and any payment to a beneficiary who has not reached the age of twenty-one (21), may be made in any amount, either directly or through a guardian, custodian, or member of the family of the beneficiary or by payment to the beneficiary in person even though he or she has not reached the age of twenty-one (21) or is incapacitated; and the receipt of the payee shall, with respect to each such payment, be a sufficient discharge to the trustees so that they need not see to the further application thereof. Notwithstanding any other provision of this trust instrument, no payment may be made that discharges a legal obligation of support or other legal obligation of an individual serving as a disinterested trustee hereunder.

(b) *Spendthrift Clause.* The interest of each beneficiary, and all payments of income or principal to be made to or for any beneficiary, shall be free from interference or control by any creditor, spouse, or divorced former spouse of the beneficiary and shall not be capable of anticipation or assignment by the beneficiary.

(c) *Definitions.* In this trust instrument, references to "child" or "children" mean descendants in the first degree only, and references to "issue" mean descendants in the first, second, or any other degree; in each case meaning lawful descendants of the ancestor designated, whether by blood or by adoption and whether living on the date of the trust instrument or born or adopted thereafter. For purposes of the preceding sentence, a person born out of wedlock and those claiming through that person shall be treated as lawful descendants (i) of the natural mother and her ancestors, and (ii) if the natural father acknowledges paternity, of the natural father and his ancestors, in each case unless a decree of adoption terminates such natural parent's parental rights. Whenever distribution is to be made by right of representation to the then living issue of a designated ancestor, the ancestor's children shall be considered the stocks for purposes of determining the respective shares of such issue.

(d) *Investment in Common Fund.* Each of the trusts hereunder shall constitute a separate and distinct trust, but for convenience of administration the trustees may, in their discretion, mingle or combine any of the investments or property of said trusts in a common fund in which the several contributing trusts shall have undivided proportionate interests.

Practice Note

State law grants many powers of administration to trustees. To eliminate the need to refer to statutes and case law and to set forth the donor's intent explicitly, it is

---

> good drafting practice to set forth the powers expressly. This may also serve to eliminate ambiguities in local law, expand the scope of the trustees' authority, and avoid the need for court approval of certain actions. The list of powers contained in the model Article is general and should cover most situations. The cross-reference to Article SEVENTH is explained more fully in the comments in connection with that Article.

FOURTH: Trustees' Powers. In extension and not in limitation of the powers given them by law or other provisions of this trust instrument, but subject to the provisions of Article SEVENTH below, the trustees of each trust hereunder shall have the following powers with respect to the trust and its property, in each case to be exercised from time to time in the discretion of the trustees and without order or license of court:

(a) To retain indefinitely, and to invest and reinvest in, stocks, shares, obligations, partnership interests, and other securities or any other kind of personal or real property, even though any or all of the investments made or retained are of a character or size that, but for this express authority, would not be considered proper for trustees;

(b) To sell, to exchange, to lease, and to make contracts concerning real or personal property for such consideration and upon such terms as to credit or otherwise as the trustees consider advisable, which leases and contracts may extend beyond the term of the trust; to give options on real or personal property of the trust; to establish depreciation, depletion, tax, or any other reserves; to execute deeds, transfers, leases, and other instruments of any kind; and to deal with themselves or one of them as freely as with a stranger;

(c) To hold securities or other property in bearer or unregistered form or in the name of one or more of the trustees or of any other person, firm, or corporation, without indication of any fiduciary capacity;

(d) To give general or special proxies or powers of attorney (which may or may not be discretionary and with power of substitution) for voting or acting with respect to securities to any person other than a donor; to deposit securities with, or transfer them to, protective committees, voting trustees, or similar bodies; to join in any reorganization; and to pay assessments or subscriptions called for in connection with securities held by the trustees;

(e) To receive additions to the trust by gift or will or otherwise, and to hold and administer the same under the provisions hereof;

(f) To compromise or submit to arbitration and to pay before due any tax, claim or matter in dispute;

(g) If in the opinion of the trustees it is necessary or advisable to do so, to borrow money for such time and at such rate of interest or discount as the trustees deem proper; to give notes or obligations therefor binding the trust property; and as security therefor to mortgage or to pledge real or personal property with or without power of sale;

(h) To improve or develop real estate; to construct, alter, repair, or demolish buildings or structures; to settle boundary lines and easements and other rights; to partition; and to join with co-owners or others in dealing with real estate in any way;

(i) To employ investment counsel and consult with them concerning the investments of the trust and to delegate to such counsel such powers as the trustees deem appropriate; to employ agents and to delegate to such agents such powers as the trustees deem appropriate; to employ a custodian of any funds or securities and to delegate to the custodian such powers as the trustees deem appropriate; to employ legal counsel, accountants, and any special services; and, in addition to the compensation and expenses of the trustees, to pay the compensation and expenses of all such services even if rendered by a trustee;

(j) To credit particular receipts or gains, and to charge particular disbursements or losses or charges, to income or to principal of the trust or to apportion them between income and principal, whether such credits or charges relate to bonds acquired at a premium, to reserves, or to any other matter, all as the trustees consider fair and reasonable in each case; and

(k) To make any division or distribution of, or payment from, the trust, in kind by the fair and reasonable allotment and transfer of specific securities or other personal or real property or undivided interests therein, at then current values, in lieu of cash, as a part or the whole of any one or more shares or payments.

Practice Note

Article FIFTH addresses the identity of the trustees. It clarifies that any reference to the term "trustee" or "trustees" refers to the one or more trustees occupying the position at any time, regardless of whether those trustees are original, additional, or successor trustees. This Article also deals with the manner in which trustees may resign voluntarily, and the circumstances in which trustees are deemed to resign or retire. It also grants powers to remove trustees and provides for the appointment of additional and successor trustees. Successor or additional trustees can be appointed first by the donor (if she is living and is of full legal capacity), then by the donor's spouse (if he is living and is of full legal capacity), then by the remaining trustees (if any) and finally by the beneficiary of the trust.

The trusts can be administered by a single trustee or by co-trustees. In the model document, it is assumed that there will be co-trustees. In order to avoid having the property be subject to estate tax at the donor's death, the donor should not be appointed as sole trustee. While the donor can act as a co-trustee with full investment powers, she cannot participate in decisions to make discretionary distributions without causing the trust property to be part of her estate for estate tax purposes. For this reason, the model document employs the concept of a "disinterested trustee," defined as a trustee other than a donor or the beneficiary of the particular trust, and vests that trustee alone with the discretion to make distributions. In this way, the trusts can be established with the donor and another person as trustees. The disinterested trustee could be the donor's spouse, provided, of course, that he does not make gifts to the trusts. For this purpose, it should be noted that the making of a split gift election (which causes gifts to be treated for gift and estate tax purposes as if made half by the wife and half by the husband and allows the husband's annual exclusion to be applied to the wife's gifts) does not cause the husband to be treated as a donor for purposes of these rules. In other words, he could still serve as a disinterested trustee.

If a nondonor parent is appointed to act as the disinterested trustee, it is important that the trust prohibit the trust assets from being used to discharge support obligations. The reason for this is that if a parent-trustee can use trust property to discharge such obligations, the trust property is arguably includable in the parent's estate should he or she die while the trust is in existence, irrespective of whether the parent-trustee was the source of the trust contributions. To prevent this problem, the model document expressly provides under the "facility of payment" provision in Article THIRD (a) that no distributions may be made that discharge legal obligations of support owed by the disinterested trustee. Of course, prohibiting distributions for support may prevent the trust property from being used for desired purposes, such as the payment of private school bills. This should be taken into consideration in choosing whether to make the donor's spouse the disinterested trustee.

The model document permits the donor and, after her death, the donor's husband to remove trustees, including the disinterested trustee. Previously, it was thought inadvisable to permit the donor to remove a trustee who had discretion to distribute the trust property. The ability to remove and appoint a replacement trustee was thought to constitute retained control over the trust property, thereby causing the trust property to remain in the donor's estate for estate tax purposes. Since 1995, however, the Internal Revenue Service has dispelled this concern, provided that any replacement trustee controlling distributions is not related or subordinate to the donor. This restriction is included in the model document. The model document goes beyond the requirements of the 1995 ruling by imposing a similar restriction on replacement trustees appointed by the spouse.

This Article authorizes the trustees to delegate authority to each other and waives requirements of bond or surety. Other provisions that might be included would cover trustee compensation and/or a limitation on trustee liability in the absence of gross negligence or willful default.

FIFTH: Trustees. References in this trust instrument to the "trustee" or the "trustees" mean with respect to each trust hereunder the one or more trustees, whether original, additional, or successor, for the time being in office; and references to the "disinterested trustee" mean the one or more trustees *other than* a donor or the person who has a current interest in the income or principal of the particular trust.

Any trustee may resign by giving written notice to the Donor, if she is then living, or, if not, to her husband, SAM SAMPLE, if he is then living, or, if not, to the remaining trustee, if any, or, if none, to the person to whom the trustees would then render accounts of the particular trust as provided below in Article SIXTH. Any individual trustee shall be deemed to have resigned upon (i) the appointment of a legal guardian or similar legal representative for such individual or (ii) the receipt by the one or more persons (other than the particular trustee) who are then entitled to appoint successor trustees of a writing signed by the individual's regularly attending physician certifying that, in such physician's opinion, such individual is mentally or physically incapable of discharging the responsibilities of a trustee.

Any trustee may be removed by a writing delivered to the trustee and signed by the Donor, if she is then living and of full legal capacity, or, if not, by her said husband, if he is then living and of full legal capacity; *provided* that no such removal of a disinterested trustee shall take effect until a successor disinterested trustee who is not a "related or subordinate" party (within the meaning of Section 672(c) of the Internal Revenue Code of 1986, as amended) to the person effecting the removal has been appointed as a successor trustee as provided below and has accepted the office in writing.

There need not be more than one trustee for the time being in office of each trust hereunder, but there shall always be at least one disinterested trustee for the time being in office of each trust hereunder. In the case of any vacancy in the office of trustee, a successor trustee may be appointed in a writing signed by the Donor, if she is then living and of full legal capacity, or, if not, by the Donor's said husband, if he is then living and of full legal capacity, or, if not, by the remaining trustee, if any, or, if none, by the person to whom the trustees would then render accounts of the particular trust as provided below in Article SIXTH.

At any time or times, an additional trustee may be appointed to take office presently or at any future time and upon such other terms and conditions, in each case in a writing signed by the person then entitled to appoint successor trustees as provided above. Any appointment of an additional trustee may be revoked in writing by such person before it becomes effective.

Unless otherwise provided in the instrument of appointment, each appointment of an additional or successor trustee shall take effect upon written acceptance of the office.

Whenever there is more than one trustee for the time being in office, any trustee may delegate, by a writing or writings, all or any of that trustee's powers and discretions to any other trustee for a period specified in such writing, and may revoke or successively renew such delegation; *provided* that the powers and discretions given to the disinterested trustee, as such, shall be exercised by the disinterested trustee alone, exclusive of any other of the trustees, and may be delegated only to another disinterested trustee.

No trustee named herein or appointed as above provided need furnish any bond or surety. No one dealing with the trustees need inquire concerning the validity of anything the trustees purport to do or need see to the application of any money paid or property transferred to or upon the order of the trustees.

Practice Note

A trust should deal with the manner in which the trustees account to beneficiaries so that the trustees' obligations are clear. In the model form, accounts may,

> but are not required to be, rendered to the beneficiary. A trustee would ordinarily render accounts on a regular basis.

SIXTH: Accounts. The trustees of each trust hereunder may (but shall not be required to) render an account of the trust to the beneficiary of the trust to whom in the period covered by such account current income from the trust could have been paid in the discretion of the disinterested trustee and who is living and of full legal capacity or, if the beneficiary is not of full legal capacity, to his or her legal guardian or similar legal representative, if any, or, if none, to either of his or her parents if he or she is a minor. In the case of each trust hereunder, the written assent to any such account by the person of full legal capacity to whom it is rendered as provided above shall fully protect the trustees as to all matters or transactions stated in such account or shown thereby, even if such person is serving as a trustee hereunder. Any person who is not of full legal capacity shall be deemed to assent to such account if his or her legal guardian or similar legal representative assents in writing to the account or if (such beneficiary being a minor and having no such legal guardian or similar legal representative) the parent to whom the account was rendered assents in writing to the account. Nothing in this Article shall be deemed to give anyone the power to modify the terms of this trust instrument or to alter or shift any beneficial interest created hereunder.

Practice Note

Article SEVENTH states that the trust is irrevocable and is not subject to alteration or amendment. It also includes language to ensure that the "grantor trust" provisions of the Code do not apply to the trust in such a way as to cause the trust income to be attributed back to the donor. Finally, this Article contains a saving provision designed to preclude in all events the inclusion of the trust property in the gross estate of the donor for federal estate tax purposes.

The definition of donor at the end of the Article excludes the beneficiary from being treated as such because of the beneficiary's failure to exercise a withdrawal power.

SEVENTH: Irrevocable; Fiduciary Standards. This trust instrument and the trusts hereunder shall be irrevocable and shall not be subject to alteration or amendment. No income or principal of any trust hereunder shall be used for the benefit of any donor or the spouse of any donor or to pay premiums on any policy of insurance on the life of any donor or the spouse of any donor; no loans shall be made, directly or indirectly, to any donor or the spouse of any donor from any trust hereunder; and no property of any trust hereunder shall be bought from, sold to, exchanged with, or leased to or from any person for less than an adequate consideration in money or money's worth. Except in a fiduciary capacity, no donor shall have the power to control in any manner the administration of any trust hereunder. References in this trust instrument to a "donor" include the Donor but do not include any person solely by virtue of that person's right of withdrawal under paragraph (b) of Article SECOND above.

Practice Note

The trustees should make secure arrangements for the custody of all trust documentation. It is general practice today, in light of photocopying technology, to sign only one original counterpart of the trust instrument. This provision allows outside parties to rely on certified copies of the original document rather than requiring access to the original document itself.

EIGHTH: Trust Documentation. The original of each resignation, removal, or appointment of a trustee, each acceptance of appointment, and each instrument of delegation shall be kept attached to the original trust instrument, which shall be held by the trustees. Anyone may rely on a copy certified by a notary public of this trust instrument or of any writings attached thereto as fully as on the original document; and anyone may rely fully upon any statements of fact certified by anyone who appears from the original document or a certified copy thereof to be a trustee hereunder.

Practice Note

Article NINTH states which jurisdiction will govern the operation of the trust. A governing law clause will generally be upheld as long as the chosen state has some logical connection to the trust. Consideration should be given to permitting the trustees to change the governing law in the future. This might be appropriate if all connections with the originally selected jurisdiction cease to exist. This Article also contains a savings clause that the trust should be construed in light of the donor's intent that no part of any property gifted to the trust be included in the donor's estate for federal estate tax purposes.

NINTH: Governing Law. This trust instrument and the trusts hereunder shall be governed, construed, and administered in accordance with the laws of [*SPECIFY GOVERNING STATE LAW*] from time to time in force, and shall also be construed and administered in all respects so as to further the Donor's intent that no property contributed to the trusts hereunder by the Donor or any other donor by *inter vivos* gift shall be includable in the estate of the particular donor for federal estate tax purposes.

Practice Note

The document should be dated and signed by the donor and the trustees at the end. It is good practice to have the donor's signature notarized. Care should be taken to ensure that the trust is executed in accordance with all required local formalities (particularly if it is contemplated that the trust may hold interests in real estate). In

> some jurisdictions, the signatures of the donor and trustees might need to be witnessed. In other jurisdictions, all signatures must be notarized. In general, the document should be executed in accordance with the requirements of the donor's state of domicile.

SIGNED and SEALED this ___ day of _____, 20 ___.

_____

SARAH SAMPLE, Donor

_____

[*TRUSTEE #1*], Trustee

_____

[*TRUSTEE #2*], Trustee

STATE/COMMONWEALTH OF [*NAME OF STATE*]

——————, ss.

On this ——— day of —————, 20——, before me, the undersigned notary public, personally appeared the above-named SARAH SAMPLE, known to me personally or proved to me through ————— as satisfactory evidence of identification, to be the person whose name is signed on the preceding document, and acknowledged to me that she signed it voluntarily for its stated purpose.

————————————————————
Notary Public
My Commission Expires:

FORM 6
Additional Annual Exclusion Trust

Overview

The model Annual Exclusion trust instrument (Form 5) contemplates and authorizes the creation of additional trusts (e.g., for future born children) after the original document is signed. This form provides a model document establishing an additional trust.

THE SARAH SAMPLE CHILDREN'S TRUSTS
Establishment of New Trust for [*Name of Child*]

Pursuant to the provisions of Article FIRST of THE SARAH SAMPLE CHILDREN'S TRUSTS, established [*DATE*], by SARAH SAMPLE, of [*ADDRESS*], as Donor, with [*TRUSTEE #1*], of [*ADDRESS*], and [*TRUSTEE #2*], of [*ADDRESS*], as trustees (the "Trust"), the Donor hereby establishes a new trust thereunder for the benefit of the Donor's son/daughter, [*NAME OF CHILD*] (born [*DATE OF BIRTH*]), and transfers to this new trust the sum of [*AMOUNT IN WORDS*] ($___). The trust for [*NAME OF CHILD*] shall be administered and disposed of as a separate trust in accordance with the provisions of Article SECOND of the Trust.

SIGNED and SEALED this ____ day of ____, 20___.

_____
SARAH SAMPLE, Donor

The undersigned trustees hereby acknowledge receipt of the foregoing and agree to administer the new trust for [*NAME OF CHILD*] as aforesaid, all as of the date last above written.

_____
[*TRUSTEE #1*], Trustee

_____
[*TRUSTEE #2*], Trustee

STATE/COMMONWEALTH OF [*NAME OF STATE*]

_____, ss.

On this ___ day of _____, 20__, before me, the undersigned notary public, personally appeared the above-named SARAH SAMPLE, known to me personally or proved to me through _____ as satisfactory evidence of identification, to be the person whose name is signed on the preceding document, and acknowledged to me that she signed it voluntarily for its stated purpose.

_____
Notary Public
My Commission Expires:

FORM 7

Will with Pour-Over Provision

Overview

This form of will provides for the disposition of the testator's tangible personal property to the testator's spouse, or, if she is not living, equally to the testator's children. It then provides that the rest of the testator's property will be distributed to, and administered in accordance with, the terms of a living trust established by the testator prior to signing the will. This form is intended to be used in conjunction with Form 1 (Living Trust With Traditional Marital Trust and Credit Shelter Trust) or Form 2 (Living Trust with Multiple QTIP Marital Trust Options). Finally, the will names a guardian for the testator's children and a personal representative for his estate.

WILL

Practice Note

The opening paragraph is commonly referred to as the publishing clause. It identifies the person making the will. All names in which property is owned by the testator should be stated in order to help the personal representative identify, collect, and transfer the testator's property.

The residency of the testator establishes where the will is to be probated after the testator's death, assuming that the testator does not move after the date the will is signed. It also determines which state law is applicable in interpreting provisions of the will. If the testator divides time between two homes, the primary residency used for income tax purposes should be used to avoid inconsistency.

The publishing clause should state that all prior wills and codicils are revoked. Before including such a clause, however, the estate planner should confirm that this conforms to the testator's intent. There may be situations in which the testator would like to leave another will in place (e.g., if the testator has a will executed in a foreign country disposing of foreign property). If that is the intention, the will should state the limited scope of the revocation (e.g., this will revokes all prior wills and codicils only to the extent that they purport to dispose of property located within the United States of America at the time of my death).

In some jurisdictions, a will disposing of all property will exercise testamentary powers of appointment held by the testator. It is good practice to avoid this result by explicit provision. If a testator has powers of appointment, they should be reviewed carefully and exercised only by express provision.

Wills frequently include a direction to the personal representative to "pay all just debts." It is generally better form to omit this provision. By law, a personal representative is required to pay all enforceable debts of a testator. Inclusion of such a provision could imply that the testator wanted the personal representative to pay

> debts barred by the statute of limitations or to pay all mortgages associated with the testator's property.

I, SAM SAMPLE (also known as SAMUEL ARTHUR SAMPLE), of [AD-DRESS], make this my last will, hereby revoking all earlier wills and codicils. I do not by this will exercise any power of appointment.

Practice Note

Tangible personal property is palpable, susceptible to the sense of touch, capable of ownership, and endowed with intrinsic value. The term includes cars, boats, and airplanes, artwork, antiques and other collectibles, furniture and furnishings, jewelry, clothing, and pets. In most jurisdictions, it would also include property used in a trade or business unless specifically excluded.

A separate gift of tangible personal property is always desirable, even if the residuary assets are to be distributed to the same individuals. For federal income tax purposes, a specific bequest does not carry out income earned by estate assets to the recipient of the bequest. Accordingly, the recipient is not exposed to liability for income earned by investment assets upon receipt of a gift of jewelry or furniture.

If tangible personal property is given to a group of individuals, a mechanism for determining the recipients of specific items might be added to the will to deal with controversy among the beneficiaries. For example, a will could provide that the beneficiaries choose by lot. If the testator wants to give specific property to particular beneficiaries, examples of such bequests can be found in Form 8.

The model article includes precatory language that the recipients should dispose of certain items in accordance with the testator's wishes. The testator may leave a separate memorandum or letter of nonbinding guidance regarding his or her wishes. If, instead, the testator wants enforceable provisions, most jurisdictions still require that a separate memorandum be incorporated into the will by reference, meaning that the memorandum must be in existence when the will is executed, referred to explicitly in the will and not be susceptible to future change. This offers little flexibility for those of wavering intentions. In some jurisdictions (notably those that have adopted the Uniform Probate Code), it is now possible to provide that tangible personal property will be disposed of in accordance with the last dated memorandum left with the will. The estate planner should check the law of the applicable jurisdiction to determine if this option is available.

Where a beneficiary might be a minor, the will should include a mechanism for the personal representative to deliver the items to someone on behalf of the minor and obtain a receipt. The suggested language is broad and authorizes distribution to guardians, custodians, and adult relatives to hold for the minor beneficiary.

FIRST: <u>Tangible Personal Property</u>. I give all my tangible personal property (as distinguished from money, securities, and the like), wherever located, to my wife, SARAH SAMPLE, if she is living on the thirtieth day after my death, or, if she is not then living, in shares of as near equal value as possible to those of my children who are then living, or all to the survivor of them if only one of them is then living. I hope that whoever receives this property will dispose of certain items of it in accordance with my wishes, if and however made known, but I impose no trust, condition, or enforceable obligation of any kind in this regard.

Any items of my tangible personal property distributable hereunder to a child of mine who is under the age of majority may be distributed to a guardian or adult relative of or custodian for the child or to the child directly, in each case in any amount and in the discretion of my personal representative; and the receipt of the distributee shall, with respect to each such distribution, be a sufficient discharge to my personal representative who need not see to the further application thereof.

References in this will or a codicil to "child" or "children" mean all descendants of mine in the first degree, whether by blood or by adoption.

Practice Note

A will must have a residuary clause in order to avoid having property pass by intestacy. This clause disposes of property not specifically transferred by other provisions in the will. It also governs the disposition of property for which a specific bequest has failed (e.g., because the intended recipient predeceased the testator). If a will does not have a residuary clause, the testator's remaining assets would pass in accordance with the intestacy laws of the testator's domicile.

States have generally adopted the Uniform Testamentary Additions to Trusts Act, which recognizes as valid a residual bequest to an *inter vivos* or living trust, provided the trust is in existence at the time the will is signed. The trust can, however, be amended after the date of the will and the residual estate will be disposed of in accordance with the amended terms.

If the estate plan includes a living trust and a pour-over residuary disposition, it is typical to include provisions for the payment of estate taxes in the trust. The will should, however, state this fact in order to override state apportionment statutes and federal and state reimbursement rights.

If the testator has children and other issue and leaves the residuary estate to a living trust, the will should include a statement that the children and other issue have been provided for in the trust, or, in the alternative, a statement that the issue have not been provided for intentionally in the will. Such a statement overrides state laws that permit children to claim their intestate share of an estate if they can show inadvertent omission from the will.

SECOND: Residue. I give and devise the residue of all the property, of whatever kind and wherever located, that I own at my death to the then trustees of THE SAM SAMPLE [*YEAR*] TRUST established earlier this day by me, as Donor, with myself and my said wife as trustees (my "[*YEAR*] TRUST"), to be added to the principal of my [*YEAR*] TRUST and administered in accordance with the provisions thereof, as from time to time amended. I have provided in my [*YEAR*] TRUST for my children and more remote issue and for the method of paying all federal and state taxes in the nature of estate, inheritance, succession, and like taxes occasioned by my death.

Practice Note

In most states, the surviving parent is entitled to the custody of minor children. This cannot be defeated by a provision in the will of the first parent to die unless a court finds the surviving parent unfit. In contrast, a testator could specify someone other than the surviving parent to be guardian of property passing to minor children. Generally, this is not of significance, because a well-drafted estate plan will provide trust accounts for minor children or provide for property to pass to a custodial account for a minor child under the Uniform Gifts to Minors Act or Uniform Transfers to Minors Act.

Frequently, the most difficult estate planning decision is the choice of who will raise minor children should both parents die. Aging grandparents, often the most appealing choice, may not realistically be up to the challenge. If the desire is to have the children cared for by a married couple, care should be taken to spell out the consequences if the named couple divorces or if one person fails to be appointed or later ceases to serve.

The naming of a guardian in the will is not binding on the court. However, a court will generally give effect to the testator's wishes, unless the named guardian can be shown as unfit or the appointment would not be in the best interests of the child.

The will should waive any statutory requirement to furnish a surety or an official bond. This will reduce expenses incurred in the administration of the estate.

THIRD: Guardian of Children. I appoint my wife, SARAH SAMPLE, as guardian of each child of mine during minority; and if for any reason she fails to qualify or ceases to serve in that capacity, I appoint [*NAME OF ALTERNATE*], of [*ADDRESS*], as such guardian in her place. No guardian appointed in this will or a codicil need furnish any bond or surety on any official bond, as the case may be.

Practice Note

The personal representative is the person charged with carrying out the terms of the testator's will. Many jurisdictions still use the term executor, which is interchangeable with the term personal representative.

The testator can name more than one person to act as personal representative. Where more than one person is named, the personal representatives are generally required to act unanimously. This may cause delay, administrative difficulties, and additional costs if the named parties are scattered geographically. In this event, particularly if more than two persons are named to act at the same time, a majority vote provision may be added (although certain actions such as the signing of estate tax returns will always require the signature of all named personal representatives).

The testator should name at least one alternate personal representative and perhaps more if the first and second choices are advanced in age. If a professional is named as personal representative, the will could also include provisions concerning compensation. If family members are named, the testator may wish to provide for

---

their out-of-pocket expenses but otherwise waive any entitlement they may have under state law to compensation.

Dispensing with bond or sureties, as permitted by state law, is common practice to reduce administration expenses. This article further provides that, if available, the estate will be subject to independent administration only. Independent administration is a concept found in the latest version of the Uniform Probate Code and is available in some but not all jurisdictions. It allows an estate, regardless of its size, to be administered with a minimum of court supervision. The final sentence of the model article deals with virtual representation and the waiver of a guardian *ad litem* in court proceedings, including the allowance of the accounts of the personal representative. Again, these provisions are aimed at reducing expenses of administration.

FOURTH: Personal Representative. I name my wife, SARAH SAMPLE, as my personal representative; and if for any reason she fails to qualify or ceases to serve in that capacity, I name [*NAME OF ALTERNATE*], of [*ADDRESS*], as my personal representative in her place. References in this will or a codicil to my "personal representative" mean the one or more personal representatives (or executors, temporary executors, or administrators with this will annexed) for the time being in office. No personal representative named in this will or a codicil need furnish any bond or surety on any official bond, as the case may be; and, if applicable, my estate shall be subject to independent administration only. In any proceeding relating to my estate, including the allowance of an account of my personal representative, and in any jurisdiction in which either of the following is applicable, (a) I request the Court to dispense with the appointment of a guardian *ad litem* to represent any person or interest, and (b) I direct that service of process upon any person under disability shall not be made when another person not under a disability is a party to the proceeding and has the same interest as the person under the disability.

Practice Note

State laws generally grant a broad array of powers. Nevertheless, specific powers should be included to make it easier for the personal representative to deal with third parties. The powers listed in Article FIFTH are general and designed to give the personal representative broad latitude with minimal court interference or notice to beneficiaries. The Article should be modified if there are unusual situations in the testator's estate, including the continuation of an unincorporated business.

FIFTH: Personal Representative's Powers. In addition to other powers, my personal representative shall have power from time to time at discretion and without license of court: To retain, and to invest and reinvest in, any kind or amount of property; to vote and exercise other rights of security holders; to make such elections for federal and state estate, gift, generation-skipping transfer, and income tax purposes as my personal representative may deem advisable; to compromise or submit to arbitration any matters in dispute; to borrow money, and to sell, mortgage, pledge, exchange, lease and contract with respect to any real or personal property, all without notice to any beneficiary and in such manner, for such consideration and on such terms as to credit or otherwise as my personal representative may deem advisable, whether or not the effect thereof extends beyond the period of settling my estate; and in distributing my estate, to allot property, whether real or personal, at then current values, in lieu of cash.

Practice Note

The will should be dated and signed by the testator following the final effective provision. Except in very limited circumstances, a will must be witnessed by at least two competent individuals in order to be valid. The attestation clause includes a minimum recitation of the circumstances surrounding the execution. Witnesses should sign legibly and give a full residence address in case it becomes necessary to track them down at the time of probating the will (although this should not be necessary if a self-proving affidavit is also executed when the will is signed).

It is good practice to have the testator sign each of the pages of the will to safeguard against substitution of pages.

WITNESS my hand this _____ day of _____, 20__.

_____

SAM SAMPLE

Signed, published, and declared by the above-named SAM SAMPLE as and for his last will, in the presence of us two who, at his request and in his presence and in the presence of each other, hereto subscribe our names as witnesses, all on the date last above written.

Name	Residence Address
_____	_____
_____	_____

Practice Note

Most states now permit wills to be admitted to probate without further testimony or proof of execution if there is a self-proving affidavit. A self-proving affidavit is designed to take the place of in-court testimony of the witnesses and generally states that all of the requirements for valid execution have been met. The affidavit form listed here meets the baseline requirements of many jurisdictions.

STATE/COMMONWEALTH OF [*NAME OF STATE*]

_____, ss.

Before me, the undersigned authority, on this day personally appeared SAM SAMPLE, *[WITNESS #1]*, and *[WITNESS #2]*, known to me to be the testator and the witnesses, respectively, whose names are signed to the foregoing instrument, and all of these persons being by me duly sworn, SAM SAMPLE, the testator, declared to me and to the witnesses in my presence that the instrument is his last will, that he willingly signed it, and that he executed it as his free and voluntary act for the purposes therein expressed; and each of the witnesses stated to me, in the presence of the testator and in the presence of each other, that he or she signed the will as a witness at the request and in the presence of the testator and in the presence of each other, and that to the best of his or her knowledge the testator was eighteen years of age or over, of sound mind and under no constraint or undue influence.

_____
SAM SAMPLE, Testator

_____
Witness

_____
Witness

Subscribed and sworn to before me by the said testator and the said witnesses, this _____ day of _____, 20__.

_____
Notary Public
My commission
expires:_____

FORM 8
Will with Outright Dispositions

Overview

This form is a basic will with outright dispositions of property. The form is an alternative to using Form 7 (Will with Pour-Over Provision) in conjunction with a Living Trust (Form 1 or Form 2). A will with outright dispositions may be used when there is no need for a trust. This is most likely to arise if the testator has no minor children and is not survived by a spouse. This form provides for the disposition to both individuals and charities of a variety of types of property, including tangible personal property, real estate, and securities.

WILL

Practice Note

The opening paragraph is commonly referred to as the publishing clause. It identifies the person making the will. All names in which property is owned by the testator should be stated in order to help the personal representative identify, collect, and transfer the testator's property.

The residency of the testator establishes where the will is to be probated after the testator's death, assuming that the testator does not move after the date the will is signed. It also determines which state law is applicable in interpreting provisions of the will. If the testator divides time between two homes, the primary residency used for income tax purposes should be used to avoid inconsistency.

The publishing clause should state that all prior wills and codicils are revoked. Before including such a clause, however, the estate planner should confirm that this conforms to the testator's intent. There may be situations in which the testator would like to leave another will in place (e.g., if the testator has a will executed in a foreign country disposing of foreign property). If that is the intention, the will should state the limited scope of the revocation (e.g., this will revokes all prior wills and codicils only to the extent that they purport to dispose of property located within the United States of America at the time of my death).

In some jurisdictions, a will disposing of all property will exercise testamentary powers of appointment held by the testator. It is good practice to avoid this result by explicit provision. If a testator has powers of appointment, they should be reviewed carefully and exercised only by express provision.

Wills frequently include a direction to the personal representative to "pay all just debts." It is generally better form to omit this provision. By law, a personal representative is required to pay all enforceable debts of a testator. Inclusion of such a provision could imply that the testator wanted the personal representative to pay debts barred by the statute of limitations or to pay all mortgages associated with the testator's property.

I, SAMUEL A. SAMPLE (also known as SAM SAMPLE), of [*ADDRESS*], make this my last will, hereby revoking all earlier wills and codicils. I do not by this will exercise any power of appointment.

Practice Note

A testator may wish to make specific bequests of particular items of tangible personal property. Tangible personal property includes cars, boats, and airplanes, artwork, antiques and other collectibles, furniture and furnishings, jewelry, clothing, and pets. In most jurisdictions, it would also include property used in a trade or business unless specifically excluded. Tangible personal property has varied characteristics. Some tangible personal property is very valuable (such as airplanes, artwork, jewelry, or antiques), whereas other tangible personal property has only nominal value (such as clothes and household goods). Tangible personal property can also have great sentimental value (such as photo albums and family heirlooms). Since tangible personal property is such a varied class, it is likely that the testator will want to dispose of it in varied ways. This section provides several options for disposing of tangible personal property. The estate planner should review carefully the testator's property to ensure that the plan of disposition as drafted conforms to the testator's wishes.

When making a gift of specific items, the estate planner should describe adequately what is intended to be given. Vague terms such as "personal effects" should be avoided. Section (a) provides for a bequest of a specific item to an individual. The provision includes a requirement that the recipient survive the testator by 30 days in order to receive the property. The reason for this provision is that if the named recipient does not survive the testator for that period, the testator would presumably want the property to pass by the residuary clause of the testator's will rather than by the terms of the recipient's will. This section could also be drafted to provide for an alternate taker in the event that the named recipient does not survive the required period.

Section (b) provides an example of a charitable bequest of tangible personal property—in this case a bequest of a painting to a museum. In making such a bequest, it is important to determine the legal name of the entity since it may be different from the name by which it is commonly known.

Section (c) gives the personal representative general discretion to dispose of tangible personal property not specifically bequeathed. To the extent that property is sold as opposed to distributed to individuals or charities, the sale proceeds are directed to be disposed of as part of the residuary estate.

Article FIRST could also include a provision that tangible personal property not specifically bequeathed be disposed of by a memorandum. In some jurisdictions (notably those that have adopted the Uniform Probate Code), it is now possible to provide that tangible personal property will be disposed of in accordance with the last dated memorandum left with the will. In other jurisdictions, a memorandum will only be binding if it is incorporated into the will by reference. Incorporation by reference requires that the memorandum be in existence when the will is executed, and be referred to explicitly in the will. The effect of this is that, absent a codicil or new will, the memorandum is not susceptible to change. This offers little flexibility for those of wavering intentions.

If the testator believes that certain items of tangible personal property will be sold in all events, thought should be given to including a provision directing the personal representative to sell those items. This has the advantage of making the selling expenses deductible for federal estate tax purposes as expenses of administration. If there is no such direction in the will, the Internal Revenue Service may determine that the assets were sold for the beneficiaries' convenience, in which case the associated expenses will not be deductible. A direction to sell is particularly valuable for those assets that may have substantial commissions associated with sale, including artwork, airplanes, and boats.

Where tangible personal property is to be distributed to persons different from the residuary beneficiaries, it is good practice to specify that expenses associated with insuring, storing, and distributing items of tangible personal property will be paid from the residuary estate and treated as expenses of administration. Otherwise, those expenses may have to be borne by the beneficiaries of the tangible personal property. This may pose an undue burden, particularly if these beneficiaries are not receiving cash under the terms of the will.

In general, if an item of tangible personal property subject to a specific bequest is not in the possession of the testator at his death, the bequest will fail, or *adeem*, and the beneficiary will receive nothing as a result of that bequest. Some states have enacted statutes that prevent ademption in certain circumstances, but if the testator wishes to provide for an alternative bequest, it is better drafting practice to identify the alternative item explicitly in the will.

FIRST: <u>Tangible Personal Property</u>. I give all my tangible personal property (as distinguished from money, securities, and the like), wherever located, as follows:

(a) My [*DESCRIBE ARTICLE OR ARTICLES*] to [*NAME AND ADDRESS*], if he [*or* she] is living on the thirtieth day after my death.

(b) My painting entitled [*DESCRIPTION*] to [*NAME OF MUSEUM*], in [*ADDRESS*], if it is then in legal existence and a qualified charitable organization.

(c) All the residue of my tangible personal property not disposed of as provided above shall be disposed of as my personal representative, in my personal representative's discretion, sees fit, whether by gift or by sale and whether to individuals (other than my personal representative) or institutions named or not named otherwise in this will or a codicil. This power shall be exercisable by my personal representative in a personal as opposed to a fiduciary capacity. Should any items be sold, the net proceeds of sale shall be disposed of as part of my residuary estate as provided below in Article FIFTH.

The expenses of insuring, storing, packing, and delivering any items of my tangible personal property bequeathed under this Article FIRST shall be borne by my residuary estate as an expense of administration.

Practice Note

The devise of real estate should adequately identify the parcel to be given. It is good practice to check the testator's deed to ensure that the property is owned by the testator in such a way that it can be passed by will. If, for example, the property is owned by the testator with another person as joint tenants with right of survivorship, then the property will pass automatically to the surviving joint tenant and the testator may have no interest to devise should he die prior to the other joint tenant.

Vague references to devising all real estate owned in a particular location should be avoided. If a testator owns only one lot in the location at the time of executing the will but subsequently acquires an additional lot in the same location prior to death, a general devise of all real estate in that location will operate to pass title to both lots. This may not be the testator's intention. Therefore, the estate planner should describe the parcel to be devised with accuracy.

The will should indicate whether the beneficiary takes the real estate subject to mortgages or other liens. In most states, the default rule is that the testator's interest in the property passes subject to any existing mortgages. State laws also vary concerning the liability for real estate taxes assessed prior to date of death. If the testator wants the devisee to take the interest totally unencumbered, the will should state this explicitly.

If the intended beneficiaries of the real estate predecease the testator, it is generally a good practice to direct in the will that the real estate be sold (provided this conforms to the testator's wishes). By including such a direction, all expenses associated with the sale can be claimed as an expense of administration deductible for federal estate tax purposes. Without such a direction, a sale of the real estate may be treated as made for the convenience of the residuary beneficiaries of the estate, with the result that the sale expenses are not deductible for estate tax purposes.

As in the case of items of tangible personal property, specific devises of real estate are subject to ademption. Thus, if real estate specifically devised under a will is not owned by the testator at the time of his death, the devise will fail, or *adeem,* and the beneficiary will receive nothing. Some states have enacted statutes that prevent ademption in certain circumstances, but if the testator wishes to provide for an alternative devise or bequest, the better practice is to state the alternative explicitly in the will.

SECOND: Real Estate. I give and devise my real estate known as and numbered [*IDENTIFY PROPERTY*] (as more fully described in a deed dated [*DATE*] and recorded with [*COUNTY NAME*] County Registry of Deeds at Book __, Page __) to my brother, [*NAME*], if he is living on the thirtieth day after my death, free of any mortgages secured on such real estate and any real estate taxes assessed as of the date of my death. If my said brother is not then living, I direct my personal representative to sell my said real estate as soon as practicable after my death and to dispose of the net proceeds of sale as part of my residuary estate as provided below in Article FIFTH.

Practice Note

A testator may wish to provide for a simple bequest of money to family members, friends, or charities. In drafting such bequests, the amount of the gift should be stated clearly, as should the identity of the recipient and the requirement of survivorship (by a set number of days, if desired). If a joint bequest is made, for example, to a married couple, the bequest should also address what happens if only one of the recipients survives.

In the case of a charitable bequest, the proper legal name of the charity should be used. If the gift is unrestricted, the will should state simply that the bequest is for the general charitable purposes of the organization without restriction. If restrictions are required, they should be set forth in the will. It is good practice to check the type and wording of restrictions with the charity ahead of time. If the restrictions are not appropriate, the gift may have to be declined by the charity or may result in costly litigation or construction proceedings.

THIRD: Bequests of Cash. I give the following sums to the following individuals living on the thirtieth day after my death and to the following qualified charitable organization if then in legal existence:

(a) The sum of [*NUMBER IN WORDS*] Thousand Dollars ($__) to my niece, [*NAME*].

(b) The sum of [*NUMBER IN WORDS*] Thousand Dollars ($__) to [*NAMES*], of [*ADDRESS*], in equal shares if they are both then living, or all to the survivor of them if only one of them is then living.

(c) The sum of [*NUMBER IN WORDS*] Thousand Dollars ($__) to [*NAME OF COLLEGE*], in [*ADDRESS*], for [*PURPOSE*].

Practice Note

As a general matter, a bequest of a specific number of shares of stock in a publicly traded corporation should be avoided. Changes in the nature of the stock holdings and the disposition of part or all of the stock holdings by the testator before death can produce myriad problems. In general, it is better practice to have the testator substitute a pecuniary bequest. Nonetheless, clients sometimes feel strongly about making these types of bequests, in which case the estate planner needs to address a variety of issues.

The language in the model Article attempts to deal with the effect of stock splits, stock dividends, and other changes in the capital structure of the corporation identified. In some states, these issues are covered by state statutory law if not specifically addressed by the testator. In general, where a specified number of shares of stock are bequeathed in a will and at the time of death a smaller number of shares is owned by the testator, the difference in the number of shares is treated as a partial ademption of the bequest. In other words, if there is a bequest of 500 shares and if at the time of death only 300 shares of the stock are owned, there would be an ademption of 200 shares and the named beneficiary would receive the 300 shares then owned.

FOURTH: Bequest of Stock. I give [*NUMBER IN WORDS*] () shares of the common stock of [*CORPORATION NAME*], to my sister, [*NAME*], if she is living on the thirtieth day after my death. If there shall be any change in the capital structure or any consolidation or merger of [*CORPORATION NAME*] after the date of execution of this will, which affects the number and/or the identity of shares that I own or am entitled to (including, without limitation, stock dividends and stock splits and stock issued to me in exchange for or as a consequence of holding shares of common stock in [*CORPORATION NAME*]), I give such number of my shares of the common stock of [*CORPORATION NAME*] as shall in the sole judgment of my personal representative be equivalent at the time of my death to [*NUMBER IN WORDS*] (# of shares) of the common stock therein on the date of execution of this will.

Practice Note

A will must have a residuary clause in order to avoid having property pass by intestacy. This clause disposes of property not specifically transferred by other provisions in the will. It also governs the disposition of property for which a specific bequest or devise has failed (e.g., because the intended recipient predeceased the testator). If a will does not have a residuary clause, the testator's remaining assets would pass in accordance with the intestacy laws of the testator's domicile. In the model document, the residuary estate is split between a gift to family members and a gift to charity. The family distribution provides for the property to be distributed equally between the nieces and nephews of the testator. It also provides for the issue of any deceased niece or nephew to take by right of representation the share that the niece or nephew would have received if living.

The model document provides that if any property is distributable to a beneficiary who is under the age of 21, it will be distributed to a custodian under the Uniform Transfers to Minors Act or Uniform Gifts to Minors Act rather than being distributed to the beneficiary or to a guardian or other representative of the beneficiary. While there is considerable uniformity in state laws concerning custodial gifts, care should be taken (and this provision adapted if necessary) to conform with the local version of the Uniform Act.

The will should include a provision for the payment of estate taxes. Such a provision will override state apportionment statutes and federal and state reimbursement rights. In the model will, taxes on property passing under the will are directed to be paid from that portion of the residuary estate passing to the family members. Taxes will only be paid from the charitable portion if the family portion is insufficient to pay the taxes in full. Such a direction maximizes the charitable deduction available to the decedent's estate. Of course, it will have the effect that the net amount distributable to family and charity will be different. Charity will receive a gross distribution of 50 percent of the residuary estate, whereas the family's portion will be reduced by taxes on the probate assets. Sometimes, such a result thwarts the testator's intention. In that event, the tax provision should charge the estate taxes generally to the residuary estate before the division into shares. This will increase the overall estate tax liability because the charitable portion of the residuary estate—and with it the corresponding charitable deduction—will be smaller.

The tax clause in the model document picks up taxes on all property passing under the will. This means that the specific bequests and devises contained in the first four Articles will pass tax free to the named recipients. The taxes attributable to those bequests and devises will be borne by the residue. The model tax provision does not pick up taxes on property passing outside the will. It is important for the practitioner to know about the existence of such assets and to discuss the tax burden with the testator. Assets passing outside the will that can generate a tax liability include jointly held property (where the other joint owner survives the testator) and, in general, life insurance proceeds (where the policy is owned by the testator or the testator has incidents of ownership in the policy) and retirement plan assets. The latter two types of property are examples of assets that are normally disposed of by separate contractual beneficiary designations. In some circumstances, however, the probate estate of the testator may be named as the beneficiary of a life insurance policy or a retirement plan. The probate estate is also commonly the default beneficiary of such assets if the testator fails to execute a separate beneficiary designation. If that property passes under the terms of the will (as either the named or default beneficiary), then the taxes will be paid under the terms of the will.

The final provision in the model document is designed to ensure that a charitable income tax deduction will be available to the testator's estate for income earned during the period of administration that is properly allocable to the share of the residuary estate distributable to charity.

FIFTH: Residue. I give and devise the residue of all the property, of whatever kind and wherever located, that I own at my death (my "residuary estate") as follows:

(a) Fifty percent (50%) thereof in equal shares, one share to each child of my said brother, [*NAME*], and my said sister, [*NAME*], who is living on the thirtieth day after my death, and one share by right of representation to the then living issue of each such child who is then deceased with issue then living.

(b) Fifty percent (50%) thereof (or all thereof if no child of my said brother or of my said sister nor any issue of any such child is then living), to [*NAME OF CHARITY*], in [*ADDRESS*], to be held by it in a separate fund, to be known as the "THE SAM SAMPLE FUND," the income only from which may be used for [*DESCRIBE PURPOSE AND OTHER RESTRICTIONS IF ANY*]. If the said [*NAME OF CHARITY*] is not then in legal existence or if it is not then a qualified charitable organization, fifty percent (50%) (or all, as the case may be) of my residuary estate shall be distributed to such qualified charitable organizations, for such charitable purposes and in such amounts and proportions to each as my personal representative, in my personal representative's discretion, shall select and determine. Without imposing any trust, condition, or enforceable obligation, I hope that my personal representative will select as recipients those charitable organizations in which I have expressed an interest during my lifetime.

Any property distributable under this Article FIFTH to a beneficiary who has not reached the age of twenty-one (21) shall be distributed to a custodian for the beneficiary under the Uniform Transfers to Minors Act or Uniform Gifts to Minors Act of any state, instead of being distributed outright to the beneficiary. The receipt of the custodian of such property shall, with respect to each distribution, be a sufficient discharge to my personal representative who need not see to the further application thereof.

All federal and state taxes in the nature of estate, inheritance, succession, and like taxes occasioned by my death with respect to property passing under this will or a codicil shall be paid from and borne by the portion of my residuary estate disposed of under paragraph (a) of this Article; and, to the extent that such portion is insufficient to pay in full all such taxes, the unpaid balance of such taxes shall be paid from and borne by the portion of my residuary estate disposed of under paragraph (b) of this Article.

Any net income or capital gains earned or realized with respect to any property passing under this Article FIFTH that is properly allocable to the charitable distribution under paragraph (b) above shall, within one year after the close of the calendar year in which such net income or gains are earned or realized, be paid over to the recipients of the distribution or be set aside for such recipients.

Practice Note

The personal representative is the person charged with carrying out the terms of the testator's will. Many jurisdictions still use the term *executor,* which is interchangeable with the term personal representative.

The testator can name more than one person to act as personal representative. Where more than one person is named, the personal representatives are generally required to act unanimously. This may cause delay, administrative difficulties, and additional costs if the named parties are scattered geographically. In this event, particularly if more than two persons are named to act at the same time, a majority vote provision may be added (although certain actions such as the signing of estate tax returns will always require the signature of all named personal representatives).

The testator should name at least one alternate personal representative and perhaps more if the first and second choices are advanced in age. If a professional is named as personal representative, the will could also include provisions concerning compensation. If family members are named, the testator may wish to provide for their out-of-pocket expenses but otherwise waive any entitlement they may have under state law to compensation.

Dispensing with bond or sureties, as permitted by state law, is common practice to reduce administration expenses. This article further provides that, if available, the estate will be subject to independent administration only. Independent administration is a concept found in the latest version of the Uniform Probate Code and is available in some but not all jurisdictions. It allows an estate, regardless of its size, to be administered with a minimum of court supervision. The final sentence of the model article deals with virtual representation and the waiver of a guardian *ad litem* in court proceedings, including the allowance of the accounts of the personal representative. Again these provisions are aimed at reducing expenses of administration.

SIXTH: Personal Representative. I name [*NAME OF PERSONAL REPRE-SENTATIVE*], of [*ADDRESS*], as my personal representative; and if for any reason he fails to qualify or ceases to serve in that capacity, I name [*NAME OF ALTERNATE PERSONAL REPRESENTATIVE*], of [*ADDRESS*], as my personal representative in his place. References in this will or a codicil to my "personal representative" mean the one or more personal representatives (or executors, temporary executors, or administrators with this will annexed) for the time being in office. No personal representative named in this will or a codicil need furnish any bond or surety on any official bond, as the case may be; and, if applicable, my estate shall be subject to independent administration only. In any proceeding relating to my estate, including the allowance of an account of my personal representative, and in any jurisdiction in which either of the following is applicable, (a) I request the Court to dispense with the appointment of a guardian *ad litem* to represent any person or interest, and (b) I direct that service of process upon any person under disability shall not be made when another person not under a disability is a party to the proceeding and has the same interest as the person under the disability.

Practice Note

State laws generally grant a broad array of powers. Nevertheless, specific powers should be included to make it easier for the personal representative to deal with third parties. The powers listed in Article SEVENTH are general and designed to give the personal representative broad latitude with minimal court interference or notice to beneficiaries. The Article should be modified if there are unusual situations in the testator's estate, including the continuation of an unincorporated business.

SEVENTH: Personal Representative's Powers. In addition to other powers, my personal representative shall have power from time to time at discretion and without license of court: To retain, and to invest and reinvest in, any kind or amount of property; to vote and exercise other rights of security holders; to make such elections for federal and state estate, gift, generation-skipping transfer, and income tax purposes as my personal representative may deem advisable; to compromise or submit to arbitration any matters in dispute; to borrow money, and to sell, mortgage, pledge, exchange, lease, and contract with respect to any real or personal property, all without notice to any beneficiary and in such manner, for such consideration and on such terms as to credit or otherwise as my personal representative may deem advisable, whether or not the effect thereof extends beyond the period of settling my estate; and, in distributing my estate, to allot property, whether real or personal, at then current values in lieu of cash.

Practice Note

Article EIGHTH defines several terms used in the will. With respect to the terms "child," "children," and "issue," adoptive and all natural born descendants are included. A testator may wish to restrict the scope of this provision. The term "by right of representation" is defined to state how the shares are to be determined when this means of distribution is employed. The children of the person whose issue are to be benefited are considered the stocks for purposes of determining the number of distributive shares, whether or not any of those children are alive at the time of distribution. This overrides the law of several states. For example, if the deceased beneficiary had three children (Alice, Betty, and Charles) who all also predeceased the testator and who had four children (one from Alice, one from Betty, and two from Charles) all of whom survived the testator, under the terms of distribution provided in the model will, the testator's bequest to the issue by right of representation of the deceased beneficiary would be divided into three parts (one part for each child of the beneficiary who had predeceased the testator and who was survived by issue of his or her own). In this example, Alice's and Betty's children would each get one-third of the property and Charles's two children would each get one-sixth.

The final definition is of the term qualified charitable organization. This term is defined to include organizations described in Section 2055 of the Internal Revenue Code and to which bequests at the time of death are deductible for federal estate tax purposes. This is a broader group of charitable organizations than those described under the income tax deduction provisions. It would include, for example, foreign as well as domestic charities.

EIGHTH: <u>Definitions</u>. References in this will or a codicil to "child" or "children" mean descendants in the first degree only, and references to "issue" mean descendants in the first, second, or any other degree; in each case meaning all descendants of the ancestor designated, whether by blood or by adoption. Whenever distribution is to be made by right of representation to the then living issue of a designated ancestor, the ancestor's children shall be considered the stocks for purposes of determining the respective shares of such issue.

References in this will or a codicil to a "qualified charitable organization" mean an organization described at the time of my death in Section 2055 of the Internal Revenue Code of 1986, as amended, bequests to which qualify for the federal estate tax charitable deduction.

Practice Note

The will should be dated and signed by the testator following the final effective provision. Except in very limited circumstances, a will must be witnessed by at least two competent individuals in order to be valid. The attestation clause includes a minimum recitation of the circumstances surrounding the execution. Witnesses should sign legibly and give a full residence address in case it becomes necessary to track them down at the time of probating the will (although this should not be necessary if a self-proving affidavit is also executed when the will is signed).

It is good practice to have the testator sign each of the pages of the will to safeguard against substitution of pages.

WITNESS my hand this_____ day of _____, 20 ____

_____
SAMUEL A. SAMPLE

Signed, published, and declared by the above-named SAMUEL A. SAMPLE as and for his last will, in the presence of us two who, at his request and in his presence and in the presence of each other, hereto subscribe our names as witnesses, all on the date last above written.

Name	Residence Address
_____	_____
_____	_____

Practice Note

Most states now permit wills to be admitted to probate without further testimony or proof of execution if there is a self-proving affidavit. A self-proving affidavit is designed to take the place of in-court testimony of the witnesses and generally states that all of the requirements for valid execution have been met. The affidavit form listed here meets the baseline requirements of many jurisdictions.

STATE/COMMONWEALTH OF [*NAME OF STATE*]

_____, ss.

Before me, the undersigned authority, on this day personally appeared SAMUEL A. SAMPLE, [*WITNESS #1*], and [*WITNESS #2*], known to me to be the testator and the witnesses, respectively, whose names are signed to the foregoing instrument, and all of these persons being by me duly sworn, SAMUEL A. SAMPLE, the testator, declared to me and to the witnesses in my presence that the instrument is his last will, that he willingly signed it, and that he executed it as his free and voluntary act for the purposes therein expressed; and each of the witnesses stated to me, in the presence of the testator and in the presence of each other, that he or she signed the will as a witness at the request and in the presence of the testator and in the presence of each other, and that to the best of his or her knowledge the testator was eighteen years of age or over, of sound mind, and under no constraint or undue influence.

_____
SAMUEL A. SAMPLE, Testator

_____
Witness

_____
Witness

Subscribed and sworn to before me by the said testator and the said witnesses, this _____ day of _____, 20 ____.

_____
Notary Public
My commission expires:

FORM 9

Codicil

Overview

A codicil is a document that changes terms of an existing will. A codicil has the effect of republishing the will and any prior codicils, meaning that each of these documents is treated as if it had been executed on the date of the final codicil. This can have unexpected results in certain situations. For example, in many jurisdictions, a child born after the execution of a will, or a spouse from a marriage occurring after execution of a will, is entitled to share a portion of the decedent's estate as a *pretermitted child* or *pretermitted spouse*. However, if the testator executes a codicil to the will after the birth of the child or the marriage of the testator, this will have the effect of republishing the will as of the date of the codicil essentially negating the pretermitted status of the child or spouse.

CODICIL

Practice Note

The codicil should make specific reference to the will that is being amended. The estate planner should take care to ensure that the referenced will is indeed the most recent will, as the effect of the codicil will be to republish the referenced will as of the date of the codicil (thereby revoking other wills). For example, assume a testator executed one will in 2000 and then a second will in 2003. The 2003 will revokes the 2000 will. If the testator executes a codicil in 2022 that makes reference to the 2000 will (instead of the 2003 will), the effect will be to republish the 2000 will as of 2022 and effectively revoke the 2003 will.

I, SARAH SAMPLE, of [*ADDRESS*], make this first codicil to my last will dated [*INSERT DATE*], hereby ratifying, confirming, and republishing my said will as modified by this first codicil.

I make the following changes to my said will:

1.

2.

3.

WITNESS my hand this _____ day of _____, 20_____.

_____
SARAH SAMPLE

Signed, published, and declared by the above-named SARAH SAMPLE as and for the first codicil to her last will, in the presence of us two who, at her request and in her presence and in the presence of each other, hereto subscribe our names as witnesses, all on the date last above written.

Name   Residence Address

_____   _____

_____   _____

Practice Note

A codicil must be executed with the same formalities and witness requirements applicable to a will. This codicil uses the same witness attestation clause and the recommended self-proving affidavit described in the comments to the form will.

STATE/COMMONWEALTH OF [*NAME OF STATE*]

_____, ss.

Before me, the undersigned authority, on this day personally appeared SARAH SAMPLE, [*WITNESS #1*], and [*WITNESS #2*], known to me to be the testator and the witnesses, respectively, whose names are signed to the foregoing instrument, and all of these persons being by me duly sworn, SARAH SAMPLE, the testator, declared to me and to the witnesses in my presence that the instrument is a first codicil to her last will, that she willingly signed it, and that she executed it as her free and voluntary act for the purposes therein expressed; and each of the witnesses stated to me, in the presence of the testator and in the presence of each other, that he or she signed the codicil as a witness at the request and in the presence of the testator and in the presence of each other, and that to the best of his or her knowledge the testator was eighteen years of age or over, of sound mind, and under no constraint or undue influence.

_____
SARAH SAMPLE, Testator

_____
Witness

_____
Witness

Subscribed and sworn to before me by the said testator and the said witnesses, this _____ day of _____ 20 _____.

_____
Notary Public
My commission expires:

FORM 10

Durable Power of Attorney

Overview

Documents that plan for a client's incapacity are an essential part of a complete estate plan. The basic incapacity documents are a durable power of attorney and a health care proxy (Form 11) and living will (Form 12).

Powers of attorney are governed by the common law of agency. The person executing the power of attorney (the principal) nominates one or more persons (the attorney-in-fact) to act for her in a contractual manner and in other ways authorized in the instrument creating the power. A power of attorney can be general, granting broad authority in all business and contractual matters, or specific, granting limited powers.

Under common law, a power of attorney terminates upon the death or earlier incapacity of the principal. As such, the common law power of attorney is not a useful planning vehicle for incapacity. The durable power of attorney was first proposed in 1975 by the drafters of the Uniform Probate Code. Most states have now adopted the Uniform Durable Power of Attorney Act. Under this Act, the power of attorney remains effective, notwithstanding the disability or incapacity of the principal. A durable power, however, terminates at the principal's death.

The model power of attorney is drafted to be effective immediately. However, the power of attorney could instead be drafted to be effective only upon the occurrence of a specific event, such as the disability or incapacity of the principal. The term for this latter type of power of attorney is a *springing* power of attorney. To be a springing power, the document should state that it becomes "effective upon the disability or incapacity of the principal." The client often prefers the concept of a springing power, because the client may be loath to give away control over assets before it is absolutely necessary, or may be concerned that the power could be abused. A springing power, however, may not be a desirable planning tool. A third party may refuse to accept the power because the third party does not know whether it is effective. A springing provision also raises doubts about whether the principal may have regained capacity, thereby effectively revoking the authority granted under the power. Finally, some jurisdictions do not permit springing durable powers of attorney. If a springing power is used, it should spell out how incapacity is to be determined and evidenced, and state that a determination of incapacity can be relied on for a set period of time after the determination is made.

Rather than use a springing power, it may be preferable to use a durable power and set up an escrow arrangement between the drafting lawyer and the principal. Under such an arrangement, the drafting lawyer retains the original durable power of attorney and agrees with the principal that the document will not be released to the attorney-in-fact until certain conditions have been satisfied. For example, the document might be released when the lawyer is presented with a letter from a physician certifying that the principal is incompetent or when the principal, while competent, directs that the document be released.

With respect to the disclosure of medical records in particular, regulations under the Health Insurance Portability and Accountability Act of 1996 (HIPAA) that took effect in 2003 contain provisions to protect the privacy of a patient's health care records. These regulations can make it difficult for an agent to obtain necessary information or a certification of incapacity that would bring a springing power of attorney into existence. While the power to release protected health care information to an agent can appear as a specific power within a power of attorney, based on the current language of the HIPAA statute and regulations, it may be preferable to effect a release of protected health information to an agent acting for a principal through a separate document rather than within the power of attorney. *See* Form 13, HIPAA Authorization Form, for a sample of such a release.

DURABLE POWER OF ATTORNEY

Practice Note

The introductory paragraph states the name of the principal and identifies the person or persons appointed as the attorneys-in-fact. Whenever more than one person is appointed, the document must specify whether each may act alone or whether they must act jointly. Joint action may provide security to the principal, but this advantage must be weighed against the likelihood of considerable inconvenience, since all attorneys-in-fact will be required to sign or give oral authorization for transactions.

I, SAM SAMPLE, of [*ADDRESS*], hereby constitute and appoint my wife, SARAH SAMPLE, and [*NAME OF SECOND ATTORNEY HOLDER*], of [*AD-DRESS*], or either of them (either or both of them being referred to as my "attorney"), as my true and lawful attorney, for me and in my name, from time to time, and at her or his discretion, to do anything whatsoever that I may or could do in person. By this document I intend to create a Durable Power of Attorney under [*STATE STATUTORY REFERENCE*] and the document shall be governed and construed in accordance with the laws of [*GOVERNING STATE LAW*].

Practice Note

Many state statutes permit the exercise of broad powers by the attorney-in-fact but do not list specifically the acts that the attorney may perform. Other state statutes create a statutory form of durable power and provide detailed statutory explanations of the scope of the powers granted. If available, it may be preferable to use a statutory form of power of attorney since it may be more broadly accepted and understood in the marketplace.

It is good practice in a general broad form power of attorney to enumerate the primary powers given to the attorney-in-fact. This forces the client to consider the issue of whether there are powers the client does not want to give. It also may make it easier for the attorney-in-fact to deal with third parties, such as brokers and bankers. It should be noted that, despite state statutes specifically authorizing durable powers of attorney, many banks and brokerage houses are reluctant to allow action by an attorney-in-fact unless the attorney-in-fact is appointed under the bank's or broker's own form. Accordingly, it is often advisable to have the client execute a general power and in addition execute special powers on bank and brokerage house forms.

Certain powers should be spelled out if it is desired that the powers be granted to the attorney-in-fact. The most important is the power to make gifts. Unless granted specifically, state law may not permit the attorney-in-fact to make gifts. Even if state law is expansive, the Internal Revenue Service may challenge gifts made under a power of attorney otherwise silent on this matter. In granting a gift-making power, its scope should be defined carefully. If an attorney-in-fact has an unrestricted power to make gifts to herself, the power of attorney may be construed to create a general power of appointment in the attorney-in-fact. This will cause the principal's estate to be included in the estate of the attorney holder if she dies holding the power. This form grants the power to make gifts, but contains many common restrictions on gift-giving powers, including the exclusion of the attorney-in-fact as a donee, limiting the gift-giving power to gifts qualifying for the federal gift tax annual exclusion, and authorizing gifts to qualified charitable organizations.

The attorney-in-fact should be given the express power to fund the principal's revocable trust, and to withdraw income and principal from the trust. The attorney may also be given an express power to amend or revoke an existing revocable trust or to create further trusts for the benefit of the principal and/or her family.

The area in which the attorney-in-fact is likely to meet the most challenge to her authority is in dealing with tax agencies. For this reason, the document should include the power to make and file all appropriate tax returns, endorse refund checks, and otherwise represent the principal with respect to tax matters. A cautious practitioner might also want an elderly client to sign IRS Form 2848, which constitutes a formal power of attorney with respect to federal tax matters.

Other express powers that might be included are powers to deal with retirement benefits and closely held business interests, and powers to deal with personal decisions, such as health care matters. The latter are, however, more appropriately handled in a separate health care power of attorney or health care proxy. Some practitioners also include authority to deal with government benefits such as Social Security and Medicare. In general, however, the Social Security Administration will not accept powers of attorney and requires that representative payees be appointed on separate government forms.

U.S. persons that have an interest in or signature authority over any foreign account(s) must file FinCEN Form 114, Report of Foreign Bank and Financial Accounts ("FBAR") every calendar year if the aggregate maximum value of the foreign account(s) exceeds $10,000 at any time during the calendar year. There are significant penalties for failure to file this form when required. The current position of the Internal Revenue Service is that an attorney-in-fact (in addition to the principal) is subject to the FBAR filing requirements if the power of attorney gives the attorney-in-fact signature authority over foreign financial accounts that exceed the $10,000 threshold. It is therefore advisable to except from the general grant of authority any activity pertaining to foreign financial accounts, unless the principal and agent specifically intend to have the agent oversee foreign financial accounts, and the agent is aware of the related reporting requirements.

Without limiting the generality of the foregoing broad power, I expressly authorize my attorney:

(a) To endorse checks payable to me and stock certificates and other securities standing in my name;

(b) To deposit with or pay to any bank, broker, or person any money or property of mine;

(c) To draw checks on any bank and to withdraw from any bank, broker, or person any money or property belonging to me or due me;

(d) To go to any safe deposit box to which I have access and to place in it or take from it any property or papers;

(e) To buy, sell, lease, mortgage, exchange, transfer, dispose of, and deal with any stocks, bonds, or other property, real or personal;

(f) To invest and reinvest in any stocks, bonds, or other securities;

(g) To vote and give consents with respect to any stocks, bonds, or other securities and to give proxies therefor, with or without power of substitution;

(h) To make and sign all federal, state, and local income, gift, property, and excise tax returns that I may be required to file for the years 20__ through 20__ (including but not limited to federal Forms 1040 and 709); to receive and inspect confidential tax information; to receive and endorse refund checks; and to perform any and all acts that I can perform with respect to tax matters, including the execution from time to time of IRS Form 2848 (designating an attorney for federal tax matters) and the equivalent state and local forms, and the negotiation and execution of agreements, consents, and other documents;

(i) To make gifts to or in trust for the benefit of such individuals (other than my attorney) and charitable or other nonprofit organizations as my attorney thinks advisable to take advantage of the federal gift tax annual exclusion or the federal income tax charitable deduction;

(j) To transfer any property that I own to THE SAM SAMPLE [*YEAR*] TRUST, or any other revocable trust that may be established by me, and to exercise any and all rights and powers that I have in my individual capacity to withdraw income and principal from any such trust;

(k) To tender my resignation or declination to serve as trustee, personal representative or other fiduciary;

(l) To represent me in court or elsewhere in connection with any controversy;

(m) To collect, receive, and give receipt or discharge for any money, debt, or thing belonging to me or due me;

(n) To pay debts and discharge obligations owed by me (including any medical bills that my attorney determines should be paid);

(o) To make contracts and agreements, whether sealed or unsealed; and

(p) To do any one or more or all of the foregoing at discretion and from time to time, and to do any and all things, whether herein enumerated or not, which my attorney shall consider advantageous or proper in connection with my affairs, provided, however, that this grant of authority shall not extend to any activity pertaining to any account in a foreign country, as defined in 31 CFR 1010.350(c) and 1010.350(d).

Practice Note

It is advisable to include a self-dealing provision so that an attorney's actions are not challenged on the basis of self-interest.

My attorney is authorized to deal with herself or himself (or with any concern in which she or he is interested) as freely and effectually as though dealing with a stranger.

Practice Note

For maximum flexibility, the attorney should be authorized to appoint substitutes and additional attorneys. The named attorney-in-fact may not be available for a limited time period or may not be able to deal with certain matters because of conflicts of interest.

My attorney may in writing from time to time appoint one or more substitute and additional attorneys to have all or any of my attorney's powers hereunder, including this power of appointment, and may revoke any such appointments. Such substitutes and any additional attorneys, as well as my attorney above named, are included in references to my "attorney" in this power of attorney.

Practice Note

Many state laws provide that an attorney-in-fact is accountable to a guardian or conservator who is appointed after the execution of the power of attorney. A court appointed fiduciary might also revoke or amend a power of attorney. Those same laws generally permit a principal to nominate in the power of attorney the person that she would prefer to have serve as guardian or conservator. This addresses the possibility of a third party forcing a guardianship proceeding to preempt the authority of an attorney-in-fact.

If protective proceedings for my person or estate are ever commenced in any court, I hereby nominate my wife, SARAH SAMPLE, as my conservator, guardian of my estate, or guardian of my person (as the case may be); and if for any reason she fails to qualify or ceases to serve in any such capacity, I hereby nominate [NAME OF ALTERNATE], of [ADDRESS], as my conservator, guardian of my estate, or guardian of my person (as the case may be).

Practice Note

The first sentence of the following paragraph is critical. Without this statement the power of attorney will not be durable. The governing state statute should be checked to ensure that the statement is worded appropriately. In general, it is good practice to execute multiple original powers of attorney. Often a third party will require to see an original signed power of attorney before accepting the action by the attorney-in-fact. Nevertheless, the document should also include a statement that a certified copy may be relied on by third parties.

This power of attorney shall not be affected by my subsequent disability or incapacity. Anyone may rely upon a copy certified by a notary public of this power of attorney or of any appointments of substitute and additional attorneys as fully as on the original instrument.

Practice Note

A power of attorney should be dated and signed by the principal. There are few other mandatory formalities. However, it is good practice to have a power of attorney witnessed and to have the principal's signature notarized. The witnessing and notarization may be required under state law for the document to be effective for real estate transactions and to permit its recording with land records.

Some practitioners also have the attorney-in-fact sign the power. This provides a signature for later comparison and potentially easier acceptance by third parties of the power and actions taken pursuant to it.

WITNESS my hand and seal this _____ day of _____, 20____.

_____
SAM SAMPLE

Signed and acknowledged in the presence of:

_____
Witness

_____
Witness

STATE /COMMONWEALTH OF [*NAME OF STATE*]

———————, ss.

On this ———— day of ————, 20——, before me, the undersigned notary public, personally appeared the above-named SAM SAMPLE, known to me personally or proved to me through ———— as satisfactory evidence of identification, to be the person whose name is signed on the preceding document, and acknowledged to me that he signed it voluntarily for its stated purpose.

———————————————————————
Notary Public
My Commission Expires:

FORM 11
Health Care Proxy

Overview

In the last 25 years, most states have passed legislation that recognizes the validity of a health care proxy. Under a health care proxy (sometimes referred to as a health care power of attorney or appointment of health care surrogate), the principal can designate a person, such as a family member or close friend, to make medical decisions for her if she loses the ability to make or communicate those decisions for herself. A health care proxy differs from a living will (Form 12) in that the living will is a self-executing statement by the principal that certain actions and procedures not be undertaken or followed when the principal is terminally ill or permanently unconscious.

In states recognizing the validity of both, the health care proxy and living will can be incorporated into one document. In those states authorizing health care proxies but not living wills, it is possible to achieve a comparable result by incorporating specific directions in the health care proxy that describe those actions the principal wants taken by the proxy in the event of terminal illness or permanent unconsciousness. The advantage of executing both a health care proxy and a living will (either separately or within the same document) is that it enables an individual to state her wishes regarding particular situations or procedures, while designating a person to make decisions in other circumstances.

The model form sets forth a general health care proxy. Many states have required statutory forms. The statutory forms may include a detailed warning statement of the effect of the proxy. If the principal lives in a state with a required or suggested statutory form, that form should be used.

Privacy regulations promulgated by the Department of Health and Human Services under the Health Insurance Portability and Accountability Act of 1996 (HIPAA) were intended to provide safeguards against the inappropriate sharing of "protected health information" by health care providers. They have, however, had the unintended effect of complicating planning for incapacity. Health care proxies or health care powers of attorney present an inherent problem in that the agent's authority is usually springing in nature, not arising until the principal is incapable of making or communicating health care decisions for himself. The process required to establish that the principal is incapacitated may result in a delay before the agent is able to obtain important medical information on behalf of the principal. Therefore, although it is possible to have a provision within a health care proxy that references the HIPAA statute and allows the health care agent to have access to all of the patient's medical information, the better practice is to have such a release set forth in a separate document with the health care agent listed by name. *See* Form 13, HIPAA Authorization Form, for a sample of such a release.

HEALTH CARE PROXY

Practice Note

The first paragraph should identify the person making the health care proxy (the principal) and the primary health care agent. Reference should also be made to the law governing the health care proxy.

---

1. *Appointment of Health Care Agent.* I, SAM SAMPLE, of [*ADDRESS*], hereby appoint my wife, SARAH SAMPLE, as my health care agent ("agent"). By this document I intend to create a health care proxy under [*STATE STATUTORY REFERENCE*].

Practice Note

It is good practice to appoint an alternate agent in the event that the primary agent is not able to act. Since in many situations the alternate agent will not be a person living in the same household as the principal, a telephone number might be added.

Most state laws provide that certain individuals cannot act as a health care agent (particularly administrators or employees of health care facilities in which the principal is a resident or patient), unless the otherwise disqualified individual is a family member. In addition, only one person can be legally authorized to make health care decisions at any given time. It is generally not permissible to appoint joint agents. A consultation provision might be added, requesting but not mandating that the appointed agent consult with other family members before making medical decisions.

---

2. *Appointment of Alternate Agent.* In the event that my said wife, SARAH, is not available, willing, or competent to act as my agent, or is not expected to become available, willing, or competent to make timely decisions given my medical circumstances, or, if I revoke her appointment or authority to act as my agent, I hereby appoint [*NAME AND ADDRESS OF ALTERNATE*] to serve as my agent.

Practice Note

The authority of the agent is effective when the principal is no longer capable of making or communicating health care decisions for herself. Once the agent has authority, the agent may make all decisions the principal could make, subject to any specific limitations set forth in the proxy document. The specific limitations could also be set forth in a separate document referenced in the health care proxy. Several medical groups have published detailed directives outlining choices in medical care treatment in a variety of different circumstances.

---

3. *General Statement of Authority Granted.* This health care proxy shall take effect if it is determined that I lack the capacity to make or communicate health care decisions for myself. I hereby grant to my agent full power and authority to make any and all health care decisions for me that I could make if I had the capacity to do so, including, without limitation, decisions about life-sustaining treatment, care, services, and procedures. In exercising this authority, my agent shall consult with my health care providers, consider acceptable medical alternatives regarding diagnosis, prognosis, and treatments and their side effects and make health care decisions in accordance with my agent's assessment of my wishes, or, if my wishes are not known on a particular matter, in accordance with my agent's assessment of my best interests. My agent shall have the right to receive any and all medical information, including, without limitation, any and all confidential medical information, that I would be entitled to receive. For the purposes of this document, "health care decision" means consent, refusal of consent, or withdrawal of consent to any treatment, care, service, or procedure to diagnose or treat a physical or mental condition of mine.

Practice Note

The governing law should be that of the principal's state of residency. Most state statutes contain definitions of the triggering conditions for the operation of the proxy and other rules limiting or explaining the effect of the proxy. This reference clarifies that the principal intended that those statutory rules apply.

---

4. *Governing Law.* The laws of [*GOVERNING STATE LAW*] shall govern this document in all respects, including its validity, construction, interpretation, and termination, and shall be used to determine the validity of acts taken under the authority granted in this document. I intend for this health care proxy to be honored in any jurisdiction where it may be presented and for any such jurisdiction to refer to [*GOVERNING STATE LAW*] law to interpret and determine the validity of this document and any of the powers granted under this document.

Practice Note

Most state laws provide that a health care proxy may be revoked by oral or written notification to the health care agent or by the execution of a new proxy. Authority is also revoked automatically if the principal regains capacity, although the agent's authority begins again automatically with another loss of incapacity. If the named agent is a spouse, divorce or legal separation generally revokes the spouse's nomination.

---

5. *Prior Health Care Proxies Revoked.* I revoke all prior health care proxies.

Practice Note

A proxy should include a general release of the health care agent for all acts taken in good faith. It should also include a general release and indemnification provision to all health care providers who accept instructions given by the health care agent.

---

6. *Release.* I, for myself, my heirs, personal representatives, and assigns, hereby release, hold harmless, and agree to indemnify my agent for or from any liability for having exercised in good faith the authority granted under this health care proxy. I, for myself, my heirs, personal representatives, and assigns, hereby release my physicians and all health care professionals attending me and any health care provider of which I am a patient, as well as any person employed by or under contract with such health care provider, for or from all liability for having honored the consents and followed the instructions given by my agent. I direct any person entrusted with the care of my affairs or who at any time represents my interests in any capacity, including, but not limited to, the interests of my estate, to honor this release.

Practice Note

It is strongly recommended that a principal sign several copies of the health care proxy. An original should be given to the health care agent, to any successor agent, and to the regular physician. An original should also be put in the principal's medical records.

---

7. *Copies.* Anyone may rely upon a copy certified by a notary public of this health care proxy as fully as on the original document.

Practice Note

Most state laws require that a proxy be signed by or at the direction of the principal and be witnessed by two competent adults. A person designated as a health care agent is generally prohibited from acting as a witness to the signing. It is good practice to have the signatures and statements of the principal and the witnesses affirmed before a notary public.

IN WITNESS WHEREOF, I, SAM SAMPLE, declare this health care proxy to be a true statement of my wishes, and in the presence of each of the witnesses named below have hereunto set my hand and seal on this _____ day of _____, 20_____.

_____
SAM SAMPLE

We, the undersigned, affirm that on the date last above written, SAM SAMPLE, of [ADDRESS], a person known to us, and who, in our opinion, is eighteen years of age or over, of sound mind, and under no constraint or undue influence, signed the foregoing instrument in our presence and declared it to be a true statement of his wishes, and we, in his presence and in the presence of each other, have hereunto subscribed our names.

Signature   Residence Address

_____   _____

_____   _____

STATE/COMMONWEALTH OF [*NAME OF STATE*]

_____, ss.

On this _____ day of _____, 20_____, before me, the undersigned notary public, personally appeared SAM SAMPLE, personally known to me or proved to me through satisfactory evidence of identification, which was, that he is the person whose name is signed on the foregoing document, and who acknowledged to me that he signed it voluntarily for its stated purpose.

_____

Notary Public
My commission expires:

FORM 12

Living Will

Overview

A living will is a statement of the client's intentions with respect to medical treatment, generally in the case of terminal illness or permanent unconsciousness. It does not designate specific persons to make decisions on behalf of the client. The model form is very broadly drawn. It should be amended in all circumstances to reflect accurately the client's wishes, and to correspond with governing state law. Most states authorizing living wills have statutory definitions of the term "terminal condition" or "permanent unconsciousness," or their equivalents.

LIVING WILL

By this Declaration made this _____ day of _____, 20 _____, I, SARAH SAMPLE, of [*ADDRESS*], willfully and voluntarily make known my desire that my dying not be artificially prolonged under the circumstances set forth below, and I do hereby declare:

Practice Note

The model form provides a general request that "life-prolonging procedures" be withheld or withdrawn. Specific issues not included in the model form but which should be considered are:

- Withdrawal of artificial means of providing nutrition and hydration;

- Entry of "no-code" or "do not resuscitate" orders; and

- Preference for hospice care over hospitalization.

If at any time I have a terminal condition or I am in a state of permanent unconsciousness, and if my attending or treating physician and another consulting physician have determined that there is no medical probability of my recovery from such condition or state, I direct that life-prolonging procedures be withheld or withdrawn when the application of such procedures would serve only to prolong artificially the process of dying, and that I be permitted to die naturally with only the administration of medication or the performance of any medical procedure deemed necessary to provide me with comfort care or to alleviate pain.

It is my intention that this declaration be honored by my family and physicians as the final expression of my legal right to refuse medical or surgical treatment and to accept the consequences for such refusal.

I understand the full import of this declaration, and I am emotionally and mentally competent to make this declaration.

_____
SARAH SAMPLE

Practice Note

While not a uniform requirement, living wills should in general be executed with the same signing formalities as a regular dispositive will. Therefore, it is commonplace to have the living will witnessed by two disinterested individuals (not immediate family members) and to memorialize the signing ceremony with an affidavit supervised by a notary public.

Signed and declared as and for her Living Will by the said SARAH SAMPLE in the presence of us, both being present at the same time, and who in her presence and in the presence of each other, have hereunto subscribed our names as attesting witnesses as of the date first above written.

_____   _____
Witness   Address

_____   _____
Witness   Address

STATE/COMMONWEALTH OF [*NAME OF STATE*]

_____, ss.

Before me, the undersigned authority, on this day personally appeared SARAH SAMPLE, [*WITNESS #1*], and [*WITNESS #2*], known to me to be the declarant and the witnesses, respectively, whose names are signed to the foregoing instrument of Living Will, and all of these persons being by me duly sworn, SARAH SAMPLE, declared to me and to the witnesses in my presence that the instrument is her Living Will, that she willingly signed it, and that she executed it as her free and voluntary act for the purposes therein expressed; and each of the witnesses stated to me, in the presence of the declarant and in the presence of each other, that he or she signed the living will as a witness at the request and in the presence of the declarant and in the presence of each other, and that to the best of his or her knowledge the declarant was eighteen years of age or over, of sound mind and under no constraint or undue influence.

_____
SARAH SAMPLE, Declarant

_____
Witness

_____
Witness

Subscribed and sworn to before me by the said declarant and the said witnesses, this _____ day of _____, 20_____.

_____
Notary Public
My commission expires:

FORM 13

HIPAA Authorization Form

Overview

Regulations under the Health Insurance Portability and Accountability Act of 1996 (HIPAA) that took effect in 2003 contain provisions to protect the privacy of a patient's health care records. These provisions can make it difficult for an attorney-in-fact named in a durable power of attorney or a health care agent named in a health care proxy (*See* Forms 10 and 11, *supra*, respectively) to obtain the information necessary to carry out a required task for the patient. The best practice to assure that a trusted agent has easy access to the patient's medical records is to execute a separate document that releases protected health care information to a list of persons referenced by name or position. Such a release can also appear as a specific power listed within a durable power of attorney or health care proxy, but if the attorney-in-fact or health care agent's power to act is only activitated if the patient is determined to be incapacitated, the agent's access to helpful medical information may be restricted or delayed.

The model HIPAA Authorization Form authorizes all health care professionals, insurance companies, and related providers to disclose and release to the specific persons named all information that the the patient executing the document could have received in his or her individual capacity.

AUTHORIZATION TO RELEASE PROTECTED HEALTH INFORMATION
HEALTH INSURANCE PORTABILITY AND ACCOUNTABILITY ACT OF 1996 ("HIPAA")

Practice Note

The release should identify the patient and list the persons authorized to obtain protected health care information. The release should contain a statement describing the type of information that may be disclosed, the fact that it applies to past, present, and future medical and mental health conditions, and the potential that any information disclosed may be redisclosed by the recipient and no longer covered by HIPAA.

I, SARAH SAMPLE, of [*ADDRESS*], authorize any physician, health care professional, dentist, health plan, hospital, clinic, laboratory, pharmacy or other covered health care provider, any insurance company, the Medical Information Bureau Inc., or any other health care clearinghouse that has provided treatment or services to me, or has received health care information relating to me, or that has paid for or is seeking payment from me for such services ("Health Care Providers"), to give, disclose and release to any HIPAA Agent designated below, at such HIPAA Agent's request and without restriction, all of my individually identifiable health information and medical records regarding any past, present or future medical or mental health condition, including diagnosis and treatment of such condition (collectively, my "Records").

I understand that I may revoke this authorization at any time and in the manner provided below. I understand that I am not required to sign this authorization to receive health care benefits. I further understand that any information disclosed to my HIPAA Agents may be subsequently disclosed by any one or more of them and will then no longer be protected by federal health information privacy regulations.

I designate (1) my husband, SAM SAMPLE, (2) any person who is designated as my health care agent or alternate health care agent in a Health Care Proxy (or comparable document and regardless of the time of the commencement of any other powers granted to the health care agent in the health care proxy), and (3) any person appointed as my attorney-in-fact in a durable power of attorney, as my HIPAA Agents. I intend that each of them individually (without any requirement of joint action) shall stand in my place and be treated as I would be with respect to my rights regarding the use and disclosure of my Records. This release authority applies to any information governed by HIPAA and any regulations promulgated thereunder.

Practice Note

The document should specify that it supersedes any prior agreements made with health care providers to restrict access to or disclosure of such information. The regulations require either a specific expiration date, or an expiration event that relates to the patient or the purpose of the use or disclosure.

The authority given to my HIPAA Agents shall supersede any prior agreement that I may have made with my Health Care Providers to restrict access to or disclosure of my Records. The authority given to my HIPAA Agents shall expire upon the earlier of two years after the date of my death or the date upon which I revoke the authority in writing and deliver such revocation to those Health Care Providers that have received this authorization.

Date: _____   _____

                                 SARAH SAMPLE

FORM 14
Charitable Remainder Unitrust

Overview

Form 14 establishes a Charitable Remainder Unitrust (CRUT). A CRUT is an irrevocable trust that creates two distinct interests. The first is an income interest that the donor and/or one or more individual beneficiaries designated by the donor retain for life or for a term of years. In a CRUT, this income interest is determined annually by reference to the market value of the trust assets on a defined valuation date. The second interest is the remainder interest in the property that the charity will receive after the income interest ceases.

A charitable remainder trust must include a number of governing instrument provisions required by the Internal Revenue Code, Treasury Regulations, IRS rulings, and case law. To assist the practitioner (and to lessen the burden on the IRS for ruling requests), the IRS has from time to time published sample documents. In August 2005, the IRS issued a variety of inter vivos and testamentary CRUT forms in Revenue Procedures 2005-52 through 2005-59. These supersede sample forms issued in 1989 and 1990. In general, they provide a very useful drafting guide and are accompanied by thorough annotations explaining the documents and outlining possible variations and additional provisions. While a great improvement on past model forms, the new CRUT documents do not necessarily adopt as default provisions all those that most practitioners will want to use and are somewhat sparse when it comes to basic trust provisions.

The CRUT is one of the two forms of a charitable remainder trust sanctioned by the Internal Revenue Code. The other is the Charitable Remainder Annuity Trust (CRAT).[1] A CRAT differs from a CRUT in several respects:

1. In a CRAT, the income interest paid to the individual beneficiaries is fixed at inception. The distribution does not vary from year to year with underlying asset values.

2. Only one type of income distribution is permitted from a CRAT- the annual fixed annuity. The trust cannot be drafted to pay out the lesser of net income and the annuity amount. As described more fully below, there are different payout options in a CRUT.

3. No additional contributions are permitted to be made to a CRAT after the initial funding. In contrast, a CRUT can accept further funding, and the payout will be adjusted to reflect the value of the additional assets.

Other than those differences, CRATs and CRUTs share many drafting require-ments, and are both governed by Section 664 of the Internal Revenue Code. For further discussion of these vehicles and other types of "split interest" charitable gifts, *see* Chapter 10.

---

[1]Forms for a charitable remainder annuity trust (CRAT) were issued in 2003 in Revenue Procedures 2003-53 through 2003-60, 2003-31 I.R.B. 230-274.

Practice Note

Charitable Remainder Trusts—whether CRUTs or CRATs—have two distinct tax characteristics. First, the donor is entitled to a deduction for income, gift, and/or estate tax purposes for the present value of the remainder interest given to charity. Second, the trust itself is a tax-exempt entity for federal income tax purposes (although a 100 percent tax is applied to any unrelated business taxable income earned or realized by the trust).

THE SARAH SAMPLE CHARITABLE REMAINDER UNITRUST

Practice Note

The opening paragraph identifies the settlor of the trust (the "donor"). The donor's full legal name should be used, and a statement of the donor's residence included. Any person or entity can be the donor of a CRUT. While it is generally accepted that spouses may act as joint donors, it is otherwise inadvisable, however, to have multiple donors. In a much-criticized 1995 Private Letter Ruling, 199547004, the IRS concluded that a charitable remainder trust with multiple *inter vivos* donors should be treated as a taxable association rather than a qualified exempt trust.

The opening paragraph should also identify the initial trustee or trustees by name. There are no requirements regarding who may act as a trustee of a CRUT or the number of trustees. The donor could serve as the sole trustee; by the same token, the charitable remainder beneficiary may be the trustee. Other potential trustees include family members, banks, and trust companies.

There are certain circumstances in which a donor should not serve as the sole trustee. If a donor does not retain an interest in the trust (in other words, the income interest is payable to individuals other than the donor), the donor should not be the trustee if the trust permits the income interest to be distributed in discretionary amounts among a class of beneficiaries, or gives the trustee discretion over the identity of the eventual charitable remainder beneficiary. Either of these powers will cause the trust property to be includable in the donor's estate for estate tax pur-poses, in circumstances in which the trust property would not otherwise be includable.

Finally, the introductory paragraph should identify the funding assets. As in the model document, this can be done on a separate schedule.

SARAH SAMPLE, of [*ADDRESS*] (the "Donor"), herewith transfers the property described in Schedule A attached hereto to [*TRUSTEE #1*], of [*ADDRESS*], and [*TRUSTEE #2*], of [*ADDRESS*], as Trustees hereunder; and the Trustees hereby acknowledge receipt thereof and agree, for themselves and all successors in office, to hold and manage such property [, *together with any additions thereto*,] IRREVOCABLY IN TRUST, upon the following terms and provisions:

Practice Note

Article FIRST sets forth the name of the trust. It then provides all the operative dispositive provisions of the CRUT.

The model document assumes that the donor will be the initial beneficiary and that her spouse will be the successor beneficiary in the event that he survives her. Many alternate individual beneficiary structures are possible. The donor can name herself as the sole income beneficiary. She could provide that another person, such as a child, would be the initial and perhaps only beneficiary. Furthermore, the trust could be created for a class of beneficiaries (such as the donor's children). It is important to note, however, that unitrust income beneficiaries must be alive at the creation of the trust if they are to receive an interest payable to them for life. For example, if the donor wishes to provide a stream of payments to her three living children, she can name each of them as beneficiaries and provide that they will receive payments for their respective lifetimes. If, however, the donor wishes to provide for later-born children as well, the unitrust payout can only be made for a term of years not to exceed 20.

In addition to naming individual beneficiaries of the percentage unitrust amount, the CRUT may provide for the percentage amount to be paid to corporations, partnerships, charitable organizations, or trusts for the benefit of individuals. However, several points must be noted. First, charitable organizations cannot be the sole unitrust beneficiaries. Second, when such beneficiaries are named, the trust term must ordinarily be a term of years. The only exception applies to a trust for an individual beneficiary who is "financially incompetent." In that circumstance, the CRUT can last for the trust beneficiary's lifetime.

If the donor names someone other than herself as a beneficiary of the percentage amount, there may be gift and eventually estate tax consequences for the donor. If, for example, the donor retains no interest in the CRUT and names her child as the sole individual beneficiary, the donor will make a taxable gift equal to the present value of the child's unitrust interest when the CRUT is funded. Part of that taxable gift may be offset by the gift tax annual exclusion. Provided the donor retains no control over the beneficial interests in the trust, the trust property will not, however, be includable in her estate for estate tax purposes in this situation. In contrast, if the donor retains the percentage amount interest for herself for the rest of her lifetime and names her child as the successor beneficiary after the donor's death, both gift and estate tax issues must be addressed. First, the donor will make a taxable gift of the present value of the child's successor interest (with no offset provided by the annual exclusion) unless the donor retains the right to revoke the child's interest. Furthermore, at the donor's death the trust property will be includable in the donor's estate because of the donor's retained beneficial interest in the trust. Although an estate tax charitable deduction will be available for the charity's interest, the child's income interest will be a taxable transfer. As explained more fully below in the comments to Article NINTH, any estate tax liability must be paid from other assets of the donor or by the child; it cannot be paid from the trust.

There are no gift or estate tax consequences attributable to a spouse's successor interest because of special gift and estate tax marital deduction provisions. It is critical to note, however, that the special deductions are only available if the spouse is the only other individual beneficiary. If a CRUT is set up by a donor with her spouse as first successor beneficiary and her daughter as second successor beneficiary, the marital deduction is not available to shield the spouse's interest in the trust (due to the terminable interest rule). This is frequently overlooked and can cause an entirely unexpected tax liability.

FIRST: Name of Trust; Payment of Percentage Amount. This trust shall be known as "THE SARAH SAMPLE CHARITABLE REMAINDER UNITRUST," and shall be administered as follows:

Practice Note

There are three basic annual payment options for the non-charitable beneficiary's interest in a CRUT: (1) a fixed percentage of trust assets (called a standard CRUT); (2) the lesser of net income earned by the trust assets and a fixed percentage of trust assets (called a NICRUT if there is no makeup provision and a NIMCRUT if there is a makeup provision); and (3) the lesser of net income and the percentage amount, until the occurrence of a triggering event, at which time the beneficiary's interest changes to a standard CRUT (called a FLIPCRUT). These options are set forth in the model document as Options 1, 2, and 3. Numerous tax and non-tax considerations bear on the decision of which type of payout to use. These are discussed in Chapter 10. It is important to note, however, that the income tax charitable deduction available to the donor is always calculated with reference to the percentage amount; a larger deduction is not available even if the charity receives more due to the net income limitation.

[OPTION 1—STRAIGHT PERCENTAGE PAYOUT]

Practice Note

The first option is a standard CRUT. Under this payout option, the distribution to the "income beneficiary" is measured by a fixed percentage of the value of the trust assets, determined each year on a fixed valuation date. This amount is distributed to the income beneficiary, regardless of the actual income earned by the trust assets. If income is less than the distribution amount, principal is distributed to make up the shortfall. This is the pure unitrust distribution, referred to throughout these notes as the "percentage amount."

The requirement to make annual distributions under the first option may be problematic in the situation where the donor transfers assets that, at the time of transfer, are illiquid and do not produce sufficient income to meet the annual payments. This commonly occurs when the donor transfers an interest in a closely held business or in non-income-producing land. The payout options in Option 2 and 3 are designed to address this situation.

(a) *Payment of the Percentage Amount.* For each taxable year through that in which the Termination Date occurs, the Trustees shall pay the Percentage Amount to the Donor, if she is living at the time of payment, or if not, to the Donor's husband, SAMUEL SAMPLE. Payments for each taxable year shall be made from income and, to the extent that income is not sufficient, from principal.

Practice Note

Under the second option, the income beneficiary receives the lesser of two distribution amounts. The first is the percentage amount. The second is the net income earned by the trust assets. This type of unitrust is frequently referred to by the acronym NICRUT (net income charitable remainder unitrust). There is a further variant to this option provided in the bracketed language that deals with deficiencies in distributions. If this option is selected, a makeup account is created in any year in which net income is less than the percentage amount. In a subsequent year, if net income is greater than the percentage amount, the excess income can be paid out to the beneficiary to the extent of the balance in the makeup account. An example will illustrate. Assume that a CRUT is funded with $1,000,000 on January 1, 2022. The percentage amount is 6 percent of asset value, or $60,000 for 2022. During 2022, the trust earns net income of $25,000. In 2022, the income beneficiary receives $25,000, the lesser of the two distribution amounts. The $35,000 difference between the percentage amount and the net income is recorded in the makeup account. Assume that, at the beginning of 2023, the trust assets are worth $1,100,000. The percentage amount for 2023 will be $66,000. If the trust earns net income in 2023 of $80,000, the income beneficiary will receive the entire $80,000. The 2023 distribution consists of the percentage amount ($66,000) plus an additional makeup distribution of $14,000. The makeup account will carry over a balance of $21,000 ($35,000 minus $14,000) to 2024. This type of unitrust is frequently referred to by the acronym NIMCRUT (net income makeup charitable remainder unitrust).

[OPTION 2—NET INCOME (WITH OPTIONAL MAKEUP)]

(a) *Payment of the Percentage Amount.* For each taxable year through that in which the Termination Date occurs, the Trustees shall pay the lesser of the net income of the trust and the Percentage Amount to the Donor, if she is living at the time of payment, or if not, to the Donor's husband, SAMUEL SAMPLE [; *provided* that if in any taxable year the net income of the trust exceeds the Percentage Amount, the amount to be paid shall be that amount equal to the sum of (i) the Percentage Amount and (ii) the amount of such excess to the extent of the Deficiency Amount for that year. No provision of this trust instrument shall be construed to require that the Trustees invest the trust property to produce sufficient net income to make up the Deficiency Amount].

Practice Note

The third option is the so-called FLIPCRUT. The FLIPCRUT starts as a lesser of net income unitrust (Option 2) but, after a triggering event, switches (or flips) to a straight percentage amount unitrust (Option 1). A FLIPCRUT can be useful because an individual can contribute illiquid, non-income-producing property to the trust, and then receive the higher unitrust amount (without regard to the actual income earned by the trust assets) once the trust has sufficient liquidity. The flip event can occur on any triggering date (referred to as the conversion date) that is not within the control of the donor, beneficiary, trustee, or any other person. For example, the conversion date could be the closing date of sale of unmarketable funding assets (e.g., commercial or residential real estate), the date of removal of sale restrictions on trust assets (e.g., rule 144 limits), the beneficiary's marriage or divorce, the beneficiary's reaching a certain age, the birth or death of a family member, or simply a fixed date. It cannot, however, be the date of sale of marketable assets, the making of a request to flip by the beneficiary, or an event such as the beneficiary's retirement. Once the conversion date occurs, the actual change in the payout method occurs on January 1 of the following year. The bracketed language provides for a makeup account to handle the problem raised by deficiencies in distributions. This is similar to Option 2, discussed above. However, in the event that the trust had a makeup account while it was a net income unitrust, any deficiency amount remaining in the makeup account is forfeited after the year in which the conversion date occurs.

[OPTION 3—FLIP (WITH OPTIONAL MAKEUP)]

(a) *Payment of the Percentage Amount.* For each taxable year through that in which the Conversion Date occurs (or, if earlier, through that in which the Termination Date occurs), the Trustees shall pay the lesser of the net income of the trust and the Percentage Amount to the Donor, if she is living at the time of payment, or if not, to the Donor's husband, SAMUEL SAMPLE [; *provided* that if in any such taxable year the net income of the trust exceeds the Percentage Amount, the amount to be paid shall be that amount equal to the sum of (i) the Percentage Amount and (ii) the amount of such excess to the extent of the Deficiency Amount for that year. No provision of this trust instrument shall be construed to require that the Trustees invest the trust property to produce sufficient net income to make up the Deficiency Amount]. For each taxable year beginning with the first taxable year after that in which the Conversion Date occurs and continuing through that in which the Termination Date occurs, the Trustees shall pay the Percentage Amount to the Donor, if she is living at the time of payment, or if not, to the Donor's said husband. Payments for all taxable years after that in which the Conversion Date occurs shall be made from income and, to the extent that income is not sufficient, from principal.

Practice Note

When the income interest terminates, the remaining trust property must be irrevocably transferred to one or more charities. The donor can name the charities in the trust instrument or retain the right to designate the charities by a later executed document. The three versions of paragraphs (b) and (c) of Article FIRST deal with possible alternative remainder distributions. The first is to a single named charity; the second is to multiple named charities; and the third is to later designated charities.

The most important issue at termination is that the charities to whom the property is distributed must qualify at that time as organizations described in Sections 170(c), 2055, and 2522 of the Internal Revenue Code. If a charity named or designated by the Donor qualifies at the time the trust instrument is signed or the designation is made, but is not so qualified at the termination of the trust, the trust instrument must provide for one or more qualified alternate charitable beneficiaries or for a mechanism to select qualified alternate charitable beneficiaries. The model document sets forth a selection mechanism and gives the trustees the power to name the alternate recipients. That decision could, however, be placed in the hands of family members or other individuals.

The term "qualified charitable organization" used in paragraphs (b) and (c) is defined later in the document. *See* paragraph (g) of Article TWELFTH. In that definition, reference is also made to Section 170(b)(1)(A) of the Code. This reference should be included, except in the limited circumstance where the donor names or desires the flexibility to later designate a private foundation as a remainder beneficiary. By including the reference to the additional section, distributions are limited to public charities, and, as a consequence, the donor's available income tax deduction will be measured with reference to the more favorable limits that apply to gifts to public charities. These deduction limits are discussed in Chapter 10.

The designation option provides that the designation is to be made by a separate written instrument delivered to the trustees as opposed to by the donor's will. In the author's experience, this is the preferable approach. It permits a designation to be made irrevocable, a necessary requirement if a donor is seeking gift credit from the charity for the remainder gift (for example, toward a reunion campaign). It is also helpful if a donor wants to terminate the trust prematurely by assigning the percentage amount to the same charity that will eventually receive the remainder.

[OPTION 1—DISTRIBUTION TO ONE CHARITY]

(b) *Termination and Distribution of Remainder to Designated Charity.* Upon the Termination Date, the trust shall terminate and the then trust property shall be distributed to [CHARITY #1], in [ADDRESS], for its general charitable purposes.

(c) *Distribution of Remainder if Designated Charity is not a Qualified Charitable Organization.* If on the Termination Date [CHARITY #1] is not a Qualified Charitable Organization, the Trustees shall instead distribute the then trust property to such one or more Qualified Charitable Organizations, for such charitable purposes and in such proportions to each as the Trustees, in their absolute discretion, shall then in writing select and determine.

[OPTION 2—DISTRIBUTIONS TO TWO OR MORE NAMED CHARITIES]

(b) *Termination and Distribution of Remainder to Designated Charities.* Upon the Termination Date, the trust shall terminate and the then trust property shall be distributed to the following named organizations for the purposes specified below:

   (i) *[PERCENTAGE AMOUNT IN WORDS]* percent (_____%) thereof to *[CHARITY #1]* in *[ADDRESS]*, to establish an endowment fund in the name of the Donor, for the support of its educational programs.

   (ii) *[PERCENTAGE AMOUNT IN WORDS]* percent (_____%) thereof to *[CHARITY #2]*, in *[ADDRESS]*, for its general charitable purposes.

(c) *Distribution of Remainder if Either Designated Charity is not a Qualified Charitable Organization.* If on the Termination Date either of the organizations named in paragraph (b) above is not a Qualified Charitable Organization, the share of the then trust property distributable to such organization shall be distributed instead to the other organization named in paragraph (b) above if it is then a Qualified Charitable Organization. If on the Termination Date neither organization named in paragraph (b) above is a Qualified Charitable Organization, the then trust property shall be distributed instead to such one or more Qualified Charitable Organizations, for such charitable purposes and in such proportions to each as the Trustees, in their absolute discretion, shall then in writing select and determine.

[OPTION 3—DISTRIBUTIONS TO CHARITIES SUBSEQUENTLY DESIGNATED BY DONOR]

(b) *Termination and Distribution of Remainder to Designated Charities; Power to Amend Charitable Beneficiary Designation.* Upon the Termination Date, the trust shall terminate and the then trust property shall be distributed to such one or more Qualified Charitable Organizations, for such charitable purposes and in such proportions to each as may be designated in the last-dated writing referring to this paragraph and signed by the Donor and delivered to the Trustees during the Donor's lifetime. Except to the extent that the Donor states in a particular designation that all or any part of its provisions are irrevocable, the Donor shall have the right at any time or times, by a writing (other than a will or a codicil) signed and delivered to the Trustees on or prior to the Termination Date, to amend or revoke any such designation, with the result that the last-dated designation (as it may be amended) on file with the Trustees on the Termination Date with respect to any portion of the then trust property shall control the distribution of that portion. A designation shall be considered delivered to the Trustees at such time that the Trustees acknowledge its receipt in writing.

(c) *Disposition of Remainder in Default of Designation of Charitable Beneficiaries by Donor.* If on the Termination Date there is no written designation of charitable beneficiaries filed with the Trustees pursuant to paragraph (b) above, or if any designation so filed does not dispose of all the trust property, or if any organization so designated is not then a Qualified Charitable Organization and no effective alternate disposition has been provided for, that part or all of the trust property not effectively designated shall be distributed instead to such one or more Qualified Charitable Organizations, for such charitable purposes and in such proportions to each as the Trustees, in their absolute discretion, shall then in writing select and determine.

Practice Note

Paragraph (d) sets forth the percentage amount payout. This is the percentage of the trust assets that will be paid to the noncharitable beneficiaries in paragraph (a) of Article FIRST. The percentage amount has lower and upper limits. At the lower end, it must be at least 5 percent of the fair market value of the trust assets. At the upper end, there are two limitations. First, it cannot exceed 50 percent of the fair market value of the trust assets. Second, the value of the remainder interest must be at least 10 percent of the fair market value of the property transferred to the trust on the date of contribution. Whether this test is satisfied will depend on all the factors used in the actuarial valuation of the remainder, including the term of the trust, the interest rate factor, the frequency and timing of payments to the income beneficiaries, and the size of the percentage amount. A careful calculation must be made when the trust is funded to ensure that the 10 percent rule is not violated.

Paragraph (d) also sets forth the date for valuing the trust assets each year to determine the current distribution. Regulatory requirements will be satisfied provided that the trust instrument adopts a consistent method for making the valuation. The form uses the first business day of the year. It could instead prescribe another fixed date, or it could require that valuation be based on an average of values on several dates (e.g., a rolling average method that looks to the valuation of trust assets on the first business day of the preceding three years).

(d) *Percentage Amount.* Subject to Article SECOND below, the Percentage Amount shall be, for each taxable year of the trust, that amount equal to [*PERCENTAGE AMOUNT IN WORDS*] percent (_____%) of the net fair market value of the trust assets determined as of the first business day of such taxable year.

Practice Note

Paragraph (e) sets forth the termination date of the trust. The trust may last for the life or lives of the beneficiary or beneficiaries, or it may be for a term of years. It cannot be for both. The regulations indicate, however, that the trust may be for a term of years or the life or lives of beneficiaries alive at the creation of the trust, whichever is the shorter period. This type of arrangement is illustrated in the second

---

option to paragraph (e). When a trust term is based on lives, the lives used must be those of the trust beneficiaries. For example, a CRUT cannot make payments to the donor's son during the lifetime of the donor's daughter.

(e) *Termination Date.* The Termination Date shall be [the date of death of the survivor of the Donor and her said husband] or [the earlier of (i) [INSERT SPECIFIC DATE] and (ii) [the date of death of the survivor of the Donor and her said husband].

Practice Note

Paragraph (f) is only applicable to FLIPCRUTs, since it contains a definition of the conversion date. This concept was discussed more fully above in the note to paragraph (a).

(f) *Conversion Date.* [For flip trusts only] The Conversion Date shall be [INSERT SPECIFIC DATE] or [the date on which occurs {DESCRIBE TRIGGERING EVENT}] or [the first date on which the trust owns no interest (whether as the result of the closing of a single sale, exchange or like transaction or the closing of the final of a series of such transactions or otherwise) in the assets described in Schedule A attached hereto.]

Practice Note

Article SECOND sets forth various rules that apply to the timing and calculation of the distributions made to the individual beneficiaries under Article FIRST.

SECOND: Payment to the Unitrust Recipients. Payments to the Donor and the Donor's said husband under Article FIRST above shall be subject to the following provisions, notwithstanding any other provisions of this trust instrument:

Practice Note

Paragraph (a) states that payments will be made in arrears and in equal calendar quarterly installments. It could instead provide for monthly, semiannual, or annual payments, and could provide for the installments to be made at the beginning of the payment period. The frequency and timing of payments have a modest impact on the size of the donor's charitable deduction. Assuming all other variables are constant, the largest deduction is available if the percentage amount distributions are to be made in arrears and only once at the end of the year.

This paragraph also deals with the proration of payments in the event of the death of a beneficiary. Treasury regulations either permit daily proration (with any part payment due a beneficiary's estate after the beneficiary's death) or payments to terminate with the installment for the full period prior to the beneficiary's death. The model document adopts the latter approach, which is generally the most convenient for the trustees. It may not, however, be appropriate if the installments are to be made at less frequent intervals than quarterly.

(a) *Frequency of Payments.* Payments for each taxable year shall be made in installments at the end of each calendar quarter. Payments shall be prorated so as to terminate with the regular installment for the quarter next preceding the death of the Donor or her said husband, as the case may be, and the full amount for the quarter in which the Donor's death occurs shall be paid (without daily proration) to the Donor's said husband if he is living at the end of such quarter.

(b) *Proration for Short Taxable Year.* In determining the amount payable for a short taxable year other than the taxable year in which all payments terminate, the Trustees shall prorate the Percentage Amount on a daily basis.

(c) *Excess Net Income.* Any net income not required to be distributed shall be added to principal at the end of each taxable year and at the Termination Date.

Practice Note

Paragraph (d) deals with additional contributions. A CRUT must either prohibit additional contributions or include the detailed provisions set forth in the model document calculating the percentage amount in the event of additions. Note that if the first option is selected (no additions), appropriate changes need to be made by removing the bracketed language in the introductory paragraph to the trust, in paragraph (e) of Article SECOND, and in paragraph (e) of Article FOURTH.

(d) *Additional Contributions Prohibited.* No additional contributions shall be made to this trust after the initial contribution.

[OR]

(d) *Adjustment to Percentage Amount for Additional Contributions.* For any taxable year in which an additional contribution is received, the Percentage Amount shall (subject to proration as provided in paragraph (b) above, if required) be [PERCENTAGE AMOUNT IN WORDS] percent (_____%) of the sum of (1) the net fair market value of the assets of the trust as of the first business day of such taxable year (excluding the additional contribution and any income from, or appreciation on, the additional contribution) and (2) that proportion of the net fair market value of the additional contribution as of the date of its transfer to the Trustees which the number of days in the period beginning with the date of such transfer and ending with the earlier of the last day of the taxable year or the Termination Date bears to the number of days in the period beginning with the first day of the taxable year and ending with the earlier of the last day of the taxable year or the Termination Date. In the event that any such addition to this trust is made as a result of the death of an individual, notwithstanding any other provisions hereof:

(i) Such addition shall be deemed to have been made on the date of death of such individual;

(ii) The obligation to make the payment provided for under Article FIRST above with respect to such addition shall commence with the date of death of such individual, but the Trustees may defer or may estimate the amount of payments due the Donor or her said husband on account of such addition for the period from the date of death until the end of the taxable year of the trust in which occurs the earlier of the end of a reasonable period of administration or settlement of the estate of such individual or complete funding of such addition; and

(iii) In case the Trustees defer or estimate the amount of payments due the Donor or her said husband as the result of such addition, the amount which is payable on account of such addition for the period described in clause (ii) above shall be retroactively determined within a reasonable period of time after the end of such period, and the Trustees shall pay to (in the case of an underpayment) or shall be repaid by (in the case of an overpayment) the Donor, her said husband, or his or her estate, as the case may be, any difference between (aa) the amount actually paid, plus interest computed in accordance with the applicable Regulations, and (bb) the amount properly payable determined in accordance with the special method provided in Regulation Section 1.664-1(a)(5)(ii).

Practice Note

Paragraph (e) deals with errors in calculating the percentage amount. It requires that additional payments be made to (or reimbursement be sought from) the individual beneficiaries in the event that the assets have been incorrectly valued and the wrong amount distributed.

(e) *Adjustment for Incorrect Valuation of Trust Property.* In the event that the net fair market value of the trust assets [*or of any additional contribution*] has been incorrectly determined and as a result the payments to the Donor or her said husband exceed or are less than the payments required to be made hereunder, then within a reasonable period of time after the final determination of the correct net fair market value the Trustees shall pay to (in the case of an undervaluation) or shall be repaid by (in the case of an overvaluation) the Donor, her said husband, or his or her estate, as the case may be, an amount equal to the difference between the amount which the Trustees should have paid if the correct valuation had been used and the amount which the Trustees actually paid.

Practice Note

Article THIRD states that the trust is intended to qualify as a CRUT and that no discretion or power given to the trustees can be exercised in a way that would cause the trust to lose its qualification. It also sets forth the private foundation rules to which a CRUT is subject. First, a CRUT that has no charitable income beneficiaries is subject to the rules pertaining to self-dealing and expenditures for prohibited purposes. In general, the self-dealing rules prevent the donor and persons related to the donor (known as "disqualified persons") from engaging in certain transactions with the trustees of the CRUT (e.g., renting or buying from, or selling or lending to, the trust). If there is an act of self-dealing, both the disqualified person and the CRUT are subject to penalty taxes. One particularly important application of the self-dealing rules arises in connection with pledges; a donor cannot use an existing CRUT to discharge a personal pledge with a charitable organization later entered into by the donor. Similarly, a donor cannot transfer residential real estate to a CRUT and then continue to live in that real estate. In this situation, there is a disqualifying act of self-dealing even if the donor pays a fair market rental for use of the premises.

THIRD: Intent of Trust; Private Foundation Restrictions. This trust is intended to qualify as a charitable remainder unitrust within the meaning of Section 664(d) of the Code, the Regulations thereunder and decisional law, and at no time may the Trustees exercise any power granted herein or otherwise act in such a manner as to defeat this intent. In addition, the following provisions shall apply to this trust and to all actions taken by the Trustees:

(a) *Self-Dealing.* Except for any payment under Article FIRST above, the Trustees shall not engage in any act of self-dealing as defined in Section 4941(d) of the Code, nor make any taxable expenditures as defined in Section 4945(d) of the Code.

(b) *Excess Business Holdings.* For any period for which Sections 4943 and 4944 of the Code are applicable to this trust, the Trustees shall not retain any excess business holdings as defined in Section 4943(c) of the Code, nor make any investments which would subject the trust to tax under Section 4944 of the Code.

(c) *Jeopardizing Investments and Taxable Expenditures.* Whenever the trust hereunder is subject to Section 4942 of the Code, the Trustees shall make distributions at such time and in such manner as not to subject the trust to tax under said Section.

Practice Note

Paragraph (d) reflects a regulatory requirement that no provision in the trust instrument can restrict the trustees from selling trust assets and realizing gains.

(d) *Investments to Provide Reasonable Income.* No provision of this trust instrument shall be construed to restrict the Trustees from investing the trust assets in a manner which could result in the annual realization of a reasonable amount of income or gain from the sale or disposition of trust assets.

Practice Note

Paragraph (e) adopts a provision required by the IRS in other split interest vehicles and mandates that depletion and depreciation reserves be maintained whenever assets subject to depletion or depreciation are held in the trust.

(e) *Reserve for Depreciation or Depletion.* If the Trustees accept gifts of depreciable or depletable property or make investments in such property, the Trustees shall establish and maintain for as long as such property is held in the trust hereunder a depreciation or depletion reserve in accordance with Generally Accepted Accounting Principles (GAAP) as established by the Financial Accounting Standards Board (FASB) or any successor thereto.

Practice Note

Paragraph (f) deals with the valuation of trust assets. In order to prevent possible manipulation of the amount distributable to the income beneficiaries, Treasury Regulations require that assets without a readily ascertainable market value be valued either by an independent trustee or by a qualified appraiser in a qualified appraisal. All these terms are defined in Treasury Regulations, and are referred to in Article TWELFTH.

(f) *Valuing Unmarketable Assets.* Whenever there is an Independent Trustee in office hereunder, the net fair market value of all Unmarketable Assets shall be determined by that Trustee. If there is no Independent Trustee in office, the net fair market value of all Unmarketable Assets shall be determined by a current Qualified Appraisal from a Qualified Appraiser.

Practice Note

Article FOURTH sets forth the powers of the trustees. While state law frequently grants a series of default powers to trustees, it is good drafting practice to set forth the powers expressly. This eliminates ambiguities in local law, may expand the scope of the trustees' authority, and may avoid the need for court approval of certain actions. The list of powers is general and should cover most situations. The only special provision for CRUTs is contained in paragraph (j). This provides that, in making distributions in kind, the trustees must distribute assets that are fairly representative of the adjusted bases of all assets available for distribution. Ordinarily, this will not be relevant; it does not apply to the percentage amount distributions and is of no consequence when the trust terminates in full and the charitable remainder beneficiaries receive the trust property. However, if a CRUT has multiple individual beneficiaries (e.g., the donor's children) and is structured so that as each individual beneficiary dies a portion of the trust assets is immediately distributable to charity (a so-called "peel off" distribution), this requirement means that the trustees must not manipulate the selection of assets in making the partial distribution to the charitable beneficiaries.

FOURTH: Trustees' Powers. In addition to other powers, the Trustees shall have the following powers with respect to the trust and its property, in each case to be exercised from time to time at the discretion of the Trustees and without order or license of the court:

(a) To retain indefinitely, and to invest and reinvest in, without notice to any beneficiary, stocks, shares, general or limited partnership interests, obligations and other securities or any other kind of personal or real property, even though any or all of the investments made or retained are of a character or size which, but for this express authority, would not be considered proper for trustees;

(b) To sell, to exchange, to lease and to make contracts concerning real or personal property, for such consideration and upon such terms as to credit or otherwise as the Trustees consider advisable, which leases and contracts may extend beyond the term of the trust; to give options on real or personal property of the trust; to establish depreciation, depletion, tax or any other reserves; and to execute deeds, transfers, leases and other instruments of any kind;

(c) To hold securities or other property in bearer or unregistered form or in the name of any one or more of the Trustees or of any other person, firm or corporation without indication of any fiduciary capacity;

(d) To give general or special proxies or powers of attorney (which may or may not be discretionary and with power of substitution) for voting or acting with respect to securities; to deposit securities with, or transfer them to, protective committees, voting trustees or similar bodies; to join in any reorganization; and to pay assessments or subscriptions called for in connection with securities held by the Trustees;

(e) [To receive additions to the trust by gift or will or otherwise, and to hold and administer the same under the provisions hereof;]

(f) To compromise or submit to arbitration any claim or matter in dispute;

(g) To credit particular receipts and gains, and to charge particular disbursements or losses or charges, to income or to principal of the trust or to apportion them between income and principal, whether such credits or charges relate to bonds acquired at a premium, to reserves or to any other matter, all as the Trustees consider fair and reasonable in each case;

(h) To employ investment counsel and consult with them concerning the investments and management of the trust and to delegate to them such powers as the Trustees deem appropriate; to employ a custodian of any funds or securities and to delegate to it such powers as the Trustees deem appropriate; to employ investment bankers or other appraisal services to value securities or other investments which are not publicly traded and to render advice and provide services in connection with the sale of any such securities or other investments; to employ legal counsel, accountants and other special services; and, in addition to the compensation and expenses of the Trustees, to pay the compensation and expenses of all such services, even if rendered by a Trustee;

(i) To improve or develop real estate; to construct, alter, repair or demolish buildings or structures; to settle boundary lines, easements or other rights; to partition; and to join with co-owners, or others in dealing with real estate in any way; and

(j) To make any division or distribution of, or payment from, the trust in kind by the fair and reasonable allotment and transfer of specific securities or other personal or real property or undivided interests therein, at then current values, in lieu of cash, as a part or the whole of any one or more shares or payments. The adjusted basis for federal income tax purposes of any trust property which the Trustees distribute in kind to charity must be fairly representative of the adjusted basis for such purposes of all trust property available for distribution on the date of distribution.

Practice Note

Article FIFTH states that the trust is irrevocable but then gives the trustees the ability to amend the trust so that it qualifies as a charitable remainder trust. In addition, Article FIFTH gives the donor the right to terminate the successor interest of her spouse. Retention of this right used to be necessary because of an anomaly in the federal gift tax marital deduction. This anomaly was cured many years ago. Nevertheless, the donor may want to retain the revocation right for non-tax reasons. In the event that a successor beneficiary to the donor is someone other than the spouse, the retention of the revocation right is important. Without it, the donor will be treated as making a taxable gift of the present value of the successor interest at the time the trust is funded.

FIFTH: Irrevocable; Limited Amendment. This trust shall be irrevocable and shall not be subject to alteration or amendment, except that the Trustees may in writing amend this trust instrument at any time or times to enable the trust hereunder to continue to qualify as a charitable remainder unitrust under Section 664(d) of the Code, the Regulations thereunder and decisional law. Notwithstanding the foregoing, the Donor shall have the power, exercisable solely by will duly admitted to probate, to revoke and terminate the interest of her said husband, in which case, any other provisions of this trust instrument notwithstanding, the trust property shall be paid over and distributed at the Donor's death as if her said husband had died immediately prior thereto.

Practice Note

Article SIXTH contains a spendthrift clause. It provides that creditors cannot reach the interest of the successor beneficiary. It also prevents the donor and her spouse from assigning their interests (other than to a qualified charity).

SIXTH: Spendthrift Clause. The interest of the Donor's said husband, and all payments to be made to or for him, shall be free from interference or control by any creditor, spouse or divorced former spouse. In addition, no interest of or payment to or for the Donor and her said husband shall be capable of anticipation or assignment (except in the case of a voluntary transfer of part or all of such interest to any Qualified Organization [*named in*] or [*designated pursuant to*] Article FIRST above).

Practice Note

Article SEVENTH deals with the trustees. It provides for voluntary and involuntary resignations. It also gives the donor and her spouse the right to remove trustees. No estate tax problems are caused by the retention and granting of the removal right. The model document names a specific successor to one of the initially named trustees and then creates a mechanism for appointing further successors. By making reference to the accounting article, the model document gives the power to appoint trustees first to the donor and then to her spouse.

The Article waives the requirements of bond or surety. Finally, it provides that a third party dealing with the trustees need not look into the validity of the trustees' actions but can assume that the trustees are authorized to act as they purport to.

SEVENTH: Trustees. Any Trustee may resign by giving written notice to the one or more persons then entitled to request an account of the Trustees as provided below in Article EIGHTH. Any individual Trustee (including the Donor) shall be deemed to resign (i) if a legal guardian or similar legal representative has been appointed for such individual or (ii) if the one or more persons (other than the particular Trustee) to whom written notice of a resignation would then be given receive a writing signed by the individual's regularly attending physician certifying that, in the physician's opinion, such individual is mentally or physically incapable of discharging the responsibilities of a Trustee. Any Trustee may be removed by a writing delivered to the Trustee and signed by the Donor, if she is then living and of full legal capacity, or, if not, by her said husband, if he is then living and of full legal capacity.

If for any reason [*TRUSTEE #1*] ceases to serve as Trustee hereunder, [*TRUSTEE #3*], of [*ADDRESS*], shall become a successor Trustee, upon written acceptance of the office. If for any reason [*TRUSTEE #3*] declines to accept the appointment or, having accepted, later ceases to serve as a Trustee hereunder, and in case of any other vacancy in the office of Trustee not filled as provided above, a successor Trustee may be appointed in a writing signed by the person then entitled to request an account of the Trustees as provided below in Article EIGHTH. Each such appointment shall take effect upon written acceptance of the office. There need not be more than one Trustee for the time being in office hereunder.

No Trustee named herein or appointed as provided above shall be required to furnish a bond or surety on a bond. No one dealing with the Trustees need inquire concerning the validity of anything the Trustees purport to do or need see to the application of any money paid or property transferred to or upon the order of the Trustees.

Practice Note

Trust instruments should deal with the manner in which trustees account to the beneficiaries. Article EIGHTH clarifies the trustees' obligations. In the model form, accounts are to be rendered first to the donor and, after her death, to her spouse. In the event that either of them is incapacitated, accounts will be rendered to the legal guardian or similar legal representative. The model provision attempts to bring finality to the accounting procedure by providing protection to the trustees after the accounts are assented to.

EIGHTH: Accounts. Upon written request, the Trustees shall render an account of the trust hereunder to the Donor during her lifetime, and after the Donor's death to her said husband and, if either of them is not of full legal capacity, to his or her legal guardian or similar legal representative; and without any request, the Trustees may also at any time render an account for any period during which the Donor or her said husband is entitled to receive payments under Article FIRST above to him or her, or to his or her legal guardian or similar legal representative. The written assent to any such account by the person of full legal capacity to whom it is rendered as provided above shall fully protect the Trustees as to all matters or transactions stated in such account or shown thereby. Nothing in this Article shall give anyone the power to modify the terms of this trust instrument or to alter or to shift any beneficial interest created hereunder.

Practice Note

Whenever there is a succeeding non-charitable income interest following the death of the donor, the trust agreement must provide that no death taxes attributable to the inclusion of the trust property in the donor's estate will be allocated to or recoverable from the trust. If there is any possibility that a CRUT can bear a share of the donor's estate taxes, whether because of a state apportionment statute or otherwise, the trust will not be a qualified charitable remainder trust. To address this requirement, the model document first contains a covenant from the donor that she will provide for any such taxes to be paid from her estate. If the donor fails to make

---

adequate provision, the trustees are then authorized to enforce a claim against the donor's estate. If that is not successful, the successor beneficiary's interest only takes effect if the beneficiary pays the estate taxes. If the beneficiary refuses, he or she is deemed to have predeceased the donor, meaning that the trust property passes to charity at the donor's death and any estate tax liability is avoided by the availability of the charitable deduction.

It is advisable to include this provision in every CRUT, even if the spouse is the successor beneficiary. While federal estate tax laws grant a marital deduction for the surviving spouse's interest, state estate or inheritance tax laws may not.

NINTH: Estate Taxes. No part of any federal or state estate, inheritance, succession or like tax imposed by reason of the Donor's death on any interest in property of this trust shall be paid from property of the trust. The Donor covenants with the Trustees that she will provide by will or otherwise for the payment of any such taxes from sources other than property of the trust; and if for any reason the Donor fails to do so, the Donor directs that the Trustees shall recover from her estate the amount of any such taxes imposed on the trust, as an obligation of her estate.

Notwithstanding any other provisions of this trust instrument, if for any reason the trust hereunder becomes liable for any such taxes and the Trustees are unable to recover such taxes from the Donor's estate and such taxes are not paid otherwise, the interest of the Donor's said husband if he survives the Donor shall take effect only if he furnishes the funds to pay such taxes; and if he fails to furnish those funds, he shall be deemed for all purposes of this trust instrument to have died immediately prior to the Donor's death.

Practice Note

Article TENTH deals generally with trust documentation. It places an obligation on the trustees to establish secure arrangements for the custody of all documents that are related to the trust. It also provides that outside parties may rely on certified copies of the original documentation.

TENTH: Trust Documentation. The original of each alteration or amendment of this trust instrument by the Trustees, each resignation, removal or appointment of a Trustee, and each acceptance of appointment, shall be kept attached to the original trust instrument, which shall be held by the Trustees. Anyone may rely on a copy, certified by a notary public, of this trust instrument or of any writings attached thereto as fully as on the original document; and anyone may rely fully upon any statements of fact certified by anyone who appears from the original document or a certified copy thereof to be a Trustee hereunder.

Practice Note

Article ELEVENTH sets forth the jurisdiction that will govern the operation of the trust. A governing law clause will generally be upheld as long as the state chosen has some logical connection to the trust. In appropriate circumstances, it might be advisable to permit the trustees to change the governing law with respect to the administration of the trust (if, for example, no individual beneficiary or trustee has any connection with the originally specified jurisdiction).

ELEVENTH: Governing Law. This trust instrument and the trust hereunder shall be governed, construed and administered in accordance with the provisions of the Code from time to time applicable thereto and by the laws of [*SPECIFY GOVERNING STATE LAW*] from time to time in force.

Practice Note

Article TWELFTH sets forth definitions that apply to the CRUT. As noted, paragraphs (b) and (c) only apply to the net income variants and FLIPCRUT, and not to the standard CRUT. Obviously, the determination of net income is critical to these types of CRUT, because each permits payouts based on trust income. The definition set forth in the document refers to Section 643(b) of the Code, under which income is determined in accordance with applicable local law or the terms of the governing instrument. Ordinarily, trust accounting income includes only interest, dividends, and rents. It does not include all items that may be subject to income tax, such as capital gains. While state law may permit gains in some circumstances to be allocated to income, the charitable remainder trust regulations provide that gain may only be included to the extent that it is attributable to appreciation that occurs after an asset has been contributed to the trust. Built-in appreciation at the time of contribution is required in all circumstances to be treated as principal. This restriction has been criticized; its requirements are nevertheless reflected in paragraph (c).

TWELFTH: Definitions. The following terms used in this trust instrument shall have the following meanings:

(a) "Code" shall mean the Internal Revenue Code of 1986, as amended, or any successor provisions thereto.

(b) [*Use with NIMCRUT/FLIP with makeup only:*] "Deficiency Amount" shall mean, for any particular year, the amount by which the aggregate of the Percentage Amounts for years prior to the year in question exceeds the aggregate distributions actually made during those years.

(c) [*Use with NICRUT/NIMCRUT/FLIP only:*] "Income" shall have the meaning set forth in Section 643(b) of the Code and the Regulations under Section 664 of the Code. [*Optional inclusion of capital gains as income:*] Notwithstanding the foregoing, the Trustees shall include as an item of income in any particular taxable year net capitalized income recognized in that year (reduced but not below zero by net capitalized loss recognized in that year). For this purpose, "net capitalized income" and "net capitalized loss" shall mean the difference between the net proceeds received on the sale or exchange of a particular asset (reduced by any expenses incurred in the transaction) and the cost basis amount of the asset. The "cost basis amount" shall mean the original acquisition price (plus any expenses of acquisition), in the case of an asset acquired by the Trustees, and fair market value at the date of contribution, in the case of an asset contributed to the trust by any donor, reduced or increased, in either case, by any adjustments to basis occurring after acquisition or contribution ordinarily required to be made in determining gain or loss for federal income tax purposes.

(d) "Independent Trustee" shall mean a person who is not a donor to or a non-charitable beneficiary of this trust or a related or subordinate party (within the meaning of Section 672(c) of the Code and the Regulations thereunder) to the Donor, the Donor's said husband, or any non-charitable beneficiary of this trust.

(e) "Qualified Appraisal" shall have the meaning set forth in Section 170(f)(ii)(E) of the Code and in Regulation Section 1.170A-13(c)(3).

(f) "Qualified Appraiser" shall have the meaning set forth in Section 170(f)(ii)(E) of the Code and in Regulation Section 1.170A-13(c)(5).

(g) "Qualified Charitable Organization" shall mean an organization which, at the time any distribution is to be made to such organization, is then in legal and operational existence and is described in Sections [170(b)(1)(A),] 170(c), 2055(a) and 2522(a) of the Code.

(h) "Regulations" shall mean the United States Treasury Regulations as from time to time in force, or any successor provisions thereto.

(i) "Trustee" or "Trustees" shall mean the one or more Trustees, whether original or successor, for the time being in office.

(j) "Unmarketable Assets" shall mean assets other than cash, cash equivalents, or other assets that can be readily sold or exchanged for cash or cash equivalents.

SIGNED and SEALED this _____ day of _____, 20 _____.

_____
SARAH SAMPLE, Donor

_____
[*TRUSTEE #1*], Trustee

_____
[*TRUSTEE #2*], Trustee

COMMONWEALTH/STATE OF [*NAME OF STATE*]

_____, ss.

On this _____ day of _____, 20__, before me, the under-signed notary public, personally appeared the above-named SARAH SAMPLE, known to me personally or proved to me through _____ as satisfac-tory evidence of identification, to be the person whose name is signed on the preceding document, and acknowledged to me that she signed it voluntarily for its stated purpose.

_____
Notary Public
My Commission Expires:

FORM 15

Qualified Personal Residence Trust (QPRT)

Overview

This form establishes a Qualified Personal Residence Trust (QPRT). A QPRT is an irrevocable trust to which a donor transfers ownership of a primary or secondary residence. A QPRT creates two distinct trust interests. First, the donor retains the right to use the trust property for a specified term of years. Second, at the end of the specified term, the trust property passes outright to (or in further trust for) one or more remainder beneficiaries other than the donor.

A QPRT must include certain provisions required by Internal Revenue Code Section 2702(a)(3)(A) and Treasury Regulation Section 25.2702-5(c). In 2003, the IRS issued a sample QPRT in Revenue Procedure 2003-42. A trust that is substantially similar to the sample QPRT issued by the IRS will be recognized by the IRS as a QPRT that meets the necessary requirements.

The goal of a QPRT is to enable the donor to transfer property to the remainder beneficiaries at a reduced value for gift tax purposes. The remainder beneficiaries receive the property if and when the Donor survives the specified term; however, the value of the gift is calculated based on the present, discounted value of the remainder interest in the property as of the month in which the QPRT is established. If the donor survives the specified term, the property will be removed from his or her estate through a favorably valued taxable gift. If the donor does not survive the specified term, the QPRT will not achieve the anticipated tax savings, and the trust property will be included in the donor's estate for estate tax purposes because the donor will have a retained interest in the trust. However, the donor will be in no worse position than if he had never established the QPRT in the first place.

THE [*SARAH SAMPLE*] [*YEAR*] QUALIFIED PERSONAL RESIDENCE TRUST

Practice Note

The opening paragraph identifies the settlor of the trust (the "donor") and the initial trustee or trustees. The donor's full legal name should be used, and a statement of the donor's residence included. There are no requirements regarding who may act as a trustee of a QPRT or the number of trustees. The donor could serve as the sole trustee during the specified term, but should resign prior to the end of the specified term to prevent the trust property from being includable in the donor's estate for estate tax purposes where the trust property would not otherwise be includable.

The donor may transfer either complete ownership of a personal residence to the QPRT, or only a fractional interest in such a residence. The residence transferred may include appurtenant structures used by the donor for residential purposes, and adjacent land not in excess of that which is reasonably appropriate for residential purposes. If the donor does not currently own the personal residence that will constitute the trust corpus, the donor may transfer cash to the QPRT for the purchase of the initial residence, so long as a contract to purchase that residence exists. However, if this occurs, the purchase of the residence must take place within three months from the date that the trust is created.

[*SARAH SAMPLE*], of [*CITY*], [*STATE*] (the "Donor"), herewith transfers (by separate deed) all her right, title and interest in and to the residence located at [*ADDRESS*], in said [*CITY*] (the "Residence"), to herself and her husband, [*NAME*], as trustees hereunder, to be held in trust under Article FIRST below; and the Donor also herewith transfers the nominal sum of One Dollar ($1) to herself and her said husband, as trustees hereunder, to be held in trust under Article FOURTH below; and in each case the trustees hereby acknowledge receipt thereof and agree, for themselves, any additional trustees and all successors in office, to hold the Residence and such nominal sum and all additions thereto permitted by this trust instrument, IRREVOCABLY IN TRUST, upon the following terms and provisions:

Practice Note

This provision sets forth the name of the trust and provides that the donor will retain the right to live in the residence transferred to the trust for the specified term. The donor will be solely responsible for those expenses associated with the residence that would be the responsibility of a holder of a legal life estate in the property, including expenses such as real estate taxes and the cost of ordinary repairs. If the donor transfers only a fractional interest in a personal residence to the QPRT, the trust should include language regarding the proration of expenses relating to the residence.

FIRST: Name of Trust; Donor's Retained Use During Trust Term. The trust under this Article FIRST shall be known as "THE SARAH SAMPLE [*YEAR*] QUALIFIED PERSONAL RESIDENCE TRUST". From the date this trust is established until the termination date, the Donor shall be entitled to occupy the Residence for personal use and shall be solely responsible for real estate taxes, insurance, costs of maintenance and repair and all other costs in connection with the Residence which would be the responsibility of the holder of a legal life estate in such property.

Practice Note

Selecting the length of the term interest is important when drafting a QPRT. The longer the specified term, the smaller the value of the donor's taxable gift, because

---

the remainder interest will be more remote and will therefore have a lower present value. However, the donor must survive the specified term to achieve the estate tax objective of the QPRT. As the length of the donor's retained term increases, the probability that the donor will not survive the specified term (and the associated probability that the estate tax benefit will be lost) also increases.

If the donor survives the specified term, the model document provides that the residence will be held in trust for the donor's issue and others as provided in Article FOURTH. If the donor wishes to continue to live in the property after the specified term, the donor must pay rent to the remainder beneficiaries, unless the donor's spouse is a remainder beneficiary.

If the donor does not survive the specified term, the dispositive provisions of the model document are designed to take advantage of the estate tax marital deduction. The model document gives the donor the right, by so providing in his or her will, to direct the disposition of the remaining trust property. To the extent that the donor does not exercise this power of disposition, the model document provides that the trust property will be distributed to the donor's spouse, thus deferring any estate taxes attributable to the trust property until the death of the donor's spouse. If the donor's spouse is not then living, the model document provides that the remaining trust property will be held in trust for the donor's issue and others as provided in Article FOURTH.

The termination date of the trust under this Article FIRST shall be the xxxth (XXth) anniversary of the date on which this trust instrument is executed, or if sooner, the date of the Donor's death. If the termination date is the xxxth (XXth) anniversary of the date of execution of this trust instrument, the then remaining trust property shall, except as otherwise provided in Article SECOND below, be held in trust for the Donor's issue and others as provided in Article FOURTH below. If the termination date is the date of the Donor's death, the then remaining trust property shall be disposed of as the Donor appoints by her will, executed at any time after the date of this trust instrument and referring specifically to this power of appointment, to or for the benefit of any one or more persons or objects, including the Donor's estate. This power shall be exercisable for such estates, on such trusts and subject to such terms, conditions, general or special powers and restrictions as the Donor so appoints. In default of or subject to appointment by the Donor as aforesaid if the termination date is the date of the Donor's death, the then remaining trust property shall, except as otherwise provided in Article SECOND below, be distributed to the Donor's said husband, if he is then living, or if not, held in trust for the Donor's issue and others as provided in Article FOURTH below.

Practice Note

To qualify as a QPRT, the trust instrument must contain all the provisions required under the applicable Treasury Regulations, and these provisions must continue to be in effect during the specified term. Most of the paragraphs in Article SECOND are required provisions for a QPRT. In general, during the specified term, except for small amounts of cash, sale proceeds, or insurance policies or proceeds, the QPRT cannot hold any asset other than one residence (or a portion thereof), which must be used or held for use as a personal residence of the donor.

SECOND: Governing Instrument Requirements. The trust under Article FIRST above is intended to be a qualified personal residence trust within the meaning of Treasury Regulation Section 25.2702-5(c) (or any successor regulation thereto), and this trust instrument shall be construed in all respects in accordance with this intent. The trust under Article FIRST above shall be subject to the following additional provisions, which shall continue in effect throughout the term of the trust:

(a) *Distributions from the Trust.* No distributions of income or corpus may be made to any beneficiary other than the Donor prior to the termination of the Donor's interest as provided in Article FIRST above. In addition, any income of the trust must be distributed to the Donor at least as often as annually.

(b) *Assets Held in the Trust.* Except as otherwise provided in this Article, the trustees may not hold any asset, including without limitation any tangible personal property, other than one residence to be used as a personal residence by the Donor. For purposes of this trust instrument, the term "personal residence" shall have the meaning given to it by Treasury Regulation Section 25.2702-5(c)(2) (or any successor regulation thereto).

(c) *Assets Other Than Personal Residence Held in the Trust.* The trustees may accept additions of cash to the trust, and may hold such additions in a separate account, each in an amount which, when added to the cash already held in the account for such purposes, does not exceed the amount required (i) for payment of trust expenses already incurred or reasonably expected to be paid by the trust within six (6) months from the date the addition is made, (ii) for improvements to the Residence to be paid by the trust within six (6) months from the date the addition is made, or (iii) for the purchase by the trust of a personal residence for the Donor to replace the Residence previously held hereunder within three (3) months after the addition is made; *provided* that no addition may be made for this last purpose, and the trust may not hold any such addition, unless the trustees have previously entered into a contract to purchase the replacement personal residence. Any improvements to the Residence made pursuant to this paragraph (c) must not cause the Residence to fail to meet the requirements of a personal residence as herein defined.

(d) *Distributions of Excess Cash.* If any addition of cash is made to the trust under paragraph (c) above, the trustees must determine, at least quarterly, the amounts held by the trust for payment of expenses in excess of the amounts permitted by said paragraph (c), and such amounts must be distributed immediately thereafter to the Donor. In addition, upon termination of the Donor's interest, any amounts held by the trustees for the purposes permitted by said paragraph (c) that are not used to pay trust expenses due and payable on the termination date (including expenses directly related to termination) must be distributed outright to the Donor, if she is then living or, if the trust terminates by reason of the Donor's death, to the Donor's executor or administrator, to be disposed of as part of the Donor's estate, in either case within thirty (30) days after the termination date.

Practice Note

If the residence is sold during the specified term, the trustees may use the sale proceeds to purchase a replacement residence. Under the Treasury Regulations, if the trustees decide to purchase a replacement residence, they must purchase the replacement residence by the earlier of (1) the second anniversary of the date the residence was sold, or (2) the end of the QPRT term. If the trustees do not purchase a replacement residence within this time period (or if the trustees purchase a replacement residence that costs less than the sale proceeds), the trust will cease to be a QPRT with respect to the remaining sale proceeds at the end of this time period.

(e) *Sale of Personal Residence; Sale Proceeds.* The Residence may be sold, and the trustees may hold the proceeds from such sale in a separate account. However, the trust shall cease to be a qualified personal residence trust, and paragraph (g) below shall apply, with respect to any such proceeds of sale and any proceeds of insurance held as provided in paragraph (f) below, in either case, which are held by the trustees on the first to occur of (i) the second anniversary of the date of sale (or damage or destruction, as the case may be), (ii) the termination date, and (iii) the date on which a new Residence is acquired by the trust (or on which the replacement or repair of the Residence is completed, as the case may be).

Practice Note

The QPRT may hold insurance policies relating to the residence. Under the applicable Treasury Regulations, if damage or destruction renders the residence unusable as a residence and the trustees decide to repair or replace the residence, they must complete the repairs (or the purchase of the replacement residence) by the earlier of (1) the second anniversary of the date the residence was damaged or destroyed, or (2) the end of the QPRT term. If the trustees do not complete the repairs (or the purchase of a replacement residence) within this time period or if the repairs (or the purchase of a replacement residence) cost less than the insurance proceeds, the trust will cease to be a QPRT with respect to the remaining insurance proceeds at the end of this time period.

(f) *Damage to or Destruction of Personal Residence.* The trustees may hold one or more policies of insurance on the Residence. In addition, the trustees may hold, in a separate account, proceeds of insurance payable to the trust as a result of damage to or destruction of the Residence. For purposes of this paragraph, amounts (other than insurance proceeds payable to the trust as a result of such damage or destruction) received as a result of the involuntary conversion (within the meaning of Section 1033 of the Internal Revenue Code of 1986, as amended, or any successor provision thereto (the "Code")) of the Residence shall be treated as proceeds of insurance. However, if damage or destruction renders the Residence unusable as a personal residence, the trust shall cease to be a qualified personal residence trust, and paragraph (g) below shall apply, on the second anniversary of the date of damage or destruction (or on the termination date, if earlier) unless, prior to such date, the replacement or repair of the Residence is completed or a new Residence is acquired by the trustees.

Practice Note

The trust instrument must provide that the trust ceases to be a QPRT if the residence ceases to be used or held for use as a personal residence of the donor. Under the Treasury Regulations, a residence is "held for use" as a personal residence of the donor if the residence is not occupied by any other person (other than the spouse or a dependent of the donor) and is available at all times for use by the donor as a personal residence.

Within thirty days after the trust has ceased to be a QPRT with respect to any assets, either: (1) those assets must be distributed outright to the donor; (2) those assets must be converted to and held for the balance of the specified term in a separate share of the trust meeting the requirements of a grantor retained annuity trust (GRAT); or (3) the trustee may be given discretion to comply with either (1) or (2). The model document provides for the conversion to a GRAT.

(g) *Disposition of Trust Assets on Cessation of Qualified Personal Residence Trust.* Within thirty (30) days after the trust ceases to be a qualified personal residence trust with respect to all or certain trust assets, the trustees shall hold such assets for the balance of the term provided in Article FIRST above in a separate trust for the Donor under Article THIRD below.

(h) *Commutation.* The Donor's interest in the trust may not be commuted.

Practice Note

Any improvements made to the residence will constitute additional gifts to the remainder beneficiaries.

(i) *Improvements.* Improvements to the Residence may be added to the trust and the trust may hold such improvements; *provided* that the Residence as improved remains a personal residence as herein defined.

(j) *Replacement Personal Residence.* All references in this trust instrument to the Residence shall include any replacement personal residence of the Donor which may be purchased by the trustees pursuant to this Article.

(k) *Specific Powers Relating to Residence.* The trustees shall have the power, in the trustees' discretion and without order or license of any court, to sell, improve, maintain, mortgage, lease or otherwise deal with or dispose of the Residence, and to hold and deposit any cash contributed to or held hereunder in one or more bank, money market or similar accounts or to invest such cash in common stocks or in any other form of investment to the extent permitted by applicable Treasury regulations; *provided* that no such power shall be exercised or exercisable in a way which would cause the trust to fail or cease to qualify as a qualified personal residence trust (except by reason of the sale or damage or destruction of the Residence as provided in paragraphs (e) and (f) above).

Practice Note

Article THIRD provides that, if the trust ceases to qualify as a QPRT, the assets will be held as a separate GRAT, and a qualified annuity interest will be paid to the donor until the end of the QPRT term.

THIRD: Contingent Annuity Trust. All property provided in Article SEC-OND above to be held in a separate trust for the Donor under this Article THIRD shall in each case be administered as follows:

Practice Note

The first sentence of paragraph (a) reflects regulatory requirements for the payment of the annuity to the donor. The model document prohibits reimbursement of income taxes paid by the donor. This is the more conservative position to take based on Situation 3 of Rev. Rul. 2004-64, 2004-2 C.B. 7.

(a) *Right to Receive Annuity; Donor's Income Taxes.* The annuity amount, as hereinafter defined, shall be paid to the Donor at least as often as annually. Payments for a particular year may be made after the close of the taxable year; *provided* that any such payment shall be made no later than April 15 of the succeeding year. In no event may the trustees make any distribution to the Donor in order to reimburse the Donor for any income taxes incurred by the Donor attributable to the undistributed net income and capital gains of the trust. The Donor shall have no right to seek reimbursement for any such income taxes.

Practice Note

If the donor survives the specified term, the model document provides that the remaining trust property will be held in trust for the benefit of the donor's issue and others as provided in Article FOURTH. If the donor dies before the end of the specified term, the model document gives the donor the right, by so providing in his or her will, to direct the disposition of the remaining trust property. To the extent that the donor does not exercise this power of disposition, the model document provides that the remaining trust property will be distributed to the donor's spouse, thereby deferring any estate taxes attributable to the remaining trust property until the death of the donor's spouse. If the donor's spouse is not then living, the model document provides that the remaining trust property will be held in trust for the donor's issue and others as provided in Article FOURTH.

(b) *Termination Date.* The termination date of the trust under this Article THIRD shall be the xxxth (XXth) anniversary of the date on which this trust instrument is executed, or if sooner, the date of the Donor's death. If the termination date is the xxxth (XXth) anniversary of the date of execution of this trust instrument, the then remaining principal and any balance of net income shall be held in trust for the Donor's issue and others as provided in Article FOURTH below. If the termination date is the date of the Donor's death, the then remaining principal and any balance of net income shall be disposed of as the Donor appoints by her will, executed at any time after the date of this trust instrument and referring specifically to this power of appointment, to or for the benefit of any one or more persons or objects, including the Donor's estate. This power shall be exercisable for such estates, on such trusts and subject to such terms, conditions, general or special powers and restrictions as the Donor so appoints. In default of or subject to appointment by the Donor as aforesaid if the termination date is the date of the Donor's death, the then remaining principal and any balance of net income shall be distributed to the Donor's said husband, if he is then living, or if not, held in trust for the Donor's issue and others as provided in Article FOURTH below.

Practice Note

The trust instrument must provide that the donor's right to receive the annuity amount begins on the date of the sale of the residence, the date of damage to or destruction of the residence, or the date on which the residence ceases to be used or held for use as a personal residence (or in certain limited cases, a later date, with the payment of interest).

(c) *Payment of Annuity.* The Donor's right to receive the annuity amount shall begin on the date of sale of the Residence, the date of damage to or destruction of the Residence or the date on which the Residence ceases to be used or held for use as a personal residence, as the case may be (the "Cessation Date"). The trustees may, however, defer payment of any annuity amount otherwise payable after the Cessation Date until a date up to thirty (30) days after the assets are transferred to the trust under this Article THIRD pursuant to paragraph (g) of Article SECOND above (the "Conversion Date"); *provided* that any such deferred payment must bear interest from the Cessation Date at the rate in effect under Section 7520 of the Code on the Cessation Date. In addition, the trustees may reduce the aggregate deferred annuity payments by the amount of income or principal actually distributed by the trustees to the Donor during the deferral period.

Practice Note

Paragraph (d)(i) of the model document provides a formula for determining the annuity amount if the entire trust is converted to a GRAT. Paragraph (d)(ii) of the model document provides a formula for determining the annuity amount if only a portion of the trust is converted to a GRAT.

(d) *Determination of Annuity Amount.* The annuity amount for purposes of this Article THIRD shall be determined as follows:

   (i) *Entire Trust Ceases to be a Qualified Personal Residence Trust.* If on the Conversion Date the assets of the trust under Article FIRST above do not include a residence used or held for use as a personal residence, the annuity amount shall be that amount determined by dividing the lesser of the value of all interests retained by the Donor as of the date of the original transfer or transfers to that trust and the value of all the assets of that trust (as of the Conversion Date) by an annuity factor determined for the original term of the Donor's interest under Article FIRST above, at the rate (determined under Section 7520 of the Code) used in valuing the Donor's retained interests at the time of the original transfer or transfers.

   (ii) *Portion of Trust Continues as a Qualified Personal Residence Trust.* If on the Conversion Date the assets of the trust under Article FIRST above include a residence used or held for use as a personal residence, the annuity amount shall be the amount determined under clause (i) above multiplied by a fraction, the numerator of which is the excess of the fair market value of the assets of the trust under Article FIRST above on the Conversion Date over the fair market value of the assets as to which the trust continues as a qualified personal residence trust, and the denominator of which is the fair market value of the assets of the trust under Article FIRST above on the Conversion Date.

(e) *Additional Contributions Prohibited.* No additional contributions shall be made to the trust under this Article THIRD.

(f) *Proration for Short Taxable Year.* In determining the amount payable for a short taxable year and for the year in which all payments terminate, the trustees shall prorate the annuity amount on a daily basis. Payments of the annuity amount shall be made from income and, to the extent that income is not sufficient, from principal. Any income for a taxable year in excess of the annuity amount shall be added to principal.

(g) *Adjustment for Incorrect Valuation of Trust Property.* If the initial annuity amount is incorrectly determined and as a result a payment to the Donor exceeds or is less than the payment required to be made hereunder, then within a reasonable period after the final determination of the correct annuity amount the trustees shall pay to the Donor (in the event of an underpayment) or shall be repaid by the Donor (in the event of an overpayment) an amount equal to the difference between the amount which the trustees should have paid and the amount which the trustees actually paid.

(h) *Prohibited Distributions.* No distributions may be made to or for the benefit of any person other than the Donor prior to the expiration of the Donor's interest as provided in paragraph (b) above.

(i) *Commutation.* The Donor's interest in the trust may not be commuted.

(j) *Use of Debt Instruments to Satisfy Payment of Annuity Amount Prohibited.* The trustees are prohibited from issuing a note, other debt instrument, option or similar financial obligation in satisfaction of the obligation to pay the annuity amount.

(k) *Intent of Trust.* The Donor's interest in the trust under this Article THIRD is intended to meet all the requirements of and to function exclusively as a qualified annuity interest within the meaning of Treasury Regulation Section 25.2702-3 (or any successor regulation thereto) and also to meet all the requirements of Treasury Regulation Section 25.2702-5(c)(8)(ii) (or any successor regulation thereto). This trust instrument shall be construed in all respects in accordance with this intent.

Practice Note

Article FOURTH establishes a trust for the benefit of the donor's issue and others. The trust will be the remainder beneficiary of the QPRT or GRAT, as applicable.

Paragraph (a) provides that, as long as the trust holds any interest in residential real estate, the donor and/or the donor's spouse will have the right to rent the real estate from the trust for fair market rent, subject to any reasonable terms and conditions that the independent trustee deems advisable. To the extent that the donor and/or the donor's spouse do not occupy the real estate, paragraph (a) provides that any one or more of the donor's issue may occupy the real estate upon such terms and conditions, and with or without the payment of rent, as the disinterested trustee may deem advisable. Paragraph (a) also provides for discretionary distributions of income and principal among the donor's issue, subject to the rights of the donor and the donor's spouse described above.

Given that a donor's generation-skipping transfer (GST) exemption cannot be fully allocated until the donor's term interest in the QPRT expires, the dispositive provisions of the trust should take into account the potential GST tax consequences under Section 2601 of the Internal Revenue Code. The model document addresses the potential GST tax consequences in two ways. First, it gives the trustees the power to add charitable or educational organizations as beneficiaries of the trust under Article FOURTH (thus avoiding direct skips and taxable terminations). Second, it provides that the remaining trust property will be retained in a "spray" trust under Article FOURTH for the benefit of the donor's issue and others and recites that the donor hopes that the disinterested trustee will give due consideration to the donor's wishes as may be expressed outside of the trust instrument. The donor could express his or her wishes that the trustees would distribute the trust property to the donor's then living children, in equal shares, thus avoiding a generation-skipping transfer since the donor's children are not skip persons.

FOURTH: Family Trust. The nominal initial funding amount and any other property provided under any Article of this trust instrument to be held in trust under this Article FOURTH shall be combined and administered (together with any additions thereto) in a single, separate trust to be known as "The [*SARAH SAMPLE*] [*YEAR*] TRUST", to be administered as follows:

(a) *Use and Management of Residential Real Estate; Distributions.* If and so long as the trust property includes any interest in residential real estate, the Donor and the Donor's said husband (or either of them alone) shall be entitled to occupy such real estate during their lifetimes subject to the payment of fair market rent and subject to such other reasonable terms and conditions as the disinterested trustee, in the disinterested trustee's discretion, thinks advisable; and if and to the extent that such real estate is not so occupied by the Donor or the Donor's said husband, any one or more of the Donor's issue may be permitted, in the discretion of the disinterested trustee, to occupy such real estate, upon such terms and conditions and with or without the payment of rent, all as the disinterested trustee, in the disinterested trustee's discretion, thinks advisable. In addition, subject to the rights of the Donor and her said husband as aforesaid, all or any part of the net income and principal may be paid to any one or more of the Donor's issue, in such amounts and at such time or times as the disinterested trustee, in the disinterested trustee's discretion, thinks advisable for any purpose, including to terminate the trust hereunder. Any net income not so paid may be added to principal at any time or times. In extension and not in limitation of the disinterested trustee's authority to make payments of net income and principal as aforesaid, the disinterested trustee, in the disinterested trustee's discretion, is hereby authorized:

(i) To make any distribution of all or any portion of the net income and principal of the trust hereunder subject to such terms, conditions and restrictions (including, without limitation, terms, conditions or restrictions regarding use or transfer) as the disinterested trustee thinks advisable; and

(ii) To distribute all or any portion of the net income and principal of the trust hereunder to (and to form or otherwise participate in the formation of) any general or limited partnership, limited liability company, business or nominee trust or other entity, all the beneficial interests in which are owned by any one or more of the trusts hereunder, the Donor's issue and any other beneficiaries under this paragraph (a) added by the disinterested trustee pursuant to paragraph (b) below.

The Donor hopes, without limiting the discretion of the disinterested trustee, that, in the exercise of the foregoing authority to make payments of net income and principal, the disinterested trustee will give due consideration to the Donor's wishes as may be expressed outside this trust instrument, if and however made known, but the Donor imposes no trust, condition or enforceable obligation of any kind in this regard.

Practice Note

Under Section 674(c) of the Internal Revenue Code, a trust will be a grantor trust with respect to the donor if an independent trustee has the power to add a beneficiary other than after-born or after-adopted children of the donor. Paragraph (b) of Article FOURTH is a provision that maintains grantor trust status after the expiration of the specified term. It gives the independent trustee the power to add one or more of the spouses of the donor's issue and charitable or educational organizations as beneficiaries and also gives the disinterested trustee the right to release this power. If the trust is a grantor trust with respect to the donor, then, for federal income tax purposes, the donor will be treated as the owner of any property (including real estate) owned by the trust. Therefore, any rent payments made by the donor would not be subject to income tax because the donor would be deemed to be making the rent payments to himself/herself. In addition, if the real estate is sold, the donor would be responsible for the payment of any tax relating to a capital gain on the sale.

(b) *Power to Add Beneficiaries.* The disinterested trustee shall have the right at any time or times, by a writing or writings delivered to the trustees, to add any one or more of the spouses of the Donor's issue and charitable or educational organizations as beneficiaries of the trust under paragraph (a) above to whom distributions of income and/or principal may be made from all or any fractional share of the trust thereunder. The disinterested trustee may also alter or amend the terms and conditions of any such beneficial interest previously given pursuant to the previous sentence, and may eliminate it entirely. The disinterested trustee may release the power given under this paragraph (b), and any such release shall be binding on all successor disinterested trustees. Any such release shall not affect the validity of any prior exercise of the power.

Practice Note

Paragraph (c) is a provision designed to ensure that the trust does not violate the rule against perpetuities.

(c) *Rule Against Perpetuities.* The trust shall terminate (if not sooner terminated as provided above) twenty (20) years after the death of the survivor of the Donor, her said husband, and the Donor's issue and the spouses of the Donor's issue, in each case who are living on the date of this trust instrument, whereupon the then remaining principal and any balance of net income shall be distributed to any one or more of the Donor's then living issue and any other beneficiaries under paragraph (a) above added by the disinterested trustee pursuant to paragraph (b) above, in such amounts or proportions to each, as the disinterested trustee, in the disinterested trustee's discretion, thinks advisable.

FIFTH: General Administrative Provisions. The trust under Article FOURTH above is subject to the following provisions:

Practice Note

Article FIFTH contains general administrative provisions. Paragraph (b) contains a spendthrift clause. It provides that creditors cannot reach the interest of a beneficiary. It also prevents a beneficiary from assigning his or her interest.

(a) Whenever a payment of income or principal is to be made to any beneficiary but the beneficiary has not reached the age of twenty-one (21) or is ill or away or because of other circumstances it is impracticable or undesirable, in the opinion of the disinterested trustee, to make such payment directly to the beneficiary, the disinterested trustee, in the disinterested trustee's discretion, may apply such payment for the beneficiary's benefit in such manner as the disinterested trustee thinks best for the beneficiary, regardless of the beneficiary's other resources. Such application for the beneficiary's benefit and any payment to a beneficiary who has not reached the age of twenty-one (21) may be made in any amount, either directly or through a guardian, custodian or member of the family of the beneficiary or by payment to the beneficiary in person even though he or she has not reached the age of twenty-one (21) or is incapacitated; and the receipt of the payee shall, with respect to each such payment, be a sufficient discharge to the trustees so that they need not see to the further application thereof. Notwithstanding any other provisions of this trust instrument, no payment may be made hereunder which discharges a legal obligation of the Donor or of an individual serving as a disinterested trustee.

(b) The interest of each beneficiary, and all payments of income or principal to be made to or for any beneficiary, shall be free from interference or control by any creditor, spouse or divorced former spouse of the beneficiary and shall not be capable of anticipation or assignment by the beneficiary.

(c) In this trust instrument, references to "issue" mean descendants in the first, second or any other degree; in each case meaning lawful descendants of the ancestor designated, whether by blood or by adoption (finalized while the adoptee is under the age of twenty-one (21)) and whether living on the date of this trust instrument or born or adopted thereafter. For purposes of the preceding sentence, a person born out of wedlock and those claiming through that person shall be treated as lawful descendants (i) of the natural mother and her ancestors and (ii) if the natural father acknowledges paternity, of the natural father and his ancestors, in each case unless a decree of adoption terminates such natural parent's parental rights. References in this trust instrument to a "spouse" or to "spouses" include a widow or widower, whether or not remarried, but do not include a divorced former spouse.

(d) The disinterested trustee, in the disinterested trustee's discretion, may divide the trust under Article FOURTH above into two or more separate trusts of equal or unequal value, to be administered in the aggregate on the same terms as the original trust.

Practice Note

Article SIXTH sets forth the powers of the trustees of the trusts under Article THIRD and FOURTH, and recites that these powers cannot be exercised in a manner which would disqualify the trust under Article THIRD as a GRAT. While state law frequently grants a series of default powers to trustees, it is good drafting practice to set forth the powers expressly. This eliminates ambiguities in local law, may expand the scope of the trustees' authority, and may avoid the need for court approval of certain actions. The list of powers is general and should cover most situations.

SIXTH: Trustees' Powers. In extension and not in limitation of the powers given the trustees by law or other provisions of this trust instrument, the trustees of the trusts under Articles THIRD and FOURTH above shall have the following powers with respect to the trust and its property, in each case to be exercised from time to time in the discretion of the trustees and without order or license of court; *provided* that, with respect to any trust under Article THIRD above, each such power shall be subject in all respects to the provisions of paragraph (k) of Article THIRD above and shall not be exercised or exercisable in a way which would cause the Donor's interest in that trust to fail or cease to qualify as a qualified annuity interest:

(a) To retain indefinitely, and to invest and reinvest in, stocks, shares, general or limited partnership interests, obligations and other securities or any other kind of personal or real property (including any entity described in paragraph (a)(ii) of Article FOURTH above), even though any or all of the investments made or retained are of a character or size which, but for this express authority, would not be considered proper for a trustee; and, in addition, to associate and to become and act as a partner, general or limited, or as a joint venturer in any partnership, venture or enterprise, or as a member of a limited liability company with and at the risk of any and all of the assets of the trust;

(b) To sell, to exchange, to lease and to make contracts concerning any real or personal property, for such consideration and upon such terms as to credit or otherwise as the trustees consider advisable, which leases and contracts may extend beyond the term of the trust; to give options on real or personal property of the trust; to establish depreciation, depletion, tax or any other reserves; to execute deeds, transfers, leases and other instruments of any kind;

(c) To hold securities or other property in bearer or unregistered form or in the name of one or more of the trustees or of any other person, firm or corporation, with or without indication of any fiduciary capacity;

(d) To give general or special proxies or powers of attorney (which may or may not be discretionary and with power of substitution) for voting or acting with respect to securities to any person other than the Donor; to deposit securities with, or transfer them to, protective committees, voting trustees, or similar bodies; to join in any reorganization; and to pay assessments or subscriptions called for in connection with securities held by the trustees;

(e) To compromise or submit to arbitration any tax, claim or matter in dispute;

(f) If in the opinion of the trustees it is necessary or advisable to do so, to borrow money for such time and at such rate of interest or discount as the trustees deem proper; to give notes or obligations therefor binding the trust property; and as security therefor to mortgage or to pledge real or personal property with or without power of sale;

(g) To credit particular receipts or gains, and to charge particular disbursements or losses or charges, to income or to principal of the trust or to apportion them between income and principal, whether such credits or charges relate to bonds acquired at a premium, to reserves or to any other matter, all as the trustees consider fair and reasonable in each case;

(h) To manage, improve or develop real estate; to construct, alter, repair or demolish buildings or structures; to settle boundary lines and easements and other rights; to partition; and to join with co-owners or others in dealing with real estate in any way; to investigate, prevent and remediate violations or possible violations of federal, state or local law regarding substances posing a hazard to the environment or to human health which may be applicable to any property held by the trustees and to undertake such actions prior to the formal enforcement of such laws by any federal, state or local agency against trust property; and to charge all expenses associated with any such investigation, prevention or remediation, including the fees of consultants and counsel, against the income or principal of the trust holding the property;

(i) To employ investment counsel and consult with them concerning the investments and management of the trust and to delegate to such counsel such powers as the trustees deem appropriate; to employ agents and to delegate to such agents such powers as the trustees deem appropriate; to employ legal counsel, accountants and any special services; to employ a custodian of any funds or securities and to delegate to the custodian such powers as the trustees deem appropriate; and, in addition to the compensation and expenses of the trustees, to pay the compensation and expenses of all such services, even if rendered by a trustee;

(j) To participate as a seller or purchaser in private placements, secondary offerings and other regulated or special transactions, and to execute and deliver such instruments and take such action as is customary or, in the opinion of the trustees, appropriate in connection therewith, including investment representations, indemnity agreements, pledges and guarantees binding the trust property;

(k) To organize a corporation, limited liability company, limited partnership, real estate trust or other suitable entity under the laws of any state or country at any time prior to the final distribution or sale of all of the trust property and to transfer thereto all or any part of any interest in real property or other property held in this trust (including such property which in the disinterested trustee's discretion is necessary in order to maintain, improve and pay for the management of said real property) and to receive in exchange therefor such stocks, bonds, certificates of beneficial interest and other securities in such manner and amounts as they deem appropriate; and

(l) To make any division or distribution of, or payment from, the trust in kind, by the fair and reasonable allotment and transfer of specific securities or other personal or real property or undivided interests therein, at then current values, in lieu of cash, as a part or the whole of any one or more shares or payments.

In addition, in the case of the trust under Article FOURTH above (and no other trust under this instrument), the trustees shall have the power from time to time, in their discretion and without order or license of court, to accept additions to the trust, whether by gift or will or transfer from any other trust established by the Donor or her said husband or otherwise.

Practice Note

This paragraph is required for all QPRTs. The trust instrument must prohibit the trustees from selling or transferring the residence directly or indirectly to the donor, the donor's spouse, or an entity controlled by the donor or the donor's spouse, during the specified term or at any time after the expiration of the specified term when the trust is a grantor trust. A sale or transfer to another grantor trust of the donor or the donor's spouse is considered a sale or transfer to the donor or the donor's spouse.

This prohibition does not apply to a distribution for no consideration either: (1) to another grantor trust of the donor or the donor's spouse, if the distributee grantor trust includes the same prohibition against a sale or transfer; (2) to the donor's spouse after the term of the QPRT; or (3) if the donor dies prior to the expiration of the specified term, to any person pursuant to the trust instrument or the exercise of the donor's retained power of appointment.

Notwithstanding any other provisions of this trust instrument, the trustees are prohibited from selling or transferring the Residence, directly or indirectly, to the Donor, any spouse of the Donor or any entity controlled by the Donor or by any spouse of the Donor, including any trust which is a grantor trust (as defined in Sections 671 through 677 of the Code) with respect to the Donor or any spouse of the Donor. This prohibition shall continue after the termination date, for so long as the Residence is held in a trust hereunder which is a grantor trust (as defined) with respect to the Donor or any spouse of the Donor.

Practice Note

Article SEVENTH includes a number of provisions relating to the trustees. It provides for voluntary and involuntary resignations. It also gives the donor, the donor's spouse, and the donor's adult children the right to remove trustees. No estate tax problems are caused by the retention and granting of the removal right. The model document names additional trustees to serve under the trust under Article FOURTH when it is funded, and creates a mechanism for appointing successor trustees of each trust under the trust instrument.

The Article also waives the requirements of bond or surety. Finally, it provides that a third party dealing with the trustees need not look into the validity of the trustees' actions but can assume that the trustees are authorized to act.

SEVENTH: Trustees. References in this trust instrument to the "trustees" mean, with respect to each trust hereunder, the one or more trustees, whether original, additional or successor, for the time being in office; and references to the "disinterested trustee" mean the one or more trustees other than the Donor and her said husband having no beneficial interest, whether vested or contingent, in the income or the principal of any trust hereunder. If the Donor shall serve as a trustee of any trust hereunder, the Donor shall cease to serve as a trustee thirty (30) days prior to the xxxth (XXth) anniversary of the date on which this trust instrument is executed, or upon the Donor's earlier resignation.

Any trustee may resign by giving written notice to the Donor, if she is then living, or if not, to her said husband, if he is then living, or if not, to the remaining trustees, if any, or if none, to the one or more persons to whom the trustees would then render accounts of the particular trust as provided in Article EIGHTH below. Any individual trustee (including the Donor) shall be deemed to have resigned and any named individual successor trustee shall be deemed unable to serve if a legal guardian or similar legal representative is or has been appointed for such individual or upon the receipt by the one or more persons (other than such trustee) then entitled to appoint successor trustees as provided below of a writing signed by the individual's regularly attending physician certifying that, in the physician's opinion, such individual is mentally or physically incapable of discharging the responsibilities of a trustee.

Any trustee may be removed by a writing delivered to such trustee and signed by the Donor, if she is then living and of full legal capacity, or if not, by her said husband, if he is then living and of full legal capacity. After both the Donor and her said husband have died, any trustee may be removed by a writing delivered to such trustee and signed by a majority of the Donor's children who are then living and of full legal capacity. Notwithstanding the foregoing, (a) no such removal of a disinterested trustee, other than by the Donor prior to the xxxth (XXth) anniversary of the date on which this trust instrument is executed, shall be effective until a successor disinterested trustee who is not a "related or subordinate party" (within the meaning of Section 672(c) of the Code) with respect to any person effecting such removal has been appointed by the one or more persons effecting the removal and has accepted the office in writing, and (b) no such removal of a disinterested trustee by any one or more of the Donor's children shall be effective unless such successor disinterested trustee is a professional trustee (meaning a national bank, a trust company or an individual who is a member of a partnership or other association the members of which are engaged regularly in the management of trusts and have collectively under active trust administration assets of at least One Billion Dollars ($1,000,000,000)).

Upon and following the funding of the trust under Article FOURTH above (not including the nominal initial funding thereof), there shall regularly be at least one disinterested trustee of such trust; and upon the funding of such trust (not including such nominal initial funding), [NAME OF TRUSTEE], of [CITY], [STATE], and [NAME OF TRUSTEE], of [CITY], [STATE], shall become additional trustees thereof. If for any reason either of them fails to accept the office or, having accepted, later ceases to serve as a trustee, and in case of any other vacancy in the office of trustee of any trust hereunder not filled as provided above, a successor trustee may be appointed by a writing signed by the Donor, if she is then living and of full legal capacity, or if not, by her said husband, if he is then living and of full legal capacity, or if not, by the remaining trustees, if any, or if none, by the one or more persons of full legal capacity to whom the trustees would then render accounts of the particular trust as provided in Article EIGHTH below.

One or more other additional trustees may be appointed at any time or times, to take office presently or at any future time and upon such other terms and conditions, all as specified in a writing signed by the Donor, if she is then living and of full legal capacity, or if not, by her said husband, if he is then living and of full legal capacity, or if not, by the trustees then in office. Any such appointment may be revoked in writing by the one or more persons having made the appointment at any time before it becomes effective. No appointment of a successor trustee or an additional trustee shall take effect without written acceptance of the office.

Pending the filling of a vacancy, the surviving or remaining trustee shall have, and may exercise, all the powers and discretions of the trustees; *provided* that the powers and discretions given to the disinterested trustee, as such, shall be exercised by the disinterested trustee alone, exclusive of any other of the trustees, and may be delegated only to another disinterested trustee. Except as otherwise provided above, whenever there is more than one trustee in office, any trustee may delegate in writing all or any of that trustee's powers and discretions to any other trustee for a period specified in such writing, and may revoke or successively renew such delegation.

No trustee named herein or appointed as above provided need furnish any bond or surety. No one dealing with the trustees need inquire concerning the validity of anything the trustees purport to do or need see to the application of any money paid or property transferred to or upon the order of the trustees. No trustee shall be liable for any loss that may occur by reason of depreciation in the value of any assets of any trust hereunder, or for any other type of loss that may occur to the trust, absent a showing of gross negligence or intentional wrongdoing. No trustee shall be liable for the acts or omissions of any agent, custodian or other person or entity to which the trustee's duties have been delegated properly, provided that such agent, custodian or other person or entity was retained and is supervised with due care. No trustee shall be liable or responsible for the acts or omissions within the sole power and discretion of any other trustee, and no trustee shall have any duty or liability for, or duty or liability for failure to rectify, the acts or omissions of any predecessor trustee. No trustee shall incur any personal liability to any third party who deals with the trustee in the administration of any trust hereunder. Each trustee shall be entitled to reimbursement from the trust property for any liability incurred in the administration of any trust hereunder in accordance with the provisions hereof and shall be entitled to contract in the administration of any such trust in a form as to exempt the trustee from any personal liability and to cause such liability to be limited to the assets of the trust.

Practice Note

Trust instruments should address the manner in which trustees account to the beneficiaries. Article EIGHTH clarifies the trustees' obligations. In the model form, accounts for a trust are to be rendered to each beneficiary who is eligible to receive a distribution from the trust. In the event that a beneficiary is not of full legal capacity, accounts will be rendered to the beneficiary's legal guardian or representative or, if none, to either of the beneficiary's parents if the beneficiary is a minor.

EIGHTH: Accounts. The trustees of each trust hereunder other than the trust under Article FIRST above shall render an account of the trust at least as often as annually to each beneficiary to whom in the period covered by such account distributions were required to be made or could be made in the discretion of the disinterested trustee, if the beneficiary is living and of full legal capacity, or if the beneficiary is not of full legal capacity, to his or her legal guardian or similar legal representative, if any, or if none, to either of his or her parents if he or she is a minor. In the case of each trust hereunder, the written assent to any such account by each person of full legal capacity to whom it is rendered as provided above shall fully protect the trustees as to all matters or transactions stated in such account or shown thereby, even if such person is serving as a trustee hereunder. Any person who is not of full legal capacity shall be deemed to assent to such account if his or her legal guardian or similar legal representative assents in writing to the account or if (such beneficiary being a minor and having no such legal guardian or representative) the parent to whom the account was rendered assents in writing to the account. Nothing in this Article shall be deemed to give anyone the power to modify the terms of this trust instrument or to alter or shift any beneficial interest created hereunder.

Practice Note

A QPRT must be irrevocable. However, a modification of a QPRT to comply with the QPRT requirements set forth under the Treasury Regulations is possible under certain circumstances.

NINTH: Irrevocable; Limited Amendment. This trust instrument and the trusts hereunder shall be irrevocable and shall not be subject to alteration or amendment; *provided* that the trustees other than the Donor may in writing amend this trust instrument at any time or times solely (a) to enable the trust under Article FIRST above to qualify or continue to qualify as a qualified personal residence trust, or to enable the Donor's interest in any trust under Article THIRD above to qualify or continue to qualify as a qualified annuity interest under Treasury Regulation Section 25.2702-3 and Treasury Regulation Section 25.2702-5(c)(8)(ii), or (b) to the extent consistent with clause (a) above, to take advantage of any additional powers and discretions, not granted under this trust instrument, which may be given to the trustees of a qualified personal residence trust under future applicable Treasury Regulations or amendments to Section 2702 of the Code; *provided* that nothing in this Article shall be deemed to give anyone the power to alter or shift any beneficial interest created hereunder.

Practice Note

Article TENTH addresses trust documentation. It places an obligation on the trustees to establish secure arrangements for the custody of all documents that are related to the trust. It also provides that outside parties may rely on certified copies of the original documentation.

TENTH: Trust Documentation. The original of each amendment of this trust instrument by the trustees as provided in Article NINTH above, each resignation, removal or appointment of a trustee, each acceptance of appointment and each instrument of delegation shall be kept attached to the original of this trust instrument, which shall be held by the trustees. Anyone may rely on a copy certified by a notary public of the original of this trust instrument or of any writings attached thereto as fully as on the original document; and anyone may rely fully upon any statements of fact certified by anyone who appears from the original document or a certified copy thereof to be a trustee hereunder.

Practice Note

Article ELEVENTH sets forth the jurisdiction that will govern the operation of each trust under the trust instrument. A governing law clause will generally be upheld as long as the state chosen has some logical connection to the trust. This Article also gives the disinterested trustee the power to change the situs of administration of any trust under the instrument to another jurisdiction that has a connection to the trust, and provides that if the situs of administration of a trust is changed, the laws of the new jurisdiction will govern the administration of the trust (but not the validity of the trust or the construction of its language, which will remain governed by the laws of the original jurisdiction).

ELEVENTH: Governing Law. This trust instrument and the trusts hereunder shall be governed, construed and administered in accordance with the laws of [NAME OF STATE] from time to time in force. The disinterested trustee may from time to time by a writing change the situs of administration of any trust hereunder from one jurisdiction to another that has a connection to the trust, in which case the laws of such other jurisdiction shall govern the administration of the trust (but not the validity of the trust or the construction of the language of this trust instrument, both of which shall always be governed by [STATE] law).

SIGNED and SEALED this _____ day of _____, 20 _____.

_____
[*SARAH SAMPLE*], Donor and Trustee

_____
[*NAME*] _____, Trustee

STATE/COMMONWEALTH OF [*NAME OF STATE*]

_____, ss.

On this _____ day of _____, 20_____, before me, the undersigned notary public, personally appeared [SARAH SAMPLE], who proved to me through satisfactory evidence of identification, which was _____, that she is the person whose name is signed on the foregoing document, and who acknowledged to me that she signed it voluntarily for its stated purpose.

_____

Notary Public
My Commission Expires:

FORM 16
Grantor Retained Annuity Trust (GRAT)

Overview

This form establishes a grantor retained annuity trust (a "GRAT"). A GRAT is an irrevocable trust to which a donor contributes assets and retains the right to receive annual payments (the "annuity") from the trust for a specified term of years. A GRAT creates two distinct interests. First, the donor retains the right to receive an annuity interest for a fixed period of years. Second, at the end of the specified term, the trust property passes outright to (or in further trust for) one or more remainder beneficiaries other than the donor.

A GRAT must include certain provisions required by Internal Revenue Code Section 2702(a)(2)(B) and Treasury Regulation Section 25.2702-3(b).

The goal of a GRAT is to enable the donor to transfer property to the remainder beneficiaries at a low gift tax cost (or no gift tax cost). The remainder beneficiaries receive the property at the end of the specified term; however, for gift tax purposes, the value of the donor's gift is equal to the value of the property when it is transferred to the GRAT minus the present value of the donor's retained right to receive the annuity payments. The present value of the donor's retained annuity depends upon a number of factors, including the annuity payment rate, the term of the donor's retained annuity, and the applicable discount rate (the Section 7520 rate) in the month in which the GRAT is funded. For a GRAT to be successful, the donor must survive the specified annuity term, which should be a consideration when selecting the annuity term.

This form can be used to establish a "zeroed-out" GRAT, where the donor retains an annuity interest with a present value that is approximately equal to the value of the assets transferred to the GRAT. This will produce a minimal taxable gift, and thus result in the use of only a small amount of the donor's gift tax exemption amount or a small payment of gift tax. If the donor survives the specified term, the remainder interest will be transferred to the remainder beneficiaries and removed from the donor's estate with no further payment of estate or gift tax. If the donor does not survive the specified term, or if there is no property remaining in the trust after the annuity payments are made to the donor, the GRAT will not achieve the anticipated tax savings, and all (or substantially all) of the trust property will be included in the donor's estate for estate tax purposes; however, other than transaction costs, the donor will be in no worse position than if he or she had never established the GRAT.

THE SARAH SAMPLE [*YEAR*] ANNUITY TRUST

Practice Note

The opening paragraph identifies the settlor of the trust (the "donor") and the initial trustee or trustees. The donor's full legal name should be used, and a statement of the donor's residence included. There are no requirements regarding who may act as a trustee of a GRAT or the number of trustees. The donor could serve as the sole trustee during the specified term, but should resign prior to the end of the specified term to prevent the trust property from being includable in the donor's estate for estate tax purposes where the trust property would not otherwise be includable.

The donor may transfer most types of assets to a GRAT; however, GRATs are most effective when the current value of the assets is low (for example, because of a downturn in the market or the availability of valuation discounts) and significant future appreciation is expected. When these elements are present, it is likely that the trust assets will appreciate more than the Section 7520 rate in effect at the time of the GRAT's establishment, and as a result, assets will remain in the GRAT at the end of the donor's annuity term and pass to the remainder beneficiaries without the payment of any gift tax at that time.

A donor should be aware that funding a GRAT with some types of business assets can create certain business problems or problems under Section 16(b) of the Securities Exchange Act of 1934 ("Section 16(b)") (with respect to interests in public companies), Section 2036(b) of the Internal Revenue Code (with respect to transfers of voting stock in a controlled corporation), or Section 2701 of the Internal Revenue Code (which for certain interests in a corporation or partnership requires a gift tax value that is significantly more than fair market value). If the donor is transferring assets of a closely held entity, the donor should also confirm that the transfer of assets to the GRAT satisfies any applicable transfer restrictions imposed by the entity.

SARAH SAMPLE, of [*ADDRESS*] (the "Donor"), herewith transfers the property described in Schedule A annexed hereto to [*NAME OF TRUSTEE #1*], of [*ADDRESS*], and [*NAME OF TRUSTEE #2*], of [*ADDRESS*], as trustees hereunder; and the trustees hereby acknowledge receipt thereof and agree, for themselves, any additional trustees and all successors in office, to hold said property, IRREVOCABLY IN TRUST, upon the following terms and provisions:

FIRST: Annuity Trust.

(a) *Name of Trust.* The trust under this Article FIRST shall be known as "THE SARAH SAMPLE [*YEAR*] ANNUITY TRUST."

Practice Note

This provision provides that the donor will retain the right to receive an annuity for the specified term. The annuity for the first year is expressed as a fraction of the initial fair market value of the assets transferred to the GRAT, as finally determined for federal gift tax purposes.

Each subsequent annuity payment will be 120% of the amount of the payment for the preceding year. The regulations permit the annuity to increase by up to 20% each year. Using a graduated annuity will often be advantageous from a gift tax perspective, particularly when the donor expects the assets contributed to the GRAT to appreciate rapidly after the transfer to the GRAT. Lower annuity payments in the early years will give the GRAT assets a greater opportunity to appreciate in value in the early years.

The regulations also permit the annuity amount to be defined as a stated dollar amount, but the percentage formula is preferable for hard-to-value assets. If a stated dollar amount is used for the annuity amount and the IRS is able to establish a higher value for the assets contributed to a GRAT than the value the donor reports on his or her gift tax return, the amount of the donor's taxable gift will increase by the excess. With a GRAT that uses the percentage methodology, if the IRS establishes a higher value for the assets contributed to the GRAT, there is a commensurate increase in the value of the donor's retained annuity, because each annual annuity payment is a specified percentage of the initial value of the trust assets as finally determined for federal gift tax purposes. As a result, the amount of the donor's taxable gift will not increase.

Selecting the length of the annuity term is important when drafting a GRAT. As the length of the term increases, the length of the period to outperform the Section 7520 hurdle rate for the month the GRAT was funded increases and the size of the annuity payments required to minimize (or zero out) the taxable gift made on funding the GRAT decreases. However, the donor must survive the specified term to achieve the estate tax objective of the GRAT. If the donor dies before the expiration of the term, substantially all of the GRAT's assets will be includable in the donor's estate for estate tax purposes. A shorter term provides the donor with the greatest likelihood of surviving the term and removing the appreciation in the GRAT assets from his or her estate and also minimizes the risk that a few years of poor investment performance will eliminate the gains from other years. With a shorter term, the donor may use a "rolling GRAT" strategy by transferring each annuity payment received from the existing GRAT to a new GRAT.

If the donor dies during the annuity term, the document provides that any annuity payments payable after the donor's death must be paid to the donor's estate for the balance of the term. This is required to comply with the *Walton* decision, 115 T.C. 589 (2000) and Treasury Regulation Section 25.2702-3(e), example 5.

(b) *Annuity Amount; Term of Trust.* Until the expiration of the annuity trust term, the trustees shall pay to or apply for the benefit of the Donor, from the assets of the trust, an annuity equal to the "annuity amount", calculated in the following manner. For the first year of the annuity trust term, the "annuity amount" shall be an amount equal to [XX] percent ([XX]%) of the "initial net fair market value" of the property transferred to the trust. For each succeeding year of the annuity trust term, the "annuity amount" shall be an amount equal to one hundred twenty percent (120%) of the annuity amount for the preceding year of the annuity trust term. The "annuity trust term" shall be the [YY] ([YY]) year period commencing on the date on which the property listed on Schedule A shall be irrevocably assigned, transferred, and conveyed to the trustees (the "Funding Date"). If the Donor shall die during the annuity trust term, the annuity shall be paid to the Donor's estate for the balance of such term. For purposes of determining the annuity amount, the "initial net fair market value" of the property transferred to the trust shall be the fair market value of such property on the Funding Date, as determined by the disinterested trustee (based upon such information as such trustee shall determine to be appropriate), or such other amount as may finally be determined for federal gift tax purposes.

Practice Note

The annuity amount must be payable to the donor at least annually for each taxable year of the term. The annuity amount may be payable based on the anniversary date of the creation of the GRAT or on the taxable year of the GRAT. If the annuity amount is payable based on the anniversary date of the creation of the GRAT, it must be paid no later than 105 days after the anniversary date. An annuity amount payable based on the taxable year of the GRAT may be paid after the close of the taxable year, provided that it is made by the due date of the GRAT's federal income tax return (determined without regard to extensions). It is generally preferable to use a 12-month period ending on the anniversary date of the creation of the GRAT because this allows the assets in the GRAT to increase in value for as long as possible before each annuity payment must be made.

(c) *Payment of Annuity Amount.* The annuity amount shall be payable to or for the benefit of the Donor or to the Donor's estate, as applicable, annually during the annuity trust term, on the day before each anniversary of the Funding Date (each, an "anniversary date"). An annuity payment may be made after the anniversary date, provided the payment is made no later than one hundred five (105) days after the anniversary date. The annuity shall be paid from the income and, to the extent that income is not sufficient, from the principal of the trust. Except as otherwise provided in paragraph (b) of Article NINTH of this instrument, any income of the trust in excess of the annuity amount for any year during the annuity trust term shall be added to principal. The trust under this article is sometimes hereinafter referred to as the "annuity trust" and is expressly subject to the provisions of Article SIXTH of this instrument.

Practice Note

The donor must decide how to structure the remainder interest in the GRAT after the expiration of the specified term. The remaining GRAT assets may either pass outright to the remainder beneficiaries or be held in trust for the benefit of the remainder beneficiaries.

If the donor survives the specified term, the model document provides that the remaining GRAT assets will be paid to a separate free-standing grantor trust for the benefit of the donor's children and their issue. Using a separate trust will avoid any argument that the donor retained any interest in the remainder that would cause estate tax inclusion in the donor's estate. Structuring the separate trust as a grantor trust will enable the donor to continue to pay the income taxes attributable to the trust income without making additional taxable gifts to the remainder beneficiaries. To

---

prevent a taxable termination for generation-skipping transfer tax purposes, the beneficiaries of the separate trust should include the donor's children and/or individuals who, for generation-skipping transfer tax purposes, are assigned to generations higher than the donor's children (such as the donor's spouse).

If the donor does not survive the specified term, substantially all of the value of the GRAT assets will be includable in the donor's estate for estate tax purposes. The *Walton* decision and Treasury Regulation Section 25.2703-3(e), example 5 require that the annuity payments must be made to the donor's estate for the balance of the specified term. If the donor wishes to obtain a marital deduction in this circumstance, special guidelines exist as to how to obtain this result.

If the donor does not survive the specified term and if the donor's spouse survives the donor, the model document provides that the fractional share of the remaining GRAT assets that are includable in the donor's estate for estate tax purposes will be distributed outright to the donor's spouse (or the spouse's estate if the spouse shall not be living on the expiration of the specified term), thereby deferring any estate taxes attributable to the includable GRAT assets until the spouse's later death. If the donor's spouse does not survive the donor, the model document provides that the remaining GRAT assets will be disposed of as though the donor had survived the specified term.

SECOND: Disposition of Trust Property Upon Expiration of Annuity Trust Term. Upon the expiration of the annuity trust term, the trustees shall dispose of the remaining trust property (other than any amount due the Donor or the Donor's estate) as follows:

(a) *Donor Living.* If the Donor shall then be living, the trustees shall pay over such property to the trustees then acting under the SARAH SAMPLE [*YEAR*] FAMILY TRUST, established by a Trust Agreement made the [*DATE*] day of [*MONTH*], [*YEAR*] between SARAH SAMPLE, as Donor, and [*TRUSTEE 1*] and [*TRUSTEE 2*], as trustees, to be added to the property held in trust thereunder, and to be held, administered and distributed in accordance with the provisions of said Trust Agreement.

(b) *Donor Not Living; Donor's Husband Living.* If the Donor shall not then be living, but the Donor's husband, [*NAME*], shall have survived the Donor, the trustees shall pay over the remaining trust property to the Donor's said husband (or his estate, if he shall not then be living). Notwithstanding the provisions of the preceding sentence, if less than the entire value of the property of the annuity trust is includable in the value of the Donor's gross estate as finally determined for federal estate tax purposes, the trustees shall pay over to the Donor's said husband the "Marital Share" (as hereinafter defined) of the remaining trust property, and the trustees shall dispose of the "Excluded Share" (as hereinafter defined) of the remaining trust property as provided in paragraph (a) of this article, as if the Donor had then been living. The "Marital Share" and the "Excluded Share" shall be determined in the following manner: as of the date of the Donor's death, the trustees shall divide the trust property into two shares, an Excluded Share and a Marital Share. The Excluded Share shall consist of that fraction of the trust property which is not includable in the value of the Donor's gross estate as finally determined for federal estate tax purposes, and the Marital Share shall consist of the balance of the trust property. To the extent the Marital Share shall have sufficient assets, all remaining payments to the Donor's estate under Article FIRST of this instrument and clause (i) of paragraph (b) of Article NINTH of this instrument during the annuity trust term shall be made from the Marital Share until the Marital Share has been exhausted and then from the Excluded Share.

(c) *Donor and Donor's Husband Not Living.* If the Donor shall not then be living and if the Donor's said husband shall not have survived the Donor, the trustees shall pay over the remaining trust property as provided in paragraph (a) of this article, as if the Donor had then been living.

Practice Note

Article THIRD includes a number of provisions relating to the trustees. It provides for voluntary and involuntary resignations. It also gives the donor, the donor's spouse, and the donor's adult children the right to remove trustees.

The article also waives the requirement of bond or surety. Finally, it provides that a third party dealing with the trustees need not look into the validity of the trustees' actions but can assume that the trustees are authorized to act.

THIRD: Trustees. References in this trust instrument to the "trustees" mean, with respect to each trust hereunder, the one or more trustees, whether original, additional or successor, for the time being in office; and references to the "disinterested trustee" mean the one or more trustees other than the Donor and her said husband who have no beneficial interest, whether vested or contingent, in the income or the principal of any trust hereunder or under the aforementioned SARAH SAMPLE [YEAR] FAMILY TRUST. If the Donor shall serve as a trustee of any trust hereunder, the Donor shall cease to serve as a trustee thirty (30) days prior to the expiration of the annuity trust term, or upon the Donor's earlier resignation.

Any trustee may resign by giving written notice to the Donor, if she is then living, or if not, to her said husband, if he is then living, or if not, to the remaining trustees, if any, or if none, to the one or more persons to whom the trustees would then render accounts of the particular trust as provided in Article EIGHTH below. Any individual trustee (including the Donor) shall be deemed to have resigned and any named individual successor trustee shall be deemed unable to serve if a legal guardian or similar legal representative is or has been appointed for such individual or upon the receipt by the one or more persons (other than such trustee) then entitled to appoint successor trustees as provided below of a writing signed by the individual's regularly attending physician certifying that, in the physician's opinion, such individual is mentally or physically incapable of discharging the responsibilities of a trustee.

Any trustee may be removed by a writing delivered to such trustee and signed by the Donor, if she is then living and of full legal capacity, or if not, by her said husband, if he is then living and of full legal capacity. After both the

Donor and her said husband have died, any trustee may be removed by a writing delivered to such trustee and signed by a majority of the Donor's children who are then living and of full legal capacity. Notwithstanding the foregoing, (a) no such removal of a disinterested trustee, other than by the Donor prior to the expiration of the annuity trust term, shall be effective until a successor disinterested trustee who is not a "related or subordinate party" (within the meaning of Section 672(c) of the Code) with respect to any person effecting such removal has been appointed by the one or more persons effecting the removal and has accepted the office in writing, and (b) no such removal of a disinterested trustee by any one or more of the Donor's children shall be effective unless such successor disinterested trustee is a professional trustee (meaning a national bank, a trust company or an individual who is a member of a partnership or other association the members of which are engaged regularly in the management of trusts and have collectively under active trust administration assets of at least One Billion Dollars ($1,000,000,000)).

There need not be more than one trustee for the time being in office of each trust hereunder, but there shall regularly be at least one disinterested trustee of each such trust. In the event of the first vacancy in the office of trustee, [*TRUSTEE 3*] of [*ADDRESS*], shall become a successor trustee, upon written acceptance of the office. If for any reason [*TRUSTEE 3*] fails to accept the appointment or, having accepted, later ceases to serve, and in the event of any other vacancy in the office of trustee of any trust hereunder not filled as provided above, a successor trustee may be appointed by a writing signed by the Donor, if she is then living and of full legal capacity, or if not, by her said husband, if he is then living and of full legal capacity, or if not, by the remaining trustees, if any, or if none, by the one or more persons of full legal capacity to whom the trustees would then render accounts of the particular trust as provided in Article EIGHTH below.

One or more other additional trustees may be appointed at any time or times, to take office presently or at any future time and upon such other terms and conditions, all as specified in a writing signed by the Donor, if she is then living and of full legal capacity, or if not, by her said husband, if he is then living and of full legal capacity, or if not, by the trustees then in office. Any such appointment may be revoked in writing by the one or more persons having made the appointment at any time before it becomes effective. No appointment of a successor trustee or an additional trustee shall take effect without written acceptance of the office.

Pending the filling of a vacancy, the surviving or remaining trustee(s) shall have, and may exercise, all the powers and discretions of the trustees; *provided* that the powers and discretions given to the disinterested trustee, as such, shall be exercised by the disinterested trustee alone, exclusive of any other of the trustees, and may be delegated only to another disinterested trustee. Except as otherwise provided above, whenever there is more than one trustee in office, any trustee may delegate in writing all or any of that trustee's powers and discretions to any other trustee for a period specified in such writing, and may revoke or successively renew such delegation.

No trustee named herein or appointed as above provided need furnish any bond or surety. No one dealing with the trustees need inquire concerning the validity of anything the trustees purport to do or need see to the application of any money paid or property transferred to or upon the order of the trustees. No trustee shall be liable for any loss that may occur by reason of depreciation in the value of any assets of any trust hereunder, or for any other type of loss that may occur to the trust, absent a showing of gross negligence or intentional wrongdoing. No trustee shall be liable for the acts or omissions of any agent, custodian or other person or entity to which the trustee's duties have been delegated properly, provided that such agent, custodian or other person or entity was retained and is supervised with due care. No trustee shall be liable or responsible for the acts or omissions within the sole power and discretion of any other trustee, and no trustee shall have any duty or liability for, or duty or liability for failure to rectify, the acts or omissions of any predecessor trustee. No trustee shall incur any personal liability to any third party who deals with the trustee in the administration of any trust hereunder. Each trustee shall be entitled to reimbursement from the trust property for any liability incurred in the administration of any trust hereunder in accordance with the provisions hereof and shall be entitled to contract in the administration of any such trust in a form as to exempt the trustee from any personal liability and to cause such liability to be limited to the assets of the trust.

Practice Note

Article FOURTH provides general administrative provisions and recites that these powers cannot be exercised in a manner which would disqualify the GRAT. While state law frequently grants a series of default powers to trustees, it is good drafting practice to set forth the powers expressly. This eliminates ambiguities in local law, may expand the scope of the trustees' authority, and may avoid the need for court approval of certain actions. The list of powers is general and should cover most situations.

FOURTH: Trustees' Powers. In extension and not in limitation of the powers given the trustees by law or other provisions of this trust instrument (but subject to the provisions of this instrument applicable to the annuity trust), the trustees shall have the following powers with respect to the trust and its property, in each case to be exercised from time to time in the discretion of the trustees and without order or license of court:

(a) To retain indefinitely, and to invest and reinvest in, stocks, shares, general or limited partnership interests, obligations and other securities or any other kind of personal or real property, even though any or all of the investments made or retained are of a character or size which, but for this express authority, would not be considered proper for a trustee; and, in addition, to associate and to become and act as a partner, general or limited, or as a joint venturer in any partnership, venture or enterprise, or as a member of a limited liability company with and at the risk of any and all of the assets of the trust;

(b) To sell, to exchange, to lease and to make contracts concerning any real or personal property, for such consideration and upon such terms as to credit or otherwise as the trustees consider advisable, which leases and contracts may extend beyond the term of the trust; to give options on real or personal property of the trust; to establish depreciation, depletion, tax or any other reserves; to execute deeds, transfers, leases and other instruments of any kind;

(c) To hold securities or other property in bearer or unregistered form or in the name of one or more of the trustees or of any other person, firm or corporation, with or without indication of any fiduciary capacity;

(d) To give general or special proxies or powers of attorney (which may or may not be discretionary and with power of substitution) for voting or acting with respect to securities to any person other than the Donor; to deposit securities with, or transfer them to, protective committees, voting trustees, or similar bodies; to join in any reorganization; and to pay assessments or subscriptions called for in connection with securities held by the trustees;

(e) To compromise or submit to arbitration any tax, claim or matter in dispute;

(f) If in the opinion of the trustees it is necessary or advisable to do so, to borrow money for such time and at such rate of interest or discount as the trustees deem proper; to give notes or obligations therefor binding the trust property; and as security therefor to mortgage or to pledge real or personal property with or without power of sale;

(g) To credit particular receipts or gains, and to charge particular disbursements or losses or charges, to income or to principal of the trust or to apportion them between income and principal, whether such credits or charges relate to bonds acquired at a premium, to reserves or to any other matter, all as the trustees consider fair and reasonable in each case;

(h) To manage, improve or develop real estate; to construct, alter, repair or demolish buildings or structures; to settle boundary lines and easements and other rights; to partition; and to join with co-owners or others in dealing with real estate in any way; to investigate, prevent and remediate violations or possible violations of federal, state or local law regarding substances posing a hazard to the environment or to human health which may be applicable to any property held by the trustees and to undertake such actions prior to the formal enforcement of such laws by any federal, state or local agency against trust property; and to charge all expenses associated with any such investigation, prevention or remediation, including the fees of consultants and counsel, against the income or principal of the trust holding the property;

(i) To employ investment counsel and consult with them concerning the investments and management of the trust and to delegate to such counsel such powers as the trustees deem appropriate; to employ agents and to delegate to such agents such powers as the trustees deem appropriate; to employ legal counsel, accountants and any special services; to employ a custodian of any funds or securities and to delegate to the custodian such powers as the trustees deem appropriate; and, in addition to the compensation and expenses of the trustees, to pay the compensation and expenses of all such services, even if rendered by a trustee;

(j) To participate as a seller or purchaser in private placements, secondary offerings and other regulated or special transactions, and to execute and deliver such instruments and take such action as is customary or, in the opinion of the trustees, appropriate in connection therewith, including investment representations, indemnity agreements, pledges and guarantees binding the trust property;

(k) To organize a corporation, limited liability company, limited partnership, real estate trust or other suitable entity under the laws of any state or country at any time prior to the final distribution or sale of all of the trust property and to transfer thereto all or any part of any interest in real property or other property held in this trust (including such property which in the disinterested trustee's discretion is necessary in order to maintain, improve and pay for the management of said real property) and to receive in exchange therefor such stocks, bonds, certificates of beneficial interest and other securities in such manner and amounts as they deem appropriate; and

(l) To make any division or distribution of, or payment from, the trust in kind, by the fair and reasonable allotment and transfer of specific securities or other personal or real property or undivided interests therein, at then current values, in lieu of cash, as a part or the whole of any one or more shares or payments.

Practice Note

Article FIFTH contains provisions regarding the investment and retention of securities and sales or distributions of securities to fund annuity payments. It authorizes the retention of various types of business interests, whether incorporated or not, and gives the trustees the authority to diverge from the general fiduciary duty to diversify trust investments. Without this language, interests in certain closely-held entities may not be proper trust investments.

FIFTH: Investment and Retention of Securities.

(a) Without limitation of the powers, authorities or discretion conferred on the trustees elsewhere in this instrument (but subject always to the restrictions applicable to the annuity trust), the trustees are expressly authorized to receive the property described in Schedule A, or shares of stock of any class, bonds, notes, options, general or limited partnership interests, limited liability company interests, beneficial interests or other interests of any kind in any corporation, partnership, limited liability company, business or nominee trust, sole proprietorship or other venture owned by the Donor or in which the Donor had an interest at any time during the Donor's lifetime, or in any organization or concern succeeding to or carrying on all or any substantial part of the business or activities of any of the foregoing (collectively, "Securities"); to retain any of the Securities for such period or periods of time as the trustees may deem appropriate in the trustees' absolute discretion; to purchase or otherwise acquire additional Securities; to distribute any of the Securities in kind; to sell all or any part of the Securities at public or private sale to any person or concern for such consideration and on such terms as the trustees may deem reasonable in light of the conditions then existing; to exchange one kind of Securities for any other kind, to enter into agreements with other holders of Securities, to participate in any reorganization, merger, consolidation, recapitalization, liquidation or any other change with respect to the Securities and to vote and deal with the Securities as fully and effectively as if owned outright and free of trust.

(b) Any trustee may serve as an officer, director, partner, manager, member, employee, trustee or in any other capacity with any entity the Securities of which are held by the trustees and may be compensated for so acting. A trust as such may serve as an owner-manager or the sole owner-manager of a limited liability company.

(c) No trustee shall incur any liability to any person because of the character or amount of the investment of trust property in the Securities (and the consequent failure to diversify trust assets) or because of any action taken or omitted to be taken in good faith in accordance with the provisions of this article with respect to the Securities. No trustee shall incur any liability to any person because such trustee may be interested in the Securities in such trustee's own right or may have an interest in any action taken by the trust with respect to the Securities. No trustee shall be disqualified from serving as such nor shall any action taken by any trustee be voidable or invalid by reason of such trustee's individual ownership of Securities, such trustee's status as an officer, director, partner, manager, member, employee, or trustee of any entity the Securities of which are held by the trustees, or any other interest, real or apparent, in the transaction.

(d) During the annuity trust term, the trustees are authorized to sell assets of the trust to the Donor or the Donor's estate in order to realize funds with which to pay the annuity amount or for any other reason in their sole discretion. The trustees may also distribute assets in kind (including the Securities) to the Donor or the Donor's estate to pay the annuity amount. Any such sales or distributions shall be at fair market value as reasonably determined by the disinterested trustee. The provisions of this paragraph shall not in any way limit the Donor's right during the annuity trust term to reacquire trust assets as provided in Article SEVENTH of this instrument.

(e) No trustee shall incur any liability to any person as a result of any determination made by the disinterested trustee in good faith of the initial net fair market value of the property transferred to the trust or of the value of any assets (including Securities) sold or distributed to the Donor or the Donor's estate in payment of the annuity amount.

Practice Note

In order to qualify as a GRAT, the trust instrument must contain all the provisions required under the applicable Treasury Regulations, and these provisions must continue to be in effect during the specified term. Most of paragraphs in Article SIXTH are required provisions for a GRAT.

SIXTH: Other Provisions Relating to Annuity Trust. The provisions of this article shall apply to the annuity trust established under Article FIRST of this instrument.

Practice Note

If the annuity amount is stated in terms of a fraction or percentage of the initial fair market value of the property transferred to the GRAT, the GRAT must provide for adjustments to the annuity payments for any incorrect determination of the fair market value of the property of the trust. The adjustment clause must satisfy the requirements of Treasury Regulation Section 1.664-2(a)(1)(iii).

(a) *Adjustment for Incorrect Valuation of Trust Property.* If the initial net fair market value of the property used in determining the annuity amount is determined, for federal gift tax purposes, to be an amount other than the amount initially determined by the disinterested trustee as provided in paragraph (b) of Article FIRST of this instrument, then, within a reasonable period after the final determination of the correct value for such purposes, the trustees shall pay to the Donor, or to the Donor's estate, as applicable, in the case of an undervaluation, or shall be repaid by the Donor, or by the Donor's estate, as applicable, in the case of an overvaluation, an amount equal to the difference between the amount which the trust should have paid the Donor or the Donor's estate, as applicable, if the correct value were used and the amount which the trust actually paid the Donor or the Donor's estate, as applicable, in accordance with Treasury Regulation Section 1.664-2(a)(1)(iii). Interest, if any, shall be paid with such amount as may from time to time be required by the Code and the regulations thereunder.

Practice Note

The GRAT must provide for proration of the annuity amount payable for any short year.

(b) *Proration for Short Taxable Year.* If any period during which the annuity is payable to the Donor is less than twelve (12) months, in determining the annuity amount for such period, the trustees shall prorate the same, on a daily basis, in accordance with Treasury Regulation Section 25.2702-3(b)(3).

(c) *Taxable Year.* The taxable year of the trust shall end on December 31 of each year.

Practice Note

The GRAT must prohibit additional contributions to the trust. In the event an additional contribution is inadvertently made to the trust, this paragraph contains a savings clause which directs the trustees to hold the additional contribution as the initial contribution to a separate annuity trust upon the terms specified in the trust instrument.

(d) *Additional Contributions Prohibited.* During the annuity trust term, no additional contribution shall be made to the trust after the initial contribution on the Funding Date. If, notwithstanding the foregoing, an additional contribution is made to the trust during the annuity trust term, such additional contribution shall not be part of the initial annuity trust, but shall be held by the trustees as the initial contribution to a separate annuity trust upon the terms herein specified (except that the annuity amount of the separate annuity trust shall be determined based upon the Section 7520 rate on the date of such additional contribution and the annuity trust term of the separate annuity trust shall be the [YY] [(YY)] year period commencing on the date of such additional contribution).

Practice Note

The trust instrument must prohibit distributions to or for the benefit of any person other than the donor during the specified term.

(e) *Prohibited Distributions.* No distributions from the annuity trust shall be made to or for the benefit of any person other than the Donor (or the Donor's estate) during the annuity trust term. The foregoing shall not limit the Donor's right to pledge or assign as security for a loan to the Donor the Donor's right to receive the annuity under paragraph (b) of Article FIRST of this instrument.

Practice Note

The GRAT must prohibit commutation (prepayment) of the donor's annuity interest.

(f) *Commutation.* The interest of the Donor (or the Donor's estate) in the annuity trust shall not be subject to commutation (prepayment).

(g) *Investments to Provide Reasonable Income.* Nothing in this instrument shall be construed to restrict the trustees from investing the annuity trust assets in a manner which could result in the annual realization of a reasonable amount of income or gain from the sale or disposition of trust assets.

Practice Note

The GRAT must prohibit the trustees from using a note, other debt instrument, option, or other similar financial arrangement to satisfy the trustees' obligation to pay the annuity amount at least annually.

(h) *Use of Debt Instruments to Satisfy Payment of Annuity Amount Prohibited.* The trustees shall not issue a note, other debt instrument, option, or other similar financial arrangement in satisfaction of any payment of the annuity amount.

(i) *Determinations of Value.* All determinations of the value of the assets of the annuity trust during the annuity trust term shall be made solely by the disinterested trustee or trustees.

(j) *Code and Regulations.* References in this instrument to the Code or the federal income tax regulations ("Reg. §" or "Treasury Regulation Section") shall be deemed to mean the Internal Revenue Code of 1986 or the regulations thereunder as now in force or hereafter amended, and to include corresponding provisions of any subsequent federal tax laws and regulations.

Practice Note

This paragraph references Internal Revenue Code Section 2702 and Treasury Regulation Section 25.2702-3, which establishes governing instrument requirements applicable to GRATs.

(k) *Donor's Intention.* It is the Donor's intention that the interest of the Donor (or the Donor's estate) in the annuity trust shall meet the requirements of a qualified annuity interest within the meaning of Code § 2702 and the regulations thereunder and that the value of such interest for federal tax purposes on the date hereof shall be approximately equal to the initial net fair market value of the property transferred to the trust. Accordingly, the provisions of this instrument shall be construed, and the annuity trust created under this instrument shall be administered, solely in accordance with such intention and in a manner consistent with the Code and regulations.

Practice Note

During the specified term, the trust will be treated as a grantor trust and the donor will be treated as the owner of the trust property for income tax purposes. As a result, the donor will be taxed on any income realized by the GRAT during the specified term. This will enable the donor to pay the income tax incurred on the GRAT's income or capital gains without making additional taxable gifts to the remainder beneficiaries. It will also enable the trustees to distribute appreciated assets to the donor in satisfaction of the donor's annuity obligation without recognizing any gain.

This article is included for income tax reasons, to further assure that the trust will qualify as a grantor trust for income tax purposes.

SEVENTH: Donor's Right to Reacquire Trust Assets; Donor's Income Taxes.

(a) *Donor's Right to Reacquire Trust Assets.* Notwithstanding any other provision of this instrument, the Donor shall have the right at any time during the annuity trust term, exercisable in a non-fiduciary capacity and without the approval or consent of the trustees or any other person acting in a fiduciary capacity, to reacquire the trust principal (or any part thereof) by substituting other property of equivalent value. The Donor may exercise such right by an instrument in writing delivered to the trustees specifying the property to be reacquired and tendering the property of equivalent value to be substituted for such property. Upon receipt of such writing and such substituted property and after confirming that such properties are of equivalent value, the trustees shall promptly transfer the property to be reacquired to the Donor.

(b) *Annuity Trust as Grantor Trust.* During so much of the annuity trust term as the Donor shall be living, it is the Donor's intention that the annuity trust will be treated in its entirety as a so-called grantor trust of the Donor for federal income tax purposes.

Practice Note

The model document prohibits reimbursement of income taxes paid by the donor. This is the more conservative position to take based on Situation 3 of Rev. Rul. 2004-64, 2004-2 C.B. 7.

(c) *Donor's Income Taxes.* In no event may the trustees make any distribution to the Donor in order to reimburse the Donor for any income taxes incurred by the Donor attributable to the undistributed net income and capital gains of the trust. The Donor shall have no right to seek reimbursement for any such income taxes.

Practice Note

Trust instruments should address the manner in which trustees account to the beneficiaries. Article EIGHTH clarifies the trustees' obligations. In the model form, accounts for the annuity trust during the annuity trust term are to be rendered to the donor, if she is then living and competent, or if not, to her legal representative, if any, and to the trustees then acting under the separate grantor trust which is designated as the remainder beneficiary in the event the donor survives the specified term. If the donor survives the specified term, the model form provides that, after the expiration of the specified term, accounts are to be rendered to the donor's husband, if he shall then be living, or if not, to the trustees then acting under the separate grantor trust which is designated as the remainder beneficiary.

EIGHTH: Accounts. The trustees of each trust hereunder shall render an account of the trust at least as often as annually (i) during the annuity trust term, to the Donor, or, if she is not then living and of full legal capacity, to the Donor's legal representative, if any, and (ii) if the Donor survived the annuity trust term, after the expiration of the annuity trust term, to the Donor's said husband, if he shall then be living and of full legal capacity, or if not, to the trustees then acting under the aforementioned SARAH SAMPLE [*YEAR*] FAMILY TRUST. In the case of each trust hereunder, the written assent to any such account by each person of full legal capacity to whom it is rendered as provided above shall fully protect the trustees as to all matters or transactions stated in such account or shown thereby, even if such person is serving as a trustee hereunder. Any person who is not of full legal capacity shall be deemed to assent to such account if his or her legal guardian or similar legal representative assents in writing to the account. Nothing in this Article shall be deemed to give anyone the power to modify the terms of this trust instrument or to alter or shift any beneficial interest created hereunder.

Practice Note

Article NINTH includes provisions to assure the allowance of a marital deduction in the event that the donor dies during the specified term.

NINTH: Tax Considerations.

(a) *Estate Tax Marital Deduction.* The Donor intends that the value of any property which passes to the Donor's said husband under paragraph (b) of Article SECOND of this instrument shall qualify for the estate tax marital deduction in the Donor's estate for estate tax purposes. All questions arising with respect to such disposition shall be resolved and all powers and discretions conferred upon the trustees by this instrument shall be exercised accordingly.

(b) *Rules for Payments to Donor's Husband.* If the Donor shall die prior to the expiration of the annuity trust term, then, to the extent of any property which otherwise passes to the Donor's said husband under paragraph (b) of Article SECOND of this instrument, from the date of the Donor's death until the expiration of the annuity trust term: (i) notwithstanding the provisions of Article FIRST of this instrument, the trustees shall pay to the Donor's estate, on each anniversary date in accordance with paragraph (c) of Article FIRST of this instrument, all net income of the trust (or, if less than the entire value of the property of the annuity trust was includable in the value of the Donor's gross estate as finally determined for federal estate tax purposes, of the Marital Share) in excess of the annuity amount; (ii) any non-income producing property held by the trust or the Marital Share, as the case may be, shall be made productive or converted within a reasonable time at the request of the Donor's said husband; and (iii) no allocation of any receipt to principal or of any expense to income shall be made if such allocation would result in the Donor's estate receiving less than the whole amount of net income from the trust or the Marital Share, as the case may be, to which the income beneficiary of a trust would be entitled under applicable rules of law.

(c) *Definition of Marital Deduction.* The term "marital deduction" as used in this instrument shall mean the marital deduction available under federal or state law, as appropriate, at the time of the Donor's death, but if such term shall have no operative meaning under the applicable law at the time of the Donor's death, it shall have the meaning provided by federal or state law, as appropriate, in effect at the date of execution of this instrument.

> **Practice Note**
>
> A GRAT must be irrevocable. However, a modification of a GRAT to comply with the GRAT requirements set forth under the Treasury Regulations is possible under certain circumstances.

TENTH: Irrevocable; Limited Amendment. This trust instrument and the trusts created by it shall be irrevocable. However, the disinterested trustee shall have the power, acting alone, at any time or from time to time, by written instrument, to amend this instrument in any manner required for the purpose of ensuring that the Donor's interest or the interest of the Donor's estate, as applicable, in the annuity trust qualifies as a qualified annuity interest under applicable provisions of Section 2702 of the Code and the regulations thereunder.

> **Practice Note**
>
> Article ELEVENTH sets forth the jurisdiction that will govern the operation of the trust. A governing law clause will generally be upheld as long as the state chosen has some logical connection to the trust.

ELEVENTH: Governing Law. The validity and effect of this instrument and the administration of the trusts created by it shall be determined in accordance with the laws of [*NAME OF STATE*].

TWELFTH: Acceptance. The trustees, by joining in the execution of this instrument, hereby accept the trust and agree to carry out the provisions of this instrument.

IN WITNESS WHEREOF, the undersigned have executed this instrument the day and year first above written.

> **Practice Note**
>
> The document should be dated by the donor on the first page and signed by the donor and trustees at the end of the document. Care should be taken that the trust is executed in accordance with the requirements of the donor's state of domicile. In some jurisdictions, the signatures of the donor and trustees should be witnessed. In other jurisdictions, all signatures must be notarized.

_____
SARAH SAMPLE, Donor

_____
[*TRUSTEE 1*], Trustee

_____
[*TRUSTEE 2*], Trustee

STATE/COMMONWEALTH OF [*NAME OF STATE*]
County of [*NAME OF COUNTY*]

On this _____ day of _____, 20_____, before me, the undersigned notary public, personally appeared SARAH SAMPLE, proved to me through satisfactory evidence of identification to be the person whose name is signed on the preceding or attached document, and acknowledged to me that she signed it voluntarily for its stated purpose.

_____
Notary Public

SCHEDULE A

TO

SARAH SAMPLE [*YEAR*] ANNUITY TRUST

Assets Transferred to Trust

[INSERT DESCRIPTION OF ASSETS TRANSFERRED TO TRUST]

Index

H

I